Logic Works

Logic Works is a critical and extensive introduction to logic. It asks questions about why systems of logic are as they are, how they relate to ordinary language and ordinary reasoning, and what alternatives there might be to classical logical doctrines.

The book covers classical first-order logic and alternatives, including intuitionistic, free, and many-valued logic. It also considers how logical analysis can be applied to carefully represent the reasoning employed in academic and scientific work, better understand that reasoning, and identify its hidden premises. Aiming to be as much a reference work and handbook for further, independent study as a course text, it covers more material than is typically covered in an introductory course. It also covers this material at greater length and in more depth with the purpose of making it accessible to those with no prior training in logic or formal systems.

Online support material includes a detailed student solutions manual with a running commentary on all starred exercises, and a set of editable slide presentations for course lectures.

Key Features

- Introduces an unusually broad range of topics, allowing instructors to craft courses to meet a range of various objectives
- Adopts a critical attitude to certain classical doctrines, exposing students to alternative ways to answer philosophical questions about logic
- Carefully considers the ways natural language both resists and lends itself to formalization
- Makes objectual semantics for quantified logic easy, with an incremental, rule-governed approach assisted by numerous simple exercises
- Makes important metatheoretical results accessible to introductory students through a discursive presentation of those results and by using simple case studies

Lorne Falkenstein is Professor Emeritus at Western University in London, Canada.

Scott Stapleford is Professor of Philosophy at St. Thomas University in Fredericton, Canada.

Molly Kao is Assistant Professor of Philosophy at the University of Montreal, in Montreal, Canada.

Logic Works

A Rigorous Introduction to Formal Logic

Lorne Falkenstein, Scott Stapleford, and Molly Kao

NEW YORK AND LONDON

Cover image: Martin Shoesmith

First published 2022
by Routledge
605 Third Avenue, New York, NY 10158

and by Routledge
2 Park Square, Milton Park, Abingdon, Oxon OX14 4RN

Routledge is an imprint of the Taylor & Francis Group, an informa business

Library of Congress Cataloging-in-Publication Data
A catalog record for this title has been requested

ISBN: 978-0-367-46030-3 (hbk)
ISBN: 978-0-367-46029-7 (pbk)
ISBN: 978-1-003-02653-2 (ebk)

DOI: 10.4324/9781003026532

Typeset in Bembo
by Newgen Publishing UK

Access the Support Material: www.routledge.com/9780367460297

Contents

Preface

Logic Works takes what might be called a philosophical approach to logic. It does not cover philosophy of logic as currently conceived, but it does ask questions about why systems of logic are as they are, how they relate to ordinary language and ordinary reasoning, and what alternatives there might be to classical logical doctrines. It covers classical first-order logic, and introduces supervaluations, many-valued logics, paraconsistent logic, intuitionistic logic, modal sentential logic, free logic, and description theories. It also covers mathematical induction, completeness and soundness proofs, and formal semantics. In addition to these field-specific topics, it considers how logical analysis might be applied to carefully represent the reasoning employed in academic and scientific work, better understand that reasoning, and identify its hidden premises. *Logic Works* deals with this material from the ground up, aiming to make it accessible to those with no prior background in logic, mathematics, or formal systems. It aims to be as much a reference work and a handbook for further, independent study as a course text. To this end, it covers more material than is typically covered in an introductory course, and it covers introductory material at greater length and in more depth. Course instructors will teach only a portion of the material presented here and will teach that portion by way of abbreviation, highlighting, and alternative explanation rather than supplementation. More advanced material is separated from foundational material by being placed in appendices, in a separate sequence of "advanced topics" chapters, and in chapter sections that build on advanced material introduced in earlier chapters. There are numerous answered exercises to facilitate self-instruction.

An outline of classical sentential logic with some nonclassical variants is completed by the close of chapter 7. Later chapters repeatedly cycle through the material originally presented over chapters 2–7, both reinforcing and embellishing that original learning. Alterations to previously presented material are highlighted, to focus attention on what is new and to make clear what is being retained with each step to a higher level.

Chapters interrupt exposition with exercises. Details are often worked out in running comments on the solutions to the selected exercises. It is necessary to work through the exercises and consult the solutions to get the full story.

Logic is learned by doing exercises. Language can be too ambiguous for the precise applications logic demands and details too small to be noticed at first can be crucial. Even the most clearly written English prose will be understood differently by different people, and the attempt to explain everything in the detail it deserves can produce an account that frustrates its own purpose by being too long and tedious. To grasp the meaning behind the language it is necessary to work on the exercises. The theory of logic is abstract. We are better at understanding concrete examples than abstract concepts. Exercises are the examples. *Logic Works* makes working through the exercises even more essential by including important portions of the expository material in the solutions to selected exercises.

Exercises that are prefaced by an asterisk (⋆) are answered. Answers can be downloaded from the textbook's product page at www.routledge.com/9780367460297. The answers should be used to check on the correctness of work, not as a substitute for it. Often, the solution to an exercise will make no sense to someone who has not first struggled to solve the exercise on their own. A history of failed attempts makes it clear why the answer is as it is. The exercises are progressive. Earlier ones teach things needed to handle later ones. Looking up answers to earlier exercises without working on them first makes it harder to remember the solution when needed for more advanced applications. A poor grasp of the solutions to earlier exercises makes engagement with the later exercises more difficult and time consuming. Time spent struggling with the earlier exercises is repaid by time saved dealing with the later ones.

Understanding the text is not a prerequisite for doing the exercises. Doing the exercises produces understanding. Trying to give an answer, even in the absence of understanding, is the beginning of understanding. Every second exercise is answered to serve as a prompt. An incorrect idea can be corrected by consulting a neighbouring, answered question. Neighbouring answered questions illustrate how to deal with similar cases. Sometimes only minor changes to an answered question are required to solve an unanswered one. Uncertainty over how to answer an exercise will prompt a review of important portions of the preceding text. When the text is reread with a particular difficulty in view, it will be found to say more than it did the first time through.

Instructors' Preface

Logic Works contains more material than can be taught in a single course. It does so with the aim of offering students a book that will continue to have value as a reference work and a guide for independent study. Instructors can focus on abbreviating, condensing, highlighting, sidelighting, answering questions, and taking up examples and exercises. Students can be referred to the text for more detailed explanations.

There are two sequences of chapters, a principal sequence (chapters 1–17) and an advanced sequence (chapters A-1–A-6). The advanced chapters are placed at points where they can be studied by those who have mastered the preceding principal chapters. They are not necessary for understanding the principal chapters that follow them. Later principal chapters sometimes refer to results established in earlier advanced chapters, but they do not demand understanding of how those results are established. The advanced chapters are progressive among themselves. It is necessary to have mastered the material in the earlier advanced chapters before taking up later advanced chapters.

Chapters 1, 3, 5, 7, 16, and 17 section some material off into appendices. This is done for different reasons. The appendix to chapter 1 is a summary presentation of basic concepts, better assigned for reading and reference than taken up in a class or lecture. Chapter 1 itself raises a philosophical problem with the foundations of logic and sets up an opposition between formalist and intuitionist answers to that problem that is explored throughout the subsequent chapters, and resolved (in one way and to some extent) in the advanced chapters. Otherwise, the chapter offers an introduction to methods and foundational concepts that can be quickly summarized or assigned as reading.

Instructors must decide whether to begin a course on formal logic by discussing how to formalize a natural language or by presenting a largely uninterpreted formal language. Neither approach is a happy one. The first can be confusing for many, who find that the formal language does not mesh with their intuitions about how their natural language is used. The second tries the patience of many, who do not see the point of studying a formal system that is not clearly related to their natural language. Even more unfortunately, those who are confused by the first approach are most likely to be the ones who are impatient with the second.

Logic Works begins with two brief chapters on formal syntax and semantics and only relates the formal language to English in chapter 4. The aim is to familiarize students with how the formal language works before asking them to associate it with a natural language. Relating the formal language to a natural language is very important, but it requires caution to minimize confusion and frustration. *Logic Works* is designed on the principle that introducing the formal language as a way of capturing the form of natural language sentences and demonstrations invites too many misapprehensions to be pedagogically effective. At the risk of trying students' patience, the formal language needs to first be sketched on its own terms. It can then be presented as a tool that might be used to formalize *a part* of what is said in natural languages, with due regard for the fact that the fit is not always exact.

The appendix to chapter 3 proves the expressive completeness of a formal language for sentential logic containing just five (or two or one) connectives. In passing, it introduces the concepts of disjunctive normal form and of a lean formal language. These are topics that can be skipped in an introductory course but that instructors might want to consider wedging in, depending on course objectives. The notion of a lean language is alluded to at the outset of chapter 6 to motivate introducing an abbreviated system of derivation rules. The derivation of disjunctive normal forms is discussed both in chapter 6 on derivations and chapter 7 on trees, where it serves as a hint that derivations, trees, and semantic techniques can be expected to establish the same results. The fact of expressive completeness is brought up when discussing how much of what is said in English lends itself to formalization (in chapter 4), and again in the appendix to chapter 5 when discussing what multi-valued logics aim to achieve.

The material on multi-valued logics is put in appendices to chapters 5 and 7 because it can be skipped, depending on course objectives. There are special reasons to include it in a course that aims to take a critical and philosophical approach to introductory logic. Students can find it liberating to be exposed to alternative ways in which logic might be conceived, some of which hearken back to non-Western traditions, and the alternative approaches help to strengthen their understanding of the foundations of the classical approach and of what is involved in designing an alternative system of logic.

Supervaluations are introduced in appendix 5.1. Those interested in exposing students to free logic and the philosophical problems attendant on definite descriptions and discourse concerning nonexistent objects will want to include appendix 5.1 on their course syllabi. It is foundational for sections 11.7.7 and 14.4.4.

Chapter 4, on formalization (or translation) devotes special attention to the formalization of natural language conditionals. In conformity with standard practice, it discusses the reasons why the material conditional cannot adequately formalize causal and subjunctive conditionals and presents the paradoxes of material implication. Unusually, this chapter also draws attention to special contexts where natural language conditionals are intuitively captured by material conditionals. It further offers a unique analysis of how conditionals are expressed in English and of the types of English conditionals.

Logic Works makes no attempt to "sell" the study of logic to students on the ground that it will improve their reasoning skills. In part, this is because the sales pitch is inconsistent with the appeals to intuitive foundations that are made in many chapters. In part, it is because we are sceptical of the ability of any training in logic to overcome the psychological factors that induce resistance to counterdemonstrations. But *Logic Works* does make a case that the study of logic is both intrinsically philosophically interesting and that sentential logic is instrumentally valuable for students of philosophy. Familiarity with valid and invalid sentential forms aids in the analysis of philosophical arguments. While it rarely uncovers invalid arguments, it reveals implicit premises and questionable premises, assisting in crafting rigorous, critical papers. This makes section 4.12 and the attached exercises an important component of any course for philosophy students.

Logic Works inserts chapter 4 between two chapters on formal semantics. Chapter 3 deals with the essentials of sentential semantics, as illustrated by truth tables. Chapter 5 introduces a short table method for discovering models and discusses how to establish validity and invalidity by direct appeal to the connective rules. Chapter 4 interrupts the sequence to relate the formal language to natural language sentences and demonstrations as soon as is pedagogically feasible, but also because chapter 5 can be skipped, depending on time constraints and course objectives. Courses designed to present accepted decision procedures without digressing too far to discuss what justifies those procedures will pass directly from chapter 4 to chapter 6 or 7. Chapter 5 is important for a course that aims to teach formal semantics for more advanced systems of logic (it is presupposed by chapters 9, 11, 15, and 16) and for those wanting to expose students to the techniques for demonstrating metatheoretic results (there called "informal demonstrations," and treated as such). Chapter 5 also quietly introduces natural deduction techniques in an informal context. Those planning on covering the material in chapter 6 will find that sections 5.2–3 and 5.5 prepare the way, though the material in chapter 6 does not depend on any prior knowledge of chapter 5.

Some instructors may find it preferable to pass over the material on discovering models in section 5.1 in favour of using trees. *Logic Works* opts to present trees as derivational structures, albeit structures based on semantic rules rather than intuitively consequential forms. In keeping with that approach, it treats tree models as subject to verification. As usual, the verification procedure is to climb the path, appealing to the connective rules to demonstrate how truth flows up the tree from literals to the givens. That procedure is described in section 5.1 in the context of verifying models drawn from short tables. But instructors should find little difficulty in inverting the textbook order, taking up chapter 7 in place of section 5.1, and drawing on the relevant parts of section 5.1 to explain how to verify tree models.

Chapters 6 on natural deduction derivations, and 7, on reduction trees, have been designed so that either one may be taken up in the absence of the other. Those planning to take up soundness and completeness demonstrations for more advanced systems are advised that chapters A-4, A-5, and A-6 only demonstrate the soundness of derivations and the completeness of trees. Appeal to a method for converting trees to derivations replaces the demonstration of the soundness of trees and the completeness of derivations. The reliability of that method is not rigorously demonstrated.

Chapter 6 follows up on the distinction drawn in chapter 1 between formal and intuitionistic approaches to solving the problems of logic. Derivations are there presented as a distinct approach to solving the problems of logic, grounded in intuitively obvious equivalences and entailments rather than a theory of the meaning of the sentential connectives. Chapter 5 prepared for this move by informally relying on the rules of indirect proof, conditional proof, modus ponens, and proof by cases when giving semantic demonstrations. At the outset of chapter 6, this fact is invoked to counter the prejudice that semantic theory sits in judgement of the correctness of the derivation rules. Not all instructors will agree, and whether they do or not, the observation is not offered as dogma, but as an invitation for philosophical consideration. Those who have the time to go further will find that the following advanced chapter, A-2, presents soundness and completeness demonstrations as an answer. This is an important reason for making the advanced material available. It addresses the fundamental problem exposed in chapter 1.

Though the derivation rules are justified by appeal to intuition, they are nonetheless classical. This makes recognition and discussion of alternative intuitions, prominently those labelled as "intuitionist," a topic that cannot be merely relegated to an appendix. Many courses will not have the time for this material, but it is at least there as a source for the many readers who naturally question the identification of double negatives with positives.

Those who choose to take up the study of derivations will find two differences from other treatments. *Logic Works* tends to present the more complex and restrictive derivation rules first. Learning to apply derivation rules is not like physical training. It is not necessary to start easy and build up from there. It may in fact be counterproductive. The simpler rules are in no sense components of the more complex and restrictive rules. On the contrary, giving the impression that the more complex and restrictive rules are somehow developments of the simpler and more powerful ones makes it more tempting to take liberties with the application of the more complex rules, or to imagine that they can be replaced with the simpler ones. Those who learn the more restrictive rules first are less likely to abuse them.

Secondly, *Logic Works* cautions readers that while the rules are individually intuitive, the manner in which they are to be applied to obtain an assigned result is often quite difficult to discern. The approach taken to this problem is regimented and not at all left to "intuition." *Logic Works* provides heuristics for the application of each rule. "Topdown" thinking is restricted to the application of particular rules, a "bottom-up" method is inculcated for the remainder, and a flow chart for the sequence in which rules are to be applied is followed. To mitigate indecision due to multiplicity of choice, instruction begins with a derivation system designed for a "lean language" that recognizes only atomic sentences, negations, conditionals, and the associated derivation rules. This reduces the number of rules to be juggled from 11 to five without compromising the completeness of the system. Rewriting disjunctions, conjunctions, and biconditionals as the equivalent $\sim/\rightarrow$ sentences makes for many challenging and instructive exercises, providing instruction in everything it is most important to know about doing derivations.

The lean derivation system is given a different name from the full derivation system, but chapter 6 does not teach two distinct systems. The names notwithstanding, there is one 11-rule system. It is just presented over two stages. Instructors feeling time pressure have the option of just teaching the lean system (possibly backed up with instruction on how to convert disjunctions, conjunctions, and biconditionals to $\sim/\rightarrow$ sentences, summarized in section 6.5.1). This reveals everything that is most important to learn about doing derivations. The remainder can be left to independent study. Much of the material in chapter 6.5 can also be sacrificed to time constraints. Those who do take up sections 6.5.2–4 will find that it establishes how derivations can be used to establish invalidity, by way of deriving the disjunctive normal form of the iterated conjunction of the premises and the negation of the conclusion. Anyone planning to say more about the soundness of the derivation system should consider section 6.5.6 and making the comparison with exercise 5.12. This makes it possible to assign section A-2.1 as supplementary reading for those who have studied A-1.1.

Logic Works does not aim to offer a full course in modal logic. It does aim to provide enough of an introduction to normal sentential modal logics to give readers a sense of the scope of the field, and enough background to understand Kripke semantics for intuitionistic logic and the associated tree method. Treatment of quantified modal logic is confined to an appendix to chapter A-6, which discusses theoretical and philosophical questions to the exclusion of presenting a theory. The treatment of semantics for intuitionistic logic is extended to quantified logic with identity in chapter 14, which goes out on a limb in offering an intuitionistic identity theory, echoed by the treatment of "substances" in the appendix to chapter A-6.

Somewhat idiosyncratically, *Logic Works* treats the logic of terms, predicates, and identity as a preliminary to quantificational logic, through to providing a semantics, derivations rules, and a tree method, as well as soundness and completeness results (the latter in the associated advanced topics chapter). This is done to provide a gradual introduction to the complexities of the semantics for quantified logic. It also provides an occasion to discuss definite descriptions (considered as terms) and a range of non-Russellian approaches to improper terms. Those in philosophy departments that offer courses touching on discourse concerning nonexistent objects will be interested in this material. Others can study sections 10.1–2 and 11.1–3 (and possibly 4) without taking up the following sections. The treatment of functional terms and definite descriptions in the remainder of chapters 10 and 11 takes place in two separate, supplementary modules, either of which can be studied independently of reference to the other. The module on definite descriptions gives special attention to supervaluations and to Meinongian semantics. This material is recommended for anyone going on to consider the treatment of trees for free description theory in chapter 14. Chapters 13 and 14, on derivations and trees for quantified predicate logic, place the treatment of derivations and trees for complex terms in separate subsections which can be skipped by those who chose not to study the prior material in chapters 10 and 11.

There are also two idiosyncrasies in the approach that *Logic Works* takes to quantified modal logic. One has to do with the treatment of formalization of natural language sentences in chapter 12. Many logic textbooks are oddly silent about scope ambiguities in quantified sentences of natural language. Readers of these textbooks are told that whichever unary operator happens to be mentioned first has scope over the unary operator mentioned second. Work by linguists and philosophers of language has made it clear that this is false. "There is a fork by every plate" does not have to mean that the plates are all stacked up in a pile with a single fork beside them.[1] "Someone loves everyone" is – the declarations of many textbooks notwithstanding – ambiguous. Rather than contradict those who have different intuitions about the parsing of quantified sentences, *Logic Works* identifies scope ambiguities in English and proposes policies for dealing with them. This takes some time and effort. It is necessary.

An immediate implication for those who recognize that natural languages are deeply infected with scope ambiguities is that it is hopeless to attempt to teach predicate semantics informally, by appeal to the declared meaning of natural language instantiations of formalized sentences. Many students will simply not intuit that the natural language sentence means what the instructor says it does, and they will have every right to think differently. Attempts on the part of the instructor to brow beat them into submission only leave them feeling stupid and confused and no better able to intuit the justification for the parsing the instructor insists on. This leaves no alternative but to teach the semantics for quantified logic as formal semantics. (This is one reason why *Logic Works* places chapter 3 before chapter 4. Even when doing sentential semantics it is important to establish the principle that the semantics for the formal language has to be understood independently of reference to the complex and ambiguous meanings invested in associated terms of the natural language.) The difficulty of doing this in an introductory course is not to be underestimated, and may explain why so many textbooks abandon the effort to teach modern predicate semantics in favour of recourse to syllogisms or circle diagrams or an emphasis on monadic predicate logic.

In contrast, one of the principal aims of *Logic Works*, initiated with the apparently tedious verbal semantic demonstrations of chapter 5 and steadily pursued over the ensuing semantics chapters, is to make formal semantics for quantified logic easy. This is where the second idiosyncrasy comes in. It is common in logic to distinguish between monadic and polyadic systems. This is a distinction founded on the "arity" of predicates, and it has no relation to the complexity of sentences. $\forall xGxx$ and $\forall xGax$ are not significantly more complex than $\forall xGx$. The treatment of predicate logic without quantification in chapter 11 regards all predicates as satisfied by lists of objects. In that context the added complexity that comes from dealing with lists of two or more as compared to lists of one is not worth remarking on. (This is one reason why *Logic Works* contains two preliminary chapters on unquantified predicate logic.) With that preparation, derivations, trees, and tree model semantics can all be dealt with without having to remark on a distinction between monadic and polyadic logic. Formalization is another matter. Chapter 12 deals with it by appealing to the concept of an instance to illustrate how formal language sentences must be parsed. Because the concept of an instance is syntactic, this can be done without appeal to a formal semantics. But that recourse will not serve to explain why the quantifier rules (for either derivations or trees) are sound, and it cannot explain why the quantifier rules are intuitive, which two of the four flatly are not. Failing a further appeal to instructor authority, a formal semantics is necessary.

Logic Works does this over chapters 15 and 16, the first devoted to singly quantified sentences and connective compounds of such sentences, and the second to sentences containing quantifiers with overlapping scope. This reflects a truly substantive step up in complexity, since sentences of the former sort can be dealt with by a semantics that works with variable assignments whereas those of the latter sort require appeal to variants. Both chapters provide numerous, progressive assignments training students first in the application of individual valuation rules, then in the application of sequences of those rules to establish the value of a formula on a given model, and finally in the application of the rules to discover and verify models or demonstrate that there can be no model. After this training, chapter 15 is able to conclude with two metatheorems (there simply called "principles") that lay the foundations for a soundness demonstration. Chapter 16 provides similarly careful instruction in how to step up and step down through chains of variants on variants. The appendix could have been included in the following advanced topics chapter, but is so obviously demanded by the definition of truth of a quantified sentence that it is better that it be specially selected for attachment at that point.

Logic Works does not deal with higher-order logic, undecidability, or incompleteness. However, it concludes with a brief treatment of second-order logic designed to introduce the topic in a way that conforms with the style of the earlier chapters.

Logic Works is backed up with a set of slide presentations, useful for classroom or video conference presentation, and a set of answers to ★ exercise questions, both available from the book's product page at www.routledge.com/9780367460297. Editable copy of the answers to the remaining exercises questions, which can be cut and pasted to reduce labour when correcting student exercises or crafting lectures, is available to instructors on request.

Sample course syllabus for a one semester, basic introduction to classical bivalent logic.

Chapter 1.1–5
Chapter 2
Chapter 3.1–4
Chapter 4
Chapter 5.1–4 (possibly replacing 5.1 with 7)
Chapter 6.1–2 and 6.6 or Chapter 7
Chapter 10.1–2
Chapter 11.1–3 (and 11.4 if Chapter 14.1–2 will be done)
Chapter 12
Chapter 13.1 and 13.2.2 or Chapter 14.1–2
Chapter 15
Other materials by choice and interest as time permits

Note

1 We owe this observation to conversations with our colleague, Robert Stainton.

Acknowledgements

Logic Works has been influenced by numerous introductory and intermediate treatments of logic, especially Beall and van Fraassen (2003); Bell, DeVidi, and Solomon (2001); Bencivenga, Lambert, and van Fraassen (1991); Bergmann, Moore, and Nelson (2014); Bostock (1997); Garson (2013); Hunter (1996); Jeffrey (1991); Kalish, Montague, and Mar (1980); Lambert and van Fraassen (1972); Nolt (1997); Prior (1962); and Sider (2010). John L Bell and Robert Stainton kindly corrected some of the more egregious errors in the treatment of intuitionistic logic and the relation between logic and ordinary language. The errors that doubtless remain are found in portions of the text they will not have seen. Jeff He read very carefully through the opening chapters and suggested a number of improvements. Special thanks to John Lehmann. We are indebted to anonymous referees for the press, whose astute observations and advice have prompted significant improvements. Very special thanks to Andrew Beck, Marc Stratton, Edward Gibbons, Lesley Hay, Kelly Winter and other members of the Taylor & Francis and Newgen production teams, who patiently accommodated a distressingly large number of corrections. Our greatest debt is to those of our students who have had the most difficulty learning logic.

References

Beall, JC and van Fraassen, Bas C, 2003, *Possibilities and Paradox,* Oxford University Press, Oxford.

Bell, John L, DeVidi, David, and Solomon, Graham, 2001, *Logical Options: An Introduction to Classical and Alternative Logics,* Broadview, Peterborough, ON.

Bencivenga, Ermanno, Lambert, Karel, and van Fraassen, Bas C, 1991, *Logic, Bivalence and Denotation,* 2nd edition, Ridgeview, Atascadero, CA.

Bergmann, Merrie, Moor, James, and Nelson, Jack, 2014, *The Logic Book,* 6th edition, McGraw-Hill, New York.

Bostock, David, 1997, *Intermediate Logic,* Clarendon Press, Oxford.

Garson, James W, 2013, *Modal Logic for Philosophers,* 2nd edition, Cambridge University Press, New York.

Hunter, Geoffrey, 1996, *Metalogic: An Introduction to the Metatheory of Standard First Order Logic,* University of California Press, Berkeley.

Jeffrey, Richard, 1991, *Formal Logic: Its Scope and Limits,* 3rd edition, McGraw-Hill, New York.

Kalish, Donald, Montague, Richard, and Mar, Gary, 1980, *Logic: Techniques of Formal Reasoning,* 2nd edition, Harcourt Brace Jovanovich, San Diego.

Lambert, Karel and van Fraassen, Bas C, 1972, *Derivation and Counterexample,* Dickenson, Encio, CA.

Nolt, John, 1997, *Logics,* Wadsworth, Belmont, CA.

Prior, Arthur, 1962, *Formal Logic,* 2nd edition, Clarendon Press, Oxford.

Sider, Theodore, 2010, *Logic for Philosophy,* Oxford University Press, Oxford.

Symbol Summary

This summary is available to download from the book's product page at www.routledge.com/9780367460297

Symbol	Name	Meaning		Symbol	Name	Meaning
′	(prime)	placeholder				
^{1}	(the one)	definite description symbol				
∀	(universal)	each		α	(alpha)	assignment
A		sentence/predicate symbol		a		object name
B		sentence/predicate symbol		b		object name
C		sentence/predicate symbol		c		object name
Γ	(gamma)	set				
Δ	(delta)	secondary set		δ	(delta)	denotes
D		object domain		d		object name
𝔻	(hollow D)	outer domain				
∃	(existential)	at least one				
E		exists		e		object name
F		false		f		object name
G		sentence/predicate symbol		f		function variable
H		sentence/predicate symbol				
I		interpretation				
J		secondary interpretation				
K		sentence/predicate symbol		k		closed term
L		list				
M		secondary list		m		object metavariable
N		neither true nor false		n		object metavariable
Ω	(omega)	domain of worlds		o		object metavariable
P		sentence/predicate metavariable		p		name metavariable
Q		sentence/predicate metavariable		q		name metavariable
R		sentence/predicate metavariable		r		name metavariable
S		sees		s		term metavariable
T		true		t		term metavariable
				u		world
				v		world
				w		world
X		predicate variable		x		object variable
				χ	(chi)	variable variable
Y		predicate variable		y		object variable
				ψ	(psi)	variable variable
Z		predicate variable		z		object variable
				ζ	(zeta)	variable variable
⊥	(con)	contradiction symbol		∪		union
=	(identity)	is		⊢		yields
~	(tilde)	not		−|−		interderivable
&		conjunction		⊨		entails
∨		disjunction		=|=		equivalence

$\rightarrow$	conditional	$\varnothing$		empty set
$\equiv$	biconditional	|		replace each
$\square$	necessarily	┆		replace one or more
$\diamond$	possibly	$\Gamma\ /\ P$		demonstration
(,)	primary punctuation	$\uparrow$	(nand)	not-and
[,]	secondary punctuation	$\downarrow$	(nor)	not-or
{,}	set	#	(hash)	both true and false
<,>	list	?		nonevident

1 Introduction to the Study of Logic

Contents

1.1 Demonstration and Interpretation

Logic is the theory of what makes demonstration work. Metalogic is the theory of what makes logic work. This is a textbook of deductive logic, as illuminated by basic metalogic.

Demonstrations work with sentences of various sorts. Declarations, observations, commands, promises, and even questions[1] can figure in demonstration. Logic comes into play insofar as sentences have values that can be determined by the values of their parts or the values of other sentences. Paradigmatically, the sentences logic is concerned with are declarative sentences and their logically salient values are "true," "false," "neither," "both," "undetermined," and so on. These values are determined by more fundamental values ascribed to the parts of sentences. They can also be affected by larger contexts in which sentences are stated. Logic studies both how the more fundamental values determine truth and falsity (see chapters 10–11 below) and how contexts affect truth and falsity (see chapters 8–9 below). It also studies other kinds of sentences with other kinds of values – for example, "evident" and "nonevident"; "obeyed" and "disobeyed"; "upheld" and "violated"; "answerable" and "unanswerable." The question of whether the conditions of a contract (which is a type of promise) have been upheld or violated can be a matter for protracted dispute in a court of law. The same holds for the deduction of rights and duties (which are a kind of law) from other laws. Whatever else the lawyers and judges are doing, they are demonstrating what actions are required, prohibited, or allowed by contracts and legal commands. Those demonstrations are examined and systematized by logic.

A demonstration consists of a collection of sentences, called the premises of the demonstration, and a further sentence, purported to be a consequence of the premises, called the conclusion of the demonstration.

Authors and speakers will often flag what they mean to assert as a conclusion, what they mean to assert as premises, or both. Words like "therefore," "hence," "so," and "consequently," or phrases like "it follows that," and "it can be concluded that," alert the reader or the listener to expect that what is about to be stated is a conclusion. In contrast, words or phrases like "for," "since," "because," "from the fact that," "for the reason that," "given that," or "supposing that" alert the reader to expect that what is about to be stated is a premise.

In ordinary speaking and writing, premises and conclusions may be presented in any order: conclusion first, followed by premises, premises first followed by conclusion, or conclusion interspersed among premises. The demonstration may be interrupted by comments on other topics. The conclusion may be omitted if it is assumed that it will be sufficiently obvious to the audience. Important premises may be omitted, on the assumption that the audience will presuppose them. Indicator words may be omitted, on the assumption that the audience can tell

DOI: 10.4324/9781003026532-1

what the conclusion is and what its premises are. These assumptions may be mistaken. When they are, the author's intended meaning needs to be determined by questioning or, in the author's absence, reconstructed by the exercise of interpretative skills. The art of interpretation, or hermeneutics, is not strictly part of logic. Logic proceeds on the assumption that the premises and the conclusion of a demonstration have already been identified, and that all questions about what sentences mean have been resolved. However, some aspects of the art of interpretation are taken up in chapters 4, 8, 10 and 12 below.

When demonstrations are critically examined, the premises and the conclusion are isolated and numbered for ease of reference. The conclusion is marked with an indicator word or symbol and placed last, as in the following demonstration, loosely based on Sextus Empiricus, *Outlines of Pyrrhonism* 1.87. Here, the indication of the conclusion is a line placed after the last numbered premise. (In this textbook, displayed demonstrations and sentences will often be numbered for possible future reference, as with 1.1 below.)

1.1
1. Either we should have confidence in all people or only in some.
2. Having confidence in all is impossible since all are in disagreement.
3. Having confidence in some means we need to decide which ones.
4. Deciding which ones requires having a criterion for picking them out.
5. Having a criterion means putting confidence in someone's opinion of what that criterion should be.
6. But whom to have confidence in is precisely what is in question.

We are in no position to have any confidence in anyone.

Sextus did not present his reasoning in this fashion. Instead, he wrote (in the translation of Inwood and Gerson [1988: 330]),

1.2   Either we shall have confidence in all men or in some. But if in all we shall be undertaking impossibilities and admitting opposing statements. But if in some, let them tell us to whom we are supposed to give assent. For the Platonist will say to Plato, the Epicurean to Epicurus, and the others analogously, and so being in an undecidable conflict they will induce suspension of judgement in us.

A philosopher, seeking to analyse Sextus's demonstration, will isolate and number his premises, omit strictly irrelevant illustrative details, asides, and other interjections, supply missing premises judged from other parts of Sextus's writings to have been intended, and separate the conclusion from the premises. It is not the business of logic to do this. It is the business of hermeneutics. Once the hermeneutical task has been performed, and the premises and conclusion have been laid out, logic takes over.

This having been said, the dependence between logic and hermeneutics is mutual. One of the fundamental hermeneutical principles, the principle of charity, dictates that where there are two or more ways of understanding what someone said, the option that is most charitable, in the sense of being more likely to be true, interesting, or consequential, ought to be preferred. Logic has something to say about that.

1.2 Deductive and Inductive Demonstrations

Insofar as the conclusion of a demonstration is purported to have a value that is determined by the values of its premises, there is, as people say, "a logic" to the demonstration. That logic is concerned with whether and how the values of the premises determine the value of the conclusion.

Logic is not always concerned with determining the values of premises. Common experience and testimony, or, where that is inadequate, the investigations of the various sciences, determine such things as whether premises are true or false, or evident or nonevident, and whether promises were made, contracts signed, laws legislated, or questions asked. Logic is concerned with how contexts and the values of parts determine the values of premises, whether the value of the conclusion is indeed determined by the values of the premises, and with why it is so determined or fails to be so determined.

The relations between the premises and the conclusion of a demonstration are of two main sorts, probabilistic and deductive. Inductive demonstrations make a case for the likelihood of the conclusion. This case may be based on such things as

- experience and a supposition that things will continue to be the way they have been
- analogy with other, less controversial cases
- the measurement of frequencies or the use of sampling techniques considered to be statistically sound, and a further appeal to the laws of statistics or a theory that specifies how to calculate probability given evidence

Deductive demonstrations make a case for the certainty of the conclusion.

The study of inductive demonstrations, also called inductive logic, is not taken up in this textbook. This textbook deals with deductive demonstrations.

1.3 The Principle of Noncontradiction

Deductive demonstration is based on the principle of noncontradiction: the principle that nothing can be both affirmed and denied.[2] A deductive demonstration makes a case for the certainty of a conclusion by attempting to set up a situation in which anyone who accepts the premises of the reasoning would be forced into a contradiction were they to deny the conclusion. No reasonable, honest person wants to contradict themselves, that is, to say at one and the same time, of one and the same thing, that it both has and does not have a certain value: that it both is and is not evident; must and must not be done; will and will not be done; is and is not questionable; even that it is "both true and false" (supposing "both true and false" to be a value that some sentences can have) and not "both true and false." That is the hallmark of being illogical, duplicitous, or reckless. When presented with deductive reasoning, the honest, reasonable listener must either

- accept the conclusion
- deny one or more of the premises
- find a way to reject the logic of the reasoning, that is, to evade the charge that there is a contradiction in denying the conclusion while still accepting the premises

While the principle of noncontradiction offers a short answer to the question of what makes deductive demonstration work, there is much to be said about what is responsible for producing or preventing contradictions, particularly in less obvious cases. It helps to begin with some definitions.

A contradiction arises when the same sentence is both affirmed and denied. Classically, the sentence is a declarative sentence that is ascribed presumably incompatible values, such as "true" and "false." But incompatible values can be more generally understood to be any pair of values that should not both be attributed to the same sentence, such as "obeyed" and "ignored" for commands; "kept" and "broken" for promises; or "answerable" and "not answerable" for questions. Taken yet more generally, nonlinguistic entities can have one or other of incompatible sets of values. States of affairs can be evident or nonevident; collections and lists can contain an element or an item or not contain it; electrical switches can be on or off; objects can be the same or different, or be and not be. These incompatible states of things are the ground of the incompatible values of sentences and hence of the contradictions that arise when incompatible values are attributed to the same sentence. Logic does not stop with considering sentences to be true or false. It recognizes other values sentences can have some of which are "designated" (like "true" or "neither true nor false") as values we are particularly concerned to establish or demonstrate. More fundamentally, logic is concerned with how the values of sentences are determined by nonsentential values like "is" or "is not," and "is in" or "is not in" as said of things.

A sentence is, as the grammarians say, a series of one or more words that expresses a complete thought. Insofar as deductive logic is concerned with demonstrations that are based on the principle of noncontradiction, its focus is on those sentences that can have a value. (This concern spills over into consideration of sentences that might have more than one value, or none; and eventually spills over into consideration of how to handle sentences that have intermediate or alternative values.) A good way to identify such sentences, though not a perfectly reliable one, is by considering whether they can be denied. "It is raining," can be denied by "It is not raining"; "Eat the fruit of the tree of knowledge" by "Do not eat the fruit of the tree of knowledge"; "I will be on time" by "I will not be on time." It is not so clear that a question can be denied, but even questions can have values, like "answerable" and "not answerable" that might be attributed to them as a consequence of the values of other sentences appearing in a demonstration.

A demonstration is anything that is apparently intended by the author to convince an audience to accept a conclusion (be it by way of believing it, acting on it, obeying it, or in some other such way). A demonstration need not succeed in this enterprise. Unsuccessful attempts at giving demonstrations are still demonstrations. They are just ineffective demonstrations.

Effective demonstrations are of two sorts. Some are rhetorically effective. They have the intended effect of convincing the intended audience. Others are logically effective. They compel anyone who accepts their premises to also accept the conclusion, on pain of contradicting themselves.

It is possible for demonstrations to be both rhetorically and logically effective, or neither, or one but not the other.

Logically effective deductive demonstrations are traditionally said to be "valid." Logically ineffective deductive demonstrations are traditionally said to be "invalid."

A demonstration is deductively *valid* if and only if anyone who affirms the premises but denies the conclusion would be caught in a contradiction.

A demonstration is deductively *invalid* if and only if anyone who affirms the premises can deny the conclusion without contradicting themselves.

(The English term, "valid" comes from the Latin, "vel," which means "true," and that historical sense has never been abandoned. In ordinary language, "valid" is still used as a synonym for "true." That makes it a bad word to use to describe the relation between the premises and the conclusion of a demonstration. Truth is a value some sentences can have, not a relation between a collection of premises and a conclusion. It would be more appropriate to describe logically effective deductive demonstrations as "consequential" and logically ineffective demonstrations as "nonconsequential." This having been said, standard practice *in logic* is to use the more misleading expressions, "valid" and "invalid." That usage is followed here, with the coda that, as used by logicians, "valid" means "consequential." It does not mean "true.")

For any demonstration, there is a collection or "set" of sentences that corresponds to that demonstration: the set comprised of the premises of the demonstration and the *denial* of its conclusion. 1.1, for instance, has the following "corresponding set":

1.3   {Either we should have confidence in all people or only in some,
      Having confidence in all is impossible since all are in disagreement,
      Having confidence in some means we need to decide which ones,
      Deciding which ones requires having a criterion for picking them out,
      Having a criterion means putting confidence in someone's opinion of
          what that criterion should be,
      Whom to have confidence in is precisely what is in question,
      It is not the case that we are in no position to have any confidence in
          anyone}

Here, the sentence that appeared as the conclusion of the demonstration is denied, and that denial is included along with the premises to make up a set of sentences. (It is standard practice in logic to mark the start and end of a set with braces, as above.)

A demonstration is valid if and only if the corresponding set comprised of its premises and the denial of its conclusion is contradictory. This makes sense given that a demonstration is valid if and only if affirming its premises while denying its conclusion produces a contradiction.

When the sentences in a set of sentences cannot all be affirmed without contradiction the set is said to be "unsatisfiable." It cannot be "made good," so to speak.

A set of sentences is *unsatisfiable* if and only if anyone who affirms all the sentences in the set would be caught in a contradiction.

A set of sentences is *satisfiable* if and only if someone can affirm all the sentences in the set without contradicting themselves.

In applying the definitions of validity and satisfaction, it is important to distinguish between being contradictory and being false, and being noncontradictory and being true. Not everything that is false is contradictory. Many things that are false are simply contrary to fact. They could be made true, or be true in other circumstances. What is satisfiable could somehow be satisfied (that is, made to be or found to be true or evident, or to have been "obeyed" or "upheld"), even though it is not satisfied as a matter of current, local fact. What is unsatisfiable could not possibly be satisfied, where the bar for being "not possible" is placed very high: as involving a contradiction. What is contradictory is not simply contrary to fact, but contrary to itself or to other things that are accepted along with it. The sentence,

"The sky is green" is false. But it is not contradictory. "The sky is green but it is not" is contradictory. It is not contradictory because it attributes both truth and falsity to "the sky is green." It is contradictory because, supposing "true" and "false" are incompatible values, it both affirms and denies that "the sky is green" has the value "true."

Similarly, the set {The sky is green, The Antarctic is in the Tropics} contains two false sentences. But there is no contradiction in affirming both of the sentences in that set.

Exercise 1.1

State whether the following sets of sentences are unsatisfiable. If they are unsatisfiable, identify one thing that anyone who believes all of them must both affirm and deny. Be careful to ensure that this thing is something that they are committed to accepting just insofar as they accept the sentences in the set and not insofar as they hold other background beliefs not described by sentences included in the set. If the sets are not unsatisfiable, describe a circumstance in which all would be true. In all exercises sets in this textbook, answers to questions marked with a star can be found online at www.routledge. com/9780367460297.

- a. {Robert Walpole was British Prime Minister on 7 May 1731, Spencer Compton was British Prime Minister on 7 May 1731}
- b. {Robert Walpole was British Prime Minister on 7 May 1731, Spencer Compton was British Prime Minister on 7 May 1731, Only one person was British Prime Minister on 7 May 1731}
- ★c. {Robert Walpole was British Prime Minister on 7 May 1731, Spencer Compton was British Prime Minister on 7 May 1731, Only one person was British Prime Minister on 7 May 1731, Robert Walpole was not Spencer Compton}
- d. {The Earth is flat, The Earth is not flat}
- ★e. {The Earth is flat, The Earth is round}
- f. {The Earth is flat, The Earth is round, Nothing can be both flat and round at the same time}
- ★g. {The ball is either red or green, The ball is red, The ball is green}
- h. {The ball is either red all over or green all over, The ball is red all over, The ball is green all over}
- ★i. {The ball is either red all over or green all over, The ball is red all over, Nothing can be both red all over and green all over, The ball is green all over}
- j. {You can have either ice cream or cake, You had ice cream, You can have cake}

1.4 Abstraction, Variables, and Formalization; Logical and Nonlogical Elements; Formal Contradiction

To make what is responsible for producing or preventing a contradiction stand out, logicians abstract the other aspects of a sentence or set of sentences. This is done by replacing these nonlogical elements with variables. A variable is a symbol that stands in for what can vary, that is, for any of a number of different things. In the case at hand, it stands for what can vary without affecting whether the sentence or set of sentences gives rise to a contradiction.

To take a simple case, the sentences

> 1.4   It is raining
> 1.5   It is not the case that it is raining

are contradictory. Any two sentences, one of which is the same as the other but for being prefaced by the words "it is not the case that" must be contradictory. Here, the logical element is the phrase "it is not the case that," whereas the variable element is whatever is said to both be and not be the case. The latter can be replaced with a variable. Take the capital letters of the English alphabet, A, B, C, G, H, K, to be variables for sentences ("sentence variables" for short). If more are needed, put numerical subscripts on A's to get an infinite supply, $A_1, A_2, A_3, \ldots$ (The other capitals are reserved for other uses.)

In the case at hand, the result is:

> 1.6   A
> 1.7   It is not the case that A

Though variables stand in the place that can be occupied by a variety of things, within any given context (within the same discussion, example, exercise, or case), no one variable can replace two or more different variants. If the variable, A, is put in the place of one occurrence of the sentence, "It is raining," it may not elsewhere be put in the place of some other sentence, such as "Pigs have wings." The two occurrences of A in the case displayed above must therefore replace the same sentence.[3] It need not be specified what sentence that is. It is allowed that it could be *any* sentence (e.g., "I promise to be on time"). But it must be the same sentence in each place the variable occurs.

Sameness is understood very strictly.

> One *sentence* is the *same* as another if and only if the two sentences consist of the same words, placed in the same order.

Replacing variants with variables produces a form. In the case just given, the form is a form for a pair of contradictory sentences. This example of abstraction defines the notion of a formal contradiction.

> A *formal contradiction* is a set of two sentences of the form {A, It is not the case that A}

The form contains the logical element, "it is not the case that," and the variable, A, which here stands for any sentence. Putting any deniable sentence in the place of the two occurrences of A in the form produces two contradictory sentences. (Caution needs to be exercised to ensure that when a sentence replaces a variable, the result is still a complete thought. "Is it raining?" and "Close the door!" become ungrammatical when prefaced by "It is not the case that." In some cases, an appropriate rewrite can serve instead. "Close the door" can be replaced by "The last person out is hereby commanded to close the door," which is a deniable sentence.)

There are many other contradictory forms. The sentence

> 1.8   It is raining but it is not raining

is by itself a contradictory sentence. Here, the logical elements are "but" and "not." The sentence that is repeated before and after these logical elements can vary. Many sentences, first stated on their own and then repeated under the word "not" and conjoined with their initial statement by the word "but," build a compound sentence that must be contradictory. Abstracting from what can vary without affecting whether a contradiction arises gives rise to

> 1.9   A but not A

which is one form that a self-contradictory sentence can have.

The definition of a formal contradiction can be extended to include this alternative.

> A *formal contradiction* is either a set of two sentences of the form {A, It is not the case that A} or a single sentence of the form A but not-A or the form not-A but A.

This having been said, not all contradictions are formal, and hermeneutics plays a large role in identifying those that are not by showing how they can be identified with formal contradictions. As noted earlier, what people say or write can often need to be interpreted, that is, rewritten in other words to make the intention more explicit. This happens with reasoning, so it necessarily happens with the sentences that figure in reasoning. It would be absurd to insist that someone who says

> 1.10   The ball is red yet it isn't

has not contradicted themselves. Technically, "The ball is red" and "It isn't" are not two sentences that consist of the same words placed in the same order except for the fact that one is prefaced with the word "not" and the two are conjoined with "but." Nonetheless, this sentence is implicitly contradictory because it can be interpreted as formally contradictory. It can be rewritten as

> 1.11   The ball is red but [yet] it is not ['nt] the case that the ball [it] is red

Provided the rewrite accurately represents what the author meant, the original sentence counts as being implicitly contradictory.

Rewrites must be done with care. One of the fraught issues in logic concerns the scope of negations. "It is not the case that you are commanded to …" and "It is not the case that I promise to …" do not mean the same thing as "You are commanded to not …" and "I promise to not …" The account that has just been given of a formal contradiction captures what is called a "wide scope" denial. There are also "narrow scope" denials, exemplified by commands or promises to not do something. Capturing the forms of narrow scope denials is a project for later chapters. Now it only matters to be sensitive to the possibility that rewriting a sentence to replace prefatory "it is not the case that" with internal "not" needs to ensure the original meaning is preserved.

Exercise 1.2

1. *State whether the following pairs of sentences are the same or different.*
    ⋆a. Dr Jekyll is Mr Hyde. Mr Hyde is Dr Jekyll.
    b. The coffee has sugar in it. The coffee is sugared.
    ⋆c. Either there will be a sea battle tomorrow or there will not be a sea battle tomorrow. Either there will not be a sea battle tomorrow or there will be a sea battle tomorrow.
    d. Some doctors are lawyers. Some lawyers are doctors.
    ⋆e. Some doctors are lawyers. It is not true that no doctors are lawyers.
    f. Some doctors are lawyers. At least one doctor is a lawyer.

2. *State whether the following sentences or pairs of sentences are formally contradictory.*
    ⋆a. Dr Jekyll is Mr Hyde. It is not the case that Mr Hyde is Dr Jekyll.
    b. All bankrupts are despicable. No bankrupts are despicable.
    ⋆c. All bankrupts are despicable. Not all bankrupts are despicable.
    d. All bankrupts are despicable. Some bankrupts are not despicable.
    ⋆e. It is not the case that all bats are rabid, but they are.
    f. It is not the case that all bats are rabid, but some are.

3. *State whether the following pairs of sentences are implicitly contradictory. Justify your answers.*
    ⋆a. The light is red. The light is green.
    b. The coffee is hot. The coffee is not hot.
    ⋆c. There are bats in the belfry. It is not the case that there are flying mammals in the belfry.
    d. Some doctors are lawyers. Some doctors are not lawyers.
    ⋆e. Dr Jekyll is Mr Hyde. It is not the case that Mr Hyde is Dr Jekyll.
    f. Some doctors are lawyers. No doctors are lawyers.

As noted earlier, within any one case (exercise, example, etc.) repeated occurrences of the same variable designate the same variant. However, occurrences of different variables need not designate different variants. This is part of what it means for variables to stand for what can vary. When a variable is used, one of the things it could stand for is the same thing that some other variable stands for.

Different variables certainly may stand for different things. It is always considered that they could just as well stand for different things as for the same thing. Consequently, (i) someone who wants different variables to be understood to stand for the same thing must say so; (ii) someone who wants to rule out the possibility that different variables stand for the same thing must say so; (iii) someone who says nothing either way must be understood to include both possibilities. (iii) is the default, so those in the third group are never obliged to remark on it. The reader is expected to assume that (iii) is meant when neither (i) nor (ii) is stated. Therefore,

> 1.6   A
> 1.12   It is not the case that B

and

> 1.13   A but not B

are not formal contradictions. This is not because A and B could not possibly stand for the same sentence, but because there is no promise that A stands for the same sentence as B.

This having been said, in important cases it is permissible to underscore the default, with phrases like, "where A and B are any two (not necessarily distinct) sentences."

1.5 A Fundamental Problem

Contradictions do not just arise when one sentence explicitly denies another, or when a single sentence contains formally contradictory components, or even when one sentence lends itself to being interpreted in a way that makes it deny another sentence. Consider the set of sentences found in exercise 1.1(c).

> 1.14   {Robert Walpole was British Prime Minister on 7 May 1731,
> Spencer Compton was British Prime Minister on 7 May 1731,
> Only one person was British Prime Minister on 7 May 1731,
> Robert Walpole was not Spencer Compton}

A contradiction arises from considering all these sentences to be true. This contradiction has nothing to do with who Walpole or Compton were or how the British government worked in 1731. It arises from certain logical elements contained in these sentences. These logical elements have to do with attribution, quantification (saying how many), and identification (or its opposite, differentiation). To bring them out, use lower-case letters a, b, c, as variables for objects and use upper-case G, H, K as variables for attributes that objects might be said to have.[4] Take the variable "a" to stand for Robert Walpole, b to stand for Spencer Compton and G to stand for being British Prime Minister on 7 May 1731.[5] Then the set has the form,

> 1.15   {a is G,
> b is G,
> Only one object is G,
> a is not b}

The first two sentences attribute something, G, to some objects, "a," and b. The third says how many objects have the G attribute. The fourth denies an identity, saying that object "a" is not the same object as object b. What the attribute is and what the objects are does not matter. What matters is that only one thing is said to have the attribute and yet two things that are not the same are said to have it.

When "formalized" in this way, the set is intuitively contradictory. The original English set may not have seemed so when doing exercises 1.1(a) and 1.1(b). Those exercises may have inspired the question of whether there is yet some further trick preventing 1.1(c) from being contradictory. There is not, and the formalization makes it intuitively obvious why.

But though the formalized set is intuitively contradictory, it is not formally contradictory. It does not contain two sentences, one of the form A (or "a is G," or "only one object is G," or "a is b") and one of the form not-A (or the corresponding denial of any of the other sentences mentioned). This poses a problem: What if someone does not share the intuition that this set is contradictory? What if they cannot "see" it? One recourse appeals to other things the person accepts to reduce the implicitly contradictory sentences to a formal contradiction. This amounts to demonstrating that the set really is contradictory.[6] In this case, the other things the person accepts might be ways of restating the given sentences in equivalent terms, or they might be beliefs the person has about what sentences are entailed by what other sentences.

For instance, it can be said that the sentences

> 1.16   a is G
> 1.17   b is G
> 1.18   a is not b

are equivalent to the sentence

> 1.19   At least two different objects are G

and that this entails that

> 1.20   It is not the case that only one object is G

which does formally contradict

1.21   Only one object is G

(The difference between equivalence and entailment is that equivalence goes both ways, from what is given to what it is equivalent to, and from that back to what is given. Entailment need go only one way, from what is given to what it entails. If object "a" has attribute G and object b has attribute G and object "a" is not object b, then there must be at least two objects that have attribute G. The reverse is also the case: if at least two things have attribute G, then at least one object, "a," has attribute G, and at least one object, b, has attribute G and object "a" is not object b. In contrast, from the fact that at least two different objects are G it follows that it is not the case that at least one object is G. But it does not go the other way. If it is not the case that at least one object is G, it does not follow that at least two are. It might instead be that none are.)

Hopefully, anyone who cannot "see" why the original set is contradictory will be able to see it when the point is demonstrated by appeal to intermediate equivalences and entailments. Otherwise, a vicious regress threatens. The threat becomes apparent when considering how equivalence and entailment are defined.

> Two sentences are *equivalent* if and only if there is a contradiction in affirming either one while denying the other.
>
> Two sentences are *not equivalent* if and only if there is no contradiction in affirming one of them while denying the other.

> A sentence is *entailed* if and only if it is the conclusion of a valid demonstration, that is, if and only if there is a contradiction in denying it while affirming the premises that entail it.

There is no problem if the contradictions spoken of in these definitions are formal contradictions. Determining whether two sentences are formally contradictory is easy. It only requires looking to see if they are the same but for the fact that one of them is prefaced by "it is not the case that" or words to that effect. But when the contradictions are only implicit there is a problem. Implicit contradictions are made explicit (demonstrated to lead to formal contradictions) by appealing to equivalences and entailments. But equivalences and entailments are themselves established by appealing to the impossibility of denying them without getting caught in a contradiction. When a contradiction is only implicit, any equivalence or entailment invoked to expose it must also be only implicit, and so equally in need of demonstration. (Working only with formal contradictions never gets beyond affirming and denying the same thing. The only equivalences and entailments that are established by appeal to formal contradictions are those with forms like "A if and only if A," "A is A," and "A entails A," which are trivial. An equivalence or entailment used to establish an implicit contradiction could not be trivial and so would need its own demonstration.) A vicious regress threatens.

There are two ways to block the regress: (i) recognize that we intuitively accept certain equivalences and entailments, even though the contradiction that arises from rejecting them is only implicit, and trust that those intuitions are correct, or (ii) develop a theory of the meaning of the logical elements that explains why equivalences and entailments are contradictory. As an example of (i), it might be claimed that demonstrations like

1.22
1. a is G.
2. b is G.
3. a is not b.
   _____
   At least two objects are G.

or

1.23
1. A.
2. If A then B.
   _____
   B.

are just obviously valid. The contradiction in accepting the premises while denying the conclusion is so obvious that any attempt to demonstrate it from more fundamental principles would be less obvious.

Undaunted, a champion of (ii) might nonetheless attempt to explain the meaning of the logical elements involved in these sentences and attempt to show how an explicit contradiction follows from those meanings.

Both approaches to what makes logic work are explored in the chapters that follow. An application of (ii) is explored in chapters 3 and 5; one of (i) in chapter 6. Later chapters alternate between the two, and some, like the optional chapter A-2, explore the extent to which the two approaches can be trusted to deliver the same results.

It might be thought that (ii) is obviously superior to (i). But there is a problem with it. Different theories of the meaning of the logical elements can be proposed. These theories yield different results, some of which sit better with our intuitions than others. In this respect, type (ii) accounts are like geometry. There are various geometries, Euclidean and non-Euclidean, and it is a question which best describes physical space, or visual space, or tactile space. Chapters 8 and 9 show how a similar situation arises in modal logic. Even in the comparatively simple sentential logic of chapters 2–7 there are theoretical disputes. Some of them are taken up in what follows, beginning with the appendix to chapter 5. A very important issue, centred on the role of intuition in demonstration, is explored beginning in section 6.6.

In fairness, the same problem might be raised with (i). Even fundamental principles of logic such as the law of the excluded middle (either A or not-A), the reduction of double negations (if not-not-A then A), and the principle that anything follows from a contradiction might be (and have been) denied to be intuitively obvious. These concerns are also taken up, beginning with the appendix to chapter 5 and continuing with section 6.6.

1.6 Chapter Outline

In addition to using variables to stand for the nonlogical elements in a sentence or a set of sentences, logicians will often use special symbols for the logical elements. For example, the logical element, "not" or "it is not the case that," is symbolized by the tilde (~) in some logic textbooks and by the corner sign (¬) or the minus sign (–) in others. "But" and "and" are symbolized by the ampersand (&) in some textbooks and the hat (∧) or dot (•) in others. There is no standardized way of doing this. But (as this textbook is written in English), there is something to be said for using symbols that are readily accessible on the English keyboard.

A system of variables and logical symbols constitutes a formal language, that is, a language used to represent the forms of sentences and sets of sentences of a natural language. An increasingly enhanced formal language for demonstrative logic is developed over the chapters that follow.

A language for formalizing some basic deductive demonstrations is presented in chapter 2. In chapters 3 and 5, an account is given of why forms described using this system are equivalent or not equivalent, and contradictory or noncontradictory. In chapters 5, 6, and 7, procedures for testing for validity, unsatisfiability, entailment, and equivalence are presented. In the optional chapters A-2 and A-3, these test procedures are shown to agree.

Initially, the formal language is presented on its own terms. Its symbols are only incidentally related to ordinary language. The relation between the formal language and English is discussed in chapter 4, after the workings of the formal language have been discussed in chapters 2 and 3. This may seem disorienting, but it is important to bear with it. The formal language is a power tool, designed for application to the materials provided by natural languages. Like the power tools of the construction trade, its use and limitations need to be understood before it is applied, to avoid damage and injury.

Procedural Note

It is natural to attempt to understand what is unfamiliar (the formal language) by analogy with what is familiar (the natural language), just as it is natural to think that the way to learn to use a power saw is to pick it up and start hacking away at something. An early attempt to relate formal languages to sentences and demonstrations in ordinary language can cause more confusion than illumination. The correspondence between logical systems and natural languages is not exact, in part because natural languages carry elements of meaning that basic logical systems are not designed to formalize, and in part because expressions in natural languages need to be understood in context. Those beginning the study of logic know their natural language better than they know the formal language. When they are presented with natural language interpretations of the symbols in a basic formal system, they invest the symbols with too much meaning. This causes them to misapply the formal tool, producing material damage. When the material damage is discovered, it produces upset and confusion, which are cognitive injuries. Proper advance training in the workings of the formal language can avoid both.

In chapter 4, it is shown that there are limitations to the formal language that has been developed over chapters 2–3. Some of the limitations serve as the occasion for the presentation of refinements to the system. This is done repeatedly in chapters 8–17, with the introduction of formal languages of increasing complexity, each adding to what was done by the previous one to extend the system to cases it previously could not handle.

At various points, the textbook presentation of this material is interrupted with chapters on advanced topics, labelled A-1 through A-6. These chapters are inserted at the point where enough has been said to understand the material taken up in the chapter, but they can be skipped or reserved for a more advanced course or for independent study. Results proven in the advanced chapters are often mentioned in subsequent chapters, but it is in no case necessary to understand how those results were proven. The material contained in appendices is also optional.

Technical Appendix: Elements of a Theory of Demonstrative Logic

The following concepts are fundamental and common to all the languages that will be studied. Later chapters will make them more familiar and provide opportunity to become experienced in their application. They need not be memorized or fully understood at this point. This appendix is intended as a useful summary and reference for later work.

A *sentence* is any sequence of one or more symbols that the language in question recognizes as a sentence. As such a sentence must:

(i) consist of elements included in the vocabulary of the language
(ii) list those elements in an order approved by the grammar of the language.

Two sentences are the same if and only if they consist of the same symbols, placed in the same order.

Two sentences are *different* if and only if they are not the same.

Two sentences are *opposite* if and only if they are the same but for the fact that one of them is preceded by "it is not the case that," or other words or phrases to that effect, or symbols recognized by the language in question as symbolizing words or phrases to that effect.

In addition to sentences, all systems of logic are concerned with three main groups of sentences: sets, lists, and demonstrations. They are also concerned with a special relation that can be defined in terms of sets and lists, that of a function.

(1) A *set* consists of 0 or more *different* members (for now, the set members are sentences), collected in no particular order.

A set with no members in it, called the empty set, counts as a set, as does a set with only one member in it, called a unit set.

By convention, sets are identified by being enclosed in braces with the members of the set separated from one another by commas. In the case where the set contains only one member, and context makes it clear that the member is being considered as the member of a unit set, the braces may be omitted. The empty set may be designated either by { } or by the symbol, Ø, or simply by a blank space in a place where a set would otherwise be identified. When the intention is to speak about some set or other, without specifying what members it contains, or without having any one set in mind, the Greek capital, Γ (gamma), is used. (Γ is L flipped, and L is later used to stand for a related concept, that of a list. Some flipped symbols [⊥, Γ, ∀, ∃] are so pleasingly evocative that they are used in this text even though they are not readily accessible on the keyboard.) On occasions where more than one set must be referred to, numerical subscripts or primes (′) may be employed, as below. On some (rare) occasions, the Greek capital, Δ (delta), may also be used.

A further symbol, ∪ (union), is used to represent the set that results from combining two sets or from adding a sentence to a set. Γ ∪ Γ′ is the set of everything in Γ supplemented with everything in Γ′. Γ ∪ A is the set of everything in Γ with the addition of A. Some writers will insist that only sets may be united and hence that Γ ∪ A should be written Γ ∪ {A}, where {A} is the unit set containing A. In keeping with a general policy to reduce clutter whenever no mistake can arise from doing so, *Logic Works* is not so scrupulous. Since ∪ is understood to be preceded by a set, braces may even be omitted on the left when the set is a unit set. However, they are retained to delimit the contents of sets that contain more than one member.

> Two sets are *different* if and only if there is at least one member that is in one set but not in the other; otherwise they are *the same*.
>
> One set, Γ, is a *subset* of another, Γ′, if and only if every member of Γ is in Γ′. There may, but need not be members of Γ′ that are not in Γ (so every set is a subset of itself). As a special case, Ø is a subset of every set.
>
> One set, Γ, is a *superset* of another, Γ′, if and only if every member of Γ′ is in Γ. There may, but need not be members of Γ that are not in Γ′ (so every set is also a superset of itself).

Sets can themselves be members of sets. There can be sets of sets, sets of sets of sets, and so on.

(2) A *list* consists of 0 or more *not necessarily different* items (for now, the list items are sentences) listed one after another. By convention, lists are identified by being enclosed in angle brackets with the items on the list separated from one another by commas. The ordinary sense of the term notwithstanding, a list of no items counts as a list, as does a list of just one item. In the case where the list consists of a single item, the angle brackets may be omitted. The empty list is designated by < > or by Ø or simply by a blank space. On lists, it is often only the last item on the list that matters. In that case, the English capital, L, is used to designate whatever earlier items there might be on the list. Since the appearance of L by itself indicates the presence of a list, the angle brackets may be omitted when L is used. For example, L,A designates a list that begins with the items on the list, L, and ends with A.

In addition to standing for the earlier items on a list, L may be used when the intention is to speak of some list or other, without specifying what items it contains, or what item it ends with. On the rare occasions where more than one such list must be referred to, numerical subscripts or primes (′) may be employed. On some occasions, M may also be used to designate a second list.

> Two lists are *different* if and only if the same items do not occur in the same order on each list; two lists are *the same* if and only if they consist of the same items listed in the same order.

Both conditions must be satisfied; a list, L, that consists of the same items found on another list, M, but that does not list those items in the same order as they are on M is not the same as M.

Lists can themselves be items on lists, as can sets. There can be lists of lists, lists of sets, lists of lists and sets, and so on. There can also be sets of lists.

Both sets and lists might metaphorically be described as bags of members or items. The difference is that a set is like a bean bag whereas a list is like an egg carton. The members of a set are just there, in no order, whereas each item has its own place on a list. On a list, the same item can occur two or more times in different places, whereas in a set this makes no sense. The set {1,1,2} is no different from the set {1,2,1} or from the set {2,1} since what defines a set is just what members it contains. But on a list, the list items have place relative to one another, which makes it possible for the same item to occur more than once, in different places. The lists, <1,1,2>, <1,2,1>, <1,2>, and <2,1> are all different from one another. Some of these lists contain three items, others two, and some contain the same number of the same items but differ from one another in how the items are ordered on the list.

In the examples just given, numbers make up the set members and list items. But anything (and for present purposes notably sentences) can appear in a set or on a list, as suggested by the example of a task list or a bag of groceries. Numerals are often used as names for list items or set members that it would be irksome to have to describe or name in other ways. When numerals appear in examples in *Logic Works*, they only rarely stand for mathematical objects. They most often designate list items or set members that are not worth identifying beyond being called "member/item 1," "member/item 2," and so on.

(3) A *demonstration* is a list, <Γ,A>, consisting of a set of 0 or more sentences, Γ, followed by a further sentence, A. The sentences in Γ are called the premises of the demonstration and A is called its conclusion.

Notwithstanding the oddity of doing so, a demonstration with no premises is recognized as a demonstration.

Γ is a (possibly empty) set, not a list. The list is the list of the set, Γ, followed by the sentence, A.

As noted in section 1.1 above, one form for presenting a demonstration assigns numbers to a finite subset of the sentences in Γ and lists these numbered sentences above a horizontal line, below which the sentence A is placed. *Logic Works* also uses the briefer notation, Γ / A, to represent demonstrations. When Γ is empty, / A by itself indicates that A is the conclusion of a demonstration that has no premises. (Presumably, A is such a good conclusion that it is valid all by itself.) Where appropriate, Γ may have the appearance of a set of sentences separated from one another by commas. The forward slash (/) is used in place of a comma between the last sentence in Γ and A. It serves as a conclusion indicator. Because the forward slash by itself indicates that what lies to the left is a set of premises of a demonstration and what lies to the right is a conclusion, the angle brackets and the braces are omitted.

When Γ / A is valid, A is said to be *entailed* by Γ. When Γ / A is invalid, Γ does not entail A. A special symbol, the double turnstile (⊨) is used to represent entailment. A slash through the double turnstile (which for purposes of work at the keyboard can be approximated by the bar symbol followed by the not equals symbol, |≠) represents nonentailment. Γ ⊨ A is read as "gamma entails A," Γ ⊭ A as "gamma does not entail A." Like /, ⊨ is understood to be preceded by a set and followed by a sentence. When Γ is a unit set, the braces may be omitted.

When Γ / A is valid, the corresponding set, Γ ∪ not-A, is unsatisfiable. When Γ / A is invalid, Γ ∪ not-A is satisfiable.

(4) A *function* is a special relation between a set of lists, called the *arguments* of the function, and another set, called the *range* of the function. The lists in the first set must all have the same length, and they cannot be empty. If the lists are lists of one thing, the function is called a one-place function, if they are lists of two things, the function is called a two-place function, and so on. The second set, the range, is a set of one or more *values*.

Functions are commonly notated in the form $f(L)$ is x, where f is a symbol used to designate the function, L is an argument (a list), and x is a value drawn from the range. Though the argument is always a list, even if only a list of one, it is customary to put parentheses around it, rather than angle brackets. Functions are ubiquitous in mathematics and mathematicians like to use = in place of "is." An example drawn from mathematics is +(1,2)=3, read as "the sum of 1 and 2 is 3," where + is the "sum of" function. (In the case of two-place functions, it is common to put the function between the list items. This produces the more common 1 + 2 = 3.) An example drawn from everyday life is f(Alma) is Boda, read as "the mother of Alma is Boda," where f is the "mother of" function, "Alma" is one of the arguments for that function, and Boda (who is, incidentally, Alma's mother) is the value that argument takes under that function.

The set of lists comprising the arguments of a function is based on a more remote set, called the *domain* of the function. (When the domain and the range are discussed together, the range is often called the *co-domain* instead.) The domain specifies what objects are to be used to make lists. For each function of n places (where n may be 1, 2, 3, or whatever number), the set of lists must include every list of n objects that it is possible to form from objects in the domain. When the function is a one-place function, the set of argument lists is just the set of each object in the domain. When it is a two-place function the set of argument lists contains each ordered pair that it is possible to form using (not necessarily distinct) members of the domain.

For example, consider a domain that has two members. It does not matter what the members are, so just consider the domain to be {A, B} where A and B are labels for these two members. Consider also a co-domain or range of values, say the set {T, F}. (In principle, the co-domain might include some or all of the members of the domain or it might include none. The aim at this point is to cover all bases, so nothing hangs on what is considered to be in the domain or what is considered to be in the co-domain.) Now consider a three-place function that relates (or "maps") this domain to (or onto) these values. The function must assign exactly one value from the set of values in the range to each list of three that it is possible to form from members of the domain. In the case at hand, this means that it must make an assignment of exactly one of T or F to each of the following lists:

1.24   <A,A,A>
        <A,A,B>
        <A,B,A>
        <A,B,B>
        <B,A,A>
        <B,A,B>
        <B,B,A>
        <B,B,B>

Each of these lists is an argument that the function uses to determine a value. Given the domain and the values specified, there will be as many different three-place functions as there are different ways of assigning exactly one value from the range to each list. Here is a list of the values assigned to each of these lists by a function that can be symbolized as, 1/a, and that is defined as the function that assigns T to each argument that contains exactly one A and otherwise assigns F.

1.25   1/a(A,A,A) is F
1/a(A,A,B) is F
1/a(A,B,A) is F
1/a(A,B,B) is T
1/a(B,A,A) is F
1/a(B,A,B) is T
1/a(B,B,A) is T
1/a(B,B,B) is F

There are of course many other ways of assigning exactly one of T or F to each list in 1.24. Each of them is a different function, beginning with the function that assigns T to each list and F to none and continuing through a total of 256 different ways of assigning exactly one of T and F to each of these eight lists. Were A, B, and C considered to be sentence variables and T and F to designate the values, true and false, these functions would represent various ways of assigning a single truth value to each different list of the three sentences in the domain.

Exercise 1.3

★**a.** Specify a possible domain and a range for the function, "square of."
★**b.** Specify a possible domain and a range for the function, "mother of."
★**c.** Why is "square root of" not functional over the domain of rational numbers and the range of real numbers?
★**d.** Why is "brother of" not functional over the domain and range of human beings?
★**e.** Specify a domain and a range over which the relation "spouse of" is functional.

Notes

1   Questions can set the task for reasoning or challenge it. The answerability of questions can be a topic for reasoning. Hamami and Roelofsen (2015) offer introductory comments on the logic of questions.
2   Immanuel Kant (1724–1804) identified the principle of noncontradiction as "the highest principle of all analytic judgments," which for Kant are sentences asserting the containment of predicate concepts under subject concepts. For Kant, contradictions accordingly affirm and deny that one thing falls under a concept. On this account, contradiction has more to do with relations of containment under a concept than truth and falsity. Truth and falsity are derivative from the more fundamental relation of being in or not in. Arthur (2011: 26) traces the thesis that deductive reasoning is based on "incompatibility" back to the Stoic logician Chrysippus (279–206 BCE).
3   Those who are concerned to flag cases where a term is mentioned might want to see A put in quotes. *Logic Works* is not so scrupulous. It does not employ any special means for distinguishing between *use* and *mention*, except in those cases where a reader might initially confuse an expression that is only being mentioned with one that is being used. In that case the mentioned term is put in double quotes.
4   There is a shift here between using variables to stand for linguistic entities (sentences) and using them to stand for non-linguistic entities (objects and predicates of objects). This is in order. The shift is discussed in chapter 10.
5   The use of "a" as a variable has a drawback. It is both a lower-case letter of the English alphabet and a word of English (an indefinite article). Consider, for instance the three stand-alone occurrences of the first lower-case letter of the English alphabet in the sentence, "The use of a as a variable has a drawback." In many contexts, inserting the variable in a sentence without further ado could lead a reader to confuse it with the definite article at first glance, forcing a double-take when the rest of the sentence does not fit with that assumption. Throughout this work occurrences of "a" will often be quoted to ease the reading when the letter is used as a variable. This caution is not necessary with other variables.
6   The implication is noteworthy: demonstrations are only called for when intuition fails us.

References

Arthur, Richard TW, 2011, *Natural Deduction*, Broadview, Peterborough, ON.
Hamami, Yacin and Roelofsen, Floris, 2015, "Logics of Questions," *Synthese* 192: 1581–4.
Inwood, Brad and Gerson, LP, 1988, *Hellenistic Philosophy: Introductory Readings*, Hackett, Indianapolis.

Part I
Sentential Logic

2 Vocabulary and Syntax

2.1 Introduction

Deductive logic seeks to identify the factors responsible for producing or preventing a contradiction. This is done by constructing a formal language, that is, a language that contains variables to stand for the nonlogical parts of sentences or sets of sentences, and special symbols to stand for the logical parts. The nonlogical parts are the parts that can vary without creating or eliminating a contradiction. The logical parts are the parts that play a role in creating or preventing a contradiction.

Formal languages can be constructed at various levels of specificity, incorporating more or fewer of the elements responsible for giving rise to contradictions. It is best to start with fewer. This and the following chapters start with those elements that give rise to contradictions when sentences are compounded with one another, be it in demonstrations, sets, or compound sentences. The study of these elements comprises the logic of sentences, also called sentential logic.

Some sentences are atomic, which is to say that they do not consist of parts that are themselves sentences. "Pigs have wings" is an atomic sentence. Other sentences are built up from atomic sentences using connective expressions.

A connective may be unary, in which case it is attached to one sentence. "It is not the case that pigs have wings" is a compound sentence, compounded from the atomic sentence "Pigs have wings" and the unary connective "It is not the case that …"

A binary connective connects two sentences. "Pigs have wings but they cannot fly" is a compound sentence, compounded from the atomic sentence "Pigs have wings" and a further sentence "Pigs cannot fly," using the connective expression "but." In this example, "but" connects an atomic sentence with a sentence that is already a compound of an atomic sentence, "Pigs can fly," and a unary connective, "not." "But" is nonetheless still a binary connective because it connects only two sentences, even though one of them is itself compound.

There are also connective expressions that are used to connect three or more sentences. "At least one but no more than two of Alma, Boda, and Crumb were advised by Gear" uses the higher-place connective "at least one but

DOI: 10.4324/9781003026532-3

no more than two of …" to connect the sentences "Alma was advised by Gear," "Boda was advised by Gear," and "Crumb was advised by Gear."

Exercise 2.1

State whether the following sentences are atomic or compound. If they are compound, identify their atomic components. An atomic component of a compound sentence must be a part that is a sentence in its own right. As a special case, some compound sentences may consist of one atomic component and a connective expression.

★a. Active power is what enables someone to bring about an effect.

　b. It is the soul that sees, and not the eye; and it does not see directly, but only by means of the brain.

★c. Bodies produce ideas in us by impulse, as that is the only way we can conceive bodies to operate in.

　d. Our ideas are adequate representations of the most minute parts of extension.

★e. If morality has some influence on human actions, it is right to try to inculcate it; and that multitude of rules, with which all moral writings abound, is not pointless.

　f. A succession of ideas constitutes time, and is not only the sensible measure of time.

Some connective expressions are of interest to logicians and others are not. Most systems of sentential logic include symbols for five connectives, though systems vary in which symbols are used for these five connectives.

There are more than five connectives that are of interest to logicians and many more that are not of interest to logicians. The question of how to identify and deal with all the logically interesting ones is taken up in the appendices to chapters 3 and 5.

Some systems of sentential logic, including the one presented here, also use a special symbol, $\perp$, to stand for contradiction. This is appropriate given the central role of contradiction in deductive logic (see chapters 1.4–1.6). $\perp$ has various names: "up tack," "falsum," and "bottom" or "bot" are some. "Con" is a memorable name that alludes to the precise meaning the symbol has in this textbook while avoiding troublesome associations with a sentential value and irrelevant associations with its shape. The symbol is best entered at the English keyboard with "space," "capital I," "space," all underlined: $\underline{\ I\ }$.

$\perp$ and symbols for the five chosen connectives make up the logical vocabulary of a formal language for sentential logic, called SL. The language is further outfitted with an infinite stock of variables, to stand for sentences, and a pair of punctuation marks.

Vocabulary of SL

(The commas that appear below are not included in the vocabulary; they serve to separate those items that are.)

Sentence letters:	$A, B, C, G, H, K, A_1, A_2, A_3, \ldots$
Contradiction symbol:	$\perp$
Connectives:	$\sim, \&, \lor, \rightarrow, \equiv$
Punctuation marks:	$), ($

The infinity of the stock of sentence letters is provided for by placing numerical subscripts on A's. The subscripts are considered part of the A's they are attached to, so numerals do not need to be added as separate vocabulary items. The six unscripted capitals are unnecessary. They are included to make the language easier to read and use. Six sentence letters are more than are needed for most purposes. There is something to be said for working with a logical vocabulary that uses characters that are readily accessible on the keyboard, thereby facilitating electronic submission of work. Ideally, those characters would also be mnemonic. Using just six English capitals as sentence letters frees the remainder for other purposes. (D, E, F, and I, for instance, are later used for "domain," "exists," "false," and "interpretation." J is reserved for a second interpretation in those cases where more than one interpretation is under consideration.) When this approach is not always followed, it is out of respect for conventions, because the symbol is only infrequently used in student exercises, because the best mnemonic English character has already been put to other uses, or because the symbol is especially evocative of what it stands for.

The names of the connective symbols are tilde (~), ampersand (&), wedge (∨), arrow (→), and triple bar (≡). At the keyboard, arrow can be produced with "hyphen," "right angle bracket": ->. Triple bar should be rendered with "left angle bracket," "hyphen," "right angle bracket": <->. The names for the connectives are intentionally descriptive only of the shape, not of the meaning. At this point, only the shape matters. Meaning is taken up in chapter 3.

When the sentence letters of SL are interpreted by having sentences of English or other natural languages assigned to them, and natural language connective expressions are assigned to the connectives of SL, SL can be used to represent the forms of sentences, sets of sentences, and demonstrations of natural languages. The use of SL to formalize English sentences, and the techniques for instantiating sentences of SL in English (coming up with an English sentence that is an instance of the form described by a sentence of SL) are taken up in chapter 4.

The remainder of this chapter deals just with how the vocabulary elements of SL are arranged.

Any vocabulary element or sequence of vocabulary elements constitutes an expression of SL.

In this and the preceding chapter, some symbols are introduced that do not appear in the vocabulary of SL (P, Q, R, ∅, Γ, Δ, L, M, ∪, /, ⊨, ⊢, {, }, <, >). On the following pages, these symbols are often mixed with vocabulary elements of SL. The resulting formulas are not expressions of SL. Expressions of SL consist only of the vocabulary elements listed earlier.

Even lower-case letters of the English alphabet, or upper-case letters in boldface, italics, or other fonts, or upper-case letters other than A, B, C, G, H, and K in the font used here, or upper-case B, C, G, H, and K when followed by numerical subscripts are not vocabulary elements of SL.

Ellipses and commas are also not vocabulary elements, even though they may be mixed in with vocabulary elements, as in the description of the vocabulary of SL given above. There, the ellipses indicate that "A" may have numerical subscripts that go to infinity. Commas are used to separate listed items from one another.

Exercise 2.2

State whether the following symbol sequences are expressions of SL. Justify your answers.

★**a.** ~⊥
  b. [A ∨ B]
  c. ⊥ A
★**d.** ((A ≡ B$_7$()
  e. ~)A & B(
  f. ¬ A ∧ B
  g. (***A*** ∨ C)
  h. (A ≡ (D & C))

While any vocabulary element or sequence of vocabulary elements is an expression of SL, not just any vocabulary element or sequence of vocabulary elements is a sentence. To be a sentence, the vocabulary elements need to be arranged in the right way. This way is defined by a brief system of formation rules. The rule system is recursive, which means that longer sentences can be built by reapplying the rules to sentences constructed by previous applications of the rules.

According to the rules, ⊥ is a sentence and each of the sentence letters is a sentence. The rules further specify that the result of putting ~ in front of a sentence is a sentence. For example, because ⊥ is a sentence, ~⊥ is a sentence, and thus so are ~~⊥ and ~~~⊥. The rules finally specify that taking any two sentences, putting a binary connective between them, and enclosing the result in parentheses produces a sentence. Because A and ~A are sentences, (A & ~A) is a sentence. And because rules may be applied on top of rules, the fact that ~⊥ and (A & ~A) are sentences means that ~(A & ~A) and (~(A & ~A) ∨ ~⊥) are sentences.

Meaning is not at issue at this point. Only form and formation are at issue. It does not matter whether arranging vocabulary elements in accord with the formation rules produces a form that might be taken to mean something absurd or contradictory. On the contrary, it would be a bad thing if the formation rules of SL prohibited constructing a formally contradictory sentence, since SL is supposed to identify some of the factors responsible for generating contradictions. What is invalid or unsatisfiable needs as much to be symbolized as what is valid or satisfiable.

The formation rules constitute the grammar or, in more technical language, the syntax of the language.

The syntax for SL can be more precisely formulated by using the symbols P and Q (and later, R and numerically subscripted P's) as variables for expressions of SL. Because SL is itself a language built around variables that stand for sentences of a natural language, this makes P and Q variables for variables, or what are called metavariables.

Syntax of SL

An *expression* is any vocabulary element or sequence of vocabulary elements.
A *sentence* is any expression formed in accord with the following rules:

(SL):	If P is ⊥ or a sentence letter, then P is a sentence.
(~):	If P is a sentence, then ~P is a sentence.
(bc):	If P and Q are two (not necessarily distinct) sentences, then (P & Q), (P ∨ Q), (P → Q), and (P ≡ Q) are sentences.
(exclusion):	Nothing is a sentence unless it has been formed by one or more applications of the preceding rules.

In what follows, the expression (~) is used to name the second of the formation rules given above. It is not used as an expression of SL. Similarly (SL), (bc), and (exclusion) are names of the first, third, and fourth of the formation rules.

According to the rules, a tilde may only be added to the front of a sentence, a binary connective may only be placed between two sentences, and punctuation marks may only be used in left and right pairs, placed on either side of the sentences conjoined by a binary connective. Punctuation is never placed around ⊥ or the sentence letters, and never used when adding a tilde to a sentence. ~(A) is not a sentence. ~(~A) is not a sentence. (A & (~B)) is not a sentence. And so on. The only rule that adds punctuation is (bc). For each pair of corresponding parentheses, there must be exactly one binary connective that is dedicated to that pair of parentheses. Where there is no corresponding binary connective there should be no parentheses. Where there is a binary connective there must be exactly one pair of parentheses. No pair of parentheses may be shared by more than one binary connective, no binary connective may use more than one pair of parentheses, and no pair of parentheses may appear that is not dedicated to exactly one binary connective.

Exercise 2.3

State whether the following expressions are sentences of SL. Justify your answers, following the example of the answers linked to the ★ questions. Be careful to appeal to (exclusion) when justifying the claim that an expression is not a sentence.

- **★a.** AB
- b. A~B
- **★c.** (A & (~B))
- d. (A & ~B)
- **★e.** (A & ~(~B))
- f. (A & ~(~B ∨ C))
- **★g.** (A & A)
- h. (A & ~A)
- **★i.** ((~⊥) & B)
- j. ~(⊥ & B)
- **★k.** ~(~A & B)
- l. ((A & ~(B ∨ C))
- **★m.** ((A & B & C) ∨ ⊥)
- n. ((A & B) & C ∨ ⊥)
- o. (((A & B) & C) ∨ ⊥)
- p. (⊥ → ~⊥)
- **★q.** (~((~A → A) ≡ ~(A & ~A)) ∨ (~A → A))
- r. (A ∨ (~(B ∨ C)))

Understanding the syntactic rules requires an ability to relate expressions containing the metavariables P, Q, and R to sentences of SL that instantiate those expressions. Expressions containing metavariables, like P, ~P, and P & Q, have the status of forms that various sentences of SL can share. Relating metalinguistic expressions and sentences of SL means recognizing which sentences of SL are instances of which forms.

> An *instance* is any result of replacing the variables in a form with objects that the variables could stand for, doing so in such a way that the same object is put in the place of each occurrence of the same variable.

Instances are not always direct. ~(A & B) is an instance of ~(P & Q), but so are:

2.1	~(A & A)
2.2	~(⊥ & A)
2.3	~(~A & B)
2.4	~(A & ~B)
2.5	~(~A & ~B)
2.6	~(((~B → ~G) ∨ K) & ~(B ≡ ~K))

Like all variables, P and Q could stand for arbitrarily complex sentences of SL. They could also stand for the same sentence of SL.

Exercise 2.4

1. *State whether the following sentences are instances of the form, ~P. If they are, identify the sentence that instantiates P. If they are not, say why not.*
   ⋆**a.** ~⊥
   b. ~~B
   ⋆**c.** (~C & ~G)
   d. ~(C & ~G)
   ⋆**e.** ~((~A & B) ∨ C)
   f. (~(~A & B) ∨ C)

2. *State whether the following sentences are instances of the form, (P & Q). If they are, identify the sentences that instantiate P and Q. If they are not, say why not.*
   ⋆**a.** (A & A)
   b. (⊥ & B)
   ⋆**c.** ((A & B) & ⊥)
   d. (A & ~A)
   ⋆**e.** ~(A & B)
   f. (~A & B)
   ⋆**g.** ((~A & B) ≡ C)
   h. (~A & (B ≡ C))

3. *State whether the following sentences are instances of the form, ~(P → ~Q). If they are, identify the sentences that instantiate P and Q. If they are not, say why not.*
   ⋆**a.** ~(~A → ~B)
   b. ~(A → ~A)
   ⋆**c.** (~A → ~⊥)
   d. ~(~A → ~~⊥)
   ⋆**e.** ~(A → ~(B → C))
   f. ~(A → (~B → C))

4. *State whether the following sentences are instances of the form, (~P → Q). If they are, identify the sentences that instantiate P and Q. If they are not, say why not.*
   ⋆**a.** ~(A → B)
   b. (~A → ~B)
   ⋆**c.** (~~A → B)
   d. (~(~A → B) → ~(C → A))

⋆**e.** (∼⊥ → ⊥)
  f. ((∼A → B) ≡ C)

5. *State whether the following sentences are instances of the form,* (P → (Q ∨ ∼P)). *If they are, identify the sentences that instantiate P and Q. If they are not, say why not.*
   ⋆**a.** (A → (A ∨ ∼A))
     b. (A → (∼A ∨ ∼A))
   ⋆**c.** (∼A → (B ∨ ∼A))
     d. (∼A → (B ∨ ∼∼A))
   ⋆**e.** (∼(A ∨ B) → (B ∨ ∼∼(A ∨ B)))
     f. (∼B → (A ∨ B))

6. *(This question draws on material presented in chapter 1.3 and point 1 of the technical appendix to chapter 1. Please review those sections before proceeding and consult the solutions to the ⋆ questions before attempting those that are unanswered. This having been said, the solutions demonstrate that it is possible to answer these questions without knowing anything about what* Γ, *"set,"* ∪, *or* { } *stand for. Forms can be instantiated without knowing anything about the meanings of the elements used to construct either the form or the items plugged into it. This is the most valuable lesson to take away from this exercise.)*
   State whether the following are instances of the form, Γ ∪ ∼P, *where* Γ *is a set of sentences and P is a sentence. If they are, identify the set of sentences that instantiates* Γ *and the sentence that instantiates P. If they are not, say why not. Keep the following points in mind: Braces ({ }) are put around the members of a set. No other symbols are used for this purpose. A set may contain only one sentence, in which case the braces before* ∪ *may be omitted. A set may also be empty, in which case it can be designated by* Ø, *by* { }, *or by nothing at all.*
   ⋆**a.** {(A → B), A} ∪ ∼B
     b. {(A → B), (B → C)} ∪ ∼(A → C)
   ⋆**c.** A ∪ ∼A
     d. A ∪ A
   ⋆**e.** {(A → B), ∼B} ∪ ∼∼A
     f. ∼B ∪ ∼B

2.2 Conventions

The vocabulary of SL contains just two punctuation marks, and the third syntactic rule requires the use of parentheses with each binary connective. The ensuing forest of punctuation marks can make sentences hard to read. To improve the appearance of sentences, two conventions are adopted.

   (b)   Brackets may be substituted for parentheses.
   (op) Outermost parentheses may be coloured out (they are still there).

These are conventions in the sense that they are not officially included in the vocabulary or allowed by the syntax of the language. In strictness, brackets should be understood to really be poorly drawn parentheses, and outer parentheses should be understood to really be there, written in ink too pale to see.

   (op) only allows colouring out outer parentheses if they really are outer. To be outermost the left parenthesis must be the first vocabulary element of the sentence. In accord with this definition

   2.7   ∼(A → A)

has no outermost parentheses.

   Outermost parentheses may only be coloured out if they remain outer. If a further vocabulary element is added to either the front or the back of a sentence, the outermost parentheses must be coloured back in before the addition occurs.

   In the chapters that follow, frequent mention is made of the negation, ∼P, of a sentence, P, and it is often necessary to construct negations.

> The *negation*, ~P, of a sentence, P, is constructed by applying (~) to P.
>
> *Caveat:* If (op) has been applied to P, the outer punctuation must be coloured back in before applying (~).

In accord with the caveat, the negation of A ∨ B is ~(A ∨ B). ~A ∨ B cannot be constructed by negating A ∨ B. It must be constructed by disjoining ~A and B.

~A ∨ B and ~(A ∨ B) are not the same. Sentences are not the same unless they consist of the same vocabulary elements presented in the same order. Parentheses are vocabulary elements. They are officially present even when not coloured in. Parentheses serve to define the "scope" or extension of the associated binary connective. In ~(A ∨ B) the leftward scope of "∨" is A. In ~A ∨ B, otherwise written as (~A ∨ B), the leftward scope of ∨ is ~A. This is a significant syntactic difference. It is a separate question whether there is also a difference in meaning. (In this case, there is.) For now, the only question is whether sentences are the same or different, and that question is decided by the appearance, not by the meaning.

> Two *sentences* are not *the same* unless they consist of the same vocabulary elements, presented in the same order.
>
> **Caveat:** When determining whether two sentences are the same, disregard the effect of applying any informal notational conventions.

Exercise 2.5

1. *State whether the sentences in each of the following pairs are the same. Give reasons to justify your answer.*
   * **a.** A, ~~A
   b. A & B, B & A
   * **c.** A & (B & C), (A & B) & C
   d. A → B, (A → B)
   * **e.** (A ≡ [C ∨ B]), [A ≡ (C ∨ B)]
   f. ~(A & B), (~A & ~B)

2. *Construct the negation of each of the following sentences.*
   * **a.** ~A
   b. ~(A ∨ B)
   * **c.** ~A ∨ B
   d. A → ⊥
   * **e.** A → (B → ⊥)
   f. (A → B) → ⊥

2.3 Syntactic Demonstrations and Trees

An expression can be demonstrated to be a sentence by showing how it is built in accordance with the formation rules. For example, ~A ∨ B is demonstrated to be a sentence as follows:

> Since A is a sentence by (SL), ~A is a sentence by (~). B is also a sentence by (SL), so since it has just been established that ~A is also a sentence, it follows by (bc) that (~A ∨ B) is a sentence. So, by (op), ~A ∨ B is a sentence.

This demonstration is given in the conversational style of everyday discourse. Another style of demonstration says the same things, but numbers the different assertions and separates justifications from assertions.

1. A and B are sentences (by (SL)).
2. ~A is a sentence (from line 1 by (~)).

3.   (~A ∨ B) is a sentence (from lines 2 and 1 by (bc)).
4.   ~A ∨ B is a sentence (from line 3 by (op)).

Numbering assertions is useful for referring to what was established at earlier points. As demonstrations grow longer, it can become difficult for the reader to remember all their parts. This makes it useful to have an indexing system to allow the reader to quickly look up what was established earlier.

To take another example, the entirely different expression, ~(A ∨ B), is demonstrated to be a sentence by an appeal to a different sequence of steps. Since it is tedious to write "is a sentence" and "from … by" on every line, and since after seeing one demonstration written in this way everyone should understand how it goes, an abbreviated format may be adopted.

1.   A   (SL)
2.   B   (SL)
3.   (A ∨ B)   1,2 (bc)
4.   ~(A ∨ B)   3 (~)

At line 3 (bc) is applied to A and B rather than (~) to A, setting the course for building ~(A ∨ B) rather than ~A ∨ B.

Another way of demonstrating that an expression is a sentence is by means of syntactic trees, which diagram how the parts are put together, step by step, to form the sentence. Here are syntactic trees for the two sentences discussed previously.

1.	A B	(SL)		1.	A B	(SL)
2.	~A	1 (~)		2.	(A → B)	1,1 (bc)
3.	(~A → B)	2,1 (bc)		3.	~(A → B)	2 (~)
4.	~A → B	3 (op)				

Whereas living trees grow from the bottom up, these syntactic trees are drawn from the top down. There is one branch at the top of the tree for each occurrence of ⊥ or a sentence letter, taken in order from left to right as they appear in the sentence. If ⊥ or a sentence letter occurs more than once in a sentence, they are listed more than once on the first line. The first line of the tree is always justified by (SL). If (op) is applied, it may only be applied on the last line of the tree or demonstration. The intermediate lines depict how the sentence is built from its parts. Where there are differences between sentences, their trees look different.

The trees above are simple. When sentences get more complex, it can be unclear how to proceed with the tree, and there can be different ways of doing so. If it is not obvious how to proceed, it can help to box off the parts of the sentence in the following order:[1]

1.   Draw a box around each sentence letter and each ⊥. This identifies each application of (SL).
2.   Draw the box defined by each pair of corresponding punctuation marks. This identifies applications of (bc). Where the corresponding punctuation marks are brackets it also identifies applications of (b).
3.   If a tilde is followed by a box, draw the box that contains that tilde and the box that follows it. Repeat as necessary if this creates a new case of a tilde being followed by a box. This identifies each application of (~).
4.   If the previous steps have not put the whole sentence in a box, draw the box that contains the whole sentence. This identifies an application of (op).

For example, the sentence,

2.8   ~[(~A → A) ≡ ~(A & ~⊥)] ∨ (~A → A)

can be boxed off in the following stages. Step 1 produces six boxes:

$$\sim [\,(\sim\boxed{A}\!\rightarrow\!\boxed{A}\,)\equiv\,\sim(\boxed{A}\,\&\sim\boxed{\perp})\,]\vee(\sim\boxed{A}\!\rightarrow\!\boxed{A})$$

$$\begin{array}{ccccccc}1 & 2 & & 3 & 4 & & 5 & 6\end{array}$$

Step 2 produces four more:

$$\sim[\,\boxed{(\sim\boxed{A}\!\rightarrow\!\boxed{A}\,)}\equiv\,\sim\boxed{(\boxed{A}\,\&\sim\boxed{\perp})}\,]\vee\boxed{(\sim\boxed{A}\!\rightarrow\!\boxed{A})}$$

$$\begin{array}{ccc}7 & 8 & 9\end{array}$$

and

$$\sim\boxed{[\,(\sim\boxed{A}\!\rightarrow\!\boxed{A}\,)\equiv\,\sim\boxed{(\boxed{A}\,\&\sim\boxed{\perp})}\,]}\vee(\sim\boxed{A}\!\rightarrow\!\boxed{A})$$

10

Step 3 produces:

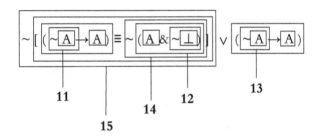

$$\begin{array}{ccccc}11 & & & 12 & 13\\ & & 14 & & \\ & 15 & & &\end{array}$$

Step 4 produces:

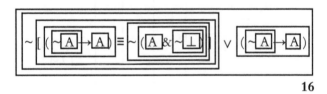

16

The boxes exhibit how the sentence's atomic parts are put together to make compounds that are put together to make larger compounds. (The atomic parts are ⊥ and the sentence letters.) When producing a syntactic tree, work from innermost boxes out to the boxes that contain those boxes, to the boxes that contain those boxes, and so on. For example, work from box 1 to box 11, from boxes 11 and 2 to box 7, from 4 to 12, from 3 and 12 to 8, from 8 to 14, and so on. When a larger box contains two smaller boxes separated by a binary connective, there can be a choice whether to start with the smallest boxes on the left side, or those on the right. For example, when constructing the contents of box 10, it is just as good to start by going from 4 to 12, 3 and 12 to 8, and 8 to 14 as it is to start from 1 to 11, and 11 and 2 to 7. Going from left to right incrementally generates the following tree for $\sim[(\sim A \rightarrow A) \equiv \sim(A \& \sim\perp)] \vee (\sim A \rightarrow A)$:

$$1.\quad A\quad A\qquad A\quad \perp\quad A\quad A\quad\text{(SL)}$$

The first line of the tree always lists the atomic components as they appear from left to right. They are sentences according to (SL). Starting with the leftmost of the innermost boxes and going out means going from the sentence in box 1 to the sentence in box 11, which is done by (∼).

$$\begin{array}{llllllll}1.\quad & A & A & A & \perp & A & A & \text{(SL)}\\ & | & | & | & | & | & | & \\ 2.\quad & \mathbf{\sim A} & & & & & & 1\,(\sim)\end{array}$$

Box 11 is contained in box 7, which joins the sentence in box 11 to the one in box 2 with an arrow, so the next step is to apply (bc) to generate the contents of box 7.

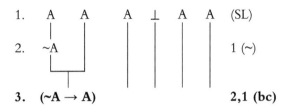

Box 7 is contained in box 10, which joins the sentence in box 7 to the one in box 14 with a triple bar. Since the sentence in box 14 is compound, the tree needs to show how it is constructed before joining it to the sentence in box 7. The leftmost of the innermost boxes in box 14 is box 3. The sentence in that box is joined to the one in box 12 with an ampersand. Since the sentence in box 12 is again compound, the tree must first show how it is constructed before joining it to box 3. This means the next step on the tree is to start with the sentence in box 4. Stepping up from it to what is contained in box 12 means applying (~):

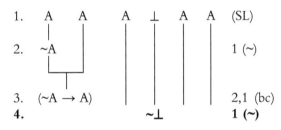

Now (bc) can be applied to the sentences in boxes 3 and 12 to generate the sentence in box 8:

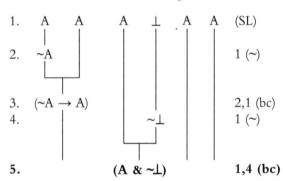

Now it is possible to go from the sentence in box 8 to the one in box 14.

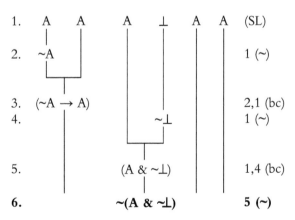

And now it is possible to go from the sentences in boxes 7 and 14 to the one in box 10. When the sentences in boxes 7 and 14 are conjoined, it must be by applying (bc), which always introduces parentheses. However, the sentence being constructed contains brackets. This necessitates a subsequent application of (b) to convert the parentheses to brackets.

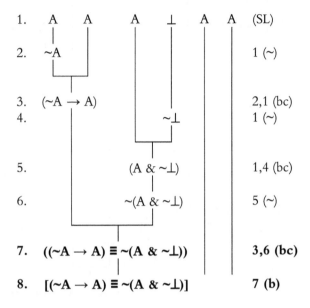

Now it is possible to go up to box 15.

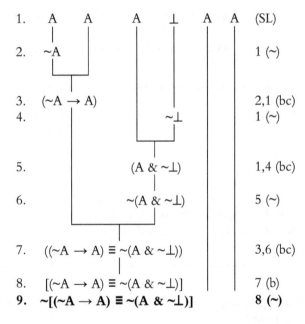

Box 15 is contained in box 16, which joins the sentence in box 15 to the one in box 9 with a wedge. Since the sentence in box 9 is again compound, it must first be built up from its components. Once this has been done over lines 10 and 11 applying (bc) and (op) completes the tree.

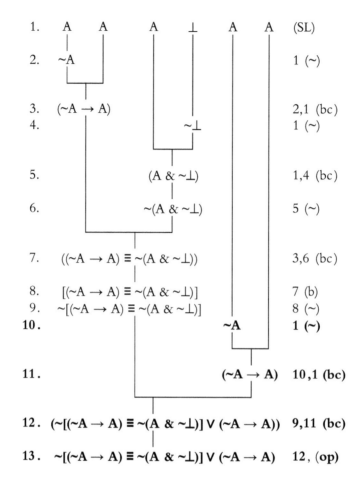

1.	A A A ⊥ A A	(SL)
2.	~A	1 (~)
3.	(~A → A)	2,1 (bc)
4.	~⊥	1 (~)
5.	(A & ~⊥)	1,4 (bc)
6.	~(A & ~⊥)	5 (~)
7.	((~A → A) ≡ ~(A & ~⊥))	3,6 (bc)
8.	[(~A → A) ≡ ~(A & ~⊥)]	7 (b)
9.	~[(~A → A) ≡ ~(A & ~⊥)]	8 (~)
10.	**~A**	**1 (~)**
11.	**(~A → A)**	**10,1 (bc)**
12.	**(~[(~A → A) ≡ ~(A & ~⊥)] ∨ (~A → A))**	**9,11 (bc)**
13.	**~[(~A → A) ≡ ~(A & ~⊥)] ∨ (~A → A)**	**12, (op)**

Because there are only five formation rules (including (op) and (b)), and their application is obvious, it is permissible to omit the line numbers and justifications and just draw the tree.

However, it is not permissible to omit the applications of (op) and (b). (bc) does not add brackets, and it never fails to add parentheses, so it would not be permissible to skip line 7 above and declare line 8 to be obtained by (bc), or to skip line 12 and declare line 13 to be obtained by (bc).

(op) may only be applied on the last line. It is used to remove outer punctuation and no punctuation has the status of being outer before the entire sentence has been constructed.

With practice, it becomes unnecessary to draw boxes to determine how to construct a tree. The punctuation marks and the positions of the tildes by themselves define where the boxes should go, making it possible to see how a sentence falls into parts and sub-parts without needing to draw boxes.

Exercise 2.6

Draw syntactic trees to prove that the following are sentences, being careful to apply the conventions when called for. Line numbers and justifications may be omitted.

★a. ⊥ → [A & ~A]
  b. ~~~B
  c. (A ≡ ~A) ∨ ~B
  d. ⊥ ≡ (~A ∨ ~B)
  e. ~[~(A & B) & C]
★f. ~([~A → B] ∨ [C & (G ∨ ⊥)]) ≡ ~G
  g. [(⊥ → ⊥) → [⊥ → (A & ~A)]]
★h. [A → (C ∨ ~C)] & [~A → (C ∨ ~C)]
  i. ~(⊥ & A) ≡ (~⊥ ∨ ~A)

2.4 Scope; Main Connective and Immediate Components; Named Forms

The concepts of the scope or extension of a connective and of the main connective of a sentence are foundational for many other syntactic concepts. Intuitively, the scope of a connective is the sentences that the connective connects to (or together). On the line of a syntactic tree where a connective is added to a sentence, the scope of the connective is the prior sentence or sentences the new connective is added to. The main connective of a sentence is the last connective to be added in the process of generating the sentence. It is the only connective to have scope over the whole sentence. More rigorously, scope is defined as follows:

- when ~ is followed by an atomic sentence (⊥ or a sentence letter), its scope is that atomic sentence
- when ~ is followed by an opening punctuation mark, its scope is everything from that mark up to the corresponding closing punctuation mark, inclusive of those marks
- when ~ is followed by a tilde, its scope is the following tilde and whatever falls within the scope of that following tilde
- the scope of a binary connective (&, ∨, →, or ≡) begins and ends with the punctuation marks added to the sentence in conjunction with that connective, excluding that connective, but including its punctuation marks

---

Exercise 2.7

1. *Number the tildes in each of the following sentences from left to right. Beside the number for each tilde, write down the sentence that falls within that tilde's scope.*

   ⋆**a.** ~⊥
   b. ~~⊥
   ⋆**c.** ~⊥ ∨ B
   d. ~(⊥ ∨ B)
   ⋆**e.** ~(~⊥ ∨ ~B)
   f. ~~~A
   ⋆**g.** ~(A & B) → ⊥
   h. ~C ∨ A
   ⋆**i.** ~(C → ~A)
   j. ~[~(~A & B) & C]

2. *Number the binary connectives in each of the following sentences from left to right. Beside the number for each binary connective, write down the sentence that falls within the leftward scope of that binary connective, followed by the sentence that falls within the rightward scope of that binary connective.*

   ⋆**a.** ~~A ≡ B
   b. ~(~A ≡ B)
   ⋆**c.** A → (B → A)
   d. (A → B) → A
   ⋆**e.** (A & B) ∨ (B ≡ C)
   f. [(A ∨ B) → C] & G
   ⋆**g.** A ≡ [(A & H) ∨ K]
   h. B ∨ [A ∨ (C ∨ G)]

The main connective of a sentence is rigorously defined as a connective with a scope that ranges over all the other parts of the sentence. Some sentences, those comprised of a single sentence letter or ⊥, have no main connective. The rest can only have one. A demonstration that no sentence can have more than one main connective can be found in chapter A-1.1.

The immediate components of a sentence are the sentences that remain after the main connective and its associated punctuation, if any, have been removed from the sentence. Since sentences can only have one main connective, and the connectives are only unary or binary, and the binary connectives conjoin two sentences whereas the unary attach to one, sentences can have at most two immediate components and as few as none (none if they have no main connective).

Each sentence is considered a component of itself, as are its immediate components (if any), and the immediate components of anything previously identified as a component. For example, the components of ~[(A → ~B) & C] are:

- ~[(A → ~B) & C]
- (A → ~B) & C
- A → ~B
- C
- A
- ~B
- B

Sentences and their immediate components are given special names depending on what their main connective is. The names hint at the meaning of the connectives. Those hints should be disregarded for now.

Named Forms

A sentence that has no main connective is an *atomic sentence*. Atomic sentences have no immediate components. In particular, ⊥ is an atomic sentence, as is each sentence letter.

A sentence with ~ as its main connective is a *negation*. Negations have the form ~P, where P is the immediate component of the negation. P is called the *nullation* of ~P.

The atomic sentences and the negations of atomic sentences are *literals*. A negation is not a literal unless its nullation is atomic. So ~~A is not a literal, though ~A and A are.

A sentence with & as its main connective is a *conjunction*. Conjunctions have the form P & Q, and the immediate components, P and Q, are called *conjuncts*.

A sentence with ∨ as its main connective is a *disjunction*. Disjunctions have the form P ∨ Q, and the immediate components, P and Q, are called *disjuncts*.

A sentence with → as its main connective is a *conditional*. Conditionals have the form P → Q. The left immediate component is called the *antecedent* and the right immediate component is called the *consequent*.

A sentence with ≡ as its main connective is a *biconditional*. Biconditionals have the form P ≡ Q.

Arbitrarily more specific forms can be described using combinations of these names: conditionals with negated antecedents, conjunctions with a first conjunct that is a negated conditional and a second conjunct that is a disjunction of a biconditional and a negation, and so on.

Alternatively, more specific forms can be pictured using metavariables for the unanalysed components. A negated disjunction has the form ~(P ∨ Q), a disjunction with a negated first disjunct has the importantly different form ~P ∨ Q, and a conjunction with a first conjunct that is a negated conditional and a second conjunct that is a disjunction of a biconditional and a negation has the form ~(P → Q) & [(R ≡ P₁) ∨ ~P₂].

The ability to *parse* a sentence is the ability to identify its main connective, its immediate component(s), the main connective of each immediate component, the immediate component(s) of each immediate component and so on up the syntactic tree to atomic components.

Exercise 2.8

State whether each of the following sentences is a negation, conjunction, disjunction, conditional, or biconditional. Then identify its immediate component or components and say whether that immediate component is atomic or is a negation, conjunction, disjunction, conditional or biconditional.

★**a.** ~A ∨ B

 b. ~(A ∨ B)

★**c.** A ∨ ~(B ≡ A)

 d. ~(A ∨ B) ≡ A

★**e.** K ∨ (~[G ∨ ~(B ≡ K)] → A)

 f. K → ~([G ∨ ~(B ≡ K)] → A)

★**g.** (K ∨ G) ∨ [~B ≡ (K → A)]

 h. ~[(K ∨ G) → [~B ≡ (K → A)]]

★**i.** [~(A & B) → (B ≡ (H &C))] & ~⊥

 j. [(A ∨ ~A) & ⊥] ≡ ~(C ≡ A)

2.5 Formal Properties

> Sameness
> No expression or sentence of SL is *the same* as any other unless it consists of the same vocabulary elements, placed in the same order.
>
> Two expressions or sentences are *distinct* if and only if they are not the same.
>
> *Caveat:* The effects of applying informal notational conventions are to be disregarded when determining whether two expressions or two sentences are the same.
>
> Negation
> The *negation*, ~P, of a sentence, P, is constructed by applying (~) to P. If (op) has been applied to P, P's outer punctuation must be replaced before applying (~).
>
> Opposition
> Two sentences are *opposites* if and only if one of them is the negation of the other.
>
> Formal Contradiction
> A *formal contradiction* is either two sentences, one of the form P, the other of the form ~P, or the sentence ⊥, or any sentence of the form (P & ~P), or any sentence of the form (~P & P).
>
> Converse, Inverse, and Contrapositive
> Given a conditional sentence, P → Q,
> > the *converse* of P → Q is Q → P
> > the *inverse* of P → Q is ~P → ~Q
> > the *contrapositive* of P → Q is ~Q → ~P.

Exercise 2.9

1. *State whether the sentences in each of the following pairs are opposites. Give reasons to justify your answer. If the sentences are not opposites, identify the true opposite of each.*

    ★**a.** ~A, ~~A

     b. A, ~~~A

    ★**c.** A & B, ~A & ~B

     d. ~(A ∨ B), ~~(A ∨ B)

    ★**e.** ~(A ∨ B), [A ∨ B]

     f. A → (B ∨ C), ~A → (B ∨ C)

2. *Construct the converse, inverse, and contrapositive of each of the following conditionals.*

   ⋆**a.** A → (B & C)

   b. ~A → ⊥

   ⋆**c.** ~⊥ → ~~⊥

   d. A → (B → C)

   ⋆**e.** (⊥ → ~⊥) → ~~⊥

   f. ~(A → B) *(trick question)*

Note

1 Not everyone has difficulty seeing how sentences are constructed. They should skip to the concluding four paragraphs of this section.

3 Semantics

Contents

3.1 Semantics for ⊥ and the Sentence Letters

Whereas the syntax for SL specifies how the vocabulary elements can be arranged, the semantics specifies the meaning of the vocabulary elements and of their various arrangements.

The sentence letters of SL are used as variables for sentences of English or other natural languages. As such, their meaning is not fixed, but varies from case to case. A case might be an example, an exercise question, or a discussion in a textbook section.

Consider all the sentences of English to be lined up in a column. In a column to their left are all the sentence letters of SL. Now imagine each sentence letter as the terminus of exactly one arrow originating from an English sentence. Each sentence letter must be pointed to by an arrow. No sentence letter can be pointed to by more than one arrow. But the same English sentences can send arrows to multiple different sentence letters. And some English sentences can send no arrows.

DOI: 10.4324/9781003026532-4

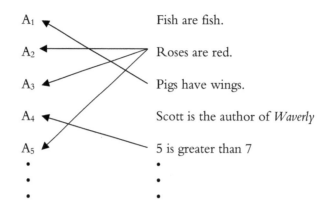

This scheme illustrates the central semantic notion of an interpretation (hereafter often designated with the symbol, "I"). An interpretation is one way of interpreting or assigning sentences of a natural language to sentence letters. There are infinitely many others. Imagine all the different ways an arrow could be drawn to each of the sentence letters in the left column from any sentence in the right column. Each way of drawing exactly one arrow to each sentence letter is an interpretation.

Another way to put this point is to say that interpretations are one-place functions in the sense discussed at the close of chapter 1. Each sentence letter is an "argument" the function assigns a value (an English sentence) to. The sentence letters are the things up for valuation or the "arguments." The sentences of English are the "values" that the function assigns to them. Any one interpretation is any one way of assigning exactly one value (English sentence) to each argument (sentence letter).[1]

While the sentence letters can be interpreted in infinitely many ways, there are two constraints on any one interpretation:

- Logic does not tolerate ambiguity. No sentence letter can have two different meanings on any one interpretation. This means no interpretation can assign two different sentences to a sentence letter. It does not hold the other way. There is nothing wrong with assigning the same English sentence to two different sentence letters. That just means that different sentence letters are names or symbols for the same sentence. The meaning of each sentence letter is still unambiguous.
- No sentence letter can be meaningless. Each must have exactly one sentence assigned to it. Again, it does not hold the other way. Some sentences can go unsymbolized. In the extreme, one sentence might be assigned to all the sentence letters, leaving all the remaining sentences unsymbolized.

Granting that these two constraints have been met, a question arises about values. There are many values that might be ascribed to sentences: true, false, both true and false, neither true nor false, indeterminate, evident, nonevident, possibly true, true to degree *x*, obeyed, disobeyed, kept, broken, answered, unanswered, answerable, unanswerable, and the list goes on. A simple place to start is with just two values, true and false. (Other values will be introduced after learning how things work with just these two.) Confining consideration to just those English sentences that can bear exactly one of these two values means placing a further (temporary) restriction on interpretations. They may only assign those English sentences that bear exactly one of the two values to sentence letters. Paradigmatically, these are assertions. But the range of English sentences up for consideration may be broadened to include sentences that do other things in addition to making an assertion. Someone who makes a promise might be said to perform the act of bringing an obligation into being. But part of making a promise is declaring that an event within the agent's control will occur at a certain time provided the right circumstances have been met, and this is an assertion about the future course of events that can prove to be true or false. Someone who issues a command or asks a question simultaneously makes a (necessarily true) autobiographical report ("I order you to …"; "I would like to ask you whether …"). That report can be picked up and anonymously reissued by others ("It is required that …"; "It is questionable whether …"), and these restatements may be true or false depending on how accurately they represent what was originally commanded or asked.

By assigning sentences that make an assertion to sentence letters, interpretations invest those sentence letters with values. A sentence letter acquires the value true if the sentence assigned to it is true, and false if the sentence is false. Often, these values are symbolized as T and F. However, it is not uncommon to use other symbols (1 and 0 are popular but are needed for other purposes in this textbook), and to associate those symbols with other pairs of opposed values, such as "switched on" and "switched off." For now, T means "true" and F means "false," but in later chapters these symbols will be extended to stand for other values and taken to be determined by other values.

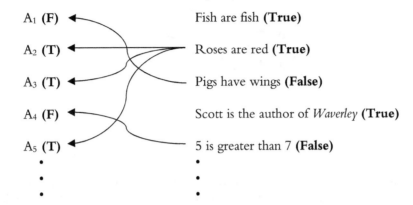

For sentence letters, truth is relative. There are infinitely many ways of drawing a single arrow to each sentence letter from one of the sentences of a natural language like English. Each corresponds to a different interpretation. The value of the sentence letters changes depending on how they are interpreted. A sentence letter is always true or false *on an interpretation*. No sentence letter is absolutely true or false.

The discussion so far has not mentioned ⊥, and ⊥ has not appeared on any of the columns of sentences and sentence letters displayed above. ⊥ is not a variable. It is a part of the logical vocabulary of SL, like the connectives. This makes it an exception. It has a meaning that is not open to interpretation. The meaning of ⊥ is F.[2]

When speaking of the values of sentences it is common to use expressions like "A is true on I," "B is true on J," "C is false on I," where A, B, and C are sentence letters and I and J are interpretations. In writing, it saves time and effort to employ a more abbreviated form: I(A) is T, J(B) is T, I(C) is F.

It is also common to display interpretations on a table.

	A	B	C	G	H	K	A_1	A_2	...
I	T	T	F	F	T	T	F	T	...

On this table the sentence letters are listed in alphanumeric order on the top row and the values I assigns to each sentence letter are listed on the bottom row. ⊥ is not listed as it is not up for interpretation.

When two interpretations, I and J, are under consideration they can be compared on the same table.

	A	B	C	G	H	K	A_1	A_2	...
I	T	F	F	F	T	T	F	T	...
J	T	T	F	F	T	T	F	T	...

The table shows that J is like I but for assigning T to B, and perhaps in other ways as well that do not make it onto the displayed portion of the table.

The difference in the assignments that I and J make to B would be explained by the fact that they assign different sentences of English to B. Perhaps I assigns "snow is green" to B and J assigns "grass is green" to it.

In logic, it is often unimportant what sentence is assigned to a sentence letter. It only matters whether it is assigned to a true sentence or a false one. It is irksome to have to make the connection between sentence letters and values by appeal to sentences. The truth or falsity of sentences is often dependent on the facts or the context in which the sentence is uttered, and that requires that these facts and contexts be known or ascertained. To get around this, logicians often skip over identifying which sentence is assigned to which sentence letter. Instead, they just consider whether a sentence letter has one of the true sentences or one of the false ones assigned to it. This is tantamount to treating the sentence letters as if they were each assigned one of the values, rather than assigned sentences with these values.

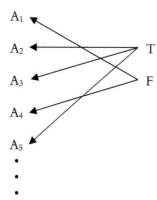

This gives rise to two ways of understanding an interpretation: as an assignment of sentences of a natural language to sentence letters of SL that results in an assignment of values to sentence letters of SL, or as a direct assignment of values to sentence letters of SL, ignoring the intermediate assignment of sentences of English. An interpretation that works in the second of these ways is called a valuation.

> A *valuation* is an assignment of values to the nonlogical vocabulary elements of a formal language.
>
> A *valuation for SL* is an assignment of exactly one of T and F to each sentence letter. Notation: I(P) is T or I(P) is F, where P is a sentence letter.

A valuation for SL is a function on the domain of sentence letters. It specifies a co-domain, V, of values, {T,F}. It takes each sentence letter as an argument and returns exactly one of T or F as value. There are infinitely many different ways of assigning exactly one of T and F to each sentence letter. Each of these ways is a different valuation and so a different interpretation. Different interpretations return different values in the case of at least one sentence letter.

Exercise 3.1

1. *Identify what value the following interpretations assign to the specified sentence letter.*
    *   ★**a.** I(A) is "The Sun is an astronomical object."
    *   b. I(B) is "The Eiffel Tower is an astronomical object."
    *   ★**c.** I(C) is "The Eiffel Tower is a terrestrial object."
    *   d. I(G) is "The Sun is the Eiffel Tower."
    *   ★**e.** I(H) is "The Sun is the Sun."
    *   f. I(K) is "The Eiffel Tower is not the Eiffel Tower."
    *   ★**g.** Is it possible for the same interpretation to make all of the assignments described in (a)–(f)? Why or why not?

2. *Identify a sentence that I might assign to the indicated sentence letter or sentence letters in order to assign the identified value. Draw on sentences that are generally well known to be true or false, not those that are controversial or that others would have to research to learn about. In cases where questions identify assignments to two or more sentence letters, consider whether one sentence could do the job for more than one sentence letter and make identifications accordingly. Consult the answered questions for further guidance.*
    *   ★**a.** I(A) is F
    *   b. I(B) is T
    *   ★**c.** I(A) is T and I(C) is T
    *   d. I(A) is F and I(C) is T
    *   ★**e.** I(A) is T, I(B) is T, I(C) is F
    *   f. I(A) is F, I(B) is T, I(C) is T

Logicians are not concerned which of the infinitely many interpretations is the correct one. It is standard practice to consider all of them.

This is not always as big a job as it might seem. When considering one sentence letter, A, the infinitely many interpretations reduce to two: the ones that assign T to A and the ones that assign F to A. After all, if the interest is just in A, all that needs to be considered is whether an interpretation assigns it T or F, regardless of how values are assigned to all other sentence letters.

Similarly, when considering two sentence letters, A and B, the infinitely many interpretations reduce to four, the ones that assign T to both A and B, the ones that assign T to A but F to B, the ones that assign F to A but T to B, and the ones that assign F to both.

When considering three sentence letters, there are 8 interpretations; four, 16; five, 32; and so on, though for practical purposes more than five will rarely be considered. The number of different interpretations is 2^n, where n is the number of different sentence letters under consideration.

When the number of sentence letters is not too great, there is a standard form for listing interpretations. The interpretations are presented on a table. On the top row of the table, the sentence letters are listed in alphanumeric order (A–K first, followed by the subscripted A's). Below this row is the appropriate number of rows for that number of sentence letters (2^n where n is the number of atomic sentences). In the rightmost column, the one for the last sentence letter in the alphanumeric order, T and F alternate for the appropriate number of rows. In the next column to the left, two T's alternate with two F's, then four with four, eight with eight, and so on out to the first sentence letter in the alphanumeric order.

The alteration is based on the following considerations: For a single sentence letter, A, there are just two kinds of interpretations: those that assign T and those that assign F.

	A
I_T	T
I_F	F

When two sentence letters, A and B, are under consideration, each of these cases splits into two. The interpretations that assign T to A divide into those that assign T to B and those that assign F to B, and likewise for the interpretations that assign F to A.

	A	B
I_{T1}	T	T
I_{T2}	T	F
I_{F1}	F	T
I_{F2}	F	F

When three sentence letters, A, B, and C, are under consideration, each of these four cases again splits into two. The interpretations that assign T to A and B divide into those that assign T to C and those that assign F to C, and likewise for the other three groups of interpretations, producing 4×2 or 8 groups:

	A	B	C
I_{T1-1}	T	T	T
I_{T1-2}	T	T	F
I_{T2-1}	T	F	T
I_{T2-2}	T	F	F
I_{F1-1}	F	T	T
I_{F1-2}	F	T	F
I_{F2-1}	F	F	T
I_{F2-2}	F	F	F

Each time a further sentence letter is added to the table, each of the previously listed types of interpretation splits into two groups, thereby continually doubling the number of listed interpretations.

Exercise 3.2

1. *Tabulate the possible interpretations for the following collections of sentence letters in standard form.*
   - ⋆**a.** $A, \perp$
   - b. C, A
   - ⋆**c.** A_1, B
   - d. G, A, C
   - ⋆**e.** C, A, A_3, B
   - f. A_1, A_4, G, A_{10}, A_2

2. *State what is wrong with the following tables of interpretations (each has something wrong with it).*

⋆**a.**

	A	$\perp$
I_1	T	F
I_2	T	F
I_3	F	F
I_4	F	F

b.

	A	B
I_1	T	T
I_2	F	T
I_3	T	F
I_4	F	F

⋆**c.**

	A	B	C
I_1	T	T	T
I_2	T	T	F
I_3	T	F	T
I_4	F	F	F
I_5	F	F	T
I_6	F	T	F
I_7	T	F	F
I_8	F	T	T

d.

	A_1	B	C
I_1	T	T	T
I_2	T	T	F
I_3	T	F	T
I_4	T	F	F
I_5	F	T	T
I_6	F	T	F
I_7	F	F	T
I_8	F	F	F

⋆**e.**

	C	G
I_1	T	T
I_2	F	T
I_3	T	F
I_4	F	F
I_5	T	T
I_6	F	T
I_7	T	F
I_8	F	F

f.

	A	B	C
I_1	T	T	T
I_2	T	F	F
I_3	T	T	T
I_4	F	F	F
I_5	F	T	T
I_6	F	F	F

3.2 Semantics for the Connectives

The connectives of SL build compound sentences that have a value that is completely determined by the values of their immediate components. Each connective does this in a different way. The meaning of each connective is given by the way it does this. $\perp$ can be treated as if it were a connective.

- $\perp$ builds an atomic sentence that is false on any interpretation
- $\sim$ builds a compound sentence that has the opposite value of its immediate component
- & builds a compound sentence that is true if and only if both immediate components are true and otherwise is false
- $\vee$ builds a compound sentence that is true if and only if at least one immediate component is true and otherwise is false
- $\rightarrow$ builds a compound sentence that is false if and only if its antecedent is true but its consequent is false and otherwise is true
- $\equiv$ builds a compound sentence that is true if and only if its immediate components have the same value and otherwise is false

Keeping in mind that truth is truth on an interpretation, the connectives are symbols for rules that an interpretation follows in assigning values to compound sentences, depending on what connective is used to build the compound. These rules can be called valuation rules.

Valuation Rules

(⊥): I(⊥) is F
(~): I(~P) is T if and only if I(P) is F; otherwise I(~P) is F
(&): I(P & Q) is T if and only if I(P) and I(Q) are T; otherwise, I(P & Q) is F
(∨): I(P ∨ Q) is T if and only if at least one of I(P) and I(Q) is T; otherwise I(P ∨ Q) is F
(→): I(P → Q) is F if and only if I(P) is T and I(Q) is F; otherwise I(P → Q) is T
(≡): I(P ≡ Q) is T if and only if I(P) is the same as I(Q); otherwise I(P ≡ Q) is F

This statement of the valuation rules is optimized for both use and concision. Though the format is different from the informal statement given earlier, the two versions come to the same thing.

(~) was used in chapter 2 as a label for a syntactic formation rule. It is reused here as a label for a semantic rule. There is no danger of confusing the two.

The valuation rules might be more expansively presented by unpacking the phrases, "if and only if" and "otherwise."

"Otherwise" means "in all other cases." At this point only two cases are under consideration, so specifying the "other" cases gives rise to a statement of both the conditions under which I assigns a T to a compound and the conditions under which it assigns an F.

(T~) I(~P) is T if and only if I(P) is F	**(F~)** I(~P) is F if and only if I(P) is T
(T&) I(P & Q) is T if and only if I(P) and I(Q) are T	**(F&)** I(P & Q) is F if and only if at least one of I(P) and I(Q) is F
(T∨) I(P ∨ Q) is T if and only if at least one of I(P) and I(Q) is T	**(F∨)** I(P ∨ Q) is F if and only if I(P) and I(Q) are F
(T→) I(P → Q) is T if and only if at least one of the following: (i) I(P) is F; (ii) I(Q) is T	**(F→)** I(P → Q) is F if and only if I(P) is T and I(Q) is F
(T≡) I(P ≡ Q) is T if and only if I(P) are I(Q) are the same	**(F≡)** I(P ≡ Q) is F if and only if I(P) and I(Q) are different

---

These rules can be further expanded by unpacking their "if and only if" clauses. An English sentence of the form, "A if B" asserts that B is sufficient for A. B's being the case is all that is needed for A to be the case.

An English sentence of the form, "A only if B" says something else: that B is necessary for A. B's being the case is one thing (not necessarily the only thing) that is required for A to be the case.

While "A if B" says that B is all that is needed for A, it does not rule out other ways of getting A than by having B. So, it does not say that B is necessary for A. By contrast, while "A only if B" says that B is one thing that is required for A, it does not say that B is the only thing that is required for A. So, it does not say that B is sufficient for A.

While "A only if B" does not mean the same thing as "A if B," it does mean the same thing as "If A then B." "If A then B" says that A is all that is needed to get B. "A" suffices for B. So, having A means having B. "A only if B" says that having A requires having B. B is necessary for A. So, having A again means having B.

In light of these points, "A if and only if B" can be seen to assert two different things:

- "A if B," which is the same as "if B, A" or "if B then A"
- "A only if B," which is the same as "if A then B"

Using terminology that was introduced in chapter 2, "A if and only if B" asserts both "if A then B," and its converse, "if B then A." It is like a conditional that goes both ways, from left to right, so to speak (from A to B), and from right to left (from B back to A).

Because the valuation rules are stated using "if and only if," they can be read "in reverse," so to speak. They do not just specify the conditions under which I assigns a T or an F to compound sentences of different sorts. They also specify what assignments I must have earlier made to the components to be able to make the assignment it did to the compound.

Unpacking the "if and only if" clauses into an "if" clause and an "only if" clause gives the following, compound to component and component to compound statement of the rules:

Compound to Component	
(for making short tables and demonstrating that there is no model)	
(T~) If I(~P) is T then I(P) is F	**(F~)** If I(~P) is F then I(P) is T
(T&) If I(P & Q) is T then I(P) is T If I(P & Q) is T then I(Q) is T	**(F&)** If I(P & Q) is F then at least one of I(P) and I(Q) is F
(T∨) If I(P ∨ Q) is T then at least one of I(P) and I(Q) is T	**(F∨)** If I(P ∨ Q) is F then I(P) is F If I(P ∨ Q) is F then I(Q) is F
(T→) If I(P → Q) is T then at least one of the following: i) I(P) is F; ii) I(Q) is T	**(F→)** If I(P → Q) is F then I(P) is T If I(P → Q) is F then I(Q) is F
(T≡) If I(P ≡ Q) is T then I(P) are I(Q) are the same	**(F≡)** If I(P ≡ Q) is F then I(P) and I(Q) are different

In the case of (T&), (F∨), and (F→), one or both of the listed inferences may be drawn.

Component to Compound	
(for making long tables and verifying that there is a model)	
(T~) If I(P) is F then I(~P) is T	**(F~)** If I(P) is T then I(~P) is F
(T&) If both I(P) and I(Q) are T then I(P & Q) is T	**(F&)** If I(P) is F then I(P & Q) is F If I(Q) is F then I(P & Q) is F
(T∨) If I(P) is T then I(P ∨ Q) is T If I(Q) is T then I(P ∨ Q) is T	**(F∨)** If both I(P) and I(Q) are F then I(P ∨ Q) is F
(T→) If I(P) is F then I(P → Q) is T If I(Q) is T then I(P → Q) is T	**(F→)** If I(P) is T and I(Q) is F then I(P → Q) is F
(T≡) If I(P) is the same as I(Q) then I(P ≡ Q) is T	**(F≡)** If I(P) is different from I(Q) then I(P ≡ Q) is F

In the case of (F&), (T∨), and (T→), one or both of the listed inferences may be drawn.

Exercise 3.3

1. *State what, if anything, follows from each of the following by each of the valuation rules. Answers to these questions require applying the valuation rules by reasoning from values of components to values of compounds. Consult the answered questions for further illustration of how to do this.*

    ⋆**a.** I(P) is T
      b. I(P) is F
    ⋆**c.** I(P) is T and I(Q) is T
      d. I(P) is T and I(Q) is F
    ⋆**e.** I(P) is F and I(Q) is T
      f. I(P) is F and I(Q) is F
    ⋆**g.** I(P) is the same as I(Q)
      h. I(P) is not the same as I(Q)

2. *State what, if anything, follows from each of the following by a* single *application of the appropriate valuation rule. Answers to these questions require applying the valuation rules by reasoning from values of compounds to values of* immediate *components. (Do not draw conclusions for components of immediate components.) Consult the answered questions for further illustration of how to do this.*

    ⋆**a.** I(~P) is T
      b. I(~P ∨ Q) is F
    ⋆**c.** I(~P & Q) is F
      d. I(~P) is F
    ⋆**e.** I(P & ~Q) is T
      f. I(~P & Q) is F
    ⋆**g.** I(~(P & Q)) is F
      h. I(~(P ∨ Q)) is T
    ⋆**i.** I(~P ∨ Q) is T
      j. I(P ∨ ~Q) is F
    ⋆**k.** I(P → (Q ∨ R)) is T
      l. I(~P → Q) is F
    ⋆**m.** I((P → Q) ≡ (Q → P)) is T
      n. I(~(P → Q) ≡ (~Q → P)) is F
    ⋆**o.** I(~[(P → Q) ≡ (~Q → P)]) is T
      p. I((P → Q) ≡ ~R) is F

3. *State what follows from each of the following by first reasoning from the given value of the given compound to the value(s) of its component(s) and then reasoning from the given value of the sentence to the value of a negation, conjunction, disjunction, conditional, or biconditional containing that sentence as one of its immediate components. Consult the answered questions for further illustration of how to do this.*

    ⋆**a.** I(~P) is T
      b. I(~P) is F
    ⋆**c.** I(P & Q) is F
      d. I(P & Q) is T
    ⋆**e.** I(P ∨ Q) is T
      f. I(P ∨ Q) is F
    ⋆**g.** I(P → Q) is T
      h. I(P → Q) is F
    ⋆**i.** I(P ≡ Q) is F
      j. I(P ≡ Q) is T

Over the course of this section, the valuation rules have been defined in two ways, first concisely, then expansively. There is a third way the valuation rules might be defined: as functions. The valuation rules can be considered in a very abstract way, one that does not even mention sentence letters, let alone sentences of English or other natural languages. Considered at this level of abstraction, the valuation rules are operations that assign exactly one of the values, T and F, to lists of the values T and F. ~ is a one-place function from lists of one value onto one of the values. In other words, it assigns exactly one of T and F to each list of one T or one F. Each of the binary connectives is a different two-place function. Each assigns exactly one of T and F to each list of two of the values. Each connective does this in a different way, in accord with its own valuation rule. ~ assigns F to the list <T> and T to the list <F>. & assigns T to the list <T,T> and F to the three remaining lists of two values, <T,F>, <F,T>, and <F,F>.

$$\sim(<T>) \quad \text{is} \quad F$$
$$\sim(<F>) \quad \text{is} \quad T$$

&(<T,T>) is T	∨(<T,T>) is T	→(<T,T>) is T
&(<T,F>) is F	∨ (<T,F>) is T	→(<T,F>) is F
&(<F,T>) is F	∨ (<F,T>) is T	→(<F,T>) is T
&(<F,F>) is F	∨ (<F,F>) is F	→(<F,F>) is T

$$\equiv(<T,T>) \quad \text{is} \quad T$$
$$\equiv(<T,F>) \quad \text{is} \quad F$$
$$\equiv(<F,T>) \quad \text{is} \quad F$$
$$\equiv(<F,F>) \quad \text{is} \quad T$$

While this abstract way of understanding how the valuation rules work is important, and will be brought up again in the appendix to this chapter, it will not be used for the time being. Functions go from arguments to values. In the case at hand, they go from previously made assignments to components to values that are then assigned to compounds. But in sentential logic, it is equally important to go in the other direction – that is, to think about what values the components must or might have in order to account for why the compound has the value it does. Even when going from components to compounds, the functional statement is more specific than it needs to be. In many cases, it is not necessary to know the values of both components in order to determine the value assigned to the compound. If either conjunct is false, the conjunction is false, regardless of the value of the other conjunct. If either disjunct is true, the disjunction is true regardless of the value of the other disjunct, and likewise for conditionals with a false antecedent and conditionals with a true consequent. If a biconditional is false, often all that matters is that the components have different values, not which is the one that gets the T.

Similar problems infect a further way of understanding the valuation rules. The effects of applying four of the five valuation rules can be represented on "characteristic tables." Characteristic tables combine the function tables given above, with tables of interpretations. Whereas tables of interpretations list all the ways of making assignments to the sentence letters, characteristic tables list all the ways of making assignments to immediate components. They then go on to specify the value that a valuation rule determines for the compound on each of those assignments.

According to (~) a negation receives the opposite value of its nullation. This is illustrated by the characteristic table for ~.

P	~P
T	F
F	T

According to (&) a conjunction receives a T if and only if both conjuncts get T and otherwise receives an F. This is illustrated by the characteristic table for &.

P	Q	P & Q
T	T	T
T	F	F
F	T	F
F	F	F

According to (∨) a disjunction receives a T if and only if at least one of its disjuncts gets a T and otherwise receives an F. This is illustrated by the characteristic table for ∨.

P	Q	P ∨ Q
T	T	T
T	F	T
F	T	T
F	F	F

And according to (≡) a biconditional receives a T if and only if its immediate components receive the same value and otherwise receives an F. This is illustrated by the characteristic table for ≡.

P	Q	P ≡ Q
T	T	T
T	F	F
F	T	F
F	F	T

Setting the different characteristic tables alongside one another provides an aerial view of how the valuation rules work. A glance shows how the assignments made by (&) differ from those made by (∨), or (≡).

P	Q	P & Q	P ∨ Q	P ≡ Q
T	T	T	T	T
T	F	F	T	F
F	T	F	T	F
F	F	F	F	T

Despite their utility for various purposes, characteristic tables are, like functional definitions of the valuation rules, underdetermined in one respect and overdetermined in another.

Using tables makes it easy to work from components to compounds: just identify the row with the given pair of component values on the table and scan across to see the value assigned to the compound in that case. But working with tables makes it harder to go in the reverse direction, since compounds can receive the same value on multiple rows, leading to multiple different conclusions about the values of the components. For example, if a conjunction is false, the characteristic table makes it false on three different rows that reveal three different pairs of values its two conjuncts could have. It seems like there are three different alternatives that have to be juggled. In fact, there is only one. A conjunction is false if and only if at least one component is false. The characteristic table does not reveal that rule. The valuation rule does.

A characteristic table for (→) has so far been neglected because it is misleading. The spatial arrangement of T's and F's on the table adds information that is not entailed by the rule. A table that does not facilitate misinterpretation would have to be incomplete.

			P → P′
row 1	T	T	T
row 2	T	F	
row 3	F	T	
row 4	F	F	T

This table puts nothing above the two left columns of values. It also makes no assignments to → on rows 2 and 3. This is not because the values are unknown or nonexistent. They are just not determined by the information that is present on the table. To fill in the blanks, it must be known which of P and P′ is the component receiving which column of values. Deciding that question and assigning T's and F's to P → P′ accordingly, and then presenting this information on a table as if it were *the* characteristic table for →, can invite the mistaken inference that the assignment is determined by which row of the table the F appears on rather than by the assignments made to P and P′ on that row. The confusion does not matter for any of the other connectives. In no other case does the order of the immediate components make any difference to the assignment to the compound.

Covering both alternatives at once can also be confusing.

	P	P′	P′ → P	P → P′
row 1	T	T	T	T
row 2	**T**	**F**	**T**	**F**
row 3	**F**	**T**	**F**	**T**
row 4	F	F	T	T

This table gives a false appearance of variety. It makes it look like the rule reverses the way it assigns T and F between rows 2 and 3. In fact, the rule always puts F in the same place, the place where the antecedent gets T and the consequent gets F. (This happens on both row 2 last column, and row 3 second last column.) The apparent variety arises only because, when P and P′ are flipped between antecedent and consequent positions, they carry their values along with them and that changes the row on which there is a true antecedent and a false consequent. The change results from a change in the place where the true component is put relative to the false component, not a change in the values of the components or a change in how (→) applies.

3.3 Semantics for Compound Sentences

The sentences of SL have two sorts of meaning: extensional meaning and intensional meaning.

> The *extensional* meaning of a sentence on an interpretation, I, is its value on I.
>
> The *intensional* meaning of a sentence is its value on each possible interpretation.

Intensional meaning is uninteresting for atomic sentences. Since an interpretation is any way of assigning exactly one of T and F to each sentence letter, and ⊥ is F on any interpretation, there could always be an interpretation on which any sentence letter is assigned a different value from ⊥ or on which any two sentence letters are assigned different values. Thus, each sentence letter is intensionally distinct from ⊥ and from each other sentence letter. This does not hold for compound sentences. Different compound sentences can have the same intensional meaning, that is, they can have the same value on each interpretation. Some can have other, noteworthy forms of intensional meaning. Extensional meaning must be considered first, however, as the range of extensional meanings determines intensional meaning.

3.3.1 Extensional Meaning

The extensional meaning of a sentence on an interpretation, I, is determined by working up from the values I assigns to its atomic components using the valuation rules. The atomic components are ⊥ and the sentence letters. The value of ⊥ is F on all interpretations. On any one interpretation, I, the value of the sentence letters is assigned by I. The value (on I) of any compound that has ⊥ or the sentence letters as its immediate components is determined by the values (on I) of those components and the rule for the compound's connective. The value (on I) of any compound that has those compounds as its immediate components is determined by their values (on I) and the rule for the main compound's connective. And so on, up to the main connective, which gives the sentence its value (on I).

When determining values on an interpretation, it is important to be able to see the architecture of the sentences of SL at a glance. This means seeing what the main connective is, what the immediate components are, what the main connective of each immediate component is, and so on down to atomic components. The ability to parse sentences of SL (to be able to identify main connectives and immediate components, and break sentences down into their component structure) is essential for further progress in the study of logic. If the parsing is unclear, drawing the architecture boxes described in chapter 2.3 should help. As a reminder, boxes are drawn by following these steps, in the order they are written:

- Draw a box around each atomic component.
- Draw the box defined by each pair of corresponding punctuation marks.
- Where there is a tilde that is followed by a box, draw the box that contains that tilde and the following box. Repeat this step as necessary when applying it puts boxes in front of further tildes.
- Draw the box containing the whole sentence, if prior steps have not already produced it.

The boxes illustrate how the sentence is compounded from its innermost parts (those in the innermost boxes) to its outermost.

Exercise 3.4

Box the parts of the following sentences following the instructions just given.
★a. ~(~A ∨ B)
  b. ~~A ∨ B
★c. ~~(A & B) → (~A ≡ B)
  d. ~[(A & B) → (~A ≡ B)]
★e. ⊥ ≡ [(~A & B) ∨ [C → (G ≡ H)]]
  f. ~[⊥ & ~(A & B)] ∨ (~A ∨ ~B)

Values are calculated by working from the innermost boxes out. The smallest boxes contain ⊥ or sentence letters. ⊥ is always F and the sentence letters have values that are given by I. Larger boxes contain either one immediately smaller box preceded by a tilde, or two immediately smaller boxes separated by a binary connective. The "right-to-left" (component to compound) version of the valuation rule together with the values in the immediately smaller boxes determines the value of the next box up. When the rule requires that only one of two components have a specified value and the component in the appropriate box has that value, only the value in that box need be considered when assigning a value to the larger box.

Exercise 3.5

Proceeding from innermost boxes out, enter values in the boxes created for the sentences in exercise 3.4 using the interpretation that assigns T *to* A, C *and* H, *and* F *to* B *and* G.

Answers for **a, c,** and **e**

Once the ability to parse a sentence of SL has been developed, questions can be answered without drawing boxed sentences. The value of a sentence can instead be demonstrated from a given assignment to the atomic components.

For example, the value of ~(A → ~B) → ~⊥ on I is determined by looking up what values I assigns to A and B. Once those values have been determined, the value of I(~B) and I(~⊥) can be determined. Given values for I(A) and I(~B), the value of I(A → ~B) can be determined. (In some cases, the value of I(A → ~B) can be determined from just one of I(A) and I(~B).) Given a value for I(A → ~B), the value of I(~(A → ~B)) can be determined. And given values for I(~(A → ~B)) and I(~⊥), the value of I(~(A → ~B) → ~⊥) can be determined. (Though this is one case where both values do not need to be known for the rule to deliver a result.)

There are many equally good ways to do this. Two are discussed here: using syntactic trees, and using skeletal semantic trees. To use the method of syntactic trees, first make the syntactic tree.

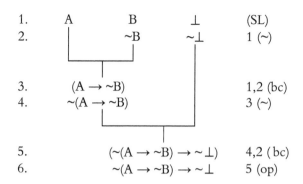

Then go to the first line and convert the atomic components that appear on that line to the assignments I makes to those components. Suppose I assigns T to A and F to B. By (⊥), ⊥ gets F on any interpretation. These can be notated as the assignments that are "given."

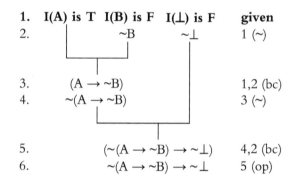

Now go down the tree applying the valuation rules in the place of the formation rules. For example, if the syntactic rule (~) is used to add ~ to a sentence, instead apply the semantic rule (~) to calculate the value of the negation given the value previously assigned to its nullation.

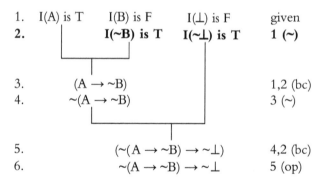

If (bc) is used to conjoin two previously formed sentences with a binary connective, instead apply the semantic rule for that connective to calculate the value of the compound given the values previously assigned to its components.

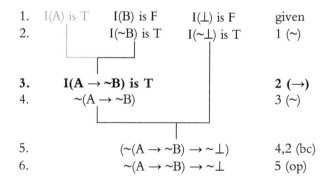

In the tree above, the left branch has been pruned and the result at line 3 has been said to follow by 2 (→), not 1,2 (→). It takes two components to apply (bc) to generate a compound sentence. But it only takes one to determine that a conditional is true, and it may be that only one of the two serves the purpose. Line 1 says that I(A) is T and that is information that is compatible with I(A → ~B) being F. It would be important to cite line 1 if I(A → ~B) were F, but it is irrelevant when other considerations lead to the conclusion is that I(A → ~B) is T. When I(A) is T, I(A → ~B) could be either T or F depending on how I(~B) turns out. But when I(~B) is T, I(A → ~B) must be T regardless of what I(A) is. Since line 2 is alone relevant to the result, it alone is mentioned in the justification, and the tree reflects that this branch alone determines the result.

After a further application of (~) at line 4, a further instance of pruning occurs at line 5.

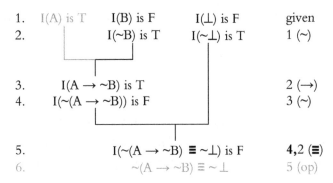

In this case, both the sentence at line 4 and the sentence at line 2 justify the conclusion at line 5. But each of them suffices by itself to justify the conclusion, without the help of the other. In these cases, the more complex of the two branches is pruned (or, one is simply picked for pruning if both are equally complex). Pruning develops the skill of identifying which way of arriving at a result requires the least work. That skill is needed for multiple tasks taken up in later chapters.

Line 6 is omitted because the value of the sentence has been determined as of line 5.

Of course, it is not always possible to prune branches. When conjunctions turn out to be true, when disjunctions or conditionals turn out to be false, and when biconditionals are given either value, both branches are needed to justify the result. A tree for ~(A → ~B) ≡ ~⊥ would have turned out differently.

1.	I(A) is T	I(B) is F	I(⊥) is F	given
2.		I(~B) is T	I(~⊥) is T	1 (~)
3.	I(A → ~B) is T			2 (→)
4.	I(~(A → ~B)) is F			3 (~)
5.		I(~(A → ~B) ≡ ~⊥) is F		**4,2 (≡)**
6.		~(A → ~B) ≡ ~⊥		5 (op)

The valuation rules guide whether to prune a path. Where a rule specifies that "at least one" component must get an assignment for an assignment to be made to a compound, it is only necessary to follow one path. Following the second path is at best redundant (if it also leads to the needed result) and at worst pointless (if it does nothing to establish the result).

The unpruned portions of the tree done earlier for ~(A → ~B) → ~⊥ define a skeletal semantic tree.

	~	(A	→	~	B)	→	~	⊥	
1.		T			F			F	given
2.							T		1 (~)
3.						T			2 (→)

On the skeletal tree, values are placed underneath the main operator of the component that receives the value, or the atomic sentence if the component is atomic. So F is placed directly under ⊥ and T under the ~ in ~⊥.

The course of reasoning sketched on the skeletal tree might be more explicitly written up using numbered lines and justifications.

1.	I(⊥) is F	(⊥)
2.	I(~⊥) is T	1 (~)
3.	I(~(A → ~B) → ~⊥) is T	2 (→)

The written demonstration is offered by laying out the sequence of inferences taken on one path of the tree down to the node where it joins a second, then going back to the top of the tree and following what appears on that second path down to the node. As illustrated above, it is not always necessary to follow each path that appears on the syntactic tree. When it is, various routes might be followed to give a demonstration by numbered lines and justifications.

Here is the skeletal semantic tree for the biconditional given earlier.

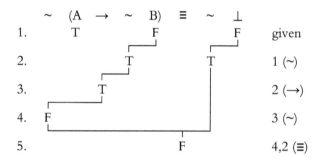

Various written demonstrations (all of the same result) might be based on this tree. One would follow the left path down to line 4, then follow the right path to line 2, and then conclude with line 5. Another would do the right path before the left. A third would go line by line down the tree, from left to right where there are two results on a line

Left path then right				**Line by line down the tree**	
1.	I(B) is F	given	1.	I(B) is F	given
2.	I(~B) is T	1 (~)	2.	I(⊥) is F	(⊥)
3.	I(A → ~B) is T	2 (→)	3.	I(~B) is T	1 (~)
4.	I(~(A → ~B)) is F	3 (~)	4.	I(~⊥) is T	2 (~)
5.	I(⊥) is F	(⊥)	5.	I(A → ~B) is T	3 (→)
6.	I(~⊥) is T	5 (~)	6.	I(~(A → ~B)) is F	5 (~)
7.	I(~(A → ~B) ≡ ~⊥) is F	4,6 (≡)	7.	I(~(A → ~B) ≡ ~⊥) is F	6,4 (≡)

Other variants will all take up the same number of lines and contain the same sentences, differing just in the order of those sentences. Any variant must, however, proceed in a downward direction through the tree, deriving what appears on lower lines from what appears on higher lines of the same path.

Skeletal semantic trees might be made even more elegant by omitting the columns of line numbers and justifications. Since there are so few rules, and their application is obvious, justifications are only required when addressing a beginning audience.

Exercise 3.6

1. *Use skeletal semantic trees to determine the value of the following sentences on the interpretation,* I, *that assigns* T *to* A *and* C *and* F *to* B. *Line numbers and justifications may be omitted, but be careful to place values under the vocabulary elements that receive those values. Use architecture boxes and make a preliminary syntactic tree if you are uncertain how to proceed. Questions have been designed so that the value of each sentence can be determined in three lines or less.*

    ⋆a. $(\sim A \equiv B) \vee (\bot \rightarrow \sim C)$

    b. $\sim C \mathrel{\&} A$

    ⋆c. $\sim(A \vee C) \rightarrow C$

    d. $\sim\sim B \vee (B \rightarrow \sim B)$

    ⋆e. $[(B \vee A) \vee (\sim B \vee A)] \rightarrow \sim B$

    f. $(A \rightarrow C) \vee (A \rightarrow B)$

2. *Use skeletal semantic trees to determine the value of the following sentences on the interpretation,* I, *that assigns* T *to* A *and* C *and* F *to* B. *Line numbers and justifications may be omitted, but be careful to place values under the vocabulary elements that receive those values. Use architecture boxes and make a preliminary syntactic tree if you are uncertain how to proceed.*

    ⋆a. $(A \rightarrow \bot) \equiv B$

    b. $\sim(A \rightarrow \bot) \equiv B$

    ⋆c. $\sim[(A \rightarrow \bot) \equiv \sim B]$

    d. $\sim\sim A \vee [\sim B \rightarrow (C \mathrel{\&} A)]$

    ⋆e. $[\sim A \vee (A \rightarrow \bot)] \mathrel{\&} C$

    f. $([(B \rightarrow A) \vee (A \rightarrow B)] \mathrel{\&} \sim(B \equiv A)) \rightarrow \bot$

While skeletal semantic trees are more elegant, and can be done more quickly than demonstrations by numbered lines and justifications, they cannot be applied to higher systems of logic, and they cannot be used to establish general principles of sentential logic. For this reason, it is important to be comfortable with the more verbose, but also more perspicacious and powerful technique of giving semantic demonstrations. With practice, it becomes possible to write up demonstrations without first constructing syntactic or skeletal semantic trees. This is an important ability to develop for working with the semantics for more advanced systems of logic.

Exercise 3.7

Use semantic demonstrations to establish the values of the sentences in exercise 3.6 on the interpretation, I, *that assigns* T *to* A *and* C *and* F *to* B. *Questions in 3.6#1 have been designed so that the value of each sentence can be determined in four lines or less.*

Answers for 3.6#**1a, c, e**, #**2a, c, e**

3.3.2 *Intensional Meaning*

After what has been said about determining extensional meaning, the task of determining intensional meaning may appear overwhelming. It requires doing all the work that needs to be done to determine meaning on just one interpretation for each interpretation. However, once the techniques of parsing sentences and applying the valuation rules to determine the value of a sentence on an interpretation have been learned, it is possible to work expeditiously, by entering assignments to connectives on what is called a long table. Long tables are based on the skeletal semantic trees discussed earlier, except the entries on the skeletal tree are collapsed onto a single line.

A long table is drawn up by first listing all the possible interpretations of the sentence letters contained in the collection of sentences under consideration, using the approved form discussed in section 3.1. The component to compound versions of the valuation rules are then used to calculate the values of compounds made from atomic components, compounds made from those compounds, and so on up. Only the results of those calculations are entered on the table.

A long table for the sentence assigned in exercise 3.6#2f is set up as follows.

	A	B	([[(B	→	A)	∨	(A	→	B)]	&	~	(B	≡	A))	→	⊥
I₁	T	T														
I₂	T	F														
I₃	F	T														
I₄	F	F														

The table above begins with A, even though B is the first sentence letter in the sentence. Sentence letters are listed in alphanumeric order, not order of first appearance in the sentences being considered.

In the columns under the list of sentence letters, all the different interpretations are listed on successive rows, in the manner outlined in section 3.1. Where there are just two atomic components, there are four possible interpretations.

Once set up, work on long tables proceeds by entering the values each interpretation assigns to the atomic components wherever those atomic components appear on the row for that interpretation. This produces columns of T's and F's under each atomic component. At this stage, F is also assigned to ⊥ wherever it appears.

	A	B	([[(B	→	A)	∨	(A	→	B)]	&	~	(B	≡	A))	→	⊥
I₁	T	T	T		T		T		T			T		T		F
I₂	T	F	F		T		T		F			F		T		F
I₃	F	T	T		F		F		T			T		F		F
I₄	F	F	F		F		F		F			F		F		F

The next step is to apply the valuation rules to make assignments to those components that have only atomic sentences as their immediate components. When → is the main connective of such a component, first look at the column of values under the antecedent and assign T to → wherever the antecedent gets F.

	A	B	([[(B	→	A)	∨	(A	→	B)]	&	~	(B	≡	A))	→	⊥
I₁	T	T	T		T		T		T			T		T		F
I₂	T	F	F	⇒ **T**	T		T		F			F		T		F
I₃	F	T	T		F		F	⇒ **T**	T			T		F		F
I₄	F	F	F	⇒ **T**	F		F	⇒ **T**	F			F		F		F

Next, look at the column of values under the consequent and assign T to → wherever the consequent gets T. (Some places may already have T's.)

	A	B	([[(B	→	A)	∨	(A	→	B)]	&	~	(B	≡	A))	→	⊥
I₁	T	T	T	**T** ⇐	T		T	**T** ⇐	T			T		T		F
I₂	T	F	F	T ⇐	T		T		F			F		T		F
I₃	F	T	T		F		F	T ⇐	T			T		F		F
I₄	F	F	F	T	F		F	T	F			F		F		F

Finally assign F in all the remaining places. This conforms to (T→) which says that a conditional gets a T if and only if its antecedent is false or its consequent is true. The same results are obtained by using (F→) as a guide. This means assigning F wherever the antecedent is true and the consequent is false. While (F→) is simpler, applying it requires looking in two places at once, which is more likely to lead to clerical errors.

	A	B	(B	→	A)	∨	(A	→	B)]	&	~	(B	≡	A))	→	⊥
I₁	T	T	T	T	T		T	T	T			T		T		F
I₂	T	F	F	T	T		T	**F**	F			F		T		F
I₃	F	T	T	**F**	F		F	T	T			T		F		F
I₄	F	F	F	T	F		F	T	F			F		F		F

When ≡ is the main connective there is no recourse but to look at both immediate components. Assign T where both are the same.

	A	B	(B	→	A)	∨	(A	→	B)]	&	~	(B	≡	A))	→	⊥
I₁	T	T	T	T	T		T	T	T			T ⇒	**T**	⇐ T		F
I₂	T	F	F	T	T		T	**F**	F			F		T		F
I₃	F	T	T	**F**	F		F	T	T			T		F		F
I₄	F	F	F	T	F		F	T	F			F ⇒	**T**	⇐ F		F

Assign F everywhere else. This conforms to (≡) which says that a biconditional gets T if and only if both immediate components have the same value. Otherwise, it gets F.

	A	B	(B	→	A)	∨	(A	→	B)]	&	~	(B	≡	A))	→	⊥
I₁	T	T	T	T	T		T	T	T			T	T	T		F
I₂	T	F	F	T	T		T	**F**	F			F	**F**	T		F
I₃	F	T	T	**F**	F		F	T	T			T	**F**	F		F
I₄	F	F	F	T	F		F	T	F			F	T	F		F

The next step is to calculate values for those connectives that have had values calculated for their immediate components. To avoid clerical errors, it helps to erase or cross out any values that are not used in the calculation. No further reference to these values will be necessary.

	A	B	(B	→	A)	∨	(A	→	B)]	&	~	(B	≡	A))	→	⊥
I₁	T	T	T	T	T		T	T	T			T	T	T		F
I₂	T	F	F	T	T		T	F	F			F	F	T		F
I₃	F	T	T	F	F		F	T	T			T	F	F		F
I₄	F	F	F	T	F		F	T	F			F	T	F		F

When ∨ is the main connective, first look at the column of values under the left immediate component and assign T to ∨ wherever the component gets T.

	A	B	(B	→	A)	∨	(A	→	B)]	&	~	(B	≡	A))	→	⊥
I₁	T	T	T	T	⇒	⇒ **T**	T	T	T			T	T	T		F
I₂	T	F	F	T	⇒	⇒ **T**	T	F	F			F	F	T		F
I₃	F	T	T	F	F		F	T	T			T	F	F		F
I₄	F	F	F	T	⇒	⇒ **T**	F	T	F			F	T	F		F

Then look at the column of values under the right immediate component and assign T to ∨ wherever the component gets T.

Formula: ([(B → A) ∨ (A → B)] & ~ (B ≡ A)) → ⊥

	A	B	B	→	A	∨	A	→	B	&	~	B	≡	A	→	⊥
I_1	T	T	T	T	T	T ⇐⇐	T	T	T			T	T	T		F
I_2	T	F	F	T	T	T	T	F	F			F	F	T		F
I_3	F	T	T	F	F	**T** ⇐⇐	F	T	T			T	F	F		F
I_4	F	F	F	T	F	T ⇐⇐	F	T	F			F	T	F		F

Assign F everywhere else. (Or nowhere else if no places are left, as in this case.) This accords with (∨), which says that a disjunction gets T if and only if either disjunct gets T. Otherwise it gets F.

Now a syntactic tree or a box diagram will show that it is not possible to determine the values under & because it has an immediate component, ~(B ≡ A), that has not yet had values assigned to it. However, B ≡ A has had values assigned to it, so it is possible to determine the value of its negation on each interpretation. (~) dictates reversing the value of the nullation.

Formula: ([(B → A) ∨ (A → B)] & ~ (B ≡ A)) → ⊥

	A	B	B	→	A	∨	A	→	B	&	~	B	≡	A	→	⊥
I_1	T	T	T	T	T	T	T	T	T		**F** ⇐	T	T	T		F
I_2	T	F	F	T	T	T	T	F	F		**T** ⇐	F	F	T		F
I_3	F	T	T	F	F	T	F	T	T		**T** ⇐	T	F	F		F
I_4	F	F	F	T	F	T	F	T	F		**F** ⇐	F	T	F		F

Now it is possible to determine the values under &. To do this, first cross out the irrelevant values and then look at the values under the left immediate component and assign F to & wherever the component gets F. In this case, there is nothing to do on that score.

Formula: ([(B → A) ∨ (A → B)] & ~ (B ≡ A)) → ⊥

	A	B	B	→	A	∨	A	→	B	&	~	B	≡	A	→	⊥
I_1	T	T	T	T	T	T	T	T	T		F	T	T	T		F
I_2	T	F	F	T	T	T	T	F	F		T	F	F	T		F
I_3	F	T	T	F	F	T	F	T	T		T	T	F	F		F
I_4	F	F	F	T	F	T	F	T	F		F	F	T	F		F

Then turn to the column of values under the right immediate component and assign F to & wherever the right immediate component gets F.

Formula: ([(B → A) ∨ (A → B)] & ~ (B ≡ A)) → ⊥

	A	B	B	→	A	∨	A	→	B	&	~	B	≡	A	→	⊥
I_1	T	T	T	T	T	T	T	T	T	**F** ⇐	F	T	T	T		F
I_2	T	F	F	T	T	T	T	F	F		T	F	F	T		F
I_3	F	T	T	F	F	T	F	T	T		T	T	F	F		F
I_4	F	F	F	T	F	T	F	T	F	**F** ⇐	F	F	T	F		F

Insert T everywhere else. This is in accord with (&), which takes & to receive T in all cases other than those where it receives F. The outcome would be the same were (T&) used as a guide to the assignment of T's and all other cases relegated to F, but that requires looking at two things at once. It is best to perfect the habit of making decisions about the value of binary connectives based on consulting just one component, in those cases where a single component determines the result: ((F&), (T∨), and (T→)).

	A	B	(B	→	A)	∨	(A	→	B)]	&	~	(B	≡	A))	→	⊥
I₁	T	T	T	T	T	T	T	T	T	F	F	T	T	T		F
I₂	T	F	F	T	T	T	T	F	F	**T**	**T**	F	F	T		F
I₃	F	T	T	F	F	T	F	T	T	**T**	**T**	T	F	F		F
I₄	F	F	F	T	F	T	F	T	F	F	F	F	T	F		F

It is finally possible to determine the value under the main connective, and so of the sentence, on each possible interpretation. First assign T wherever the antecedent gets F.

	A	B	(B	→	A)	∨	(A	→	B)]	&	~	(B	≡	A))	→	⊥
I₁	T	T	T	T	T	T	T	T	T	F	⇒	⇒	⇒	⇒	**T**	F
I₂	T	F	F	T	T	T	T	F	F	T	T	F	F	T		F
I₃	F	T	T	F	F	T	F	T	T	T	T	T	F	F		F
I₄	F	F	F	T	F	T	F	T	F	F	⇒	⇒	⇒	⇒	**T**	F

Then assign T wherever the consequent gets T (in this case, nowhere).

	A	B	(B	→	A)	∨	(A	→	B)]	&	~	(B	≡	A))	→	⊥
I₁	T	T	T	T	T	T	T	T	T	F		T	T	T	T	F
I₂	T	F	F	T	T	T	T	F	F	T		F	F	T		F
I₃	F	T	T	F	F	T	F	T	T	T		T	F	F		F
I₄	F	F	F	T	F	T	F	T	F	F		F	T	F	T	F

Finally, assign F everywhere else.

	A	B	(B	→	A)	∨	(A	→	B)]	&	~	(B	≡	A))	→	⊥
I₁	T	T	T	T	T	T	T	T	T	F	F	T	T	T	T	F
I₂	T	F	F	T	T	T	T	F	F	T	T	F	F	T	**F**	F
I₃	F	T	T	F	F	T	F	T	T	T	T	T	F	F	**F**	F
I₄	F	F	F	T	F	T	F	T	F	F	F	F	T	F	T	F

The table illustrates that the sentence is true on I₁ and I₄ and false on all other interpretations. So it is true on any interpretation on which A and B get the same value, and false on any interpretation on which they get different values. This is the intensional meaning of the sentence or what might be called the concept of the sentence. Someone who grasps the concept understands what it takes to make the sentence true or false. They can identify the sort of interpretation on which the sentence is true and the sort on which it is false.

The multiple tables given above are only for purposes of giving incremental snapshots of the stages in the development of a single table. In practice, only one table is drawn for each sentence.

Exercise 3.8

Draw up long tables to determine the intensional meaning of each of the following sentences. Highlight the column of values under the main connective for the sentence. If it is possible to summarize the intensional meaning with a sentence or a rule do so. (Consulting the answered questions will give you some idea how to do this. There are multiple correct as well as multiple incorrect ways of summarizing the intensional meaning.) The answers given to the ★ questions do not black out preliminary assignments. However, a cross out procedure is recommended to minimize clerical errors. Should work be submitted for correction, crossed out values should be legible to allow the marker to pinpoint the source of any mistakes.

★**a.** $A \to \bot$
 b. $\bot \to A$
★**c.** $A \to A$
 d. $\sim\sim A \to A$ *(double negation elimination)*
★**e.** $A \equiv \sim A$
 f. $A \lor \sim A$ *(law of excluded middle)*
★**g.** $\sim(A \ \& \sim A)$ *(principle of noncontradiction)*
 h. $(B \to A) \equiv (A \to B)$
★**i.** $(A \to B) \equiv (\sim B \to \sim A)$ *(equivalence of contrapositives)*
 j. $\sim(B \to A) \equiv (\sim B \to A)$
★**k.** $([(A \lor B) \to C] \ \& \sim A) \ \& \sim(B \lor C)$
 l. $[([A \to (\sim B \to C)] \ \& \ A) \ \& \sim C] \ \& \sim B$
★**m.** $[(A \to B) \ \& \ A] \to (B \lor C)$
 n. $[(A \to B) \ \& \ (B \lor C)] \to A$

3.4 Intensional Concepts

Exercise 3.8 shows that there are some sentences of SL that are true on each interpretation. There is a column of T's under their main connective on the long table. It also shows that there are some sentences that are false on each interpretation. There is a column of F's under their main connective on the long table. And it shows that there are sentences that are true on at least one interpretation and false on at least one interpretation. There are T's and F's mixed in the column under the main connective. These are the three main forms of intensional meaning for sentences of SL: true on all interpretations, false on all interpretations, and true on some interpretations but false on others. The first two of these forms of intensional meaning recall the informal concepts of validity (cannot be denied without contradiction) and unsatisfiability (cannot be affirmed without contradiction) that were introduced in chapter 1. However, in SL the concepts of validity and satisfaction are defined in terms of the two values that SL works with, truth and falsity. The difference is recognized by tagging the concepts with an "s."

> A sentence is *s-valid* if and only if there is no interpretation on which it is false.
>   A sentence is *s-invalid* if and only if there is at least one interpretation on which it is false.
>
> A sentence is *s-unsatisfiable* if and only if there is no interpretation on which it is true.
>   A sentence is *s-satisfiable* if and only if there is at least one interpretation on which it is true.
>
> A sentence is *s-contingent* if and only if it is true on at least one interpretation and false on at least one interpretation.

These definitions complement those given in chapter 1 by considering an interpretation to be a noncontradictory state of affairs. In SL, this means that no interpretation can assign the values, true and false, which SL declares to be incompatible, to the same sentence letter. Under this condition, the long table presents an exhaustive list of all the interpretations there are, that is, all the ways of assigning exactly one of T and F to each sentence letter. Taking these factors into account, when there is no row of the long table (no interpretation) on which a sentence is false, anyone who maintains the sentence is false would have to either break one of the valuation rules or ascribe both T and F to at least one sentence letter, thereby contradicting fundamental principles of SL. A similar consequence follows when there is no interpretation on which a sentence is true. In chapter 5, these contradictions are made explicit by a "short table" method for reasoning from the valuation rules.

Some of the sentences in Exercise 3.8 are biconditionals. A biconditional is s-valid (true on each interpretation) if and only if its immediate components have the same value on each interpretation. On some rows, the immediate components may be both true. On others they may be both false. The salient point is that there can be no interpretation on which they have different values. Now consider the two components as if they were independent sentences, but both present on the same long table (as if they were the immediate components of a biconditional with the ≡ column erased). This defines the test for what can be called the s-equivalence of two sentences. If there is no interpretation on which the two sentences have different values they are s-equivalent. If there is such an interpretation, they are not s-equivalent.

	P	≡	Q	
I_1	F	T	F	✓
·	F	T	F	✓
·	F	T	F	✓
·	T	T	T	✓
I_k	**T**	**F**	**F**	✗
·	T	T	T	✓
·	F	T	F	✓
·	T	T	T	✓
I_n	**F**	**F**	**T**	✗
·	T	T	T	✓
·	T	T	T	✓
·	...	...	...	

	P	Q	
I_1	F	F	✓
·	F	F	✓
·	F	F	✓
·	T	T	✓
I_k	**T**	**F**	✗
·	T	T	✓
·	F	F	✓
·	T	T	✓
I_n	**F**	**T**	✗
·	T	T	✓
·	T	T	✓
·	...	...	

Determining whether two sentences are s-equivalent is like determining whether a biconditional is s-valid. The two sentences are put on the same long table. A single row on which they get different values (which would be a row on which their biconditional gets F), proves they are not s-equivalent. All rows must check out (the sentences must have the same value on each row) for them to be s-equivalent.

> Two sentences are *s-equivalent* if and only if there is no interpretation on which one receives a different value from the other.
>
> Two sentences are not *s-equivalent* if and only if there is at least one interpretation on which they have different values.
>
> The *corresponding sentence* to two sentences, P and Q, is P ≡ Q. P and Q are s-equivalent if and only if P ≡ Q is s-valid. P and Q are s-nonequivalent if and only if P ≡ Q is s-invalid.

Some of the sentences in Exercise 3.8 are iterated conjunctions. An iterated conjunction is made by using an ampersand to conjoin two sentences, using another ampersand to conjoin a third, and so on, producing a sentence of the form $(...(P_1 \& ...) \& P_n$. Falsity is infectious in iterated conjunctions. If any one of the conjuncts is false, it makes the conjunction of which it is an immediate component false. That conjunction makes the conjunction of which it is an immediate component false, and so on. The whole iterated conjunction ends up with an F. The same holds in reverse. If an iterated conjunction is false on an interpretation, I, at least one of its conjuncts must be false on I, that conjunct must have at least one conjunct that is false on I, and so on down to at least one conjunct that is not itself a conjunction. It follows that when an iterated conjunction is s-unsatisfiable, and so false on each interpretation, at least one of its conjuncts must be false on each interpretation. It need not be the same conjunct that is false on each interpretation. One conjunct may be false on one interpretation, another on another. But one or other must be false on each.

What holds for the conjuncts of an iterated conjunction holds for the sentences in a set, Γ. Take an iterated conjunction and remove all the ampersands between its conjuncts and the columns of values under those ampersands. Any interpretation that assigns an F to any one of the conjuncts is now an interpretation that assigns an F to one of the sentences in the set of all the conjuncts. When no interpretation assigns a T to each conjunct, and so when the iterated conjunction is s-unsatisfiable, no interpretation assigns a T to each sentence in the set of all the conjuncts. This is what it means for a set to be s-unsatisfiable.

	(P	&	Q)	&	R			P	Q	R	
I_1	**F**	F	F	F	T	✓	I_1	F	F	T	✓
.	**F**	F	F	F	T	✓	.	F	F	T	✓
.	**F**	F	F	F	F	✓	.	F	F	F	✓
.	T	T	T	F	**F**	✓	.	T	T	**F**	✓
.	T	F	**F**	F	F	✓	.	T	F	F	✓
.	T	T	T	F	**F**	✓	.	T	T	**F**	✓
.	**F**	F	F	F	T	✓	.	F	F	T	✓
.	T	T	T	F	**F**	✓	.	T	T	**F**	✓
.	**F**	F	T	F	T	✓	.	F	T	T	✓
.	T	T	T	F	**F**	✓	.	T	T	**F**	✓
.	T	T	T	F	**F**	✓	.	T	T	**F**	✓
.	...	...	...				.	...	...	...	

Determining whether a set of sentences is s-unsatisfiable is like determining whether an iterated conjunction is s-unsatisfiable. The sentences are put on the same long table. A single row on which they are all true (which would be a row on which their iterated conjunction is true), proves the set is s-satisfiable. All rows must check out (at least one sentence must be false on each row) for the set to be s-unsatisfiable.

> A set of sentences is *s-unsatisfiable* if and only if there is no interpretation on which each sentence in that set is true.
>
> A set of sentences is *s-satisfiable* if and only if there is at least one interpretation on which each sentence in that set is true.
>
> The *corresponding sentence* to a finite set, $\{P_1,...,P_n\}$ is the iterated conjunction, $(...(P_1 \ \& \ ...) \ \&$ P_n. $\{P_1,...,P_n\}$ is s-unsatisfiable if and only if $(...(P_1 \ \& \ ...) \ \& \ P_n$ is s-unsatisfiable. $\{P_1,...,P_n\}$ is s-satisfiable if and only if $(...(P_1 \ \& \ ...) \ \& \ P_n$ is s-satisfiable.

Up to now, the values, T and F, have been considered to be on a par. However, the intensional concept of satisfaction elevates or, as it is said, "designates" truth as a value of special concern. We care whether there is an interpretation on which all the sentences in a set are true or on which the iterated conjunction of those sentences is true, not whether there is an interpretation on which all the sentences in a set are false or on which the iterated disjunction of those sentences is false. (Where unsatisfiability is concerned, having just one false set member or conjunct, that is, not having all true, is already bad enough.) Earlier, an interpretation was said to specify a co-domain, V, of values. It also specifies a subset, V_d, of V, containing "designated values." These are the values that "satisfy" sets. In SL, V_d is $\{T\}$. In other systems, V may include other values and more than one value may be designated.

Two special cases call for comment, the case of a unit set of sentences, and the case of the empty set of sentences. As noted in other contexts, logicians like to consider the unit case and the null case as just other instances of the multiple case. Accordingly, iterated conjunctions with only one conjunct are still considered to be iterated conjunctions, even though they may not contain an ampersand. A unit set, like {P}, is therefore no exception to the definitions boxed above. The corresponding sentence to {P} is P, and {P} is s-unsatisfiable if and only if P is s-unsatisfiable. The case of the empty set is not as easy to deal with. The empty set is s-satisfiable, for reasons discussed in section 5.5 and alluded to in exercise 3.9#7b.

Some of the s-invalid sentences in exercise 3.8 are conditionals that have iterated conjunctions as their antecedents. They have forms like $[(P_1 \& P_2) \& P_3] \rightarrow Q$. A conditional is s-valid if and only if there is no interpretation on which its antecedent gets a T and its consequent gets an F. When the antecedent is an iterated conjunction, there is no interpretation on which each of the component conjuncts gets a T.

Conditionals with iterated conjunctions as their antecedents correspond to demonstrations. The antecedent iterated conjuncts correspond to the premises of the demonstration and the consequent corresponds to the conclusion. Take a demonstration, form the iterated conjunction of the premises, and make that iterated conjunction the antecedent of a conditional that has the conclusion as its consequent. That conditional is s-valid if and only if there is no interpretation that assigns a T to each conjunct in the iterated conjunction (thereby making the iterated conjunction true) and an F to the conclusion. Now remove the ampersands between the conjuncts of the iterated conjunction and the arrow between the antecedent and the consequent and consider the iterated conjuncts and the consequent to be separate sentences comprising the premises and conclusion of a demonstration, all placed on the same long table. Then the demonstration is s-valid if and only if there is no interpretation on which each premise is true and the conclusion is false.

	[(P₁	&	P₂)	&	P₃]	→	Q				P₁	P₂	P₃	Q	
I₁	F	F	F	F	T	T	T	✓		I₁	F	F	T	T	✓
.	F	F	F	F	T	T	T	✓		.	F	F	T	T	✓
.	F	F	F	F	F	T	T	✓		.	F	F	F	T	✓
.	T	T	T	T	T	T	T	✓		.	T	T	T	T	✓
.	T	F	T	F	F	T	F	✓		.	T	T	F	F	✓
.	T	T	T	F	F	T	F	✓		.	T	T	F	F	✓
.	F	F	F	F	T	T	T	✓		.	F	F	T	T	✓
.	T	T	T	T	T	T	T	✓		.	T	T	T	T	✓
.	F	F	F	F	T	T	F	✓		.	F	F	T	F	✓
.	T	T	T	F	F	T	F	✓		.	T	T	F	F	✓
.	T	T	T	T	T	F	F	✗		.	T	T	T	F	✗
.	...	...	...	...	...					.	...	...	...		

Determining whether a demonstration is s-valid is like determining whether taking the iterated conjunction of its premises as antecedent of a conditional that has the conclusion as its consequent is s-valid. The premises and conclusion are put on the same long table. A single row on which each premise is true and the conclusion is false (which would be a row on which the corresponding conditional is false) proves the demonstration is s-invalid. All rows must check out (each row must have at least one false premise or a true conclusion) for the demonstration to be s-unsatisfiable.

> A demonstration is *s-valid* if and only if there is no interpretation on which each premise is true and the conclusion is false.
>
> A demonstration is *s-invalid* if and only if there is at least one interpretation on which each premise is true and the conclusion is false.
>
> The *corresponding sentence* to a demonstration, $P_1, \ldots P_n$ / Q, is $(\ldots (P_1 \& \ldots) \& P_n) \rightarrow Q$. $P_1, \ldots P_n$ / Q is s-valid if and only if $(\ldots (P_1 \& \ldots) \& P_n) \rightarrow Q$ is s-valid. $P_1, \ldots P_n$ / Q is s-invalid if and only if $(\ldots (P_1 \& \ldots) \& P_n) \rightarrow Q$ is s-invalid.

Any demonstration must demonstrate something, and so must have a conclusion, but just as demonstrations may have three premises or two or only one, so they may have none. In the case where there are no premises, (...(P₁ & ...) & Pₙ) → Q is just Q, but the rule still holds: Ø / Q is s-valid if and only if the corresponding sentence, Q, is s-valid.

This definition also "designates" truth as a value of special concern in SL. We want to see true premises combined with a true conclusion, and declare the demonstration invalid if there is even one interpretation where the premises are true, but the conclusion is not true. We have no similar concern that there be no interpretation on which all the premises are false but the conclusion is not false.

Exercise 3.9

1. *Based on the long tables drawn up in answer to exercise 3.8, say whether each of those sentences is s-valid, s-unsatisfiable, or s-contingent. Justify your answer by appeal to what appears on the long table.*

   Answers for a, c, e, g, i, k, m

2. *Use a long table to determine whether the sentences in each of the following pairs are s-equivalent. In each case, say what the table proves and why. Put both sentences up on the same table, not two different ones!*
   ★a. ~(A ∨ B), ~A ∨ ~B
    b. ~(A & B), ~A & ~B
   ★c. A & (B ∨ C), (A & B) ∨ (A & C) *(distribution of & over ∨)*
    d. A ∨ (B & C), (A ∨ B) & (A ∨ C) *(distribution of ∨ over &)*
   ★e. A → (B & C), (A → B) & (A → C)
    f. A & (B → C), (A & B) → (A & C)
   ★g. A → (B ∨ C), (A → B) ∨ (A → C)
    h. A ∨ (B → C), (A → B) ∨ (A → C)

3. *Use a long table to determine whether each of the following sets is s-satisfiable. (One long table for each set!) In each case, say what the table proves and why.*
   ★a. {A → B, B → ~C, A & C}
    b. {A ≡ (~B ∨ C), C & ~A}
   ★c. {A → (B → C), ~C → A}
    d. {A ∨ B, ~(C → A), ~B}
   ★e. {A ∨ ~A, B → B, C ≡ ~C}
    f. {A ∨ B, A → C, B → ~C},

4. *Use a long table to determine whether each of the following demonstrations is s-valid. (One long table for each demonstration!) In each case, say what the table proves and why.*
   ★a. A → B, A / B *(modus ponens)*
    b. A → B, B / A *(fallacy of affirming the consequent)*
   ★c. A ∨ B, A → C, B → C / C *(proof by cases)*
    d. A → B, A → ~B / ~A *(indirect proof)*
   ★e. A → C, B → C / C *(fallacy of incomplete enumeration of cases)*
    f. A ≡ ~B, (A & B) ∨ ~(A ∨ B) / A → C
   ★g. A, ~A / B *(ex falso quodlibet – EFQ)*
    h. C / A → A

5. *Explain why each of the following is true. Appeal to how the intensional concepts are defined in terms of values on interpretations (rows) on the long table and how the valuation rules dictate assignments to the components.*
   ★a. If a set contains an s-unsatisfiable sentence, that set must be s-unsatisfiable.
    b. If an iterated conjunction is s-contingent, the set of its conjuncts must be s-satisfiable.
   ★c. If two different sentences, P and Q, are s-equivalent, ~(P ≡ Q) must be s-unsatisfiable.
    d. If P / Q and Q / P are s-valid, P and Q must be s-equivalent
   ★e. If P / Q is s-valid, {P, ~Q} must be s-unsatisfiable.
    f. If P / ⊥ is s-valid, P must be s-unsatisfiable.

6. *Give a counterexample to each of the following claims.*

   *a. If a set contains an s-valid sentence, that set must be s-satisfiable.

   b. If a set is s-unsatisfiable, at least one of the sentences in that set must be s-unsatisfiable.

   *c. If P and Q are both s-contingent, they cannot be s-equivalent.

   d. If the sentence letters in P are different from the sentence letters in Q, P and Q cannot be s-equivalent.

   *e. If P and Q are not s-equivalent, {P, ~Q} must be s-satisfiable.

   f. If {P, Q} is s-satisfiable, P / Q must be s-valid.

7. ***a.** Why would it be a bad idea to attempt to determine whether P and Q are s-equivalent by doing two different long tables, one for P and one for Q, and attempting to determine whether they receive the same value assignments on each row? *(Hint: try to think of a counterexample: two sentences that are obviously not s-equivalent but that would pass such a test, or two that obviously are s-equivalent but that would fail such a test.)*

   *b. Why would it be catastrophic if the empty set were in fact s-unsatisfiable? *(Hint: consider the implications of the fact that any demonstration has a corresponding conditional. What does (&) say about iterated conjunctions that do not have a conjunct that is true on any interpretation? What does (→) say about conditionals that have such iterated conjunctions as their antecedents?)*

   *c. Suppose {~Q} is s-unsatisfiable. What, if anything can be inferred about Ø / Q?

Appendix Expressive Adequacy; Disjunctive Normal Form; The Lean Language

In section 3.2 the valuation rules were presented in five different ways: informally, elegantly, expansively, functionally, and on characteristic tables. Considered as functions, the valuation rules assign one of T and F to lists of T's and F's. (~) is a one-place function. It assigns exactly one of the two values to each list of one value.[3]

$$\sim(<T>) \quad \text{is} \quad F$$

$$\sim(<F>) \quad \text{is} \quad T$$

The binary rules are two-place functions. Each assigns exactly one of the two values to each list of two values. Each binary rule does this in a different way.

&(<T,T>)	is	T	v(<T,T>)	is	T	→(<T,T>)	is	T	≡(<T,T>)	is	T
&(<T,F>)	is	F	v(<T,F>)	is	T	→(<T,F>)	is	F	≡(<T,F>)	is	F
&(<F,T>)	is	F	v(<F,T>)	is	T	→(<F,T>)	is	T	≡(<F,T>)	is	F
&(<F,F>)	is	F	v(<F,F>)	is	F	→(<F,F>)	is	T	≡(<F,F>)	is	T

Exercise 3.10

1. *Represent the assignments that are made by* ***&**, ∨, ***→**, *and* ≡ *in the case where they are used to connect a sentence to itself (so, the assignments are made to* P & P, P ∨ P, P → P, *and* P ≡ P*). These are cases where* &, ∨, →, *and* ≡ *function as though they were unary connectives. Only one sentence is involved (though it occurs twice), and there are only two possible assignments to the one sentence.*

2. *When so understood, do any of* &, ∨, →, *or* ≡ *make a different assignment from* ~? *Do any of them make a different assignment from one another?*

Considered from this point of view, the valuation rules are a small and apparently arbitrary selection from among all the possible functions from lists of T's and F's onto T and F. (~) does not symbolize the only way of assigning exactly one of T and F to each of <T> and <F>. There are four ways to do this. Represented on a combined characteristic table they are:

	1	2	~	4
\<T\>	T	T	F	F
\<F\>	T	F	T	F

(&), (∨), (→), and (≡) are a similarly small and arbitrary selection from among all the ways of assigning exactly one of T and F to each ordered pair of T's and F's. There are 16 ways to do this. The four symbolized in SL are identified.

	1	∨	3	4	→	6	≡	&	9	10	11	12	13	14	15	16
\<T,T\>	T	T	T	T	T	T	T	T	F	F	F	F	F	F	F	F
\<T,F\>	T	T	T	T	F	F	F	F	F	T	T	T	T	F	F	F
\<F,T\>	T	T	F	F	T	T	F	F	T	T	F	F	T	T	F	F
\<F,F\>	T	F	T	F	T	F	T	F	T	F	T	F	T	F	T	F

There are 256 different ways of assigning exactly one of T and F to each ordered triplet of T's and F's. None of them are recognized as valuation rules or symbolized with sentential connectives by SL. As the number of places increases, the number of different functions from lists of the two values onto exactly one of the two values increases by 2 to the power of 2^n, where n is the number of values listed.

This raises the question of whether SL has enough connectives. Might it be missing something by not having more symbols for ways of connecting sentences to make a compound that has a value that is a function of the value of its components? This is called the question of expressive adequacy.

This question cannot be dismissed by claiming that English does not use expressions that compound sentences in accord with any other functions than those symbolized in SL. It does use others. For instance, the English expression "unless" can be used to make a compound sentence, "I will take the bananas unless you want them," that has a value that is determined by the values of its two component sentences in accord with two-place function #10.

I take the bananas	You want the bananas	I will take the bananas unless you want them
T	T	F
T	F	T
F	T	T
F	F	F

English can come up with expressions that connect two sentences to make a compound that has a value that is determined by any of the 16 binary functions. "Neither … nor …" builds a compound sentence that has its values determined by the values of its components in the way described by function #15. "A regardless of B" does the job of function #4 when the English sentence symbolized by A is the one that gets T on the first two rows of the table, or of function #6 when it is the one that gets T on the first and third rows. And so on. (It is an amusing exercise to come up with English words and phrases that build compound sentences that have values that are determined by the values of their components in accord with each of the four unary and 16 binary functions.) English is also capable of building compound sentences that have values that are a function of three or more components, such as "At least one but not more than two of Alma, Boda, and Crumb are in the room." (The components are "Alma is in the room," "Boda is in the room," and "Crumb is in the room." The English sentence contains them in abbreviated form.) The question of the expressive adequacy of SL cannot, therefore, be set aside on the grounds that natural languages do not compound sentences in accord with any other functions than those symbolized in SL.

To be an expressively adequate language for sentential logic, SL need not have a symbol for each of the infinitely many different ways of building a compound sentence that has a value that is a function of the values of its components. It would be enough if, given the symbols it has, it could build a sentence that is s-equivalent to any compound sentence with a value determined in accord with any of those functions. For example, ~(A ≡ B) is s-equivalent to any compound sentence that has a value determined in accord with function #10, and hence to any English sentence compounded using the strong sense of "unless" that figures in "I will take the bananas unless you want them." On any interpretation on which #10 assigns a T, ~(A ≡ B) gets a T, and on any interpretation on which

#10 assigns an F, ~(A ≡ B) assigns an F. ~(A ∨ B) is similarly s-equivalent to any compound sentence that has a value determined in accord with function #15 and English "Neither … nor …." Taking A to be the sentence that gets the first value in an ordered pair of values, and B to be the one that gets the second, A & (B ∨ ~B) is s-equivalent to compound sentences with values determined in accord with function #4 whereas B & (A ∨ ~A) is s-equivalent to those with values determined in accord with #6. B → A serves for function #3.

In fact, SL has more connectives than it needs to build sentences that are s-equivalent to any sentence that receives one of two values as a function of which of those two values is assigned to each of the sentences from which it is compounded. It can build any such sentences using just ~, &, and ∨.

To see why, consider that any function, *f*, from each list of *n* T's and F's onto exactly one of T and F can be described by a characteristic table of the sort used above to describe the four unary and the 16 binary functions. The table lists all the *n*-place lists of T's and F's on the left. On the right it makes assignments of exactly one of T and F to each list. For example, *f* might be a three-place function with the following characteristic table.

$$f(<T,T,T>) \quad \text{is} \quad F$$

$$f(<T,T,F>) \quad \text{is} \quad F$$

$$f(<T,F,T>) \quad \text{is} \quad F$$

$$f(<T,F,F>) \quad \text{is} \quad T$$

$$f(<F,T,T>) \quad \text{is} \quad F$$

$$f(<F,T,F>) \quad \text{is} \quad F$$

$$f(<F,F,T>) \quad \text{is} \quad T$$

$$f(<F,F,F>) \quad \text{is} \quad F$$

A sentence of SL that is s-equivalent to any sentence that is compounded from three components and that has values determined by the values of those components in accord with function *f* can be generated as follows. First, use the first *n* sentence letters to label the first *n* values on the list. E.g., for three-place lists, take A to have the first value on the list, B the second, and C the third. The job is then to make a sentence, P, of SL, containing A, B, and C, that has the same column of T's and F's under its main connective. (⊥ might or might not be a component of P, but exactly three sentence letters must be, otherwise the table will not have the right number of rows.)

f( ) is		A	B	C	P
$f(<T,T,T>)$ is	**F**	<T	T	T>	**F**
$f(<T,T,F>)$ is	**F**	<T	T	F>	**F**
$f(<T,F,T>)$ is	**F**	<T	F	T>	**F**
$f(<T,F,F>)$ is	**T**	<T	F	F>	**T**
$f(<F,T,T>)$ is	**F**	<F	T	T>	**F**
$f(<F,T,F>)$ is	**F**	<F	T	F>	**F**
$f(<F,F,T>)$ is	**T**	<F	F	T>	**T**
$f(<F,F,F>)$ is	**F**	<F	F	F>	**F**

Finding a sentence of SL that has the same column of T's and F's under its main connective that P does is not a merely academic exercise. The function, *f*, is named by an English connective expression that can be used to construct a compound English sentence. An example would be "Exactly one of Alma and Crumb out of all of Alma, Boda, and Crumb are in the room," which compounds the sentences, "Alma is in the room," "Boda is in the room," and "Crumb is in the room." That English sentence is true when only Alma is in the room, and true when only Crumb is in the room, and false in all other cases, reflecting the assignments made by function *f* in these cases. Because English can compound sentences with "exactly one of A and C out of all of A, B, and C," and such sentences could figure in reasoning that is valid solely in virtue of the meaning of that expression, SL had better be able to formalize sentences compounded using that expression, on pain of not being adequate to capture all of sentential logic. In this case, at least, it can.

The procedure for coming up with such a sentence is best explained over three stages.

Stage 1

The procedure works with the notions of an iterated conjunction and an iterated disjunction. As noted in section 3.4, an iterated conjunction is made by adding conjuncts to conjuncts to produce a sentence of the form

3.1 $(...(A_1 \& ...) \& A_n$

An iterated disjunction is made by adding disjuncts to disjuncts to produce a sentence of the form

3.2 $(...((A_1 \vee ...) \vee A_n$

As noted in section 3.4, falsity is infectious in iterated conjunctions. If any one conjunct is false, it makes the conjunction of which it is an immediate component false, that conjunction makes the conjunction of which it is an immediate component false, and so on up to the main connective. Truth is similarly infectious in iterated disjunctions.

Stage 2

As a reminder, the term literal, originally defined in chapter 2, is used to refer to those sentences that are either atomic or are negations of atomic sentences. A "literal" conjunct of an iterated conjunction is either an atomic conjunct or the negation of an atomic conjunct.

Any interpretation of the first n sentence letters, I, can be described by an iterated conjunction that has as its literal conjuncts those sentence letters that receive a T on I and those negations of atomic sentences that receive an F on I. This iterated conjunction is true on I and false on all other interpretations of the first n sentence letters. Such a sentence is called a characteristic sentence.

For example, consider the interpretation, I, that assigns T to A, B, and C and F to G and H. I is described by the iterated conjunction that has A, B, C, ~G, and ~H as its literal conjuncts (A, B, and C because I assigns T to each of them; ~G and ~H because I assigns F to G and H).

3.3 $(((A \& B) \& C) \& {\sim}G) \& {\sim}H$

Where there are five atomic components there are $2^5 = 32$ different interpretations. $(((A \& B) \& C) \& {\sim}G) \& {\sim}H$ has the unique property of being true on and only on I. Any of the other interpretations must differ from I by assigning a different value to at least one of A, B, C, G, or H. But in that case, the other interpretation must make at least one of the conjuncts of the iterated conjunction false. Because falsity is infectious in iterated conjunctions, the whole sentence will be false on that interpretation.

This is the case for any interpretation of any finite number of atomic sentences. The characteristic sentence for that interpretation is true only on that interpretation and false on all the alternatives.

Exercise 3.11

Following the example that has just been given, form iterated conjunctions of literals that describe the following assignments to A, B, C, G, *and* H.

⋆**a.** T to A, B, C, G, and H
  b. T to A, C, H, and F to B and G
⋆**c.** T to B and G, and F to A, C, H
  d. F to all of A–H
⋆**e.** F to A and G; T to B, C, and H
  f. F to A, B, H; T to C and G

Stage 3

So far, the discussion has focused on interpretations of literals. Now consider the assignments those interpretations make to compound sentences.

As an example, consider how to make a sentence compounded from two sentence letters that does the work of two-place function #10 on the table of two-place functions given earlier. The characteristic table is:

	A	B	10
I_1	<T	T>	F
I_2	<T	F>	T
I_3	<F	T>	T
I_4	<F	F>	F

When A and B are used to head off the two columns of values on the left, the list of each two-place list of values is converted to a list of the possible interpretations of A and B. Each of I_1–I_4 is described by its own characteristic sentence. I_1 is described by A & B, I_2 by A & ~B, and so on. Consider just those interpretations on which a T is assigned in the rightmost column. They are I_2 and I_3. The characteristic sentences that describe those interpretations, A & ~B and ~A & B are true only on I_2 and I_3 respectively, and false on all other interpretations.

Now consider the iterated disjunction of these two sentences

3.4   (A & ~B) ∨ (~A & B)

Because truth is infectious in iterated disjunctions, 3.4 is true on either I_2 or I_3, but false on any other interpretation. It therefore has the same column of T's and F's under its main connective (∨) that function #10 assigns.

In general, because a characteristic sentence is true on and only on the interpretation for which it was written, and an iterated disjunction of characteristic sentences is true on and only on any of the interpretations described by the characteristic sentences it disjoins and false on all others, an iterated disjunction of characteristic sentences can be written that will receive the values assigned by *almost* any *n*-place function.

The one exception is the case where the interpretation assigns only F's. The instructions so far given specify making an iterated disjunction of the characteristic sentences describing *n*-place lists of values that are assigned a T. But in this case no T's are assigned.

In all such cases, ⊥ can serve as a sentence of SL that receives the values assigned by the function. A long table for ⊥ accommodates any number of rows.

With this final addendum, it is established that there is a sentence of SL that has the values determined by any function from the values of its components onto T and F. SL is therefore adequate to formalize any sentence of English or any other language that has been compounded using any expression that is similarly functional. It can do so, moreover, using sentences that contain just tilde, ampersand, wedge, the sentence letters, punctuation marks, and, in the exceptional cases, ⊥.

The iterated disjunctions of iterated conjunctions of literals produced by the procedure outlined above are said to be in "perfect" disjunctive normal form or "perfect dnf." They are also called "perfect dnf's." To be "in dnf" a sentence must either be ⊥, or a sentence letter, or a literal, or an iterated conjunction of literals, or an iterated disjunction of iterated conjunctions of literals. (The first four clauses of this definition are redundant for a reason given earlier: an iterated disjunction with just one disjunct is still an iterated disjunction, and an iterated conjunction with just one conjunct is still an iterated conjunction. ~A is simultaneously a literal, an iterated conjunction of literals, an iterated disjunction of iterated conjunctions, and an iterated disjunction of literals.)

To be in perfect dnf the disjuncts must be in "long table order" (the order they are defined on the long table from the top down), the literals in each disjunct must be in alphanumeric order, any atomic sentence that is present in any one disjunct must be present (in negated or unnegated form) in each other disjunct, no literal can be repeated within any one disjunct, and no disjunct can occur more than once. A ∨ B is in dnf (because it is a disjunction of iterated conjunctions that contain just one literal, but not in perfect dnf (because the disjuncts do not contain occurrences of the same sentence letters). The perfect dnf for A ∨ B is (A & B) ∨ (A & ~B) ∨ (~A & B).

Exercise 3.12

Give the perfect dnf that has the same column of values under its main connective as the functions identified by the following tables.

★a.

A	B	
T	T	F
T	F	T
F	T	F
F	F	F

b.

A	B	
T	T	T
T	F	F
F	T	T
F	F	T

★c.

A	B	
T	T	F
T	F	F
F	T	F
F	F	F

d.

A	B	C	
T	T	T	T
T	T	F	F
T	F	T	T
T	F	F	F
F	T	T	T
F	T	F	F
F	F	T	T
F	F	F	F

★e.

A	B	C	
T	T	T	T
T	T	F	T
T	F	T	F
T	F	F	F
F	T	T	F
F	T	F	F
F	F	T	T
F	F	F	T

f.

A	B	C	
T	T	T	F
T	T	F	F
T	F	T	F
T	F	F	F
F	T	T	F
F	T	F	F
F	F	T	F
F	F	F	F

SL would be expressively adequate even without the ~, &, and ∨ connectives. All it needs is →. For any negation, conjunction, or disjunction, there is an s-equivalent sentence of SL that uses only →, ⊥, and the sentence letters and punctuation marks.

Any sentence of the form	is s-equivalent to
~P	P → ⊥
P & Q	[P → (Q → ⊥)] → ⊥
P ∨ Q	(P → ⊥) → Q

Any instance of these equivalences can be verified using a long table.

This means that any dnf can be rewritten as an s-equivalent sentence that uses just the → connective. → is therefore the only connective SL needs to be expressively complete. The other connectives need not have been included in the vocabulary. Everything that is done could be done with s-equivalent sentences that use just the → connective. Admittedly, such sentences would be considerably longer. However, there are certain purposes for which it would be better not to recognize any more connectives than are necessary. This makes it useful to introduce what will be called the lean language. The lean language for SL drops the ~, &, ∨, and ≡ connectives from the list of vocabulary elements. It instead expands the list of informal notational conventions to declare that sentences of the form (P → ⊥) may be abbreviated as ~P, that sentences of the form ((P → (Q → ⊥)) → ⊥) may be abbreviated as (P & Q), that sentences of the form ((P → ⊥) → Q) may be abbreviated as (P ∨ Q), and that sentences of the form (((P → Q) → ((Q → P) → ⊥)) → ⊥) may be abbreviated as (P ≡ Q).

The lean language can get by with only the arrow connective because ⊥ is in the language. Not all systems of sentential logic use ⊥. There are other ways of formulating a lean language. As can be verified by using a long table, P ≡ Q and (P → Q) & (Q → P) are s-equivalent. The triple bar could therefore be omitted from the vocabulary and all sentences containing triple bars could be replaced with equivalent sentences using arrow and ampersand.

P → Q is likewise s-equivalent to ~P ∨ Q and to ~(P & ~Q), so all conditionals could be dropped from the language in favour of using disjunctions with negated first disjuncts or negated conjunctions of the antecedent and the negation of the consequent in their place.

Again, P & Q is s-equivalent to ~(~P ∨ ~Q) and P ∨ Q is s-equivalent to ~(~P & ~Q), so conjunctions could all be replaced with equivalent disjunctions or disjunctions with equivalent conjuncts.

The other connectives could not be omitted in favour of &. Because falsity is infectious in compounds that contain only ampersands, no sentence compounded using only ampersands gets a T when any of its atomic components gets an F, so none can do the job of any function that assigns a T to a list of values that contains one or more F's (as ~ does). Similarly, because truth is infectious in compounds that contain only wedges, no sentence compounded using only wedges gets an F when any of its atomic components gets a T, so none can do the job of any function that assigns an F to a list of values that contains one or more T's (as ~ again does). The same holds for any combination of triple bars, ⊥, and sentence letters, but the result is not so easily demonstrated. (It must wait for exercise A-1.2#2.) Even sentences built from any combination of &, ∨, →, ≡ and sentence letters (without ~ or ⊥) cannot express all the functions. (This is another difficult result to establish. It must wait for exercise A-1.2#1.)

To be expressively adequate, SL need only contain ~ and & (without ⊥), or ~ and ∨ (without ⊥), or → and ⊥. (≡ and ~ could not do the job alone, for reasons given in exercise A-1.2#2c.) Including all five connectives is not necessary for the expressive adequacy of SL. They are included in the vocabulary because they represent connectives that perform functions that logicians consider to be particularly important: making a dnf and making the corresponding sentences for a demonstration, a set, or an s-equivalent pair.

As a curiosity, even if ⊥ were not included in the language, it would be possible to use just one connective for all of sentential logic, though none of those symbolized in SL could do that job. There are exactly two others that will, often symbolized by the up arrow (↑) and the down arrow (↓). They are sometimes called nand and nor, respectively. "Nor" abbreviates "not-or" or ~(P ∨ Q), and "nand" abbreviates "not-and" or ~(P & Q).

Valuation Rules for ↑ and ↓

(↑):   I(P ↑ Q) is T if and only if at least one of I(P) and I(Q) is F; otherwise I(P ↑ Q) is F

(↓):   I(P ↓ Q) is T if and only if I(P) and I(Q) are F; otherwise I(P ↓ Q) is F

Exercise 3.13

1. *Give the characteristic tables for (↑) and (↓). Which functions are these on the list of 16 two-place functions given earlier?*

2.

   ⋆**a.** Give a sentence containing just A and ↑ that is s-equivalent to ~A.

   b. Give a sentence containing just A and ↓ that is s-equivalent to ~A.

   ⋆**c.** Give a sentence containing just A, B, and ↑ that is s-equivalent to A & B.

   d. Give a sentence containing just A, B, and ↓ that is s-equivalent to A & B.

   ⋆**e.** Give a sentence containing just A, B, and ↑ that is s-equivalent to A ∨ B.

   f. Give a sentence containing just A, B, and ↓ that is s-equivalent to A ∨ B.

Exercise 3.13#2 shows that SL would be expressively adequate even without ⊥, ~, ∨, &, or →, provided it contains one of nand or nor. This is because SL would be expressively complete if it contained just ~ and ∨, and exercise 3.13#2 shows that either one of nand and nor can do the job of each of ~ and ∨.

Nand and nor are the only binary connectives that are individually sufficient to make SL expressively complete in the absence of ⊥. Exercise A-1.2#1 demonstrates that sentences compounded using only binary connectives that assign T when both immediate components get a T could never receive an F on the first row of any long table, and so could not do the job of functions that assign F to <T,T>. A variant on the demonstration of exercise A-1.2#1 would demonstrate that sentences compounded using only binary connectives that assign F when both immediate components get F would have the corresponding defect. It follows that the only binary connectives that would suffice by themselves to make SL expressively adequate are ones that assign F to <T,T> and T to <F,F>. That leaves only four candidates.

	↑	11	13	↓
<T,T>	F	F	F	F
<T,F>	T	T	F	F
<F,T>	T	F	T	F
<F,F>	T	T	T	T

The first candidate is nand (originally introduced as two-place function #9) and the fourth is nor (originally introduced as two-place function #15). Neither of the other two, two-place functions (##11 and 13 from the table given earlier), is a successful candidate. The second candidate makes an assignment that is a function just of the second value on the list. (It assigns F when the second value is T, regardless of what the first value is, and T when the second value is F, regardless of what the first value is.) It corresponds to the English connective, "not-B regardless of A." The third makes an assignment that is a function just of the first value on the list and corresponds to English "not-A regardless of B." A binary connective that disregards one of two immediate components when making its assignments cannot do the work of a function that makes assignments depending on how both turn out.

Notes

1   The arrows that appear in the diagram above and in similar diagrams later in this chapter are sometimes drawn pointing in the other direction, from items in the column of arguments to items in the column of values. In that case the arguments are often spoken of as being "mapped" or "projected" onto the values. Arrows going from values to arguments instead describe how values are "assigned" to arguments. Unfortunately, the terminology of "mapping," "projecting," and "assigning" is not very fixed or uniform. The important thing is that for each argument there is exactly one line, never none, and never more than one, and that the line connects the argument with a value. For each value, there can be multiple lines, or none. In this textbook, "assignment" always means assignment of values to arguments. Paradigmatically, the arguments up for assignment are variables and the values assigned to them are variants. The assignment interprets the variables as unambiguous signs for variants.

2   It would be in order to supplement the vocabulary for SL with a logical symbol that means T. But the discussion that follows has no use for such a symbol.

3   Here and throughout this section, references to two values should be taken to designate references to any two unspecified values. The only constraints are that there be only two of them and that each sentence under consideration have exactly one of the two. The values continue to be designated as T and F, but the symbols could stand for any opposed values: true / false; on / off; in / out; is / is not; satisfies / does not satisfy; evident / nonevident; upheld / broken; observed / ignored, and so on. The point is that the demonstration of expressive adequacy applies regardless of what the values are taken to be, not just when they are taken to be "true," and "false."

4 Formalization

Contents

4.1 Looseness of Fit

Logicians do their work by using variables to stand for the nonlogical elements of sentences (the parts that can vary without affecting whether a sentence is contradictory) and using special symbols to stand for the logical elements. This produces a formal language, which can be used to represent the forms of sentences and demonstrations of natural languages.

In chapters 2 and 3, a formal language for sentential logic, SL, is presented and studied on its own terms. A technique is developed for appealing to the semantics of that language to determine which of its sentences are equivalent, which of its sets are unsatisfiable, and which of its demonstrations are valid. These results carry over to those sentences, sets, and demonstrations of natural languages that have these forms. Natural language sentences and demonstrations that have the form of valid sentences and demonstrations of SL are themselves valid; natural language sentences and sets of sentences that have the form of unsatisfiable sentences and sets of sentences of SL are

DOI: 10.4324/9781003026532-5

themselves unsatisfiable, and natural language sentences that have the form of equivalent sentences of SL are themselves equivalent.

For these inferences to be drawn, the form of natural language demonstrations, sets, and sentences must be correctly identified. Unfortunately, this is not just a matter of assigning natural language sentences to sentence letters and directly converting natural language connective expressions to connectives of SL. The fit between sentences of SL and sentences of English is not tight for many reasons.

In what follows, formalization is considered at two levels, a core semantic level, and a pragmatic level. Core semantics identifies preferred contexts for understanding connective expressions of English. In these preferred contexts there is an affinity between speakers' intuitions about the meaning of English connective expressions and the valuation rules for associated connectives of SL. Pragmatics considers how the core meaning changes with shifts away from these preferred contexts. Pragmatics does not fit SL to English (SL is not pliable). It instead identifies circumstances in which what is said in English needs to be rewritten to better lend itself to formalization in SL. Discussion of core semantic meaning takes up most of sections 4.1–4.10, though there are ongoing remarks on how pragmatic considerations affect formalization. Pragmatic considerations are paramount in sections 4.11 and 4.12.

4.1.1 Formalization of Sentences as Sentence Letters

SL is designed to capture the forms of functionally compound sentences. These are sentences that have simpler sentences as their components and that have values, like "true" and "false" or "satisfied" and "not satisfied," that are determined by the values of their components. SL is not designed to capture the form of simple sentences (sentences that do not have parts that are themselves sentences). It can use sentence letters to stand for simple sentences, and so formalize them in this minimal sense. But even this much is only possible if the sentence has some value that is functionally related to the value of a compound sentence. A sentence that has no such value ("Hello" might be an example) cannot be formalized, even as a sentence letter.

The semantics for SL recognizes just two values, exactly one of which must be possessed by each sentence letter. This restriction to two values is not necessary. The sentence letters could be taken to stand for sentences that have more than two values, and the connectives could be reinterpreted as functions over more than two values. (This will be done in one way in the appendix to chapter 5 and in another in section 6.6). However, there are many English sentences that can be treated as possessing exactly one of two values (assertions as either true and false, promises as kept or broken, commands as obeyed or ignored) so this restriction will continue to be observed for now. Sentences that do not bear exactly one of two values (perhaps because they sit on the borderline between the two, as when someone who has not shaved in the past day is said to have a beard) or that manage to lay claim to both at once (such as "This sentence is a lie") will not be formalized in SL.

Some sentences have a value that changes with context. "It is raining" changes value depending on where and when it is uttered, "I am confused" depending on who is speaking. These sentences can be formalized, but enough of the intended context needs to be specified to justify the assignment of a value.

Up to now, the values have been designated T and F and associated with "true" and "false." But nothing that has been said so far requires any understanding of what T and F stand for beyond two values, exactly one of which must be possessed by each sentence under consideration. There is no reason why T and F might not be taken to stand for "evident" and "nonevident"; "observed" and "broken" (as with commands); "upheld" or "violated" (as with promises); or "answerable" and "not answerable" (as with questions).

Within the confines of any one case (any one discussion, example, or exercise) any one sentence letter may be used to formalize one and only one sentence of a natural language. This raises the question of how sentences are to be identified. Speakers will sometimes express the same thought using slightly different strings of words, e.g., "the dog bit the ball" and "the ball was bitten by the dog." Strictly, these are different sentences, since sentences are only the same if they consist of the same vocabulary elements listed in the same order. But if the speaker presumes the audience will understand different formulations to be equivalent, and the audience does in fact understand them that way, it is better to be lax and formalize the different sentences using the same sentence letter.

In some of the cases discussed in this chapter, more than one sentence is under consideration. As in sections 3.1–2, an interpretation is any way of assigning exactly one of the natural language sentences under consideration to each sentence letter. When only a finite number, n, of English sentences is under consideration, the default is to assign them to the first n sentence letters, taking the English sentences in the order in which they appear.

In this chapter, interpretations are described by listing some of the sentence letters and specifying which sentence is assigned to each of them.

4.1.2 *Formalization of Connective Expressions*

As discussed in chapters 2 and sections 3.1–2, SL contains symbols for five connectives. These connectives are functional.

A connective is *functional* if and only if, for each combination of values assigned to the component(s), the connective assigns a unique value to the compound.

A connective is *nonfunctional* if and only if it builds a compound sentence that has a value that is not determined by the value of its components in at least one case.

A compound sentence is *functionally compound* if and only if it has a value that is a function of the value of its immediate components.

English uses many connective expressions. Not all of them are functional. An example is the connective "before" in "He left the room before she finished speaking."

He left the room	before	she finished speaking
T	?	T
T	T	F
F	F	T
F	F	F

In three of four cases, the value of this sentence is determined by the values of its component parts. If it is true that he left the room and false that she finished speaking, then he must have left before she finished, and the sentence is true. If he never left the room, then whether she finished speaking or not, the sentence is false. But if it is true that he left the room and true that she finished speaking, then it could be either true or false that he left before she finished. One failure is all it takes to establish that "before" is not a functional connective.

When a connective is not functional, no connective of SL can symbolize it. An English compound expression that has been compounded using a nonfunctional connective might still have exactly one of the two salient values. "He left the room before she finished speaking" is either true or false. But because its value is not determined by the value of its components in all possible cases, it must be formalized as an atomic sentence of SL.

Complications arise when sentences contain both functional and nonfunctional connectives. This is an issue taken up in section 4.11.

Even when English uses functional connective expressions, it does not always use the same expressions in the same ways.

> 4.1   You won't get a bonus unless you volunteer for special events

is false if you don't volunteer for any special events but get a bonus anyway, but it falls short of promising that you will get a bonus if you do, and so is not false in that case. But

> 4.2   I will lead with hearts unless you raise your eyebrow

is false both if you don't raise your eyebrow and I don't lead with hearts, and if you do raise your eyebrow and I lead with hearts anyway. In 4.1 a sentence compounded using the English functional connective "unless," is false if and only if the condition (volunteering) is not met but the threatened consequence (not getting a bonus) fails to occur, whereas in 4.2 a similarly compounded sentence is false both if the condition (raising an eyebrow) is not met and the consequence (leading with hearts) fails to occur and if the condition and the result both occur. The conclusion to draw is not that English "unless" is some sort of fuzzy connective that does not always determine the same result. It is rather that English uses the same word for two different functional connectives.

English can also use different functional expressions to connect simple sentences in the same way.

> 4.3   Although Alma was not the fastest sprinter, she was the smartest

and

> 4.4   Alma was not the fastest sprinter but she was the smartest

are compound sentences that have values that are a function of the values of their components. Moreover, their values are the same function of the values of their components, notwithstanding that different English expressions are used to name that function and that the English expressions occur in different positions relative to the two sentences they connect. Unlike SL, English does not need to place binary connectives between the two sentences it connects. Sentences that are compounded using functional connectives of English do not always have a syntax that meshes with SL syntax. In SL, components may need to be differently ordered from the way the components they formalize are ordered in English, or they may need to be differently punctuated, or connectives and components may need to be repeated in SL where they do not appear in English. In the extreme, English can form functionally compound sentences without using any connective expressions at all.

> 4.5   No shirt, no shoes, no service

is a compound of three sentences of English. It is, moreover, functionally compound. It has a value that is determined by the values of its components. The sentence has the same truth conditions as

> 4.6 $(\sim A \lor \sim B) \to \sim C$

but the SL connectives are not expressed by any English words.

English can also use the same expression as both a functional connective and a nonfunctional connective.

> 4.7   Alma and Boda were a happy couple

does not contain a functional connective;

> 4.8   Alma and Boda were sprinters

can be rewritten as "Alma was a sprinter and Boda was a sprinter," which is a compound sentence that has a value that is a function of the value of its two components (the same function symbolized by &). In contrast, "Alma was a happy couple and Boda was a happy couple" is nonsense.

An English connective expression can also carry extra meaning in addition to its functional meaning.

> 4.9   Alma went for a walk and met Boda

uses "and" to suggest the temporal sequence in which the events occurred as well as to conjoin the claims that they did occur.

This makes formalization challenging. The dangers are multiple: attempting to symbolize a connective expression that cannot be symbolized because it is not functional; symbolizing a connective expression in the wrong way because its interpretation depends on context and the context is not properly consulted or is unknown; or symbolizing a connective expression in the wrong way because a hopeless attempt is made to capture added meaning that does not lend itself to symbolization.

These difficulties can be addressed by performing a valuation test. The test identifies cases where a connective is being used functionally. Sentences that fail the test cannot be formalized as compounds (they may still be formalized as atomic sentences of SL). When a sentence passes the test, the test will indicate how to formalize it.

Valuation Test

To formalize a compound English sentence in SL:

- identify its simple components
- draw up a long table that identifies what value the English compound intuitively receives on each possible combination of values to the simple components

- if there is a row on the table where it is uncertain which value the compound has on a valuation of its components, formalize the entire compound as a sentence letter
- otherwise, assign A to the first simple component, B to the second, and so on, and formalize the sentence as any compound based on these sentence letters that has the same column of T's and F's under its main connective as appear on the table
  - it is wise to use the simplest such compound; otherwise
  - following the procedure for constructing a "dnf" (sentence in disjunctive normal form, detailed in the appendix to chapter 3) will always identify one

The valuation test has already been applied to determine that the English compound sentence, "He left the room before she finished speaking" is compounded using a nonfunctional connective. It could equally well have been used to identify sentences of SL that formalize "No shirt, no shoes, no service"; "If you don't volunteer for special events, you won't get a bonus"; and the other sentences displayed above.

Further applications of the test lead to the discovery that there are certain English prefixes, words, and phrases that correspond, in preferred contexts, to ~, &, and ∨. Because the valuation table test is cumbersome to employ, these correspondences may be used instead. However, context alters meaning. When connective expressions do not appear in preferred contexts, recourse to the valuation table test is called for.

In what follows, the valuation test is applied to discover principles for formalizing English conditionals, which pose the greatest challenges.

4.2 Conditional Sentences of English

Whereas English uses prefixes, words, and phrases that correspond roughly to the tilde, ampersand, and wedge connectives of SL, it has no expression that corresponds to the arrow connective of SL.

Technical Note

English words like "implies," "yields," and "entails" are no exception. They are not sentential connectives. To say that A implies, yields, or entails B is to say that the sentence, A → B, is a theorem or is valid. Alternatively, it is to say that the demonstration, A / B, is derivable or valid. (The concepts of a theorem and of derivability are discussed in chapter 6.)

Similarly, to say that A *is equivalent to* B is not to utter a sentence that can be formalized in SL, not even as A ≡ B. It is to say something *about* the sentence, A ≡ B: that it is a theorem or valid.

It has already been noted that English is capable of compounding sentences without using connectives to do so. The sentences are simply stated one after another and context is relied on to say how they are connected. This is always the case with conditionals. Conditionals combine two sentences, one of which describes a result, and the other of which places a condition on the occurrence of that result. It is usually obvious which is the result and which the condition, so no special expression is needed to identify which is which, and English does not bother to do so. It simply states one after the other, and it is happy to do that in either order: result first and condition second, or condition first and result second.

However, there are different kinds of conditions that can be placed on results, and English is sensitive to those kinds of condition. But it does not express them with connectives. It instead attaches an inflection to the condition. The inflection is a special word or phrase that indicates what kind of condition it is.

    4.10   Competition will start at 10 if the track is dry

is a conditional sentence of English. It conjoins two sentences, "Competition will start at 10" and "The track is dry." Background knowledge makes it obvious which states the result, and which states the condition placed on that result. The sentences stating the result and the condition are simply stated one after the other, without any connective word or phrase, and they can be stated in either order, with the condition first and the result second,

4.11　If the track is dry competition will start at 10

or with the result first and the condition second, as in 4.10.

The term "then," which is sometimes used along with "if" does not denote a connective. It is a verbal punctuation mark, serving to denote a right parenthesis closing off the conditional clause.

When English concatenates clauses describing conditions and results, it uses special words or phrases to inflect the condition, that is, to stipulate what kind of condition it is.

4.10　Competition will start at 10 if the track is dry
4.12　Competition will start at 10 only if the track is dry
4.13　Competition will start at 10 unless the track is dry
4.14　Competition will start at 10 if and only if the track is dry
4.15　Competition will start at 10 unless the track is dry in which case it will not start at 10

Each of these sentences says something different from the others, even though each places the same condition on the same result. In each case, reversing the order, so that the condition is stated first and the result second, does not change the meaning. But inflecting the condition differently, with "if" rather than "only if," or "if and only if" rather than "if" or "only if" alone, etc., does change the meaning.

The examples given illustrate five main kinds of condition that can be placed on a result: a necessary condition, a sufficient condition, an exception, a condition that is both necessary and sufficient, and a strong exception. English uses various words and phrases to inflect the different kinds of condition. Some of them are listed on the following table.

When condition is inflected as:	Words or phrases used to do so can be:
Necessary	only if only provided that it is necessary that it is requisite that just in the case that
Sufficient	if provided that supposing/assuming that it is sufficient that in the case that
Exception	Unless Except in the case that
Necessary and sufficient	If and only if provided and only provided that in case and just in case It is necessary and sufficient that
Strong exception	Unless … in which case not … Except in the case that … in which case not …

Exercise 4.1

1. *State whether the following sentences place a condition on the occurrence of a result. If they do, identify the result, and the condition placed on it. (Just identify the condition, don't yet say what sort of condition it is inflected as being. That is the job of the next exercise.)*
   ⋆**a.** Leaving a higher tip will get you better service.
   　b. The food is good; however the service is not.
   ⋆**c.** The only way to get attention is to make a lot of noise.
   　d. You must pay attention or you will cause a serious accident.

*e. The greatest degree of caution and the most reasonable assumptions led, in this case, to the most unfortunate results.

f. If each tree for Γ is open then each tree in the canonical series of trees for Γ is open.

2. *Each of the following sentences places a condition on the occurrence of a result. Identify the condition. Then say whether it is inflected as being sufficient, necessary, both necessary and sufficient, an exception, or a strong exception. A sufficient condition is one that suffices for or guarantees a result, but that is not required for it. A necessary condition is one that is required for a result but that may not be all that is required. An exception is a circumstance in which a result need not occur, and a strong exception is a circumstance in which a result cannot occur. Use the previous table of words and phrases to help you decide.*

*a. Proper fuelling before competition is necessary for a good result.

b. Unless new evidence is brought forward, the court will decline to hear the case.

*c. This matter should not be raised unless it is raised discreetly.

d. A conjunction is false provided either conjunct is false.

*e. A conjunction is false unless both conjuncts are true, in which case it is true.

f. A conditional is true as long, and just as long, as either its antecedent is false or its consequent is true.

g. [Answer this question for any of exercise 4.1#1a-f identified as conditional sentences.]

Necessary, sufficient, exceptional, necessary and sufficient, and strongly exceptional conditions may be stated in a great variety of contexts. Two kinds of context (by no means the only two there are) bear scrutiny, the one because conditional claims made in it are often not functional, the other because they generally are. These are the causal and the contractual contexts. In causal contexts, there is a dependence discovered to hold in nature between a condition and a result. In contractual contexts, a dependence is imposed on things that are intrinsically independent of one another.

Causal claims are ubiquitous, with one particularly prominent example being their use in scientific reasoning. Consider the following case.

4.16	If someone with strep throat takes antibiotics		their symptoms will clear up within two days.
	T	?	T
	T	?	F
	F	?	T
	F	?	F

This sentence posits a causal connection between two events, namely a person's taking antibiotics and the abatement of their symptoms. In none of the four possible cases does the value of the components determine the value of the compound. Suppose a person with strep throat takes antibiotics and their symptoms do clear up within two days. This might be taken to establish the causal connection, and thus make the sentence true. But sometimes, strep throat symptoms clear up on their own in this timeframe and would have done so without any intervention. The fact that both things happened in succession does not by itself mean that the first caused the second. To draw any such conclusion apart from a series of experiments with similar conditions and treatments is to commit the "post hoc ergo propter hoc" fallacy (the fallacy of supposing that simply because one thing happened after another on one occasion, the first must have been the cause of the second).

Suppose instead that someone with strep throat takes antibiotics and their symptoms do not clear up in two days. This might be taken to falsify the causal sentence. But not by itself. For example, it could be the case that the person also has another illness that is causing those symptoms to continue. In the absence of this further illness, their symptoms would have abated within two days. The bare fact of taking antibiotics and not seeing symptoms clear up is not enough by itself to render the causal sentence false. There is a background, unstated presupposition that all other conditions have remained equal. That further presupposition is difficult to verify, as it presupposes total knowledge of what all the relevant background conditions are, as well as of whether they obtain. Failing that total knowledge, theorists have recourse to statistical correlations. But relying on statistical correlations means that causal sentences can no more be disconfirmed than established by a single instance.

Suppose, finally, that someone with strep throat does not take antibiotics. Then the causal sentence has been neither established nor falsified, and its value remains open to question.

The foregoing discussion might be taken only to apply in cases where causal claims are being made in terms of statistical correlations. Perhaps a causal claim that posits a more direct relationship between two events would be functional, such as "Alma slipped because he stepped on ice." But upon reflection, it can be seen that a positive instance of Alma slipping and stepping on ice cannot establish that the first event occurred because of the second. He may instead have had a clumsy moment occasioned by a sudden loud noise nearby or an earlier glass of wine. And as discussed in section 4.1.2, if there is even a single combination of assignments to components such that it is uncertain which value the compound has, the connective is not functional.

Though causal sentences do not have values that are determined by the values of their components, when it is accepted that they are true, inferences in the other direction, from compound to component, are sometimes possible, but they are not functional. If it is true that unsupported heavy bodies fall, and true that Alma has lost his footing, it can be inferred that in the absence of any other support Alma will fall. If it is true that unsupported heavy bodies fall, and false that Alma fell, it can be inferred Alma managed to keep his balance or was supported in some other way. However, in these sorts of cases both the truth of the causal sentence and an appropriate value for one of the components (true cause or false effect) must be known before the value of the remaining component can be determined. When the causal sentence is true but the antecedent is false, no inference can be drawn about the consequent, and likewise for the antecedent when the causal sentence is true and the consequent is true. Even in the cases where an inference can be drawn, it only comes close to being deductive in the case of fundamental laws of nature confirmed by exceptionless past experience (the Alma case appeals to our willingness to accept universal gravitation). In other cases, the inferences are only likely true, depending on the extent to which other causes or irreducibly probabilistic phenomena have a role to play. The fact that causal sentences can sometimes figure in inferences that are almost as good as certain means that there are special contexts in which they can be formalized as conditional sentences of SL. Paradigmatically, these are the contexts provided by a demonstration where causal sentences are accepted as premises (and so as true) and further statements are premised concerning either the cause or the effect. When taken out of these contexts (as when displayed alone on a page or in an exercise), causal sentences should be formalized as atomic sentences.

Unlike causal conditionals, contractual conditionals generally are functional. This makes the contractual context a preferred context for using SL to formalize conditional sentences of English.

Whereas causal conditionals report on a dependence discovered to hold in nature, contractual conditionals impose a dependence on things that are intrinsically unrelated to one another. This is what happens when parties sign a contract, or someone makes a promise or a threat, or lays down a rule, or stipulates how they want a term or phrase to be understood. (Stipulative definitions are a kind of contract set up between a writer and a reader.) The thing being promised or threatened may be unrelated to the condition under which it is promised or threatened, but the speaker undertakes to make it so. No natural law dictates that things must happen in a certain sequence, but a rule of human making is laid down enjoining people to bring them about in that way.

Consider the following contractual sentence:

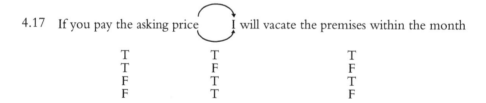

4.17   If you pay the asking price   I will vacate the premises within the month

T	T	T
T	F	F
F	T	T
F	T	F

There is no intrinsic, natural, or causal relation between these activities. But the persons involved draw up a contract that brings such a connection into existence. The contract is upheld or violated depending on the value of the components. It might be objected that contracts and promises cannot properly be said to be true or false, but that is a quibble. Anyone who did not balk at the attribution of T's and F's to the promise, "I will take the bananas unless you want them," which appeared in the appendix to chapter 3, or to the promises, "You wont' get a bonus unless you volunteer for special events," and "I will lead with hearts unless you raise your eyebrow," which appeared earlier in this chapter, will have already shown themselves willing to accept that promises and contracts do have values – and not only values but *truth* values. However, there is no need to quibble over words. What matters is that the compound sentence can be ascribed one of two values as a function of the values ascribed to its components. T and F merely stand for those values. The values can be given any name at pleasure without affecting what matters. "Satisfied" and "unsatisfied" (which, as of chapter 15, will largely supplant "true" and "false" in this textbook) will do. Depending on whether the condition is met or not met, the condition is satisfied or not satisfied. Depending on whether the result occurs or does not occur, the result is satisfied or not satisfied. Depending on the satisfaction of the condition and the result, the contract is satisfied or not satisfied, and its satisfaction is in each possible case determined by the satisfaction of the condition and the result. If the buyer pays the requested sum (and so satisfies the condition) and the seller vacates the premises (and so satisfies the result), the contract has been satisfied. If the buyer pays the requested sum and the seller does not vacate the premises, the contract has not been satisfied. If the buyer does not pay the requested sum and the seller vacates the premises anyway, something strange has happened, but whatever is going on the contract has been satisfied (it has certainly not been violated and contracts are either one or the other). And if the buyer does not pay the requested sum and the seller does not vacate the premises, the contract has likewise been satisfied. The buyer is in this case in no position to take the seller to court on a charge of breach of contract.

It has been objected that there is something paradoxical about the values ascribed to conditional sentences on the above table. The standard way of motivating this objection is to craft an example of a conditional with a false antecedent and a consequent that is intuitively incompatible with the antecedent such as, "If I live for a thousand years I will die tomorrow." Were the antecedent satisfied, the consequent could not possibly be satisfied. But because the antecedent cannot be satisfied the conditional defaults to being satisfied. That a conditional should be satisfied when its antecedent is incompatible with its consequent is said to be paradoxical. However, the only applications of this strategy that produce paradoxical results are those that appeal to noncontractual conditionals. "If I live for a thousand years then I will die tomorrow" is satisfied since there is no chance that the sufficient condition, living for a thousand years, placed on the result, dying tomorrow, will be satisfied. However, the conditional is only paradoxically true if it is interpreted as asserting an intrinsic or natural connection between living for a thousand years and dying tomorrow. Interpreted as a contract, stating a condition under which the contractor undertakes to bring about a specified result, it is a variant on contracts of the form "I will do that if hell freezes over." There is nothing paradoxical about such contracts. Placing a condition that could not possibly be satisfied on the execution of a contract is unparadoxically interpreted as a colourful way for the contractor to refuse to be bound to produce the result.

When a sufficient condition a contractor places on producing the result is not satisfied, the contractor is released from the obligation to produce the result. This does not mean that the contractor is released from the contract. To repeat, it means that under the terms of the contract the contractor is released from the obligation to produce the result stipulated in the contract. The terms of the contract must remain in effect for the contractor to be released from the obligation to deliver the result in accord with the terms of the contract. The contract has accordingly been satisfied in any case where the condition is "if I live for a thousand years," or "if hell freezes over," even though it is satisfied by default rather than by operation.

Promises and threats are a kind of contract and work the same way. Rules or laws like "if you are the last one out, close the door" are similarly satisfied or not satisfied, and so verified or falsified depending on whether someone is the last one out and whether they close the door.

Stipulative definitions are a special case. They are functional. But they are also performative in the sense that the person who stipulates a definition makes it so. The performance of making it be the case that something is defined or understood in certain terms does not itself have a truth value. But the definition this performance creates is inherently valid: it cannot be false given that the stipulation is in effect. The sentence,

4.18   A sentence is s-valid if and only if there is no interpretation on which it is false

stipulates a meaning for the term, "s-valid." S-validity could have been defined differently, or not defined at all. A different author could stipulate differently. But speakers have a claim to be understood on their own terms. Listeners need not employ the definition in their own work. But, provided the definition is not self-contradictory, listeners are obliged to observe it in interpreting the work of the person who stipulates it, and the person who stipulates it makes a promise to abide by that stipulation. The stipulation is a contract between speaker and listener governing the terms of their mutual expression and understanding.

Unlike promises, contracts, commands, etc., which can be broken or violated, once a stipulation has been laid down and accepted, there can be no cases where it is false. It licenses inferring the truth of one component from the truth of the other, and the falsity of one from the falsity of the other.

Exercise 4.2

Determine whether the following sentences are causal or contractual. Give reasons for your answers.

*a. If a body approaches a strongly gravitating body at sufficient speed and an oblique angle, it will orbit that body.

  b. If you approach an oncoming vehicle on a dirt road, you must move to the right.

*c. If it rains, I will bring an umbrella.

  d. If there is one interpretation on which a sentence is true and another on which it is false, the sentence is s-contingent.

*e. Water will boil at 100 degrees Celsius only if it is at sea level.

  f. Reid would not have rejected Berkeley's immaterialism if he had not read Hume's *Treatise*.

4.3 Necessary Conditions

As noted earlier, there are five main kinds of conditional sentence of English. There are correspondingly five main kinds of contractual conditional. Over the remainder of this and the sections that follow, each is considered in turn.

When someone says,

> 4.19   You can win only if you play

they declare that there is a condition, playing, that those dispensing the winnings place on winning. The context is a legalistic one, which can be considered either as a promise made by the administrators of the game, or as a rule that they declare they intend to observe. The promise or obligation concerns a result, winning, and a condition is placed on this result, playing. This condition is tagged or inflected with the words "only if." These words convey that satisfying the condition, playing, is necessary for the result to be satisfied. It is the *only* way to get the result. Not everyone who plays wins, and it is not promised that playing is all that is needed to win. But it is said that playing is something that must be done to have a chance of winning. And it is promised that there is no case in which winnings will go to someone who has not played. If someone wins, but they did not play, the promise has not been satisfied, but if they play, but don't win, it is satisfied because there is no promise to give winnings to anyone, only a promise not to give winnings to certain people. And, of course, if they play and do win, or don't play and don't win the promise has also been satisfied. These results can be summarized on the following table.

Condition x plays	Result x wins	Sentence x wins **only if** x plays
T	T	T
T	F	T
F	T	F
F	F	T

The table illustrates that "You can win only if you play," has a value that is in each case uniquely determined by the value of its component parts. For every possible combination of values its component sentences might have, there is exactly one value assigned to the compound. The values are here designated T and F, which, as noted earlier, are symbols that can be used for any pair of mutually exclusive values, including satisfied/unsatisfied and kept/broken. But, in the case of promises, T and F can also be taken to stand for "true" and "false." A broken promise is a false promise. The person who breaks a promise is accused of having told a lie, that is, of having said something false, whereas a person who keeps their promises is "honest" in the sense of having told the truth.

It might be objected that if someone doesn't play and doesn't win, then the promise is neither satisfied nor not satisfied but rather untested. Even if someone plays and does win, it may be merely by accident. They might have been given the winnings even if they hadn't played, so here too the promise is untested. And if someone does play and doesn't win, then perhaps that is because the game is fixed in favour of the house so that no one who plays wins, and it is at least misleading to say that you can win only if you play.

These objections are valid only when the sentence is understood causally, rather than contractually. Understood causally, the sentence says that playing is a necessary, even if not sufficient, cause of winning. On that understanding, the statement is not functionally compound and its value is not determined by the value of its component parts.

But the objections are not appropriate when the statement is understood contractually, as a promise made by the administrators of the game to potential clients. (Suppose the game is a lottery and the administrators are making a promise to potential ticket purchasers). In this case, the connection between playing and winning is not asserted to be intrinsic to the nature of playing and winning, but is instead something that a third party, the administrators of the game, undertake to bring about as a matter of contractual obligation. When it is read in this way, as a promise or contract, the question to ask is not: Has the right sort of intrinsic relation between playing and winning been established by seeing the components get these values? It is rather: Have the administrators acted in accord with the provisions of their contract when the component clauses are satisfied or not satisfied under the specified conditions? The promise is just that playing is *necessary* (not *sufficient*) for winning, so that no one will be allowed to walk away with the winnings if they have not played. If someone either plays or does not win, the promise has been satisfied in that case. Even if someone does not play, the promise is not "untested" but satisfied by the fact that no winnings have gone to that nonplayer. Failing to satisfy a promise is a serious matter. It can have legal consequences and always has consequences for the reputation of the person accused of failing to satisfy the promise. It would be highly unjust if someone could be accused of failing to satisfy a promise on the basis of speculation or something as difficult to verify as a hypothetical or counterfactual allegation. A promise that has so far not failed to be satisfied is a promise that has so far been satisfied, and it continues to be satisfied with each passing case (or each passing moment) until such time as a case arises where it is not satisfied. If there are no cases it has been satisfied by default. As long as no one wins, the promise that no winnings will go to those who have not played has been satisfied. It only fails to be satisfied when someone wins who has not played. Just as the accused is innocent until proven guilty, so a promise has been satisfied up to such time as it fails to be satisfied. A third value (untested) has no place in any regular, evidence-based finding of guilt or innocence on the charge of having broken a contractual obligation.

Context and the art of interpretation play a role here, though it is the minimal role of establishing just that the case at hand is a contractual one. It needs to be intended and understood that the sentence is a promise. On that supposition, the sentence has a value that is a function of the value of its components.

4.4 Sufficient Conditions

Whereas a necessary condition is one that must be met to obtain the result, but that may not be all that is needed for the result, a sufficient condition is all that needs to be done to obtain the result. However, unlike a necessary condition, it is not required for the result. While it suffices for the result, there may be other, equally sufficient means of obtaining the result. This is the difference between a condition that is both necessary and sufficient and one that is merely sufficient. When a condition is both necessary and sufficient, it is both needed and all that is needed. When it is merely sufficient, it is all that is needed, but it may be dispensed with in favour of some alternative.

English promises that place a sufficient condition on a result are broken if and only if the condition is satisfied but the result does not occur. If the condition is not satisfied but the result occurs the promise is not broken, because the promise does not rule out other ways of getting the result. And, of course, if both the condition and the result occur, or neither does, the promise is once again satisfied.

Consider the following sentence:

4.20   Your package will be delivered by 4 p.m. if you get it in by noon

This sentence identifies a condition that those running the courier company place on delivering a package by 4 p.m. the same day. The context is again a legalistic one, which can be considered either as a promise made by the courier company, or as an obligation laid by them on their customers. The promise or obligation concerns a result, getting a package delivered by 4 p.m. that same day, and a condition placed on this result, getting the package in to the pickup location by noon. This condition is tagged or inflected with the word "if." This word serves to convey that satisfying the condition is *sufficient* to obtain the result. It is all that is required to get the result. There may also be other ways to get the result. The sentence does not rule out the possibility that the parcel might be delivered by 4 p.m. even if it comes in later than noon. It is not promised that no one who fails to meet the deadline will ever get their package delivered by 4 p.m. The company could not be accused of having told a lie if someone brought their parcel in at 2 p.m. and the company still managed to deliver it by 4. The promise is that if the package is given to them by noon they will not fail to deliver it by 4. So if the package is in by noon, but it is not delivered by 4, the promise is not satisfied, but if it is in after noon, and it is still delivered by 4, the promise has been satisfied. Delivering more than what was promised is one way of keeping a promise. And, of course, if it is in by noon and it is delivered by 4, or not in by noon and it isn't, the promise has been satisfied. It would be absurd if someone who got the package in late where to take the company to court on a charge of breach of contract based on the claim that, due to some speculative circumstances, even if the package *had been* in by noon the company *would not* have delivered it by 4pm. There would be no point to placing conditions on the execution of promises if people could be successfully charged with failing to satisfy a promise in the very cases where the contract says they are released from satisfying it, and it is unlikely that the institution of promising would survive in any jurisdiction that countenanced such proceedings. This is so much the case that people who have no intention of performing a certain act will make their unwillingness clear by promising to perform the act under a condition that could never be satisfied. Someone who says "I will do that when hell freezes over" is not considered to have told a lie or made a false promise, even though it is clear to everyone that they have no intention of performing the act. Placing an unsatisfiable sufficient condition on a performance makes it certain that the promise to do the act in that circumstance will always be satisfied. It will always be satisfied because it can never fail to be satisfied and it is clear to everyone that it can never fail to be satisfied because the circumstance in which it could fail to be satisfied cannot arise.

These results can be summarized on the following table.

Condition Package is in by noon	Result Package is delivered by 4pm	Sentence Package is delivered by 4pm **if** it is in by noon
T	T	T
T	F	F
F	T	T
F	F	T

The table again illustrates that the sentence, "Your package will be delivered by 4 p.m. if you get it in by noon" has a value that is a function of the value of its components. For each possible combination of values its component sentences might have, there is a unique value determined for the compound.

4.5 Necessary and Sufficient Conditions; The Principle of Charity

People are not always careful about the distinction between a condition that is merely necessary (required but not all that is required) or merely sufficient (enough to get the result but not the only way to get it) and one that is both (all and only what is required). Sometimes they will use words that flag a condition as necessary or as sufficient when they really mean to flag it as both necessary and sufficient. A parent might say to their child,

> 4.21   You won't get dessert if you don't finish your vegetables.[1]

In this case, the parent inflects the condition with "if," which in preferred contexts is an inflection that attaches to a merely sufficient condtion. Going by the second row of assignments on the table for merely sufficient conditions given in section 4.4, when the condition (not eating vegabales) is satisfied and the result does not occur (the parent relents and gives the child dessert anyway), the promise is not satisfied. This is intuitively the right result. But, according to the third row, when the condition is not satisfied (the child finishes their vegetables) and the result occurs anyway (no dessert is forthcoming) the promise has been satisfied, for the reason given in section 4.4: the condition placed on not giving dessert is only sufficient. It is guaranteed that there will be no dessert in the case where the vegetables are not finished. No promise is made about what will happen if they are. However, many would insist that the promise has also been broken in this case.

There is good reason for this sentiment. Even though the same inflection, "if," is attached to the condition in both 4.20, "The package will be delivered by 4 p.m. if it is in by noon" and 4.21 "You won't get dessert if you don't finish your vegetables," the promises are made in different contexts. In 4.20, all that needs to be known about the context is that a sufficient condition is being attached to a promise. In any such case, the promise is not satisfied when the condition is satisfied but the result does not occur, and otherwise satisfied. But in 4.21, there is a special context that supplies extra information that affects how the condition is understood. The remark is clearly intended to give the child an incentive to finish the vegetables. Given that context, there would be no point to warning the child that not finishing the vegetables suffices for not getting any dessert unless this also meant promising that finishing them will evade that result. The promise is not explicit in words. But it is at least consistent with them, and it is strongly suggested by the context. Saying that not finishing your vegetables suffices for getting no dessert does not rule out that it might also be necessary for getting no dessert (thereby implying that dessert will otherwise be given). Recognizing that implicit implication means treating the condition as if it were inflected as both sufficient and necessary.

Condition You do not eat your vegetables	Result You do not get dessert	Sentence You won't get dessert if *(implicit: and only if)* you don't finish your vegetables
T	T	T
T	F	F
F	T	F
F	F	T

This valuation test reflects the conditions under which a promise made under a condition that is both sufficient and necessary has been satisfied or not satisfied. If the child finishes the vegetables and the parent does not give dessert (row 3) then "You won't get dessert if *(implicit: and only if)* you don't finish your vegetables" is not satisfied because not finishing the vegetables was implied by context to be necessary for not getting dessert and yet that threatened result occurred even though the act that was purportedly necessary to make it happen did not occur. If the child does not finish the vegetables but the parent gives dessert anyway (row 2) then "You won't get dessert if you don't finish your vegetables" is again not satisfied, because the parent explicitly said that doing just that one thing, not finishing their vegetables, would mean no dessert and it turned out not to be so. Of course, in the cases where the child does not finish the vegetables and gets no dessert, or does finish them and gets it (rows 1 and 4), the promise has been satisfied.

This case would have been straightforward had the parent only said, "You won't get dessert if and only if you don't finish your vegetables." The parent's use of "if" calls for an appeal to the implications of the context of utterance that would have been unnecessary had "if and only if" been used instead. Cases like this one are by no means uncommon, and they illustrate the importance of the distinction between preferred context and special context.

When the same word or phrase of a natural language is used for two different purposes, as when "if" is used to designate both a condition that is merely sufficient and a condition that is necessary as well as sufficient, logic steps in and demands that the usage be disambiguated. At bottom, it may not matter which of the two contesting readings is designated the preferred one (though often there are practical reasons for preferring one to the other). But logic demands that some choice be made to resolve the ambiguity. One way of understanding the word or phrase must be designated as the preferred reading and the other identified as a variant, implied by special circumstances. In the case at hand the choice is to identify the preferred meaning of "if" with the one instanced by 4.20, and the special meaning with 4.21. For 4.21, a distinction between what is explicitly said and what is implicitly meant is drawn accordingly: the parent is considered to *explicitly say* "if" as that term is understood in the preferred case, but *implicitly mean* "if and only if."

The fact that people will sometimes say "if" when they really mean "if and only if," or "only if" when they really mean "if and only if," fosters misunderstanding. Misunderstandings can be exploited by less scrupulous individuals or cause innocent mistakes and consequent disputes over who meant what or who ought to have understood what.

Consider the case of the student of logic and the law who promises a roommate, "I will do your laundry only if you buy me a coffee." The roommate buys the coffee, the student drinks it, and when the roommate asks why the student hasn't done the laundry the student says there was never any promise to do the laundry *if* a coffee was purchased. Doing the laundry was instead promised *only if* a coffee was purchased. All the student ever said was that buying a coffee was necessary for doing the laundry, not that it was *all* that was necessary. Having said that much, the student would have told a lie if the roommate had *not* bought a coffee and the student had gone ahead and done the laundry anyway, because then the condition that was said to be necessary for the result would not have turned out to be necessary. But as it is, the student told no lie, the student broke no promise, and the student would win in a court of law, because the student never said "I will do your laundry *if* you buy me a coffee" which would imply that buying the coffee is all the roommate needs to do, but instead said "only if" which implies that it is just one thing that needs to be done.

At this point, the roommate may be inclined to feel they have been tricked, and the student may be inclined to feel that the roommate has only been taught a life lesson about the importance of understanding contracts in accord with the strict meaning of terms. In many cases (though not this one), people can honestly mean something other than what they are understood to mean, making it unclear who is to blame: the person who purportedly uses misleading language or the person who is not duly sensitive to what is meant in preferred contexts. When there is more at stake than a household chore, the dispute may become so intense that the parties have recourse to a court of law. There is a moral to be drawn. It is better to be clear about the wording of a contract than to have to make a case in a court of law and throw a large sum to the mercy of a judge's decision on whether the context was pre-ferred or special and, if the latter whether the context was sufficient to make the implication obvious in the absence of more explicit wording.

Where reasoning is concerned, there is a background principle that can be used to resolve problem cases, the principle of charity. The principle of charity dictates that whenever there is a question of what the speaker means, the speaker should be understood to have meant the thing that is more likely to be true. Adherence to this principle is dictated by the project of reasoning. Reasoning is only interesting in the case where the premises are accepted, so when there is any question of how a premise is to be understood, those concerned with discovering truths will want to understand it in the way most likely to be true.

In the case at hand, what is most likely to be true is what gets a T on the most of rows of the long table. As illustrated by the valuation tests given over the course of this and the two prior sections, a promise made under an "if and only if" condition is false in more circumstances than a promise made under either an "if" or an "only if" condition. The principle of charity therefore dictates that no one should be assumed or understood to mean "if and only if" when all that they say is "only if" or "if." Of course, there are cases where context dictates otherwise. But as this is a textbook in logic and not in hermeneutics, further instruction in how to assess the implications of context is not provided here. Policy for the remainder of this textbook is to consider "if" and similar words or phrases to mean "is sufficient for," and "only if" and similar words or phrases to mean "is necessary for." Anyone meaning to designate a condition as both necessary and sufficient must inflect it with "if and only if," or similar words or phrases. (See the **list** given in section 4.1.)

4.6 Formalizing Necessary and Sufficient Conditions

The effects of placing necessary, sufficient, and both necessary and sufficient conditions on promises are compared on the following table:

Condition	Result	Result **only if** condition	Result **if** condition	Result **if and only if** condition
T	T	T	T	T
T	F	T	F	F
F	T	F	T	F
F	F	T	T	T

Even though "only if," "if," and "if and only if" are not connectives but inflections attached to conditions, they work like connectives of SL. They help to build a compound sentence that has exactly one of the two values for each pair of values its two components could take. Conditionalized promises, commands, requests, and other contractual sentences of English that use conditions inflected in any of these ways are expressible in SL. The valuation test for necessary and sufficient conditions corresponds to the characteristic table for ≡, so contractual sentences that place a necessary and sufficient condition on a result can be formalized as biconditionals. The remaining conditional sentences of English can be formalized as conditional sentences of SL, on the following principle:

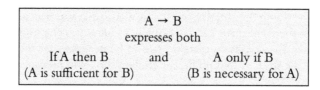

$$A \rightarrow B$$
expresses both

If A then B   and   A only if B
(A is sufficient for B)   (B is necessary for A)

This might be confusing. How can one sentence of SL, A → B, formalize both necessary and sufficient conditions?

When formalizing either necessary or sufficient conditions, it is important to remember that → does not do the work. It does not formalize "if" and it does not formalize "only if." → is a functional connective of SL that has no counterpart in any English word or phrase. Likewise, English "if" and English "only if" are not sentential connectives. They are two different inflections that attach to English conditions.

Rather than be formalized by a *connective*, "if" and "only if" are formalized by the antecedent and consequent *positions* in the arrow sentence. The antecedent position formalizes sufficiency, the consequent position formalizes necessity.

The antecedent position formalizes sufficiency because, when the antecedent gets a T, it is assured that the consequent gets a T (otherwise the conditional is false) whereas when the antecedent gets an F the consequent can still get a T without falsifying the conditional as a whole. This replicates the situation with (merely) sufficient conditions on results, where results must arise if the condition is met but can arise for other reasons when the condition is not met.

The consequent position formalizes necessity because, without the consequent (when the consequent gets an F), there can be no antecedent (the antecedent cannot get a T), otherwise the conditional is false. However, when the consequent gets a T the antecedent can still get an F without making the conditional as a whole false. This replicates the situation with (merely) necessary conditions on results, where the result cannot arise if the condition is not met, and may not arise even if it is met.

Formalizing conditionals by focusing on the position (antecedent or consequent) rather than the connective can be challenging because it can require altering the order of the components, and altering it in different ways in different circumstances. English can state the result first and the condition second, or the condition first and the result second, without altering the meaning of what is said. But a formalization in SL must put the result first, if the condition is a necessary condition, and must put the result second if the condition is a sufficient condition.

Formalizing Necessary and Sufficient Conditions

When formalizing a conditional sentence of English, first determine which part of the sentence states the result and which part places a condition on that result. Then look for the words or phrases that indicate whether the condition is necessary, sufficient, or both. Consult the **list** of these words and phrases given earlier.

Put necessary conditions in the consequent position of an arrow sentence and results in the antecedent position.

Put sufficient conditions in the antecedent position of an arrow sentence and results in the consequent position.

Put necessary and sufficient conditions in either position of a triple bar sentence, depending on whether the English sentence states the condition before or after stating the result. (The English order need not be followed, but it might as well be when there is no good reason not to.)

It might be objected that there is something wrong with expressing necessary conditions by putting the condition in the consequent position of a conditional sentence of SL. But, the (unfortunate) name, "conditional," notwithstanding, there is no condition in an arrow sentence of SL. The left component of an arrow sentence is no more a condition on the right component than the right component is a condition on the left. The components of arrow sentences are antecedents and consequents (names that are themselves misleading), not conditions and results. The distinction between antecedent and consequent is a distinction that is based solely on position. A sentence like ~A → A is a perfectly well-formed conditional sentence of SL. It is even true on any interpretation on which A is true. But the antecedent, ~A, is not a condition on the consequent, A. Neither is the consequent, A, a condition on ~A. So called "conditionals" and "biconditionals" of SL do not assert any special relation of conditionality to hold between the component sentences. The only meaning arrow sentences have is the meaning given by the valuation rule for arrow sentences, which says that the sentence is true if and only if either the antecedent is false or the consequent is true and is otherwise false. That valuation rule enables the consequent position to formalize necessary conditions and the antecedent position to formalize sufficient conditions.

Exercise 4.3

1. *State whether the following promises are satisfied or not satisfied in the specified circumstances.*
    ⋆**a.** Competition will start at 10 a.m. only if the track is dry. *(The track is not dry. Competition does not start.)*
    b. Competition will start at 10 a.m. only if the track is dry. *(The track is dry. Competition does not start.)*
    ⋆**c.** Competition will start at 10 a.m. if the track is dry. *(The track is not dry. Competition starts.)*
    d. Competition will start at 10 a.m. only if the track is dry. *(The track is not dry. Competition starts.)*
    ⋆**e.** Competition will start at 10 a.m. if the track is dry. *(The track is dry. Competition does not start.)*
    f. Competition will start at 10 a.m. if the track is dry. *(The track is not dry. Competition does not start.)*

2. *Specify the one set of circumstances under which each of the following promises is not satisfied. (Use T to stand for "satisfied" and F for "not satisfied".) Then formalize the sentence in SL, using A to stand for "Competition will start at 10 am" and B to stand for "the track is dry." Verify that the formalization gets an F under and only under that one condition.*
    ⋆**a.** Competition will start at 10 a.m. only if the track is dry.
    b. If the track is dry, competition will start at 10 a.m.
    ⋆**c.** Only if the track is dry will competition start at 10 a.m.
    d. Competition will start at 10 a.m. provided that the track is dry.
    ⋆**e.** For competition to start at 10 a.m. it is necessary that the track be dry.
    f. For competition to start at 10 a.m. it is sufficient that the track be dry.

An alternative way to meet the challenges of formalizing necessary and sufficient conditions is to rewrite sentences that use them in a standard form. There are two standard forms: "If A then B," and "A only if B." Rewriting a sentence in one or other of these forms, being careful to pick the one that produces a rewrite that says the same thing as the original, produces a sentence that can be formalized in the order it is written: first clause in the antecedent position, second in the consequent.

**Formalizing Necessary and Sufficient Conditions
Using Standard Forms**

Rewrite the sentence in one or the other of the following standard forms, choosing the one that produces a rewrite that says the same thing as the original:

If … then …

… only if …

Formalize the sentence putting whichever clause is stated first in the standard form rewrite in the antecedent position and whichever is stated second in the consequent position.

For example,

4.22   Competition will start at 10 a.m. provided that the track is dry

can be formalized in SL by first noting that it can be rewritten as,

4.23   If the track is dry then competition will start at 10 a.m.

without changing the meaning. (The other choices obviously do not say the same thing. "If competition will start at 10 a.m. then the track is dry," and, "The track is dry only if competition will start at 10 a.m." turn "competition will start at 10 a.m." into the condition rather than the result. "Competition will start at 10 a.m. only if the track is dry" treats the condition as being necessary for the result rather than sufficient for it.)

Once the correct rewrite has been chosen, the sentence is formalized in SL in the order it is written. Taking "A" to stand for "Competition will start at 10 a.m.," and "B" to stand for "the track is dry" gives

4.24   B → A

In contrast,

      4.25   It is necessary that the track be dry for competition to start at 10 a.m.

is formalized in SL by first noting that it can be rewritten as

      4.26   The competition will start at 10 a.m. only if the track is dry

without any change in meaning. The sentence is then formalized in SL in the order it is written. Using "A" and "B" as before gives

      4.27   A → B

Exercise 4.4

Rewrite the following sentences in standard form and then formalize them in SL using the specified sentence letters to stand for the components. State whether each sentence is true or false.

⋆a. A conditional is true provided that its antecedent is false. *(A: A conditional is true; B: The antecedent of the conditional is false.)*

  b. A set is s-satisfiable just in case there is an interpretation on which each sentence in that set is true. *(A: A set is s-satisfiable; B: There is an interpretation on which each sentence in that set is true.)*

⋆c. For a conditional to be true it is necessary that its antecedent be false. *(A: A conditional is true; B: the antecedent of the conditional is false.)*

  d. It suffices to have an s-valid conclusion for a demonstration to be s-valid. *(A: The conclusion is s-valid; B: A demonstration is s-valid.)*

⋆e. P and Q are s-equivalent if there is no interpretation on which P is true and Q is false. *(A: P and Q are s-equivalent; B: There is no interpretation on which P is true and Q is false.)*

  f. P and Q are s-equivalent only if there is no interpretation on which P is true and Q is false. *(A: P and Q are s-equivalent; B: There is no interpretation on which P is true and Q is false.)*

The opposite of formalization is instantiation. Sentences of SL are forms that many different sentences of English and other natural languages may exhibit. Instantiation is coming up with one English sentence that is an instance of a sentence of SL. This is done by providing an interpretation of the sentence letters, and reading back what the interpretation produces when the connectives are associated with preferred connective expressions or inflections of English. For example, on the interpretation of "A" as symbolizing "a resident complains," and B as symbolizing, "the owner of a vehicle parked on the street overnight will be given a ticket,"

      4.27   A → B

might be instantiated as

      4.28   If a resident complains the owner of a vehicle parked on the street overnight
               will be given a ticket

Instantiation poses a problem that does not arise when English sentences are formalized in SL. Considered just as a form, A → B can be read as either "If A then B," or "A only if B." The readings are equivalent, since "If A then B" says that having A means having B (since A is all that is needed for B), and "A only if B" also says that having A means having B (since B is required for A). But while A → B can be read either as "If A then B" or "A only if B," the English instantiation,

      4.29   A resident complains only if the owner of a vehicle parked on the street overnight
               will be given a ticket

sounds odd, and may even be taken as saying something entirely different: not that a resident who is put off by others parking on the street overnight will get satisfaction, but that residents will complain only if they learn that someone has been ticketed for parking on the street overnight, and that this is the only thing they will ever complain about.

Logically, the two sentences are equivalent. Each is false only in the case where a resident complains and the owner of a vehicle parked on the street overnight is not given a ticket. In the one case this is because complaining is said to guarantee that result; in the other because complaining is said to never occur except in that sort of case. But there is a significant difference. In the odd, second case, the inflection, "only if" is attached to what is clearly the result, rather than to the condition placed on its occurrence. English does not inflect results. It only inflects conditions. SL does not distinguish between conditions and results. A → B has an antecedent and a consequent, but a condition can occur in either the antecedent or the consequent position. Because SL is indifferent to the distinction between condition and result, it considers "If A then B" and "A only if B" to be equivalent. But English does care about the difference between condition and result, and that is an issue that must be managed when instantiating arrow sentences of SL. When instantiating conditionals using sentences that are clearly related as condition and result, it is important to inflect the condition, not the result, and to inflect it appropriately for its position.

For example, had the interpretation used in this section been applied to

4.24   B → A

the instantiation would need to be "The owner of a vehicle parked on the street overnight will be given a ticket only if a resident complains." The instantiation is dictated by the fact that what is clearly the result in this case, issuing a ticket, occurs in the antecedent and the condition on that result occurs in the consequent. That means that the condition must be inflected as necessary rather than sufficient, in accord with the position it occupies.

The issue does not arise when formalizing English sentences in SL because then the English condition is clearly distinguished from its result by being inflected as either necessary or sufficient, and its position in the formalization is determined by how it is inflected.

This topic is further examined in exercise 4.5#2.

4.7 Exceptions and Strong Exceptions

In addition to placing necessary or sufficient conditions on promises, speakers will sometimes attach exceptions to promises. Exceptions make a promise, but then attach a rider that specifies that the obligation to keep the promise is lifted in the case where a condition is met. *Not* meeting the condition assures the result. Meeting the condition means the obligation to bring about the result is suspended. For example,

4.30   Tax refunds will be received within two weeks unless reports are filed after the deadline

makes a promise to do something, send out tax refunds within two weeks, but attaches an exception to the promise, here tagged or inflected with the word, "unless," indicating that provided the condition is *not* satisfied the promised result will be forthcoming. The possibility of receiving a refund within two weeks is not ruled out, even if the report is late. Strictly, it is only promised to get refunds out within two weeks in all other cases while saying nothing about what happens in cases where the report is submitted late. These results are summarized on the following table.

Condition Report submitted late	Result Refund sent out within two weeks	Sentence [result] unless [condition]
T	T	T
T	F	T
F	T	T
F	F	F

At row 1 the report is submitted late, but the refund is sent out within two weeks anyway. No one could say that the promise was not satisfied in this case. On the contrary, people got more than was promised. At row 2 the report is submitted late, and the refund is not received within two weeks. Again, no one could justly say the promise was not satisfied, since it is precisely in this case that people are advised that the result is not promised. At row 3 the report is not submitted late, and the refund is sent out within two weeks. This is exactly what was promised, so the promise has again been satisfied. At row 4, the report is not submitted late, but the refund is not received within two weeks. In this circumstance, the promise is not satisfied.

An exception is equivalent to a negated sufficient condition. To make a promise, A, by attaching a rider that says that should a certain circumstance, C, arise the promise is waived is the same as saying that *if* the exceptional case does *not* arise, the promised result will be delivered: "if not-C, then A."

Exception	Result				
C	A	A unless C	~C	→	A
T	T	T	F	T	T
T	F	T	F	T	F
F	T	T	T	T	T
F	F	F	T	F	F

English conditionals that place an exception on a result should accordingly be formalized by negating the exception and placing it in the antecedent of an arrow sentence of SL.

But the rule must be exercised with caution. English exceptions can be intended in a strong form. The strong form not only promises that the result *will* occur provided the condition is *not* met but also suggests that the result will *not* occur if the condition *is* met. For example, suppose *x* promises *y* that,

> 4.31 I will take any unsold merchandise unless you tell me you want it

y wants the unsold merchandise and says so, but *x* takes it anyway. Most would think that *x* has not satisfied the promise. In this case, the promise is not just to take the unsold merchandise if the condition is not met, but also to *not* take it if the condition *is* met.

Exception *y* wants the unsold merchandise	Result *x* takes the unsold merchandise	Sentence [result] unless [condition]
T	T	F
T	F	T
F	T	T
F	F	F

As this table illustrates, strong exceptions are still functional. For every combination of values for the condition and the result, there is a unique value for the compound.

Sentences of this sort can be formalized by negating the condition and placing it in a biconditional, rather than a conditional.

Exception	Result				
C	A	A unless C (in which case not C)	A	≡	~C
T	T	F	T	F	F
T	F	T	F	T	F
F	T	T	T	T	T
F	F	F	F	F	T

English weak and strong exceptions make use of the same words to name two, different functions. Sometimes, context can help distinguish which sense a speaker might intend. "A fire extinguisher shall be placed on each floor unless the structure is a single family dwelling" would not be taken by most English speakers to mean that owners of single family dwellings would have broken the law were they to put a fire extinguisher on each floor. But "Four electrical outlets shall be evenly spaced throughout each room unless such placement would be within one metre of a water source" would be taken by most people to mean that an electrician who evenly spaced the fourth outlet within a metre of a water source would not have satisfied the code. Sentences like "Non-members will not be admitted unless they pay a fee" fall into a grey area. Is it meant that paying a fee is all that is required to gain admission, or might admission still be refused in this case because the only promise is to the members, that no non-members will be allowed in unless they do at least that much?

Where ambiguity enters, a distinction between preferred and special contexts is called for, and the principle of charity can be used to decide which should be the preferred context. Because strong exceptions are not satisfied in two of four possible cases whereas weak ones are not satisfied in only one, charity demands that speakers be presumed to mean the exception in the weak sense unless they either make it explicit that they mean the exception to be taken in the strong sense, or some special feature of the context dictates that they ought to be understood accordingly. Exceptions can be made explicitly strong by attaching the words "in which case not …" as in "Non-members will not be admitted unless they pay a fee, in which case they will [not not] be admitted."

As already noted, this is a textbook in logic and not in hermeneutics. As such it does not provide instruction on how to assess the implications of context. Instead, it stipulates policies for the resolution of hard cases. Policy for what follows is to take exceptions in the weak sense unless explicit wording is attached to make it clear that they are intended in the strong sense.

Review of Principles for Formalizing Conditionals

There are five different ways in which English inflects conditions. Because there are only two conditional connectives in SL, the SL connectives must be used in different ways to express each of the five different English contractual conditionals. It makes a difference whether the condition is placed in the antecedent or the consequent position of an arrow sentence of SL (A $\rightarrow$ B is not s-equivalent to B $\rightarrow$ A). It makes a difference whether the condition is negated or not negated. And it makes a difference whether the connective between the condition and the result is an arrow or a triple bar. These differences give rise to five variants that correspond to the five kinds of English conditionals.

Necessarily C (only if C):	$\rightarrow$ C
It is sufficient that C (if C):	C $\rightarrow$
Except in the case that C (unless C):	~C $\rightarrow$
It is both necessary and sufficient that C (if and only if C):	$\equiv$ C
"Strong" except in the case that C (unless C, in which case not):	$\equiv$ ~C

This review shows that English has neglected to name an alternative, $\rightarrow$ ~C, which makes a promise while stipulating that for the promise to be satisfied it is necessary that a certain condition not be satisfied. (C $\equiv$ and ~C $\equiv$ are not neglected, because inverting the order does not change the characteristic table for biconditionals.) English can still place negated necessary conditions on promises (e.g., with the words "only if not"), just as SL can formalize them. The neglect may have arisen because conditionals of the form "[result] only if not [condition] are intuitively equivalent to the contrapositive, if [condition] then not [result]," which turns the negated necessary condition into a sufficient condition for failing to get the result. It may be that listeners pick up on the point as conveyed by the latter formulation more quickly and easily, and speakers find it rhetorically more effective for that reason.

Exercise 4.5

1. *Formalize the following sentences in SL using the specified sentence letters to stand for the components. Rewrite sentences containing sufficient, necessary, or exceptional conditions in standard form prior to formalization.*
   A: *You may write the exam.*
   B: *You have preregistered.*
   C: *You show up more than 10 minutes late.*
      ★a. You may write the exam if you have preregistered.
      b. You may write the exam only if you have preregistered.
      ★c. You may write the exam if and only if you have preregistered.
      d. If you have preregistered, you may write the exam.
      ★e. You may write the exam unless you show up more than ten minutes late.
      f. You may write the exam unless you show up more than ten minutes late, in which case you may not write.
      ★g. Unless you show up more than ten minutes late, you may write the exam provided you have preregistered.

h. Supposing you preregistered you may write the exam, except if you show up more than ten minutes late.

A: *There is a passing average on the examinations.*
B: *The course is passed.*

    *i. A passing average on the examinations is necessary to pass the course.

    j. A passing average on the examinations is sufficient to pass the course.

    *k. A necessary condition for passing the course is a passing average on the examinations.

    l. To pass the course it is necessary to get a passing average on the examinations.

    *m. It suffices to get a passing average on the examinations to pass the course.

    n. A sufficient condition for passing the course is getting a passing average on the examinations.

    *o. A disjunction is false unless at least one of its disjuncts is true. (A: *A disjunction is false;* B: *At least one of the disjuncts is true.*)

    p. A conjunction is true unless one of its conjuncts is false, in which case it is not true. (A: *A conjunction is true;* B: *a conjunct is false.*)

A: *A conditional is false.*
B: *Its consequent is false.*
C: *Its antecedent is true and its consequent is false.*

    *q. For a conditional to be false it is necessary for its consequent to be false.

    r. For a conditional to be false it is not sufficient for its consequent to be false. *(Careful!)*

    *s. For a conditional to be false it is necessary and sufficient that the antecedent be true and the consequent false.

The following exercises illustrate that it is not necessary to understand the atomic components in order to be able to formalize a compound sentence. All that matters is the connective expressions and what sentence letters are assigned to the atomic sentences.

    t. The conclusion of a demonstration is derivable from the set of its premises only if it is s-valid, unless Ds is unsound. (A: *The conclusion of a demonstration is derivable from the set of its premises;* B: *the demonstration is s-valid;* C: *Ds is sound.*)

    *u. Except in the case where a sentence is s-contingent, it has an s-model if and only if its opposite does not have an s-model. (A: *a sentence is s-contingent;* B: *a sentence has an s-model;* C: *its opposite does not have an s-model.*)

    v. If Ts is complete, then Γ / P is s-invalid provided $\Gamma \cup$ ~P has at least one tree with at least one exhausted path. (A: Ts *is complete;* B: Γ / P *is s-invalid;* C: $\Gamma \cup$ ~P *has at least one tree with at least one exhausted path.*)

2. *Instantiate the following sentences on the interpretation provided, and under the constraint indicated.*

    *a. ~A $\rightarrow$ B (A: *An opponent appeals the result within 10 minutes of the end of the race;* B: *An award will be final; do not use "if.")*

    b. A $\rightarrow$ B (A: *A rider shall be relegated;* B: *The chief commissaire approves the decision;* "A" *is clearly the result in this case and the instantiation should reflect that.)*

    *c. B $\rightarrow$ A (A: *The leading rider shall be relegated;* B: *The leading rider drops below the measuring line; note that* "A" *is clearly the result in this case and the instantiation should reflect that.)*

    d. A $\rightarrow$ [B $\rightarrow$ (~C $\rightarrow$ ~G)] (A: *Rider 1 starts a sprint outside the sprinter's lane;* B: *The opponent is in the sprinter's lane;* C: *Rider 1 has a clear lead;* G: *Rider 1 enters the sprinter's lane; do not use "if" more than once.)*

    *e. B $\rightarrow$ A (A: *Rider 1 shall be relegated;* B: *Rider 1 passes on the left within the sprinter's lane.)*

    f. ~A $\rightarrow$ B (A: *The result is considered a foregone conclusion;* B: *A rider who drops below the measuring line shall be relegated; note that* "A" *is clearly the condition in this case and the instantiation should reflect that.)*

Exercise 4.5#1(r) brings up an issue with the scope of negations in English conditionals. When English means to negate a conditional, it will not always begin with a negation, but may wait until halfway through the sentence before inserting the negation. This frequently happens when the condition is only stated after the result, as in "For A it is not necessary that C," or "For A it is not sufficient that C." The position of "not" makes it tempting to think that the English only means to negate the condition. But there is a difference between saying "For A it is not necessary that C" and "For A it is necessary that not C." The same is true of "For A it is not sufficient that C" and "For A it is sufficient that not C." "For A it is not necessary that C" means that it is not the case that C is necessary for A, which is formalized as ~(A $\rightarrow$ C). It does not mean that not-C *is* necessary for A, which would be formalized as A → ~C. Likewise, "For A it is not sufficient that C" means that it is not the case that having C is enough to get A, which is formalized as ~(C → A).

4.8 Disjunction

In addition to formalizing contractual conditionals, SL can be used to formalize those English sentences that deny, conjoin, disjoin, or count. These include the kinds of sentences that say that each is or is not the case, or that none is, or that at least one is, or all but one, and so on (though the number cannot become very great before becoming unmanageably complex). These sorts of sentences are formalized using combinations of tilde, ampersand, and wedge. & symbolizes "both are" (or other words or phrases to that effect, such as "each is"), ∨ symbolizes "at least one is" (or other words or phrases to that effect), and ~ handles the denials.

"At least one is," builds a compound sentence that is true if and only if at least one of its components is true, and is otherwise false, as does the wedge connective of SL. English also uses a phrase, "exactly one is," that builds a compound sentence that is true if and only if exactly one of its components is true and otherwise is false. This phrase builds compound sentences of SL that are true or false under the same conditions as negated biconditionals. Less elegantly, but more literally, they might be formalized as saying that at least one but not both are the case: (A ∨ B) & ~(A & B).

A	B	At least one	A ∨ B	Exactly one	~	(A ≡ B)	(A ∨ B)	&	~	(A & B)
T	T	T	T	F	F	T	T	F	F	T
T	F	T	T	T	T	F	T	T	T	F
F	T	T	T	T	T	F	T	T	T	F
F	F	F	F	F	F	T	F	F	T	F

The meaning of English "or" is controversial. Suppose a forensic investigator testifies in court that the murderer was either over six feet tall or over 120 kg. Suppose the lawyer for the accused responds, "then by your own testimony my client could not possibly be the one who did it, because my client is both over six feet tall and over 120 kg." It is not likely that such a defence would succeed. Suppose an employer says to an employee, "Either get to work or go home." If the employee gets to work and the employer, remaining dissatisfied, fires the employee anyway, the employer cannot be accused of having made a false promise, because there was only ever a threat to fire if no work was done. There was no promise to refrain from firing if it was. English sentences of the form, "either A or B" are often true if and only if at least one of A and B is true and are otherwise false, in conformity with the truth conditions for wedge.

It is widely claimed that English "or" is also used in what is called an "exclusive" sense, to say that exactly one of A or B is the case. But this has been disputed (Barrett and Stenner, 1971). According to those who deny that "or" has a strong or exclusive sense, the examples that have been put forward to prove that "A or B" can mean "exactly one of A and B" are of two sorts: (i) cases in which context implies that A and B cannot both be true; (ii) cases in which "or" occurs under the scope of a nonfunctional connective or within a question, request, offer, or other nonassertoric sentence. In the first case, the impossibility of having both A and B is a consequence of background knowledge rather than a special sense of "or." For example, in "Art took the make-up exam on Tuesday or on Wednesday" (Hausman, Kahane, and Tidman, 2013: 30), the use of "the" indicates that there is only one exam and background knowledge about the length of make-up exams and the times of day at which they start suffices to rule out the possibility that Art wrote on both days. The exclusivity is expressed by "the" and background knowledge rather than "or." (Was the exam a take home? Was it scheduled at 11:30 p.m. on Tuesday? The background presumptions imported into the context are what makes the disjunction exclusive.) In the second case, the sentence needs to be rephrased before it can be formalized as a sentence that has a value that is a function of a component disjunction. But cases where this can be done without changing the meaning of the original sentence are, it is charged, not to be found. For example, when the purportedly exclusive and inclusive questions "Tea or coffee?" or "Cream or sugar?" are rephrased as assertions, "Tea is available or coffee is available"; "Tea is a choice or coffee is a choice"; "You can have tea if you ask for it or you can have coffee if you ask for it," the rewrite invites the response, "Well, which is it? You ought to know." A decisive assertion would use "and" in place of "or," which would make it merely informative of what is in stock. Embellishing the bald disjunction with information about whether the statement is made by a clerk coming out of the stock room of a grocery store, the salesperson for a catering company, or a server in a restaurant makes the disjuncts compatible or exclusive in virtue of background context, failing to establish that any ambiguity attaches to "or."

As observed by Grice (1989: 44–6), if "or" had its own exclusive sense, it ought to carry that sense with it from context to context and in particular into sentences where it appears as the immediate component of a negation. But the denial of an exclusive "or" is equivalent to "It is not the case that exactly one of A and B is the case," which (by double negation) is equivalent to "A if and only if B." There do not appear to be any instances where "It is not the case that A or B" is taken to mean "A if and only if B." Bencivenga, Lambert, and van Fraassen (1991: 26) suggest that a variant on "Either Alma will go out with Boda or she will go to the party" is plausibly construed as using "or" exclusively and so as meaning that Alma will do exactly one of the two. But "It is not the case that either Alma will go out with Boda or she will go to the party" is not plausibly construed as saying that Alma will go out with Boda if and only if she goes to the party, which it would have to be if "or" were used exclusively. This is a compelling reason for thinking that any exclusive sense of "or" arises from special contexts in which (unnegated) "or" appears rather than any alternative meaning that attaches to the word "or" itself.

Whether this is the correct analysis or not, the widespread opinion that "or" can mean "exactly one" is tongue tying. It deprives those who want to say "at least one" of a word, forcing them to use circumlocutions and add extra clauses. This textbook is a case in point. Up to now, "at least one" has been used instead of "or." This is not always easy to do. Were "or" not considered by many people to be ambiguous, the truth condition for conditional sentences could be stated elegantly.

> 4.32   A conditional, P → Q, is true if and only if P is false or Q is true; otherwise it is false

Supposing that "or" is ambiguous forces speakers and writers to employ comparatively convoluted expressions to make it clear which sense they intend:

> 4.32.1   A conditional, P → Q, is true if and only if at least one of the following is the case: (a) P is false; (b) Q is true
>
> 4.32.2   A conditional, P → Q, is true if and only if (a) P is false or (b) Q is true or (c) P is false and Q is true
>
> 4.32.3   A conditional, P → Q is false if and only if P is true and Q is false otherwise it is true

Perspicuity requires brevity. Whatever diminishes brevity forces speakers to communicate their ideas in a suboptimal fashion. (4.32.3 is as brief as 4.32, but it requires a disruptive appeal to the inverse case.) The penalties only start here. One of the most necessary and frequently employed forms of demonstration (one assigned in numerous exercises in this and following chapters) is proof by cases, which involves enumerating all the possibilities and demonstrating that each has the same result. When the truth conditions on a conditional or a disjunction, or the falsity conditions on a conjunction can be reduced to two cases (as in, "either P is false or Q is true"), a proof by cases requires two demonstrations. But if "or" is not understood by default to mean "at least one of," "either P is false or Q is true or both" must be used instead, and the required number of demonstrations expands to three, making for unnecessary additional work.

Logic is in no position to dictate how English speakers should express themselves. But being forced to complicate statements and make demonstrations half as long again is undesirable. As a remedy, the following practice governs the understanding and use of "or" in this textbook and work associated with it.

> **Rule Governing the Use and Meaning of English "Or" and "Either ... Or ..."**
>
> English "A or B" and "either A or B," where A and B are any English component sentences, are in all contexts to be understood to mean "at least one of A and B."
>
> The writer or speaker who uses "A or B" or "either A or B" is under no obligation to add "or both" or other words or phrases to make it clear that the sentence remains true when both A and B are true. By a stipulation that henceforth has effect throughout this book, the case where both A and B are true is always included in any claim to the effect that A "or" B is true or that "either" A "or" B is true.
>
> All the obligation is on those who want to say "exactly one of A or B" to make their claim explicit. They may not use a standalone occurrence of "A or B" or "either A or B" to express their thought. Instead, they must employ a circumlocution and say "exactly one of A or B" or "A or B but not both."

This rule is not instituted simply to make explanations in the textbook less verbose, or textbook exercises easier to complete. It is also dictated by the principle of charity. As illustrated by the tables given earlier, "at least one" is true in three of four cases, whereas "exactly one" is true in only two of four. On the principle that the speaker should be understood to say what is more likely to be true (unless explicit words to the contrary are uttered), "A or B" should be understood to mean "at least one of A and B."

A similar rule was earlier instituted for "unless." But whereas the rule for "or" is needed to combat an unfortunate popular opinion, a rule for "unless" is required because there clearly are cases in which occurrence of the exceptional circumstance not only releases the agent from the obligation to act, but imposes a contrary obligation not to act. Consider, "I will lead with hearts unless you raise your eyebrow"; "Applications will not be considered unless they are posted before the deadline"; "The vehicle in the turning lane shall turn unless there is a pedestrian in the intersection." And so on. Others were mentioned in section 4.7.

The difference between "unless" and "or" may be due to the fact that "unless" is primarily used to specify conditions under which an agent is released from an obligation, whereas "or" is primarily used when listing alternatives. In the former case, an agent makes things be a certain way; in the latter, things just are a certain way. The former case draws attention to what the agent has undertaken or been obliged to do, and that obligation can be taken in a stronger or weaker sense. The latter case draws attention to the alternatives themselves and so to whether they are intrinsically compatible or incompatible. When alternatives are obviously incompatible, there is no need to take their incompatibility to be asserted by a special sense of "or." When alternatives are not made incompatible by background knowledge, it is incumbent on the speaker to explicitly state that they are so. That means adding "but not both" or words to that effect.

Exercise 4.6

1. *Formalize the following compound sentences in SL. Provide a preliminary interpretation for the sentence letters you choose to use. (The instructions for question 2 below provide an example of what an interpretation should look like.) Use the alphanumerically first sentence letter to stand for the first simple sentence to appear in the compound, the second for the second, and so on. Part of the exercise is to demonstrate that you are correctly identifying each simple component from start to finish, so be sure to assign complete sentences of English (not single words or abbreviated phrases) to each sentence letter.*

    ★a. "No, [we are not going on a hike in the morning and to the theatre in the afternoon]; we are going on a hike or we are going to the theatre." (Tarski, 1941: 21).

    ★b. "Either [John] goes out with Mary or he goes to the party." (Bencivenga, Lambert, and van Fraassen, 1991: 26)

      c. You may contact me either to ask questions about the assignment or to discuss the material more generally.

    ★d. If you misrepresent or provide incomplete information, this will result in cancellation of the insurance or denial of a claim.

      e. Your insurance will reimburse 80% of your expenses if your flight is delayed or you are denied boarding.

    ★f. The insurance company will only reimburse you if you can prove you were not at fault or if you purchased complete coverage.

      g. A conjunction is false only if either the left conjunct is false or the right conjunct is false.

    ★h. A disjunction is true if and only if either the left disjunct is true or the right disjunct is true.

      i. A conditional is true if the antecedent is false or the consequent is true.

2. *Instantiate the following sentences of SL using the following interpretation:*
    A: Your insurance claim will be denied.
    B: Your insurance claim will be investigated.
    C: You make a claim regarding a car accident.
    G: You make a claim regarding theft of your property.
    H: Your insurance plan will be cancelled.
    K: You misrepresent information on an insurance claim.

Try your best to make your instantiations sound natural. Do your best to follow the guidelines after each question. Feel free to adjust verb tenses and moods to improve the reading.

★**a.** K → (A ∨ H)

  b. (C ∨ G) → B

★**c.** ~C ≡ G *(devise a correct instance that does not use the word "not")*

  d. (B ∨ H) → K *(treat the consequent as a type of condition)*

★**e.** ~H → (A ∨ B) *(try not to use the word "if")*

  f. ~H → (~C ≡ G) *(devise a correct instance that uses "if" and "or")*

4.9 Negations and Conjunctions

English has various means of denying a sentence. Paramount among them are negative words and phrases like "not" and "it is not the case that." But English can also deny a sentence by adding negative prefixes like "an-," "in-," "non-," or "un-" to words. "Alma is unmotivated" has the same meaning as "Alma is not motivated," which in turn has the same meaning as "it is not the case that Alma is motivated." Because the tilde builds a compound sentence that asserts that the nullation has an opposite value, English denials can generally be formalized using the tilde. This requires some caution, as it can be easy to miss the negative prefix and treat "Alma is unmotivated" as if it were a simple sentence rather than a negation.

English will sometimes deny a sentence without meaning to affirm that it has an incompatible value. This is often the case with double denials. "Alma is not unmotivated" may mean that Alma is something less than fully motivated rather than that Alma is motivated. SL is not equipped to handle this nuance. Such double denials must be formalized as atomic sentences.

English also uses various expressions to conjoin sentences to build a compound sentence that is true if and only if both of its components are true. Some of these expressions carry added meaning. Some of them are not always used functionally.

The paradigm English expression used to conjoin sentences is "and," but it and its cognates can be entirely omitted in favour of using a comma or semicolon, and it can be used for other purposes, some functional, others nonfunctional. In "Leave a higher tip and you will get better service," or "Get better service and you must have left a better tip," "and" separates the condition and the result of a conditional sentence. In, "Price and Priestley were English," "and," is used to connect the objects named Price and Priestley, not two sentences. "Price and Priestley were English" can be rewritten as "Price was English and Priestley was English," which does use "and" as a sentential connective, and which preserves the meaning of the original. But this is not always possible. "Price and Priestley played whist on many occasions" cannot be rewritten as "Price played whist on many occasions" and Priestley played whist on many occasions" if the intention is to affirm that Price and Priestly played whist with one another on those occasions. In such cases "and" is being used as what might be called an "objectual" rather than a sentential connective. Rather than connect one sentence to another sentence it connects the objects that make up a compound object or fall under a relation. The assertion that the objects constitute that compound or stand in that relation must be formalized as an atomic sentence of SL.

Even when used as a sentential connective, "and" can carry extra meaning. "The thief stole the key and gained access to the building," not only conjoins two sentences but suggests that one occurred before the other and that the two are causally related. When this extra meaning affects the value of the compound (suppose the thief took the key from the building after having gained access in some other way), the sentence must be formalized as an atomic sentence of SL, because the value of the English compound is not a function of the value of its components. (An alternative is to rewrite the sentence as "First the thief stole the key, and then used it to gain access to the building.") In contexts where the extra meaning is not intended, the sentence can safely be formalized as a conjunction.

The issue of additional meaning also arises with expressions like "but," "yet," and "however." These expressions sometimes function as conjunctive connectives, but they also convey the further thought that there is something surprising or exceptional or inevitable about the case, as in "I am a lazy fool, but I have done very well for myself," or "But for my laziness, I could have accomplished much." This is an element of nonfunctional meaning that novices will sometimes attempt to capture by mixing ampersands with tildes in their formalizations. While it is tempting to think of "but" and cognates like "yet" or "however" as being halfway towards a denial, they are not. They still affirm both components. The additional expression of surprise or contrariety to expectations is made by way of comment on the fact of the conjunction. & only captures the functional meaning and so formalizes "but," "however," "yet," etc., as if they were simple conjunctions. Unlike the cases of additional meaning discussed earlier, this additional meaning does not affect the value of the compound, so it can safely be formalized as a conjunction of SL.

Many other English connectives can be formalized using combinations of tilde, ampersand, and wedge. This job is made easier by the fact that English uses phrases or contractions that make the relative placement of the corresponding connectives of SL explicit. For example, "none," "nor," and "neither," are all, in a way, contractions that have lost their apostrophes: "n'one," "n'or," and "n'either," that is, not-one, not-or, and not-either. When English mentions two connectives, the first one to be mentioned tends to have scope over the second. Accordingly, "none of A or B" or "neither A nor B," which really mean "not (either) one of A or B" and "not-either A or B," are formalized just as they are written: $\sim(A \lor B)$. However, "none of A and B" is, intuitively, "not any one of A and B" which is directly formalized as $\sim A \& \sim B$, though SL semantics demonstrates this to be equivalent to $\sim(A \lor B)$.

Similarly, "not both A and B" is formalized by giving the first connective to be mentioned, "not," scope over the second connective to be mentioned, "and": $\sim(A \& B)$.

A formalization of "not both" can be employed as the second part of a formalization of "Either A or B but not both": $(A \lor B) \& \sim(A \& B)$. This has the force of "exactly one of A and B."

Between them, $A \& B$, $A \lor B$, $(A \lor B) \& \sim(A \& B)$, $\sim(A \& B)$, and $\sim(A \lor B)$ say "both A and B," "at least one of A and B," "exactly one of A and B," "at most one of A and B," and "none of A and B" respectively.

$A \& B$:	both A and B
$A \lor B$:	at least one of A and B
$(A \lor B) \& \sim(A \& B)$:	exactly one of A and B
$\sim(A \& B)$:	at most one of A and B
$\sim(A \lor B)$:	none of A and B

"Exactly one of A and B" is intuitively formalized by the dnf, "either A and not-B or not-A and B": $(A \& \sim B) \lor (\sim A \& B)$. More elegant formalizations are $\sim(A \equiv B)$, $A \equiv \sim B$ and $\sim A \equiv B$. The fact that the triple bar can be used to say "exactly one" belies the label "biconditional." It is only in some contexts that $\equiv$ formalizes "is necessary and sufficient for." In other contexts, it can mean "exactly one of." Attention needs to be paid to this fact, both in formalization and instantiation.

With three sentences in play, combinations of tilde, ampersand, and wedge can be used to express all, at least two, at least one, exactly two, exactly one, at most two, at most one, or none.

The formalizations that follow omit internal punctuation from iterated conjunctions and iterated disjunctions. Culling the forest of punctuation makes the more important, larger-scale groupings more readily apparent.

All of A, B, and C:	$A \& B \& C$
At least two of A, B, and C:	$(A \& B) \lor (A \& C) \lor (B \& C)$
At least one of A, B, and C:	$A \lor B \lor C$
Exactly two of A, B, and C:	$(A \& B \& \sim C) \lor (A \& \sim B \& C) \lor (\sim A \& B \& C)$
Exactly one of A, B, and C:	$(A \& \sim B \& \sim C) \lor (\sim A \& B \& \sim C) \lor (\sim A \& \sim B \& C)$
Not all of A, B, and C:	$\sim(A \& B \& C)$
At most two of A, B, and C:	$\sim(A \& B \& C)$
At most one of A, B, and C:	$(\sim A \& \sim B) \lor (\sim A \& \sim C) \lor (\sim B \& \sim C)$
None of A, B, and C:	$\sim(A \lor B \lor C)$

The most challenging of these formalizations are the "at most" sentences, which require formalizing what in English is positive using negatives. The temptation is to consider "at most one of A, B, and C," to mean that it might be possible to have any one of A, B, or C or to have none of them. This would come out as $(A \lor B \lor C) \lor \sim(A \lor B \lor C)$, but as a long table will show, such a sentence is true on an interpretation on which all of A, B, and C are true, and the English sentence is false under that condition. The key to getting the correct formalization is recognizing that "at most one of three are" means "at least two of three are not."

"At least two" can also cause problems. "At least two" includes the possibility that all three are the case, suggesting that a further clause, "… ∨ (A & B & C)." ought to be added to the recommended formalization. But the formalization given on the table is already true on an interpretation that assigns T to each sentence letter, so no further clause is needed.

A formalization is not acceptable unless it passes the valuation test. It is wise to use the test to confirm whether "at least *x*" and "at most *x*" sentences have been correctly formalized.

Exercise 4.7

1. *Formalize the following sentences in SL. If the sentence contains a conditional, rewrite it in standard form first. When formalizing, identify the simple component sentences in each compound sentence (a simple sentence will not contain a functional connective) and provide a formalization key that shows which simple sentences have been assigned to which sentence letters. Each sentence letter must have a complete sentence assigned to it, not a word or phrase. This means writing out the sentence as a whole when specifying the formalization key. Consult the answered questions for further guidance.*

    ⋆a. Roses are red and violets are blue.

    b. Roses are not blue, but violets are.

    ⋆c. Either roses are red or violets are.

    d. Neither roses nor violets are attractive to butterflies.

    ⋆e. Roses and violets are not both red.

    f. Either roses or violets are red, but they are not both red.

    ⋆g. Carrots are not unhealthy, but they are unappetizing.

    h. Carrots are healthy but not appealing, sugar is appealing but not healthy, and cheese is neither.

    ⋆i. A disjunction is true if and only if at least one of its disjuncts is true.

    j. A biconditional is true if both the left immediate component and the right immediate component are false.

    ⋆k. A conjunction is true only if neither the left conjunct nor the right conjunct is false.

    l. A disjunction is true if and only if the left disjunct and the right disjunct are not both false.

    For the following exercises in this set, internal punctuation may be omitted in iterated conjunctions and iterated disjunctions.

    ⋆m. For an interpretation, I, to satisfy a set of three sentences, it is necessary that none of the first sentence, the second sentence, or the third sentence be false on I. *(Use the following formalization key: A: an interpretation, I, satisfies a set of three sentences; B: the first sentence is false on I; C: the second sentence is false on I; G: the third sentence is false on I.)*

    n. Provided an iterated conjunction with three conjuncts is true, all of the first conjunct, the second conjunct, and the third conjunct are true.

    ⋆o. An iterated conjunction with three conjuncts is true unless one of the first conjunct, the second conjunct, or the third conjunct is false.

    p. If at least two of Alma, Boda, and Crumb will receive a settlement then at most one of them will not be charged.

    ⋆q. If at most two of Alma, Boda, and Crumb will receive a settlement then at least one of them will not be charged.

    r. If exactly one of Alma, Boda, and Crumb will receive a settlement then exactly two of them will not be charged.

2. *Instantiate the following sentences of SL using the following interpretation:*

    A: Alma's artwork was effective.

    B: Boda's artwork was effective.

    C: Crumb left the auditorium in disgust.

    G: Crumb will have to pay a bonus.

    H: Crumb will have to extend the appointment.

Try your best to make your instantiations sound natural. Instantiations in stilted, quasi-English logicalese are to be avoided. Do your best to follow the guidelines after each question. Feel free to adjust verb tenses and moods to improve the reading.

★a. ~~A *(devise a correct instance that uses "not" at most once)*

b. ~(A ∨ B) *(devise a correct instance that does not begin with "it is not the case that")*

★c. ~A & B *(devise a correct instance that does not use the words "not" or "and")*

d. ~(B & A) *(be careful of the order of the English connectives; make a valuation table for your English instantiation and compare it to a valuation table for ~(B & A))*

★e. A & C *(devise a correct instance that begins with the connective and lists the component sentences afterwards)*

f. (~B ∨ ~A) & C *(be careful to generate an instance that is functionally compound; claims about causes of effects are not)*

★g. (A & B) & C *(do not use "and" or "inspiring" more than once)*

h. ~(A & B) → ~(G ∨ H) *(give two equivalent answers, one using "if" and at most one occurrence of "not"; the other using "unless" and no occurrences of "not"; do not begin with "unless")*

★i. ~(G ∨ H) → (~A ∨ ~B) *(give two equivalent answers, one using "if" the other using "it is necessary that"; do not use "or" in either answer)*

j. (A ∨ B) & ~(A & B) *(do not use "or")*

★k. H → ~(A ≡ B) *(give an instantiation that represents G as a result depending on a condition that is stated without using "not")*

l. A ≡ ~B *(devise an instance that does not represent either one of A and ~B as a condition on the other)*

4.10 Punctuation

Spoken English needs punctuation as much as written. Punctuation is often expressed by emphases or stops, but English also uses special words as punctuation marks. The words are paired with a connective or inflection and serve as the equivalent of an opening or closing parenthesis:

either	...	or
neither	...	nor
both	...	and
if	...	then

In each of these cases, a functionally compound sentence can occur within the ellipses. The operation can be iterated to punctuate arbitrarily compound sentences, e.g., "If neither ... nor ... then both ... and either ... or ...," which is formalized in SL as ~(... ∨ ...) → [... & (... ∨ ...)].

An advantage of having a word to designate the opening (as opposed to closing) punctuation mark is that it permits taking the scope of an initial "not" to extend through to the corresponding closing punctuation mark, so "either," "neither," "both," and "if" do double duty. They both indicate the scope of the first component of their corresponding connective (in the case of "either," "neither," and "both") or the condition being inflected (in the case of "if") and widen the scope of a prior "not" over the associated connective.

When the intention is to negate only the first component, "not" must follow the verbal punctuation mark, in accord with the principle that English mentions the connective with the widest scope first, as in "either not ... or ..."; "both not ... and ..."; or "if not ... then ..."

English can also use "or," "nor," and "and" as higher-place connectives, as in "either ... or ... or ...," "neither ... nor ... nor ...," "all of ... and ... and ... and ...," for arbitrarily many iterations. The formal syntax of SL requires the corresponding formalizations to be punctuated with an increasingly thick forest of punctuation marks. This can do more to obscure than assist understanding. When many simpler sentences are linked with conjunctions, it is permissible to omit the internal punctuation around pairs of conjuncts, and likewise for disjunctions and their disjuncts. This is a liberty that will not be exercised for the time being, because its legitimacy is only fully demonstrated in chapter 5. In the meantime, situations that require the forest of punctuation marks are avoided.

In writing, English has further resources. They should be respected. By default, periods separate English sentences. Whatever falls between two periods should be formalized as a sentence, not split into two or more sentences, or amalgamated with another sentence. The only exception is when an English sentence contains both a premise and the conclusion of a demonstration. In that case, the conclusion must be formalized as a distinct sentence. Within

English sentences, commas, semicolons, and colons should be taken as a guide to how a compound sentence has been built up from its components. Not all compounds are functionally compound, but where they are, punctuation marks indicate the main breaks, and so the locations of the main connectives. A colon indicates a stronger break (and so a more widely separated pair of parentheses) than a semicolon and a semicolon a stronger break than a comma.

Exercise 4.8

1. *Formalize the following sentences in SL. When formalizing, identify the simple component sentences in each compound sentence (a simple sentence will not contain a functional connective) and assign these simple sentences to sentence letters. Rely on both verbal signs and punctuation marks to identify which connectives fall within the scope of which others. Consult the answered questions for further guidance.*

   *a. A director may be removed from office provided a resolution to that effect is passed by two-thirds of the members of the corporation, but this may be done only if notice specifying the intention to pass such a resolution has been given. *(Hint: read "this may be done" as repeating a claim made earlier.)*

   b. The whole board of directors shall retire at the annual general meeting, but a retired director shall be eligible for re-election, except when the provisions of this by-law forbid that action.

   *c. The board may meet as often as it sees fit unless the executive committee is authorized to fix its quorum, in which case the quorum shall not be less than six members. *(Hint: supply the appropriate unstated connective at the point of the comma; do not confuse "in which case" with "in which case not"; read "in which case" as other words for a claim made earlier and as having the force of "in the case that.")*

   d. At most one of the president, the treasurer, and the chair of the board may be absent from a meeting, unless the purpose of the meeting is to replace the absent officers.

   *e. Provided neither the president nor the treasurer is absent the board may rule on any motion involving a financial expenditure.

   f. Unless the goods are picked up by 6 p.m., either a storage fee will be levied or they will be sold or destroyed.

   *g. If neither Alma nor Boda are present for the hearing, they will not both be able to make the application to the court.

   h. Provided I am able to sell my present residence for the asking price I will buy the house, except in the case where I don't receive the inheritance.

   *i. For an extraordinary membership meeting to be convened, it is necessary that either the president and the treasurer resign, or the Board reject the budget.

   j. It is not necessary for a person to have a record of service in order to obtain certification, but it is necessary for that person to not have been convicted of a criminal offence. *(There is an obviously intended but unexpressed repetition of a claim that must be included in the formalization.)*

2. *Instantiate the following as idiomatic English sentences using the following interpretation:*
   A: I will buy the house.
   B: I will buy the yacht.
   C: I will take a vacation.
   G: I receive the inheritance.
   H: Hell freezes over.
   K: I am able to sell my present residence for the asking price.

   *a. A ∨ (B ∨ C) *(Devise a correct instantiation that does not use "or.")*
   b. G → (B & C)
   *c. (G → B) & C
   d. (A → G) & (H → B) *(The instantiation should reflect what are clearly the conditions in this case.)*
   *e. G → (K → A)
   f. (~C → A) → (G & K) *(Devise a correct instantiation that does not begin with "if if.")*
   *g. ~(A ∨ C) → (~G & ~K)
   h. ~(G ∨ K) → ~A *(Devise a correct instantiation that does not use "if" or "neither.")*
   *i. A & [~G ≡ ~(B ∨ C)]
   j. ~H → [(A & B) ∨ C]
   *k. (A ≡ G) & ~(A ≡ B)
   l. [(G & K) → (B & C)] & [~(G & K) → ~(B ∨ C)]

4.11 Limits of Formalization

This chapter opened by identifying some limits on what can be formalized in SL. To summarize the main points of that discussion, there are some sentences that cannot be formalized, even as sentence letters, because they do not have a functional value, and there are many sentential connectives that cannot be formalized because they are nonfunctional. (They do not build a compound with a value that is a function of the values of its components.) Sentences compounded using nonfunctional connectives can still be formalized as atomic sentences of SL, provided they bear exactly one of two values.

Difficulties arise with certain cases, such as conditionals, where the connective (or the inflection that takes its place), is only functional in certain contexts. In earlier sections of this chapter the formalization of conditionals was restricted to contractual cases, because these are cases that intuitively reflect the valuation rules for → and ≡. Contractual conditionals were contrasted with causal conditionals, which are not functional. There is another kind of conditional to watch out for, conditionals that talk about what would have happened if things had turned out otherwise, for example, "if I had more money I would buy you a balloon." Such conditionals are called counterfactuals, because their antecedents are contrary to what is in fact the case. They can take the form of promises (or quasi promises), as above, or causal sentences, such as "if it had not rained, there would not have been as many crashes in the junior race" and "If Caesar had not crossed the Rubicon, Rome would have remained a republic." Counterfactuals, of whatever sort, generally cannot be formalized in SL. Someone who knows how stingy I am may doubt whether it is true that I would have bought you a balloon, even if I had more money. Someone who thinks that juniors will crash regardless of the circumstances will doubt that the rain would have made any difference. And historians may think that Caesar would have seized power at some point anyway, even if he had heeded the Senate's order that fateful day. But if any counterfactual is formalized in SL, it must be true, because, by definition, a counterfactual has a false antecedent. This cannot be right, since if the counterfactual is at all controversial, its truth can be questioned.

Like causal sentences, counterfactuals are either true or false, and so and so make assertions. (Their truth or falsity is just not a function of the values of their components.) When it is generally accepted that a counterfactual is true, and it is premised in a demonstration, it can be rewritten in the indicative and formalized as if it were a promise made under a sufficient condition. Counterfactual conclusions drawn from counterfactual premises by what is called "hypothetical syllogism" can be similarly formalized. (See the discussion of material conditionals in section 4.12). But when considered in isolation counterfactuals must be treated as atomic sentences, which have a truth value that is not a function of the truth value of their components. They may only be formalized as conditionals in special contexts.

Exercise 4.9

Identify what values the following sentences might take. If they are compound, determine whether the values of the components determine the values of the compounds in all possible cases. If they do, suggest how the compound might be formalized in SL.

- **★a.** Do you take cream or sugar in your coffee?
- b. Leave your application in the box and go to the registration area.
- **★c.** I left my application in the box and went to the registration area.
- d. Either process the forms in order or I will report you.
- **★e.** I wish I had left sooner.
- f. If you had left sooner you would not have embarrassed yourself.
- **★g.** Any attempt to bypass the normal registration process will result in your being moved to the bottom of the list.
- h. If you raise the temperature of a substance to its critical point, you will observe all kinds of unexpected behaviour.
- **★i.** If you hadn't injured your knee in practice last month, you would have been able to play in the final playoff game and we would surely have won the championship.

Issues arise with a class of expressions that look like unary connectives but are better described as operators. They include, "it is possible that," "it is necessary that," and "it was said / hoped / believed / asked / desired / wished / feared / willed / intended that" (this list could be embellished at much greater length). These operators can be attached to a sentence to make a compound. But they are not functional. The value of the component does not always determine the value of the compound. It might be true that there is milk in the refrigerator, but that does not determine whether it is true that I believe that there is milk in the refrigerator. And while it might be false that there is beer in the refrigerator or true that there is milk, that does not determine whether it is possible that there is beer in the refrigerator or whether it is necessary that there be milk there instead.

Sometimes a sentence containing a functional connective will occur within the scope of a nonfunctional operator, as in

4.33   Alma hopes the game has not been cancelled

Whether the game has been cancelled or not does not determine whether Alma hopes it has not been cancelled. But the sentence does contain a functional connective. This raises the question of whether it might be rewritten in an equivalent form that brings the functional connective, "it is not the case that" out from under the scope of the nonfunctional operator, "hopes that," permitting the sentence to be formalized as a functional compound.

4.34   It is not the case that Alma hopes the game has been cancelled

The acceptability of this approach depends on whether hoping that something is not the case is equivalent to not hoping that it is the case, which is doubtful. Hoping it is and hoping it is not are both states of mind. Not hoping means not being in a state of mind of either sort. The safest approach is to accept that when "it is not the case that" (or words or phrases to that effect) occurs within the scope of "it was said / asked / hoped / feared / wished / intended that" and so forth, the claim must be formalized as a sentence letter. A rewrite that brings the negation outside of the scope of the operator does not obviously preserve the meaning. This is clearly the case with the operator, "said that."

4.35   Alma said that the game has not been cancelled

does not entail

4.36   Alma did not say that the game has been cancelled

"It is possible that" and "it is necessary that" are exceptions to this policy. They bear a special relation to one another, often called *"duality."* With duals, an internal negation can be made an external negation provided the operator is replaced with its dual. "It is *possible* that the game has *not* been cancelled" is intuitively equivalent to "It is *not necessarily* the case that the game has been cancelled," and "It is *necessary* that the game *not* be cancelled" is intuitively equivalent to "It is *not possible* that the game is cancelled." In this case, "it is possible/necessary that A is not the case" can be rewritten as "it is not necessary/possible that A is the case" and formalized in SL as a negation.

Duality also applies to "all" and "some." "Some of the apples are not ripe," is intuitively equivalent to "not all of the apples are ripe. Unfortunately, "All of the apples are not ripe" does not lend itself to similar treatment. It is inherently ambiguous. It might be read as saying either "All of the apples are unripe" or "It is not the case that all of the apples are ripe." This frustrates what would otherwise be a straightforward application of the principle of duality. Chapter 12.3.3 adopts the policy of declaring sentences of the form "all are not" to be ungrammatical.

Rewrites are also sometimes possible when binary connectives are placed under the scope of nonvalutional operators. "And" is a very strong connective. When it occurs under the scope of a nonfunctional operator the sentence can generally be rewritten as an equivalent conjunction. "Alma knows that there is milk and beer in the refrigerator" is intuitively equivalent to "Alma knows that there is milk in the refrigerator and Alma knows that there is beer in the refrigerator" and the same holds for "said that," "asked whether," "believes that," "hopes that," and so on. In contrast, "or" is a weak connective. If Alma knows that there is either milk or beer in the refrigerator, it does not follow that either Alma knows that there is milk in the refrigerator or Alma knows that there is beer in the refrigerator, and the same tends to hold for the other nonfunctional operators.

Exercise 4.10

Determine whether the following English sentences can be formalized in SL. If they can be, determine whether they can be formalized as functional compounds or must be formalized as sentence letters. Give reasons for your answers.

> ***a.** Hume said that justice applies only if there is limited abundance and limited generosity.
>
> b. Hume believed that all objects that are separable are distinguishable and that there can be no necessary connections between separable objects.
>
> ***c.** Hume believed that causal claims must be either matters of fact or relations of ideas.
>
> d. This sentence is false.
>
> ***e.** The sentence "this sentence is false" is false.
>
> f. It is necessary that there will either be a sea battle tomorrow or not be a sea battle tomorrow.
>
> ***g.** It is possible that Locke and Newton were both Antitrinitarian.
>
> h. Hume published the *Enquiry Concerning Human Understanding* before the failed attempt to get the appointment at the University of Glasgow, but not before the failed attempt to get the appointment at Edinburgh.
>
> ***i.** Mary Wollstonecraft argued that women are just as capable of rational thought as men are and should be given the opportunity to be educated in the same way.
>
> j. Although Alma has studied the history of education, she is not aware that Mary Wollstonecraft argued that women should be educated.
>
> ***k.** While Alma knows that Boda wrecked her car, she does not believe that it was his fault because it was the best course of action at the time.
>
> l. Although the city was neither able to provide an adequate explanation for why the inspection had not been performed nor say when one would take place it was able to say when work would resume.
>
> ***m.** If I freely raised my arm, it must have been possible for my arm not to rise even though it did rise and it will never be true that it did not rise. *(loosely based on an observation made by Diodorus Cronus (d. 284 BCE), quoted by Epictetus in Discourses ii.19.1)*

4.12 Formalizing Demonstrations

The formalization of demonstrations brings its own challenges. These challenges are hermeneutical rather than logical, though logic plays an ancillary role in overcoming them.

The sort of demonstrations that occur in philosophy and in ordinary language are short and simple. They employ familiar, intuitively valid forms. Demonstrations containing multiple premises and unfamiliar forms are largely confined to mathematics, logic, and student exercises. (The same thing is true of "natural arithmetic." The sort of calculating done in the grocery store or at a restaurant is very simple by comparison with what is found in a university textbook.) Protracted demonstrations do not occur naturally, even in philosophy, and for good reason. Audiences will not tolerate them. An author who wants to be understood will not employ long, convoluted reasoning but will instead split the demonstration into multiple parts, employ lemmas, perform the derivation for the audience, and use whatever other devices ingenuity can suggest to make the reasoning obvious.

Logic textbook exercises notwithstanding, the purpose of formalization is not primarily to identify highly complex demonstrative forms prior to testing those forms for validity. Formalization does not just serve as an aid to identifying instances of invalid reasoning. As illustrated by academic journal articles in philosophy and pub or coffee house disputations in ordinary language, it is more often used as a necessary preliminary to critical scrutiny of the premises of valid demonstrations. Such scrutiny requires correctly identifying which valid form the author means to use. This makes the premises precise, and aids in the discovery of unstated but intended premises.

Given that most demonstrations are short, simple, and familiar, it might be assumed that formalizing them should be easy. Challenges are posed by the facts that demonstrations in natural language are rarely laid out as neatly as they are in logic, with numbered premises followed by a clearly separated and identified conclusion. Demonstrations in natural language could contain the conclusion at the start, in the middle or at the end. The conclusion might be stated more than once, in different places and in different but equivalent forms. When the logic of the argument is particularly obvious, the conclusion might even be unstated, on the assumption that the audience will draw it for themselves. Alternatively, obviously true or commonly accepted premises may be omitted. (Audiences can find it irritating and pedantic if an author goes through all the obvious premises for a conclusion.) More rhetorically, authors might adopt an air of profundity by way of making audiences feel ashamed of not being clever or informed enough to see all the unstated premises, thereby shifting the burden of proof from themselves onto their audiences (a deplorable trick that is, unfortunately, all too effective).

Perhaps the greatest challenge to formalizing demonstrations is posed by the fact that they are comparatively rare. Even in philosophy and other academic work, where one might expect to find them in abundance, they can be few and far between. Much of what is said in most academic work is said by way of reporting or explaining, not by way of demonstration, and most demonstrations are inductive rather than deductive. The task of identifying the deductive demonstrations is complicated by the fact that explanations look very much like demonstrations. Explanations speak of consequences, offer reasons for those consequences, and use the same indicator words and phrases to tag reasons and consequences that deductive demonstrations use to tag premises and conclusions. (The same is true of inductive demonstrations, but inductive demonstrations can be more easily distinguished by the fact that they only purport to establish the likelihood, as opposed to the certainty, of their conclusions.)

A useful heuristic for distinguishing demonstrations from explanations is based on the distinction between what is better known and what is less well known. Demonstrations tend to go from what is better known (the premises) to what is less well known (the conclusion). Even demonstrations by what is called "reduction to absurdity" ask the audience to provisionally accept certain premises (something the audience is often quite disposed to do) by way of deriving a contradiction and so demonstrating that at least one of the premises must be rejected.

In contrast, explanations go from what is less well known to what is better known. The consequences that explanations are concerned with are accepted, and the reasons explanations offer for them are not offered to convince the audience that what they already accept is the case. Explanations are instead offered to help the audience understand why it is the case. If this were obvious, no explanation would be necessary, so explanations are only called for in cases where the explanation being offered is, of its nature, less well known than the event it purports to explain.

To say "the accident occurred because the driver was either inattentive or following too closely" is to explain an event. Presumably, all are agreed that an accident did occur and do not need to be convinced of this. The question is instead what produced this consequence. Two alternative explanations are offered: that the driver was either inattentive or following too closely. These explanations may be contentious. Those who agree that the consequence occurred may disagree over why it occurred. Perhaps the sight lines were blocked. Perhaps the brakes failed. But everyone agrees that the consequence did in fact occur. Even when the explanation is not contentious, it appeals to things that are not as widely known or accepted as the fact being explained.

In contrast, "the length of the skid marks indicates that the driver was either inattentive or following too closely" offers a reason for a conclusion. In this case, what is inferred or concluded is not something that is accepted but something that is more difficult to determine, that the driver was either inattentive or following too closely. This can be hard to know after the fact, especially if there are no independent, reliable witnesses. But a photograph of a tape measure laid alongside the skid marks is available for all to see. Here, the inference is from what is better known to what is less well known.[2]

Even when deductive demonstrations have been correctly identified, it should not be supposed that everything that is said is part of the demonstration. In the process of giving a demonstration, an author could digress to comment on matters that are irrelevant to the demonstration. The conclusion of the demonstration could be found in only one part of an English sentence, the remainder of which contains premises or irrelevant material. Reports and explanations might be mixed in with demonstrations, interspersed with the premises by way of commenting on or further illustrating the premises. Sometimes, authors will report the demonstrations of others, as a prelude to criticizing those demonstrations, or conjecture about objections others might raise as a prelude to refuting those objections. Alternatively, a demonstration might be interrupted for the sake of demonstrating one of its premises. Long passages might be merely stage-setting, preliminary to the presentation of the actual demonstration. Even when demonstrations are deductive, the deduction might turn on a more advanced logic, so that a formalization in SL will appear invalid.

Those who have studied sentential logic have the advantage of being better able to recognize simple, intuitively valid demonstrations in sentential logic when they are being employed. They are like experienced bird watchers, who are better able to see the bird through the underbrush. This makes them better able to identify and criticize an author's premises.

Being able to recognize simple, intuitively valid demonstrative forms is not enough, however. A critic needs to be skilled in the art of interpretation. Though this is a textbook in logic and not in hermeneutics, some basic hermeneutic principles need to be followed.

1. Each English sentence should be formalized as a sentence of SL. When one English sentence contains multiple unrelated assertions, ampersands should be used to conjoin them. Sometimes a sentence may contain material that is not relevant to the demonstration. It should be omitted from the formalization.

2. Where the same claim is stated multiple times using different words, the different wordings should be assigned to the same sentence letter. What decides whether different wordings should be assigned to the same sentence letter is whether it would be possible for them to have different values. When this is not possible, they are the same. An important exception to this policy is when it is part of the author's purpose to demonstrate that the different wordings have the same meaning. In such cases, the audience will not automatically assume that the different wordings mean the same thing.

3. Principle 1 notwithstanding, when the conclusion of a demonstration occurs in the same English sentence as one or more of the premises, the conclusion must be formalized as a separate sentence of SL.

4. Whether any given sentence is meant to serve as a premise or as a conclusion, or whether it is irrelevant to the demonstration, must be distinguished by (i) understanding the speaker's intentions and (ii) making the default assumption that the speaker means to use a simple, valid form.

   4.i.   Speakers will sometimes explain themselves by inflecting their sentences with words or phrases that indicate the presence of a premise list or a conclusion. Among conclusion indicators are words like "therefore," "so," "implies," "entails," "yields," and "it follows that." Among premise indicators are "for the reason that," "from," "since," and "because."

   4.ii. In the absence of other indications, the speaker should be assumed to be using the simple, valid form that most closely fits with the passage. This is a defeasible assumption. It is only to be applied in cases where there is some question what the speaker means to say. In cases where the speaker makes their intentions explicit, the form for the demonstration must be assigned accordingly, even if it is invalid.

   4.iii. 4.ii notwithstanding, if the actually stated form can be made valid by adding further premises, those premises should be added subject to the following considerations: the added premises need to be ones that would have been accepted both by the speaker and the speaker's audience (which is not to say they must be true), and they need to be consistent with the speaker's intentions.

5. Conditionals should normally be formalized. In earlier sections of this chapter, formalization was limited to contractual conditionals and stipulative definitions. However, in demonstrations, a third type of functional conditional, called the material conditional, is ubiquitous.[3] Material conditionals are expressed in English using the same inflections that are placed on causal and contractual conditions, and they are formalized in SL in the same way as English contractual conditionals. But they do not place conditions on results. A material "conditional," so called, asserts that it is impossible for one sentence, P, to be accepted while simultaneously denying another Q. It need not assert that this is the case because P causes Q, nor need it undertake to bring Q about on the condition that P occurs. It simply asserts that it is unacceptable to deny Q while accepting P. $P \rightarrow Q$ is in this case an abbreviation for what is more fully, but less elegantly expressed by $\sim(P\ \&\ \sim Q)$ or $\sim P \lor Q$. When P is a premise or some other sentence that can be inferred from the premises, the material conditional, $P \rightarrow Q$, serves to advance the demonstration by establishing that Q must also be the case. Alternatively, when $\sim Q$ is a premise or some other sentence that can be inferred from the premises, $P \rightarrow Q$ serves to advance the demonstration by establishing that $\sim P$ must also be the case.

Though causal conditionals and counterfactual conditionals were earlier set aside because they are not functional, when they appear the context of a demonstration they are often asserted only with "material" intent, to advance the demonstration from one claim to another. In that case, they can be formalized as if they were material conditionals. This is especially advisable when treating a causal or counterfactual conditional as if it were a material conditional would impose one of the three classically valid forms of conditional inference on the demonstration.

Classically Valid Forms of Conditional Inference	
Modus ponens:	A. If A then B. / B.
Modus tollens:	Not-A. If B then A. / Not-B.
Hypothetical syllogism:	If A then B. If B then C. / If A then C.

Of course, once having been formalized in these terms, the demonstration remains open to critical scrutiny. Any material conditionals figuring among the premises need to be acceptable or justified somehow.

Sometimes, sentences that are not explicitly conditional can be rewritten as equivalent conditionals. This is useful when dealing with classifications or subsumptions, where it is claimed that all things of sort A are things of sort

B. Paraphrasing the claim as "If a thing is an A then it is a B" can make a demonstration that would otherwise require formalization in a more advanced system of logic tractable in SL.

Consider the following brief demonstration, drawn from David Hume, *A Treatise of Human Nature*, Volume 3 (London: Thomas Longman, 1740), 102:

> The act of the mind, exprest by a promise, is not a *resolution* to perform any thing: For that alone never imposes any obligation.

The first clue to formalizing this demonstration is the word "for," which is a premise indicator. Going by this clue, the first sentence appears to be the conclusion, the second a premise.

A next step to formalizing the demonstration is to paraphrase it in standard form, with premises first, followed by conclusion under a horizontal line. In making the paraphrase, sentences (or, in this case, sentential components) that are repeated in slightly different terms (or alluded to on a different occasion) are rewritten in the same terms, and information judged to be peripheral to the demonstration is omitted. Here is one way of doing that.

> A resolution to do something never imposes any obligation to do that thing.
> _____
> A promise to do something is not a resolution to do that thing.

In generating this paraphrase, the words "alone" and "the act of the mind expressed by" are judged to be peripheral to the demonstration. This judgement might be mistaken. But a start must be made somewhere.

When the demonstration is paraphrased as above, it is obvious that it is invalid. It is also obvious that it can be made valid by adding a further premise. Moreover, that further premise comes so easily to mind and is so plausible, that it is very likely it was intended and was omitted merely in order to avoid prolixity and the appearance of being unduly pedantic. Logic, however, demands that it be added.

> A resolution to do something never imposes any obligation to do that thing.
> [*implicit:*] A promise to do something imposes an obligation to do that thing.
> _____
> A promise to do something is not a resolution to do that thing.

Now the demonstration is intuitively valid, but because the premises and the conclusion are each simple sentences, they can only be formalized using three different sentence letters. No such formalization is valid in SL. However, the premises and the conclusion lend themselves to being conditionalized. The reference to "acts of the mind" earlier elided from the paraphrase proves useful for this purpose.

> If an act of the mind takes the form of a resolution to do something, it is not an act that imposes an obligation to do something.
>
> [*implicit*] If an act of the mind takes the form of a promise to do something, it is an act that imposes an obligation to do something.
> _____
> If an act of the mind takes the form of a promise to do something, it is not an act that takes the form of a resolution to do something.

When conditionalizing sentences, it is important to be sure that the conditionalized sentence means the same thing as the original. If it does not, the attempt to formalize the demonstration must be abandoned. Formalization cannot come at the cost of making authors say something other than what they clearly meant to say.

Granting that the conditionalizations proposed above are acceptable, the premises and the conclusion can be formalized as conditional sentences of SL. The resulting demonstrative form is s-valid. Taking "A" to formalize "an act of the mind takes the form of a resolution to do something," B to formalize "an act of the mind imposes an obligation to do something," and C to formalize "an act of the mind takes the form of a promise to do something" yields

4.37 $A \rightarrow \sim B, C \rightarrow B \ / \ C \rightarrow \sim A$

As a long table will show, this is a valid form, but that merely confirms what is intuitively evident when considering the paraphrase. If there is anything controversial about this demonstration, it is the first premise, not the implicit premise. Implicit premises ought, as here, to be ones any auditor would think of and accept, though this particular requirement is not always met.

The passage just cited continues with a second demonstration.

> <u>Nor is it a *desire* of such a performance</u>: FOR we may bind ourselves without such a desire, ~~or even with an aversion~~, declar'd ~~and avow'd~~.

The quotation has been marked up in preparation for formalization. Words or phrases that indicate that a passage is a premise or a conclusion have been put in all caps. The sentence that is presumed to be the conclusion has been underlined. Content that is judged to be merely illustrative, ampliative, repetitive, or otherwise peripheral has been crossed out. A possible paraphrase is:

> We may promise [i.e., bind ourselves] to do something without declaring a desire to do that thing.
>
> [*implicit*] If we may promise to do something without declaring a desire to do that thing, a promise to do something is not a declared desire to do that thing.
> _____
> A promise to do something is not a declared desire to do that thing.

In this case, the implicit premise is a material conditional that links the explicit premise and the conclusion to make a valid demonstration. Taking "A" to stand for "We may promise to do something without declaring a desire to do that thing," and B to stand for "A promise to do something is not a declared desire to do something," the resulting formalization is:

$$4.38 \quad A, A \rightarrow B \ / \ B$$

Making a demonstration valid by inserting an implicit conditional that has the explicitly stated premise as its antecedent and the conclusion as its consequent is a technique that should be avoided whenever possible. Anyone who is inclined to doubt that B can be inferred from A will be equally inclined to doubt that $A \rightarrow B$ is true. That makes appealing to $A \rightarrow B$ to make the demonstration valid question-begging. It is only legitimate when there can be no question of the truth of the implicit conditional. (In other words, it is only legitimate when the inference from A to B is already intuitively obvious.) That is the case here, so the formalization can stand.

Hume's text continues as follows:

> <u>Neither is it the *willing* of that action, which we promise to perform</u>: FOR a promise always regards some future time, and the will has an influence only on present actions.

In paraphrasing, the principle that same sentences of English should carry over to same sentences of SL should be respected, the sole exception being sentences that contain both the conclusion and a premise.

> A promise always regards some future time and the will has an influence only on present actions.
>
> [*implicit*] If the will has an influence only on present actions it cannot regard any future time.
>
> [*implicit*] If a promise always regards some future time and the will cannot regard any future time, promising to do something is not willing to do what we promise.
> _____
> Promising to do something is not willing to do what we promise.

In this case, two implicit premises are needed to make the inference from the stated premise to the conclusion valid. Following the usual practice of assigning sentences to sentence letters in the order in which the sentences first appearance in the paraphrase, the formalization is:

$$4.39 \quad A \ \& \ B, B \rightarrow \sim C, (A \ \& \sim C) \rightarrow G \ / \ G$$

The conclusions of the three demonstrations that have just been surveyed occur in a larger demonstration.

The act of the mind, exprest by a promise, is not a *resolution* to perform any thing. ~~For that alone never imposes~~ ~~any obligation.~~ Nor is it a *desire* of such a performance. ~~For we may bind ourselves without such a desire, or even~~ ~~with an aversion, declar'd and avow'd.~~ Neither is it the *willing* of that action, which we promise to perform. ~~For~~ ~~a promise always regards some future time, and the will has an influence only on present actions.~~ IT FOLLOWS, THEREFORE, THAT ~~SINCE~~ the act of the mind, which enters into a promise, and produces its obligation, ~~is neither~~ ~~the resolving, desiring, nor willing any particular performance,~~ it <u>must necessarily be the *willing* of that *obligation*,</u> <u>which arises from the promise.</u>

The three premises that earlier served to justify the conclusions of the three prior demonstrations are struck out, leaving the conclusions to stand as premises of the larger demonstration. This larger demonstration contains a conclusion indicator, "it follows, therefore," immediately followed by a premise indicator, "since." The following sentence contains both a premise and the conclusion. In this case, the premise restates all three of the premises stated in the earlier part of the passage. They should all be struck out (being repetitions of what is said earlier), producing the following paraphrase.

> The act of the mind that produces the obligation of a promise is neither resolving, desiring, nor willing.
> ___
> The act of the mind that produces the obligation of a promise is that of willing the obligation that arises from the promise.

The demonstration is once again invalid. A further implicit premise is required.

> The act of the mind that produces the obligation of a promise is neither resolving, desiring, nor willing.
>
> [*implicit*] The act of the mind that produces the obligation of a promise is either resolving, desiring, willing, or willing the obligation that arises from the promise.
> ___
> The act of the mind that produces the obligation of a promise to do something is that of willing the obligation that arises from the promise.

The formalization is:

4.40 $\sim[(A \lor B) \lor C], [(A \lor B), \lor C] \lor G / G$

While the resulting formalization is s-valid, the implicit premise required to make it so is not obviously true. Why accept that G is the only alternative to A, B, or C? Implicit premises should be obvious. If they are not, they can be inserted, provided they are needed to make the demonstration valid. But it needs to be determined whether the audience would have accepted them (that is at least questionable in this case) or, failing that, whether there is further reasoning that justifies the implicit premise. The surrounding passages need to be searched. In this case, Hume did not go on to justify the implicit premise. The passage quoted is followed by four and a half paragraphs that offer a further argument for rejecting G, and then concludes that a promise could not be any sort of act of mind. It must be an act of different sort, like waving hello, which can only be performed in a certain social context that invests the arm motion with a meaning it could not have otherwise. This is surprising. What appeared to be the conclusion of the demonstration (G) turned out to be not a conclusion at all but merely a way of introducing a further unacceptable alternative. The real conclusion is justified by rejecting all four alternatives with an argument of the following form, where K is: "a promise is a human invention, founded on the necessities and interests of society."

4.41   1. $\sim[(A \lor B) \lor C]$
      2. $\sim[(A \lor B) \lor C] \to (G \lor K)$
      3. $\sim G$
      ___
      K

But this is no improvement. The demonstration is still valid, but only the first and third premises are justified. The second remains implicit and questionable. Why accept that A, B, C, and G are the only acts of mind that might constitute a promise? When there is no reason to be found in the surrounding passages, Hume's other works need to be consulted. If there is still no reason to be found, works of others known to have influenced him need to be consulted. Might the eighteenth-century literature on promises have fixed on the notion that a promise is an act of willing an obligation? Quite independently of that research project, it is permissible to speculate and to criticize. Might Hume have thought that it is simply obvious that resolving, desiring, and willing are the only acts of the mind that could plausibly be taken to constitute promising, so that if none of them is eligible the only alternative is some desperate, impossible concoction, "willing the obligation?" If he was wrong about that, what is the alternative act of mind that he failed to consider? Is it relevant that Hume's harshest contemporary critic, Thomas Reid, who thought Hume's position on promising to be nothing less than irresponsibly subversive, felt obliged to invent the notion that there are mental acts that can only be performed by two or more minds working in concert in order to address Hume's argument?

Pursuing these issues is going far beyond the task of formalizing Hume's demonstration. The relevant point for current purposes is that formalizing the demonstration is the essential first step that sets the subsequent project of historical research and philosophical criticism on its course. It does not show that the demonstration is invalid. It makes the premises precise, in the process highlighting a questionable implicit premise and thereby focusing further inquiry into Hume's reasoning.

This discussion does not suggest, and should not be taken as attempting to suggest, that there is a faultless procedure that can be followed to come up with the correct formalization of a demonstration. Rewriting an author's words and inserting implicit premises are highly suspect enterprises, even when performed to construct a formally valid demonstration. Living authors can always be asked for further clarification (though their answers can sometimes fail to be as illuminating as one might like). But when dealing with historical figures, there is no choice but to do one's best to capture the logic of the demonstration. This is so difficult and so controversial an undertaking that the resulting attempts can take months of research, are made the subject of academic journal articles, and are often matters for protracted dispute. There are no firm answers to the following exercises. There are, however, some clearly better and worse ones. Those who have learned sentential logic will find it easier to discover the better ones.

Exercise 4.11

Circle any premise or conclusion indicators in the following passages. Underline the conclusion. Cross out any irrelevant comments. If the conclusion is stated more than once, underline each occurrence. If the conclusion is unstated, write it in. Also write in any further premises that you consider to be intended, but unstated because obvious. Formalize the demonstration, providing a formalization key.

★a. But while I agree with [the author of the *Treatise of Human Nature*] in his reasoning, I would make a different application of it. He takes it for granted, that there are ideas of extension in the mind; and thence infers, that if it is at all a substance, it must be an extended and divisible substance. On the contrary, I take it for granted, upon the testimony of common sense, that my mind is a substance, that is, a permanent subject of thought; and my reason convinces me, that it is an unextended and indivisible substance; and hence I infer, that there cannot be in it any thing that resembles extension. (Thomas Reid, *An Inquiry into the Human Mind on the Principles of Common Sense*, London, A. Millar, 1764: 538–9)

b. But let us observe what use the Bishop [Berkeley] makes of this important discovery [that nothing can be like an idea but another idea]: Why, he concludes, that we can have no conception of an inanimate substance, such as matter is conceived to be, or of any of its qualities … But how does this follow? Why thus: We can have no conception of any thing but what resembles some sensation or idea in our minds; but the sensations and ideas in our minds can resemble nothing but the sensations and ideas in other minds; therefore, the conclusion is evident. (Thomas Reid, *An Inquiry into the Human Mind on the Principles of Common Sense*, 2nd edition, London, A. Millar, 1765: 117)

★c. To which I could add, if I thought it good *Logick*, the *inconvenience* of denying *necessity*, as that it destroyeth both the *decrees* and the *prescience* of *God Almighty*; for whatsoever *God* hath *purposed* to bring to pass by *man*, as an instrument, or foreseeth shall come to pass, a man, if he have *Liberty* (such as his Lordship affirmeth) from *necessitation*, might frustrate and make not to come to pass, and *God* should either not *foreknow* it, and not *decree* it, or he should *foreknow* such things shall be, as shall never be, and *decree* that which shall never *come to pass*. (Thomas Hobbes, *Of Libertie and Necessitie*, London, F. Eaglesfield, 1654: 79–80. "His Lordship" is Hobbes's interlocutor, Bishop Bramhall)

d. [I would] ask you to explain how the soul can determine the spirits of the body to produce voluntary actions (being naught but a thinking substance). For it seems that any determination of movement comes about by the impulsion of the object being moved, according to the way in which it is pushed by that which is moving it, or depending on the qualification and shape of the surface of the latter. Contact is required for the first two conditions, and extension for the third. You exclude contact ["celui-ci"] entirely from your notion of the soul, and extension ["celui-là"] appears to me to be incompatible with something immaterial. This is why I ask you to provide a more precise definition of the soul than in your Metaphysics, that is, of its substance, separate from its action of thinking. (Elisabeth of Bohemia, Letter to René Descartes of 6 May 1643, trans. Molly Kao) *(Attribute an implicit conclusion to this passage. Passages need to be interpreted in context. The relevant context in this case is the mores and customs observed in correspondence between women and men in seventeenth-century Europe. Elisabeth's correspondence with Descartes was unfailingly polite and self-deprecating. The correspondence of Descartes's male contemporaries Thomas Hobbes and Pierre Gassendi is abusive and condescending, and Descartes's replies to them are even more so. The logician must abstract from the customs of the time and focus on the logical implications of the assertions. Though they are expressed as questions and requests for clarification rather than counterarguments, Elisabeth's observations are no less critical than Hobbes's or Gassendi's.)*

★e. Whatever is extended consists of parts; and whatever consists of parts is divisible, if not in reality, at least in the imagination. But 'tis impossible any thing divisible can be *conjoin'd* to a thought or perception, which is a being altogether inseparable and indivisible. For supposing such a conjunction, wou'd the indivisible thought exist on the left or on the right hand of this extended divisible body? On the surface or in the middle? On the back- or fore-side of it? If it be conjoin'd with the extension, it must exist somewhere within its dimensions. If it exist within its dimensions, it must either exist in one particular part; and then that particular part is indivisible, and the perception is conjoin'd only with it, not with the extension: Or if the thought exists in every part, it must also be extended, and separable, and divisible, as well as the body; which is utterly absurd and contradictory. For can any one conceive a passion of a yard in length, a foot in breadth, and an inch in thickness? Thought, therefore, and extension are qualities wholly incompatible, and never can incorporate together into one subject. (David Hume, *A Treatise of Human Nature* Vol. 1, London, John Noon, 1739: 408–9)

f. It is evident to any one who takes a Survey of the Objects of Human Knowlege, that they are either Ideas actually imprinted on the Senses, or else such as are perceiv'd by attending to the Passions and Operations of the Mind, or lastly Ideas formed by help of Memory and Imagination … That neither our Thoughts, nor passions, nor Ideas formed by the Imagination, Exist without the Mind, is what every Body will allow. And to me it is no less evident that the various Sensations or Ideas imprinted on the Sense, however Blended or Combin'd together (that is whatever Objects they compose) cannot Exist otherwise than in a Mind perceiving them … It is indeed an Opinion strangely prevailing amongst Men, that Houses, Mountains, Rivers and in a word all sensible Objects have an Existence Natural or Real, distinct from their being perceiv'd by the Understanding. … Yet whoever shall find in his Heart to call it in Question may, if I mistake not, perceive it to involve a manifest Contradiction. For what are the foremention'd Objects but the things we perceive by Sense, and what … do we perceive besides our own Ideas or Sensations, and is it not plainly repugnant that any one of these or any Combination of them shou'd Exist unperceiv'd? (George Berkeley, *A Treatise Concerning the Principles of Human Knowledge*, Dublin, Aaron Rhames, 1710: 41–5)

★g. Indeed, the fallacy, on which [Hume's] whole sceptical doctrines are *built,* may be seen at the very outset of his first Essay [section IV of *An Enquiry Concerning Human Understanding*]. He imagines it [is] impossible to conceive the *contrary* to any *known relation* in quantities; but that we may *conceive* the *contrary of every matter of fact as possible* … Mr. Hume did not perceive that all [effects of] objects whatever in relation to us, are but masses of certain qualities, elicited from [those objects in] certain prevening circumstances, and therefore incapable of … showing [diversity] … whilst yet they remain [effects of] similar objects *born under like circumstances.* …[C]onceiving the nature of the operation of this [productive principle or cause] to be wholly unknown, he imagined and alleged all things to be only *"conjoined, and not connected.* ([Mary Shepherd], *An Essay upon the Relation of Cause and Effect*, London, T. Hookham, 1824: 83–4)

h. We can thus see that objects are not lodged in us according to their form and their essence, and that they do not make their entrance by their own force and authority: for if this were the case, we would receive them in the same way; wine would be the same in the mouth of one who is sick as in the mouth of one who is well; one whose fingers are chapped, or numb, would find the same hardness when touching wood or iron as any other. External objects thus enter us at our mercy; we accept them as we please. (Michel de Montaigne, *An Apology for Raymond Sebond*, 1588, trans. Molly Kao)

★i. Moral Necessity may be as absolute, as natural Necessity. That is, the Effect may be as perfectly connected with its moral Cause, as a natural [*sic*] necessary Effect is with it's [*sic*] natural Cause. Whether the Will in every Case is necessarily determined by the strongest Motive, or whether the Will ever makes any Resistance to such a Motive, or can ever oppose the strongest present Inclination, or not; if that Matter should be controverted, yet I suppose none will deny, but that, in some Cases, a previous Bias and Inclination, or the Motive presented, may be so powerful, that the Act of the Will may be certainly and indissolubly connected therewith. When Motives or previous Bias are very strong, all will allow that there is some *Difficulty* in going against them. And if they were yet stronger, the Difficulty would be still greater. And therefore, if more were still added to their Strength, to a certain Degree, it would make the Difficulty so great, that it would be wholly *impossible* to surmount it; for this plain Reason, because whatever Power Men may be supposed to have to surmount Difficulties, yet that Power is not infinite; and so goes not beyond certain Limits. If a Man can surmount ten Degrees of Difficulty of this Kind, with twenty Degrees of Strength, because the Degrees of Strength are beyond the Degrees of Difficulty; yet if the Difficulty be increased to thirty, or an hundred, or a thousand Degrees, and his Strength not also increased, his Strength will be wholly insufficient to surmount the Difficulty. As therefore it must be allowed, that there may be such a Thing as a *sure* and *perfect* Connection between moral Causes and Effects; so this only is what I call by the name of *moral Necessity*. (Jonathan Edwards, *A Careful and Strict Enquiry into the Modern Prevailing Notions of That Freedom of Will, Which is Supposed to be Essential to Moral Agency, etc.* reprint of the Boston edition of 1754, London, Thomas Field, 1762: 30–1)

  j. It is one of Mr. HUME'S maxims, That we can never have reason to believe that any object, or quality of an object, exists, of which we cannot form an idea. But, according to this astonishing theory of power, and causation, we can form *no idea* of power, nor of any being endowed with any power, MUCH LESS of one endowed with infinite power. The inference is — what I do not chuse to commit to paper. But our elegant author is not so superstitious. He often puts his readers in mind, that this inference, or something very like it, is deducible from his doctrine: — for which, no doubt, every friend to truth, virtue, and human nature, is infinitely obliged to him! (James Beattie, *Essays on the Nature and Immutability of Truth, in Opposition to Sophistry and Scepticism*, 5th edition corrected, London, Edward and Charles Dilly; Edinburgh, William Creech, 1774: 300)

  k. If I freely raised my arm, it must have been possible for my arm not to rise even though it is both the case that it did rise and that it will never be true that it did not rise. Because the possible cannot follow from the impossible, if an event is possible even though it did not happen and it will never be true that it did happen, then it cannot be impossible, from which it follows that whatever is past and true is not necessary. So, freedom of the will implies that the past can be changed. (*loosely based on the "master argument" of Diodorus Cronus, as cited by Epictetus, Discourses II.19.1) (Hard. Read "Because" as both asserting the truth of the clause that immediately follows it and asserting that clause as the antecedent of a conditional that has a conditional as its consequent. That is, take the second sentence up to "from which it follows that" to have the form, C, C → (B → G). On this formalization of the second sentence, G contains a reference to "an event." Replace this reference with the specific event, "not raising my arm." Take the remainder of the second sentence, beginning "from which it follows that" to be a further premise, where "from which it follows that" refers to taking H as the antecedent of a further conditional. The entire second sentence is therefore C, C → (B → G), G → H. Preserving the apparent validity of the demonstration depends on what G is taken to stand for. There is also an implicit premise: If whatever is past and true is not necessary then the past can be changed.*

Notes

1 Thanks to a referee for the press for suggesting this example.

2 As important as it is, distinguishing between demonstrations, reports, and explanations, and between deductive and inductive demonstrations is a matter of hermeneutics rather than logic. Deductive logic takes over only once the deductive demonstrations have been identified. The exercises at the close of this section all contain deductive demonstrations.

3 The qualification, "material" does not import any meaning of its own. It appears to have been coined to designate any conditional that is not "formal," where a formal conditional is a conditional that asserts a relation between kinds of objects that is true in virtue of a necessary connection between the forms of the antecedent objects and those of the consequent objects. For details see Tarski (1995: 24–8).

References

Barrett, Robert B and Stenner, Alfred J, 1971, "The Myth of the Exclusive 'Or,'" *Mind* 80: 116–21.

Bencivenga, Ermanno, Lambert, Karel, and van Fraassen, Bas C, 1991, *Logic, Bivalence and Denotation*, Ridgeview, Atascadero, CA.

Grice, P, 1989, *Studies in the Way of Words*, Harvard University Press, Cambridge, MA.

Hausman, Alan, Kahane, Howard, and Tidman, Paul, 2013, *Logic and Philosophy*, 12th edition, Wadsworth, Boston.

Tarski, Alfred, 1995, *Introduction to Logic and to the Methodology of Deductive Sciences*, trans. Olaf Helmer, Dover, New York.

5 Working with SL Semantics

Contents

Long tables are an effective way of determining the intensional properties of sentences, sets, and demonstrations of SL. But they have limitations, some practical, others theoretical. Practically, long tables become unwieldy when more than three sentence letters are involved. They can also require more work than is necessary. S-invalidity, s-satisfiability, and s-nonequivalence are established by a single interpretation. Doing an eight- or sixteen-row table to find a single row is unnecessary work, and the number of unnecessary rows increases exponentially with the number of sentence letters involved. The situation is only somewhat better where s-validity, s-unsatisfiability, and s-equivalence are concerned. These intentional properties are established by showing that there is no interpretation of a certain sort. Long tables do this by the brute force method of polling each interpretation. A more direct alternative would uncover why there can be no such interpretation.

The theoretical limitations are more serious. Long tables are premised on the possibility of listing each possible interpretation. This can be done in SL, provided only a finite number of sentence letters need to be considered. But

DOI: 10.4324/9781003026532-6

in more advanced systems of logic there are too many ways for interpretations to vary for it to be feasible to list them all in even simple cases. Even within SL, long tables are not useful for establishing general principles.

More general and powerful techniques for determining the intensional status of sentences, sets, and demonstrations are needed. This chapter provides instruction in three such techniques, the short table technique, the technique of providing demonstrations by appeal to valuation rules and definitions of intensional properties, and the technique of refutation by counterexample. Each technique is used for a different purpose. Short tables are used to discover at least one interpretation that establishes s-invalidity, s-satisfiability, or s-nonequivalence. Demonstrations are used to verify the discoveries made on short tables, to establish that there is no interpretation to be found, and to establish general principles. Refutation by counterexample is used to falsify general principles.

In passing, this chapter also provides instruction in four important informal demonstrative techniques: indirect proof, proof by cases, conditional proof, and biconditional proof.

5.1 Identifying and Verifying Interpretations

The intensional concepts defined in section 3.4 are defined by the presence or absence of an interpretation or interpretations (never more than two) that achieves a specific result. What might be called the "no interpretation" concepts are defined by the absence of an interpretation that does the job. (What that job is varies depending on which property is in question.)

"No Interpretation" Concepts

- Γ / P is s-valid
  there is no interpretation on which each premise in Γ is true and P is false
- Γ is s-unsatisfiable
  there is no interpretation on which each sentence in Γ is true
- P is s-valid
  there is no interpretation on which P is false
- P is s-unsatisfiable
  there is no interpretation on which P is true
- P and Q are s-equivalent
  there is no interpretation on which P and Q have different values

---

The opposites of these concepts, which might be called the "interpretation" concepts, are defined by the presence of an interpretation that does the job.

"Interpretation" Concepts

- Γ / P is s-invalid
  there is at least one interpretation on which each premise in Γ is true and P is false
- Γ is s-satisfiable
  there is at least one interpretation on which each sentence in Γ is true
- P is s-invalid
  there is at least one interpretation on which P is false
- P is s-satisfiable
  there is at least one interpretation on which P is true
- P is s-contingent
  there is at least one interpretation on which P is true and at least one interpretation on which P is false
- P and Q are s-nonequivalent
  there is at least one interpretation on which P and Q have different values

Exercise 5.1

State what interpretation or interpretations need to be discovered to establish each of the following claims.

★a. A → (B & C), ~C ∨ G / ~A → (B & G) is s-invalid
  b. ~(A & ~B) is s-satisfiable
★c. {A ≡ B, ~(~B & A)} is s-satisfiable
  d. (C ∨ A) & ~B is s-invalid
★e. ~(A ≡ ~B) is s-contingent
  f. ~A & ~B and ~(A & B) are s-nonequivalent

This section is devoted to presenting a method, called the short table method, for directly identifying the one or two interpretations needed to establish s-invalidity, s-satisfiability, s-nonequivalence, and s-contingency – thereby bypassing the need to survey all the possible interpretations on a long table.

Short tables work backwards from the desired result (an interpretation of the right sort) to the values that interpretation must assign to the atomic components of the sentences under consideration. When there is no such interpretation this enterprise fails. But when there is, the short table discovers at least one of them. Short tables are long tables in reverse. Long tables start by listing each possible interpretation and apply the valuation rules to go from component to compound. Short tables begin with just one assignment to the main connective of the sentence or sentences at issue and apply the valuation rules to go from compounds to components. The aim is to discover an interpretation (if there is one) in a more efficient way than by constructing a long table. The assignment to the sentence letters is the last thing to be discovered on a short table, rather than the first to be given, and the short table aims to determine if there is even one interpretation that does the job, not to produce an exhaustive survey of what each interpretation determines.

For example, the demonstration, A → B, B ∨ C / B, is s-invalid. Demonstrating this to be the case requires finding an interpretation on which the premises, A → B and B ∨ C, are true and the conclusion, B, is false. On a short table, this begins with a single row. The sentences in the demonstration are placed on top of the table and a T is assigned to each premise while an F is assigned to the conclusion.

A	B	C	A	→	B	B	∨	C	B
I				**T**			**T**		**F**

Because the valuation rules are stated in the form of "if and only if" sentences, they apply in both directions. When filling in long tables, the rules are applied from right to left, that is, from assignments to components to assignments to compounds. But the rules can also be applied from left to right. Given an assignment to the compounds, it is possible to work back to an assignment to the components, and so discover an interpretation without having to draw up a long table.

Reasoning from values of compounds to values of components is not as straightforward as reasoning from components to compounds. Whereas any given combination of values to the components determines a unique value for the compound, any given value for a compound does not always determine unique values for the components. There are two ways to make a disjunction or a conditional true, two ways to make a conjunction false, and two ways to make a biconditional either true or false. (There are not three. Doing more than is required is not a further way of doing what is required.)

In other cases, there is no choice. The idea is to begin filling in the table by adding those values that are determined by already assigned values. According to (→) when I(A → B) is T either I(A) is F or I(B) is T. According to (∨) when I(B ∨ C) is T at least one of I(B) and I(C) is T. Each of these consequences leaves some choice over what to say next. But according to the definition of an interpretation no sentence can be assigned both T and F. Once it is determined that I(B) is F, that value must be entered everywhere B appears on the table.

A	B	C	A	→	B	B	∨	C	B
I	**F**			T	**F**	**F**	T		**F**

These new assignments foreclose choices that were previously open. According to (→), a conditional with a false consequent can only be true if it has a false antecedent. And according to (∨), a disjunction with a false disjunct can only be true if its other disjunct is true.

A	B	C	A	→	B	B	∨	C	B
I	**F**	F	**T**	**F**	T	F	**F**	T	T	**T**	F

The long table has revealed that the interpretation,

	A	B	C
I	F	F	T

assigns a T to each premise and F to the conclusion. This demonstration is therefore s-invalid. This result has been discovered in a briefer and more interesting fashion than by doing a long table.

The short table has only served to *discover* an interpretation on which the premises are true and the conclusion is false. It does not serve as a *demonstration* that the interpretation does so. Verification that the interpretation discovered on the table does assign T to the premises and F to the conclusion is given by the sort of demonstration discussed in section 3.3 and practiced in exercise 3.7. The interpretation discovered above, for example, is "verified" (that is, demonstrated to be an interpretation that assigns T to each premise and F to the conclusion) as follows:

1. I(A) is F   given
2. I(A → B) is T   1 (→)

3. I(C) is T   given
4. I(B ∨ C) is T   3 (∨)

5. I(B) is F   given

8. A → B, B ∨ C / B is s-invalid   2,4,5 def s-validity

Over the course of this demonstration, each of the premises is shown to be true on I, while the conclusion is shown to be false on I. Gaps are introduced to section off the parts of the demonstration concerned with each sentence. A final section applies the definition of s-validity to arrive at the main conclusion, that the demonstration is s-invalid.

It might be objected that this result is already evident from the short table and should not need to be demonstrated. This is true. Where tables for sentences of SL are concerned it is generally obvious that the table has uncovered the correct result. However, as systems of logic become more complex, the means used to discover interpretations become more difficult to work with, and their results are not as obviously correct. This makes verification important. Practicing the technique in the current, simplified context makes it easier to step up to using it in more advanced contexts.

Exercise 5.2

1. *Identify and verify interpretations that show that the following sentences are s-invalid.*
    ★a. (⊥ → A) → ~A
      b. (A ≡ ⊥) → A
    ★c. ~(A & B) → ~A
      d. (A ∨ B) → A
    ★e. (~A ∨ ~B) ∨ [A ≡ (B → C)]
      f. ~(A ≡ B) ∨ (A → C)

2. *Identify and verify interpretations that show that the following demonstrations are s-invalid.*
    ★a. A → B, B / A *(fallacy of affirming the consequent)*
      b. A → B, ~A / ~B *(fallacy of denying the antecedent)*
    ★c. A → B / B → A *(conversion fallacy)*
      d. A → B / ~A → ~B *(inversion fallacy)*
    ★e. A → C, B → C / C *(fallacy of incomplete enumeration of cases)*
      f. A → C, B → ~C / A ∨ B

Not all short tables are as direct as the ones just considered. Sometimes, starting with an assignment to each of the sentences only opens a variety of choices. This is a good thing. The more choice, the more ways of finding an interpretation. But not all ways may work. Making the wrong choice can lead to consequences that culminate in assigning T to ⊥ or both T and F to a sentence letter. No interpretation can do either of those things, which means that either there is none to discover or that a wrong course was taken when constructing the table. When assignments are not compelled but made by choice, the wrong choice might have been made, and the only recourse is try a different one. There is a way to reduce the chances of making the wrong choice. Choose the alternative that has the fewest repercussions. If one choice has a cascade of consequences and another does not, choose the latter.

For example, the set, {(~A & B) ≡ C, A ∨ ~C} is s-satisfiable. Putting it up on a short table and assigning T to the main connective of each sentence yields

A B C	(~ A & B) ≡ C	A ∨ ~ C
I	T	T

There are two ways for a biconditional to be true and two ways for a disjunction to be true. In this situation, the wisest course of action is to pick the alternative that has the fewest repercussions, that is, that maximizes choice for the remaining assignments. For example, attempting to make the biconditional true by making both of its immediate components true is a bad choice.

A B C	(~ A & B) ≡ C	A ∨ ~ C
I	T? T T?	T

There is nothing intrinsically wrong with assigning T's rather than F's to the immediate components of true biconditionals. The choice is made wrong by the features of this case. In this case, assigning T's means making a conjunction true. This is a bad choice because it has numerous repercussions. Assigning a T to a conjunction requires assigning a T to both of its conjuncts. Since a T is also assigned to C, this one choice forces an assignment to all the atomic components, leaving no alternatives. Assigning a T to C means that C must be T everywhere, since a sentence letter cannot have two different values. That in turn means that ~C must be false.

A B C	(~ A & B) ≡ C	A ∨ ~ C
I	T	T? T T?	T F T

Assigning a T to ~A & B means that its conjuncts must be true. Since ~A is one of the conjuncts, that in turn means that its nullation, A, must be false.

A B C	(~ A & B) ≡ C	A ∨ ~ C
I	T	T F T? T T?	T F T

But, for A ∨ ~C to still be true, A must be true. So, A has ended up with two different values.

A B C	(~ A & B) ≡ C	A ∨ ~ C
⊦ T/F	T	T F T? T T?	T T F T ✗

This is impossible. But it does not mean that there is no interpretation on which all the sentences in the set are true. It just means that the choice that was made to start has not found one. That choice must be scratched in favour of exploring an alternative option: making both components of the biconditional false, or making one of the disjuncts of the second sentence true.

A B C	(~ A & B) ≡ C	A ∨ ~ C
~~T/F~~	~~F~~ ~~F~~ ~~F~~ ~~T?~~ ~~F~~ ~~F~~ ~~T?~~	~~F~~ ~~F~~ ~~F~~ ~~F~~ ✗
I		T	T

When this happens, the earlier choice is not erased. It is kept as a record for future reference. One thing the record shows is that it is not possible to make the biconditional true by making both of its immediate components true. But by (≡) a biconditional is also true when both immediate components are false.

A	B	C	(~	A	&	B)	≡	C	A	∨	~	C	
T̶/F̶		T̶	T̶	F̶	T̶?	T̶	T̶	T̶?	T̶	T̶	F̶	T̶	✗
I				**F**			T	**F**		T			

This is a better alternative than the first one. While it still assigns F to C, it leaves the assignments to A and B open. At least one of them must be false. But now it is possible to choose which one in light of what proves most useful. Moreover, assigning F to C means assigning T to ~C which by itself preserves the assignment of T to A ∨ ~C, leaving it open what to assign to A.

A	B	C	(~	A	&	B)	≡	C	A	∨	~	C	
T̶/F̶		T̶	T̶	F̶	T̶?	T̶	T̶	T̶?	T̶	T̶	F̶	T̶	✗
I	**F**					F		T	F		T	**T**	**F**

Now there are different ways of finding an interpretation. The truth of the second sentence has already been secured without needing to make any assignment to A. The truth of the first can be secured by assigning F to B, though this is just one option.

A	B	C	(~	A	&	B)	≡	C	A	∨	~	C	
T̶/F̶		T̶	T̶	F̶	T̶?	T̶	T̶	T̶?	T̶	T̶	F̶	T̶	✗
I	**F**	F				F	**F**	T	F		T	T	F

The long table has revealed that the interpretation

	A	B	C
I		F	F

assigns a T to each sentence in {(~A & B) ≡ C, A ∨ ~C}. Though A occurs in this set, it does not matter what value it gets as long as B and C are both assigned F. It is not always necessary to find an assignment for each sentence letter. Provided a demonstration can be written with assignments to fewer sentence letters, the assignment to the remainder need not be specified. Work on the short table also suggests that there are other interpretations that would do the job: for instance, one based on assigning T to A and F to C regardless of the assignment to B.

The result is verified by the following demonstration.

1. I(B) is F   given
2. I(~A & B) is F   1 (&)
3. I(C) is F   given
4. I((~A & B) ≡ C) is T   2,3 (≡)

5. I(~C) is T   3 (~)
6. I(A ∨ ~C) is T   5 (∨)

7. {(~A & B) ≡ C, A ∨ ~C} is s-satisfiable   4,6 def s-satisfiability

Short tables are best constructed in two stages. First make all assignments that are forced by assignments that have already been made. Once only assignments that require choice are left, begin by making the assignment that has the fewest repercussions for determining the remaining assignments.

This having been said, fretting over which option has the fewest repercussions can sometimes take more time than just picking one and forging ahead. Use question marks to indicate the point where a choice was made. That way, if a choice fails, it is possible to go back to the point where it was made and choose differently.

Work on short tables will come to nothing unless the table begins by searching for the right sort of interpretation. Just what interpretation that is changes with the question being asked. Some questions require looking for interpretations that assign F to some sentences and T to others. Some require looking for two different interpretations rather than just one. It is essential to review the definitions of the intensional properties both prior to making the table and when justifying the final line of its verification.

Exercise 5.3

1. *Identify and verify interpretations that show that the following sentences are s-satisfiable. These are interpretations that assign a T to the sentence.*

   ★a. A → ~A
   b. (A ∨ B) → (~A & ~B)
   ★c. ~(A & B) & (A ∨ B)
   d. (A → B) & (~B → ~A)
   ★e. [(A & B) → C] → [(A → C) & (B → C)]
   f. (A ≡ ~B) ≡ (~B → A)

2. *Identify and verify interpretations that show that the following sets are s-satisfiable. These are interpretations that assign a T to each sentence in the set.*

   ★a. {(A → B), (~A ∨ ~B)}
   b. {~A, B → C, ~[(A → B) ≡ C]}
   ★c. {A → B, A → ~B, ~A → B}
   d. {~(A & B), B → (A ∨ C)}
   ★e. {A ∨ (B → C), ~C ∨ (B ≡ A)}
   f. {~[A ≡ (B ∨ C)], C ∨ (~A & ~B)}

3. *Identify and verify interpretations that show that the following sentences are s-invalid. These are interpretations that assign an F to the sentence.*

   ★a. (~A ≡ B) ≡ (~B → A)
   b. (A ≡ ~B) → ~(A ∨ B)
   ★c. ~A ≡ [(A → B) & (B → ⊥)]
   d. [(A & ~B) → C] ≡ [(~C ∨ ~A) & (~A ∨ B)]
   ★e. ~(A ≡ B) ≡ (A & ~B)
   f. [A ≡ (B ∨ C)] ≡ [(A ≡ B) ∨ (A ≡ C)]

4. *Identify and verify interpretations that show that the following demonstrations are s-invalid. These are interpretations that assign a T to each premise and an F to the conclusion.*

   ★a. (A & B) ∨ (C & G), ~(A & G) / B & ~C
   b. (A → B), ~(A & C) / (B ∨ C) ≡ ~A
   ★c. (A ≡ B) ∨ (C ≡ B), B → C / A & ~C
   d. A ≡ ~(B ∨ C), ~A → (G ∨ H) / (~G → ~C) & (~H → ~B)
   ★e. A ≡ (B & C) / (A ≡ B) & (A ≡ C)
   f. A ∨ (B → C), ~G → ~(B & A), ~(B ∨ C) → H / G ∨ H

5. *Identify and verify interpretations that show that the following sentences are s-contingent. This means finding two interpretations for each sentence, one that assigns a T, another that assigns an F.*

   ★a. A ∨ (A & ~A)
   b. (A & B) ∨ (~A & ~B)
   ★c. [(A → B) & (B → C)] → (C → A)
   d. ~(A & B) ∨ ~(A ≡ B)
   ★e. [~A & (B ∨ C)] → (B ∨ G)
   f. [A → (B ≡ ~B)] ≡ (B & A)

6. *Identify and verify interpretations that show that the sentences in the following pairs are not s-equivalent. These are either interpretations that assign T to the first sentence and F to the second or interpretations that assign T to the second sentence and F to the first. Begin by considering the assignment that has the fewest repercussions. Be prepared to scratch that effort should it prove to be unsuccessful, and try the alternative.*

  ★**a.** ~(A ∨ B), ~A ∨ ~B
    b. ~(A & B), ~A & ~B
  ★**c.** A & (B ∨ C), (A & B) ∨ C
    d. ~~(B → ~A) → B, ~[~(B → ~A) → B]
  ★**e.** ~(A ≡ B), ~(A → ~B) ∨ ~(B → ~A)
    f. (A → B) → (C → G), A → [(B & C) → G]

5.2 Demonstrating That There Is No Interpretation

Sometimes, every option that can be explored on a short table proves to be unworkable. This ought to happen when there is no interpretation that does the job called for by the intensional property. But it can also happen because the person drawing up the short table made a mistake. Short tables that crash need as much to be verified as tables that discover an interpretation. But when the table crashes, there no interpretation to verify. In these cases, a special form of demonstration can be used to verify that there is no interpretation of the sort being sought. Such demonstrations proceed by supposing, to the contrary, that there is such an interpretation, and then establishing that this supposition leads to a contradiction and so must be abandoned. This is what is known as a demonstration by indirect proof or *reductio ad absurdum*.[1]

The introduction of demonstration by indirect proof finally integrates the theory of sentential logic with the claim made in chapter 1, that deductive reasoning is based on the principle of noncontradiction. The valuation rules and the definitions of intensional concepts make no mention of contradiction. But its central role comes out when demonstrating how those rules and concepts apply.

The contradiction in question must be either the assignment of T to ⊥ or of both T and F to a sentence letter. It is not sufficient to find that both a T and an F are assigned to a compound sentence or a compound component. By definition, no interpretation can assign T to ⊥ or two different values to a sentence letter, but it has not been demonstrated that no compound sentence could have more than one value. Until it is (in section A-1.2), it will not be presumed.

In exercise 3.8(c) a long table was used to establish that A → A is s-valid. By the definition of s-validity given in terms of interpretations, this means that there is no interpretation on which A → A is false. A short table that begins by assigning F to A → A should therefore find a contradiction at every turn. The following demonstration by indirect proof verifies that there is no such interpretation and explains why neither the long table nor the short table could find one: because the supposition that there is such an interpretation requires assigning both T and F to "A," contrary to the definition of an interpretation.

  1. Suppose to the contrary that A → A is not s-valid.
    2. By definition of s-validity, there is an interpretation, I, such that I(A → A) is F.
    3. By (→), I(A) is T and I(A) is F.
    4. No I can assign both T and F to the same sentence letter.
  5. Since the supposition at line 1 leads to a contradiction at lines 3 and 4, that supposition must be rejected: A → A is s-valid.

This demonstration may seem cumbersome, but it reflects the way demonstrations are informally given in English and other natural languages. In ordinary reasoning, people do not establish their points with long or short tables. They use demonstrative forms like indirect proof. This makes it worthwhile to reflect on how this and other informal means of demonstration work.

The indirect proof just given exhibits stylistic elements that are employed in all the demonstrations that follow. When reading the bulleted list below, look at the demonstration to see how it illustrates each item on the list.

- When something is supposed, it is not known for sure whether it is true or false. "Suppose" means "suppose for the sake of seeing what follows from this supposition." Everything that follows from accepting the supposition is indented under the supposition, to indicate that it rests on the supposition. When something is inferred that does not rely on the truth of the supposition, it is outdented.
- The phrase "suppose to the contrary" indicates that the supposition is contrary to what is believed to be true, and is made only to demonstrate that it leads to a contradiction and so must be rejected. When a demonstration

is indented under "suppose to the contrary," it always aims to find a contradiction, and it is always outdented by a sentence that concludes that the supposition has been shown to lead to a contradiction and so must be rejected.

- The demonstration uses numbered lines and justifications. Usually the assertion that comes next in a demonstration is a consequence of the assertion that has just preceded it. When that is the case, the justification for inferring the subsequent assertion from the prior assertion is preceded by "by." However, in some cases, an assertion is not inferred from the immediately prior assertion, but from a yet earlier assertion. In these cases, the line number for the earlier assertion is given and the justification has the form "from line [#] by ..."
- Demonstrations tend to open with minor variations on the first few assertions and to close with minor variations on the last few assertions. There is a boilerplate for the opening and closing lines of demonstrations that can be extracted from the answers to the ⋆ questions.
- Justifications for the boilerplate sections tend to apply definitions of intensional properties. Those for the middle section of the demonstration tend to apply the valuation rules. The valuation rules should always be used to draw inferences from values of compounds to values of their components with the aim of arriving at a contradiction in the interpretation of atomic components. A proper demonstration never appeals to the value of components to draw an inference about the value of compounds.

Boilerplate for a Demonstration by Indirect Proof
(This boilerplate lays out the clauses that will generally appear in any indirect proof.)

    1. Suppose to the contrary that A.
       ...
    k. B.
       ...
    n. not-B.
    n+1. Since the supposition at line 1 leads to a contradiction at lines k and n that supposition must be rejected: not-A.

In the demonstrations that follow, two ways of applying (→) are distinguished, called *modus ponens* (MP) and *modus tollens* (MT).

Modus ponens (MP): from I(P) is T and I(P → Q) is T infer that I(Q) is T

Modus tollens (MT): from I(Q) is F and I(P → Q) is T infer that I(P) is F

As discussed in chapter 3.2, compound to component applications of (→) take one of two forms:

- (T→): from I(P → Q) is T infer that either I(P) is F or I(Q) is T (as noted in section 4.8, nothing more should be added)
- (F→): from I(P → Q) is F infer that I(P) is T and I(Q) is F (drawing both (F→) inferences is not necessary when just one will do)

Modus ponens and *modus tollens* are specific applications of (T→). *Modus ponens* applies when it has been established that both I(P → Q) and I(P) are T. In this case, it must be concluded that I(Q) is T. *Modus tollens* applies when it has been established that I(P → Q) is T but I(Q) is F. In this case, it must be concluded that I(P) is F.

(T→), (F→), (MP), and (MT) are all instances of compound to component applications of (→). They are distinguished from one another to assist the reader in following the reasoning.

There is more to giving demonstrations than has been discussed so far. The rest is best illustrated over the course of solutions to exercises. Solutions to the ⋆ exercises will be better appreciated if a few minutes are taken to attempt to answer the question before consulting the solution.

Exercise 5.4

1. *Demonstrate that the following sentences are s-valid. Compare the ★ questions to extract boilerplate for the opening and closing lines of the demonstration.*

   ★**a.** A ∨ ~A *(law of excluded middle)*

   b. A ≡ A

   ★**c.** ⊥ → A

   d. A → (B → A)

   ★**e.** [A → (B → C)] → [(A → B) → (A → C)] *(Note the use of (MP) and (MT) in this exercise.)*

   f. (A ∨ A) → (A & A)

2. *Demonstrate that the following demonstrations are s-valid. Compare the ★ questions to extract boilerplate for the opening and closing lines of the demonstration.*

   ★**a.** A / ~~A *(double negation introduction)*

   b. ~~A / A *(double negation elimination)*

   ★**c.** ~A / A → B *(false antecedent yields true conditional)*

   d. B / A → B *(true consequent yields true conditional)*

   ★**e.** (A & B) → C / A → (B → C) *(conditional proof)*

   f. A, A → B / B *(modus ponens)*

   ★**g.** A → B, A → ~B / ~A *(indirect proof)*

   h. A ∨ B, A → C, B → C / C *(proof by cases; hint: use (MT))*

   ★**i.** A ∨ B, ~A / B *(disjunctive syllogism)*

   j. A ∨ B, A → G, B → H / G ∨ H *(constructive dilemma)*

   ★**k.** ~B, A → B / ~A *(modus tollens)*

   l. A → B, B → C / A → C *(hypothetical syllogism)*

3. *Demonstrate that the following sentences are s-unsatisfiable. Compare the ★ questions to extract boilerplate for the opening and closing lines of the demonstration.*

   ★**a.** A & ~A

   b. (A → ⊥) & A

   ★**c.** ~(A ≡ B) & (~A & ~B)

   d. ~(A → B) & B

   ★**e.** ~(A → B) & ~A

   f. ~(A ∨ B) & B

4. *Demonstrate that the following sets are s-unsatisfiable. Compare the ★ questions to extract boilerplate for the opening and closing lines of the demonstration.*

   ★**a.** {~(A ≡ B), ~(A → ~B)}

   b. {A & (B ∨ C), A → ~B, ~C}

   ★**c.** {A, (A ∨ B) → C, C → ⊥}

   d. {A → (B → C), ~[B → (A → C)]}

   ★**e.** {A → B, A, B → ⊥}

   f. {A ≡ B, ~(~A ≡ ~B)}

5. *Demonstrate that the sentences in the following pairs are s-equivalent. Compare the ★ questions to extract boilerplate for the opening and closing lines of the demonstration.*

   ★**a.** A & ~A, ⊥ *(definition of ⊥)*

   b. ~A, A → ⊥ *(lean language definition of ~)*

   ★**c.** A & B, [A → (B → ⊥)] → ⊥ *(lean language definition of &)*

   d. A ∨ B, (A → ⊥) → B *(lean language definition of ∨)*

   ★**e.** A & B, B & A *(commutation)*

   f. A ∨ B, B ∨ A *(commutation)*

   ★**g.** ~~A, A *(double negation)*

   h. ~(A & B), ~A ∨ ~B *(De Morgan's theorem)*

*i. ~(A ∨ B), ~A & ~B *(De Morgan's theorem)*
  j. A → B, ~A ∨ B *(implication)*
*k. A → B, ~B → ~A *(contraposition)*
  l. A → B, ~(A & ~B) *(implication)*
*m. A ≡ B, ~(A ≡ ~B)
  n. A ∨ (B ∨ C), (A ∨ B) ∨ C *(∨ association)*
  o. A & (B & C), (A & B) & C *(& association)*

Not all demonstrations are as straightforward as those assigned in exercise 5.4. As when employing short tables, sometimes reasoning from the assignment to a compound to the assignments to its components opens multiple possibilities. When looking for a contradiction, each possibility must be explored and found to result in a contradiction. This calls for a form of demonstration called proof by cases.[2]

A proof by cases begins by showing that at least one of a limited number of alternatives must be true. These alternatives are the cases in question. It is not known which of them is the true one. But it is known that at least one of them is true. The demonstration then proceeds by showing that the same consequence follows from each alternative. This means that the consequence must be accepted. Because the list of alternative cases is exhaustive, at least one of them is true. Since the consequence follows from each alternative, it does not matter which is the true one. Whichever turns out to be the true one, the consequence follows.

For example, {(A → B) → ~A, B & A} is s-unsatisfiable. But reasoning from values of compounds to values of components does not lead directly to a contradiction.

1. Suppose to the contrary that {(A → B) → ~A, B & A} is s-satisfiable.
2. By definition of s-satisfiability, there is an interpretation, I, such that I((A → B) → ~A) and I(B & A) are T.
3. By (&) I(B) and I(A) are T.
4. From line 2 by (→) either I(A → B) is F or I(~A) is T.
5. By (~) either I(A → B) is F or I(A) is F.
6. By (→) either I(A) is T and I(B) is F or I(A) is F.

At this point, two alternatives have opened without a contradiction having been uncovered. The claim at line 6 that at least one of the two alternatives must be the case is the initial step for a proof by cases. After line 6 the demonstration proceeds as follows.

7. Suppose for purposes of proof by cases on line 6 that I(A) is T and I(B) is F.
8. From lines 3 and 7, I(B) is both T and F.
10. Now suppose, for further purposes of proof by cases on line 6, that I(A) is F.
11. From lines 3 and 9, I(A) is both T and F.

As of this point, the demonstration seems once again to have stalled. When pursuing a proof by cases it very often turns out that each case yields a different result. As of line 8, the consequence of the first case is that I(B) is both T and F. As of line 11, the consequence of the second case is that I(A) is both T and F. Since the two cases lead to different results, the proof by cases is in danger of collapse. The same conclusion needs to follow from both cases. Otherwise no inference can be drawn from either one.

The collapse of the demonstration can be prevented by generalizing the results. Proceeding once again from line 8:

7. Suppose for purposes of proof by cases on line 6 that I(A) is T and I(B) is F.
8. From lines 3 and 7, I(B) is both T and F.
9. I assigns both T and F to the same sentence letter.

10. Now suppose, for further purposes of proof by cases on line 6, that I(A) is F.
11. From lines 3 and 10, I(A) is both T and F.
12. I assigns both T and F to the same sentence letter.

Even though one case leads to the conclusion that I(B) is both T and F and the other case leads to the different conclusion that I(A) is both T and F, both cases lead to the general conclusion that at least one sentence letter is both T and F on I, and that is all that is needed to complete the proof by cases.

Lines 9 and 12 of the example given above illustrate a further important feature of proof by cases: generalization. Overspecification is the bane of proof by cases. Many a proof by cases fails or is drawn out at too great a length because the author is too deeply involved in concrete thinking and so only sees differences where a view from a higher level would uncover the underlying general principle that all the cases instantiate.

Finding the common conclusion that all the cases lead to can be difficult. To facilitate this, it is permissible to use parallel columns to explore both parts of the demonstration alongside one another, as follows:

7. Suppose for purposes of proof by cases on line 6 that I(A) is T and I(B) is F.	10. Suppose, for purposes of proof by cases on line 6, that I(A) is F.
8. From lines 3 and 7, I(B) is both T and F.	11. From lines 3 and 10, I(A) is both T and F.
9. I assigns both T and F to the same sentence letter.	12. I assigns both T and F to the same sentence letter.

The demonstration can now be concluded.

13. Since according to line 6 one of the cases supposed at lines 7 and 10 must be true and, either way, the same result follows, that result can be asserted outside of those suppositions: I assigns both T and F to the same sentence letter.

14. No I can assign both T and F to the same sentence letter.

15. Since the supposition at line 1 has led to a contradiction at lines 13 and 14 that supposition must be rejected: {(A → B) → ~A, B & A} is s-unsatisfiable.

The proof by cases runs over lines 6 to 13. It uses the following boilerplate, which is exhibited by any proof by cases.

> **Boilerplate for a Demonstration by Proof by Cases**
>
> 1. Either A or B.
> 2. Suppose for purposes of proof by cases at line 1 that A.
>
>   ...
>
>   *i*. Then C.
>
> *i*.+1 Suppose for further purposes of proof by cases at line 1 that B.
>
>   ...
>
>   *k*. Then C.
>
> *k*.+1 Since according to line 1 at least one of the cases supposed at lines 2 and *i*+1 is true and, either way, the same result follows, that result can be asserted outside of those suppositions: C.

The claim at line *k*+1 is justified by the claims at all of lines 1, 2 to *i*, and *i*+1 to *k*. The claim at line 1 is that there are just two alternatives. The claim over lines 2 to *i* is that the first alternative leads to a certain result. The claim over lines *i*+1 to *k* is that the second alternative leads to the same result. So even though it is not known which of the two alternatives is true, since the same result follows either way, and at least one of the alternatives must be true, that result can be affirmed.

Exercise 5.5

Demonstrate that the following sentences are s-equivalent. Look for an occasion to apply proof by cases. Some cases may need to be generalized to yield a common result.

★**a.** A ≡ B, ((A → B) → [(B → A) → ⊥]) → ⊥ *(lean language definition of* ≡*)*
 b. A → (B → C), (A & B) → C *(exportation)*
★**c.** A ≡ B, (A → B) & (B → A) *(equivalence)*
 d. A ≡ B, (A & B) ∨ (~A & ~B) *(equivalence)*
★**e.** A & (B ∨ C), (A & B) ∨ (A & C) *(&/∨ distribution)*
 f. A ∨ (B & C), (A ∨ B) & (A ∨ C) *(∨/& distribution)*

5.3 Demonstrating General Principles

The sentence letters of SL are variables used to stand for sentences of English or other natural languages. This gives them the status of forms common to many natural language sentences. Sets of sentences of SL and demonstrations in SL correspondingly have the status of forms common to many sets of natural language sentences and many demonstrations in natural languages.

In this chapter and chapter 3, long tables, short tables, and demonstrations have been used to establish that a number of these forms are valid, invalid, or equivalent. These results hold for all the sentences, sets, or demonstrations in English or other natural languages that instantiate the relevant forms. Among the most important results are that

- sentences with following forms are s-valid
    ~(A & ~A) *(principle of noncontradiction; exercise 3.8g)*
    A ∨ ~A *(law of excluded middle; exercises 3.8f and 5.4#1a)*
- demonstrations of the following forms are s-valid:
    A / ~~A *(double negation introduction; exercise 5.4#2a)*
    ~~A / A *(double negation elimination; exercise 5.4#2b)*
    A → ⊥ / ~A *(indirect proof; read A → ⊥ as "A is absurd"; exercises 3.9#2a and 5.4#5a)*
    A → B, A → ~B / ~A *(indirect proof; exercises 3.9#4d and 5.4#2g)*
    A ∨ B, A → C, B → C / C *(proof by cases; exercises 3.9#4c and 5.4#2h)*
    A ∨ B, A → C, B → G / C ∨ G *(constructive dilemma; exercise 5.4#2j)*
    A → B, A / B *(modus ponens; exercises 3.9#4a and 5.4#2f)*
    A → B, ~B / ~A *(modus tollens; exercise 5.4#2k)*
    A → B, B → A / A ≡ B *(biconditional proof; exercise 3.9#2f)*
    A → B, ~A → ~B / A ≡ B *(biconditional proof; exercise 3.9#2g)*
    A ∨ B, ~A / B *(disjunctive syllogism; exercise 5.4#2i)*
    A ∨ B, ~B / A *(disjunctive syllogism)*
    A → B, B → C / A → C *(hypothetical syllogism; exercise 5.4#2l)*
- demonstrations with the following forms are s-invalid:
    A → B, B / A *(fallacy of affirming the consequent; exercises 3.9#2b and 5.2#2a)*
    A → B, ~A / ~B *(fallacy of denying the antecedent; exercise 5.2#2b)*
    A → C, B → C / C *(fallacy of incomplete enumeration of cases; exercises 3.9#2e and 5.2#2e)*
    A → B / B → A *(conversion fallacy; exercise 5.2#2c)*
    A → B / ~A → ~B *(inversion fallacy; exercise 5.2#2d)*
- sentences with the following forms are s-equivalent:
    A; ~~A *(double negation; exercise 5.4#5g)*
    A → B; ~B → ~A *(equivalence of contrapositives; exercises 3.8i and 5.4#5k)*
    A & B; B & A *(&commutation; exercise 5.4#5e)*
    A ∨ B; B ∨ A *(∨ commutation; exercise 5.4#5f)*
    (A & B) & C; A & (B & C) *(& association; exercise 5.4#5o)*
    (A ∨ B) ∨ C; A ∨ (B ∨ C) *(∨ association; exercise 5.4#5n)*
    ~(A & B); ~A ∨ ~B *(De Morgan's theorem; exercise 5.4#5h)*
    ~(A ∨ B); ~A & ~B *(De Morgan's theorem; exercise 5.4#5i)*
    A → B; ~A ∨ B *(implication; exercise 5.4#5j)*

When these results are read using "not" in place of ~, "and" in place of &, "or" in place of ∨, "only if" in place of →, and "if and only if" in place of ≡, they state intuitively obvious forms of validity, invalidity, and equivalence. SL semantic results capture many of our most basic intuitions about what is logical or illogical. SL semantics also provides a theory of what accounts for the distinction. According to this theory, validity, invalidity, and equivalence are determined by the way the valuation rules for the connectives determine assignments to compounds given assignments to their atomic components.

In addition to applying SL to formalize natural languages, sentences of SL can be treated as objects that themselves share certain forms, and so fall under their own general principles. There is an obvious utility to doing so. For example, in exercises 3.8f and 5.4#1a it is shown that A ∨ ~A is s-valid. This only applies to that sentence, not to (A → B) ∨ ~(A → B), ~[G ∨ ~(K ≡ H)] ∨ ~~[G ∨ ~(K ≡ H)], or even to B ∨ ~B. Clearly, any disjunction that has a sentence and its negation as its disjuncts is s-valid. (More elegantly expressed, all sentences of the form P ∨ ~P are s-valid.) But exercises 3.8f and 5.4#1a do not prove this, and it is undesirable to have to rewrite those demonstrations for each different instance of P ∨ ~P that might come up.

General principles cannot be demonstrated using long or short tables. Because they talk about all (arbitrarily complex) sentences of certain forms, no one table could cover all the instances of the principle. However, with two small tweaks, the techniques of section 5.2 can be used to demonstrate them. For example, the claim of exercise 3.8g, that A ∨ ~A is s-valid can be demonstrated by rewriting the original demonstration for A ∨ ~A, replacing A with the metavariable, P, which stands for any sentence of SL.

   1. Suppose to the contrary that P ∨ ~P is not s-valid.
   2. By definition of s-invalidity, there is an interpretation, I, such that I(P ∨ ~P) is F.
   3. By (~), I(P ∨ ~P) is F.
   4. By (∨) I(P) is F and I(~P) is F.
   5. By (~) I(P) is F and I(P) is T.

The demonstration stalls at this point. Since P is a metavariable, it need not stand for an atomic sentence, so it cannot be said that I(P) cannot be both T and F. While I cannot assign both T and F to any sentence letter, it has not been demonstrated that no compound sentence can be both T and F. Anticipating what will only be proven in chapter A-1.2, the thesis that each sentence of SL must have exactly one of the two values can be invoked as a lemma, called the "bivalence" lemma. A lemma is a claim that still needs to be proven. Calling it a lemma is a way of signalling that it is provable and will be proven later.

   6. By the bivalence lemma, no I can assign both T and F to the same sentence.
   7. Since the supposition at line 1 leads to a contradiction at lines 5 and 6, that supposition must be rejected: P ∨ ~P is s-valid.

As noted in section 2.1.2, A ∨ ~A is what is called an *instance* of P ∨ ~P.

> An *instance* is any result of replacing the metavariables in a form with either atomic or compound sentences, in such a way that the same sentence is put in the place of each occurrence of the same metavariable.

For example,

- B ∨ ~B
- (A → B) ∨ ~(A → B)
- ~[G ∨ ~(K ≡ H)] ∨ ~~[G ∨ ~(K ≡ H)]

are all instances of P ∨ ~P.

Once it has been demonstrated that P ∨ ~P is s-valid, the point holds for any instance of that claim.

Exercise 5.6

1. *State which of the following forms are instances of* P → Q, ~Q / ~P. *If a form is an instance, identify the sentence of SL that is being put in the place of each occurrence of* P *and each occurrence of* Q. *If a form is not an instance, say why not.*
   ★a. ~(A → B), ~C → (A → B) / ~~C
    b. ~(A → B), ~B / ~A
   ★c. B → ~A, ~A / ~B
    d. ~B → ~A, ~~A / B
   ★e. ~C → ~(A → B), A → B / C
    f. ~B, B → A / ~A

2. *State which of the following forms are instances of* $\Gamma \cup \sim(P \vee \sim Q)$. *If a form is an instance, identify the sentence of SL that is being put in the place of each occurrence of* P *and each occurrence of* Q, *and the set of sentences of SL, if any, that is put in the place of* Γ. *If a form is not an instance, say why not.*

　★a. $\{\sim(A \equiv B), \sim(\sim C \vee \sim C)\}$
　　b. $\{\sim A, B \vee C\} \cup \sim(A \vee \sim A)$
　★c. $A \cup \sim[(B \mathbin{\&} C) \vee \sim G]$
　　d. $\{A, B \rightarrow \sim C, G\} \cup \sim\sim(H \vee \sim K)$
　★e. $\sim(A \vee \sim B)$
　　f. $\{A, B \rightarrow \sim C, G\} \cup \sim(\sim H \vee \sim K)$

3. *Following is a list of important forms of equivalence between sentences of SL. Some of them can be demonstrated by making small changes to the demonstration of atomic instances found in earlier exercises. (They are tagged with the exercise numbers where they were demonstrated.) Others are new. Demonstrate those that are new.*

	Equivalence Principles of SL				
5.4#5e.	P	$=\mid=$	$\sim\sim P$	(DN)	*(double negation)*
★a.	P	$=\mid=$	$P \mathbin{\&} P$	(idem)	*(idempotence)*
b.	P	$=\mid=$	$P \vee P$	(idem)	*(idempotence)*
★c.	P	$=\mid=$	$(P \mathbin{\&} Q) \vee (P \mathbin{\&} \sim Q)$	(elab)	*(elaboration)*
d.	P	$=\mid=$	$(P \vee Q) \mathbin{\&} (P \vee \sim Q)$	(elab)	*(elaboration)*
5.4#5a.	$P \mathbin{\&} \sim P$	$=\mid=$	$\bot$	(con)	*(contradiction)*
★e.	$P \vee \sim P$	$=\mid=$	$\sim\bot$	(em)	*(excluded middle)*
5.4#5b	$\sim P$	$=\mid=$	$P \rightarrow \bot$	(def $\sim$)	*(definition of $\sim$)*
f.	$P \mathbin{\&} \bot$	$=\mid=$	$\bot$	(inf)	*(infection)*
★g.	$P \vee \sim\bot$	$=\mid=$	$\sim\bot$	(inf)	*(infection)*
h.	$P \mathbin{\&} \sim\bot$	$=\mid=$	P	(imm)	*(immunity)*
★i.	$P \vee \bot$	$=\mid=$	P	(imm)	*(immunity)*
5.4#5e.	$P \mathbin{\&} Q$	$=\mid=$	$Q \mathbin{\&} P$	(com)	*(& commutation)*
5.4#5f.	$P \vee Q$	$=\mid=$	$Q \vee P$	(com)	*($\vee$ commutation)*
5.4#5n.	$P \vee (Q \vee R)$	$=\mid=$	$(P \vee Q) \vee R$	(assoc)	*($\vee$ association)*
5.4#5o.	$P \mathbin{\&} (Q \mathbin{\&} R)$	$=\mid=$	$(P \mathbin{\&} Q) \mathbin{\&} R$	(assoc)	*(& association)*
5.5e.	$P \mathbin{\&} (Q \vee R)$	$=\mid=$	$(P \mathbin{\&} Q) \vee (P \mathbin{\&} R)$	(dist)	*(&/$\vee$ distribution)*
5.5f.	$P \vee (Q \mathbin{\&} R)$	$=\mid=$	$(P \vee Q) \mathbin{\&} (P \vee R)$	(dist)	*($\vee$/& distribution)*
5.4#5h.	$\sim(P \mathbin{\&} Q)$	$=\mid=$	$\sim P \vee \sim Q$	(DeM)	*(De Morgan's theorem)*
5.4#5i.	$\sim(P \vee Q)$	$=\mid=$	$\sim P \mathbin{\&} \sim Q$	(DeM)	*(De Morgan's theorem)*
5.5b.	$(P \mathbin{\&} Q) \rightarrow R$	$=\mid=$	$P \rightarrow (Q \rightarrow R)$	(exp)	*(exportation)*
5.4#5j.	$P \rightarrow Q$	$=\mid=$	$\sim P \vee Q$	(impl)	*(implication)*
5.4#5l.	$P \rightarrow Q$	$=\mid=$	$\sim(P \mathbin{\&} \sim Q)$	(impl)	*(implication)*
j.	$P \mathbin{\&} Q$	$=\mid=$	$\sim(P \rightarrow \sim Q)$	(impl)	*(implication)*
5.4#5k.	$P \rightarrow Q$	$=\mid=$	$\sim Q \rightarrow \sim P$	(contra)	*(contraposition)*
5.5c.	$P \equiv Q$	$=\mid=$	$(P \rightarrow Q) \mathbin{\&} (Q \rightarrow P)$	(equiv)	*(equivalence)*
k.	$P \equiv Q$	$=\mid=$	$(P \rightarrow Q) \mathbin{\&} (\sim P \rightarrow \sim Q)$	(equiv)	*(equivalence)*
5.5d.	$P \equiv Q$	$=\mid=$	$(P \mathbin{\&} Q) \vee (\sim P \mathbin{\&} \sim Q)$	(equiv)	*(equivalence)*
★l.	$\sim(P \equiv Q)$	$=\mid=$	$(P \mathbin{\&} \sim Q) \vee (Q \mathbin{\&} \sim P)$	($\sim$equiv)	*($\sim$ equivalence)*
m.	$\sim(P \equiv Q)$	$=\mid=$	$(P \vee Q) \mathbin{\&} \sim(P \mathbin{\&} Q)$	($\underline{\vee}$)	*(exclusivity)*

It is also possible to demonstrate general principles that are not so readily formalized, such as that if a set is s-unsatisfiable any superset of that set must be s-unsatisfiable. Many such claims, this one included, are conditionals. When the job is to demonstrate that a conditional is true, a special argumentative strategy is called for, conditional proof.

A conditional proof aims to establish that a conditional is true by supposing that its antecedent is true and showing that anyone who accepts this supposition is also committed to accepting that the consequent is true.

Conditional proof is not as intuitive as indirect proof or proof by cases. People are reluctant to make a supposition unless they are given a reason why that supposition should be accepted. Making a supposition "to the contrary," that is, precisely in order to demonstrate that it should not be accepted, assures people that they are not being asked to simply accept something. On the contrary, they are being shown why they should not do so. A pair of suppositions made for purposes of proof by cases is always backed up by an "either … or …" clause that promises that at least one of the two suppositions must be correct. But suppositions for purposes of conditional proof seem to have no excuse. Conditional proof proceeds by supposing the antecedent is true and then drawing a consequence from that supposition, and this seems suspicious. What if the supposition is false?

This worry is unfounded, because a conditional only makes a claim about what happens in the case where its antecedent is true. It makes no claim about what happens in the case where its antecedent is false. And it does not claim that its antecedent is true. It only makes a claim about what would be the case *if* its antecedent *were* true. The conditional claims that were such a case to arise the consequent would have to be true as well. But it does not claim that this case actually arises. Investigating the truth of a conditional requires supposing the antecedent and determining whether it is still possible to deny the consequent under this supposition. There is no danger to making this supposition, because its falsity is not precluded. Indeed, the case where the antecedent proves to be false is a case that does nothing to refute the conditional claim. The way to refute a conditional is to assume that the antecedent is true and then show that it remains possible for the conditional to be false under this supposition. But if it can be established that supposing the antecedent makes it impossible to deny the consequent without getting caught in a contradiction, then the *conditional* (not its consequent and not its antecedent) is true.

Boilerplate for a demonstration by conditional proof makes this explicit by indenting what follows under the assumption of the antecedent and then outdenting the conditional, showing that all that is demonstrated is the truth of the conditional.

Boilerplate for a Demonstration by Conditional Proof

  1. Suppose for purposes of conditional proof that A.

     …

     k. B.

  k+1. Since the claim at line *k* is demonstrable directly under the supposition at line 1, it follows that if the supposition at line 1 is accepted the claim at line *k* must also be accepted: If A then B.

Conditional proof is often combined with indirect proof. When doing this, the initial assumption of the antecedent is immediately followed by a further supposition to the contrary, that the consequent is not the case. The demonstration then proceeds to show that a contradiction follows under this further assumption, which means that the consequent follows by indirect proof, and the conditional follows by conditional proof.

Boilerplate for a Demonstration by Conditional Proof Supplemented by Indirect Proof

  1. Suppose for purposes of conditional proof that A.

    2. Suppose further, to the contrary, that not-B.

       …

       i. C.

       …

       k. not-C.

  k+1. Since the further supposition at line 2 leads to a contradiction at lines *i* and *k*, under the initial supposition at line 1, the further supposition at line 2 cannot be sustained under the supposition at line 1. Provided the supposition at line 1 is sustained: B.

  k+2. Since the claim at line *k* is demonstrable directly under the supposition at line 1, it follows that if the supposition at line 1 is accepted the claim at line *k* must also be accepted: If A then B.

A combination of conditional proof and indirect proof is used to demonstrate the claim mentioned earlier, that if a set is s-unsatisfiable, any superset of that set must be s-unsatisfiable.

1. Suppose for purposes of conditional proof that a set, Γ, is s-unsatisfiable.
   2. Suppose further, to the contrary, that there is a superset, Γ', of Γ that is s-satisfiable.
      3. By definition of s-satisfiability, there is an interpretation, I, on which each sentence in Γ' is true.
      4. By definition of a superset, each sentence in Γ is in Γ'.
      5. From lines 3 and 4 each sentence in Γ is true on I.
      6. From line 1 by definition of s-satisfiability, at least one sentence in Γ is false on any interpretation, including I.
      7. From lines 5 and 6, at least one sentence in Γ is both true and false on I.
      8. By the bivalence lemma, no sentence can be both true and false on any I.
   9. Since the further supposition at line 2 leads to a contradiction at lines 7 and 8, the further supposition at line 2 cannot be sustained under the supposition at line 1. Provided the supposition at line 1 is sustained, any superset, Γ', of Γ is s-unsatisfiable.
10. Since the claim at line 9 is demonstrable directly under the supposition at line 1, it follows by conditional proof that if the supposition at line 1 is accepted, the claim at line 9 must be accepted: if Γ is s-unsatisfiable, then any superset, Γ', of Γ is s-unsatisfiable.

This demonstration makes use of a further demonstrative technique, the employment of abbreviations. There are two principal ways of referring to things: by means of descriptions and by means of names. References by description can require many words. The forest of words can impede discovery and understanding. It can require awkward and tediously repetitive grammatical constructions. The more words that are used, the harder it is to follow what is being said, and the more ways there are for what is said to be misunderstood. Names, i.e., symbols, get around all these difficulties. Many people are symbol shy. It helps to think that symbols are just very short names. The symbol, Γ, can look foreign and be intimidating. But it is just a name for any set that might be considered. Using it reduces the forest of words, making the point clear.

It is easy to name things by putting them in apposition. The first time a thing is mentioned, it is described, and then, following the description, an apposition is added, giving the thing a name. For example,

- an interpretation, I, …
- a set, Γ, …
- a superset, Γ', …
- a conjunction, P & Q, …
- a demonstration, Γ / P, …
- a set comprised of the premises of a demonstration and the negation of its conclusion, $\Gamma \cup \sim P$, …

Exercise 5.7

1. *Demonstrate the following, using apposition to name repeatedly mentioned objects. Use conditional proof and indirect proof as needed. Compare the answered questions to get a better idea of how to do this.*
   *a. If a sentence is s-contingent, its negation must be s-contingent.
   b. If a conjunction has an s-unsatisfiable conjunct, it must be s-unsatisfiable.
   *c. If a disjunction has two opposite disjuncts, it must be s-valid.
   d. If a conditional has an s-unsatisfiable antecedent, it must be s-valid.
   *e. If a conditional has an s-valid consequent, it must be s-valid.
   f. If a biconditional has two s-equivalent immediate components, it must be s-valid.

5.4 Falsifying General Claims

General principles are verified, and so elevated to the status of principles, by giving a demonstration. Falsifying a general claim calls for a different approach. Maintaining that the claim must be false because it cannot be demonstrated is not acceptable. Demonstration can require ingenuity. If a demonstration has not been discovered, the failure may be due to a lack of ingenuity rather than the falsity of the claim. Attempting to demonstrate that it is impossible to give a demonstration is a poor alternative. Such demonstrations are commonly difficult to discover and so complex that they are prone to error and unconvincing. There is a quicker and easier way to refute a general claim: give a counterexample. A counterexample is one case that does not turn out the way the general claim says it should. Presenting such a case is all that needs to be done.

Consider the claim that if two sentences, P and Q, are s-contingent, the set comprised of those two sentences, {P, Q} must be s-satisfiable.

This claim is false. The way to prove that it is false is to give a counterexample. Compare the following two efforts to see why.

> *Effort 1 (demonstration):* If P is s-contingent then it must be true on at least one interpretation, and if Q is s-contingent then it must be true on at least one interpretation, but this does not mean that there has to be any one interpretation on which both are true. So it does not follow that {P, Q} must be s-satisfiable.
>
> *Effort 2 (counterexample):* As a long table will show, both A and ~A are s-contingent. But, as a long table will further show, {A, ~A} is s-unsatisfiable.

Effort 1 is considerably longer and considerably harder to follow than effort 2. It took more time to produce. And it is ultimately question-begging. It does not get beyond asserting the very point that stands in need of proof: that even though P and Q are s-contingent, there may be no interpretation on which both are true. Why not?

A common failure of attempts to demonstrate that a general claim is false is that they never get beyond establishing the possibility that things could be otherwise than claimed. A counterexample, in contrast, presents a case where things do turn out to be otherwise than the claim says they should. Once a counterexample has been presented, no further demonstration of what makes it possible is called for. Whatever is actual is possible.

To be effective, a counterexample needs to have two features. Firstly, a counterexample should be an individual. It should not contain metavariables. Metavariables designate a group, not an individual. The counterexamples called for when refuting general claims about sentences, sets, or demonstrations of SL are always sentences, sets, or demonstrations of SL. They should contain only the vocabulary elements of SL.

Secondly, a counterexample needs to be to the point. It must be a case of the sort the general claim is talking about, albeit a case that does not turn out as the claim says all cases of that sort should. A common error is coming up with an example that does not turn out as the general claim says it should but that is not of the right sort. A less common, but still frequent error is coming up with an example that is of the right sort but does turn out just as the general claim says it should.

> *Effort 3 (bad counterexample – not a case of the right sort):* This cannot be true because {A, ⊥} is s-unsatisfiable.
>
> *Effort 4 (bad counterexample – not contrary to what is claimed):* This cannot be true because A and B are both s-contingent.

A good counterexample has two parts. It first makes a case that the individuals cited constitute a case of the right sort. It then makes a case that these individuals do not turn out as the general claim says they should. The bad efforts made above do only one of these things. Effort 3 does not begin by saying that A and ⊥ are both cases of the right sort, that is, s-contingent sentences. They are not (⊥ is s-unsatisfiable), so even though {A, ⊥} is s-unsatisfiable, this fails to be a case of the right sort. Effort 4 does not conclude by claiming that {A, B} is s-unsatisfiable – or if it did, it would say something false.

Demonstration and counterexample are used for different purposes and may not be substituted for one another. Demonstrations establish general rules and falsify particular claims. Examples falsify general rules and establish particular claims. No finite number of examples is sufficient to establish a general rule. That requires a demonstration from fundamental concepts and rules. And no demonstration from fundamental concepts and rules is needed to establish either what may be the case or what need not be the case. That is best done by giving an example.

Sometimes, it is not obvious whether a claim is true or false, and so not obvious whether it needs to be established by a demonstration or refuted with a counterexample. In such cases, it is best not to mull over things, but to pick one alternative and work at it. When an attempt to construct an example is picked, and each example that is attempted fails, it is often possible to isolate some factor responsible for the failure. This factor can then serve as the basis for a demonstration of why no example can be constructed. Alternatively, when an attempt at giving a demonstration breaks down, it is often because some counterexample presents itself. In logic, it rarely happens that anything is lost by making the wrong choice. Discovering why the wrong choice does not work is tantamount to proving the right choice.

Exercise 5.8

1. *Give a counterexample to each of the following claims. (Think of a sentence of SL that is not the way the claim says that all sentences of that sort must be.)*

    ⋆a. If P and Q are s-satisfiable, P & Q is s-satisfiable.

    b. If P and Q are s-contingent, P ∨ Q is s-contingent.

    ⋆c. If P ≡ Q is s-contingent, P → Q is s-contingent.

    d. If {P, Q} is s-unsatisfiable, P ≡ Q is s-unsatisfiable.

    ⋆e. If {P, Q} is s-satisfiable, P / Q is s-valid.

    f. If P and Q are s-equivalent, {P, Q} is s-satisfiable.

2. *Establish that the following claims are either true or false by means of a demonstration or an example as appropriate.*

    ⋆a. If P s-valid, ~P is s-unsatisfiable.

    b. If P is s-satisfiable, ~P is s-unsatisfiable.

    ⋆c. If P is s-satisfiable, P ∨ Q must be s-satisfiable.

    d. If P and Q are not s-equivalent, P & Q is s-unsatisfiable.

    ⋆e. If P and Q are opposite, P → Q is s-contingent.

    f. If Γ / P is s-valid, and Γ is s-satisfiable, then P is s-valid.

5.5 Relations between Intensional Concepts; Models; Entailment; Biconditional Proof

In section 3.4 it was noted that for any pair of sentences, for any set, and for any demonstration there is a corresponding sentence. The corresponding sentence, P ≡ Q is s-valid if and only if P and Q are s-equivalent. The corresponding sentence, (…(P₁ & …) & Pₙ), is s-unsatisfiable if and only if {P₁,…,Pₙ} is s-unsatisfiable, and the corresponding sentence, (…(P₁ & …) & Pₙ) → Q is s-valid if and only if P₁,…,Pₙ / Q is s-valid. In section 3.4 these correspondences were justified in a less than ideal way, by appeal to intuitions about how any instance of these forms would appear on a long table. Now that demonstrative techniques have been explained, they can be used to rigorously establish these results. This provides an occasion to introduce a final demonstrative technique, specific to cases where an "if and only if" principle needs to be established.

As discussed in section 3.3, sentences of the form "A if and only if B" are conditionals that go both ways. They assert that if A is the case then B is the case, and that if B is the case then A is the case. Exercises that ask for the demonstration of a principle that is formulated as an "if and only if" proposition should accordingly be approached as if they were two exercises collapsed into one: demonstrating that if A then B, and then demonstrating its converse, that if B then A.

Alternatively, "A if and only if B" can be demonstrated by demonstrating that if A then B, and then demonstrating its inverse, that if not-A then not-B. This works because "if not-A then not-B" is the contrapositive of "if B then A," and conditionals are equivalent to their contrapositives. If it is not immediately clear why, consider that granting "if not-A then not-B" and accepting B means having to accept A as well (because it is granted that when A is not the case B could not be the case either). So, "if not-A then not-B" entails "if B then A." Conversely, granting "if B then A" and accepting that A is not the case means having to accept that B is not the case either (because it is granted that if B were the case A would have to be as well). So "if B then A" reciprocally entails "if not-A then not-B."

In some cases, a demonstration of "A if and only if B" might take the form of a chain of "if and only if" propositions: "A if and only if A₁"; "A₁ if and only if A₂"; "A₂ if and only if …"; up to: "Aₙ if and only if B." Supposing such a chain of "if and only if" propositions can be set up, it follows that the first link is the case if and only the last link is the case.

The first two ways of demonstrating a biconditional are called biconditional proof (BP); the third is called biconditional syllogism (BS).

> Boilerplate for Proving "If and Only If" Principles
>
> 1. Boilerplate for proving "if and only if" principles can take one or other of three main forms. The first form is based on the fact that a biconditional means to assert both a conditional and its converse. Each must be independently demonstrated.
>
>   1. Suppose for purposes of biconditional proof that A.
>
>   …
>
>   k. B.

k+1. Now suppose, for purposes of the second half of biconditional proof that B.

 ...

 n. A.

n+1. From lines 1 to k and k+1 to n by (BP), A if and only if B.

2. The second form is also based on the fact that a biconditional means to assert both a conditional and its converse, but rather than demonstrate the converse directly, it demonstrates it indirectly, by demonstrating its contrapositive instead.

 1. Suppose for purposes of biconditional proof that A.

  ...

 k. B.

 k+1. Now suppose, for purposes of the second half of biconditional proof that not-A.

  ...

 n. not-B.

 n+1. From lines 1 to k and k+1 to n by (BP), A if and only if B.

3. The third form uses biconditional syllogism (BS) rather than biconditional proof (BP). It consists of a chain of if and only if propositions.

 1. A if and only if A_1.
 2. A1 if and only if A_2.
 3. A2 if and only if A_3.
  ...
 n+1. A_n if and only if B.
n+2. From lines 1 to n+1 by (BS), A if and only if B.

Biconditional syllogisms are more elegant, which makes them the preferred way of demonstrating "if and only if" propositions. But it is not always possible to offer biconditional syllogisms. Sometimes the intermediate biconditionals are not available, making it necessary to employ other means.

The first of the principles mentioned at the outset of this section, that two sentences, P and Q are s-equivalent if and only if P $\equiv$ Q is s-valid, can be demonstrated by biconditional syllogism.

1. By definition of s-equivalence, two sentences, P and Q are s-equivalent if and only if there is no interpretation on which they have different values, that is, if and only if they have the same value on each interpretation.
2. By ($\equiv$) P and Q are the same on each interpretation if and only if P $\equiv$ Q is true on each interpretation.
3. By definition of s-validity, P $\equiv$ Q is true on each interpretation if and only if it is s-valid.
4. From lines 1–3 by biconditional syllogism, P and Q are s-equivalent if and only if P $\equiv$ Q is s-valid.

A demonstration by biconditional syllogism should read just as well in reverse. In this case, it would say that P $\equiv$ Q is s-valid if and only if it is true on each interpretation. P $\equiv$ Q is true on each interpretation if and only if P and Q are the same on each interpretation, that is, if and only if there is no interpretation on which they have different values. There is no interpretation on which P and Q have different values if and only if they are s-equivalent.

The intermediate chain of biconditionals is not available to use biconditional syllogism to demonstrate the third of the principles mentioned at the outset of this section, that a demonstration is s-valid if and only if the corresponding conditional is s-valid. The second form of biconditional proof is used here instead.

1. Suppose for purposes of biconditional proof that a demonstration, $P_1,...P_n$ / Q is s-valid.
 2. By definition of s-validity, there is no interpretation on which $P_1,...,P_n$ are true and Q is false, that is, on any interpretation, I, either at least one of $P_1,...,P_n$ is false or Q is true.
 3. Suppose for purposes of proof by cases on line 2 that at least one of $P_1,...,P_n$ is false on I.

4. By iterated applications of (&), (…(P₁ & …) & Pₙ, that is, the iterated conjunction of P₁,…,Pₙ, is false on I. (Since at least one of P₁,…,Pₙ is false on I, whichever one it is, the conjunction of which it is an immediate conjunct must be false, the conjunction of which that conjunction is an immediate conjunct must be false, and so on up to the main conjunction.)

5. By (→), (…(P₁ & …) & Pₙ) → Q is true.

6. Now suppose, for purposes of the second half of proof by cases on line 2, that I(Q) is T.

7. By (→), (…(P₁ & …) & Pₙ) → Q is true.

8. Since at least one of the alternatives listed at line 2 must be the case on any interpretation, and since, as shown by lines 3–5 and 6–7 the same consequence follows either way, that consequence can be affirmed unconditionally: (…(P₁ & …) & Pₙ) → Q is true on any interpretation.

9. By definition of s-validity, (…(P₁ & …) & Pₙ) → Q is s-valid.

10. Now suppose for purposes of the second half of biconditional proof that P₁,…Pₙ / Q is s-invalid.

11. By definition of s-validity, there is at least one interpretation, I, on which P₁,…,Pₙ are true and Q is false.

12. By iterated applications of (&), I(…(P₁ & …) & Pₙ) is T. (Since each of I(P₁) … I(Pₙ) is T, I(P₁ & P₂) must be T, its conjunction with P₃ must be T, and so on up to the main conjunction.)

13. From lines 11 and 12 by (→) I(…(P₁ & …) & Pₙ) → Q) is F.

14. By definition of s-validity, (…(P₁ & …) & Pₙ) → Q is s-invalid.

15. From lines 1–9 and 10–14 by biconditional proof, P₁,…Pₙ / Q is s-valid if and only if (…(P₁ & …) & Pₙ) → Q is s-valid.

Exercise 5.9

Demonstrate the second principle, that a set, {P₁,…,Pₙ} is s-unsatisfiable if and only if (…(P₁ & …) & Pₙ is s-unsatisfiable. Use the first form of (BP). Neither this principle nor the third principle can be rigorously demonstrated without using a demonstrative technique called mathematical induction (to be introduced in chapter A-1) to establish that falsity is infectious in iterated conjunctions. However, you should be able to give the idea of how such a demonstration would go, following the example given at line 4 above.

The fact that pairs of sentences, sets, and demonstrations have corresponding sentences means it would be possible to determine all intensional properties just by considering the intensional properties of sentences. Interestingly, the same holds for sets and demonstrations. Just as there are corresponding sentences, so there are corresponding sets and corresponding demonstrations. All intensional properties can be determined just by considering the intensional properties of sets, or just by considering the intensional properties of demonstrations.

Corresponding sets are best described by appeal to a further notion, that of a model. A model is a special kind of interpretation.

> A *model* for a set, Γ, is an interpretation on which each of the sentences in Γ is T.
>
> An *s-model* is an interpretation on which each of the sentences in a set of sentences of SL is T.

The concept of a model figures in an alternative definition of the satisfiability of sets.

> A *set*, Γ, is *s-unsatisfiable* if and only if it does not have an s-model.
>   It is *s-satisfiable* if and only if it has an s-model.

For any sentence, P, there are two corresponding sets, {~P} and {P}. For any pair of sentences, P and Q, there are also two corresponding sets {P, ~Q} and {Q, ~P}. And for any demonstration, Γ / P, there is a corresponding set, Γ ∪ ~P. The validity, satisfaction, equivalence, and contingency of sentences and demonstrations can be defined in terms of whether their corresponding sets have s-models.

A sentence, P, is s-valid if and only if it is not false on any interpretation, that is, if and only if it is true on each interpretation. By (~) this is the case if and only if its opposite, ~P, is false on each interpretation, that is, if and only if there is no interpretation on which it is true. So, a sentence, P, is s-valid if and only if {~P} does not have an s-model.

> A *sentence*, P, is *s-valid* if and only if {~P} does not have an s-model.
> It is *s-invalid* if and only if {~P} has an s-model.

In contrast, P is s-unsatisfiable if and only if it is not true on any interpretation and so has no s-model.

> A *sentence*, P, is *s-unsatisfiable* if and only if {P} does not have an s-model.
> It is *s-satisfiable* if and only if {P} has an s-model.
> It is *s-contingent* if and only if both {P} and {~P} have s-models.

Two sentences, P and Q, are not s-equivalent if and only if there is at least one interpretation on which P and Q have different values, that is, if and only if either P is true and Q is false, or Q is true and P is false. By (~), this is the case if and only if there is at least one interpretation that assigns a T to each sentence in at least one of {P, ~Q} and {Q, ~P}, that is, if and only if at least one of {P, ~Q} and {Q, ~P} has an s-model.

> *Two sentences*, P and Q, are *s-equivalent* if and only if neither {P, ~Q} nor {Q, ~P} has an s-model.
> They are *s-nonequivalent* if and only if at least one of {P, ~Q} and {Q, ~P} has an s-model.

Γ / P is s-valid if and only if there is no interpretation that assigns T to each sentence in Γ and F to P. By (~) this is the case if and only if there is no interpretation that assigns T to each sentence in Γ and T to ~P, that is, if and only if the set that results from adding ~P to the sentences in Γ does not have an s-model.

> A *demonstration*, Γ / P is *s-valid* if and only if Γ ∪ ~P does not have an s-model.
> It is *s-invalid* if and only if Γ ∪ ~P has an s-model.

Exercise 5.10

1. *Restate the results of exercise 3.9##1–4 in terms of s-models. In some cases, this requires appealing to the effect of (~) in generating an additional column of values on the tables done when answering the original questions. Follow the example of the answered exercises.*

   Answers for **3.9#1**a, c, e, g, i, k, m; **#2**a, c, e, g; **#3**a, c, e; **#4**a, c, e, g

2. *Demonstrate the following. Use biconditional syllogism.*
   a. P is s-valid if and only if {~P} is s-unsatisfiable.
   *b. P and Q are s-equivalent if and only if both {P, ~Q} and {Q, ~P} are s-unsatisfiable.
   c. Γ / P is s-valid if and only if Γ ∪ ~P is s-unsatisfiable.

Corresponding demonstrations are also best described by appeal to a further notion, that of entailment.

Entailment, symbolized with the double turnstile (⊨) and called s-entailment (⊨ₛ) where sentential logic is concerned, is the relation between the premises and the conclusion of a valid demonstration. The subscripted "s" is dropped when it is obvious that s-entailment is meant.

> Γ *s-entails* P if and only if there is no interpretation on which each sentence in Γ is true and P is false (equivalently, if and only if, on any interpretation on which all sentences in Γ are true, P is true).
> Γ *does not s-entail* P if and only if there is at least one interpretation on which each sentence in Γ is true and P is false.

> Alternatively,
> Γ *s-entails* P if and only if $\Gamma \cup {\sim}P$ does not have an s-model. In abbreviated notation: $\Gamma \vDash P$
>> Γ *does not s-entail* P if and only if $\Gamma \cup {\sim}P$ has an s-model. In abbreviated notation: $\Gamma \nvDash P$

For any sentence, P, there are two corresponding demonstrations, $\emptyset$ / P and P / $\perp$. For any pair of sentences, P and Q, there are two corresponding demonstrations, P / Q and Q / P. And for any set, Γ, there is a corresponding demonstration, Γ / $\perp$. The intensional properties of sentences and sets can be defined in terms of whether their corresponding demonstrations have premises that s-entail their conclusions.

Suppose a sentence, P, is s-valid. By definition, there is no interpretation on which it gets an F. Then regardless of what sentences there are in a set, Γ, there can be no interpretation on which all the sentences in Γ get a T *and* P gets an F. The contents of Γ do not matter. In particular, if there are no contents, that is, if Γ is $\emptyset$, there is still no interpretation on which all the sentences in the set are true and P is false. So by definition of s-validity $\emptyset \vDash P$.

Now suppose that $\emptyset \vDash P$. By definition of s-entailment, there is no interpretation on which all the sentences in $\emptyset$ are true and P is false. This means that each interpretation must be such that either there is at least one sentence in $\emptyset$ that is false on that interpretation or P must be true on that interpretation. Since there are no sentences in $\emptyset$ to be false, P must be true on each interpretation, that is, it must be s-valid.

> A *sentence*, P, is *s-valid* if and only if the empty set s-entails P. In abbreviated notation, "$\emptyset \vDash P$" or "$\{\ \} \vDash P$" or just "$\vDash P$."
>> P, is *s-invalid* if and only if the empty set does not s-entail P. In abbreviated notation, $\nvDash P$.

Like any other set, the unit set, $\{P\}$, s-entails a sentence if and only if there is no interpretation on which each sentence in $\{P\}$ is true and that sentence is false. But by ($\perp$), the sentence $\perp$ is false on each interpretation. It follows that $\{P\}$ s-entails $\perp$ if and only if the one sentence in $\{P\}$ is false on each interpretation, that is, if and only if P is s-unsatisfiable.

> A *sentence*, P, is *s-unsatisfiable* if and only if $P \vDash \perp$.
>> P is *s-satisfiable* if and only if $P \nvDash \perp$.
>> A *sentence*, P is *s-contingent* if and only if $\emptyset \nvDash P$ and $P \nvDash \perp$.

The s-satisfiability and s-unsatisfiability of sets is defined in the same way as for sentences. Entailment requires that there be no interpretation where all the premises are true and the conclusion is false. Since $\perp$ is false on any interpretation, entailing $\perp$ requires that at least one premise be false on each interpretation (the one that is false on one interpretation need not be the same as the one that is false on another). This is the case if and only if the set of premises is s-unsatisfiable.

> A *set*, Γ, is *s-unsatisfiable* if and only if $\Gamma \vDash \perp$;
>> it is *s-satisfiable* if and only if $\Gamma \nvDash \perp$.

Finally, P and Q are s-equivalent if and only if there is no interpretation on which they receive different values, that is if and only there is no interpretation on which P receives a T and Q receives an F (so, $P \vDash Q$) and if and only if there is no interpretation on which Q receives a T and P receives an F (so, $Q \vDash P$). s-equivalence can therefore be defined in terms of mutual entailment. A special symbol is employed to designate mutual entailment, the double-double turnstile, $=\!|\!=$. Whereas entailment is a relation between a set and a sentence, mutual entailment is a relation between two sentences.

> *Two sentences*, P and Q, are *s-equivalent* if and only if $P =\!|\!= Q$.
>> They are *not s-equivalent* if and only if either $P \nvDash Q$ or $Q \nvDash P$.

→ versus ⊨; ≡ versus =|=

The definition of s-entailment resembles the truth conditions for arrow. s-equivalence is defined in terms of the absence of an interpretation on which sentences have different values, which resembles the truth conditions for the triple bar. This raises the question of whether sentences of the form $(\ldots(P_1 \ \& \ \ldots) \ \& \ P_n) \to Q$ mean the same thing as assertions of the form $\{P_1,\ldots,P_n\} \vDash Q$, and whether $P \equiv Q$ asserts the s-equivalence of P and Q. Neither is the case. Suppose I(A) and I(B) are true. Then $I(A \equiv B)$ is true. But A is not s-equivalent to B. Suppose I(A) is false. Then $I(A \to B)$ is true. But A does not s-entail B. It is only when $P \equiv Q$ is s-valid that P and Q are s-equivalent, and only when $P \to Q$ is s-valid that P s-entails Q (and in either case that never happens when P and Q stand for different sentence letters).

→ and ≡ are connectives of SL. ⊨ and =|= are symbols of English used to stand for intensional relations between a set and a sentence (⊨) or between two sentences (=|=). → does not say that $P \to Q$ cannot be false, and ≡ does not say that $P \equiv Q$ cannot be false. On the contrary, → assigns an F to $P \to Q$ on any interpretation on which P is true and Q is false, and ≡ assigns an F to $P \equiv Q$ on any interpretation on which P and Q have different values. The assignments that → and ≡ make are interpretation-relative. Assigning T on one interpretation does not preclude assigning an F on another.

⊨ and =|=, in contrast, make a claim about what all the interpretations are like. ⊨ claims that there is no interpretation on which all the sentences in Γ are true and Q is false (hence, none on which $(\ldots(P_1 \ \& \ \ldots) \ \& \ P_n) \to Q$ is false), and =|= claims that there is no interpretation on which P and Q get different values (hence, none on which $P \equiv Q$ is false).

Exercise 5.11

1. *Restate the results of exercise 3.9#1–4 in terms of entailment. Follow the example of the answered exercises.*

   Answers for **3.9#1**a, c, e, g, i, k, m; **#2**a, c, e, g; **#3**a, c, e; **#4**a, c, e, g

2. *Many of the claims below were informally presented above. Demonstrate them by appeal to the definitions of the intensional concepts given in chapter 3.4 and either of the following definitions of ⊨ as appropriate: Γ ⊨ P if and only if there is no interpretation on which each sentence in Γ is true and P is false; Γ ⊨ P if and only if, on any interpretation on which each sentence in Γ is true, P is true. Use the boilerplate for biconditional syllogism wherever possible (it is not always possible).*

   ★**a.** Γ is s–unsatisfiable if and only if Γ ⊨ ⊥

   b. P is s–unsatisfiable if and only if P ⊨ ⊥ *(Hint: use (BP) and indirect proof.)*

   ★**c.** Γ ⊨ P if and only if Γ ∪ ~P ⊨ ⊥

   d. Γ / P is s–valid if and only if Γ ⊨ P

   ★**e.** P is s–valid if and only if ⊨ P

   f. ⊨ P if and only if ~P ⊨ ⊥. *(Hint: use 5.11#2c.)*

   g. P and Q are s–equivalent if and only if P ⊨ Q and Q ⊨ P

   ★**h.** P ⊨ Q and Q ⊨ P if and only if ⊨ P ≡ Q

   i. If Γ ⊨ P and P and Q are s–equivalent then Γ ⊨ Q

   ★**j.** $\{Q_1,\ldots,Q_n\} \cup$ ~P, is s–unsatisfiable if and only if $(\ldots(Q_1 \ \& \ \ldots) \ \& \ Q_n) \ \& \ $~P ⊨ ⊥

   k. $\{Q_1,\ldots,Q_n\} \vDash$ P if and only if ⊨ $(\ldots(Q_1 \ \& \ \ldots) \ \& \ Q_n) \to$ P *(Hint: it was proven in the text of section 5.5 that $P_1,\ldots P_n$ / Q is s-valid if and only if $(\ldots(P_1 \ \& \ \ldots) \ \& \ P_n) \to Q$ is s-valid. Appeal to this principle together with 5.11#2d, read right to left, and 5.11#2e.)*

As illustrated in answers to some of these exercises, previously established principles can be used to abbreviate a demonstration. They can also assist in discovering one. An example is the demonstration that the empty set is s-satisfiable. This is an important result, but it is not only hard to discover but perplexing when working from the definition of s-satisfiability. A set is s-satisfiable if and only if there is an interpretation on which each sentence in the set gets a T. But there are no sentences in the empty set to get T's. This might make it seem like the empty set could not be s-satisfiable. But, by that same line of reasoning, a set is s-unsatisfiable if and only if, on each interpretation, at least one of the sentences in the set gets an F. And there are no sentences in the empty set to get F's. It appears as if there is just as much reason to say that the empty set cannot be s-unsatisfiable.

In this case, a demonstration is easier to discover by appealing to the superset principle established towards the close of section 5.3.

    1. Suppose, to the contrary, that Ø is s-unsatisfiable.
      2. By the superset principle proven at the close of section 5.3, any superset of Ø is s-unsatisfiable, including the superset Ø ∪ ~⊥.
      3. Since there are no sentences in Ø, Ø ∪ ~⊥ is just {~⊥}.
      4. From lines 2 and 3, {~⊥} is s-unsatisfiable.
      5. By definition of s-satisfaction, there is no interpretation on which the one sentence in {~⊥}, namely ~⊥, is true.
      6. By (~), there is no interpretation on which ⊥ is false.
      7. By definition of an interpretation, ⊥ is false on any interpretation.
    8. Since the supposition at line 1 has led to a contradiction at lines 7 and 8, that supposition must be rejected: Ø is s-satisfiable.

Exercise 5.12

Demonstrate the following.

★a. If P is in Γ then Γ ⊨ P
  b. If Γ ⊨ P and Γ′ is a superset of Γ, then Γ′ ⊨ P *(Hint: use the superset principle and results 5.11#2a and c.)*
★c. If Γ ⊨ both P and ~P then Γ ⊨ ⊥ *(Hint: establish that Γ is s-unsatisfiable, then appeal to 5.11#2a.)*
  d. If Γ ∪ P ⊨ ⊥, then Γ s-entails any opposite of P *(Hint: make a supposition for conditional proof, then suppose for purposes of conditional proof that there is an interpretation on which all the sentences in Γ are true.)*
★e. If Γ ∪ P ⊨ Q then Γ ⊨ P → Q
  f. If (i) Γ ⊨ P and (ii) Γ ⊨ P → Q then Γ ⊨ Q
★g. If (i) Γ ⊨ P ∨ Q and (ii) Γ ∪ P ⊨ R and (iii) Γ ∪ Q ⊨ R then Γ ⊨ R
  h. If Γ ⊨ P then Γ s-entails both P ∨ Q and Q ∨ P
★i. If (i) Γ ⊨ P and (ii) Γ ⊨ Q then Γ ⊨ P & Q
  j. If Γ ⊨ P & Q then Γ ⊨ P and Γ ⊨ Q *(Hint: run the demonstration of (i) in reverse.)*
★k. If (i) Γ ∪ P ⊨ Q and (ii) Γ ∪ Q ⊨ P then Γ ⊨ P ≡ Q
  l. If (i) Γ ⊨ P ≡ Q and (ii) Γ s-entails either one of P and Q then Γ s-entails the other one of P and Q
★m. If ⊨ P and P ⊨ Q, then ⊨ Q
  n. If Γ is s-satisfiable and Γ′ is a subset of Γ, then Γ′ is s-satisfiable

---

Appendix Alternatives to Bivalence

The system of logic that has been presented so far is bivalent. It assumes that there are only two values and that each sentence has exactly one of them. This assumption was made to keep things simple. By this point, enough has been learned about how bivalent logic works to consider the effects of allowing that some sentences might have other values, or none, or both. Classical Indian logic recognizes four values: true, false, both, and neither. The treatment that follows distinguishes between systems that recognize value gaps, systems that recognize an intermediate or indeterminate value, and systems that recognize sentences that possess both of two opposed values.

There are various reasons for recognizing other values, or allowing sentences with no value or both values. Declarative sentences about future events, like "rain will begin at noon tomorrow," acquire a value when the time comes, but might be thought to lack it at the present time. Sentences that refer to nonexistent objects, like "Pegasus has wings," might be supposed to lack a value, but they can figure in reasoning. Sentences asserting vague predicates, like "x is bald," seem to be neither true nor false in borderline cases. The problem is not that people lack the expertise to apply them correctly. They are not well enough defined for precise application. Sentences like "this sentence is false" seem to bear both values at once. Some have turned to many-valued logics in the hope of finding a connective that might better reflect conditional sentences of English, avoiding the paradoxes that are thought to result when → or ≡ are used to formalize conditionals (see section 4.2). Others are discontent with the fact that the definition of validity allows irrelevant conclusions to be drawn in special cases (any conclusion can be the consequence of contradictory premises and any demonstration with a valid conclusion is valid regardless of its premises). The project of formulating an alternative "relevance" logic tinkers with the definition of validity in ways that dovetail with the way validity is defined in some many-valued logics. More radically yet, it might be charged that "true" and "false" are not the fundamental semantic categories. We should instead be concerned with the evident and what is not (yet) evident. On this view, both what is true and what is false are varieties of what has become evident, and are opposed to what is nonevident.

For introductory purposes, six positions on sentential values can be distinguished:

- *Classicism:* There are exactly two values, true and false, and any sentence that does not have exactly one of them does not fall within the scope of sentential logic.
- *Supervaluationism:* There are some sentences that have no value but that can still be considered by sentential logic. Sentences mentioning future contingencies or nonexistent objects are paradigm cases.
- *Three-valued logic:* There are some sentences that have a third value. Sentences mentioning "fuzzy" or vague predicates are paradigmatic. The value in such cases seems to be "neither" or "indeterminate."
- *Infinite-valued logic:* There are infinitely many values sentences could bear, paradigmatically reflecting cases where it makes sense to consider truth to come in degrees. Sentences mentioning "fuzzy" or vague predicates are again paradigmatic but considered as having values that fall somewhere between true and false.
- *Paraconsistent logic:* There are some sentences that have both truth values, paradigmatically the liar sentence.
- *Intuitionism:* The basic values are evident and not (yet) evident; truth and falsity are different forms of evidence.

This appendix focuses on supervaluationist, three-valued, and paraconsistent logics. Infinite-valued logic is considered only by way of considering three-valued logic. Intuitionism is taken up later and at greater length, beginning in section 6.6.

Appendix 5.1 Supervaluations

Supervaluationist semantics, first formulated by Bas C. van Fraassen (1941–), allows interpretations to make only partial assignments of values to sentence letters. Any interpretation may leave any one or more or even all sentence letters without an assignment. Where there are only two sentence letters under consideration, A and B, there are nine, rather than four possible interpretations. Five of them are partial interpretations.

	A	B
I_1	T	T
I_2	T	
I_3	T	F
I_4		T
I_5		
I_6		F
I_7	F	T
I_8	F	
I_9	F	F

I_5, which makes no assignment to either sentence letter, still counts as an interpretation.

Were there three sentence letters under consideration, there would be twenty-seven different interpretations. The nine given above would be repeated three times over, once to make all the interpretations on which the third sentence letter gets T, then to make all the interpretations where it gets F, and finally to make all the interpretations where it gets no assignment. Adding a fourth sentence letter would mean repeating each of those twenty-seven (or 3^3) interpretations three times over (for a total of 3^4 or 81). As the number of sentence letters increases, the number of interpretations increases by three to the power of n (or 3^n) where n is the number of sentence letters.

The blank spaces that appear on interpretation tables do not represent a third value. They represent a value gap. Proponents of multi-valued logics will often speak of sentences that are neither true nor false, but then they designate "neither true nor false" with a symbol, like N, and consider what values should be ascribed to compound sentences that contain a component with the value N. This is not the case with supervaluationism. On supervaluationist semantics, the gap is a true gap because it plays no role in determining the value of compound sentences.

Interpretations for classical sentential logic are just valuations made by assigning T and F directly to the sentence letters, or by assigning sentences of English or other natural languages that have one or other of two values (designated T and F or 1 and 0) to the sentence letters. On supervaluationist semantics, for each of I_1–I_9 there is a second interpretation, called a superinterpretation or "supervaluation," labelled SI_1–SI_9. The value of a sentence, P, on a supervaluation, SI, based on a valuation, I, is determined by first considering all the ways of filling the gap or gaps left behind by I. (If I leaves no gaps, there is just one way of filling the gaps, namely I itself.) If P ends up being true regardless of how the gaps left by I are filled, it is true on the supervaluation based on I or "supertrue." In brief, SI(P) is T. If P ends up being false regardless of how the gaps left by I are filled, it is "superfalse." SI(P) is F. If P is true on some ways of filling the gaps, but false on others, it continues to have no value on the supervaluation. (SI) P is undetermined.

On this account, there are three things to consider: (i) the original valuation, I, which may be partial, and so may leave some atomic sentences without a value; (ii) all the different ways filling each gap left by I with exactly one of T or F, called the "completions" of I; (iii) the supervaluation on I, which is T, F or "undetermined" depending on whether the completions agree on T, agree on F, or disagree.

For example, the gap in I_6 on the previous table might be filled in two ways.

	A	B
I_6		F
I_{6T}	T	F
I_{6F}	F	F

The different ways of filling the gaps on a partial interpretation such as I_6 are not just "extensions" of I. An extension fills some gaps; a completion is an extension that fills all the gaps.

Each completion makes assignments to compound sentences in the usual way. For example, the two completions of I_6 make the following assignments to the following sentences.

	A	B	~A	~B	A & B	A ∨ B	A → B	B → A	B → B	...
I_6		F		T	F			T	T	
I_{6T}	T	F	F	T	F	T	F	T	T	...
I_{6F}	F	F	T	T	F	F	T	T	T	...

The "supervalues" assigned by SI_6 depend on how these completions turn out. If each of I_{6T} and I_{6F} assigns a T to a sentence, then that sentence gets a T on SI_6. If each completion of I_6 assigns an F, the sentence gets an F on SI_6. But if different completions assign different values, SI_6 continues to leave a gap.

	A	B	~A	~B	A & B	A ∨ B	A → B	B → A	B → B
I_6		F		T	F			T	T
I_{6T}	T	F	F	T	F	T	F	T	T
I_{6F}	F	F	T	T	F	F	T	T	T
SI_6		F		T	F			T	T

The supervalues of compound sentences are not a function of the values or the supervalues of their components. For example, A and B have no value on SI_5, but A → A has a value even though A → B does not.

		A	B	A → B	A → A
	I_5				
	I_{5TT}	T	T	T	T
	I_{5TF}	T	F	F	T
	I_{5FT}	F	T	T	T
	I_{5FF}	F	F	T	T
SI_5					T

This illustrates the point made earlier, that value gaps are true gaps. When a component has no value, the fact that it has no value plays no role in the determination of the value of any compound in which it appears. The fact that A and B each have no value on SI_5 does not determine the value of A → B or A → A on SI_5. If it did, they would each get the same value, but they do not. To take another example, a long table for (A → ⊥) → (A → B) begins like this:

	A	B	(A	→	⊥)	→	(A	→	B)
I_1	T	T	T	F	F	T	T	T	T
I_2	T		T	F	F	T	T		
I_3	T	F	T	F	F	T	T	F	F
I_4		T			F	T		T	T
I_5					F				
I_6		F			F				F
I_7	F	T	F	T	F	T	F	T	T
I_8	F		F	T	F	T	F	T	
I_9	F	F	F	T	F	T	F	T	F

I_1, I_3, I_7, and I_9 are already complete interpretations, so the completions of those interpretations just are those interpretations, and the supervalue of a sentence on each of those interpretations just is the values already determined by that interpretation.

		A	B	(A	→	⊥)	→	(A	→	B)
	I_1	T	T	T	F	F	T	T	T	T
SI_1		T	T	T	F	F	T	T	T	T
	I_2	T		T	F	F	T	T		
	I_3	T	F	T	F	F	T	T	F	F
SI_3		T	F	T	F	F	T	T	F	F
	I_4		T			F	T		T	T
	I_5					F				
	I_6		F			F				F
	I_7	F	T	F	T	F	T	F	T	T
SI_7		F	T	F	T	F	T	F	T	T
	I_8	F		F	T	F	T	F	T	
	I_9	F	F	F	T	F	T	F	T	F
SI_9		F	F	F	T	F	T	F	T	F

But the remaining interpretations are partial interpretations. The supervalues of the compounds on those interpretations can only be determined by inserting completions of those interpretations on the table and consulting those completions. The supervalue of the whole sentence on an interpretation is not determined by first calculating the supervalues of its components and then using them to determine the compound. The completions must be consulted to calculate the value of the main connective of the whole sentence. For instance, the values on I_6 are determined as follows.

	A	B	(A	→	⊥)	→	(A	→	B)
I_1	T	T							
I_2	T								
I_3	T	F							
I_4		T							
I_5									
I_6		F			F				F
I_{6T}	T	F	T	F	F	T	T	F	F
I_{6F}	F	F	F	T	F	T	F	T	F
SI_6		F			F	T			F
I_7	F	T							
I_8	F								
I_9	F	F							

Each of I_{6T} and I_{6F} makes an assignment to $(A \to \bot) \to (A \to B)$ as well as to $A \to \bot$ and $A \to B$. SI_6 for its part makes an assignment to $(A \to \bot) \to (A \to B)$ based on what I_{6T} and I_{6F} assign to $(A \to \bot) \to (A \to B)$, not on what it itself assigns to $A \to \bot$ or $A \to B$. SI_6 assigns F to B because I_{6T} and I_{6F} both assign F to B. It assigns nothing to $A \to \bot$ because I_{6T} and I_{6F} make different assignments to $A \to \bot$. It might be thought that the fact that SI_6 assigns no value to either $A \to \bot$ or $A \to B$ would mean that it should assign no value to $(A \to \bot) \to (A \to B)$. But the value of $(A \to \bot) \to (A \to B)$ on SI_6 is not determined by the value of its immediate components on SI_6. It is determined by the value of $(A \to \bot) \to (A \to B)$ on I_{6T} and I_{6F}.

Completing the table for the remaining partial interpretations, I_2, I_4, I_5, and I_8 reveals that $(A \to \bot) \to (A \to B)$ is neither false nor undetermined on any of SI_1–SI_9. It is therefore supervaluationally valid.

In saying this, the definition of validity given in section 3.4 has been slightly adjusted. Section 3.4 says, "A sentence is s-valid if and only if there is no interpretation on which it is *false*." But, on supervaluational semantics,

> A sentence is *supervalid* (S-valid, with a capital "S") if and only if there is no supervaluation on which it is *not true*, that is, if and only if there is no supervaluation on which it is either false or undetermined.

The adjustment is required because, with the introduction of value gaps, "false" is no longer the opposite of "true." The opposite of "true" is "not true," which means "either false or undetermined."

The definitions of the other intensional concepts are adjusted accordingly.

> A sentence is *superunsatisfiable* if and only if there is no supervaluation on which it is true; it is supersatisfiable if and only if there is such a supervaluation.
>
> A sentence is *supercontingent* if and only if there is a supervaluation on which it is true and a supervaluation on which it is not true.
>
> Two sentences are *superequivalent* if and only if there is no supervaluation on which one is true and the other is not true; they are not superequivalent if and only if there is such a supervaluation.
>
> A set of sentences is *superunsatisfiable* if and only if there is no supervaluation on which each sentence in that set is true; it is supersatisfiable if and only if there is such a supervaluation.
>
> A demonstration is *supervalid* if and only if there is no supervaluation on which its premises are true and its conclusion is not true; it is superinvalid if and only if there is such a supervaluation.

These definitions follow those of classical satisfiability and validity in "designating" truth as a value of special concern. There are sentences that are false on each supervaluation. But the definitions are not written to highlight them or focus on any property involving them. They only mention truth on all supervaluations.

Exercise 5.13

Use a long table to determine whether each of the following is the case.

★**a.** A ∨ ~A is supervaluationally valid.

 b. A ≡ ~A is supervaluationally unsatisfiable.

★**c.** A → (B → A) is supervaluationally valid.

 d. A ∨ B, ~A / B is supervaluationally valid.

★**e.** A → ⊥ and ~A are supervaluationally equivalent.

 f. A → B and ~A ∨ B are supervaluationally equivalent.

As suggested by this exercise set, supervaluational semantics preserves classical results. Whatever is s-valid, s-unsatisfiable, s-equivalent, or s-contingent is S-valid, S-unsatisfiable, S-equivalent, or S-contingent, respectively, and vice versa.

The thesis that the two sets of categories do deliver the same results can be demonstrated for the case of S-contingency and s-contingency (supercontingency and classical contingency) as follows.

1. Suppose for purposes of biconditional proof that a sentence, P, is S-contingent.
   2. By definition of S-contingency there is a supervaluation, SI, on which P is true and a supervaluation, SJ, on which P is not true.
   3. By definition of a supervaluation, P is true on every completion of I and so on at least one completion, I_C, of I.
   4. By definition of a completion, I_C leaves no gaps in any assignments it makes, so it is a classical interpretation.
   5. From lines 3 and 4, P is true on at least one classical interpretation.
   6. From line 2 by definition of a supervaluation, if P is false on SJ, it must be false each completion of J and so on at least one completion, J_C, of J; and if P is undetermined on SJ it must be false on at least one completion, J_C, of J, so either way it must be false on at least one completion, J_C, of J.
   7. By definition of a completion, Jc leaves no gaps in any assignments it makes, so it is a classical interpretation.
   8. From lines 6 and 7, P is false on at least one classical interpretation.
   9. From lines 5 and 8, P is s-contingent.
10. Suppose for further purposes of biconditional proof that a sentence, P, is s-contingent.
   11. By definition of s-contingency there is at least one classical interpretation, I, on which P is true and at least one classical interpretation, J, on which P is false.
   12. By definition of a partial interpretation, each classical interpretation is a partial interpretation that just happens to leave no gaps.
   13. By definition of a completion of a partial interpretation, each classical interpretation is its own, sole completion.
   14. By definition of a supervaluation if the one and only completion of I, and so each completion of I, assigns T to P, SI(P) is T, and if the one and only completion of J, and so each completion of J, assigns F to P, SJ(P) is F.
   15. From lines 11 and 14, there is at least one supervaluation on which P is T and at least one on which it is not T.
   16. By definition of S-contingency, P is S-contingent.
17. From lines 1–9 and 10–16 by biconditional proof, a sentence is S-contingent if and only if it is s-contingent.

The point can be demonstrated for the validity of demonstrations as follows.

1. Suppose for purposes of biconditional proof that a demonstration, Γ / P, is S-invalid.
   2. By definition of S-validity there is a supervaluation, SI, on which each sentence in Γ is true but P is not true.

3. By definition of a supervaluation, if each sentence in Γ is true on SI, each sentence in Γ must be true on each completion of I and so on at least one completion, I_C, of I; and if P is not true on SI it must be false on at least one completion, I_C, of I (it can only be undetermined on SI if it is false on at least one completion of I, and can only be false on SI if it is false on each completion, and so at least one completion of I).

4. By definition of a completion, I_C leaves no gaps in any assignments it makes, so it is a classical interpretation.

5. From lines 3 and 4, each sentence in Γ is true and P is false on at least one classical interpretation.

6. By definition of s-validity, Γ / P is s-invalid.

7. Suppose for further purposes of biconditional proof that Γ / P is s-invalid.

8. By definition of s-invalidity, there is at least one classical interpretation, I, on which each sentence in Γ is true and P is false.

9. By definition of a partial interpretation, each classical interpretation is a partial interpretation that just happens to leave no gaps.

10. By definition of a completion of a partial interpretation, each classical interpretation is its own, sole completion.

11. By definition of a supervaluation if the one and only completion of I, and so each completion of I, assigns T to each sentence in Γ but F to P, SI assigns T to each sentence in Γ but F to P.

12. From lines 8 and 11, there is at least one supervaluation on which each sentence in Γ is T but P is not T.

13. By definition of S-validity, Γ / P is S-invalid.

14. From lines 1–7 and 8–13 by biconditional proof, a demonstration is S-invalid if and only if it is s-invalid.

15. By contraposition, a demonstration can be S-valid if and only if it is s-valid.

Demonstrations for the remaining intensional concepts are left as an exercise.

Supervaluational semantics allows logicians to expand interpretations to include sentences that have no assigned value, such as those describing future contingencies or mentioning nonexistent objects. Brilliantly, this can be done without having to revise assessments of what is valid, unsatisfiable, equivalent, or contingent in sentential logic or invent new techniques for detecting these qualities. Classical decision procedures (long tables, short tables, and demonstrations) can be used without emendation to determine supervaluational as well as classical validity, unsatisfiability, and other intensional properties, but a range of sentences that fall outside of the purview of classical logic, because they lack values, can be brought under logical scrutiny.

Appendix 5.2 Three-Valued Logic

Three-valued systems of logic make room for a third value, assigned to sentences that are supposed to be neither true nor false. On one construal, they are neither true nor false because they fall somewhere between "true" and "false," perhaps because they describe an object as falling somewhere on a spectrum where there is no clear dividing line between opposites. The value might be designated as N, for "neutral." (This having been said, three-valued logic could lend itself to many interpretations. Nothing in what follows depends on taking the third value to be "neutral" as opposed to "indefinite," "imprecise," "undetermined," or some other value.)

Where two sentence letters are under consideration, an interpretation table for three-valued logic might look like this:

	A	B
I_1	T	T
I_2	T	N
I_3	T	F
I_4	N	T
I_5	N	N
I_6	N	F
I_7	F	T
I_8	F	N
I_9	F	F

As with supervaluation tables, for three sentence letters the table would list 27 different interpretations; for four sentence letters it would list 81 interpretations. For any given number, n, of sentence letters it would list 3^n interpretations.

Three-valued logic resurrects the question of expressive adequacy, considered in appendix 3. There are 27 different ways of assigning one of the three values to each list of one of the three values.

	T									S									~								
T	T	T	T	T	T	T	T	T	T	N	N	N	N	N	N	N	N	N	F	F	F	F	F	F	F	F	F
N	T	T	T	N	N	N	F	F	F	T	T	T	N	N	N	F	F	F	T	T	T	N	N	N	F	F	F
F	T	N	F	T	N	F	T	N	F	T	N	F	T	N	F	T	N	F	T	N	F	T	N	F	T	N	F

(The assignments designated T, S, and ~ are of special interest and are mentioned later.)

The number of ways of assigning one of the three values to each list of two of the three values is already unmanageable: three to the power of 3^n, where n is the number of places or 19,683. To see how this number is determined, consider that there are nine two-place lists drawn from three values. (See the leftmost column on the table below.) Any way of assigning exactly one of the three values to each of these nine lists would be like a nine-digit number, read along one of the columns from top down, each of whose digits could be 1 (=T), 2 (=N), or 3 (=F). Counting in base 3 for nine digits (111111111, 111111112, 111111113, 111111121, …) from 111111111 to 333333333 takes 3^9 steps.

<T,T>	1	1	1	1	1	1	1	1	1	1	1	1	1	1	1	1	1	1	1	1	…
<T,N>	1	1	1	1	1	1	1	1	1	1	1	1	1	1	1	1	1	1	1	1	…
<T,F>	1	1	1	1	1	1	1	1	1	1	1	1	1	1	1	1	1	1	1	1	…
<N,T>	1	1	1	1	1	1	1	1	1	1	1	1	1	1	1	1	1	1	1	1	…
<N,N>	1	1	1	1	1	1	1	1	1	1	1	1	1	1	1	1	1	1	1	1	…
<N,F>	1	1	1	1	1	1	1	1	1	1	1	1	1	1	1	1	1	1	1	1	…
<F,T>	1	1	1	1	1	1	1	1	1	2	2	2	2	2	2	2	2	3	…		
<F,N>	1	1	1	2	2	2	3	3	3	1	1	1	2	…							
<F,F>	1	2	3	1	2	3	1	2	3	1	2	…									
			3							*9*										*27*	

The number of ways of assigning exactly one of the three values to each of the twenty-seven lists of three of the three values is much greater, that to each list of four of the three values much greater yet, and so on. Nevertheless, it has been established that there are expressively complete vocabularies for three-valued logic. Jerzy Słupecki (1904–87) demonstrated the expressive completeness of a language using the ~ and S functions from the table of one-place functions given earlier, and three two-place functions figuring in a system proposed by Jan Łukasiewicz (1878–1956).)

It is more of a question which of the 19,683 functions to symbolize with &, ∨, →, and ≡. It might be objected that this question makes no sense: Assigning &, ∨, →, and ≡ to four of the 19,683 functions does not cause the rest to disappear. Moreover, using &, ∨, →, or ≡ to stand for any of the 19,683 functions may seem pointless at best, and confusing at worst, as it presumes that there is some relevant similarity that is being captured by using the same symbol in both three-valued and two-valued contexts. Those functions for three-valued logic that are judged to be particularly important could simply be given their own symbols.

The answer to this concern is that the project is really to determine how conjunctive, disjunctive, and conditional expressions of English are best understood when English sentences are recognized to bear a third value. This question is particularly intriguing for natural language conditionals, which conform to the valuation rules for two-valued logic in only a limited range of contexts.

One way to approach this question is to begin with the less controversial English connectives, "and" and "at least one." "And" is often used to build a compound sentence that is true if and only if both of its components are true and false if and only if at least one component is false. "At least one" correspondingly builds a compound sentence that is true if and only if at least one of its components is true and false if and only if both are false. These facts have led many logicians to suppose that any three-valued "and" and "or" valuation rules ought to track the classical rules of chapter 3.2 in the cases where each component is assigned one or other of T and F. Granting that much leaves it undecided what assignments to make to the compound when at least one component is assigned N.

As stated in section 3.2 the classical valuation rules for & and ∨ are:

> (&): I(P & Q) is T if and only if I(P) and I(Q) are T; otherwise, I(P & Q) is F
> (∨): I(P ∨ Q) is T if and only if at least one of I(P) and I(Q) is T; otherwise I(P ∨ Q) is F

Were these rules used as is for three-valued logic, their "otherwise" clauses would rule out any assignment of N to conjunctions or disjunctions, defeating the purpose of introducing a three-valued logic. One remedy is to rewrite "otherwise ... is F" as "otherwise ... is not T." This raises the question of which of the other cases should assign an F and which an N. A conservative answer to this question would take the two-valued (F&) and (F∨) rules (see chapter 3.2) as a guide to the assignment of F, and leave the assignment of N to the remaining cases. This gives the following form to the rules:

> (&): I(P & Q) is:
>> (i): T if and only if I(P) and I(Q) are T;
>> (ii): F if and only if at least one of I(P) and I(Q) is F;
>> (iii): otherwise N.

> (∨): I(P ∨ Q) is:
>> (i): T if and only if at least one of I(P) and I(Q) is T;
>> (ii): F if and only if I(P) and I(Q) are F;
>> (iii): otherwise N.

Following the pattern established for (&) and (∨), (→) and (≡) would be:

> (→): I(P → Q) is:
>> (i): T if and only if I(P) is F or I(Q) is T;
>> (ii): F if and only if I(P) is T and I(Q) is F;
>> (iii): otherwise N.

> (≡): I(P ≡ Q) is:
>> (i): T if and only if I(P) and I(Q) are either both T or both F
>> (ii): F if and only if one of I(P) and I(Q) is T and the other is F
>> (iii): otherwise N.

These rules can be called the Kleene rules, after Stephen C. Kleene (1909–94), to whom they are due. The characteristic tables defined by the Kleene rules are:

	P	Q	P & Q	P ∨ Q	P → Q	Q → P	P ≡ Q
I_1	T	T	T	T	T	T	T
I_2	T	N	N	T	N	T	N
I_3	T	F	F	T	F	T	F
I_4	N	T	N	T	T	N	N
I_5	N	N	N	N	N	N	N
I_6	N	F	F	N	N	T	N
I_7	F	T	F	T	T	F	F
I_8	F	N	F	N	T	N	N
I_9	F	F	F	F	T	T	T

The extent to which the Kleene (→) and (≡) rules follow the pattern of the (&) and (∨) rules might be questioned. Why not consider I(P → Q) to be T provided I(P) is not T (so, either N or F)? Why not consider

I(P ≡ Q) to be T in all cases where I(P) and I(Q) are the same (so, including when both are N)? In one sense there is no answer to these questions, because these alternatives are among the 19,683 functions from lists of two of the three values onto one of the three values, and they all conform to some extent with the two-valued rules. They just do so in different ways. Making both changes (considering I₅ and I₆ to assign T to P → Q, I₅ and I₈ to assign T to Q → P, and I₅ to assign T to P ≡ Q would make P ≡ Q and (P → Q) & (Q → P) nonequivalent. A biconditional should be equivalent to the conjunction of a conditional and its converse. Leaving I₆ and I₈ as they are on the Kleene table but adjusting I₅ to assign T to all of P → Q, Q → P, and P ≡ Q avoids this problem. This alternative, which was proposed by Łukasiewicz, prior to Kleene's presentation of his approach, will be considered further below.

These are not the only ways to come up with three-valued rules that track the classical rules to some extent. It seems halfhearted to go to the trouble of introducing a third value and then dutifully follow the bivalent versions of (&) and (∨) in all cases where they make a decision, allowing N to appear only in the unclaimed rump (the "otherwise N" clauses). A more radical alternative to bivalence would let N rule the "at least one" clauses and relegate F (in the case of (&)) or T (in the cases of (∨) and (→)) to the "otherwise" clauses. This gives the following form to the rules:

(&): I(P & Q) is:
    (i):   T if and only if I(P) and I(Q) are T;
    (ii):   N if and only if at least one of I(P) and I(Q) is N;
    (iii):   otherwise F.

(∨): I(P ∨ Q) is:
    (i):   F if and only if I(P) and I(Q) are F;
    (ii):   N if and only if at least one of I(P) and I(Q) is N;
    (iii):   otherwise T.

Analogously, for (→) and (≡),

(→): I(P → Q) is:
    (i):   F if and only if I(P) is T and I(Q) is F;
    (ii):   N if and only if at least one of I(P) and I(Q) is N;
    (iii):   otherwise T.

(≡): I(P ≡ Q) is:
    (i):   T if and only if I(P) and I(Q) are either both T or both F
    (ii):   N if and only if at least one of I(P) and I(Q) is N;
    (iii):   otherwise F.

These rules can be called the Bochvar rules, after DA Bochvar (1903–90), who first formulated them. The characteristic tables defined by the rules are

	P	Q	P & Q	P ∨ Q	P → Q	Q → P	P ≡ Q
I₁	T	T	T	T	T	T	T
I₂	T	N	N	N	N	N	N
I₃	T	F	F	T	F	T	F
I₄	N	T	N	N	N	N	N
I₅	N	N	N	N	N	N	N
I₆	N	F	N	N	N	N	N
I₇	F	T	F	T	T	F	F
I₈	F	N	N	N	N	N	N
I₉	F	F	F	F	T	T	T

The difference between the Kleene and Bochvar rules can be summarized by saying that, for Kleene, N has no effect in those cases where an assignment of T or F to just one component would classically determine the value of the compound (when one conjunct gets F or one disjunct T or the antecedent F or the consequent T). For Bochvar whenever a component is assigned N, the compound gets N as well. Both systems track the classical rules to some extent. They make the same assignments to compounds that classical logic does in cases where neither component gets an N. The two systems also deal with the case where both components get N in the same way. The differences are confined to I_2, I_4, I_6, and I_8.

The Bochvar rules do not track the classical rules as far as the Kleene rules. But this does not make the Kleene rules patently better than the Bochvar rules. Bochvar considered N to designate "nonsense" rather than "neutral," and he further considered the nonsense of a component to infect the compound. It is plausible to maintain that if P is nonsense, "Both P and Q" and "At least one of P and Q" are nonsense, regardless of whether Q is false or true.

Another consideration in Bochvar's favour might be raised by those who do not like the classical → rule. According to the Bochvar rules, a false antecedent does not suffice to make a conditional true, and a true consequent does not suffice to make a conditional true, thereby mitigating the irrelevant consequences mentioned in chapter 4.2.

Both Kleene's and Bochvar's systems have a disturbing feature, which can be brought out by taking note of a generally accepted way of rewriting (~) for three-valued logic.

(~): I(~P) is T if and only if I(P) is F and F if and only if I(P) is T; otherwise, I(~P) is N

	P	~P
I_1	T	F
I_2	N	N
I_3	F	T

Compare I_5 on the Kleene and Bochvar tables with I_2 on the ~ table. Each of these interpretations assigns N to any compound sentence in the case when its immediate component(s) receive N. Taking "s-valid" to mean "true on all interpretations," means that there can be no s-valid sentences in Kleene or Bochvar logic (supposing ⊥ is not included in the language, which would allow for exceptions compounded with ⊥ such as ~⊥).[3] On any interpretation on which any sentence letter is N, any compound containing that sentence letter, however complex it may become, must be N. For example, A → A, which was shown to be s-valid in exercise 3.8c, is invalid in Kleene and Bochvar logic. The same holds for ~(A & ~A), A ∨ ~A, and A ≡ A. The infection only spreads upwards from there. As long as ⊥ does not appear, no compound will escape having components that are N on at least one assignment.

Łukasiewicz's system, alluded to earlier, avoids some of these consequences. It is like Kleene's but for using the following valuation rules for conditionals and biconditionals:

(→): I(P → Q) is:
    (i): T if and only if either: (a) I(P) is F, (b) I(P) and I(Q) are N, (c) I(Q) is T;
    (ii): F if and only if I(P) is T and I(Q) is F;
    (iii): otherwise N.

(≡): I(P ≡ Q) is:
    (i): T if and only if I(P) and I(Q) are the same;
    (ii): F if and only if at least one of I(P) and I(Q) is T and the other is F;
    (iii): otherwise N.

On the characteristic table, sentences get the same columns of values they do on the Kleene table, except for a T to P → Q, Q → P, and P ≡ Q on I_5. This change enables Łukasiewicz logic to recognize the validity of sentences of the forms P → P and P ≡ P, as well as of many other sentences containing → or ≡. However, it is still treats sentences in which there are no occurrences of →, ≡, or ⊥ as invalid. Whatever might be said against this, the Łukasiewicz valuation rules describe three of the 19,683 functions from lists of two of the three values onto one of the three values. In that sense, they are as eligible for symbolization by → and ≡ as those proposed by Kleene or Bochvar.

Bochvar proposed a different way of working around the consequence that no sentences are s-valid. He introduced a further symbol for one of the unary valuations (designated T̲ on the table of unary valuations given earlier). Sentences or sentential components that have T̲ as their main connective are either true or false. They get a T if the immediate component gets a T and an F if the immediate component gets either N or F. When the atomic components of classically valid sentences are prefaced with the T̲ connective, they become valid. For instance, while A → A is invalid, T̲A → T̲A is valid. This is unsurprising, since the use of T̲ in front of atomic sentences erases all further occurrences of N from the characteristic table. This is not tantamount to giving up on three-valued logic, since T̲ does not have to be used.

A third way of avoiding the result that no sentences are valid is to invoke the definition of validity in the new light in which it is cast by three-valued logic. As stated in section 3.4, a sentence is s-valid if and only if there is no interpretation on which it is *false*. But, in three-valued logic, what is not false is either true or neutral. Abiding by this definition, A → A *is* valid because, even though there are interpretations on which it is not true, there is no interpretation on which it is false. Taking this approach involves recognizing both T and N as "designated values" (see section 3.4).

Up to now, only T has been designated. When both T and N are designated a sentence is satisfied if and only if there is at least one interpretation that does not assign an F to it and a set of sentences is satisfied if and only if there is at least one interpretation that does not assign F each sentence in the set (and so assigns either a T or an N to each sentence in the set). A model continues to be defined as an interpretation that satisfies a set. Provided the valuation rule for negations is taken to be the one given earlier, according to which I(~P) is N if and only if I(P) is N, when P is satisfied {~P} can also be satisfied (by an interpretation that assigns N to P and so to ~P), so validity can no longer be defined in terms of corresponding sets that include negations. Revised definitions of validity (distinguished as "para-validity") are called for.

- P is para-valid if and only if there is no interpretation that is not a model for {P}
  - that is, if and only if each interpretation assigns either T or N to P
- Γ / P is para-valid if and only if there is no interpretation that is a model for Γ but not a model for {P}
  - that is, if and only if there is no interpretation on which each premise is not F and the conclusion is F
  - alternatively, on each interpretation either at least one premise is F or the conclusion is T or N

(The account of the validity of demonstrations does not countenance moving from premises with either of the designated values, T and N, to a conclusion with the undesignated value, F. This is another way of understanding the concept of a designated value. It is a value that is designated as being "preserved" in definitions of validity and entailment.)

Designating both T and N makes all and only classically valid sentences valid on Kleene's and Bochvar's systems as well. As an inspection of the Kleene and Bochvar characteristic tables shows, classical logic, Kleene logic, and Bochvar logic all make the same assignments on "classical" interpretations, that is, interpretations that do not assign N to any sentence letter. So, if Kleene and Bochvar do not assign an F to a sentence on any interpretation, classical or nonclassical, classical logic will not assign an F to that sentence on any classical interpretation. The converse also holds. If a sentence does not receive an F on any classical interpretation, it will not receive an F on any Kleene or Bochvar interpretation. Bochvar only assigns F to compound sentences on classical interpretations (any compound is N on any interpretation that assigns N to any sentence letters in that compound), and while Kleene does assign F to compounds when a component is N, it is only in the case when one of the conjuncts of a conjunction is assigned F. Those cases are tracked by classical interpretations. Any classical interpretation must assign either T or F to the remaining conjunct, and either way the classical interpretation must also assign F to the conjunction.[4] Thus, for Kleene, no compound gets an F on any nonclassical interpretation unless it also gets an F on each classical interpretation.

This might be viewed as a welcome outcome, or it might be viewed as going too far in the direction of accepting classical results. It all depends on one's attitude to classically valid sentences like (A & ~A) → B, which instantiates the tenet that a conclusion may be drawn from irrelevant (albeit contradictory) premises, or A ∨ ~A, which might be read as affirming that the future is "closed" because statements about what will be are already either true or false today.

The remainder of this section works with a definition of validity, called 3-validity, that designates only T. Para-validity is further investigated in the following section.

A *sentence* is *3-valid* if and only if there is no interpretation on which it is not T.

A *demonstration* is *3-valid* if and only if there is no interpretation on which its premises are T and its conclusion is not T.

While Kleene's and Bochvar's systems do not recognize any 3-valid sentences compounded from sentence letters, they do recognize many 3-valid demonstrations. While they deny that A → A and [A & (A → B)] → B are 3-valid, they establish that A / A and A, A → B / B are. Kleene's system recognizes the validity of more classically valid demonstrations than Bochvar's. On Bochvar's system, if ⊥ does not occur, and a sentence letter, P, occurs in the conclusion that does not occur in the premises, the conclusion will be N on any interpretation that assigns N to P. The only way the demonstration could be 3-valid, in this case, is if the set of premises is 3-unsatisfiable (that is, when there is no interpretation on which each sentence in the set of premises is true). Kleene's system is not so restrictive. Notably, it recognizes that A / A ∨ B, B / A → B, and ~A / A → B are 3-valid.

This does not demonstrate the superiority of Kleene's system. The notion that a three-valued system ought to respect all the two-valued assignments to the fullest extent presumes that the two-valued rules for &, ∨, and → do a perfect job of capturing the meaning of the associated natural language connectives. As noted in section 4.2, it has been charged that there is something paradoxical about taking a conditional to be s-entailed by the negation of its antecedent or by the bare assertion of its consequent. From this perspective, it is a point in favour of Bochvar's system that it does not countenance ~A / A → B or B / A → B.

Exercise 5.14

1. *Use three-valued long tables to determine whether the following sentences are 3-valid on each of Kleene's, Łukasiewicz's, and Bochvar's systems.*

   ★**a.** A → A
   b. A ∨ ~A
   ★**c.** TA ∨ ~TA
   d. TA ∨ T~A
   ★**e.** ~(A & ~A)
   f. [A & (A → B)] → B
   ★**g.** A → (B → A)
   h. A → (B ∨ ~B)

2. *Use three-valued long tables to determine whether the following demonstrations are 3-valid on each of Kleene's, Łukasiewicz's, and Bochvar's systems.*

   ★**a.** A → B, A / B
   b. ~~A / A
   ★**c.** A → B / ~A ∨ B
   d. A / A ∨ B
   ★**e.** ~A / A → B
   f. B / A → B
   ★**g.** A / B → B
   h. A, ~A / B
   ★**i.** A / B ∨ ~B
   j. A → B, A → ~B / ~A
   ★**k.** A → B / A → (A & B)
   l. A → B / ~B → ~A

3. *Review the answers to questions 1 and 2 above and say whether the sentence or the demonstration is para-valid (valid according to the third of the three alternative ways of defining validity identified earlier). You need not redo the tables. Just inspect the work already done and apply the alternative definition. Do this only for Bochvar and Łukasiewicz logic (results in Kleene logic are the topic for a later exercise).*

   Answers for ★ questions in **5.14#1**; **5.14#2**

Appendix 5.3 Paraconsistent Logic

Since antiquity, philosophers and logicians have been perplexed by the liar sentence, "What I am now saying is a lie," and variants on it like, "this sentence is false." Such sentences seem to bear both truth values. If "What I am now saying is a lie" is true, then "What I am now saying is a lie" is not a lie but a true sentence, which means that what it says (that it is a lie) must be false. But if "What I am now saying is a lie" is false, then since saying that I am lying when it is false that I am lying is telling a lie, it turns out that "What I am now saying is a lie" says what is true. If it is true it is false, and if it is false it is true. Whether or not what it says is absurd, it seems to have both truth values.

The liar sentence is not the only motive for considering some sentences to be both true and false. Practically, the circumstance often arises, sometimes with catastrophic results. A computer database might be designed to assign either 1 or 0 to a certain cell, depending on what information is fed into it. Sometimes, the information can come from different sources and one source might feed in a 1 while another feeds in a 0. Human beings are not that different. In our everyday lives we must deal with multiple sources of information, some of it equally good but nonetheless leading to opposite results. In such cases, like a computer, we can "crash," that is, have some sort of breakdown, manifested by confusion and an inability to proceed with the task at hand, again with occasionally catastrophic results. This makes developing a logic for dealing with conflicting values something more than an academic exercise.

Classical sentential logic explains why computers and human beings can break down when fed inconsistent information. Exercise 3.9#4g is an instance of the general principle that anything follows from a contradiction. The principle is called EFQ, from the Latin, *ex falso quodlibet*, where the "falso" refers to premises that cannot all be true. The breakdown in human and machine reasoning is caused by the fact that the presence of a contradiction in the set of the premises allows anything whatsoever to be inferred. If a contradiction could be true, anything could be. A machine might, in such a case, proceed to infer one random thing after another. A human being might proceed to do one irrational thing after another.

Paraconsistent logic (logic that goes beyond the situation in which the available information is consistent) is motivated on the one hand by the recognition that inconsistencies in the available information can arise, and on the other by the project of preventing what paraconsistent logicians call "explosion," the consequent tendency to infer anything and everything. This requires finding a way to reject EFQ. One proposal, due to Priest (1979), who calls it the "logic of paradox (LP)," proceeds by making the following changes to classical sentential logic.

A third value, # (hash), is recognized. It stands for "both true and false." The reading of T and F must be modified, since # is a way of being both true and false. T means "simply true," F "simply false." The Kleene valuation rules are intuitively plausible when considered as rules for assigning values to sentences that have a component or components with the value "both true and false" (#), so the Kleene rules can be rewritten as valuation rules for LP. (# replaces N in the rule statements and on the tables.)[5]

Both T and # are designated values. The implicated concept of validity is called para-validity. Para-valid demonstrations are "simple falsity" avoiding. They do not permit the derivation of a "simply false" conclusion when none of the premises is "simply false." The fact that none of the premises of a para-valid demonstration is simply false guarantees that the conclusion is not simply false (but not that it is "simply true"). This makes sense in the context where conflicting information is entered into a system. Conflicting information offers some evidence of truth, in contrast to information that delivers a uniform verdict of "false."

> A *sentence* is *para-valid* if and only if there is no interpretation on which it is F.
>
> A *demonstration* is *para-valid* if and only if there is no interpretation on which its premises are not F and its conclusion is F.

On this account of validity, a demonstration is para-valid if and only if, on each row of the Kleene table, either at least one premise is F or the conclusion is either # or T. Inversely, a demonstration is para-invalid if and only if there is at least one interpretation on which each premise is *either* T *or* #, but the conclusion is F.

This way of defining validity countenances inferences to conclusions that are both true and false (#). But it prevents explosion from such conclusions or from premises that have the value #. EFQ is not a principle of this system. Consider the instance, A, ~A / B, of EFQ, and consider an interpretation, I, on which A is # and B is F. By the Kleene version of (~), I(~A) is also #. So, the demonstration has premises that are both "not-false" on I but a conclusion that is false on I. It is therefore para-invalid. The inference to just anything (B) is blocked.

Exercise 5.15

Review the Kleene tables offered in solutions to exercise 5.14. Consider # to replace N and state whether the table shows the sentence or demonstration to be para-valid. It is not necessary to redo the tables.

Answers for 5.14**#1a, c, e, g; #2a, c, e, g, i**

The solutions to exercise 5.15 support the observation that LP recognizes all classically valid sentences as para-valid. The same does not hold of demonstrations. Strikingly, modus ponens is not para-valid. (Exercise 5.15 for 5.14#2a is an instance of that failure.) This is hard to avoid. The failure arises on interpretations where both premises are assigned #, and the project is to prevent inferences from # to just anything. B is not just anything in the case of A, A → B / B. But it would take a strong arm to open the door to modus ponens without enabling other, less acceptable inferences to press in afterwards.

Notes

1 The label, "indirect proof" has been used before. In exercise 3.9#4d the demonstration,

A → B, A → ~B / ~A

was labeled "indirect proof." As it is being used now, however, "indirect proof" does not refer to a demonstration formalized in SL but to an informal demonstrative technique. There is an affinity between the informal technique and the formalization in SL, but the demonstrative technique is intuitively valid and does not gain its authority from anything established in SL.

2 The remark made in the previous note applies here as well. The label, "proof by cases," is being used for an intuitively valid, informal demonstrative technique, not for the demonstration in SL this label is attached to in exercises 3.9#4c and 5.4#2h.

3 In keeping with (⊥), which defines ⊥ as a sentence that is F on any interpretation, were ⊥ included in the language it could not be identified with P & ~P, since P & ~P is N on any interpretation on which P is N, as dictated by the versions of (~) and (&) used by any of the Kleene, Łukasiewicz, and Bochvar systems. This raises the question of how a contradiction is identified in these systems. As more fully explored in the appendix to chapter 7 on trees for three-valued logics, a contradiction arises when the same sentence is ascribed any two of the three values, and on trees ⊥ is used to designate that result. P cannot be assigned both T and F, or both T and N, or both N and F. It is just that the version of (~) used by Kleene, Łukasiewicz, and Bochvar does not assign two different values to P and ~P when P is N. As in classical logic, where asserting one of the two values is equivalent to denying the other, in these logics asserting one of the three values is equivalent to denying the other two.

4 This cannot be said of Łukasiewicz logic. Łukasiewicz logic makes assignments of T to conditionals and biconditionals (and hence of F to their negations) that are not tracked by all possible classical interpretations. An example is ~(A ≡ ~A).

5 Though the paraconsistent approach recognizes sentences that are both true and false and designates both T and #, treating "both T and F" as a third value, #, means that it can still maintain that no sentence can be both "simply true" and "both true and false," or "simply false" and "both true and false." It need not go so far as to say there are sentences that can simultaneously bear two (or more) of the three values, "simply true," "simply false," and "both true and false." And it can still recognize that no sentence can be both affirmed to have any one of these three values and denied to have that value.

References

Priest, Graham, 1979, "Logic of Paradox," *Journal of Philosophical Logic* 8: 219–41.

A-1

Advanced Topics Concerning SL Semantics

This is the first of a sequence of brief chapters on advanced topics in logic. The advanced chapters, designated A-1 through A-6, form a separate series from the others. It is not necessary to take up the advanced chapters to understand any of the others. They are placed where they are because they presuppose familiarity with the chapters that precede them, but not with those that follow them.

This chapter deals with a technique for demonstrating results that is employed throughout the following sequence of advanced chapters, mathematical induction, and goes on to examine some foundational features of the syntax and semantics of SL. It justifies the principle of bivalence (that sentences of SL must have exactly one of two values), which had to be assumed in some of the demonstrations in chapter 5. The justification for the principle of bivalence in turn makes two assumptions, that sentences of SL cannot be infinitely long and that each can only have one main connective. These assumptions are justified in section 6.1, which also justifies two assumptions that were made in the appendix to chapter 3, that truth is infectious in iterated disjunctions, and falsity infectious in iterated conjunctions. The chapter concludes by demonstrating that SL is extensional and compact. The first means that compound sentences of SL do not change their meaning as a result of substitution of components that have the same meaning (for example, replacing occurrences of ~~A with occurrences of A does not change the value of a sentence containing A). The second says that in SL no demonstration needs infinitely many premises. The first of these principles supports an expansion to the derivation system studied in chapter 6 and the second establishes that the system is adequate to do its job.[1]

Most of the principles established in this and the following advanced chapters will seem intuitively obvious and so not in need of justification. From a logical point of view, where nothing is obvious unless it wears a contradiction on its face when it is denied, they are not obvious. But because they are intuitive, it is quite possible to grant that they are correct and move on to other work, particularly when pressed for time. Those of a more scrupulous or critical disposition may look to these advanced chapters to see their questions answered.

A-1.1 Mathematical Induction

Chapters 2 and 3 describe a formal language used to isolate some of the factors responsible for producing a contradiction. In chapter 5 various features of this formal language are informally demonstrated. These informal demonstrations make use of intuitively valid styles of demonstrative reasoning, such as indirect proof, conditional proof, and proof by cases. Another informal style of reasoning is needed to establish claims such as one asserted, but not demonstrated, in section 5.3: that each of the compound sentences of SL has exactly one of two values. A common feature of such claims is that they make an assertion about infinitely many things. This makes them

DOI: 10.4324/9781003026532-7

difficult to justify. It is not possible to go through all the sentences of SL and demonstrate the point for each one. But it is possible to do this by reasoning by what is misleadingly called mathematical induction.

Mathematical induction is neither mathematical nor inductive. The reasoning is deductive, and even though it is often used to demonstrate results in mathematics, it is not based on mathematical principles.

Mathematical induction is possible in any circumstance with the following three features:

- the objects under consideration can be lined up
- the first thing in line has some property
- it is of the nature of this property to be transmitted down the line

Reasoning by mathematical induction amounts to no more than drawing the conclusion that, under these circumstances, all the objects in line must have the property. This is based on the reasoning that if the first thing has the property, and one thing's having the property means the next thing in line must have it as well, then all the things must have the property, even if there are infinitely many of them.

> Suppose all the birds in a flock are sitting on a power line.
> Suppose it is a law of nature that if one bird flies off the line the next one after it flies off as well.
> Suppose the first bird flies off the line.
> Then it follows by "mathematical induction" that all the birds fly off the line.

This demonstration appeals to a law of nature. Strictly, demonstrations by mathematical induction appeal to laws of logic or mathematics. But aside from this detail, the same pattern of demonstration is used to arrive at the conclusion.

A single demonstration by mathematical induction can sometimes be quite involved, and can go on for pages. When this happens, it is not because the conclusion needs any further support. The extra work is devoted to demonstrating the truth of the premises: that the property in question really does carry on down the line and that the first object in line has the property. The former can be particularly difficult to justify. However, the genius behind reasoning by mathematical induction often consists in figuring out how to line the objects up.

Figuring out how to line things up is something that happens in the background. The discovery is often the product of trial and error. One line-up does not have the features necessary to demonstrate that a property must be passed on to all the objects, so another one must be tried instead. None of that background work is revealed. The demonstration simply begins by saying: "Consider these things to be lined up in this way." What led to the idea to line them up that way is not explained.

Because determining the proper line-up can be so difficult, most student exercises begin with directions about how things should be lined up. The idea of how to line them up only comes with example, practice, and intimate knowledge of the subject matter.

Supposing a line-up has been given, the reasoning proceeds by establishing that the first thing in line has the property. This is known as demonstrating the basis clause or simply the "basis" of the reasoning. The reasoning then proceeds to establish that the property in question passes on down the line. This is known as establishing the inductive step or simply the "induction" of the reasoning. Once the basis clause and the inductive step have been established, the conclusion is obvious and needs no further support.

For example, it was claimed in section 3.4 that if any conjunct in an iterated conjunction is false on an interpretation, the whole iterated conjunction must also be false on that interpretation. That claim, which could not be rigorously demonstrated there, can be demonstrated by appeal to mathematical induction.

An iterated conjunction is made by adding conjuncts to conjuncts to produce a sentence of the form

> A-1.1 $(\ldots(P_1 \ \& \ \ldots) \ \& \ P_n$

To demonstrate by mathematical induction that falsity is infectious in iterated conjunctions, it is first necessary to come up with a way of listing the parts of an iterated conjunction, beginning with any one that is supposed to be false on an interpretation.

Consider any conjunct, P_i, in an iterated conjunction, $(\ldots(P_1 \ \& \ \ldots) \ \& \ P_n$. Call it Q_1. Either Q_1 is the whole iterated conjunction (by definition, an iterated disjunction can have just one conjunct) or it is one of the two immediate components of a conjunction, Q_2. Either Q_2 is the whole iterated conjunction or it is one of the two immediate components of a conjunction, Q_3. This can go on for indeterminately many iterations until the whole iterated conjunction is arrived at. Call the whole iterated conjunction Q_m. (Q_m could be Q_1, Q_2, Q_3, or some other Q with an arbitrarily large subscript.) The aim is to demonstrate that if Q_1, that is, P_i, is false on an interpretation, I, Q_m, that is $(\ldots(P_1 \& \ldots) \& P_n$, must be false on I.

Having set up this list, the demonstration by mathematical induction can be given as follows:

Basis:	$I(Q_1)$ is F.
Induction:	If $I(Q_k)$ is F, $I(Q_{k+1})$ is F.
Conclusion:	$I(Q_m)$ is F.

The conclusion is certain given the truth of the basis clause and the inductive step. If Q_1 is false on I, it follows by the inductive step that Q_2 is false on I, which, by the inductive step, means that Q_3 is false on I, which, by the inductive step, means that Q_4 is false on I, and so on for as many steps as there are to be made.

It still needs to be demonstrated that the basis clause and the inductive step are true. It is common practice to state the demonstration by mathematical induction first, as was done above, and then follow up with separate demonstrations of the basis and the induction. In the case at hand this might be done as follows:

Demonstration of the basis: The basis is true by supposition. (The project at hand is to assume that there is an interpretation on which one of the conjuncts in an iterated conjunction is false on an interpretation, I, and see what that means for the whole iterated conjunction.)

Demonstration of the induction: By definition, Q_{k+1} is a conjunction that has Q_k as one of its conjuncts. In that case by (&), if $I(Q_k)$ is F, $I(Q_{k+1})$ is F.

At this point nothing more needs to be said. It has been established that if any of the conjuncts of an iterated conjunction is false on an interpretation, the whole iterated conjunction must be false on that interpretation.

Exercise A-1.1

Following the example that has just been given, write up a demonstration in three parts to show that if any disjunct, P_i in an iterated disjunction, $(\ldots(P_1 \lor \ldots) \lor P_n$, is true on an interpretation, I, then that disjunction must also be true on I. Part 1 should explain how to list the items for the demonstration, part 2 should give the demonstration, and part 3 should explain why the basis and the induction are justified (it suffices to say that the basis is true by supposition).

There are two main versions of mathematical induction, the weak and the strong. So far, mathematical induction has only been considered in its weak form. The difference between the two forms is in the inductive step. In weak induction, the inference is from one item on the list to the next one. In strong induction, the list is a list of sets, and the inference is from all the prior members of all the prior sets on the list to all the members of the next set on the list.

Form of a demonstration by weak mathematical induction

Basis:	The first list item has the property.
Induction:	If the kth item has the property, the $k+1$ item also has it.
Conclusion:	All the items have the property.

Form of a demonstration by strong mathematical induction

Basis:	All the members of the first set have the property.
Induction:	If all the members of all the sets from the first to the kth have the property, all the members of the $k+1$ set also have it.
Conclusion:	All the members have the property

The terms "weak" and "strong" are again misnomers. The conclusions of both sorts of demonstration are equally certain. So called "strong" induction is "strong" because it appeals to a more extensive connection between the things under consideration. There is a set of predecessors, and a set of immediate successors. Some successors get the property from one of the immediate predecessors, others from a different one, or from more than one. Other successors may not get it from any of the immediate predecessors, but from predecessors in more remote sets. Each successor still gets the property from some predecessor or predecessors, but the inheritance relations are more like a web than a line.

weak induction

*The property passes from the immediately prior individual in line
to the next one in line. So, if the immediately prior one has it,
the next one must have it.*

strong induction

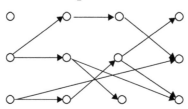

*The property passes from one or more individuals anywhere in the earlier series to one or
more later individuals. It needs to be established that all the earlier ones have it before it
can be inferred that any of the next ones must have it.*

For example, it can be proven by strong induction on the number of occurrences of connectives in sentences of SL that no sentence of SL contains infinitely many vocabulary elements. "Number of occurrences of connectives" means how many times connectives occur in a sentence, not how many different connectives there are. So ~~A contains two occurrences of connectives, though each is an occurrence of the same connective. This induction is based on a list of sets of sentences, not a list of individuals. The first set on the list contains all the sentences of SL that contain no occurrences of connectives (all the atomic sentences). In logic it is common to begin with the zero case. Here, the zero case is not the "no sentence" case but the case of sentences that have no occurrences of connectives, which are the atomic sentences. The next set consists of all the sentences that contain exactly one occurrence of a connective, like ~A and A & A. The third group contains sentences like ~~A, A ∨ (B → C), A & ~B, ~(A ≡ B). And so on. Given this list, the demonstration, by strong induction, is as follows:

> *Basis:* No sentence with zero occurrences of connectives contains infinitely many vocabulary elements.
>
> *Induction:* If no sentence with 0 to k occurrences of connectives contains infinitely many vocabulary elements, no sentence with $k+1$ occurrences of connectives contains infinitely many vocabulary elements.
> ───
> *Conclusion:* No sentence contains infinitely many vocabulary elements.

The demonstration is completed by demonstrating the truth of the basis and the truth of the induction.

> *Demonstration of the basis:* The sentences of SL that have zero occurrences of connectives are the atomic sentences: ⊥ and the sentence letters. Since each of them consists of a single vocabulary element, none of them contains infinitely many vocabulary elements.

Strong induction is necessary to demonstrate the inductive step. Sentences containing $k+1$ connectives may have a binary connective as their main connective. In that case, each of their immediate components may contain fewer than k connectives. For example, (A → B) ∨ ~A, which contains three occurrences of connectives, is built from two sentences that each contain only one occurrence of a connective. An induction that goes from all the sentences with two occurrences of connectives to all the sentences with three occurrences of connectives would fail to cover it. The induction must go from all the sentences in all the earlier groups to each sentence in the next group.

Demonstration of the induction: Suppose for purposes of conditional proof that no sentence containing from 0 to k occurrences of connectives contains infinitely many vocabulary elements. According to the formation rules, a sentence of SL containing k+1 occurrences of connectives is formed by either prefacing a sentence with k occurrences of connectives with a tilde or conjoining two sentences that each contain k or fewer connectives with a binary connective and enclosing the result in punctuation marks. The first operation adds one vocabulary element to a sentence that contains a finite number of vocabulary elements, and the second operation adds three vocabulary elements to two sentences that each contain a finite number of vocabulary elements. Either way, since the sum of finite quantities is finite, the result is a sentence that contains only finitely many vocabulary elements. By conditional proof, if it is supposed that no sentence that contains from 0 to k occurrences of connectives contains infinitely many vocabulary elements, it must be accepted that no sentence that contains k+1 occurrences of connectives contains infinitely many vocabulary elements.

Strong inductions like this one can seem question-begging. The demonstration of the basis does nothing but prove the trivial point that sentences that consist of a single vocabulary element cannot contain infinitely many vocabulary elements. The induction then appears to make an unjustified leap to asserting that sentences containing any arbitrarily large number, k, of occurrences of connectives cannot contain infinitely many vocabulary elements.

In fact, the demonstration does not *assert* that no sentences containing from 0 up to k occurrences of connectives can be infinitely long. It *supposes* this for purposes of conditional proof. As noted in section 5.3, a conditional proof aims to establish the truth of a conditional sentence. Such sentences do not make a claim about what is the case. They only make a claim about what would be the case if their antecedents were true. The best way to demonstrate such a claim is to show that anyone who *supposes* that the antecedent is true is compelled by that supposition to accept the truth of the consequent. This is not the same thing as *asserting* that the antecedent is true. It is simply doing what is necessary to establish the truth of the *conditional,* which says that *if* the antecedent is true *then* the consequent is true.

In the case at hand, demonstrating the inductive step only establishes that *if* none of the sentences containing from 0 to k occurrences of connectives is infinitely long, none of the sentences containing $k+1$ occurrences of connectives are infinitely long. It does not establish *that* none of the sentences containing from 0 to k occurrences of connectives is infinitely long. It does not even establish that none of the sentences containing one occurrence of connectives is infinitely long. The basis clause is needed to establish that all the sentences in the first group in fact have the property. Only when this has been established can the inductive step be invoked to infer that all the sentences in the second group must have the property, that, as a consequence, all the sentences in the third group must have the property, and so on, for however many groups there are, or forever if they are endless. (Even if there are infinitely many sentences, it has been established that none of them can be infinitely long.)

To take another example, strong induction on the number of occurrences of connectives in sentences of SL can be used to justify the claim made in section 2.4 that no sentence of SL has more than one main connective.

Basis:	No sentence that contains 0 occurrences of connectives contains more than one main connective.
Induction:	If none of the sentences that contain from 0 to k occurrences of connectives contains more than one main connective, none of the sentences containing $k+1$ occurrences of connectives contains more than one main connective.
Conclusion:	No sentence contains more than one main connective.

The basis needs no demonstration. The induction does. Even though none of the formation rules adds more than one connective each time it is applied, it needs to be demonstrated that the added connective satisfies the definition of a main connective: it has scope over the rest of the sentence whereas no pre-existing connective has scope over it.

It often happens that the demonstration of an inductive step requires running through a number of cases. Since inductive steps are commonly demonstrated by conditional proof, the overall demonstration has the form of a conditional proof with a proof by cases nested inside of it. Sometimes, demonstrating one of the cases might require running through a number of subcases, leading to proofs by cases being nested inside of proofs by cases. Since conditional proof involves assuming the antecedent in order to demonstrate that the consequent must follow, the assumption of the antecedent must often be repeated in the ensuing demonstration of multiple cases. To avoid having to repeatedly write the assumption out, it is given a name, the inductive hypothesis. This name is frequently employed in demonstrations of inductive steps. It always denotes the antecedent of the inductive step.

Demonstration of the induction: Suppose for purposes of conditional proof that **none of the sentences that contain from 0 to k occurrences of connectives contains more than one main connective**.

Any sentence, P_{k+1} that contains $k+1$ occurrences of connectives must contain at least one connective. By (exclusion) nothing is a sentence unless it has been formed by iterated applications of (SL), (~) and (bc). Since (SL) adds no connectives, any sentence that contains $k+1$ occurrences of connectives must have been formed by applying either (~) or (bc) to one or two previously formed sentences. So there are two cases to consider:

Case one: Suppose for purposes of proof by cases that P_{k+1} arises from applying (~) to a previously constructed sentence, Q. Since (~) only adds a single tilde to the front of a sentence, P_{k+1} must have the form ~Q. Since Q contains only k occurrences of connectives it follows from the inductive hypothesis (highlighted above) that it does not contain more than one main connective. Consequently, Q must either contain no connective, in which case it is ⊥ or a sentence letter, or it must have a tilde as its one main connective, or it must have a binary connective as its one main connective. So there are three cases to consider:

Case one(a): If Q is ⊥ or a sentence letter then by the definition of scope (see section 2.4), a ~ preceding Q has scope over Q and so, by the definition of a main connective, is a main connective of ~Q. Moreover, since Q contains no connectives, ~ must be the only main connective in ~Q.

Case one(b): By the definition of scope, the scope of a ~ extends only to its right, so if the main connective in Q is a tilde then, Q must have the form ~R (otherwise there would be vocabulary elements in Q that fall outside of the scope of the tilde, meaning it could not be a main connective). By the definition of a main connective, the leading tilde in ~R must have scope over all of R. By the definition of scope, a ~ immediately preceding ~R must have scope over the initial tilde in ~R and everything that falls within that tilde's scope (namely R), and so, by the definition of a main connective, is a main connective. Moreover, since the initial tilde in ~R does not have scope that extends back to its left over a tilde that precedes it, and since, by the inductive hypothesis, no other connective in R is a main connective, ~ must be the only main connective in ~Q (that is, in ~~R).

Case one(c): If Q has a binary connective as its main connective then by (bc) and the definition of a main connective Q must begin with a left parenthesis and end with a right parenthesis. By the definition of scope, a tilde preceding Q must have scope that extends from one of these parentheses to the other and so must have scope over all of Q. By the definition of a main connective it is therefore a main connective. But, again by the definition of scope, the scope of the main connective in Q cannot extend beyond its leftmost parenthesis, and so cannot extend over a ~ preceding Q, and by the inductive hypothesis no other connective in Q is a main connective. So if Q has a binary connective as its main connective, ~ must be the only main connective in ~Q.

It follows that if P_{k+1} has the form ~Q, then regardless of whether Q contains no occurrences of connectives, has a ~ as its main connective, or has a binary connective as its main connective, the initial tilde in ~Q must be its only main connective, that is P_{k+1} has no more than one main connective in this case.

Case two: Now suppose for further purposes of proof by cases that P_{k+1} arises from applying (bc) to two sentences, Q and R. Since (bc) adds only a single binary connective, P_{k+1} must have the form (Q (bc) R) where (bc) is any of the binary connectives. By the definition of scope the scope of (bc) must extend from the opening parenthesis in (Q (bc) R) to the closing parenthesis, excluding only (bc) itself, and so must extend over all the remainder of P_{k+1}. By the definition of a main connective, (bc) is a main connective of (Q (bc) R). Moreover, no connective in Q or R can be a main connective of (Q (bc) R).

Case two(a): Since tildes do not have scope that extends to the left, no tilde in R could have scope that extends left of R and no tilde in Q could have scope that extends over the left parenthesis preceding Q. By the definition of a main connective, no tilde in Q or R could be a main connective of (Q (bc) R).

Case two(b): Since R existed as a sentence of SL before being combined with Q, any binary connective in R must have been added to R along with punctuation marks confined to R. For the same reason any binary connective in Q must have been added to Q along with punctuation marks confined to Q. By the definition of scope, no binary connective in either Q or R can have scope over all the rest of (Q (bc) R). By the definition of a main connective, no binary connective in either Q or R could be a main connective of (Q (bc) R).

It follows that if P_{k+1} has the form (Q (bc) R), (bc) must be its only main connective, that is P_{k+1} has no more than one main connective in this case.

It follows that regardless of whether it was formed by (~) or by (bc), no sentence, P_{k+1}, that contains $k+1$ occurrences of connectives can have more than one main connective.

It follows by conditional proof that if **none of the sentences that contain from 0 to k occurrences of connectives contains more than one main connective, no sentence containing $k+1$ occurrences of connectives can contain more than one main connective**.

Exercise A-1.2

These exercises complement the claims of the appendix to chapter 3. The first shows that a language for sentential logic that does not contain ⊥, and only recognizes the &, ∨, →, and ≡ connectives could not contain a sentence that is F on any interpretation on which all the sentence letters are T. The second shows that a language for sentential logic that does contain ⊥, but recognizes only the ≡ connective could not contain a sentence that receives an odd proportion of T's and F's over all possible interpretations (so none that is T on three of four interpretations, for example).

1. *Consider a positive sentence to be a sentence that contains no occurrences of ⊥ or ~. Demonstrate by strong induction on the number of occurrences of connectives in sentences from 0 (atomic sentences) on that all the positive sentences are true on I_T, the interpretation that assigns T to each sentence letter. Proceed as follows:*
    ★a. *Give a summary demonstration by mathematical induction for the conclusion that all the positive sentences are true on I_T. (The demonstration should consist of a basis clause, an inductive step, and a conclusion.)*
    ★b. *Demonstrate the basis. (Appeal to the definitions of I_T and a positive sentence. Remember that the basis concerns sentences that have no occurrences of connectives, which are the atomic sentences.)*
    ★c. *Demonstrate the inductive step. (Assume the inductive hypothesis. Consider what forms any positive sentence with $k+1$ occurrences of connectives could have. Remark on the fact that the immediate components of any such sentence must fall under the inductive hypothesis. Draw the consequence from this remark for the positive sentence.)*

2. *Consider a ⊥≡ sentence to be a sentence that contains no connectives other than triple bar connectives. Demonstrate by strong induction on the number of occurrences of connectives in ⊥≡ sentences from 0 on that no ⊥≡ sentence receives an odd proportion of T's and F's over all possible interpretations, where an odd proportion is any proportion other than 0:100, 50:50, and 100:0. Proceed as follows:*
    a. State and demonstrate the basis clause. Consider two basic cases: ⊥ and the sentence letters. Note that since ⊥ is F on any interpretation it does not have an odd proportion of T's and F's on any interpretation.
    b. State the inductive step. Proceed to demonstrate it by supposing the inductive hypothesis. Go on to note that since any sentence can have only one main connective, any ⊥≡ sentence with $k+1$ occurrences of connectives must be of one of the forms ⊥ ≡ P, P ≡ ⊥ or P ≡ Q where P and Q contain k or fewer connectives.
    c. Demonstrate that the inductive step holds in the first two cases. Appeal to (≡) and the inductive hypothesis.
    d. Demonstrate that the inductive step holds in case three. Note that a supposition to the contrary would require that P and Q have the same values on an odd number of interpretations. Appeal to the inductive step.
    ★e. Following the example of the answers to 1a–c, integrate the answers to a–d in a single demonstration leading to the conclusion that no ⊥≡ sentence receives an odd proportion of T's and F's over all possible interpretations.

A-1.2 Bivalence

The definition of a valuation given in chapter 3 is "classical" in the sense that it stipulates that any valuation must assign exactly one of T and F to each sentence letter of SL. Leaving some sentence letters without an assignment or assigning something other than one of T and F to some of them is not allowed. However, stipulating that each sentence letter must be assigned exactly one of T and F does not entail that each *compound* sentence must be assigned exactly one of T and F. Strong induction can be employed to demonstrate that, if it is supposed that each atomic sentence has exactly one of the values, the same must hold for each compound sentence. None can be without a value, and none can have both.

In what follows, the cumbersome phrase, "has exactly one of the two values on any interpretation" is replaced by "is bivalent."

The induction is based on the number of occurrences of connectives in sentences.

Basis:	Every sentence with 0 occurrences of connectives is bivalent.
Induction:	If every sentence with *k* or fewer occurrences of connectives is bivalent, then every sentence with *k*+1 occurrences of connectives is bivalent.

Conclusion:	Every sentence is bivalent.

Demonstration of the basis: The sentences with 0 occurrences of connectives are ⊥ and the sentence letters. ⊥ is F on any interpretation, and by definition of a valuation each interpretation must assign exactly one of T and F to each sentence letter. So, every sentence with 0 occurrences of connectives is bivalent.

Demonstration of the induction: Suppose for purposes of conditional proof that every sentence with *k* or fewer occurrences of connectives is bivalent. Any sentence with *k*+1 occurrences of connectives must contain at least one connective. **Given that no sentence can have more than one main connective**, sentences that contain at least one connective must have either the form ~P or the form (P (bc) Q), where (bc) is a binary connective. Given that ~ or (bc) is the *k*+1 connective, P (and Q) must (each) contain *k* (or fewer) connective(s). It follows by the inductive hypothesis, that P and Q are bivalent, that is, each has exactly one of the two values on any interpretation. Given exactly one value for P on each interpretation, (~) dictates exactly one value for ~P on each interpretation, and given exactly one value for P and Q on each interpretation (&), (∨), (→), and (≡) dictate exactly one value for P (bc) Q on each interpretation. So, every sentence with *k*+1 occurrences of connectives must be bivalent. It follows by conditional proof that if every sentence with *k* or fewer occurrences of connectives is bivalent, every sentence with *k*+1 occurrences of connectives must be bivalent as well.

This demonstration presupposes that each sentence has exactly one main connective. If it were possible to form a sentence with two or more main connectives, then even though the valuation rules dictate that for each possible combination of values to the components, the compound must have a unique value, there could be more than one compound getting a value, and the values could be different. This presupposition was justified in section 6.1.

Bivalence depends on another presupposition, the presupposition, also justified in section 6.1, that there are no infinitely long sentences of SL. There are infinitely many sentences of SL, but each of them is only finitely long. Their infinite number is a consequence of being able to iterate the formation rules, to continually add further connectives to previously formed sentences and combine previously formed sentences. But, as demonstrated in 6.1, though there is no end to the number of times these operations can be performed, and so an infinity of sentences can be constructed, no infinitely long sentence is ever constructed. Otherwise, ~~~…A could be constructed, and that would pose a challenge for bivalence.

A-1.3 Extensionality

Extensionality is the property of invariance in meaning under substitution of parts that have the same meaning. In SL, parts are components and the only elements of meaning retained by components are the values, T and F. These values vary with interpretations. So in SL, the notion of sameness of meaning of two components, P and Q, reduces to that of P having the same value as Q on an interpretation. SL is extensional in the sense that substituting components that have the same value on an interpretation, I, will not change the value of the compound on I. For example, if I(A) and I(~C) are T, substituting ~C for A in any sentence in which A occurs, such as A & B, will not produce a sentence that has a different value on I. I(~C & B) will have the same value as I(A & B).

(def extensional)

A sentence, P, is extensional if and only if, if Q is a component of P and I(Q) is I(R), then I(P) is I(P(R|Q)), where P(R|Q) is the sentence that results from replacing one or more occurrences of Q in P with occurrences of R.

Extensionality is not trivial. To take a famous example, everyone knows that Walter Scott is Walter Scott, even those who do not know who Walter Scott was. Walter Scott was the author of the anonymously published novel, *Waverley*. But even though "Scott" and "the author of *Waverley*" name the same person, and so have the same meaning, substituting "the author of *Waverley*" for the second occurrence of "Scott" in the sentence, "Everyone knows that Scott is Scott" does not produce a sentence that has the same value as the original.

The fact that SL is extensional, whereas English is not, does not entail that SL is a bad tool for representing the forms of English sentences, sets of sentences, and demonstrations. It just means that it does not formalize everything that is of logical interest in some English sentences. It was never claimed that it could.

Because extensionality is nontrivial, it needs to be demonstrated.

The demonstration is given by strong induction on the number of occurrences of connectives in sentences of SL.

Basis:	All sentences of SL with 0 occurrences of connectives are extensional.
Induction:	If all sentences of SL with zero to k occurrences of connectives are extensional, then all sentences with $k+1$ occurrences of connectives are extensional.
Conclusion:	All the sentences of SL are extensional.

Demonstration of the basis: The sentences with 0 occurrences of connectives are the atomic sentences. Since atomic sentences have no components other than themselves, the only way a sentence, Q, could be a component of a sentence P is if P is Q. In that case, the result, P(R|Q) of putting R in the place of one or more occurrences of Q in P is R. It follows that if Q is a component of P and I(Q) is I(R), I(P) must be I(P(R|Q)), simply because P is Q and P(R|Q) is R. By (def extensional), P is extensional.

In demonstrating the induction there are three cases to consider: Since every sentence is a component of itself, Q may be P, or Q may be what is called a "proper" component of P (a component other than P itself). In the first of these cases, P must be extensional for the reason already given when demonstrating the basis clause. In the second case, P must either be the result, ~P$_1$, of prefacing some proper component, P$_1$, with a "~," or it must be the result of connecting two proper components, P$_1$ and P$_2$, with a binary connective.

Demonstration of the induction:

1. Suppose for purposes of conditional proof that each of the sentences of SL with from 0 to k occurrences of connectives is extensional.
2. Suppose further that Q is a component of P and that I(Q) is I(R).
   3. Then there are three cases to consider:
      i. P may be Q
      ii. P may have the form ~P$_1$, or
      iii. P may have the form, (P$_1$ (bc) P$_2$), where (bc) is a binary connective.
   4. Suppose for purposes of proof by cases that the component, Q, of P that R replaces just is P.
      5. Then **I(P) is I(P(R|Q))** because P is Q, which means P(R|Q) is R, and it is being supposed that I(Q) is I(R).
   6. Suppose for further purposes of proof by cases that P has the form ~P$_1$.
      7. Then P$_1$ has only k connectives (the ~ in ~P$_1$ is the $k+1$ connective).
      8. By the inductive hypothesis (line 1), P$_1$ is extensional.
      9. By def extensional, I(P$_1$) is I(P$_1$(R|Q)).
      10. By (~), I(~P$_1$) is I(~P$_1$(R|Q)). That is, **I(P) is I(P(R|Q))** in this case.
   11. Suppose for final purposes of proof by cases that P has the form, (P$_1$ (bc) P$_2$).
      12. Since (P$_1$ (bc) P$_2$) has $k+1$ occurrences of connectives, each of its immediate components, P$_1$ and P$_2$, must contain k or fewer occurrences of connectives.
      13. By the inductive hypothesis (line 1), each of P$_1$ and P$_2$ is extensional.
      14. By def extensional I(P$_1$) is I(P$_1$(R|Q)) and I I(P$_2$) is I(P$_2$(R|Q)). Consequently, regardless of whether R is put for Q in P$_1$, P$_2$, or both, or whether Q is a proper component of P$_1$ or P$_2$ or one or other of P$_1$ or P$_2$, the result will be a sentence with a left immediate component that has the same value as P$_1$ on I, and a sentence with a right immediate component that has the same value as P$_2$ on I.

15. The value of $(P_1 \mathbin{\&} P_2)$, $(P_1 \lor P_2)$, $(P_1 \to P_2)$, and $(P_1 \equiv P_2)$ is in each case determined by the value of its immediate components. Since the substitution of R for Q results in no changes to the values of the immediate components on I, $I(P_1 \text{ (bc) } P_2)$ is $I(P_1 \text{ (bc) } P_2)(R \,|\, Q)$. That is, **I(P) is I(P(R $\,|\,$ Q)) in this case**.

16. From line 3 (where the three cases were laid out), lines 4–5 (demonstration for case (i)), lines 6–10 (demonstration for case (ii)), and lines 11–15 (demonstration for case (iii)) by proof by cases, I(P) is $I(P(R \,|\, Q))$.

17. From lines 2–16 by conditional proof, if Q is a component of P and I(Q) is I(R), then I(P) is $I(R \,|\, Q)$.

18. By def extensional, P is extensional.

19. From lines 1–18 by conditional proof, if each of the sentences of SL with from 0 to k occurrences of connectives is extensional, any sentence, P, that contains $k+1$ occurrences of connectives is extensional.

The extensionality of the sentences of SL has an important corollary.

Substitution Principle

If Q is s-equivalent to R and P contains 1 or more occurrences of Q, then P is s-equivalent to $P(R \,|\, Q)$.

The substitution principle is an immediate consequence of the extensionality of the sentences of SL. If Q is s-equivalent to R then they have the same values on each interpretation. It follows by extensionality that if P contains one or more occurrences of Q, P must have the same value as $P(R \,|\, Q)$ on each interpretation, and so must be s-equivalent to $P(R \,|\, Q)$.

The substitution principle facilitates a significant expansion to the demonstrative techniques that can be employed to establish claims about sentences of SL. It means that the equivalence principles listed on the table of section 5.3 can be used to transform sentences of SL into equivalent forms making it possible to demonstrate some results simply by transforming sentences. For example, $[(A \to B) \mathbin{\&} (A \mathbin{\&} {\sim}B)]$ might be demonstrated to be s-equivalent to $\bot$ and so, like $\bot$, s-unsatisfiable by running through a chain of substitutions rather than by a demonstration of the sort performed in exercise 5.4#3.

$(A \to B) \mathbin{\&} (A \mathbin{\&} {\sim}B)$	given
$({\sim}A \lor B) \mathbin{\&} (A \mathbin{\&} {\sim}B)$	(impl)
$[({\sim}A \lor B) \mathbin{\&} A] \mathbin{\&} {\sim}B$	(assoc)
$[A \mathbin{\&} ({\sim}A \lor B)] \mathbin{\&} {\sim}B$	(com)
$[(A \mathbin{\&} {\sim}A) \lor (A \mathbin{\&} B)] \mathbin{\&} {\sim}B$	(dist)
$[\bot \lor (A \mathbin{\&} B)] \mathbin{\&} {\sim}B$	(con)
$[(A \lor B) \lor \bot] \mathbin{\&} {\sim}B$	(assoc)
$(A \mathbin{\&} B) \mathbin{\&} {\sim}B$	(imm)
$A \mathbin{\&} (B \mathbin{\&} {\sim}B)$	(assoc)
$A \mathbin{\&} \bot$	(con)
$\bot$	(inf)

Another useful corollary of extensionality is based on the fact that (assoc) may be applied to demonstrate the s-equivalence of any two different ways of punctuating sentences compounded from multiple conjuncts and the s-equivalence of any two different ways of punctuating sentences compounded from multiple disjuncts. This demonstrates that internal punctuation does not affect the meaning of sentences compounded from multiple conjuncts or sentences compounded from multiple disjuncts and so can be omitted. A new informal notational convention, (ip) can be instituted to this effect.

(ip): internal punctuation may be omitted from sequences of conjuncts and sequences of disjuncts

A-1.4 Compactness

When a set of sentences is unsatisfiable, adding more sentences to that set will do nothing to change that fact. The sentence or sentences that give rise to the contradiction are still there and still make it possible to demonstrate that the larger set is unsatisfiable, even if it is made infinitely large.

With SL the converse is also the case. If an infinitely large set of sentences of SL is s-unsatisfiable, it must have at least one finite subset that is already s-unsatisfiable. SL satisfies what is called the compactness principle.

Compactness: A set is unsatisfiable if and only if it has a finite, unsatisfiable subset.

Of course, since every set is a subset of itself, there is nothing surprising about saying that a *finitely* large set cannot be unsatisfiable unless it contains at least one unsatisfiable subset. But the claim that an *infinitely* large s-unsatisfiable set needs to have a *finite* subset that is already s-unsatisfiable is surprising.

In general, removing sentences from an unsatisfiable set risks removing the sentences responsible for creating the contradiction, and in English there are some infinitely large unsatisfiable sets that have no finite unsatisfiable subsets. The set

$$\Gamma: \{ \text{There are only finitely many stars in the sky,}$$
$$\text{There is at least one star in the sky,}$$
$$\text{There are at least two stars in the sky,}$$
$$\text{There are at least three stars in the sky,}$$
$$\ldots \}$$

is unsatisfiable. Anyone who accepts all of them would be caught in a contradiction. But any finite subset of this set is satisfiable.

But while not all infinitely large sets of English sentences are compact, all infinitely large sets of sentences of SL are. Compactness fails for reasons that SL is not equipped to formalize, and consequently it fails only for systems of logic able to formalize those features. This is indicated by the fact that none of the sentences in the set just given contains any sentential connectives. What is responsible for the unsatisfiability of the set is subsentential and so beyond anything formalized by SL.

Compactness is worth demonstrating because it entails that no s-valid demonstration need have more than finitely many premises. The demonstration from a set of premises, Γ, to a conclusion, P, is valid if and only if $\Gamma \cup$ ~P is unsatisfiable. According to the compactness principle, if this larger set, $\Gamma \cup$ ~P, is infinite, it must have a finite subset that is already unsatisfiable. When compactness holds, a conclusion, P, is entailed by a set of premises, Γ, if and only if P is entailed by a *finite* set of the premises in Γ.

The compactness principle can be demonstrated by contraposition. As originally defined in chapter 2, the contrapositive of a conditional sentence is the sentence that results from inverting the order of the immediate components and negating each (so the contrapositive of A $\rightarrow$ B is ~B $\rightarrow$ ~A). Without drawing on the results of exercises 5.4#5k and 5.6#3 (which are specific to the formal language SL), any conditional is intuitively equivalent to its contrapositive. Suppose it is the case that if A is true, then B is true, and suppose further that B is not true. Then A could not be true either, since if it were, it would follow from the initial supposition that B must be true, contradicting the claim that it is not. So, if it is supposed that if A is true B must be true, it must be accepted, on pain of contradiction, that if B is not true, A cannot be true either. Alternatively, suppose that if B is not true then A is not true, and suppose further that A is true. Then B must be true, because if it were not true it would follow from the first supposition that A is not true, contradicting the second supposition. So, if it is supposed that if B is not true then A is not true, then it must be accepted, on pain of contradiction, that if A is true then B is true.

A perfectly good way of demonstrating a conditional, therefore, is to proceed by instead demonstrating its contrapositive. The frame for a contrapositive demonstration of compactness is as follows:

1.   Suppose for purposes of conditional proof that each finite subset of an infinitely large set, $\Gamma\star$ is s-satisfiable.

   •   •

   •   •

   •   •

n. $\Gamma\star$ is s-satisfiable.

n+1.   It follows from lines 1 to *n* by conditional proof that if each finite subset of $\Gamma^\star$ is s-satisfiable $\Gamma^\star$ is s-satisfiable.

n+2.   By contraposition, if $\Gamma^\star$ is s-unsatisfiable it has at least one finite subset that is s-unsatisfiable.

Line *n* is demonstrated by showing that if each finite subset of $\Gamma^\star$ is s-satisfiable, as supposed at line 1, then there is a way to construct a single interpretation on which all the sentences in each of those finite subsets is true. It is then shown that all the sentences in $\Gamma^\star$ must be true on this interpretation from which it follows that $\Gamma^\star$ must be s-satisfiable.

This is not easily established. For any finite subset, Δ, of Γ, if that finite subset is s-satisfiable then there must be at least one interpretation on which all the sentences in that set are true. But it is not immediately obvious why the interpretation that works for one finite subset should work for any other.

To show why there must be a common interpretation, it helps to introduce four preliminary notions, the notions of a total order for the atomic sentences of SL, of a partial interpretation, of an extension of a partial interpretation, and of the satisfaction of a set by a partial interpretation.

(i) A total order for the atomic sentences of SL is a way of listing the atomic sentences of SL without leaving any out. Not every way will work. The list, $<A_2, A_4, A_6, \ldots>$ goes on forever but still manages to leave out infinitely many atomic sentences of SL.

It is intuitively obvious that each atomic sentence of SL will eventually appear somewhere on the following list:

$$<\bot, A, B, C, G, H, K, A_1, A_2, A_3, \ldots>$$

However, to simplify the exposition that follows, it is useful to scratch A, B, C, G, H, and K from the vocabulary and work with the following list:

$$<\bot, A_1, A_2, A_3, \ldots>$$

(ii) A partial interpretation, I_n, is a valuation of the first *n* sentence letters on the list. A partial interpretation leaves some sentence letters without any value and leaves any compound sentences that depend on the values of those sentence letters without any value. In contrast, a complete interpretation, $I^\star$, assigns a value to each sentence of SL.

(iii) An extension I_{n+x}, of a partial interpretation, I_n, is an interpretation that assigns all the same values that I_n does, but that also assigns further values to the sentence letters in the next *x* places. *x* could have the value 0. (It is desirable to be able to consider each partial interpretation to be an extension of itself.)

The union of all the partial interpretations is a complete interpretation. It assigns a value to each sentence letter. (The union is complete rather than the last extension in the sequence, because there is no last extension in the sequence.)

(iv) A partial interpretation, I_n, satisfies a set, Δ, if and only if there is an extension of that interpretation on which all the sentences in Δ are true. Δ may contain atomic sentences that do not have a value under I_n. Even though I_n leaves these atomic sentences, and any compounds in Δ that contain them without values, it still satisfies Δ if there is an extension of I_n on which all the sentences in Δ are true.

For example, even though the partial interpretation that assigns F to A_1 and A_2 makes no assignment to A_3, it satisfies $\{\sim A_2, A_3 \equiv A_2\}$ whereas the partial interpretation that assigns F to A_1 and T to A_2 does not.

Exercise A-1.3

1.   *Explain why the partial interpretation that assigns F to A_1 and A_2 satisfies $\{\sim A_2, A_3 \equiv A_2\}$ whereas the partial interpretation that assigns F to A_1 and T to A_2 does not.*

2.   *What would make it wrong to say that the partial interpretation that assigns F to A_1 and A_3 satisfies $\{\sim A_2, A_3 \equiv A_2\}$? (Hint: appeal to the definition of a partial interpretation.)*

3.   *State whether the partial interpretation, I_3, that assigns F to A_1, T to A_2 and F to A_3 satisfies each of the following sets. Justify your answers with an example (of an extension on the partial interpretation that does the job) or a demonstration (of why it would be impossible for there to be such an extension) as appropriate.*

   ★a. { }

   b. $\{A_4\}$

   ★c. $\{\bot\}$

   d. $\{(A_2 \lor A_3) \rightarrow A_4, \sim A_4 \lor A_5\}$

*e. $\{A_4 \rightarrow A_2, \sim A_4, A_4 \rightarrow A_3\}$
  f. $\{A_2 \rightarrow \perp, \sim\perp, A_2 \rightarrow A_3\}$

This exercise notwithstanding, it is not necessary to know whether any given partial interpretation satisfies any given set. The demonstration that follows does not require that knowledge. It starts from the supposition that each finite subset of $\Gamma^\star$ is s-satisfiable, from which it follows that for each finite subset there is at least one complete interpretation that assigns a T to each sentence in that subset, from which it follows that at least one partial interpretation must satisfy the subset. This is a consequence of the fact that the subset is finite, which means it can only contain finitely many sentence letters, which means that one of them must be the last of all the others to occur on the approved list. Any partial interpretation that goes up that high will assign values to each sentence in the finite subset.

Consider a sequence of extensions on a partial interpretation defined as follows:

I_0 assigns a value to all the sentence letters in the empty set (it does not assign a value to any sentence letter).

I_1 assigns T to A_1 provided that doing so satisfies each finite subset of $\Gamma^\star$; otherwise I_1 assigns F to A_1. (It does not matter what happens as a consequence of assigning F to A_1. This is just what I_1 does when assigning a T does not allow I_1 to satisfy each finite subset of $\Gamma^\star$.)

I_2 keeps whatever assignments I_1 makes and assigns T to A_2 provided that doing so satisfies each finite subset of $\Gamma^\star$; otherwise I_2 assigns F to A_2.

In general, I_{n+1} keeps whatever assignments I_n makes and assigns T to A_{n+1}, provided that doing so satisfies each finite subset of $\Gamma^\star$; otherwise I_{n+1} assigns F to A_{n+1}.

Remark 1

This construction is based on assignments made to sentence letters. $\Gamma^\star$, and all its finite subsets, may contain only compound sentences. When assignments are made to sentence letters, assignments are not necessarily made to any sentence in $\Gamma^\star$. The sentences in $\Gamma^\star$ may not contain sentence letters that have been assigned values, and even if they do, assignments to some of the remaining sentence letters may need to be determined before assignments to any of the compounds can be determined.

Remark 2

By supposition, each finite subset of $\Gamma^\star$ is s-satisfiable. So, for each finite subset, Δ, there is an interpretation on which all the sentences in that subset are true. The question is just whether it is the same interpretation for all of them.

Remark 3

I_0 must satisfy each finite subset of $\Gamma^\star$.

I_0 makes no assignment to any sentence letter, so it can be expanded to any interpretation whatsoever. Since each finite subset of $\Gamma^\star$ is supposed to be s-satisfiable, and so consists of sentences that are all true on some interpretation or other, and all are extensions of I_0, it follows that I_0 must satisfy each finite subset of $\Gamma^\star$.

(Since $\perp$ is F on any interpretation, and each finite subset of $\Gamma^\star$ is supposed to be s-satisfiable, $\perp$ cannot stand alone in $\Gamma^\star$. It may well figure as a component of other sentences.)

Remark 4

Given any sentence in any finite subset of $\Gamma^\star$, I_1 must either assign a T to that sentence or leave that sentence without any assignment.

This must be the case even if I_1 assigns an F to A_1. Suppose assigning a T to A_1 would make some sentence in some finite subset of $\Gamma^\star$ false (perhaps because $\{\sim A_1\}$ is a finite subset of $\Gamma^\star$). According to the way I_1 was defined above, this is a condition under which I_1 must assign an F to A_1. If assigning that F to A_1 also made some sentence in some finite subset of $\Gamma^\star$ false (perhaps because $\{A_1 \vee A_1\}$ is a finite subset of $\Gamma^\star$), then $\Gamma^\star$ would contain a finite subset – the one consisting of the sentence made false by assigning T to A_1 and the one consisting of the sentence made false by assigning F to A_1 (e.g., a finite subset like $\{\sim A_1, A_1 \vee A_1\}$) – that contains sentences that are not true on any interpretation (since all must assign exactly one of T and F to A_1 and neither assignment makes all the sentences in this finite subset true). But then $\Gamma^\star$ would have to contain at least one s-unsatisfiable subset, contrary to the initial supposition that it has no such finite subset. So I_1 cannot make any sentence in any finite subset of $\Gamma^\star$ false, regardless of what it ends up doing. If assigning a T to A_1 would make at least one sentence in one finite subset of $\Gamma^\star$ false, assigning an F to A_1 instead cannot make any sentence in any finite subset false. Given any sentence in any finite subset, I_1 must either assign a T to that sentence or leave it without an assignment.

This result can be applied to all the extensions on I_1 by mathematical induction. Not only must each sentence in $\Gamma^\star$ either be assigned a T by I_1 or be left without an assignment, there must be at least one way of extending I_1 to satisfy each finite subset of $\Gamma^\star$ (though it is not being claimed just yet that *the same* extension will work for all of them), and the same must hold for each subsequent extension in the series.

> *Basis:* I_0 satisfies each finite subset of $\Gamma^\star$.
>
> *Induction:* If I_n satisfies each finite subset of $\Gamma^\star$, then I_{n+1} satisfies each finite subset of $\Gamma^\star$.
>
> ---
>
> *Conclusion:* Each extension satisfies each finite subset of $\Gamma^\star$.

The demonstration of the basis clause has already been given. Since each finite subset is s-satisfiable and so true on some interpretation, and since I_0 does not make an assignment to any sentence letter and so can be expanded to any interpretation, it can be expanded to any interpretation on which all the sentences in any finite subset of $\Gamma^\star$ are true. So, it satisfies each finite subset.

The demonstration of the inductive step generalizes on the one given in remark 4 above.

Suppose that I_n satisfies each finite subset of $\Gamma^\star$, but that, contrary to what is being proposed, I_{n+1} does not satisfy at least one finite subset, Δ. Then by the way I_{n+1} is defined, I_{n+1} must assign an F to A_{n+1}. (By definition, this is what I_{n+1} does in cases where assigning a T to A_{n+1} fails to satisfy each finite subset of $\Gamma^\star$. If assigning a T to A_{n+1} would have satisfied each finite subset of $\Gamma^\star$, I_{n+1} would have made that assignment. What must have happened is that assigning a T to A_{n+1} failed to satisfy at least one finite subset, Δ', and because of that, I_{n+1} assigned an F to A_{n+1}, which results in some other finite subset, Δ, not being satisfied.) But now note that I_{n+1} inherits all the assignments it makes from I_n, except for the assignment of F to A_{n+1}. This means that I_n expanded by the assignment of a F to A_{n+1} would fail to satisfy Δ. Not only this, but rather more interestingly, I_n, expanded by the opposite assignment of a T to A_{n+1} would also have to fail to satisfy at least one finite subset, Δ', of $\Gamma^\star$. (If it didn't, then by definition I_{n+1} would have had to assign a T to A_{n+1}, as doing so would have satisfied each finite subset.) But this leads to a contradiction. Because Δ and Δ' are each finite subsets of $\Gamma^\star$, all the sentences in the set produced by combining them, $\Delta \cup \Delta'$, is a finite subset of $\Gamma^\star$, and the sentences in this finite subset are not true either on an interpretation that assigns T to A_{n+1} or on an interpretation that assigns F to A_{n+1}. But every extension of I_n must assign either a T or an F to A_{n+1}. It follows that no extension of I_n satisfies each finite subset of $\Gamma^\star$, contradicting the original supposition that I_n satisfies each finite subset of $\Gamma^\star$. (Recall preliminary notion #iv (p.158), which defines what it means for a partial interpretation to satisfy a set.) If that original supposition is correct (if I_n really does satisfy each finite subset of $\Gamma^\star$) then there is no way I_{n+1} can fail to do so as well. And that is just what was proposed: that *if* I_n satisfies each finite subset of $\Gamma^\star$, *then* I_{n+1} satisfies each finite subset of $\Gamma^\star$. So that point has been demonstrated.

This subtle and beautiful demonstration is due to Adolf Lindenbaum (1904–41).

Given these demonstrations of the basis clause and the inductive step, it follows by mathematical induction that all the extensions in the series must satisfy each finite subset.

It further follows that the union of all the partial interpretations in the series must be a single, complete interpretation, $I^\star$, that satisfies each finite subset (it must be single because no later partial interpretation makes any changes to assignments made by any earlier one; each only adds something else to what was done by the previous one; it must be complete because it is the union of all the partial interpretations). All the sentences in each finite subset of Γ must be true on $I^\star$.

It is now straightforward to demonstrate that, given that each finite subset of $\Gamma^\star$ is satisfied by $I^\star$, $\Gamma^\star$ must be satisfied by $I^\star$ and so must be s-satisfiable. Suppose for purposes of indirect proof that $\Gamma^\star$ is not s-satisfiable. Then there can be no interpretation on which all the sentences in $\Gamma^\star$ are true. So, consider any sentence, P, in $\Gamma^\star$ that is false on $I^\star$ (by supposition, there must be at least one), and consider the atomic component, A_n with the highest "catalogue number" of all the atomic components in P.

(The catalogue number of the atomic sentences can be defined as follows: $\bot$ has number 0 and $A_1, A_2, A_3, \ldots$ have the number of their subscripts. Even though there are infinitely many sentence letters, the subscript of each of them is a finite number. Consequently, however many atomic components P contains, each of them has a finite catalogue number. As was demonstrated in section 6.1, no sentence of SL contains infinitely many vocabulary elements, so one of these catalogue numbers must be the highest.)

A_n would have been assigned its value by the partial interpretation, I_n. But the set $\{P\}$ is a finite subset of $\Gamma^\star$ and it has been established that I_n must make an assignment to A_n that satisfies each finite subset of $\Gamma^\star$ and in particular that satisfies $\{P\}$. I_n must therefore have assigned a value to A_n that makes P true. But $I^\star$ makes all the assignments made by any partial interpretation in the series. Since it has been established that I_n must assign T to P, $I^\star$ must assign T to P, contradicting the original inference that $I^\star$ must assign an F to P. Since this inference only arose because it was supposed that $\Gamma^\star$ is s-unsatisfiable, that assumption has been exposed as contradictory and so must be rejected. That means accepting that if all the finite subsets of $\Gamma^\star$ are s-satisfiable, $\Gamma^\star$ must be s-satisfiable as well.

It follows that if $\Gamma^\star$ is not s-satisfiable then it must have at least one finite subset that is s-unsatisfiable.

It follows that the language SL is compact. A set of sentences of SL can be s-unsatisfiable only if (and, trivially, if) it has a finite subset that is already s-unsatisfiable.

Note

1 A technical note: Many authors treat compactness as a consequence of completeness. The first of the versions of the completeness demonstration given in chapter A-2 presupposes semantic compactness and so requires that it be independently established. The demonstration follows Hunter (1996: 114–16).

References

Hunter, Geoffrey, 1996 *Metalogic: An Introduction to the Metatheory of Standard First Order Logic*, University of California Press, Berkeley.

6 Derivations

Contents

Chapter 1 drew attention to a problem at the foundations of logic. Not all contradictions are formally contradictory. Demonstrating that apparent contradictions really are contradictory involves appealing to equivalences and entailments. But equivalence and entailment are themselves demonstrated by appeal to contradictions. Because

DOI: 10.4324/9781003026532-8

formal contradictions never get beyond affirming and denying the same thing, it seems impossible to demonstrate that an apparent contradiction entails or is equivalent to a formal one.

Chapter 1 proposed two ways to block this regress: (i) trust our intuitions that certain sentences have equivalent forms and certain demonstrations have valid forms, and use these intuitive equivalences and entailments to establish equivalences and entailments that are not as obvious, or (ii) develop a theory of the meaning of logical terms that can explain why denying certain equivalences and entailments is tantamount to accepting a formal contradiction. The second of these ways is explored in chapters 3 and 5. This chapter explores the first. It focuses on entailments. (Equivalences are just entailments that go both ways.) In section 6.1 five intuitively obvious forms of entailment are identified. A system for using these entailments to demonstrate other, less intuitive entailments is also developed. While the five forms of entailment are intuitively obvious, applying them to demonstrate other entailments can be challenging. Section 6.2 presents strategies for doing this. Section 6.3 identifies six more intuitive forms of entailment and section 6.4 provides further strategies for using them to demonstrate other entailments. After considering some further features of the system in section 6.5, section 6.6 turns to consider how uniform and reliable our intuitions are, and whether some of them might be used to challenge some classically accepted entailments.

This is not a merely academic exercise, rendered unnecessary by what is said in chapters 3 and 5. Many of the intuitive entailments presented in this chapter are familiar. They are employed in the informal demonstrations that are used to establish semantic results in chapter 5. Chapter 5 does not just appeal to connective rules and definitions of fundamental logical concepts and relations. The demonstrations of chapter 5 invoke the rules of indirect proof, proof by cases, conditional proof, biconditional proof, and biconditional syllogism. These rules describe intuitively obvious forms of entailment. They are not justified by the valuation rules and definitions of intensional concepts of chapters 3 or 5. They could hardly be justified by the valuation rules and definitions of intensional concepts when reasoning from valuation rules and definitions of intensional concepts rests on them. In chapter 5, these rules are invoked as a higher-order set of principles that make it possible to reason from valuation rules and definitions of intensional concepts. The ultimate authority for these rules is the intuition that they must be accepted on pain of contradiction. It is intuitive, for example, that anyone who accepts that at least one of A and B is the case, and that A and B are each sufficient for C, would get caught in a contradiction were they to deny C. This makes proof by cases an intuitively obvious form of entailment.

This chapter does not investigate whether our intuitions about what is entailed agree with what the semantic theory of chapters 3 and 5 says about what is entailed. That is the job of chapter A-2. Before that can be done, it is necessary to identify our most basic intuitions on this matter and systematize them. That is the only job of this chapter.

In taking this task on, it is important not to assume that our intuitions about what is entailed agree with what semantic theories, like that of chapters 3 and 5, say is entailed. To forestall any such confusion, this chapter uses different terms: instead of speaking of what is entailed, it speaks of what is derivable; instead of referring to "equivalence," it refers to "interderivability"; instead of "demonstration," "derivation"; instead of "valid," "derivable"; instead of "unsatisfiable," "inconsistent." This may be disorienting at first, but it is necessary to avoid begging important questions. "Demonstration" is replaced with "derivation" because demonstrations have been associated with the application of valuation rules and definitions of intensional concepts, which are features of SL semantics. Because validity, equivalence, and unsatisfiability are defined semantically, in terms of interpretations, s-models, and s-entailment, they are replaced with appeals to what is intuitively derivable. A new symbol, the single turnstile ($\vdash$), read as "yields" or "is derivable from," replaces the entailment symbol ($\vDash$). It is not assumed that whatever is entailed according to the semantic theory of chapters 3 and 5 is, as it is now put, "derivable" in accord with our intuitions, or that what is intuitively derivable is entailed. Only one claim is made about the intuitively valid forms of inference studied in this chapter: there is at least one conclusion that cannot be derived from the empty list of premises using these forms of inference. This is a minimal constraint on an acceptable derivation system. Were there no sentences that are underivable, there would be no point to establishing that other sentences are.

6.1 D_L: A Lean Derivation System

This section presents five intuitively derivable results, called "derivation rules," and provides instruction in their application to derive further results. The rules are used with sentences formalized in SL, which is why five are all that are needed. It is possible to do everything using only five rules by only dealing with three sorts of sentences of SL: atomic sentences, negations, and conditionals. Nothing is lost by leaving out conjunctions, disjunctions, and biconditionals. For any sentence of SL that contains occurrences of &, ∨, or ≡ there is an s-equivalent (and interderivable) sentence that contains only occurrences of ~, →, ⊥, sentence letters, and punctuation marks. (This is established in section 6.5.2 and exercise 6.15. Compare exercises 5.4#5b–d and 5.5a.)

Three of the derivation rules presented here will be familiar to those who have studied chapters 5.3 and 5.5. They are versions of the rules of indirect proof, conditional proof, and modus ponens, rewritten for use with sentences of SL. The remaining rules are a rule for deriving ⊥, called ⊥ introduction (⊥I) and a reiteration rule. Together these rules comprise a system, called D_L, the lean derivation system.

The intuitions behind the lean derivation rules are drawn from meanings associated with ⊥, ~, and →.

- ⊥ means "there is an absurdity"
- ~P means "not P" or "deny P"
- P → Q means "P is sufficient for Q," that is, "If P is the case, Q is the case" or equivalently, "Q is necessary for P," that is, "P is the case only if Q is the case." Either way, having P means having Q, be it because having P is all that is needed for having Q or because Q is a condition that must be satisfied to have P. (And either way, having Q does not mean having P, be it because having P is not the only way to get Q or because Q may not be all that is needed to have P.)

The meaning of "if" and "only if," and of "is sufficient for" and "is necessary for" can also be taken from the following diagram, when it is understood as depicting the conditions on the location of a point in nested circles. Take the inner circle to represent the antecedent (P) and the outer circle to represent the consequent (Q).

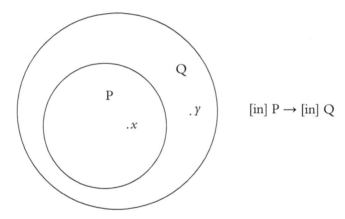

[in] P → [in] Q

Since the P circle is contained in the Q circle, a point, x, can be in the P circle only if it is in the Q circle. Being in Q is *necessary*, but not *sufficient* for being in P. (y is in Q but not in P.)

Again, if a point, x, is in the P circle, then it is in the Q circle. Being in P is one way of being in Q, though, again, it is not the only way. So, while being in the P circle *suffices* for being in the Q circle, it is not *necessary* for being there. (y is in Q but not in P.)

These meanings are not further defined. Notably, they are not related to sentential values or valuation rules. Even "not" refers only to the operation of denying a sentence, not to the assignment of a value to the denied sentence. Affirming and denying one and the same sentence constitutes an absurdity prior to any theorizing about truth, falsity or other values.

As presented in chapter 5, indirect proof is based on the intuitively compelling reasoning that if a supposition or, as it will now be called, an assumption, yields something absurd, that assumption should be denied. Yielding something absurd is represented as yielding ⊥. And denying a supposition is represented using ~. If the assumption is a sentence, P, its denial is its negation, ~P. If the assumption is a negation, ~P, it can be denied with either its nullation, P, or its negation, ~~P. To cover all the bases, the expression, "P-opposite" is used. If P is Q, P-opposite is ~Q. If P is ~Q, P-opposite is either of Q and ~~Q.

Were the rule of indirect proof stated as an entailment, it would be

(IP): if Γ ∪ P ⊨ ⊥, then Γ ⊨ P-opposite (see exercise 5.12(d))

In other words, if adding the supposition, P, to a (possibly empty) set of premises, Γ, produces a set, Γ ∪ P, that entails an absurdity, ⊥, then P must be denied provided all the premises in Γ continue to be affirmed. That is, any opposite of P must be affirmed provided all the sentences in Γ continue to be affirmed.

However, in order to avoid begging any questions about the affinity between what is intuitively derivable and what is entailed according to SL semantics, the rule needs to be stated in terms of what is derivable, rather than what is entailed.

$$\boxed{\text{(IP): If } L,P \vdash \bot, \text{ then } L \vdash P\text{-opposite.}}$$

In this statement, the derivability symbol ($\vdash$) replaces the entailment symbol ($\vDash$), the list symbol, L, replaces the set symbol, Γ, and L,P designates a list supplemented by the sentence, P, replacing $\Gamma \cup P$, which represents a set to which P has been added. The reason for talking about lists rather than sets, which will happen from now on, is given shortly.

The idea is the same notwithstanding the revised terminology. L is a possibly empty list of premises. L,P represents the result of supplementing L with the assumption of P. (IP) states that if adding assumption P to L makes it possible to derive $\bot$, then if the premises on list L are asserted, P must be denied. Denying P is the equivalent of asserting P-opposite.

Though the idea is the same, this is more than a merely notational alteration. What is derivable is cashed out in terms of what can be done using the derivation rules, not in terms of how values are assigned to sentences.

As presented in chapter 5, conditional proof is based on the intuitively compelling reasoning that if supposition, P, yields a sentence, Q, then having P means having Q. As a detail, if P is supposed subsequently to making other suppositions, and Q is derivable as a result, then provided those prior assumptions continue to be accepted, having P means having Q. This gives the following form to the rule of conditional proof, (CP), in D_L. (Those wondering what the corresponding entailment would look like can consult exercise 5.12(e).)

$$\boxed{\text{(CP): If } L,P \vdash Q, \text{ then } L \vdash P \rightarrow Q.}$$

The rule says that if adding an assumption, P, to a (possibly empty) list, L, of premises makes it possible to derive a further (not necessarily distinct) sentence, Q, then $P \rightarrow Q$ is derivable from the premises on L alone (or derivable from nothing if L is the empty list).

In chapter 5, when a claim was supposed for purposes of indirect proof or conditional proof subsequent work was indented under that supposition up to the point where a contradiction or the intended consequent was derived. The subsequent inference drawn by indirect proof or conditional proof was then outdented from the prior line of proof. Indenting and outdenting served to distinguish what follows only under the supposition from what follows independently of that supposition. D_L employs the same convention, using large brackets, called assumption brackets, to make the indents and outdents explicit. When an assumption is made for purposes of indirect proof or conditional proof, D_L inserts an assumption bracket. The idea is to bracket off the assumption, and everything that follows from it, from the main line of derivation. The assumption is written on the first line of the assumption bracket, above a horizontal line. (The horizontal line helps to highlight the assumption for later reference.) The assumption bracket continues down to the point where P-opposite or $P \rightarrow Q$ is inferred. Those inferences are outdented. Once they are outdented, no further appeal can be made to the sentences contained within the assumption bracket. The bracketed off sentences only serve to establish [P-opposite] or $P \rightarrow Q$. They may not be used for other purposes.

D_L uses a further notation to designate assumptions. Assumptions made for purposes of indirect proof are notated as (A/IP) and assumptions made for purposes of conditional proof are notated as (A/CP). (A/IP) and (A/CP) are not independent rules. They are part of what is involved in an application of (IP) and (CP), respectively.

This gives the following forms to the rules of indirect proof and conditional proof.

(IP)			(CP)		
	(L)			(L)	
...	...		...	...	
i.	P	(A/IP)	*i.*	P	(A/CP)
...	...		...	...	
k.	$\bot$	lemma for (IP)	*k.*	Q	lemma for (CP)
...	...		...	...	
...	...		...	...	
n.	P–opposite	*i–k* (IP)	*n.*	$P \rightarrow Q$	*i–k* (CP)

(L) is used to indicate that there may be prior premises or prior assumptions. Whether there are or not, they play no role in the application of the rule. (L) only serves to indicate where they would be located. Line i represents L,P, the addition of assumption P to premise list L. The indentation of the assumption and its consequences is made explicit by inserting an assumption bracket. Line k represents the claim that L,P $\vdash \perp$, in the case of (IP), or that L,P $\vdash$ Q, in the case of (CP). Line n represents the consequence that L $\vdash$ P-opposite, or that L $\vdash$ P $\rightarrow$ Q, by outdenting P-opposite or P $\rightarrow$ Q from the assumption bracket. The assumption bracket marks the boundaries of a subsidiary derivation, called a subderivation. As was the case in chapter 5, P-opposite and P $\rightarrow$ Q are derived from the whole subderivation. P-opposite is not derived from $\perp$. It is derived from a subderivation (headed off by the assumption of P) that derives $\perp$ immediately to the right of its assumption bracket. Similarly, P $\rightarrow$ Q is not derived from Q. It is derived from a subderivation (headed off by the assumption of P) that derives Q immediately to the right of its assumption bracket. The justifications at line n are accordingly not k, but i–k, citing the entire subderivation that runs from lines i to k.

Deriving P-opposite requires first deriving $\perp$ inside the assumption bracket, and deriving P $\rightarrow$ Q requires first deriving Q within the assumption bracket. Neither (IP) nor (CP) says how that happens. This is why $\perp$ and Q are designated as lemmas in the justification columns. Recall that a lemma is a claim that needs to be justified but that has not yet been justified. It represents a promise to pay off a debt. In this case the promise is to go on to derive the lemma. (IP) and (CP) only say what follows if $\perp$ and Q can be derived. Deriving them is a task for other rule applications.

While (IP) and (CP) formalize intuitively compelling forms of reasoning, their associated assumptions, (A/IP) and (A/CP), can seem counterintuitive. They create an assumption bracket and allow a sentence to be inserted at the head of that assumption bracket. This might seem suspicious. How can it be right to just insert a sentence into a derivation? What if the sentence is deniable?

This is an issue that has come up before, when conditional proof was first introduced in chapter 5.3, and again when discussing the use of conditional proof to justify inductions in chapter A-1.1. The point that was made on those occasions bears repeating. It is not permitted to simply insert a sentence into a derivation. But (A/IP) and (A/CP) allow no such thing. They only allow sentences to be assumed for purposes of indirect proof or conditional proof. The deniability of the assumption is not an issue in either case. When assuming P for indirect proof, the whole point is to prove that P yields $\perp$ and so must be denied. When assuming P for purposes of conditional proof, the point is only to establish that P suffices for Q, not to assert that P is the case. Intuitively, a good way to establish that P suffices for Q is to show that if P is assumed, Q must be accepted (that is, Q is derivable under the assumption of P). This only establishes that P suffices for Q, formalized as P $\rightarrow$ Q, and P $\rightarrow$ Q is all that (CP) derives. It does not derive P or anything else. This is clear from the fact that only P $\rightarrow$ Q is derived from the subderivation, not P. Once the assumption bracket terminates with the derivation of P $\rightarrow$ Q, no sentence lying within that bracket may be used to derive any further sentence.

D_L allows multiple assumptions to be added to the end of a list. When assumption brackets are used, each new assumption must have its own assumption bracket. Because each further assumption is part of a commitment to apply either (IP) or (CP), most recent (rightmost) assumption brackets must achieve that purpose (they must be terminated or "closed" by an application of (IP) or (CP)) before work under earlier assumptions can continue. Importantly, only one assumption bracket, the rightmost one, can be closed by any one application of (IP) or (CP), and it must be by an application of (IP) for an assumption made for purposes of (IP), and by (CP) for (A/CP). There is an intuitive reason for this restriction, explained in the solutions to exercise 6.1#1k and l and related exercises below.

These features of D_L explain why the list symbol, L, replaces the set symbol, Γ in almost all contexts. In D_L it matters in what order assumptions are made, because the project associated with the most recent assumption must be completed before continuing with the project of prior assumptions. The rules therefore presuppose that earlier assumptions have been listed in the order in which they were made.

The forms depicted above are templates that can be used to determine whether (IP) and (CP) have been applied correctly. No deviation from the templates is permitted. This means:

> Guidelines for Conforming to a Template
>
> - a sentence that replaces P at one location in the template must replace P at each other location where P occurs on the template, and likewise for Q
> - the sentence put in the place of P must occur in the same location relative to connectives (in this case, $\sim$ and $\rightarrow$) that P occurs in on the template, and likewise for the sentence that replaces Q

- assumption brackets must appear as they appear on the template, except that other assumption brackets may lie to the left of, above, or below the ones depicted
- the sentence put in the place of P must occur in the same location relative to these assumption brackets that P occurs in on the template, and likewise for Q
- where ⋯ appears, 0 or more lines with other sentences on them may intervene

Because P, Q, *i*, and *k* are variables, and a variable can stand for any of the things that vary underneath it, it is possible that:

- P and Q could be same sentence, and either could be ⊥
- *i* and *k* could be the same line, and (because L could be empty) *i* could be line 1

Exercise 6.1

1. *State whether each of the following is an instance of (IP). If it is not, say why not.*

★a.
i. | A   (A/IP)
⋯
k. | ⊥   lemma
n. ~A   *i–k* (IP)

b.
i. | ~B   (A/IP)
⋯
k. | ⊥   lemma
n. ~~B   *i–k* (IP)

★c.
i. | ~C   (A/IP)
⋯
k. | ⊥   lemma
n. C   *i–k* (IP)

d.
i. | ~A → B   (A/IP)
⋯
k. | ⊥   lemma
n. A → B   *i–k* (IP)

★e.
i. | A → B   (A/IP)
⋯
k. | ⊥   lemma
n. ~A → B   *i–k* (IP)

f.
i. | A   (A/IP)
⋯
k. | ~A   lemma
n. ⊥   *i–k* (IP)

★g.
i. | ⊥   (A/IP)
⋯
k. | ~⊥   lemma
n. ~⊥   *i–k* (IP)

h.
k. | ⊥   (A/IP)
n ~⊥   *k–k* (IP)
careful!
see comment on 2c
below

★i.
| A
i. | ~B → C   (A/IP)
⋯
k. | ⊥   lemma
n. | ~(~B → C)   *i–k* (IP)

j.
i. | A   (A/IP)
⋯
k. | ⊥   lemma
n. | ~A   *i–k* (IP)

★k.
| A
i. | ~B → C   (A/IP)
⋯
k. | ⊥   lemma
n. ~(~B → C)   *i–k* (IP)
pay careful attention to the explanations
for this answer and the next one

★l.
i. | A   (A/IP)
⋯
⋯
k. | ⊥   lemma
n. ~A   *i–k* (IP)

*m.

```
       ┌ ┌ A
   i.  │ │ ~B → C        (A/IP)
  ...  │ │ ...
   k.  │ │ ⊥              lemma
   n.  │ ~(~B → C)       i–k (IP)
```

n.
```
   i.  ┌ ┌ A          ?
  ...  │ │ ...
   k.  │ │ ⊥           lemma
   n.  │ ~A           i–k (IP)
```

2. *State what follows from each of the following by (IP). If nothing follows say why not. If more than one thing follows state each one. Also state which assumption bracket it follows under. Do this by naming the assumption that heads off the assumption bracket. If the consequence follows under more than one assumption bracket, name each of them.*

*a.
```
┌ A
│ ┌ B
│ │ ┌ ~C
│ │ │ ...
│ │ │ ⊥
```

b.
```
┌ A
│ ┌ B
│ │ ┌ ~C
│ │ │ ...
│ │ ⊥
```

*c.
```
┌ A
│ ┌ ⊥
```

d.
```
┌ A
│ ┌ ~B
│ │ ...
│ │ C
│ │ ...
│ │ ⊥
```

*e.
```
┌ A
│ ...
│ ┌ B
│ │ ...
│ │ ⊥
```

f.
```
┌ A
│ ┌ B
│ │ ...
│ │ ⊥
│ │ C
```

3. *State whether each of the following is an instance of (CP). If it is not, say why not.*

*a.
```
   i.  ┌ ┌ B         (A/CP)
  ...  │ │ ...
   k.  │ │ A          lemma for (CP)
   n.  │ B → A       i–k (CP)
```

b.
```
   i.  ┌ ┌ B         (A/CP)
  ...  │ │ ...
   k.  │ │ A          lemma for (CP)
   n.  │ A → B       i–k (CP)
```

*c.
```
   i.  ┌ ┌ C         (A/CP)
  ...  │ │ ...
   k.  │ │ ~A         lemma for (CP)
   n.  │ C → ~A      i–k (CP)
```

d.
```
   i.  ┌ A           (A/CP)
  ...  │ ...
   k.  │ C            lemma for (CP)
   n.  │ A → C       i–k (CP)
```

*e.
```
       ┌ A          ?
  ...  │ ...
   i.  │ ┌ C → A      (A/CP)
  ...  │ │ ...
   k.  │ │ G          lemma for (CP)
   n.  │ A → G       i–k (CP)
```

f.
```
       ┌ ┌ A          ?
  ...  │ │ ...
   i.  │ │ ┌ B        (A/CP)
  ...  │ │ │ ...
   k.  │ │ │ C        lemma for (CP)
   n.  │ B → C       i–k (CP)
```

*g.
```
   k.  ┌ ┌ A          (A/CP)
   n.  │ A → A       k–k (CP)
```

h.
```
       ┌ A
  ...  │ ...
   i.  │ ┌ B          (A/CP)
  ...  │ │ ...
   k.  │ │ C          lemma for (CP)
   n.  │ B → A       i–k (CP)
```

*i.

i.	A	(A/CP)
...	...	
k.	⊥	lemma for (CP)
n.	A → ⊥	*i–k* (CP)

*j.

	A	
...	...	
i.	B	(A/CP)
	...	
	C	
...	...	
k.	G	lemma for (CP)
n.	B → G	*i–k* (CP)

4. State what follows from each of the following by (CP), providing line numbers and justifications. If nothing follows say why not. If more than one thing follows state each one. Also state which assumption bracket it follows under. Do this by naming the assumption that heads off the assumption bracket. If the consequence follows under more than one assumption bracket, name each of them.

*a.
1. A
2. B
3. C
4. G
...
k. H

b.
1. A
2. B
3. C
4. G
...
k. H

*c.
1. A
2. B
3. C
4. G
...
k. H

d.
1. A
2. B
...
k. C
...
n. G

*e.
1. A
2. B
3. C
...
B
k. C → B

f.
1. A
2. B
...
k. ~B

5. State what would have to be assumed, and what would have to be entered as a lemma under that assumption for each of the following sentences to be derived by (CP). Display how each of these items (assumption, lemma, resultant conditional) would have to be placed relative to assumption brackets and how each of them would be justified. Designate line numbers with letters i, k, n and lines that need not be immediately successive with an intervening line containing three dots.

*a. ~A → A
b. (A → B) → C
*c. A → ~(B → C)
d. (A → B) → (B → A)
*e. ~[(A → B) → C] *(trick question)*
f. A → (B → C) *(take it to the second level)*

The remaining rules of D_L, (⊥I), (MP), and (R), draw intuitively obvious consequences from previously given sentences (premises or assumptions) or previously derived sentences. According to (⊥I), if P and ~P have both been derived, then ⊥ is derivable.

> (⊥I): If L ⊢ P and L ⊢ ~P, then L ⊢ ⊥

Little needs to be said about the intuition behind this inference. ⊥ stands for whatever is absurd, and it is absurd to simultaneously assert and deny the same thing, so ⊥ is derivable from the combination of P and ~P. (A corresponding entailment follows from exercise 5.12c.)

According to (MP), if P and P → Q have both been derived, then Q is derivable.

> (MP): If L ⊢ P and L ⊢ P → Q, then L ⊢ Q

The intuitive basis for (MP) is given by the meaning of P → Q as "P is sufficient for Q" / "Q is necessary for P" or as illustrated by the circle diagram presented earlier. P → Q says that P is sufficient for Q, or, alternatively, that Q is necessary for P. So, if P is the case, and it is further the case that P suffices for Q, it can be inferred that Q is the case (if a point is in the P circle and being in the P circle suffices for being in the Q circle, that point must be in the Q circle). Again, if P is the case, and it is further the case that Q is necessary for P, it can be inferred that Q must also be the case (if a point is in the P circle and being in the Q circle is necessary for being in the P circle that point must be in the Q circle). A corresponding entailment was demonstrated in exercise 5.12f.

The inference only goes in the direction the arrow is pointing, from the antecedent of the conditional to its consequent. If Q is the case, and it is further the case that Q is necessary for P, P can still fail to be the case, because Q may not be all that is necessary for P (a point can be in the Q circle without being in the P circle). Again, if Q is the case, and it is further the case that P suffices for Q, P can still fail to be the case because other things could suffice for Q, and Q may be the case in virtue of one of those other things (just because a point is not in the P circle, it does not follow it is not somewhere else in the Q circle). Either way, <Q, P → Q> does not yield P.

The rules have the following templates.

	(⊥I)			(MP)	
	(L)			(L)	
...	...		...	...	
k.	P	?	*k.*	P	?
...	...		...	...	
k★.	~P	?	*k★.*	P → Q	?
...	...		...	...	
n.	⊥	*k,k★* (⊥I)	*n.*	Q	*k,k★* (MP)

The templates depicted above are overdetermined in one respect. Line numbers *k* and *k★*, along with the sentences on them, may occur in either order. Whichever occurs first, the sentence on line *k* (P) is cited first in the justification.

The dashed line depicted above also does not appear in instances of the templates. It is inserted in the templates to distinguish what must be the case before the rule can be applied from what follows in accord with the rule. The sentences at lines *k* and *k★* have question marks in their justification columns because (⊥I) and (MP) do not say how these sentences come to be there. They only say what follows once they are. The other sentences must already have been given or derived somehow.

All sentences involved in an application of (⊥I) or (MP) must lie alongside the same assumption bracket. Other brackets may lie to the left of that bracket, but neither they nor any sentences they contain are involved in the rule application.

Exercise 6.2

1. *State whether each of the following is an instance of (⊥I). If it is not, say why not.*

★a.	*i.*	A → B		b.	*i.*	~(A → B)		★c.	*i.*	A		
	...	...			...				...		...
	k.	~A → B			*k.*	A → B			*k.*		~A
	...	...			...				...		...
	n.	⊥ *i,k* (⊥I)			*n.*	⊥ *k,i* (⊥I)			*n.*		⊥ *i,k* (⊥I)

d.
```
i. | A   |
.. |     | ...
k. |     | ~A
.. |     | ...
n. | ⊥         i,k (⊥I)
```

*e.
```
   | A   |
   |     | ...
i. |     | B
   |     | ...
k. |     | ~B
n. | ⊥         i,k (⊥I)
```

f.
```
i. | ~C
.. | ...
k. | ~~C
.. | ...
n. | ⊥     i,k (⊥I)
```

2. *State whether each of the following is an instance of* (MP). *If it is not, say why not.*

*a.
```
k. | A → B
.. | ...
n. | A        k (MP)
```

b.
```
i. | C → B
.. | ...
k. | C
.. | ...
n. | B        i,k (MP)
```

*c.
```
i. | C → B
.. | ...
k. | C
.. | ...
n. | B        k,i (MP)
```

d.
```
i. | C → B
.. | ...
k. | B
.. | ...
n. | C        k,i (MP)
```

*e.
```
i. | B
.. | ...
k. | ~(B → C)
.. | ...
n. | C        i,k (MP)
```

f.
```
i. | ~B
.. | ...
k. | ~(B → C)
.. | ...
n. | ~C       i,k (MP)
```

*g.
```
i. | B
.. | ...
k. | A → (B → C)
.. | ...
n. | C        i,k (MP)
```

h.
```
k. | A → B
.. | ...
n. | B        k (MP)
```

*i.
```
i. | A → B  |
.. |        | ...
k. |        | A
.. |        | ...
n. |        | B    k,i (MP)
```

j.
```
i. |   | A
   |   | ...
k. |   | A → B
n. | B        i,k (MP)
```

*k.
```
i. | A → B
.. | ...
k. | B            i,n (MP)
.. | ...
n. | A
```

As noted, applications of (⊥I) and (MP) require that all sentences involved lie alongside the same assumption bracket. The remaining rule, (R), facilitates the application of (⊥I) and (MP) by specifying when a sentence may be repeated (or "reiterated") alongside another assumption bracket.

(R) is based on the intuition that adding further information does nothing to detract from what is derivable from less information. If L yields P, whatever reasons there were for deriving P from L continue to be in effect when L is supplemented by the addition of Q_1, Q_2, etc. More abstractly expressed, if P has been derived from a list, L, and one or more assumptions are subsequently added to the end of that list, making an expanded list, L,M, then P must be derivable from L,M as well. (The corresponding entailment is found in exercise 5.12(b).)

> (R): If L ⊢ P then L,M ⊢ P

If this seems counterintuitive, it is because the counterexamples come from the field of inductive logic. Many inductive inferences are only made likely by a survey of past cases. That likelihood can be diminished or overturned in the light of new information. In deductive logic, conclusions are derived from premises on pain of contradiction. The discovery of further information can do nothing to change the fact that affirming the previous information while denying the conclusion leads to a contradiction. The most new information can do is contradict some of the previous information, raising the question of whether that previous information should be denied or retracted. (R) applies to a circumstance where the later information, M, is added to L without any retraction of what is on L.

Adding an assumption to a list is the equivalent of starting an assumption bracket inside of an assumption bracket. Accordingly, (R) allows reiterating sentences from outer assumption brackets to inner ones, that is, from derivations into their subderivations. It does not allow reiterating from inner (contained) assumption brackets to outer (containing) ones. That would be the equivalent of supposing that if a longer list of assumptions yields P, a shorter list must still yield P. That is intuitively unacceptable. What follows from more information need not follow from less.

The template for (R) presented below imposes two further restrictions on reiterations.

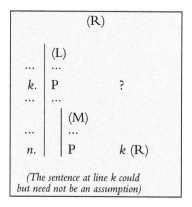

Exercise

What else does the template depicted above require in addition to requiring that the assumption bracket containing P *at line k contain the assumption bracket containing* P *at line n?*

The template prohibits reiterating sentences within the same assumption bracket. It further prohibits reiterating more than one step in. This is visually apparent on the template, which depicts P being reiterated alongside the next assumption bracket to the right. The two assumption brackets are depicted as lying immediately alongside one another, which means that no others can come in between. And the left assumption bracket is depicted as continuing down to line *n*, which means the right assumption bracket must be inside it. Were the right bracket not inside the left one, but below it, or left of it, or on top of it, reiteration would also be impermissible.

The additional restrictions on reiteration are motivated by two considerations. First, reiteration is only needed to facilitate ($\perp$I) and (MP). Since ($\perp$I) and (MP) place no restrictions on the order of the sentences at lines *k* and *k*★, or on their distance above the sentence derived from them, there is no call to reiterate sentences within the same subderivation. Second, once sentences have been reiterated into the next assumption bracket in, there is nothing to prevent them from being reiterated into the next assumption bracket in from there. Just as (R) allows that if L ⊢ P then L,M ⊢ P so it allows that if L,M ⊢ P then L,M,L′ ⊢ P. Direct reiteration from L ⊢ P to L,M,L′ ⊢ P could be allowed. But the possibility of continually reiterating into the next subderivation is a feature of D_L. More advanced derivation systems place roadblocks to reiteration. "One step at a time" reiterations are instituted now, in D_L, to develop a cautious approach needed when working in more advanced systems. Those who do not plan to study the derivation system of section 8.3 may allow reiteration directly into a subderivation that lies two or more brackets to the inside, provided the assumption bracket at line *k* continues unbroken down to line *n*. Solutions to exercises abide by the more restrictive version of (R).

Exercise 6.3

State whether each of the following is (strictly!) an instance of (R). If it is not, say why not.

*a. k. | A
   ... | ...
   n. | A   k (R)

b. k. | B
   ... | ...
   ... | | ...
   n. | | ∼∼B   k (R)

*c. k. | C
   ... | ...
   ... | | ...
   ... | | | ...
   n. | | | C   k (R)

d. ... | | ...
   k. | | G
   ... | | ...
       | ...
   n. | G   k (R)

*e. ... | | ...
   k. | | H
   ... | | ...
       | | A
   ... | | ...
   n. | | H   k (R)

f. k. | K
   ... | ...
       | | A
   ... | | ...
       | | B
   ... | | ...
   n. | | K   k (R)

Now that the rules of D_L have been introduced, something can be said about how they may be used to establish other, less intuitively obvious results. The main idea is to apply the rules in sequence to given sentences of SL to show that those sentences yield other sentences by means of a chain of intuitively obvious, intermediate steps.

> A *derivation in* D_L is a list of sentences of "lean" SL, each of which is either given to start with or entered on the list in accord with a rule of D_L.
>
> A *sentence*, P, is *derivable in* D_L from a (possibly empty) list of sentences, L, (alternatively expressed, L *yields* P) if and only if there is a derivation in D_L that yields the "lean" equivalent of P immediately to the right of an assumption bracket headed off by all and only the "lean" equivalents of the sentences on L. Notation: L ⊢ P
>
> A sentence, P, is a *theorem* of D_L if and only if the empty list yields the "lean" equivalent of P. Notation: ⊢ P
>
> A *sentence*, P, is *inconsistent* in D_L if and only if the "lean" equivalent of P yields ⊥. Notation: P ⊢ ⊥
>
> Two sentences, P and Q, are *interderivable* in D_L if and only if <P> ⊢ Q and <Q> ⊢ P. Notation P ⊣⊢ Q
>
> A *set*, Γ, is *inconsistent* in D_L if and only if ⊥ is derivable in D_L from a finite list, L, of the sentences in Γ. Notation: L ⊢ ⊥
>
> A *demonstration*, Γ / P, has a conclusion that is *derivable* in D_L from its premises if and only if P is derivable in D_L from a finite list, L, of the premises in Γ. Notation: L ⊢ P

Remark 1: The definitions speak of the "lean" equivalents of sentences of SL rather than of sentences of SL because D_L only works with atomic sentences, negations, and conditionals. Sentences containing ampersands, wedges, or triple bars are rewritten as s-equivalent sentences containing only ⊥, ∼, →, sentence letters, and punctuation marks. These s-equivalent sentences are called "lean" equivalents. "Lean" is put in quotes because strictly, the lean language for SL does not contain negations, either. (See the appendix to chapter 3, where the lean language is introduced.) The definitions of interderivability and of the inconsistency and derivability of sets and demonstrations do not require further qualification because they are stated in terms of derivability.

Remark 2: When a conclusion is derived from a nonempty list of premises, the derivation begins by putting a finite subset of the premises on that list on successive lines at the head of a single assumption bracket. The premises are notated as "given." Not all the premises need to be listed. But in the case where Γ is finite, leaving some out risks making the conclusion underivable. Most exercises do not include redundant or unnecessary premises, so it is wise to list them all.

The reference to a finite list acknowledges that conclusions are not derived from infinite premise lists. Sentences are entered in derivations by means of a successive series of rule applications. If a derivation continues forever without ever arriving at a conclusion, that conclusion has not been derived. To be derived it must be derived after some finite number of rule applications. Since no rule is justified by an infinite list, only finitely many premises can figure in the rule applications, so only they need to appear at the head of the derivation. There is no need to worry that this might mean that there are some s-valid demonstrations that are underivable because it was demonstrated in section A-1.4 that SL is compact: any s-unsatisfiable set must have at least one s-unsatisfiable subset. In particular, the corresponding set to any s-valid demonstration with infinitely many premises must have an s-unsatisfiable finite subset. (See chapters 1.3 and 5.5 for a discussion of corresponding sets.)

Remark 3: The derivational concepts defined above correspond only to the "no interpretation" cases of SL semantics (s-validity, s-unsatisfiability, s-equivalence). There is a way to use D_L to establish that demonstrations are underivable, that sets are consistent, that pairs of sentences are not interderivable, and that sentences are neither theorems nor inconsistent. It is discussed in section 6.5.

A → B is derivable from the list, <~B → ~C, A → C>. (This claim is notated as ~B → ~C, A → C ⊢ A → B. As with braces around unit sets before ⊨, angle brackets before ⊢ may be omitted.) According to the definition of derivability, this means that there must be a derivation using the five rules of D_L that yields A → B immediately to the right of an assumption bracket headed off by the sentences on this list. The derivation must therefore begin and end like this:

1.	~B → ~C	given
2.	A → C	given
...	...	
20.	A → B	?

There is nothing sacrosanct about line numbers. There is no telling in advance how many lines a derivation will take up, and there is no point to having an accurate count. It is important, however, to give a bottom to the derivation, and to put a last number and the conclusion on this last line. This serves as a guide to how to proceed with the derivation.

The remainder of the derivation proceeds both from the top down and from the bottom up. There are three derivation rules that work from the top down: (R), (MP), and (⊥I). In the case at hand, none is applicable. There are two derivation rules that work from the bottom up, (IP) and (CP). Both are applicable. Applying (IP) would mean entering ~(A → B) at the head of an assumption bracket entered at line 3 and entering ⊥ at the bottom of this assumption bracket at line 19. Applying (CP) would mean entering A at the head of an assumption bracket entered at line 3 and entering B at the bottom of this assumption bracket at line 19. When it is possible to apply (CP), it should be preferred to (IP).

1.	~B → ~C	given
2.	A → C	given
3.	**A**	**(A/CP)**
...	...	
19.	**B**	**lemma for (CP)**
20.	A → B	**3–19 (CP)**

Once (CP) has been applied, no further attention needs to be paid to A → B at line 20. The question mark beside it is removed and replaced with a justification. It is ghosted to show that it has become unimportant. (This is not an appearance that needs to be replicated in exercise submissions.) It is no longer the conclusion that the derivation aims to justify. The job of the derivation has shifted to justifying the lemma for (CP) that was introduced on line 19.

Doing a derivation is like starting up a business. It is necessary to take out a loan to cover the expenditures that must be made before the business generates income. The loan is the assumption. The debt to be paid off is the associated lemma. Taking out the loan purchases the conclusion, which is no longer an item of concern. The concern shifts to paying off the debt.

There are many derivations that cannot be completed without taking out multiple loans. This requires keeping a record of which debts need to be paid off and in what order they come due. That record is given by the bottom half of the derivation.

The greatest difficulty encountered by those doing derivations for the first time is knowing what to assume. It seems like anything can be assumed and too much choice makes it hard to choose. But this is a false appearance. In D_L there are at most two answers to the question of what to assume and often only one: either assume the antecedent of the sentence that needs to be derived (supposing the sentence that needs to be derived is a conditional) or assume an opposite of the sentence that needs to be derived. It is, however, impossible to identify what the antecedent or an opposite is without looking down at the bottom of the derivation to see what sentence currently needs to be derived. Since each new assumption pays off a loan and creates a new debt, the sentence that needs to be derived changes with each new assumption. Identifying it requires working from the bottom up.

The greatest obstacle to finding derivations is neglecting to enter a lemma on the last line of each new assumption bracket. It is necessary to associate each assumption with a lemma that needs to be derived under that assumption. An assumption is not a further premise for deriving the conclusion. It is a premise for deriving the new lemma under that assumption. The addition of the subderivation headed off by the assumption and concluding with the lemma solves the problem of how to derive the conclusion, but it incurs a debt to derive the lemma. That debt must be discharged. This requires entering the lemma and considering how to derive it. This is not extra work. It is essential work that achieves the original project, but at the cost of setting a new (easier) project.

In the case at hand, the project is now to derive B at line 19. The addition of the assumption at line 3 has made it possible to do a significant amount of work from the top of the derivation down. It is not worth fretting over how much of that work needs to be done and how much can be avoided. The rules that work from the top down, (R), (MP), and ($\perp$I), are all finite. They either move sentences down from containing brackets to contained brackets – and there are only ever finitely many sentences to be moved down through finitely many brackets – or they derive shorter sentences from longer ones – which can only be done finitely many times before only atoms or inapplicable sentences are left. Unless it is clear what needs to be done to complete the derivation, the task of applying each of (R), (MP), and ($\perp$I) to exhaustion is not only feasible but advisable. A dentist or a surgeon lays out all their instruments before getting to work. Exhaustively applying top-down rules is like that. It brings out all the sentences that might be of use. It is optimal to do this by making each possible application of (R), followed by each of (MP), followed by each of ($\perp$I). In the case at hand, the task is to derive B which is located inside the assumption bracket that starts at line 3. That means moving all the reiterable sentences into the new assumption bracket, and making all possible (MP) and ($\perp$I) applications to reveal what further sentences might be available for use, and repeating these procedures to exhaustion.

1.	~B → ~C	given
2.	A → C	given
3.	A	(A/CP)
4.	**~B → ~C**	**1 (R)**
5.	**A → C**	**2 (R)**
6.	**C**	**3,5 (MP)**
...	...	
19.	B	lemma for (CP)
20.	A → B	3–19 (CP)

At this point there is no more work that can be done from the top down. Work must therefore proceed from the bottom up. There are only two bottom-up rules, (IP) and (CP), and (CP) does not apply to B. Moreover, B only has one opposite. So in this case there is only one way to proceed: derive B at line 19 by entering a new assumption bracket at line 7 headed off by B's one opposite, ~B, and enter $\perp$ as a lemma at line 18.

1.	~B → ~C	given
2.	A → C	given
3.	A	(A/CP)
4.	~B → ~C	1 (R)
5.	A → C	2 (R)
6.	C	3,5 (MP)
7.	**~B**	**(A/IP)**
...	...	
18.	**⊥**	**lemma for (IP)**
19.	B	lemma for (CP) **7–18 (IP)**
20.	A → B	3–19 (CP)

Once (IP) has been applied to provisionally derive B at line 19, it ceases to be a lemma. The debt incurred by making the assumption at line 3 has been paid off (in this case by taking out a new loan). The debt is discharged by replacing the claim that the sentence derived at line 19 is a lemma with a justification, and it is ghosted (because it has been derived and is no longer a concern). The project of the derivation shifts to deriving the new lemma at line 18.

The addition of the further assumption at line 7 has once again created work that can be done from the top down. And again, there is no need to fuss over what needs to be done and what can be avoided. There is so little of it that time spent mulling over what to do next generally outlasts the time it takes to do everything.

1.	~B → ~C	given
2.	A → C	given
3.	A	(A/CP)
4.	~B → ~C	1 (R)
5.	A → C	2 (R)
6.	C	3,5 (MP)
7.	~B	(A/IP)
8.	**A**	**3 (R)**
9.	**~B → ~C**	**4 (R)**
10.	**A → C**	**5 (R)**
11.	**C**	**6 (R)**
12.	**~C**	**7,9 (MP)**
...	...	
18.	⊥	lemma for (IP) **11,12 (⊥I)**
19.	B	lemma for (CP) 7–18 (IP)
20.	A → B	3–19 (CP)

A solution to the question of how to derive ⊥ on line 18 has emerged without really thinking about it. Just making all possible top-down rule applications uncovers a way to justify the lemma. Upon inspection, it turns out that the sentences on lines 8 and 10 were unnecessary. But they do not detract from the derivation and it took almost no time to enter them. Of course, if observation or practice shows that there is no need to derive a sentence, it may be omitted. But when the way to derive the lemma is unclear, it generally saves time to do everything.

A derivation will typically have a large gap between the work done from the top down and the work done from the bottom up, and it will have interrupted line numbers or sentences that have been squeezed in between other sentences on decimal or alpha expansions on line numbers. Line numbers are not used for purposes of mathematical calculation but only as an index to enable the reader to easily ascertain what justifies entering a sentence on a line.

> General Note to Section 6.1: Understanding vs. Applying a Rule
>
> This section has justified the derivation rules by appeal to intuition. It has incidentally shown how the rules are applied. Grasping the intuition behind a rule and applying that rule are two different things. It is possible to get the intuition behind a rule but still misapply it. It is also possible to reliably apply a rule with no understanding. Computers apply rules reliably with no understanding. Applying a rule is a matter of following a template. The rules presented in this section all have templates. The templates contain variables and constants. The variable parts stand for what can vary. The constant parts stand for what must be there just as it is depicted. In the templates given in this section, the constant parts are the assumption brackets, the connectives, and the rule names. The metavariables identify the locations where sentences must be repeated: the same sentence for each occurrence of the same metavariable. The other variable parts are the number of lines each ⋯ takes up, the number of assumption brackets to the left of, above, or below (not between!) the ones depicted, the line number variables, the question marks, and the contents of (L), if any.
>
> All the templates are collected in one place in the Appendix. They should be consulted while working on derivations. In addition to serving as guidelines for correct rule application, they can supply hints for what rules to apply next.
>
> A template is a kind of picture. It consists of elements placed at locations relative to one another in space. An instance of a rule application is another picture. It should consist of corresponding elements situated in the same way relative to one another. Determining whether a rule has been correctly applied is more a matter of perception than a matter of understanding. It requires lining the template and the instance up with one another and determining whether the one can be overlaid on the other.

Exercise 6.4

1. *Establish each of the following using* (MP).
   ⋆a. $B \rightarrow A, B \vdash A$
   b. $B, B \rightarrow (B \rightarrow A) \vdash A$
   ⋆c. $A, B \rightarrow C, A \rightarrow B \vdash C$
   d. $\sim(A \rightarrow B) \rightarrow (B \rightarrow A), \sim(A \rightarrow B) \vdash B \rightarrow A$
   ⋆e. $A \rightarrow B, A, B \rightarrow \perp \vdash \perp$
   f. $A \rightarrow \perp, \sim B \rightarrow A, \sim B \vdash \perp$
   g. $(A \rightarrow \perp) \rightarrow \sim C, (B \rightarrow \perp) \rightarrow (A \rightarrow \perp), B \rightarrow \perp, \sim C \rightarrow A \vdash \perp$

2. *Establish each of the following using* (MP) *and* (⊥I).
   ⋆a. $C, A \rightarrow B, C \rightarrow \sim B, A \vdash \perp$
   b. $\sim A, \sim C, \sim A \rightarrow \sim\sim B, \sim C \rightarrow \sim B \vdash \perp$
   ⋆c. $\sim B, A \rightarrow (\sim B \rightarrow \sim A), A \vdash \perp$
   d. $\sim C \rightarrow B, A \rightarrow \perp, (A \rightarrow \perp) \rightarrow \sim C, (A \rightarrow \perp) \rightarrow \sim B \vdash \perp$
   ⋆e. $\sim\sim\sim A, A, A \rightarrow (B \rightarrow \sim\sim A), A \rightarrow C, C \rightarrow B \vdash \perp$
   f. $\sim A \rightarrow [(C \rightarrow \perp) \rightarrow A], C \rightarrow \perp, (C \rightarrow \perp) \rightarrow \sim A \vdash \perp$

3. *Establish each of the following using* (A/CP) *to start,* (MP) *and* (⊥I) *to continue (as needed), and* (CP) *to finish. Use* (R) *as necessary to facilitate* (MP) *and* (⊥I). *Always assume the antecedent of the conditional sentence you are attempting to derive. Always enter the consequent of that conditional as a lemma under this assumption.*
   ⋆a. $A \rightarrow B, B \rightarrow C \vdash A \rightarrow C$ *(hypothetical syllogism)*
   b. $\sim A \vdash A \rightarrow \perp$
   ⋆c. $A \rightarrow (B \rightarrow C), B \vdash A \rightarrow C$
   d. $(A \rightarrow B) \rightarrow (B \rightarrow C), B \vdash (A \rightarrow B) \rightarrow C$
   ⋆e. $A \vdash (A \rightarrow B) \rightarrow B$
   f. $G \rightarrow (B \rightarrow C), G \vdash A \rightarrow (B \rightarrow C)$
   g. $B \vdash [\sim(G \rightarrow K) \rightarrow A] \rightarrow B$

4. *Establish each of the following using two applications of (A/CP). Consult the conditional sentences you are attempting to derive to determine what to assume and what to enter as a lemma under each assumption.*

    ⋆**a.** $A \rightarrow (B \rightarrow C) \vdash B \rightarrow (A \rightarrow C)$

    b. $\vdash A \rightarrow [(B \rightarrow \perp) \rightarrow A]$ *(when nothing appears to the left of the turnstile, the sentence to the right must be derived from nothing. (A/CP) and (A/IP) each make this possible.)*

    ⋆**c.** $\vdash A \rightarrow [(A \rightarrow \perp) \rightarrow \perp]$

    d. $A \rightarrow (B \rightarrow C) \vdash (A \rightarrow B) \rightarrow (A \rightarrow C)$

    ⋆**e.** $C \rightarrow G \vdash A \rightarrow [(A \rightarrow C) \rightarrow G]$

    f. $C \rightarrow \perp, B \rightarrow C \vdash (A \rightarrow \perp) \rightarrow (B \rightarrow \perp)$

5. *Establish each of the following using (A/IP) to start, (MP) and (⊥I) to continue (as needed), and (IP) to finish. Use (R) as necessary to facilitate (MP) and (⊥I). Always assume an opposite of the sentence you are attempting to derive and enter ⊥ as a lemma under this assumption.*

    ⋆**a.** $A -\!|\!- \sim\sim A$ *(i.e., establish both $A \vdash \sim\sim A$ and $\sim\sim A \vdash A$) (double negation introduction (DNI) and double negation elimination (DNE))*

    b. $\perp \vdash \sim\sim(G \rightarrow K)$

    ⋆**c.** $A \rightarrow B, \sim B \vdash \sim A$ *(modus tollens)*

    d. $A \rightarrow \perp -\!|\!- \sim A$ *(definition of ~)*

    ⋆**e.** $A, \sim B \vdash \sim(A \rightarrow B)$

    f. $A \rightarrow \sim C, A \rightarrow B, B \rightarrow C \vdash \sim A$

6. *Establish each of the following using (A/CP) followed by (A/IP). Consult the sentences you are attempting to derive to determine what to assume and what to enter as a lemma under each assumption.*

    ⋆**a.** $A \rightarrow \sim B \vdash B \rightarrow \sim A$

    b. $\sim A \vdash A \rightarrow B$

    ⋆**c.** $B \rightarrow \perp \vdash A \rightarrow \sim B$

    d. $A \rightarrow \perp \vdash A \rightarrow \sim B$

    ⋆**e.** $A \vdash (A \rightarrow \sim B) \rightarrow \sim(\sim B \rightarrow \sim A)$

    f. $A \rightarrow B, C \vdash A \rightarrow \sim(C \rightarrow \sim B)$

    g. $\vdash \perp \rightarrow A$

    h. $\vdash A \rightarrow \sim\perp$

6.2 Strategies for Doing Derivations in D_L

As so far presented, derivations in D_L proceed by alternating between "top-down" and "bottom-up" sets of rules. (R), (MP) and (⊥I), are applied to do whatever can be done from the top down. When that is exhausted, one of (CP) and (IP) is applied. That application adds a new assumption to the top of the derivation and sets a new lemma to be derived at the bottom. However, even when work cycles back and forth between these stages, there will be cases where the derivation cannot be completed unless further lemmas, based on bottom-up applications of (MP) and (⊥I), are identified and derived. Even (MP) and (⊥I), it turns out, are not purely "top-down" derivation rules. This makes D_L as much a "method of discovery" as it is a method of derivation.

Method of Discovery vs. Method of Demonstration

The English politician and philosopher, Francis Bacon (1561–1626), was no friend to the Aristotelian logic of his day. Writing at the time of a religious reformation antipathetic to the idolatry that was perceived to have infected the Roman Catholic Church, Bacon described the use of logic as the adoration of an idol. Logic, for Bacon, is a specifically theatrical idol. It does not teach us new things. It is not a "method of discovery." It is nothing more than a "method of demonstration" for things already learned by other means. And it is a particularly theatrical method. It serves the rhetorical purpose of dressing up merely purported knowledge in an imposing appearance of formal rigour, which serves more to intimidate the audience and conceal its weaknesses from their critical scrutiny than to reveal the foundations of its truth. Bacon attempted to provide a new logic of discovery that would replace the old, Aristotelian demonstrative logic.

> D_L is a method of discovery as well as a method of demonstration. It discovers lemmas and assumptions.

Considered as rules of discovery, (CP), (MP), ($\bot$I), and (IP) are each employed along with its own strategy. The strategies are "bottom-up" as opposed to "top-down" strategies. They work up from the conclusion and the lemmas. There is also a preliminary, "top-down" strategy.

> **Top-Down Strategy**
> Make all possible applications of (R), (MP), and ($\bot$I).
>
> **(CP) Strategy**
> When the aim is to derive a conditional, $P \rightarrow Q$, assume P and enter Q as a lemma for (CP) under this assumption.
>
> **(MP) Strategy**
> If the sentence that needs to be derived, Q, could be derived by (MP) but for the fact that the antecedent, P, needed to derive Q from $P \rightarrow Q$ is missing, enter P as a lemma for (MP) and attempt to derive it.
>
> **($\bot$I) Strategy**
> When $\bot$ cannot be derived by ($\bot$I), (MP), (R) or by the (MP) strategy, look up at the sentences that have so far been derived, enter the opposite of one of those sentences as a lemma for ($\bot$I), and attempt to derive it. The best choice is a lemma that is easily derivable. Otherwise pick a lemma that demands making further assumptions and entering other lemmas. (This is called a "pregnant" lemma.)
>
> **(IP) Strategy**
> When no other way of deriving a sentence, P, is obvious, assume P-opposite and enter $\bot$ as a lemma for (IP) under this assumption.

There is a preferred order for the application of these strategies.

> **Stage 1 (Top-Down)**
> Make all possible applications of (R) followed by all possible applications of (MP), followed by all possible applications of ($\bot$I). Proceed to stage 2.
>
> **Stage 2 (CP)**
> Apply the (CP) strategy once and return to stage 1. When a cycle through stages 1 and 2 has no effect, proceed to stage 3a.
>
> **Stage 3a (MP)**
> Apply the (MP) strategy once and return to stage 1. When a cycle through stages 1–3a has no effect, proceed to stage 3b.
>
> **Stage 3b ($\bot$I)**
> Apply the ($\bot$I) strategy once and return to stage 1. When a cycle through stages 1–3b has no effect, proceed to stage 4.
>
> **Stage 4 (IP)**
> Apply the (IP) strategy. Return to stage 1.

The (IP) strategy is the strategy of last resort. It is only to be used when all other strategies are inapplicable. Being the strategy of last resort also makes it the strategy of first resort in special cases. When running through the entire flow chart, including making terminal applications of the (IP) strategy, still fails to discover a way to complete the derivation, it can be necessary to scratch the entire effort and begin again, this time making the (IP) strategy the first strategy to be applied. The solution to exercise 6.8#3e includes a detailed discussion of such a case. That discussion is best postponed until after obtaining practice with easier derivations. In the meantime, it is worth noting that an early application of (IP) will never block a derivation. The worst it can do is add unnecessary lines.

As an illustration of an easier case, consider the derivation that establishes that $(\bot \rightarrow A) \rightarrow \bot \vdash B$.

Since derivations are best done from both the top down and the bottom up and it is not known in advance how many lines they will take up, they should begin by making an ample assumption bracket (20 lines or a page worth is not too many) headed off by the givens and ending with the conclusion.

$$
\begin{array}{lll}
1. & (\bot \rightarrow A) \rightarrow \bot & \text{given} \\
\ldots & \ldots & \\
20. & B & ?
\end{array}
$$

There are two main impediments to success at doing derivations. One is failure to follow the template for the rule, which produces derivations that break the rules. The other is reluctance to use large amounts of space. This makes it impossible to work from the bottom up, making the solution much more difficult to discover. The second impediment is often assisted by arrogance. There is nothing to be gained by fancying oneself smart enough to think it through from the top down without needing to use the paper to work it out from the bottom up.[1] Nor is it helpful in this context to value aesthetic order over problem solving techniques. These attitudes only waste time and increase frustration and mental fatigue. The extra paper more than pays for itself.

Once the framework has been laid out, the first step is to look for applications of (R), (MP), or ($\bot$I). In this case, there are none, so the second step is to cycle through the remaining strategies. The (CP) strategy does not apply because the conclusion is not a conditional. The (MP) strategy does not apply because the conclusion is not the consequent of a conditional. The ($\bot$I) strategy does not apply because the conclusion is not $\bot$. That leaves the strategy of last resort, the (IP) strategy, which dictates assuming the opposite and making $\bot$ a lemma under this assumption.

$$
\begin{array}{lll}
1. & (\bot \rightarrow A) \rightarrow \bot & \text{given} \\
2. & \quad \sim B & \text{(A/IP)} \\
\ldots & \quad \ldots & \\
\mathbf{19.} & \quad \bot & \textbf{lemma for (IP)} \\
20. & B & \textbf{2--19 (IP)}
\end{array}
$$

Applying the (IP) strategy offers a provisional solution to the question of how to derive the conclusion, meaning it can be ghosted in favour of focusing attention on how to derive the sentence on line 19. As a bonus, the (IP) strategy adds a further sentence to the top of the derivation to help with this new project.

Each time a strategy has been applied, go back to the beginning and ask the series of strategic questions again. Are there any possible applications of (R), (MP) or ($\bot$I)? There is one application of (R) possible.

$$
\begin{array}{lll}
1. & (\bot \rightarrow A) \rightarrow \bot & \text{given} \\
2. & \quad \sim B & \text{(A/IP)} \\
\mathbf{3.} & \quad (\bot \rightarrow A) \rightarrow \bot & \textbf{1 (R)} \\
\ldots & & \\
19. & \quad \bot & \text{lemma for (IP)} \\
20. & B & \text{2--19 (IP)}
\end{array}
$$

There are no possible applications of (MP) or ($\bot$I). (MP) requires a conditional and its antecedent, and while there is a conditional, its antecedent is missing. ($\bot$I) requires a sentence and its opposite, and while there is a negation, its opposite is missing.

Since nothing more can be done by top-down reasoning using (R), ($\bot$I), or (MP), the next step is to cycle through the remaining strategies. The (CP) strategy does not apply because the lemma that needs to be derived, $\bot$, is not a conditional. However, the (MP) strategy does apply because $\bot$ does occur as the consequent of the conditional sentence on line 3. According to the (MP) strategy, when the sentence that needs to be derived occurs as the consequent of a conditional but the antecedent is missing, the antecedent should be entered as a lemma, setting a new goal to derive that higher lemma.

```
1.  | (⊥ → A) → ⊥        Given
2.  |  | ~B             (A/IP)
3.  |  | | (⊥ → A) → ⊥  1 (R)



18. |  | | ⊥ → A        lemma for (MP)
19. |  | | ⊥            lemma for (IP) 18,3 (MP)
20. |  | B              2–19 (IP)
```

Entering ⊥ → A as a lemma on line 18 solves the problem of how to justify the lemma on line 19. That justification can now be entered and the sentence can be ghosted. With both line 20 and line 19 justified, attention turns to deriving the new lemma on line 18.

Since ⊥ → A is a conditional, the (CP) strategy applies. Derive it by assuming its antecedent and entering its consequent as a lemma under this assumption.

```
1.  | (⊥ → A) → ⊥        Given
2.  |  | ~B             (A/IP)
3.  |  | | (⊥ → A) → ⊥  1 (R)
4.  |  | | | ⊥          (A/CP)



17. |  | | | A          lemma for (CP)
18. |  | | ⊥ → A        lemma for (MP) 4–17 (CP)
19. |  | | ⊥            lemma for (IP) 18,3 (MP)
20. |  | B              2–19 (IP)
```

Inserting the subderivation from line 4 to 17 solves the problem of how to derive ⊥ → A on line 18. That sentence is now justified by 4–17 (CP) and can be ghosted. Attention turns to how to derive A on line 17.

Review the strategic questions: Are there any possible applications of (R), (MP), or (⊥I)? There are two possible applications of (R), but none of (MP) or (⊥I).

```
1.  | (⊥ → A) → ⊥        Given
2.  |  | ~B             (A/IP)
3.  |  | | (⊥ → A) → ⊥  1 (R)
4.  |  | | | ⊥          (A/CP)
5.  |  | | | (⊥ → A) → ⊥ 3 (R)
6.  |  | | | ~B         2 (R)



17. |  | | | A          lemma for (CP)
18. |  | | ⊥ → A        lemma for (MP) 4–17 (CP)
19. |  | | ⊥            lemma for (IP) 18,3 (MP)
20. |  | B              2–19 (IP)
```

Since nothing more can be done by top-down reasoning, the next step is to cycle through the remaining strategies. Is the current conclusion a conditional? No. Is it the consequent of a conditional? No. Is it ⊥? No. That leaves the strategy of last resort, the (IP) strategy: Assume its opposite and enter ⊥ as a lemma under this assumption.

1.	$(\bot \to A) \to \bot$	Given
2.	~B	(A/IP)
3.	$(\bot \to A) \to \bot$	1 (R)
4.	$\bot$	(A/CP)
5.	$(\bot \to A) \to \bot$	3 (R)
6.	~B	2 (R)
7.	**~A**	**(A/IP)**
16.	$\bot$	**lemma for (IP)**
17.	A	lemma for (CP) **5–16 (IP)**
18.	$\bot \to A$	lemma for (MP) 4–17 (CP)
19.	$\bot$	lemma for (IP) 18,3 (MP)
20.	B	2–19 (IP)

Inserting the subderivation from lines 7–16 solves the problem of how to derive A on line 17. That sentence is now justified by 7–16 (IP) and can be ghosted. Attention turns to how to derive $\bot$ on line 16. The first step to doing this is to return to stage 1 and do whatever can be done by top-down rule applications. The first of those applications is a reiteration of $\bot$ from line 4, which justifies the lemma on line 16, thereby completing the derivation. In this case, the derivation is discovered principally by working from the bottom up. It would have been very difficult to discover it just by reasoning from the top down. Someone wanting to save space and think it through in advance might give up in frustration or solve it at the cost of so much time and effort that an assignment to answer four or five such questions would seem impossibly time consuming and exhausting. Using the paper to work from the bottom up makes it possible to answer questions easily, quickly, and in the numbers needed to enhance learning.

When submitting the completed question for marking there is no need to renumber the lines, close the gap, or take measures to replicate the effect of ghosting. Retaining the gaps and nonconsecutive line numbers in submission proves that the assignment was done in the proper way, by using the paper it takes to work from the bottom up.

A review of the completed derivation reveals unnecessary work. As it turned out, the reiterations at lines 3, 5, and 6 proved to be unnecessary. It is permissible to either cross them out or simply leave them as they are. With practice it becomes easier to tell when reiterations will prove to be necessary and when not. Sometimes, a reiteration that was ignored or overlooked proves to be needed. It is acceptable to squeeze reiterations in between already completed lines of derivation. Simply amplify the inserted line numbers with decimal or alpha extensions to facilitate reference.

Exercise 6.5

Establish each of the following by means of a derivation in D_L *constructed by cycling through the stages.*

★a. $A, B \to \bot \vdash \sim(A \to B)$

  b. $A \to B, B \to \bot \vdash A \to \bot$

★c. $\sim C, A \to B, B \to C \vdash \sim A$

  d. $A \to B, B \to C, (A \to C) \to G \vdash G$ *(Hint: using the (MP) strategy, make* $A \to C$ *a lemma.)*

★e. $\sim A, (A \to \bot) \to B \vdash B$ *(Hint: using the (MP) strategy, make* $A \to \bot$ *a lemma.)*

  f. $\sim(A \to \sim B) \to C \vdash A \to (B \to C)$ *(conditional proof) (Hint: use the (CP) strategy twice, then the (MP) strategy, then the (IP) strategy.)*

Showing that a sentence is a theorem of D_L (the analogue of an s-valid sentence of SL) is done by deriving it from nothing, that is, from the empty list of givens. (IP) and (CP) make this possible. For example, the demonstration that $A \to (B \to A)$ is a theorem of D_L, notated as $\vdash A \to (B \to A)$ or as $\varnothing \vdash A \to (B \to A)$, can be given by two successive applications of (CP).

```
0.  |
1.  |  | A                    (A/CP)
2.  |  |  | B                 (A/CP)
... |  |  | ...
18. |  |  | A                 1 (R)
19. |  | B → A                lemma for (CP) 2–18 (CP)
20. |  A → (B → A)            1–19 (CP)
```

Line 0 is omitted from demonstrations of theorems. It is included above for one time only to illustrate that the derivation really begins from the empty list of givens. Since there is no point in writing down nothing, conventional format chops off the head of the first assumption bracket.

```
1.  |  | A                    (A/CP)
2.  |  |  | B                 (A/CP)
... |  |  | ...
18. |  |  | A                 1 (R)
19. |  | B → A                lemma for (CP) 2–18 (CP)
20. |  A → (B → A)            1–19 (CP)
```

Exercise 6.6

Establish each of the following by means of a derivation in D_L *constructed by cycling through the stages.*

★a. ⊢ ⊥ → (~(~A → B) →[~G → ~(K → A)])
  b. ⊢ (~(~A → B) →[~G → ~(K → A)]) → (H → H) *(Like ★a, this is easier than it looks.)*
★c. ⊢ [A → (B → C)] → [(A → B) → (A → C)] *(metatheorem 3)*
  d. ⊢ ~A → (A → B) *(Hint: apply the (CP) strategy twice followed by the (IP) strategy.)*
★e. ⊢ ~(A → B) → A
  f. ⊢ ~(A → B) → ~B *(Hint: using the (⊥I) strategy, make A → B a lemma.)*

Showing that a sentence or a set of sentences is inconsistent in D_L is a minor variant on showing that a conclusion is derivable in D_L. In a derivation of inconsistency, the conclusion is always ⊥, and the inconsistent sentence or a finite list of sentences from the inconsistent set comprise the givens. For example, a demonstration that {A, A → B, A → ~B} is inconsistent in D_L, notated as A, A → B, A → ~B ⊢ ⊥, can be given as follows.

```
1.  | A                 given
2.  | A → B             given
3.  | A → ~B            given
4.  | B                 1,2 (MP)
5.  | ~B                1,3 (MP)
6.  | ⊥                 4,5 (⊥I)
```

A derivation establishing that ~(A → A) is inconsistent in D_L, notated as ~(A → A) ⊢ ⊥, begins as follows.

```
1.  | ~(A → A)          given
... | ...
20. | ⊥                 ?
```

This derivation is discovered by applying the ($\perp$I) strategy: when the goal is to derive $\perp$, and there is no way to do so by ($\perp$I), (MP), (R), or the (MP) strategy, enter an opposite of one of the sentences above the gap (there is only one to choose from in this case) as a lemma and attempt to derive it.

1.	$\sim(A \to A)$	given
...	...	
19.	$A \to A$	lemma for ($\perp$I)
20.	$\perp$	19,1 ($\perp$I)

The derivation is readily completed by using the (CP) strategy.

1.	$\sim(A \to A)$	given
2.	A	(A/CP)
...	...	
19.	$A \to A$	lemma for ($\perp$I) 2–2 (CP)
20.	$\perp$	19,1 ($\perp$I)

Exercise 6.7

1. *Establish each of the following by means of a derivation in D_L constructed by cycling through the stages.*
   $\star$**a.** $B, \sim A \to \sim B, \sim\sim\sim A \vdash \perp$
   b. $B, \sim(\sim B \to A) \vdash \perp$ (*Hint: using the ($\perp$I) strategy, make $\sim B \to A$ a lemma.*)
   $\star$**c.** $(A \to \perp) \to \perp, \sim A \vdash \perp$
   d. $\sim(A \to \perp), \sim A \vdash \perp$ (*Hint: using the ($\perp$I) strategy, make $A \to \perp$ a lemma.*)
   e. $(A \to B) \to \sim B, B \vdash \perp$
   f. $A \to (B \to C), \sim\sim A, \sim(B \to C) \vdash \perp$

2. *Establish each of the following by means of a derivation in D_L constructed by cycling through the stages.*
   $\star$**a.** $\sim(\sim A \to \sim A) \vdash \perp$
   b. $\sim(A \to \sim\sim A) \vdash \perp$
   $\star$**c.** $\sim(\sim\sim A \to A) \vdash \perp$
   d. $\sim[(A \to \perp) \to (A \to B)] \vdash \perp$ (*Hint: using the ($\perp$I) strategy, make the opposite of the premise a lemma.*)
   $\star$**e.** $(B \to (A \to B)) \to \perp \vdash \perp$
   f. $[(\sim A \to A) \to A] \to \perp \vdash \perp$ (*Hint: using the (MP) strategy, make $(\sim A \to A) \to A$ a lemma; then use the (IP) strategy.*)

Showing that two sentences are interderivable in D_L is also a variant on showing that the conclusion of a demonstration is derivable from its premises. In this case, there are two derivations, one showing that the second sentence is derivable from the first, the other that the first is derivable from the second. For example, a demonstration that $A \to B$ and its contrapositive, $\sim B \to \sim A$ are interderivable, notated as $A \to B -|- \sim B \to \sim A$, might be given as follows.

1.	$A \to B$	given	1.	$\sim B \to \sim A$	given
2.	$\sim B$	(A/CP)	2.	A	(A/CP)
3.	$A \to B$	1 (R)	3.	$\sim B \to \sim A$	1 (R)
4.	A	(A/IP)	4.	$\sim B$	(A/IP)
5.	$A \to B$	3 (R)	5.	$\sim B \to \sim A$	3 (R)
6.	$\sim B$	2 (R)	6.	A	2 (R)
7.	B	4,5 (MP)	7.	$\sim A$	4,5 (MP)
...	...		...	...	
18.	$\perp$	lemma for (IP) 7,6 ($\perp$I)	18.	$\perp$	lemma for (IP) 6,7 ($\perp$I)
19.	$\sim A$	lemma for (CP) 4–18 (IP)	19.	B	lemma for (CP) 4–18 (IP)
20.	$\sim B \to \sim A$	2–19 (CP)	20.	$A \to B$	2–19 (CP)

Exercise 6.8

1. *Establish each of the following by means of a derivation in* D_L *constructed by cycling through the stages.*

   ★**a.** A −|− ~A → A

   b. ~A −|− A → (A → ⊥)

   ★**c.** A −|− (A → ⊥) → ⊥ *(lean language (DNI) and DNE))*

   d. ~A → B −|− (A → ⊥) → B *(lean language definition of* ∨*)*

   ★**e.** A → B −|− (B → ⊥) → (A → ⊥) *(lean language equivalence of contrapositives; this exercise calls for an important embellishment to the (MP) strategy, discussed in the solutions)*

   f. ~(A → ~B) −|− [A → (B → ⊥)] → ⊥ *(lean language definition of* &*)*

2. *As established by exercise 6.4#5d,* ~A *and* A → ⊥ *are interderivable. This means that, like conjunctions, disjunctions, and biconditionals, negations need not have been included in a lean derivation system. How would* D_L *have to be changed if negations were not included in the language? In answering this question, consider that not including negations would mean rewriting all sentences containing* ~ *as the corresponding conditionals. Supposing that were done, answer the following questions.*

   a. What would the rule form for (⊥I) look like if all negations were rewritten as the corresponding arrow sentences? Would there be any need for (⊥I) in this case or could all instances of its application be replaced by applications of one or more of the other rules?

   b. What would the application of (IP) to derive ~P from the assumption of P look like if all negations were rewritten as the corresponding arrow sentences? Would there be any need for (IP) in this case or could all instances of this way of applying (IP) be replaced by applications of one or more of the other rules?

   c. What would the application of (IP) to derive P from the assumption of ~P look like if all negations were rewritten as the corresponding arrow sentences? Could all instances of this way of applying (IP) be replaced by applications of one or more of the other rules or is there an inference drawn here that could not otherwise be drawn and that therefore requires its own rule if it is to be drawn?

   ★**d.** In the light of the answers to a–c, how would the rules of D_L have to be stated if all negations were rewritten as the corresponding arrow sentences?

3. *Establish the following assertions by cycling through the stages. Write a brief account of how your derivation instantiates the instructions on the strategy chart.*

   ★**a.** [A → (B → ⊥)] → ⊥ ⊢ B *(lean language (&E))*

   b. [(A → B) → (A → ⊥)] → ⊥ ⊢ B *(lean language modus ponens)*

   ★**c.** [A → (B → ⊥)] → ⊥ ⊢ A *(lean language (&E))*

   d. (A → ⊥) → B, A → C, B → G ⊢ (C → ⊥) → G *(lean language constructive dilemma)*

   ★**e.** (A → ⊥) → B, A → C, B → C ⊢ C *(lean language proof by cases)*

   f. A, B ⊢ ((A → B) → [(B → A) → ⊥]) → ⊥ *(lean language (&I))*

   ★**g.** A → (B → ⊥), A → B, C → A ⊢ C → ⊥

   h. ~[(A → B) → ~(A → ~B)] ⊢ A → C *(indirect proof)*

   ★**i.** [(A → C) → ⊥] → (B → C) −|− ([A → (B → ⊥)] → ⊥) → C

   j. [(A → B) → ⊥] → (A → C) −|− A → [(B → ⊥) → C]

   k. A → ⊥, C → A, (C → ⊥) → (B → ⊥) ⊢ B → ⊥

4. *Some of the following assertions are not derivable. Others are. In each case follow the instructions on the strategy chart to make as much progress with the derivation as possible. If this does not produce a successful derivation, try applying the (IP) strategy at the outset of the derivation. Should a claim still not be derivable, determine using the methods of chapter 5.2 whether there is an interpretation on which the premises are true and the conclusion is false.*

   ★**a.** A, B → ⊥ ⊢ (A → B) → ⊥

   b. A → (B → ⊥) ⊢ B → ~A

   ★**c.** (A → B) → C, B ⊢ C

   d. (A → A) → B ⊢ B

   ★**e.** (A → B) → (A → C), B, A → B ⊢ C

   f. B, B → (C → ~A), ~A ⊢ C

   ★**g.** ~B → ~(A → A), B → C ⊢ C

   h. ⊢ A → ~[(B → A) → ~A]

   ★**i.** ⊢ ~[(A → A) → ⊥]

    j. $(\sim B \to A) \to C, \sim A \to \perp \vdash C$

★k. $(A \to \perp) \to \perp, A \to B, [(A \to \perp) \to \perp] \to A \vdash \perp$

    l. $\sim(B \to A), \sim B, A \to \perp \vdash \perp$

    m. $(A \to \perp) \to (B \to \perp), B \vdash \perp$

6.3 Ds: A Derivation System for SL

D_L can be expanded to Ds, a derivation system for all the sentences of SL. This is done by supplementing the rules of D_L with six more rules, three for deriving conjunctions, disjunctions, and biconditionals, and three for deriving information from conjunctions, disjunctions, and biconditionals. The intuitions behind these rules draw on nonvaluational meanings associated with these connectives. Wedge means "at least one of," ampersand means "both of," and triple bar means "is both necessary and sufficient for."

Two of the new rules were introduced and informally employed in chapter 5, the rule of proof by cases (PC), and the rule of biconditional proof (BP). According to the first, if it is known that at least one of two alternatives, P and Q, is the case, then as long as both alternatives yield the same consequence, R, that consequence must be the case. The second rule is based on the thought that a biconditional, $P \equiv Q$ affirms that P is necessary for Q, which means that having Q requires having P, and that P is sufficient for Q, which means that having P requires having Q. The former can be established by showing that the supposition of Q yields P, the latter by showing that the supposition of P yields Q. These considerations give the following forms to the rules of proof by cases and biconditional proof:

> (PC): If $L \vdash P \vee Q; L, P \vdash R$; and $L, Q \vdash R$, then $L \vdash R$.
>
> (BP): If $L, P \vdash Q$ and $L, Q \vdash P$, then $L \vdash P \equiv Q$.

Templates for using these rules with assumption brackets are:

(PC)				(BP)		
	(L)				(L)	
...	...			...	...	
i.	P ∨ Q	?		*k.*	P	(A/BP)
...	...			...	...	
k.	P	(A / *i*.PC)		*n.*	Q	lemma for (BP)
	...			...	...	
n.	R	lemma for (PC)		*k.★*	Q	(A/BP)
...	...			...	...	
k.★	Q	(A / *i*.PC)		*n.★*	P	lemma for (BP)
	...			...	...	
n.★	R	lemma for (PC)			P ≡ Q	*k–n*, *k★–n★* (BP)
...	...					
n★+m.	R	*i,k–n,k★–n★* (PC)				

The form for (PC) illustrates that for a sentence, R, to be derived by (PC) three things must all lie immediately to the right of the same assumption bracket: a disjunction at line *i*, plus two subderivations, succeeding one below the other over lines *k* to *n* and *k★* to *n★*. One subderivation must be headed off by the assumption of the first disjunct, the other by that of the second, and R must occur immediately to the right of the assumption bracket for each subderivation. Under these conditions, R can be derived outside of the two subderivations, alongside the same assumption bracket that includes the disjunction.

P ∨ Q at line *i* may be either a given, an assumption or a derived line. The absence of a horizontal bar in the form is not meant to rule out any of these options. Lines *k–n* and *k★–n★*, along with the sentences on them, may occur in the reverse order, but whichever is first, the subderivation headed off by the first disjunct is cited first in the justification.

The assumptions of P at line k and Q at line $k\star$ are justified as (A/PC), further notated by the line number for P ∨ Q. The additional notation is helpful in situations where multiple assumptions for purposes of (PC) are nested inside one another. Having a note about which assumption comes from which disjunction helps keep track of what can become a complex operation.

Assumptions for (PC) are legitimated by the disjunction at line i, which promises that at least one of the two assumptions is the case. It is not known whether both are, but it does not matter if one is not the case provided the same sentence is derivable under each. Since that sentence is derivable either way, it is derivable independently of knowing which of the two is the case.

This line of reasoning only works insofar as P ∨ Q has been given, assumed, or derived somehow. (PC) takes it for granted that it has been, hence the question mark in the justification column. Removing this question mark is never a problem. (PC) is a top-down rule. It is only ever applied after a disjunction has been given, assumed, or derived somehow.

(PC) also presumes that some way can be found to derive R under each of the two subderivations. This is why the lemmas appear in the justification column. (PC) does not say how to derive R at lines n and $n\star$. It simply demands that this be managed somehow. Supposing it has, (PC) says what is derivable in that circumstance.

Because all the work goes into finding a way to complete the two subderivations it is easy to slip into thinking that they are what justifies applying (PC) to derive R. They are not enough. The two subderivations only establish that P yields R and Q yields R. All that follows from that is P → R and Q → R and those sentences are compatible with denying R. Before R can be derived it needs to be known that at least one of P and Q is the case. That makes the disjunction, P ∨ Q, essential. R at line $n\star+m$ only follows from all three of the things specified as being necessary for (PC): the disjunction at line i and the subderivations over lines k to n and $k\star$ to $n\star$.

(BP) is comparatively straightforward. It is just two successive applications of (CP), deriving a conditional, P → Q, and its converse, Q → P. But rather than derive the conditional from each (CP) subderivation, a biconditional is derived from the two in succession. The two subderivations can be presented in either order. Lines $k\star$ to $n\star$, along with the sentences on them, could come either before or after lines k to n. But when justifying P ≡ Q, the subderivation that goes from the left immediate component to the right is cited first.

Exercise 6.9

1. *State whether each of the following is an instance of (PC). If it is not, say why not. Assume question marked sentences have been properly derived.*

★a.
1.	A ∨ A	given
2.	A	(A/1 PC)
3.	A	1,2–2,2–2 (PC)

b.
h.	A ∨ B	?
i.	A	(A/h PC)
$k+1$.	B	(A/h PC)
...	...	
n.	A	?
	A	$h, i{-}i, k{+}1{-}n$ (PC)

★c.
h.	A ∨ B	?
i.	A	(A/h PC)
...	...	
k.	C	?
$k+1$.	B	(A/h PC)
...	...	
n.	C	?
	C	$i{-}k, k{+}1{-}n$ (PC)

d.
i.	A	(A/h PC)
...	...	
k.	C	?
$k+1$.	B	(A/h PC)
...	...	
n.	C	?
	C	$i{-}k, k{+}1{-}n$ (PC)

*e.

h.	A ∨ B	?	
i.	⎢A	(A/*h* PC)	
...	...		
k.	⎢C	?	
k+1.	⎢⎢B	(A/*h* PC)	
...	...		
n.	⎢⎢C	?	
	C	*h,i–k, k*+1–*n* (PC)	

f.

h.	A ∨ B	?	
i.	⎢A	(A/*h* PC)	
...	...		
k.	⎢C		
k+1.	⎢⎢B	(A/*h* PC)	
...	...		
n.	⎢⎢C	?	
	C	*h,i–k, k*+1–*n* (PC)	

*g.

h.	A ∨ B	?	
	...		
i.	⎢A	(A/*h* PC)	
...	...		
k.	⎢C	?	
k+1.	⎢⎢B	(A/*h* PC)	
...	...		
n.	⎢⎢C	?	
	C	*h,i–k, k*+1–*n* (PC)	

h.

e.	A ∨ B	?	
...	...		
f.	C ∨ D	?	
g.	⎢C	(A/*f* PC)	
h.	⎢A ∨ B	*e* (R)	
i.	⎢⎢A	(A/*h* PC)	
	...		
k.	⎢⎢G	?	
k+1.	⎢⎢⎢B	(A/*h* PC)	
	...		
n.	⎢⎢G	?	
	G	*h,i–k, k*+1–*n* (PC)	

2. *State whether each of the following is an instance of* (BP). *If it is not, say why not. Assume question marked sentences have been properly derived.*

*a.

1.	⎢A	(A/BP)	
2.	A ≡ A	1–1 (BP)	

b.

i.	⎢A	(A/BP)	
...	...		
k.	⎢C	?	
m.	⎢C	(A/BP)	
...	...		
n.	⎢A	?	
	C ≡ A	*i–k,m–n* (BP)	

*c.

i.	⎢A	(A/BP)	
...	...		
k.	⎢C	?	
m.	⎢C	(A/BP)	
...	...		
n.	⎢A	?	
	...		
	A ≡ C	*m–n, i–k* (BP)	

d.

i.	⎢A	(A/BP)	
...	...		
k.	⎢B	?	
m.	⎢⎢B	(A/BP)	
...	...		
n.	⎢A	?	
	A ≡ B	*i–k,m–n* (BP)	

⋆e.

i.	A	?	
...	...		
k.	B	?	
...			
m.	B	?	
...	...		
n.	A	?	
	A ≡ B	*i,k,m,n* (BP)	

f.

i.	A	(A/BP)	
...	...		
k.	B	?	
	C	(A/?)	
m.	B	(A/BP)	
	...		
n.	A	*i* (R)	
	A ≡ B	*i,k,m,n* (BP)	

Logic Works recognizes an alternative orientation for (PC) subderivations, parallel orientation. In parallel orientation, the two (PC) subderivations are done alongside one another. (The other orientation is serial orientation.)

(PC) in parallel orientation	(PC) in serial orientation
i. P ∨ Q	*i.* P ∨ Q
... ...	... ...
k. P Q (A/ *i* PC)	*k.* P (A/ *i* PC)
... ...	... ...
n. R ?	*n.* R ?
... ...	...
n⋆. R ?	*k.⋆* Q (A/ *i* PC)
... ...	...
R *i,k−n⋆,k−n* (PC)	*n.⋆* R ?
	... ...
	R *i,k−n,k⋆−n⋆* (PC)

In the parallel form R on line *n* right could come before, after, or coincidentally with line *n⋆*, depending on how much work it takes to derive R in each subderivation.

The parallel form uses just one number column and one justification column for both subderivations. When a sentence derived in one subderivation does not have the same justification as the sentence derived in the other, a sentence can be derived in one of the two subderivations and the line left blank in the other. This policy is waived when similar sentences are derived for similar reasons. In that case, the two different justifications are separated by a slash. One reason for doing (PC) in parallel is that same or similar sentences are often derived for same or similar reasons in the two subderivations, reducing the lines of demonstration. (BP) is not done in parallel because this tends not to be the case with (BP) subderivations.

In addition to being more elegant than serial orientation, parallel orientation makes the parallel case structure of a proof by cases more obvious. It is also used for tree conversions, discussed in chapter A-3.

Unfortunately, parallel orientation gives the appearance that the list of assumptions at line *i* is supplemented by both P and Q, which would invite appealing to sentences in one subderivation to justify sentences derived in the other, or reiteration from the P subderivation into the Q subderivation. Neither is legitimate. Parallel subderivations need to be treated as if they had a wall between them. (A wall is drawn in the template given above, but this is not normally done.) What lies above the start of that wall can be reiterated into what lies on either side of the wall. But nothing can be allowed to cross the wall, be it by reiteration from the P–R subderivation into the Q–R subderivation, or reiteration from the Q–R subderivation into the P–R subderivation.

Exercise 6.10

State whether each of the following is an instance of (R). *If it is not, say why not.*

*a. $k.$ | A ∨ B   ?
         … | …
         $n.$ | C   ?
              | | A | B | (A/k PC)
              | | C | … | n (R)

b. $k.$ | A ∨ B   ?
        … | …
        $n.$ | C   ?
             | | A | B | (A/k PC)
             | | … | C | n (R)

*c. $i.$ | A ∨ B   ?
         $k.$ | | A | B | (A/i PC)
              | | | C | (A/?)
         n | | | A | k (R)

d. $i.$ | A ∨ B   ?
        $k.$ | | A | B | (A/i PC)
             | | | C | (A/?)
        $n.$ | | | B | k (R)

*e. $i.$ | A ∨ B   ?
         $k.$ | | A | B | (A/i PC)
              | | … | A | k (R)

f. $i.$ | A ∨ B   ?
        $k.$ | | A | B | (A/i PC)
             | | … |
        $n.$ | | C | … | ?
             | | | C | n (R)

Ds uses four more rules. P ≡ Q says that P is both necessary and sufficient for Q. So, if P has been derived, because it suffices for Q, Q must be derivable; and if Q has been derived, because P is necessary for it, P must be derivable. Likewise, if P has been derived and Q has been derived, both have been derived, so P & Q must be derivable. These rules are called biconditional modus ponens (BMP) and conjunction introduction (&I). They have the following forms:

> (BMP): If L ⊢ P and L ⊢ either P ≡ Q or Q ≡ P then L ⊢ Q.
>
> (&I): If L ⊢ P and L ⊢ Q then L ⊢ P & Q

Templates for the use of these rules with assumption brackets are:

(BMP)		(&I)	
(L)		(L)	
… …		… …	
$k.$ P	?	$k.$ P	?
… …		… …	
$k.\star$ P ≡ Q [or Q ≡ P]	?	$k.\star$ Q	?
… …		… …	
$n.$ Q	$k,k\star$ (BMP)	$n.$ P & Q	$k,k\star$ (&I)
(The sentence on line k★ could occur before the sentence on line k.)			

As with (⊥I) and (MP), the forms depicted above are unavoidably overdetermined in one respect. Lines k and $k\star$, along with the sentences on them, may occur in either order. Whichever occurs first, however, the sentence on line k is cited first in justification. In the case of (&I) that means the sentence that is the left conjunct of the conjunction.

The dashed line depicted above also does not appear in instances of the forms. It is inserted above to distinguish what must be the case before the rule can be applied from what follows in accord with the rule. The sentences at lines k and $k\star$ have question marks in their justification columns because (BMP) and (&I) do not say how these sentences come to be derived. They only say what follows should they be derived.

All three of the sentences involved in (BMP) and (&I) must lie alongside the same assumption bracket. Other brackets may lie to the left but neither they nor any sentences they contain figure in the rule application.

The two remaining rules are conjunct extraction (&E) and "wedge in" (∨I). (&E) is based on the intuition that if both P and Q are the case, either one of must be the case. So, if P & Q has been derived, either P or Q is derivable. (∨I) is based on the intuition that if P has been derived then at least one of P and any other sentence has been derived. So, if P is derivable, P ∨ Q and Q ∨ P are derivable, where Q is any sentence of SL. The rules have the following forms:

> (&E): If L ⊢ P & Q then L ⊢ P and L ⊢ Q
>
> (∨I): If L ⊢ P then L ⊢ P ∨ Q and L ⊢ Q ∨ P

Templates for the use of these rules with assumption brackets are:

(&E)			(∨I)		
	(L)			(L)	
...	...		...	...	
$k.$	P & Q	?	$k.$	P	?
...	...		...	...	
$n.$	P [or Q]	k (&E)	$n.$	P ∨ Q [or Q ∨ P]	k (∨I)

(∨I) might seem suspicious. Given a sentence, P, (∨I) allows wedging any sentence onto either the front or the back of P, and then wedging any other sentence onto the front or the back of that sentence, and so on without end.

There is something illogical about (∨I). But it is not that (∨I) allows bringing something in out of nowhere. This would only be a problem if there were some way of extracting the arbitrarily wedged on component from the disjunction. But the only rule that allows deriving information from a disjunction is (PC), and (PC) only allows deriving things that can be demonstrated to be independently derivable from each disjunct. The power to bring things in out of nowhere and wedge them onto sentences is no power at all. Rather than produce something more than what was there to start with, it produces something less, because it is twice as much work to derive a consequence from each disjunct as from just one of them. Worse, if what is arbitrarily wedged on to a sentence does not independently yield the same consequences as the sentence it was wedged onto, the wedge sentence becomes useless. This is where the illogical aspect comes in.

(∨I) weakens and obscures what is known. Suppose someone knows for a fact that A is true. But instead of saying what they know to be the case, that A is true, the person instead says that *either* A is the case *or* B is the case. This *is* implied by what the person knows. But to wedge something on to what is known also weakens what is known. When someone asserts A ∨ B, they only assert that at least one of A or B is the case without saying which it is. In effect, they bring the previously established assertion of A into doubt. Knowledge is hard to come by, and should not be allowed to degrade. Someone who has established that A is the case, but only says that A ∨ B is the case is casting doubt on what is known, and that is not logical. It suggests duplicity or foolishness.

This is the real problem with (∨I). In one sense, it is logical. It is valid. But in another sense, it is bad. It has the effect of weakening what is known, which is not something that is ordinarily excusable.

There are two exceptions. (∨I) does not just weaken. It generalizes. When (∨I) is used in natural demonstration (as opposed to academic exercises) it is used to support (PC), the way (⊥I) is used to support (IP). As noted in chapter 5, when demonstrating by cases, generalization is often necessary. Overspecification is the bane of proof by cases. It makes it look like what follows from one case is different from what follows from another case, so that no common conclusion can be reached. But often, this is just an appearance resulting from over specification. When the conclusions from the cases are generalized, it is revealed that they are the same after all. One case may yield A. Another case may yield B (or, to take a more striking example, ~A). So (PC) cannot be applied. But apply (∨I) first to derive A ∨ B (or A ∨ ~A) from each case, and (PC) can be applied after all.

The second exception is similar. When a disjunction is *negated*, (∨I) can be used to derive the negation of either disjunct. (Assume one disjunct, wedge on the other, and apply (IP).)

In natural contexts (∨I) is used along with (PC) and (IP) in one of the ways just mentioned. It is only in student exercises (or journal articles in analytic epistemology) that one sees it being used to derive conclusions on its own, outside of a larger application of (PC) or (IP).

Exercise 6.11

1. State whether each of the following is an instance of (BMP). If it is not, say why not.

★a.
$$
\begin{array}{ll}
i. & C \\
\ldots & \ldots \\
k. & C \equiv G \\
& G \qquad k,i \text{ (BMP)}
\end{array}
$$

b.
$$
\begin{array}{ll}
i. & C \equiv G \\
\ldots & \ldots \\
k. & G \\
& C \qquad k,i \text{ (BMP)}
\end{array}
$$

★c.
$$
\begin{array}{ll}
i. & \sim C \\
\ldots & \ldots \\
k. & \sim(C \equiv G) \\
& \sim G \qquad i,k \text{ (BMP)}
\end{array}
$$

d.
$$
\begin{array}{ll}
i. & A \equiv (B \equiv C) \\
\ldots & \ldots \\
k. & B \\
& C \qquad k,i \text{ (BMP)}
\end{array}
$$

★e.
$$
\begin{array}{lll}
i. & C & \qquad ? \\
\ldots & \ldots & \\
k. & \quad| G \equiv C & \qquad ? \\
& \quad| G & \qquad i,k \text{ (BMP)}
\end{array}
$$

f.
$$
\begin{array}{lll}
i. & \quad| G \equiv C & \text{(A/?)} \\
\ldots & \quad| \ldots & \\
k. & \quad| C & \qquad ? \\
& G & \qquad k,i \text{ (BMP)}
\end{array}
$$

2. State whether each of the following is an instance of (&I). If it is not, say why not.

★a.
$$
\begin{array}{ll}
i. & A \qquad\qquad ? \\
& A \,\&\, A \quad\; i \text{ (&I)}
\end{array}
$$

b.
$$
\begin{array}{ll}
i. & A \qquad\qquad ? \\
\ldots & \ldots \\
k. & B \qquad\qquad ? \\
& B \,\&\, A \quad\; i,k \text{ (&I)}
\end{array}
$$

★c.
$$
\begin{array}{ll}
i. & B \qquad\qquad ? \\
\ldots & \ldots \\
k. & A \qquad\qquad ? \\
& A \,\&\, B \quad\; k,i \text{ (&I)}
\end{array}
$$

d.
$$
\begin{array}{ll}
i. & \sim A \qquad\qquad ? \\
\ldots & \ldots \\
k. & \sim B \qquad\qquad ? \\
& \sim(A \,\&\, B) \quad\; i,k \text{ (&I)}
\end{array}
$$

★e.
$$
\begin{array}{ll}
i. & \sim A \qquad\qquad ? \\
\ldots & \ldots \\
k. & \quad| B \\
& \quad| B \,\&\, \sim A \quad\; k,i \text{ (&I)}
\end{array}
$$

f.
$$
\begin{array}{ll}
i. & A \qquad\qquad ? \\
\ldots & \ldots \\
k. & \sim A \qquad\qquad ? \\
& \sim A \,\&\, A \quad\; k,i \text{ (&I)}
\end{array}
$$

3. State whether each of the following is an instance of (&E). If it is not, say why not.

★a.
$$
\begin{array}{ll}
n. & A \,\&\, (B \to C) \qquad ? \\
\ldots & \ldots \\
& B \to C \qquad\qquad n \text{ (&E)}
\end{array}
$$

b.
$$
\begin{array}{ll}
n. & (A \,\&\, B) \to C \qquad ? \\
\ldots & \ldots \\
& A \qquad\qquad\qquad n \text{ (&E)}
\end{array}
$$

★c.
$$
\begin{array}{ll}
n. & A \,\&\, (B \,\&\, C) \qquad ? \\
\ldots & \ldots \\
& B \qquad\qquad\qquad n \text{ (&E)}
\end{array}
$$

d.
$$
\begin{array}{ll}
n. & (A \,\&\, B) \,\&\, \sim C \qquad ? \\
\ldots & \ldots \\
& \sim C \qquad\qquad\qquad n \text{ (&E)}
\end{array}
$$

*e. $n.$ | $\sim$(A & B)   ?
... | ...
| A n (&E)

f. $n.$ | | A & B   ?
| A n (&E)

4. *State whether each of the following is an instance of ($\vee$I). If it is not, say why not.*

*a. $n.$ | A $\rightarrow$ C   ?
... | ...
| (A $\vee$ B) $\rightarrow$ C n (VI)

b. $n.$ | A   ?
... | ...
| A $\vee$ A n (VI)

*c. $n.$ | B   ?
... | ...
| B $\vee$ $\sim$A n (VI)

d. $n.$ | A $\vee$ B   ?
... | ...
| A $\vee$ (A $\vee$ B) n (VI)

*e. $n.$ | A $\vee$ B   ?
... | ...
| C $\vee$ (A $\vee$ B) n (VI)

f. $n.$ | | A   ?
... | A $\vee$ A n (VI)

6.4 Strategies for Doing Derivations in Ds

The four stage procedure recommended for doing derivations in D_L is expanded for Ds. A new stage, called stage 0, is devoted to a new (BP) strategy. Stage 1, the "top-down" reasoning stage, is rewritten to recommend beginning with applications of (R), followed by (&E), (MP), (BMP), and ($\perp$I). A further strategy associated with (PC) is recommended for use after all other top-down work has been completed. (&I) and ($\vee$I) are not recognized as top-down rules. They derive longer sentences from shorter ones, so there is no end to how often they can be applied. Their application needs to be guided by what sentences are being derived, so they figure at stage 3.

Stage 2, the (CP) strategy, is unchanged.

Stages 3a and 3b are collapsed into a single stage, called the "bottom-up" reasoning stage. This stage is further expanded with strategies for (BMP), (&I), ($\vee$I), and a special ($\sim$bc) strategy, to be used in situations where a negated binary, or $\sim$bc sentence, exists above the gap.

Stage 0 (BP)

When the aim is to derive a biconditional, P $\equiv$ Q, split the derivation into two serial subderivations. Head the first off with the assumption of P and enter Q as a lemma for (BP) under this assumption. Head the second off with the assumption of Q, and enter P as a lemma for (BP) under this assumption. Should either P or Q be a biconditional repeat this strategy for it; otherwise, proceed to stage 1.

Stage 1 (Top-Down)

Make all possible applications of (R), **except for the cases noted below, followed by all possible applications of (&E),** (MP), **(BMP),** and ($\perp$I). Return to stage 0. When a complete cycle through **stages 0 and** 1 produces no changes to the derivation, proceed to stage **1a.**

> **Exceptions to (R):**
> i. If a subderivation is justified by (A/nPC), do not reiterate the disjunction at line n into that subderivation (that is, do not reiterate disjunctions into their own (PC) subderivations
> ii. Do not reiterate sentences into (BP) subderivations if it is clear they are not needed to derive the lemma

Stage 1a (PC)

Make one application of the (PC) strategy, then return to stage 0. When a complete cycle through stages 0 to 1a produces no changes to the derivation, proceed to stage 2.

(PC) strategy:
When a disjunction appears above the gap, split the derivation into two, serial or parallel subderivations, each headed off by the assumption of one of the disjuncts. Enter the sentence that currently needs to be derived as a lemma for (PC) on the last line of each assumption bracket.

Stage 2 (CP)

When the aim is to derive a conditional, P → Q, assume P and enter Q as a lemma for (CP) under this assumption. Return to stage **0**. When a complete cycle through stages **0** to 2 produces no changes to the derivation, proceed to stage 3.

Stage 3 **(Bottom-Up)**

Make one application of one of the following strategies and return to stage **0**:
- (MP): If the sentence that needs to be derived, Q, could be derived by (MP) but for the fact that the antecedent, P, needed to derive Q from P → Q is missing, enter P as a lemma for (MP) and attempt to derive it.
- **(BMP): If the sentence that needs to be derived, Q, could be derived by (BMP) but for the fact that the other immediate component needed to derive it is missing, enter the missing immediate component as a lemma for (BMP) and attempt to derive it.**
- **(&I): If the sentence that needs to be derived is P & Q and one or both of P and Q are missing, enter it or them as lemmas for (&I) and attempt to derive it or them.**
- **(∨I): If the sentence that needs to be derived is P ∨ Q, enter one of P or Q as a lemma for (∨I) and attempt to derive it.**
- (⊥I): If the sentence that needs to be derived is ⊥, and ⊥ cannot be derived by (⊥I), (MP), (R), or by the (MP/BMP) strategies, look up at the sentences that have so far been derived, enter the opposite of one of those sentences as a lemma for (⊥I), and attempt to derive it. The best choice is a lemma that is easily derivable. Otherwise, pick a lemma that demands making further assumptions or entering other lemmas.

  (~bc) supplement:
  When the negation of a binary sentence, ~(P & Q), ~(P ∨ Q), ~(P → Q), or ~(P ≡ Q), exists above the gap, consider using it and its opposite for (⊥I).

When a complete cycle through stages **0** to 3 produces no changes to the derivation, proceed to stage 4.

Stage 4 (Indirect Proof)

When no other way of deriving a sentence, P, is obvious, assume P-opposite, enter ⊥ as a lemma for (IP), and return to stage 0.

The main innovations are the introduction of the (BP), (PC), and (~bc) strategies. The (BP) strategy is put in first place because deriving a biconditional is like doing two independent derivations. The givens and derived sentences used to complete the one (BP) subderivation can be different from the givens and derived sentences used to complete the other. Splitting the derivation at the start makes it possible to reiterate just the relevant givens and derived sentences into each (BP) subderivation. This can be especially expedient when the givens and derived lines include disjunctions. Applications of the (PC) strategy to disjunctions that are not required to complete a (BP) subderivation will not block the derivation, but they will considerably complicate it.

Applications of the (PC) strategy look like the form for the rule.

1.	P_1		given
2.	$P_2 ∨ P_3$		given
3.	P_4		given
...	...		
8.	P_2	P_3	(A/2PC)
...	...	...	
19.	P_5	P_5	?
20.	P_5		2,8–19,8–19 (PC)

The strategy should be applied at the end of stage 1, but before going on to any of the other stages. If applying the strategy makes further applications of the strategy possible, they should be performed as well, but only after cycling through stages 0 and 1 and making any (R), (&E), (MP), (BMP), and (⊥I) applications made possible by the creation of the two initial (PC) subderivations. Importantly, the disjunction that was used to make the (PC) subderivations should not be reiterated under its own subderivations. That would create an unending series of cycles through stages 1 and 1a.

According to the (PC) strategy, seeing a disjunction anywhere above the gap is a sign that the sentence that currently needs to be derived will need to be derived twice – once under each disjunct. Sometimes, the sentence that needs to be derived is itself a disjunction. In that case, it often happens that one of the disjuncts is derivable under one (PC) subderivation, the other under the other. This needs to be kept in mind should an occasion to apply the (∨I) strategy arise.

The (~bc) supplement is a special case of the (⊥I) strategy. Whereas the (⊥I) strategy makes only vague recommendations about what lemmas to use, the (~bc) strategy makes a specific recommendation: When a negated binary sentence (that is, a sentence of the form ~(P & Q), ~(P ∨ Q), ~(P → Q) or ~(P ≡ Q)) exists above the gap, that negated binary and its opposite should be used to derive ⊥. An example is provided by the derivation that establishes that ~(A ∨ B) ⊢ ~B.

$$
\begin{array}{ll}
1. & \quad \sim(A \vee B) \qquad \text{given} \\
& \\
\ldots & \quad \ldots \qquad\qquad\quad \ldots \\
20. & \quad \sim B \qquad\qquad\quad ?
\end{array}
$$

At the outset, there is nothing to do at stages 1, 2, or 3, so the (IP) strategy is indicated.

$$
\begin{array}{ll}
1. & \sim(A \vee B) \qquad \text{given} \\
2. & \quad B \qquad\qquad (A/IP) \\
\ldots & \quad \ldots \qquad\qquad \ldots \\
19. & \quad \bot \qquad\qquad \text{lemma for (IP)} \\
20. & \sim B \qquad\qquad 2\text{–}19 \text{ (IP)}
\end{array}
$$

The (~bc) strategy says that when negated binary sentence exists above the gap, it and its opposite should be first choice for deriving ⊥. In this case, this means reiterating the negated binary sentence under the assumption, and entering its opposite as a lemma.

$$
\begin{array}{ll}
1. & \sim(A \vee B) \qquad\qquad \text{given} \\
2. & \quad B \qquad\qquad\qquad (A/IP) \\
3. & \quad\quad \sim(A \vee B) \qquad 1 \text{ (R)} \\
\ldots & \quad\quad \ldots \qquad\qquad\qquad \ldots \\
18. & \quad A \vee B \qquad\qquad \text{lemma for (⊥I)} \\
19. & \quad\quad \bot \qquad\qquad\qquad \text{lemma for (IP) } 18,3 \text{ (⊥I)} \\
20. & \sim B \qquad\qquad\qquad 2\text{–}19 \text{ (IP)}
\end{array}
$$

In case it is not obvious what to do next, apply the strategies: There is nothing to be done at stages 0, 1, or 2. At stage 3, since the current lemma is a disjunction, the (∨I) strategy needs to be applied: enter one of the disjuncts as a lemma for (∨I) and aim to derive it. Pick the one that looks to be the easiest to derive. That would be B, which has already been derived, allowing "lemma for (⊥I)" to be ghosted and replaced with 2 (∨I). The derivation of ~A from ~(A ∨ B) uses a similar strategy.

Further and more detailed illustrations of the strategies for doing derivations in Ds are given over the course of solved exercises.

Exercise 6.12

1. *The following derivations call for one or more applications of the (PC) strategy. Cycle through stages 1 and 1a (stage 0 is not called for in any of these exercises) until there is nothing left to do after a cycle through both stages. Do not complete the derivations beyond this point. Use this exercise just as practice setting up (PC) subderivations and identifying the right lemmas. Refer to the answered questions for further illustration.*

    ★a. ~A ∨ B ⊢ A → B *(implication)*
    b. ~A ∨ B, (C ≡ B) & A ⊢ C
    ★c. (A → B) ∨ (A → C) ⊢ A → (B ∨ C)
    d. A ∨ (B ∨ ~C) ⊢ (~C ∨ A) ∨ B *(compare e below)*
    ★e. ~A ∨ (K ∨ B), (A ≡ C) & (G → ~B) ⊢ ~K → (~C ∨ ~G)
    f. A → G, B → (G ∨ C) ⊢ (A ∨ B) → (C ∨ G)

2. *Returning to the partially completed derivations of question 1, continue by cycling through stages 2, 1, and 1a until there is nothing left to do after a cycle through just these stages. Identify those derivations containing (PC) subderivations that end with lemmas that are themselves disjunctions. Apply the (∨I) strategy to these cases.*

    Answers to **a, c, e**

3. *The following derivations call for one or more applications of the (BP) strategy. Cycle through stages 0 to 2 until there is nothing left to do after a cycle through these stages. Do not complete the derivations beyond this point. Use this exercise just as practice setting up (BP) subderivations. Refer to the answered questions for further illustration.*

    ★a. ~A, ~B ⊢ A ≡ B
    b. A ≡ B ⊢ ~B ≡ ~A
    ★c. (~A ∨ B) & (~B ∨ A) ⊢ A ≡ B
    d. ⊢ (A ≡ ⊥) ≡ (A → ⊥)
    ★e. ~(A ≡ B) ⊢ ~A ≡ B
    f. A ≡ (B ≡ C), C ⊢ A ≡ B

4. *The following derivations call for one or more applications of the (~bc) supplement to the (IP) strategy. Cycle through the stages up to the point where an initial application of the strategy is called for. Do not complete the derivations beyond this point. Use this exercise just as practice setting up an initial (~bc) subderivation. Refer to the answered questions for further illustration.*

    ★a. ~(~A & ~B) ⊢ A ∨ B
    b. ~(A & B) ⊢ ~A ∨ ~B *(De Morgan's theorem)*
    ★c. ~(~A ∨ B) ⊢ ~(A → B)
    d. ~(A → B) ⊢ A & ~B *(implication)*
    ★e. ~(A ∨ B) ⊢ ~A & ~B *(De Morgan's theorem)*
    f. ~(~A ∨ ~B) ⊢ A & B

5. *Complete all the partially completed derivations of questions 2–4.*

    For 3f, use the (BMP) strategy in the second half
    For 4b and 4f look for a second application of the (~bc) strategy. Compare 4a, c, and e.
    Answers to **#2a, c, e; #3a, c** *(apply the (BP) strategy before the (PC) strategy)*, **e** *(use the result of 3a);* **#4a, c, e**

6. *Establish the following.*

    ★a. ⊢ [C → (A & B)] → [~(B & A) → ~C]
    b. ⊢ [(B ∨ A) → C] → (A → C)
    ★c. ⊢ [(A ≡ G) & ~B] → (B → A)
    d. ⊢ [B → (C ∨ A)] ≡ [~C → (B → A)]
    ★e. ⊢ (A & B) ∨ (~A ∨ ~B)
    f. ⊢ (A → B) ∨ (B → A)

7. *Establish the following.*

    ★a.   A → A –|– B ∨ ~B
    b.   ⊥ –|– ~(A ≡ A)
    ★c.   (A → ⊥) → B –|– A ∨ B

    d. $(A \to C) \lor (B \to C)$ $-|-$ $(A \& B) \to C$

★e. $(A \to B) \& (C \to B)$ $-|-$ $(A \lor C) \to B$

    f. $(A \to B) \& (A \to C)$ $-|-$ $A \to (B \& C)$

8. *Establish the following.*

  ★a. $(C \& H) \to B, C \lor H, (C \equiv A) \& (H \equiv A)$ $\vdash$ $A \equiv B$

    b. $\sim(G \lor C), \sim A \to C, A \equiv B$ $\vdash$ B *(use the (BMP), (IP), (~bc) strategies)*

  ★c. $\sim K \to \sim H, (G \& H) \equiv C$ $\vdash$ $C \to K$

    d. $(A \& \sim C) \equiv \sim B, (A \to C) \lor G, G \equiv H$ $\vdash$ $B \lor H$

  ★e. $(A \to \sim B) \lor C, (A \lor G) \& \sim C, \sim(B \equiv G)$ $\vdash$ G

    f. $H \equiv \sim(A \to K), \sim C \lor K$ $\vdash$ $(C \& H) \to (A \to B)$

          (apply the (CP) strategy before the (PC) strategy)

9. *Establish the following.*

  ★a. $B \to \sim A, \sim(C \lor \sim A), \sim(\sim C \& \sim B)$ $\vdash$ $\bot$

    b. $\sim(A \to \sim B), \sim(B \lor C)$ $\vdash$ $\bot$

  ★c. $\sim(A \& \sim B) \to (A \& C), A \& B, \sim B \equiv C$ $\vdash$ $\bot$

    d. $\sim A \to A, A \equiv \sim(B \lor C), \sim C \to B$ $\vdash$ $\bot$

  ★e. $\sim(A \lor B), (\sim A \lor C) \equiv B$ $\vdash$ $\bot$ *(use the (~bc) strategy*

        and try to derive the opposite of a given negated binary sentence)

    f. $\sim(K \lor \sim H), \sim C \lor \sim G, (A \to B) \to C, (B \equiv A) \& (G \equiv H)$ $\vdash$ $\bot$

6.5 Extensions of Ds; Bracket Free Notation

6.5.1 Systematic Overview; Adequacy of D_L

The rules of Ds comprise a system. Each of the binary connectives has two rules associated with it: a rule used for deriving a sentence with that connective as its main connective – (CP), ($\lor$I), (BP), (&I) – and a rule for deriving something from a sentence with that connective as its main connective – (MP), (PC), (BMP), and (&E). $\bot$ similarly has two rules associated with it, one for deriving $\bot$ ($\bot$I), and one for deriving something from $\bot$ (IP). This leaves atomic sentences and negations. They can be derived by using the (IP) strategy, and information can be derived from them using the same strategy.

	Deriving	Deriving from
$\to$	(CP)	(MP)
$\lor$	($\lor$I)	(PC)
$\equiv$	(BP)	(BMP)
$\&$	(&I)	(&E)
$\bot$	($\bot$I)	(IP)
$\sim$	(IP)	(IP)
A_n	(IP)	(IP)

The systematic character of the rules of Ds might make it look as if the rules are all necessary, but they are not. In section 6.1, it was asserted that the rules for conjunctions, disjunctions, and biconditionals are unnecessary. The lean language equivalent of anything that can be derived in Ds can be derived in D_L. More radically, it can be derived in a reduced version of D_L, which does not use tildes or ($\bot$I), and uses only the following version of (IP), called (IP~E):

$$\text{If } L, P \to \bot \vdash \bot \text{ then } L \vdash P$$

(See exercise 6.8#2 for further details.)

The ability of (R), (MP), (CP), and (IP~E) to replace all the other rules can be demonstrated in two steps: First, consider sentences of the forms ~P, P & Q, P ∨ Q, and P ≡ Q to be abbreviations for the following more verbose sentences:

$$\sim P: \quad P \to \bot$$
$$P \lor Q: \quad (P \to \bot) \to Q$$
$$P \& Q: \quad [P \to (Q \to \bot)] \to \bot$$
$$P \equiv Q: \quad ((P \to Q) \to [(Q \to P) \to \bot]) \to \bot$$

Second, do exercise 6.13.

Exercise 6.13

Replacing disjunctions, negations, conjunctions, and biconditionals with the sentences they abbreviate, rewrite each of the templates for (PC), (∨I), (&E), (&I), (BMP), and (BP), in the lean language (use metavariables). Then show how to derive the sentence derived by each of these rules, using just (R), (MP), (CP), and (IP~E). ((⊥I) is omitted from this set because the exercise is too trivial.) Note that many of these derivations require extensive use of the (MP) strategy. Consult the answered questions for further help.

⋆a. (PC) *(use serial orientation)*
  b. (∨I) *(a separate derivation is required for each of the two forms in which (∨I) is stated in the lean language:* P ⊢ (P → ⊥) → Q *and* P ⊢ (Q → ⊥) → P)
⋆c. (&E) *(a separate derivation is required for each of the two forms of (&E))*
  d. (&I)
⋆e. (BP)
  f. (BMP) *(a separate derivation is required for each of the two forms of (BMP)):* P, ((P → Q) → [(Q → P) → ⊥]) → ⊥ ⊢ Q *and* Q, ((P → Q) → [(Q → P) → ⊥]) → ⊥ ⊢ P

6.5.2 Metatheorems and Derived Rules for Ds

Shorter derivations often occur over the course of longer ones. When the shorter derivation has already been done in an earlier exercise, there is no point repeating it. The earlier exercise can be cited as a justification for deriving the conclusion of the shorter derivation from its premises, provided that all occur within the same subderivation in the later exercise. An example is exercise 6.12#5 for 3a, which is used to justify a step in exercise 6.12#5 for 3e. This can considerably abbreviate a derivation. But it is only possible when the shorter derivation and the longer one use the same sentences. Exercise 6.12#8e did not lend itself to similar abbreviation, because the sentences use different sentence letters.

Derivations can be generalized to get around this problem. It is possible to do derivations that put metavariables in the place of sentence letters. These derivations are done in the same way, using the same rules. But they have a different status. A derivation of P from one or more sentences, Q, R, … has the status of a routine sequence of steps that can be applied to derive any instance of P from the corresponding instances of Q, R, …. Similarly, a derivation of P from the empty list has the status of a routine sequence of steps that can be used to derive any instance of P at any point in any derivation.

For example, exercise 6.12#5 for 3a establishes that ~A, ~B ⊢ A ≡ B. Rewriting the derivation of this claim putting P for A and Q for B produces a routine sequence of steps that can be followed to derive any biconditional from the negation of its immediate components.

Similarly, exercise 6.1#3g establishes that A → A is a theorem. Rewriting that derivation putting P for A produces a routine sequence of steps that can be followed to derive any sentence of the form P → P at any point in a derivation.

Exercise 6.14

1. *Exhibit the routines for deriving any sentence of the following forms.*
    ★a. P → P *(metatheorem 1 (M1))*
     b. P ∨ ~P *(law of the excluded middle (em))*
    ★c. ~(P & ~P) *(law of noncontradiction (nc))*
     d. ⊥ → P *(ex falso quodlibet (EFQ))*
    ★e. P → (Q → P) *(metatheorem 2 (M2))*
     f. [P → (Q → R)] → [(P → Q) → (P → R)] *(metatheorem 3 (M3))*
     g. ~⊥ *(tilde con (~⊥))*

2. *Exhibit the routines for performing the following operations.*
    ★a. P → Q, Q → R ⊢ P → R *(hypothetical syllogism (HS))*
     b. ~P, Q → P ⊢ ~Q *(modus tollens (MT))*
    ★c. ~(P → Q) ⊢ P *and* ~(P → Q) ⊢ ~Q *(tilde arrow (~→))*
     d. ~P ⊢ P → Q *and* Q ⊢ P → Q *(T-arrow (T→))*
    ★e. P ⊢ ~~P *(double negation introduction (DNI))*
     f. ~~P ⊢ P *(double negation elimination (DNE))*
    ★g. P ∨ Q, ~P ⊢ Q *and* P ∨ Q, ~Q ⊢ P *(disjunctive syllogism (DS)); it suffices to derive just one of these)*
     h. Q ∨ R, Q → P₁, R → P₂ ⊢ P₁ ∨ P₂ *(constructive dilemma (CD))*
    ★i. ~(P ∨ Q) ⊢ ~P *and* ~(P ∨ Q) ⊢ ~Q *(tilde wedge (~∨)); it suffices to derive just one of these)*
     j. ~P, P ≡ Q ⊢ ~Q *and* ~Q, P ≡ Q ⊢ ~P *(biconditional modus tollens (BMT)); it suffices to derive just one of these)*
    ★k. P, ~(P ≡ Q) ⊢ ~Q *and* Q, ~(P ≡ Q) ⊢ ~P *(negated biconditional modus ponens (~BMP)); it suffices to derive just one of these)*
     l. ~P, ~(P ≡ Q) ⊢ Q *and* ~Q, ~(P ≡ Q) ⊢ P *(negated biconditional modus tollens (~BMT)); it suffices to derive just one of these)*
     m. ⊥ ⊢ P *(ex falso quodlibet (EFQ))*

Once the routine for deriving a "metatheorem" (a theorem with metavariables in the place of sentences of SL) has been mastered, there is nothing more to be gained from repeating it. When the situation arises where it would expedite the progress of a demonstration to derive an instance of that metatheorem, that instance can simply be inserted, justified by the recognized name for the metatheorem. Technically, the instance of the metatheorem is justified by reiteration. Since the instance is derivable from the empty list, it can be reiterated under any other list. In practice, the justification is the exercise set number where the metatheorem was demonstrated or an assigned name, if the metatheorem has been assigned a name.

For example, it is moderately challenging to establish that A ≡ (C ∨ G), ~(C ∨ G) ≡ B ⊢ A ∨ B using the 11 basic rules of Ds. The derivation is more straightforward if instances of metatheorems can be inserted at any point. The derivation below exploits this permission by inserting an instance of the metatheorem (em) at line 3.

1.	A ≡ (C ∨ G)	given
2.	~(C ∨ G) ≡ B	given
3.	(C ∨ G) ∨ ~(C ∨ G)	(em)
4.	C ∨ G ~(C ∨ G)	(A/3PC)
5.	A ≡ (C ∨ G) ~(C ∨ G) ≡ B	1/2 (R)
6.	A B	4,5 (BMP)
7.	A ∨ B A ∨ B	6 (VI)
8.	A ∨ B	3,5–7,5–7 (PC)

Similarly, when a routine has been established for deriving P from one or more sentences, Q, R, … and instances of Q, R, … have been derived within the same subderivation, the corresponding instance of P can be derived by appeal to that routine. In this case the justification is referred to as a derived rule. For example, it would be moderately challenging to establish that A → B, G → A, ~B, C ∨ G ⊢ ~C → K. The derivation is more straight-forward if derived rules can be used. The derivation below uses derived rules established in exercise 6.14#2: (HS), (MT), (DS), (DNI), and (T→).

1.	A → B	given
2.	G → A	given
3.	~B	given
4.	C ∨ G	given
5.	G → B	2,1 (HS)
6.	~G	5,3 (MT)
7.	C	4,6 (DS)
8.	~~C	7 (DNI)
9.	~C → K	8 (T→)

The sentences on lines 2 and 1, G → A and A → B, are instances of P → Q and Q → R. Since these sentences both lie immediately to the right of the same assumption bracket, (HS) can be applied to derive G → B, which is the corresponding instance of P → R. Again, the sentences on lines 5 and 3, G → B and ~B, are instances of P → Q and ~Q. Since they both lie immediately to the right of the same assumption bracket, (MT) can be applied to derive ~G, which is the corresponding instance of ~P. The sentences on lines 4 and 6, C ∨ G and ~G, are instances of P ∨ Q and ~Q. Since these sentences both lie immediately to the right of the same assumption bracket, (DS) can be applied to derive C, which is the corresponding instance of P.

Lines 7–9 illustrate an important point about applying derived rules. Wherever a tilde appears in a derived rule, a tilde must appear in any instance of that derived rule. For example, (T→) specifies that P → Q is derivable from ~P. It does not specify that ~P → Q is derivable from P. This is why the application of (DNI) is necessary at line 8. When the instance of P → Q is ~C → K, the corresponding instance of ~P is ~~C.

Care must also be taken to apply derived rules to whole sentences. It is tempting to ignore this stipulation in applications of (DNI) and (DNE). A → ~~B yields ~~(A → ~~B) by (DNI). But it does not yield A → B by (DNE). (DNE) can only be applied to a whole sentence. All of the derived rules are like this. The issue of replacing proper components of a sentence with interderivable components is taken up later.

The introduction of metatheorems and derived rules makes Ds very powerful. Results that would require many lines of demonstration can be derived in a single line, and results that would require multiple subderivations can often be derived without needing to introduce any subderivations. In many cases, there will be many different ways to derive the result, using different rules or same rules in different orders. But while metatheorems and derived rules shorten derivations, they do not make it possible to derive anything that could not be derived using just the 11 basic rules. Each of them is based on a routine sequence of steps made using just the 11 basic rules, and serves only to abbreviate that routine.

Exercise 6.15

1. *Establish the following using named theorems and derived rules to abbreviate the derivation. Aim to do each derivation using as few subderivations as possible, and in as few lines as possible. (These exercises are drawn from those in exercise 6.5#1 and 2. You may want to compare those answers and do what you can to ensure that these are shorter.)*

   ★a. A, B → ⊥ ⊢ (A → B) → ⊥

   b. ~B → ~(A → A), B → C ⊢ C

   ★c. ⊢ A → ~[(B → A) → ~A]

   d. (~B → A) → C, ~A → ⊥ ⊢ C

   ★e. [(A → B) → (A → ⊥)] → ⊥ ⊢ B

   f. [A → (B → ⊥)] → ⊥ ⊢ B

   ★g. (A → ⊥) → B, A → C, B → G ⊢ (C → ⊥) → G

   h. (A → ⊥) → B, A → C, B → C ⊢ C

   ★i. A, B ⊢ ((A → B) → [(B → A) → ⊥]) → ⊥

   j. A → (B → ~C), B ⊢ C → (A → ⊥)

2. *Redo any of exercises 6.12#6–9 that lend themselves to solution using any of the theorems or derived rules.*

Answers for #6★a, ★c ★e; #7★a, ★c, ★e; #8★a, ★c, ★e; #9★a, ★c, ★e

6.5.3 Substitution Principles

Some metatheorems are biconditionals. In that case, if one of the immediate components of an instance of the metatheorem occurs within a subderivation, inserting the instance would permit deriving the other immediate component. For instance, $(P \rightarrow Q) \equiv (\sim P \vee Q)$ is a metatheorem. Label it (impl). Suppose $(A \& B) \rightarrow C$ occurs in a subderivation. Then inserting the instance, $[(A \& B) \rightarrow C] \equiv [\sim(A \& B) \vee C]$ of (impl) in the subderivation permits deriving $\sim(A \& B) \vee C$ by (BMP).

Where a biconditional metatheorem has been demonstrated and named, it is permissible to skip the intermediate step of inserting the instance of the metatheorem and appealing to (BMP). One immediate component of an instance of (impl) can be directly derived from the other by appeal to (impl). $(A \& B) \rightarrow C$, for example, can be immediately derived from $\sim(A \& B) \vee C$ by (impl). This amounts to treating (impl) as if it were an interderivability principle, $(P \rightarrow Q) -|- (\sim P \vee Q)$. The principle permits deriving a sentence of either of these forms from one of the other form.

The following forms of interderivability are recognized and named.

				Substitution Principles of Ds		
★a.		P	−|−	~~P	(DN)	*(double negation)*
b.		P	−|−	P & P	(idem)	*(idempotence)*
★c.		P	−|−	P ∨ P	(idem)	*(idempotence)*
d.		P	−|−	(P & Q) ∨ (P & ~Q)	(elab)	*(elaboration)*
★e.		P	−|−	(P ∨ Q) & (P ∨ ~Q)	(elab)	*(elaboration*
f.		P & ~P	−|−	⊥	(con)	*(contradiction)*
★g.		P ∨ ~P	−|−	~⊥	(em)	*(excluded middle)*
h.		P ∨ ~⊥	−|−	~⊥	(inf)	*(infection)*
★i.		P & ⊥	−|−	⊥	(inf)	*(infection)*
j.		P ∨ ⊥	−|−	P	(imm)	*(immunity)*
★k.		P & ~⊥	−|−	P	(imm)	*(immunity)*
l.		P ∨ Q	−|−	Q ∨ P	(com)	*(commutation)*
★m.		P & Q	−|−	Q & P	(com)	*(commutation)*
n.	P & (Q & R)		−|−	(P & Q) & R	(assoc)	*(association)*
★o.	P ∨ (Q ∨ R)		−|−	(P ∨ Q) ∨ R	(assoc)	*(association)*
p.	P ∨ (Q & R)		−|−	(P ∨ Q) & (P ∨ R)	(dist)	*(distribution)*
★q.	P & (Q ∨ R)		−|−	(P & Q) ∨ (P & R)	(dist)	*(distribution)*
r.	~(P ∨ Q)		−|−	~P & ~Q	(DeM)	*(De Morgan's theorem)*
★s.	~(P & Q)		−|−	~P ∨ ~Q	(DeM)	*(De Morgan's theorem)*
t.	P → Q		−|−	~P ∨ Q	(impl)	*(implication)*
★u.	P → Q		−|−	~(P & ~Q)	(impl)	*(implication)*
v.	P → Q		−|−	~Q → ~P	(contra)	*(contraposition)*
★w.	(P & Q) → R		−|−	P → (Q → R)	(exp)	*(exportation)*
x.	P ≡ Q		−|−	(P → Q) & (~P → ~Q)	(equiv)	*(equivalence)*
★y.	P ≡ Q		−|−	(P → Q) & (Q → P)	(equiv)	*(equivalence)*
z.	~(P ≡ Q)		−|−	(P & ~Q) ∨ (Q & ~P)	(~equiv)	*(~ equivalence)*
★aa.	P ≡ Q		−|−	(P & Q) ∨ (~P & ~Q)	(equiv)	*(equivalence)*
bb.	~(P ≡ Q)		−|−	(P ∨ Q) & ~(P & Q)	(∨̲)	*(exclusivity)*

Ds can be made yet more powerful by introducing a set of substitution principles permitting interderivable sentences to be substituted for one another wherever they occur as components of larger sentences. This presumes that Ds supports a kind of extensionality, D-extensionality.

> *D-extensionality:* If P contains one or more occurrences of some component, Q, and Q and R are interderivable, then P and P(R|Q) are interderivable, where P(R|Q) is the sentence that results from replacing one or more occurrences of Q in P with occurrences of R.

D-extensionality makes it permissible to derive P(R|Q) directly from P, provided it has been previously established that Q and R are interderivable. (D-extensionality is demonstrated by defining a routine for deriving P(R|Q) from P using "whole sentence" substitutions. The routine is explained in the solution to exercise 6.16#3a.)

For example, supposing (DN), P −|− ~~P is recognized as an interderivability principle, D-extensionality permits deriving A ∨ B from ~~A ∨ B, or A ∨ ~~B from A ∨ B. This does not just hold for atomic components. R and Q could be arbitrarily complex, making it permissible to derive ~~(A & C) ∨ B from (A & C) ∨ B, or A ∨ ~~(B & G) from A ∨ (B & G).

In applying the substitution principles, care must be taken to ensure that both sentences involved are instances of the forms. For example, (contra) allows deriving a sentence of the form P → Q from one of the form ~Q → ~P. It does not allow deriving A → ~B from B → ~A, though it would allow deriving A → ~B from ~~B → ~A. Of course, (DN) can be applied to turn B → ~A into ~~B → ~A. But it does need to be applied. It cannot be integrated with the application of (contra).

1.	(B → ~A) ≡ C	given
2.	(~~A → ~B) ≡ C	1 (contra)
3.	(A → ~B) ≡ C	2 (DN)

To take another example, (B & C) ∨ (A & C) cannot be derived from (A ∨ B) & C by (dist).

1.	(A ∨ B) & C	given
✗ 2.	**(B & C) ∨ (A & C)**	**(dist)**

(A ∨ B) & C does not have the form P & (Q ∨ R), and (B & C) ∨ (A & C) does not have the form (P & Q) ∨ (P & R), so (dist) cannot be applied. Working around this requires applications of (com):

1.	(A ∨ B) & C	given
2.	C & (A ∨ B)	1 (com)
3.	C & (B ∨ A)	2 (com)
4.	(C & B) ∨ (C & A)	3 (dist)
5.	(B & C) ∨ (C & A)	4 (com)
6.	(B & C) ∨ (A & C)	5 (com)

The correct derivation illustrates a further point: it is only permissible to make one substitution at a time. Line 2 could not be omitted in favour of deriving line 3 directly from line 1, because flipping the conjuncts at line 2 and flipping the disjuncts at line 3 are two different forms of (com), based on different equivalences. For clarity, they need to be demonstrated separately. The equivalences are both called "commutation," but they are as different from one another as any two substitution principles on the table. Even when what really is the same rule is applied, and only conjuncts are flipped, as at lines 5 and 6, it is strictly only permissible to flip one at a time, not two at once. So line 6 cannot be directly inferred from line 4.

Applications of (dist) are challenging when the sentence being distributed is itself compound. A & (B ∨ C) obviously distributes as (A & B) ∨ (A & C). (A & B) ∨ (C & G) is not so obvious. The solution is to treat (A & B) as a unit, in which case it has the form P ∨ (Q & R), and distributes as

$$[(A \& B) \lor C] \& [(A \& B) \lor G].$$

Treating (A & B) as a unit will not help in the case of

$$(A \& B) \lor (C \lor G)$$

since distribution must be of a disjunct over the conjuncts comprising a second disjunct or a conjunct over the disjuncts comprising a second conjunct. Disjuncts cannot be distributed over disjuncts or conjuncts over conjuncts. However, there are still various ways this sentence could be distributed. One is by means of a prior application of (com) to produce (C ∨ G) ∨ (A & B). This allows (C ∨ G) to be treated as a unit, producing

$$[(C \lor G) \lor A] \& [(C \lor G) \lor B]$$

Another is by applying (assoc) to (A & B) ∨ (C ∨ G) to produce [(A & B) ∨ C] ∨ G, and then applying (com) to produce [C ∨ (A & B)] ∨ G. Now C can be distributed over (A & B).

$$[(C \lor A) \& (C \lor B)] \lor G$$

If desired, a further application of (com) will permit distribution of G over each of the conjuncts.

Once the principles higher up on the list have been demonstrated, they can be used to demonstrate some of the principles lower down on the list. An example can be taken from the last principle on the list, the exclusivity principle, ~(P ≡ Q) –|– (P ∨ Q) & ~(P & Q). Establishing the interderivability of the two forms is possible using just the 12 basic rules of Ds, but it can be more quickly done by appealing to the earlier interderivability principles.

1.	~(P ≡ Q)	given	1.	(P ∨ Q) & ~(P & Q)	given
2.	~[(P & Q) ∨ (~P & ~Q)]	1 (equiv)		[repeat lines 2–6	1 (DN)
3.	~(P & Q) & ~(~P & ~Q)	2 (DeM)		in reverse order]	2 (DN)
4.	~(~P & ~Q) & ~(P & Q)	3 (com)			3 (DeM)
5.	(~~P ∨ ~~Q) & ~(P & Q)	4 (DeM)			4 (com)
6.	(P ∨ ~~Q) & ~(P & Q)	5 (DN)			5 (DeM)
7.	(P ∨ Q) & ~(P & Q)	6 (DN)	7.	~(P ≡ Q)	6 (equiv)

This example illustrates two commonly occurring features of derivations that employ substitution of interderivable components: (i) The derivation often requires only one assumption bracket; (ii) Where the aim is to demonstrate interderivability it often suffices to do the derivation in just one direction. The substitution principles are all reversible. Provided they are the only rules used in the derivation, repeating the sequence of derived sentences in the reverse order, and repeating the sequence of justifications in the reverse order, derives the premise from the conclusion. Doing the derivation in just one direction makes it clear enough how to do the second half, allowing that part of the exercise to be omitted.

Exercise 6.16

1. *Supply routines for deriving the substitution principles listed above. Feel free to use theorems and derived rules and substitution principles justified by answering questions higher up on the list to solve questions lower down on the list. The posted solution to (aa) is important.*

2. *Derive the following claims in Ds using the theorems, derived rules, and substitution principles introduced in this chapter to abbreviate the derivation.*
   ⋆a. ⊢ [A → (B ∨ C)] ≡ [(A → B) ∨ (A → C)]
   b. ⊢ [(A → B) & (~A → ~B)] ≡ [(A & B) ∨ (~A & ~B)]
   ⋆c. ⊢ [(B & C) ∨ ~A] ≡ [(~B → ~A) & (C ∨ ~A)]
   d. ⊢ ~[~(A ∨ B) & C] ≡ [(~B & C) → A]
   ⋆e. ⊢ [(~B → A) ∨ ~(~A & ~B)] → (~~A ∨ B)
   f. ⊢ ~[(B → A) ∨ (A ∨ B)] → ~A
   ⋆g. ⊢ [([B & (A & ⊥)] ∨ (A → ⊥)) & A] → ⊥
   h. ⊢ [(A & B) ∨ (~A & ~B)] → [(~A ∨ B) & (~B ∨ A)]

3. *Establish the following by applying substitution principles, (&E), (A/PC), (&I), (∨I), and (PC) to whole sentences.*

  ★a. ~[(C & A) ∨ (A → ~B)] ⊢ ~[(C & ~~A) ∨ (~~A → ~B)]

  b. [(A → B) & A] → (B ∨ C) ⊢ [(~A ∨ B) & A] → (B ∨ C)

6.5.4 Disjunctive Normal Form

The substitution principles introduced in the previous section make it possible to transform any sentence of SL into a sentence in disjunctive normal form ("dnf"). This in turn makes it possible to define a mechanical procedure for doing any derivation: one that requires no ingenuity in the choice of what rules to apply, that yields P whenever P is derivable from Γ, and that discovers a counterexample (a model on which all the sentences in Γ are true and P is false) whenever P is not derivable from Γ. The procedure can take many more lines to apply than a free style derivation, making it impractical. But the fact that it exists makes an important point about the affinity between derivations and the semantic procedures of chapters 3 and 5.

As noted in the appendix to chapter 3, a sentence of SL is said to be in disjunctive normal form when it is a disjunction of conjunctions of literals.

- → and ≡ do not appear, no ∨ occurs within the scope of an &, and ~ only appears when immediately followed by a sentence letter or by ⊥
- the atomic components of each iterated conjunction occur in alphanumeric order
- each disjunct contains each atomic sentence to occur in any other disjunct, so the disjuncts are composed of conjunctions of the same atomic sentences
- ⊥ does not occur unless it or ~⊥ is the whole sentence

As a special case, a lone atomic sentence is an iterated disjunction with just one disjunct. It is also an iterated conjunction with just one conjunct. A lone iterated conjunction of arbitrarily many conjuncts is likewise an iterated disjunction with just one disjunct. So, A, A & ~B, and (~A & B) & ~C all count as iterated disjunctions as well as iterated conjunctions.

Sentences in disjunctive normal form can be hard to read through the forest of punctuation around iterated conjunctions and iterated disjunctions. Since (assoc) proves that it makes no difference how iterated disjunctions and iterated conjunctions are internally punctuated, a new informal notational convention, (ip) is adopted.

- internal punctuation may be removed from iterated conjunctions and iterated disjunctions

For example, [(A & ~B) & (C & ~G)] and ([(A & ~B) & C] & ~G) can be rewritten as (A & ~B & C & ~G). Only the internal punctuation can be omitted. The punctuation at the start and the end of the iterated conjunction or disjunction must be retained, unless the (op) convention applies.

As with all other informal notational conventions, this convention may be adopted or omitted at will. No rule application is called for to apply it or remove it, and internal punctuation that has been removed from one copy of a sentence can be inserted in a subsequent copy without any special notice. When it is reinserted, it can be inserted in any way that suits the present purpose. Thus, A & B & C can be recopied as either (A & B) & C or A & (B & C).

There is an effective procedure for conversion to dnf.

Stages of Conversion to dnf

 (i) Apply (imp) and (equiv-aa) to convert all conditionals to disjunctions and all biconditionals to disjunctions of conjunctions; proceed to step (ii).

 (ii) Wherever ~ is followed by ~, apply (DN); proceed to step (iii).

 (iii) Wherever ~ is followed by a punctuation mark, apply (DeM); return to stage (ii); after a cycle through stages ii–iii produces no changes, proceed to stage (iv).

 (iv) Wherever a conjunction has a disjunction as one of its immediate components, apply (dist-q) (or (com) and (dist-q) if the disjunction is the left immediate component); repeat until there are no more such instances; proceed to stage (v).

 (v) Wherever conjuncts are not in alphanumeric order, apply (com) to put them in order; proceed to stage (vi).

> (vi) Apply (idem) to eliminate repetition of the same conjunct; proceed to stage (vii).
>
> (vii) Using (com) as necessary to facilitate this, apply (con) from left to right only (that is, to produce rather than remove ⊥'s); proceed to stage (viii).
>
> (viii) Wherever ⊥ occurs in an iterated conjunction, apply (inf) assisted by (com) where necessary to convert the whole iterated disjunction to ⊥; proceed to stage (ix).
>
> (ix) Wherever some disjunct other than ⊥ or ~⊥ lacks a sentence letter that is present in other disjuncts, apply (elab-d), then apply (com) to put the sentence letters in alphanumeric order and arrange the disjuncts in "long table" order; apply (idem) to remove duplicates; if the resulting dnf is not ⊥, apply (imm) to remove any occurrences of ⊥.

As an example, consider how to convert [(A → B) & A] & ~B into dnf. Stage 1 is to convert conditionals and biconditionals into wedge/ampersand sentences by applying (impl) and (equiv).

1.	[(A → B) & A] & ~B	given
2.	[(~A ∨ B) & A] & ~B	1 (impl)

Stages 2–3 are to work to ensure that any tildes are followed by sentence letters by applying (DeM) and (DN). In this case, there is nothing to do at this stage. Stage 4 is to apply (dist), or (com) and (dist) as necessary to make all ampersands fall under the scope of a wedge. (The earlier remarks on some of the complexities of applying (dist) are worth reviewing prior to doing this.)

1.	[(A → B) & A] & ~B	given
2.	[(~A ∨ B) & A] & ~B	1 (impl)
3.	**[A & (~A ∨ B)] & ~B**	**2 (com)**
4.	**[(A & ~A) ∨ (A & B)] & ~B**	**3 (dist)**
5.	**~B & [(A & ~A) ∨ (A & B)]**	**4 (com)**
6.	**[~B & (A & ~A)] ∨ [~B & (A & B)]**	**7 (dist)**

Stage 5 is to to reorder the conjuncts of each disjunct in alphanumeric order. Stage 6 does not apply in this case.

1.	[(A → B) & A] & ~B	given
2.	[(~A ∨ B) & A] & ~B	1 (impl)
3.	[A & (~A ∨ B)] & ~B	2 (com)
4.	[(A & ~A) ∨ (A & B)] & ~B	3 (dist)
5.	~B & [(A & ~A) ∨ (A & B)]	4 (com)
6.	[~B & (A & ~A)] ∨ [~B & (A & B)]	5 (dist)
7.	**[(A & ~A) & ~B] ∨ [~B & (A & B)]**	**6 (com)**
8.	**[(A & ~A) & ~B] ∨ [(A & B) & ~B)]**	**7 (com)**

Stages 7 and 8 are to apply (con) and (inf). At line 9, advantage is taken of the permission to silently omit internal punctuation in order to skip an application of (assoc).

1.	[(A → B) & A] & ~B)	given
2.	[(~A ∨ B) & A] & ~B)	1 (impl)
3.	[A & (~A ∨ B)] & ~B	2 (com)
4.	[(A & ~A) ∨ (A & B)] & ~B	3 (dist)
5.	~B & [(A & ~A) ∨ (A & B)]	4 (com)

6.	[~B & (A & ~A)] ∨ [~B & (A & B)]	5 (dist)
7.	[(A & ~A) & ~B] ∨ [~B & (A & B)]	6 (com)
8.	[(A & ~A) & ~B] ∨ [(A & B) & ~B]	7 (com)
9.	**(⊥ & ~B) ∨ (A & B & ~B)**	**8 (con)**
10.	**(⊥ & ~B) ∨ (A & ⊥)**	**9 (con)**
11.	**⊥ ∨ (A & ⊥)**	**10 (inf)**
12.	**⊥ ∨ ⊥**	**11 (inf)**

Work at this stage illustrates why it was said earlier that ⊥ either does not appear in dnf or the dnf reduces to ⊥. ⊥ is infectious in iterated conjunctions. If it occurs as a conjunct, (inf) converts the conjunction in which it appears into ⊥. (inf) then converts any larger conjunction in which the new ⊥ appears into ⊥, and so on until the whole iterated conjunction is converted into ⊥. On the other hand, iterated disjunctions are immune to infection by ⊥. If one of the disjuncts is ⊥, (imm) makes it disappear, leaving the other disjunct. The only way ⊥ can continue to appear in an iterated disjunction is if all disjuncts are ⊥, in which case applications of (idem), required at stage 9, convert the whole disjunction into ⊥.

1.	[(A → B) & A] & ~B)	given
2.	[(~A ∨ B) & A] & ~B)	1 (impl)
3.	[A & (~A ∨ B)] & ~B	2 (com)
4.	[(A & ~A) ∨ (A & B)] & ~B	3 (dist)
5.	~B & [(A & ~A) ∨ (A & B)]	4 (com)
6.	(~B & A & ~A) ∨ (~B & A & B)	5 (dist)
7.	(A & ~A & ~B) ∨ (~B & A & B)	6 (com)
8.	(A & ~A & ~B) ∨ (A & B & ~B)	7 (com)
9.	(⊥ & ~B) ∨ (A & B & ~B)	8 (con)
10.	(⊥ & ~B) ∨ (A & ⊥)	9 (con)
11.	⊥ ∨ (A & ⊥)	10 (inf)
12.	⊥ ∨ ⊥	11 (inf)
13.	**⊥**	**12 (idem)**

(The reverse would happen with ~⊥, though ~⊥ would only appear in a dnf if it were a component of the original sentence being converted to dnf. Iterated conjunctions are immune to ~⊥, so it drops out of them by (imm). But when it appears in an iterated disjunction, it is infectious and converts the whole disjunction to ~⊥.)

The derivation that has just been done illustrates how the routine for deriving a dnf might be used to complete any derivation. Any derivation has the form of a list of premises, <P₁,...,Pᵢ>, yielding a conclusion, Q.

1.	P₁	given
...	...	given
i.	Pᵢ	given
...	...	
n.	Q	?

Begin the derivation by assuming the opposite, ~Q. Then reiterate all the premises under this assumption. Then apply (&I) multiple times to form a single sentence that is the iterated conjunction of the premises and the negation of the conclusion.

```
 1.  | P₁                                        given
...  | ...                                       given
 i.  | Pᵢ                                        given
i+1. |  | ~Q                                     (A/IP)
...  |
 k.  |  | (...(P₁ & ...) & Pₙ) & ~Q              [multiple (R)'s and (&I)'s]
...  |  | ...
n−1. |  | ⊥                                      dnf construction on k
 n.  | Q                                         i+1 to n−1 (IP)
```

Now apply the procedure for constructing the dnf of the sentence at line k. If the dnf collapses to ⊥, (IP) can be applied to derive Q, and the derivation has been completed.

The derivation that was done earlier yields this outcome for A → B, A ⊢ B. Conjoining the two premises with the negation of the conclusion produces [(A → B) & A] & ~B, which, when converted to dnf, becomes ⊥. Of course, the derivation of the conclusion from the premises could be done in one line by applying (MP). But in cases where ingenuity fails, the procedure for constructing a dnf serves as a foolproof, automatic routine for coming up with one, supposing there is one to come up with (not everything is derivable).

When there is no derivation, constructing a dnf proves that the demonstration is invalid. For example, the claim that A → B, B ⊢ A is an instance of the fallacy of affirming the consequent. No correct way of deriving the conclusion from the premises has yet been discovered. Converting the iterated conjunction of the premises and the negation of the conclusion to dnf does not prove that none will ever be discovered, but it does discover an interpretation on which the premises are true and the conclusion is false, thereby establishing that the derivation is s-invalid.

```
 1.  | [(A → B) & B] & ~A                        given
 2.  | [(~A ∨ B) & B] & ~A                        1 (impl)
 3.  | [B & (~A ∨ B)] & ~A                        2 (com)
 4.  | [(B & ~A) ∨ (B & B)] & ~A                  3 (dist)
 5.  | ~A & [(B & ~A) ∨ (B & B)]                  4 (com)
 6.  | (~A & B & ~A) ∨ (~A & B & B)               5 (dist)
 7.  | (~A & ~A & B) ∨ (~A & B & B)               6 (com)
 8.  | (~A & B) ∨ (~A & B & B)                    7 (idem)
 9.  | (~A & B) ∨ (~A & B)                        8 (idem)
10.  | ~A & B                                     9 (idem)
```

The derivation does not yield ⊥ and so cannot be plugged into a demonstration that A → B, B ⊢ A. But the sentence it yields is what the appendix to chapter 3 describes as a characteristic sentence. It is an iterated conjunction of literals. As noted in that appendix, such sentences are true on exactly one interpretation, the interpretation that assigns a T to each literal. ~A & B is true on exactly the interpretation that assigns F to A and T to B. As a long table test shows, the original sentence, [(A → B) & B] & ~A, is also true on exactly that interpretation.

As proven in section A-2.8, this holds in general. Each disjunct of the dnf for a sentence describes a unique interpretation on which the sentence is true, and as a group the disjuncts pick out every such interpretation. The exception is the case where the dnf collapses to ⊥, in which case the sentence is false on each interpretation.

This means that dnf's can be used to discover a model for a sentence (an interpretation on which the sentence is true), indeed, all the models that a sentence can have. When a sentence is s-valid, that is, true on each interpretation, the dnf for the sentence will prove it by having exactly 2^n disjuncts, where n is the number of different sentence letters in the sentence. Since that is exactly the number of interpretations on the long table for the sentence, the dnf proves that the sentence gets a T on each interpretation and so is s-valid.

When a derivation seems impossible to complete, a recourse (though often a laborious one) is to derive the dnf for the iterated conjunction of the premises and the negation of the conclusion. If that dnf is not ⊥, it identifies one or more interpretations on which the premises are true and the conclusion is false. This does not prove that the derivation is impossible to complete, but it does establish that the demonstration is s-invalid. In section A-2.1, it is shown that this means there can be no derivation.

Exercise 6.17

1. *Derive dnf's for each of the following sentences. Follow the nine-stage conversion procedure. Resist the temptation to apply rules that are not mandated by the procedure or not mandated at that stage, even if those applications would shorten sentences or reduce the number of lines of demonstration. Part of the purpose of this exercise is to gain insight into how the nine-stage procedure automatically ensures that a dnf will be produced.*

   ★**a.** $(A \rightarrow B) \equiv (\sim B \rightarrow \sim A)$
   b. $\sim[(A \rightarrow \bot) \rightarrow \sim A]$ *(careful!)*
   ★**c.** $([(A \lor B) \rightarrow C] \;\&\; \sim A) \;\&\; \sim(B \lor C)$
   d. $\sim(A \;\&\; B) \rightarrow \sim A$
   ★**e.** $[(A \rightarrow B) \;\&\; A] \rightarrow (B \lor C)$
   f. $A \rightarrow (B \rightarrow B)$

★**2.** *Construct long tables for each of the sentences in exercise 1 and compare the dnf's constructed in answer to question 1 to those tables. What does the comparison show?*

3. *Following the nine-stage procedure, derive dnf's for each of the following claims.*

   ★**a.** $A \rightarrow B \vdash B \rightarrow A$
   b. $A \rightarrow B, A \rightarrow \sim B \vdash \sim A$
   ★**c.** $A \rightarrow (B \rightarrow \bot) \vdash B \rightarrow \sim A$
   d. $(A \rightarrow A) \rightarrow B \vdash B$
   ★**e.** $A \rightarrow C, B \rightarrow C \vdash A \lor B$
   f. $(A \rightarrow B) \rightarrow \sim A \vdash \sim B$

4. *Describe how the method of deriving dnf's might be adapted to determine each of the following. In each case describe both how to set up the test, and what test results (yielding $\bot$ as opposed to yielding an iterated disjunction of other literals) establish which assertions. Consult the answered questions for further illustration.*

   ★**a.** Whether a sentence is a theorem of Ds or is s-invalid.
   b. Whether a sentence is inconsistent in Ds or is s-satisfiable.
   ★**c.** Whether a sentence is s-contingent.
   d. Whether a finite set is inconsistent in Ds or is s-satisfiable.
   ★**e.** Whether two sentences are interderivable in Ds or are s-nonequivalent.

6.5.5 Relations between Intensional Concepts

At the outset of this chapter it was remarked that it cannot be assumed that derivability ($\vdash$) and entailment ($\vDash$) are the same. That is, it cannot be assumed either that whatever is derivable is entailed, or that whatever is entailed is derivable. However, over the course of this chapter, same sentences have been derived and same demonstrations have been shown to be derivable that were shown in chapters 3 and 5 to be valid. A striking instance is the long list of substitution principles identified earlier, which correspond to the entailment principles identified in section 5.3. And it has just been shown that, in those cases where a derivation proves to be so difficult as to be impossible to find, deriving the dnf instead reveals a model that establishes that there is no entailment. At a more fundamental level, the rules of Ds, stated in terms of lists and $\vdash$, parallel the entailment principles demonstrated in exercise 5.12b–l.

This correspondence between results obtained in Ds and semantic results extends to the correspondences identified in chapters 3 and 5. There it was shown that for any pair of sentences, for any set of sentences, and for any demonstration there is a corresponding sentence. Similarly, for sentences, pairs of sentences, and demonstrations there are corresponding sets, and for sentences, pairs of sentences, and sets there are corresponding demonstrations. Similar correspondences hold in Ds.

Corresponding Sentences
1. P and Q are interderivable if and only if $P \equiv Q$ is a theorem.
2. $<P_1,\ldots,P_n>$ is inconsistent if and only if $P_1 \;\&\; \ldots \;\&\; P_n$ is inconsistent.
3. $\Gamma \vdash Q$ if and only if and only if $(P_1 \;\&\; \ldots \;\&\; P_n) \rightarrow Q$ is a theorem, where $<P_1,\ldots,P_n>$ is a finite list of the sentences in Γ.

> **Corresponding Lists**
>
> 4. P is a theorem if and only if <~P> is inconsistent.
> 5. P and Q are interderivable if and only if both <P,~Q> and <Q,~P> are inconsistent.
> 6. $\Gamma \vdash Q$ if and only if L,~Q is inconsistent, where L is a finite list of the sentences in Γ.

Demonstrations of some of these principles follow. The rest are set as exercises.

Principle 4: $\vdash$ P if and only if ~P $\vdash \perp$.

Suppose $\vdash$ P. Then there is a derivation that looks like this:

$$
\begin{array}{ll}
1. & \\
\cdots & \\
n. & P
\end{array}
$$

This derivation can be transported into a derivation that is headed off by the assumption of ~P and completed as follows.

$$
\begin{array}{lll}
0. & \text{~P} & \text{given} \\
1. & & \\
\cdots & & \\
n. & P & \\
n+1. & \perp & 0,n\ (\perp\text{I})
\end{array}
$$

So if $\vdash$ P then ~P $\vdash \perp$. This is half of what needs to be demonstrated. Now suppose that ~P $\vdash \perp$. Then there is a derivation that looks like this (lines 1 to *n*−1 will have sentences on them that result in $\perp$ at line *n*):

$$
\begin{array}{lll}
1. & \text{~P} & \text{given} \\
\cdots & \cdots & \\
n. & \perp & \#,\#\ (\perp\text{I})
\end{array}
$$

But this derivation has a demonstration that $\vdash$ P as its immediate consequence.

$$
\begin{array}{lll}
1. & \text{~P} & \text{given} \\
\cdots & \cdots & \\
n. & \perp & \#,\#\ (\perp\text{I}) \\
n+1. & P & 1-n\ (\text{IP})
\end{array}
$$

So $\vdash$ P if and only if ~P $\vdash \perp$

Principle 6: L $\vdash$ P if and only if L,~P $\vdash \perp$.

Suppose that L $\vdash$ P. Then there is a derivation beginning with an assumption bracket headed off by the sentences on L ($Q_1 \ldots Q_k$) that derives P immediately to the right of this assumption bracket.

$$
\begin{array}{ll}
1. & Q_1 \\
\cdots & \cdots \\
k. & Q_k \\
\cdots & \cdots \\
n. & P
\end{array}
$$

Now suppose that ~P is added to the list of givens for this derivation at line *k*+1. Then after deriving P at (now) line *n*+1, $\perp$ can be derived by *n*+1,*k*+1 ($\perp$I).

$$
\begin{array}{rl}
1. & Q_1 \\
\cdots & \cdots \\
k. & Q_k \\
k+1. & \sim P \\
\cdots & \cdots \\
n+1. & P \\
n+2. & \bot \qquad n+1, k+1 \;(\bot I)
\end{array}
$$

But this means that the list of sentences on L supplemented by the addition of ~P is inconsistent.

So if L ⊢ P then L,~P ⊢ ⊥. This is half of what needs to be demonstrated. To demonstrate the other half, suppose that L,~P ⊢ ⊥. Then starting with a derivation that begins by taking the sentences on L (Q₁...Qₖ) as givens and adding the assumption of ~P must yield ⊥.

$$
\begin{array}{rl}
1. & Q_1 \\
\cdots & \cdots \\
k. & Q_k \\
k+1. & \quad \sim P \\
\cdots & \quad \cdots \\
n. & \quad \bot \qquad \text{(because } \langle Q_1\ldots Q_k, \sim P\rangle \text{ yields } \bot\text{)}
\end{array}
$$

But it is an immediate consequence of this derivation that L ⊢ P.

$$
\begin{array}{rl}
1. & Q_1 \\
\cdots & \cdots \\
k. & Q_k \\
k+1. & \quad \sim P \\
\cdots & \quad \cdots \\
n. & \quad \bot \\
n+1. & P \qquad k+1-n \;(\mathrm{IP})
\end{array}
$$

So L ⊢ P if and only if L,~P ⊢ ⊥.

Exercise 6.18

Following the examples just given, demonstrate principles 1–3 and 5 above. For 3 use the demonstration of 6 and note that if a derivation is headed off by the initial assumption of the iterated conjunction, $(P_1 \& \ldots P_n)$, repeated applications of (&E) will obtain each of $P_1, \ldots, P_n$ immediately to the right of the assumption bracket for this assumption. Similarly, if a derivation is headed off by $P_1, \ldots, P_n$, repeated applications of (&I) will obtain $(P_1 \& \ldots P_n)$ under this assumption.

6.5.6 *Bracket Free Notation*

When the rules of D_L and Ds were first presented in sections 6.2 and 6.4, they were supplemented with templates depicting how to apply the rules using assumption brackets. The templates are not the rules. They are an interface that makes it easier to work with the rules. It is possible to do derivations without assumption brackets. Derivations done without using assumption brackets are done in bracket free notation.[2] The notation that has been used up to now is standard notation. In bracket free notation, derivations appear as lists of sentences of English that state what lists of sentences of SL yield what sentences of SL. Such sentences are sometimes called sequents.

> A *derivation in bracket free notation* is a list of sequents, where each sequent on the list is entered in accord with a derivation rule.

In bracket free notation, each sequent begins with a list of assumptions, followed by a turnstile. The sentence that is derived in standard notation follows the turnstile. This gives a sequent the form of a claim that a list of assumptions yields a sentence. Later sequents are derived from earlier ones in accord with the derivation rules rather than their templates. The rules are well suited to this purpose since they relate forms for sequents.

(R):	If L ⊢ P then L,M ⊢ P
(IP):	If L,P ⊢ ⊥ then L yields any opposite of P
(⊥I):	If L ⊢ P and L ⊢ ~P then L ⊢ ⊥
(CP):	If L,P ⊢ Q then L ⊢ P → Q
(MP):	If L ⊢ P and L ⊢ P → Q then L ⊢ Q
(PC):	If (i) L ⊢ P ∨ Q; (ii) L,P ⊢ R; and (iii) L,Q ⊢ R, then L ⊢ R
(∨I):	If L ⊢ P then L ⊢ P ∨ Q and L ⊢ Q ∨ P
(&E):	If L ⊢ P & Q then L ⊢ P and L ⊢ Q
(&I):	If L ⊢ P and L ⊢ Q then L ⊢ P & Q
(BP):	If L,P ⊢ Q and L,Q ⊢ P then L ⊢ P ≡ Q
(BMP):	If L ⊢ P and L ⊢ P ≡ Q or Q ≡ P then L ⊢ Q

The difference between derivations in standard notation and derivations in bracket free notation is largely notational. Same sentences still appear on same lines for same reasons. They are just written down differently. In bracket free notation, each sentence is prefaced by the list of assumptions it is derived from. That list corresponds to the assumptions that head off the assumption brackets, taken from left to right, that continue down to the line where the sentence appears. Applications of (IP), (CP), (PC), and (BP) are justified by prior sequents rather than completed subderivations.

Eliminating assumption brackets requires one modification to the rules. (A) appears as an independent rule, used not only to make assumptions, but to derive givens. The parallel entailment principle is given in exercise 5.12a.

$$(A): L,P \vdash P$$

(A) expresses the intuitively obvious principle that if P is the last sentence on a list, then that list yields P. As a special case, when L is the empty list, P added to the empty list yields P, that is P ⊢ P. (A) complements (R), which says that if a sentence occurs prior to last place on a list, then the list also yields that sentence. Unlike the other rules of Ds, which describe what sentences may be derived from what other sentences, (A) is an axiom. It is the form for a sequent that can be inserted at any point, without needing to be derived from any prior sequents. It enables derivations in Ds to get started.

To illustrate how derivations are done in bracket free notation, consider how ~(A → B) → A might be demonstrated to be a theorem using "standard" notation.

1.		~(A → B)	(A/CP)
2.		~A	(A/IP)
3.		A	(A/CP)
4.		~A	2 (R)
5.		~B	(A/IP)
6.		A	3 (R)
7.		~A	4 (R)
8.		⊥	6,7 (⊥I)
9.		B	5–8 (IP)
10.		A → B	3–9 (CP)
11.		~(A → B)	1 (R)
12.		⊥	10,11 (⊥I)
13.		A	2–12 (IP)
14.		~(A → B) → A	1–13 (CP)

To rewrite this derivation in bracket free notation, consider each line to assert that the sentence on that line is yielded by the list of assumptions that head off assumption brackets, taken from left to right, that continue unbroken down to that line. The sentence at line 1 is ~(A → B). There is also only one sentence heading off one of the two assumption brackets that descend unbroken down to that line, ~(A → B). The true form of the derivation at line 1 is therefore:

$$0. \qquad\qquad\quad \vdash$$

$$1. \quad \sim(A \to B) \quad \vdash \quad \sim(A \to B) \quad (A/CP)$$

Line 0 represents the leftmost assumption bracket, which is headed off by nothing. It is the line at which nothing is derived from the empty list. It could just as well have been written as ∅ ⊢ . But because this line contains no useful information, it can be omitted, as is the case in what follows.

Line 1 no longer says that ~(A → B) is being assumed for purposes of conditional proof. It asserts that the sequent, ~(A → B) ⊢ ~(A → B) is an instance of the (A) axiom. (In this case it is an instance of (A) that will be used in a later application of (CP).) (A) says that L,P ⊢ P. In this case, L is the empty list and P is ~(A → B). Line 1 could just as well have been written as ∅,~(A → B) ⊢ ~(A → B), but again this variant adds no useful information.

At line 2, there is one sentence, ~A. There are also two sentences heading off two of the three assumption brackets that descend unbroken down to line 2. Going from the left to the right, they are ~(A → B) and ~A. The true form of the derivation at line 2 is:

$$1. \quad \sim(A \to B) \qquad\qquad \vdash \quad \sim(A \to B) \quad (A/CP)$$

$$\mathbf{2. \quad \sim(A \to B), \sim A \quad \vdash \quad \sim A \qquad (A/IP)}$$

The sequent at line 2 is once again an instance of (A), this time one being asserted for purposes of an eventual application of (IP). In this case L is <~(A → B)> and P is ~A.

At line 3 of the derivation in standard notation, a new subderivation is added, with a further application of (A). Bracket free notation for the derivation at line 3 adds the assumption to the list:

$$1. \quad \sim(A \to B) \qquad\qquad \vdash \quad \sim(A \to B) \quad (A/CP)$$

$$2. \quad \sim(A \to B), \sim A \qquad \vdash \quad \sim A \qquad (A/IP)$$

$$\mathbf{3. \quad \sim(A \to B), \sim A, A \quad \vdash \quad A \qquad (A/CP)}$$

At line 4 of the derivation in standard notation, no new subderivations are added, and none have been removed, so the list from which the sentence at line 4 is derived is the same list from which the sentence at line 3 is derived.

$$1. \quad \sim(A \to B) \qquad\qquad \vdash \quad \sim(A \to B) \quad (A/CP)$$

$$2. \quad \sim(A \to B), \sim A \qquad \vdash \quad \sim A \qquad (A/IP)$$

$$3. \quad \sim(A \to B), \sim A, A \quad \vdash \quad A \qquad (A/CP)$$

$$\mathbf{4. \quad \sim(A \to B), \sim A, A \quad \vdash \quad \sim A \qquad 2 \; (R)}$$

The justification at line 4, 2 (R), should again be read differently. It is not saying that ~A is being reiterated from line 2. It is saying that the sequent at line 4 is justified by (R) applied to the sequent at line 2. The sequent at line 2 has the form L ⊢ P, where L is <~(A → B), ~A> and P is ~A. The sequent at line 4 has the form L,M ⊢ P, where M is <A> and L and P are (of course) as before. This is precisely the form (R) takes. It says that if L ⊢ P then L,M ⊢ P, that is, if a list yields a sentence, that list followed by any other list yields that sentence.

A new assumption bracket is introduced at line 5. For as long as this assumption bracket continues, which is up to line 8, the list from which sentences are derived adds the sentence that heads off this assumption bracket.

$$1. \quad \sim(A \to B) \qquad\qquad\quad \vdash \quad \sim(A \to B) \quad (A/CP)$$

$$2. \quad \sim(A \to B), \sim A \qquad\quad \vdash \quad \sim A \qquad (A/IP)$$

$$3. \quad \sim(A \to B), \sim A, A \quad \vdash \quad A \qquad (A/CP)$$

$$4. \quad \sim(A \to B), \sim A, A \quad \vdash \quad \sim A \qquad 2 \; (R)$$

5.	~(A → B), ~A, A, ~B	⊢	~B	(A/IP)
6.	~(A → B), ~A, A, ~B	⊢	A	3 (R)
7.	~(A → B), ~A, A, ~B	⊢	~A	4 (R)
8.	~(A → B), ~A, A, ~B	⊢	⊥	6,7 (⊥I)

Now the justification at line 8 should be read as saying that the sequent at line 8 follows from those at lines 6 and 7 by (⊥I). (⊥I) says that if L ⊢ Q and L ⊢ ~Q then L ⊢ ⊥. In this case, L is <~(A → B), ~A, A, ~B > and Q is A. Line 6 has the form L ⊢ Q, line 7 the form L ⊢ ~Q, and line 8 the form L ⊢ ⊥.

At line 9, the rightmost assumption bracket ends. This is the equivalent of dropping the last sentence from the list.

1.	~(A → B)	⊢	~(A → B)	(A/CP)
2.	~(A → B), ~A	⊢	~A	(A/IP)
3.	~(A → B), ~A, A	⊢	A	(A/CP)
4.	~(A → B), ~A, A	⊢	~A	2 (R)
5.	~(A → B), ~A, A, ~B	⊢	~B	(A/IP)
6.	~(A → B), ~A, A, ~B	⊢	A	3 (R)
7.	~(A → B), ~A, A, ~B	⊢	~A	4 (R)
8.	~(A → B), ~A, A, ~B	⊢	⊥	6,7 (⊥I)
9.	**~(A → B), ~A, A**	⊢	**B**	**8 (IP)**

The justification at line 9 is again different. Line 9 no longer has the form of a sentence, B, being derived from a prior subderivation running over lines 5–8. It instead says that the sequent at line 9 is justified by the sequent at line 8 by (IP). The sequent at line 8 has the form L,~P ⊢ ⊥, where L is <~(A → B), ~A, A> and ~P is ~B. (IP) properly says that if L,~P ⊢ ⊥ then L ⊢ P, which in this case means that <~(A → B), ~A, A> ⊢ P, which is just what the sequent at line 9 says.

At each of lines 10, 13, and 14 in the derivation in standard notation another assumption bracket ends. This is the equivalent of dropping yet other assumptions from the end of the list in the derivation in bracket free notation. The sequents on these lines are again not justified by appeal to prior subderivations (there are none) but by reference to prior sequents.

For instance, the justification for line 14 is 13 (CP). Line 13 has the form L,P ⊢ Q, where L is the empty list and P is ~(A → B). According to (CP), if L,P ⊢ Q then L ⊢ P → Q. In this case that means that the empty list yields P → Q, which is what the sequent at line 14 says. Offering a similar analysis for the justifications at lines 10 and 13 is left as an exercise.

1.	~(A → B)	⊢	~(A → B)	(A/CP)
2.	~(A → B), ~A	⊢	~A	(A/IP)
3.	~(A → B), ~A, A	⊢	A	(A/CP)
4.	~(A → B), ~A, A	⊢	~A	(R)
5.	~(A → B), ~A, A, ~B	⊢	~B	(A/IP)
6.	~(A → B), ~A, A, ~B	⊢	A	3 (R)
7.	~(A → B), ~A, A, ~B	⊢	~A	4 (R)
8.	~(A → B), ~A, A, ~B	⊢	⊥	6,7 (⊥I)
9.	~(A → B), ~A, A	⊢	B	8 (IP)
10.	**~(A → B), ~A**	⊢	**A → B**	**9 (CP)**
11.	**~(A → B), ~A**	⊢	**~(A → B)**	**1 (R)**
12.	**~(A → B), ~A**	⊢	**⊥**	**10,11 (⊥I)**
13.	**~(A → B)**	⊢	**A**	**12 (IP)**
14.		⊢	**~(A → B) → A**	**13 (CP)**

At line 14 of the derivation as written in standard notation there is only a single assumption bracket headed off by the empty list. This is made explicit in the corresponding line of the derivation as written in bracket free notation.

Given a derivation written down in bracket free notation, like the one above, a derivation in standard notation can be readily reconstructed. Take each column of sentences in the assumption list to mark an assumption bracket,

1.	~(A → B)			⊢	~(A → B)
2.	~(A → B)	~A		⊢	~A
3.	~(A → B)	~A	A	⊢	A
4.	~(A → B)	~A	A	⊢	~A
5.	~(A → B)	~A	A	~B ⊢	~B
6.	~(A → B)	~A	A	~B ⊢	A
7.	~(A → B)	~A	A	~B ⊢	~A
8.	~(A → B)	~A	A	~B ⊢	⊥
9.	~(A → B)	~A	A	⊢	B
10.	~(A → B)	~A		⊢	A → B
11.	~(A → B)	~A		⊢	~(A → B)
12.	~(A → B)	~A		⊢	⊥
13.	~(A → B)			⊢	A
14.				⊢	~(A → B) → A

delete the repetitions of assumptions in each column and remove the intermediate column of turnstiles,

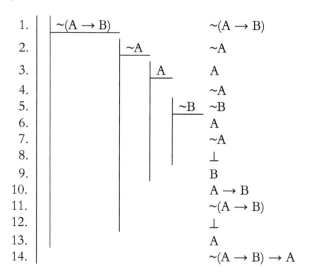

then shove each sentence on the far right to the left, up to the first assumption bracket it butts into, overwriting the sentence at the head of that assumption bracket if there is one.

```
 1. |  ~(A → B)   ←    ←    ←      ← ~(A → B)
 2. |         ~A   ←    ←      ← ~A
 3. |              A    ←      ← A
 4. |                   ←    ← ~A
 5. |              ~B     ← ~B
 6. |                   ←    ← A
 7. |                   ←    ← ~A
 8. |                   ←    ← ⊥
 9. |                   ←    ← B
10. |         ←    ←    ←      ← A → B
11. |         ←    ←    ←      ← ~(A → B)
12. |         ←    ←    ←      ← ⊥
13. |  ← ← ←   ←    ←    ←      ← A
14. |  ← ← ← ←    ←    ←    ←      ← ~(A → B) → A
```

Reverse this procedure to turn a derivation in standard notation into one in bracket free notation.

This makes it obvious that bracket free notation is simply a different way of writing down derivations in Ds, not a different derivation system. All the derivations in this chapter could have instead been done in bracket free notation without having to change anything but the appearance of the derivation. No extra line of derivation would need to be added, and none removed.

Standard notation has been used up to now because bracket free notation requires rewriting each sentence on the assumption list on each subsequent line, which is irritating and time consuming, and which produces unnecessary clutter. Bracket free notation nonetheless reveals the derivation in its true form, as a series of sequents. Any derivation written down in standard notation should be understood to be merely an abbreviation of a bracket free derivation that more accurately expresses what is happening: each sequent makes an assertion that some list of sentences yields some particular sentence. *Sentences* are not really being derived from other sentences or from subderivations. *Sequents* are being derived from other sequents.

It is quite possible to do derivations in bracket free notation, though it takes some practice, and those who have become accustomed to standard notation may find it more difficult to discover derivations. This is merely an effect of custom. Had bracket free notation been learned first, the switch to standard would have been equally difficult.

When derivations are done from scratch in bracket free notation, there are some further details to note about the use of (A), and about the growth and diminution of lists. Conversion from standard to bracket free notation ensures these details will be observed. Without that guide, care must be taken to ensure that each time (A) is used to add a sentence to a list, the sentence is added to the right end of the list. Sentences that were added earlier may not be removed from the list. Once they have been added to a list, sentences must stay there, and they must stay there in the order they were added. They cannot be shifted to a different position on the list, and they cannot be removed, except by applications of (IP), (CP), (PC), or (BP). Those applications remove them in the reverse order to the order they were added, from the right end to the left.

In bracket free notation all derivations start with an application of (A). The justification "given" is no longer employed. Instead, givens are derived by successive applications of (A). Account needs to be taken of this in converting a derivation in bracket free notation into standard notation. In standard notation, the givens are all stacked up in the top right quadrant of a single assumption bracket. Separate assumption brackets are not introduced for each given. Givens are distinguished from other assumptions by the fact that they continue to be on the list (i.e., stated to the left of the turnstile) on the last line of the derivation. Other assumptions are removed by applications of (IP), (CP), (PC), or (BP).

Justifying (PC) requires citing three prior line numbers, one for a sequent of the form L ⊢ P ∨ Q, one for a sequent of the form L,P ⊢ R, and one for a sequent of the form L,Q ⊢ R. Justifying (BP) requires citing two prior line numbers, one for a sequent of the form L,P ⊢ Q, the other for a sequent of the form L,Q ⊢ P.

(PC) subderivations must be oriented serially. Parallel orientation is a further abbreviation that is not countenanced in bracket free notation. When converting from standard to bracket free notation, any parallel applications of (PC) must first be converted to serial orientation.

Because derivations in bracket free notation are merely an alternative way of writing down derivations in standard notation, the same strategies apply for discovering derivations. Work proceeds both from the top down and from the bottom up, by applying (A) to generate the list of givens, if any, entering the conclusion some 20 lines down, and then cycling through stages 1–4.

Exercise 6.19

1. *Convert the solutions given in exercises 6.12#1a,c; #3a,c; and #4a,c into bracket free notation. Where the standard derivation does (PC) in parallel orientation, be careful to convert it to serial orientation before making the conversion to bracket free notation.*

    Answers for **6.12#1a**, and **#4a**

2. *Formulate bracket free versions of* (T1), (T2), (DN), (MT), (HS), (T→), (~→), (DS), *and* (~∨). *It is not necessary to redo the derivations of any of these theorems or derived rules.*

    Answers for (T1), (DN), (HS), and (~→)

3. *Establish the following directly by means of a derivation in bracket free notation. Do not first create or consult a derivation in standard notation.*
    - ★**a.** $[A \rightarrow (B \rightarrow \bot)] \rightarrow \bot \vdash B$
    - **b.** $[(A \rightarrow B) \rightarrow (A \rightarrow \bot)] \rightarrow \bot \vdash B$
    - ★**c.** $[A \rightarrow (B \rightarrow \bot)] \rightarrow \bot \vdash A$
    - **d.** $(A \rightarrow \bot) \rightarrow B, A \rightarrow C, B \rightarrow G \vdash (C \rightarrow \bot) \rightarrow G$
    - ★**e.** $(A \rightarrow \bot) \rightarrow B, A \rightarrow C, B \rightarrow C \vdash C$
    - **f.** $A, B \vdash ((A \rightarrow B) \rightarrow [(B \rightarrow A) \rightarrow \bot]) \rightarrow \bot$
    - ★**g.** $A \rightarrow (B \rightarrow \bot), A \rightarrow B, C \rightarrow A \vdash C \rightarrow \bot$
    - **h.** $A \rightarrow (B \rightarrow \bot), A \rightarrow B, A \vdash C$
    - **i.** $A \rightarrow \bot, C \rightarrow A, (C \rightarrow \bot) \rightarrow (B \rightarrow \bot) \vdash B \rightarrow \bot$

6.6 Intuition and "Intuitionism": Derivation in Intuitionistic Logic

The derivation rules that have been presented in this chapter rest on no higher authority than intuition. Intuition means just "seeing" that something is so, the way one just sees that the sky is blue. This is a firm enough foundation provided that everyone sees it that way. But the foundation crumbles if there are others who do not see it that way and cannot be inspired to see it that way.

Of all the derivation rules presented in this chapter the one that is most frequently challenged is (IP). Deriving ~~P from P is not questioned. If P is the case it is intuitive that not-P should be denied. Deriving P from ~~P is another matter. Denying denying P is not so obviously the same as affirming P. Saying that someone's work is "not uninteresting" need not imply that it is interesting. It may be simply a polite way of pointing out that it does not quite manage to be very interesting. There are many other cases where a double negative does not clearly yield a positive: saying that someone is not incompetent, not unhealthy, not inconsiderate, and so on. Rejecting the inference from a double negative to a positive has far-reaching consequences. For reasons given below, maintaining that ~~P does not entail P challenges the principle of the excluded middle (em), along with many of the substitution principles of section 6.5.3. Those raising the challenges to these principles cannot be dismissed. They include some of the most notable mathematicians and philosophers of the early twentieth century. And whether it is telling or whether it is merely ironic, their theories have seized the label of "intuitionism."

Intuitionism raises an obvious problem, which is equally pressing both for what might be called the "classical" derivation theory presented so far in this chapter and for its "intuitionist" detractors. How can either theory claim a foundation in intuition if there is, apparently, no agreement about what our intuitions are? Are our intuitions narrower than has been claimed over the course of this chapter? Do they really support only some of the derivation rules or only some of their consequences or only consequences obtained in certain cases? More seriously, might there be no intuitions to be had on these matters? Intuitionism as a foundation for mathematics was first proposed in the early twentieth century by L.E.J. Brouwer (1881–1966) and then developed into a formal system of intuitionistic logic by his student Arend Heyting (1898–1980) in 1930. If it took this long for claims about the intuitive status of ~~P ⊢ P to be contested, might there be yet other classically accepted principles that are not clearly intuitive? Might none be? There are no easy answers to these questions.

Intuitionists do not just declare that they do not see the logic of ~~P ⊢ P. When others do not share your intuitions, it is sometimes possible to say things that can bring them to see it your way, or at least convince them that their view is less obvious than they thought. Intuitionists have compelling reasons for their position. Classical logic is based on the supposition that the truth is out there, waiting to be discovered. Our ignorance of the truth of a sentence does not have any bearing on whether that sentence is true or false. But intuitionists balk at the idea that sentences can be true even though no one has established that they are true. Without getting too deeply into the reasons for this, it is incontestable that in many cases (perhaps in all), we cannot get beyond making claims about what is evident to us. This makes it worthwhile to develop a logic based on the distinction between what is evident or established and what is not (yet) evident or established,[3] as opposed to what is independently true or false.

Intuitionists do not understand "evidence" in weak kneed terms. Seeing the evidence for a claim is not just having a hunch or considering it to be fifty-one out of a hundred times more likely than its opposite. Brouwer was principally concerned with the evidence of mathematical truths, which is provided by demonstration and leaves no room for doubt once it has been provided. Other forms of evidence are current, personal, direct sensory experience obtained under optimal conditions and further confirmed by multiple, independent observers, or deductions from such experience in accord with established laws of nature. For intuitionists, we either have evidence or we do not. There is no such thing as having only some evidence and no such thing as a partially evident claim. A partially evident claim is a nonevident claim. An evident claim is nothing less than a totally evident claim, and a totally evident claim is one that has been proven to be true or false. In mathematics or logic, it is a demonstratively evident claim. In the realm of matters of fact, it is a "moral certainty," that is, a claim that allows for no reasonable doubt. Intuitionism is therefore still a bivalent system of logic. But the bivalence takes a different form. Sentences are either evident or nonevident.

Supposing evidence is as close to truth as we can get, all references to truth must really be references to evidence. There can be no truth where there is no evidence, because truths distinct from evidence are not encountered and are not what "truth" names for us. The notion that there is some background reality that is only temporarily hidden and can be revealed by further and better experience must be replaced with the notion that evidence increases over time. When new evidence emerges, it is not because a truth that was there all along reveals itself. That would imply that we somehow managed to get access to a truth behind the evidence, but no such truth exists. Rather, evidence that did not exist before has been newly created.

Consider a closed, opaque pot. It is not evident what it contains. Suppose that upon opening it coffee beans are seen inside. At that point evidence emerges that was not there before. With that, the sentence "there are coffee beans in the pot" becomes true. It was not evident before and there is no truth behind evidence that we can access or that we can presume to talk about. At the same time, the sentence "there are no coffee beans in the pot" is refuted. Falsity also emerges with the right sort of evidence.

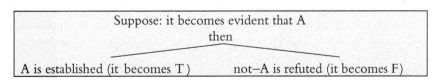

What was the value of "there are coffee beans in the pot" before the pot was opened? No intuitionist would want to say that, before the pot was opened, "there are coffee beans in the pot" was true but that its value was unknown. The whole point is to get away from talking about truth as if it were something that could exist apart from evidence. Before the pot is opened, the sentence cannot be true, given that evidence is as close as we can get to truth and it is not (yet) evident that there are coffee beans in the pot. Neither can it be false. Just as it has not been established that it is true, so it has not been established that it is false, and it would be just as contrary to the intuitionist approach to consider falsity to exist apart from evidence (in this case, evidence for the truth of the negation "there are no coffee beans in the pot"). But intuitionists do not want to say that, before the pot was opened, "there are coffee beans in the pot" had no value or that it had a third value.

This looks like an impossible situation to deal with, but it is not. The solution to the conundrum is that "false" is not a basic value. The basic values are true (that is, "evident") and "nonevident." "False" does not mean "nonevident," but this does not make it a third, basic value in addition to "true/evident" and "nonevident." It is a derivative value. It arises when the negation becomes evident. Evidence does not just take the form of evidence of truth. There is also evidence of falsity, which is cashed out in terms of evidence of the impossibility of something ever becoming evident. Of course, whatever is false must be in some sense nonevident. There can be no evidence for it – in the strong intuitionist sense of "evidence" – if it is false. But what is false has to be more than just nonevident. There must be evidence "behind" the nonevidence, so to speak: evidence for the impossibility of it ever becoming evident. Falsity is evidence of the negation. As such, falsity is bound up with a revised semantic rule for negations, one that demands more than that P not be true or evident. This revised valuation rule is the key to the intuitionist approach. Unfortunately, going further into intuitionistic semantics presupposes material that can only be taken up after studying basic modal semantics in chapter 9.1–2. In the meantime, it is best to think of the intuitionist values as 0 and 1, where 0 means "nonevident" or "not (yet) true (or false)," or "not (yet) evaluated." T can be identified with 1, but F cannot be identified either with 0 or with a third value. The assignment of F to P is a consequence of the assignment of 1 to ~P, and making that assignment requires more than just assigning 0 to P.

Some nonevident things are nonevident because they have not yet been made either evident or evidently nonevident. Prior to the point at which evidence emerges, "there are coffee beans in the pot" is in that class. It is *simply* nonevident or not (yet) established. Both the sentence "there are coffee beans in the pot" and its negation "there are no coffee beans in the pot" are nonevident (they both have the value 0).

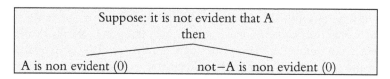

If this seems odd, it is due to the persistent conviction that truth and falsity exist in the things themselves independently of evidence. That erroneous conviction – assuming the intuitionists are right – is what gives intuitionistic semantics a whiff of unfamiliarity. Many people are inclined to suppose that there is a real world that is the way it is independently of how it appears to us, and that we can bump into that world and so come to know how it is in itself. But intuitionistic logic is designed for contexts where those beliefs are put aside. Brouwer developed intuitionism to complement his rejection of Platonism in mathematics. (Platonism is the view that mathematical objects and mathematical truths exist independently in a perfect, intelligible world, accessible to the eyes of reason). Brouwer was committed to a rival, "constructivist" account of mathematical objects and mathematical truths. According to that account, there are no mathematical truths that have not been demonstrated and so made evident. Like buildings, mathematical truths do not exist prior to being constructed. (This is not to say that they can be constructed in any way whatsoever. Buildings cannot be constructed in just any way, and mathematical intuition, like physical space, imposes severe constraints on what is constructible.) Intuitionistic logic is written for contexts where there is nothing we can bump into before it becomes or is made evident. Because a truth behind evidence is inaccessible, all references to truth and falsity must be references to evidence and evident impossibility of evidence. What is nonevident is not (yet) true and not (yet) false, up to such a point in time at which evidence emerges. Then, if the evidence is positive, the sentence becomes true, like a building that only comes to be once it has been constructed. If the evidence takes the form of a refutation, the sentence becomes false, like a building that cannot be constructed because the design is physically impossible to realize.

Suppose that the pot has just been excavated from a long-abandoned dwelling on a coffee plantation. It is closed and has never been seen before, let alone opened, by any living person. Establishing that "there are coffee beans in the pot" is false is equivalent to establishing that "there are no coffee beans in the pot" is true. Either way, it requires more than the nonevidence of "there are coffee beans in the pot." It requires one or other of two things: obtaining direct evidence (for example, opening the pot and seeing that there are none inside), or, failing that, obtaining evidence that there could be no evidence (for example, discovering that the pot belongs to a prehistoric site and was in use and abandoned at a time prior to the cultivation of coffee). The first of these alternatives reduces to the second: seeing that there are now no beans in the pot is one way of making it evident that there could be no evidence that there are now any in there.

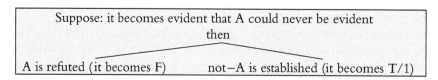

Evidence either exists or it does not. And sentences are either evident (1) or nonevident (0). But the nonevidence of sentences is impermanent. A sentence that is nonevident today could become true tomorrow (though never the reverse – evidence does not decay, so long as "evidence" is understood in the intuitionist way as *conclusive* evidence).

And both a sentence and its negation could be nonevident. An assignment of 1/T to A determines an assignment of 0 (and an assignment of F) to not-A, and an assignment of 1/T to not-A determines an assignment of 0 (and an assignment of F) to A. But an assignment of 0 to A does not *by itself* determine any assignment to not-A and an assignment of 0 to not-A does not by itself determine any assignment to A. (An assignment of 0 to A is compatible with an assignment of either 1 or 0 to not-A, and likewise for an assignment of 0 to not-A.) It is not that there is a value gap in these cases. When A is assigned 0, not-A must be assigned exactly one of 1 and 0 and likewise for not-A and A. But both A and not-A could get 0. Which of 1 and 0 is assigned to not-A when A gets 0 is determined by further details. For now, consider only the assignment of 1 to be an assignment in the proper sense, where someone does something to make it so (gives a demonstration or discovers evidence). 0 is a kind of default state. It takes something positive, the discovery of evidence, to determine an assignment of 1. It takes nothing to determine an assignment of 0 which is just the way sentences are in the absence of evidence. The assignment of 0 is not actively determined or decided upon. It designates the value "not yet evaluated." Further details must wait for section 9.3. But enough has been said to account for an intuitionist derivation system, the topic of this chapter.

The ideas sketched here explain why intuitionists reject (em): ⊢ P ∨ ~P, and (DNE): ~~P ⊢ P. When it is nonevident that P, ~P could also be nonevident, so both disjuncts in P ∨ ~P could be 0. But (em) requires that P ∨ ~P have at least one true disjunct in all cases. So (em) fails. It is easy to see why (DNE) fails as well. For it to be evident that ~P is the case it must be evident that there could be no evidence that P is the case. In other words, P must have been refuted.

Now suppose that ~P is denied. (That is, ~~P is asserted.) To deny ~P is to say that it is evident that P cannot be refuted. (It is evident that there could be no evidence for the claim that it is evident that there could be no evidence that P.) But establishing that there could be no refutation of P is not the same thing as establishing that P. Put differently, evidence that there could be no disproof is not the same thing as proof. The inference from ~~P to P breaks down.

While these inferences fail, many other classical inferences do not. Most notably, (DNI): P ⊢ ~~P is still acceptable. If P is evident then P is not evidently impossible, which is another way of saying that ~~P is evident. Intuitionists also accept (EFQ): ⊢ ⊥ → P. Q → P is read as asserting that either Q is not evident, or P is. When Q is ⊥, it is evidently impossible for there to be evidence for Q, so any sentence of the form ⊥ → P must be true.

One derivation system that is acceptable to intuitionists accepts the basic rules of Ds except for (IP), which is replaced with (IP~I) and (EFQ). Metatheorems, derived rules, and the interderivability principles on which substitution principles are based must be reconfirmed before being used. (Not all of them can be reconfirmed.)

The Derivation System Dis

(A), (R), (⊥I), (CP), (MP), (&I), (&E), (∨I), (PC), (BP) and (BMP) along with:

(IP~I): If L,P ⊢ ⊥, then L ⊢ ~P

(EFQ): If L ⊢ ⊥ then L ⊢ P

(IP~I) is based on the intuition that yielding a contradiction makes it evident that what is responsible for producing the contradiction could never become evident. It also legitimates inferring L ⊢ ~~P from L,~P ⊢ ⊥, but it does not allow inferring L ⊢ P from L,~P ⊢ ⊥ and so does not justify ~~P ⊢ P. The version of (EFQ) stated above is an obvious consequence (by (MP)) of being able to insert the (EFQ) axiom, ⊥ → P, at any point in a derivation.

Exercise 6.20

Derive the following in Dis.

⋆**a.** P ⊢ ~~P
   b. ~~~P ⊢ ~P *(Do not use (DNI).)*
⋆**c.** ~P –|– P → ⊥
   d. ⊢ ~~(P ∨ ~P) *(Do not use (~∨).)*
⋆**e.** ~P ∨ Q ⊢ P → Q *(Hint: use (EFQ).)*
   f. ~(P ∨ Q) –|– ~P & ~Q
⋆**g.** ~P ∨ ~Q ⊢ ~(P & Q)
   h. P → Q ⊢ ~Q → ~P
   i. P ∨ Q, ~P ⊢ Q *(Do not use (DS).)*

As shown by exercises 6.20(b) and (d), though intuitionists reject (DNE) and (em), they do accept some of their instances. These are just two examples of a general outcome: if the inference from P to Q is classically derivable but intuitionistically unacceptable, the inference from ~P to ~Q will still be intuitionistically derivable.

Not surprisingly, given that (IP~I) and (EFQ) are also rules of Ds, whatever is derivable in Dis is derivable in Ds. But because Dis lacks (IP~E) (that is, if L,~P ⊢ ⊥ then L ⊢ P), not everything that is derivable in Ds is derivable in Dis. In particular, 6.20(e), (g), and (h), which are interderivable in Ds, are only derivable in one direction in Dis. (Section 9.3 shows that the other direction is invalid on intuitionistic semantics.) It follows that the connectives cannot be defined in terms of one another, that sentences cannot be reduced to dnf's, that contrapositives are not equivalent, and that there can be no lean language for intuitionistic logic. This makes intuitionistic logic a significant departure from classical logic.

This section began by raising the question of whether disagreements over which derivation rules are correct undermine the project of appealing to intuition to justify derivation rules. By now it has been established that intuitionists accept all the classical derivation rules but for (IP~E), and that they do not recognize any derivation rules that are not recognized by classical logic. In this light, intuitionism is more a corrective than a challenge, one that charges that classical logic involves an extension that cannot be properly justified by intuition. It would be contrary to the "intuitionist" project if "intuitionism" were understood as anything else.

Intuitionism is based on the rejection of the Platonist thesis that mathematical objects and mathematical truths exist independently of being constructed by mathematical operations. It is echoed by antirealist views in metaphysics and epistemology, and by ordinary people's reluctance to take the denial of a negation to be the same thing as the affirmation of the nullation. The thesis that evidence is as close as we can get to truth is undeniable in many contexts. Respected thinkers from Democritus, Pyrrho, and Carneades to Berkeley and Kant (the last of whom influenced Brouwer) have maintained that evidence is as good as it gets, and some interpretations of quantum mechanics carry the same implication. This is not to say that these thinkers are correct or that (IP~E) should be rejected in all contexts. But it is to acknowledge that a strong case has been made against the intuitive status of one derivation rule, and for a cascade of consequent revisions.

Notes

1   This fancy is further supported by the belief that working from the top down exercises ingenuity or superior reasoning abilities. There is nothing ingenious or rational about working from the top down. It is nothing more than hacking. Hacking is a randomized version of what is called a "brute force" approach to a problem. Brute force procedures systematically (and mindlessly) test each possible option until a solution eventually emerges. Hacking randomly (and so even more mindlessly) tests options until a solution accidentally emerges. This is the antithesis of reasoning, which is goal directed and which employs strategies. In the context of derivations, hacking consists in making unmotivated assumptions in the hope they will lead somewhere. If they do, the accidental discovery is attributed to ingenuity. To the extent that it is at all ingenious, it is only because the hacker has unconsciously learned bottom-up reasoning strategies and is unconsciously employing them to discover what assumptions to make and what lemmas to aim to derive.

2   The account of bracket free notation given here and its later application in chapter A-2 are inspired by Garson, who calls it "horizontal notation."

3   In drawing the distinction in these terms, we follow John L. Bell (1945–), whose various works on intuitionistic logic have inspired much of what is said here.

References

Garson, James W, 2013, *Modal Logic for Philosophers*, 2nd edition, Cambridge University Press, New York.

A-2

Advanced Topics Concerning the Soundness and Completeness of Ds

This is the second of a sequence of brief chapters on advanced topics in logic. The advanced chapters, designated A-1 through A-6, form a separate series from the others. It is not necessary to take up the advanced chapters to understand any of the others. They are placed where they are because they presuppose familiarity with the chapters that precede them, but not with those that follow them.

This chapter shows that results obtained using the derivation rules of chapter 6 and results obtained using the valuation rules of chapters 3 and 5 fall into line with one another. Whatever is derivable is s-entailed (this is called soundness), and whatever is s-entailed is derivable (this is called completeness). As a consequence, whatever is a theorem is s-valid and vice versa, whatever is inconsistent is s-unsatisfiable and vice versa, and whatever is interderivable is s-equivalent and vice versa.

In passing, this chapter also shows that Ds has other desirable features. As promised at the outset of chapter 6, it is consistent in the sense that there is at least one sentence that is not a theorem of Ds. It will not allow anything whatsoever to be derived. Ds can also be supplemented with a set of instructions that make it decidable. Following the instructions ensures that whatever is derivable will be derivable in a finite number of lines.

Terminological Note

The terms, soundness and completeness, make it sound like Ds must live up to the semantics of chapters 3 and 5. Ds is only "sound" if everything it derives is s-entailed and only "complete" if it can derive everything that is s-entailed. But, historically, logicians have first codified intuitively sound rules of inference and have only later developed a semantic system to reflect those rules. Sometimes it can look like the semantics is foundational. But the semantic system may have been engineered to legitimate our intuitions about which derivation rules are sound. A difference between what is derivable and what is entailed can just as well lead theorists to demand an alternative semantics as to revise their intuitions about what derivation rules ought to be employed.

DOI: 10.4324/9781003026532-9

A-2.1 Soundness

The soundness demonstration establishes that Ds will not permit the derivation of an s-invalid conclusion. If P is derivable from a (possibly empty) list using the rules of Ds, then the set of sentences on that list s-entails P.

Soundness
If $L \vdash P$ then $\Gamma_L \vDash P$
where Γ_L is the set of the sentences on L

This is not a trivial or obvious result. What is derivable is a function of what can be done using the derivation rules, which are based on intuitions concerning what is implicitly contradictory or noncontradictory. But what is s-entailed is determined by a theory of the factors responsible for the assignment of values on an interpretation. It needs to be demonstrated that these two different accounts justify the same inferences.

The demonstration that follows applies to derivations done in bracket free notation using just the 12 basic derivation rules. As noted in chapter 6.5.6, assumption brackets are merely an abbreviated way of writing down what appears in bracket free notation. Strictly, derivations are done in bracket free notation, even when they appear on the page using assumption brackets. The soundness of the other rules of Ds is a consequence of the soundness of the 12 basic rules.

The demonstration of the soundness of the 12 basic rules draws on the notion of an instance of a derivation rule. An instance of a derivation rule is the result of replacing the variables P, Q, R, L, and M in the statement of the rule with sentences or lists of sentences of SL. For example, (R)

$$\text{If } L \vdash P \text{ then } L, M \vdash P$$

has as its instances such sequents as

$$B \vdash B$$
[therefore, on some later line]
$$B, A \vdash B$$

$$A, A \rightarrow B \vdash B$$
[therefore, on some later line]
$$A, A \rightarrow B, C \vdash B.$$

And (CP),

$$\text{If } L, P \vdash Q \text{ then } L \vdash P \rightarrow Q,$$

has as its instances such successions of sequents as

$$A \lor C \vdash B$$
[therefore, on some later line]
$$\vdash (A \lor C) \rightarrow B$$

$$A \& B, {\sim}C \rightarrow A \vdash {\sim}B$$
[therefore, on some later line]
$$A \& B \vdash ({\sim}C \rightarrow A) \rightarrow {\sim}B$$

The demonstration also puts the phrase, "is sound" to a special use. $L \vdash P$ "is sound," means that Γ_L, the set of sentences on L, s-entails P. If $L \vdash P$ "is sound," $\Gamma_L \vDash P$.

The demonstration of the soundness of Ds can be briefly given by appeal to two lemmas.

1. Suppose that $L \vdash P$ in Ds.
   2. By definition of derivability in Ds, there is a derivation in Ds that ends with $L \vdash P$.
   3. The sequent on the first line of any derivation in Ds is sound. *(Lemma 1)*

4. If the sequents on lines 1 to k of a derivation in Ds are sound, the sequent on line $k+1$ is sound. *(Lemma 2)*

5. From lines 3 and 4 by mathematical induction, the sequent on the last line of any derivation in Ds is sound.

6. From lines 5 and 2, L ⊢ P is sound, that is, $\Gamma_L \vDash P$.

7. From lines 1–6 by conditional proof, if L ⊢ P, then $\Gamma_L \vDash P$.

Demonstration of the lemmas:

Lemma 1: The sequent on the first line of any derivation in Ds is sound.

1. Because the only derivation rule that does not appeal to sequents established on prior lines is (A), the sequent on the first line of any derivation in Ds must be justified by (A).

2. By (A), the sequent on the first line of any derivation in Ds has the form, P ⊢ P.

3. By the solution to exercise 5.12(a), if a set, Γ, contains a sentence, P, then $\Gamma \vDash P$.

4. As a special case of this general principle, when Γ is {P}, P ⊨ P.

5. From lines 2 and 4, the sequent derived on the first line of any derivation in Ds is sound.

Lemma 2: If the sequents on lines 1 to k of a derivation in Ds are sound, the sequent on line $k+1$ is sound.

Because the sequent on line $k+1$ must be derived by one of the 12 derivation rules, the demonstration of lemma 2 splits into 12 cases. Each of these cases except for the first (which does not need it) is established under the supposition of the inductive hypothesis: the supposition that each of the sequents on lines 1 to k is sound. In the demonstration for each case, consider P_i to be the sentence yielded by L_i on line i of a derivation in bracket free Ds and Γ_i to be the set of the sentences on L_i.

Case one: The sequent on line $k+1$ is derived by (A).
Then it must have the form $L, P_{k+1} \vdash P_{k+1}$ (or it would not be justified by (A)). By the solution to exercise 5.12(a), Γ_{k+1}, the set of sentences on the list at line $k+1$ (which is $\Gamma_L \cup P_{k+1}$), s-entails P_{k+1}. So, the sequent on line $k+1$ is sound in this case.

Case two: The sequent on line $k+1$ is derived by (R).
Then it must have the form $L_i, M \vdash P_{k+1}$ and the earlier lines 1 to k must include a line, i, of the form $L_i \vdash P_{k+1}$ (otherwise (R) could not be applied as it requires that the sentences derived on lines i and $k+1$ be the same and that the list at line $k+1$ consist of the list at line i supplemented by the sentences on M).

Consequently:

1. Because line i is prior to line $k+1$, it follows from the inductive hypothesis that $\Gamma_i \vDash P_{k+1}$.

2. Γ_{k+1}, the set of sentences on the list at line $k+1$ (which is L_i, M), is by definition a superset of Γ_i, the set of sentences on the list at line i.

3. From 1 and 2 by the solution to exercise 5.12(b), $\Gamma_{k+1} \vDash P_{k+1}$.

So, the sequent on line $k+1$ is sound in this case.

Case three: The sequent on line $k+1$ is derived by ($\bot$I).
Then it must have the form $L_{k+1} \vdash \bot$ and the earlier lines 1 to k must include a line, h, of the form $L_{k+1} \vdash Q$ and a line, i (coming before or after h), of the form $L_{k+1} \vdash \sim Q$ (otherwise ($\bot$I) could not be applied, as it requires that the list at each of these lines be the same: L_h must be the same list as L_{k+1}, and likewise for L_i).

Consequently:

1. Because lines h and i are prior to line $k+1$, it follows from the inductive hypothesis that Γ_{k+1} s-entails Q and $\sim Q$.

2. By the solution to exercise 5.12(c), Γ_{k+1} s-entails $\bot$, which is P_{k+1} in this case.

So, the sequent on line $k+1$ is sound in this case.

Case four: The sequent on line $k+1$ is derived by (IP). Then it must have the form $L_{k+1} \vdash$ [Q-opposite] and the earlier lines 1 to k must include a line, i, of the form $L_{k+1}, Q \vdash \bot$. (Were the list preceding Q at line i not the same as L_{k+1} at line $k+1$, (IP) could not be applied.)

Consequently:

1. Because line i is prior to line $k+1$, it follows from the inductive hypothesis that $\Gamma_{k+1} \cup Q$ (which is the set of sentences on the list at line i, namely those on L_{k+1} supplemented by Q) s-entails $\perp$.
2. By the solution to exercise 5.12(d), $\Gamma_{k+1} \vDash$ [Q-opposite], which is P_{k+1} in this case.

So, the sequent on line $k+1$ is sound in this case.

Case five: The sequent on line $k+1$ is derived by (CP). Then it must have the form $L_{k+1} \vdash Q \rightarrow R$ and the earlier lines 1 to k must include a line, i, of the form $L_{k+1}, Q \vdash R$. (Were the list preceding Q at line i not the same as L_{k+1} at line $k+1$, (CP) could not be applied.)

Consequently:

1. Because line i is prior to line $k+1$, it follows from the inductive hypothesis that $\Gamma_{k+1} \cup Q$ (which is the set of sentences on the list at line i, namely those on L_{k+1} supplemented by Q) s-entails R.
2. By the solution to exercise 5.12(e), $\Gamma_{k+1} \vDash Q \rightarrow R$, which is, P_{k+1} in this case.

So, the sequent on line $k+1$ is sound in this case.

Exercise A-2.1

Demonstrate the remaining seven cases. The demonstrations of the (PC) and (BP) cases are patterned on those for cases four and five. The demonstrations of the other cases are patterned on that for case three.

Answers for the (PC) and (BMP) cases

A-2.2 Corollary Results

The fact that Ds is sound makes it possible to briefly demonstrate some important corollary results.

Corollary 1. *The derived rules and substitution principles of Ds are sound.*

> Since each derived rule, and each substitution principle states the result of a routine sequence of applications of the 12 basic rules, and those rules are sound, the derived rules and substitution principles are sound as well.

Corollary 2. *If P is a theorem then P is s-valid.*

> Suppose for purposes of conditional proof that P is a theorem. By definition, this means that $\varnothing \vdash P$. By soundness, it follows that $\varnothing \vDash P$. By one half of the solution to exercise 5.11#2(e), P is s-valid. By conditional proof, if P is a theorem, then P is s-valid.

Corollary 3. *If L is inconsistent then Γ_L is s-unsatisfiable as is any superset of Γ_L. As a special case (the case where L is the unit set, <P>), if P is inconsistent then P is s-unsatisfiable.*

> Suppose for purposes of conditional proof that L is inconsistent. By definition of inconsistency, $L \vdash \perp$. By soundness, $\Gamma_L \vDash \perp$. By exercise 5.12(b), any superset of $\Gamma_L \vDash \perp$. By one half of the solution to exercise 5.11#2(a), Γ_L and any superset of Γ_L are s-unsatisfiable. By conditional proof, if L is inconsistent, Γ_L and any superset of Γ_L are s-unsatisfiable.
>
> In the case where L is <P> the same consequence holds for the same reason, citing exercise 5.11#2(b) in place of 5.11#2(a).

Corollary 4. *If P and Q are interderivable then they are s-equivalent.*

Corollary 5. *Ds is consistent.*

> Suppose to the contrary that A is a theorem of Ds. It follows from corollary 1 that A is s-valid. By definition of s-validity, there is no interpretation on which ~A is true. But the assignment of F to each atomic sentence of SL satisfies the definition of an interpretation and by (~), ~A receives a T on any such interpretation. So there is an interpretation on which ~A is true, contradicting what was just demonstrated. Since this

contradiction arises from the initial supposition that A is a theorem of Ds, that supposition must be rejected. So, there is at least one sentence that is not a theorem of Ds. By definition of consistency, Ds is consistent.

Corollary 6. *Ø is consistent.*

Exercise A-2.2

Demonstrate corollaries 4 and 6. The demonstration of corollary 4 appeals to one half of the solution to exercise 5.11#2(g). To demonstrate corollary 6 suppose the opposite and arrive at a contradiction.

Corollary 7. *The substitution principles of Ds are sound.*

A dedicated demonstration of the soundness of the substitution principles is not given here. Since exercise 6.18#3a defines a routine for performing subsentential substitutions using "whole sentence" substitutions, Corollary 2 is already sufficient for this purpose. (It is necessary to appeal to the routine because the completeness demonstration of section A-2.8 requires that the substitution principles be derived from the fundamental rules of Ds, not borrowed from SL semantics by way of an appeal to the extensionality of SL. Those relying on the completeness demonstration of sections A-2.3-7 can bypass this approach in favour justifying the soundness of the substitution principles by appeal to corollary 4 and the substitution principle of chapter A-1.3.)

A-2.3 Henkin Completeness

Whereas the soundness demonstration establishes that whatever is derivable in Ds is s-entailed, the completeness demonstration establishes that whatever is s-entailed is derivable in Ds. If a (possibly empty) set, Γ, s-entails P, there is a way of deriving P from a finite list of the sentences in Γ using the rules of Ds.

> **Completeness**
>
> If $\Gamma \vDash P$ then $L \vdash P$
> where L is a finite list of sentences in Γ

The demonstration of this principle can be given in a more abbreviated form than was the case with the soundness proof. It is important to demonstrate the soundness of each of the rules of Ds because each rule introduces a risk that its application could produce an invalid result. This is not necessary with the completeness proof. If a more limited set of rules can be demonstrated to be complete, then it is not necessary to consider the others. Adding yet more rules to a complete set does nothing to change the fact that all the s-valid results can already be derived from the leaner set.

Ds has more rules than it needs because SL has more connectives than it needs. As shown in the appendix to chapter 3, negations, conjunctions, disjunctions, and biconditionals can all be replaced by s-equivalent sentences that use only the arrow connective. The equivalences are demonstrated in exercises 5.4#5(b)–(d) and 5.5a, though the demonstrations given there need to be rewritten using metavariables and appeals to bivalence.

$$\sim P \quad =|= \quad P \to \bot$$
$$P \lor Q \quad =|= \quad (P \to \bot) \to Q$$
$$P \,\&\, Q \quad =|= \quad [P \to (Q \to \bot)] \to \bot$$
$$P \equiv Q \quad =|= \quad ((P \to Q) \to [(Q \to P) \to \bot]) \to \bot$$

Exercise A-2.3

Show that the principles listed above are also interderivability principles of Ds. Do not use metatheorems, derived rules, or substitution principles. However, once $[P \to (Q \to \bot)] \to \bot \vdash P \,\&\, Q$ has been established, it is legitimate to use it as a derived rule when demonstrating the interderivability involving $P \equiv Q$.

For purposes of the completeness proof, sentences made using ~, ∨, &, and ≡ connectives can be treated as abbreviations of sentences made using just →, ⊥, and the sentence letters. As in the appendix to chapter 3, this thinned out language for sentential logic is called the lean language.

Exercise A-2.4

1. *Identify the sentences of the lean language that are abbreviated by the following sentences of* SL.
   ★a. A → ~B
    b. ~(A → B)
   ★c. ~(A & B)
    d. ~~A
   ★e. ~A ∨ ~B
    f. A ≡ ~B

2. *(For those who have read section 6.6.) There is no lean language for intuitionistic logic. Why not?*

Without wedge, ampersand, and triple bar in the language, there is no use for derivation rules involving disjunctions, conjunctions, or biconditionals, so (PC), (∨I), (&I), (&E), (BP), and (BMP) can be left out of account. As will already have been discovered by those who did exercise 6.8#2, (⊥I) can also be eliminated. When rewritten for the lean language, (⊥I) is stated as the rule that if L ⊢ P and L ⊢ P → ⊥ then L ⊢ ⊥, and that follows by (MP).

In lean language derivations (IP) takes a different form, called (IP~E):

$$\text{(IP~E): If } L, P \rightarrow \bot \vdash \bot \text{ then } L \vdash P$$

(The soundness demonstration of section A-2.1 did not cover (IP~E). It did not need to, because (IPE) is an instance of (IP). (IP) allows deriving L ⊢ P from L,~P ⊢ ⊥. In the lean language, this is deriving L ⊢ P from L, P → ⊥ ⊢ ⊥.)

The completeness demonstration can therefore be given by showing that the lean language equivalent of whatever is s-valid can be derived using just (A), (R), (CP), (MP), and (IP~E). In what follows, this lean derivation system is called D_L. The name D_L was used for a slightly expanded system in sections 6.1–2 one that uses full (IP) and includes ~ in the vocabulary. It is appropriated for a yet leaner system here.

It might be expected that completeness would be demonstrated by showing how to use the rules of D_L to derive the conclusion of any s-valid demonstration. There are such demonstrations. One is based on the procedure for deriving a dnf (chapter 6.5.4). Another is based on a procedure for converting the reduction trees studied in chapter 7 to derivations. Both methods are impractical. Derivations discovered by following the strategies of chapter 6 are considerably shorter than those constructed by following automatic procedures. They can be done more quickly, even allowing for the time taken puzzling over hard cases. They are also more reliable, due to the length and complexity of the automatic procedures, which invites clerical errors. The point of formulating algorithms for deriving any s-valid result is not to assist in discovering derivations, but to demonstrate that there is a way of deriving any s-valid conclusion. A demonstration that establishes completeness without giving an algorithm is therefore as good as one that does.

This chapter's discussion of completeness begins with a demonstration, due to Leon Henkin (1921–2006), that focuses on establishing a contrapositive version of the completeness principle. The canonical version of the completeness principle then follows as a corollary. The contrapositive of the completeness principle is

If no finite list, L, of sentences in Γ yields P then Γ does not s-entail P

Because contrapositives are intuitively equivalent to the conditionals they are based on (see p.157), establishing the contrapositive of a principle is as good as establishing the principle.

Henkin focused on establishing the corresponding point for lists and sets.

> ### Henkin Completeness Principle
>
> If any finite list, L, of sentences in Γ is consistent then Γ is s-satisfiable.

(Recall that a demonstration is derivable if and only if the corresponding list is inconsistent [section 6.5.5], which means that it is not derivable if and only if the corresponding list is consistent. Similarly, a demonstration is s-valid if and only if the corresponding set is s-unsatisfiable [exercise 5.10#2c], which means that it is s-*invalid* if and only if the corresponding set is s-*satisfiable*. Assertions of underivability and invalidity are merely specific instances of assertions of inconsistency and satisfiability. The Henkin principle trades on this result. Supposing it is possible to establish the general principle that if a finite list, L, of sentences in Γ is consistent then Γ is s-satisfiable, it follows that if L,~P is consistent then Γ ∪ ~P is s-satisfiable, and hence that if L does not yield P, Γ does not s-entail P.)

Taking this approach means supposing the antecedent for purposes of conditional proof and then establishing that making this supposition requires accepting the consequent. This approach avoids the need to come up with a procedure for giving a derivation. It supposes that there is no derivation, that is, no derivation of ⊥ from any finite list of sentences in Γ. Supposing this is the case, the task is to show that there must be an interpretation on which all the sentences in Γ are true, which means that Γ must be s-satisfiable. If this can be done, it follows that if Γ is *not* satisfiable then there must be a derivation of ⊥ from at least one finite list of sentences in Γ.

The demonstration can be given briefly, with the aid of a few lemmas:

1. Suppose for purposes of conditional proof that any finite list, L, of sentences in a set, Γ, is consistent in D_L.
2. The sentences on L belong to a set, Γ⋆ that is maximally consistent. *(Lemma 1)*
3. The assignment, I⋆, of T to each atomic sentence in Γ⋆ and F to all other atomic sentences satisfies the conditions for being an interpretation. *(Lemma 2)*
4. Each sentence in Γ⋆ is true on I⋆. *(Lemma 3)*
5. By definition of s-satisfaction, Γ⋆ is s-satisfiable.
6. From line 2 by exercise 5.12n (any subset of an s-satisfiable set must be s-satisfiable), $Γ_L$, the set of sentences on L, is s-satisfiable.
7. From the initial supposition, L is *any* finite list of sentences in Γ, and so $Γ_L$ is *any* finite subset of Γ. By compactness (chapter A-1.4), Γ is s-satisfiable.
8. By conditional proof, if any finite list, L, of sentences in a set, Γ, is consistent in D_L then Γ is s-satisfiable.

Lemma 1 is the Lindenbaum lemma. A variant on the lemma was applied in the compactness proof of chapter A-1.4. It is developed in this alternative context below.

Lemma 2 refers to each atomic sentence that stands alone in Γ⋆, not to atomic sentences that occur as components of compound sentences. Lemma 2 follows from lemma 1 and the definition of an interpretation. An interpretation must assign exactly one of T or F to each sentence letter and so to each atomic sentence other than ⊥, which gets an F by (⊥). It is trivial that each atomic sentence must either be in a set or not be in that set. So, assigning a T to each atomic sentence in Γ⋆ and an F to each other atomic sentence satisfies the definition of an interpretation, on the further condition that ⊥ could not be in Γ⋆. It will be shown presently that lemma 1 entails this further condition.

Lemma 3 follows by mathematical induction on the number of arrows (the only connectives there are) in sentences in Γ⋆.

Since the solutions to exercise A-2.3 demonstrate that the additional rules of Ds are adequate to convert negations, disjunctions, conjunctions, and biconditionals back and forth between the lean language and SL, it follows further that if any finite list of sentences in Γ is consistent in Ds, then Γ is s-satisfiable.

Two corollaries complete the demonstration of the canonical version of the completeness principle, that if Γ ⊨ P then L ⊢ P in Ds, where L is a finite subset of sentences in Γ.

It remains to demonstrate the Lindenbaum lemma, lemmas 2 and 3, and these corollaries.

A-2.4 Demonstration of the Lindenbaum Lemma

According to the Lindenbaum lemma the sentences on any list, L, that is consistent in D_L (that does not yield ⊥) can be expanded to make a set, Γ⋆, that is maximally consistent.

A maximally consistent set is a set that is as big as it can get without coming to contain a sentence that would cause it to yield ⊥.

> **(def max)**
>
> Γ⋆ is maximally consistent if and only if (i) no finite list of sentences in Γ⋆ yields ⊥, and (ii) any sentence, P, is either in Γ⋆ or Γ⋆,P ⊢ ⊥.

Strictly speaking, only lists yield sentences. However, in a derivative sense, a set can be said to yield a sentence if it contains the sentences appearing on a list that yields that sentence. When sets appear to the left of ⊢ in what follows, that is what is intended.

The set of sentences on the consistent list, L, is expanded to a maximally consistent set by considering each of the sentences of the lean language in turn. Though there are infinitely many of them, and though they have an unlimited variety of increasingly complex forms, each can be assigned a unique catalogue number, determined by a two-digit numeral assigned to its vocabulary elements (including outer parentheses, even if not coloured in).

Symbol	Numeral	Symbol	Numeral	Symbol	Numeral
⊥	10	0	20	A	30
→	11	1	21	B	31
(	12	…		C	32
)	13	9	29	G	33
				H	34
				K	35

According to this scheme, the catalogue number for ⊥ is 10. That for ⊥ → ⊥ is 1210111012 (outer parentheses must be included). That for A_3 is 3023. That for A → ⊥ is 1230111013.

This scheme permits lining up all the infinitely many sentences in numeric order so that they can each be considered in turn without running the risk of omitting any. The process of considering sentences one after another in the order they are listed will go on forever, but because each sentence is only finitely long (as demonstrated in chapter A-1.1), and so has a finite catalogue number, the turn of each will come up at some finite point.

$\Gamma\star$ is a union of extensions, $\Gamma_1, \Gamma_2, \Gamma_3, \ldots$, defined as follows:

- Γ_1 is the set of sentences on L, the consistent list being expanded to $\Gamma\star$.
- Γ_2 is the product of adding the numerically first sentence, P_1, not already in Γ_1 to Γ_1, provided doing so will not bring Γ_2 to contain a finite list that is inconsistent in D_L (otherwise Γ_2 just is Γ_1).
- Γ_3 is the product of adding the numerically second sentence, P_2, not already in Γ_2 to Γ_2, provided doing so will not bring Γ_3 to contain a finite list that is inconsistent in D_L (otherwise Γ_3 is Γ_2),.
- In general, Γ_n is the product of adding the $n-1$ sentence, P_{n-1}, not already in Γ_{n-1} to Γ_{n-1}, provided doing so will not bring Γ_n to contain a finite list that is inconsistent in D_L (otherwise Γ_n is Γ_{n-1}).

This is a definition, not an exercise. Adding a sentence, P_n, to a set, Γ_n, either makes it possible to derive ⊥ from a finite list of the sentences in Γ_n or it does not. If it does, then P_n is by definition not in Γ_{n+1}. If it does not P_n is by definition in Γ_{n+1}. No one is being tasked with determining whether it does, or with adding or not adding it accordingly. It is enough that there be a fact of the matter, even if no one knows what it is or has demonstrated it or has acted on it before going on to consider the next step in the construction. As it turns out, nothing in the demonstration that follows requires knowledge of the contents of any extension in the series.

As thus defined, each extension in the series must be consistent in D_L. This is because Γ_1 is defined as the set that consists just of the sentences on some consistent list, L, and each other set in the sequence of extensions on Γ_1 either replicates the one before it, or includes one additional sentence on the condition that adding that sentence does not produce an inconsistent list. Though $\Gamma\star$ is not any of the sets in the series, not even the last one (there is no last one), it can be demonstrated that it must also be consistent.

1. Suppose to the contrary that $\Gamma\star$ is inconsistent.
    2. By definition of inconsistency in Ds, $\Gamma\star$ must contain some finite list, L′, that yields ⊥.
    3. Consider the sentence, P_n, that has the highest catalogue number of all the sentences on L′. (There must be such a sentence because, as established by the demonstration for Corollary 6 of the soundness proof, the empty list is consistent, so any inconsistent list must contain at least one item.)
    4. By lines 2 and 3 and the definition of how $\Gamma\star$ is constructed, Γ_{n+1} must have added P_n to Γ_n.
    5. Since P_n has the highest catalogue number of all the sentences in L′, adding P_n to Γ_n would have completed the contents of L′, contents that constitute an inconsistent finite subset of $\Gamma\star$.
    6. By definition Γ_{n+1} cannot have added P_n to Γ_n in this case.
7. Since the supposition at line 1 leads to a contradiction at lines 4 and 6, that supposition must be rejected: $\Gamma\star$ is consistent in D_L.

The second premise of this demonstration may seem opportunistic. Why not liberalize the definition of inconsistency in Ds to allow the derivation of ⊥ from infinite lists? Without this restriction, the demonstration would fail, since there need be no sentence with a highest catalogue number on an infinite list of sentences.

There can be derivations that go on forever. (To take a simple example, start with A ⊢ A and apply (&I) or (∨I) infinitely many times). But any sequent that is derived over the course of an infinite derivation is derived at some finite point, after only finitely many prior sequents have been derived and only finitely many, finitely long sentences have been generated. For the derivation to go to infinity "before" L ⊢ ⊥ is derived is for the derivation to go on to infinity without ever deriving L ⊢ ⊥.

This "finitude of derivations" does not prove the *incompleteness* of D_L. The compactness demonstration of chapter A-1.4 establishes that $\Gamma \vDash P$ if and only if some finite subset of $\Gamma \vDash P$, so anything that is s-entailed in SL is s-entailed by a finite set of premises. There are no demonstrations requiring an infinite premise set, and so none from a premise set that D_L could not possibly use to derive that result.

In addition to being consistent, $\Gamma^\star$ must be maximally consistent.

1. Suppose to the contrary that $\Gamma^\star$ is not maximal.
    2. Then by definition of maximality, there is a sentence, P, that is neither in $\Gamma^\star$ nor such that $\Gamma^\star,P \vdash \bot$.
    3. P has some catalogue number, n.
    4. Since P is not in $\Gamma^\star$, it follows from the definition of how $\Gamma^\star$ is constructed that P must not have been admitted into Γ_n.
    5. According to that definition, P can only have been excluded from Γ_n on the ground that $\Gamma_{n-1},P \vdash \bot$.
    6. Γ_{n-1} is a finite subset of $\Gamma^\star$.
    7. From lines 5 and 6 by definition of derivability, $\Gamma^\star,P \vdash \bot$.
8. Since the supposition at line 1 leads to a contradiction at lines 2 and 7, that supposition must be rejected. $\Gamma^\star$ is maximal.

A-2.5 Demonstration of Lemma 2

Lemma 2: The assignment, I★, of T to each atomic sentence in $\Gamma^\star$ and F to each other atomic sentence satisfies the conditions for being an interpretation.

The only part of lemma 2 that is not trite is the claim that ⊥ could not stand alone in $\Gamma^\star$ (it could occur as a component of a compound sentence) and so could not receive a T on I★. This follows because, were ⊥ in $\Gamma^\star$, there would be a finite list of sentences in $\Gamma^\star$, <⊥> that yields ⊥ (by (A)). But then $\Gamma^\star$ would be inconsistent. Since the Lindenbaum lemma demonstrates that $\Gamma^\star$ is not inconsistent, it follows that ⊥ could not be in $\Gamma^\star$.

A-2.6 Demonstration of Lemma 3

Lemma 3: Each sentence in $\Gamma^\star$ is true on I★.

Lemma 3 is demonstrated by mathematical induction on the number of connectives (arrows) in sentences in $\Gamma^\star$. In demonstrating the inductive step, it turns out to be necessary to establish not just that each lean language sentence with k or fewer connectives in $\Gamma^\star$ is true on I★, but also that each such sentence that is not in $\Gamma^\star$ is false on I★. (Lines 6 and 14 of the demonstration given below require this supposition.) As a result, the entire demonstration needs to establish a stronger conclusion than the principally desired one, that all the sentences in $\Gamma^\star$ are true on I★.

> *Basis:* Each sentence with 0 connectives is in $\Gamma^\star$ if and only if it is true on I★.
>
> *Induction:* If each sentence with k or fewer connectives is in $\Gamma^\star$ if and only if it is true on I★ then each sentence with $k+1$ connectives is in $\Gamma^\star$ if and only if it is true on I★.
> _____
> *Conclusion:* Each sentence is in $\Gamma^\star$ if and only if it is true on I★.

Demonstration of the basis: The sentences with 0 connectives are the atomic sentences. By definition, I★ is the interpretation that assigns a T to each atomic sentence in $\Gamma^\star$ and an F to all other atomic sentences other than ⊥, which is F by (⊥). So, if an atomic sentence receives a T on I★ it is in $\Gamma^\star$ and if it is in $\Gamma^\star$ it receives a T on I★, that is an atomic sentence receives a T on I★ if and only if it is in $\Gamma^\star$.

The demonstration of the induction relies at various points on two supporting principles and a derivation. They are laid out now for future reference. (Recall that when $\Gamma^\star$ appears to the left of $\vdash$ it means that some of the sentences in $\Gamma^\star$ comprise a finite list that yields the sentence on the right of $\vdash$.)

(i) If P is not in $\Gamma^\star$, then $\Gamma^\star \vdash P \rightarrow \bot$. *Demonstration:* By (def max), if P is not in $\Gamma^\star$ then $\Gamma^\star, P \vdash \bot$, from which it follows **by (CP)** that $\Gamma^\star \vdash P \rightarrow \bot$.

(ii) If $\Gamma^\star \vdash P$, P is in $\Gamma^\star$. *Demonstration:*
1.   Suppose that $\Gamma^\star \vdash P$.
    2.   Suppose, to the contrary, that P is not in $\Gamma^\star$.
        3.   By principle (i), $\Gamma^\star \vdash P \rightarrow \bot$.
        4.   From (1) and (3) **by (MP)**, $\Gamma^\star \vdash \bot$.
        5.   By the Lindenbaum lemma, $\Gamma^\star$ is consistent.
    6.   Since the supposition at line 2 has led to a contradiction (at lines 4 and 5) under the initial supposition at line 1, it must be rejected as long as the supposition at line 1 is sustained: P is in $\Gamma^\star$.
7.   From lines 1 to 6 by conditional proof, if $\Gamma^\star \vdash P$, P is in $\Gamma^\star$.

(iii) The derivation establishes a version of (EFQ), that if $\Gamma^\star \vdash P \rightarrow \bot$ then $\Gamma^\star \vdash P \rightarrow Q$.

1.	$\Gamma^\star$	$\vdash$ $P \rightarrow \bot$	given
2.	$\Gamma^\star, P$	$\vdash$ P	**(A)**
3.	$\Gamma^\star, P, Q \rightarrow \bot$	$\vdash$ $Q \rightarrow \bot$	**(A)**
4.	$\Gamma^\star, P, Q \rightarrow \bot$	$\vdash$ $P \rightarrow \bot$	1 **(R)**
5.	$\Gamma^\star, P, Q \rightarrow \bot$	$\vdash$ P	2 **(R)**
6.	$\Gamma^\star, P, Q \rightarrow \bot$	$\vdash$ $\bot$	5,4 **(MP)**
7.	$\Gamma^\star, P$	$\vdash$ Q	6 **(IPE)**
8.	$\Gamma^\star$	$\vdash$ $P \rightarrow Q$	7 **(CP)**

Demonstration of the induction:
1.   Suppose for purposes of conditional proof that each sentence with k or fewer occurrences of connectives is in $\Gamma^\star$ if and only if it is true on I*.
    2.   The sentences with $k+1$ occurrences of connectives must contain at least one connective, and since $\rightarrow$ is the only connective, they must be sentences of the form $P \rightarrow Q$, where $\rightarrow$ is the $k+1$ connective, and so where each of P and Q contains k or fewer connectives.
    3.   Suppose for purposes of biconditional proof that $P \rightarrow Q$ is in $\Gamma^\star$.
        4.   Suppose to the contrary that I*($P \rightarrow Q$) is F.
            5.   By ($\rightarrow$), I*(P) is T and I*(Q) is F.
            6.   Since P and Q contain k or fewer connectives it follows from line 1 that P must be in $\Gamma^\star$ and Q must not be in $\Gamma^\star$.
            7.   By lines 3 and 6 both $P \rightarrow Q$ and P are in $\Gamma^\star$.
            8.   **By (MP)** $<P \rightarrow Q, P> \vdash Q$.
            9.   From lines 7 and 8 $\Gamma^\star \vdash Q$.
            10.   By supporting principle (ii) Q is in $\Gamma^\star$.
        11.   Since the supposition at line 4 leads to a contradiction at lines 6 and 10, that supposition must be rejected: $P \rightarrow Q$ is T on I*.
    12.   Suppose for further purposes of biconditional proof that $P \rightarrow Q$ is T on I*.
        13.   By ($\rightarrow$) either I*(P) is F or I*(Q) is T.
        14.   Since P and Q contain k or fewer connectives it follows from lines 1 and 13 that either P is not in $\Gamma^\star$ or Q is in $\Gamma^\star$.
        15.   Suppose for purposes of proof by cases that P is not in $\Gamma^\star$.
            16.   By supporting principle (i), $\Gamma^\star \vdash P \rightarrow \bot$.
            17.   By supporting derivation (iii) $\Gamma^\star \vdash P \rightarrow Q$.
        18.   Suppose for further purposes of proof by cases that Q is in $\Gamma^\star$.
            19.   **By (R)** $\Gamma^\star, P \vdash Q$ from which it follows **by (CP)** that $\Gamma^\star \vdash P \rightarrow Q$.

20. From lines 12, 13–15, and 16–17 it follows that, either way, $\Gamma^\star \vdash P \rightarrow Q$.
21. By supporting principle (ii), $P \rightarrow Q$ is in $\Gamma^\star$.
22. From lines 3–11 and 12–21 by biconditional proof, any sentence with $k+1$ connectives is in $\Gamma^\star$ if and only if it is true on $I^\star$
23. From lines 1–22 by conditional proof, if each sentence with k or fewer occurrences of connectives is in $\Gamma^\star$ if and only if it is true on $I^\star$, each sentence with $k+1$ connectives is in $\Gamma^\star$ if and only if it is true on $I^\star$.

It is noteworthy that each of the rules of D_L, (A), (R), (CP), (MP), and (IPE) is needed for this demonstration of the inductive step to carry through. Each is used at least once, either in the demonstration proper or in the demonstration of supporting principles (i) and (ii), or in the supporting demonstration, (iii). This is an indication that D_L would not be complete without each of these rules.

The demonstration is also a good example of a sad, but instructive fact. The most elegant or straightforward demonstration is often one that conceals the reasoning that led to its discovery, and one that can do more to perplex than enlighten the learner. All that needs to be demonstrated is that $\Gamma^\star$ is satisfiable, that is, that each sentence in $\Gamma^\star$ is true on $I^\star$. But the demonstration opens by proposing to prove more than that: not just that if a sentence is in $\Gamma^\star$ then it is true on $I^\star$, but that each sentence is in $\Gamma^\star$ if and only if it is in $I^\star$. The scrupulous learner ought to be perplexed by this move, yet the demonstration provides little indication of why it was made.

The demonstration is discovered by setting out normally, to establish that if a sentence is in $\Gamma^\star$ then it is true on $I^\star$. But when this is set as a project the demonstration runs into a roadblock at line 6. To proceed from line 6, it needs to first be established that since $I^\star(Q)$ is F, Q is not in $\Gamma^\star$. An inductive hypothesis that reads "each sentence with k or fewer occurrences of connectives is in $\Gamma^\star$ only if it is true on $I^\star$" is inadequate for that job. The inverse consequence that a sentence that is *not* in $\Gamma^\star$ is false on $I^\star$ also needs to be supposed (and established both as part of the demonstration of the basis and when completing the demonstration of the inductive step over lines 12–22). This background reasoning is concealed.

A-2.7 Corollary Results

Corollary 1: *If Γ is s-unsatisfiable then L is inconsistent in Ds, where L is at least one finite list of sentences in Γ.*

The corollary follows from the Henkin completeness principle by contraposition. (Note that the negation of "any finite list is consistent" is "at least one finite list is inconsistent.)

Corollary 2: If $\Gamma \vDash P$, then $L \vdash P$ in Ds, where L is a finite list of sentences in Γ.

1. Suppose for purposes of conditional proof that $\Gamma \vDash P$.
   2. By exercises 5.11#2(a) and (c), $\Gamma \cup \sim P$ is s-unsatisfiable.
   3. By corollary 1, $L,\sim P$ is inconsistent in Ds, where L is a finite list of sentences in Γ.
   4. By definition of inconsistency, $L,\sim P \vdash \bot$.
   5. By (IP$\sim$E), $L \vdash P$
6. From lines 1–5 by conditional proof, if $\Gamma \vDash P$, then $L \vdash P$, where L is a finite list of sentences in Γ.

Corollary 2 is the canonical statement of the completeness principle. Establishing it satisfies the promise made at the outset of this section, to show how the Henkin version of the principle establishes the canonical version. To close this discussion, two more pertinent corollaries are mentioned.

Corollary 3: If P is s-valid then it is a theorem of D_L.

Demonstration: Suppose P is s-valid. Then, by one half of the solution to exercise 5.11#2(e), $\emptyset \vDash P$. So, by corollary 2, $\emptyset \vdash P$, that is, P is a theorem of D_L.

Corollary 4: If P and Q are s-equivalent then they are interderivable in D_L.

Exercise A-2.5

Prove corollary 4. Appeal to one half of the solution to exercise 5.11(g) and corollary 2.

A-2.8 Post/Hilbert–Ackermann Completeness

(The following paragraph is repeated here for those who may have chosen to skip study of sections A-2.3–7. Those who have not done so are advised that the completeness demonstrations given here and in exercise A-2.6 do not use the lean language.)

Whereas the soundness demonstration establishes that Ds will not yield anything that is not s-entailed, the completeness demonstration establishes that whatever is s-entailed is derivable in Ds. If a (possibly empty) set, Γ, s-entails P, there is a way of deriving P from a finite list of the sentences in Γ using the rules of Ds.

Completeness

If $\Gamma \models P$ then $L \vdash P$ in Ds
where L is a finite list of sentences in Γ

Completeness can be demonstrated by devising an automatic procedure for deriving any s-valid result. One such procedure, devised by Emil Post (1897–1954) has already been presented in section 6.5.4. A variant on this procedure is made the subject for exercise A-2.6, and a different procedure is based on the reduction trees of chapter 7 and is presented in chapter A-3.4. Post's procedure uses the substitution principles of Ds to derive a disjunctive normal form (dnf) of the iterated conjunction of the premises of a demonstration and the negation of its conclusion. A dnf is an iterated disjunction of iterated conjunctions of literals. An iterated conjunction of literals is a characteristic sentence. Except in the case where literals of the forms P and ~P are both among the iterated conjuncts, it describes the one interpretation on which it itself is true. In the case where there is no interpretation on which the iterated conjunction is true, P and ~P are both among the iterated conjuncts, and the iterated conjunction itself reduces to $\bot$ by (con) and (inf). Provided each disjunct of a dnf is elaborated to include each sentence letter to appear in any other disjunct, the dnf characterizes each interpretation on which it is true.

As illustrated in section 6.5.4, there is a way of deriving a sentence's dnf from that sentence. If the dnf for the conjunction of the premises and the negation of the conclusion reduces to $\bot$, a derivation that starts with the premises as givens, follows up with the assumption of the negation of the conclusion, conjoins all these sentences in an iterated conjunction, and continues with the sequence of steps for deriving the dnf of this iterated conjunction under the assumption of the negation of the conclusion, will yield the conclusion under the givens by (IP).

But will this procedure always be effective? In particular, if $\Gamma \models P$, in which case there can be no interpretation on which all the sentences in $\Gamma \cup {\sim}P$ are true, will the procedure for deriving a dnf from the iterated conjunction of at least one finite list of premises drawn from Γ and ~P always yield $\bot$? Post explained why the answer to these questions must be "yes."

Post's Completeness Principle

If P is s-unsatisfiable then P is inconsistent in Ds.

In other words, if there is no interpretation on which a sentence, P, is true, then there will always be a way of deriving $\bot$ from P in Ds. What holds for sentences holds for demonstrations since any demonstration has a corresponding sentence.

1. Suppose for purposes of conditional proof that P is s-unsatisfiable.
    2. $P = | = P_{dnf}$. *(lemma 1)*
    3. From lines 1 and 2, P_{dnf} is s-unsatisfiable.
    4. $P \vdash P_{dnf}$. *(lemma 2)*
    5. If P_{dnf} is s-unsatisfiable the procedure for deriving it yields $\bot$. *(lemma 3)*
    6. From lines 3, 4 and 5, $P \vdash \bot$.
7. From lines 1–6 by conditional proof, if P is s-unsatisfiable, then it is inconsistent in Ds.

Demonstration of the lemmas:

Lemma 1: Any sentence, P, is s-equivalent to its dnf, P_{dnf}.

> *Demonstration:* As demonstrated in the appendix to chapter 3, except in the case where a sentence, P, is s-unsatisfiable, its dnf is read off the rows of its long table on which it is assigned a T. On each such row, any

sentence letter that is assigned an F is negated, and the iterated conjunction of these negations and the remaining sentence letters is formed, taking the sentence letters in alphanumeric order. Such iterated conjunctions are true only on the row they are written for. P_{dnf} is the iterated disjunction of these iterated conjunctions. Consequently, P_{dnf} gets a T on all and only those rows on which its component disjuncts (which are the conjunctions just described) get a T. P is similarly true on all and only those rows. So, in these cases, there is no interpretation on which P and P_{dnf} have different values. This leaves the case in which P is not true on any row. In that case, P_{dnf} is stipulated to be ⊥ which is also F on any row. So, in this case as well, there is no interpretation on which P and P_{dnf} have different values. Either way, P and P_{dnf} have the same value on any interpretation, so they are s-equivalent.

Lemma 2: Any sentence, P, yields its dnf, P_{dnf}.

Demonstration: In what is called a "perfect" dnf, (i) the literals in each disjunct are in alphanumeric order with all repetitions deleted, (ii) each disjunct contains each sentence letter to appear in any other disjunct, (iii) each disjunct is listed in long table order (each disjunct corresponds to an interpretation of its sentence letters; these disjuncts are listed in the order the interpretations are entered from top to bottom of a long table), and (iv) all repetitions of disjuncts have been deleted. To demonstrate lemma 2 it suffices to demonstrate (i) that the procedure specified in chapter 6.5.4 will always yield a perfect dnf after a finite number of steps, and (ii) that this dnf must be P's dnf as defined by P's long table (see lemma 1).

The procedure begins by applying (imp) and (equiv) to convert conditionals to disjunctions and biconditionals to disjunctions of conjunctions. When a sentence contains no arrows or triple bars it has already passed this stage for reduction to dnf. When it does contain them, each application of each of these rules removes an arrow or triple bar and replaces it only with some combination of tilde, ampersand, and wedge. So no application of either of these rules creates more work to be done by either of these rules. Since any sentence of SL is only finitely long and so contains only a finite number of connectives, it can only contain a finite number of arrows or triple bars. So work at this stage must come to an end after a finite number of (imp) and (equiv) applications.

When a sentence that has passed the (imp)/(equiv) stage is found to contain a tilde that is followed by another tilde or by a punctuation mark, (DNE) and (DeM) are applied to remove those tildes. When this is not possible, the sentence has already passed this stage for reduction to dnf. When it is possible, each application of (DNE) reduces the number of tildes in the resulting sentence without adding any other connectives, and each application of (DeM) removes a tilde that has other connectives within its scope and replaces it with two tildes each of which has fewer connectives within its scope, again without adding any other connectives. Since doubling the number of tildes still leaves a finite number of tildes, any round of applications of (DeM) leaves only a finite task for (DNE). Even if a second round of (DNE) does not remove all cases of tildes followed by punctuation marks, a further round of (DeM) applications will remove those tildes and replace them with two tildes each of which has fewer connectives within its scope. Since sentences are only finitely long, only a finite number of rounds of (DNE) and (DeM) applications can be performed before the only tildes that remain are those that have no other connectives within their scope. Once this happens, work at this stage must terminate. Moreover, since (DNE) and (DeM) do not introduce arrows or triple bars, work at this stage does not require a return to the previous, (imp)/(equiv) stage.

When a sentence has passed the (dist) stage, (com) and (assoc) are applied to rearrange the component literals of each iterated conjunction in alphanumeric order. (idem) is then applied to eliminate any repetitions of the same conjunct, (con) is applied to reduce any conjunctions of a conjunct and its opposite to ⊥, and, in that case, (inf) is applied to reduce the entire iterated conjunction to ⊥. Since the iterated conjunctions and disjunctions existing at this stage are only finitely long (the original sentence was only finitely long and work at the prior stages has only added a finite number of vocabulary elements) and any application of these rules merely reorders vocabulary elements or produces a shorter sentence, work at this stage must terminate. As work at this stage does not introduce arrows or triple bars, cause tildes to fall outside of tildes or punctuation marks, or bring wedges under the scope of ampersands, it terminates without requiring a return to any of the earlier stages.

Should work at the (con)/(inf) stage produce an iterated disjunction of ⊥'s, (idem) would be applied to reduce the dnf to a single ⊥. As the sentence in question can only be finitely long (as demonstrated in the previous paragraph), it could contain only finitely many ⊥'s, so work at this stage would terminate after a finite number of steps. Otherwise (when a sentence has passed the (con)/(inf) stage without being reduced to an iterated disjunction of ⊥'s), (elab) is applied to add missing sentence letters to each disjunct that is not ⊥, (com) and (assoc) are applied to rearrange disjuncts in long table order, (idem) is applied to remove any repetitions of disjuncts, and (imm) is applied to remove any disjuncts that are ⊥. Since the sentence in question is still only finitely long (as demonstrated in the previous paragraph), only a finite number of disjuncts need to be rearranged/eliminated. So, work at this stage must eventually come to an end. Moreover, since (com), (assoc), (idem) and (imm) add nothing new and (elab) only adds new literals other than $\perp$ and $\sim\!\perp$ to existing iterated conjunctions, and since it does not add arrows, triple bars, tildes that are followed by other tildes or punctuation marks, wedges with ampersands within their scope, or $\perp$, work at this stage terminates without requiring a return to any of the earlier stages. It also results in a perfect dnf: there are no arrows or triple bars, all tildes are followed by a sentence letter, no disjunction lies within the scope of a conjunction, each sentence letter to occur (negated or unnegated) in any disjunct occurs in each other disjunct, the conjuncts of each conjunction are in alphanumeric order, and the disjuncts are in truth table order.

It follows that a perfect dnf can be derived from any sentence using the procedure outlined in section 6.5.4.

It remains to demonstrate that this perfect dnf must be that sentence's dnf, as defined by its long table. The dnf's derived by the procedure outlined in section 6.5.4 are derived using only the substitution principles, (impl), (equiv), (DN), (DeM), (dist), (con), (inf), (com), (assoc), (elab), and (idem), and each of these substitution principles is also an equivalence principle. As demonstrated by exercise 5.6#3, sentences that are derived by any of these principles are s-equivalent to the sentences they were derived from. Since s-equivalence is transitive (if P is s-equivalent to Q and Q is s-equivalent to R then P is s-equivalent to R) the perfect dnf resulting from applying a sequence of substitution principles to a sentence, P, must be s-equivalent to P. For the same reason, by lemma 1, it must also be s-equivalent to the dnf defined by P's long table, which is automatically a perfect dnf. Since any change in a perfect dnf either makes it imperfect or creates a nonequivalent perfect dnf, two perfect dnf's that are s-equivalent must be the same sentence. So the perfect dnf yielded by applying the procedure of chapter 6.5.4 to P must be P's dnf as defined by its long table.

Lemma 3: If P_{dnf} is s-unsatisfiable the procedure for deriving it must yield $\perp$.

Demonstration: Suppose P_{dnf} is s-unsatisfiable. In that case, the procedure of chapter 6.5.4 must reveal that each disjunct derived on the way to deriving P_{dnf} contains either $\perp$ or the combination of a sentence letter and its negation among its iterated conjuncts. (The alternative would be that at least one disjunct, Q_1 & ... & Q_n, is such that none of $Q_1 ... Q_n$ is $\perp$ and no two of them are a sentence letter and its opposite. In that case, by definition of an interpretation, the assignment, I, of T to each of $Q_1 ... Q_n$ that is a sentence letter and F to all other sentence letters is an interpretation. By ($\sim$) it is, moreover, an interpretation on which each of $Q_1 ... Q_n$ is true and so, by (&) on which Q_1 & ... & Q_n is true, and so, by ($\vee$), an interpretation on which P_{dnf}'s imperfect ancestor is true. Given that, as noted in the second half of lemma 2, each of P_{dnf}'s ancestors is s-equivalent to it, this is contrary to the supposition that P_{dnf} is s-unsatisfiable.)

Since each disjunct derived on the way to deriving P_{dnf}'s imperfect ancestor must contain either $\perp$ or the combination of a sentence letter and its negation among its iterated conjuncts, applications of (con) and (inf) will derive $\perp$ from each disjunct, and applications of (idem) will derive $\perp$ from that result.

So, if P_{dnf} is s-unsatisfiable, the procedure for deriving it must yield $\perp$.

The following corollary substantiates a claim made towards the close of chapter 6.5.4.

Corollary of Lemma 1

If P is s-satisfiable, then for each interpretation, I, that assigns a T to P there is a disjunct of P_{dnf} that characterizes I. As a special case, if P is s-valid, then P_{dnf} has as many disjuncts as there are rows on the long table for P, and each of those disjuncts characterizes one of those rows.

This corollary is a direct consequence of the demonstration of lemma 1. Since lemma 2 establishes that any sentence's dnf is derivable from that sentence, it follows that the intensional properties of any sentence can be inferred by deriving its dnf. If the dnf is $\perp$ (or if each disjunct contains either $\perp$ or the combination of a sentence letter and its negation among its disjuncts) the sentence is unsatisfiable. If the sentence has n sentence letters and the dnf hs 2^n disjuncts, the sentence is s-valid. Otherwise it is s-contingent.

Exercise A-2.6

This exercise explores a modified version of Post's approach to demonstrating completeness, due to David Hilbert (1862–1943) and Wilhelm Ackermann (1896–1962). Hilbert and Ackermann's approach to completeness is based on an alternative normal form, called conjunctive normal form or cnf.

A sentence's cnf is derived in the same way as its dnf except that, at the stage where (dist) is applied, disjunctions are distributed over conjunctions to create an iterated conjunction of iterated disjunctions of literals.

Disjunctive vs. Conjunctive Normal Form	
(dnf)	$(A_1 \, \& \, ... \, \& \, A_i) \lor ... \lor (A_k \, \& \, ... \, \& \, A_n)$
(cnf)	$(A_1 \lor ... \lor A_i) \, \& \, ... \, \& \, (A_k \lor ... \lor A_n)$

Like Post's approach, the Hilbert–Ackermann approach does not demonstrate the canonical completeness principle, that if $\Gamma \vDash P$ then $L \vdash P$, where L is a finite list of the sentences in Γ. Instead, it demonstrates a variant on the canonical principle. For Post, the variant is "if P is s-unsatisfiable then it is inconsistent in Ds," whereas for Hilbert–Ackermann it is "if P is s-valid, then it is a theorem of Ds."

Whereas the crucial step in Post's approach is demonstrating that each disjunct in the imperfect dnf of an s-inconsistent sentence must have a sentence letter and its negation among its component conjuncts, the crucial step in the Hilbert–Ackermann approach turns on the showing that each conjunct in the cnf for any s-valid sentence must have at least one sentence letter and its negation among its component disjuncts, making it a theorem. This central thesis is then employed a demonstration of the variant completeness principle that if P is s-valid then it is a theorem of Ds. It figures, again, as lemma 3 of that larger demonstration.

Using the demonstration that has just been given of Post's completeness principle as a guide, write up a demonstration of the Hilbert–Ackermann principle: If P *is s-valid, then* P *is a theorem. Demonstrate the lemmas as well. The demonstration of lemma 2 still falls into two parts, but the demonstration of the* (impl)/(equiv) *and* (DN)/(DeM) *stages can be omitted from the first part, as it is unchanged from Post's version, except for replacing references to dnf's with references to cnf's and inverting references to disjunctions/disjuncts and references to conjunctions/conjuncts.*

7 Reduction Trees

Contents

In this and the following chapter, a final method of answering the questions of sentential logic is investigated, the reduction tree method, called Ts (for sentential trees). The method is variously labelled in other textbooks. Alternatives include "truth trees," and "semantic tableaux." The label used here is chosen to distance the method both from the semantic methods of chapter 5 and from the syntactic trees of chapter 2.

Reduction trees are a recent addition to the techniques of logic. Derivation rules were codified by the ancients. Semantic theories were developed in the late nineteenth and early twentieth centuries. Reduction trees were only invented in the mid twentieth century, independently by Evert Willem Beth (1908–64) and Jaakko Hintikka (1929–2015). They occupy a middle ground between derivations and semantic theories. Like derivations, they derive sentences from (or reduce sentences to) other sentences based on their form. But whereas derivation rules are based on intuition, reduction rules are based on valuation rules. Values do not appear on the trees presented in this chapter. (They do in versions of the method presented in some other textbooks.) But the sentences that do appear are supposed to be true, and longer sentences are reduced to shorter ones in accord with what valuation rules say about the values components can take given the values of compounds.

Even though reduction rules are based on valuation rules there is a question whether reduction trees establish the same results as semantic theories. Like derivations using assumption brackets, reduction trees work with a spatial structure. In the case of derivations in standard notation, the structure is a subderivation structure. In the case of reduction trees, it is a branching structure. Sentences are distributed or copied to different locations within this structure in ways that are not simply a function of semantic results.[1] For this reason, this and subsequent chapters do not treat reduction trees as if they were methods for directly discovering semantic results. They are instead presented as methods for deriving sentences. They are accordingly treated as methods for directly establishing derivability, inconsistency, and interderivability, and only indirectly establishing validity, unsatisfiability, and equivalence.

DOI: 10.4324/9781003026532-10

7.1 Method and Strategies

In chapter 2, syntactic trees are used to depict how compound sentences are built up from their component parts. The reduction trees examined in this chapter are in many ways the opposite of the syntactic trees of chapter 2. Rather than converge downwards from many branches on top, they diverge downwards from a common trunk on top. Rather than illustrate how compound sentences are built up from their component parts, they reduce compound sentences to shorter sentences. The shorter sentences are not components of the sentences being reduced. They are instead derived from the sentences being reduced, though by means of rules that are in most cases different from those of Ds.

Reduction trees are used to determine whether sets are inconsistent, that is, whether they yield ⊥. Because any sentence, any pair of sentences, and any demonstration has a corresponding set or sets, reduction trees can also be used to determine whether sentences are theorems or are inconsistent, whether pairs of sentences are interderivable, and whether demonstrations have derivable conclusions.

Reduction trees work by reducing the sentences in a set to literals. The reduction produces a branching structure, called a tree. A set is "inconsistent according to the reduction tree" if and only if ⊥ is derived on each path through the tree. If there is even one path on which each sentence in the set is reduced to literals without yielding ⊥, the set is "consistent according to the reduction tree," and the literals on the path characterize an interpretation that satisfies the set.

Reduction trees are canonically constructed by reducing the sentences in a set one by one, in order of the catalogue numbers defined in chapter A-2.4, but this manner of proceeding tends to produce unnecessarily complex trees. When sets are finite, it is more practical to begin the tree with a list of all the sentences in the set, placed one below the other on successive lines, and to reduce sentences following a method designed to minimize complexity.

A sentence is reduced by applying a rule specific to its form. There is no choice over which rule to apply. And sentences of SL are only reduced once (though the rules can require that multiple copies of the reduction results be entered at different places). It helps to keep track of which sentences have been reduced and which remain to be reduced. On some reduction tree systems, sentences must be reduced in a prescribed order (for instance, from the top down). This ensures that none will be omitted, and none dealt with more than once. *Logic Works* allows sentences to be reduced in any order, but an optimal selection procedure is recommended. A record of which have been reduced and which remain to be reduced is kept by checking off those sentences that have been reduced.

While there are six basic forms for sentences of SL (atomic, negation, conjunction, disjunction, conditional, biconditional) there are ten rules of Ts, further supplemented by a principle and two definitions. Literals (atomic sentences and their negations) use one rule, (⊥I), familiar from chapter 6, and reintroduced here. The remaining negations use five different rules, memorably called (DN), (~&), (~∨), (~→), and (~≡) depending on whether they are double negations or negations of conjunctions, disjunctions, conditionals or biconditionals. Rules for disjunctions, conjunctions, conditionals and biconditionals, called (T∨), (T&), (T→), and (T≡), make up the rest.

Those who have worked with (⊥I) in Ds should note that while (⊥I) is a rule of Ts as well as of Ds, in Ts its application is restricted to literals. On trees, it is not permitted to derive ⊥ from a compound sentence and its negation, not even ~A and ~~A.

Four of the ten rules, (T∨), (⊥I), (DN), and (T&), a placement principle, and two definitions are foundational for Ts. The remaining rules are consequences of the foundational ones. (T∨) takes pride of place because it is what gives trees their name. It is stated here in a crude form, to be refined in a moment.

(Preliminary T∨): Given a sentence of the form P ∨ Q, derive P on a left path and Q on a right path.

Schematically (T∨) is:

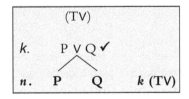

The scheme depicts P ∨ Q as given at some line, *k*. When (T∨) is applied at some later line, *n*, P ∨ Q at line *k* is checked off. Two lines, called paths, are drawn diverging from one another below P ∨ Q. P is entered on the left path and Q on the right. The justification cites the line number for the sentence (T∨) was applied to and the rule that was applied.

Having been checked off, P ∨ Q at line 1 may never be reduced again. Each sentence is reduced only once. Some may never be reduced.

The idea behind (T∨), and all the other reduction rules, is to reduce compound sentences to shorter sentences that must be true supposing the compounds are true. This accounts for why the split paths appear. When a disjunction is true, all that follows is that at least one of its disjuncts is true. The rule attempts to accommodate this by depicting what might metaphorically be called a split in the river of truth. When truth flows from above down to a disjunction, making it true, it might flow on to only one of the disjuncts. To represent that the truth could go either way, the rule splits the path. It is assured that truth will flow down along at least one of the paths, but not assured which one or ones. The main thing is that it must go down somehow and, however it is, that way is represented on the tree.

(T∨) gives reduction trees their name. Applications of (T∨) create a branching structure that looks like an inverted tree.

This raises the question of where the results of subsequent reductions should be placed on the branching structure. That question is answered by the placement principle.

Placement Principle

The results of reducing a sentence are to be completely and repeatedly entered on each path running up to its location, provided that ⊥ has not been derived on that path. They are not to be entered on any path that does not run up to its location or on any path that yields ⊥.

The placement principle prohibits adding to a path with ⊥ on it because trees are supposed to depict the paths taken by the river of truth on its downward flow. ⊥ can never be true, so it is like a dam in the river. Truth cannot flow through it, so no sentences can be added below it.

To reflect the placement principle, (T∨) is precisely stated as follows:

(T∨)

P ∨ Q reduces to P on a left path extension and Q on a right path extension of each path selected by the placement principle.

The precise statement of (T∨) implies that sentences may need to be reduced on multiple paths. Though each sentence is only reduced once, the one reduction can require copying the reduction results multiple times on different paths.

Trees can get complex by growing many paths. The placement principle recognizes this complexity by demanding that a sentence be *completely* and *repeatedly* reduced on each path running up to it. "Repeatedly" means that the reduction of any one sentence must be finished before doing anything else. When multiple paths run up to a sentence, it is not permitted to reduce it on just some of them and wait for a later occasion to do the rest. There is enough to do without having to worry about remembering to complete unfinished tasks.

The application of the placement principle can be illustrated by considering a tree used to determine whether the set, {(A ∨ ⊥) ∨ C, ~B ∨ ~C, (~A ∨ C) ∨ (B ∨ G)} is inconsistent. The first step in making the tree is to list the sentences in the set as givens on successive numbered lines.

> 1.   (A ∨ ⊥) ∨ C   given
> 2.   ~B ∨ ~C   given
> 3.   (~A ∨ C) ∨ (B ∨ G)   given

The next step is to pick a sentence and reduce it to simpler sentences by applying the rule specific to its form. While there are no rules governing which sentence to pick, and the same result will be obtained regardless of which is picked in what order, careful selection can prevent trees from becoming too complex. The placement principle dictates that results of a single rule application must be completely entered on each path that runs up to the sentence. This makes it advisable to do the longer sentences first. That minimizes the number of times their longer reduction results must be entered.

Since line 3 contains the longer sentence, it is advisable to reduce it first. Since it is a disjunction, only the (T∨) rule may be applied to it.

$$
\begin{array}{lll}
1. & (A \vee \bot) \vee C & \text{given} \\
2. & \sim\!B \vee \sim\!C & \text{given} \\
3. & (\sim\!A \vee C) \vee (B \vee G)\checkmark & \text{given} \\[4pt]
4. & \quad \sim\!A \vee C \qquad B \vee G & 3 \ (T\vee)
\end{array}
$$

(T∨) dictates entering the left disjunct on the left path and the right disjunct on the right path. As defined by punctuation, ∼A ∨ C is the left disjunct of (∼A ∨ C) ∨ (B ∨ G). Likewise for B ∨ G and the right disjunct.

The results of reducing a sentence are themselves subject to reduction. So, while the sentence at line 3 has been checked off, there are now four sentences remaining on the tree that are subject to reduction, those on lines 1 and 2, that on line 4 left, and that on line 4 right.

Since the sentence on line 1 is longer, it is advisable to make it the next target for reduction.

Now the placement principle comes into play. The placement principle dictates that the results of reducing the sentence on line 1 must be completely entered on each path running up to it, provided that path does not yield ⊥. As there are two paths running up to the sentence on line 1 and neither of them yields ⊥, the results of applying (T∨) to the sentence on line 1 must be entered twice – once on each path. For them to be *completely* entered on *each* path is not for half the result to be entered on one path and half the result to be entered on the other path. It is for the complete results of the reduction to be entered on each path. Since (T∨) dictates making two paths, that means two paths must be made on each existing path.

$$
\begin{array}{lll}
1. & (A \vee \bot) \vee C\checkmark & \text{given} \\
2. & \sim\!B \vee \sim\!C & \text{given} \\
3. & (\sim\!A \vee C) \vee (B \vee G)\checkmark & \text{given} \\[4pt]
4. & \quad \sim\!A \vee C \qquad\qquad B \vee G & 3 \ (T\vee) \\[4pt]
5. & A \vee \bot \quad C \quad A \vee \bot \quad C & 1 \ (T\vee)
\end{array}
$$

It might seem like each rule application only expands the amount of work remaining to be done. Here, one sentence was checked off only to add four more.

In Ts, reduction trees always end. They do so for one or both of two reasons. When a path yields ⊥, the placement principle prohibits adding any further results to that path. ("Yields ⊥" means that ⊥ stands alone on a line on the path, not that it occurs as a component of a compound. No path of the tree above yields ⊥.) Each rule application also produces sentences that are shorter than the one that is checked off. (The checked off sentence is never reduced a second time and its reduction results are always shorter than it is.) Given finitely many, finitely long sentences to start with, there must come a point at which only literals are left unchecked. There is only one rule that applies to literals (⊥I); it only serves to close paths by putting ⊥ on them, and it does not always apply. When it does not apply, there is nothing left to be done. When it does apply, there is still nothing left to do because it adds ⊥ to a path.

The continuation of the tree started earlier illustrates each of these outcomes. As of line 5 this tree contains unchecked sentences on lines 2, 4 left, 4 right, 5 left-left, 5 left-middle, 5 middle-right, and 5 right-right. There is nothing to be done with C at 5 left-middle and 5 right-right, as no rule applies to it. All of the remaining sentences are almost equally long. However, 5 left-left and 5 middle-right will produce a path with ⊥ on it, and no further work can be done on such paths. That makes it advisable to make them targets for reduction sooner rather than later, as they leave only the original four paths for later work whereas reducing other sentences multiplies the number of paths.

Exercise 7.1

Continue the tree started above by applying (T∨) to line 2, illustrating why it leaves eight paths on which any further work must be done. Then redo the tree, this time continuing it by instead applying (T∨) to the sentence on the left path at line 4, illustrating why it leaves six paths on which any further work must be done.

Before applying (T∨) to line 5, the placement principle should be reviewed. The placement principle requires entering the results of applying a reduction rule *completely* on *each* path that runs up to the location of the sentence the rule is being applied to. But the principle also says that the results of applying a rule are not to be entered on any path that does not run up to the sentence's location.

Up to now an intuitive understanding of a path has been relied upon. But it may be useful to have a definition in place.

(def path)

A *path* is a line that runs from a sentence on the bottom of a tree to the sentence on the top of that tree, following lines inserted on the tree as a consequence of applying reduction rules. The path line is considered to pass through any sentences that lie in its way.

(def bottom)

A sentence is on the *bottom* of a tree if and only if there is no line below it that runs down to any other sentence.

Paths can converge as they run up to the top of the tree. In the tree given above, there are four paths on line 5, but as of line four the two leftmost and the two rightmost have converged, and as of line 3 (still reading up from the bottom) the two remaining ones have converged as well. There are nonetheless four paths on the tree as of line 3. The paths may converge, but they do not combine. Think of them as lying on top of one another as of the point of their convergence.

Paths are distinguished by where they end, not where they start. Paths are different if they descend to different places.

A correct understanding of the notion of a path is necessary for the correct application of (⊥I) as well as for the correct application of the placement principle. (⊥I) stipulates that ⊥ must be entered when an atomic sentence and its negation have both been derived *on the same path*. When they have not been derived on the same path, (⊥I) does not apply. For example, a tree for {A ∨ ~A} looks like this:

1.   A ∨ ~A ✔   given

2.   A   ~A   1 (T∨)

This tree is unextendible. No further rule may be applied to it. In particular (⊥I) may not be applied. Though the tree contains an atomic sentence and its negation, they do not occur on the same path, so ⊥ may not be entered on either path.

Keeping the definition of a path in mind for the application of the placement principle, (T∨) is applied to the sentence on line 5 left-left as follows

1.   (A ∨ ⊥) ∨ C ✔   given
2.   ~B ∨ ~C   given
3.   (~A ∨ C) ∨ (B ∨ G) ✔   given

4.   ~A ∨ C   B ∨ G   3 (T∨)

5.   A ∨ ⊥ ✔   C   A ∨ ⊥   C   1 (T∨)

6.   **A   ⊥**   **5 (T∨)**

The results of reducing A ∨ ⊥ on line 5 left-left are not entered on any path that does not run up to its location. Of the four paths on the tree as of line 5, none run up to this location. The sentence itself lies on the leftmost of the four, but it lies on the bottom of the path, with nothing else leading up to it. The results of applying (T∨) to it are therefore only entered on its own path and not on any other.

The remaining paths do not contain ⊥, and there are unchecked nonliterals on all of them, so they should be represented as continuing down through line 6. Paths need not have occupants at each line.

```
1.              (A ∨ ⊥) ∨ C✔              given
2.                ~B ∨ ~C                  given
3.          (~A ∨ C) ∨ (B ∨ G) ✔          given
                    ╱   ╲
4.       ~A ∨ C              B ∨ G         3 (T∨)
             ╱  ╲            ╱  ╲
5.     A ∨ ⊥✔  C    A ∨ ⊥   C              1 (T∨)
          ╱ ╲
6.      A    ⊥        │       │            5 (T∨)
```

There is an infelicity on this tree. At line 6, (T∨) is applied only to the sentence on the leftmost path at line 5. However, there is another sentence on the middle-right path at line 5 to which (T∨) applies.

When a single rule applies to sentences that lie on different paths on the same line, the rule should be applied to each of those sentences at once. This is the case even if the sentences are not identical; only the rule need be the same.

This practice is helpful but not necessary. Trees will still yield the correct result if rules are not applied on each path where they can be applied. But they will require more work.

After "5 (T∨)" is applied everywhere that it is applicable, the tree looks like this:

```
1.              (A ∨ ⊥) ∨ C✔              given
2.                ~B ∨ ~C                  given
3.          (~A ∨ C) ∨ (B ∨ G) ✔          given
                    ╱   ╲
4.       ~A ∨ C              B ∨ G         3 (T∨)
             ╱  ╲            ╱  ╲
5.     A ∨ ⊥✔  C    A ∨ ⊥✔  C              1 (T∨)
          ╱ ╲        ╱ ╲
6.      A    ⊥     A    ⊥     │            5 (T∨)
```

Though there appear to be six paths on this tree, there are only four. The placement principle prohibits adding anything more to the paths on which ⊥ stands alone.

At this point, no rules apply to any of the sentences on line 6. And everything that can be done to the sentences on line 5 has been done. The only unchecked sentences left are the two on line 4 and the one on line 2. There is not much difference between them in terms of complexity. But applying (T∨) to the two wedge sentences on line 4 will leave nine paths without ⊥ on them whereas applying it to the sentence on line 2 will leave only eight.

When applying (T∨) to ~B ∨ ~C on line 2, a further component of the placement principle needs to be kept in mind. The results of reducing ~B ∨ ~C must not be entered on paths that yield ⊥. The resulting tree is:

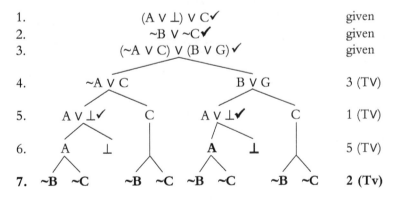

Applying (T∨) to line 2 has created paths that contain both C and ~C. This is a situation in which the second foundational rule (⊥I) must be applied.

(⊥I)

When both an atomic sentence and its negation have been derived on the same path, add ⊥ to that path at the first opportunity.

Schematically, (⊥I) is:

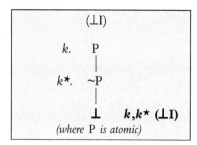

(where P is atomic)

P and ~P must be literals, which means that P must be an atomic sentence.

They must lie on the same path. ~P at line *k*★ may come before P at line *k*. However, in the justification the line with the negation is cited second.

Check marks are not used with (⊥I). Check marks are used to verify that nonliterals have been reduced. Literals cannot be further reduced and it is obvious when a sentence is a literal, so there is no point in checking off those to which (⊥I) applies.

Applications of (⊥I) are not optional. It must be applied immediately after finishing the rule application that adds the later of P or ~P to the path. Since some of the reduction rules add two lines to a path, ⊥ will not always appear immediately after the last of P and ~P. But it will always appear within a line of the last of them to appear.

Exercise

Continue the tree started above by applying (⊥I) wherever appropriate.

In keeping with what was said earlier, when a rule is applied on a line, it should be applied to each sentence on any path on that line to which it is applicable. (⊥I) cites two lines, and strictly it ought to cite the line with the shorter sentence first, but when multiple pairs of two opposite sentences occur on the same two lines on different paths it would pointlessly prolong the tree to be fastidious about observing this requirement. Applying 5,7 (⊥I) on all the paths where it applies produces the following tree.

```
1.                    (A ∨ ⊥) ∨ C✔                        given
2.                     ~B ∨ ~C✔                            given
3.                  (~A ∨ C) ∨ (B ∨ G)✔                    given

4.            ~A ∨ C                    B ∨ G              3 (TV)

5.        A ∨ ⊥✔      C            A ∨ ⊥✔      C           1 (TV)

6.        A     ⊥               A     ⊥                    5 (TV)

7.    ~B  ~C    ~B  ~C    ~B  ~C    ~B  ~C                 2 (Tv)
8.    |   |     |   ⊥     |   |     |   ⊥                  5,7 (⊥I)
```

⊥ does not appear on any other path.

Exercise

Why does ⊥ not appear on any other path?

Fortuitously, only one application of (⊥I) is necessary because the opposite sentences occur on the same line on each path. Had some paths contained their opposite sentences on different lines from other paths, multiple applications of (⊥I) would have been required. As with (PC) subderivations done in parallel orientation, when justifications are different, either in the lines they cite or in the rules they use, results should normally be entered on different lines. When being fastidious about this policy would unduly prolong the tree without making it any clearer to the reader, multiple justifications may be used on the same line.

No more work may be done on the paths that contain ⊥, so only six paths remain open on the tree.

At this point the sentences on line 4 remain unchecked. The literals appearing lower down on the tree are not reducible. Since both the sentences on line 4 are disjunctions, both should be reduced simultaneously. But for the sake of seeing how the placement principle applies, consider just the result of reducing the left sentence on line 4.

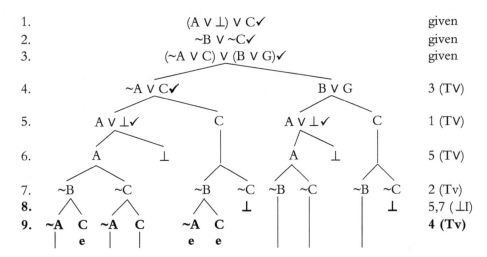

Each path that runs up to ~A ∨ C on line 4 splits into two paths, with ~A on the left and C on the right. But this is not done on paths on which ⊥ has been derived or on paths that do not run through the location that ~A ∨ C occupies.

At this point, there is nothing more to be done on the second path from the left. Each nonliteral has been checked off, and the literals that remain do not contain an opposite pair to which (⊥I) could be applied. This path is said to be exhausted. The same holds for paths 6 and 7 counting from the left. An exhausted path can be considered to yield the iterated conjunction of the literals on that path. (An iterated conjunction of literals is a characteristic sentence. It characterizes an interpretation.) The leftmost exhausted path yields (A & ~B) & C. (The literals are conventionally conjoined in alphanumeric order.) Paths 5 and 8 are said to be closed. A path is closed when ⊥ stands alone on it. (⊥ stands alone on lines 6 and 8 above. It does not stand alone on lines 1 or 5. To stand alone it cannot occur as a component of a compound.) Closed paths do not yield any literals, not even ⊥. Paths 1, 3 and 4, in contrast, are unfinished. Rules, in this case (⊥I), may still be applied on these paths.

There is no point to continuing with this tree. Trees are done to derive ⊥ on each path. If a single path is exhausted without yielding ⊥, ⊥ is considered underivable, and no further work will change that result. However, while there is no point to continuing with the tree, it is not permissible to stop halfway through a rule application. When the decision to apply (T∨) to line 4 is made, that project must be fully executed. This means applying (T∨) to each wedge sentence on line 4, and applying it completely (on any one path) and repeatedly (on each path). It is only permissible to stop after that has been done.

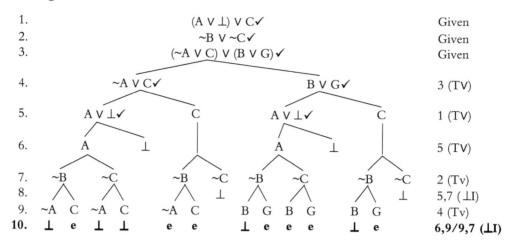

1.	(A ∨ ⊥) ∨ C✓	Given
2.	~B ∨ ~C✓	Given
3.	(~A ∨ C) ∨ (B ∨ G)✓	Given
4.	~A ∨ C✓ B ∨ G✓	3 (T∨)
5.	A ∨ ⊥✓ C A ∨ ⊥✓ C	1 (T∨)
6.	A ⊥ A ⊥	5 (T∨)
7.	~B ~C ~B ~C ~B ~C ~B ~C	2 (T∨)
8.		5,7 (⊥I)
9.	~A C ~A C ~A C B G B G B G	4 (T∨)
10.	⊥ e ⊥ ⊥ e e ⊥ e e e ⊥ e	6,9/9,7 (⊥I)

In this case, completing the 4 (T∨) project ended up either closing or exhausting each path. This does not always happen. Had any path been left unfinished, it would not be necessary to finish it. Once a single path has been exhausted, and the rule application that produces it has been completed, there is no point to continuing with the tree.

Some of the paths on this tree close because a rule application other than (⊥I) yields ⊥ on the path. Others close because they come to contain opposite literals, at which point an application of (⊥I) is required to derive ⊥ on the path. The remaining paths are exhausted. All the rules that could be applied are applied, resulting in a situation where each sentence on the path is either a literal other than ⊥ or checked off. Paths of the last sort are annotated with the "exhausted" sign, e, which indicates that all work that could possibly be done on that path has been done without causing ⊥ to appear.

To be exhausted, a path must have three features:

> (def ex)
>
> A tree path is *exhausted* if and only if:
>
> (i)   each sentence in the set the tree is made for has been placed on top of the tree
>
> (ii) ⊥ does not stand alone on any line of the path
>
> (iii) each sentence on the path is either a literal or a nonliteral that has been reduced (checked off).

For a path to be exhausted, it is not enough that it end with a literal. It is necessary to go up the path, sentence by sentence from the bottom, and verify that each nonliteral has been checked off, that ⊥ does not appear alone, and that a literal and its opposite (which would require entering ⊥) do not appear. It is also necessary to verify that each sentence in the set is on the top of the tree.

Trees look for ⊥ on each path. When they find it, they establish that the set of given sentences at the top of the tree is inconsistent in Ts.

> A set of sentences of SL is *inconsistent in* Ts if and only if it has at least one tree that yields ⊥ on each path.

Care needs to be taken with using this definition to determine that a tree is consistent in Ts. A tree might not have ⊥ on each path simply because it is unfinished. It needs to be established that no amount of work that is done on a tree will turn it into a tree that has ⊥ on each of its paths. Practically, this means establishing that the tree has at least one exhausted path.

> A set of sentences of SL is *consistent in* Ts if and only if it has at least one tree with an exhausted path.

These definitions are troubling. Inconsistency and consistency are opposites. They ought therefore to be defined in opposite terms. The opposite of having a tree that yields ⊥ on each path is lacking a tree that yields ⊥ on each path. Why should lacking a tree that yields ⊥ on each path mean having a tree with an exhausted path?

The second definition was said to be "practical" for this reason. It can be hard to verify that a set lacks a tree that yields ⊥ on each path. Trees for the same set can be done in different ways. In many cases, it is not practical to check each different way of producing a tree to verify that none yields ⊥ on each path. The practical definition asserts that, for practical purposes, finding even one tree with even one exhausted path is good enough. For reasons to be given in section 7.3, this is an adequate definition.

As noted at the outset of this chapter, trees do not directly establish semantic results. They yield sentences. When a tree yields ⊥ on each path, it establishes that the set of givens at the head of the tree yields ⊥. When a tree produces an exhausted path, it establishes that the set of givens at the head of the tree yields the conjunction of the literals on that path. However, given the affinity between the reduction rules and the valuation rules, there is reason to expect that these derivational results correspond to semantic results. If a tree yields ⊥ on each path, hopefully it means that the sentences that were given at the head of the tree cannot all be true and so must compose an s-unsatisfiable set. If a tree produces an exhausted path, hopefully it means that the conjunction of the literals characterizes an interpretation that satisfies the set of givens at the head of the tree.

A demonstration that this correspondence really does hold is given in chapter A-3. In the meantime, it can be verified, on a case-by-case basis, that on any occasion where a tree produces an exhausted path, the sentence letters that stand alone on lines of that path define a model, called a tree model, for the set of givens at the head of the tree. (Recall that a model for a set is an interpretation on which all the sentences in that set are true.) Tree models are easily constructed.

Method for Constructing a Tree Model

(i)   Look only at the leftmost exhausted path.

(ii) Assign a T to each sentence letter that stands alone on a line of that path and an F to each other sentence letter.

T's are assigned to sentence letters that stand alone on a line of the leftmost exhausted path. The "A" in "A ∨ ⊥" does not stand alone. Each of the "A's" that appear on line 6 of the tree above does stand alone on its path.

Each sentence letter must either stand alone on a path or not stand alone on it. So, assigning a T to each sentence letter that stands alone on an exhausted path and an F to all other sentence letters is tantamount to assigning exactly one of T and F to each sentence letter. This assignment therefore satisfies the definition of an interpretation.

On the tree just done, the leftmost exhausted path (the second path from the left) defines the following tree model:

A	B	C	G
T	F	T	F

All other atomic sentences are F on this model. A, B, C, and G are specified because they are the atomic components of the three given sentences at the top of the tree. A and C receive T because A and C occur on the path. B and G get F because they do not occur on the path.

~B occurs on the path, and it is legitimate to think that if truth flows down the path to ~B, that means that B must get F. But just thinking that B gets F because it is not on the path is simpler, and yields the same result. Of course, if B were there along with ~B, ⊥ would have to be added to the path, the path would not be exhausted and there would be no tree model to extract.

Constructing a tree model is one thing. Verifying that it really does assign T to all the givens is another. It is easy to verify that the tree model produced above is a model for {(A ∨ ⊥) ∨ C, ~B ∨ ~C, (~A ∨ C) ∨ (B ∨ G)}.

1.   I(C) is T   given
2.   I(~A ∨ C) is T   1 (∨)
3.   I((~A ∨ C) ∨ (B ∨ G)) is T   2 (∨) verifying the given on line 3

4.	I(B) is F	given
5.	I(~B) is T	4 (~)
6.	I(~B ∨ ~C) is T	5 (∨) verifying the given on line 2
7.	I(A) is T	given
8.	I(A ∨ ⊥) is T	7 (∨)
9.	I((A ∨ ⊥) ∨ C) is T	8 (∨) verifying the given on line 1

This demonstration is not as elegant as it could be. (Line 9 could have been derived by 1 (∨), for example.) It has been designed to illustrate that truth flows up an exhausted tree path from the literals on that path to the sentences those literals were reduced from, and so on up to the givens. The demonstration starts from the last literal on the path, C on line 9. It then proceeds to the sentence it was reduced from, the one on line 4, and then to the sentence that one was reduced from, the one on line 3.

The justification then goes back to the next lowest literal on the path, ~B on line 7 of the tree, explains why it is true on the model, and then goes up to the sentence it was reduced from, which is the one on line 2 of the tree.

Finally, the justification goes back to the third lowest literal on the path, A on line 6, and goes up from it to the sentence it was reduced from, and then to the sentence that sentence was reduced from.

This verification was straightforward. In other cases, negations can require special treatment. Sometimes, when climbing the path to a negation, ~P, it needs to be established that I(~P) is T (or F, as the case may be) before proceeding further. But at other times, it only needs to be established that I(P) is F (or T, as the case may be), and going on to establish the value of I(~P) turns out to be beside the point. Which to establish depends on what the value of P or ~P is used to establish and that is made obvious as the verification proceeds. The matter is taken up in solutions to ★ exercises.

Exercise 7.2

Use Ts to determine whether the following sets are inconsistent. Be careful to observe the closure and placement principles and to apply (⊥I) at the first opportunity to do so. If a tree yields an exhausted path, identify and verify the tree model defined by that path. Be sure to use the conventionally appropriate path when doing so.

Begin each tree on the top centre of a new page. There is no telling how long or how wide the tree will become, and working in cramped spaces will cramp thought. Reduction trees are generated mechanically, and do not require insight or ingenuity. But they do take up space, and they require spatial organization and clarity. If they are cramped or messy, it becomes difficult to keep track of what is going on. Whereas failures in Ds are chiefly due to unwillingness to work from the bottom up, failures in Ts are largely due to slovenliness and to attempts to cram the tree into too small a space. An unwillingness to use large amounts of paper is at the root of failures in both systems.

★a. {A ∨ ⊥, ~A ∨ ~A}
b. {A ∨ B, ~A ∨ ~B}
★c. {A ∨ ~A, ~⊥ ∨ ⊥}
d. {~A, A ∨ B, ~B}
★e. {(B ∨ B) ∨ ⊥, (A ∨ B) ∨ C, ~B ∨ ~B}
f. {(~A ∨ ~C) ∨ (~A ∨ C), B ∨ ~B, A ∨ C}

There are two more foundational rules, (DN) and (T&).

(DN)
~~P reduces to P on each path selected by the placement principle
(T&)
P & Q reduces to P over Q on each path selected by the placement principle

Schematically, the rules are:

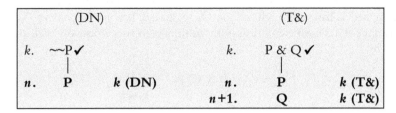

These rules are obvious consequences of the notion that compound sentences should be reduced to simpler sentences that must be true if the compounds are true. As with all the rules, the placement principle applies. The results of applying a rule to a sentence must be reiterated on each path that runs up to that sentence, unless ⊥ has been derived on that path, in which case the results may not be entered on that path. The results also may not be entered on any path that does not run up to the sentence.

In the case of (T&) both results must be entered on successive lines in the order indicated: first conjunct on the first line, second conjunct on the second line, each with its own justification. It is not permissible to enter only one of the two or to pause to do something else between entering the first and entering the second. This holds even if the first conjunct is ⊥ or a literal with an opposite on the path. Completing the application of (T&) does not violate the placement principle as that principle comes into effect only after the rule application that causes ⊥ to appear on a path has been completed.

For example, a tree for {A ∨ (~~B & C), ~A ∨ ~B} begins by listing the members of the set on successive lines.

$$1. \quad \text{A} \lor (\sim\sim\text{B} \,\&\, \text{C}) \qquad \text{given}$$
$$2. \quad \sim\text{A} \lor \sim\text{B} \qquad \text{given}$$

The sentence on line 1 is a disjunction. So neither (DN) nor (T&) may be applied to it. For any given sentence, there is only one rule that may be applied. That rule is determined by the sentence's form. When the sentence is a disjunction, the only rule that can be applied is (T∨).

(T∨) applies to both sentences. The outcome will be the same whichever is reduced first. But the amount of work required to obtain that outcome will vary. To minimize work, rules should be applied in an order that keeps the number of open paths as low as possible for as long as possible. When that consideration does not determine a choice, the longest sentences should be dealt with first. In this case, the sentences on lines 1 and 2 each produce two open paths, so the first consideration does not apply. The second consideration dictates dealing with the sentence on line 1 first.

1.   A ∨ (~~B & C) ✔   given
2.   ~A ∨ ~B   given

3.   A   ~~B & C   1 (T∨)

At this point, the first consideration comes into play. Of the two unchecked nonliterals currently on the tree, the one on line 2 would produce three open paths (four in the first instance, but one of them would immediately close after (⊥I)). The other, ~~B & C on line 3 right, produces only one open path. It is reduced by a nonbranching rule. And the placement principle dictates that the results of reducing it may not be entered on the left-hand path, as that path does not run up to it.

Exercise

What is the only rule that may legitimately be applied to ~~B & C? What determines that it is the one that applies rather than any other? What are the results of applying this rule?

Since the sentence on line 3 right is a conjunction, the only rule that may legitimately be applied to it is the rule for conjunctions, (T&).

Just as (DN) may not be applied before (T&), so it may not be applied at the same time. The results that emerge by applying (T&) are sentences that are the same as the conjuncts of the conjunction.

(DN) may not be applied halfway through, either. Once started, the application of (T&) must be completed before anything else is done. This means entering both conjuncts in succession on each path that runs up to the conjunction.

1.	A ∨ (~~B & C) ✓		given
2.	~A ∨ ~B		given
3.	A ~~B & C ✓		1 (TV)
4.	**~~B**		**3 (T&)**
5.	**C**		**3 (T&)**

Now (DN) may be applied.

1.	A ∨ (~~B & C) ✓		given
2.	~A ∨ ~B		given
3.	A ~~B & C ✓		1 (TV)
4.	~~B ✓		3 (T&)
5.	C		3 (T&)
6.	**B**		**4 (DN)**

At this point, the only sentence left that is not either a literal or checked off is the one on line 2. As both the left and the right path run up to it, and neither has ⊥ on it, the complete results of its reduction must be fully entered on each path.

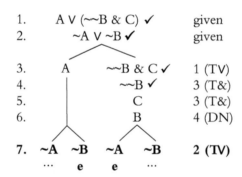

This rule application has produced two exhausted paths, so there is no point doing any more work on the tree. It has been established that at least one path does not yield ⊥, which is presumed to mean that the set is s-satisfiable.

This can be demonstrated by recovering the tree model from the leftmost exhausted path and verifying that it is in fact a model for the original set.

```
          A  B  C
          T  F  F
```

1.	I(B) is F	given
2.	I(~B) is T	1 (~)
3.	I(~A ∨ ~B) is T	2 (∨) verifying the given on line 2
4.	I(A) is T	given
5.	I(A ∨ (~~B & C)) is T	4 (∨) verifying the given on line 1

Consistently with expectations, both sentences in the set are true on this interpretation.

Exercise 7.3

Use Ts to determine whether the following sets are inconsistent. Be careful to observe the closure and placement principles and to apply (⊥I) at the first opportunity to do so. If the tree yields an exhausted path, identify and verify the tree model defined by that path. Be sure to use the conventionally appropriate path when doing so.

★a. {~~A ∨ ⊥, (A ∨ B) & (C ∨ ~B), ~A & C}
  b. {(A & B) ∨ (A & C), (~A ∨ ⊥) ∨ ~B}
★c. {A ∨ [(~A & ⊥) ∨ B]}
  d. {~~A & ~⊥, ~~B ∨ C, (~B ∨ ~A) ∨ ~C}
★e. {C ∨ ~A, ~B ∨ A, ~B & ~~~C, ~⊥ ∨ B}
  f. {~~~~A, C ∨ B, C ∨ (~⊥ & A), ~A ∨ ~⊥}

The remaining reduction rules are likewise consequences of the principle that compound sentences should be reduced to simpler sentences that must be true if the compounds are true. P → Q, is true only if either P is false or Q is true, and so only if at least one of ~P and Q is true.

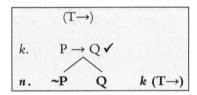

~(P & Q), is true only if P & Q is false, which is the case only if at least one of P and Q is false and so only if at least one of ~P and ~Q is true.

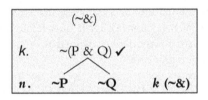

~(P ∨ Q) is true only if P ∨ Q is false, which is the case only if both P and Q are false, and so only if both ~P and ~Q are true. Likewise, ~(P → Q) is true only if P → Q is false, which is the case only if P is true and Q is false, and so only if P and ~Q are both true.

(~∨)				(~→)		
k.	~(P ∨ Q) ✔			*k.*	~(P → Q) ✔	
n.	~P	*k* (~∨)		*n.*	P	*k* (~→)
n+1.	~Q	*k* (~∨)		*n*+1.	~Q	*k* (~→)

P ≡ Q is true only if P and Q are the same, which means that either they are both true or they are both false. In the second of these cases, ~P and ~Q are both true. In contrast, ~(P ≡ Q) is true only if P and Q are different, which means that either P is true and Q is false (in which case P and ~Q are both true) or Q is true and P is false (in which case Q and ~P are both true).

(T≡)				(~≡)		
k.	P ≡ Q ✔			*k.*	~(P ≡ Q) ✔	
n.	P ~P	*k* (T≡)		*n.*	P Q	*k* (~≡)
n+1.	Q ~Q	*k* (T≡)		*n*+1.	~Q ~P	*k* (~≡)

The rules could just as well be seen to be consequences of applying (T∨) and (T&) to known equivalences:

- P → Q is s-equivalent to ~P ∨ Q, so it is reduced the way ~P ∨ Q is reduced.
- ~(P & Q) is s-equivalent to ~P ∨ ~Q, so it is reduced the way ~P ∨ ~Q is reduced.
- ~(P ∨ Q) and ~(P → Q) are s-equivalent to ~P & ~Q and P & ~Q, respectively, so they are reduced the way their respective conjunctions are reduced.
- P ≡ Q is s-equivalent to (P & Q) ∨ (~P & ~Q) and ~(P ≡ Q) to (P & ~Q) ∨ (Q & ~P), so they are likewise reduced accordingly.

The placement principle applies to each of these rules. The form must be followed exactly. When the form specifies adding a tilde to a component, a tilde must be added to that component. Removing a tilde from the component is not an acceptable substitute. For example, when (T→) is applied to ~A → B, it produces ~~A on the left path.

The form for (~≡) reflects the way s-equivalence is defined in terms of models (section 5.5): P and Q are s-equivalent if and only if neither {P, ~Q} nor {Q, ~P} has a model. It also reflects the procedure to be specified in section 7.2 below for using trees to determine the interderivability of P and Q: two trees are to be done, one for <P, ~Q> and the other for <Q, ~P>, and both must close to demonstrate interderivability. The second tree is headed off by Q and followed by ~P to facilitate converting trees to derivations, as discussed in chapter A-3.4.

When a form specifies that a component be placed on the left, or above, that component must be placed on the left or above. (~≡) requires that the first immediate component of the biconditional be unnegated on the left and negated on the right. Reversing the layout will not affect the outcome. But in cases where exercises are submitted to a marker, the marker's time is best spent assisting those who are making mistakes rather than verifying results that do not conform to a template.

The application of these rules and policies can be illustrated by a tree for {~[~(A & B) ≡ (B → ~A)]}.

1. ~[~(A & B) ≡ (B → ~A)]   given

As the tree has only one sentence on it, there is no question what to do next. (~≡) must be applied. This means correctly identifying the left immediate component and the right immediate component, and getting them in the right layout: left immediate component over negation of right immediate component on the left; right immediate component over negation of left immediate component on the right.

Negating means adding a tilde, not removing one.

1. ~[~(~A ∨ B) ≡ (B → ~A)] ✔   given

2.   ~(~A ∨ B)   B → ~A   1 (~≡)
3.   ~(B → ~A)   ~~(~A ∨ B)   1 (~≡)

At this point, a decision must be made about which path to begin working on. While the wisest policy is normally to apply rules that will not multiply the number of paths before applying rules that will, the case at hand is an exception. The two paths are unrelated, because there is no unchecked nonliteral above them. This makes working on them equivalent to doing two separate trees. Should one of those trees end up with an exhausted path, there would be no need to do the other, as a single exhausted path decides the question. Should one of them produce all closed paths, it would be necessary to go on to do the other, as the other might still prove to have an exhausted path.

In this circumstance, it is wisest to begin work on the path that seems least likely to close. That path is the one that is most likely to produce the greatest number of further paths. When rule applications only prolong a single path, the chances of opposite literals appearing are much greater than when the literals are scattered over multiple paths.

On the partially completed tree above, both sentences on the left-hand path use rules that prolong a single path. The right-hand path, by contrast, quickly produces four paths.

Work on this path should nonetheless commence with applying (DN) to the sentence on line 3 right. That way, it need only be reduced once, rather than twice over as would be the case were it postponed until after performing (T→) on the sentence on line 2 right.

1.   ~[~(~A ∨ B) ≡ (B → ~A)] ✓   given

2.   ~(~A ∨ B)   B → ~A   1 (~≡)
3.   ~(B → ~A)   ~~(~A ∨ B) ✓   1 (~≡)
4. | **~A ∨ B**   **3 (DN)**

Now the consequences are the same whether the sentence on line 2 right or line 4 right is done first, so it is just as well to proceed from the top down.

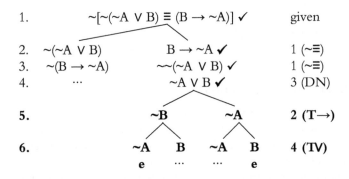

1.   ~[~(~A ∨ B) ≡ (B → ~A)] ✓   given

2.   ~(~A ∨ B)   B → ~A ✓   1 (~≡)
3.   ~(B → ~A)   ~~(~A ∨ B) ✓   1 (~≡)
4.   …   ~A ∨ B ✓   3 (DN)

5.   ~B   ~A   2 (T→)

6.   ~A   B   ~A   B   4 (TV)
                e   …   …   e

After applying (T→) to line 2 right and (TV) to line 4 right, two exhausted paths have appeared, so there is no point in doing any further work on the tree. The tree model that comes off the leftmost exhausted path assigns F to A and F to B. Verification is:

1.   I(A) is F   given
2.   I(~A) is T   1 (~)
3.   I(~A ∨ B) is T   2 (∨)
4.   I(~(~A ∨ B)) is F   3 (~)

5.   I(B) is F   given
6.   I(B → ~A) is T   5 (→)

7.   I(~(~A ∨ B) ≡ (B → ~A)) is F   4,6 (≡)
8.   I(~[~(~A ∨ B) ≡ (B → ~A)]) is T   7 (~) verifying the given on line 1

The verification establishes that assigning F to A and F to B is indeed a model for {~[~(A & B) ≡ (B → ~A)]}. Since this set does have a model, it is s-consistent, as predicted by the tree.

The following strategies abbreviate the amount of work required, both for authors and readers.

Strategies for Applying Reduction Rules
(i)   Apply a rule that will close a path before applying any rule that will retain or increase the number of open paths.
(ii)   Apply nonbranching rules ((⊥I), (DN), (T&), (~∨), and (~→)) first.
(iii)   Apply branching rules ((T∨), (T→), (T≡), (~&), and (~≡)) that produce at least one closed path before applying those that produce two open paths.
(iv)   Apply branching rules that produce two open paths to longer sentences before applying them to shorter sentences.
(v)   Focus work on paths most likely to yield an exhausted path. When paths are independent (there are no unchecked nonliterals above them), work on the path that splits the most first.
(vi)   When all other considerations are equal, work from the top down.

Exercise 7.4

Use Ts to determine whether the following sets are inconsistent. Be careful to observe the closure and placement principles and to apply (⊥I) at the first opportunity to do so. If the tree yields an exhausted path, identify and verify the tree model defined by that path. Be sure to use the conventionally appropriate path when doing so.

★a. {A → B, ~(B → ~C), ~(~A & C)}
  b. {~(~A ∨ ~B), ~(A ≡ ~B), ~A → (B & C)}
★c. {~[~(A ∨ C) ≡ B], ~(C → ~A), B → C}
  d. {~(A → B) ≡ (C ∨ ~⊥), A ∨ B}
★e. {(A → ⊥) → A, ~(B & A), A → B}
  f. {A ≡ (B ∨ C), B → ~A, ~(~B → ~C)}

7.2 Using Trees to Determine Derivability

In addition to being used to determine whether sentences and sets of sentences are inconsistent, Ts can be used to determine whether sentences and demonstrations exhibit a special form of derivability, called derivability in Ts. A sentence, P, is derivable in Ts from a set of premises, Γ, when the corresponding set, Γ′ ∪ ~P, is inconsistent in Ts, where Γ′ is at least one finite subset of Γ. Two sentences, P and Q, are interderivable in Ts when the corresponding sets, {P,~Q} and {Q,~P} are inconsistent in Ts. A sentence, P, is a theorem of Ts when it is derivable in Ts from the empty set, that is, when the corresponding set {~P}, is inconsistent in Ts.

These definitions are not just arbitrarily stipulated. It is hoped that what is derivable in Ts would coincide with what is derivable in Ds, and with what is s-valid and s-equivalent. But that cannot be assumed without demonstration, which is only given in chapter A-3. In the meantime, the distinctive label "in Ts" is attached to avoid begging the question of whether what yields ⊥ on each path of at least one tree also proves to be inconsistent in Ds and s-unsatisfiable; derivable in Ds and s-valid; or interderivable in Ds and s-equivalent. Exercises also provide an opportunity to verify the coincidence on a case-by-case basis.

7.2.1 Theorems; Inconsistent and Contingent Sentences

> A sentence, P, is:
>
> - a *theorem* of Ts if and only if {~P} is inconsistent in Ts
> - *inconsistent* in Ts if and only if {P} is inconsistent in Ts
> - *contingent* in Ts if and only if both {P} and {~P} are consistent in Ts

It often turns out that both a sentence and its negation have a tree that has at least one exhausted path. To take a simple example, consider a tree for A and a tree for ~A. There is only one way to do each of these trees, and each produces an exhausted path as soon as it starts. The exhausted path for the tree for A yields a tree model according to which A is T, and the exhausted path for the tree for ~A yields a tree model according to which A is F and ~A is T, thus establishing that both A and its opposite have an s-model and hence that A is s-contingent, as well as that it is contingent in Ts.

A → ~A, which says that if A is the case then it is not the case, is (perhaps surprisingly) not inconsistent in Ts, though A ≡ ~A is.

1.	A → ~A ✓		given
2.	~A ~A		1 (T→)
	e e		

1.	A ≡ ~A ✓		given
2.	A ~A		1 (T≡)
3.	~A ~~A ✓		1 (T≡)
4.	⊥ |		2,3 (⊥I)
5.	A		3 (DN)
6.	⊥		5,2 (⊥I)

Recovering and verifying the tree model defined by the leftmost exhausted path for the tree on the left incidentally establishes that the given is s-satisfiable. The tree model is one that assigns F to each sentence letter. On that model, A → ~A has a false antecedent and so is true.

The tree on the right yields ⊥ on each path, which, by definition, proves that the sentence is inconsistent in Ts. A derivation would also establish that A ≡ ~A yields ⊥ in Ds.

In contrast, A → (B → A), which is s-valid and a theorem of Ds, can be demonstrated to be a theorem of Ts by doing a tree for the corresponding set, {~[A → (B → A)]}.

1.	~[A → (B → A)] ✓	given
2.	A	1 (~→)
3.	~(B → A) ✓	1 (~→)
4.	B	3 (~→)
5.	~A	3 (~→)
6.	⊥	2,5 (⊥I)

The apparently similar (A → B) → A is not a theorem of Ts as shown by a tree for its negation.

1.	~[(A → B) → A] ✓	given
2.	A → B ✓	1 (~→)
3.	~A	1 (~→)
4.	~A B	2 (T→)
	e e	

The tree shows that the corresponding set, {~[(A → B) → A]} has at least one tree with at least one exhausted path. That path defines a tree model.

Exercise

What is the tree model defined by the leftmost exhausted path?

On that model, all the sentence letters of SL, including B, are F. Paths must not be concatenated when determining the tree model. The tree model is taken only from the atomic sentences on the leftmost exhausted path. There are no atomic sentences on the leftmost exhausted path of the tree above, so the tree model assigns F to all the other atomic sentences of SL.

Since A is F on the model, A → B is T, making (A → B) → A false, and so making its opposite true. (A → B) → A is therefore s-invalid, since its opposite has a model.

When determining whether a sentence, P, is a theorem of Ts, inconsistent in Ts, or contingent in Ts, it is wise to begin by working on the corresponding set, {P} or {~P}, that produces trees with the fewest paths (supposing strategies for preventing unnecessary path-splitting have been properly applied). When reduction results are concatenated on a single path, there is a greater chance the path will close than when they are spread out over multiple paths. If one of the corresponding sets turns out to have a tree that yields ⊥ on each path, it is unnecessary to do a tree for the other set. But if one set turns out to have a tree with at least one exhausted path, the status of the sentence remains undecided. If {P} has a tree with at least one exhausted path, a second tree for {~P} is required to determine whether P is contingent in Ts or a theorem of Ts. Likewise, if {~P} has a tree with at least one exhausted path, a second tree for {P} is required to determine whether P is contingent in Ts or inconsistent in Ts. When a tree produces one or more exhausted paths, there is no way to determine, just from that one tree, whether the opposite set must have a tree that yields ⊥ on each path.[2] (This issue is further investigated in exercise 7.5#4a–d.) The best policy is to begin by working on the set that is most likely to produce a tree that yields ⊥ on each path.

Consider ⊥ → A. This might look like a sentence that ought to be inconsistent in Ts, meaning it should have a closed tree. But a tree for the sentence must begin with a path split whereas a tree for the negation will go straight down. On that supposition, it would be unwise to begin by doing a tree for the sentence. And so it is.

1. ⊥ → A ✔   given

2.   ~⊥   A   1 (T→)
       e   e

The tree defies expectations and produces at least one exhausted path. In such cases, the work ought to be checked. Each sentence on the path is either a literal or checked off. There are no opposite literals on the path. The leftmost exhausted path defines an interpretation, I, on which each sentence letter is assigned F. By (⊥), ⊥ is F on any interpretation, meaning I(⊥ → A) is T. The tree checks out, establishing that ⊥ → A is not inconsistent in Ts, and leaving the question whether it is contingent in Ts or instead a theorem of Ts.

Had a tree for the negation been done first, the labour invested in doing a tree for the sentence could have been saved. (In this case, it is not a great deal of labour, but in other cases it is.)

1. ~(⊥ → A) ✔   given
2.   ⊥   1 (~→)
3.   ~A   1 (~→)

This tree is closed, as ⊥ stands alone on line 2 of its single path. By itself it establishes that ⊥ → A is a theorem.

7.2.2 Demonstrations

> A demonstration, Γ / P, is *derivable* in Ts if and only if the corresponding set, Γ′ ∪ ~P, where Γ′ is at least one finite subset of Γ, is inconsistent in Ts.
>
> Γ / P is *not derivable in* Ts if and only if Γ′ ∪ ~P is consistent in Ts.

Though this definition speaks of at least one finite subset of Γ, when Γ is finite and small, the tree should begin by listing all the sentences it contains. The alternative (entering one sentence from Γ at the head of a tree, reducing it to literals, then, if the tree has not closed, entering another and reducing it to literals, and proceeding in this fashion) can produce unmanageably complex trees. That alternative must, however, figure in the definition of derivability for reasons given in the completeness demonstration of chapter A-3.2.

One half of the principle of the equivalence of contrapositives, A → B / ~B → ~A, can be demonstrated to be derivable by starting a tree for the premise and the negation of the conclusion.

1.   A → B   given
2.   ~(~B → ~A)   given

Finishing the tree requires strategizing to minimize unnecessary work. Line 1 contains a conditional and so is reduced by (T→), whereas line 2 contains the negation of a conditional and so is reduced by (~→). Since (T→) splits the path, everything done after applying it must be done twice (unless one or both paths close, which they do not). Since (~→) does not split the path, whatever is done after applying it must be done only once.

1.   A → B ✔   given
2.   ~(~B → ~A) ✔   given
3.   ~B   2 (~→)
4.   ~~A ✔   2 (~→)
5.   A   4 (DN)

6.   ~A   B   1 (T→)
7. | ⊥   6,3 (⊥I)
8.   ⊥   5,6 (⊥I)

Since ⊥ is derived on each path, the corresponding set {A → B, ~(~B → ~A)} is inconsistent, and the demonstration is derivable in Ts.

In contrast, A ∨ B, (~A ∨ C) & ~B / ~C is not derivable in Ts, as is demonstrated by completing a tree for the corresponding set, {A ∨ B, (~A ∨ C) & ~B} ∪ ~~C.

1.	A ∨ B	given
2.	(~A ∨ C) & ~B	given
3.	~~C	given

The tree proceeds by applying nonbranching rules first to avoid needlessly doubling the amount of work to be done.

1.	A ∨ B ✓	given
2.	(~A ∨ C) & ~B ✓	given
3.	~~C ✓	given
4.	~A ∨ C ✓	2 (T&)
5.	~B	2 (T&)
6.	C	3 (DN)
7.	A B	1 (TV)
8.	~A C ~A C	4 (TV)

Because the corresponding set has at least one tree with an exhausted path, the demonstration is not derivable in Ts. The tree model defined by the exhausted path verifies this result.

As trees become more complex, it is important to verify that exhausted paths really are exhausted. This is best done by following the path from the bottom up and confirming that each sentence encountered on the way is either a literal or checked off. It is also necessary to confirm that there are no contradictions on the path. This is best done by recording values for each literal encountered on the way, assigning T's to atomic sentences and F's to negations of atomic sentences. The exhausted path for the tree produces the record C: true; A: true; C: true; B: false. This establishes that no contradictions have been inadvertently overlooked.

Verifying this tree model provides a further check on the correctness of the work and also establishes that the demonstration is invalid: {A ∨ B, (~A ∨ C) & ~B} ∪ ~~C has an s-model (namely, the tree model).

1.	I(C) is T	given
2.	I(~A ∨ C) is T	1 (∨)
3.	I(A) is T	given
4.	I(A ∨ B) is T	3 (∨), verifying the given on line 1
5.	I(~C) is F	1 (~)
6.	I(~~C) is T	5 (~) verifying the given on line 3
7.	I(B) is F	given
8.	I(~B) is T	7 (~)
9.	I((~A ∨ C) & ~B) is T	2,8 (&) verifying the given on line 2

As remarked earlier, verification goes up the exhausted tree path from literals to the sentences they were reduced from. This verification illustrates two anomalies. The lowest literal is C. It was derived from the sentence on line 4, and its value is used to determine the value of the sentence on line 4. That sentence was derived from the sentence on line 2, but a true conjunct does not suffice to determine the value of a conjunction, so further upward progress must wait for verification of the second conjunct.

Verification therefore proceeds to the next literal up from the bottom, A on line 7. It was derived from line 1, which was a given, and it verifies that given.

Verification then proceeds to the next literal up the path, which is C again. When the same literal appears multiple times on a path, it was reduced from different sentences. C on line 6 was reduced from ~~C on line 3. However, it is not necessary to repeat that I(C) is T. That information is cited from line 1 when going on to verify ~~C on line 3. Verification of double negations typically calls for an intermediate step, noting that the single negation gets F. This is the second of the two anomalies. ~C does not appear on the exhausted path, and verification is supposed to show how truth flows up the path from the literals to the givens. But in the case of double negations, that means taking a step to remark on the falsity of the negation.

Verification proceeds to the next literal up, which is ~B on line 5. This discovers the value of the second conjunct at line 2, allowing the last given to be verified.

7.2.3 Interderivability

> Two sentences, P and Q, are *interderivable* in Ts if and only if each of the corresponding sets, {P, ~Q} and {Q, ~P}, is inconsistent in Ts.
>
> P and Q, are *not interderivable in* Ts if and only if at least one of {P, ~Q} and {Q, ~P} is consistent in Ts.

Since both sets need to be inconsistent in Ts to establish interderivability in Ts, and only one needs to have a tree with an exhausted path to establish the opposite, it is wise to pick the set most likely to produce a tree with an exhausted path, and work on that set first in the hope it will do so and make work on the second set unnecessary. The set most likely to do that is the one that produces trees with the greatest number of paths. There is less chance of trees closing when the literals are distributed over multiple paths, and more chance when they are concatenated on a single path. Paths created by not following the strategies for applying the reduction rules do not count. Branching must be forced even while following all recommended strategies for keeping the tree trim.

Consider the question of whether ~(A ∨ B) and ~A ∨ ~B are interderivable in Ts. The corresponding sets are {~(A ∨ B), ~(~A ∨ ~B)} and {~A ∨ ~B, ~~(A ∨ B)}. After an initial application of (DN), a tree for the second set requires two applications of path-splitting rules, whereas a tree for the first begins with only one. That makes the second tree the one to prefer.

```
1.      ~A ∨ ~B ✓        given
2.      ~~(A ∨ B) ✓      given
3.        A ∨ B ✓        2 (DN)
              /\
4.      ~A        ~B      1 (TV)
        /\        /\
5.    A   B    A   B      3 (TV)
      ···   e    ···
```

The single tree proves that ~(A ∨ B) and ~A ∨ ~B are not interderivable in Ts. It is worth noting that had the tree for the other set been done first, it would have closed.

```
1.      ~(A ∨ B) ✓       given
2.    ~(~A ∨ ~B) ✓       given
3.        ~A             1 (~∨)
4.        ~B             1 (~∨)
5.        ~~A ✓          2 (~∨)
6.        ~~B            2 (~∨)
7.         A             5 (DN)
8.         ⊥             7,3 (⊥I)
```

The tree closes even before all compound sentences have been checked off. But all it proves is that {~(A ∨ B), ~(~A ∨ ~B)} is inconsistent in Ts. It does not prove that the kindred set is also inconsistent. And only one of the two needs to be consistent to establish that the sentences are not interderivable in Ts. A look at the two trees confirms the general point. The one that produces the most path splits is the one that is most likely to produce an exhausted path; the one with the fewest paths is the one most likely to close.

Exercise 7.5

1. *Determine whether the following sentences are theorems of Ts, inconsistent in Ts, or contingent in Ts. Say what the tree proves and why. Do the tree likely to produce the* fewest *paths first.*

   *a. (A ∨ C) ∨ (~A ∨ B)
   b. ~A → A
   *c. ~A → (A → ⊥)
   d. ~(A ≡ B) & (~A ∨ ~B)
   *e. [A & (B → C)] → [(A → B) & (A → C)]
   f. [(A ∨ B) & C] → [~(B → ~A) ∨ ~(A → ~C)]
   *g. [(~B → ~A) & (~~B → ~A)] → ~A
   h. [(A → B) & (A → ~B)] → (C → ⊥)
   *i. (A → ⊥) → [(~A → ⊥) → ~(A ∨ ~A)]
   j. (A ≡ ~B) → (~A ∨ B)
   *k. ~[~[(A → B) → A] ∨ A]
   l. [(~B ∨ C) & (A ∨ B)] → (A ∨ C)

2. *Determine whether the following demonstrations have corresponding sets that are inconsistent in Ts. If a tree has an exhausted path, recover and verify the tree model from the leftmost such path to appear. Say what the tree proves and why.*

   *a. A ≡ ~B, C ∨ A, ~C ∨ ~B ⊢ A
   b. A → B, B ⊢ A
   *c. ~A → B, A → C, ~B & C ⊢ A ≡ ~[C ∨ (~B → A)]
   d. A ≡ (B ∨ C), C ⊢ A
   *e. (~C ≡ A) & A, A → (B ∨ C) ⊢ A & B
   f. ~(A → ~B), C ∨ ~A ⊢ C → ~B
   *g. B → (C → K), ~A ∨ B ⊢ ~K → (C → ~A)
   h. ~(A ∨ B) → (~C ∨ ~~K), (~A & ~K) ⊢ C → B
   *i. A → C, ~A → B, ~B ⊢ C ∨ A
   j. B & C, ~B → ~A, K ≡ C ⊢ ~(A ∨ K)
   *k. (~B → ~A) & (C ∨ A), (~C ∨ K) & ~(~A & ~C) ⊢ K ∨ B
   l. (A & B) → C, C → ~B ⊢ A & (B → C)

3. *Determine whether the following pairs of sentences are interderivable in Ts. Say what the tree or trees prove and why. Do the tree likely to produce the* most *paths first.*

   *a. ~(A & B); ~A & ~B
   b. A ∨ B; ~A ∨ ~B
   *c. (A ∨ B) → C; (A → C) & (B → C)
   d. (A & B) → C; B → (~C → ~A)
   *e. (A → B) & (~A → ~B); ~(A ≡ ~B)
   f. (A & B) → C; (A → C) & (B → C)
   *g. ~(A & ~A) ∨ ⊥; (⊥ → K) & ~K
   h. (A ∨ ~C) & (B ∨ ~C); C → ~(B → ~A)
   *i. ~(A & B) ∨ C; (~C ∨ A) → (~B ∨ C)
   j. (A ≡ B) → A; (A ≡ B) → B
   *k. (~A ∨ C) ∨ B; (~A & B) ∨ (~A → B)
   l. (A & B) ≡ ~A; (~A & ~B) ≡ B

4. *Give a counterexample to each of the following claims. A "closed" path is one that yields* ⊥.
   *a. If a sentence has a tree with all exhausted paths, it must be a theorem of Ts.
   b. If a sentence, P, has a tree with all exhausted paths, ~P must be inconsistent in Ts.
   *c. If a sentence, P has a tree with at least one closed path, ~P cannot be inconsistent in Ts.
   d. If a sentence has a tree with at least one closed path, it cannot be a theorem of Ts.
   *e. If a sentence has a tree with at least one closed path, and at least one exhausted path, it must be contingent in Ts.
   f. If there is an interpretation on which a sentence is false, it must have at least one tree with a closed path.

5. *Turn the following shells into theorems by plugging A's, B's and* ⊥*'s into the blanks. Any combination is permissible, but with one restriction: Use* at most one ⊥ *per sentence. Construct a tree to prove that the resulting sentence is a theorem.*
   *a. _ → (_ → _)
   b. _ → (_ & _)
   *c. (~~~_ ∨ ~_) ∨ ~_
   d. (_ ∨ ~_) & ~_
   *e. (_ → _) → ~ _
   f. ~ (_ ≡ _) ≡ (~_ ≡ _)
   *g. ~ (_ ∨ _) → ~ (_ ≡ ~_)
   h. (_ ≡ _) & (~_ → ~_)
   *i. (_ → _) & [(_ → _) → (_ ∨ ~_)]
   j. ~ [(_ ∨ _) → _] ≡ (_ & _)
   *k. (_ & _) ≡ [~_ & ~ (~_ ∨ ~_)]
   l. [(~_ ∨ ~~_) ∨ ~~~_] → (~_ & ~_)

7.3 Theory and Definitions

A tree is as much a tree after writing down a single sentence on a line as after creating a complex, branching structure. The trees that have been produced on the previous pages and in exercises are sequences of trees.

> A *tree* is any result of one or more of the following operations:
> - adding one of the sentences in a set to the head of a tree
> - applying a rule of Ts to a sentence on a tree.

When these operations are repeatedly performed on the trees resulting from prior applications of these operations the result is a series of "extensions" of trees.

> A *one-step extension* of a tree is a tree produced by either adding another sentence from a set to the top of a tree or applying a rule of Ts to a sentence on that tree.
>
> A tree for a set is *extendible* if and only if it has at least one one-step extension.

Identifying what makes a tree extendible requires running through some prior definitions.

> A *literal* is either an atomic sentence or the negation of an atomic sentence. All other sentences are *nonliterals*.
>
> A nonliteral sentence has been *reduced* if and only if the results of applying the reduction rule specific to its form appear on each path that runs through it, except for paths on which ⊥ stands alone on a line.

Check marks and justifications are not strictly part of trees. The definition of "reduced" is given in terms of what strictly appears on a tree.

The definition allows that a sentence need not be the target of a dedicated application of a reduction rule to be reduced. All that is required is that its reduction results appear on each path that runs through the sentence, except for paths on which ⊥ stands alone. For example, after one application of (~∨), a tree for {~(A ∨ B), ~A & ~B } is exhausted.

$$
\begin{array}{lll}
1. & \text{~(A ∨ B) ✓} & \text{Given} \\
2. & \text{~A \& ~B ✓}_{3,4} & \text{Given} \\
3. & \text{~A} & 1\ \text{(~∨)} \\
4. & \text{~B} & 1\ \text{(~∨)} \\
 & e &
\end{array}
$$

Here, both the sentence on line 1 and the sentence on line 2 are reduced by the one-step extension that takes up lines 3 and 4. Even though lines 3 and 4 are justified as the product of applying (~∨) to line 1, the justifications and the check marks are not strictly part of the tree. On the tree, the one-step extension over lines 3–4 reduces both the sentence on line 1 and the sentence on line 2. There is therefore no call for a further extension, and both sentences can be checked off. On more complex trees, it can be hard to notice that this has happened. If the author notices, adding a parenthetical remark to the checkmark can help the reader. If even the author does not notice, inadvertently reducing sentences that have already been reduced will not corrupt the result. It just unduly extends the tree.

To take another example, {(A ∨ B) & ~~(A ∨ B)} is exhausted in four lines:

$$
\begin{array}{lll}
1. & \text{(A ∨ B) \& ~~(A ∨ B) ✓} & \text{given} \\
2. & \text{A ∨ B} & 1\ \text{(T\&)} \\
3. & \text{~~(A ∨ B) ✓}_{2} & 2\ \text{(T\&)} \\
\end{array}
$$

$$
\begin{array}{lcl}
4. & \quad\quad A \qquad\qquad B & 2\ \text{(T∨)} \\
 & \quad\quad e \qquad\qquad e &
\end{array}
$$

Even though the sentence on line 2 occurs above the sentence on line 3, the one-step extension of the tree that occurs over lines 2–3 places the result of applying (DN) to the sentence on line 3 on each of the two paths that run up to that sentence. It just places the result higher up on these paths, above their intersection point. The sentence has still been reduced on each path that runs up to it. No dedicated application of (DN) is required.

Caution must be taken with sentences that are reduced by path-splitting rules. When a sentence is reduced by a path-splitting rule, a dedicated application of the rule to that sentence could only be avoided if all its reduction results already appear on each path that runs through it. For example, the disjunctions on line 7 of the following partially completed tree have not been reduced.

$$
\begin{array}{lll}
1. & \text{A \& ~(B \& C) ✓} & \text{given} \\
2. & \text{G \& (~B ∨ ~C) ✓} & \text{given} \\
3. & \text{A} & 1\ \text{(T\&)} \\
4. & \text{~(B \& C) ✓} & 1\ \text{(T\&)} \\
\end{array}
$$

$$
\begin{array}{lll}
5. & \text{~B} \qquad\qquad \text{~C} & 4\ \text{(~\&)} \\
6. & \text{G} \qquad\qquad\ \text{G} & 2\ \text{(T\&)} \\
7. & \text{~B ∨ ~C} \quad \text{~B ∨ ~C} & 2\ \text{(T\&)} \\
 & \quad\ \text{...} \qquad\qquad\ \text{...} &
\end{array}
$$

~B ∨ ~C is reduced by ~B on a left path extension and ~C on a right path extension. Were both ~B and ~C to occur on each path that runs through the occurrence of ~B ∨ ~C on line 7 left, that occurrence would be reduced and could be checked off, and likewise for the occurrence of ~B ∨ ~C on line 7 right. (If ~B and ~C both lie on the path above ~B ∨ ~C, it is as good as ~B lying on a left path extension and ~C on a right path extension below ~B ∨ ~C since both extensions run through ~B ∨ ~C and lie on top of one another above it.) But ~C does not lie on any path that runs through the occurrence of ~B ∨ ~C on line 7 left, and ~B does not lie on any path that runs through the occurrence of ~B ∨ ~C on line 7 right. So neither of the occurrences on line 7 has yet been reduced.

This tree was produced by ineptly reducing the sentence at line 4 before the sentence at line 2. But inept reduction sequences still produce trees that yield the right results. They just do so in a less elegant fashion. In this case, the added complexity does not just arise from the fact that the sentence on line 2 must be reduced twice, but from the fact that the sentences on line 7 require reduction, adding yet more complexity to the tree. Had the sentence on line 2 been reduced before the sentence on line 4, ~B ∨ ~C would have occurred above the path split, and in that case both ~(B & C) and ~B ∨ ~C would have been reduced by the same one-step extension.

A *path* is *closed* if and only if ⊥ stands alone on that path.

A *path* is *open* if and only if it is not closed.

Closed paths could contain nonliterals that have not been reduced. This would happen if a rule application causes ⊥ to be derived on the path before all nonliteral sentences on the path have been reduced. Therefore, a tree might be unextendible even though it contains a sentence to which a reduction rule could be applied.

Open paths could likewise contain nonliterals that have not been reduced, in which case they are unfinished. But paths could also be open even after all nonliterals on the path have been reduced. Whether a path is open depends on whether ⊥ stands alone on the path. If it does not, the path is open.

An open path is *exhausted* if and only if:

   (i)   each sentence in the set the tree is made for has been added to the top of the tree
  (ii)   ⊥ does not stand alone on any line of the path
 (iii)   each sentence on the path is either a literal or has been reduced.

An open path is *extendible* (or *unfinished*) if and only if it is not exhausted.

An extendible path is *finitely extendible* if and only if it will either close or be exhausted after a finite number of one-step extensions.

An extendible path is *infinitely extendible* if and only if it will neither close nor be exhausted after any finite number of one-step extensions.

A *path* is *unextendible* (or *finished*) if and only if it is either closed or exhausted.

---

s-trees do not have infinitely extendible paths, except in the case where the set the tree is based on is both infinite and consistent. But even finite sets can have trees with infinitely extendible paths in other systems, so room is made for that eventuality now.

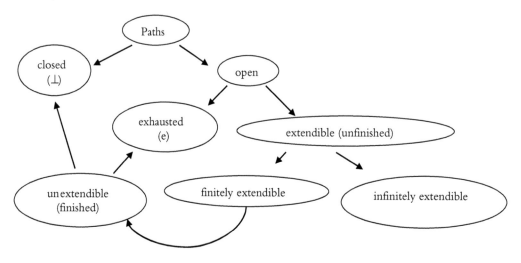

Trees are open or closed, extendible or unextendible depending on their paths.

> A *tree* is *closed* if and only if each of its paths is closed.
>
> A *tree* is *open* if and only if it is not closed.
>
> A *tree* is *unextendible* (*finished*) if and only if each of its paths is either closed or exhausted.
>
> A *tree* is *extendible* (*unfinished*) if and only if it has at least one extendible path.

Ts is designed to determine whether a set is inconsistent. It does this by producing a tree that yields ⊥ on each path.

> A set is *inconsistent in* Ts if and only if it has at least one closed tree.
>
> A set is *consistent in* Ts if and only if it does not have a closed tree.

(As noted in section 7.2, other derivational concepts are defined in terms of the inconsistency of corresponding sets.)

As stated here, what is consistent in Ts is defined by a criterion that seems hard to determine in many cases: lacking even one tree that yields ⊥ on each path. Since any one-step extension of a tree is a tree, and the result of applying reduction rules in a different order is a tree, might this mean having to survey dozens of different ways of doing trees before being able to say that a set is consistent?

In sections 7.1 and 7.2, where practical considerations were paramount, this question was avoided by proposing a practical criterion: if even one tree for a set has an exhausted path, no tree for that set could be closed. This criterion needs to be justified. What rules out getting an exhausted path by reducing the sentences in a set in one way, while getting a closed tree while reducing it in another?

It is shown in section A-3.2 that both exhausted paths and infinitely extendible paths define a tree model, that is, an interpretation on which all the sentences in the set the tree was done for are true. It is further proven in section A-3.1 that if a set has a tree model, it cannot have a closed tree. Combining these two results, if a set has even one tree with an exhausted or an infinitely extendible path, no tree for that set can be closed. Conversely, if no tree is closed each must be open, which means each must have at least one open path. The only way this could be true of *each* tree for the set is if each tree has either an infinitely extendible path or a finitely extendible path that is extendible to an exhausted path.

Demonstrating these two results, that if a set has even one tree with even one exhausted or infinitely extendible path it must have a tree model, and that if a set has a tree model it cannot have a closed tree, is tantamount to demonstrating what is called the "completeness" and the "soundness" of reduction trees. The results are usually stated in the contrapositive, which brings them into alignment with similar completeness and soundness results for derivations.

For trees, the contrapositive of the soundness principle is: if a set has even one closed tree, that is, if it is inconsistent in Ts, it cannot have a tree model. A tree model, like any other model, is an interpretation on which all the sentences in a set are true. So not having a tree model means being s-unsatisfiable. Ts is a "sound" method for answering the questions of SL in the sense that it never declares a set to be inconsistent unless that set is s-unsatisfiable.

> *Soundness:* If a set of sentences is inconsistent in Ts, then it is s-unsatisfiable.

Inconsistency in Ts is defined as having "even one" closed tree because any one-step extension of a tree is a tree. Therefore, s-unsatisfiable sets can have numerous open trees: all the one-step extensions of trees prior to the one that is closed. What distinguishes inconsistent sets from consistent ones is not that inconsistent sets do not have open trees, but that they have at least one closed tree.

For trees, the contrapositive of the completeness principle is: if a set is not s-satisfiable (and so does not have a tree model), it cannot have even one tree with an exhausted or infinitely extendible path. It must, therefore, have at least one closed tree, and so must be inconsistent in Ts. (All of its trees could not be finitely extendible. A finitely extendible tree is one that can be extended to make another tree. If *all* the trees were finitely extendible, each of them could be extended to make another tree, entailing that each tree must have an infinitely extendible path and so contradicting the supposition that *all* the trees are only finitely extendible.)

> *Completeness:* If a set of sentences is s–unsatisfiable, then it is inconsistent in Ts.

In addition to being sound and complete, Ts is decidable.

> *Decidability:* Any tree for any finite set of sentences becomes unextendible after a finite number of one-step extensions.

In other words, Ts will "decide" whether any finite set is inconsistent in a finite number of rule applications. It will not go on reducing sentences forever without reaching a verdict. s-trees do not have infinitely extendible paths, except in the case where the infinite extension is a consequence of adding sentences from an infinite set to the head of a tree. Decidability is demonstrated in section 10.3. Importantly, it is an ancillary result, not needed to establish either the soundness or the completeness of Ts.

The soundness and completeness of Ts have some noteworthy corollary results.

> *Corollary 1:* If a set, Γ, has a closed tree, a long table or a demonstration from the valuation rules will show that there is no interpretation that assigns a T to each sentence in Γ.
>
> *Corollary 2:* If Γ has a tree with an exhausted path, θ, the interpretation that assigns T to each atomic sentence on θ and F to all other atomic sentences is an s-model for Γ.

Corollary 1 is an immediate consequence of soundness, which says that if at least one tree for Γ is closed it must be s-unsatisfiable. Corollary 2 is an immediate consequence of completeness. Taken together, the corollaries entail that the semantic procedures of chapter 5 can be used as a check on trees. If a tree closes but a long table or a demonstration from the valuation rules establishes that there is a model for the set, then something must have gone wrong somewhere, either in drawing up the tree or the table, or in reasoning from the valuation rules.

> *Corollary 3:* If a set, Γ, has a closed tree, there is a derivation in Ds that derives $\bot$ from that set.
>
> *Corollary 4:* If Γ has a tree with an exhausted path, there is a derivation in Ds that derives a dnf that contains the literals on that path in at least one of its disjuncts.

Corollaries 3 and 4 entail that derivations can also be used as a check on trees. Corollary 3 follows because, by the soundness principle for trees, if a set has a closed s-tree, it must be s-unsatisfiable, and by corollary 1 of the completeness principle for derivations (chapter A-2.7), if a set is s-unsatisfiable it must be inconsistent in Ds.

Corollary 4 follows because, by the completeness principle for trees, if a set, Γ, has at least one s-tree with at least one exhausted path, it must be s-satisfiable. By chapter A-2.8, if Γ is s-satisfiable it yields a dnf other than $\bot$ in Ds. Each disjunct of that dnf is a characteristic sentence, which describes the interpretation used by a model for Γ, and the complete dnf identifies all the possible models for Γ. At least one of those models must coincide with any tree model for Γ.

The connection between Ts and Ds is so close that there is a systematic way of converting any closed tree into a derivation of $\bot$. This is explained in chapter A-3.4.

> *Corollary 5:* Any unextendible tree can be systematically converted into a derivation in Ds that either yields $\bot$ (if the tree is closed) or a dnf other than $\bot$ (if the tree has one or more exhausted paths).

Exercise 7.6

Say whether the following statements are true or false. Justify your answer with an example or a demonstration appealing to the claims made in this section, as appropriate. Where a claim is justified in whole or in part by appeal to the completeness, soundness, or decidability of Ts or by one of the corollaries, be sure to specify which it is.

★a. If a set is s-satisfiable, it cannot have a closed tree. *(Hint: consider the contrapositive of the soundness principle.)*

b. If a set has a tree with an exhausted path, it is s-satisfiable.

★c. If a sentence, P, has a tree with at least one exhausted path, ~P cannot be a theorem of Ts.

d. If a sentence, P, has a closed tree, ~P cannot be contingent in Ts.

★e. If a sentence has a tree with an unextendible open path, it cannot be inconsistent in Ts.

f. A set may have some closed trees and some unextendible open trees. *(Hint: What sort of path must an unextendible open tree have? Appeal to corollary 2 and the soundness principle.)*

Appendix Trees for Three-Valued and Paraconsistent Logic

Ts can be modified for use with many-valued logics. This section shows how this is done for the systems proposed by Kleene, Łukasiewicz, Bochvar, and Priest. (See appendices 5.2–3. Since supervaluational semantics for sentential logic establishes the same results as classical sentential semantics, supervaluational semantics does not require any modifications to classical derivations or trees. Trees for intuitionistic logic are discussed in section 9.4.)

As noted at the outset of this chapter, in Ts, longer sentences are reduced to shorter ones in accord with what the valuation rules say about the values components can take given the value of compounds. In Ts, values can be read off of negations. The occurrence of a sentence, P, indicates that P is assumed to receive a T on an interpretation, I, on which all the givens are true. The occurrence of ~P indicates that P is assumed to receive an F on I. The reduction rules are designed to reduce P accordingly. Three-valued logics introduce a third value (designated N or # in the appendix to chapter 5). This puts a strain on the accepted vocabulary for SL, which contains a vocabulary element that designates that a sentence is not true (or perhaps that it is false, depending on how strongly ~ is read), but none that discriminates between N and F (or T and N, if ~ is taken to mean "false" rather than "not true").

The symbol N/ (N slash; later #/) can be used on trees to make up for this defect.[3] N/ is not a unary connective or other new vocabulary element. It does not officially appear in sentences of SL and so has no formal syntax. Informally, it is a metalinguistic symbol that precedes the occurrence of a sentence without being a part of that sentence. It serves as a tag to indicate that the sentence is assumed to have the value N on I. N/ may never occur inside or after a sentence and its occurrence before a sentence does not call for any syntactic modification to that sentence. Where the main connective is a binary connective, the sentence's outer punctuation may of course be entered, but this is not necessary because N/ is not a unary connective and may only apply to the entire sentence that follows it.

The addition of N/ requires an extension of the conditions on closure. In three-valued logic, no sentence can receive more than one value on any interpretation. (Even in paraconsistent logic, no sentence can receive the value, "both T and F," and either the value "simply T" or the value "simply F.") ($\perp$I) is revised to capture this consequence.

The special case arises when $\perp$ appears as a component of a sentence. This makes it possible for the application of a rule to cause N/ $\perp$ to stand alone on a path. Since $\perp$ must be F on any interpretation, it cannot be N on any interpretation, so the path must close.

Some of the reduction rules for Kleene's system of three-valued logic can be read directly off the Kleene valuation rules.

(&): I(P & Q) is:

    (i)   T if and only if I(P) and I(Q) are T
    (ii) F if and only if at least one of I(P) and I(Q) is F
    (iii) otherwise N

(∨): I(P ∨ Q) is:

    (i)   T if and only if at least one of I(P) and I(Q) is T
    (ii) F if and only if I(P) and I(Q) are F
    (iii) otherwise N

(→): I(P → Q) is:

    (i)   T if and only if I(P) is F or I(Q) is T
    (ii) F if and only if I(P) is T and I(Q) is F
    (iii) otherwise N

(≡): I(P ≡ Q) is:

    (i)   T if and only if I(P) and I(Q) are either both T or both F
    (ii) F if and only if one of I(P) and I(Q) is T and the other is F
    (iii) otherwise N

(~) I(~P) is T if and only if I(P) is F and F if and only if I(P) is T; otherwise, I(~P) is N

Clause (i) of (&) dictates that (T&) must reduce P & Q to P over Q, while clause (ii) dictates that (~&) must reduce ~(P & Q) to ~P on a left path and ~Q on a right path. This replicates the familiar (T&) and (~&) rules. The first two clauses of the other binary connective rules likewise implicate the familiar (T∨), (~∨), (T→), (~→), (T≡) and (~≡) rules, and the first two clauses of (~) implicate the familiar (DN). However, the implications of the third, "otherwise," clauses are hard to gather just from the rule statements. They are better collected by filling the blanks left in the Kleene characteristic tables after all the T's and F's have been assigned.

The Kleene and Łukasiewicz tables are recopied below. (Though Łukasiewicz trees are not now under consideration, the tables are combined for ease of future reference. They differ in only three spots, I_5 for P → Q, Q → P and P ≡ Q.)

	P	Q	~P	P & Q	P ∨ Q	P → Q	Q → P	P ≡ Q
I_1	T	T	F	T	T	T	T	T
I_2	T	N	F	N	T	N	T	N
I_3	T	F	F	F	T	F	T	F
I_4	N	T	N	N	T	T	N	N
I_5	N	N	N	N	N	$N_K/T_Ł$	$N_K/T_Ł$	$N_K/T_Ł$
I_6	N	F	N	F	N	N	T	N
I_7	F	T	T	F	T	T	F	F
I_8	F	N	T	F	N	T	N	N
I_9	F	F	T	F	F	T	T	T

The tables make it clear that (~) assigns N to P in exactly one case, that in which P is assigned N. (&) assigns N to P & Q in three cases, when P is T and Q is N, when both are N, and when Q is T and P is N. These cases cannot be further reduced. It would not do, for instance, to say that & assigns N to P & Q whenever either P or Q gets N, because assignments of F to P and N to Q, or F to Q and N to P, are not assignments on which P & Q gets N. By similar reasoning, (∨) assigns N to P ∨ Q and (→) assigns N to P → Q in three cases. In contrast, the five cases in which (≡) assigns N to P can be reduced to two, since in these cases the compound gets N if and only if at least one of the immediate components gets N. This produces the following new rules for the N cases:

	(N~)			(N&)				(N∨)		
				N/ P & Q✓				N/ P ∨ Q✓		
k.	N/ ~P✓									
n.	N/ P k (N~)	n.	P N/ P Q k (N&)				n.	~P N/ P ~Q k (N∨)		
				N/ Q N/ Q N/ P k (N&)				N/ Q N/ Q N/ P k (N∨)		

	(N→)				(N≡)		
k.	N/ P → Q✔			*k.*	N/ P ≡ Q✔		
n.	P N/ P ~Q *k* (N→)			*n.*	N/ P N/ Q *k* (N≡)		
n+1.	N/ Q N/ Q N/ P *k* (N→)						

(N&), (N∨), and (N→) have been designed to be memorable. The middle paths are always N/ P and N/ Q. The "*n*" lines on the extreme paths invert the way the familiar path-splitting rules work and the last lines enter the N/ of the second component.

Łukasiewicz's valuation rules are like Kleene's but for expanding the conditions under which conditionals and biconditionals are assigned T.

(→): I(P → Q) is:

(i)   T if and only if either: (a) I(P) is F, (b) I(P) and I(Q) are N, (c) I(Q) is T
(ii) F if and only if I(P) is T and I(Q) is F
(iii) otherwise N

(≡): I(P ≡ Q) is:

(i)   T if and only if I(P) and I(Q) are the same
(ii) F if and only if at least one of I(P) and I(Q) is T and the other is F
(iii) otherwise N

The first clauses of each rule specify three cases under which a T is assigned to conditionals and biconditionals. The "otherwise" clauses are unpacked by consulting the characteristic table and seeing two cases where conditionals get N and four where biconditionals get N.

	(ŁT→)		(ŁT≡)
k.	P → Q✔	*k.*	P ≡ Q✔
n.	~P N/ P Q *k* (T→)	*n.*	P N/ P ~P *k* (T≡)
n+1.	N/ Q *k* (T→)	*n*+1.	Q N/ Q ~Q *k* (T≡)

	(ŁN→)		(ŁN≡)
k.	N/ P → Q✔	*k.*	N/ P ≡ Q✔
n.	P ~Q *k* (N→)	*n.*	N/ P N/ Q *k* (N≡)
n+1.	N/ Q N/ P *k* (N→)	*n*+1.	Q ~Q P ~P *k* (N≡)

(ŁN≡) might just as well have required a four-way split. The chosen format may be easier to remember.

Exhausted paths are defined in the familiar way for both Kleene and Łukasiewicz trees. A path is exhausted if and only if (i) each sentence in Γ has been added to the head of the tree, (ii) ⊥ does not stand alone on any line of the path, and (iii) each sentence is either a literal or has been reduced. An exhausted path still defines a tree model. But sentences of the form N/ P, where P is a sentence letter, are also literals. And tree models are not necessarily models on which the givens are true. They are models on which all the givens except those tagged with N/ are true. Givens tagged with N/ must be N. Tree models are verified by appealing to the semantic rules to show how both T and N/ flow up the path from the literals to the sentences from which they were reduced, and from those sentences on up to the givens, which must end up with the value T if not tagged with N/, and must get N otherwise.

There is no third value for the verdicts delivered by reduction trees. As in Ts, there are only two possible outcomes: at least one tree is closed or not even one is closed. As with classical trees, for practical purposes, it can be assumed that if Γ has at least one tree with at least one exhausted path, then no tree for Γ is closed.

The definitions of consistency and inconsistency, of derivability and interderivability, of a theorem, and of contingency must be revised to take account of N/ sentences. The definitions that follow suppose that T is the only designated value.

A *set* is *inconsistent* if and only if it has at least one closed tree.
A set is *consistent* if and only if it does not have a closed tree.

A conclusion, P, from a demonstration, Γ / P is *derivable* from the set of its premises, Γ, ($\Gamma \vdash P$) if and only if **both $\Gamma \cup \sim$P and $\Gamma \cup$ N/ P are** inconsistent.
A conclusion, P, is *not derivable* from a set of premises, P, (Γ does not yield P) if and only if **either $\Gamma \cup \sim$P or $\Gamma \cup$ N/ P** is consistent.

A *sentence*, P, is a *theorem* if and only if **both $\{\sim$P$\}$ and $\{$N/ P$\}$ are** inconsistent.
A sentence, P, is *inconsistent* if and only if $\{$P$\}$ is inconsistent.
A sentence, P, is *contingent* if and only if $\{$P$\}$ and **either $\{\sim$P$\}$ or $\{$N/ P$\}$** are consistent.

Two sentences, P and Q, are *interderivable* if and only if both $P \vdash Q$ and $Q \vdash P$ are derivable.
P and Q are *not interderivable* if and only if either Q is not derivable from P or P is not derivable from Q.

These definitions explain something that would otherwise be impossible: how N/ sentences can appear on Kleene trees. N/ is not in the vocabulary, so no set of sentences of SL contains an N/. And none of the Kleene reduction rules derives an N/ sentence from a sentence that is not already an N/ sentence. The only way N/ sentences come to appear on Kleene trees is by being added to givens at the start, as required by the definitions of derivability, of a theorem, and so on.

Demonstrating that $\Gamma \vdash P$ and that P is a theorem requires doing two trees. Demonstrating that P and Q are interderivable requires four. However, when there are no N/ sentences among the givens, the Kleene trees are identical to classical trees. If the classical trees have already been done as part of a previous exercise, that exercise may be cited in preference to redoing the tree.

In cases where a test requires that only one of two sets not have a closed tree (practically, that one have at least one tree with at least one exhausted path), consider which set to try first. The added complexity of the N/ rules needs to be weighed against the fact that the more paths a tree produces, the greater the chances it will produce an exhausted path.

Were both T and N designated, the consistency definitions would require considering as many trees as there are ways of assigning T and N to the sentences in the set. For example, each of $\{$P, Q$\}$, $\{$P, N/ Q$\}$, $\{$N/ P, Q$\}$, and $\{$N/ P, N/ Q$\}$ would need to have at least one closed tree to establish the inconsistency of $\{$P, Q$\}$, while consistency would require that at least one of the four sets not have a closed tree. The derivability definitions would only mention trees for $\Gamma \cup \sim$P, but there would again be multiple trees to consider if there is more than one premise in Γ. The concluding section of this appendix explores an alternative approach.

Exercise 7.7

1. *Determine whether the following sentences are theorems of TK. Say what your tree or trees prove and why. If an N/ tree is not closed, extract and verify the tree model defined by the leftmost exhausted path. Use the Kleene valuation rules.*

 *a. $A \rightarrow A$
  b. $A \vee \sim A$
 *c. $(A \And B) \rightarrow A$
  d. $\sim\sim A \equiv A$
 *e. $A \rightarrow (B \rightarrow A)$
  f. $(A \rightarrow B) \vee (B \rightarrow A)$

2. *Determine whether the following demonstrations are derivable in* TK. *Say what your tree or trees prove and why. If an* N/ *tree is not closed, extract and verify the tree model defined by the leftmost exhausted path.*

 *a. ~A / A → B
 b. B / A → A
 *c. B / A ∨ ~A
 d. A / A ∨ B
 *e. A, ~A / B
 f. ~~A / A
 *g. A & ~A / B & ~B
 h. ~A & ~B / ~(A ∨ ~~B)
 *i. A → B / ~A ∨ B
 j. A → B, A / B
 *k. A ∨ B, ~A / B
 l. A → (B → C) / (A & B) → C

3. *Redo exercises 1 and 2 for* TŁ, *giving verifications (where called for) using the Łukasiewicz valuation rules. These are the Kleene valuation rules but for the first clauses of* (→) *and* (≡), *given earlier.*

Answers for **1a, c, e, 2a, c, e, g, i, k**

Bochvar's system of three-valued logic uses the same valuation rule for negations and biconditionals, and so the same versions of (DN), (N~), (T≡) and (~≡) as does Kleene's. The valuation rules for the remaining binary connectives,

 (&): I(P & Q) is:
   (i) T if and only if I(P) and I(Q) are T
   (ii) N if and only if at least one of I(P) and I(Q) is N
   (iii) otherwise F

 (∨): I(P ∨ Q) is:
   (i) F if and only if I(P) and I(Q) are F
   (ii) N if and only if at least one of I(P) and I(Q) is N
   (iii) otherwise T

 (→): I(P → Q) is:
   (i) F if and only if I(P) is T and I(Q) is F
   (ii) N if and only if at least one of I(P) and I(Q) is N
   (iii) otherwise T

have first clauses that preserve the familiar "straight" rules: (T&), (~∨), and (~→). The second clauses all specify the same condition for the assignment of N. This is also the condition under which Bochvar and Kleene assign N to biconditionals. Effectively, there is only one N reduction rule for TB. Where (bc) is any binary connective:

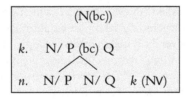

The Bochvar valuation rules relegate false conjunctions, true disjunctions, and true conditionals to the "otherwise" clauses, so the implied reduction rules need to be gathered from the Bochvar characteristic table.

	P	Q	~P	P & Q	P ∨ Q	P → Q	Q → P	P ≡ Q
I₁	T	T	F	T	T	T	T	T
I₂	T	N	F	N	N	N	N	N
I₃	T	F	F	F	T	F	T	F
I₄	N	T	N	N	N	N	N	N
I₅	N	N	N	N	N	N	N	N
I₆	N	F	N	N	N	N	N	N
I₇	F	T	T	F	T	T	F	F
I₈	F	N	T	N	N	N	N	N
I₉	F	F	T	F	F	T	T	T

As the table makes clear, when & gets F, ∨ gets T, or → gets T, the value of a single component does not suffice to determine the value of the compound. Both must be specified to rule out the possibility of an N assignment to a component, which would dictate the assignment of N to the compound as well.

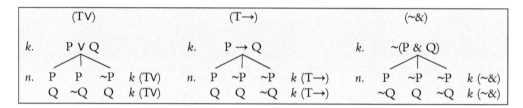

To make the rules easier to remember, the paths read from left to right in the way that the characteristic tables read from the top down. For example, P ∨ Q gets a T on I₁, I₃, and I₇; the left path of (T∨) characterizes I₁, the middle path I₃, and the right I₇.

Exercise 7.8

Redo exercise 7.7#1 and #2 for TB, giving verifications (where called for) using the Bochvar valuation rules. If the Bochvar result is the same as the Kleene or Łukasiewicz result, just explain why no changes are required to the earlier answer.

Answers for **1a, c, e, 2a, c, e, g, i, k**

Reduction trees do not fit well with the project of paraconsistent logic. They search for ⊥, and when they find it they consider a path to be closed. But paraconsistent logic does not want contradictions to impede further inferences. The concern is only to prevent anything whatsoever from being inferred from a contradiction.

Early attempts to use reduction trees in paraconsistent logic were based on a variant method, known as the "coupled tree" method. A coupled tree is created by doing two trees, one for the premises, and one for the conclusion. The tree for the conclusion is then turned upside down, set below the tree for the premises, and further criteria are invoked to determine whether each path of the upper tree can be "coupled" with a path of the lower tree. The coupled tree method is suited to what is called "relevance logic," which demands that the premises of a valid demonstration be relevant to the conclusion. Demanding relevance entails rejecting demonstrations that go from inconsistent premises to any conclusion whatsoever. This makes relevance logic of interest to paraconsistent logicians, who want to prevent contradictions from "exploding" to any conclusion whatsoever.

More recent work takes a different approach, which more closely resembles the classical tree method.[4] It will be called T_LP (tree method for paraconsistent logic). T_LP requires only one tree to determine derivability, but at the cost of introducing two parallel sets of reduction rules, one that handles inferences from simply true sentences and another that handles inferences from sentences that are either simply true or "both true and false" (#). ⊥ can close paths on these trees, and there are still three closure rules (the same ones used by Kleene, Łukasiewicz, and Bochvar), but this variety of means notwithstanding, there are ways to get exhausted paths that contain sentences that have the value # (both true and false).

T_{LP} increases the number of "tags" used on trees from one to four. The tags do not indicate values. This is still a three-valued logic where the intermediate value, #, is read as "both T and F." The remaining values, T and F, are read as "simply true," and "simply false." "Simply true" and "simply false" each have a dedicated tag, T! and F!. But the remaining tags are signs for categories of values. T and # are both designated as being "at least T" (tagged as T/) # and F are both designated as being "at least F" (tagged as F/).

$$
\begin{array}{l}
\text{T}-\text{T!} \;\;\}\; \text{T/} \\
\#<^{\text{T}}_{\text{F}} \\
\text{F}-\text{F!} \;\;\}\; \text{F/}
\end{array}
$$

The value, #, is, insofar as it includes T, a species of the general category, T/. Insofar as it also includes F, it is also a species of the general category, F/. T/ includes both T and #. F/ includes both F and #.

T! P	P is simply true (it cannot also be false)
T/ P	P is at least true (it could also be false, but not necessarily)
F/ P	P is at least false (it could also be true, but not necessarily)
F! P	P is simply false (it cannot also be true)

T_{LP} is sometimes formulated using F-overbar (for "definitely not false") rather than (as here) T! (for "simply true"), and T-overbar (for "definitely not true") rather than F!. But things are complex enough without throwing in double negatives. As noted in other contexts, there is also something to be said for using symbols that are readily accessible on the keyboard.

With these tags in place, para-derivability is defined as follows:

A conclusion, P, from a demonstration, Γ / P is *para-derivable* from the set of its premises, Γ, ($\Gamma \vdash$ P) if and only if $\Gamma_{T/} \cup$ F! P is inconsistent.

A conclusion, P, is *not para-derivable* from a set of premises, P, (Γ does not para-yield P) if and only if $\Gamma_{T/} \cup$ F! P is consistent.

$\Gamma_{T/}$ is the set resulting from tagging each sentence in Γ with T/. In accord with this definition, the trees for Γ / P will have as their givens the conclusion, tagged with F!, and each sentence in Γ tagged with T/ (or as many of them as need to be added to the head of the tree to produce closure). If at least one of the trees is closed, Γ / P is para-derivable. If none are (practically, if at least one has at least one exhausted path), Γ / P is not para-derivable, and the exhausted path should define a tree model on which each sentence in Γ is not simply false but P is simply false.

Though para-derivability is defined by appeal to just two of the four tags, the remaining tags are still necessary. They get created in the process of applying the ~, → and ≡ reduction rules.

(T!~)	(T/~)	(F/~)	(F!~)
T! ~P	T/ ~P	F/ ~P	F! ~P
|	|	|	|
F! P	F/ P	T/ P	T! P

(T!&)	(T/&)	(F/&)	(F!&)
T! P & Q	T/ P & Q	F/ P & Q	F! P & Q
|	|	∧	∧
T! P	T/ P	F/ P F/ Q	F! P F! Q
T! Q	T/ Q		

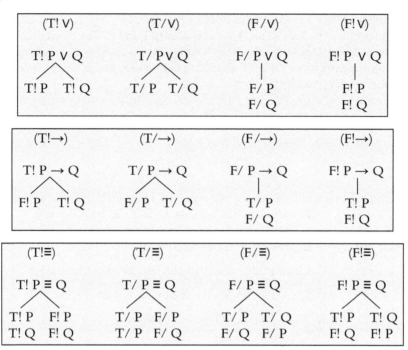

These are just the familiar rules, written down twice over, once for ! and once for /. This is what would be expected. A compound is *at least* true or false as a function of its components being *at least* true or false in the same way that a compound is *simply* true or false as a function of the *simple* truth or falsity of its components. ((DN) is not included. All sentences are tagged, so ∼∼P is reduced in accord with the ∼ rule for its tag.)

The closure rules are based on the consideration that T/ P and F/ P are compatible (this is the point of paraconsistent logic), and that T! P and F! P are species of T/ P and F/ P respectively. The incompatible combinations are:

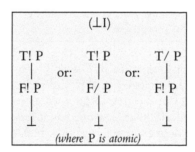

No literal can be both simply true and simply false, or simply true and at least false, or at least true and simply false. ⊥ is simply false, and so should be tagged F! if it comes to stand alone on a tree path for some other reason than an application of (⊥I). This makes it unnecessary to recognize a fourth, special closure case. ∼⊥ is similarly simply true.

To extract a tree model from an exhausted T_{LP} path,

- assign T to each sentence letter on the path tagged by T!
- assign F to each sentence letter on the path tagged by F!
- assign # to each sentence letter not tagged by either T! or F!

When writing up a verification, givens prefaced by T/ on the tree are verified if reasoning from the tree model using the Kleene rules establishes that the given receives either T or #. Givens tagged with F! must get F.

Exercise 7.9

1.★ *Explain why all theorems of* Ts *must be theorems of* T_{LP}.

2. *Redo exercise 7.7#2 to determine whether the demonstrations are derivable in* T_{LP}. *Also do the following exercises. Say what your tree proves and why. If the tree is not closed, extract and verify the tree model defined by the leftmost exhausted path using the Kleene valuation rules.*

★**m.** $A \vee B, A \to C, B \to G \ / \ C \vee G$

   n. $A \to B, B \to C \ / \ A \to C$

Answers for **a, c, e, g, i, k**

Notes

1 This is confirmed by the role played by a non-semantic "placement principle" in both the soundness and the completeness demonstrations of chapter A-3.

2 To be more precise, there is no way that does not presuppose that the exhausted paths on a fully completed tree must define all the models for the givens, a principle that is not demonstrated here or in chapter A-3 (but see the concluding discussion of chapter A-2.8). It generally requires as much or more work to fully complete a single tree, and recover and count up the models defined by its exhausted paths, as it does to do a second tree.

3 This approach is adopted from Bell, DeVidi, and Solomon (2001).

4 Presented by Bloesch (1993). Bloesch cites the principal prior work on coupled trees and remarks on drawbacks with that method.

References

Bell, John L, DeVidi, David, and Solomon, Graham, 2001, *Logical Options: An Introduction to Classical and Alternative Logics*, Broadview, Peterborough, ON.

Bloesch, Anthony, 1993, "A Tableau Style Proof System for Two Paraconsistent Logics," *Notre Dame Journal of Formal Logic* 34: 295–301.

A-3

Advanced Topics Concerning the Soundness and Completeness of Ts

Contents

A test is sound when it never detects anything it shouldn't. Whenever it says that something has the property being tested for, it does. A test is complete when it detects everything it should. Whenever something has the property being tested for, the test says it does. A test is decidable when it delivers unambiguous results before it is too late to do anything about it.

Ts is designed to detect s-unsatisfiable sets by producing at least one closed tree. So, it is sound if, whenever it produces at least one closed tree for a set of sentences, that set is s-unsatisfiable. It is complete if, whenever a set is s-unsatisfiable, it produces at least one closed tree. And it is decidable if any tree for any finite set will turn into a closed tree or a tree with an exhausted path after a finite number of one-step extensions.

Each of these results is demonstrated over the course of this chapter. In doing so the chapter demonstrates how each of the rules of Ts plays a necessary role in providing for the soundness and the completeness of the system. It also illustrates why two of the provisions of the placement principle, (i) that the results of applying a rule to a sentence are not to be entered on any path that does not lead to that sentence, and (ii) that they are to be entered on each open path that does, are essential for the soundness and completeness of Ts. The chapter concludes by showing how to convert closed trees into derivations. This allows the completeness of the tree method to be used in an alternative demonstration of the completeness of Ds.

A-3.1 Soundness of Ts

The soundness principle

> If Γ has at least one closed tree, then Γ is s-unsatisfiable

is demonstrated by contraposition. The demonstration proceeds by showing that if Γ is s-satisfiable then it cannot have even one closed tree. From this it follows that if it does have a closed tree, it could not be s-satisfiable.

The frame for the soundness demonstration is:

> 1. Suppose for purposes of conditional proof that Γ is s-satisfiable.
>
> ...
>
>   *n*. By [?], Γ cannot have a closed tree.

DOI: 10.4324/9781003026532-11

    n+1. From lines 1 to *n* by conditional proof, if Γ is s-satisfiable it cannot have
      a closed tree.

    n+2. By contraposition, if Γ has a closed tree it is s-unsatisfiable.

The gap is filled by noting that since Γ is s-satisfiable there must be an interpretation, I, on which all the sentences in Γ are true. This means that the first one-step extension of any tree for Γ, the one that places one of the sentences in Γ on the top of the tree, must consist of sentences that are all true on I. The demonstration then calls in the aid of mathematical induction to establish that this must hold for all the sentences on at least one path, call it θ, of any subsequent one-step extension. The consequence is that, for however long a tree for Γ can be extended, θ must consist of sentences that are all true on I. Since ⊥ is not true on any interpretation, θ cannot contain ⊥. So, it must be an open path. So, no one-step extension for any tree for Γ can contain all closed paths, and hence Γ cannot have a closed tree.

The frame given above is filled in as follows. T_1 is the first one-step extension of any tree for Γ. By definition, the first one-step extension of a tree for Γ consists of one of the sentences in Γ. T_2 is any one-step extension of T_1, that is, any result of either adding another sentence from Γ to the head of the tree or applying a rule of Ts to an unreduced sentence in T_1. T_3 is any one-step extension of T_2 and so on. There will be many different series of T's, since later ones depend on decisions made about what rule to apply next. All the different series of trees are all the possible trees for the sentences in Γ. From lines 3–6, the demonstration applies to any tree in any series of trees for Γ.

    1. Suppose for purposes of conditional proof that Γ is s-satisfiable.
    2. By def. satisfaction, there is an interpretation, I, on which all the sentences in Γ are true.
    3. By lemma 1, all the sentences on at least one path, θ, in T_1 are true on I.
    4. By lemma 2, if all the sentences on θ in T_k are true on I, all the sentences on at least one extension of θ in T_{k+1} are true on I.
    5. From lines 3 and 4 by mathematical induction, all the sentences on at least one path of any tree for Γ are true on I.
    6. By lemma 3, a path with sentences on it that are all true on an interpretation cannot be a closed path.
    7. By definition of closure, Γ cannot have a closed tree.
    8. From lines 1–7 by conditional proof, if Γ is s-satisfiable, it cannot have a closed tree.
    9. By contraposition, if Γ has a closed tree it is s-unsatisfiable.

Lemma 1 is the basis clause and lemma 2 the inductive step for the induction at line 5. (The induction is strong, even though lemma 2 only speaks of T_k, not of T_1 to T_k. T_k includes all of T_1 to T_{k-1}.) Lemma 3 is a direct result of the definition of a closed path, as a path on which ⊥ stands alone, and (⊥), which says that ⊥ is F on any interpretation. So, it only remains to demonstrate lemmas 1 and 2.

Demonstration of lemma 1 (the basis): Ts dictates that T_1 must contain a single path with a single line on which is written one of the sentences in Γ, and by supposition each of those sentences is true on I. So, all the sentences on at least one path in T_1 are true on I.

Demonstration of lemma 2 (the induction): As usual, the demonstration of the induction begins by assuming the inductive hypothesis: **Suppose for purposes of conditional proof that all the sentences on at least one path, θ, in T_k are true on I.** The aim is to prove that making this supposition requires accepting that all the sentences on at least one extension of θ in T_{k+1} are true on I. To see why this must be the case, consider that T_{k+1} is a one-step extension of T_k. As such, it results from either adding another sentence from Γ to the head of the tree, or applying a rule of Ts to some unreduced nonliteral on a path in T_k. There are 10 different rules that could be applied, and the rule could be applied either to a sentence that lies on θ or to a sentence that lies on some other path. So there are 12 cases to consider.

    Case one: (A sentence from Γ is added to the head of the tree.) Since all paths run to the head of any s-tree, θ runs to the head of the tree. So adding a sentence from Γ to the head of the tree extends θ one line upwards in T_{k+1}. Since the added sentence comes from Γ and each sentence in Γ is by supposition true on I, T_{k+1} must in this case contain at least one extension of θ that consists of sentences that are all true on I.

    Case two: (A reduction rule is applied to a nonliteral sentence on some other path than θ.) In this case, since **the placement principle dictates that sentences be reduced only on paths that run up to them,** and θ is by supposition not one of those paths, the rule application produces no changes to θ. This means that the only extension of θ in T_{k+1} is θ itself. By the inductive hypothesis, θ in T_k consists of sentences that are all true on I. So T_{k+1} must in this case contain at least one extension of θ that consists of sentences that are all true on I.

Case three: ((⊥I) is applied to two sentences on θ in T_k.) This case cannot arise, since by the inductive hypothesis all the sentences on θ in T_k are true on I. Since no interpretation can assign a T to both an atomic sentence and its negation, θ cannot contain the sentences that would permit an application of (⊥I).

Case four: ((DN) is applied to a sentence on θ in T_k.) Any sentence that (DN) applies to must have the form ~~P. Since ~~P lies on θ in T_k it follows by (DN) and the placement principle that θ must be extended by a single path, on which P stands alone. By the inductive hypothesis, θ in T_k consists of sentences that are all true on I, so I(~~P) is T. By two applications of (~), I(P) is T as well. So T_{k+1} must in this case contain at least one extension of θ that consists of sentences that are all true on I.

Case five: ((T&) is applied to a sentence on θ in T_k.) Any sentence that (T&) applies to must have the form P & Q. Since P & Q lies on θ in T_k it follows by (T&) and the placement principle that θ must be extended by the addition of a single path on which a sentence of the form P occurs above a sentence of the form Q. By the inductive hypothesis, θ in T_k consists of sentences that are all true on I, so I(P & Q) is T. By (&), I(P) and I(Q) are T. So T_{k+1} must in this case contain at least one extension of θ that consists of sentences that are all true on I.

Case six: ((T∨) is applied to a sentence on θ in T_k.) Any sentence that (T∨) applies to must have the form P ∨ Q. Since P ∨ Q lies on θ in T_k, it follows by (∨) and the placement principle that θ must be extended by a left path extension with P on it and a right path extension with Q on it. By the inductive hypothesis, θ in T_k consists of sentences that are all true on I, so I(P ∨ Q) is T. By (∨), at least one of I(P) and I(Q) is T. So T_{k+1} must in this case contain at least one extension of θ that consists of sentences that are all true on I.

Exercise A-3.1

Prove the remaining six cases using either case five or case six as a template, as appropriate.

Since all 12 possible cases lead to the same consequence, it follows by proof by cases that this consequence holds regardless of what rule is applied to extend θ. So, if it is supposed that all the sentences on at least one path in T_k are true on I, it must be accepted that T_{k+1} contains at least one extension of θ that consists of sentences that are all true on I.

A-3.2 Completeness of Ts

Like the soundness principle, the completeness principle

If Γ is s-unsatisfiable then it has at least one closed tree

is demonstrated by contraposition. The demonstration proceeds by showing that if each tree for Γ is open then Γ must be s-satisfiable. From this it follows that if Γ is s-unsatisfiable then it must have at least one closed tree. Otherwise (if it did not have at least one close tree) each of its trees would be open in which case it would have to be s-satisfiable.

The frame for the completeness demonstration is:

1. Suppose for purposes of conditional proof that each tree for Γ is open.
   ...
   n. By [?], Γ is s-satisfiable.
   n+1. From lines 1 to *n* by conditional proof, if each tree for Γ is open it is s-satisfiable.
   n+2. By contraposition, if Γ is s-unsatisfiable it must have a closed tree.

Standard practice up to now has been to go on to give the entire demonstration in summary form, with the aid of lemmas. The lemmas are then justified. However, in this case the short form demonstration introduces so many new notions that presenting it at this point would not be very helpful. Instead, the full demonstration is completed incrementally, with comments on each line of demonstration as it is introduced. To begin, it follows from the first premise that:

Each tree in the canonical series of trees for Γ is open.

This can be said independently of knowing what the canonical series of trees for Γ is. If all the trees are open, then any trees that are considered, in whatever order they are considered, are each open. However, it is important for the rest of the demonstration that the canonical series of trees, in particular, be open.

The canonical series of trees, T_1, T_2, T_3, ..., is a series of one-step extensions of trees produced by following a canonical method. The method begins by selecting the sentence in Γ with the lowest catalogue number and placing it on the head of a tree.

The catalogue number for a sentence is generated by assigning a two-digit number to each of the vocabulary elements of SL, as follows:

Symbol	Numeral	Symbol	Numeral	Symbol	Numeral
$\perp$	10	0	20	A	30
$\rightarrow$	11	1	21	B	31
(	12	...		C	32
)	13	9	29	G	33
~	14			H	34
&	15			K	35
$\vee$	16				
$\equiv$	17				

The catalogue number of a sentence is the number that results from replacing each vocabulary element in the sentence with its associated numeral. For this purpose, informal notational conventions are disregarded. Outer parentheses must be included, and brackets converted to parentheses. For example the catalogue number for $\sim A \rightarrow B$ is 121430113113 and that for $\sim(A \rightarrow B)$ is 141230113113. Since sentences are different if they do not consist of the same vocabulary elements, placed in the same order, each different sentence must have its own catalogue number. This allows all the sentences of SL, as infinitely various as they are, to be listed in a linear order.

The canonical method generates the canonical series, T_1, T_2, T_3, ..., as follows:

T_1 consists of the sentence in Γ with the lowest catalogue number. (No one needs to know which sentence that is. It is not important for purposes of the completeness demonstration that a canonical tree be constructed by anyone. It only matters that there is such a thing. And for any set there is a catalogue number for each sentence in that set and an order for those sentences determined by their catalogue numbers.) If the sentence on line 1 in T_1 is not a literal, T_2 is the one-step extension produced by applying the appropriate reduction rule to it. If any sentence on line 2 in T_2 is not a literal, T_3 is the one-step extension produced by applying the appropriate reduction rule or rules to each of those sentences.

(When different nonliterals occur on different paths on the same line they are reduced simultaneously, even when this means applying different rules on the same line. Trees in the canonical series are ideal creations. It is not intended that they would ever be physically produced. Line numbers, check marks, and justifications are not expressions of SL and so not strictly part of trees. On an ideal consideration, the architecture of trees need not be modified to accommodate them.)

Each subsequent tree in the series is a one-step extension of the previous one produced by applying rules of Ts to nonliterals (or applying ($\perp$I) to literals as the occasion calls for) in the order in which they occur on line to line from the top down.

When no more nonliterals are left and no more applications of ($\perp$I) can be made, the next tree in the series is the one-step extension that has the sentence in Γ with the next lowest catalogue number added to the top of the tree. The one-step extensions then continue with the application of tree rules to any resulting nonliterals. As the series proceeds, the tree grows in both directions, downwards on lengthening and possibly diverging paths, and upwards on an increasingly tall trunk.

Given that a series of trees for any set can be generated by the canonical method, the completeness demonstration can be advanced as follows:

1. Suppose for purposes of conditional proof that each tree for Γ is open.
2. Each tree in the canonical series of trees for Γ is open.
3. **Each tree in the canonical series of trees for Γ must contain at least one path, call it θ, that has the following three features:**
   (a) **⊥ does not stand alone on θ.**
   (b) **For each nonliteral on θ, at least one of the up to two paths of reduction results for that sentence appears on at least one extension of θ in at least one of the subsequent trees in the series.**
   (c) **Each sentence in Γ appears on θ in at least one of the subsequent trees in the series.**

Feature (a) follows from line 1 by the definition of what it means for each tree for Γ to be open.

Features (b) and (c) are a consequence of following the canonical method **and of the placement principle.**

The canonical method ensures that each nonliteral on θ will get reduced in one of the trees in the series and thereby that the turn of each sentence in Γ to be added to the head of the tree will come up. Closed paths may contain nonliterals that were not reduced before the path closed. But θ is open and paths that are open can only contain unreduced nonliterals because those nonliterals have either been overlooked or because their turn has not come up yet. When following the canonical method, no nonliteral can be overlooked, because each must be reduced in the order in which they appear from the top of the tree down. And the turn of each *will* come, because the sentences on the tree before them are reduced only once (and not at all if their reduction results already occur on the path), and because the results of reducing a sentence are always finite. As demonstrated in chapter A-1.1, each sentence is only finitely long, and is reduced to a finite number of sentences (never more than four) that are shorter than it is, entered on a finite number of new paths (never more than two), on each of a finite number of pre-existing paths. Trees start with only one path, each one-step extension never does more than double the number of prior paths, and the product of finite quantities is always finite. So, the situation where there is an infinite task to complete before going on to reduce the next sentence, or add a new sentence from Γ to the head of the tree, never arises. Even if Γ is infinite, since each of the infinitely many sentences in Γ is only finitely long, each has a finite catalogue number, which means that its turn will come up.

The placement principle dictates that the results of reducing a sentence on θ must be entered on each open path that runs up to that sentence. Since the extensions of θ in each subsequent tree in the series are such a path, the results must appear on it.

θ defines the canonical tree model, I★. Where P is atomic, I★(P) is T if and only if P stands alone on a line of θ; otherwise I★(P) is F. Because any sentence letter either stands alone on a line of θ in at least one tree in the series, or does not stand alone on a line of θ in any tree in the series, the assignment of T to those that do and F to those that do not is an interpretation of the sentence letters. I★ is not just a tree model, but also an interpretation of SL.

The demonstration of the completeness of Ts continues by appealing to induction on the length of sentences of SL to establish that I★ is an s-model for the givens. The demonstration begins with a basis clause:

1. Suppose for purposes of conditional proof that each tree for Γ is open.
2. Each tree in the canonical series of trees for Γ is open.
3. Each tree in the canonical series of trees for Γ must contain at least one path, call it θ, that has the following three features:
   (a) ⊥ does not stand alone on θ.
   (b) For each nonliteral on θ, at least one of the up to two paths of reduction results for that sentence appears on at least one extension of θ in at least one of the subsequent trees in the series.
   (c) Each sentence in Γ appears on θ in at least one of the subsequent trees in the series.
4. **Each sentence on θ of length 1 is true on the canonical interpretation, I★.**

The length of a sentence is defined as the number of vocabulary elements it contains, excluding numerical subscripts. Defining length in this way ensures that all atomic sentences have equal length, and are shorter than any compound sentence.

Exercise A-3.2

Calculate the length of the following sentences.

⋆**a.** A
  b. ~A
⋆**c.** ~~A
  d. A & B *(Outer parentheses must be included in the count even if not coloured in!)*
⋆**e.** $(\sim A_{27} \lor (C \& D))$
  f. ~(A ∨ (C & D))

The sentences of length 1 are ⊥ and the sentence letters. By feature (a) of θ, ⊥ cannot stand alone on any line of θ. So the only sentences on θ of length 1 are sentence letters. By definition of I⋆, those sentences are true on I⋆. The next two premises are the inductive step and the conclusion of the appeal to mathematical induction.

1. Suppose for purposes of conditional proof that each tree for Γ is open.
2. Each tree in the canonical series of trees for Γ is open.
3. Each tree in the canonical series of trees for Γ must contain at least one path, call it θ, that has the following three features:
   (a) ⊥ does not stand alone on θ.
   (b) For each nonliteral on θ, at least one of the up to two paths of reduction results for that sentence appears on at least one extension of θ in at least one of the subsequent trees in the series.
   (c) Each sentence in Γ appears on θ in at least one of the subsequent trees in the series.
4. Each sentence on θ of length 1 on θ is true on the canonical interpretation, I⋆.
5. **If each sentence on θ of lengths 1 to k is true on I⋆, each sentence on θ of length $k+1$ is true on I⋆. *(lemma)***
6. **From lines 4 and 5 by mathematical induction, each sentence on θ is true on I⋆.**

As usual, the demonstration of the inductive step (the claim on line 5) begins by assuming **the inductive hypothesis: Suppose for purposes of conditional proof that each sentence on θ of lengths 1 to k is true on I⋆.** The aim is to prove that making this supposition requires accepting that each sentence on θ with length $k+1$ is true on I⋆. To see why this must be the case, consider that the sentences of length $k+1$ must have at least length 2, and so must contain at least one connective. This means that they must be either disjunctions, conjunctions, conditionals, biconditionals, or negations, and if negations, either negations of atomic sentences or negations of negations, disjunctions, conjunctions, conditionals, or biconditionals. So, there are 10 cases to consider.

Case one: (The sentence on θ with length $k+1$ is a negation of an atomic sentence.) Negations of atomic sentences have the form ~P, where P is ⊥ or a sentence letter. Since ~P occurs on θ, **it follows from feature (a) of θ** that P cannot occur on θ (because if it did, then either ⊥ would occur on θ or (⊥I) would have to be applied, placing ⊥ on θ, and by feature (a) of θ, ⊥ does not occur on θ). Either way (whether P is ⊥ or a sentence letter), I⋆(P) is F, in the former case by (⊥) and in the latter in virtue of the way I⋆ is defined (as an interpretation that assigns F to any sentence letter that is not on θ). By (~), I⋆(~P) is T. So, if the sentence on θ with length $k+1$ is a literal, it must be true on I⋆.

Case two: (The sentence on θ with length $k+1$ is a sentence of the form ~~P.) **By feature (b) of θ,** ~~P must have been reduced by (DN). By (DN), P occurs on at least one extension of θ in at least one of the subsequent trees in the canonical series. Since ~~P has length $k+1$, P must have length $k-1$. **By the inductive hypothesis, any sentence on θ with length k or less is true on I⋆, so** P is true on I⋆. By two applications of (~), ~~P is true on I⋆. So, in this case the sentence on θ with length $k+1$ is true on I⋆.

Case three: (The sentence on θ with length $k+1$ is a sentence of the form P & Q.) By **feature (b) of θ,** P & Q must have been reduced by (T&). By (T&), P and Q occur on at least one extension of θ in at least one of the subsequent trees in the canonical series. Since P & Q has length $k+1$, each of P and Q must have length less than $k+1$. **By the inductive hypothesis, any sentence on θ with length k or less is true on $I^\star$, so** P and Q are true on $I^\star$. By (&), P & Q is true on $I^\star$. So, in this case the sentence on θ with length $k+1$ is true on $I^\star$.

Case four: (The sentence on θ with length $k+1$ is a sentence of the form P ∨ Q.) By **feature (b) of θ**, P ∨ Q must have been reduced by (T∨). By (T∨), either P or Q occurs on at least one extension of θ in at least one of the subsequent trees in the canonical series. Since P ∨ Q has length $k+1$, each of P and Q must have length less than $k+1$. **By the inductive hypothesis, any sentence on θ with length k or less is true on $I^\star$, so** whichever one of P and Q is on θ, it is true on $I^\star$. By (∨), P ∨ Q is true on $I^\star$. So, in this case the sentence on θ with length $k+1$ is true on $I^\star$.

The remaining cases are left as an exercise. Since all ten cases lead to the same result, that result follows by proof by cases: the sentence on θ with length $k+1$ is true on $I^\star$. To sum up, it follows by conditional proof that if all the sentences with lengths from 1 to k on θ are true on $I^\star$, each sentence on θ with length $k+1$ is true on $I^\star$.

Having justified the inductive step at line 5, and so the induction at line 6, the remainder of the completeness demonstration can be filled in as follows:

1. Suppose for purposes of conditional proof that each tree for Γ is open.
2. Each tree in the canonical series of trees for Γ is open.
3. Each tree in the canonical series of trees for Γ must contain at least one path, call it θ, that has the following three features:
   (a) $\perp$ does not stand alone on θ.
   (b) For each nonliteral on θ, at least one of the up to two paths of reduction results for that sentence appears on at least one extension of θ in at least one of the subsequent trees in the series.
   (c) Each sentence in Γ appears on θ in at least one of the subsequent trees in the series.
4. Each sentence on θ of length 1 on θ is true on the canonical interpretation, $I^\star$.
5. If each sentence on θ of lengths 1 to k is true on $I^\star$, each sentence on θ of length $k+1$ is true on $I^\star$.
6. From lines 4 and 5 by mathematical induction, each sentence on θ is true on $I^\star$.
7. **From line 3(c), all the sentences in Γ are true on $I^\star$.**
8. **By def. satisfaction, Γ is s-satisfiable.**
9. **From lines 1 to 8 by conditional proof, if each tree for Γ is open, Γ is s-satisfiable.**
10. **By contraposition, if Γ is s-unsatisfiable, it must have at least one closed tree.**

Exercise A-3.3

1. *Demonstrate the remaining six cases for the inductive step using either case three or case four as a template, as appropriate. Be careful with the negations. ★Also explain why the demonstration of some of the cases would have failed had the induction been based on the number of connectives in sentences, rather than on their length.*

2. *The demonstration of the completeness of Ts given here takes the long way around by not relying on the lean language, which would allow lemma 2 to be demonstrated with just three cases. Rewrite the demonstration of lemma 2 for the lean language. To do this, first revise (T→) and (⊥I) for the lean language (compare the solution to exercise 6.8#2 and how the lean language was used in the Henkin completeness demonstration in chapter A-2). Explain why disaster would ensue were sentences of the form P → ⊥ reduced with (T→). Propose a remedy for this disaster. (Hint: treat P → ⊥ as a literal when P is atomic, and develop an alternative rule, (→⊥), for reducing P → ⊥ when P is compound (in this case, P → ⊥ has the form (Q → R) →⊥). This alternative rule resembles (∼→) and is the second case for the demonstration of lemma 2. The first case is the current case one rewritten for P → ⊥ when P is atomic. The demonstration of the revised (T→) case is the third case and is very difficult, requiring appeal to the results established in the previous two cases. Does the induction for the lean language demonstration still need to be based on the length of sentences or can it instead be based on the number of connectives in sentences?*

★3. *(For those who have studied the appendix to chapter 7. Prior completion of exercise A3.3#2 will also make this easier). Revise the completeness proof to demonstrate the completeness of Bochvar trees. It is not necessary to restate all the background details. Just give the definition of I★ for a three-valued logic, modify lines 4 and 5 accordingly, and update the justifications for lines 4 and 5. Bochvar's logic accepts the interderivability of ~P and P → ⊥; P & Q and [P → (Q → ⊥)] → ⊥; and P ∨ Q and (P → ⊥) → ⊥; so line 5 can be justified using the technique developed in answering question 2 above. Alternatively, explore enough cases to make it clear that the remainder will continue to justify the proof by cases.*

4. *("Devil tree" project)* Ts *is designed to ensure that truth flows down along at least one path of a tree. Supposing that there is an interpretation,* I, *on which all the givens are true, the reduction rules require checking those sentences off and replacing them with sentences that are true on* I *on at least one path extension.*

   But the devil always lies and is very concerned that no truths be derived from his lies. He would therefore prefer to have a tree method that starts off with the assumption that there is an interpretation, J, *on which all the givens are false and that proceeds to reduce these sentences into sentences that must be false on* J *along at least one path. Design an alternative tree method,* Td, *for the devil to use. As part of this job, do each of the following:*

   (a) Design an alternative set of reduction rules for the devil to use when constructing trees. These rules should ensure that if a sentence is false on an interpretation, then the sentence or sentences it is reduced into will be false along at least one path. As part of this, define an exhausted path and state how an exhausted path would be used to define a tree model for the devil (a model on which all the givens are false), and the conditions under which a path would close. In doing this, consider whether the closure symbol for trees should be amended, to replace ⊥ with ~⊥. (~⊥ is true on all interpretations, just as ⊥ is false on all interpretations.) Would it make any difference if ⊥ or ~⊥ were used to designate closed paths or would paths still close under the same circumstances?

   (b) Formulate an account of what the Td tests for inconsistency, derivability, interderivability, and contingency in Td would have to be like. For example, when testing for interderivability, what sentence or sentences should be put on top of a devil tree and what conclusions should be drawn if the tree turns out to be closed or to have an exhausted path? Work on the tests for sentences first.

   (c) Do the answered exercises in exercise 7.5#1–3 using the Td rules and the revised tests. Compare the results with those that are posted for s-trees. What does this comparison show?

   (d) The devil does not like the way human logicians have designated truth in their definitions of s-validity and s-unsatisfiability. He uses an alternative pair of concepts called d-nulidity/nontailment and d-antisatisfiability. These alternative concepts are defined in terms of a d-model. A d-model is an interpretation on which all the sentences in a set are false.

   (i) a demonstration, Γ / P, is d-nulid iff Γ ∪ ~P does not have a d-model, that is, if and only if there is no interpretation on which all the premises in Γ are false and P is true (so, no interpretation on wihich each sentence in Γ ∪ ~P is false); otherwise the demonstration is d-innulid.
   When Γ / P is d-nulid, Γ is said to d-nontail P

   (ii) a set, Γ, is d-antisatisfiable iff it has a d-model, that is, if and only if there is an interpretation on which all the sentences in the set are false; otherwise (if there is no interpretation on which each sentence in the set is false) it is not d-antisatisfiable.

   Accepting that an exhausted path of a d-tree defines an interpretation on which the givens are false, and that a closed d-tree established that there is no such interpretation, describe what a tree or trees would have to look like to determine whether a demonstration is d-nullid or d-innulid and whether a set is d-antisatisfiable or not d-antisatisfiable (specify which result is established by a tree with an exhausted path, which by a closed tree).

   (e) Establish the soundness and completeness of Td (that is, that a set has a closed d-tree if and only if it is s-unsatisfiable). This can be done by rewriting the demonstrations given in sections A-3.1 and A-3.2, making the appropriate minor modifications.

A-3.3 Decidability of Ts

The demonstrations of the soundness and completeness of Ts allow for the possibility that trees might go on forever. s-trees for finite sets do not. But that is not a consequence of either the soundness or completeness demonstrations, which neither establish nor presuppose that result. Decidability is an additional feature of s-trees for finite sets, established by further considerations.

The decidability principle states that any s-tree for a finite set of sentences becomes unextendible after a finite number of one-step extensions.

The demonstration falls into two parts. The first part establishes what is known as the Kőnig lemma, after its author, Dénes Kőnig (1884–1944). Suppose to the contrary that there is a finite set, Γ, that has only unfinished trees, that is, trees to which it is always possible to add yet more sentences by further reducing sentences already on the tree. When a set has only unfinished trees, there are infinitely many one-step extensions that can be added to any of its trees and so infinitely many sentences that can be added to any of its trees, since any one-step extension adds at least one sentence. It follows that Γ must have some trees that contain infinitely many sentences.

According to the Kőnig lemma, a tree for a set of sentences of SL could contain infinitely many sentences only if it had at least one path that has infinitely many sentences on it. To see why, consider that on any tree, all the paths grow out of a common trunk at the top of the tree. There must be at least one sentence on this trunk, at line 1. If there are infinitely many sentences on the tree this initial sentence must itself have infinitely many sentences below it (an infinite number minus one is still an infinite number). Now consider the sentence or sentences on the next line down from line 1, if any. Since no single rule application creates more than two paths, there will either be one sentence directly below the first one, or two below it – one on a left path extension and one on a right path extension. If both sentences have only finitely many sentences below them, the original sentence could not have infinitely many sentences below it. By supposition, the first sentence does have infinitely many sentences below it, so at least one of the sentences on the next line down must have infinitely many sentences below it. Now consider any one that does. Obviously, the same considerations that have just been surveyed apply to it, entailing that there must be at least one sentence below it that has infinitely many sentences below it. As this can never end, there must be at least one path with infinitely many sentences below it. This completes the demonstration of the Kőnig lemma.

The second part of the demonstration appeals to the fact that each of the reduction rules removes a sentence from further consideration (it reduces it, and reduced sentences may not figure in any subsequent rule application), and extends the path with an addition that contains fewer vocabulary elements (not counting numerical subscripts) than the sentence that was removed.

The worst case is (T≡), which removes a sentence containing $3 + x + y$ vocabulary elements (a left parenthesis, a right parenthesis, a triple bar, and the sum of the vocabulary elements in the two immediate components) and replaces it with a path containing $2 + x + y$ vocabulary elements (the right-hand path, which contains two tildes plus the sum of the vocabulary elements in the two immediate components.)

Exercise A-3.4

Verify that, for each of the rules of Ts, neither of the up to two paths added by the rule contains more vocabulary elements, not counting numerical subscripts, than the sentence that was reduced.

It follows that, with each rule application, the number of vocabulary elements in unreduced sentences on any given path diminishes, even though the path grows longer, and the total number of unreduced sentences may increase. Given a finite number of vocabulary elements to start with (due to having a finite number of finitely long givens) this cannot go on forever. As each path loses vocabulary elements, the remaining unreduced sentences on the path must become shorter until only literals are left, at which point the path becomes unextendible.

But if no path can be infinitely long, then by the argument of Part 1 above, no tree can contain infinitely many sentences, which means that every tree must become unextendible after a finite number of steps.

As a corollary of this result, the tree method for SL always produces either a closed tree or a tree with an exhausted path after a finite number of one-step extensions.

A-3.4 Tree Conversion; Completeness and Decidability of Ds

It is possible to convert trees into derivations. Any unfinished (extendible) tree can be converted into a derivation that gets as far as the tree does. Any finished (unextendible) tree can be converted into a derivation of the disjunctive normal form (dnf) of the iterated conjunction of the givens. When an unextendible tree is closed, the dnf is ⊥, and the derivation takes the form of a derivation of ⊥ from the givens.

For conversions to be efficient, some changes need to be made to the rules of both systems. The modified systems are called Tsd (sentential reduction trees for derivations) and Dst (sentential derivation system for reduction trees). The modified systems are not (and must not be) significantly different from their parents. Whatever is derivable in Ts is derivable in Tsd, and whatever is derivable in Dst is derivable Ds.

The following modifications are made to Ts:

- (T→) reduces P → Q to ~P ∨ Q
- (~&) reduces ~(P & Q) to ~P ∨ ~Q
- (T≡) reduces P ≡ Q to (P & Q) ∨ (~P & ~Q)
- (~≡) reduces ~(P ≡ Q) to (P & ~Q) ∨ (Q & ~P)

These modifications apply to each of the path-splitting rules, other than (T∨). Each modification rewrites a path-splitting rule to require it to transform the target sentence into a disjunction that, when reduced by (T∨), produces the same result that the original reduction rule produced when applied to the original sentence. For example, in Ts, applying (T→) to P → Q splits the path and puts ~P on the left and Q on the right. In Tsd applying (T→) to P → Q enters ~P ∨ Q on the same path, but a subsequent application of (T∨) then splits the path and puts ~P on the left and Q on the right, reinstating the result obtained by Ts. It is the same with the other three modifications. None of the modifications changes what results are derived on trees. Each creates an s-equivalent disjunction and then uses (T∨) to reduce that s-equivalent disjunction in just the way the original sentence would have been reduced in Ts. This is done to facilitate conversion of the tree to a derivation.

The following derived rules (first introduced in Chapter 6.5.2, or as substitution principles in 6.5.3) are added to Dst:

(impl):	derive ~P ∨ Q from P → Q
(DeM):	derive ~P ∨ ~Q from ~(P & Q)
(equiv):	derive (P & Q) ∨ (~P & ~Q) from P ≡ Q
(~equiv):	derive (P & ~Q) ∨ (Q & ~P) from ~(P ≡ Q)
(DNE):	derive P from ~~P
(~∨):	derive each of ~P and ~Q from ~(P ∨ Q)
(~→):	derive each of P and ~Q from ~(P → Q)

As a reminder, any derived rule is derivable in Ds. It just takes a routine sequence of steps (sometimes more than a dozen) using the 11 rules of Ds to create the derivation.

It is no accident that the first four of these rules replicate the modifications to Ts and that the last three import rules of Ts into Dst.

These modifications produce an exact correspondence between the rules used on trees and the derivation rules.

Tree Rule	Derivation Rule
(T→)	(impl)
(T≡)	(equiv)
(~&)	(DeM)
(~≡)	(~equiv)
(T∨)	(A/PC)
(DN)	(DNE)
(T&)	(&E)
(~→)	(~→)
(~∨)	(~∨)
(⊥I)	(⊥I)

Corresponding rules derive the same sentences or situations in derivations that they produce on trees. The (T→)/(impl), (T≡)/(equiv), (~&)/(DeM), and (~≡)/(~equiv) rules convert all sentences that are reduced by path-splitting rules, other than disjunctions, into disjunctions. (A/PC) creates two parallel (PC) subderivations in all cases where (T∨) creates two paths. (DN)/(DNE), (T&)/&E, (~→), (~∨), and (⊥I) derive same sentences from same sentences in same circumstances, both on trees and in derivations.

Because of these modifications, derivations can be drawn up that almost exactly correspond to trees. Same sentences appear on same lines, justified by corresponding rules, but appear in adjacent subderivations rather than on adjacent paths. To facilitate this, some (R) applications are omitted. In Ds, one use of (R) is to govern when sentences may be used to justify top-down rules. Since Dst follows the tree, that check is unnecessary. The placement principle requires that sentences not be reduced on paths that do not run up to them, effectively prohibiting use of the wrong sentences in justification.

Since it has been shown that Tsd produces all the same results as Ts, since exercises 6.14#2 and 6.16#1 demonstrate that anything that can be derived in Dst can be derived in Ds, and since it has just been established that Tsd and Dst are merely notational variants on one another, displaying the same sequence of sentences, in the one case on paths, in the other in parallel subderivations, it follows that any tree can be converted into a derivation of ⊥.

The operation is best understood by example and exercise. In the following example, it is shown that $\{[A \rightarrow (B \& C)]$ & $[\sim(A \rightarrow B) \vee \sim(A \rightarrow C)]\}$ is inconsistent in both Tsd and Dst. In Ds this is done by deriving ⊥ from the single sentence in this set. To base the derivation on the corresponding tree, a tree for the sentence is first done in Tsd.

```
1.     [A → (B & C)] & [~(A → B) ∨ ~(A → C)] ✔      given
2.               A → (B & C) ✔                       1 (T&)
3.            ~(A → B) ∨ ~(A → C) ✔                  1 (T&)
4.               ~A ∨ (B & C) ✔                      2 (T→)
                    /        \
5.      ~(A → B) ✔              ~(A → C) ✔           3 (T∨)
6.          A                      A                 5 (~→)
7.         ~B                     ~C                 5 (~→)
         /    \                 /     \
8.     ~A    B & C ✔          ~A    B & C ✔         4 (T∨)
9.     ⊥       |              ⊥       |              6,8 (⊥I)
10.            B                      B              8 (T&)
11.            C                      C              8 (T&)
12.            ⊥                                     10,7 (⊥I)
13.                                   ⊥              11,7 (⊥I)
```

This sd-tree looks like an s-tree, but for the application of the Tsd version of (T→) at line 4. The Tsd version of (T→) converts the conditional at line 2 to the corresponding disjunction, leaving it to an application of (T∨) at line 8 to establish what an s-tree would more directly derive. This is done to facilitate conversion to the derivation, which appears below.

```
1.   | [A → (B & C)] & [~(A → B) ∨ ~(A → C)] |        given
2.   | A → (B & C)                           |        1 (&E)
3.   | ~(A → B) ∨ ~(A → C)                    |        1 (&E)
4.   | ~A ∨ (B & C)                          |        2 (Impl)
5.   |  | ~(A → B)        |  | ~(A → C)       |        A/3 (PC)
6.   |  | A              |  | A               |        5 ~→
7.   |  | ~B             |  | ~C              |        5 ~→
8.   |  | | ~A | B & C   |  | | ~A | B & C    |        A/4 (PC)
9.   |  | | ⊥  |         |  | | ⊥  |          |        6,8 (⊥I)
10.  |  |      | B       |  |      | B        |        8 (&E)
11.  |  |      | C       |  |      | C        |        8 (&E)
12.  |  |      | ⊥       |  |                 |        10,7 (⊥I)
13.  |                   |  |      | ⊥        |        11,7 (⊥I)
```

Over lines 1–13 of the derivation, same sentences appear in the same configuration and are justified by the application of the corresponding rules. Lines 4, 6, and 7 are not reiterated. Instead, they are cited from the higher derivations in which they appear.

When a tree is unextendible, like the one above, the corresponding derivation in Dst continues for a few lines after the tree ends. On closed trees, again like the one above, (PC) is repeatedly applied to derive ⊥ outside the scope of the various (PC) subderivations. The derivation exhibited earlier, for example, continues as follows:

1.	[A → (B & C)] & [~(A → B) ∨ ~(A → C)]	given
2.	A → (B & C)	1 (&E)
3.	~(A → B) ∨ ~(A → C)	1 (&E)
4.	~A ∨ (B & C)	2 (Impl)
5.	~(A → B) ~(A → C)	A/3 (PC)
6.	A A	5 ~→
7.	~B ~C	5 ~→
8.	~A ∣ B & C ~A ∣ B & C	A/4 (PC)
9.	⊥ ⊥	6,8 (⊥I)
10.	B B	8 (&E)
11.	C C	8 (&E)
12.	⊥	10,7 (⊥I)
13.	⊥	11,7 (⊥I)
14.	⊥	**4,8–9,8–13 (PC)**
15.	⊥	**4,8–9,8–12 (PC)**
16.	⊥	**3,5–15,5–14 (PC)**

Over lines 14–16, (PC) is repeatedly applied to derive ⊥ under the givens, thus completing the derivation. Where there are multiple paths on a tree, and consequently multiple (PC) subderivations nested inside of one another, providing justifications can be a confusing operation unless (A/PC) assumptions are notated with the line number of the disjunction that the subderivations are based on.

The opening and closing lines are slightly different for trees that are used to prove derivability and interderivability.

When a closed tree for ~P is used to establish that P is a theorem, the corresponding derivation begins by entering ~P as an assumption for (IP). It closes by applying (PC) only as far as necessary to derive ⊥ under ~P and then ends by deriving P by (IP).

Consider the conversion of the tree that is used to demonstrate that the principle of immunity, [(A ∨ B) ∨ ⊥] → (A ∨ B), is a theorem:

1.	~([(A ∨ B) ∨ ⊥] → (A ∨ B))✓	1.	~([(A ∨ B) ∨ ⊥] → (A ∨ B)) (A/IP)
2.	(A ∨ B) ∨ ⊥✓	2.	(A ∨ B) ∨ ⊥ 1 (~→)
3.	~(A ∨ B)✓	3.	~(A ∨ B) 1 (~→)
4.	~A	4.	~A 3 (~∨)
5.	~B	5.	~B 3 (~∨)
6.	A ∨ B✓ ⊥	6.	A ∨ B ⊥ (A/2PC)
7.	A B	7.	A ∣ B (A/6PC)
8.	⊥ ⊥	8.	⊥ ∣ ⊥ 7,4/5 (⊥I)
		9.	⊥ 6,7–8,7–8 (PC)
		10.	⊥ 2,6–9,6–6 (PC)
		11.	[(A ∨ B) ∨ ⊥] → (A ∨ B) 1–10 (IP)

Establishing that (A ∨ B) ∨ ⊥ ⊢ A ∨ B is a minor variant on this procedure. In that case, the derivation would start on line 2 (line 1 would not exist), (A ∨ B) ∨ ⊥ would have been entered as given, immediately to the right of the leftmost assumption bracket, and the negation of the consequent, ~(A ∨ B), would have been entered on the following line as an assumption for (IP). The rest of the derivation proceeds as laid out above.

Left derivation:

2.	(A ∨ B) ∨ ⊥ ✓	given
3.	~(A ∨ B) ✓	given
4.	~A	3 (~∨)
5.	~B	3 (~∨)
6.	A ∨ B ✓ ⊥	2 (TV)
7.	A B	6 (TV)
8.	⊥ ⊥	7,4/5 (⊥I)

Right derivation:

2.	(A ∨ B) ∨ ⊥	**given**
3.	~(A ∨ B)	**(A/IP)**
4.	~A	3 (~∨)
5.	~B	3 (~∨)
6.	A ∨ B ⊥	(A/2PC)
7.	A B	(A/6PC)
8.	⊥ ⊥	7,4/5 (⊥I)
9.	⊥	6,7–8,7–8 (PC)
10.	⊥	2,6–9,6–6 (PC)
11.	[(A ∨ B) ∨ ⊥] → (A ∨ B)	1–10 (IP)

To establish that (A ∨ B) ∨ ⊥ and A ∨ B are interderivable, the conversion just given would be the first of two. The second would begin with A ∨ B as given and enter ~[(A ∨ B) ∨ ⊥] as an assumption for (IP) and follow the corresponding tree from there.

Exercise A-3.5

Convert all the closed trees obtained in solutions to answered exercises in chapter 7 into derivations.

Answers for 7.5#1*a, *g; #2*a, *g; #3*c

The concluding lines for derivations that correspond to trees with exhausted paths are more involved. Under each subderivation that does not yield ⊥, (&I) is applied to derive the iterated conjunction of the literals occurring in that subderivation, in alphanumeric order. In many cases, this produces a variety of different results. Some subderivations end with ⊥, others end with iterated conjunctions, and those that end with iterated conjunctions end with different iterated conjunctions. This frustrates any application of (PC). The difficulty can be overcome by using (∨I) to wedge the results derived under any one subderivation onto the results derived under its parallel partner. Iterated applications of this procedure make it possible to derive an iterated disjunction of the results of all the (PC) subderivations under the givens.

By way of illustration consider an sd-tree for {~(A ≡ B), ~(~B & C)}.

1.	~(A ≡ B) ✓	given
2.	~(~B & C) ✓	given
3.	(A & ~B) ∨ (B & ~A) ✓	1 (~≡)
4.	~~B ∨ ~C ✓	2 (~&)
5.	A & ~B ✓ B & ~A ✓	3 (TV)
6.	A B	5 (T&)
7.	~B ~A	5 (T&)
8.	~~B ~C ~~B ~C	4 (TV)
9.	B e B e	8 (DN)
10.	⊥ e	9,7 (⊥I)

Whereas an s-tree would be finished as of line 8, with two exhausted paths, all paths of the sd-tree must be finished. The corresponding derivation in Dst is:

1.	~(A ≡ B)	given
2.	~(~B & C)	given
3.	(A & ~B) ∨ (B & ~A)	1 (~≡)
4.	~~B ∨ C	2 (~&)
5.	A & ~B B & ~A	(A/3PC)
6.	A B	5 (&E)
7.	~B ~A	5 (&E)
8.	~~B ~C ~~B ~C	(A/4PC)
9.	B B	8 (DN)
10.	⊥	9,7 (⊥I)

The derivation continues beyond this point to use (&I), (∨I), and (PC) in cycles to derive an iterated disjunction of all the results under the givens.

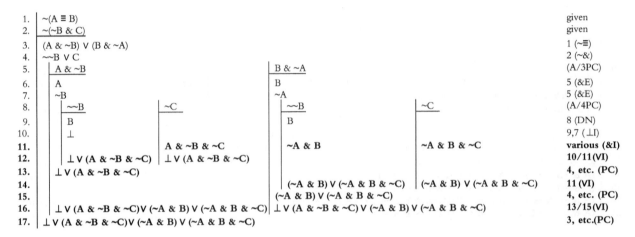

At line 11, (&I) is used to derive the iterated conjunction of all the reiterable literals in each of the (PC) subderivations that do not yield ⊥. (⊥ is infectious in iterated conjunctions in the sense that for any iterated conjunction, P_1 & ... & P_n & ⊥, P_1 & ... & P_n & ⊥ ⊢ ⊥, so there is no point to conjoining literals that will only be removed by subsequent applications of (inf).) At lines 12 and 14, results obtained in parallel subderivations are wedged onto one another. At lines 13 and 15, (PC) is applied to derive the results obtained from the lower-level (PC) subderivations. Results obtained under the higher-level subderivations are then wedged onto one another at line 16, and a final application of (PC) derives that combined result under the givens.

There were four paths at the bottom of the tree, and there are four corresponding disjuncts in the iterated disjunction that is ultimately derived under the givens, each of them representing what that subderivation yielded: either ⊥, or an iterated conjunction of reiterable literals.

The resulting iterated disjunction is what is called an "imperfect" dnf. In an imperfect dnf, some disjuncts may be repeated, others may be ⊥ (⊥ will only appear in a perfect dnf if it is the entire dnf), and yet others may lack sentence letters that appear elsewhere.

Turning an imperfect dnf into a perfect dnf requires a further modification to Dst. The use of five of the substitution principles introduced in chapter 6.5.3 must be allowed.

idempotence (idem): P ∨ P −|− P
(repeat occurrences of the same disjunct drop out of an iterated disjunction)

elaboration (elab): P −|− (P & Q) ∨ (P & ~Q)
(if a sentence letter is missing from an iterated conjunction it can be added in this way, where P
is the iterated conjunction and Q is the missing sentence letter)

immunity (imm): P ∨ ⊥ −|− P
(⊥ drops out of any iterated disjunction that contains it)

commutation (comm): P & Q −|− Q & P *and* P ∨ Q −|− Q ∨ P
(*sentence letters in iterated conjunctions can be placed in alphanumeric order;*
disjuncts in iterated disjunctions can be placed in long table order)

association (assoc): P & (Q & R) −|− (P & Q) & R
(*iterated conjunctions may be punctuated in any way*)

The association principle legitimates omitting internal punctuation in iterated conjunctions. (This has already been done to facilitate readability of the derivation given above.)

Application of these principles completes the derivation started earlier.

1.	~(A ≡ B)	given
2.	~(~B & C)	given
3.	(A & ~B) ∨ (B & ~A)	1 (~≡)
4.	~~B ∨ C	2 (~&)
5.	A & ~B / B & ~A	(A/3PC)
6.	A / B	5 (&E)
7.	~B / ~A	5 (&E)
8.	~~B / ~C / ~~B / ~C	(A/4PC)
9.	B / B	8 (DN)
10.	⊥	9,7 (⊥I)
11.	A & ~B & ~C / ~A & B / ~A & B & ~C	various (&I)
12.	⊥ ∨ (A & ~B & ~C) / ⊥ ∨ (A & ~B & ~C)	10 / 11 (VI)
13.	⊥ ∨ (A & ~B & ~C)	4, etc. (PC)
14.	(~A & B) ∨ (~A & B & ~C) / (~A & B) ∨ (~A & B & ~C)	11 (VI)
15.	(~A & B) ∨ (~A & B & ~C)	4, etc. (PC)
16.	⊥ ∨ (A & ~B & ~C) ∨ (~A & B) ∨ (~A & B & ~C) / ⊥ ∨ (A & ~B & ~C) ∨ (~A & B) ∨ (~A & B & ~C)	13 / 15 (VI)
17.	⊥ ∨ (A & ~B & ~C) ∨ (~A & B) ∨ (~A & B & ~C)	3, etc. (PC)
18.	**(A & ~B & ~C) ∨ (~A & B) ∨ (~A & B & ~C) ∨ ⊥**	**17 (comm)**
19.	**(A & ~B & ~C) ∨ (~A & B) ∨ (~A & B & ~C)**	**18 (imm)**
20.	**(A & ~B & ~C) ∨ (~A & B & C) ∨ (~A & B & ~C) ∨ (~A & B & ~C)**	**19 (elab)**
21.	**(A & ~B & ~C) ∨ (~A & B & C) ∨ (~A & B & ~C)**	**20 (idem)**

Line 21 is a perfect dnf: there are no occurrences of ⊥, each disjunct contains each sentence letter to occur in any other disjunct, and the literals in each disjunct are in alphanumeric order. The disjuncts are also in long table order (that is, the interpretations they describe are listed in the order they would be listed from the top down on a long table).

As a long table will show, each disjunct describes an interpretation on which the givens on lines 1 and 2 are true, and there are no other interpretations that do that.

Knowing how to convert trees to derivations can be of use in discovering derivations. But the main lessons to be drawn from the affinity between Ts and Ds are theoretical. In section A-3.1, Ts was shown to be sound, in the sense that whenever it says that a set, Γ, is s-unsatisfiable (by producing a closed tree), Γ does not have an s-model.

If Γ is inconsistent in Ts, then Γ is s-unsatisfiable.

In section A-3.2, it was also shown to be complete, in the sense that it never fails to identify an s-unsatisfiable set.

If Γ is s-unsatisfiable, then Γ is inconsistent in Ts.

A similar pair of claims was shown in chapter A-2 to hold of Ds, except that the primary focus of Ds is establishing derivability.

Soundness: If L ⊢ P, then Γ_L ⊨ P, where Γ_L contains the sentences on L.

Completeness: if Γ ⊨ P, then L ⊢ P, where L is a finite list of the sentences in Γ.

Soundness is a matter of what the rules of Ds will *not* allow it to do (they will not allow it to derive anything that is not s-entailed). It therefore depends on what the rules of Ds are, and as those rules are different from the rules of Ts, Ts is irrelevant to establishing the soundness of Ds.

In contrast, completeness is a matter of what the rules of Ds *will* allow it to do (they will allow it to derive anything that is s-entailed). Since Ts is complete, if $\Gamma \models P$, that is, if $\Gamma \cup \sim P$ is s-unsatisfiable, then $\Gamma \cup \sim P$ is inconsistent in Ts, that is, it has a closed tree. Since it has just been shown that any closed tree for $\Gamma \cup \sim P$ can be converted into a derivation of P from Γ, it follows that the completeness of Ts can be used to establish the completeness of Ds. Somewhat more rigorously:

1. Suppose for purposes of conditional proof that $\Gamma \models P$.
2. By compactness, at least one finite subset, Γ', of sentences in Γ s-entails P.
3. By def $\models$, there is no interpretation on which each sentence in Γ' is T and P is F, which means that $\Gamma' \cup \sim P$ is s-unsatisfiable.
4. By completeness of Ts, $\Gamma' \cup \sim P$ is inconsistent in Ts (it has at least one closed tree).
5. Any closed tree for a finite set, Γ, can be converted into a derivation of $\bot$ from L in Ds, where L is any list of each of the sentences in Γ.
6. From lines 4 and 5, L, $\sim P \vdash \bot$ in Ds, where L is any list of each of the sentences in Γ'.
7. By (IP), $L \vdash P$.
8. By conditional proof, if $\Gamma \models P$, then $L \vdash P$ where L is a finite list of the sentences in Γ.

The possibility of converting trees to derivations also establishes the decidability of Ds. Since any tree for any finite set of sentences can be turned into an unextendible tree after a finite number of one-step applications, any tree for the corresponding set for any derivation of a conclusion from a finite list of premises can likewise be turned into an unextendible tree after a finite number of one-step applications. Since any such tree can be converted into a derivation, there is a way of applying the rules of Ds to determine, in a finite number of lines, whether a conclusion is derivable from a finite list of premises or not. If it is, the corresponding derivation will yield the conclusion; if it is not, the corresponding derivation will yield the dnf of the iterated conjunction of the premises and the negation of the conclusion.

Tree conversions reciprocally make it possible to establish the soundness of Ts by appeal to the soundness of Ds.

1. Suppose for purposes of conditional proof that Γ is inconsistent in Ts.
2. By definition, Γ has at least one closed tree.
3. By definition, Γ has at least one tree that yields $\bot$ on each path, which means that tree does not have an infinitely extendible path. Accordingly, only a finite subset, Γ', of the sentences in Γ heads off the tree.
4. Any closed tree for a finite set, Δ, can be converted into a derivation of $\bot$ from L in Ds, where L is any list of each of the sentences in Δ.
5. From lines 3 and 4, $L \vdash \bot$ in Ds, where L is a finite list of the sentences in Γ'.
6. By soundness of Ds, $\Gamma' \models \bot$.
7. By exercise 5.12b, $\Gamma \models \bot$.
8. By exercise 5.11#2a Γ is s-unsatisfiable.
9. From lines 1–7 by conditional proof, if Γ is inconsistent in Ts, it is s-unsatisfiable.

These relations hold in any system where tree conversions are possible. In subsequent chapters they are exploited to obviate the need to provide further demonstrations of the soundness of trees or the completeness of derivations.

Part II

Modal Sentential Logic

8 Vocabulary, Syntax, Formalization, and Derivations

Contents

Modal logic is the logic of intensional contexts. It is sometimes referred to as "intensional logic" or "contextual logic," but as of the time of writing those titles have not gained currency. The more popular label, "modal" describes an older conception of the subject. On that conception, modal logic is the logic of "modes of assertion" or of ways in which an assertion can be "modified." Classical sentential logic recognizes only one way in which an assertion can be modified: by being denied. But there are other modifications. Traditionally, "it is possible that" and "it is necessary that" have captured the most attention, but the list includes "it is always the case that," "it is sometimes the case that," "it is everywhere the case that," "it is somewhere the case that," "it is obligatory that," "it is permissible that," "it is known/believed/doubted/said that," "it is hoped/feared/anticipated that," and so on.

According to the more recent conception, modal logic is the logic of those contexts in which extensionality fails. These are called "intensional" contexts, by way of contrast with "extensional." Extensionality is the property of invariance in meaning under substitution of parts that have the same meaning. For example, if "Cicero" names the same person as "Tully," then replacing "Cicero" with "Tully" in the sentence "Cicero wrote *de Officiis*" is replacing one part of a sentence with another part that has the same meaning. In this case, the substitution produces a sentence with the same meaning as the original, so extensionality holds. It likewise holds in the case of "It is not the case that Cicero wrote *de Officiis*." But there are contexts in which it does not hold. Replacing "Cicero" with "Tully" in "It is widely known that Cicero wrote *de Officiis*" is an example, and it is an example even granting the truth of "Cicero is Tully."

Classical sentential logic ignores the fact that there are contexts in which extensionality fails. In classical sentential logic, sentences are considered to have exactly one of two values, paradigmatically, "true" and "false." But a sentence like "it is raining" may be true in one place at one time and false in another place at another time. Someone may know, believe, or doubt that it is raining in a place at a time, or hope or fear that it is, or think that it could or could not, or (perhaps metaphorically) ought or ought not to be doing so, while someone else might not share these attitudes. When "it is raining" is formalized in SL, the influence of these contexts on the value of the sentence is not considered, even though changes in the context can change that value. This chapter introduces some of the ways in which SL might be extended to capture the influence of contexts on the value of sentences. As a group, the extensions are referred to as comprising modal sentential logic, or MSL.

DOI: 10.4324/9781003026532-13

In this chapter, affirming across contexts and limiting to at least one are formalized by supplementing SL with two further symbols, the box, □, and the diamond, ◇. (For purposes of work at the keyboard, □ can be replaced with facing square brackets ([ ]) and ◇ with facing angle brackets (<>)).

□ is called the strong modal operator and ◇ the weak modal operator. Semantically, □ strengthens an assertion by extending it over all relevant contexts. ◇ weakens it by limiting it to at least one relevant context. For example, if the contexts under consideration are times, □ might extend an assertion over all times (e.g., "It is always raining") and ◇ limit it to some times (e.g., "It sometimes rains.") If the context under consideration is what is morally acceptable, □ is used to say that an action is obligatory (that it ought to occur in all relevant contexts) and ◇ that it is permissible (that it may occur in a relevant context). If the context under consideration is what is true, □ is used to say that something not only is true in the current context, but is true in all relevant contexts, whereas ◇ is used to say that something is true in at least one relevant context, even if not the current one. Syntactically, □ and ◇ function in the same way as the tilde, but, for reasons explored in chapter 9, they do not create a compound that has a value that is a function of the values of its components. They are called operators rather than connectives.

8.1 Vocabulary and Syntax

The following statement of the vocabulary and syntax of MSL highlights new elements for ease of comparison with the statement of the vocabulary and syntax of SL found in chapter 2. As well as adding □ and ◇ and making the requisite changes to accommodate them, the syntax for MSL takes a lesson from the associativity principles demonstrated in chapter 5. Since P & (Q & R) and (P & Q) & R are s-equivalent, and since the same holds for P ∨ (Q ∨ R) and (P ∨ Q) ∨ R, MSL syntax allows the omission of internal punctuation in iterated conjunctions and iterated disjunctions. The informal notational convention applied for this purpose is called (ip) for "internal punctuation."

Punctuation is informally loosened up in another way as well. According to a new informal notational convention, → and ≡ outrank & and ∨. The convention for this is called (sc) for "strong conditionals." → and ≡ have default scope over & or ∨, unless punctuation indicates otherwise. Thus, A & B → C should be read as (A & B) → C. Punctuation remains necessary to define the scope of → relative to ≡ and of & relative to ∨. It is also necessary to extend the scope of & or ∨ over → or ≡. The effect of both changes is to reduce what can become a forest of punctuation marks. However, in simpler contexts, past practices will often be retained.

Vocabulary of MSL

Sentence letters:	A, B, C, G, H, K, $A_1, A_2, A_3, \ldots$
Contradiction symbol:	⊥
Operators:	~, &, ∨, →, ≡, □, ◇
Punctuation marks:	), (

Syntax of MSL

An *expression* is any vocabulary element or sequence of vocabulary elements.

A *sentence* is any expression formed in accord with the following rules:

(SL):	If P is ⊥ or a sentence letter then P is a sentence.
(uo):	If P is a sentence, then **~P, □P, and ◇P are** sentences.
(bc):	If P and Q are two (not necessarily distinct) sentences, then (P & Q), (P ∨ Q), (P → Q), and (P ≡ Q) are sentences.
(exclusion):	Nothing is a sentence unless it has been formed by one or more applications of the preceding rules.

Scope

When a ***unary operator*** (~,□, or ◇) is followed by an atomic sentence (⊥ or a sentence letter), its scope is that atomic sentence.

When a **unary operator** is followed by an opening punctuation mark, its scope extends to the corresponding closing punctuation mark.

When a **unary operator** is followed by another unary operator, its scope is that other unary operator plus that other unary operator's scope.

The scope of a *binary operator* (&, ∨, →, or ≡) begins and ends with the punctuation marks used in conjunction with that operator but excludes that operator.

In MSL, as in SL, punctuation marks never appear unless there is a binary operator between the two punctuation marks. Even though there are three different unary operators, punctuation is not required to determine their scope. When multiple unary operators are lined up at the start of a sentence, the leftmost is always the main operator, the next to the right is the main operator of the immediate component, the next the main operator of the immediate component of the immediate component, and so on. When punctuation intervenes on a list of unary operators, it always belongs to a binary connective occurring further to the right.

Named Forms

- ~, &, ∨, →, and ≡ are *connectives*.
- **□ and ◇ are *modal operators*.**
- The *main operator* of a sentence is the **operator** that has scope over all the other parts of the sentence (each sentence can have at most one main operator).
- The *immediate components* of a sentence are the sentences that remain after the main **operator** and its associated punctuation, if any, have been removed from the sentence.
- A sentence that has no main **operator** is an *atomic sentence*. Atomic sentences have no immediate components. In particular:
  - ⊥ is an atomic sentence.
  - each sentence letter is an atomic sentence.
- A sentence with ~ as its main **operator** is a *negation*. Negations have the form ~P, where P is the immediate component of the negation. The immediate component of a negation is its *nullation*.
- The atomic sentences and the negations of atomic sentences are *literals*.
- A sentence with & as its main **operator** is a *conjunction*. Conjunctions have the form (P & Q), where P and Q are the immediate components of the conjunction. The immediate components of a conjunction are its *conjuncts*.
- A sentence with ∨ as its main **operator** is a *disjunction*. Disjunctions have the form (P ∨ Q), where P and Q are the immediate components of the disjunction. The immediate components of a disjunction are its *disjuncts*.
- A sentence with → as its main **operator** is a *conditional*. Conditionals have the form (P → Q), where P and Q are the immediate components of the conditional. The left immediate component is the *antecedent* of the conditional, and the right immediate component is the *consequent*.
- A sentence with ≡ as its main **operator** is a *biconditional*. Biconditionals have the form (P ≡ Q), where P and Q are the immediate components of the biconditional.
- **A sentence with □ as its main operator is a *box sentence*. Box sentences have the form □P, where P is the immediate component of the box sentence.**
- **A sentence with ◇ as its main operator is a *diamond sentence*. Diamond sentences have the form ◇P, where P is the immediate component of the diamond sentence.**
- Each sentence is a *component* of itself, as are its immediate components (if any), the components of those immediate components (if any), and so on down to *atomic components* (these are ⊥ and the sentence letters).

Definitions of sameness, contradiction, opposition, converse, inverse, and contrapositive are unchanged from SL.

Informal notational conventions:
(when building sentences, conventions should be applied in the order listed)

    (b) Brackets may be substituted for parentheses.

    (ip) **Punctuation may be omitted around conjunctions that are conjuncts of conjunctions and disjunctions that are disjuncts of disjunctions.**

    (sc) **Punctuation used to extend the scope of → or ≡ over & or ∨ may be omitted.**

    (op) Outermost parentheses may be coloured out (they are still there).

Exercise 8.1

1. *State which of the following are sentences of MSL. Provide a syntactic tree (see section 2.3) for those that are. Explain why those that are not violate the formation rules.*

    ★**a.** ◇(□A)
    b. □A◇B
    ★**c.** ◇~B
    d. □◇□A
    ★**e.** □[◇(□A)]
    f. □~◇A
    ★**g.** □□□A
    h. □A◇
    ★**i.** A → □B
    j. □A → B
    ★**k.** □(A → B)
    l. □(~A → ~◇B)
    ★**m.** □~(A → ~◇B)
    n. □[~(A → ~◇B)]

2. *State which of the following are sentences of MSL. Explain why those that are not violate the formation rules and conventions. Provide a syntactic tree (see section 2.3) for those that are. Be careful to apply informal notational conventions in the order listed above.*

    ★**a.** A & B → C
    b. A → B ∨ C
    ★**c.** A & B & C ≡ G
    d. A ∨ B → C & G & H
    ★**e.** A ∨ B & C ≡ G
    f. A → B ∨ C ≡ G
    ★**g.** A ∨ B ∨ C → G → H ∨ K
    h. A ∨ B ∨ (C → G) → H ∨ K

3. *Rewrite the following sentences, circling (paper submission) or reddening (electronic submission) any unnecessary punctuation. Some questions may not contain any unnecessary punctuation.*

    ★**a.** [(A → B) ∨ ~(C ∨ G)]
    b. ~(A → [B ∨ (~C ∨ G)])
    ★**c.** (A ∨ [(B ∨ C) → (G → H)])
    d. ([A ∨ (B ∨ C)] → (G ∨ H))
    ★**e.** [([(A & B) ∨ C] ∨ G) & (H → K)]
    f. [([(A & B) & (C ∨ G)] & H) → K]

8.2 Formalization

□ permits formalizing discourse about what is the case in all relevant contexts. It is always so, but need not be logically necessary, in virtue of the law of noncontradiction. Examples are occurrences that are necessitated by laws of nature, claims made about what (brute factually) always was or always will be the case, or claims made about what people are legally obliged to do. In contrast, ◇ allows formalizing discourse about what is the case in at least one relevant context, though it need not be the current context. Examples are claims about human capabilities, legally permissible alternatives, and chance occurrences.

To revert to a classical conception of modal logic for purposes of comparison, being outfitted with □ and ◇ allows MSL to formalize four modes of assertion, in contrast to the two recognized by SL:

$$\Box A \quad - \text{ necessarily A}$$
$$A \quad - A$$
$$\Diamond A \quad - \text{ possibly/permissibly A}$$
$$\sim A \quad - \text{ not A}$$

Further combining these assertions with tilde captures expressions like:

Not necessarily A ($\sim\Box A$),
Possibly not A ($\Diamond\sim A$),
Not possibly A ($\sim\Diamond A$), and
Necessarily not A ($\Box\sim A$)

"Not necessarily A" is intuitively equivalent to "possibly not A," and "not possibly A" to "necessarily not A." The equivalence reduces these four combinations to two. Combining these two mixed modes with the original four produces a fuller hierarchy of modal assertions:

$$\Box A \quad - \text{ necessarily A}$$
$$A \quad - A$$
$$\Diamond\sim A \quad - \text{ possibly not A}$$
$$\Diamond A \quad - \text{ possibly/permissibly A}$$
$$\sim A \quad - \text{ not A}$$
$$\Box\sim A \quad - \text{ necessarily not A}$$

When ◇A and ◇~A are conjoined, in ◇A & ◇~A, the resulting sentence says that it is both the case that A is possible and the case that not-A is possible. This is tantamount to saying that A is contingent in a new sense of that term. The contingency is not just logical contingency, defined as there being no contradiction in the affirmation of a sentence and no contradiction in its denial. It is contingency that arises from some more robust sense of possibility, such as physical possibility or moral permissibility.

A & ◇~A says that A is the case, but need not be the case. It might be true in some special context but false in others, or done but not obligatory, or something that did happen but that need not always happen, or that exists at one place but not at another, and so on. ~A & ◇A similarly says that A is not the case, but could be.

When two different sentences are brought under a diamond operator, as in ◇(A & B), the resulting sentence expresses the thought that the two could coexist or coincide or co-occur or both be true or permissible. Otherwise put, they are compatible with one another. One or both may not be the case, but it is possible that both could be.

Modal operators can also be combined with one another to form such expressions as:

Possibly necessarily A ($\Diamond\Box A$)
Necessarily possibly A ($\Box\Diamond A$)
Necessarily necessarily A ($\Box\Box A$)
Possibly possibly A ($\Diamond\Diamond A$)

These iterated modes might seem redundant. From a certain point of view, saying that something is necessarily necessary adds nothing to saying that it is necessary. And saying that something is possibly necessary seems nonsensical, because if the necessity is merely possible, it is just a possibility and not a necessity. Similar concerns might be raised with saying that something is possibly possible or necessarily possible. But anyone who holds that laws, be they laws of nature or laws of posited legal systems, could have been otherwise will consider it to be meaningful to say that what is necessitated by a law is only possibly necessitated, or to recognize that there are some things that are not up for revision and so not only possibly necessitated but necessarily necessitated.

Formalization of iterated modal operators or modal operators mixed with connectives generally conforms with English syntax. English will state the main operator first, and will use punctuation or expressions like "If ... then," "either ... or," "neither ... nor," and "not both ... and" to indicate scope. For example:

8.1.1   "Ought" implies "can," but it does not imply "is"
8.1.2 $(\Box P \rightarrow \Diamond P)$ & $\sim(\Box P \rightarrow P)$

8.2.1   What must be is and what is, is possible
8.2.2 $(\Box P \rightarrow P)$ & $(P \rightarrow \Diamond P)$

8.3.1   Just because it happened that doesn't make it acceptable
        (It is not the case that if it happens then it is permissible)
8.3.2 $\sim(P \rightarrow \Diamond P)$

8.4.1   Just because it happened that doesn't mean it ought to be permitted
8.4.2 $\sim(P \rightarrow \Box\Diamond P)$

8.5.1   If it is raining, it is necessarily possible that it is raining
8.5.2 $P \rightarrow \Box\Diamond P$

8.6.1   If it is possible that it is raining then it is necessarily possible that the corners are slippery
8.6.2 $\Diamond P \rightarrow \Box\Diamond Q$

8.7.1   Necessarily, if it is raining then it is possible that the corners are slippery
8.7.2 $\Box(P \rightarrow \Diamond Q)$

These examples are more than merely illustrative. They use metavariables, rather than sentence letters to show, in passing, that our intuitions about one and the same form vary depending on whether $\Box$ and $\Diamond$ are read as referring to necessary and possible truth or to what is morally necessary (obligatory) or permitted. We intuitively accept that if something is necessarily true then it must be true as a matter of fact, and that if something is in fact true then it must be possibly true, that is, that $\Box P \rightarrow P$ and $P \rightarrow \Diamond P$. But we do not think that everything that ought to happen does happen (the world is not morally perfect), or that just because something does happen that makes it permissible. We deny $\Box P \rightarrow P$ and $P \rightarrow \Diamond P$ when $\Box$ and $\Diamond$ are read as referring to what is obligatory and permitted, but affirm them when $\Box$ and $\Diamond$ are read as referring to necessary and possible truth. Again, we intuitively accept that if something is the case, then it is necessarily possible that it be the case, so $P \rightarrow \Box\Diamond P$, but we deny that whatever happens ought to be permitted, and so deny $P \rightarrow \Box\Diamond P$ when $\Box$ and $\Diamond$ are taken to refer to obligation and permission.

As these examples illustrate, it makes a difference whether $\Box$ and $\Diamond$ are used to formalize "ought" and "can," respectively, and whether they are used to formalize necessary truth and possible truth, respectively, and the same might be said of other ways of reading the modal operators, like "always" and "everywhere." Our intuitions about the modal validity (or "m-validity") of same forms differ depending on which reading we adopt. This means that different derivation rules and a different semantics are required for different readings of $\Box$ and $\Diamond$, even though the symbols are the same. The one that deals with the obligatory and the permissible is called deontic modal logic. The one that deals with necessary and possible truth is called alethic modal logic. As far as syntax and formalization are concerned, the various systems can be considered together. But they must be separated when considering derivations, trees, and semantics.

When deontic and alethic modal logic are used in the same context, it is common to resolve the ambiguity by using bold **O** and **P** to stand for "obligatory" and "permissible" and reserve $\Box$ and $\Diamond$ for "necessarily true" and "possibly true."

The slippery corner statements formalized earlier suggest that modal operators might be used to formalize causal sentences. Part of what modal logic aims to do is formalize other kinds of necessity than strictly logical necessity (defined as what cannot be denied on pain of contradiction). Physical necessity, as codified in causal laws, is a prime candidate for a nonlogical form of necessity. Historically, thought about causality drove the development of modal logic. One of the pioneers of modal logic, C.I. Lewis (1883–1964), formalized causal sentences in a way that corresponds to $\Box(P \rightarrow Q)$, and proposed different ways of understanding the implications of modal statements, two of which, systems 4 and 5, continue to be widely discussed.

The formalization of causal claims poses some challenges. English is not careful about distinguishing between cases where a necessary condition is being placed on a result and cases where the connection between the condition and the result is affirmed to be one that holds of necessity. Necessary *conditions* are formalized as the consequents of arrow sentences (section 4.2). Necessary *connections* are formalized by boxing a sentence that places the (causal) condition in the antecedent position. English is not of much help here, because it likes to attach the necessity operator to the inflection rather than the sentence. This makes it look like the necessity operator is being attached to the consequent. The following sentence is straightforward,

> 8.8.1   Necessarily, if it is raining then the corners are slippery
>
> 8.8.2 $\Box(A \to B)$

But English does not like to put it this way. English will say,

> 8.9   If it is raining the corners must be slippery

which looks very much like

> 8.10   If you are to be admitted, then you must pay the fee

The intention in 8.9 to attach "must" to the connective, which is hard to do because, as explained in section 4.1, English does not use a connective for conditionals but instead inflects conditions. So, 8.9 ends up looking more like a promise or a rule that places a necessary condition on a result than a causal claim. Because "must" occurs inside the sentence the temptation is to formalize 8.9 as either

> 8.11 $A \to \Box B$

or simply as

> 8.12 $A \to B$

Either formalization would be acceptable for 8.10. ($A \to \mathbf{O}B$ is even better, as the condition in this case clearly creates an obligation.) But 8.11 is not plausibly what is intended by 8.9. 8.11 says that if it is raining anywhere at any time, all corners everywhere must be slippery for eternity. And, interpreted as placing a necessary condition on a result, 8.12 formalizes "it is raining only if the corners are slippery," which is most likely not what the speaker intends.

Following the usual practice of interpreting ambiguous sentences in the way that is most likely for them to be true dictates that $\Box(A \to B)$ should be preferred, even though idiomatic English places the necessity operator inside the consequent. Fluent English speakers will have a sense that the "must" in "if it is raining the corners must be slippery" could be intended to attach either to the whole sentence or just to the consequent. And as $A \to \Box B$ says something that is more likely to be false, the principle of charity dictates the more modest formalization, $\Box(A \to B)$.

The situation with $\Box$ recalls a similar situation encountered in chapter 4.2 when discussing the formalization of sentences that negate necessary or sufficient conditions. English expressions of the form, "for A it is not necessary that B" and "for A it is not sufficient that B" are not formalized by negating the condition but by negating the entire conditional sentence. "For A it is not necessary that B" is formalized as $\sim(A \to B)$ rather than $A \to \sim B$ (which says that for A it is necessary that not B. Similarly, "for A it is not sufficient that B" is formalized as $\sim(B \to A)$ rather than $\sim B \to A$, which says that not-B is sufficient for A.

Exercise 8.2

1. *Formalize the following sentences in MSL. Provide an interpretation, specifying what sentence letters of MSL stand for what sentences of English. Do not use a sentence letter to stand for a sentence that contains a modal operator.*
   - ⋆**a.** Though pigs do not have wings, they could have.
   - b. Though roses are red, they are not necessarily red.
   - ⋆**c.** It is necessary that tomorrow it shall rain or not rain.
   - d. If it be not necessary it shall rain, it is necessary it shall not rain.

*e. Though pigs do not have wings, if they did, that would be compatible with them not being able to fly.

　f. If roses are red, then it is necessarily possible that they are red, possibly necessary that they are red, and possibly not necessary that they are red.

*g. If roses are contingently red, then, necessarily, they are possibly red; but if they are contingently red then it is not the case that they are necessarily possibly red.

　h. If oil is lighter than water, then oil must float on water.

*i. If oil is lighter than water then oil must float on water, but it is not the case that if it is lighter than water then it necessarily floats on water. *(Provide a formalization that is not inconsistent.)*

　j. If it is impossible that pigs have wings then they do not have wings and this is not merely contingently the case.

2. *Identify the English sentence being formalized by the following sentences of MSL, taking "A" to be "Roses are red,"* B *to be "Pigs have wings," and* C *to be "Pigs can fly."*

*a. [□A → A & ◇A] & ~[(◇A → A) ∨ (A → □A)]

　b. ~B & ◇B & A & ◇~A & ◇(A & B)

*c. □(B → C)

　d. ~◇B ≡ □~B

*e. (~◇B → ~B) & ~(~B → ~◇B)

　f. □(A → [□A ∨ (A & ◇~A)])

8.3 Derivations

Because our intuitions about the validity of modal sentences vary, no one system of derivation rules can accommodate all of them. This section opens with a basic system, called Dk.[1] That system is later extended to include three increasingly contentious modal principles, giving rise to systems called Dt, Ds4, and Ds5. Ds4 and Ds5 are named after "system 4" and "system 5," the last of five increasingly strong systems of modal logic codified by C.I. Lewis. The derivation rules presented here differ from the principles proposed by Lewis, but are equivalent in the sense that they establish the same results.

In what follows, the expression "Dm" is used to refer to any modal derivation system.

Dk includes all the rules of Ds, including the metatheorems and derived rules, but not the substitution principles. The rules, metatheorems, and derived rules of Ds are unchanged but for the fact that they are extended to include sentences of MSL. This means that the following is a correct derivation in Dk and all stronger systems.

1.	□B	given
2.	□A ≡ □B	given
3.	□A	2,1 (BMP)

But the following is not.

1.	□B	given	
2.	□ (A ≡ B)	given	
3.	□A	2,1 (BMP)	**✗ WRONG!**

(BMP) can only be applied to a biconditional. The sentence on line 2 is a box sentence.

Before any rules of Ds can be applied to box sentences, the boxes must be stripped off. Derivations in Dk use a new feature for this purpose: a boxed subderivation. The immediate components of box sentences are placed in a subderivation marked by a box rather than an assumption bracket. Derivations can proceed as normally done in Ds within the box, but work done within the box may only be justified by other sentences or subderivations located within the box. Further sentences can be assumed inside the box, along with their own assumption brackets, but any sentences not assumed can only be put there because they are the immediate components of box sentences or derived from sentences already in the box. Because the boxed subderivation functions as a special place where results are derived from the immediate components of box sentences, and box sentences state necessities, whatever is brought back out of the box is also necessary and must be boxed.

On this scheme, the derivation of □A from <□B, □(A ≡ B)> is:

1.	□B	given
2.	□(A ≡ B)	given
3.	B	1 (□RE)
4.	A ≡ B	2 (□RE)
5.	A	4,3 (BMP)
6.	□A	5 (□I)

Over lines 3–5 a special space is boxed off for work on the immediate components of the □ sentences on lines 1 and 2. Once that work has been completed, its result is brought out of the box and boxed, at line 6. The rules that allow the immediate components of box sentences to be put into boxes and results obtained in boxes to be taken back out of those boxes constitute the two main derivation rules of Dk. They are box sentence reduction, (□RE), and box sentence introduction, (□I). The rules use the following templates:

(□RE)		(□I)	
k. □P ?		k. ⌐P lemma	
... ...		... ...	
... ...		... ...	
n. P	k (□RE)	n. □P	k (□I)

The template makes it look like (□RE) creates a box, the way (A) creates an assumption bracket, but this is not the case. (□RE) is more like a reiteration rule than an assumption rule. Just as (R) can copy multiple different sentences into the same subderivation, so (□RE) can copy multiple different immediate components of box sentences into the same box, as seen in the derivation given above.

In Dk, boxes are created by bottom-up reasoning. When a box sentence needs to be derived, a box is created extending from the line just above that box sentence up to the lowest unoccupied line at the top of the derivation, and the immediate component of the box sentence being aimed for is entered as a lemma at the bottom of the box.

Exercise 8.3

1. *State whether each of the following is an instance of (□RE). If it is not, say why not.*

⋆a.
k. □A → B   ?
n. A → B   k (□RE)

b.
□A
k. □B   ?
A
n. B   k (□RE)

⋆c.
k. □A   ?
n. A   k (□RE)

d.
k. □□A   ?
n. A   k (□RE)

⋆e.
k. □□A   ?
n. □A   k (□RE)

f.
i. □□A   ?
k. □A   i (□RE)
⋆g n. A   k (□RE)

h.
k. □A   ?
n. □A   k (□RE)

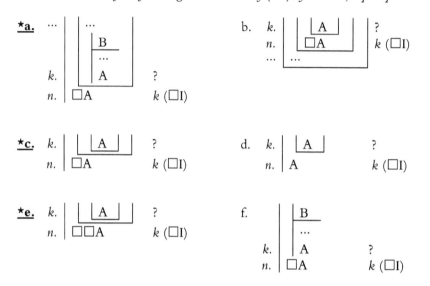

2. State whether each of the following is an instance of (□I). If it is not, say why not.

(□RE) and (□I) have so far only been depicted as templates, not stated as rules. The statement of the rules is given in terms of what lists yield what sentences, but a special embellishment is needed to represent boxed subderivations: A boxed subderivation represents the start of a new list. The rules for (□RE) and (□I) are accordingly:

$$
\begin{array}{ll}
(\Box \text{RE}): & \text{If } L \vdash \Box P, \text{ then } L, <\ > \vdash P \\
(\Box \text{I}): & \text{If } L, <\ > \vdash P, \text{ then } L \vdash \Box P
\end{array}
$$

(□RE) says that if a list yields a box sentence, then that list, supplemented by the empty list, yields the immediate component of that box sentence. This makes sense when it is considered that the immediate component of a box sentence is something like a theorem. It is true across multiple contexts, the way a theorem is true on all interpretations. A theorem is derivable from the empty list. Correspondingly, if a list yields a box sentence, that list followed by the empty list should yield the immediate component of that box sentence by (□RE), and if a list followed by the empty list yields the immediate component of a box sentence, the list should yield that box sentence by (□I).

The rules make it clear that □P is not *exactly* like a metatheorem. Unless L is itself empty, the P in the claim that L, < > ⊢ P is not derived from the empty list alone but from some other list followed by the empty list. □P only earns its box by being a consequence of this antecedent list, L. A theorem, in contrast, is not dependent on any antecedent list. But the analogy is close enough to underwrite the rules.

Stating the rules in this way makes it clear that derivations in Dk are not just derivations from lists of assumptions, but from lists of lists of assumptions. For each new box in standard notation, Dk starts a new list in bracket free notation. When (A) is applied to enter an assumption in a box, the corresponding list acquires that assumption as a new member. When (□I) is applied to take a sentence out of a box in standard notation, the corresponding empty list is removed from the end of the list of lists in bracket free notation. (The corresponding list must always be empty when (□I) is applied, as both the template and the rule make clear.)

The derivation done earlier would be written out as follows in bracket free notation:

1.	<□B>	⊢	□B	(A)
2.	<□B,□(A ≡ B)>	⊢	□(A ≡ B)	(A)
3.	<□B,□(A ≡ B)>	⊢	□B	1 (R)
4.	<□B,□(A ≡ B)>,< >	⊢	B	3 (□RE)
5.	<□B,□(A ≡ B)>,< >	⊢	A ≡ B	2 (□RE)
6.	<□B,□(A ≡ B)>,< >	⊢	A	4,5 (BMP)
7.	<□B,□(A ≡ B)>	⊢	□A	6 (□I)

Unfortunately, the clutter of angle brackets around lists can no longer be avoided, because derivations in Dk are no longer derivations from a single list of assumptions, and it needs to be clear where one list stops and another starts. Even though the added list at lines 4–6 is empty, it must still be written in to indicate that the sentence to the right of the turnstile is derived from a list supplemented by the empty list.

Considering the results of exercise 8.3 in light of the principled statement of the rules can further enhance the appreciation of what the rules allow, what they forbid, and why.

Exercise 8.4

Restate the inferences drawn in exercise 8.3 in bracket free notation. Explain why each exercise that fails to instantiate the form for the rule also violates the rule as stated in bracket free notation.

Answers for 8.3#**1b, d, f, h, j, l**; #**2b, d, f**

There is one merely apparent exception to the rule that only (i) assumptions, (ii) the immediate components of box sentences, and (iii) the sentences that can be derived from (i) or (ii) can be placed in boxed subderivations. Sometimes the immediate component of a box sentence is a negation, so the box sentence has the form □~P. Intuitively, "necessarily not P" means the same thing as "not possibly P." A tilde diamond sentence is a box tilde sentence in disguise. So (□RE) and (□I) can be reformulated as follows:

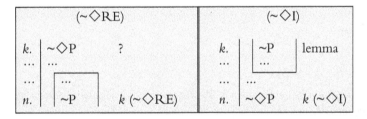

In the template on the right, it would have been equally legitimate to derive □~P by (□I) at line *n*. When the sentence in the boxed subderivation is a negation, either (□I) or (~◇I) can be applied.

Exercise 8.5

Following the example of how this was done for (□RE) and (□I) formulate (~◇RE) and (~◇I) as rules specifying what sentences may be derived from what lists of lists of sentences.

The new rules for box and ~◇ sentences involve a restriction on (R). Up to now, reiteration has been transitive. Reiterating a sentence from a higher derivation into one of its immediate subderivations permits going on to reiterate it into any of that subderivation's subderivations. But boxes get in the way of doing that. Only (□RE) and (~◇RE) can be used to put sentences into boxes, and neither they nor (R) can be used to reiterate sentences into boxes. (□RE) and (~◇RE) *reduce;* they do not *reiterate.* They put the immediate components of □ and ~◇ sentences in the box. When a box is started, no sentence outside the box can be reiterated into it. Should a subderivation be started in the box, no sentence outside of the box can be reiterated into that subderivation. The following application of (R) is incorrect:

```
1. | A                  given
2. | □(A → B)           given
   |  ┌─────────┐
3. |  │ A → B   │       2 (□RE)
4. |  │ A       │       1 (R)        WRONG!
5. |  │ B       │       3,4 (MP)
   |  └─────────┘
```

Here is another version of the same mistake:

```
1. | □A                 given
2. | □(□A → B)          given
   |  ┌─────────┐
3. |  │ □A → B  │       2 (□RE)
4. |  │ □A      │       1 (R)        WRONG!
5. |  │ B       │       3,4 (MP)
   |  └─────────┘
```

If a sentence needed to justify a rule application within a box is not in that box, it must be put there by (□RE), (~◇RE) or one of the (A/) rules.

A revised rule statement of (R) for Dk makes this restriction explicit:

$$(R): \text{If } <L> \vdash P \text{ then } <L,\mathbf{Q_1,...,Q_n}> \vdash P$$

The angle brackets are important. $Q_1,...,Q_n$ follow the sentences on L on the same list, and that list must be the last list on a list of lists. If another list, even an empty list, intervenes between $<L>$ or $<L,Q_1...Q_n>$ and the turnstile, or any of $Q_1...Q_n$ fall on a different list, (R) cannot be used to derive P. Even though $<L,Q_1...Q_n> \vdash P$, $<<L,Q_1...Q_n>,< >>$ does not yield P by R.

With the rules so far discussed in hand, $\Box(P \to Q) \to (\Box P \to \Box Q)$ and $\Box P \to \Box\sim\sim P$ can be proven to be theorems of Dk. The first of these is an important basic theorem of Dk. It will be referred to again and so is given its own name: (k).

Exercise

Derive each of the following.

a. $\vdash \Box P \to \Box\sim\sim P$
b. $\vdash \Box(P \to Q) \to (\Box P \to \Box Q)$

In attempting these exercises, begin by applying the (CP) strategy as often as possible, just as with derivations in Ds. But do not finish by applying the (IP) strategy. Instead, use the following, new stage 3 strategy.

(□I) *strategy: when the aim is to derive* □P, *create a boxed subderivation and enter* P *as a lemma for* (□I) *on its last line.*

After an application of the (□I) *strategy, continue with a new supplement to the top-down strategy:*

Make all possible applications of (□RE). *Note: Only apply* (□RE) *to put sentences in a box that was previously created for some other reason. Do not create a box simply for the sake of applying* (□RE).

Try to apply these strategies to solve the exercises before reading further.

At the commencement of the first derivation, there is nothing on any initial line, so nothing can be done at stage 1.

```
... |  ...
20. | □P → □~~P    ?
```

Work commences with an application of the (CP) strategy.

```
1.  | | □P                    (A/CP)
... | |     ...
19. | | □~~P                  lemma for (CP)
20. | □P → □~~P               2–19 (CP)
```

After an application of a stage 2 strategy, work reverts to stage 1. But even though a sentence has been added to the head of the derivation, there is nothing that can be done from the top down. (□RE) should not be applied. There should be some other reason to create a boxed subderivation before (□RE) is used to populate it. In the absence of work to be done at stage 1, work proceeds to stage 2, the (CP)/(BP) stage. Since there is also nothing to be done at that stage, work proceeds to stage 3. An application of the new (□I) strategy produces:

```
1.  | | □P                    (A/CP)
... | |     ...
18. | |   ~~P                 lemma for (□I)
19. | | □~~P                  lemma for (CP)  18 (□I)
20. | □P → □~~P               2–19 (CP)
```

Now that a reason has been discovered for creating a boxed subderivation, work can continue from the top down.

```
1.  | | □P                    (A/CP)
2.  | |   P                   1 (□RE)
... | |     ...
18. | |   ~~P                 lemma for (□I)
19. | | □~~P                  lemma for (CP)  18 (□I)
20. | □P → □~~P               2–19 (CP)
```

Now the derivation can be completed with the derived rule, (DNI).

```
1.  | | □P                    (A/CP)
2.  | |   P                   1 (□RE)
... | |     ...
18. | |   ~~P                 lemma for (□I)  2 (DNI)
19. | | □~~P                  lemma for (CP)  18 (□I)
20. | □P → □~~P               2–19 (CP)
```

The derivation of (k) opens in the same way.

```
... |  ...                                        ...
20. | □(P → Q) → (□P → □Q)    ?
```

Since there is nothing to do at stage 1, work proceeds at stage 2. In this case, two successive applications of the (CP) strategy are possible.

```
1.  | | □(P → Q)              (A/CP)
2.  | |  | □P                 (A/CP)
... | |  |   ...                 ...
18. | |  | □Q                 lemma for (CP)
19. | |  □P → □Q              lemma for (CP)  2–18 (CP)
20. | □(P → Q) → (□P → □Q)    1–19 (CP)
```

Work now reverts to stage 1.

1.	$\Box(P \to Q)$	(A/CP)
2.	$\Box P$	(A/CP)
3.	$\Box(P \to Q)$	1 (R)
...	...	...
18.	$\Box Q$	lemma for (CP)
19.	$\Box P \to \Box Q$	lemma for (CP) 2–18 (CP)
20.	$\Box(P \to Q) \to (\Box P \to \Box Q)$	1–19 (CP)

At this point there is nothing more to do at stage 1, and there is also nothing to do at stage 2, so work proceeds at stage 3, where the ($\Box$I) strategy is applicable.

1.	$\Box(P \to Q)$	(A/CP)
2.	$\Box P$	(A/CP)
3.	$\Box(P \to Q)$	1 (R)
...	...	...
17.	Q	lemma for ($\Box$I)
18.	$\Box Q$	lemma for (CP) 17 ($\Box$I)
19.	$\Box P \to \Box Q$	lemma for (CP) 2–18 (CP)
20.	$\Box(P \to Q) \to (\Box P \to \Box Q)$	1–19 (CP)

After each application of a stage 3 strategy, work reverts to stage 1, and now applications of ($\Box$RE) are permissible.

1.	$\Box(P \to Q)$	(A/CP)
2.	$\Box P$	(A/CP)
3.	$\Box(P \to Q)$	1 (R)
4.	$P \to Q$	3 ($\Box$RE)
5.	P	2 ($\Box$RE)
...	...	...
17.	Q	lemma for ($\Box$I)
18.	$\Box Q$	lemma for (CP) 17 ($\Box$I)
19.	$\Box P \to \Box Q$	lemma for (CP) 2–18 (CP)
20.	$\Box(P \to Q) \to (\Box P \to \Box Q)$	1–19 (CP)

Now the remaining lemma can be derived.

1.	$\Box(P \to Q)$	(A/CP)
2.	$\Box P$	(A/CP)
3.	$\Box(P \to Q)$	1 (R)
4.	$P \to Q$	3 ($\Box$RE)
5.	P	2 ($\Box$RE)
...	...	...
17.	Q	lemma for ($\Box$I) 5,4 (MP)
18.	$\Box Q$	lemma for (CP) 17 ($\Box$I)
19.	$\Box P \to \Box Q$	lemma for (CP) 2–18 (CP)
20.	$\Box(P \to Q) \to (\Box P \to \Box Q)$	1–19 (CP)

These derivations could just as well have been done in bracket free notation.

Exercise

Rewrite the two derivations given earlier in bracket free notation. Do not redo the derivations. Transform the answers given above into bracket free notation.

Bracket free notation for each of the derivations given earlier is as follows. Justifications are of course the same as for standard notation.

1.	$<\Box(P \to Q)>$	⊢	$\Box(P \to Q)$
2.	$<\Box(P \to Q), \Box P>$	⊢	$\Box P$
3.	$<\Box(P \to Q), \Box P>$	⊢	$\Box(P \to Q)$
4.	$<\Box(P \to Q), \Box P>,< >$	⊢	$P \to Q$
5.	$<\Box(P \to Q), \Box P>,< >$	⊢	P
...	...		...
17.	$<\Box(P \to Q), \Box P>,< >$	⊢	Q
18.	$<\Box(P \to Q), \Box P>$	⊢	$\Box Q$
19.	$<\Box(P \to Q)>$	⊢	$\Box P \to \Box Q$
20.		⊢	$\Box(P \to Q) \to (\Box P \to \Box Q)$

1.	$<\Box P>$	⊢	$\Box P$
2.	$<\Box P>,< >$	⊢	P
...	...		...
18.	$<\Box P>,< >$	⊢	$\sim\sim P$
19.	$<\Box P>$	⊢	$\Box\sim\sim P$
20.		⊢	$\Box P \to \Box\sim\sim P$

The rules so far introduced are enough to demonstrate that if P is a metatheorem of Ds then $\Box$P must be a theorem of Dk. As an example, consider the theorem, $P \to P$.

1.	P	(A/CP)
...	...	...
19.	$P \to P$	1–1 (CP)
20.	$\Box(P \to P)$	19 ($\Box$I)

The derivation of any theorem, P, of Ds, can be put in a box, and $\Box$I can be applied to derive $\Box$P outside of the box.

1.		
...	...	
k.	P	
n.	$\Box P$	k ($\Box$I)

For the same reasons, if P is a theorem of Dk, $\Box$P is a theorem of Dk. $\Box\Box(P \to P)$, for instance, is a metatheorem of Dk.

Bracket free notation for derivations like that of $\Box(P \to P)$ has a feature that has not so far been seen.

1.	$<P>$	⊢	P	(A)
...	...		...	...
19.	$< >$	⊢	$P \to P$	1 (CP)
20.		⊢	$\Box(P \to P)$	19 ($\Box$I)

A boxed subderivation need not begin with a sentence derived by ($\Box$RE) or ($\sim\Diamond$RE). It may begin with an assumption. In that case, the corresponding list in bracket free notation is not the empty list, but the list of the assumption. Creation of a new box in standard notation need not correspond to the addition of an empty list in bracket free notation. It just corresponds to the start of a new list, whether empty or already filled with an assumption.

As practised in solutions to exercise 8.3, P must occur immediately to the right of the left side of the box, not next to any further box or assumption bracket. In the derivation below, for example, it is not permissible to derive $\Box$(A & A) outside of the box because A & A does not lie immediately to the right of the left side of the box.

```
1. │ ┌──┬─────┐        (A/□I)
   │ │  │  A  │
2. │ │  │ A & A │       1,1 (&I)
   │ └──┴─────┘
3. │ □(A & A)          2 □I  WRONG!
```

Bracket free notation makes this clearer. At line 2, <A> ⊢ A & A. But (□I) says that for ⊢ □(A & A) to be derived by (□I), it must be the case that < > ⊢ A & A.

Intuitively, the sentences in the pairs, □P / ~◇~P; □~P / ~◇P; ~□P / ◇~P; and ~□~P / ◇P say the same thing as each other. The sentences comprising each pair are also interderivable in Dk.

Exercise

Derive each of the following.

   a. <□P> ⊢ ~◇~P

   b. <◇P> ⊢ ~□~P

These exercises both appear to call for an initial application of the (IP) strategy. But in the case of the first, an alternative stage 3 strategy takes priority, the (~◇I) strategy. This strategy is a variant on the (□I) strategy.

   (~◇I) strategy: When the aim is to derive ~◇P, create a boxed subderivation and enter ~P as a lemma for (~◇I) on its last line.

A new strategy is also called for in approaching the second exercise, which has a diamond sentence as its given. Diamond sentences are the Dk analogues of (~bc) sentences of Ds. There is almost nothing that can be done with them, other than to use them as one of two opposites for (⊥I). They are best used with a variant on the (~bc) strategy:

   (◇) strategy: When ◇P exists above the gap, assume the opposite of the sentence that needs to be derived, reiterate ◇P under this assumption, and enter ~◇P as a lemma for (⊥I).

The (◇) strategy has a cousin, the (~□) strategy:

   (~□) strategy: When ~□P exists above the gap, assume the opposite of the sentence that needs to be derived, reiterate ~□P under this assumption, and enter □P as a lemma for (⊥I).

Try to apply the (~◇I) and (◇) strategies to solve the exercises before reading further.

The first derivation begins with nothing to do at stages 1 and 2. At stage 3, an application of the new (~◇) strategy is called for.

```
 1. │ □P                    given
    │   ┌──────┐
... │   │  ...  │            ...
19. │   │  ~~P │            lemma for (~◇I)
    │   └──────┘
20. │ ~◇~P                  19 (~◇I)
```

Note that the strategy calls for entering the negation of the immediate component of the ~◇ sentence. If the component is already negated, this means entering the negation of that negated component. Had P been entered at line 19 instead, the sentence would have the wrong form for deriving ~◇~P.

The work done at stage 3 creates an opportunity for work at stage 1, and that work makes it possible to derive the lemma, completing the derivation.

```
 1. │ □P                    given
    │   ┌──────┐
 2. │   │  P    │            1 (□RE)
... │   │  ...  │            ...
19. │   │  ~~P │            lemma for (~◇I) 2 (DNI)
    │   └──────┘
20. │ ~◇~P                  19 (~◇I)
```

The second derivation begins with nothing to do at any of stages 1, 2, or 3, so work commences at stage 4.

1.	◇P	given
2.	□~P	(A/IP)
...	...	...
19.	⊥	lemma for (IP)
20.	~□~P	2–19 (IP)

This work creates something to do at stage 1.

1.	◇P	given
2.	□~P	(A/IP)
3.	◇P	1 (R)
...	...	...
19.	⊥	lemma for (IP)
20.	~□~P	2–19 (IP)

Now there is nothing to do at stages 1 and 2, so work proceeds to stage 3. Since the aim is to derive ⊥, the (⊥I) strategy should be employed. Whenever a ~bc or ◇ sentence exists above the gap, its opposite should be given special consideration as a lemma for (⊥I).

1.	◇P	given
2.	□~P	(A/IP)
3.	◇P	1 (R)
...	...	...
18.	~◇P	lemma for (⊥I)
19.	⊥	lemma for (IP) 3,18 (⊥I)
20.	~□~P	2–19 (IP)

This lemma is pregnant. It suggests a further use of the (~◇) strategy.

1.	◇P	given
2.	□~P	(A/IP)
3.	◇P	1 (R)
...	...	
17.	~P	lemma for (~◇I)
18.	~◇P	lemma for (⊥I) 17 (~◇I)
19.	⊥	lemma for (IP) 3,18 (⊥I)
20.	~□~P	2–19 (IP)

Now the lemma can be derived by 2 (□RE), completing the derivation. Bracket free notation for each of these derivations is as follows:

1.	<□P> ⊢ □P		(A)
2.	<□P>,< > ⊢ P		1 (□RE)
...	...	...	...
19.	<□P>,< > ⊢ ~~P		2 (DN)
20.	<□P> ⊢ ~◇~P		19 (~◇I)

1.	<◇P> ⊢ ◇P		(A)
2.	<◇P,□~P> ⊢ □~P		(A)
3.	<◇P,□~P> ⊢ ◇P		1 (R)
...	...	...	...
17.	<◇P,□~P>,< > ⊢ ~P		2 (□RE)
18.	<◇P,□~P> ⊢ ~◇P		17 (~◇I)
19.	<◇P,□~P> ⊢ ⊥		3,18 (⊥I)
20.	<◇P> ⊢ ~□~P		2–19 (IP)

Exercise 8.6

1. *Prove the other half of the interderivability of* $\Box P$ *and* $\sim\Diamond\sim P$ *and of* $\Diamond P$ *and* $\sim\Box\sim P$ *in Dk:* *that* $\sim\Diamond\sim P \vdash \Box P$
   and that $\sim\Box\sim P \vdash \Diamond P$.

2. *Prove the following in Dk.*
   a. $<\Box\sim P> \dashv\vdash \sim\Diamond P$
   b. $<\sim\Box P> \dashv\vdash \Diamond\sim P$

3. *Prove the following in Dk. Note that i–l in conjunction with exercise 8.8#3c and d demonstrate the distribution rules*
   for $\Box/\Diamond$ *and* &/$\lor$ *sentences. Consult both the prior and the subsequent answered questions for hints.*
   ★a. $<\Box(A \to B)> \vdash \Box\sim B \to \Box\sim A$
   b. $\vdash \Box(A \to B) \to (\Diamond A \to \Diamond B)$
   ★c. $\vdash \sim\Diamond(A \to B) \to \sim\Diamond B$
   d. $\vdash \Box B \to \Box(A \to B)$
   ★e. $\vdash \sim\Diamond A \to \Box(A \to B)$
   f. $\vdash \sim\Diamond(A \& \sim A)$
   ★g. $\vdash \Box(A \to A)$
   h. $\vdash \Diamond A \to \Diamond(A \lor B)$
   ★i. $<\Box(A \& B)> \dashv\vdash \Box A \& \Box B$
   j. $<\Diamond(A \& B)> \vdash \Diamond A \& \Diamond B$ *(Hint: assume* $\sim\Diamond A$; *derive* $\sim(A \& B)$ *inside a box; apply* $(\sim\Diamond I)$; *repeat.)*
   ★k. $<\Diamond(A \lor B)> \dashv\vdash \Diamond A \lor \Diamond B$
   l. $<\Box A \lor \Box B> \vdash \Box(A \lor B)$

Intuitively, "necessarily P" yields P. But this intuitive result is not derivable using the rules that have so far been given. Given $\Box P$, ($\Box$RE) allows putting P in a box, but there is no way to get it back out without boxing it. Paradoxically (given an understanding of $\Box$ as asserting universal necessity), P cannot be derived from $\Box P$. (There is no paradox when $\Box$ is understood as asserting an obligation. In an imperfect world, the fact that P is obligatory does not entail that it will occur. Even in an imperfect world, however, nothing can be called obligatory unless it is permissible. But $\Diamond P$ can no more be derived from $\Box P$ than can P using the rules so far presented.)

The rules so far supplied are limited in another way as well. Boxed subderivations have been presented as special places reserved for those sentences asserted to be necessarily true: the immediate components of box sentences and the negated immediate components of $\sim\Diamond$ sentences. But, it might be maintained, box sentences are themselves necessarily true. Intuitively, "necessarily P" says that P is true in all contexts. It might be proposed that the truth of P in all contexts makes $\Box P$ true in any one of them. Yet, while ($\Box$RE) permits putting P in a box given $\Box P$, it does not permit putting $\Box P$ in that box. Paradoxically (perhaps), $\Box P$ cannot be treated as itself necessarily true. (Here as well, though, there may be no paradox when $\Box$ is understood deontologically. Perhaps you ought to be punished for what you did, but it does not follow that you ought to put yourself in a situation where you ought to be punished.)[2] These (uncertain) weaknesses can be addressed by expanding Dk with two further rules:

$$\boxed{\begin{array}{l} (\Box E)\text{:} \quad \text{If } L \vdash \Box P, \text{then } L \vdash P \\ (\Box R)\text{:} \quad \text{If } L \vdash \Box P, \text{then } L, <\ > \vdash \Box P \end{array}}$$

Adding the first of these rules to Dk produces the derivation system Dt. Adding both the first and the second produces Ds4. ($\Box E$) allows P to be derived in the same assumption bracket or box as the assumption bracket or box that includes $\Box P$, which ($\Box$RE) does not. And ($\Box R$) allows $\Box P$ to be reiterated into a box, which ($\Box$RE) does not.

($\Box E$) and ($\Box R$) could each have been complemented with a $\sim\Diamond$ rule, but there are enough rules already, and the existing ones, in combination with ($\Box E$) and ($\Box R$), provide for ways of obtaining the analogous results for $\sim\Diamond$ sentences by means of a routine sequence of steps.

Augmenting Dt with a different rule produces Ds5.

$$\boxed{(\Box\Diamond I)\text{:} \quad \text{If } L \vdash \Diamond P, \text{then } L \vdash \Box\Diamond P}$$

This rule is based on the intuition that if P is the case in at least one relevant context, then from the perspective of each relevant context, there is at least one relevant context in which P is the case.

These rules are used with the following templates:

	(□E)			(□R)			(□◇I)	
k.	□P	?	*k.*	□P	?	*k.*	◇P	?
...	...		...	...		...	...	
n.	P	*k* (□E)	...	...		*n.*	□◇P	*k* (□◇I)
			n.	□P	*k* (□R)			

(□E) permits deriving □P from <□□P> in a single step. (□R) makes it possible to derive the reverse.

```
1. | □P        given

2. |   | □P |   1 (□R)
3. | □□P       2 (□I)
```

It follows that "necessarily" and "necessarily necessarily" are interderivable in Ds4. (□E) and (□R) can be used to show that ◇P and ◇◇P are also interderivable.

Exercise

(□E) and (□R) are top-down rules. They should be applied as part of work at stage 1. However, there is a trick. ~◇ sentences are □ sentences in disguise and should be treated in the same way. This means that, at stage 1, ~P could also be derived from ~◇P, and ~◇P could be derived in any box lying immediately to the right of an assumption bracket or box that contains ~◇P. (□E) and (□R) do not directly permit these inferences, but they do make them possible using routine sequences of steps. Try to discover these routines, that is, try to establish the following:

a.   <~◇P> ⊢ ~P

b.   <~◇P>,< > ⊢ ~◇P *(that is, do a partial derivation that starts with the assumption of ~◇P and ends with ~◇P in a box, just like the template for (□R))*

The solutions to (a) and (b) reveal routines that can be used to establish

c.   ◇P –|– ◇◇P

Try to do this before reading further.

The key to this exercise is the solution to exercise 8.6#2a, which shows how to convert ~◇P into □~P and how to convert □~P back into ~◇P. Each conversion can be done in two lines. They are applied as follows.

The routine for deriving ~P from ~◇P begins as any other derivation would.

```
1. | ~◇P   ?
...| ...    ...
 ? | ~P     ?
```

The first step is to use the right-to-left solution to exercise 8.6#2a to convert ~◇P to □~P.

```
1. | ~◇P          ?
2. |   | ~P |     1 (~◇RE)
3. | □~P          2 (□I)
...| ...          ...
 ? | ~P           ?
```

Now, (□E) can be applied to derive ~P.

```
1. | ~◇P        ?
2. |   [ ~P ]   1 (~◇RE)
3. | □~P        2 (□I)
4. | ~P         3 (□E)
```

The second routine aims to move ~◇P into a box.

```
1. | ~◇P              ?
...|  ...             ...
...|    ...           ...
?. |  |  ~◇P  |       ?
```

The first step is once again to use the right-to-left solution to exercise 8.6#2a to convert ~◇P to □~P.

```
1. | ~◇P             ?
2. |   [ ~P ]        1 (~◇RE)
3. | □~P             2 (□I)
...|   ...
?. |  |  ~◇P  |      ?
```

Now, (□R) can be used to put □~P into the box.

```
1. | ~◇P             ?
2. |   [ ~P ]        1 (~◇RE)
3. | □~P             2 (□I)
4. |  | □~P  |       3 (□R)
...|  |  ...         ...
?. |  |  ~◇P  |      ?
```

Now that □~P is in the box, the left to right solution to exercise 8.6#2a can be inserted to convert □~P back into ~◇P.

```
1. | ~◇P             ?
2. |   [ ~P ]        1 (~◇RE)
3. | □~P             2 (□I)
4. |  | □~P  |       3 (□R)
5. |  |  [ ~P ]      4 (□RE)
6. |  |  ~◇P         5 (~◇I)
```

While these routines are straightforward, they require some work. When working from the top down, it costs little to apply (□E) and (□R) as a matter of course, without considering whether the result will be of use for the ensuing derivation. It is better to pause to consider if an application of the ~◇ routines will yield a result that is needed for the remainder of the derivation.

One case where the routines are called for is the demonstration of the interderivability of ◇P and ◇◇P. The derivation from left to right begins with nothing to do at stages 1, 2, or 3, so work begins by assuming the opposite and returning to stage 1.

```
1. | ◇P            given
2. |  | ~◇◇P       (A/IP)
3. |  | ◇P         1 (R)
   |  | ...        ...
19.|  | ⊥          lemma for (IP)
20.| ◇◇P           2–19 (IP)
```

At this point, stage 1 has not been completed. A ~◇ sentence, ~◇◇P, exists above the gap at line 2. Moreover, running through the routine to reduce it to ~◇P is clearly relevant, since that would complete the derivation.

```
1. | ◇P            given
2. |  | ~◇◇P       (A/IP)
3. |  | ◇P         1 (R)
4. |  | | ~◇P |    2 (~◇RE)
5. |  | □~◇P       4 (□I)
6. |  | ~◇P        5 (□E)
   |  | ...        ...
19.|  | ⊥          lemma for (IP) 3,6 (⊥I)
20.| ◇◇P           2–19 (IP)
```

The derivation from right to left opens with an application of the (IP) strategy followed by the (◇) strategy.

```
1. | ◇◇P           given
2. |  | ~◇P        (A/IP)
3. |  | ◇◇P        1 (R)
   |  | ...        ...
18.|  | ~◇◇P       lemma for (⊥I)
19.|  | ⊥          lemma for (IP) 3,18 (⊥I)
20.| ◇P            2–19 (IP)
```

Now there is nothing to be done at stages 1 or two. At stage 3, an application of the (~◇I) strategy is called for.

```
1. | ◇◇P           given
2. |  | ~◇P        (A/IP)
3. |  | ◇◇P        1 (R)
   |  | ...        ...
17.|  | | ~◇P |    lemma for (~ ◇I)
18.|  | ~◇◇P       lemma for (⊥I) 17 (~ ◇I)
19.|  | ⊥          lemma for (IP) 3,18 (⊥I)
20.| ◇P            2–19 (IP)
```

Reiteration into boxes is impermissible, so line 17 cannot be derived from line 2 by (R). Failing that, applying the routine for turning a ~◇ sentence into a □~ sentence would clearly be useful, as it would justify the lemma.

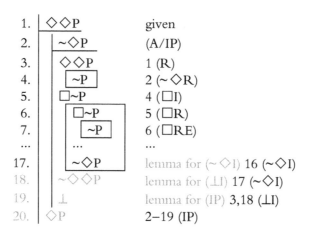

```
 1.  │◇◇P              given
 2.  │ │~◇P            (A/IP)
 3.  │ │◇◇P            1 (R)
 4.  │ │ │~P │         2 (~◇R)
 5.  │ │□~P            4 (□I)
 6.  │ │ │□~P │        5 (□R)
 7.  │ │ │ │~P │       6 (□RE)
 ...      ...          ...
17.  │ │ │~◇P          lemma for (~◇I) 16 (~◇I)
18.  │ │~◇◇P           lemma for (⊥I) 17 (~◇I)
19.  │ │⊥              lemma for (IP) 3,18 (⊥I)
20.  │◇P              2–19 (IP)
```

The interderivability of ◇◇P and ◇P shows that, just as Ds4 does not recognize any difference between "necessarily" and "necessarily necessarily," so it does not recognize any difference between "possibly" and "possibly possibly." Reiterating these modal operators is pointless in Ds4.

(□E) and (□R) each directly establish a metatheorem, which is considered the characteristic metatheorem of the corresponding systems, Dt and Ds4. For Dt the metatheorem is (t): □P → P; for Ds4 it is (4): □P → □□P. It is interesting that the rule that establishes each metatheorem also establishes the converse of the diamond version of that result. (□R), which establishes □P → □□P, also establishes ◇◇P → ◇P. (□E), which establishes □□P → □P (an instance of □P → P), also establishes ◇◇P → ◇P. And just as it establishes □P → P, so it establishes P → ◇P.

Exercise

Show that <P> ⊢ ◇P. Use the (IP) strategy followed by the (□E) strategy. Try this before reading further.

The derivation opens with nothing to do at stages 1, 2, or 3, so the (IP) strategy is applied. This creates work to do at stage 1.

```
 1.  │P               given
 2.  │ │~◇P           (A/IP)
 3.  │ │P             1 (R)
 ...     ...          ...
19.  │ │⊥             lemma for (IP)
20.  │◇P             2–19 (IP)
```

At this point, the routine for deriving ~P from ~◇P can be used to complete the derivation.

```
 1.  │P               given
 2.  │ │~◇P           (A/IP)
 3.  │ │P             1 (R)
 4.  │ │ │~P │        2 (~◇RE)
 5.  │ │□~P           4 (□I)
 6.  │ │~P            (□E)
 ...     ...          ...
19.  │ │⊥             lemma for (IP)  3, 6 (⊥I)
20.  │◇P             2–19 (IP)
```

The converse relations between $\Box P \rightarrow P$ and $P \rightarrow \Diamond P$, between $\Box\Box P \rightarrow \Box P$ and $\Diamond P \rightarrow \Diamond\Diamond P$, and between $\Box P \rightarrow \Box\Box P$ and $\Diamond\Diamond P \rightarrow \Diamond P$ are not special to these cases. They are instances of a relation that holds in general, that of duality.

Provided that P and Q do not contain any occurrences of $\sim$, $\rightarrow$, or $\equiv$, the dual of a conditional, $P \rightarrow Q$, or a biconditional, $P \equiv Q$, is obtained by (i) reversing the order of P and Q; (ii) interchanging any occurrences of $\Box$ and $\Diamond$ in P and in Q; and (iii) interchanging any occurrences of & and $\lor$ in P and Q. (The symbols, $\forall$ and $\exists$, to be introduced in later chapters, would also be interchanged.) According to this definition, the dual of $\Box P \rightarrow P$ is $P \rightarrow \Diamond P$, and the dual of $\Box P \rightarrow \Box\Box P$ is $\Diamond\Diamond P \rightarrow \Diamond P$. Another metatheorem, the deontic metatheorem or (D), $\Box P \rightarrow \Diamond P$, which says that whatever is obligatory is permissible, is its own dual.

When a sentence that has a dual is a theorem, its dual is also a theorem. Like ($\Box$E) and ($\Box$R), ($\Box\Diamond$I) directly establishes a metatheorem, (5), which is the characteristic metatheorem of Ds5. (5) is $\Diamond P \rightarrow \Box\Diamond P$. The dual of (5), $\Diamond\Box P \rightarrow \Box P$, is also a metatheorem. (The derivation is difficult and approached over stages in what follows.) In contrast, (k), the characteristic metatheorem of Dk, $\Box(P \rightarrow Q) \rightarrow (\Box P \rightarrow \Box Q)$, does not have a dual.

There are two forms of duality. In addition to the form just discussed, which may be called conditional duality, there is an oppositional form. Sentences that do not contain any occurrences of $\rightarrow$ or $\equiv$ have oppositional duals. These duals are obtained by interchanging occurrences of $\lor$ and &, interchanging occurrences of $\Box$ and $\Diamond$, and interchanging occurrences of atomic sentences and their negations. (Again, $\forall$ and $\exists$ would also be interchanged.) According to this definition, the dual of A is $\sim$A, the dual of $\sim$A is A, the dual of A & B is $\sim$A $\lor$ $\sim$B, the dual of A $\lor$ B is $\sim$A & $\sim$B, the dual of a dnf is a cnf, the dual of a cnf is a dnf, the dual of $\Box$A is $\Diamond\sim$A, and the dual of $\Diamond$A is $\Box\sim$A. Whereas conditional duals are both theorems if either one is a theorem, oppositional duals are inconsistent. In the oppositional sense, a sentence and the *negation* of its dual are interderivable.

Exercise 8.7

1. *State the duals, if any, of the following sentences (not all of them have duals). If the sentence has a dual, also state whether it is conditional or oppositional.*

   ★a. $\Diamond A \rightarrow \Box\Diamond A$

   b. $\Diamond\Box A \equiv A$

   ★c. $\Box\Diamond A \rightarrow \sim A$

   d. $\Box(A \lor B) \rightarrow (\Diamond A \ \& \ \Diamond B)$

   ★e. $\sim\Diamond\sim A$

   f. $\Box\Diamond A$

   ★g. $\Box(A \lor B) \ \& \ (\Diamond\sim A \lor \Diamond\sim B)$

   h. $\Box A \equiv \sim\Diamond\sim A$

★2. *Why does (k) not have a dual?*

Duals can help to discover derivations. A case in point is the demonstration of what is called the B metatheorem: $P \rightarrow \Box\Diamond P$.

1.	P	given
...	...	...
19.	$\Box\Diamond P$	lemma for (CP)
20.	$P \rightarrow \Box\Diamond P$	1–19 (CP)

At this point in the derivation, there is nothing to be done at stage 1 or 2. But the addition of ($\Box\Diamond$I) to the repertoire of rules has created a new stage 3 strategy, the ($\Box\Diamond$I) strategy: make $\Diamond P$ a lemma for deriving $\Box\Diamond P$.

1.	P	given
...	...	...
18.	$\Diamond P$	lemma for ($\Box\Diamond$I)
19.	$\Box\Diamond P$	lemma for (CP) 18 ($\Box\Diamond$I)
20.	$P \rightarrow \Box\Diamond P$	1–19 (CP)

Now it helps to remember that applying (□E) is tantamount to appealing to (t), and that the dual of (t), □P → P, is P → ◇P. P →◇P ought therefore to be derivable, and as demonstrated earlier, it is. That earlier derivation can be inserted to complete the current one.

1.	P	given
2.	~◇P	(A/IP)
3.	P	1 (R)
4.	~P	2 (~◇RE)
5.	□~P	4 (□I)
...	...	
16.	~P	lemma for (⊥I) 5 (□E)
17.	⊥	lemma for (IP) 3,16 (⊥I)
18.	◇P	lemma for (□◇I) 2–17 (IP)
19.	□◇P	lemma for (CP) 18 (□◇I)
20.	P → □◇P	1–19 (CP)

The principle that the dual of a theorem is a theorem has some surprising results. (5), which asserts that whatever is possible is necessarily possible, is at least plausible. The same holds of the B metatheorem, which asserts that whatever is actual is necessarily possible. But the dual of B is ◇□P → P, and the dual of (5) is ◇□P → □P. B-dual might be read as saying that if it is merely possible that P is necessary then P is the case, and (5)-dual as saying that if it is merely possible that P is necessary then it is necessary. These claims are not intuitive when "necessary" and "possible" are taken to refer to necessary and possible truth. But they are derivable in Ds5. A derivation of P from ◇□P begins with an application of the (IP) strategy followed by the (◇) strategy.

1.	◇□P	given
2.	~P	(A/IP)
3.	◇□P	1 (R)
...	...	
18.	~◇□P	lemma for (⊥I)
19.	⊥	lemma for (IP) 3,18 (⊥I)
20.	P	2–19 (IP)

~◇□P might be obtained by (~◇I), but after a further application of (IP) it is unclear how to proceed.

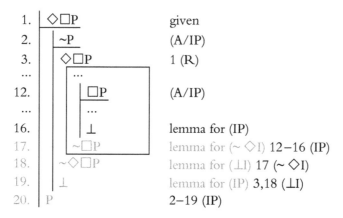

1.	◇□P	given
2.	~P	(A/IP)
3.	◇□P	1 (R)
...	...	
12.	□P	(A/IP)
...	...	
16.	⊥	lemma for (IP)
17.	~□P	lemma for (~◇I) 12–16 (IP)
18.	~◇□P	lemma for (⊥I) 17 (~◇I)
19.	⊥	lemma for (IP) 3,18 (⊥I)
20.	P	2–19 (IP)

A partial solution to the difficulty is to consider that the oppositional dual of □P is ◇~P, meaning that ~□P and ◇~P are interderivable. A way to derive the one from the other has already been discovered.

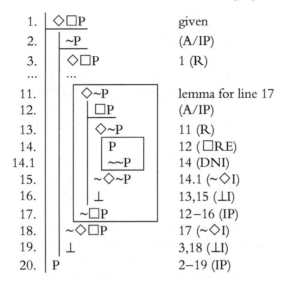

◇~P could be derived in the box at line 11 if □◇~P were available at line 10, and that sentence could be derived by (□◇I) if ◇~P were available at line 9.

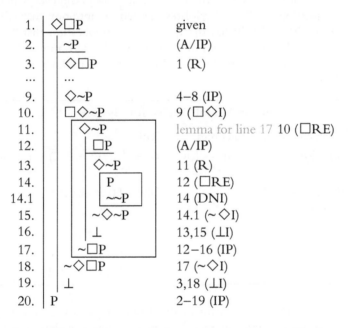

Now the derivation can be completed by appeal to the routine for deriving ◇P from P. In this case that means deriving ◇~P from ~P.

1.	◇□P	given
2.	~P	(A/IP)
3.	◇□P	1 (R)
4.	~◇~P	(A/IP)
5.	~P	2 (R)
6.	~~P	4 (~◇RE)
7.	□~~P	6 (□I)
7.1	~~P	7 (□E)
8.	⊥	5,7.1 (⊥I)
9.	◇~P	4–8 (IP)
10.	□◇~P	9 (□◇I)

11.	◇~P	10 (□RE)
12.	□P	(A/IP)
13.	◇~P	11 (R)
14.	P	12 (□RE)
14.1	~~P	14 (DNI)
15.	~◇~P	14.1 (~◇I)
16.	⊥	13,15 (⊥I)
17.	~□P	12–16 (IP)
18.	~◇□P	17 (~◇I)
19.	⊥	3,18 (⊥I)
20.	P	2–19 (IP)

It only requires a slight variant on this derivation to establish that ◇□P yields □P. Place □P at line 20 and ~□P at line 2. Reiterate ~□P at line 5. After line 6, apply (DNE) to obtain P. Then apply (□I) to obtain □P, which together with line 5 yields ⊥ on line 8. The remainder of the derivation is unchanged.

◇□P → P and ◇□P → □P are therefore both derivable. If they are objectionable, the objections carry over to their duals, P → □◇P and ◇P → □◇P. And perhaps those duals might be objectionable. ◇P → □◇P might be read as asserting that possibilities cannot change, which is not intuitively obvious. P → □◇P might be read as the similarly questionable assertion that what is currently the case must always and everywhere be possible.

(t) and (4) might also be questioned □P → P violates the deontic intuition that what is obligatory need not always be what happens. And □P → □□P, has the questionable implication that "necessarily" means "necessarily necessary," and "possibly possible" nothing less than "possibly." The derivation rules have been associated with different systems, denominated Dk, Dt, Ds4, and Ds5, to allow choice over which derivation rules to countenance. Some systems are charted below.

Some Modal Derivation Systems		
System	Characteristic metatheorem	Rule
Dk:	(k): □(P → Q) → (□P → □Q)	Ds + (□RE) + (□I) + (~◇RE) + (~◇I)
D:	(D): □P → ◇P	Dk + (D) as axiom
Dt:	(t): □P → P	Dk + (□E)
Ds4:	(4): □P → □□P	Dk + (□E) + (□R)
DB:	(B): P → □◇P	Dk + (□E) + (B) as axiom
Ds5:	(5): ◇P → □◇P	Dk + (□E) + (□◇I)

According to the chart, system D, the system for modal deontic logic, arises from using (D) as an axiom. (An axiom is a principle that is taken for granted. A metatheorem, in contrast is derived, even though only from the empty list. Instances of an axiom can be entered on any line of a derivation, making axioms alternatives to using derivation rules. For example, system Dt might just as well use (t) as an axiom as use (□E). Whenever an instance of P is derived from □P by (□E), the corresponding instance of □P → P could be entered, and P could be derived by (MP) instead.)

Dt is a stronger system that adds (□E) to Dk. ((□E) makes it possible to derive (D), so (D) does not need to be added when (□E) is present.)

Ds4 arises from adding both (□E) and (□R) to Dk. Earlier, DB was not recognized as a system because (B) can be derived from Dk, (□E), and (□◇I). But there is some choice here. (5) might just as well be derived from Dk supplemented by (□E), (□R), and (B).

Some of these systems fit better with intuitions about certain matters, such as obligation, others with intuitions about other matters, such as truth or temporality. Each of them is provably sound and complete for its semantics, so from that perspective they are all equally correct. Logic does not dictate which derivation system is the correct one for a given use. Instead, derivation systems and corresponding semantic systems are invented to capture our intuitions. The intuitions vary depending on how □ is understood (as necessary truth, permanence over time, omnipresence, obligation, etc.) Some systems are simpler, others more complex. Some can prove things that others cannot, but the question of which best conforms to our intuitions is complicated by the fact that we have different intuitions for different understandings of □. The question of which system of modal logic is the best one for a certain use is not up to logic to decide. Geometry, another formal system, is the same in this respect. There are various non-Euclidean geometries. Some are useful for describing relations between astronomical objects, others for describing spaces that human beings can easily conceive, others for spaces that lend themselves to a simplified geometry. It is not up to geometry, but to physics and psychology to decide which of various geometries is optimal for these different applications.

Exercise 8.8

Derive the following in Ds5.

★**a.** <◇P> –|– <□◇P>

b. <□P> –|– <◇□P> *(Hint: the derivation from left to right is an instance of* P → ◇P; *the text gives instructions for the derivation from right to left.)*

★**c.** <◇P> –|– <◇□◇P> *(For the derivation from left to right, use (b) as a metatheorem; for the derivation from right to left use (b) as a metatheorem, then use (a) as a metatheorem.)*

d. <□P> –|– <□◇□P> *(For the derivation from left to right, use (b) as a metatheorem then use (a) as a metatheorem; for the derivation from right to left use (a) as a metatheorem, then use (b) as a metatheorem.)*

★**e.** <◇P> –|– <□□◇P>

f. <□P> –|– <◇◇□P>

★**g.** ◇□A ⊢ □◇A *(Try to do this without relying on result (b). Hint: make ◇A a lemma for (□◇I); use the (◇) strategy to derive the lemma; use the (~◇I) strategy; then make a further use of (IP); look for an occasion to apply (~◇RE), (R), and (□E).)*

h. Show that it is possible to derive the k-metatheorem, □(P → Q) → (□P → □Q), in Ds4 without using (□RE).

★**i.** Show that it is possible to derive (5), ◇P → □◇P, in Ds4 + B. *(Hint: assume the antecedent. Insert an instance of the B axiom that has this assumption as its antecedent; use the routine for deriving ◇P from ◇◇P.)*

j. Show that it is possible to derive (4), □P → □□P, in Ds5, which uses just the k-rules, (□E), and (□◇I) *(Hint: assume the antecedent; use the (□I) strategy to derive □□P; exercise 8.8(b) right to left shows how to derive □P from ◇□P without using (□R), so that result can be cited; derive ◇□P from □◇□P by (□RE); obtain □◇□P from ◇□P by (□◇I); to derive ◇□P, use result 8.8b left to right.)*

It was noted earlier that Ds4 does not recognize any difference between sentences that begin with a string of boxes and sentences that begin with a single box, and likewise for diamonds. Exercise 8.8a–f illustrate that Ds5 does not recognize any difference between sentences that begin with a string of any mixture of boxes and diamonds and sentences that begin with the last (rightmost) box or diamond on that string. In Ds5, the iteration of modal operators, whether the same or different, is pointless.

Notes

1 Not to be confused with DK (upper-case K), a system of relevance logic developed by Richard Routley (1935–96) and Robert Meyer (1932–2009).

2 The example, an interesting variant on the "good Samaritan paradox," is due to Graham Priest.

9 Semantics and Trees for Modal and Intuitionistic Sentential Logic

Contents

9.1 Semantics for Modal Sentential Logic

It is not obvious how to give a semantics for MSL within the confines of classical (bivalent) logic. Confining consideration to the values "true" and "false" for the moment, $\Box$P seems to say that P is somehow more than true, whereas $\Diamond$P seems to say that P is something between true and false. But following this path would require recognizing more than two values.

An alternative way of understanding $\Box$ and $\Diamond$, due to Gottfried Wilhelm Leibniz (1646–1716), is to take what is possible to be what is the case in at least one context, and to take what is necessary to be what is the case in all contexts. Famously, Leibniz referred to worlds, rather than contexts. He maintained that, at the time of creation, God surveyed all the different worlds that might be produced. He considered this world (in the abstract) and all the ways it would have been different had its physical laws, objects, initial conditions, etc., been different. He then chose to create the best of all these possible worlds.

On a fully Leibnizian semantics, sentences describing objects or events in the world God chose to create have the special status of being actually true. But there are other sentences that are not only true in the actual world but that would have to be true in any possible world. These are the sentences that are necessarily true. Yet other sentences are true in some world other than the actual world. These are the sentences that are possibly true. Modern modal semantics abstracts from the metaphysical and theological commitments that motivated Leibniz to paint this picture. It identifies worlds with regions, contexts, or circumstances, leaving the question of the metaphysical status of "worlds" to others to address. Some versions, including the one presented here, do not recognize any one of these "worlds" as being the actual world.

There is a further difference. On Leibnizian semantics, all possible worlds are equally possible. God could have created any one of them. Rather than work with a "God's eye" view of the possible worlds, modern modal semantics works with a "world bound" view. From a world bound view, not all worlds may be equally possible. For example,

DOI: 10.4324/9781003026532-14

it was not possible for early civilizations to use the technology at their disposal to create machines that were more powerful than the ones they already had. That only became possible with the invention of water mills and windmills. In this case, a later possibility, using a nuclear reactor to electrify a city, only became "accessible" by first realizing an earlier possibility, harnessing the power of water and wind in a special way. Many developmental possibilities are like this. A later developmental stage, in effect, a different possible world, cannot be "seen" or "accessed" from a much earlier world, though it can be from a later world. Modern modal semantics generalizes this point by incorporating the notion that one possible world may only be able to "see" or "access" some (but not all) of the other possible worlds. (In what follows "sees"/"accesses" and "visible"/"accessible" are used interchangeably.)

For modern modal logic, truth is triply relative. It is not just relative to interpretations, as it is in SL. It is relative to worlds of interpretations, and relative to which worlds see or have access to which other worlds. A sentence that is true in all worlds of one interpretation may be false in at least one world of another interpretation. A sentence that is true in one world of one interpretation may be false in a different world of that interpretation. The truth of some sentences in a world of an interpretation is further relative to the values of their immediate components in other accessible worlds.

Consider the sentences of SL compounded from one or more occurrences of three atomic sentences, A, B, and C. In SL, there is a single, eight row long table for these sentences. Each row of the table specifies one of the eight unique valuations for three atomic sentences, and then goes on to specify the assignments to compounds of those atoms. Each interpretation of SL uses exactly one row.

	A	B	C
I_1	T	T	T
I_2	T	T	F
I_3	T	F	T
I_4	T	F	F
I_5	F	T	T
I_6	F	T	F
I_7	F	F	T
I_8	F	F	F

In SL, values of compound sentences are determined exclusively horizontally. The value of $C \rightarrow A$ on I_1 is determined by looking just at the values of A and C on I_1, not at any other interpretation.

In contrast, an interpretation for MSL corresponds (in part) to an entire table. But the table can omit one or more rows. Omitting one or more rows is tantamount to overlooking a logical possibility and thereby to treating the remaining rows as if they were a survey of something other than the purely logical possibilities. Not everything that is logically possible is physically possible or morally permissible or temporally possible.

On these tables, the rows represent possible worlds of a single interpretation, rather than different interpretations.

I_1	A	B	C	$C \rightarrow A$
w_1	T	T	T	T
w_2	T	T	F	T
w_3	T	F	T	T
w_4	T	F	F	T
w_6	F	T	F	T
w_8	F	F	F	T

The table above omits rows 5 and 7 from the table given earlier. One effect of this change is to elevate $C \rightarrow A$ from being true on some rows and false on others to being true on all. (The valuation rule for $\rightarrow$ does not change. The rows on which the rule assigns an F are just omitted.) A different table, omitting different lines from the long table, would not have this effect. But on the table given above, $C \rightarrow A$ has the status of a necessary truth. This is not to say it is valid. That would mean it is true in all worlds of all interpretations, and other "world tables" can readily be drawn up on which $C \rightarrow A$ is false on at least one row. $C \rightarrow A$ has the status of a necessary truth just on I_1.

Different interpretations may make different assignments on at least one row. Alternatively, they may include different numbers of worlds, and omit different rows.

Each interpretation of MSL uses a world table. Any interpretation must keep at least one row (that is, recognize at least one world). The one that keeps all of them is just the SL table, which does not recognize any necessities other than merely logical ones. It has already been studied. The interesting interpretations are the ones that use world tables that omit an intermediate number of rows.

The number of world tables, even for just three sentence letters, is quite large. There is 1 eight-line table. There are 8 one-line tables and 8 seven-line tables. There are 8!/2!(8−2)! = 28 two-line tables and an equal number of six-line tables. Calculating the number of three-, four-, and five-line tables using the combinatorial formula n!/r!(n−r)!, where n is the number of alternatives (8) and r is the number of choices made among the alternatives (3, 4, or 5) brings the sum to 255 tables where just three sentence letters are in play. This number does not come close to exhausting the number of different interpretations that there are for sentences containing just three sentence letters, because in addition to how many worlds they use and what assignments they make to sentence letters in each world, interpretations differ in what worlds are taken to see what other worlds.

On world tables, the values of functionally compound sentences (those that have connectives of SL as their main operators) are still determined horizontally. The value of C → A on a row (that is, in a world) of the world table is determined by the values of the immediate components, C and A, in that world. But the values of box and diamond sentences are determined vertically. The value of □(C → A) in w_1 is not just determined by the value of C → A in w_1. It is determined by the value of C → A in the accessible worlds.

Accessibility relations are often specified by using a map. Worlds appear as dots on the map, and which worlds see which other worlds is indicated by drawing arrows between them. It can get complicated with as many as six worlds. An accessibility map for just three worlds, w, v, and u, might look like this.

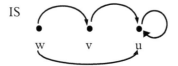

This is just one way of stipulating accessibility relations between worlds. According to this map, w sees v and u, v only sees u, and u only sees itself. Neither w nor v see themselves. The notation, IS, in the upper left corner stands for the accessibility relation, S (for "sees"), that interpretation I posits between the worlds. Other interpretations recognizing exactly three worlds and using the same world table will differ from one another in how many arrows they draw in what directions between what worlds. The choices vary from no world seeing any world, even itself, to each seeing itself and all the others. This is why the 255 different world tables mentioned earlier do not correspond to the number of different interpretations for three sentence letters. That number has to be multiplied by the number of different ways of drawing accessibility arrows between the worlds. Obviously, it is not feasible to answer the questions of modal logic by drawing up tables of world tables.

The features that have just been discussed entail that interpretations for MSL must include more than is found in interpretations for SL. An interpretation for SL is nothing more than a valuation of the sentence letters. Interpretations for MSL involve three things. Each interpretation works with a set, IΩ, of worlds, a map, IS, of the accessibility relations between the worlds, and a valuation, now separated from the other components of I and designated Iα, of each sentence letter in each world.

(Many textbooks use W rather than Ω, but experience has shown that when (lower-case) w is also used to designate a world, as it is in this text, verbal lectures and discussion can be inadvertently misleading for listeners. The common association of Ω (omega) with large quantities makes it an attractive alternative. For purposes of work at the keyboard, an underscored capital O (O) can be used as Ω and the "at" symbol (@) as α.)

Given a set of worlds, a specification of the accessibility relations between those worlds, and a valuation of the sentence letters in each world, the values of box and diamond sentences on I can be determined. □P means "necessarily P." Accordingly, □P is true in w_1 if and only if P is true in all relevant contexts, which means true in any world w_1 can see. It is false in w_1 if there is even one counterexample: one accessible world in which P is false. The reverse holds for the truth or falsity of ◇P in w_1. ◇P means "possibly P." Accordingly, ◇P is true in w_1 if and only if P can be true, which means that it is true in at least one of the possible worlds that w_1 can see. It is only false in w_1 if there is no possible world in which it is true, that is, if it is false in each world accessible to w_1.

This means that determining the value of box and diamond sentences in a given world requires consulting the accessibility map and looking up and down the world table to determine the values of the immediate components in each visible world, not just looking at the value of the immediate component in that world. (If the world does not see itself, the value of the immediate component in that world would be irrelevant; if it does, it might still not determine the value of the compound provided there are other visible worlds).

To keep things simple for the moment, return to the world table given earlier and assume that IS specifies that each of the six possible worlds on that table is accessible to each world, including itself (this is called the assumption of universal access, or just "universality"). On that supposition, on the table given above, $\Box(A \& B)$ is false in each world. It is not just false in some worlds, w_3–w_8. It is false in each world, even w_1 and w_2, in which its immediate component, A & B is true. This is because there are some worlds accessible from w_1 and w_2, namely w_3–w_8, in which at least one of the conjuncts of A & B is false, making A & B false in those worlds. According to possible worlds semantics, if A & B is false in even one world, v, $\Box(A \& B)$ is false in all worlds that have access to v, even those in which A & B is true.

In contrast, assuming universality, $\Diamond(A \& B)$ is true in all worlds, even w_3–w_8, in which A & B is false. This is because there are some worlds in which both A and B are true, making A & B true in those worlds. And according to possible worlds semantics, if A & B is true in even one world, v, then $\Diamond(A \& B)$ is true in all worlds that have access to v, even those in which its immediate component, A & B, is false. Some other interpretation might be devised on which $\Diamond(A \& B)$ is false in all worlds, but on the interpretation that uses the world table given above, and is universal, $\Diamond(A \& B)$ is true in all worlds.

Considering these remarks, the world table given above can be further completed as follows:

IS: universal

	A	B	C	C → A	A & B	$\Box$(A & B)	$\Diamond$(A & B)	A ∨ B	$\Box$(A ∨ B)	$\Diamond$(A ∨ B)
w_1	T	T	T	T	T	F	T	T	F	T
w_2	T	T	F	T	T	F	T	T	F	T
w_3	T	F	T	T	F	F	T	T	F	T
w_4	T	F	F	T	F	F	T	T	F	T
w_6	F	T	F	T	F	F	T	T	F	T
w_8	F	F	F	T	F	F	T	F	F	T

On any world table for a universal interpretation, box and diamond sentences will always have either a column of T's or a column of F's under their main connectives. This is a consequence of how their value is determined when all worlds have access to all worlds. But box and diamond sentences that are true on all rows of one world table need not be true on all the rows of a different world table, that is, on a different interpretation.

For example, $\Box(C \to A)$ is true in all worlds of the world table given above, because there is no world in which C → A is false. This does not mean that either C → A or $\Box(C \to A)$ is modally valid or m-valid. In SL, C → A is not s-consequential if there is even one interpretation on which it is false. C → A and $\Box(C \to A)$ are not m-valid in MSL, either. They are not true in all worlds of all interpretations. Even though $\Box(C \to A)$ is true in all worlds of the interpretation given above, it is not true in all worlds of other interpretations. This is as it should be, because the aim is to capture other kinds of necessity than logical necessity. The project of possible worlds semantics is to do this by understanding necessity *on an interpretation* as truth in all worlds *of that interpretation*. Box sentences are not, therefore, the equivalent of s-valid sentences of SL.

There are sentences that meet the high bar MSL sets for validity, as further discussed below.

The following, rigorous statement of the semantics for MSL reflects what has been said so far. Changes from the statement of the semantics for SL are in bold.

Interpretations for MSL

An *interpretation*, I, of **MSL** consists of **three components: a set, Ω, (omega) of worlds; a two-place relation, S, on the worlds of Ω; and a world-relative valuation, α, of the sentence letters.**

    (i) Ω is a nonempty and possibly (but not necessarily) infinite set of worlds, $\{w_1, w_2, w_3, \ldots\}$, called the worlds of I.

> (ii) **S is a two-place *accessibility relation* on the members of Ω. It specifies which worlds of Ω see which worlds of Ω.**
>
> (iii) **α assigns exactly one of T and F to each sentence letter in each world of Ω. More rigorously, α assigns exactly one of T and F to each pair, <P,w>, where P is a sentence letter and w is a world.** Notation: $\alpha_w(P)$ is T or $\alpha_w(P)$ is F. **Informally: P is T in w on α; P is F in w on α.**

In addition to Ω, S, and α, interpretations for MSL work with a co-domain, V, of values and a subset, V_d, of designated values. These components have not been listed because variations in values and designated values are not considered. All interpretations considered in sections 9.1 and 9.2 work with the same co-domain, {T,F}, and the same value, T, is designated. In sections 9.3 and 9.4 the co-domain is {0,1} and 1 is designated.

Valuation Rules

Abbreviation: If P is a sentence letter, Iw(P) is $I\alpha_w(P)$

(⊥): Iw(⊥) is F

(~): Iw(~P) is T if and only if Iw(P) is F; otherwise Iw(~P) is F

(&): Iw(P & Q) is T if and only if Iw(P) and Iw(Q) are T; otherwise Iw(P & Q) is F

(∨): Iw(P ∨ Q) is T if and only if at least one of Iw(P) and Iw(Q) is T; otherwise Iw(P ∨ Q) is F

(→): Iw(P → Q) is F if and only if Iw(P) is T and Iw(Q) is F; otherwise Iw(P → Q) is T

(≡): Iw(P ≡ Q) is T if and only if Iw(P) is the same as Iw(Q); otherwise Iw(P ≡ Q) is F

(□): Iw(□P) is T if and only if for each world, v, if w sees v, then Iv(P) is T; otherwise, Iw(□P) is F

(◇): Iw(◇P) is T if and only if for at least one world, v, w sees v and Iv(P) is T; otherwise Iw(◇P) is F

(□) and (◇) have been stated in their elegant form. The "otherwise" clauses are unpacked on the following chart.

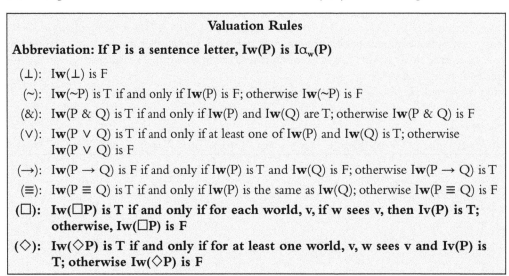

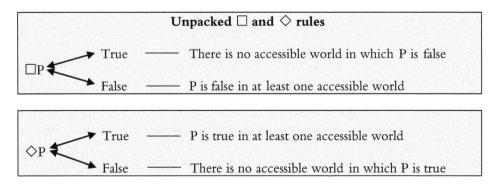

Read the chart from left to right to draw the correct inference from the fact that □P or ◇P is true or false. Read it from right to left to infer what value □P or ◇P must have in the circumstance specified on the right. When reading from left to right, consider □P or ◇P to be true or false in some mentioned world.

On this semantics, the sentences of MSL are not extensional. Extensionality is the property of invariance in meaning under substitution of parts that have the same meaning. A sentence, P, is extensional if and only if, if P contains one or more occurrences of Q, and I(Q) is I(R) (Q and R have the same value on an interpretation I), then I(P) is I(P(R ¦ Q)) (putting R in the place of one or more of the occurrences of Q in P does not produce a sentence that has a different value on I). Extensionality fails for box and diamond sentences of MSL. Suppose Iv(A) is true in each world, v, that w sees. Then Iw(□A) is true. Suppose further that Iw(A) and Iw(B) are both T, but that Iv(B) is F in at least one of the worlds, v, that w sees. Then Iw(□B) is F. So even though □A contains an occurrence of A, and Iw(A) is Iw(B), the result, □B, of replacing an occurrence of A in □A with an occurrence of B, does not have the same value on Iw as $\Box$A. Extensionality fails. As noted at the outset of chapter 8, this failure of extensionality is the defining feature of modal logic, as currently conceived.

Exercise 9.1

1. *State what follows from each of the following by a single left to right application of* ($\Box$).
   - ⋆**a.** Iw($\Box$A) is T
   - b. Iw($\Box$~A) is T
   - ⋆**c.** Jv($\Box$A) is F
   - d. Jv($\Box$(A & B)) is F
   - ⋆**e.** Iv($\Box\Diamond$A) is F
   - f. Iv($\Box\Box$A) is T
   - ⋆**g.** Jw($\Box$(A → B)) is T
   - h. Jw($\Box$(A → B)) is F

2. *State what follows from each of the following by a single left to right application of* ($\Diamond$).
   - ⋆**a.** Iw($\Diamond$A) is T
   - b. Iw($\Diamond$~A) is T
   - ⋆**c.** Iw($\Diamond$A) is F
   - d. Iw($\Diamond$(A ∨ B)) is T
   - ⋆**e.** Iw($\Diamond\Box$A) is F
   - f. Iw($\Diamond$~$\Diamond$A) is T
   - ⋆**g.** Iw($\Diamond$(A → B)) is F
   - h. Iw($\Diamond$(A → B)) is T

3. *State what, if anything, follows from each of the following by a single right to left application of* ($\Box$) *in each of the following cases:*
   - i.   IΩ *is* {w, v}, w *sees* v *but not itself, and* v *sees nothing;*
   - ii. IΩ *is* {w, v} *and* IS *is universal (*w *sees itself and* v, *and* v *sees itself and* w).
   - ⋆**a.** Iw(A) is T
   - b. Iv(A) is T
   - ⋆**c.** Iw(A) is F
   - d. Iv(A) is F
   - ⋆**e.** Iw(A) and Iv(A) are T
   - f. Iw(~A) and Iv(~A) are T *(the inference is from right to left only)*
   - ⋆**g.** Iw(A) is T and Iv(A) is F
   - h. Iw(A) is F and Iv(A) is T
   - ⋆**i.** Iw($\Box$A) is T
   - j. Iv($\Diamond$A) is T
   - ⋆**k.** Iw($\Diamond$A) is F
   - l. Iv($\Box$A) is F

4. *State what, if anything, follows from each of the following by a single right to left application of* ($\Diamond$) *in each of the following cases:*
   - i.   IΩ *is* {w, v}, w *sees* v *but not itself, and* v *sees nothing;*
   - ii. IΩ *is* {w, v} *and* IS *is universal (*w *sees itself and* v, *and* v *sees itself and* w).
   - ⋆**a.** Iw(A) is T
   - b. Iv(A) is T
   - ⋆**c.** Iw(A) is F
   - d. Iv(A) is F
   - ⋆**e.** Iw(A) and Iv(A) are T
   - f. Iw(A) and Iv(A) are F
   - ⋆**g.** Iw(A) is T and Iv(A) is F
   - h. Iw(A) is F and Iv(A) is T
   - ⋆**i.** Iw($\Box$A) is T
   - j. Iv($\Diamond$A) is T
   - ⋆**k.** Iw($\Diamond$A) is F
   - l. Iv($\Box$A) is F

5. *Suppose* IΩ *is* {w,v,u} *and* Iα *assigns* F *to* A *in* w *and* v *but* T *to* A *in* u. *What minimal accessibility map does* IS *have to provide for the following results? (Do not include more arrows than needed on the map. They can have unintended results.)*

    ★**a.** Iw($\Box$A) is T

    b. Iv($\Diamond$A) is T

    ★**c.** Iu($\Box$A) is F

    d. Iu($\Diamond$A) is F

    ★**e.** Iw($\Box\Diamond$A) is F

    f. Iẇ($\Diamond\Box$A) is T

6. *Consider the interpretations,* I_k, I_t, I_4, *and* I_5. Ω *is* {w, v, u} *for all interpretations.* α *is also as follows for all interpretations:*

α:	A	B	C
w	T	T	T
v	F	T	F
u	T	F	F

On I_kS, w *sees only v, v sees only u, and u sees nothing.*
I_tS *is the same as* I_kS *except for adding that each world sees itself.*
I_4S *is the same as* I_tS *except for adding that w sees u.*
I_5S *is universal (all worlds see all worlds including themselves).*

Determine the following by appeal to the valuation rules.

    ★**a.** I_kw(A & B)

    b. I_Kv($\Diamond$(A & B))

    ★**c.** I_kw($\Box$(A → B)) *and* I_kv($\Box$(A → B))

    d. I_ku($\Box$~A) *and* I_ku($\Diamond$A) *(Careful!)*

    ★**e.** I_ku($\Box$(A & ~A)) *and* I_ku($\Diamond$(A ∨ ~A))

    f. I_kv($\Diamond$A) *and* I_ku($\Diamond$A)

    ★**g.** I_kw($\Diamond$~(B ∨ C)), I_tw($\Diamond$~(B ∨ C)), *and* I_4w($\Diamond$~(B ∨ C))

    h. I_kv($\Box$A → A)

    ★**i.** I_tv($\Box$A → A)

    j. I_kw($\Box\Box$B) *(What worlds does w see on* I_kS? *What is* I_k($\Box$B) *in each of those worlds?)*

    ★**k.** I_kw($\Box$B → $\Box\Box$B), I_tw($\Box$B → $\Box\Box$B), I_4w($\Box$B → $\Box\Box$B)

    l. I_tw($\Box\Diamond$C), I_5w($\Box\Diamond$C)

    ★**m.** I_kw($\Diamond$C → $\Box\Diamond$C), I_tw($\Diamond$C → $\Box\Diamond$C), I_4w($\Diamond$C → $\Box\Diamond$C), I_5w($\Diamond$C → $\Box\Diamond$C)

    n. I_ku($\Diamond$(A ∨ ~A)) *and* I_5u($\Diamond$(A ∨ ~A))

These exercises have some surprising results. They show that any box sentence is true in a world that sees no worlds, even $\Box$(A & ~A). Likewise, any diamond sentence is false in a world that sees no worlds, even $\Diamond$(A ∨ ~A). (See exercise 6e.) (t) and (4) are false in some worlds of some interpretations. (See 6h and k.) And (5) is false in some worlds of some interpretations. (See 6m.) Does this mean that there are no m-unsatisfiable or m-valid sentences, and that possible worlds semantics considers Dt, Ds4, and Ds5 to be unsound?

There are m-valid sentences, but the notions of m-validity and of the other intensional concepts need to be further refined. An interpretation's set of worlds, Ω, and its accessibility relation, S, constitute a "frame" for an interpretation. Interpretations that use the same frame, and differ from one another only in their valuations, form a family. These families are principally distinguished from one another by features that can be imposed on S. The family that includes all interpretations whatsoever is the k-family. It is defined as the family of interpretations that are not restricted in how they interpret S. They can impose as many or as few accessibility relations on their worlds as they please, and those relations can go in any direction around or between worlds.

Though exercise 6e correctly establishes that $\Diamond$(A ∨ ~A) is not k-valid, A ∨ ~A is k-valid, as is $\Box$(A ∨ ~A). No interpretation can contain a world on which one and the same atomic sentence of MSL is both true and false, and no world can contain an atomic sentence that does not receive a value. "A" must therefore be exactly one of true or false in each world of each interpretation. Whichever it is, A ∨ ~A must be true in that world. So, A ∨ ~A must be true in each world of each interpretation. Moreover, for any world, w, of any interpretation, I, w either sees one or more worlds, or it does not see any worlds. Either way w does not see any worlds in which A ∨ ~A is false. So □(A ∨ ~A) must also be true in each world of each interpretation. This makes A ∨ ~A and □(A ∨ ~A) k-valid.

Similarly, even though □(A & ~A) is true in any world that does not see any world, A & ~A is still false in that world and ◇(A & ~A) is false in all worlds. This makes A & ~A and ◇(A & ~A) k-unsatisfiable. The other intensional concepts are formulated in similar terms.

Intensional Concepts for All Modal Interpretations

A sentence, P, is *m-valid* if and only if there is no **world of any** m-interpretation **in** which it is false.

P is **m-invalid** if and only if there is at least one world of at least one m-interpretation in which it is false.

P is *m-unsatisfiable* if and only if there is no **world of any** m-interpretation **in** which it is true.

P is m-satisfiable if and only if there is at least one world of at least one m-interpretation in which it is true.

P is *m-contingent* if and only if it is true **in at least one world of** at least one **m**-interpretation, and false **in at least one world of** at least one **m-interpretation (the interpretations need not be the same)**.

Two sentences, P and Q, are *m-equivalent* if and only if there is no **world of any** **m-interpretation in** which they have different values.

P and Q are not **m**-equivalent if and only if there is at least one **world of at least one m**-interpretation **in** which they have different values.

A set of sentences, Γ, is *m-unsatisfiable* if and only if it there is no **world of any** **m**-interpretation **in** which each sentence in that set is true.

Γ is *m-satisfiable* if and only if there is at least one **world of at least one** **m**-interpretation **in** which each sentence in that set is true.

A demonstration, Γ / P is *m-valid* if and only if there is no **world of any** **m**-interpretation **in** which each premise in Γ is true and P is false.

Γ / P, is **m**-invalid if and only if there is at least one **world of at least one** **m**-interpretation **in** which each sentence in Γ is true and P is false.

By these definitions, and by the results of exercise 9.1#6h, k, and m alluded to earlier, □P → P, □P → □□P, and ◇P → □◇P are not k-valid. Furthermore, because □P is true in any world that does not see any world, whereas ◇P is false in any such world, □P → ◇P is not k-valid. This does not mean that something has gone wrong with the semantics that has just been given. While □P → ◇, □P → P, □P → □□P, P → □□P, and ◇P → □◇P are invalid in the k-family, they become valid in families that, unlike k, place restrictions on S. It was noted when discussing formalization that intuitions about the validity of some modal statements are conflicting, depending on what kind of necessity □ is read as designating (necessary truth, moral necessity, temporal persistence, etc.). For this reason, the derivation rules were sectioned into different, progressively stronger systems, Dk, Dt, Ds4, and Ds5. Possible worlds semantics reflects this by recognizing corresponding families, characterized by progressively more restrictive conditions on S. (The idea of modifying possible worlds semantics with an accessibility relation, and the insight that different restrictions on the accessibility relation can capture different intuitions about what modal sentences are axiomatic is due to Saul Kripke [1940–], after whom Dk and k-semantics are named.)

Suppose someone is interested in applying modal logic to ethics. Such a person would not want to accept (□E) or □P → P. In the deontic context, □P → P says that whatever is obligatory is the case, which is false in this world (and this world is the principal one such a person would be concerned with). However, that person would want to accept (D): □P → ◇P, which says that whatever is obligatory is permissible. What is obligatory may not happen, but it must be something that is allowed to happen. Possible worlds semantics translates "Something is allowed to happen" as there is at least one possible world where it does happen ("ought" implies "can"). But as long as there can be worlds that see no worlds, "ought implies can" is invalid. $\Box P \rightarrow \Diamond P$ is false in such worlds. (As noted earlier, any box sentence is true in such worlds, and any diamond sentence false.) A deontic logic needs to rule out the possibility that there could be such worlds. This can be done by imposing a special condition on the accessibility relation. Deontic logic specifies that S must be serial, that is, that each world must see at least one world. (Other arrows could be present as well, but serial ones must be.)

Requiring that S be serial ensures the truth of $\Box P \rightarrow \Diamond P$. By ($\Box$), if $Iw(\Box P)$ is T, P must be T on I in any world that w sees. Provided IS is serial, there must be at least one such world. By ($\Diamond$), if w sees a world in which P is true on I, $\Diamond P$ must be true in w on I. So $\Box P \rightarrow \Diamond P$ cannot be false on any interpretation with a serial frame. A semantics for modal logic that builds on k-semantics by stipulating that S must be serial is called D-semantics (for "deontic").

Similar restrictions can be imposed on S to create systems of modal logic that validate $\Box P \rightarrow P$, $\Box P \rightarrow \Box\Box P$, $P \rightarrow \Box\Diamond P$, and $\Diamond P \rightarrow \Box\Diamond P$. To validate (t): $\Box P \rightarrow P$, stipulate that S is reflexive, that is, that each world must see itself.

Since ($\Box$) says that if $Iw(\Box P)$ is T then P is true on I in any world that w sees, stipulating that each world sees itself entails that P must be true in any world in which $\Box P$ is true. $\Box P \rightarrow P$ is therefore valid on interpretations with reflexive frames. Reflexive frames are a minimal way k must be extended to capture intuitions about necessity when necessity is understood as necessary truth.

To validate (4): $\Box P \rightarrow \Box\Box P$, stipulate that S is transitive, that is, that a world must see any world seen by a world that it sees (if w sees v and v sees u, w must see u).

To understand why this works, suppose $Iw(\Box P)$ is T. By ($\Box$), P must be true on I in any world, v, that w sees. By transitivity, w must not only see v, but any world, u, that v sees. Since w sees all those u's, P must be true on I in them as well, and so true in all the worlds that v sees. Since P is true in all the worlds that v sees, it follows by ($\Box$) that $\Box P$ must be true in v. But v is *any* world that w sees. So $\Box P$ is true in any world that w sees, which means $\Box\Box P$ must be true in w. Thus, imposing a transitivity condition on IS ensures that any instance of $\Box P \rightarrow \Box\Box P$ must be true in any world of I. Frames that are both reflexive and transitive are said to rank their worlds. Higher worlds see themselves and lower ones. Lower ones do not see higher ones. Rankings are important for the semantics for intuitionistic logic.

To validate (B): $P \rightarrow \Box\Diamond P$, stipulate that S is symmetric, that is, that any world is seen by any world it sees (if w sees v then v sees w).

To understand why this works, suppose P is true in w. Now consider any world, v, that w sees. By symmetry, each of those worlds sees w and so sees at least one world in which P is true, so $\Diamond P$ must be true in any world that w sees. But that means $\Box\Diamond P$ must be true in w.

To validate (5): $\Diamond P \rightarrow \Box\Diamond P$, stipulate that S is transverse, that is, that any two worlds that a world sees must see one another (if w sees both v and u, v and u must see one another; as a special case, if w sees v and w sees v, v must see v, that is, itself).

To understand why this works, suppose Iw($\diamond$P) is T. By ($\diamond$), w must see at least one world, v, in which P is T on I. But w could see other worlds as well. As long as IS is transverse, those other worlds must all see v (and v must see itself). So, by ($\diamond$), $\diamond$P must be true on I in each of those worlds. So $\diamond$P must be true in each world seen by w, which by ($\square$) means that Iw($\square\diamond$P) must be T. So any instance of $\diamond$P $\rightarrow$ $\square\diamond$P must be true in any world of any interpretation with a transverse frame.

A semantics for modal logic that builds on k-semantics by requiring that S be reflexive is called t-semantics. One that builds on k-semantics by stipulating that S must be both reflexive and transitive is called s4 semantics. One that builds on k-semantics by stipulating that S must be both reflexive and symmetric is called B-semantics. And one that builds on k-semantics by stipulating that S must be reflexive and transverse is called s5 semantics. A frame that is both reflexive and transverse is symmetric and transitive. (If any two worlds that are seen by w see one another, and w sees itself, then if w sees v, because w sees both itself and v, v sees w. And given that w's seeing v means v sees w, if v also sees u, then because v sees w and u, w and u must see one another, which means that if w sees v and v sees u, w must see u.) Frames that are reflexive, symmetric, and transitive are universal. All worlds see all other worlds. s5 semantics is a semantics for universal frames.

Systems of Modal Semantics (Frame Conditions)

k – k-semantics places no restrictions on S.

Deontic Systems

D – D semantics requires that S be serial.
  (Seriality: for each world, w, there is a world, v, such that w sees v)

Alethic Systems

t – t-semantics requires that S be reflexive.
  (Reflexivity: each world sees itself)

s4 – s4 semantics adds the requirement that S be transitive to t-semantics. This is
  tantamount to requiring that S be a ranking.
  (Transitivity: if w sees v and v sees u then w sees u)

B – B semantics adds the requirement that S be symmetric to t-semantics.
  (Symmetry: if w sees v then v sees w)

s5 – s5 semantics adds the requirement that S be transverse to t-semantics. This is
  tantamount to requiring that S be universal.
  (Transverse: if w sees v and w sees u then v and u see one another)
  (Universality: each world sees each world)

There are valid and unsatisfiable sentences, valid demonstrations, unsatisfiable collections, and equivalent sentences on each of these systems. Since m-interpretations are infinite, it is impossible to use long tables to identify them. But the techniques developed in chapter 5 continue to be applicable. Invalidity, satisfaction, contingency, and nonequivalence are defined by the existence of an interpretation of the right sort. To demonstrate that these properties hold of sentences, sets, or demonstrations, discover and verify such an interpretation. Validity, unsatisfiability, and equivalence are defined by the impossibility of an interpretation. To demonstrate that these properties hold, suppose to the contrary that there is an interpretation and demonstrate by appeal to the valuation rules and definitions of intensional concepts that this leads to a contradiction. Both techniques are now more involved.

9.1.1 Discovering Interpretations

In section 5.1, short tables were used to discover interpretations. While it is possible to devise a short table method for discovering m-interpretations, tables are used here only to assist in describing an interpretation discovered by reasoning from the valuation rules. There is a further difference. The revised definitions of the intensional concepts make it necessary to discover worlds in which sentences have certain values on interpretations, not just interpretations on which they have those values.

Worlds of interpretations can be discovered using the same method that is used to demonstrate that there is no world of an interpretation. Assume that there is at least one world of at least one interpretation. Only in this case the assumption will not lead to a contradiction, but to a description of the world and the interpretation.

To demonstrate that:	assume that:
• P is invalid	• there is a world of an interpretation in which P is false
• P is satisfiable	• there is a world of an interpretation in which P is true
• P is contingent	• there is a world of an interpretation in which P is true and a world of an interpretation in which P is false
• Γ / P is invalid	• there is a world of an interpretation in which each sentence in Γ is true but P is false
• Γ is satisfiable	• there is a world of an interpretation in which each sentence in Γ is true
• P and Q are not equivalent	• there is a world of an interpretation on which one of P and Q is true but the other is false

As when attempting to demonstrate validity, unsatisfiability, or equivalence, apply the valuation rules to reason from assignments to compounds to assignments to components. When the sentence, demonstration, set, or pair of sentences is not valid, unsatisfiable, or equivalent (respectively), this reasoning will not uncover a contradiction. Instead, it will uncover a set of restrictions on an interpretation. Where there are multiple restrictions it can be difficult to get a grip on all of them at once and a vision of how to reconcile them. Drawing up a table that identifies worlds, assignments to sentences in worlds, and accessibility relations between worlds can help to keep track of the requirements and make it more evident how to reconcile them. As the reasoning proceeds, the table should be gradually filled in with requirements that must be met. Decisions about how to meet conditions that might be met in multiple different ways should be postponed for as long as possible.

Consider how to identify and verify an interpretation that demonstrates that $\Box\Diamond A$ / $\Diamond\Box A$ is t-invalid. By definition of validity, there must be at least one world, w, of at least one interpretation, I, on which the premise $\Box\Diamond A$ is true and the conclusion, $\Diamond\Box A$ is false. Moreover, because the question concerns t-validity, any world of IΩ must see itself, so w must see itself. These requirements can be collected on a preliminary table that looks like this:

	A	□ ◇ A	◇ □ A
↻ w		T	F

The left side of the table describes the interpretation. It has a row for each world added to IΩ, arrows to represent any accessibility relations that hold between those worlds, a list of atomic sentences occurring in the sentences under consideration, and spaces to enter assignments to those atomic sentences, as they are discovered. The right side of the table is a space for entering assignments that must be made to the compound sentences and their components.

Reasoning back from assignments to compounds to assignments to components proceeds as follows.

(1) By (□), $\Diamond A$ must be T in each world, v, that w sees. By (◇) each world, v, that w sees would have to see at least one world, u, in which A is true. Since t requires that w see itself, it follows in particular that $\Diamond A$ must be T in w, but it does not follow that A must be T in w. It only follows that w see at least one world in which A is true.

	A	□ ◇ A	◇ □ A
↻ w		T T	F

(2) By (◇), $\Box A$ must be F in each world, v, that w sees. Since t requires that w see itself, it follows in particular that $\Box A$ must be F in w.

	A	□ ◇ A	◇ □ A
↻ w		T T	F F

At first blush, this might seem like a contradiction with (1), which says that $\Diamond A$ must be T in w. But there is no contradiction because, by (◇), $\Diamond A$ is true in w provided w sees at least one world in which A is true, and, by (□),

□A is false in w provided w sees at least one world in which A is false. It does follow, however, that w must see at least two different worlds, one in which A is true, and one in which it is false. w could itself be one of these worlds and a second world, v, the other. Capturing this requirement means adding a further line to the table, with a new world and the implied accessibility relations and assignments. Suppose (subject to revision if necessary) that Iw(A) is T, that Iv(A) is F, and that w sees v.

	A	□	◇	A	◇	□	A
w	T	T	T	T	F	F	
v	F						F

But this is supposed to be a t-interpretation. Each world must see itself.

	A	□	◇	A	◇	□	A
w	T	T	T	T	F	F	
v	F		F	F		F	F

Since v sees itself but does not see w, ◇A is F in v and, of course, □A is F in v.

	A	□	◇	A	◇	□	A
w	T	**T**	T	T	F	F	
v	F		**F**	**F**		F	F

But this is a problem because □◇A needs to be T in w, which it is not if w sees v and ◇A is F in v.

Fortunately, the contradiction can be evaded. One way is to add a third world that v sees in which A is true. But it is cheaper to just let v see w. Then it sees that A is T in w, and that makes ◇A (but not □A) T in v, preserving the truth of □◇A in w. (The "cheap" solution incidentally shows that the demonstration is not just t-invalid, but s5 invalid as well, since all worlds end up seeing all worlds. This is not cheating, but doing more than was asked for since the more arrows there are between worlds the harder it is to avoid a contradiction and so to discover an interpretation.)

	A	□	◇	A	◇	□	A
w	T	T	T	T	F	F	F
v	F		**T**	F		F	F

This reasoning has been so involved that the result calls for confirmation with a demonstration.

1.	w sees itself	given
2.	Iw(A) is T	given (second column from the left)
3.	Iw(◇A) is T	2,1 (◇)
4.	v sees w	given
5.	Iv(◇A) is T	4,2 (◇)
6.	w and v are all the worlds of IΩ that w sees	given
7.	Iw(□◇A) is T	3,5,6 (□)
8.	w sees v	given
9.	Iv(A) is F	given
10.	Iw(□A) is F	9,8 (□)
11.	v sees itself	given
12.	Iv(□A) is F	9,11 (□)
13.	Iw(◇□A) is F	10,12,6 (◇)
14.	□◇A / ◇□A is t-invalid	7,13 def. t-invalid

9.1.2 *Demonstrating That There Is No Interpretation*

Because interpretations for modal logic are so much more complex, there are more ways for an interpretation to be contradictory. There can be a contradiction in IΩ, which takes the form of there both being and not being at least one world of a certain sort. There can be a contradiction in IS, which takes the form of a world both seeing and not seeing another world. There can be a contradiction in Iα, which is the assignment of both T and F to the same sentence letter in the same world of the interpretation, or (⊥) can be contradicted by the result that I(⊥) is T. As before, reasoning should proceed from assignments to compounds to assignments to components. Contradictions should take one of the four forms just described. They should not take the form of an assignment of T and F to the same compound sentence. As modal systems get *weaker* (as they require fewer accessibility relations between worlds), it becomes more difficult to discover a contradiction, so it is again important to be clear about which system is under consideration. The answered questions to exercise 9.2#2 provide further illustration.

Exercise 9.2

1. *Establish the following by constructing and verifying an interpretation with the frame specified.*
   - **★a.** ~◇A / ~A is k-invalid
   - b. □□~A / □~A is k-invalid
   - **★c.** ◇A & ◇B / ◇(A & B) is k-invalid
   - d. □(A ∨ B), ~A / □B is t-invalid
   - **★e.** □◇(A ∨ B), ◇~B / ◇A is B-invalid
   - f. □(A → B) / A → □B is s5-invalid
   - g. □~□A / ~◇A is s4-invalid

2. *Establish the following.*
   - **★a.** ◇A =|=$_k$ ~□~A
   - b. □A =|=$_k$ ~◇~A
   - **★c.** If A is k-valid then □A is k-valid
   - d. □(A → B) / □A → □B is k-valid
   - **★e.** □A → A is t-valid
   - f. A → ◇A is t-valid
   - **★g.** □A → □□A is s4-valid
   - h. A → □◇A is s5-valid
   - **★i.** ◇□A → □A is s5-valid
   - j. ◇(A & B) / ◇A & ◇B is k-valid
   - **★k.** □(A & B) =|=$_k$ □A & □B
   - l. □A ∨ □B / □(A ∨ B) is k-valid
   - **★m.** ◇(A ∨ B) =|=$_k$ ◇A ∨ ◇B
   - n. ~◇(A & ~B) =|=$_k$ □(A → B)
   - **★o.** {~□◇A, ~◇□~A} is k-inconsistent

3. *Formalize the following demonstrations in MSL using the interpretation provided. Then show that each is s5-invalid by constructing and verifying an s5 model for the corresponding set. To ensure a correct start on the remainder of the exercise, answers are provided for the formalization.*
   - **★a.** "In the like manner it may be proved that every other accident, how contingent soever it seem, or how voluntary soever it be, is produced necessarily; which is that JD [John Bramhall, 1594–1663] disputes against. The same also may be proved in this manner. Let the case be put for example, of the weather. *It is necessary, that to-morrow it shall rain or not rain.* If therefore it be not necessary it shall rain, it is necessary it shall not rain. Otherwise it is not necessary that the proposition, *it shall rain or it shall not rain,* should be true." Thomas Hobbes, *Questions Concerning Liberty, Necessity, and Chance* #34. (A – it shall rain [tomorrow]; *just formalize the italicized sentence and the one following it.*)
   - **★b.** "If God foresees that I will sin, it must be that I will sin (because his foresight is infallible, meaning that it is not possible that what he foresees will fail to come to pass). God did foresee that I would sin (because God knows all things and the future is present to him just like the past.) It is therefore necessary that I would sin and it was not within my power to abstain from it." Based on Gottfried

Wilhelm von Leibniz, "Dialogue on Human Freedom and the Origin of Evil." The speaker is not Leibniz but an interlocutor. (A – God foresees [foresaw] that I will [would] sin. B – I will [would] sin; *recall the remarks made in section 8.2 on the misleading infixing of the necessity operator in idiomatic English*.)

9.2 Reduction Trees for Modal Sentential Logic

Reduction trees for modal logic use the rules of Ts and four new rules to cover the reduction of box and diamond sentences and their negations. (⊥I) is also modified. As with derivations, there is a basic system, Tk, and extensions, Tt, Ts4, and Ts5. The extensions differ from Tk in their architecture rather than in their rules. "Tm" is used to refer to any of these systems.

m–trees have two new architectural features: they have a box structure and an arrow structure in addition to a path structure. The givens are placed in an initial box. The application of two of the new rules, (T◇) and (~□), requires creating new boxes with arrows indicating the sentence responsible for generating each new box.

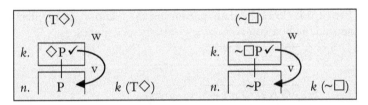

Semantically, ◇P says that P is true in at least one accessible world. That world need not be the "home" world in which ◇P is true. (T◇) accordingly dictates that ◇P be reduced to P on a portion of each open path running up to ◇P that has been boxed off from the portion of the path containing ◇P. The boxed off portions are the analogues of separations between worlds. ~□P is intuitively equivalent to ◇~P and so (~□) works in the way (T◇) would work if it were applied to ◇~P. When the new boxes are created, an arrow, called a "k arrow," is drawn from the sentence in the box containing ◇P or ~□P to the top line of the new box, where P, or ~P is entered. The arrow should originate from the sentence responsible for forming the new box. When a box contains paths, it makes a difference what path a box forming sentence is on, and the arrow needs to make that clear.

In accord with the placement principle, ◇P and ~□P must be reduced on all paths that run up to them. As with the rules of Ts, all of these reductions must be done at once. It is not permissible to reduce ◇P or ~□P on only some paths and return later to reduce them on others. They are reduced once, everywhere they can be reduced, and checked off.

Each application of (T◇) or (~□) creates a new box. Boxes are labelled w, v, u, w_1, w_2, … The letters t and s may be appropriated for this purpose as well.

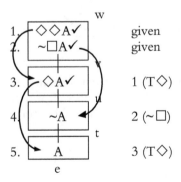

given
given

1 (T◇)
2 (~□)
3 (T◇)

If ◇◇A occurs on one line of a path and ~□A occurs on another, the resulting tree will contain three successive boxes sectioned off on each path that runs up to ◇◇A or ~□A. In the example above, the sentences were reduced from the top down, but the sentence on line 2 could just as well have been reduced first, in which case box u would have come before boxes v and t. Alternatively, the sentence on line 3 could have been reduced before that on line 2, in which case box t would have come before box u. Any way the tree is done, there will be two arrows exiting box w, to boxes v and u, and one arrow exiting box v to box t.

Likewise, any way the tree is done, the path does not close. On m-trees, contradictory literals yield ⊥ only if they are in the same box on the same path.

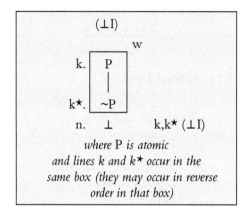

When (⊥I) can be applied, it still closes the path, preventing the addition of any further sentences or boxes. To indicate this, it is derived outside the box containing the contradictory literals.

The following tree for ◇A & ◇~A is incorrect.

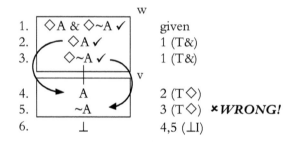

The results of reducing ◇~A at line 3 must go in a new box.

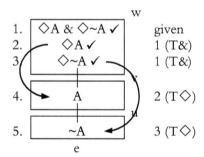

Placing u underneath v may seem wrong for a different reason: it suggests that box u is produced by v, when in fact both u and v are produced by diamond sentences in w. It is tempting to try to show their dependence on sentences in w by putting them on different paths, but this is also wrong.

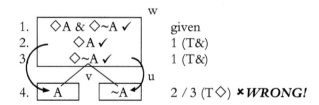

(T◇) is not a path-splitting rule. The job of representing relations between parent and child boxes is done by the arrow structure. On the earlier tree, the fact that the arrows to v and u both originate in w indicates that both v and u are produced by sentences in w. The fact that there is no arrow from v to u indicates that u is not produced by any sentence in v. But u and v still lie on the same path.

In the following case, different boxes correctly lie on different paths.

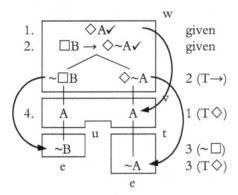

This tree illustrates the two importantly different layouts that can arise: multiple paths within the same box, and multiple boxes on the same path. When a path-splitting rule is applied to a sentence in a box, it produces two paths within that box. When two different box generating sentences lie on the same path, reducing them puts two boxes on that path. In the case where an unreduced box generating sentence lies above a path split, as at line 3 above, it makes no difference whether the sentence is reduced in a single box that stretches across both paths (as above) or is put in separate boxes on each path. In the latter case, it also makes no difference whether the same or different lower-case letters are assigned to each box. Path structure trumps box structure. What appears on other paths has no bearing on whether a given path closes or on the tree model it defines if it does not close. The principal advantage of the configuration chosen at line 4 above is that it requires only one arrow and makes it clear that both paths are extended by the same rule application. The principal disadvantage is that it masks the fact that, from the perspective of any one path, what appears on another path might as well not exist.

As before, the rules could be applied in a different order. The sentence on line 3 right could have been reduced at line 4, creating a box only on the left path at line 4. The sentence on line 1 could have been reduced at line 5, creating either a lower box that extends across both paths or different lower boxes on each path.

Exercise 9.3

Determine whether the following sets are inconsistent in Tk.

★**a.** {A & ◇(B & ~B)}

b. {◇~~A, ◇~(A ∨ ~A)}

★**c.** {◇(~A ∨ B), A & ~□B}

d. {~□A, ◇(B & ~(B ∨ A))}

★**e.** {◇(B & ~□(A → (B → □A)))}

f. {~□⊥, ◇(A & ◇(~A ∨ ⊥)}

The remaining new rules, (T□) and (~◇), require previously created arrows to previously created boxes.

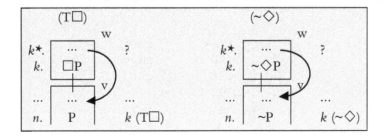

The following tree is therefore exhausted in Tk.

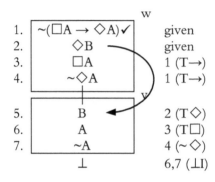

Since there is no arrow running from any sentence on the path containing □A or ~◇A, (T□) and (~◇) cannot be applied. In this case, it would make all the difference if there were a sentence on the path that is reduced by a box forming rule. The tree below closes because there is a sentence on line 2 that creates an arrow for the sentences on lines 3 and 4.

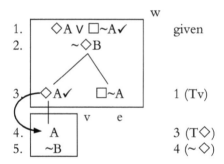

Importantly, the arrow must originate from a sentence on the same path and in the same box.

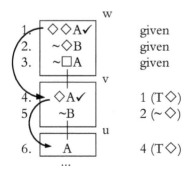

The tree above still has an exhausted path. Even though there is an arrow from w to v, □~A cannot be reduced in v (sentences can only be reduced on paths that run through them) and ~◇B cannot be reduced on the right path (though both paths run through ~◇B there is no arrow exiting from the right path).

□ and ~◇ sentences do not get checked off. As a tree grows, and more ◇ and ~□ sentences are reduced, more arrows grow out of paths. Each time an arrow is added to a path, all the □ and ~◇ sentences that are on that path in the same box as the sentence the produces the arrow need to be reduced again on each continuation of the path in the box the arrow points to. Consider the following partially completed tree.

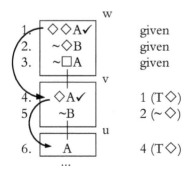

Because there is an arrow from a sentence on ~◇B's path and in ~◇B's box, ~◇B must be reduced on the portion of each path that runs down from it into the box the arrow points to. This occurs on line 5 on the tree above. Because there is no such arrow from w to u, a similar reduction is not allowed in u. But this tree is unfinished. The sentence on line 3 is checkable and has not yet been reduced. When it is reduced, it produces a new arrow from w, so ~◇B must be reduced again.

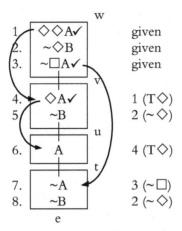

The definition of an exhausted path is revised to reflect this requirement.

(def ex)

A path of an m-tree is exhausted if and only if:

  (i) each sentence in the set the tree was made for has been placed on top of the tree **in the initial box**

  (ii) ⊥ does not stand alone on any line of the path

  (iii) each sentence on the path is either (i) a literal, (ii) a nonliteral, **non-□, non-~◇** sentence that has been reduced (checked off), **or (iii) a □ or ~◇ sentence that has been reduced on the portions of each path that runs through it that lie in each box pointed to by an arrow originating from a sentence on its path and in its box.**

Since check marks are useless for verifying whether □ and ~◇ sentences have been reduced, paths and boxes must be inspected for reduction results. On more complex trees, it can help to subscript □ and ~◇ sentences with the labels for the boxes in which they have so far been reduced.

The remaining nine rules of Ts must be applied within the same box. Once a new box has been created by one of the two box forming rules, the only sentences that may occur in it are those resulting from (T□), (~◇), or the reduction of sentences already in that box. The following tree is incorrect:

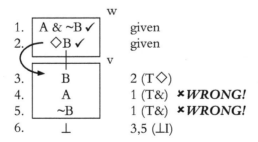

The results of an application of (T&) cannot be placed in a box that does not contain the sentence being reduced. The same holds for (T∨), (DN), or any of the other reduction rules of Ts. Once the bad choice to reduce the sentence on line 2 at line 3, and prematurely open a new box, has been made, the sentence on line 1 may not be reduced in that box. It must still be reduced. But the results of doing so must be entered in the same box that contains

A & ~B. One way to manage this after box v has been opened on the path is to draw in a "continuation" of box w around the side of v and place the reduction results in that continuation. (A continuation of w can also be drawn by making a separate, third box below v, but labelling it w. To keep things clear to start, physical continuations are drawn in this textbook wherever feasible.)

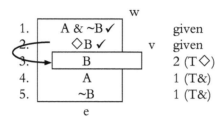

Continuations are difficult to make and difficult to follow. They should be avoided whenever possible. In the case at hand, a properly done tree avoids the continuation by reducing line 1 before line 2.

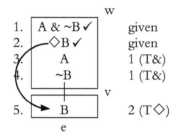

One way to reduce the need for continuations is to postpone (T◇) and (~□) applications until after all rules of Ts have been applied. Even if this means making multiple paths, the resulting tree may be less complex than one that requires continuations.

Exercise 9.4

Identify which of the following sets are inconsistent in Tk. Postpone applying the box or diamond rules until everything else that can be done has been done, regardless of how many paths are created in the process. Then make just one (T◇) or (~□) application. Draw out all the consequences that follow from that one application before making a second (T◇) or (~□) application. Make all (T◇) and (~□) applications that are possible in one box, w, before moving on to another box, v. Ensure that □ and ~◇ sentences in w are only reduced in boxes reached by k-arrows originating from the appropriate path in w. Refer to the answered questions for further guidance.

★**a.** {A & □~A}
  b. {◇A & □~A}
★**c.** {A & ~□A}
  d. {□A & □~A}
★**e.** {□A & ◇~A}
  f. {◇□A}
★**g.** {□◇A}
  h. {~□◇A}
★**i.** {~□~◇~A}
  j. {~◇~□A}
★**k.** {~(□A → A)}
  l. {~(A → □◇A)}
★**m.** {~(◇A → □◇A)}
  n. {~(◇□A → A)}
★**o.** {~(◇A → □B), □C}
  p. {~(◇A → □□B), □C}

★**q.** $\{\sim(\Diamond\Box A \rightarrow \Box A)\}$
  r. $\{\sim(\Box A \rightarrow \Box\Diamond A)\}$
★**s.** $\{\Diamond\Diamond A \mathbin{\&} \Box\sim A\}$
  t. $\{\sim(\Box A \rightarrow \Box\Box A)\}$
★**u.** $\{\sim[(A \rightarrow A) \rightarrow \Box(A \rightarrow A)]\}$
  v. $\{\sim[\Box(A \rightarrow B) \rightarrow (\Box A \rightarrow \Box B)]\}$
★**w.** $\{\sim[(\Box A \rightarrow \Box B) \rightarrow \Box(A \rightarrow B)]\}$
  x. $\{\Diamond(A \lor B), \Box\sim A, \Box\sim B\}$
★**y.** $\{\Diamond A \lor \Diamond B, \Box\sim A, \Box\sim B\}$
  z. $\{\Box A \lor \Box B, \Diamond\sim A, \Diamond\sim B\}$
★**aa.** $\{\Box(A \lor B), \Diamond\sim A, \Diamond\sim B\}$
  bb. $\{\Diamond(A \lor B), \Box(\Diamond\sim A \lor \Diamond\sim B)\}$ *(Hard.)*

Trees for t, s4, and s5 are produced by adding extra arrows to k-trees. The additional arrows require further (T□) and (~◇) reductions, often closing paths that are open on a k-tree.

> ### Arrow Structure for Enhanced Systems
>
> Tt: add a *reflexivity arrow* (also called a t-arrow) to each box (an arrow pointing from that box to itself)
>
> Ts4: add a reflexivity arrow to each box and add *transitivity arrows* (also called 4 arrows; for any three boxes, w, v, and u, if there is an arrow from w to v and v to u add an arrow from w to u)
>
> Ts5: add a reflexivity arrow to each box, and *transverse arrows* (also called 5 arrows; for any three boxes, w, v, and u, if there is an arrow from w to v and an arrow from w to u, add arrows both ways between v and u)

In Ts5, there is an arrow from each box to each other box, and from each box to itself. Rather than clog up the tree with all these arrows, it is easier and clearer to reduce □ and ~◇ sentences in all boxes on any path that runs through them, including higher as well as lower boxes. This requires some caution. Though Ts5 puts a double-headed arrow between all boxes on the same path, it does not put double-headed arrows between boxes on different paths. By way of illustration, consider how an s5 tree for $\{\Box\Diamond A \rightarrow \Diamond\Diamond\Box B, \Box C\}$ grows up from a k-tree.

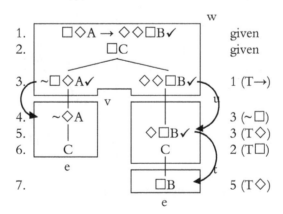

On this tree, the application of (~□) to the sentence on the left path at line 3 creates an arrow to a new box on a left path extension; the application of (T◇) to the sentence on the right path on line 3 creates an arrow to a new box on the right path extension; and the application of (T◇) to the sentence on the right path on line 5 creates an arrow to a new box on an extension of that path. Because □C on line 2 lies above both paths, and there is an arrow from the left path in w to v and an arrow from the right path in w to u, (T□) is applied in the new boxes on both paths to put C in both boxes. But because there is no further arrow from w to t, (T□) cannot be applied to put C in t.

Now consider how this k-tree would look if it were turned into a t-tree. That would mean putting reflexivity arrows on each box.

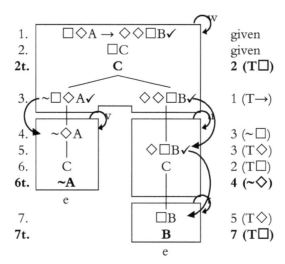

Reflexivity arrows are an exception to the rule that arrows should originate from sentences. They are placed at the head of the box and indicate that all □ and ~◇ sentences in the box must be reduced in that box, regardless of where those sentences occur in the box. The reflexivity arrows on boxes w, v and t accordingly dictate that □C be reduced in w (line 2t), that ~◇A be reduced in v (line 6t), and that □B be reduced in t (line 7t). The reflexivity arrow added to u has no effect.

Converting this t-tree to an s4 tree means adding transitivity arrows. In this case, there is only one instance where an arrow can be added. w sees u and u sees t, so an arrow from w to t is called for.

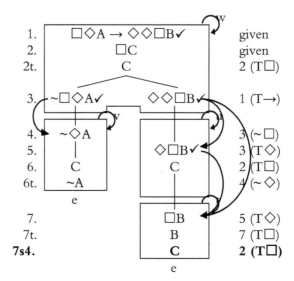

The only effect of the new arrow is to require that □C in w be reduced along the transitivity arrow in t, which is done at line 7s4.

Now consider how converting the t-tree to an s5 tree changes just the arrow structure.

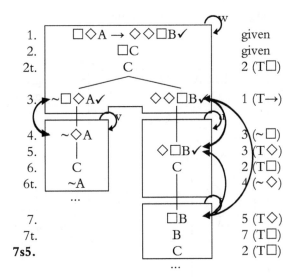

The k-arrows that were present in the t-tree become double-headed arrows. Because w sees itself and v, v must see w. Because w sees itself and u, u must see w. And because u sees itself and t, t must see u. The s5 tree also acquires a double-headed arrow where the s4 tree had a transitivity arrow. Because u sees both w and t, w and t must see one another.

But, though w sees both v and u, and both v and t, no double-headed arrows have been placed between those boxes.

Exercise

Why should a conversion of the t-tree above to an s5 tree not place double-headed arrows between v and u or v and t?

As the original k-arrows indicate, it is only because of a sentence on the left path in w that w sees v, whereas it is only because of a sentence on the right path in w that it sees u and t. Box v was created by the sentence on line 3 left. Boxes u and t were created by sentences on line 3 right and line 5 right. This is why it is important to be careful about drawing k and transitivity arrows from the sentences responsible for producing those arrows. Were transverse arrows put between v and u or v and t they would cross those paths and require that ~◇A be reduced in u and t, and that □B be reduced in v. But ~◇A does not occur on the path that contains u or t and □B does not occur on the path that contains v, so those reductions would violate the placement principle. Because □C on line 2 occurs above the path split, and w sees both v and u, it is reduced on both paths. But that does not hold for ~◇A or □B. Tree paths represent alternative ways of reducing the givens to literals. Combining results obtained on different paths risks producing false closures. Elsewhere, s5 has been characterized as implying universality, the doctrine that all worlds see all worlds. But "all worlds" is short for "all worlds of an interpretation," and different tree paths can define different tree models and so different interpretations. On s5 trees, universality only means that all boxes *on a path* have double-headed arrows to all boxes *on that path*.

s5 trees pose another problem. The double-headed arrows that must be presumed to exist between boxes on the same path (whether drawn in or not) require that □ and ~◇ sentences found in boxes lower down on the path be reduced in boxes higher up on the path. The tree given above, for example, has both paths marked as unfinished. This is because the arrow from v to w means that ~◇A must be reduced in w, and the arrows from t to u and t to w mean that □B must be reduced in u and w. This might be done by squeezing the required sentences between previously written lines, but it is unnatural to look to lower parts of a derivational structure for justifications for sentences placed higher up. It also invites mistakes. The required sentences cannot be squeezed in just anywhere in w. For example, were □B at line 7 reduced to B higher up on the path, care would have to be taken to ensure that it is not inserted above the path split. Putting B above the path split would mean entering it on both the right and the left paths, which would be tantamount to reducing □B on the left path, in violation of the placement principle. The best way to handle this challenge is with continuations. This can turn into a map maker's nightmare, as suggested by the solution below, but it keeps the right sentences on the right paths. A less theatrical alternative is to box off a lower portion of a path without using an extension arm, but designate that the lower portion is a continuation by labelling it with the same box letter.

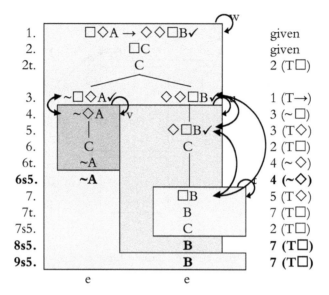

1.	□◇A → ◇◇□B✓	given
2.	□C	given
2t.	C	2 (T□)
3.	~□◇A✓ ◇◇□B✓	1 (T→)
4.	~◇A	3 (~□)
5.	◇□B✓	3 (T◇)
6.	C C	2 (T□)
6t.	~A	4 (~◇)
6s5.	**~A**	**4 (~◇)**
7.	□B	5 (T◇)
7t.	B	7 (T□)
7s5.	C	2 (T□)
8s5.	**B**	**7 (T□)**
9s5.	**B**	**7 (T□)**

The tree constructed above includes all the arrows that exist on an s5 tree: a reflexivity arrow on each box, and a double-headed arrow between any two boxes that lie on the same path. On k, t, and s4 trees, it is important to draw the arrows because they signal where (T□) and (~◇) applications need to be performed. When doing an s5 tree, they need to be performed everywhere on the path so the arrows mark nothing special and so may be omitted.

Exercise 9.5

1. *Identify the exercises in 9.4 that do not have closed trees. Redo those exercises that have different t-trees.* **Selected answers**.

2. *Identify the answers to question 1 that do not have closed trees. Redo those exercises that have different s4-trees.* **Selected answers**.

3. *Identify the answers to question 2 that do not have closed trees. Redo those exercises that have different s5-trees.* **Selected answers**.

4. *Based on the answers to questions 1–3 identify some theorems of Tt, Ts4, and Ts5. Drawing on answers to exercises 9.4, identify some theorems of Tk.* **Selected answers**.

As discussed in section 9.1, an interpretation for modal logic consists of a set of worlds, Ω, an accessibility relation S, and a valuation, α, of each sentence letter in each world. As with Ts, an exhausted path on an m-tree defines a tree model, that is, a world of an interpretation in which all the givens are true. The model must be appropriate for the tree: a k-model for k-trees, a t-model for t-trees, an s4 model for s4 trees, and an s5 model for s5 trees.

As hinted by the labels that have been used for boxes, a tree model of the appropriate sort is constructed by considering each box on the exhausted path to designate a world. Ω is defined as the set of worlds (boxes) on the exhausted path. The arrows describe the accessibility relations between the worlds. For each box on the path (world in Ω), α assigns T in that world to each sentence letter to stand alone on a line in the corresponding box, and F in that world to all other sentence letters. The values α assigns to sentence letters in one box depend only on what sentence letters appear in that box, not on those appearing in any other box. Suppose, for example, that a tree produces an exhausted path containing three boxes, w, v, and u. There are arrows from w to v and u. A, B, and C each stand alone on a line in w. B stands alone on a line in v, and A and C each stand alone on lines in u. Then I makes the following assignments:

$$
\begin{array}{cc|ccc}
S & \Omega & A & B & C \\
\hline
\curvearrowleft w & & T & T & T \\
\rightarrow v & & F & T & F \\
\rightarrow u & & T & F & T \\
\end{array} \Big\} \, \alpha
$$

Method for Constructing an M-Tree Model

(i) Look only at the leftmost exhausted path.

(ii) Consider the boxes on this path to be the worlds of Ω.

(iii) Consider the arrows between the boxes to specify which worlds see which other worlds.

(iv) Assign a T **in the world a box stands for** to each sentence letter that stands alone on a line **in that box** and an F **in that world** to all other sentence letters; **repeat for each box on the path.**

A difficulty will have been discovered by those working through the stages of the answer to exercise 9.4g. Whenever a diamond occurs within the scope of a box, it can appear that an s4 or s5 tree will continue forever.

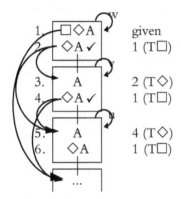

1.	□◇A	given
2.	◇A ✓	1 (T□)
3.	A	2 (T◇)
4.	◇A ✓	1 (T□)
5.	A	4 (T◇)
6.	◇A	1 (T□)
	...	

Applying (T□) to line 1 using the reflexivity arrow on w puts a diamond sentence in w, which must be reduced by opening a new box at line 3. But once the new box has been opened, (T□) must be applied to line 1 which creates a diamond sentence in the lower box. Were that diamond sentence reduced in a third box, a transitivity or transverse arrow between the first and third boxes would call for yet another application of 1 (T◇), setting the stage for an unending cycle.

The cycle can be avoided by considering that ◇A at line 4 is already reduced by A at line 3. ◇P is reduced provided there is an arrow from the box that contains it to a box that contains P. If there is no arrow to a box containing P, then (T◇) is applied to create them. But if other features of the tree have incidentally already created these results, a further application of (T◇) is not called for. ◇P can simply be checked off with a notation indicating the line at which it is reduced. Importantly, both features must already be present. There must be an arrow exiting the box that contains ◇P, if only a reflexivity arrow, and the arrow must point to a box that already contains P. When there is just an arrow and no occurrence of P, as at line 2, (T◇) must be applied to reduce ◇P in a new box.

Exercise 9.6

Describe and verify the s5 model defined by each of the exhausted paths discovered in answer to exercise 9.5#3. **Selected answers**.

There are two different strategies for doing m-trees. If it is anticipated that the tree will close, a judicious strategy is called for. It makes just those rule applications that will close the tree. If it is anticipated that the tree will produce an exhausted path, a systematic strategy is called for on that path. Since □ and ~◇ sentences are not checked off, proceeding systematically helps to ensure that no required □ or ~◇ reductions have been overlooked.

To proceed systematically, wait with applying (T◇) and (~□) until everything else that can be done (including (T□) and (~◇)) has been done, regardless of how many paths are created in the process. Call this stage 1. At stage 2 make just one (T◇) or (~□) application. It is much more trouble to draw continuations than to draw new paths, and s5 trees become unmanageable unless stage 1 is completed before stage 2 because of the multiple continuations that must be drawn when new boxes are opened prematurely. The idea is to do everything that can be done in a box before leaving that box, then open only as many new boxes as result from a single (T◇) or (~□) application, being careful to make that application on all paths selected by the placement principle. At this point, stage 3 commences: make a judicious application of (T□) and (~◇) on paths that can be closed, and a top-down application (take up (T□) and (~◇) sentences in the order in which they occur from the top down) on paths that will not close. On closed paths, the idea is to look for the quickest way to close a path using as few (T□) and (~◇) applications as possible. On paths that do not close, care must be taken to ensure that each of these rules has been applied in all possible ways to each □ or ~◇ sentence on the path. Go down the path from the top and reduce each □ or ~◇ sentence as it comes up, being sure to follow all the arrows exiting from its path in its box when doing so. It can help to keep a record of what has been done by subscripting each □ and ~◇ sentence with a list of the boxes it has already been copied into. (Keeping a record is wise, because work at this stage can create work to be done at stage 1, which can create more work to be done at this stage, at which point it can be helpful to have a record of how much has already been done.) At this point, work reverts to stage 1. When working at stage 1, do not skip to stage 2. Do not interrupt stage 1 reductions to make another (T◇) or (~□) application without finishing everything that can be done at stage 1 in all extant boxes. Otherwise, a need for extra continuations may be created. Continue cycling through the stages until the path is exhausted or the tree becomes unmanageably large.

To illustrate progress through the stages, consider an s5 tree for {◇~(~A → B) & ~□(B & A), ◇A ∨ ◇□B}. Following advice given above, arrows are omitted. It is assumed that there is a reflexivity arrow on each box and double-headed arrows between any two boxes that lie on the same path.

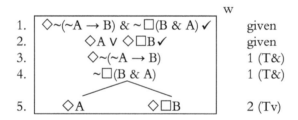

At this point, stage 1 is complete. Everything has been done in box w that can be done. Though there is an assumed reflexivity arrow on w, there are no □ or ~◇ sentences in w to reduce along that arrow. Work proceeds to stage 2. There are four stage two sentences, at lines 3, 4, and 5 left and right. Only one of them should be reduced, followed by all possible work in the box it creates. As with Ts, priority should be given to sentences that do not further split the paths. Since the sentence on line 4 reduces to a path-splitting sentence it should be set aside for now. Again, as with Ts, priority should be given to the sentence most likely to close at least one of the paths, but at this point it is not easy to see which sentence would do that. A final strategy from Ts is to prefer the sentence that will quickly produce an exhausted path, but it is not clear which one that would be.

When all other things are equal, Ts recommends reducing the more complex sentence first. But in Ts5, that is not always the shorter sentence. The shorter sentence on line 5 right is more complex than the longer one on line 3 because, as a ◇□ sentence, it will call for a continuation once it is reduced. This can be a challenging task if it is postponed. Consider the effect of reducing the longer sentence on line 3 first, and only doing the one on line 5 right after a cycle through stage 1.

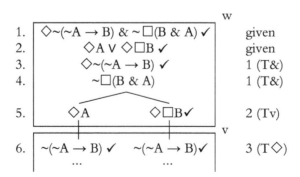

There are no □ or ~◇ sentences on the tree as of line 6, so there are no stage 3 reductions to perform at that point. Under this circumstance, it is not permissible to proceed to apply another stage 2 rule. If reducing a single stage 2 sentence does not create any work to do at stage 3, work must revert to stage 1. A further application of a stage 2 rule is only permissible after all stage 1 work created by the earlier stage 2 rule application has been completed.

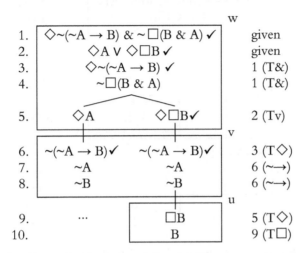

Over lines 7 and 8 work reverts to stage 1. Once that work has been completed, it is permissible to return to reduce another stage 2 sentence. This is done at line 9, where the ◇ sentence on line 5 is reduced. Work at stage three then commences with the box sentence in u (the only □ or ~◇ sentence on the tree so far) being reduced along u's assumed reflexivity arrow. Further reductions of this sentence are required by the assumed arrows from u to v and u to w.

At this point there is a choice. Proceed systematically down the right path, making all possible (T□) applications, or proceed judiciously, hoping to find just some that will close the path. The right choice is the judicious one. But for purposes of illustration, suppose it is not anticipated that the path will close and that work proceeds systematically. Because this is an s5 tree, □B on line 9 must be reduced in all boxes on the path, so B must appear in both w and v. This requires a continuation from w around to the bottom of u, and another continuation from v around to be bottom of u. It has become apparent why it was a mistake to reduce the apparently longer sentence on line 3 first. Had the actually more complex sentence on line 5 been reduced first, box u would have appeared above box v, making a continuation of v around u unnecessary.

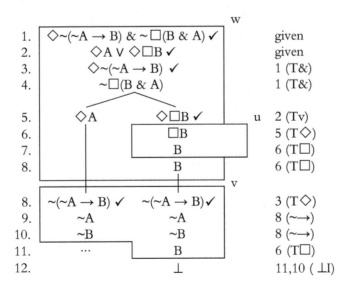

Work on the right path has been systematic. But it has turned out that the path closes. Had it been foreseen that this would happen, the (T□) applications on lines 7 and 8 could have been omitted as the path would have closed without them. Doing so simplifies the tree, eliminating the need for the continuation of w around u.

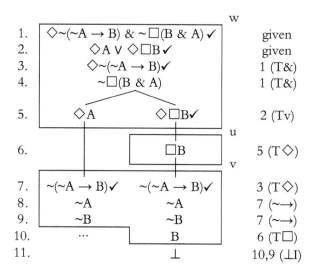

It is unfortunate that the path closed. Had it been exhausted, further work on the tree could have been abandoned in favour of extracting a tree model from the exhausted path. As it is, the left path must be completed. This requires reducing the sentences on lines 4 and 5. As the one on line 4 splits the path, it should be postponed.

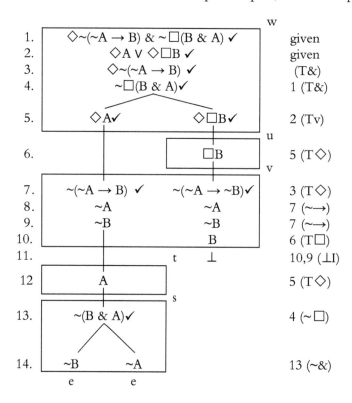

Discovering that the left path is exhausted means that some unnecessary work was done on the right path. Lines 7–9 would still have had to appear on the left path, because the sentence on line 3 stands above the path split, so its reduction results must be entered on both paths. But lines 6, 10, and 11 could have been omitted. That having been done, the sentences on lines 13 and 14 would need to be entered on the right path as well, as it is no longer closed. Entering the sentence on line 13 on the right path is required by the placement principle, since ⊥ no longer appears on the path and the path does run up to line 4. And entering the sentences on line 14 a second time is required by the principle that applying a rule on a line requires extending its results across that line, wherever they are applicable.

These modifications produce a slightly shortened tree.

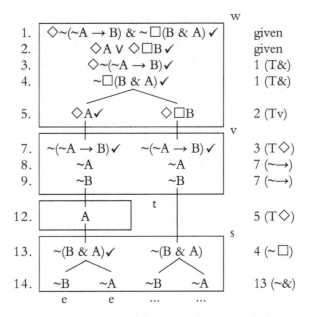

It remains to verify the tree model defined by the leftmost exhausted path.

Ω: {w, v, t, s}
S: universal

α	A	B
w	F	F
v	F	F
t	T	F
s	F	F

Verification of the tree model is as follows:

1. Is(B) is F   given
2. Is(B & A) is F and w sees s   1 (&), given
3. Iw($\Box$(B & A)) is F   2 ($\Box$)
4. Iw($\sim\Box$(B & A)) is T   3 ($\sim$)

5. It(A) is T and w sees t   given
6. Iw($\Diamond$A) is T   5 ($\Diamond$)
7. Iw($\Diamond$A $\vee$ $\Diamond\Box$B) is T   6 ($\vee$) verifying the given on line 2

8. Iv(B) is F   given
9. Iv(A) is F   given
10. Iv($\sim$A) is T   9 ($\sim$)
11. Iv($\sim$A $\to$ B) is F   10,8 ($\to$)
12. Iv($\sim$($\sim$A $\to$ B)) is T and w sees v   11 ($\sim$), given
13. Iw($\Diamond\sim$($\sim$A $\to$ B)) is T   12 ($\Diamond$)
14 Iw($\Diamond\sim$($\sim$A $\to$ B) & $\sim\Box$(B & A)) is T   4,13 (&) verifying the given on line 1

Exercise 9.7

1. *Determine whether the following demonstrations are derivable in* Ts5 *or a weaker system. Say what the tree proves and why. If a demonstration is not derivable, be sure the tree is an s5 tree, recover the tree model from the leftmost exhausted path and verify that the demonstration is s5 invalid on this model. If a demonstration is derivable, close the tree using as few arrows as possible and say whether the demonstration is already derivable in* Tk, Tt, *or* Ts4, *or only derivable in* Ts5.

   ⋆a. $\Box(A \to B) \ / \ \Box A \to \Box B$
   b. $\Box A \to \Box B \ / \ \Box(A \to B)$
   ⋆c. $\sim\Diamond A \ / \ \Box(A \to B)$
   d. $\Box B \ / \ \Box(A \to B)$
   ⋆e. $\Box\Diamond A, \Box(A \to B) \ / \ \Box\Diamond B$ *(Hint: this tree closes; look for the fastest way to get closure or it could inflate beyond workable limits.)*
   f. $\Diamond\Box A, \Diamond(A \to B) \ / \ \Diamond\Box B$
   ⋆g. $\Box A \ / \ \Diamond\Diamond A$
   h. $\Diamond A, \Diamond B \ / \ \Diamond(A \ \& \ B)$
   ⋆i. $\Diamond\Diamond A \ / \ \Diamond A$
   j. $A \lor B \ / \ \Diamond A \lor \Diamond B$
   ⋆k. $\Diamond(A \ \& \ \Box B) \ / \ \Diamond A \ \& \ \Box B$
   l. $\Box(A \lor B), \Box(A \to B) \ / \ \Box B$

2. *Following the procedure used in chapter 7, determine whether the following sentences are theorems, inconsistent, or contingent in* Ts5 *or a weaker system. Say what the tree or trees prove and why. If a sentence is contingent, be sure the tree is an s5 tree, recover two tree models and verify that it is s5 contingent on those models. Do the tree most likely to close first. If a tree does close, use as few arrows as possible to close it and say whether the sentence is already a theorem or inconsistent in* Tk, Tt, *or* Ts4, *or only has its status in* Ts5.

   ⋆a. $A \to \Box A$
   b. $A \to \Diamond A$
   ⋆c. $\Box\sim A \lor \Box\Diamond A$
   d. $A \to \Diamond\Box A$
   ⋆e. $\Diamond A \to \Diamond\Box A$
   f. $\Box[\Box(A \to B) \lor \Box(B \to A)]$
   ⋆g. $\Box\sim A \to \Box(A \to \sim A)$
   h. $\Box(\sim\Box\Diamond A \to \sim A)$
   ⋆i. $\Box\Diamond\Box A \to \Box A$
   j. $\Box\Diamond A \to \Diamond\Box\Diamond A$
   ⋆k. $\sim\Box(\sim B \to \sim A) \to \Diamond A$
   l. $\Box(\Diamond(A \ \& \ \sim A) \to B)$

3. *Following the procedure used in chapter 7, determine whether the following sentences are interderivable in* Ts5. *Say what the tree or trees prove and why. If the sentences are not interderivable, be sure the trees are s5 trees, recover a tree model from each, and verify that the corresponding sets are s5 nonequivalent on those models. Do the tree most likely to produce an exhausted path first. If both trees close, use as few arrows as possible to close them and say whether the sentences are already interderivable in* Tk, Tt, *or* Ts4, *or only have this status in* Ts5.

   ⋆a. $\Box(A \ \& \ B), \Box A \ \& \ \Box B$
   b. $\Box(A \lor B), \Box A \lor \Box B$
   ⋆c. $\Diamond(A \ \& \ B), \Diamond A \ \& \ \Diamond B$
   d. $\Diamond(A \lor B), \Diamond A \lor \Diamond B$
   ⋆e. $\Box(A \equiv B), \Box A \equiv \Box B$
   f. $\Diamond(A \equiv B), \Diamond A \equiv \Diamond B$
   ⋆g. $\Box(\sim A \to A), \Box A$
   h. $\Diamond(\sim A \to A), \Diamond A$
   ⋆i. $\Box A \to \Diamond B, \Diamond(A \to B)$
   j. $\Diamond A \to \Box B, \Box(A \to B)$
   ⋆k. $\Diamond(A \ \& \ \Diamond B), \Diamond A \ \& \ \Diamond B$
   l. $\Diamond(A \ \& \ \Diamond B), \Diamond(A \ \& \ B)$

9.3 Semantics for Intuitionistic Sentential Logic

Intuitionistic logic was originally devised as a derivation theory, based on the informal account of what is derivable that was presented in section 6.6. It was only later that Saul Kripke devised the semantics for intuitionistic logic that is presented here. That semantics is based on s4 modal semantics. Though based on s4, this semantics is not a formal semantics for intuitionistic modal logic. It is a formal semantics for intuitionistic sentential logic that uses an apparatus like that for modal sentential logic.

On this account, Ω is not a set of worlds. It is instead a set of stages in the development of evidence. Each stage affirms all the sentences that are evident as of that stage.

Introducing stages of evidence allows intuitionists to account for what it means for a sentence to be nonevident without introducing a nonevidence operator or a third value. They can instead say that a sentence, A, is nonevident at stage s if and only if s sees both a stage at which A is evident and a stage at which it is nonevident. In contrast, A is evident or true at s if and only if s does not see a stage at which A is nonevident, and A is evidently impossible or false at s if and only if s does not see a stage at which A is evident. It is as if "A is evident" meant $\Box$A, "A is false" meant $\Box{\sim}$A, and "A is nonevident" meant $\Diamond$A & $\Diamond{\sim}$A, except that the operators are absorbed into A.

As noted in section 6.6, evidence is understood as something that cannot decay or change. Like what has once been demonstrated in mathematics, what once becomes evident stays evident. More things become evident over time. This means that stages of evidence can be ranked. Later stages contain everything (all the sentences) that are evident at any earlier stage, and more besides. Each stage has a domain of sentences that it recognizes as true, and the contents of these domains can only increase, never shrink, with the passage from earlier to later stages.

Accordingly, interpretations for intuitionistic logic use s4 frames. Each stage sees itself (it sees what is evident at that stage), so there is a reflexivity arrow on each stage. And what each stage sees as evident in itself must continue to be evident in any later stage, so there are transitivity arrows carrying all the evidence down to all the later stages. There are no backwards arrows, from stages with larger domains, where more things are evident, to stages with smaller domains. The backward view is blocked. No later stage has access to the content of any earlier stage except by means of its access to itself, which copies whatever was evident at the earlier stage.

While interpretations for intuitionistic logic are in these ways like s4 interpretations, there is an important further detail. Any earlier stage, s, sees multiple, alternative, later states of evidence. For any sentence, A, that is nonevident at s, s sees at least one stage at which A is evident, and at least one stage (if only itself) at which A is nonevident. If there are two nonevident sentences at s, s will see at least four ways the evidence could turn out. Between s and these four alternative later stages there are four paths. Each of these paths leads up to a possible subsequent stage of evidence, t. s sees all the t's.

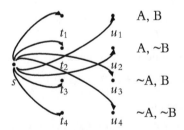

(Reflexivity arrows have not been coloured in to reduce clutter; they are still there.)

In virtue of transitivity, s also sees any stage u seen by any of the t's. But any one of the t's will not see all of the u's. Because evidence does not decay, whatever was either evident or evidently impossible at s will continue to be evident or evidently impossible at each of the t's and each of the u's that s sees. But if a sentence, say B, becomes evident at t, t will not see any stage, u, at which B is nonevident. It will only see itself and later stages at which B is true. What is evident at t cannot cease to be evident at any stage that t sees on pain of not being evident. The stages that s saw, at which B is nonevident drop off the accessibility map for t. As they drop off the map for t, so they drop off the map for any u that t sees. As far as this section of the map is concerned, it as if the rest of the map is not there. It is not going too far to say that as evidence increases, large sections of the accessibility map are erased, along with all earlier portions of the map and all the stages on them.

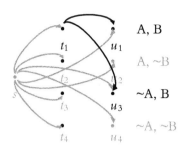

As evidence grows, the accessibility map narrows. Stages that were accessible earlier disappear. In intuitionistic semantics, possibilities (stages at which a sentence is nonevident) are not permanent, and they never increase. They only diminish as new evidence comes in.

The accessibility map is not a static picture of arrows between persisting stages. That would be the antithesis of the intuitionist tenet that there are no truths already out there waiting to be discovered. Later stages of evidence are constructed rather than discovered. Prior to being constructed there is access to a stage at which a sentence is evident and access to a stage at which it is nonevident. But the creation of evidence (be it either confirming evidence or refuting evidence) destroys this variety. One or other of the alternatives vanishes. This is not to say that it was illusory. It was a possibility at the earlier stage. But the creation of evidence at the later stage destroys it.

The formal semantics detailed below does not completely model these features. To do so, the frame conditions, Ω and S, would need to be dynamic. As new evidence is produced, earlier evidential stages would need to be deleted from Ω, and entire forward sections of the accessibility map, containing arrows to stages inconsistent with the current stage, would need to be deleted from Ω and from the map. Modelling these dynamic features is more trouble than it is worth, but keeping them in mind makes it easier to understand how the valuation rules work.

An interpretation, I, for intuitionistic sentential logic consists of:

  (i) a nonempty set, Ω, of stages of evidence $\{s_1, s_2, s_3, \ldots\}$
  (ii) a reflexive, transitive accessibility relation, S, between the stages of Ω
  (iii) A stage-relative assignment, α, of 1 (T) to a finite selection of sentence letters, $P_1 \ldots P_n$, at each stage, s, such that if s sees t and $\alpha_s(P)$ is 1, then $\alpha_t(P)$ is 1. α_s also makes a default assignment of 0 (not-T) to any sentence letter that is not assigned 1. *(Intuitionists do not recognize results that depend on the completion of infinite tasks. At each stage, s, α_s only assigns finitely many 1's to sentence letters at that stage. All other assignments are nonassignments. The default "assignment," 0, designates a nonassignment.)*

In making assignments to compound sentences, I uses the following valuation rules:

Abbreviation: if P is a sentence letter, Is(P) is Iα_s(P)

  ($\perp$): Is($\perp$) is 0 at any stage, s.

  ($\sim$): Is($\sim$P) is 1 if and only if for each stage, t, if s sees t, It(P) is 0; otherwise Is($\sim$P) is 0.

  (F): Is(P) is F if and only if Is($\sim$P) is 1.

  (&): Is(P & Q) is 1 if and only if Is(P) and Is(Q) are 1; otherwise Is(P & Q) is 0.

  ($\vee$): Is(P $\vee$ Q) is 1 if and only if at least one of Is(P) and Is(Q) is 1; otherwise Is(P $\vee$ Q) is 0.

  ($\rightarrow$): Is(P $\rightarrow$ Q) is 1 if and only if for each stage, t, if s sees t, either It(P) is 0 or It(Q) is 1; otherwise Is(P $\rightarrow$ Q) is 0.

  ($\equiv$): Is(P $\equiv$ Q) is 1 if and only if for each stage, t, if s sees t, It(P) is the same as It(Q); otherwise Is(P $\equiv$ Q) is 0.

As explained in section 6.6, interpretations for ISL assign 1's and 0's, rather than T's and F's. 1 means "evident" and is the same as T, but 0 means "nonevident" or "not-T" rather than "false" or "refuted." The (F) valuation rule is inserted to relate the values assigned by intuitionistic semantics with the classical F value. In practice, the rule has no use.

The valuation rules for conjunctions and disjunctions are like those for SL. The values of the compounds at a stage depend on the values of the components at that stage, and they do so as they did in SL. But the rules for negations, conditionals, and biconditionals are a function of assignments to components at each stage seen by the current stage.

In intuitionistic logic, ~P does not just say that there is no evidence for P. It says that it is evident that P can never become evident. Intuitionistic semantics cashes this out as meaning that P must be nonevident at each accessible stage. If ~P is 1 on I at stage s then P must be 0 at any stage that is seen by a stage that s sees. ~P must therefore continue to be 1 at any stage that s sees. This complements the truth condition on α, which ensures that if $I\alpha_s(P)$ is 1 then P must continue to be 1 on I at any stage that s sees.

It follows that even though there are only two values, 1 and 0, and even though evidence is either present or not present, there are three evidential states: the state where I(P) is 1 at s and all stages seen by s; the state where I(P) is 0 at s and all stages seen by s; and the state where I(P) is 0 at s but 1 at at least one stage seen by s. Consider any atomic sentence, P. If $Is(P)$ is 1 then if s sees a stage, t, $It(P)$ is 1, by definition of $I\alpha$. Similarly, if $Is(\sim P)$ is 1, then if s sees t, $It(\sim P)$ is 1, as a consequence of (~), as it is formulated for intuitionistic semantics. But if $Is(P)$ is 0, the value of $Is(\sim P)$ depends on a survey of all the stages that s sees, and that survey can determine two different results. If s can see a stage at which P is 1, then, because it also sees itself, it sees stages at which P is 1 and stages at which it is 0, so $Is(\sim P)$ is 0 along with $Is(P)$. It is only if P is 0 at all the stages that s can see that $Is(\sim P)$ is 1.

Intuitionists understand P $\rightarrow$ Q to assert that evidence for P constitutes evidence for Q. In keeping with this understanding if s sees a stage, t, such that $It(P)$ is 1 (evident) and $It(Q)$ is 0 (nonevident), s could not see evidence for P to constitute evidence for Q, so $Is(P \rightarrow Q)$ must be 0. But that does not mean the negation, ~(P $\rightarrow$ Q), must be 1 at s. For $Is(\sim(P \rightarrow Q))$ to be 1, s could only see stages at which P is 1 and Q is 0. If it sees any stages at which either I(P) is 0 or I(Q) is 1, then $Is(\sim(P \rightarrow Q))$ is also 0. This makes it clear what is required for $Is(P \rightarrow Q)$ to be 1: s must not see a stage at which P is 1 and Q is 0. Otherwise put, at any stage it sees, either P is 0 or Q is 1. In that case, any subsequent path on the accessibility map could close off at most one of these alternatives. Looking forward from a later state, t, P might be 1 at all subsequent stages, but then Q would have to be 1 at each of those stages as well. If, instead, looking forward from t, Q is 0 at any subsequent stage, P would have to be 0 at that stage as well.

The truth condition for biconditionals follows from that for conditionals. Biconditionals are conjunctions of converse conditionals, so the rule is the effect of conjoining the rules for converse conditionals. For both (P $\rightarrow$ Q) and (Q $\rightarrow$ P) to be evident at s, s cannot see a stage at which P is evident and Q is nonevident, and it cannot see a stage at which Q is evident and P is nonevident. At any stage s sees, either $It(P)$ and $It(Q)$ are both 1 or $It(P)$ and $It(Q)$ are both 0.

9.4 Reduction Trees for Intuitionistic Sentential Logic

While intuitionistic semantics can account for three evidential states using just two values, trees defy these simple resources. On classical sentential trees, the claim that I(P) is T appears as P and the claim that I(P) is F appears as ~P. On intuitionistic trees, the claim that I(P) is 1 can still appear as P, but ~P does not say that I(P) is 0. It instead makes the stronger assertion that I(~P) is 1. If I(~P) is 1, ~P must appear on the path in all accessible boxes; if I(P) is 0, it need not. Consequently, the classical closure rule is too weak. (If P is evident at s there can be no accessible stage at which it is nonevident. There is a contradiction if there is even one accessible stage at which it is nonevident. ~P sets the bar too high by demanding that there be no accessible stage at which P is evident.) Closure is not only warranted if P and ~P occur in the same box on the same path; it is also warranted if P and "P is nonevident" occur in the same box on the same path. SL has no way to say "P is nonevident." Since intuitionistic sentential logic uses the vocabulary for SL, this is a problem.

The resolution proposed here follows one introduced by Bell and Machover (1977). A special symbol, ?, is introduced for use on trees. "?" is not a new vocabulary element for SL. It is only generated in the process of applying tree rules, and is used as a sign that the sentence to which it is affixed is nonevident at the current stage of evidence. The occurrence of P and ?P in the same box suffices to close the path.

Syntactically, "?" is only prefaced to completed sentences, never limited to a component of a sentence. This makes punctuation redundant. "?" is always understood to have scope over the whole sentence.

With the aid of ?, and understanding that P has the same role on intuitionistic trees that $\Box$P has on modal trees (and ~P the same role as $\Box$~P), the tree rules are:

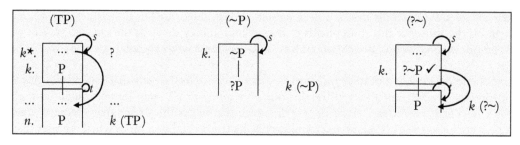

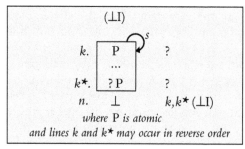

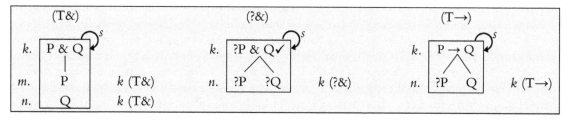

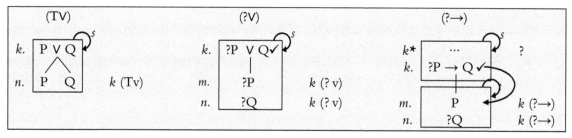

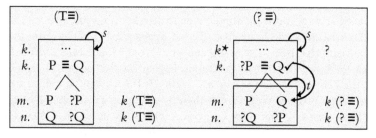

The rules resemble the rules of Ts, except that "?" replaces ~ in most cases. Except for (TP), the T rules and (~P) place their reduction results in *s*, but (TP) moves any sentence not prefaced by "?" into each accessible box. (This is why the T rules and (~P) do not check off their sentences. Any sentence not preceded by ? is the equivalent of a □ sentence for purposes of reduction in T is.) Even when a T rule derives question marked sentences, those results appear in any accessible box as a consequence of applying (TP) to the parent sentence and reducing it there. These consequences capture the principle that evidence does not decay. If a sentence is evident in one box, it must be found in any accessible box.

As with the (□) and (~◇) rules in Tm, (TP) does not create its own k-arrows. k-arrows are only created by (?~), (?→), and (?≡).

To understand why the rules are consistent with the semantics, keep in mind that P should be read as □P and ?P as saying that P is nonevident at the stage corresponding to the box where ?P occurs.

(TP) has the form that it does because P is really □P and accordingly requires that P be entered in each accessible box.

~P is really □~P. It might be expected that this would mean that (~P) would require entering ~P in each access-ible box, but (TP) already does that. (~P) has a different job to do. (⊥I) is now written to derive ⊥ only when P and ?P occur in the same box, so it is necessary to derive ?P from ~P, to avoid neglecting closures.

There is no (DN) rule. Double negations − that is, sentences of the form ~~Q − are instances of ~P, and so are reduced by (~P).

?~P is equivalent to "it is nonevident that ~P." For that to be the case, *s* must see at least one box containing P. If *s* only saw boxes containing ~P, ~P would already be evident. Between them, (~P) and (?~) reduce ~~Q in *s* to Q in at least one accessible box, *t*, preventing immediate closure in either *s* or *t* and allowing *s* to see other accessible boxes that contain ?Q.

(T&) and (T∨) work just the way they do in Ts. Because (TP) moves P & Q and P ∨ Q into each accessible box, P & Q and P ∨ Q are also reduced in each accessible box. ?P & Q and ?P ∨ Q, in contrast, only say that P & Q and P ∨ Q are nonevident at *s*, so their reduction results can only be entered in *s*.

(?→) says that if P → Q is nonevident at *s*, there must be at least one accessible box at which P is evident but Q is nonevident, that is, a box that contains P and ?Q. (T→) says that if P → Q is evident at *s*, then at any accessible stage either P cannot be evident or Q must be evident. So the path in *s* splits into branches displaying ?P and Q and, as with (T&) and (T∨), (TP) is used to move P → Q into each accessible box where (T→) is applied again. Similarly, P ≡ Q is nonevident at *s* if and only if *s* sees a stage at which one of P and Q is evident without thereby providing evidence for the other. That is a stage at which one of them is question marked and the other is not. P ≡ Q is T if and only if *s* sees no such stage, that is, if and only if at each stage either both P and Q are 1, or both are question marked. This is again provided for by reducing P ≡ Q in *s* and by using (TP) to move P ≡ Q into each accessible box, where it can be reduced again.

Intuitionistic trees can be used to confirm the fundamental intuitionist tenets that ~~P does not yield P and that P ∨ ~P is not a theorem, as well as to confirm that (DNI) and (EFQ) are "sound," and that a number of classical results continue to hold in intuitionistic logic. They can also be used to determine which equivalence principles fail in intuitionistic logic.

When setting up trees, P is demonstrated to be a theorem with a tree for ?P; P / Q is demonstrated to be derivable with a tree for P and ?Q; and P and Q are demonstrated to be equivalent with trees for P and ?Q and for Q and ?P. This is of course because the opposite of "P is evident," is "P is nonevident," symbolized on trees as ?P. In verification, question marked givens should be demonstrated to have the value 0 on the tree model.

Since sentences reduced by the T rules and (~P) are not checked off, special care needs to be taken on exhausted paths. (TP) is applicable to any sentence not preceded by ?. On an exhausted path, (TP) must be used to move each such sentence into each box pointed to by an arrow from the box containing that sentence. To verify that this has been done, it helps to keep a record by subscripting sentences with the letter designating the box in which they have been reduced after each (TP) application. If the sentence is compound, this should be followed up with visual inspection to verify that it has been further reduced in that box. The process is illustrated in solutions to ★ questions in the following exercise.

Exercise 9.8

1. *Establish the following in* Tis. *Extract and verify the tree model defined by the leftmost open path.*
    ★**a.** ~~A / A is not derivable in Tis *(do a tree for* ~~A *and* ?A, *not* ~~A *and* ~A*)*
    b. A ∨ ~A is not a theorem of Tis *(do a tree for* ?A ∨ ~A, *not* ~(A ∨ ~A)*)*

2. *Establish the following both in* Tis *and by means of a demonstration by appeal to intuitionistic semantics.*
    ★**a.** A / ~~A is derivable in Tis and is i-valid
    b. ~~~A / ~A is derivable in Tis and is i-valid
    ★**c.** ~A, ~~A / B is derivable in Tis and is i-valid
    d. ~~(A ∨ ~A) is a theorem of Tis and is i-valid
    ★**e.** A → B, A → ~B / ~A is derivable in Tis and is i-valid
    f. A → B, A → ~B / A → C is derivable in Tis and is i-valid
    ★**g.** ~(A & ~A) is a theorem of Tis and is i-valid
    h. ~A → (A → B) is a theorem of Tis and is i-valid
    i. ~~(A → B) → (~~A → ~~B) is a theorem of Tis and is i-valid *(Hard; if two* ? *sentences occur in a box, only reduce one of them; make repeated use of (TP).)*

3.   *Determine whether the following pairs of sentential forms are interderivable in* Tis. *If one tree yields an exhausted path, determine whether the other does so as well. It is worth knowing whether one of the two sentences is derivable from the other, even if they are not interderivable, and keeping track of which way the derivation can go.*

   ★a. A → B, ~A ∨ B

    b. ~(A & B), ~A ∨ ~B

   ★c. ~(A ∨ B), ~A & ~B

    d. ~(~A ∨ ~B), A & B

   ★e. A → B, ~B → ~A

    f. A ≡ B, (A → B) & (B → A)

   ★g. ~A, ~~~A

    h. A ∨ ~A, ~A ∨ ~~A

References

Bell, John L, and Machover, M, 1977, *A Course in Mathematical Logic*, Elsevier, Amsterdam.

A-4

Advanced Topics Concerning the "Soundness" and "Completeness" of Dm and Tm

Contents	

A-4.1 "Soundness" of Dm

Up to now, "soundness" has been described as the principle that if a derivation system yields a result, then the corresponding semantic system entails that result. This principle continues to be called the "soundness" principle here, but in modal logic, it really asserts that the associated semantics provides a *complete* account of what is intuitively derivable. Consider Dt and t-semantics as an example. ($\Box$E), which says that if a list yields $\Box$P then that list yields P, is intuitively plausible when "necessarily" is read as "necessarily true." In contrast, the claim that each world sees itself, which is the semantic feature that t-semantics uses to provide for ($\Box$E), has no obvious relation to truth or entailment. Its ability to verify $\Box P \to P$ is what really needs to be demonstrated. And it is demonstrated when it is established that if Dt yields a result, that result is t-entailed. Establishing this "soundness" principle is really establishing that t-semantics is complete for Dt.

The "soundness" demonstration is important for a further reason. Demonstrating that if a result is derivable then it is entailed is tantamount to demonstrating that if it is not entailed then it cannot be derivable. This establishes that modal semantics may be used to determine what is not derivable, which is a valuable resource to have in circumstances where efforts at discovering a derivation fail.

In what follows, "soundness" is first demonstrated for the basic derivation system, Dk. The soundness of Dt, Ds4, and Ds5 is then demonstrated by adding further clauses.

Demonstrating the "soundness" of Dk requires extending the concept of entailment. In Ds, sentences are derived from lists of sentences. But in Dk, sentences are derived from lists of lists. Establishing soundness is not just a matter of establishing that if $L \vdash P$ then $\Gamma_L \vDash P$. It is a matter of establishing that if $\langle L_1, \ldots L_n \rangle \vdash P$ then $\langle \Gamma_{L1}, \ldots, \Gamma_{Ln} \rangle \vDash$ P. This requires explaining what $\vDash$ means when what lies to its left is a list of sets rather than a single set. Consider the following derivation of $\Diamond \Box \sim$P from the negation, $\sim\Box\Diamond$P, of its oppositional dual.

DOI: 10.4324/9781003026532-15

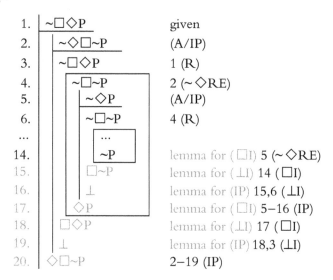

1. | ~□◇P   given

2. | | ~◇□~P   (A/IP)

3. | | ~□◇P   1 (R)

4. | | | ~□~P   2 (~◇RE)

5. | | | | ~◇P   (A/IP)

6. | | | | ~□~P   4 (R)

...

14. | | | | ~P   lemma for (□I) 5 (~◇RE)

15. | | | | □~P   lemma for (⊥I) 14 (□I)

16. | | | | ⊥   lemma for (IP) 15,6 (⊥I)

17. | | | ◇P   lemma for (□I) 5–16 (IP)

18. | | □◇P   lemma for (⊥I) 17 (□I)

19. | | ⊥   lemma for (IP) 18,3 (⊥I)

20. | ◇□~P   2–19 (IP)

Bracket free notation for lines 1–6 and 14 is

1. <~□◇P>   ⊢ ~□◇P   (A)
2. <~□◇P, ~◇□P>   ⊢ ~◇□~P   (A/IP)
3. <~□◇P, ~◇□P>   ⊢ ~□◇P   1 (R)
4. <~□◇P, ~◇□P>,< >   ⊢ ~□~P   2 (~◇RE)
5. <~□◇P, ~◇□P>,<~◇P>   ⊢ ~◇P   (A/IP)
6. <~□◇P, ~◇□P>,<~◇P>   ⊢ ~□~P   4 (R)
...
14. <~□◇P, ~◇□P>,<~◇P>,< > ⊢ ~P   5 (~◇RE)

At line 14, a sentence is derived by (~◇RE) from a list of lists, terminating with the empty list. But Ø does not k-entail ~P. Neither does the set of sentences on the prior list, {~◇P}. (See exercise 9.2#1a.)

<~◇P>,< > ⊢ ~P (which puts ~P in a boxed subderivation in Dk) asserts something that is not captured by the definition of s-entailment. Getting at the semantic analogue of <~□◇P, ~◇□~P>, <~◇P>, < > ⊢ ~P requires working up through some more basic notions: those of the satisfaction of a set by a world of an interpretation; of the satisfaction of a list of sets by a series of worlds of an interpretation; and of the serial entailment of a sentence by a list of sets.

Satisfaction

If all the sentences in a set, Γ, are true in a world, w, of an interpretation, I, then w *satisfies* Γ on I.

Serial satisfaction

If $<\Gamma_1,...,\Gamma_n>$ is a list of sets such that:

(i) for each of $\Gamma_1, ...,\Gamma_n$ there is a corresponding world, $w_1,...,w_n$, of IΩ that satisfies that set, and

(ii) each world that satisfies an earlier set on the list sees the world that satisfies the next set on the list (w_1 sees w_2, w_2 sees w_3,...,w_{n-1} sees w_n),

then I *serially satisfies* $<\Gamma_1,...,\Gamma_n>$.

Serial entailment

Take $<\Gamma_1, ...,\Gamma_n \cup {\sim}P>$ to be the list of sets, $<\Gamma_1, ...,\Gamma_{n-1}>$ supplemented by the set, $\Gamma_n \cup {\sim}P$.

Then $<\Gamma_1, ...,\Gamma_n>$ serially entails P if and only if there is no interpretation that serially satisfies $<\Gamma_1, ...,\Gamma_n \cup {\sim}P>$.

Notation: $<\Gamma_1, ...,\Gamma_n> \vDash P$ (the closing angle bracket before ⊨ suffices to indicate that the entailment is serial).

On this account, the sequent at line 14 of the derivation given above, $<\sim\Box\Diamond P, \sim\Diamond\Box\sim P>, <\sim\Diamond P>, < > \vdash \sim P$, corresponds to the assertion that $<\{\sim\Box\Diamond P, \sim\Diamond\Box\sim P\}, \{\sim\Diamond P\}, \varnothing> \vDash \sim P$, which unpacks as the claim that there is no interpretation that satisfies all four of the following conditions:

(i) All the sentences in $\{\sim\Box\Diamond P, \sim\Diamond\Box\sim P\}$ are true in a world, w;
(ii) All the sentences in $\{\sim\Diamond P\}$ are true in a world, v;
(iii) All the sentences in $\varnothing \cup \sim\sim P$, that is, $\{\sim\sim P\}$ are true in a world, u;
(iv) w sees v and v sees u.

This definition of serial entailment explains what it means to say that a sequent in bracket free D**k** is sound.

Definition of "is sound"

$<L_1,\ldots L_n> \vdash P$ is valid if and only if $<\Gamma_{L1},\ldots,\Gamma_{Ln}> \vDash P$, where $\Gamma_{L1},\ldots,\Gamma_{Ln}$ are the sets of the sentences on $L_1,\ldots L_n$.

The remainder of the demonstration that D**k** is "sound" follows that of the soundness of D**s** (section A-2.1)

1. Suppose that $L \vdash P$ in D**k**.
  2. By definition of derivability in D**k**, there is a derivation in D**k** that ends with $L \vdash P$ (L is the only member of the list of lists on this concluding line.)
  3. The sequent on the first line of any derivation in D**k** is sound. *(Lemma 1)*
  4. If the sequents on lines 1 to k of a derivation in D**k** are sound, the sequent on line $k+1$ is sound. *(Lemma 2)*
  5. From lines 3 and 4 by mathematical induction, the sequent on the last line of any derivation in D**k** is sound.
  6. From lines 5 and 2, $L \vdash P$ must be sound, that is, $\Gamma_L \vDash_k P$, where Γ_L is the set of sentences on L.
7. From lines 1–6 by conditional proof, if $L \vdash P$, then Γ_L **k-serially** entails P.

Lemma 1 is a trivial rewrite the demonstration given in chapter A-2.1.

1. Because the only derivation rule that does not appeal to sequents established on prior lines is (A), the sequent on the first line of any derivation in D**k** must be justified by (A).
2. By (A), the sequent on the first line of any derivation in D**k** has the form, $<P> \vdash P$.
3. By the solution to exercise 5.12(a), if a set, Γ, contains a sentence, P, then $\Gamma \vDash P$.
4. As a special case of this general principle, when Γ is $\{P\}$, $<\{P\}> \vDash P$.
5. From lines 2 and, 4, the sequent on the first line of any derivation in D**k** is sound.

Lemma 2 is demonstrated by establishing that whatever is yielded according to a derivation rule is k-entailed according to the valuation rules. Section A-2.1 and exercise A-2.1 demonstrated this to be the case for the rules D**k** inherits from D**s**, though the demonstrations all need trivial rewrites. That work is passed over here. It remains to show that the lemma holds for the four new rules introduced by D**k**.

This requires first establishing the following entailment principles (supplements to those established in exercise 5.12):

$(\Box RE)$ principle: If $<\Gamma_{L1},\ldots,\Gamma_{Ln}> \vDash \Box P$ then $<\Gamma_{L1},\ldots,\Gamma_{Ln}, \varnothing> \vDash P$
$(\sim\Diamond RE)$ principle: If $<\Gamma_{L1},\ldots,\Gamma_{Ln}> \vDash \sim\Diamond P$ then $<\Gamma_{L1},\ldots,\Gamma_{Ln}, \varnothing> \vDash \sim P$
$(\Box I)$ principle: If $<\Gamma_{L1},\ldots,\Gamma_{Ln}, \varnothing> \vDash P$ then $<\Gamma_{L1},\ldots,\Gamma_{Ln}> \vDash \Box P$
$(\sim\Diamond I)$ principle: If $<\Gamma_{L1},\ldots,\Gamma_{Ln}, \varnothing> \vDash \sim P$ then $<\Gamma_{L1},\ldots,\Gamma_{Ln}> \vDash \sim\Diamond P$

Demonstration of the $(\Box RE)$ principle:

1. Suppose for purposes of conditional proof that $<\Gamma_{L1},\ldots,\Gamma_{Ln}> \vDash \Box P$.
  2. By def $\vDash$, there is no interpretation that serially satisfies $<\Gamma_{L1},\ldots,\Gamma_{Ln} \cup \sim\Box P>$.
  3. Suppose to the contrary that $<\Gamma_{L1},\ldots,\Gamma_{Ln}, \varnothing> \nvDash P$.

4.   By def ⊨, there is an interpretation, I, that serially satisfies $\langle\Gamma_{L1},\ldots,\Gamma_{Ln}, \varnothing \cup \sim P\rangle$, and worlds w and v of IΩ such that w satisfies Γ_{Ln}, w sees v, and v satisfies $\varnothing \cup \sim P$, that is, $\{\sim P\}$.

5.   By (~) Iv(P) is F.

6.   Since I serially satisfies $\langle\Gamma_{L1},\ldots,\Gamma_{Ln}, \varnothing \cup \sim P\rangle$, it serially satisfies $\langle\Gamma_{L1},\ldots,\Gamma_{Ln}\rangle$.

7.   From line 2 no interpretation serially satisfies $\langle\Gamma_{L1},\ldots,\Gamma_{Ln} \cup \sim\square P\rangle$, so since by line 6, I serially satisfies $\langle\Gamma_{L1},\ldots,\Gamma_{Ln}\rangle$, Iw($\sim\square$P) must be F (w being, by line 4, the world of IΩ that satisfies Γ_{Ln}).

8.   By (~), Iw($\square$P) is T.

9.   By ($\square$), w does not see any world, v, in which P is F.

10.   From lines 5 and 9, w both does and does not see v.

11. Since the further supposition at line 3 leads to a contradiction (at line 10) under the initial supposition at line 1, as long as the supposition at line 1 is sustained the supposition at line 3 must be rejected: $\langle\Gamma_{L1},\ldots,\Gamma_{Ln},\varnothing\rangle \vDash$ P.

12.   From lines 1–11 by conditional proof, if $\langle\Gamma_{L1},\ldots,\Gamma_{Ln}\rangle \vDash \square$P then $\langle\Gamma_{L1},\ldots,\Gamma_{Ln},\varnothing\rangle \vDash$ P.

The demonstration of the (~◇RE) principle is similar and left as an exercise.

Demonstration of the ($\square$I) principle:

1.   Suppose for purposes of conditional proof that $\langle\Gamma_{L1},\ldots,\Gamma_{Ln},\varnothing\rangle \vDash$ P.

2.   By def. ⊨, there is no interpretation that serially satisfies $\langle\Gamma_{L1},\ldots,\Gamma_{Ln}, \varnothing \cup \sim P\rangle$.

3.   Now suppose to the contrary that $\langle\Gamma_{L1},\ldots,\Gamma_{Ln}\rangle \nvDash \square$P.

4.   By def ⊨, there is an interpretation, I, that serially satisfies $\langle\Gamma_{L1},\ldots,\Gamma_{Ln} \cup \sim\square P\rangle$, so there is a world, w, of IΩ such that w satisfies Γ_{Ln} and Iw($\sim\square$P) is T.

5.   By (~), Iw($\square$P) is F.

6.   By ($\square$), there is at least one world, v, of IΩ such that w sees v and Iv(P) is F.

7.   From line 4 since I serially satisfies $\langle\Gamma_{L1},\ldots,\Gamma_{Ln} \cup \sim\square P\rangle$, it serially satisfies $\langle\Gamma_{L1},\ldots,\Gamma_{Ln}\rangle$.

8.   From lines 7 and 2, w (which by line 4 satisfies Γ_{Ln}) does not see a world that satisfies $\{\sim P\}$ (otherwise, by line 7, I would serially satisfy $\langle\Gamma_{L1},\ldots,\Gamma_{Ln}, \varnothing \cup \sim P\rangle$, contrary to line 2).

9.   By (~), I(P) is T in any world that w sees.

10.   From lines 6 and 9, w both sees and does not see a world, v, such that Iv(P) is F.

11. Since the further supposition at line 3 leads to a contradiction (at line 10) under the initial supposition at line 1, as long as the supposition at line 1 is sustained the supposition at line 3 must be rejected: $\langle\Gamma_{L1},\ldots,\Gamma_{Ln}\rangle \vDash \square$P.

12.   From lines 1–11 by conditional proof, if $\langle\Gamma_{L1},\ldots,\Gamma_{Ln},\varnothing\rangle \vDash$ P then $\langle\Gamma_{L1},\ldots,\Gamma_{Ln}\rangle \vDash \square$P.

The demonstration of the (~◇I) principle is similar and is left as an exercise.

Having secured these entailment principles, lemma 2 can be demonstrated as before, by proof by cases, where the cases cover the derivation rules that might be used to justify the sequent at line *k*+1. The case for sentences derived by ($\square$RE) reads:

Case thirteen: The sequent on line *k*+1 is derived by ($\square$RE). Then it must have the form $\langle L_{1,\ldots,} L_i, \langle\ \rangle\rangle \vdash$ Q and the earlier lines 1 to *k* must include a line, *i*, of the form $\langle L_1,\ldots,L_i\rangle \vdash \square$Q. (Were the list of lists at line *i* not identical to the list at line *k*+1, but for the addition of the empty list at line *k*+1, ($\square$RE) could not be applied.) Consequently:

1.   Because line *i* is prior to line *k*+1, it follows from the inductive hypothesis that $\langle\Gamma_{L1},\ldots,\Gamma_{Li}\rangle \vDash \square$Q.

2.   By the ($\square$RE) entailment principle, $\langle\Gamma_{L1},\ldots,\Gamma_{Li},\varnothing\rangle \vDash$ Q.

So, the sequent on line *k*+1 is sound in this case.

The demonstration of the remaining three cases is closely patterned on that for ($\square$RE) and is left as an exercise.

The demonstrations that Dt, Ds4, and Ds5 are "sound" expand on lemma 2 by adding cases that establish that each of ($\square$E), ($\square$R), and ($\square$◇I) is sound. This is done be appeal to three further entailment principles.

($\square$E) principle:	If $\langle\Gamma_{L1},\ldots,\Gamma_{Ln}\rangle \vDash_t \square$P then $\langle\Gamma_{L1},\ldots,\Gamma_{Ln}\rangle \vDash_t$ P
($\square$R) principle:	If $\langle\Gamma_{L1},\ldots,\Gamma_{Ln}\rangle \vDash_{s4} \square$P then $\langle\Gamma_{L1},\ldots,\Gamma_{Ln}\rangle \vDash_{s4} \square\square$P
($\square$◇I) principle:	If $\langle\Gamma_{L1},\ldots,\Gamma_{Ln}\rangle \vDash_{s5} ◇$P then $\langle\Gamma_{L1},\ldots,\Gamma_{Ln}\rangle \vDash_{s5} \square◇$P

The demonstrations of these entailment principles are based on the special conditions each of these systems places on S.

Additional Frame Conditions

t: Reflexivity (each world sees itself)

s4: Reflexivity + transitivity (each world sees itself and each world sees any world seen by any world that it sees)

s5: Reflexivity + transverseness (each world sees itself and any two worlds seen by the same world see one another)

The demonstration of the ($\Box$E) and ($\Box$R) principles is left as an exercise (the idea for each demonstration can be gathered from the discussion of reflexivity and transitivity towards the close of section 9.1, and an exemplar for the demonstration can be gathered from the one below for the ($\Box\Diamond$I) principle).

Demonstration of the ($\Box\Diamond$I) principle:

1. Suppose for purposes of conditional proof that $\langle\Gamma_{L1},\ldots,\Gamma_{Ln}\rangle \vDash_{s5} \Diamond P$.
    2. By definition of serial entailment in s5, there is no interpretation that s5 serially satisfies $\langle\Gamma_{L1},\ldots,\Gamma_{Ln} \cup \sim\Diamond P\rangle$.
    3. Suppose to the contrary that $\langle\Gamma_{L1},\ldots,\Gamma_{Ln}\rangle \nvDash_{s5} \Box\Diamond P$.
        4. By definition of serial entailment in s5, there is an interpretation, I, that s5-serially satisfies $\langle\Gamma_{L1},\ldots,\Gamma_{Ln} \cup \sim\Box\Diamond P\rangle$.
        5. By definition of serial satisfaction, there is a world, w of $I\Omega$ such that w s5-satisfies Γ_{Ln} and $Iw(\sim\Box\Diamond P)$ is T.
        6. By ($\sim$), $Iw(\Box\Diamond P)$ is F.
        7. By ($\Box$), there is at least one world, v, of $I\Omega$ such that w sees v and $Iv(\Diamond P)$ is F.
        8. By ($\Diamond$), there is no world, u, of $I\Omega$ such that v sees u and $Iu(P)$ is T.
        9. From line 4, I s5-serially satisfies $\langle\Gamma_{L1},\ldots,\Gamma_{Ln}\rangle$, and from line 5, w is the world of $I\Omega$ that s5-satisfies Γ_{Ln}, so by line 2 $Iw(\sim\Diamond P)$ must be F (otherwise I would s5-satisfy $\langle\Gamma_{L1},\ldots,\Gamma_{Ln} \cup \sim\Diamond P\rangle$, contrary to line 2).
        10. By ($\sim$), $Iw(\Diamond P)$ is T.
        11. By ($\Diamond$), w sees at least one world, u, such that $Iu(P)$ is T.
        12. From line 7, w sees v, and from line, 11 w sees u, so by the transverse condition on IS, v sees u.
        13. From lines 12 and 11, v sees at least one world in which P is T on I, but from line 8, v sees no such world.
    14. Since the further supposition at line 3 leads to a contradiction (at line 13) under the initial supposition at line 1, as long as the supposition at line 1 is sustained the supposition at line 3 must be rejected: $\langle\Gamma_{L1},\ldots,\Gamma_{Ln}\rangle \vDash_{s5} \Box\Diamond P$.
15. From lines 1–14 by conditional proof, if $\langle\Gamma_{L1},\ldots,\Gamma_{Ln}\rangle \vDash_{s5} \Diamond P$ then $\langle\Gamma_{L1},\ldots,\Gamma_{Ln}\rangle \vDash_{s5} \Box\Diamond P$.

The demonstrations of the cases of the inductive step for ($\Box$E), ($\Box$R), and ($\Box\Diamond$I) are not worth an exercise. They simply rewrite the demonstration already given for case thirteen with the appropriate substitutions of rule names and forms.

Exercise A-4.1

1. *Demonstrate the ($\sim\Diamond$RE) and ($\sim\Diamond$I) entailment principles.*
2. *Demonstrate cases 14–16 of lemma 3 (for ($\sim\Diamond$RE), ($\Box$I), and ($\sim\Diamond$I)).*
★3. *Demonstrate the ($\Box$E) and ($\Box$R) principles, being careful to appeal to the appropriate notions of satisfaction, serial satisfaction, and entailment.*

A-4.2 Completeness of Tm

The completeness principle for reduction trees is

> If Γ is unsatisfiable then it has at least one closed tree.

For Tm, this means that if Γ is m-unsatisfiable, then it has at least one closed m-tree. As for Ts, the demonstration is given by contraposition, and by appeal to a canonical series of trees.

  1. Suppose for purposes of conditional proof that each tree for Γ is open.
      2.   Each tree in the canonical series of trees for Γ is open.
      …
      n. Γ is m-satisfiable.
  n. From lines 1 to *n* by conditional proof, if each tree for Γ is open, Γ is m-satisfiable.
  n. From line *n*+1 by contraposition, if Γ is m-unsatisfiable, it has at least one closed tree.

The opening portion of this section explains how to bridge the gap between line 2 and line *n* of the outline demonstration above. The explanation is closely patterned on the one given in chapter A-3 for s-trees. As in exercise A-3.3#2, the demonstration that follows saves work by considering just lean language trees. The lean language for MSL includes □ as well as ⊥, →, and the sentence letters, numerical subscripts, and punctuations marks. All other operators are considered to be abbreviations for sentential forms of the lean language.

- In the lean language ◇P is replaced by □(P → ⊥) → ⊥, which is the lean language equivalent of ~□~P and so of ◇P.
- Lean language trees replace (⊥I) with (MP), which must be applied as soon as possible after both P and P → ⊥ appear within the same box on a path, where P is atomic. This is the only circumstance in which (MP) is applied in Tm.
- To avoid a vicious regress, (T→) is restricted to reducing arrow sentences that do not have ⊥ as their consequents.
  - When P is atomic, P → ⊥ is treated as a literal.
  - When P → ⊥ has the form (Q → R) → ⊥ it is reduced by a modified version of (~→), called (→⊥). As would be expected, it derives Q over R → ⊥.
  - When P → ⊥ has the form □Q → ⊥, it is reduced by a modified version of (~□), called (□⊥). It derives Q → ⊥ in a new box.

As in chapter A-3, the key to bridging the gap between lines 2 and *n* is establishing that each tree in the canonical series of trees for Γ must contain at least one path, θ, that is characterized by certain features that define a canonical tree model, I★, which in this case contains a world in which all the sentences in Γ are true. Since interpretations for MSL are more complex than interpretations for SL, this requires saying more about how to base an interpretation on an exhausted or infinitely extendible path. The account of the canonical method for generating a tree needs to be extended to ensure that, even though some nonliterals are not checked off and must be reduced repeatedly as the tree continues to grow, each reducible sentence will have its complete reduction results entered on at least one extension of θ in at least one tree in the canonical series. The demonstration continues to make use of the notion of the catalogue number of a sentence, originally introduced in chapter A-2.4 and expanded as follows for the lean language:

Symbol	Numeral	Symbol	Numeral	Symbol	Numeral
⊥	10	0	20	A	30
→	11	1	21	B	31
(	12	…		C	32
)	13	9	29		
□	14				

For Tm, the canonical method produces a series of trees, T_1, T_2, T_3, …, as follows:

- T_1 places the sentence with the lowest catalogue number in box w on top of the tree.
- Each subsequent tree in the series is a one-step extension of the previous one produced by either applying reduction rules of Tm or adding sentences from Γ by repeatedly cycling through four successive stages. All work that can be done at a stage must be done before proceeding to the next stage. When all work at one stage has been exhausted, the next stage in order is taken up. When no work can be done at a stage, work must proceed to the next stage in line (stages must be cycled through in order).
- At stage 1, all possible applications of (MP), ($\rightarrow\perp$) and (T$\rightarrow$) are made to sentences taken in the order they occur from the top down, including sentences added to paths as a consequence of work at this stage. (When sentences to which any of these rules apply occur on different paths on the same line they are reduced simultaneously even if this means using different rules on the same line.) (T$\square$) applications required by reflexivity arrows are also made at this stage. Stage 1 must be completed before turning to stage 2.
- At stage 2, ($\square\perp$) is applied to each sentence to which it can be applied, proceeding from the top down. Work then proceeds to stage 3. It is not permitted to return to stage 1 after completing stage 2. Stage 1 can only be resumed after a complete cycle through the remaining stages, or verifying that there is no work to be done at those stages.
- At stage 3, all possible (T$\square$) applications that can be made along k, 4, and 5 arrows are made to each box sentence, proceeding in order from the top down. (T$\square$) should not be applied to generate sentences that already exist in a box on a path, but should be applied to $\square$ sentences generated as a consequence of work at this stage. (When a (T$\square$) application requires a sentence to be entered in a box higher up on the path, that sentence is entered in a continuation of that box on all paths selected by the placement principle. Continuation arms are not used.) Stage 3 must be completed before moving on to stage 4. It is not permitted to return to stages 1 or 2 after completing stage 3. Stage 1 can only be resumed after completing stage 4 or verifying that there is no work to be done at that stage, and stage 2 can only recommence after completing stage 1 or verifying that there is no work to be done at that stage.
- At stage 4, the sentence in Γ with the next lowest catalogue number is placed on the top of the tree in box w. The sequence of stages then recommences. Cycling through the stages continues for as long as doing so continues to produce changes to the tree (which could be forever).

The effect of following the canonical method is to take one sentence from Γ, add it to the top of the tree in w, apply all the rules that can be applied to it and the resulting products in accord with the mandate to proceed through the stages, and then add another sentence to the top of the tree in w and repeat the procedure, continuing for as many sentences as there are (forever if their number is infinite). For reasons given below, each stage comes to an end, even if cycles through the stages goes on forever.

On the supposition that each tree for Γ is open, following the canonical method ensures that any tree for Γ will contain at least one path, θ, that has the following features:

> ### Features of θ
>
> (a) $\perp$ does not stand alone on any line of θ.
> (b) For each nonliteral, nonbox sentence, P, on θ, at least one of the up to two paths of reduction results for P occurs on at least one extension of θ in at least one of the subsequent trees in the series.
> (c) For each box sentence, $\square$P, in a box, w, on θ, (i) if there is a reflexivity arrow on w, P occurs in w on at least one extension of θ, and (ii) for each box, v, on θ pointed to by an arrow that originates from a sentence that is on θ in w, P occurs in v on at least one extension of θ in at least one of the subsequent trees in the series.
> (d) Each sentence in Γ occurs in the top box on θ in at least one of the subsequent trees in the series.

Feature (a) follows from the supposition that each tree for Γ is open.

θ must have features (b), (c), and (d) because (i) the canonical method ensures that each nonliteral on θ will be reduced in one of the trees in the series and thereby that the turn of each sentence in Γ to be added to the head of the tree, will come up, and (ii) the placement principle dictates that the results of reducing a sentence on θ must be entered on each open path that runs up to that sentence. Since the extensions of θ in each subsequent tree in the series are such a path, the results must appear on it.

Following the canonical method ensures that each nonliteral on θ will get reduced in, and each sentence in Γ added to the top of, one of the trees in the series, because (1) the method dictates that each nonliteral on θ be reduced in the order it appears from the top down (so none can be overlooked), (2) reducing any one sentence is a finite process, (3) there is only a finite amount of work that can be done at each of the stages, and (4) the canonical method only allows returning to work at a prior stage by way of a complete cycle through all the stages (which, at each passage through stage 4, involves adding a further sentence from Γ to the head of the tree).

(1) is obvious. (2) is the case because (a) sentences other than □ sentences are reduced only once (and not at all if their complete reduction results already appear on the path); (b) the results of reducing a sentence are always finite; and (c) a □ sentence can only be reduced a finite number of times on any one pass through stage 3. Each sentence is only finitely long (the demonstration of this result in section A-1.1 is readily updated for MSL), and is reduced to a finite number of sentences (never more than four) that are shorter than it is, entered on a finite number of new paths (never more than two[1]), on a finite number of pre-existing paths. Trees start with only one path, each one-step extension never does more than double the number of prior ones, and the product of finite quantities is always finite. Trees also start with only one box, only the reduction of $\Box P \to \bot$ sentences creates new boxes, and each $\Box P \to \bot$ sentence only adds one box to each of the finite number of paths that runs up to it and is then checked off and not reduced again. Given a finite number of finitely long sentences on any one-step extension of a canonical tree, there can only be finitely many $\Box P \to \bot$ sentences, and even if each of them has the form $\Box\Box Q \to \bot$ and so reduces to a further $\Box P \to \bot$ sentence in a new box, that further sentence must be shorter than its parent, so the reduction of $\Box P \to \bot$ sentences must eventually come to an end, at which point only a finite number of boxes will have been added to the tree. Given a finite number of boxes as targets for reduction results, each □ sentence can be reduced only a finite number of times. So, the situation where there is an infinite task to complete before going on to reduce the next sentence never arises.

(3) Work at stage 4 must come to an end because it only involves doing one thing: adding a finitely long sentence to the head of a tree. Work at stages 1 and 2 must come to an end because, when a stage 1 or 2 sentence is reduced, it is replaced by sentences that, on any one path, contain fewer vocabulary elements than the sentence that was reduced. Thus, even though each reduction adds more sentences to be reduced by subsequent one-step extensions, only finitely many one-step extensions can occur before all available sentences are reduced to literals, leaving no more work to be done at the stage in question. $(T\to)$ is not an exception. Though there could be as many vocabulary elements in the sentence being reduced, $(P \to Q)$, as there are in the sentence on the left path, $(P \to \bot)$, either P is atomic, in which case $(P \to \bot)$ cannot be further reduced, or it has the form $((P_1 \to P_2) \to \bot)$, in which case it must be reduced by $(\to\bot)$, which replaces $((P_1 \to P_2) \to \bot)$ with P_1 over $(P_2 \to \bot)$. These second reduction results contain fewer vocabulary elements than the original $((P_1 \to P_2) \to Q)$. In this case, it simply takes two rule applications to generate the reduction in number of vocabulary elements. Work at stage 3 must come for an end for this same reason (reduction of a □ sentence produces a shorter sentence) and also for the reason given earlier, that on any given pass through stage 3, there can only be finitely many boxes on the tree for □ sentences to be reduced in, and $(T\Box)$, the only stage 3 reduction rule, does not change that number.

(4) The canonical method prohibits returning to work at a prior stage before completing all work at the current stage, and requires all work at each of the intervening stages to be completed along the way. A □ sentence may only be reduced at stage 3. A □ sentence of the form $\Box(\Box P \to \bot)$ reduces to a $\Box P \to \bot$ sentence, which is a box forming sentence but also a stage 2 sentence. A such $\Box P \to \bot$ can only be reduced after reducing all other stage 3 sentences currently on the path, then going on to do all possible work at stages 4 and 1, and then reducing any unreduced stage 2 sentences higher up on the tree than it is. Once $\Box P \to \bot$ is reduced, all other stage 2 sentences must be reduced before turning to stage 3. At stage 3, the box created by reducing $\Box P \to \bot$ may be populated with another copy of $\Box P \to \bot$ produced by reducing $\Box(\Box P \to \bot)$ in that box (though not if there are results on the path that would permit considering $\Box(\Box P \to \bot)$ to have been reduced independently of a further application of $(\Box\bot)$), but all other box sentences currently on the tree must also be reduced in turn at this stage, and the new copy of $\Box P \to \bot$ will only get its turn to be reduced after another cycle through stages 4, 1, and the higher stage 2 sentences. In this way, no sentence can be overlooked. Each stage concludes with all possible work that could have been done at that stage having been done.

As a consequence of these considerations, each nonliteral, nonbox sentence on Γ must be reduced, each box sentence must be reduced in a continuation of each box selected by an arrow originating from the box that contains that box sentence, and each sentence in Γ must be added to the head of the tree. Even if Γ is infinite, since each of the infinitely many sentences in Γ is only finitely long, each has a finite catalogue number. Because each of the stages must be completed after a finite number of one-step extensions, cycles through stage 4 must continue for as long as there are sentences in Γ to add to the tree. The turn of any given sentence in Γ to be reduced will therefore come up at some finite point. Likewise, even if new boxes are added to θ on each cycle through stage 2, only finitely many are added to a prior, finite number of boxes, which means only finitely many arrows can be directed at each of the new boxes. Consequently, at stage 3 the turn of each of those new boxes to be populated with the reduction results of each applicable box sentence will come at some finite point. Even if the cycles go on forever, and new boxes are continually added to θ, each new box will be further populated at some finite point and each box sentence will therefore be reduced in each of the infinitely many applicable boxes at some finite point. There is just no end to the finite points at which these things continue to happen.

θ determines the canonical tree model, I$\star$, which is defined as having the following properties.

Properties of I$\star$

(i) I$\star\Omega$ is the set of worlds such that for each box on θ there is a world of I$\star\Omega$.

(ii) I$\star$S is the set of accessibility relations such that for each arrow from a box, w, on θ to a (not necessarily distinct) box, v, on θ, the world of I$\star\Omega$ corresponding to w sees the world of I$\star\Omega$ corresponding to v.

(iii) Where P is a sentence letter, I$\star\alpha_w$(P) is T if and only if P stands alone on a line of θ in the box corresponding to w; otherwise I$\star\alpha_w$(P) is F.

By definition of an m-model, for I$\star$ to be not just a tree model (as defined above) but an m-model (as defined in section 9.1), and hence a justification for claims about satisfaction, (1) I$\star\Omega$ must contain at least one world, (2) I$\star$S must have the structure required by the modal system, m (k, t, s4, or s5), and (3) I$\star\alpha$ must satisfy the definition of a valuation.

(1) Because any tree starts in a box, I$\star\Omega$ contains at least one world.
(2) Arrows are added to boxes in accord with the conditions m places on S, so I$\star$S automatically has the structure required by m (it is reflexive if m is t, a ranking if m is s4, universal if m is s5, and unrestricted if m is k).
(3) Because any sentence letter must either stand alone on a line of a box on θ or not stand alone on a line of that box on θ, property (iii) ensures that I$\star\alpha$ must assign exactly one of T and F to each sentence letter relative to each box on θ, and so in each world of I$\star\Omega$. So I$\star\alpha$ is a valuation.

Enough has been said to set up a demonstration by mathematical induction to bridge the gap in the outline demonstration of the completeness of Tm given above. The bridge is made with two lemmas, which form the basis clause and the inductive step for a conclusion by mathematical induction. In the statement of the basis and the induction, the claim that a sentence is "true in its world" refers to the world corresponding to the box in which that sentence appears on θ.

1. Suppose for purposes of conditional proof that each tree for Γ is open.
   2. Each tree in the canonical series of trees for Γ is open.
   3. Each tree in the canonical series of trees for Γ must contain at least one path, call it θ, that has features (a)–(d).
   4. Each sentence on θ that contains 0 occurrences of operators is true in its world on the canonical interpretation, I$\star$. *(Lemma 1)*
   5. If each sentence on θ that contains from 0 to k occurrences of operators is true in its world on I$\star$, each sentence on θ that contains $k+1$ occurrences of operators is true in its world on I$\star$. *(Lemma 2)*
   6. From lines 4 and 5 by mathematical induction, each sentence on θ is true in its world on I$\star$.
   7. By feature (d) of θ, all the sentences in Γ are true on I$\star w_1$, where w_1 is the world corresponding to the top box on θ.
   8. By def. m-satisfiability, Γ is m-satisfiable.
9. From lines 1–8 by conditional proof, if each tree for Γ is open, Γ is m-satisfiable.
10. By contraposition, if Γ is m-unsatisfiable it must have at least one closed tree.

Demonstration of lemma 1: The sentences that contain no occurrences of operators are $\bot$ and the sentence letters. By feature (a) of θ, $\bot$ cannot stand alone on any line of θ. So the only sentences on θ that contain no occurrences of operators are sentence letters. By definition of I$\star$, those sentences are true on I$\star$.

Demonstration of lemma 2: Suppose for purposes of conditional proof that all the sentences on θ containing from 0 to k occurrences of operators are true in their worlds on I⋆. The aim is to show that making this supposition requires accepting that all the sentences on θ with $k+1$ occurrences of operators are true in their worlds on I⋆. To see why this must be the case, consider that the sentences with $k+1$ occurrences of operators must contain at least one operator. Since there are only two operators in lean MSL, → and □, this means that they must be either conditionals or box sentences, and if conditionals either (i) sentences of the form P → ⊥ where P is atomic, (ii) sentences of the form P → ⊥ where P is a compound of the form Q→ R, (iii) sentences of the form P → ⊥ where P is a compound of the form □Q, or (iv) sentences of the form P → Q where Q is not ⊥. So there are five cases to consider. (The cases are distinguished because the sentences of these forms are reduced by different rules.)

Case one: The sentence on θ with $k+1$ occurrences of operators is a sentence of the form P → ⊥ where P is atomic, that is, ⊥ or a sentence letter. Then P does not stand alone on θ in the same box, w, as P → ⊥. (If it did, an application of (MP) would be required, which would result in ⊥ occurring on θ, and that is ruled out by feature (a) of θ.) Either way (whether P is ⊥ or a sentence letter), I⋆α_w(P) is F, in the former case by (⊥) and in the latter in virtue of property (iii) of I⋆. By (→), I⋆w(P → ⊥) is T. So in this case the sentence on θ with $k+1$ occurrences of operators is true in its world on I⋆.

Case two: The sentence on θ with $k+1$ occurrences of operators is a sentence of the form (Q → R) → ⊥. It follows from feature (b) of θ that (Q → R) → ⊥ has been reduced in its box, w, by (→⊥) and consequently that Q and R → ⊥ occur on an extension of θ in w. Since (Q → R) → ⊥ contains $k+1$ occurrences of operators, each of Q and R → ⊥ must contain k or fewer occurrences of operators. Since it is being supposed that any sentence on θ that contains k or fewer occurrences of operators is true in its world, I⋆w(Q) and I⋆w(R → ⊥) are T. By (⊥), I⋆w(⊥) is F, so, by (MT), I⋆w(R) is F. Since it has been established that I⋆w(Q) is T and I⋆w(R) is F, by (→), I⋆w(Q → R) is F and I⋆w((Q → R) → ⊥) is T. So, in this case the sentence on θ with $k+1$ occurrences of operators is true in its world on I⋆.

Case three: The sentence on θ with $k+1$ occurrences of operators is a sentence of the form □Q → ⊥. It follows from feature (b) of θ that □Q → ⊥ must have been reduced by (□⊥) and consequently that Q → ⊥ occurs in some box, v, on an extension of θ, and that there is an arrow from the box, w, on θ that contains □Q → ⊥ to v. Since □Q → ⊥ contains $k+1$ occurrences of operators, Q → ⊥ must contain k occurrences of operators. And since it is being supposed that any sentence on θ that contains k or fewer occurrences of operators is true in its world, I⋆v(Q → ⊥) is T. By (⊥), I⋆v(⊥) is F, so, by (MT), I⋆v(Q) is F. Since there is an arrow from box w to box v, by property (ii) of I⋆ the corresponding world, w, sees the corresponding world, v. By (□), I⋆w(□Q) must be F. By (→), I⋆w(□Q → ⊥) is T. So in this case the sentence on θ with $k+1$ occurrences of operators is true in its world on I⋆.

Case four: The sentence on θ with $k+1$ occurrences of operators is a sentence of the form P → Q where Q is not ⊥. It follows from feature (b) of θ that P → Q has been reduced in its box, w, by (T→) and consequently that either P → ⊥ or Q occurs on an extension of θ in w.

> Suppose P → ⊥ is the sentence that occurs on the extension of θ in w. P must be either atomic or compound, and if compound either a compound of the form Q → R or a compound of the form □Q.
>
> > If P is atomic then, as established over the course of the demonstration of case one, I⋆w(P) is F.
> > Alternatively, if P has the form (Q → R) then, as established over the course of the demonstration of case two, I⋆w(Q → R), that is, I⋆w(P), is F.
> > Finally, if P has the form □Q then, as established over the course of the demonstration of case three, I⋆w(□Q), that is, I⋆w(P) is F.
> > So, whether P is atomic, an arrow sentence, or a box sentence, I⋆w(P) is F. By (→), I⋆w(P → Q) is T.
>
> Now suppose that Q is the sentence that occurs on the extension of θ in w. Because P → Q contains $k+1$ occurrences of operators, Q must contain k or fewer occurrences of operators. And since it is being supposed that any sentence that contains k or fewer occurrences of operators is true in its world on I⋆, I⋆w(Q) is T. It follows by (→) that I⋆w(P → Q) is T.

So, any way, the sentence on θ with $k+1$ occurrences of operators is true in its world on I⋆.

Case five: The sentence on θ with $k+1$ occurrences of operators is a sentence of the form □P. It follows from feature (c) of θ that (i) if there is a reflexivity arrow on the box, w, in which □P occurs, then P occurs on an extension of θ in w, and (ii) if there is an arrow from any sentence on θ in w to any box, v, on θ, P occurs in v on an extension of θ. Since □P contains $k+1$ occurrences of operators, P must contain k occurrences of operators. And since it is being supposed that any sentence on θ that contains k or fewer occurrences of operators is true in its world, each of these occurrences of P must be true in its world on I⋆. By property

(ii) of I★, w sees each of and only these worlds. It follows by (□) that I★w(□P) is true. So in this case the sentence on θ with *k*+1 occurrences of operators is true in its world on I★.

It follows that if it is supposed that all the sentences with from 0 to *k* occurrences of connectives are true in their worlds on I★, then all the sentences with *k*+1 occurrences of connectives must be true in their worlds on I★.

A-4.3 Tree Conversions

Like s-trees, m-trees can be converted to derivations. This section does not rigorously demonstrate that any m-tree can be converted. The aim is only to provide some assurance that it can be done, and to illustrate some of the principal ways it is done.[2]

As with Ts and Ds, some changes need to be made to both systems to facilitate conversion. All the modifications made in section A-2.4 to convert Ts into Tsd are made to Tm. Tm must be further modified to prevent the creation of continuations or the need for arrows.

(1) (T◇) and (~□) may not be applied until all other rule applications have been exhausted. Then one of (T◇) or (~□) is applied once, followed by all possible applications of other rules resulting from that one application. Then a second (T◇) or (~□) application is made. Work cycles back and forth between a single application of (T◇) or (~□) and drawing all the consequences of that application.

(2) Tt is modified by replacing reflexivity arrows with (□E), which is imported into Ttd from Dtt, and rewriting (~◇), which is also imported into Dkt. The rewrite for Tkd directs that ~◇P be reduced to □~P in the box containing ~◇P. In Dkt this is the rule that if L ⊢ ~◇P then L ⊢ □~P.

(3) Ts4 is further modified by replacing transitivity arrows with (□R), which is imported into Ts4d from Ds4. In the case where □P is reduced along a transitivity arrow from w to u, there must be an arrow from w to an intermediate box, v, and from v to u to permit the creation of the transitivity arrow. (□R) is used to reduce □P in w to □P in v so an application of (T□) can put P into u. The case where ~◇P occurs in w is dealt with by the new (~◇) rule supplemented by (□R).

(4) A more complicated modification is required to facilitate the removal of transverse arrows from s5 trees. At any point where (i) there is a transverse arrow from v to u, and (ii) a sentence of the form □P appears in v, there must be a "peak" box, w, (not necessarily distinct from one or other of v or u) that sends arrows to each of v and u. The goal is to find a way to get □P from v to w without using either an arrow or a continuation to do so, so that (T□) can be used to put P in u. If □P already occurs in w there is no problem. If it does not, the solution is to scrap the tree and rewrite it, adding an appropriate instance of the dual of the 5 metatheorem, ◇□Q → □Q, to the last line of w on the path that leads to □P in v. Recall that the dual of a metatheorem is itself a metatheorem, and that any instance of a metatheorem can be inserted at any line in a derivation (inserting the complete derivation of that instance prior to that line would have the same effect, and that can always be done since any instance of a metatheorem is derived from the empty list). While the insertion of a metatheorem on a tree path may seem arbitrary, all that matters is that it facilitates the production of a derivation that yields the same sentences as appear on the original tree path in a corresponding subderivation.

For example, if ~◇A appears on a path in v and there is an arrow from w to v, then the tree is scrapped and rewritten. The rewrite applies (~◇) to convert ~◇A to □~A and adds the instance ◇□~A → □~A of the dual of the 5 axiom to the last line of w on the path that leads to ~◇A in v. ◇□~A → □~A is then reduced before proceeding with the rest of the tree. Since ◇□~A → □~A is a conditional, it produces ~◇□~A on a left path and □~A on a right path. The right path has the intended effect of introducing □P (in this case □~A) into w. With □P in w, there is no longer a need for a transverse arrow from v to u. (T□) can then be used to put P in u by appeal to the occurrence of □P in w.

This operation produces a left path in w that does not exist in the original s5 tree, but that path must close because ◇□P → □P (in this case ◇□~A → □~A) was only added to the path because the path was previously discovered to produce a lower box, v, containing □P (in this case, □~A). Redoing that work recreates box v on both paths. Since box v contains □P, and the left path in w contains ~◇□P, (~◇) brings ~□P into v, and (~□) and (T□) can then be applied to close the path. (An illustration follows shortly.)

Additions of instances of the dual of the 5 theorem are justified with the notation (5D). In the corresponding derivation, the same sentence is derived by appeal to the same justification.

Dm is further altered in all the ways Ds was altered in section A-2.4. Further modifications are needed to capture (T◇) and (~□). These reduction rules open new boxes, which must be somehow reflected in derivations, both at the start, where the new box is opened, and at the finish, where the aim is to derive ⊥ from the box.

Where (T$\Diamond$) (or (~$\Box$)) are applied on trees, the corresponding derivation creates a box that begins with the assumption of the immediate component (or negated immediate component) of the $\Diamond$ (or ~$\Box$) sentence. This assumption should be notated (A / #$\Diamond\bot$) or (A / #~$\Box\bot$), where # is the number of the line where $\Diamond$P or ~$\Box$P occurs. Since all paths on the tree should close, this box should terminate in $\bot$. Dkt introduces two new derived rules for use in this situation, ($\Diamond\bot$) and (~$\Box\bot$).

$(\Diamond\bot)$: If L ⊢ $\Diamond$P and L,< P > ⊢ $\bot$, then L ⊢ $\bot$
$(\sim\Box\bot)$: If L ⊢ ~$\Box$P and L,< ~P > ⊢ $\bot$, then L ⊢ $\bot$

In standard notation, ($\Diamond\bot$) uses the following template. (~$\Box\bot$) is a minor variant on it.

$$
\begin{array}{ll}
h. & \Diamond P \\
 & \cdots \\
i. & \qquad P \qquad (A/h\Diamond\bot) \\
 & \qquad \cdots \\
k. & \qquad \bot \\
 & \cdots \\
n. & \bot \qquad h, i\text{–}k\ (\Diamond\bot)
\end{array}
$$

($\Diamond\bot$) and (~$\Box\bot$) abbreviate routine sequences of steps. The routine for ($\Diamond\bot$) is given below. That for (~$\Box\bot$) is a minor variant on it.

$$
\begin{array}{ll}
i. & \Diamond P \\
 & \cdots \\
k & \qquad P \qquad (A/IP) \\
 & \qquad \cdots \\
n. & \qquad \bot \\
n.+1 & \quad \sim P \qquad k\text{–}n\ (IP) \\
n.+2 & \sim\Diamond P \qquad n+1(\sim\Diamond I) \\
n.+3 & \bot \qquad i, n+2\ (\bot I)
\end{array}
$$

($\Diamond\bot$) and (~$\Box\bot$) achieve nothing that could not be done in a few extra lines with the original rules of Dk.

Consider, the following s5 tree for A / $\Box\Diamond$A set against a partially completed derivation of the same result.

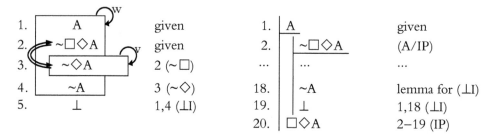

The tree contains a transverse arrow between v and w, and a $\Box$ or ~$\Diamond$ sentence on a path in v, which is the situation where the tree needs to be scrapped and rewritten to facilitate further conversion. The original tree applies (T$\Box$) to put ~$\Diamond$A in v. This creates a k arrow from w to v. Since there is a reflexivity arrow on w, and this is an s5 tree, there are arrows from w to w and w to v, so a transverse arrow between v and w is called for, effectively converting the original k arrow into a double-headed arrow. This arrow must be removed and replaced with an appeal to (5D). Since the arrow arises because there is an arrow from w to itself and an arrow from w to v, w is the "peak" box. Keeping this in mind, the original tree is scrapped and rewritten, inserting the appropriate instance of 5D, $\Diamond\Box$~A → $\Box$~A on the last line of the original segment of the "peak" box, w.

$$
\begin{array}{lll}
 & \qquad\qquad\quad \text{w} & \\
1. & A & \text{given} \\
2. & \sim\Box\Diamond A & \text{given} \\
3. & \Diamond\Box\sim A \rightarrow \Box\sim A & (5D)
\end{array}
$$

The tree continues as follows.

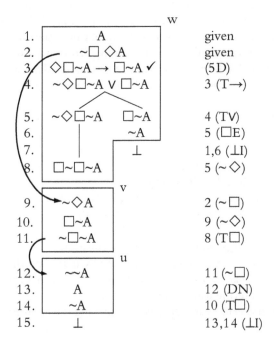

1.	A	given
2.	~□ ◇A	given
3.	◇□~A → □~A ✓	(5D)
4.	~◇□~A ∨ □~A	3 (T→)
5.	~◇□~A □~A	4 (TV)
6.	~A	5 (□E)
7.	⊥	1,6 (⊥I)
8.	□~□~A	5 (~◇)
9.	~◇A	2 (~□)
10.	□~A	9 (~◇)
11.	~□~A	8 (T□)
12.	~~A	11 (~□)
13.	A	12 (DN)
14.	~A	10 (T□)
15.	⊥	13,14 (⊥I)

The s5d tree is considerably longer, but it has no reflexivity or transverse arrows and no continuation. The reasoning of the original tree is represented on the right path, which achieves the goal of moving ~◇A (that is, □~A) from v into w as of line 5, so that ~A can be derived in w just as if it had been derived by applying (~◇) along a 5 arrow from v to w.

The s5d tree can be readily converted to a derivation. In Ds5t, the final lines are justified by (◇⊥) and (~□⊥) in addition to (PC) and a terminal application of (IP).

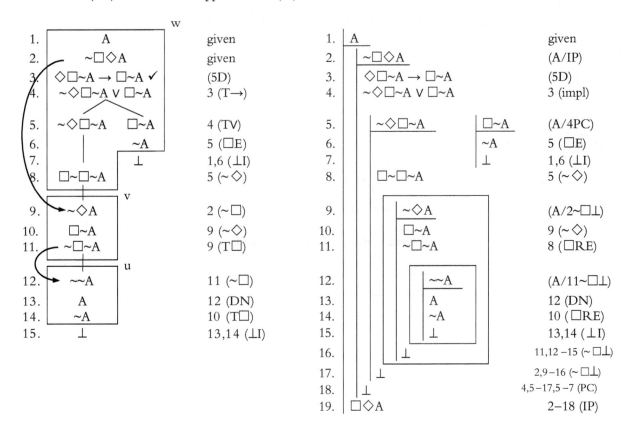

As indicated by the arrow structure for the example above, Tmd trees are k-trees. In the conversion above, there is an arrow from w to v, and an arrow from v to u. The contents of v are in the outer box on the left (PC) subderivation. The contents of u are in the box inside this outer box box. Had the second arrow gone from w to u rather than v to u, the derivation would have had to put the u box underneath, rather than inside the v box. This is the way the box structure in derivations reflects the remaining arrow structure on trees. It is why Dmt cannot tolerate continuations. Once a box, u, has been added below a box, v, in a derivation, there is no way to go back to add more sentences to v. On trees a continuation of v could wrap around u. The tree must be done to avoid that or conversion will not be possible.

By way of summary, the following is a complete list of modifications to the tree method and the derivation system. For trees:

- (T→) requires that P → Q be reduced as ~P ∨ Q
- (~&) requires that ~(P & Q) be reduced as ~P ∨ ~Q
- (T≡) requires that P ≡ Q be reduced as (P & Q) ∨ (~P & ~Q)
- (~≡) requires that ~(P ≡ Q) be reduced as (P & ~Q) ∨ (Q & ~P)
- (~◇) requires that ~◇P be reduced as □~P
- trees are to be done systematically, to avoid the need for continuations
- (T□) applications along reflexivity arrows are instead justified by (□E) and the arrows are removed
- (T□) applications along transitivity arrows are replaced by using (□R) to derive □P in the intermediate box and then applying (T□) to that intermediate occurrence of □P
- (T□) applications along transverse arrows are replaced by entering the appropriate instance of the 5D axiom on the last line of the path in the peak world

For derivations:

- (DN) is allowed for purposes of deriving P from ~~P
- (DeM) is allowed for purposes of deriving ~P ∨ ~Q from ~(P & Q)
- (Impl) is allowed for purposes of deriving ~P ∨ Q from P → Q
- (~→) is allowed for purposes of deriving P and ~Q from ~(P → Q)
- (~∨) is allowed for purposes of deriving ~P and ~Q from ~(P ∨ Q)
- (Equiv) is allowed for purposes of deriving (P & Q) ∨ (~P & ~Q) from P ≡ Q
- (~≡) is allowed for purposes of deriving (P & ~Q) ∨ (~P & Q) from ~(P ≡ Q)
- (~◇) is allowed for purposes of deriving □~P from ~◇P
- instances of the 5D metatheorem can be inserted at any point

The following derived rules are added:

- (◇⊥) – If L ⊢ ◇P and L,< P >⊢ ⊥, then L ⊢ ⊥
- (~□⊥) – If L ⊢ ~□P and L,< ~P > ⊢ ⊥ then L ⊢ ⊥
- Where (T◇) or (~□) are applied on trees to derive P or ~P in a new box, the corresponding derivation enters P or ~P as an assumption for (◇⊥) or (~□⊥) on the first line of a box

These modifications establish the following correspondence between tree rules and derivation rules:

Tree Rule	Derivation Rule
(DN)	(DN)
(T&)	(&E)
(~&)	(DeM)
(T∨)	A/(PC)
(~∨)	(~∨)
(T→)	(Impl)
(~→)	(~→)
(T≡)	(Equiv)

(~≡)	(~≡)
(T◇)	A/◇⊥
(~◇)	(~◇)
(T□)	(□RE)
(~□)	(A/~□⊥)
(□E)	(□E)
(□R)	(□R)
(5D)	(5D)
(⊥I)	(⊥I) / (◇⊥) / (~□⊥)

Exercise A-4.2

Convert all the closed trees obtained in answers to exercise 9.7 to derivations. Since conversions are based on trees constructed using the modified tree rules described in this section, it may help to first construct the modified tree. Do this at least for any tree that contains a continuation.

Solutions for **#1a, c, e, g, i, k; #2c, g, i, k; #3a, g, i, k**

A-4.4 Adequacy of Dm and Tm

The fact that m-trees can be converted to derivations can be used to establish that Dm is "complete," as it is said, and that Tm is sound, complementing the results of sections A-4.1 and A-4.2.

To begin with the former, the demonstration that Tm is complete has established that any m-unsatisfiable set must have at least one closed tree.

$$\text{If } \Gamma \text{ is m-unsatisfiable, it has at least one closed tree.}$$

By definition of $\vDash_m$, if $\Gamma \vDash_m P$, $\Gamma \cup {\sim}P$ is m-unsatisfiable. $\Gamma \cup {\sim}P$ must therefore have at least one closed tree. Necessarily, that tree must be a tree for a finite subset of the sentences in Γ. Were Γ infinite, and were it possible to go on adding sentences from Γ to any of its trees without end, it could only be because no extension is closed, contrary to the supposition. Given that closed m-trees can be turned into derivations, a derivation that starts off with the assumption of the sentences in this finite subset, continues by making the further assumption of $\sim$P, and follows the sequence of steps on the closed tree, will end up with $\bot$ under the assumption of $\sim$P, from which P follows by (IP). Consequently,

$$\text{If } \Gamma \vDash_m P \text{ then } L \vdash_m P$$
$$\text{where L is a finite list of the sentences on } \Gamma$$

That is, Dm is "complete." (Though the point might be better expressed by saying that whatever is m-entailed is verified by Dm, so m-semantics is sound.)

Turning to the latter principle, anything that can be derived in Tm can be converted to a derivation in Dm.

$$\text{If } \Gamma \vdash P \text{ in Tm then } L \vdash_m P$$
$$\text{where L is a finite list of the sentences in } \Gamma$$

In section A-4.1 it was demonstrated that whatever is derivable in Dm is m-entailed.

$$\text{If } L \vdash_m P \text{ then } \Gamma_L \vDash_m P$$
$$\text{where } \Gamma_L \text{ is the set of the sentences on L}$$

It follows that

$$\text{If } \Gamma \vdash P \text{ in Tm then } \Gamma \vDash_m P.$$

As a special case,

> If Γ has at least one closed tree (and so if $\Gamma \vdash \bot$ in Tm), $\Gamma \vDash_m \bot$, that is, Γ is m-unsatisfiable.

That is, Tm is sound.

Notes

1 Informal notational conventions are disregarded, so iterated conjunctions and iterated disjunctions are fully punctuated and reduced accordingly.
2 A rigorous demonstration can be found in Garson (2013: 164–9). The account of how to convert trees to derivations outlined here is loosely based on Garson's, which is recommended for further study.

References

Garson, James W, 2013, *Modal Logic for Philosophers*, 2nd edition, Cambridge University Press, New York.

Part III
Predicate Sentential Logic

10 Vocabulary, Syntax, Formalization, and Derivations

Contents

This and the following eight chapters consider an alternative way of extending sentential logic. To focus attention on this new material, the extensions made for modal logic are set aside. Integration of modal logic with this alternative extension is considered in the appendix to chapter A-6.

10.1 English Predication

Up to now, simple sentences have been the basic elements of logic, and values have been assigned to simple sentences on no other basis than combinatorial possibility. But there are things going on inside of simple sentences that determine their values.

Some sentences make assertions about some thing or some things. A simple assertion is true if what it says about a thing is true of that thing, or if what it says about things is true of those things. More precisely, truth is determined by whether the things spoken of satisfy what is said of or predicated of them. (Defining "true" by appeal to "true of" is question-begging. A strict definition of the technical term, satisfaction, is given in section 11.1.3.) A logic that recognizes and formalizes the relations between things and what is said of them can treat truth as something that is determined by more fundamental features, rather than as something that is simply assigned. This is the project of predicate logic. Predicate logic is the logic of how values come to be ascribed to simple sentences.

What is said of one or more things is "predicated" of them. Call what is said of them a predicate. Some of the things that have something said of them are individual objects, like the Eiffel Tower or Socrates. Others are groups

DOI: 10.4324/9781003026532-17

of objects, like the Chessmen or the Pharaohs. Predicate sentential logic (PSL) is an extension of SL that deals with those sentences that say something about individual objects. Sentences that say something about groups of objects are formalized by an extension of PSL, quantified predicate logic (QPL). The treatment of QPL begins in chapter 12. Until then, sentences that refer to groups of objects continue to be handled by SL.

The words or phrases that are used to refer to individual objects are called terms. The words or phrases that are used to refer to what is predicated of individual objects are called open sentences. Terms are of four main sorts: individual names, definite descriptions, functional terms, and variables.

An individual name is a word or list of words used as a label for an individual object. Most individual objects do not have individual names. Only those of special importance to language users (things like other language users, their pets, geographical locations, astronomical bodies) have names. The rest are lumped together in groups and labelled with group names.

Definite descriptions are lists of predicates that only one thing has, and that therefore serve to distinguish that thing from all others in its group, for example, "The plant in the third pot from the left on the top shelf."

Functional terms identify an individual object by means of a function on one or more other named or described objects, for example, "Alma's mother" or "Alma's mother's mother."

Variables can be used to designate an unspecified individual object. "Someone" in "You will find someone at the desk" is a variable.

For the sake of simplicity, the opening sections of this chapter treat definite descriptions and functional terms as if they were nothing more than verbose individual names, and postpone consideration of variables. Since the only terms to be considered for now are names, and the only names to be considered are individual names, the expressions "term" and "individual name" are dropped. "Names" will do for present purposes.

An open sentence is rigorously defined as whatever is left of a sentence after one or more names have been removed from it. Open sentences refer to predicates, so this is one way of understanding what a predicate is.

For example, the sentence "Alma is smart," says something about a named individual, Alma. The sentence can be considered to consist of the name used to denote this individual, "Alma," and what remains of the sentence after this name has been removed, the open sentence, "__ is smart." Just as the name, "Alma," denotes the individual, Alma, so the open sentence, "__ is smart," refers to the predicate of being smart.

Similarly, the sentence "Alma loves the Dragon" can be considered to consist of the name, "Alma," and what remains of the sentence after this name has been removed from it, "__ loves the Dragon." Alternatively, this sentence can be considered to consist of the name, "the Dragon," and the open sentence, "Alma loves __." Or, it can be considered to consist of a list of two names, <Alma, the Dragon> and the open sentence, "__ loves __." The open sentences "__ loves the Dragon," "Alma loves __," and "__ loves __" refer to three different predicates. A name can be left in an open sentence or separated from it. But at least one name must be removed on pain of reverting to sentential logic.

The open sentences, "__ is smart," "__ loves the Dragon," and "Alma loves __" are one-place open sentences. The open sentence, "__ loves __," is a two-place open sentence. One- and two-place open sentences refer to one- and two-place predicates. The distinction between one-place predicates and higher-place predicates is the distinction between properties of objects and relations between objects. A one-place predicate is a property of the object it is predicated of. A two- or higher-place predicate is a relation between the objects it is predicated of.

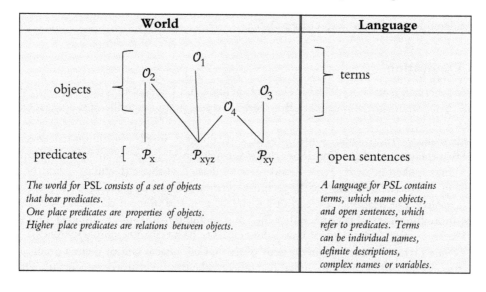

World	**Language**
$\mathcal{O}_2$ $\mathcal{O}_1$ $\mathcal{O}_3$ $\mathcal{O}_4$ objects	terms
predicates { $\mathcal{P}_x$ $\mathcal{P}_{xyz}$ $\mathcal{P}_{xy}$	} open sentences
The world for PSL consists of a set of objects that bear predicates. *One place predicates are properties of objects.* *Higher place predicates are relations between objects.*	*A language for PSL contains terms, which name objects, and open sentences, which refer to predicates. Terms can be individual names, definite descriptions, complex names or variables.*

It is often important which of the unoccupied places in a predicate is occupied by an object. The sentence "Alma loves Boda" and the sentence "Boda loves Alma" are not logically equivalent. One can be true while the other is false. The first unoccupied place in the two-place predicate "__ loves __" is occupied by the lover, the second by the beloved. In contrast, the first unoccupied place in the predicate "__ is loved by __" is occupied by the beloved, the second by the lover. These are different predicates, described by different open sentences. By contrast, in the predicate "__ plays racquetball with __," the objects in first and second place are interchangeable. By way of further contrast, where the predicate "__ is older than __" is concerned, the objects in the places are never interchangeable.

Because it sometimes matters which place an object occupies, it is best not to designate all places in the same way, by using blanks, as has just been done. From now on, lower-case letters from x to z will be used to designate places.

The sentence, "Alma loves Boda" should not be considered to contain just the two names, "Alma" and "Boda." It should instead be considered to contain the list of names <Alma, Boda>. The first name on the list goes in the first place in the open sentence, and so names the lover, and the second goes in the second place, and so names the beloved. Containing the list <Alma, Boda> rather than the list <Boda, Alma> is what distinguishes the sentence "Alma loves Boda" from the sentence "Boda loves Alma."

Lists of two objects are ordered pairs. Lists of three objects are ordered triplets. In general, lists of n objects are n-place lists.

10.2 Simple Terms

10.2.1 *Vocabulary and Syntax of Predicate Sentential Logic*

Whereas SL is constructed to represent relations between sentences, which are linguistic items, PSL is constructed to represent the predication of properties or relations of objects. Accordingly, the new vocabulary elements of PSL do not stand for sentences or sentential connectives. They do not even stand for names or open sentences. They *are* names or open sentences. With one exception, they are used to refer directly to objects and their properties and relations. The symbols of PSL may still be used to formalize sentences of English, but this is not because the symbols of PSL stand directly for English names or English open sentences. It is rather because vocabulary elements of PSL are coreferential with vocabulary elements of English.

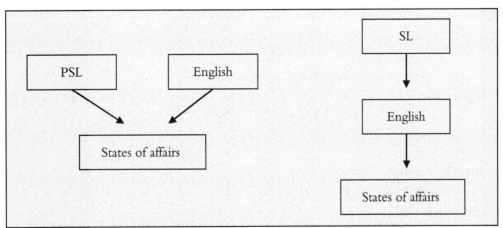

Diagram: Whereas SL formalizes English sentences, which describe states of affairs, both PSL and English describe states of affairs.

PSL uses lower-case letters a, b, c, d, e, f to denote objects. If more than six objects are under consideration, a's are numerically subscripted. These symbols are called names. Other textbooks refer to them as constants. They are "constant" because, unlike English, PSL does not tolerate ambiguity. English will use the same name to denote different objects. In PSL, each name must denote exactly one object.

PSL uses the sentence letters, A, B, C, G, H, K, now called *n*-place predicate letters, to refer to predicates. If more than six are needed, A's are numerically subscripted. *n*-place predicate letters are always followed by *n* places, where *n* could be as few as zero. These places are always filled with names. One name fills one place. The names need not be distinct. In some contexts, it is preferable not to specify what names go in the places. In those cases, x, y, z, or numerically subscripted x's are used as place holders. Predicate letters followed by these place holders are the open sentences of PSL. Open sentences are not recognized as sentences of PSL. The place holders are not included in the vocabulary. Expressions containing them are metavariables for sentences of PSL.

Because names always follow predicate letters, PSL syntax will often be different from English syntax. English can put the name in first place, as in "Alma is smart," or put the names at either end of the predicate, as in "Alma loves Boda." PSL always lines up the names after the predicates.

For example, PSL might formalize the fact that Alma is smart, as Ga, where Gx is the open sentence equivalent to the English open sentence "x is smart" and "a" names the person who goes by the English name "Alma." (It would be perfectly acceptable to use Ax rather than Gx, but the combination Aa only works in writing. To facilitate verbal discussion, constructions that combine the capital and the lower case of the same letter are avoided.)

A difference in number of places distinguishes predicates, even when the predicate letter is the same. So G, Ga, and Gab are three different predicates. When there is more than one place, the places are special, in the sense that it matters which place a name occupies. Gab is not the same sentence as Gba. The names that come after a predicate are therefore members of a list. A two-place predicate must be followed by a two-place list of names, a three-place by a three-place, and so on. For the sake of conformity with the other cases, one- and zero-place predicates are said to be followed by a one-place list of names and the empty list, respectively.

As a further example, PSL might formalize the fact that Boda loves Crumb as Hbc, taking Hxy as the open sentence that designates the relation, x loves y, b as the name for Boda, and c the name for Crumb. The nontrivially different fact that Crumb loves Boda is formalized as Hcb. The fact that Boda and Crumb love one another is formalized with the aid of symbols from SL as Hbc & Hcb. In contrast, the fact that Crumb loves herself but not Boda is formalized as Hcc & ~Hcb. Expressions like Ga and Hcb are atomic sentences of PSL, and may be related to one another or compounded using sentential connectives in all the ways provided for by SL.

A predicate letter followed by no names is a zero-place predicate. Zero-place predicates play the role that was played by the sentence letters of SL. They stand for sentences of English that do not contain any names, or none that are separately formalized.

While PSL does not allow assigning the same name to two different objects, it does allow the same object to be denoted by two or more different names. In this case, PSL uses a special symbol for the relation between the names, the identity symbol (=).

The notation =ab can be informally read as "identify 'a' with b." More accurately, it is read as "'a' and b name the same object." It should not be read as "a" is identical to b or as "a" is equal to b. "a" and b are letters of the alphabet, not quantities. Because they are different letters of the alphabet, they can not be identical. But they can designate the same object.

Vocabulary of PSL

Names:	**a, b, c, d, e, f, a$_1$, a$_2$, a$_3$, …**
***n*-place predicate letters:**	**A, B, C, G, H, K, A$_1$, A$_2$, A$_3$, … followed by 0 or more places that must be filled with names**
Contradiction symbol:	⊥
Identity symbol:	**=**
Connectives:	~, &, ∨, →, ≡
Punctuation marks:	), (

Syntax of PSL

An *expression* is any vocabulary element or sequence of vocabulary elements.

A *sentence* is any expression formed in accord with the following rules:

(P): If P is an *n*-place predicate and <q$_1$,…q$_n$> is a list of *n* not necessarily distinct names, then Pq$_1$…q$_n$ is a sentence. As a special case of (P), if P is ⊥ or a **0- place predicate** then P is a sentence.

(=): If p and q are two (not necessarily distinct) names then =pq is a sentence

(~): If P is a sentence, then ~P is a sentence.

(bc): If P and Q are two (not necessarily distinct) sentences, then (P & Q), (P ∨ Q), (P → Q), and (P ≡ Q) are sentences.

(exclusion): Nothing is a sentence unless it has been formed by one or more applications of the preceding rules.

Scope

When ~ is followed by ⊥, a 0-place predicate, an *n*-place predicate followed by *n* names, or = followed by two names the scope of ~ is those following symbols.
(There are no further changes to the definition of scope as given in chapter 2.)

Named Forms
(There are no changes to the definitions of main connective, immediate component, component, or atomic component.)

- A sentence that has no main connective is an *atomic sentence*. Atomic sentences have no immediate components. **In particular:**
  - ⊥ is an atomic sentence.
  - A sentence of the form P where P is a **0-place predicate** is an atomic sentence.
  - **A sentence of the form, $Pq_1...q_n$, where P is an *n*-place predicate and $q_1, ..., qp_n$ are *n* (not necessarily distinct) names is a** *predicate sentence*. **Predicate sentences are also atomic and do not have main connectives or immediate components.**
  - **A sentence of the form, =pq, where p and q are two not necessarily distinct names is an** *identity sentence*. **Identity sentences are also atomic and do not have main connectives or immediate components.**

(There are no further changes to the named forms.)

Sameness and Contradiction; Opposition
No expression or sentence of **PSL** is the same as any other unless it consists of the same vocabulary elements, placed in the same order.
In particular, if p and q are distinct names, =pq is not the same as =qp.
Two expressions or sentences are distinct if and only if they are not the same.
Two sentences are *opposite* if and only if they are the same but for the fact that one of them begins with ~.
Consequently, if p and q are distinct, ~=pq is not the opposite of =qp.

Informal notational conventions: *(conventions should be applied in the order listed)*
  (b): Brackets may be substituted for parentheses.
  (ip): Internal punctuation may be omitted within iterated conjunctions and iterated disjunctions.
  (sc): "Strong conditionals." Punctuation used to extend the scope of → or ≡ over & or ∨ may be omitted.
  (op): Outermost parentheses may be coloured out (they are still there).

Many textbooks "infix" rather than "prefix" the identity symbol. That practice is not followed here. Infixing the identity symbol makes it look like a sentential connective, and makes names look like sentential components, leading to such abuses as supposing that a=~b is a sentence, that ~(a=b) is a sentence, and that ~a=b means, "not-a is b." Writing "a=b" as "=ab" helps prevent these misunderstandings.

= is not a connective.
= pq is an atomic sentence. Punctuation is never placed around or within identity sentences.
Only sentences can be negated. Names cannot be negated.

Formalizations in PSL can be quite involved. They are easier to read if punctuation is reduced. This can be done in two ways, as discussed in chapter 8. Since P & (Q & R) and (P & Q) & R are s-equivalent and interderivable in Ds and Ts, and since the same holds for P ∨ (Q ∨ R) and (P ∨ Q) ∨ R, PSL syntax allows the omission of internal punctuation in iterated conjunctions and iterated disjunctions. The informal notational convention applied for this purpose is called (ip) for "internal punctuation."

Secondly, → and ≡ are taken to outrank & and ∨. The convention for this is called (sc) for "strong conditionals." → and ≡ are by default taken to have scope over & or ∨, making punctuation unnecessary to do that job. Punctuation remains necessary to define the scope of → relative to ≡ and of & relative to ∨. It is also necessary to extend the scope of & or ∨ over → or ≡. These changes thin out what can become a forest of punctuation marks. However, in simpler contexts, past practices will often be retained.

Exercise 10.1

1. *Which of the following are sentences of PSL? (Allow for all informal notational conventions.) Explain why those that are not violate the formation rules and why those that are, are in accord with the formation rules. Assume that each predicate is followed by the required number of names.*

    ★a. Ga
      b. ~Ga
    ★c. ~(Ga)
      d. G → K
    ★e. c & a
      f. ab
    ★g. G=a
      h. Gz
    ★i. G(cb)
      j. Ka & (Gacb)
    ★k. Gbbcbb
      l. ~Kab ∨ G
    ★m. ~(Gac ∨ Kb)
      n. a=c
    ★o. =aa
      p. ~=ab
    ★q. =~ab
      r. ~(=ab)
    ★s. ~(=ab → Ga)
      t. =(=ab)c
    ★u. G=ac
      v. =ab & ~=bc
    ★w. (=ab) & (=bc)
      x. ~(=ab & =bc)

2. *One of the symbol strings in question 1 is not an expression of PSL. Which one?*

3. *Produce the syntactic tree that proves that each of the following is a sentence of PSL. Assume that each predicate is followed by the required number of names.*

    ★a. ~=ac → =bd
      b. (~Gac ∨ K) & =bd
    ★c. ~(=ab ∨ Kab) → Gcad
      d. ~Ga & Ka ≡ (Hb → Ca)
    ★e. Ka & Haaa → Ga ∨ B
      f. (Ka → Gab) ≡ ~=ab

4. *If exercises 8.1#2 and 8.1#3 were not done previously, do them now.*

10.2.2 *Formalization*

The variables of PSL (the name letters and the predicate letters) stand for objects and predicates. The first task of formalization is to come up with an interpretation of the name and predicate letters. This process begins by identifying a "domain of discourse" ("domain" for short). The domain is the general group of objects under consideration. Specifying a domain might take the form of listing all the objects in the domain, e.g. D: {Alma, Boda, Crumb}, or it might be done by using a predicate that is satisfied by all and only those objects, e.g., D is the occupants of the room. (As usual, logicians do not care what is in the domain and are happy to consider all the possibilities. However, there must be something to talk about or the enterprise ceases to be predicate logic, so domains must include at least one object.) Once a domain has been specified, objects from the domain are assigned to name letters and predicates (properties and relations of objects) are assigned to predicate letters. Name letters are then combined with predicate letters to describe states of affairs.

To be useful for formalization, an interpretation must assign those objects and those predicates that are discussed in the natural language sentences being formalized to name and predicate letters. For example, the sentence "Alma is a better tipper than Boda" refers (by name) to the objects, Alma and Boda, and associates them with the relation of being a better tipper. To formalize this sentence, devise an interpretation consisting of a domain that contains these objects (for example, the customers), assign these objects to names (for example, Alma to "a" and Boda to b), and assign the relation of being a better tipper to a two-place predicate letter (for example, Gxy). Then the English sentence "Alma is a better tipper than Boda" can be formalized as Gab, which says the same thing on the interpretation. Significantly, the interpretation does not assign the English name "Alma" to "a," the English name "Boda," to b, or the English open sentence "x is a better tipper than y" to G. It assigns the object that English identifies using the name "Alma" to "a," the object that English identifies using the name "Boda" to b, and a (possibly empty) set of pairs of objects such that the first object in the pair is in fact a better tipper than the second object in the pair, to G. Unfortunately, there is no way to specify what assignments an interpretation makes without using English names and open sentences to designate or describe the objects and predicates. This makes it appear as if the variables have English expressions as their values. They do not. They have the values of the English expressions as their values. Formalization is possible when English and PSL coincide in naming the same things, not when variables of PSL are assigned to expressions of English.

Exercise 10.2

1. *Formalize the following sentences in PSL using the following interpretation:*

Domain: {Alma, Boda, Crumb}

a: Alma   Kxy: x knows y
b: Boda   Gxy: x loves y
c: Crumb   Bxyz: x knows y better than z
               Hxy: x recognizes y

  ★**a.** Alma knows Boda and Boda knows Crumb, but Alma does not know Crumb, Crumb does not know Boda, and Boda does not know herself.
   b. Alma knows Boda only if she knows him.
  ★**c.** Everyone knows themselves. *(Hint: there are only three objects in the domain; use brute force.)*
   d. Only Alma knows Boda. *(This is a new sense of "only.")*
  ★**e.** Everyone except Alma knows Boda.
   f. Alma and Boda both know Crumb, but neither of them loves him.
  ★**g.** Everyone who knows Crumb loves him.
   h. Though Alma knows Crumb better than himself, he doesn't recognize him.
  ★**i.** Everyone knows everyone but Crumb.
   j. Alma knows Crumb better than Boda, but he still will not recognize him.

2. *Rewrite the following formalizations in natural English using the following interpretation:*

Domain: {x: x is a real number}
a: 1
b: the square root of 2
c: 3
Gxy: x is greater than y

   *a.   Gab → ~Gba
    b.   ~Gac & ~Gbc & ~Gcc & Gca & Gcb
   *c.   ~(Gac ∨ Gbc) → (=ab ∨ Gab ∨ Gba)
    d.   (Gac → ~=ca) & ~(~=ca → Gac) *(use "if but not only if"; do not use "equals")*
   *e.   (Gab & Gbc) → Gac
    f.   ~=ab → Gab ∨ Gba

There are some challenges to formalization. One is being sensitive to the difference between an individual name and a group name. Name letters of SL designate individual objects. An English sentence that only names groups cannot be analysed into an open sentence and a list of individual names. Such sentences must be formalized as zero-place predicates. Sentences that contain a combination of individual names and group names must leave the group names in the open sentence. The corresponding sentence of PSL would use a predicate that involves the groups. The following exercise illustrates what this means.

Exercise 10.3

1. *List any individual names contained in each of the following sentences. Then list all the open sentences that can be formed by removing one or more names from each of them. Designate places in the open sentences with* x, y, *or* z.
   *a.   Berkeley was an Anglican.
    b.   Edwards was a Calvinist.
   *c.   Berkeley was the Dean of Derry.
    d.   The library administrators were originally opposed to appointing Hume.
   *e.   Hume and Rousseau were originally on friendly terms.
    f.   Hume was widely reputed to have been an atheist.
   *g.   Berkeley was a graduate of Trinity College.
    h.   Hume's views were strongly influenced by Bayle.

2. *Devise an interpretation and use it to formalize each of the following sentences in* PSL.
   *a.   Alma loves racquetball but he does not love Crumb.
    b.   Alma is not a good mechanic, but he knows one, and he also knows the Mayor.
   *c.   Alma's best friend is friends with Crumb.
    d.   The Police know Alma's best friend all too well.
   *e.   If Alma owns the only restaurant and the only bowling alley in town, he won't be too worried if the Mayor blocks his application for a permit to build a hotel.
    f.   Alma will come to the reception only if he is accompanied by the Mayor.

A second challenge to formalization is dealing with what are often called "improper" names. English can assign different individuals to the same individual name. English can also assign nonexistent objects, such as dead people, fictional characters, or even impossible objects, like the round square or the thing that is not identical to itself to individual names. However, PSL does not tolerate ambiguity or vacuity. Each name of PSL must denote exactly one object, never more than one, and never none. Consequently, exactly one object must be assigned to each individual name of PSL.

Where English names are ambiguous, PSL disambiguates them. Different objects that are assigned to the same English name must be assigned different names of PSL.

Names that do not denote an object are a different matter. The valuation rules to be presented in chapter 11 assign values to predicate and identity sentences depending on what objects the names appearing in those sentences denote. Were a name not to denote an object, the rules would assign an F to any predicate or identity sentence containing that name. This would make sentences of the form =pp false when p does not denote an object, with untoward effects for one of the derivation rules (see section 10.2.3). It would also make sentences of the form ~Pq (like "Pegasus is not a mythological creature") trivially true when q does not denote an object. PSL avoids these drawbacks by requiring that each name denote exactly one of the objects in the domain. This leaves two recourses for dealing with English sentences that contain names that refer to nonexistent objects: expand the domain to include those objects, or include the name in the meaning assigned to the predicate letter.

A sentence like "Pegasus is not a mythological creature" might best be formalized by including both historical and mythological objects in the domain and taking Gx to be the one-place predicate "x is a mythological creature." A sentence like "Hesiod wrote of Pegasus" might instead be formalized by restricting the domain to historical objects and taking Gx to be the one-place predicate "x wrote of Pegasus."

Expanding the domain is not obviously the best approach. Even though it is not the business of logic to tell people what they can talk about, much less determine what exists, and even though logicians are happy to consider all possible interpretations, and hence all the ways a domain might be defined, it is the business of other sciences to determine what exists, and logic is used in other sciences. If it is agreed that an English name does not identify an existing object, a PSL formalization that respects that decision may not include that object in the domain and therefore no name of PSL may denote it.

Specifying the domain of discourse is an important preliminary to formalizing any English sentence. It sets limits to what can be assigned to a name letter. This extends to deciding questions about what counts as an individual and what counts as a group. Is Beethoven's Seventh Symphony an individual or a group of notes? Or the group of its performances over time? Or the group of published copies of the score? Logic does not care. It does not decide what makes something an object or what entitles an object to admission in the domain. Its work begins after those decisions have been made and is independent of how they are made. This is so much the case that for logical purposes the members of the domain can be identified merely by catalogue numbers. Nothing more needs to be known about them, other than what predicates they satisfy, and on that score as well, logic is happy to consider all the possibilities.

Exercise 10.4

Taking the domain to be past and present persons, places, and things (broadly construed to include political and economic institutions), provide an interpretation and use it to formalize each of the following sentences in PSL. When in doubt, research things to find out if they ever existed.

★**a.** Stanley was looking for Livingston and for the source of the Nile.

 b. Franklin was looking for a northwest passage.

★**c.** George Edwards was looking for the Loch Ness Monster.

 d. Archibald Campbell was the 3rd Duke of Argyll, a member of the British House of Lords, and one of the founders of the Royal Bank of Scotland.

★**e.** Dr. Watson was the biographer of Sherlock Holmes, and Lytton Strachey was the biographer of Queen Victoria.

 f. Conan Doyle was the author of the adventures of Sherlock Holmes.

★**g.** If Archibald Stewart was the heir of Douglas then he was the son of Lady Jane, but if he was not the son of Lady Jane then James Hamilton was the heir of Douglas.

 h. If Brutus was the assassin of Caesar and Cassius was the assassin of Caesar, then Brutus is Cassius. *(Formalize this sentence in two ways: one that presumes that there was exactly one person who was the assassin of Caesar, and one that recognizes that, as a matter of historical record, there was more than one assassin. The former formalization recognizes that valid reasoning can involve references to nonexistent objects and that nonexistent objects might be included in a domain to accommodate valid reasoning that mentions them.)*

A third challenge to formalization arises in contexts where the same object has different English names. In such cases, PSL can afford to accommodate English syntax and assign the object to more than one name. But it needs to be kept in mind that the names of PSL do not denote names of English. A domain for PSL is a domain of *individual objects*, not a domain of *names*. D: {Mercury, Venus, Mars}, is not the domain of the names, "Mercury," "Venus," and "Mars" but the domain of the objects denoted by those names, the first two and the fourth planets from the Sun. When an interpretation is described by using English names to identify domain objects, the identification must be made without giving the appearance that a domain object that has more than one English name is multiple different domain objects. One way to do this is to assign the object to one name letter and use that name letter to formalize all the names that English uses to denote that object. References to "David Hume," "Mr Hume," "Le bon David," and "the author of the *Treatise*" might all be formalized as d. But sometimes, the audience does not know that the different English names denote the same object, or one of the points a speaker wants to make is that they do. These cases require assigning the object to as many different names of PSL as English assigns the object to. One way to handle this is to list all the English names for the object, linked by "aka" or "alias" opposite multiple name letters, as in

D: {x: x is a planet in the solar system}
a: Venus, aka Lucifer
b: Venus, aka Lucifer

This does not mean that the two names of PSL, "a" and b, formalize the two English names "Venus" and "Lucifer." The PSL names are two different names of the one object, the second planet from the Sun. "Venus" and "Lucifer" are likewise two different English names for that object. That having been said, the different names can be used in parallel. ("a" might appear in exactly those contexts where English uses "Venus," b in exactly those contexts where it uses "Lucifer.")

There are drawbacks to this approach. Sometimes, it is unknown whether two different names denote the same object, or, if it is known, those whose reasoning is being formalized may not know it. The issue arises when objects are named by different descriptions ("the perpetrator of the crime" and "the individual in the defendant's chair"), or names came into use at different times and places (and no one has kept an eye or hand on the object(s) across its (their) travels or throughout its (their) evolution). In these cases, it might be thought that it would be better to take name letters of PSL to stand for names of English, so as not to prejudge the outcome of the investigation. But this approach is unacceptable. It would mean that sentences of form =ab would only be true in the case where "a" and b stand for the same English name and that is too trite a matter to be worth formalizing. The interesting question is whether "a" and b name the same domain object, not whether they name the same English name.

In PSL bivalence continues to hold. Any sentence of the form =ab is either true or false. If it is true, it is because "a" and b denote the same object. If it is false, it is because they denote different objects. They either do or they do not. Cases in which it is unclear whether different names denote the same object are cases in which it is unclear which of two interpretations is the one that reflects the facts. This is not a problem for logic to address. The logician takes these matters to have been resolved by experience, testimony, or scientific investigation, and where none of those recourses is conclusive, the logician is happy to consider how things turn out on either interpretation.

This having been said, contingent identity sentences are not like contingent predicate sentences, such as "Alma is a better tipper than Boda." Gab is not contingent simply because there are interpretations on which "a" and b denote other objects than Alma and Boda. Once an interpretation has fixed the value of "a" as Alma and the value of b as Boda, it still has to fix the value of Gxy. This means deciding whether the ordered pair of objects <Alma, Boda> should be among those in the set of ordered pairs assigned to G. The assignments made to "a" and b do not determine that further valuation. In the case of identity sentences, in contrast, once the decision has been made about what values to assign to "a" and b, there is no further valuation to be made. The value of the identity sentence is already determined by the valuation of the names it contains.

Identity sentences are trite, in the sense that their meaning is determined just by the meaning of the names they contain. But they are informative (except for those of the form =pp, they could be false and whatever could be false conveys information). The information they convey has some use. As noted below (exercise 10.4#6g and chapter A-5.1), it establishes a new form of equivalence for other sentences. Other systems of logic do more to formalize claims concerning the identification and differentiation of objects, but that requires a more robust vocabulary than PSL has at its disposal and builds on features that are best learned by first studying PSL.

Exercise 10.5

Formalize the following sentences in PSL using the following interpretation:

Domain: {Samuel Clemens aka Mark Twain, Edgar Allan Poe}

a: Samuel Clemens aka Mark Twain   Gx: x is the greatest American author
b: Edgar Allan Poe   Hx: x wrote *Huckleberry Finn*
c: Samuel Clemens aka Mark Twain   Kxy: x is dining with y
                                                           Bxy: x is taller than y

*a.   If Mark Twain is Samuel Clemens, then Samuel Clemens wrote *Huckleberry Finn*.
 b.   If Mark Twain is not Samuel Clemens, then Mark Twain did not write *Huckleberry Finn*.
*c.   If Mark Twain is the greatest American author and Samuel Clemens is the greatest American author, then Mark Twain is Samuel Clemens.
 d.   If Mark Twain is taller than Samuel Clemens, then it is not the case that Mark Twain is Samuel Clemens.

*e. If Mark Twain is dining with Edgar Allan Poe then Edgar Allan Poe is dining with Mark Twain, but if Mark Twain is taller than Edgar Allan Poe then Edgar Allan Poe is not taller than Mark Twain.

   f. If Mark Twain is taller than Samuel Clemens and Samuel Clemens is taller than Edgar Allan Poe, then Mark Twain is not Samuel Clemens and he is taller than Edgar Allan Poe.

10.2.3 Derivations

The derivation system for PSL, Dp, uses all the rules of Ds plus the following two rules:

> (=I): L ⊢ =pp (where L could be the empty list)
> (=E): If L ⊢ =rq, or L ⊢ =qr, and L ⊢ P, then L ⊢ P(r ¦ q)

Templates for the use of these rules with derivation brackets are:

(=I)		(=E)	
n. =pp (=I)	*k.*	=rq [or =qr]	?
	…	…	
	k★	P	?
	…	…	
	n.	P(r ¦ q)	k,k★ (=E)

   (=I) allows any sentence of the form =pp, that is, any self-identity sentence, to be entered at any point in a derivation, including on the first line. This makes it an axiom. There is no other rule application or sequence of rule applications that yields =pp. It is independently self-evident. (=I) only applies to self-identities. =ab is not derivable by (=I). But =aa and =bb, for example, are.

   (=E) is based on the intuition that if two names denote the same object, replacing one or more occurrences of the one name with occurrences of the other makes no changes to what is being talked about. The rule statement makes use of the split bar notation, which has been used in advanced topics chapters to refer to the result of replacing zero or more occurrences of one expression with another. To begin with a simple example, consider P to be a three-place predicate sentence, Gaca and, consider P(r ¦ q) to be the result of rewriting Gaca to put b in the place of one or more of the occurrences of a. Then P(r ¦ q) could be any of Gbca, Gacb, or Gbcb. As a special case, if P does not contain any occurrences of q, then P(r ¦ q) is P. So, if P is Gce and P(r ¦ q) is the result of rewriting Gce to put occurrences of b in the place of one or more occurrences of "a" then P(r ¦ q) is just Gce.

   (=E) allows either replacing occurrences of the second name in the identity sentence with occurrences of the first, or replacing occurrences of the first with occurrences of the second. The same sentences can be derived from =ba and Gaa as from =ab and Gaa.

   A single application of (=E) suffices to put r in the place of multiple occurrences of q in P. However, it is not permissible to both replace an occurrence of q with r and replace an occurrence of r with q using a single application of (=E). That requires two applications.

   P need not be atomic. So from =ab and ~Baa any or all of ~Bba, ~Bab, and ~Bbb may be derived, and from =ab and Ba → Ca any or all of Bb → Ca, Ba → Cb, and Bb → Cb may be derived.

   It is permissible to apply (=E) to other identity sentences. =ab can be applied to =bc to obtain =ac.

   It is not permissible to apply (=E) using a negated identity sentence. ~=ab says that "a" and b do not denote the same object. In that case, Ga does not yield Gb, and Gb does not yield Ga.

   While negated identity sentences cannot be *sources* for (=E) they can be *targets* for (=E). That is, they can be the sentences of the form P within which the substitution of q for r or r for q is made, but they cannot be the sentences that say what names can be substituted for one another. =cb can be applied to ~=ab to derive ~=ac. ~=ab says that "a" does not denote the same object as b does, so of course "a" cannot be substituted for b without changing the meaning. However, if c denotes the same object as b, and b does not denote the same object as "a," then c cannot denote the same object as "a," either, so ~=ac is derivable.

   To keep things clear, when identity sentences are justified the justification takes the form *k,k*★ (=E), where *k* is the source line (the line where the identity sentence that states the terms that are going to be substituted for one another occurs) and k⋆ is the target line (the line containing the sentence where the substitution is made). Rule applications that get this justification backwards are considered incorrect. In the case where =cb is used as a source on the target ~=ab, giving the justification by citing the target line first would give the mistaken impression that negated identity sentences can be used as sources for (=E).

In addition to adding (=I) and (=E), a procedure needs to be developed for the use of (PC), (∨I), (&E) and (&I) with conjunctions and disjunctions that lack internal punctuation. The following revisions to the derivation rules are adopted for this purpose:

(PC):   If L ⊢ P₁ ∨ ... ∨ Pₙ, and L, Pᵢ ⊢ Q, where Pᵢ is each of P₁ ... Pₙ, then L ⊢ Q
(∨I):   If L ⊢ P then L yields any iterated disjunction containing P
(&E):   If L ⊢ P₁ & ... & Pₙ then L yields any of P₁ ... Pₙ
(&I):   If L ⊢ Pᵢ, where Pᵢ is each of P₁ ... Pₙ, then L ⊢ P₁ & ... & Pₙ

Exercise 10.6

1.   *State whether the following are instances of (=I).*

⋆a.   n. | =pp   (=I)   b.   n. | =cb   (=I)   ⋆c.   k. | Ga
                                                                        ...   ...
                                                                        n. | =aa   k (=I)

d.   k. | ...   ⋆e.   ... | ...
      ... | ...   n. | ⌐ =aa   (=I)
      n. | =aa   (=I)   ... | ⌐...   f.   n. | ~=aa   (=I)

2.   *State whether the following are instances of (=E).*

⋆a.   i. | | =ab   b.   i. | =ab   ⋆c.   i. | ~=ab
       ... | ...   ... | ...   ... | ...
       k. | Gb   k. | Gb   k. | =ca
       ... | ...   ... | ...   ... | ...
       n. | Ga   i,k (=E)   n. | Ga   k,i (=E)   n. | ~=cb   i,k (=E)

d.   i. | ~=ab   ⋆e.   i. | =ab   f.   i. | Ga
      ... | ...   ... | ...   ... | ...
      k. | =ac   k. | =ac   k. | ~=ba
      ... | ...   ... | ...   ... | ...
      n. | ~=cb   k,i (=E)   n. | =cb   i,k (=E)   n. | ~Gb   k,i (=E)

⋆g.   i. | =ab   h.   i. | =ab
       ... | ...   k. | =aa → ~=ba
       k. | Gca → Hbc
                              n. | =ba → ~=bb   i,k (=E)
       n. | Gcb → Hac   i,k (=E)

3. *State whether the following are instances of* (⊥I).

    ★**a.** i. │ =ab   b. k. ~=aa

          … │ …   … …

          k. │ ~=ba   n. ⊥   k (⊥I)

          … │ …

          n. │ ⊥   i,k (⊥I)

4. *Establish the following in* Dp.

    ★**a.** ⊢ ~=aa → ⊥

      b. ⊢ ⊥ → =aa

    ★**c.** ⊢ =ab → =ba

      d. ⊢ ~=ab → ~=ba

    ★**e.** ⊢ =ab & =bc → =ac

      f. ⊢ =ab & =ac → =cb

    ★**g.** ⊢ =ab → (Ga ≡ Gb)

      h. ⊢ Ga & ~Gb → ~=ab

    ★**i.** Gac, ~Gca ⊢ ~=ac

      j. Gac ⊢ =ac → Gca

    ★**k.** =ab, =ba → Kb ⊢ Ka

      l. =aa → H & Kb, ~H ⊢ ⊥

     m. Ka ≡ ~Kb ⊢ ~=ab

10.3 Complex Terms

10.3.1 Functional Terms

In addition to being denoted by a name, an object may be denoted by a relation that it uniquely bears to one or more other objects. For example, Boda might be denoted by the name "Boda," or she might instead be denoted by mentioning a relation only she bears to Alma, such as "Alma's oldest sister." Someone who does not know what Boda's name is, but who knows Alma and Alma's name, might use Alma's name to do this. Whereas names are simple terms, expressions like "Alma's oldest sister" are one kind of complex term.

Functional terms name one thing by means of a unique relation to other named things. The uniqueness of the relation is important. If many things stand in a relation to Alma, or none do, that relation will not pick out any one of them. For example, if Alma has many friends, then "Alma's friend" does not denote anyone in particular. "Alma's best friend" does, supposing only one friend can be the best, and she has at least one. But to be functional, a relation needs to relate each object in the domain to exactly one object (not necessarily the same one in each case). "Best friend of" is still not a function, because even if Alma has exactly one best friend, other people have no best friend. Even "biological mother of" is not a function. Not everything has a biological mother. This having been said, many relations become functional, when the domain is suitably restricted. "Biological mother of" is functional when the domain is restricted to higher animals, though even then the relation needs to be finessed to avoid an infinite past series of mothers, be it by ignoring the values beyond a certain point or arbitrarily denoting some sufficiently remote ancestors as their own mothers. When the domain is restricted to integers, many mathematical relations become functional, e.g., "immediate successor of," "square of." "Sum of x, y, and z" is also a function, an *n*-place function, because for any *n* integers it picks out a unique integer.

While it is necessary that an *n*-place function yield exactly one result for any *n* names that are put in its places, it need not go the other way. Different people can have the same biological mother. Different lists of integers can sum to the same result.

10.3.2 Vocabulary and Syntax of PLf; Formalization

To review what was said in chapter 1, a function is an operation that maps lists of objects drawn from one set, called the domain of the function, onto unique objects in another, not necessarily distinct set, called the range or the co-domain of the function. A one-place function takes each object from the domain and maps it onto exactly one object in the co-domain. A two-place function takes each ordered pair of (not necessarily distinct) objects in the domain and maps it onto exactly one object in the co-domain. In general, an *n*-place function takes each *n*-place list that can be made from n (not necessarily distinct) objects in the domain and assigns it to exactly one object in the co-domain. The input lists of objects are called the arguments of that function. The output object for any one argument is called the value of that argument. Same values might be assigned to multiple arguments, and some objects in the co-domain might not be the value of any argument. But each argument must have exactly one object in the co-domain as its value.

When functional terms are incorporated into PSL, the domain and the co-domain are the same: the object domain. Any n-place function must assign exactly one object from the domain to each n-place list of objects from the domain. Functional terms are formalized by adding places to the name letters.

Consider a, b, c, d, e, f, and the numerically subscripted a's to be followed by 0 or more places, like predicates. Call them function letters. Names are a special kind of function letter, a zero-place function letter. A one-place function letter is a symbol for a function that takes one object as argument and returns an object as value. A two-place function letter is a function that takes a list of two objects as arguments and returns an object as value, and so on. For example, if the domain is natural numbers, "a" denotes 2, and f is a one-place function letter standing for the "square of" function, f(a) can be taken to stand for "the square of 2." Importantly, what f(a) stands for is not the English term "the square of 2," but the object that term picks out, 4.

When predicates are followed by names, there is no punctuation around the list of names coming after the predicate. This cannot happen when function letters are followed by names. The punctuation both identifies a lower-case letter as a function letter and specifies its scope. Without punctuation, Gfab would be parsed as a three-place predicate. To represent either f or "a" as function letters requires punctuation. Gf(ab) distinguishes f as a two-place function letter and G as a one-place predicate. Gf(a)b distinguishes f as a one-place function letter, "a" as a name, and G as a two-place predicate. And Gf(a(b)) distinguishes both f and "a" as one-place function letters and G as a one-place predicate.

As this last example indicates, functional terms can have other functional terms nested inside them.

To accommodate this nesting, a functional term is recursively defined as an expression that is formed from an n-place function letter followed by n terms. Names are just one kind of term that can fill the places. Other terms can also do so. For example, b is a simple term that might be used with the function letter, f, to form the functional term, f(b). And e(abf(b)) is a functional term consisting of a three-place function letter, e, that has its first two places filled with simple terms, "a" and b, and its third place filled with another functional term, f(b).

Vocabulary of PL*f*

***n*-place function letters:**	a, b, c, d, e, f, $a_1, a_2, a_3, \ldots$ **followed by 0 or more places**
n-place predicates:	A, B, C, G, H, K, $A_1, A_2, A_3, \ldots$ followed by 0 or more places
Contradiction symbol:	$\perp$
Identity symbol:	$=$
Connectives:	$\sim, \&, \vee, \rightarrow, \equiv$
Punctuation marks:	), (

Syntax of PL*f*

An *expression* is any vocabulary element or sequence of vocabulary elements.

A *term* is any expression formed in accord with the following rules:

(ct*f*): **If *f* is an *n*-place function letter and $t_1 \ldots t_n$ are *n* (not necessarily distinct) terms, then $f(t_1 \ldots t_n)$ is a term. (As a special case of (ct*f*), if *f* is a 0-place function letter, then *f* is a term.)**

(exclusion): **Nothing is a term unless it has been formed by one or more applications of the preceding rule.**

A *sentence* is any expression formed in accord with the following rules:

(P): If P is an *n*-place predicate and $<t_1, \ldots t_n>$ is a list of *n* not necessarily distinct **terms**, then P$t_1 \ldots t_n$ is a sentence. As a special case of (P), if P is $\perp$ or a 0-place predicate then P is a sentence.

(=):	If **t** and **s** are two not necessarily distinct **terms** then =**ts** is a sentence.
(~):	If P is a sentence, then ~P is a sentence.
(bc):	If P and Q are two (not necessarily distinct) sentences, then (P & Q), (P ∨ Q), (P → Q), and (P ≡ Q) are sentences.
(exclusion):	Nothing is a sentence unless it has been formed by one or more applications of the preceding rules.

Named Forms

- An expression of the form, p, where p is a zero-place function letter, is a simple term. Simple terms are also called names.
- An expression of the form $f(t_1...t_n)$, where f is a higher-place function letter and $t_1...t_n$ are n (not necessarily distinct or simple) terms is a functional term.
- An expression of the form $f(t_1...t_n)$, where $t_1...t_n$ are each simple terms, is *a level-1 functional term*. Where each of $t_1...t_n$ are either simple terms or level-1 functional terms, $f(t_1...t_n)$ is a *level-2 functional term*, and so on.
- An expression of the form $f(t_1...t_n)$, where one or more of $t_1...t_n$ is a functional term, is a *higher-level functional term*.
- A sentence of the form $Pt_1...t_n$, where P is an n-place predicate and $t_1...t_n$ are one or more (not necessarily distinct) terms is a predicate sentence.
- A sentence of the form =ts, where t and s are two not necessarily distinct terms is an identity sentence.

All other aspects of the syntax for PSL are retained by PL*f*.

Exercise 10.7

1. *Which of the following are sentences of PLf? Explain why those that are not are not. Give a syntactic tree for those that are. Assume that each predicate and each function letter have been followed by the required number of terms.*
   ★a. G(aa)
   b. Gb(aa)
   ★c. Ga~(ca)
   d. ~Ga(a)c
   ★e. ~Gab(a)a
   f. ~Ga(b(cd))e
   ★g. =bf(a)
   h. f(a)=b
   ★i. =Gaf(b)
   j. =af(b)

2. *Formalize following in PLf using the interpretation provided.*

   D: {Alma; Boda; Crumb; the editor of anyone}; *all objects have exactly one best friend and exactly one editor (perhaps themselves).*
   a: Alma
   b: Boda
   c: Crumb
   d(x): the editor of x
   e(x): the best friend of x
   Gxy: x and y are friends
   Hxy: x works with y

   ★a. Alma works with Boda's editor.
   b. Crumb is Boda's editor.
   ★c. Boda's editor's editor is Crumb's editor.

    d. Alma's editor works with Boda's editor's editor.

*e. Alma's editor's editor and Boda's editor's editor are friends.

    f. Boda's editor works with Crumb's editor's best friend.

*g. Alma's best friend is friends with Crumb.

    h. Alma's best friend is the best friend of Crumb.

3. *Instantiate the following using the interpretation provided.*

> D: {natural numbers}
> a_1: one
> a_2: two
> a_3: three
> a_5: five
> $f(xy)$: the product of x and y
> $e(xyz)$: the sum of of x, y, and z
> Gxy: x is greater than y

*a. $Ge(a_5a_1a_5)e(a_2a_3a_5)$

    b. $\sim Gf(a_1a_2)f(a_2a_1)$

*c. $=e(a_1a_1a_3)a_5$

    d. $\sim=f(a_5a_3)a_2$

*e. $Gf(a_2e(a_3a_2a_1))e(f(a_2a_1)f(a_5a_1)f(a_1e(a_1a_1)))$

    f. $\sim=e(e(a_1a_3a_1)f(a_2a_1)f(a_2e(a_2a_2f(a_1a_3))))f(a_5a_3)$

4. *Formalize the following using the interpretation provided.*

> D: {P, Q, R}
> a: P
> b: Q
> c: R
> $d(xy)$: the disjunction of x and y
> $e(xy)$: the conjunction of x and y
> $f(x)$: the negation of x
> Gx: x is false
> Hx: x is true

*a. If P is true and Q is true, then the negation of the conjunction of P and Q is false.

    b: If the negation of P is false then the disjunction of P and Q is true.

*c. The negation of the disjunction of P and Q is false only if the conjunction of the negation of P and the negation of Q is false.

    d. The negation of the negation of the negation of P is true if and only if the negation of P is true but P is false.

*e. If the disjunction of P and Q is true, and both the disjunction of the negation of P and R and the disjunction of the negation of Q and R are true, then R is true.

    f. The conjunction of the disjunction of P and Q and R is true if but not only if the conjunction of P and R is true.

5. *The following sentence contains the term, "the son of Lady Jane." What would be wrong with formalizing this term as a functional term? (The answer has nothing to do with the contested existence of any son of Jane. It has to do with the size of the domain and the nature of the objects in it.)*

If Archibald Stewart was the heir of Douglas then he was the son of Lady Jane, but if he was not the son of Lady Jane then James Hamilton was the heir of Douglas.

10.3.3 Dpf

Dp*f* uses only the rules of Dp. However, (=I) and (=E) are expanded to include functional terms as well as names.

> (=I): L ⊢ =**tt** (where L could be the empty list **and t is any term of PL*f*)**
>
> (=E): If L ⊢ =**ts**, or L ⊢ =**st**, and L ⊢ P, then L ⊢ P(**s ¦ t**)

Derivations in Dp*f* are not instructively different from derivations in Dp or Ds, so only a few exercises are given here. One strategy is worth noting. In applying (=E), a term may be substituted for a term that figures only as a component of a more complex term. Given =af(b), "a" may not only be substituted for f(b) in Gf(b) (yielding Ga), it may be substituted for f(b) in Gf(f(b)) (yielding Gf(a)). The substitution is intuitively legitimate. If "a" denotes the same object as f(b) – if 4 is the square of 2, for example – then replacing references to the square of the square of 2 with references to the square of 4 does not make any difference as to what is being discussed.

Here is an illustration of this sort of inference, establishing that =af(a) ⊢ =f(f(a))f(f(f(a))) in Dp*f*.

1.	=af(a)	given
2.	~=f(f(a))f(f(f(a)))	(A/IP)
3.	=af(a)	1 (R)
4.	~=f(a)f(f(a))	3,2 (=E)
5.	~=af(a)	3,4 (=E)
6.	⊥	3,5 (⊥I)
7.	=f(f(a))f(f(f(a)))	2–6 (IP)

At line 4, the identity of "a" and "f(a)," asserted at line 3, is used to justify putting "a" for the two occurrences of "f(a)" in the sentence on line 2 (the first being the one in "f(f(a))," the second being the one in "f(f(f(a)))." In both cases, "f(a)" does not occur on its own, but only as a part of a more complex term. This procedure is repeated at line 5, appealing to line 1 to justify substituting "a" for each of the two occurrences of "f(a)" in line 4.

Exercise 10.8

Derive each of the following in Dp*f.*

★a. =ab, =bf(a) ⊢ Gf(a) → Gf(f(a))

  b. Gf(b) → ~Hcf(b) ⊢ (=af(b) & Hca) → ~Ga

★c. Ga → Gf(a) ⊢ Ga & =bf(a) → Gb

  d. ⊢ =ab → =f(a)f(b) *(Hint: use (=I) to derive =f(b)f(b).)*

★e. ⊢ (=f(a)b & =f(b)a) → =af(f(a))

  f. ⊢ ~=f(a)a → (=f(a)b → ~=ab)

★g. =f(e(a))b, =f(b)c, ~=f(f(e(a)))c ⊢ ⊥

  h. =ab, ~=f(a)f(b) ⊢ ⊥

10.3.4 Definite Descriptions

In ordinary language, most objects are not denoted by either simple or functional terms. They are instead denoted by descriptions that purport to pick out some feature or some collection of features that only that object possesses. Such descriptions are called definite descriptions. Superlatives are necessarily examples: the highest mountain in the world, the best student in the class, the tallest person in the room. Descriptions tagged with the qualifier "the only," such as "the only doctor in town," are another example. Other examples are provided by jobs or titles that only one person can hold, such as the Prime Minister, or the Pope. Any description that exactly one object satisfies is a definite description. In many cases, use of the word "the" by itself indicates that there is only one object that satisfies the description, at least within some limited domain intended by the speaker.

Up to now, definite descriptions have been treated as verbose names, but there is a cost to doing so because they describe as well as denote their object. The description contains information about the properties or relations the object satisfies. In some cases, this information can be consequential. Consider the following demonstration.

> The computer in the basement is broken.
> The computer you are talking about is not broken.
> _____
> The computer you are talking about is not in the basement.

This demonstration is intuitively valid. But the best that PSL can do to formalize it is with an interpretation such as the following:

> D: computers
> a: the computer in the basement
> b. the computer you are talking about
> Kx: x is broken
> Gx: x is in the basement

The resulting demonstration in PSL,

$$Ka, \sim Kb \ / \sim Gb$$

is invalid. Attempting to rectify the situation by stuttering that the computer in the basement is in the basement will not help.

$$Ka, Ga, \sim Kb \ / \sim Gb$$

This enhanced demonstration is still p-invalid. It does not assert that only one computer is in the basement and so does not rule out that the unbroken computer you are talking about is also in the basement.

The following attempt is equally unsuccessful.

$$Ka, \sim Kb \ / \sim=ba$$

This demonstration is p-consequential. But it establishes a different conclusion from the one stated in the English demonstration. The revised demonstration asserts that since one computer is broken and one is not, there are two computers. It does not draw the conclusion that the unbroken computer is not in the basement. To draw that conclusion, reference needs to be made to the word "the" in "the computer in the basement," which conveys the information that there is only one computer in the basement. Only once that information has been supplied can it be inferred that any computer that is not the broken computer could not be in the basement. The formalization given above fails to capture that information.

This is unfortunate. Most of the objects we reason about do not have names. Most of those that do have names are unknown or unfamiliar and are only made known by identifying their names with a description, which does the real work of identifying them. That work has logical consequences that are suppressed when descriptions are replaced with names. A predicate logic that cannot handle descriptions is seriously impoverished.

Without calling on the resources of quantificational logic, the information contained in definite descriptions can be unpacked by introducing a mechanism for turning an open sentence into a complex term. Begin with an open sentence, such as "x is a computer and x is in the basement." Add an expression like "the" or "the only" to create "the x such that x is a computer and x is in the basement," or more idiomatically, "the computer in the basement." This turns the open sentence into a complex name, based on a description that exactly one object is said (by using the word "the") to satisfy. "The computer in the basement" is not a sentence. It is a complex name. It denotes an object the way a name does. It can figure in predicate sentences like "x is broken" in the way a name does.

The formation of definite descriptions in English is mirrored in an extended version of PSL, called PL[1]. Take an open sentence like (Cx & Gx). Then use a symbol to convert it into a term. This is done by introducing what is called a term forming operator. Like "the" in English, a term forming operator of PL[1] turns an open sentence into a description of a unique object. This requires an amplification of the vocabulary. Lower-case x, y, and z are added, with numerical subscripts on x's if more are needed. These are the variables alluded to at the outset of this chapter. Variables are used to designate the blank spots in open sentences, the way they were informally used earlier. Now, they are needed to make terms, so they are officially written into the vocabulary for PL^1. The vocabulary is further supplemented with a definite description symbol. This is traditionally an inverted Greek letter iota, but a superscripted number 1 is easier to create on the keyboard. ^{1}, in combination with a variable, constitutes a term forming operator, ^{1}x, ^{1}y, ^{1}z, etc., read as "the one x such that ...," "the one y such that ...," "the one z such that ..." Tagging an open sentence like (Cx & Gx) with the appropriate term forming operator turns that open sentence into a definite description: ^{1}x(Cx & Gx), "the one x such that x is both C and G." Taking Cx to formalize "x is a computer" and Gx to formalize "x is in the basement," ^{1}x(Cx & Gx) formalizes "the computer in the basement."

Syntactically, term forming operators like ^{1}x constitute an inseparable unit. ^{1} cannot occur in PL^1 without being followed by a variable. It is tempting to express this union by enclosing the operator in parentheses to make (^{1}x), but this creates unnecessary clutter.

Despite its similarity to ~(Ca & Ga), which says that "'a' is not both a computer and in the basement" and ◇(Ca & Ga), which says that "'a' might be a computer in the basement," ^{1}x(Cx & Gx) is not a sentence. It has the same syntactic role as a name. It denotes (as well as describes) an object. Because it functions like a name, it could occur wherever a name could occur. =aa could be rewritten as =a^{1}x(Cx & Gx) or =^{1}x(Cx & Gx)a. Ka could be rewritten as K^{1}x(Cx & Gx).

Acquiring the expressive power that comes with introducing definite descriptions comes at a price. Derivation rules are needed to regiment how to derive information from descriptions and how to derive descriptions from information. A semantics for definite descriptions is also required. The derivation rules need to be stated using a larger vocabulary than PSL has at its disposal, so that task is postponed for chapter 13.5. The semantics is difficult to handle on any system. The mechanism for forming definite descriptions opens the door to turning any open sentence into a definite description, whether it is satisfied by exactly one object or not. "The computer in the basement" is an example. Perhaps there are other computers in the basement, or perhaps there are none. "The author of the *Treatise*" is a good definite description. It denotes exactly one object, David Hume. "The author of the *Port Royal Logic*" is not a good definite description. The *Port Royal Logic* was coauthored by Antoine Arnaud and Pierre Nicole. On one interpretation, the pairs of objects that satisfy the English open sentence "x was an author of y" might be assigned to the predicate Gxy and the *Treatise* might be assigned to the name "a." On another interpretation, the *Port Royal Logic* might instead by assigned to "a." ^{1}xGxa denotes a unique object on the first interpretation but multiple objects on the second. On one interpretation ^{1}xGx might formalize "the x such that x is Prime Minister of Canada," on another, "the x such that x is the Wizard of Oz." The same term denotes a unique object on the first interpretation, and no object on the second. Call any term that fails to denote exactly one object, but nonetheless purports to do so, an improper term. In contrast, call any term that does denote exactly one object a proper term. PSL can avoid improper terms by demanding that each name denote exactly one object in the domain. PLf does the same by requiring that any *n*-place function assign exactly one member of the domain to each *n*-place list of names. But PL^1 bases terms on open sentences and that makes it impossible to rule out improper terms. ~=aa and Ga & ~Ga must be recognized as sentences. That makes ~=xx and Gx & ~Gx open sentences. That makes ^{1}x~=xx (the non-self-identical object) and ^{1}x(Gx & ~Gx) (the self-contradictory object) terms.

This is not the place to comment on the challenges this result poses for PL^1 semantics. Syntactically, PL^1 has use for a way of specifying whether definite descriptions are proper or improper, and there are various straightforward ways of supplying one. Since names denote exactly one object, one approach is to designate those descriptions that are proper by identifying them with names, as when saying that the author of the *Treatise* is David Hume. A complementary approach takes a description that obviously cannot be satisfied by any object, such as "the object that is not identical to itself," ^{1}x~=xx, and uses it to assert that other descriptions are similarly improper. If both Arnaud and Nicole wrote the *Port Royal Logic*, for example, the delinquency of the description ^{1}xGxa, "the author of the *Port Royal Logic*," can be expressed by the sentence = ^{1}xG(xa) ^{1}x~=xx, which can be read as saying that "the author of *The Port Royal Logic* is the non-self-identical object." This does not mean that there is any such thing as a non-self-identical object. It means that the description "the author of the *Port Royal Logic*" is improper, like the description "the non-self-identical object." A third approach uses a special symbol, E, to say that a term denotes an object. E^{1}xP says that ^{1}xP is a proper description; ~E^{1}xP says that it is improper.

E might be read as "exists," and E^{1}xP as saying that "the P" exists. Some philosophers balk at doing this on the ground that it treats existence as a predicate. E is nonetheless included in the following statement of the vocabulary for PL^1. The intention is not to prejudge a controversial issue. It is rather to avoid foreclosing it. The issue is discussed in section 11.7.6.

10.3.5 Vocabulary and Syntax of PL¹; Formalization

In the statement that follows, Greek lower-case chi (χ) is used to stand for any variable ($x, y, z, x_1, \ldots$). The expression $P(\chi | q)$, read as "P chi for q," refers to the result of taking a sentence, P, that contains at least one occurrence of some name, q, and replacing each occurrence of that name with χ. For example, if P is Ga, $P(\chi | a)$ is $G\chi$. If P is Ga $\rightarrow$ Hba, $P(\chi | a)$ is $G\chi \rightarrow Hb\chi$. The converse expression, $t | \chi$, is used to designate the result of putting a term (a name, a complex term, or a variable) in the place of each occurrence of χ. So, if P is $G\chi$, $G(a | \chi)$ is Ga.

The vocabulary and syntax for PL¹ are written directly on top of the vocabulary and syntax for PSL, omitting (for the sake of focusing on the issue at hand) the extensions made in sections 10.3.1–2 to accommodate functional terms. Because descriptions are based on open sentences, and so presuppose formation of those sentences, the rules for forming terms are combined with those for forming sentences.

Vocabulary of PL¹

Names:	a, b, c, d, e, f, $a_1, a_2, a_3, \ldots$
Variables:	**x, y, z, $x_1, x_2, x_3, \ldots$**
n-place predicates:	A, B, C, G, H, K, $A_1, A_2, A_3, \ldots$ followed by 0 or more places
Contradiction symbol:	$\perp$
Identity symbol:	$=$
Existence symbol:	**E**
Connectives:	$\sim, \&, \vee, \rightarrow, \equiv$
Definite description symbol:	¹
Punctuation marks:	), (

Syntax of PL¹

An *expression* is any vocabulary element or sequence of vocabulary elements.

The *terms* and the *sentences* of PL¹ are any expressions formed in accord with the following rules:

(st): **If p is a name it is a term.**

(P): If P is an *n*-place predicate and $<t_1, \ldots t_n>$ is a list of *n* not necessarily distinct terms, then $P(t_1 \ldots t_n)$ is a sentence. As a special case of (P), if P is $\perp$ or a 0-place predicate then P is a sentence.

(=): If t and s are two not necessarily distinct terms then $=ts$ is a sentence.

(E): **If t is a term then Et is a sentence.**

(~): If P is a sentence, then $\sim$P is a sentence.

(bc): If P and Q are two (not necessarily distinct) sentences, then (P & Q), (P $\vee$ Q), (P $\rightarrow$ Q), and (P $\equiv$ Q) are sentences.

(ct¹): **If P is a sentence containing at least one occurrence of a name, q, and no χ variable then ¹χP(χ|q) is a term.**

(exclusion): Nothing is a sentence **or a term** unless it has been formed by one or more applications of the preceding rules.

Scope

When a $\sim$ is followed by $\perp$ or P, **where P is a 0-place predicate, its scope is that $\perp$ or P.**
When a $\sim$ or ¹χ is followed by an *n*-place predicate $P(t_1, \ldots, t_n)$ **its scope extends to the punctuation mark that closes the *n*-place list following P.**
When a $\sim$ or ¹χ is followed by $=$ **its scope is that** $=$ **plus the two terms following that** $=$.

When a ~ **or** $^1\chi$ is followed by an opening punctuation mark, its scope extends to the corresponding closing punctuation mark.

When a ~ **or** $^1\chi$ is followed by ~ **or** $^1\chi$, its scope is that other ~ **or** $^1\chi$ plus that other ~ **or** $^1\chi$'s scope.

Named Forms

- **Names are simple terms.**
- **Expressions of the form $^1\chi$, where χ is a variable, are term forming operators.**
- **Terms of the form $^1\chi P$ are definite descriptions.**
- **The component, P, of a definite description, $^1\chi P$, is an** *open sentence.*
- **Definite descriptions are** *complex terms.*
- **An expression of the form $^1\chi P$, where $^1\chi$ does not have scope over any term forming operators, is a** *level-1 definite description,* **and $^1\chi$ is in this case a level-1 term forming operator.**
- **An expression of the form $^1\chi P$, where $^1\chi$ has scope over at least one level-1 term forming operator, and no higher-level term forming operators, is a** *level-2 definite description* **and $^1\chi$ is in this case a level-2 term forming operator, and so on.**
- **The term forming operators and the connectives are the** *operators* **of PL^1.**
- **A sentence of the form E(t), where t is a term, is an** *existence sentence.* **Existence sentences are atomic and do not have main connectives or immediate components.**

All other aspects of the account of the syntax for PSL given in section 10.2.1 are retained, with the following substitutions:

- "term" for "name"
- "operator" for "connective" (where called for)
- "expression, term, or sentence" for "expression or sentence"

(P) requires that punctuation be placed around the lists of terms that follow predicates, even when there is only one term on the list. This is necessary to avoid ambiguity in cases where a predicate sentence is turned into a definite description and that description is inserted into another predicate sentence. For example, H^{1}xGxb, can be read in two different ways, one on which H is a one-place predicate and G a two-place predicate, the other on which H is two-place and G one-place. Requiring the term lists after predicates to be enclosed in parentheses creates either H(^{1}xG(xb)) or H(^{1}xG(x)b), removing the ambiguity.

(ip) is extended to permit omitting punctuation around term lists when doing so does not create ambiguity. The situations where ambiguity can arise are easy to identify. Whenever a term list is followed by a term that does not belong on that list, the punctuation must be retained. This only applies to predicate sentences, since only (P) adds punctuation. (=) and (E) do not. Identity symbols must be followed by exactly two terms, existence symbols by exactly one, and ambiguity is prevented by those considerations.

(ct^1) makes it possible to create expressions that look like sentences but that are terms and that can occur wherever a term would occur. This can make sentences containing such expressions hard to parse, though the difficulty disappears with practice.

(ct^1) makes it possible to base definite descriptions on other definite descriptions. Given a sentence containing occurrences of at least one name and at least one definite description, like Ga & Ha^{1}yBy, (ct^1) can be applied to convert the sentence into a term, like ^{1}x(Gx & Hx^{1}yBy). This can also be done in English. For example, "The computer in the basement is broken," which was earlier formalized as K^{1}x(Gx & Hx), contains two definite descriptions, "the computer" and "the basement." Formalizing sentences containing nested definite descriptions can be challenging. The best way to approach the task is to first write a quasi-English paraphrase, replacing occurrences of definite descriptions with "the x such that …" Taking this approach, "the computer in the basement is broken" becomes

The x such that x is a computer and x is in the y such that y is a basement is broken.

Formalize "the x such that x is a computer" as before: ^{1}xCx.

Rather than read the reference to the basement into the predicate, formalize "the x such that x is a computer and x is in …" by taking Gxy to be a two-place predicate, x is in y: ^{1}x(Cx & G(x…)).

Formalize "the basement" as ^{1}yBy, producing: ^{1}x(Cx & G(x^{1}yBy)).

"The computer in the basement is broken" comes out as $K^1x(Cx \& Gx^1yBy)$, where Kx is used as before to formalize the open sentence, "x is broken."

Syntactic trees can be used to illustrate how higher-level definite descriptions are built from lower-level definite descriptions and names, just as they can be used to illustrate how compound sentences are built from their components. The trees follow the formation rules, which begin by talking about forming simple terms, move on to forming sentences, and then permit ongoing cycles where sentences are used to form complex terms, which may then be inserted in yet further sentences. The syntactic tree for $K^1x(Gx \& Hx^1yBy)$, for example, begins by building simple terms, using those terms to build sentences, and then using those sentences to build other terms. The tree starts as follows

1.	a	a	c	(st)
2.			B(c)	1 (P)
3.			$^1yB(y)$	2 (ct^1)

As of line 3, the level-1 definite description, "the basement" has been created. A syntactic tree for the level-2 definite description, "the computer in the basement" continues as follows:

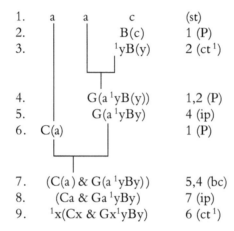

1.	a	a	c	(st)
2.			B(c)	1 (P)
3.			$^1yB(y)$	2 (ct^1)
4.			$G(a\,^1yB(y))$	1,2 (P)
5.			$G(a\,^1yBy)$	4 (ip)
6.		C(a)		1 (P)
7.		$(C(a) \& G(a\,^1yBy))$		5,4 (bc)
8.		$(Ca \& Ga\,^1yBy)$		7 (ip)
9.		$^1x(Cx \& Gx^1yBy)$		6 (ct^1)

As of line 4, it can be judged that the punctuation around the second occurrence of y can be dropped to make $G(a^1yBy)$. With or without the punctuation, it is clear that G is a two-place predicate. It would have been a different matter if the definite description had occurred in the first place. $G(^1yB(y)a)$ could not be converted to $G(^1yByb)$ without making it ambiguous whether B is a one- or a two-place predicate.

Similarly, as of line 7, it can be judged that there is no need for the punctuation around the first occurrence of "a" or around the two terms following G.

The tree finishes by inserting the one term generated at line 9 into the one place in the predicate, K.

10.	$K^1x(Cx \& Gx1yBy)$	9 (P)

The remaining punctuation may not be omitted. It was introduced by (bc), and punctuation introduced by (bc) may only be removed because it is outer, because it occurs around conjunctions that are conjuncts or disjunctions that are disjuncts, or because it falls under (sc), and none of those reasons apply in this case.

Exercise 10.9

1. *State whether each of the following is a term of* PL^1. *If it is not, explain why not; if it is, provide the syntactic tree that demonstrates why it is.*

   ★a. $\sim^1xGx$
   b. $^1x\sim Gx$
   ★c. $^1yGy^1zHz$
   d. $^1y(G \& Hy)$
   ★e. $^1y^1zH(yz)$
   f. $^1yH(y^1zHyz)$

2. *State whether each of the following is a sentence of* PL[1]. *If it is not, explain why not; if it is, provide the syntactic tree that demonstrates why it is.*

   ★**a.** ~= ¹x~=xx
     b. = ¹x=xx a
   ★**c.** = ¹x~=xa a
     d. ~= ¹x~=xx ¹x~=aa
   ★**e.** = a ¹x=ax
     f. = ¹x=ax a

3. *Formalize each of the following in* PL[1]. *Provide an interpretation of any name letters and predicates and specify the domain. Formalize improper as well as proper descriptions.*

   ★**a.** Felix is a cat.
     b. Felix is the cat.
   ★**c.** Felix is black.
     d. Felix is a black cat.
   ★**e.** The cat is black.
     f. Felix is the black cat.
   ★**g.** Felix is on a mat.
     h. Felix is on the mat.
   ★**i.** The cat is on the mat.
     j. Felix is the cat on the mat.
   ★**k.** The cat on the mat is black.
     l. The flower in the pot is blue.
   ★**m.** The pot is on the table.
     n. The pot on the table is cracked.
   ★**o.** The flower is in the pot on the table.
     p. The flower in the pot on the table is blue.
   ★**q.** The flower on the table with the pot on it is blue.
     r. Alma is not a good mechanic, but he knows one, and he also knows the Mayor.
   ★**s.** If Brutus was the assassin of Caesar and Cassius was the assassin of Caesar then Brutus was Cassius.
     t. If Arnaud authored the *Port Royal Logic*, and Nicole authored the *Port Royal Logic* and Arnaud was not Nicole, then Arnaud was not the author of the *Port Royal Logic*.
   ★**u.** If the author of the *Port Royal Logic* authored the *Port Royal Logic*, and Arnaud authored the *Port Royal Logic*, then Arnaud was the author of the *Port Royal Logic*.
     v. Russell mentioned the author of *Waverley* and the present King of France.
   ★**w.** If the author of the *Treatise* existed, then the author of either the *Treatise* or *The Adventures of Gil Blas* existed. *(Incidentally, this sentence is invalid. Why?)*

11 Semantics and Trees

Contents

In PSL, values are only directly assigned to zero-place predicate sentences. The value of a higher-place predicate sentence is determined by whether the objects it names satisfy the predicate it refers to. The value of an identity sentence is determined by whether the names it uses denote the same object. A semantics for PSL needs to explain what it means for predicates to be satisfied by objects, to account for the denotation of names, and specify how these

DOI: 10.4324/9781003026532-18

factors determine the value of predicate and identity sentences. This is done with an expansion to the concept of an interpretation.

11.1 Interpretations

In SL, interpretations did no more than assign values from a co-domain V: {T,F} to a domain of sentence letters and follow valuation rules in the assignment of these values to compound sentences. But in PSL interpretations have more work to do and the different tasks need to be distinguished. One is to define an object domain (corresponding to a domain of discourse in chapter 10). Another is to assign values, which are now not just truth values but objects from the object domain. Domain objects are assigned to names and sets of lists of domain objects are assigned to predicate letters. Interpretations for sentences of PSL accordingly consist of two things: a domain, D, which must contain at least one object, and a valuation, α, of the names and predicates. Interpretations also continue to work with a co-domain of values and a subset of this co-domain specifying designated values, but they are not specified below because they are not open to interpretation in what follows. V will only be considered to be {T,F} (except in sections on intuitionistic logic where it is {1,0}) and V_d to be {T} ({1} in sections on intuitionistic logic). Of course, nothing says it has to be this way. Systems of logic that work with other values are just not discussed here.

An *interpretation*, I, of **PSL** consists of **two components, D and α.**

(i) **D is a nonempty and possibly (but not necessarily) infinite set of objects, $\{o_1, o_2, o_3, ...\}$ called the domain of I.**

(ii) α assigns:

- exactly one of T and F to each **zero-place predicate**. Notation: $\alpha(P)$ is T or $\alpha(P)$ is F, where P is a **zero-place predicate**
- exactly one object, o, from D to each name, p. Notation: $\alpha(p)$ is o
- **where n is greater than 0, a (possibly empty) set of lists of n (not necessarily distinct) objects from D to each n-place predicate, P. Notation: $\alpha(<o_1, ..., o_n>)$ is/is not in $\alpha(P)$.**

In the interest of reducing clutter, angle brackets around one-place lists are omitted. So {<1,>, <2>, <3>} appear as {1, 2, 3}. The angle brackets are necessary for lists with more than one member, even if there is only one list in the set of lists. Even {<1,2>} cannot be abbreviated on pain of confusing the singlets satisfying a one-place predicate with the ordered pair satisfying a two-place predicate.

Each interpretation works with just one domain and one valuation. Changing the contents of D, or the value of a single sentence letter, name, or predicate is tantamount to changing the interpretation.

In SL there are only finitely many interpretations for a finite number of sentence letters. PSL takes any one valuation of the sentence letters and adds infinitely many variants on that valuation depending on how many objects there are in the domain, how objects are assigned to names, and how lists of objects are assigned to predicates. Even when there are only a few names and predicates, there can be so many interpretations that it is impractical to tabulate them.

11.1.1 Domains

The objects in the domain can be anything that can be individuated. As interests vary, so domains vary. There is no obligation to put everything that exists in the domain. Neither is there an obligation to include only properly unified substances or "objects" in some robust sense. Numbers, colours, ideas, and even fictional characters are as eligible for membership as actually existent physical objects. Moreover, the things in a domain do not all have to be of the same sort. A domain consisting of the colour red, a hamburger, the number 17, and a dog hair is as good a domain as any other. The objects can also be as few as one, and as many as transfinitely many. However, every domain must contain at least one object on pain of reverting to sentential logic.

Many domains are denumerable. Their members can be put in one-to-one correspondence with members of the set of natural numbers. The contents of these domains can be named or described, or they can simply be designated by corresponding numbers. For some applications (e.g., formalizing English sentences) the domain needs to consist of named or described individuals. But for many others it proves to be unimportant what objects are in the domain.

Work can be done simply by designating them by numbers. The first approach is the "intensional" mode of specifying a domain, the second the "extensional."

Seeing a domain that consists of numbers is not an indication that the domain is a domain of mathematical objects, much less a domain that is to be used for mathematical purposes. The numbers may only be there to designate objects that do not need to be further named or described.

11.1.2 Names

PSL does not tolerate ambiguity or vacuity. Two or more objects may not be assigned to the same name. One object must also be assigned to each name, and that object must come from the domain.

There is a countable infinity of names of PSL. However, a domain might contain only finitely many objects (as few as one) or uncountably many. So there could be many more names than there are objects to be named, or too few names for all the objects.

This is not a problem because, while a name must denote exactly one object, an object may have more than one name or may go unnamed. If there are more names than there are objects, the first object in the domain is by default assigned to the leftovers.

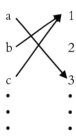

Imagine the infinitely many names of PSL lined up in a column. Opposite them are the arbitrarily many (at least one, perhaps infinitely or transfinitely many) objects. From every name there must be exactly one line that is drawn from that name to connect it with exactly one object. No name can be the point of origin for two lines. And no name can be without exactly one line leading from it to exactly one object. However, lines from multiple different names can terminate in the same object, which means that object has multiple names. And some objects can end up without any lines drawn to them, which means that member of the domain is anonymous.

11.1.3 Predicates and Satisfaction

There are two ways of understanding what a higher-place predicate is. According to the first, a higher-place predicate is something described by an open sentence, that is, a sentence from which one or more names have been removed. According to the second, it is a set of lists of objects. (One-place predicates are sets of one-place lists of objects, that is, just sets of objects. Two-place predicates are sets of lists of two objects.) The first is the intensional interpretation of a higher-place predicate, the second the extensional.

The first approach is the one naturally taken when formalizing English sentences. It is called the intensional interpretation because open sentences have a meaning or intension that lays out the conditions under which a higher-place predicate is said to be satisfied. The predicate described by the open sentence "x is large" is satisfied by all and only large objects. The predicate described by the open sentence "x loves y" is satisfied by all and only those pairs of objects such that the first object in the pair loves the second object in the pair.

The second approach is the inverse of the first. It is called the extensional approach because it considers an *n*-place predicate to be defined by a set of *n*-place lists of objects. A one-place predicate is a set of objects. Each different way of selecting zero or more domain objects to form a set is a different one-place predicate. A two-place predicate is a set of ordered pairs of objects. Each different way of selecting zero or more lists of two (not necessarily distinct) domain objects to form a set is a different two-place predicate. A domain object satisfies a one-place predicate if and only if it is in the set of objects assigned to that predicate. An ordered pair of domain objects satisfies a two-place predicate if and only if it is in the set of ordered pairs that has been assigned to that predicate.

Exercise 11.1

Which way of understanding what it means to satisfy a predicate, the intensional or the extensional, is endorsed by the third bullet point under the definition of a valuation boxed at the start of this section? How should that third bullet point have been written had the alternative been endorsed in its place? Are there any advantages or disadvantages to preferring one or the other of these accounts of satisfaction?

On any account of satisfaction, predicates can be unsatisfied. Intensionally, there are open sentences that no object satisfies, like "x is a pig with wings" or "x is a round square." Extensionally, for any number, n, one set of n-place lists of objects is the set that consists of no n-place lists.

On any account of satisfaction, zero-place predicates can also be satisfied. In this case the world is turned on its head. Truth determines satisfaction rather than the other way around. Zero-place predicates are satisfied when they are assigned T and not satisfied when they are assigned F.

11.1.4 Identity

The identity symbol is not a predicate symbol and does not have an extension assigned to it. Like $\perp$, its meaning is given by the valuation rules and is the same across interpretations.

Exercise 11.2

State whether the following are acceptable extensional interpretations of the set of sentences, {Ga → Ha, =ac, Kac}. Take for granted that the interpretations all make some acceptable assignment to all the other names of PSL. That assignment is not specified because it is irrelevant to the set of sentences under consideration.

★a. D: {1,2}
    a: 1
    c: 1
    G: {1,2}
    H: {1,2}
    K: {1,2}

b. D: {1,2}
    a: 1
    c: 1
    G: {1,2}
    H: {1,2}
    K: {<1,1>, <1,2>, <2,1>, <2,2>}

★c. D: {1,2}
    a: 1
    c: 1
    G: {1,2}
    H: {1,2}
    K: { }

d. D: {1,2}
    a: 1
    c: 2
    G: {1,2}
    H: {1,2}
    K: {<1,2>}

★e. D: {1,2,3,...}
    a: 3
    c: 2
    G: {2,4,6,...}
    H: {2,3,4,...}
    K: {<2,1>, <3,2>, <4,3>,...}

f. D: {1,2,3,...}
    a: 3
    c: 2
    G: { }
    H: { }
    K: { }

★g. D: { }
    a:
    c:
    G: { }
    H: { }
    K: { }

h. D: {1,2,3}
    a: 2
    b: 1
    c: 3
    G: {2}
    H: {2,3}
    K: {<1,1>,<2,2>}

★i. D: {1,2,3}
    a: 2
    b: 1
    G: {2}
    H: {2,3}
    K: {<2,1>,<3,2>}

j. D: {1,2,3}
    a: {1,2}
    c: 3
    G: {2}
    H: {2,3}
    K: {<2,1>,<3,2>}

★k. D: {1,2,3}
    a: 2
    c: 3
    G: {2, <1,2>}
    H: {2,3}
    K: {<2,1>,<3,2>}

l. D: {1}
    a: 1
    c: 2
    G: { }
    H: {1}
    K: { }

★**m.**   D: {1}
    a:1
    c:
    G: { }
    H: {1}
    K: { }

11.2 Valuation Rules

In PSL the values of predicate sentences are determined by whether objects satisfy or fail to satisfy predicates. An interpretation, I, assigns a T to a one-place predicate sentence, Pq, if and only if Iα assigns the name, q, to an object, o, that is in the extension of P, that is, if and only if Iα(q) is o and o is in Iα(P). Iα(q) means "object assigned to name q on interpretation I," and Iα(P) means "the extension assigned to predicate P on interpretation I."

Similarly, an interpretation, I, assigns a T to an *n*-place predicate sentence, $Pq_1...q_n$, if and only if Iα assigns the list of names $<q_1,...,q_n>$ to a list of objects $<o_1,...,o_n>$ that is in the extension of P, that is, if and only if $<o_1,...,o_n>$ is in Iα(P) and $<I\alpha(q_1),...,I\alpha(q_n)>$ is $<o_1,...,o_n>$.

The values of identity sentences are determined by whether names denote the same object. An interpretation, I, assigns a T to an identity sentence, =pq, if and only if Iα assigns the names occurring in that sentence, p and q, to the same object, that is if and only if Iα(p) is Iα(q).

The values of $\bot$ and the compound sentences are determined in accord with the familiar valuation rules of SL.

For example, Gcb is a predicate sentence made up of a two-place predicate, G, followed by two names, b and c, placed in a certain order (with c to the left of b). Any interpretation must assign some extension to G, be that extension the empty set or some set of ordered pairs of domain objects. Any interpretation must likewise assign exactly one member of its domain to b and exactly one (not necessarily distinct) member to c. All interpretations will be of one or the other of two sorts: those that assign the first member of an ordered pair of objects that is in the extension they assign to G to c and the second to b, and those that do not. In the former case, the interpretation assigns a T to Gcb; in the latter, an F.

To take another example, =bc is an identity sentence made up of the identity symbol followed by two names, b and c. Any interpretation must assign exactly one domain object to each of these names (the object assigned to one need not necessarily be distinct from the object assigned to the other). All interpretations will be of one or the other of two sorts: those that assign the same object to b and c, and those that do not. In the former case the interpretation assigns a T to =bc; in the latter, an F.

When only one interpretation is under consideration Iα is abbreviated as either I or α depending on the assignment in question. The basic assignments of objects to names, lists of objects to higher-place predicates, and truth values to zero-place predicates are made by α. All assignments made in accord with valuation rules, including the two following new valuation rules, are made by I.

> **(P):** $I(Pq_1...q_n)$ is T if and only if $<\alpha(q_1), ...,\alpha(q_n)>$ is in $\alpha(P)$; otherwise, $I(Pq_1...q_n)$ is F.
>
> **(=):** $I(=pq)$ is T if and only if $\alpha(p)$ is $\alpha(q)$; otherwise $I(=pq)$ is F.

Exercise 11.3

1. *State what conclusions follow from each of the following assertions in accord with a single application of* (P) *or* (=). *The first three questions are answered as an example.*
    a. $\alpha(c)$ is in $\alpha(G)$.
         Answer: I(Gc) is T
    b.   I(Ha) is F
         Answer: $\alpha(a)$ is not in $\alpha(H)$
    c. $\alpha(a)$ is not $\alpha(c)$
         Answer: I(=ac) is F; I(=ca) is F
    d. $<\alpha(a),\alpha(a)>$ is in $\alpha(H)$
    e. $<\alpha(b),\alpha(a)>$ is in $\alpha(K)$

f. $<\alpha(a),\alpha(b)>$ is not in $\alpha(K)$

g. $<\alpha(c),\alpha(b),\alpha(a)>$ is not in $\alpha(G)$

h. $<\alpha(a),\alpha(b),\alpha(a)>$ is in $\alpha(K)$

i. I(Gbb) is T

j. I(Hca) is T

k. I(Hac) is F

l. I(Hcac) is T

m. I(=ca) is T

n. I(=ac) is F

o. $\alpha(a)$ is $\alpha(c)$

p. $\alpha(a)$ is not $\alpha(c)$

q. $\alpha(a)$ satisfies H

r. $<\alpha(a),\alpha(b)>$ does not satisfy K

2. *Identify the features that α must have for I to assign a T to the following sentences. The first three questions are answered as an example.*

   a. ~Ha

   Answer: $\alpha(a)$ is not in $\alpha(H)$

   b. ~Hca & G

   Answer: $<\alpha(c),\alpha(a)>$ is not in $\alpha(H)$ and $\alpha(G)$ is T

   c. Ka ∨ ~Gab

   Answer: either $\alpha(a)$ is in $\alpha(K)$ or $<\alpha(a),\alpha(b)>$ is not in $\alpha(G)$

   d. Ka → Gab

   e. ~(Ka ∨ Gab)

   f. Ka ≡ Gab

   g. ~=ac ≡ G

   h. ~=aa ∨ Ha

3. *Demonstrate the value of the following sentences on the following interpretation:*

D: {1,2,3}

G: { }; H: {1,3}; K: {<1,1>, <2,2>, <1,3>}; C: F

a: 1; b: 1; d: 3

★a. Gb

  b. Hb

★c. Kda

  d. =ad

★e. =ad ∨ =da

  f. C → ~(~Ga ∨ Kda)

★g. ~=aa & ~(~Ga ∨ Kda)

  h. ~=ab → ~=ab

★i. ~Hd ≡ ~(~Ga ∨ Kda)

  j. (~Gb ≡ ~=ab) → Kad ∨ Kda

★k. Ga ∨ Gb ∨ Gd

  l. Ga ∨ ~Ga → ~=aa

★m. (Kad ≡ Kbd) & ~(Kad ≡ Kbb)

  n. ~(=ad ∨ ~Hd) & (Kdd → ~Gd)

11.3 Working with the Semantics

In PSL as in SL, invalidity, satisfaction, contingency, and nonequivalence are established by discovering and verifying an interpretation. Since p-interpretations cannot be exhaustively tabulated, long tables cannot be used to discover interpretations. A variant on the short table method of chapter 5 can still be devised, but it is suboptimal for cases where there are multiple true identity sentences. (Those cases require rewriting all literals that contain one of the identified names.) In such cases, interpretations are more reliably discovered using trees. Further discussion of how to demonstrate p-invalidity, p-inconsistency, p-contingency, and p-equivalence is accordingly postponed for the following section.

As in SL, p-validity, p-unsatisfiability, and p-equivalence are demonstrated by supposing to the contrary that there is a counterinterpretation and then demonstrating by appeal to the valuation rules that this supposition leads to a contradiction and so must be rejected. In PSL the assignment of both T and F to predicate and identity sentences does not count as a contradiction. The value of predicate and identity sentences is derived from assignments to the names and predicates, and it is a nontrivial question whether those assignments rule out the possibility of assigning both T and F to the same predicate or identity sentence. Where those sentences are concerned, contradictions must take the form of violations of the constraints on an acceptable assignment to the names and predicates.

Contradictions

- $\alpha(p)$ is not $\alpha(p)$
- $\alpha(p)$ both is and is not $\alpha(q)$
- $\langle\alpha(p_1),\ldots,\alpha(p_n)\rangle$ is both in and not in $\alpha(Q)$
- $I(\bot)$ is T
- $\alpha(P)$ is T and $\alpha(P)$ is F in the case where P is a zero-place predicate sentence

---

The set, $\{Ga, \sim Ga\}$ is p-unsatisfiable. But the following demonstration is unacceptable:

1. Suppose to the contrary that there is an interpretation, I, such that I(Ga) and I($\sim$Ga) are T.
   2. By ($\sim$), I(Ga) is F.
   3. No I can assign both T and F to the same atomic sentence.

Line 3 is wrong because it is no longer part of the definition of an interpretation that it must assign exactly one of T and F to each atomic sentence. This is only the case for zero-place predicate sentences. The contradiction, if there is one, must be found in the assignments that α makes to G and "a." The demonstration ought to proceed as follows.

1. Suppose, contrary to what it is proposed to prove that there is an interpretation, I, such that I(Ga) and I($\sim$Ga) are T.
   2. From the first conjunct of line 1 by (P), $\alpha(a)$ is in $\alpha(G)$.
   3. From line 1 by ($\sim$), I(Ga) is F.
   4. By (P), $\alpha(a)$ is not in $\alpha(G)$.
5. Since the supposition at line 1 has led to a contradiction at lines 2 and 4, that supposition must be rejected: there is no interpretation on which all the sentences in $\{Ga, \sim Ga\}$ are true.

Exercise

What does it mean to say that $\alpha(a)$ is or is not in $\alpha(G)$?

By definition, the extension of a one-place predicate, like G, is a set of objects, not a set of names. The notation, $\alpha(a)$ is an abbreviation for the phrase, "the object denoted by 'a' on α." The notation, $\alpha(G)$ is an abbreviation for "the extension assigned to G by α." Accordingly, line 2 says that the object, o, denoted by "a" is among the objects in the set, $\alpha(G)$. It does not say that the name "a" is in this set. Line 4, in contrast, says that o is not in that set. It is a clear contradiction to claim that an object is both in and not in a set. So lines 2 and 4 suffice to demonstrate that the supposition at line 1 must be rejected.

A similar move needs to be made to demonstrate that $\{=ab, \sim=ab\}$ is p-unsatisfiable. It is not enough to argue that if I($\sim$=ab) is T, I(=ab) must be F, which contradicts the claim that I(=ab) is T. The values of identity sentences are not directly assigned but determined by how objects are assigned to names, so the contradiction must be found in how objects are assigned to names. The point that needs to be made is that if I(=ab) is F then it follows by (=) that $\alpha(a)$ is not $\alpha(b)$, that is, that the object denoted by "a" on α is not the object denoted by b on α. But if I(=ab) is T then it follows by (=) that $\alpha(a)$ is $\alpha(b)$, that is, that the object denoted by "a" on α is the object denoted by b on α. That is a contradiction because the value of "a" on α cannot both be and not be $\alpha(b)$ (that is, it cannot both be and not be the object denoted by b on α).

It can sometimes be helpful to have a way of referring to unknown domain objects. If I(=ab) is T it follows that α(a) is α(b), but it does not follow which domain object that is. To facilitate direct reference to the object, lowercase o, n, m may be used as object variables. They are not part of the vocabulary of PSL. They are instead part of an informal English vocabulary used to talk about unspecified domain objects. (x, y, and z could have been used for this purpose, but they will be given another use later.)

Exercise 11.4

(For those who have studied Chapter A-1.) Using the demonstration by mathematical induction given in section A-1.2 as a model, demonstrate that all the sentences of PSL have exactly one of the two truth values. Since PSL does not use any more connectives than SL, the demonstration of the inductive step is unchanged. However, a new demonstration is required for the basis clause, covering the new kinds of atomic sentences of PSL (higher-place predicate sentences and identity sentences). In proving the case for higher-place predicate sentences, observe that an n-place list must either satisfy a predicate or not satisfy that predicate. It cannot do both and it cannot do neither. In proving the case for identity sentences draw on the stipulation that an interpretation cannot assign two different objects to the same name.

While it is provable that all the sentences of PSL have exactly one of the two truth values, forcing the contradiction down to the assignments to names and predicate letters is necessary to prepare for work using the semantic systems presented in subsequent chapters.

Exercise 11.5

1. *Demonstrate that each of the following is p-valid.*
  ★**a.** =aa
   b. =ab → (Ga ≡ Gb)
  ★**c.** Ha → Ha
   d. =ab, =ac / =cb
  ★**e.** ~Hbc ∨ Gc, ~Gb & =bc / ~Hbb
   f. Ka & ~Kb, =ab / Gc

2. *Demonstrate that each of the following is p-unsatisfiable.*
  ★**a.** ~=aa
   b. {Ka ≡ Kb, Ka & ~Kb}
  ★**c.** {(Ka ≡ ~Kb), =ab}
   d. {Gca, ~Gac, =ac}
  ★**e.** {Ha → Ka, =ba, ~Kb, Hb}
   f. {Hbc, Hcb → Gc, ~(=bc → Gb)}

3. *Demonstrate that each of the following is true.*
  ★**a.** ~=aa =|= ⊥
   b. =ab =|= =ba
  ★**c.** =ba & Kb & ~Ka =|= ~=cc
   d. =ac → Hc =|= ~Hc → ~=ca
  ★**e.** ~(=bc & Gcab) =|= ~Gbac ∨ ~=bc
   f. ~(=ab & =bc) =|= ~=ca ∨ ~=cb

★**4.** *Demonstrate that, for any name, p, ~=pp is p-unsatisfiable.*

11.4 Tp

p-trees are no longer just reduction trees. In addition to reducing nonliterals to literals, they identify the denotation of names. Tp uses a revised version of (=E) to assist in this task. It also includes all the rules of Ts. It expands the circumstances under which (⊥I) can be applied to close a path. There is a change to the definition of an exhausted path, and there are large embellishments to the method for extracting a tree model from an exhausted path.

In PSL, not all contradictions have the form P & ~P. Sentences of the form ~=pp are also contradictory and so should yield ⊥, closing any path on which they appear. In Dp, (=I) ensures that any sentence of the form ~=pp will yield ⊥, but it is more elegant to extend (⊥I) for use in Tp.

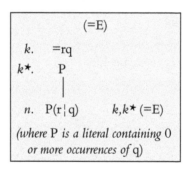

p-trees also use a revised definition of an exhausted path. The revision is required by the fact that identities can create unexpressed contradictions. For example, suppose a path contains the sentences Ga and ~Gb.

$$Ga$$
$$\sim Gb$$

So far there is no contradiction. However, if =ab is added to the path, it ought to close, because =ab says that "a" and b denote the same object, and it cannot be the case that the same object both is and is not in α(G).

$$Ga$$
$$\sim Gb$$
$$=ab$$

Yet there is no literal and its negation and no negated self-identity sentence on the path. It does not close, even though the set, {Ga, ~Gb, =ab} is p-unsatisfiable. To rectify this (=E) is applied.

$$(=E)$$

k.	=rq	
k★.	P	
	|	
n.	P(r ¦ q)	*k*,*k*★ (=E)

(where P is a literal containing 0 or more occurrences of q)

Neither the (source) identity sentence at line *k* nor the (target) literal at line *k*★ get checked off. Lines *k* and *k*★ along with the sentences on them may occur in the reverse order, though line *k* is always cited first in justification. Both must occur on the same path. The sentence on line *n* must be entered on each open path that runs up to whichever is the lowest of the sentences on lines *k* and *k*★.

As with Dp, justifications for (=E) take the form "[source],[target] (=E)," where [source] is the line number for the identity sentence that is directing what name to substitute, and [target] is the line number for the literal that contains one or more occurrences of the name being replaced.

There are two differences between the Tp version of (=E) and the Dp version. First, on trees, (=E) is only applied to literals. Second, (=E) is only applied from left to right, as if it were read in the direction it is written, "put r for q." On trees, (=E) is never used to substitute the name in second place after the identity sign for the name in first place. This eliminates unnecessary work.

(=E) is applied in conjunction with an extended definition of an exhausted path, which adds the requirement that a path is not exhausted unless (=E) has been performed in all possible ways.

> **(def ex)**
>
> A path of a p-tree is *exhausted* if and only if:
>   (i) each sentence in the set the tree is made for has been placed on top of the tree
>   (ii) ⊥ does not stand alone on any line of the path
>   (iii) each sentence on the path is either a literal or a nonliteral that has been reduced (checked off)
>   **(iv) for each sentence of the form =rq and each literal, P, each sentence of the form P(r|q) (including sentences of the form =rr), occurs on the path.**

Clause (iv) is needed because (=E) is introduced into Tp to uncover contradictions. It can only be assured that there are no contradictions if (=E) is used exhaustively. This means applying (=E) repeatedly to put r for all occurrences of q in each literal on the path, including any literals that are subsequently added to the path.

Restricting (=E) to left to right substitutions and allowing (def ex) to ignore partial substitutions (where r is put for any one or more occurrences of q) may seem contrary to the purpose of uncovering contradictions. But it is only labour saving. If the multiplicity of o's names conceals a contradiction, putting just the same name in the place of each of them must uncover it.

Exercise 11.6

State whether the following are legitimate justifications for (=E).

★a.	*i.*	Gb		b.	*i.*	Gb		**★c.**	*i.*	=ab	
	k.	=ab			*k.*	=ab			*k.*	Gb	
	n.	Ga	*i,k* (=E)		*n.*	Ga	*k,i* (=E)		*n.*	Ga	*i,k* (=E)
d.	*i.*	=ab		**★e.**	*i.*	=ab		f.	*i.*	=ab	
	k.	=bc			*k.*	=bc			*k.*	=cb	
	n.	=ac	*i,k* (=E)		*n.*	=ac	*k,i* (=E)		*n.*	=ca	*k,i* (=E)
★g.	*i.*	=ab		h.	*i.*	=ab		**★i.**	*i.*	=ab	
	k.	=cb			*k.*	=cb			*k.*	=cb	
	n.	=ac	*k,i* (=E)		*n.*	=ca	*i,k* (=E)		*n.*	=ca	*i,k* (=E)
j.	*i.*	=cb		**★k.**	*i.*	=cb		l.	*i.*	=cb	
	k.	=ab			*k.*	=ab			*k.*	=ab	
	n.	=ca	*k,i* (=E)		*n.*	=ac	*k,i* (=E)		*n.*	=ca	*i,k* (=E)
★m.	*i.*	=cb		n.	*i.*	=cb		**★o.**	*i.*	=cb	
	k.	=ab			*k.*	~=ab			*k.*	~=ac	
	n.	=ac	*i,k* (=E)		*n.*	~=ac	*i,k* (=E)		*n.*	~=ab	*i,k* (=E)

(=E) is not just used to make substitutions in sentences of the form P where P is a predicate sentence. It can also be applied to other identity sentences. This creates new identity sentences which become sources for (=E) in their turn. Infinite regress threatens, but it is blocked by the fact that none of the rules of Tp introduces names that did not previously exist on the path. Given a finite number of names, and a finite number of finitely long literals, there is necessarily only a finite number of different sentences that can be created by substituting one name in the place of the other. Tp therefore remains decidable. (=E) applications are further limited by the fact that, as with Ts, rules should not be applied to repeat sentences that already stand alone on the path.

As with Dp, (=E) can also be used to make substitutions in sentences of the form P where P is a negated identity sentence. However, negated identity sentences can only be targets for (=E) (that is, sentences containing the occurrences of q that get replaced with occurrences of r); they cannot be sources for (=E) (that is, sentences that say that r denotes the same object as q). ~=rq says that r does not denote the same object as q, and so denies that it is legitimate to substitute r for q. But =rq (considered as source) can be applied to ~=pq (considered as target) to generate ~=pr.

Exercise 11.7

State whether the following applications of (=E) are legitimate.

★a.	i.	=ab		b.	i.	=ac		★c.	i.	=ac
	k.	~=bc			k.	~=bc			k.	~=bc
	n.	~=ac	i,k (=E)		n.	=ab	k,i (=E)		n.	~=ab	k,i (=E)

d.	i.	=ab		★e.	i.	~=ab		f.	i.	~=ab
	k.	~=ac			k.	=cb			k.	=cb
	n.	~=bc	i,k (=E)		n.	~=ac	i,k (=E)		n.	=ac	k,i (=E)

Among other things, (def ex) requires applying =rq (considered as source) to itself (considered as target) to generate =rr. This may seem pointless. But self-identity sentences like =rr are needed to extract the correct tree model from an exhausted path.

Because applications of (=E) create new literals that become targets or sources for further applications of (=E), it helps to have a systematic method for applying (=E) in order to ensure that all the substitutions that are required have been done.

System for (=E) Applications

(i) Except in cases where doing so will quickly close a path or produce an exhausted path, do not apply (=E) until all nonliteral sentences have been reduced. Then focus on the path most likely to be exhausted. (When (=E) is applied, it must still be applied across the tree, on all paths where it applies, but the idea is to avoid unnecessary work on other paths.)

(ii) Starting at the top of the tree and proceeding in order from top to bottom, repeatedly apply (=E) using each *(unnegated)* identity sentence as source. Do this by going down to the first identity sentence, =rq, to appear on the path. Taking =rq as a source, go back up to the top of the path, and take in turn each literal, P, from the top of the path down as a target for one (=E) application that puts r in the place of each occurrence of q in P. Include the application of the = sentence to itself as target when its turn comes up. Be careful to make applications to each literal to occur on an open path running up to the identity sentence. Pass over applications that reproduce a literal that already exists on the path. Include literals added to paths as a consequence of work at this stage. When done, go down to the next identity sentence on the path and repeat the process, using it as source. Also use identity sentences that are entered on the bottom of paths as the result of work at this stage as sources for (=E) when their turn comes up. Continue until the lowest identity sentence on the tree has been used as source on all targets.

(iii) If all paths do not close, repeat step (ii). (This is done in case work on identity sentences lower down on the path has created literals that are subject to (=E) using identity sentences higher on the path.)

(iv) Stop when either all paths close or a complete cycle through all the identity sentences on the path discovers no further sentences to add to the path.

As with Ts, finding a single exhausted path means that the givens are p-satisfiable, so the rest of the tree does not need to be completed.

Consider a tree for the set, {Gbc ≡ ~=ab, Gaa & =ca, ~=ad & Gcc → Ha & =ba}.

1.	Gbc ≡ ~=ab	given
2.	Gaa & =ca	given
3.	~=ad & Gcc → Ha & =ba	given

The first step in extending this tree should be to reduce the sentence on line 2, as it is the only one that does not split the path.

1.	Gbc ≡ ~=ab	given
2.	Gaa & =ca✔	given
3.	~=ad & Gcc → Ha & =ba	given
4.	Gaa	2 (T&)
5.	=ca	2 (T&)

Now both the sentence on line 1 and the sentence on line 3 are path-splitting, and it is not obvious that either one will produce a closed path. This makes it better to do the more complicated one first.

1.	Gbc ≡ ~=ab✔		given
2.	Gaa & =ca✔		given
3.	(~=ad & Gcc) → Ha & =ba		given
4.	Gaa		2 (T&)
5.	=ca		2 (T&)
6.	Gbc	~Gbc	1 (T≡)
7.	~=ab	~~=ab✔	1 (T≡)
8.		=ab	7 (DN)

Reducing the ~~ sentence on line 7 makes it apparent that the right path can quickly be closed. How should that be done, and on which paths should the sentences derived on the course to doing so appear? Think about this before reading further.

1.	Gbc ≡ ~=ab ✔		given
2.	Gaa & =ca ✔		given
3.	~=ad & Gcc → Ha & =ba		given
4.	Gaa		2 (T&)
5.	=ca		2 (T&)
6.	Gbc	~Gbc	1 (T≡)
7.	~=ab	~~=ab✔	1 (T≡)
8.		=ab	7 (DN)
9.		~Gac	8,6 (=E)
10.	Gac	Gac	5,4 (=E)
11.		⊥	10,9 (⊥I)

Why does ~Gac appear on the right path but not on the left path?

Why does Gac appear on both paths?

Gac appears on both paths because both paths run up to the lowest of the two sentences involved in the (=E) application. The placement principle requires that sentences be identified on each path that runs up to them. Gac appears rather than Gcc because, though (def ex) does not require putting c for just one occurrence of "a," (=E) does allow it. The path closes either way, just not as soon.

~Gac appears only on the right path because the lowest of the sentences involved in the (=E) application only exists on that path. (In this case the higher is also on the right path, but that is irrelevant. Both sentences would need to be above the path split before ~Gac could appear on both paths.)

It remains to reduce the sentence on line 3.

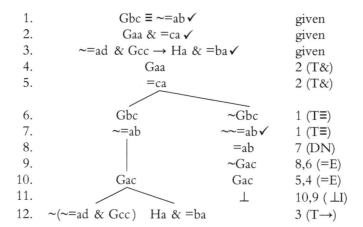

1.	Gbc ≡ ~=ab ✓		given
2.	Gaa & =ca ✓		given
3.	~=ad & Gcc → Ha & =ba ✓		given
4.	Gaa		2 (T&)
5.	=ca		2 (T&)
6.	Gbc	~Gbc	1 (T≡)
7.	~=ab	~~=ab ✓	1 (T≡)
8.		=ab	7 (DN)
9.		~Gac	8,6 (=E)
10.	Gac	Gac	5,4 (=E)
11.		⊥	10,9 (⊥I)
12.	~(~=ad & Gcc) Ha & =ba		3 (T→)

At this point it might be decided that there is no point to working further on the left path, as the right path will be exhausted. However, for any path to be exhausted, all possible identity applications must be performed on that path, and any that require entering sentences on both paths must be applied on both paths. That way, if expectations are disappointed and the path fails to be exhausted, it will not be necessary to take more lines to repeat the work a second time on the other path.

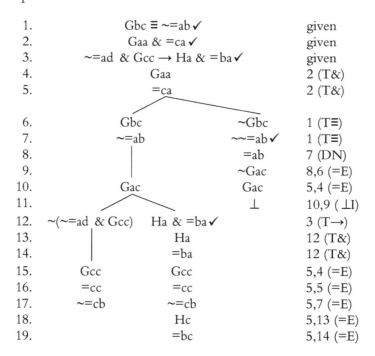

1.	Gbc ≡ ~=ab ✓		given
2.	Gaa & =ca ✓		given
3.	~=ad & Gcc → Ha & =ba ✓		given
4.	Gaa		2 (T&)
5.	=ca		2 (T&)
6.	Gbc	~Gbc	1 (T≡)
7.	~=ab	~~=ab ✓	1 (T≡)
8.		=ab	7 (DN)
9.		~Gac	8,6 (=E)
10.	Gac	Gac	5,4 (=E)
11.		⊥	10,9 (⊥I)
12.	~(~=ad & Gcc) Ha & =ba ✓		3 (T→)
13.		Ha	12 (T&)
14.		=ba	12 (T&)
15.	Gcc	Gcc	5,4 (=E)
16.	=cc	=cc	5,5 (=E)
17.	~=cb	~=cb	5,7 (=E)
18.		Hc	5,13 (=E)
19.		=bc	5,14 (=E)

So far, work has proceeded systematically. Going down the path from the top, the first identity sentence to appear is the one at line 5. This sentence is applied to each literal on the path from the top down, that is, to those on lines 4 (5,4 (=E) was already performed at line 10, but (def ex) requires replacing each occurrence of "a"), 5 (it must be applied to itself), 7 (not to line 6, because =ca only says to "put c for a" and there is no "a" in the sentence on line 6), 13 (not to line 10 because the application to that sentence produces a sentence that already exists on the path, and not to line 12 because it is not a literal, and to line 13 only on the middle path because Ha does not lie on the left path and so cannot be identified there), and 14 (not to lines 15 to 18 because those literals do not contain an occurrence of "a").

Now that the identity sentence on line 5 has been provisionally taken care of (provisionally because subsequent work may still create more sentences for it to be applied to), work proceeds by going down to the next identity sentence on the path. That is =ba on line 14, not ~=ab on line 7, because ~=ab is not an identity sentence. (def ex) only requires complete substitutions, but (=E) allows partial ones. To make a point, suppose =ba were applied to make two partial substitutions to Gaa.

1.		Gbc ≡ ~=ab ✓		given
2.		Gaa & =ca ✓		given
3.		~=ad & Gcc → Ha & =ba ✓		given
4.		Gaa		2 (T&)
5.		=ca		2 (T&)
6.		Gbc	~Gbc	1 (T≡)
7.		~=ab	~~=ab ✓	1 (T≡)
8.			=ab	7 (DN)
9.			~Gac	8,6 (=E)
10.		Gac	Gac	5,4 (=E)
11.			⊥	10,9 (⊥I)
12.	~(~=ad & Gcc)	Ha & =ba ✓		3 (T→)
13.		Ha		12 (T&)
14.		=ba		12 (T&)
15.	Gcc	Gcc		5,4 (=E)
16.	=cc	=cc		5,5 (=E)
17.	~=cb	~=cb		5,7 (=E)
18.		Hc		5,13 (=E)
19.		=bc		5,14 (=E)
20.		Gba		14,4 (=E)
21.		Gab		14,4 (=E)

What should the next step be? Lines 20 and 21 have generated sentences to which the earlier identity sentence at line 5 applies, but the application of the source on line 5 to the target on line 20 produces a sentence that already exists on the path at line 6. That application should not be made. But what about 5,21 (=E)?

1.		Gbc ≡ ~=ab ✓		given
2.		Gaa & =ca ✓		given
3.		~=ad & Gcc → Ha & =ba ✓		given
4.		Gaa		2 (T&)
5.		=ca		2 (T&)
6.		Gbc	~Gbc	1 (T≡)
7.		~=ab	~~=ab ✓	1 (T≡)
8.			=ab	7 (DN)
9.			~Gac	8,6 (=E)
10.		Gac	Gac	5,4 (=E)
11.			⊥	10,9 (⊥I)
12.	~(~=ad & Gcc)	Ha & =ba ✓		3 (T→)
13.		Ha		12 (T&)
14.		=ba		12 (T&)
15.	Gcc	Gcc		5,4 (=E)
16.	=cc	=cc		5,5 (=E)
17.	~=cb	~=cb		5,7 (=E)
18.		Hc		5,13 (=E)
19.		=bc		5,14 (=E)
20.		Gba		14,4 (=E)
21.		Gab		14,4 (=E)
22.		Gbb		14,4 (=E)
23.		=cb		14,5 (=E)
24.		⊥		23,17 (⊥I)

5,21 (=E) is not applied at line 22. It is hard enough to keep track of what needs to be done while focusing on work from the top down. Once work begins on the identity sentence on line 14, that work needs to be brought to completion and it needs to be followed by work on the next lowest identity sentence on the path. Interrupting that sequence of steps to go back and do work that pertains to one or more earlier identity sentences would make it very difficult to keep track of what needs to be done. The time to do 5,21 (=E) is after a complete cycle through all the remaining identity sentences on the path, at which point a second cycle through the sentences begins.

As it turns out, that does not happen because the path closes, contrary to expectations. On closer review, it becomes apparent that had 14,7 (=E) been performed at line 15, it would have resulted in ~=bb appearing on the path at line 15, closing it already at that point. It can be hard to notice when ⊥ can be derived. That is why it is important to follow the system to demonstrate that a path really is exhausted. (Of course, if a way to close the path is seen, that way should be taken immediately. The system is for when it does not look like the path will close.) Proceeding systematically will always uncover the contradiction if there is one. In this case, just working from the top down and applying =ba to each literal on the path containing an "a" in all possible ways eventually uncovers a contradiction, even if not the one that might have been most readily derived. Had the contradiction produced by the sentence on line 23 not been noticed, the next step would have been to derive ~=bb by 14,7 (=E), thereby arriving at the contradiction ingenuity suggests for line 15.

In this case, the cost of the unexpected closure is not as great as it could have been because foresight was exercised while working to do everything that could be done on the left path as well as the middle path. That makes it easy to continue the left path. The following extension of the tree ghosts the unnecessary (=E) applications.

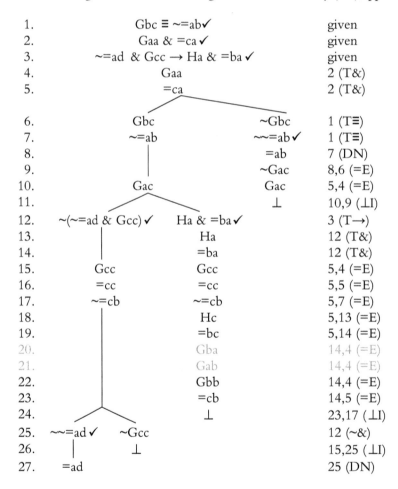

1.	Gbc ≡ ~=ab ✓	given
2.	Gaa & =ca ✓	given
3.	~=ad & Gcc → Ha & =ba ✓	given
4.	Gaa	2 (T&)
5.	=ca	2 (T&)
6.	Gbc ~Gbc	1 (T≡)
7.	~=ab ~~=ab ✓	1 (T≡)
8.	=ab	7 (DN)
9.	~Gac	8,6 (=E)
10.	Gac Gac	5,4 (=E)
11.	⊥	10,9 (⊥I)
12.	~(~=ad & Gcc) ✓ Ha & =ba ✓	3 (T→)
13.	Ha	12 (T&)
14.	=ba	12 (T&)
15.	Gcc Gcc	5,4 (=E)
16.	=cc =cc	5,5 (=E)
17.	~=cb ~=cb	5,7 (=E)
18.	Hc	5,13 (=E)
19.	=bc	5,14 (=E)
20.	Gba	14,4 (=E)
21.	Gab	14,4 (=E)
22.	Gbb	14,4 (=E)
23.	=cb	14,5 (=E)
24.	⊥	23,17 (⊥I)
25.	~~=ad ✓ ~Gcc	12 (~&)
26.	⊥	15,25 (⊥I)
27.	=ad	25 (DN)

At this point, work should continue by picking up with the system at the point where it stopped being applied on the left path. It is easy to determine what that point was. Systematic trees have a characteristic column of (=E) justifications. Looking at the justifications column above, there are repeated occurrences of the same first line number, followed by ever increasing occurrences of a second number: (5,4) (5,5) (5,7) (5,13) (5,14) (14.4) (14,5). In this case, (=E) justifications on the left path stopped with (5,7), indicating that the last systematic act to be performed on the path was applying the source on line 5 to the target on line 7. Pick up from there, applying the source on line 5 to any eligible targets after line 7. Then proceed down to the next source.

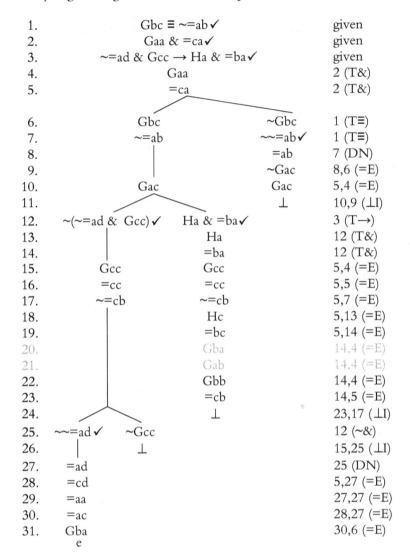

1.	Gbc ≡ ~=ab ✓	given
2.	Gaa & =ca ✓	given
3.	~=ad & Gcc → Ha & =ba ✓	given
4.	Gaa	2 (T&)
5.	=ca	2 (T&)
6.	Gbc ~Gbc	1 (T≡)
7.	~=ab ~~=ab ✓	1 (T≡)
8.	=ab	7 (DN)
9.	~Gac	8,6 (=E)
10.	Gac Gac	5,4 (=E)
11.	⊥	10,9 (⊥I)
12.	~(~=ad & Gcc) ✓ Ha & =ba ✓	3 (T→)
13.	Ha	12 (T&)
14.	=ba	12 (T&)
15.	Gcc Gcc	5,4 (=E)
16.	=cc =cc	5,5 (=E)
17.	~=cb ~=cb	5,7 (=E)
18.	Hc	5,13 (=E)
19.	=bc	5,14 (=E)
20.	Gba	14,4 (=E)
21.	Gab	14,4 (=E)
22.	Gbb	14,4 (=E)
23.	=cb	14,5 (=E)
24.	⊥	23,17 (⊥I)
25.	~~=ad ✓ ~Gcc	12 (~&)
26.	⊥	15,25 (⊥I)
27.	=ad	25 (DN)
28.	=cd	5,27 (=E)
29.	=aa	27,27 (=E)
30.	=ac	28,27 (=E)
31.	Gba	30,6 (=E)
	e	

After completing the applications using line 5 as source, which is done as of line 28, the next identity sentence on the path is =cc. It cannot be used to make any changes, so work continues with the one after that, =ad on line 27. Since d has not yet appeared in a literal, =ad can only be applied to itself, generating =aa. The next identity sentence on the path is =cd, which can only be applied to =ad to yield =ac (its application to itself has already been performed). =ac generates only slightly more work. =aa already exists on the path. Gba can be added. Gaa, =ca, ~=ab, and =ad already exist on the path, illustrating the point that adding more identity sentences cannot do much to increase the work because there are only a finite number of spaces for substitutions to be made. In this case only the addition of Gba remains. Going back to the top of the tree and checking if any of the additions made to the path have created more work for any of the earlier identity sentences reveals that there is nothing left for =ca, =ad, =cd, or =ac to do, so the path can be declared exhausted.

This tree illustrates the utility of prohibiting right-to-left (=E) applications and not requiring partial substitutions. In that case, the existence of =ad on line 25 and =cd on line 26 would require extra work, as would applications of =ba and =ca to make partial substitutions to Gaa.

Even with the aid of a systematic method of applying (=E), keeping track of what to do next can be difficult. Confirmation that a path really is exhausted can be obtained by extracting a tree model from the path. If the givens are not all true on the model, something has gone wrong somewhere.

It is not always obvious what model an exhausted path defines. The following "bin method" automates the procedure.

Bin Method for Constructing a Tree Model

(i) List the names occurring on the path in alphanumerical order and construct a bin for each name.

(ii) Provisionally assign 1 to the first name, 2 to the second, and so on down to the last.

(iii) Going up the leftmost exhausted path from the bottom, place a copy of each identity sentence that *ends* with name p in the p bin (so, all identity sentences that end with "a" go in the "a" bin, all those that end with b in the b bin, etc.).

(iv) For each bin, identify the alphanumerically earliest of the *beginning* names (the names in first place in the identity sentences), e.g., if =ca, =fa, and =ba are the identity sentences in the "a" bin, the alphanumerically earliest beginning name is b.

(v) Reassign the number that was provisionally assigned to the alphanumerically earliest name to the name the bin was made for; e.g., if =ca, =fa, and =ba are the identity sentences in the "a" bin, the alphanumerically earliest beginning name is b, so assign b's provisional number, 2, to "a." In the case where a bin is empty, continue using the provisional assignment.

(vi) Take the domain to consist just of the numbers required to make these revised assignments.

(vii) Assign the lowest number in the domain (it need no longer be 1) to all the remaining names of PSL.

(viii) To make each higher-place predicate sentence, $Pq_1...q_n$ where n is greater than 0, that stands alone on the path come out true, assign $<\alpha(q_1)...\alpha(q_n)>$ to $\alpha(P)$. Do not make any other assignments to $\alpha(P)$.

(ix) Assign the empty set to all other higher-place predicate sentences.

(x) Assign a T to any zero-place predicate sentence that stands alone on the path and an F to all other zero-place predicate sentences.

Applying these instructions to the exhausted path of the tree produced above yields the following drawing:

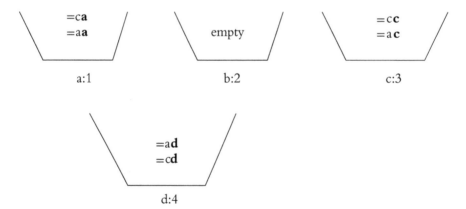

A bin was constructed for each sentence. Going up the path from the bottom and looking for identity sentences that end with the name assigned to each bin results in the contents of the different bins being filled out as specified.

Identity sentences that *end* with a name go in the bin for that name to ensure that if a name occurs in an identity sentence on the path, there will be an identity sentence in its bin. (def ex) ensures that no exhausted path can contain exactly one identity sentence, unless it has the form =pp. If =pq, occurs on a path, and q is a different name from p, (def ex) requires that =pq be used as source for an (=E) application to itself as target, causing =pp to be entered on the path. Thus, the name in second place in =pq (namely, q) will contain an identity sentence (=pq) in its bin, because by definition the identity sentence that contains that name in second place goes in its bin. And the name in first place in =pq (namely, p) will contain an identity sentence (=pp) in its bin, because by (def ex) an identity sentence containing that name in second place must be created and so must be placed in that name's bin.

Bins can still be empty. But this only happens when the names those bins are made for do not occur in any identity sentence on the path. In that case no revised denotation assignment is called for.

Populating bins serves as a check on whether all the (=E) applications required by (def ex) were made. Consider any bin that contains a name that occurs in the p bin to be a bin that is "related" to the p bin. On this understanding, if a bin contains one or more identity sentences, all the related bins ought to contain an equal number of identity sentences. For example, in the drawing above, the d bin contains the names "a," c, and d. That makes the "a," c, and d bins related bins. (It would also mean that any bins that contain an occurrence of d are related bins.) These related bins ought to each contain exactly as many identity sentences as the d bin (two). If not, either an (=E) application was missed when constructing the path or a mistake was made when populating the bins.

Supposing bins have been correctly populated, they determine a revised denotation assignment for a tree model. The alphanumerically earliest of the names to occur in first place in the identity sentences in a bin is assigned to the name the bin was made for. This is done even if that number is higher than the number that was provisionally assigned to the name the bin was made for.

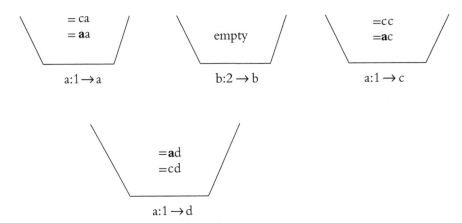

In the revised diagram above, "a" was provisionally assigned the value 1 (see the label for a's bin on the earlier diagram). It keeps that assignment because "a" is the alphanumerically earliest of the names to occur in first place in an identity sentence in a's bin. c was provisionally assigned the value 3 and d was assigned 4. But because "a" is the alphanumerically earliest of the names to occur in first place in an identity sentence in their bins, each of them is reassigned "a's" value. b keeps its provisional assignment of 2, because there are no identity sentences in its bin to say otherwise.

D is accordingly {1,2}. 3 and 4 are scratched from the domain because the names those numbers were provisionally assigned to ended up being reassigned the number 1. It does not always turn out this way. Sometimes "a" does not occur in first place in any identity sentence in its own bin, and the lowest number in the domain ends up being some other number.

As established by the completeness demonstration of chapter A-5.3, the bin method always gives consistent results, and always defines the revised denotation assignment for an interpretation on which all the givens are true. In the meantime, the reliability of the method can be empirically verified by doing exercises and seeing that the tree model the bin method always assigns a T to each of the givens – either that or a mistake was made in constructing the tree or in populating the bins.

Exercise 11.8

1. *Suppose the following are the sentences appearing on an exhausted tree path. Recover the tree model that is determined by the path.*

   ★a. {Kca, ~Kac, ~=bc, H}

   b. {~Haa, ~Hac, Hbb, ~=ab}

   ★c. {~Gb, =ba, ~Kc, =ac, =bb, =aa, =ab, =bc, ~Ka, ~Ga}

   d. {Geb, Gbe, ~=eb, Ka, =ac, =ba, Kb, =aa, =bb, =ab}

   ★e. {~Gb}

   f. {=ce, ~=eb, =bd, ~=da, =cc, =bb, ~=cb, ~=ba, ~=cd}

2. Suppose the following are the literals on an unfinished path. Complete the path by applying (=E) in the systematic fashion discussed earlier. Include justifications and ensure that these justifications cite source first and target second. Recover the tree model from each path.

★a.		b.		★c.		d.	
1.	Gab	1.	Gac	1.	=ba	1.	Gaa
2.	~=ca	2.	=ba	2.	=cb	2.	~=ab
3.	=ab	3.	=ec	3.	Gac	3.	=ca
		4.	~=ac	4.	Gcc		

★e.		f.		★g.		h.	
1.	=ab	1.	Gb	1.	=ae	1.	~Gee
2.	=cd	2.	=ab	2.	Gad	2.	=ae
3.	=bd	3.	=ca	3.	~=ab	3.	~=ce
		4.	~Kb	4.	=ca		
				5.	=bd		
				6.	~He		

3. Determine whether the following sets are inconsistent. If the tree does not close, do not apply (=E) before all other rule applications have been made, then apply (=E) in accord with the systematic method and recover and verify the tree model from the leftmost exhausted path. If the tree does close, verify the appropriate corresponding result in Dp.

    ★a. {=ca, Gab → ~=cb, Gab ≡ =ab}
    b. {Gab & ~Gaa, Gbb → =ab}
    ★c. {Kb ≡ =bc, ~=ab → ~=aa, Kc → ~=ab}
    d. {=ad & =ba, (~Gd & Gb) ∨ ~=cd}
    ★e. {=ab & Hb, Ha → Gca, Gac → ~=ab}
    f. {=ab & ~Gc, (Ga & =cb) ∨ (Gb & =da)}

4. Determine whether the conclusions of the following demonstrations are derivable from their premises. If the tree does not close, do not apply (=E) before all other rule applications have been made, then apply (=E) in accord with the systematic method and recover and verify the tree model from the leftmost exhausted path. If the tree does close, verify the appropriate corresponding result in Dp.

    ★a. ~=cb / ~=ab ∨ ~=ac
    b. Ha, ~=ab / ~Hb
    ★c. =ab, Gaa → ~(Gac & Gba) / Gbc → ~Gbb
    d. =ab ∨ =ca, Ga / Gb ∨ Gc
    ★e. Ga ∨ ~Gb → =ca & Hc, =ab / Ha
    f. =ab & ~=bc / ~=ca

5. Determine whether the following sentences are theorems, inconsistent or contingent in Tp. If the tree does not close, do not apply (=E) before all other rule applications have been made, then apply (=E) in accord with the systematic method and recover and verify the tree model from the leftmost exhausted path. If the tree does close, verify the appropriate corresponding result in Dp.

    ★a. ⊥ ≡ ~=aa
    b. Ga & ~Gb → ~=ab
    ★c. =ab → ~=ba
    d. =ab & =ac → =cb
    ★e. =ab → Ga ∨ ~Gb
    f. ~=ab → Ga ∨ Gb

6. Determine whether the following sentences are interderivable in Tp. If the tree does not close, do not apply (=E) before all other rule applications have been made, then apply (=E) in accord with the systematic method and recover and verify the tree model from the leftmost exhausted path. If the tree does close, verify the appropriate corresponding result in Dp.

    ★a. =ab, Ga ≡ Gb
    b. =ab, Gab ≡ Gba
    ★c. =ab → Ga, ~Gb → ~=ab
    d. ~(=ab ∨ Gab), ~=ab ∨ ~Gba
    ★e. ~(=ab & Gaa), ~=ab & ~Gbb
    f. ~=ab & =ac, ~(=bc ∨ =ca)

★7. *It was asserted earlier that if a bin contains one or more identity sentences, all the related bins ought to contain an equal number of identity sentences. Explain why the systematic application of (=E) on an exhausted path ensures that this must be the case. Appeal to the facts that if =pq occurs in the q bin then, by (=E), = pp must occur in the p bin, and if = pq occurs in the q bin and = qr occurs in the r bin then, by (=E), = pr must occur in the r bin.*

11.5 Semantics for Functional Terms

The semantics for PL*f* expands on PSL semantics by accounting for the meaning of function letters and functional terms. The meaning of functional terms is based on the meaning of function letters. The meaning of the function letters is accounted for by making an extension to the definition of a valuation.

> An *interpretation*, I, for PL*f* has two components, a domain, D, and a valuation, α.
>
> (i) D is a nonempty and possibly (but not necessarily) infinite set of objects, $\{o_1, o_2, o_3, \ldots\}$.
>
> (ii) α *assigns*:
>
>   (a) exactly one of T and F to each zero-place predicate
>
>   (b) exactly one object from D to each **zero-place function letter**
>
>   (c) **where *n* is greater than 0, a set of two-place lists of the form $\{<L_1, o_1>, <L_2, o_2>, <L_3, o_3>, \ldots\}$ to each *n*-place function letter, where $L_1, L_2, L_{3, \ldots}$ are each list of *n* objects that can be formed using not necessarily distinct objects from D; $o_1, o_2, o_3, \ldots$ are not necessarily distinct objects from D; and no L occurs in more than one ordered pair**
>
>   (d) where *n* is greater than 0, a (possibly empty) set of lists of *n* (not necessarily distinct) objects from D to each *n*-place predicate.

To illustrate (c), consider an interpretation with domain {1,2,3}. A two-place function from lists of two objects from D onto objects from D must assign an object from D to each two-place list of objects that it is possible to form from objects in D. Where there are three objects in D, there are nine different lists of two objects. Imagine these lists lined up in a column on the left and the objects in D lined up in a column on the right.

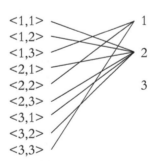

Each list on the left must be the point of origin for a line that passes from it to exactly one of the objects on the right. No list can be the origin point for more than one line. None can fail to have a line originate from it. And all lines must go to one of the objects on the right. Some of the objects on the right may not have any lines going to them. Others may have more than one.

There are many ways to draw a set of lines from each list on the left to each object on the right. Each different set of lines is a different assignment of objects in D to lists of objects in D. The diagram above illustrates one way these lines might be drawn and so illustrates one two-place function. It illustrates what "values" the function assigns to what "arguments." The arguments are the lists on the left, the values the objects on the right.

The higher-place function letters of PL*f* symbolize such functions. The assignments made by α to the higher-place function letters are like a set of instructions for drawing lines from each list of objects to exactly one object. For instance, the higher-place function diagramed above might be assigned to the two-place function letter f(xy), where x and y are used as place holders. α describes the function by following the lines from each argument to its value. Argument <1,1> gets value 2; argument <1,2> gets value 2; argument <1,3> gets value 1, and so on. More briefly, the map can be described by listing the value after each argument. Since the arguments are themselves lists, the result is a set of lists, with each list being comprised of a list followed by its value. α(f) is {<<1,1>,2>, <<1,2>,2>, <<1,3>,1>, <<2,1>,2>, <<2,2>,1>, <<2,3>,2>, <<3,1>,2>, <<3,2>,2>, <<3,3>,1>}.

Displaying assignments to higher-place function letters in this way is technically correct, but hard to read because of the forest of angle brackets. In practice, assignments to *n*-place function letters are instead displayed as sets of *n*+1 place lists. A one-place function letter is assigned a set of two-place lists, a two-place function letter a set of three-place lists, a three-place function letter a set of four-place lists, and so on. The last item on each list is the value of the list of the earlier items. On this cleaned-up presentation, α(f) is {<1,1,2>, <1,2,2>, <1,3,1>, <2,1,2>, <2,2,1>, <2,3,2>, <3,1,2>, <3,2,2>, <3,3,1>}.

For each *n*-place function letter, it is required that α make exactly one assignment to each *n*-place list that it is possible to form using objects from D. Otherwise it would be possible to form a functional term to which α either does not make an assignment or makes more than one assignment. In that case, the term would either fail to denote an object or be ambiguous. But, like PSL, PL*f* does not tolerate terms that fail to denote exactly one object. Interpretations for PL*f* therefore stipulate that α must interpret each function letter by assigning exactly one object to each list that can be formed.

Exercise 11.9

State whether the following are acceptable interpretations of the sentence Ha(d) → Gc(be). *The question is not whether the interpretations make the sentence true or false, but just whether the interpretation is a permissible interpretation of PLf.*

⋆a. D: {1}
    a:1
    b:1
    c:1
    d:1
    e:1
    G: {<1,1,1>}
    H: {<1,1>}

b. D: {1}
    a: {<1>}
    b:1
    c: {<1,1>}
    d:1
    e:1
    G: {1}
    H: {1}

⋆c. D: {1}
    a: {<1,1>}
    b:1
    c: {<1,1,1>}
    d:1
    e:1
    G: {1}
    H: {1}

d. D: {1,2}
    a: {<1,1>, <2,1>}
    b:1
    c: {<1,1,1>, <1,2,1>, <2,2,2>}
    d:1
    e:2
    G: {2}
    H: {1}

⋆e. D: {1,2}
    a: {<1,1>, <1,2>, <2,1>}
    b:1
    c: {<1,1,1>, <1,2,1>, <2,1,1>, <2,2,2>}
    d:1
    e:2
    G: {2}
    H: {1}

f. D: {1,2}
    a: {<1,2>, <2,2>}
    b:1
    c: {<1,1,1>, <1,2,2>, <2,1,2>, <2,2,1>}
    d:1
    e:2
    G: {2}
    H: {1}

⋆g. D: {1,2}
    a: { }
    b:1
    c: {<1,1,1>, <1,2,1>, <2,1,1>, <2,2,1>}

h. D: {1,2}
    a: {<1,1>, <2,2>}
    b:1
    c: {<1,1,1>, <1,2,1>, <2,1,1>, <2,1,2>, <2,2,1>}

d:1
e:2
G: {2}
H: {1}

d:1
e:2
G: {2}
H: {1}

Whereas function letters are interpreted, functional terms have values assigned to them in accord with a valuation rule. The value of a term is often called its denotation.

> (f):   The denotation of a functional term, $f(t_1 \ldots t_n)$, on an interpretation,
> I, is the object, o, in D such that $<<I/\alpha(t_1),\ldots,I/\alpha(t_n)>,o>$ is in $\alpha(f)$.
> Notation: $I(f(t_1 \ldots t_n))$ is o.

The value of a functional term is determined by the interpretation of the higher-place function letter and the interpretation of the terms that fall within its scope. Suppose $\alpha(a)$ is 1, $\alpha(b)$ is 2, $\alpha(c)$ is 3 and $\alpha(f)$ is, as in the example mapped earlier, {<1,1,2>, <1,2,2>, <1,3,1>, <2,1,2>, <2,2,1>, <2,3,2>, <3,1,2>, <3,2,2>, <3,3,1>}. Then $I(f(aa))$ is 2, $I(f(cb))$ is 2, and $I(f(bf(cc)))$ is 2. That is because $<\alpha(a),\alpha(a)>$ is <1,1> and $\alpha(f)$ assigns 2 to <1,1>; because $<\alpha(c),\alpha(b)>$ is <3,2> and $\alpha(f)$ assigns 2 to <3,2>; and because $<\alpha(c),\alpha(c)>$ is <3,3> which is assigned 1 by $\alpha(f)$, and $<\alpha(b),1>$ is <2,1> which receives 2 on $\alpha(f)$.

The last of these examples illustrates why (f) speaks of assignments being made to terms by I/α rather than simply by α. The terms in $f(t_1 \ldots t_n)$ could either be simple terms, in which case their denotation is assigned by α, or functional terms, in which case their denotation is determined by I in accord with (f). In the latter case, $f(t_1 \ldots t_n)$ is a higher-level functional term: a functional term that contains other functional terms. Its denotation is only determined by first determining the denotation of the lower-level functional terms it contains.

The remaining valuation rules for PLf are the same as those for PSL but for some minor revisions to (P) and (=).

> (P): $I(Pt_1 \ldots t_n)$ is T if and only if $<I/\alpha(t_1), \ldots, I/\alpha(t_n)>$ is in $\alpha(P)$; otherwise,
> $I(Pt_1 \ldots t_n)$ is F.
>
> (=): $I(=ts)$ is T if and only if $I/\alpha(t)$ is $I/\alpha(s)$; otherwise $I(=ts)$ is F.

Exercise 11.10

1. *State what denotation I assigns (or does not assign) to what functional term under the following conditions. The first three questions are answered as an example.*
   a. $<\alpha(a),7>$ is in $\alpha(c)$
      Answer: $I(c(a))$ is 7
   b. $<\alpha(a),\alpha(b),7>$ is in $\alpha(c)$
      Answer: $I(c(ab))$ is 7
   c. $<\alpha(e),\alpha(d),o>$ is not in $\alpha(b)$
      Answer: $I(b(ed))$ is not o
   d. $<\alpha(e),\alpha(d),\alpha(a)>$ is not in $\alpha(f)$
   e. $<\alpha(a),\alpha(a),1>$ is in $\alpha(f)$
   f. $<\alpha(a),\alpha(a)>$ is in $\alpha(f)$
   g. $<I(a(b)),\alpha(b),3>$ is in $\alpha(f)$
   h. $<I(a(b)),\alpha(b),I(c(d))>$ is not in $\alpha(f)$
   i. $<I(f(ab)),I(d(d(c))),I(e(e(b)))>$ is in $\alpha(f)$

2. *State what conditions must be met for I to assign (or not assign) the specified denotation to the specified functional term. The first three questions are answered as an example.*
   a. $I(f(a))$ is 1
      Answer: $<\alpha(a),1>$ is in $\alpha(f)$
   b. $I(f(aa))$ is 1
      Answer: $<\alpha(a),\alpha(a),1>$ is in $\alpha(f)$

   c. α(f(ab)) is not 2

      Answer: <α(a),α(b),2> is not in α(f)

   d. I(f(ab(a))) is not 2

   e. I(f(ab)) is α(c)

   f. I(f(f(a))) is o

   g. I(c(f(ab))) is not o

   h. I(e(f(a)f(b))) is α(c)

   i. I(f(e(ab)e(ba))) is I(d(bab)) *(This question has two answers depending on whether it is read from left to right or right to left.)*

3. *State whether* Ha(d) → Gc(be) *is true on interpretations c and f in exercise 11.9 above. Justify your answer by a demonstration that appeals to the semantic rules.* **Answer for c**

4. *Establish that each of the following sentences is pf-contingent. Do this by reasoning from assignments of T and F to each sentence to uncover what sort of extension the function and predicate letters must have for the sentence to be true or false. Then devise interpretations that meet these conditions. (The answers to the ★ questions illustrate how to do this.) In constructing interpretations, n-place function letters must have exhaustive sets of n-place lists of domain objects paired with domain objects as their extensions. Such sets can be very large if there are more than a few objects in the domain. Keep the domain as small as possible to get the job done! Provide a verification that demonstrates that your interpretations do in fact make the intended assignments.*

   ★a. =f(a)a

   b. =f(ab)f(ba)

   ★c. (Gaf(b) ≡ Gf(b)a) → =f(a)f(b)

   d. (=f(a)a ≡ =f(b)b) → =ab

   ★e. =f(a)f(b) → =ab

   f. =af(b) & =cf(b)

5. *Prove that each of the following is pf-valid.*

   ★a. =af(a) & =bf(a) → =ab

   b. ~=af(a) → (=bf(a) → ~=ab)

   ★c. =f(a)b & =f(b)a → =af(f(a))

   d. =ab → =f(a)f(b)

   ★e. =f(d(a))b & =f(b)c → =f(f(d(a)))c

   f. =af(a) → =f(a)f(f(a))

6. *Prove that* =tt *is pf-valid, where t is any term.*

11.6 Tp*f*

Were trees for sets of sentences of PL*f* only done to determine whether the set yields ⊥, Tp would be adequate with two minor modifications: taking ~=tt to close a path where t is any term, and extending (=E) to allow substituting identified terms of all sorts with one another.

But this is not enough to discover tree models. Exhausted paths in Tp*f* can provide very little information about how to assign extensions to higher-place function letters or even how to determine an appropriate domain for a model. A tree for the set, {~(=ab → Gf(b))}, for example, might look like this:

1.	~(=ab → Gf(b)) ✓	given
2.	=ab	1 (~→)
3.	~Gf(b)	1 (~→)
4.	=aa	2,2 (=E)
5.	~Gf(a)	2,3 (=E)
	e	

The path contains little that can be used to define an extension for f.

It might be thought that f(a) and f(b) could be treated as if they were ornamental names. In that case, following the procedure Tp uses to recover a tree model would dictate making an initial denotation assignment of 1 to "a," 2 to b, 3 to f(a), and 4 to f(b). Because =ab occurs on the path, the revised denotation assignment would assign 1 to "a" and b, 3 to f(a), and 4 to f(b). But that would be wrong. If f(a) were 3, then <1,3> would have to be in the extension of f, since "a" denotes 1. But if f(b) were 4 then <1,4> would have to be in the extension of f, since b also denotes 1. But no interpretation of a function letter can assign two different values to the same argument. Yet there is no identity sentence on the path that says that f(a) and f(b) must denote the same object, and no way of deriving one using just the rules of Tp.

Ideally, an exhausted path should dictate a tree model. No further reflection or calculation should be required. To this end, Tp*f* introduces a further rule, (T*f*).

> (T*f*): If *f*(p₁...pₙ) occurs in a literal on a path, and no sentence of the form =q*f*(p₁...pₙ), where q is any name, can be derived on that path, enter =r*f*(p₁...pₙ) on each open extension of the path, where r is the alphabetically earliest name not yet to have appeared in any sentence on the path.

(T*f*) is not a reduction rule. It is, like (=E), an identification rule. The idea behind (T*f*) is that if functional terms can be identified with names, then they will acquire the denotation α assigns to those names, permitting a tree model to be constructed by determining the denotation of names.

(T*f*) requires that the name be identified to the left of the functional term because identity substitutions are made from left to right. This ensures that the new name will replace the functional term in all literals where it occurs.

(T*f*) further requires that the name be new to the path. As a matter of policy, the alphanumerically earliest name not yet to have appeared on the path is chosen. It would be risky to presume that a functional term denotes the same object as the one denoted by a name already on the path. If it does not, a false closure could result. It is not equally risky to presume that a functional term has a new name. Same objects can have different names, and if a path does not close on account of an object having one name it will not close on account of it being given a further name entirely new to the path.

Using (T*f*) on the tree above generates the following extension:

1.	~(=ab → Gf(b)) ✓	given
2.	=ab	1 (~→)
3.	~Gf(b)	1 (~→)
4.	=cf(b)	3 (T*f*)
5.	=aa	2,2 (=E)
6.	~Gf(a)	2,3 (=E)
7.	=cf(a)	2,4 (=E)
8.	~Gc	4,3 (=E)
9.	=cc	4,4 (=E)
	e	

When a tree model is recovered from the exhausted path, 1 is provisionally assigned to "a," 2 to b, and 3 to c. The tree model does not make assignments to the functional terms, f(a) and f(b). It instead makes an assignment to the function letter, guided by the identity sentences on the path. In the identity sentences on lines 7 and 4, "a" and b are read as the names of arguments and c as the name of the value those arguments take in $\alpha(f)$. So $\alpha(f)$ includes $<\alpha(a),\alpha(c)>$, according to line 7, and $<\alpha(b),\alpha(c)>$, according to line 4. Since the revised denotation assignment assigns 1 to both "a" and b, the identity sentences on lines 7 and 4 both say both say that the extension of f includes $<1,3>$. f(a) and f(b) end up having the same value, as required. The domain contains 1 and 3. 3 is not assigned a value in the extension of f in virtue of an identity sentence containing f(c). But that is not a concern. Because f(c) does not appear on the path, it can take any value. By convention, when a functional term is not assigned to a name, its value defaults to the first object in D. In this case, that means adding $<3,1>$ to complete the extension of f.

(T*f*) is employed in accord with a new definition of an exhausted path.

(def ex)

A path of **a pf**-tree is *exhausted* if and only if:

(i)   each sentence in the set the tree was made for has been placed on top of the tree

(ii) $\perp$ does not stand alone on any line of the path

(iii)   each sentence on the path is either a literal or a nonliteral that has been reduced (checked off)

(iv)   for each sentence of the form $=q\mathbf{t}$ and each literal, P, a sentence of the form $P(q\,|\,\mathbf{t})$ (including sentences of the form $=qq$), occurs on the path

(v)   **each term of the form $f(p_1...p_n)$ to occur in a literal that stands alone on a line of the path occurs in a sentence of the form $=qf(p_1...p_n)$ that stands alone on a line of path.**

The revised definition only requires that each functional term to occur in a literal on the path be identified to the right of a name. It does not require that (T*f*) be used for this purpose. It is preferable that reduction rules or (=E) produce the identification. (T*f*) is used only as a last resort. It adds a new name to the tree and that means more work.

The fourth clause of (def ex) has been weakened. (=E) need not be applied using identity sentences beginning with a functional term. In such cases, the last clause requires that there be another identity sentence on the path that identifies that functional term to the right of a name. It suffices to apply (=E) to put that name in the place of each occurrence of the functional term. It remains permissible to use (=E) to put functional terms in the place of names if doing so would close a path. The point is just that (=E) need not be applied in this way to demonstrate that a path is exhausted.

Bin Method for Constructing a Tree Model

(i)   List the **names** occurring on the path in alphanumeric order and construct a bin for each name.

(ii)   Provisionally assign 1 to the first name, 2 to the second, and so on down to the last.

(iii)   Going up the path from the bottom, place a copy of each identity sentence that **begins with any name and** *ends* with name p in the p bin.

(iv)   For each bin, identify the alphanumerically earliest of the *beginning* names.

(v)   Assign the number that was provisionally assigned to the alphanumerically earliest name to the name the bin was made for. In the case where a bin is empty, continue using the provisional assignment.

(vi)   Take the domain to consist just of the numbers required to make these revised assignments.

(vii)   **Assign each *n*-place function letter, *f*, each *n*+1-place list, $<\alpha(p_1),...\alpha(p_n),\alpha(q)>$ determined by each identity sentence of the form $=q\,f(p_1...p_n)$ on the path.**

> (viii) Assign the lowest number in the domain to all the remaining names of **PL*f*;** **also take this number to be the value of any arguments for any function letters not specified in identity sentences that stand alone on the path.**
> (ix) For each higher-place predicate sentence, $Pt_1 \ldots t_n$, that stands alone on the path, assign $\langle \alpha/I(t_1) \ldots \alpha/I(t_n) \rangle$ to $\alpha(P)$. Do not make any other assignments to $\alpha(P)$.
>   (x) Assign the empty set to all other higher-place predicate sentences.
> (xi) Assign a T to any 0–place predicate sentence that stands alone on the path and an F to all other 0–place predicate sentences.

(T*f*) should not be used on closed paths. It is only useful for recovering a tree model. When $\bot$ is derivable, using (T*f*) will complicate that operation unnecessarily.

(T*f*) should only be applied to functional terms that contain only names (level-1 functional terms), not functional terms that contain other functional terms. For example, if Gf(af(ab)) occurs on a path, (T*f*) should not be applied to f(af(ab)). It should, however, be applied to the functional term that f(af(ab)) contains. The idea is to first identify this level-1 functional term with a name, for example, =cf(ab), then apply (=E) to transform Gf(af(ab)) into Gf(ac), and then apply (T*f*) to f(ac).

(T*f*) should only be applied to functional terms contained in literals. It needlessly complicates the tree to apply it to nonliterals, especially if subsequent work reveals that reducing the nonliterals closes the tree.

(T*f*) should only be applied once to each functional term even if it occurs in multiple sentences on that path. When the functional term occurs many times, only one of the literals containing it need be cited as a justification for (T*f*). Once the functional term has been identified with a name, all the literals that contain it can be rewritten using (=E). It is necessary, however, to ensure that each functional term is identified on each path that runs through any literal containing it.

(T*f*) should not be applied to identity sentences. If a sentence of the form =pt already exists on the path the application is pointless. If =pt does not exist on the path but =tp does, it is important to identify t to the right of a name, but in this case there is a short-cut. The principle of the symmetry of identity sentences involving a complex term and a name (sym), =tp −|− =pt, is readily demonstrable in T*pf*.

1.	=tp	given		1.	=pt	given
2.	~=pt	given		2.	~=tp	given
3.	~=tt	1,2 (=E)		3.	~=pp	1,2 (=E)
4.	$\bot$	3 ($\bot$I)			$\bot$	3 ($\bot$I)

(sym) can therefore be applied on *pf* trees to directly derive =pt from =tp.

Consider how to reduce Hf(e(a)e(b)).

1.	Hf(e(a)e(b))	given
2.	=ce(a)	1 (T*f*)
3.	=de(b)	1 (T*f*)
4.	Hf(ce(b))	2,1 (=E)
5.	=cc	2,2 (=E)
6.	Hf(e(a)d)	3,1 (=E)
7.	=dd	3,3 (=E)
8.	Hf(cd)	3,4 (=E)
9.	$=a_1 f(cd)$	8 (T*f*)
10.	Ha_1	9,8 (=E)
11.	$=a_1 a_1$	9,9 (=E)

Applying (T*f*) just to level-1 functional terms (those that contain only names) eventually results in identifying all higher-level functional terms with names as well.

This can be seen in the interpretation that comes off the path:

D: {1,2,3,4,5}
a: 1
b: 2
c: 3
d: 4
a_1: 5
(This is the provisional denotation assignment, which is unchanged by the revised denotation assignment.)
e: {<1,3>,<2,4>; the value of all other arguments is 1} *(The specified values are determined by what is seen at lines 2 and 3; the remaining values are determined by default.)*
f: {<3,4,5>; the value of all other arguments is 1} *(The specified value is determined by what is seen at line 9; the remaining values are determined by default.)*
H: {5}

On this interpretation, f(e(a)e(b)) denotes 5. This is because: (i) α(a) is 1 and <1,3> is in α(e), so I(e(a)) is 3; (ii) α(b) is 2 and <2,4> is in α(e) so I(e(b)) is 4; (iii) <3,4,5> is in α(f), so I(f(e(a)e(b))) is 5.

As the tree illustrates, when applying (=E), it is permissible to substitute names for terms that occur inside of other terms. Given a path that contains the literals,

$$=df(d)$$
$$|$$
$$Pf(f(d))$$

it is permissible to put d in the place of the occurrence of f(d) that is seen inside of f(f(d)) to derive Pf(d). This reflects how (=E) is applied in D*pf*.

The following example illustrates an important strategic consideration.

1.	~(=ab → =f(f(a))f(b)) ✓	given
2.	=ab	1 (~→)
3.	~=f(f(a))f(b)	1 (~→)
4.	=cf(b)	3 (T*f*)
5.	=cf(a)	2,4 (=E)
6.	=aa	2,2 (=E)
7.	~=f(f(a))f(a)	2,3 (=E)
8.	~=f(f(a))c	4,3 (=E)
9.	=cc	4,4 (=E)
10.	~=f(c)f(b)	5,3 (=E)
11.	~=f(c)c	5,7 (=E)
12.	=df(c)	10, (T*f*)

...

After line 3, both f(a) and f(b) must be identified to the right of a name. At line 4, a choice is made to apply (T*f*) to f(b) before applying it to f(a). This makes it possible to identify f(a) by applying (=E) rather than (T*f*). It would have been permissible to apply (T*f*) to f(a) first, but this would have required that f(b) be identified with a name by making a second application of (T*f*). This would have added an extra name on the path, demanding many extra (=E) applications. If a way can be found to identify a functional term without using (T*f*), it should be preferred.

The path above finishes with

13.	~=df(b)	12,10 (=E)
14.	~=dc	12,11 (=E)
15.	=dd	12,12 (=E)

e

D contains three objects (since there are four names and "a" and "b" have been identified). Both f(a) and f(b) have been identified with c, so the value that the argument commonly denoted by "a" and b receives in $\alpha(f)$ is $\alpha(c)$, which is 3. Similarly, since f(c) has been identified with d, the value the argument denoted by c receives in $\alpha(f)$ is $\alpha(d)$, which is 4. And since f(d) does not appear on the path its value is set by default to 1.

D: {1, 3, 4}
a: 1
b: 1 (since =ab is on the path)
c: 3
d: 4
f: {<1,3>,<3,4>,<4,1>}

11.6.1 Systematic Paths

pf trees do not produce any more paths than p-trees, but they can get involved in multiple (=E) applications, making it difficult to keep track of all the work that needs to be done on a single path before it can be declared to be exhausted. For this reason, it is helpful to specify an order in which sentences are to be reduced, and an order in which the terms in those sentences are to be identified. This order has already been silently followed in work done so far. Following it ensures that everything that needs to be done to exhaust a path is done. Work on closed paths can be done in any order. If it can be foreseen that the path will close, it must be foreseen why and only that work need be done. When closure is not foreseen it is best to proceed systematically.

On a path where the system is being followed, rules are applied over three stages. All rule applications except for (T*f*) and (=E) make up stage 1. An exception is made for (=E) applications that would quickly close a path. These are also considered to belong to stage 1. (=E) applications that identify a functional term to the right of a name and (T*f*) rule applications make up stage 2. All remaining (=E) applications make up stage 3. All work that can be done at stage 1 is completed before proceeding to stage 2, then all work that can be done at stage 2 is completed before proceeding to stage 3. Working at stage 3 can produce sentences that need to be identified at stage 2. But once stage 3 commences a return to stage 2 is not allowed. All work that can be done at stage 3 must be completed first. Only after that is it permissible to return to stage 2. Work proceeds by cycles through the final two stages. (Since stage 2 and 3 identifications do not generate new nonliteral sentences, there should be nothing more to do at stage 1 after the first time through). At the point where a complete cycle through stages 2 and 3 produces no further changes to the tree, the path is exhausted.

The Systematic Reduction Method
(to be used on paths that are not expected to close)

Stage 1 (Reduction of Nonliterals)
• Make all possible applications of rules that do not split the path.
• When no more straight rules can be applied, apply path-splitting rules that create one or more closed paths before those that create all open paths. Also apply (=E) across all open paths where it applies if doing so will close one or more of those paths.
• When no more rules that produce one or more closed paths can be applied, reduce the most complex of any remaining nonliteral sentences, and return to the start of this stage.
• Once all nonliteral sentences have been reduced and all (=E) applications that close a path have been made, proceed to stage 2.

Stage 2 (Identification of Functional Terms)
- Apply (=E) or (Tf) to each level-1 functional term, $f(p_1...p_n)$, that is, each functional term that contains only names and that does not occur to the right of a name in an identity sentence on the path. Use (=E) in preference to (Tf), and prioritize (Tf) applications that make it possible to use (=E) to identify other functional terms.
- Once all level-1 functional terms have been identified, proceed to stage 3.

Stage 3 (Identification of Names)
- Apply (sym) to = sentences that begin with a functional term and end with a name.
- Starting at the top of the tree and proceeding in order from top to bottom, repeatedly apply (=E) using each = sentence that begins with a name as source. Do this by going down to the first = sentence, =qt, that begins with a name to appear on the path. Taking that sentence as a source, go back up to the top of the path, and take in turn each literal, P, from the top of the path down as a target for one (=E) application that puts q in the place of each occurrence of t in P. Include the application of the = sentence to itself as target when its turn comes up. Be careful to make applications to each literal to occur on an open path running up to the = sentence. Pass over applications that reproduce a literal that already exists on the path. Include literals added to paths as a consequence of work at this stage. When done, go down to the next identity sentence on the path and repeat the process, using it as source. Also use = sentences that begin with names and that are entered on the bottom of paths as the result of work at this stage as sources for (=E) when their turn comes up. Continue until the lowest = sentence on the tree to begin with a name has been used as a source on all targets.
- return to stage 2.

Stop when either all paths close or a complete cycle through stages 2 and 3 produces no changes to at least one open path. In the second case, declare that path to be exhausted. Do not continue work on a tree that has produced an exhausted path.

This system is followed in the previous example. Over lines 1–3, all nonliteral sentences are reduced, constituting work at stage 1. Stage 2 begins at line 4. Both line 4 and line 5 identify functional terms, even though one uses (=E). As mentioned earlier, some art is applied here to minimize (Tf) applications.

Beginning at line 6 (=E) applications are made, starting from sentences on the top of the tree and proceeding downwards. Targets are also hit in order as they come up from the top down. Only sentences that do not already exist on the path are added to the path.

Work at stage 3 finishes as of line 11 and reverts to stage 2 at line 12. Work at stage 2 had been exhausted earlier over lines 4–5, but a new level-1 functional term was generated later, at line 10. Because new work was created to be done at stage 2, it is necessary to go back to stage 2 once all work that can be done at stage 3 has been exhausted. The new work at stage 2 is completed by the single identification at line 12. Even though there are multiple lines at which f(c) occurs, once it has been identified the first time, it is not identified again. (It does not matter which of lines 10–11 is used to justify (Tf).) Completion of the new cycle through stage 2 is followed by a return to stage 3. Importantly, work at this stage commences all over again from the top of the path, not just from the newly added source at line 12. It is possible that subsequent work will have created new targets for the higher sources. In the case at hand, no new targets for old identity sentences have been created as of line 12. Work on the new identity sentence is completed over lines 13–15. That work does not create any new functional terms, so a return to stage 2 is not called for. However, a last cycle through each identity sentence from the top of the path down should be performed, to verify that no further changes to the path are called for. None are. So, the path is exhausted.

11.6.2 *Decidability*

Tpf remains decidable. Even though (Tf) adds new terms to the path, each cycle through stages 1 and 2 generates functional terms that are shorter in length than the ones identified earlier. (In the example above, the first cycle removed "f(f(a))," replacing it with functional terms that contain only one function letter to its two.) Since sentences are finitely long, trees start off with a finite number of finitely long functional terms. The cycle of (Tf) and (=E) applications must therefore result in the production of a finite number of functional terms that contain only one function letter, and the identification of each of these terms with only a finite number of new names. Paths will therefore contain a finite number of names, and a finite number of places in which those names could be put, leaving only a finite number of identity substitutions to be performed.

Exercise 11.11

1. *Consider each of the following to be the list of literals occurring on an exhausted Tpf path. Specify the tree model that can be recovered from these literals. If necessary, apply (Tf) and (=E) to get the job done.*

   ★a. {=ab, ~Hb, Ga, ~Ha}
     b. {=cb, Gcc, Gbc, ~Hcc, ~Hbc}
   ★c. {~=df(d)}
     d. {~=f(ab)f(ba)}
   ★e. {Ga, ~Hf(a), ~=af(a)}
     f. {~=af(a), ~=bf(b)}
   ★g. {Ga, =f(c)b}
     h. {=f(a)a}
   ★i. {~=f(a)a, ~Ha, ~Gf(b), =f(f(a))f(b), ~Gf(f(a))}
     j. {Hf(e(ab)d(c)), =d(c)a₁(aa₂(a)), Hf(e(ab)a₁(aa₂(a)))}

2. *Determine whether each of the following sequents is derivable in Tpf. Verify this result with a derivation in Dpf or a semantic demonstration from a tree model defined by the leftmost exhausted path, as appropriate.*

   ★a. ⊢ =af(a) → =af(f(a))
     b. ⊢ =af(f(a)) → =af(a)
   ★c. ⊢ [Gf(a) ≡ Gf(f(a))] → =f(f(a))f(a)
     d. ⊢ =ab → =f(f(a))f(f(b))
   ★e. =bf(a), =cf(a), Gb & ~Gc ⊢ ⊥
     f. =ab, =af(a) ⊢ =bf(f(a))

11.7 Semantics for PL¹

Accounting for the meaning of definite descriptions requires explaining how to interpret the variables as well as the definite descriptions of the language. This requires an expansion to the way semantics has been done up to now, preparing the way for similar work that must be done to deal with the semantics for quantifiers, taken up in chapters 15 and 16.

The semantics for definite descriptions must deal with both proper and improper descriptions. The semantics for improper descriptions is controversial. It grapples with a long-standing debate over the nature of discourse concerning nonexistent objects in an especially rigorous context.

11.7.1 Variable Assignments

A variable is a symbol that could stand for any object. Consequently, it is not desirable for α to assign objects to variables. That would give them a fixed meaning, like names. The meaning of variables is instead supplied by something that can vary while the interpretation stays the same. This is a variable assignment.

> A *variable assignment*, δ (Greek lower-case delta, for "denotes"), on an interpretation, I, expands on the work done by I by assigning exactly one object from ID to each variable of PL¹.

(For work at the keyboard, δ may be replaced with lower-case "d," standing for "denotes." However, the English letter is suboptimal for verbal lectures and discussion, given that upper-case "D," which has the same verbal name, is also in play in contexts where variable assignments are likely to be discussed. Greek delta is pressed into service as a compromise.)

For any one interpretation, there is only one α, but there are as many different δ's as there are different ways of assigning objects to variables. If D is {1,2}, and ¹xGx is a definite description, the variable assignments that need to be considered are those that assign 1 to x and those that assign 2 to x. They are notated as δ[1/x] and δ[2/x], read "delta one for x" and "delta two for x." The reading suggests that 1 should be imagined standing in the place of x wherever x occurs in the sentence under consideration. (As a technical note, δ[1/x] and δ[2/x] are properly understood as *variants* on δ rather than as *specifications* of what δ does. δ[1/x] is the variable assignment that is just like δ except that it overwrites δ's assignment to x with a possibly but not necessarily different assignment of 1 to x.)

δ[1/x] and δ[2/x] are groups of variable assignments. Each variable assignment in the δ[1/x] group assigns 1 to x, but differs from the others in its group in assignments it makes to other variables. When the only definite description under consideration is ^{1}xGx, those other assignments are irrelevant.

When definite descriptions are nested inside of one another, variable assignments need to be expanded in the order of the nesting. The example from sections 10.3.4–5, "The computer in the basement is broken" is formalized as

$$K^1x(Cx \text{ \& } G(x^1yBy))$$

where Kx is "x is broken," Cx is "x is a computer," Gxy is "x is in y," and Bx is "x is a basement." If D is {1,2,3} then the variable assignments that need to be considered are, first, those that assign an object to x: δ[1/x], δ[2/x], and δ[3/x]. But because there is a ^{1}y operator within the scope of the ^{1}x operator, consideration of each of these variable assignments needs to be expanded by what each assigns to y, resulting in variants on each of these assignments: δ[1/x,1/y], δ[1/x,2/y], δ[1/x,3/y], δ[2/x,1/y], and so on.

As a terminological note, sometimes it is not important to specify which object a δ assigns to a variable. In such cases, o, n, m, are used as object variables, with subscripts on o's should more be needed. As in chapter 10.3.5, Greek lower-case χ (chi) is used to stand for any variable. In some rare cases, a second or third "variable variable" is called for, and in those cases ψ (phi) and ζ (zeta) are also used, with the usual caution that distinct "variable variables" need not stand for distinct variables. Each of δ, δ[o/x], and δ[o/x,n/y] is called a variable assignment. The δ[o/x]'s are also called variants on δ, and the δ[o/x,n/y]'s are called variants on δ[o/x]. The sequence might be continued.

A variable assignment inherits all the assignments to names and predicates made by the interpretation it is on. It is not allowed to change anything done by the interpretation. It only supplements that work by making an assignment to the variables – the assignment partially specified in the brackets.

11.7.2 Denotation for Variables

> (χ):   The *denotation of a variable*, χ, on a variable assignment, δ[o/χ], on an interpretation, I, is o. Notation: δ[o/χ](χ) is o.

(χ) stutters because of cases where variable assignments are expanded. When the discussion concerns δ[1/y,2/x], for example, it might need to be specified whether the assignment of immediate concern is the one to x or the one to y. <δ[1/y,2/x](x),δ[1/y,2/x](y)> is the ordered pair, <2,1>. <δ[1/y,2/x](y),δ[1/y,2/x](x)> is the ordered pair <1,2>.

11.7.3 Satisfaction

A description places a condition on objects. Objects that meet the condition are said to "satisfy" the condition. A proper definite description is satisfied by exactly one object. But which one? Were all definite descriptions based on one-place predicates, the answer would be obvious: just look at the extension α assigns to the predicate. Provided the description is proper, there should be exactly one object there, making it the one denoted by the description. But definite descriptions are not always so simple. They can be based on compound sentences and on predicates that contain places for more than one object. Some of those places might be filled by other definite descriptions. Provided they are proper, these complex descriptions still denote exactly one object.

To determine which object is denoted by a description, a new valuation rule, (^{1}) is instituted. (^{1}) specifies the conditions under which a variable assignment, δ, assigns an object, o, to a description, ^{1}χP. It does this by surveying each of its variants δ[o$_1$/χ], δ[o$_2$/χ], δ[o$_3$/χ] …, where o$_1$, o$_2$, o$_3$, … are each object in D, to determine which one or ones (if any) satisfy the description, P. Because P must be an open sentence and can be compound and can contain predicates with places for more than one object, (^{1}) cannot work alone. It needs the aid of further rules that specify the conditions under which an object satisfies an open sentence. To this end, the valuation rules are transformed from being conditions under which I assigns T to a sentence to conditions under which a variable assignment or variant on a variable assignment, δ, satisfies either an open sentence or a sentence. (δ needs to be able to satisfy sentences as well as open sentences because sentences can be components of open sentences; for example, Ga might be a component of Ga & Hx, creating a situation where δ can only satisfy Ga & Hx if it can be shown to satisfy Ga.) Because any sentence, even ⊥ or a zero-place predicate sentence, could figure in a definite description, (⊥) and assignments made by α to zero-place predicates are converted to satisfaction conditions.

In the clauses that follow, consider the expression, "α/δ(t)" to mean α(p) where the assignment is to a name and δ(t) where it is to a variable or a definite description.

Satisfaction Conditions

(⊥): **No δ satisfies ⊥ on any interpretation.**

(P): δ **satisfies** $P(t_1...t_n)$ if and only if $<\alpha/\delta(t_1),...,\alpha/\delta(t_n)>$ is in α(P); otherwise, δ **does not satisfy** $P(t_1... t_n)$ **as a special case of (P), δ satisfies a zero-place predicate sentence, P, if and only if α(P) is T; otherwise, δ does not satisfy P.**

(=): δ **satisfies =ts** if and only if α/δ(t) is α/δ(s); otherwise, δ **does not satisfy =ts.**

(~): δ **satisfies ~P** if and only if **it does not satisfy** P; otherwise δ **does not satisfy ~P.**

(&): δ **satisfies** P & Q, if and only if **it satisfies** each of P and Q; otherwise δ **does not satisfy** P & Q.

(∨): δ **satisfies** P ∨ Q, if and only if **it satisfies** at least one of P and Q; otherwise δ **does not satisfy** P ∨ Q.

(→): δ **does not satisfy** P → Q if and only if it **satisfies** P but does not **satisfy** Q; otherwise, δ **satisfies** P → Q.

(≡): δ **does not satisfy** P ≡ Q if and only if it satisfies one of P and Q but not the other; otherwise δ **satisfies** P ≡ Q.

These rules rewrite the valuation rules, substituting satisfaction by δ for truth on I. But (⊥), (P), and (=) also expand the rules to allow δ to satisfy open sentences. This is illustrated in the example taken up in the following section.

11.7.4 Denotation for Proper Descriptions

(The following statement of (¹) covers only the case where a definite description is proper. It is expanded in subsection 11.7.6 to cover cases where the description is improper.)

(¹): If $^1\chi P$ is a definite description, then if there is exactly one object, o, in D such that δ[o/χ] satisfies P, δ($^1\chi P$) is o.

Recall that a level-1 definite description begins with a term forming operator that does not have any other term forming operators within its scope. As with the higher-level functional terms of section 11.5, the denotation of higher-level definite descriptions is determined after first determining the denotation of the lower-level definite descriptions they contain. In that case, δ[o/χ] is δ[...o/χ]. The assignment to the variable belonging to the level-1 definite description is always last on the variant list. Each time (¹) is applied, it shrinks the variant list. The last variant on the list drops off. If δ[o/χ] is the only variant on δ that satisfies P, then it is just δ, not δ[o/χ], that assigns o to $^1\chi P$. Successive applications of (¹) shrink any variant list to zero, that is, to a δ that is not followed by any specification of what assignments it makes.

Given an interpretation, (¹) can be applied to determine the denotation of the description contained in the example of section 10.3, "The computer in the basement is broken," earlier formalized as $K^1x(Cx \& G(x^1yBy))$. Consider how this is done on the following interpretation:

D: {1,2,3}
d: 2
B: {3}
C: {1,2}
G: {<1,3>}
K: {1}

Since ¹x(Cx & G(x¹yBy)) is a definite description that contains another definite description, its denotation is determined by first determining the denotation of the description it contains. That is ¹yBy. Strip off the term forming operator, ¹y, and consider the resulting open sentence, By. y is a variable. It could stand for any object in the domain. Unlike a name, it is not possible to look at the interpretation to see what object α assigns to it. Instead, there are several variable assignments, each assigning a different object to it, as well as making some assignment to x. For now, the assignment to x makes no difference, so it can be designated as δ[o/x] where o is any object in D. Given that D is {1,2,3}, the assignment to y could be any of three different objects, so there are three variants to consider, δ[o/x,1/y], δ[o/x,2/y], and δ[o/x,3/y]. Given that α(B) is 3, exactly one of these variable assignments, δ[o/y,3/x], satisfies By. According to (¹), that is the condition under which the parent of δ[o/x,3/y], namely δ[o/x] assigns 3 to ¹yBy. As it is notated, δ[o/x](¹yBy) is 3 (where o is any object in D).

Now that the denotation of ¹yBy has been determined, that of ¹x(Cx & G(x¹yBy)) can be determined. As before, strip off the term forming operator, ¹x, and consider the resulting open sentence, Cx & G(x¹yBy). ¹yBy has already been found to denote 3. x is a variable. Its denotation varies with which variable assignment is being considered. Given that there are three objects in the domain, there are three variable assignments to consider. Given that x occurs in first place in a two-place open sentence, Gx¹yBy, along with a term that has already been determined to denote 3, it is pertinent that those three variable assignments figure in three different ordered pairs ending in 3 that might be found in the extension of G: <δ[1/x](x), δ[1/x](¹yBy)>, <δ[2/x](x), δ[2/x](¹yBy)>, and <δ[3/x](x), δ[3/x](¹yBy)>, that is, <1,3>, <2,3>, and <3,3>. Of these three alternatives only one, <1,3> is in α(G). So, there is exactly one variable assignment, δ[1/x], that satisfies G(x¹yBy)). Since 1 is in α(C) it further follows that δ[1/x] satisfies Cx. By the (&) satisfaction condition, δ[1/x] satisfies Cx & G(x¹yBy). 2 is also in α(C), but since neither δ[2/x] nor δ[3/x] satisfy G(x¹yBy), δ[1/x] is the only variable assignment that satisfies Cx & G(x¹yBy). According to (¹), that is the condition under which the parent of δ[1/x], namely δ, assigns 1 to ¹x(Cx & G(x¹yBy)). As it is notated, δ(¹x(Cx & G(x¹yBy))) is 1. All that remains is to note that 1 is in α(K) in order to draw the conclusion that δ satisfies K¹x(Cx & G(x¹yBy)) as well.

The reasoning might be more rigorously written up as follows, using numbered lines and justifications. "sat" abbreviates "satisfies." As before, o is any object in D.

1.	3 is the only object in D that is in α(B) and δ[o/x,3/y](y) is 3	given
2.	δ[o/x,3/y] is the only variant on δ[o/x] that sat By	1 (P)
3.	δ[o/x](¹yBy) is 3	2 (¹)
4.	<1,3> is in α(G) so <δ[1/x](x), δ[1/x](¹yBy)> is in α(G)	3 and given
5.	δ[1/x] sat G(x¹yBy)	4 (P)
6.	<2,δ[2/x](¹yBy)> and <3,δ[3/x](¹yBy)> are not in α(G)	3 and given
7.	δ[2/x] and δ[3/x] not sat G(x¹yBy)	6 (P)
8.	δ[1/x] is the only variant on δ that sat G(x¹yBy)	5,7 def D
9.	1 is in α(C)	given
10.	δ[1/x] sat Cx	6 (P)
11.	δ[1/x] sat Cx & G(x¹yBy)	5,10 (&)
12.	δ[2/x] and δ[3/x] not sat Cx & G(x¹yBy)	7 (&)
13.	δ[1/x] is the only variant on δ that sat Cx & G(x¹yBy)	11,12 def D
14.	δ(¹x(Cx & G(x¹yBy))) is 1 and 1 is in α(K)	13 (¹) and given
15.	δ sat K¹x(Cx & G(x¹yBy))	14 (P)

11.7.5 Truth Conditions

As indicated by line 15 of the demonstration above, the denotation conditions have usurped the role of the familiar truth conditions. Rather than conclude that I(K¹xG(x¹yBy)) is T, it is concluded that δ sat K¹xG(x¹yBy). The δ's and their variants were introduced just as a means for determining the denotation of terms. But they are imperious creatures. The satisfaction conditions are so broad that they entail that each δ will either satisfy or not satisfy any sentence, even if that sentence contains only names or is ⊥ or a zero-place predicate sentence. This leaves I with no work to do, other than second the verdicts of the δ's. The truth conditions that have been employed up to now have no more role to play. This result is recognized by replacing the old valuation rules with a single truth condition that forces I to countersign the verdicts of its δ's.

> **(def truth)**
>
> I(P) is T if and only if each δ on I satisfies P.
> I(P) is F if and only if no δ on I satisfies P.

The requirement that *each* δ satisfy or not satisfy P follows as a matter of course. As the demonstration that was given earlier indicates, the real work of establishing satisfaction is not done by any δ but by its variants. A variant on any one δ is a variant on all the others, so whatever decision the variants on any δ make is a decision the variants on all the δ's make, and so a decision all the δ's must adopt.

Consider some examples, continuing on the work done in the previous subsection, where it was determined that δ ^{1}x(Cx & G(x^{1}yBy)) is 1. Given that result, it is straightforward to determine the value of predicate sentences or identity sentences containing that term. B^{1}x(Cx & G(x^{1}yBy)), which says that the computer in the basement is a basement, is false. That is because δ(^{1}x(Cx & G(x^{1}yBy))) is 1 and 1 is not in α(B). But this result no longer follows directly by (P) because (P) has been rewritten as a satisfaction condition rather than a truth condition. (P) must be supplemented with def truth to get the result.

14.	δ(^{1}x(Cx & G(x^{1}yBy))) is 1 and 1 is not in α(B)	13 (^{1}) and given
15.	δ not sat B^{1}x(Cx & G(x^{1}yBy))	14 (P)
16.	I(B^{1}x(Cx & G(x^{1}yBy))) is F	15 def truth

(Strictly, a further line of demonstration should be inserted between lines 15 and 16 stating that because δ satisfies the sentence, each δ on I satisfies it. As that would be tedious, it is skipped here and elsewhere.)

In contrast ~= d ^{1}x(Cx & G(x^{1}yBy)) is true. That is because α(d) is 2 and δ(^{1}x(Cx & G(x^{1}yBy))) is 1.

15.	α(d) is 2 so α(d) is not δ(^{1}x(Cx & G(x^{1}yBy)))	given and line 14
16.	δ not sat = d ^{1}x(Cx & G(x^{1}yBy))	15 (=)
17.	δ sat ~= d ^{1}x(Cx & G(x^{1}yBy))	16 (~)
18.	I(~= d ^{1}x(Cx & G(x^{1}yBy))) is T	17 def truth

The application to other functionally compound sentences is similar.

11.7.6 *Denotation for Improper Descriptions*

Any one-place open sentence can be turned into a definite description, including Gx & ~Gx, which can become ^{1}x(Gx & ~Gx), or ~=xx, which can become ^{1}x~=xx. Even apart from these extreme consequences, on any given interpretation, there are many ways of assembling vocabulary elements to form descriptions that either are not satisfied by any object or are satisfied by more than one. This means that, on any interpretation, many definite descriptions fail to fall under (^{1}), as it has so far been formulated. Sentences containing these improper descriptions must be dealt with somehow. Logicians remain divided over how. This section surveys five different approaches.

Intuitions about the following test cases figure in the assessment of these approaches:

11.1 theorems of classical sentential logic like P → P
(instantiated with predicate sentences containing improper descriptions such as G^{1}x~=xx → G^{1}x~=xx)

11.2 sentences of the form =tt, like = ^{1}x~=xx ^{1}x~=xx

11.3 intuitively valid biconditionals like G^{1}xHx ≡ G^{1}yHy and G^{1}xHx ≡ G^{1}x~~Hx

11.4 the "characterization principle": P^{1}χP
("The author of the *Treatise* is an author of the *Treatise*"; "The god of thunder is a god of thunder")

11.5 Intuitively true sentences that contain improper descriptions
("The Loch Ness monster is believed to inhabit Loch Ness")

11.6 Sentences that are paradoxically true on the supposition that all improper descriptions denote the same object
("The present king of France is the greatest prime number")
("Von Blücher prevented the victory of the French at Waterloo, so von Blücher prevented the execution of Napoleon")

One way of dealing with improper descriptions is to hold that (^{1}) is adequate as written. It determines the value of a definite description in those cases where it has a value, and in all others the description has no value. (^{1}) can be completed by making this explicit.

> (^{1})x: If $^1\chi P$ is a definite description, then if there is exactly one object, o, in D such that $\delta[o/\chi]$ satisfies P, $\delta(^1\chi P)$ is o; **otherwise $\delta(^1\chi P)$ has no value.**

Adopting (^{1})x raises the question of what to say about the values of predicate and identity sentences that contain improper terms.

One way to answer this question is to consider predicate and identity sentences that contain improper terms to have some third value, such as N. This raises familiar questions about the status of 11.1 sentences, which are already in trouble on many three-valued semantic systems. (See appendix 5.2). In PSL, these questions extend to the 11.2 and 11.3 sentences. Attaching a third value to predicate and identity sentences that contain improper descriptions means that, when ^{1}xHx and ^{1}xKx are improper, G^1xHx $\to G^1$xHx and G^1xHx $\to G^1$xKx must have the same value, and likewise for $= {}^1$xHx ^{1}xHx and $= {}^1$xHx ^{1}xKx.

In contrast, supervaluationist semantics can preserve the validity of the 11.1 and 11.2 sentences. On supervaluationist semantics, even zero-place predicate sentences can have no value for the reason given in appendix 5.1: Supervaluationist semantics recognizes partial interpretations, which assign values to only some of the zero-place predicates. The notion of a partial interpretation can be extended for predicate logic by allowing domains to be only partially filled (in the extreme, they might be empty), and assignments to names and predicates to be only partially made. When α makes no assignment to a name or a zero-place predicate, or when no δ satisfies a description or more than one does, it creates a value gap. These gaps extend upwards from the terms to any more complex terms that contain those terms, to the predicate and identity sentences that contain those terms, and to the compound sentences containing unvalued components.

The root level gaps in assignments to terms and zero-place predicates are filled by "completions" (complete extensions) of a partial assignment. A completion arbitrarily assigns any admissible value to each gap in assignments to terms and zero-place predicates. In the case of zero-place predicate sentences, the values are T and F. In the case of terms, they are objects in D. A completion can add extra objects to D for this purpose. When it assigns values to improper descriptions, it does so in the same way that α assigns values to names. It just assigns exactly one of the objects in D to the improper description. Completions treat descriptions as if they were nothing more than verbose names, and they do not care what the verbiage says. They do not analyse the description to find out what it describes. That was the job of the δ's on the original interpretation. When the δ's fail in that project, the completions do not think twice about what to do. They just assign an arbitrarily selected object in D to the description without asking whether it is the only object to satisfy the description. Satisfaction is one thing, denotation another, and the completions are not bound by the first clause of (^{1}), which says that what a description denotes ought to be the only object to satisfy that description. Completions assign objects to descriptions like "the self-contradictory object" (^{1}x[Gx & ~Gx]) and "the non-self-identical object" (^{1}x~=xx), which are unsatisfiable on any interpretation, just as easily as they assign objects to descriptions like "the one object that is assigned to the name "a" (^{1}x=xa).

For any improper description, $^1\chi P$, every completion and so every arbitrarily selected object will give $\delta(^1\chi P)$ a value on which δ satisfies $Q^1\chi P \to Q^1\chi P$ and $= {}^1\chi P\ ^1\chi P$, regardless of what interpretation δ is on. That makes these sentences supervaluationally true ("supertrue") on any interpretation, and so "supervalid" (S-valid), preserving the validity of sentences of the form P $\to$ P and =tt. But not every completion will give $\delta(^1\chi P)$ and $\delta(^1\chi Q)$ the same value on any interpretation on which $^1\chi P$ and $^1\chi Q$ are improper, leaving $R^1\chi P \to R^1\chi Q$ and $= {}^1\chi P\ ^1\chi Q$ supervaluationally undetermined on any such interpretation, and so leaving these sentences S-invalid.

A more radical understanding of what it means for improper descriptions to have no value was proposed by Bertrand Russell (1872–1970), who maintained that descriptions are not terms (Russell, 1920). According to Russell, even proper descriptions, like "the author of the *Treatise*," do not denote objects. (^{1}) is entirely wrong.

> Russell: There is no condition under which a definite description has a value. Values can only be ascribed to sentences that include definite descriptions. Those descriptions are better formalized using the quantified predicate logic of chapters 12–16 than using term forming operators.

"The cat" in a sentence like "The cat is on the mat," is not a separable component, a term, that takes an object as its value. Isolated from the rest of the sentence, it has no meaning. It only contributes to determining the meaning of the sentence that contains it. On Russell's account, when there is no cat, or when there is more than one, "The cat is on the mat" is false. But it is not false because "the cat" is a component of the sentence that has no meaning. The cat is not a distinct component of any sort. "The cat is on the mat" is not correctly read as asserting a relation between an individual animal and an individual furnishing. It is properly read as a complex existence claim. It is really saying, "there is at least one object, x, such that x is a cat and for any object, y, either y is not a cat or y is x, and x is on at least one object, z, such that z is a mat and for any object, y, either y is not a mat or y is z." The complex sentence has a value, but it is a value that is determined by the semantics of the expressions, "for at least one," and "for any," as well as the semantics for the predicates "is a cat," "is a mat," and "is on." "The cat" and "the mat" do not figure among the sentence's valuation conditions.

On Russell's approach, even self-identity sentences are false when the identification describes an object that does not exist or that is not the only object of that sort. "The non-self-identical object is the non-self-identical object" is false (indeed, false on any interpretation and so invalid). It follows by (∼) that "the non-self-identical object is *not* the non-self-identical object" must be true. But for Russell this is not an objection. It is only what is to be expected. Since there is no non-self-identical object, of course it cannot be identical to itself, so the negation of the identity is appropriately asserted.

The same holds for predicate sentences that contain improper terms. Famously, there is no present king of France, so "The present king of France is bald," is false, according to Russell. It is natural to object that it follows by (∼) that "It is not the case that the present king of France is bald," must be true. But if there is no present king of France, how could that be?

Russell's reply was that, far from constituting an objection, this case only helps to show that definite descriptions are not terms. According to Russell, "The present king of France is bald" should not be understood as attributing a property to an object identified by means of a description. It should be read as a complex existence claim, "There is at least one person, x, such that x is a present king of France and for any y either y is not a present king of France or y is x and x is bald." When the sentence is read that way, it can be denied in two different ways. One is to deny the sentence as a whole by prefacing the whole sentence with "it is not the case that." The other is to deny the predication by prefacing "bald" with "not." In the former case, the denial says there is no bald present king of France; in the latter, it says that there is a present king of France who is not bald. Russell's preferred method of formalizing "The present king of France is not bald" (examined in section 12.3.8 below) resolves the ambiguity. It forces a choice between the two readings. In contrast, when "the present king of France" is formalized as a term, the ambiguity arises. Suppose "the present king of France" is formalized as ^1xKx where Kx is "x is a present king of France," and "The present King of France is bald" as B^1xKx, where By is "y is bald." Then PL^1 syntax only allows the sentence to be negated in one way. The fact that there are two quite different ways of denying the sentence (with different truth values in this case) points to an inadequacy. There is a way of tweaking PL^1 syntax to bring out both forms of negation,[1] but Russell's point was that the inadequacy is not just in PL^1 syntax but in the manner of thinking behind the objection. Thinking of "the present king of France" as a term invites the mistaken thought that "The present king of France is not bald" presupposes that there is a present king of France. Taking some care over how predications involving improper descriptions are to be formalized and understood makes it possible to maintain that they are all false.

This having been said, the thesis that improper descriptions cannot figure in true predicate sentences has some counterintuitive consequences, as illustrated by 11.5.

A different way of dealing with improper descriptions is based on an observation made by Gottlob Frege (1848–1925), and subsequently elaborated by Rudolf Carnap (1891–1970).[2] Frege acknowledged that languages have an incompleteness that arises from containing expressions that fail to denote an object, even though the form of the expression makes it appear to do so. But he went on to say that in a logically perfect language any expression that is grammatically constructed as if it were a proper term should in fact designate an object, even when there is no such object. He gave the example of mathematicians who stipulate that a divergent infinite series shall stand for the number 0. Following on this hint, what has been called the Frege/Carnap or "designated object" account of improper descriptions proposes that the domain be outfitted with a special object that serves the purpose of being the one object denoted by any improper description. On this account, (^{1}) is completed as follows

> (^{1})+:   If $^1\chi P$ is a level 1 definite description, then if there is exactly one object, o, in D such that $\delta[o/\chi]$ satisfies P, $\delta(^1\chi P)$ is o; **otherwise, $\delta(^1\chi P)$ is 0.**

$(^1)+$ uses 0 as the designated object, but any other symbol could be used for the purpose if it were desirable to recognize whole numbers as domain objects.

Because $^1x{\sim}{=}xx$, "the object that is not identical to itself," is clearly a description that cannot be satisfied by any object on any interpretation, it follows directly from $(^1)+$ that $\delta(^1x{\sim}{=}xx)$ must be 0 on any interpretation. Any other description that is improper on any given interpretation, I, can be identified as improper by being identified with $^1x{\sim}{=}xx$.

This result needs to be carefully understood. Because $^1x{\sim}{=}xx$ is a description that clearly cannot be satisfied by any object on any interpretation it is equally clear that any object assigned to $^1x{\sim}{=}xx$ cannot be assigned because it satisfies that description, but can only be assigned because it has been arbitrarily stipulated that it shall be the value of that description. $\delta(^1x{\sim}{=}xx)$ is not 0 because 0 satisfies the description, "the non-self-identical object." (0 is identical to itself, after all.) But though 0 does not satisfy $^1x{\sim}{=}xx$, $^1x{\sim}{=}xx$ denotes 0 in virtue of the "otherwise" clause of $(^1)+$. What a description denotes and what satisfies that description are not necessarily the same, except in the case of proper descriptions. In the case of improper descriptions either nothing satisfies the description, or more than one thing does, and that makes it possible to distinguish between what satisfies the description and what it denotes. $(^1)+$ takes it to denote a designated object, in this case 0.

While 0 need not satisfy improper descriptions (and could not satisfy some, such as $^1x{\sim}{=}xx$), it is an object in D. Like any other object in D, α could assign it to names or include it on lists assigned to the extension of predicates. Consequently, predicate and identity sentences that contain improper descriptions are not necessarily false. 11.4 is contingent on this semantics and 11.5 is satisfiable.

While 11.4 is contingent, 11.2 is valid. All improper descriptions denote the same object, 0, and all proper descriptions denote exactly one object. Frege/Carnap semantics also makes it possible to demonstrate the validity of such intuitively correct principles as $G^1xHx \equiv G^1yHy$ and $G^1xHx \equiv G^1x{\sim}{\sim}Hx$. A drawback is 11.6. The premise, "Von Blücher prevented the victory of the French at Waterloo" is true, notwithstanding that the description, "the victory of the French at Waterloo" is improper (in fact, the sentence is true precisely because the description is improper!). Since Napoleon was not executed, "the execution of Napoleon" is likewise an improper term. On Frege / Carnap semantics, all improper terms denote the same object, so it follows that "the victory of the French at Waterloo" is "the execution of Napoleon." By (=E), von Blücher must have prevented the execution of Napoleon (as well as everything else that never happened).

A final semantics for improper descriptions is associated with the work of yet another turn of the nineteenth century thinker, Alexius Meinong (1853–1920),[3] who is famous for observing that "being" is not the same thing as "being such and such." Unlike any of the description theories examined up to this point, Meinongian semantics accepts that predicate sentences, identity sentences, and so descriptions can be satisfied by objects that are not in the domain. Insofar as the domain is identified with what exists, this is tantamount to allowing that descriptions can be satisfied by objects that do not exist, and that names can be assigned objects that do not exist. The coherence of this notion was questioned by Russell, and later by Willard van Orman Quine (1908–2000),[4] but it is possible to formulate a consistent Meinongian semantics.[5]

Meinongian semantics distinguishes between a "local" domain, which is the domain of the objects that exist, and a further, "outer" domain, $\mathbb{D}$ (called "hollow D"), which is the domain of the objects of discourse. On some versions of Meinongian semantics, these domains do not overlap; on others, D is a subset of $\mathbb{D}$. Either way, objects that are not in D can be assigned to names, to the extension of predicates, and to improper descriptions. On the version of Meinongian semantics developed in this text, $(^1)$ is completed as $(^1)^\wedge$ (called "one up").

> $(^1)^\wedge$:　If $^1\chi P$ is a level 1 definite description, then if there is exactly one object, o, in D such that $\delta[o/\chi]$ satisfies P, and P does not contain any terms that denote an object that is not in D, $\delta(^1\chi P)$ is o; **otherwise, χP denotes an object in $\mathbb{D}$ that is not in D, as assigned by α_2.**

α_2 is a follow-up assignment of objects to descriptions that have been designated as improper under the first clause of $(^1)^\wedge$. (It is a follow-up assignment because $(^1)^\wedge$ needs to be applied before α_2 can be applied, and applications of $(^1)^\wedge$ in turn depend on assignments made by α.) Like a completion, and like designated object theory, α_2 treats improper descriptions as if they were verbose names, and assigns objects to them without regard for whether those objects satisfy the description. Nonetheless, any α_2 must verify the 11.1 and 11.2 sentences, so they are valid on this semantics. The 11.3, 11.4, and 11.5 sentences are at least satisfiable on this semantics, but they are not valid. Because there can be more than one object that is not in D, and α_2 can assign different such objects to different descriptions, 11.6 is invalid, but by that token so are the 11.3, 11.4, and 11.5 sentences.

11.7.7 *Free Description Theory*

The discussion thus far has explored various description theories without presenting a formal semantics for any of them. There is little more to say about multi-valued theories, Russell's theory, or the Frege/Carnap theory. Multi-valued theories use $(^1)x$ supplemented by the following rules for predicate and identity sentences:

Special Satisfaction Conditions for Three-Valued Description Theories

(P): If any item on $<\alpha/\delta(t_1),\ldots, \alpha/\delta(t_n)>$ has no value, $\delta(P(t_1\ldots t_n)$ is undetermined; otherwise, δ satisfies $P(t_1\ldots t_n)$ if $<\alpha/\delta(t_1),\ldots,\alpha/\delta(t_n)>$ is in $\alpha(P)$ and does not satisfy $P(t_1\ldots t_n)$ if $<\alpha/\delta(t_1),\ldots,\alpha/\delta(t_n)>$ is not in $\alpha(P)$.

(=): If neither $\delta(t)$ nor $\delta(s)$ has a value, $\delta(=ts)$ is undetermined; otherwise, δ satisfies $=ts$ if $\alpha/\delta(t)$ is $\alpha/\delta(s)$ and does not satisfy $=ts$ if $\alpha/\delta(t)$ is not $\alpha/\delta(s)$.

(=) requires that both $\delta(t)$ and $\delta(s)$ lack a value on the intuition that if one has a value and the other does not, they do not have the same value on δ, so δ does not satisfy $=ts$. Bochvar semantics is the most plausible completion: if any component is undetermined, the compound is undetermined; if $\delta[o/\chi](P)$ is undetermined because P contains some term other than χ that has no value, $\delta(^1\chi P)$ has no value; when a sentence is undetermined on each δ on I, I assigns N to that sentence; otherwise the standard valuation rules apply.

The Russellian theory recommends dispensing with terms formed by term forming operators and formalizing descriptions in a way that requires an enhanced logical vocabulary, to be introduced in chapter 12. It would dispense with any version of $(^1)$ and use the semantics of chapters 15 and 16. This having been said, the principal point of Russell's approach can be incorporated with PL^1 by using $(^1)x$ with the following versions of (P) and (=):

Special Satisfaction Conditions for PL^1 under Russellian Description Theory

(P): If any of $\delta(t_1),\ldots,\delta(t_n)$ has no value δ does not satisfy $P(t_1\ldots t_n)$; otherwise, δ satisfies $P(t_1\ldots t_n)$ if $<\alpha/\delta(t_1),\ldots,\alpha/\delta(t_n)>$ is in $\alpha(P)$ and does not satisfy $P(t_1\ldots t_n)$ if $<\alpha/\delta(t_1),\ldots,\alpha/\delta(t_n)>$ is not in $\alpha(P)$.

(=): If either $\delta(t)$ or $\delta(s)$ has no value, δ does not satisfy $(=ts)$; otherwise, δ satisfies $=ts$ if $\alpha/\delta(t)$ and does not satisfy $=ts$ if $\alpha/\delta(t)$ is not $\alpha/\delta(s)$.

The Frege/Carnap theory only requires $(^1)+$. No modifications to the versions of (P) or (=) given in section 11.7.3 are required.

This leaves supervaluationist and Meinongian theories. Both deny that all terms (including names as well as descriptions) must denote existing objects (that is, objects in D). They differ over whether terms that do not denote existing objects have no value, or instead denote other objects. This difference aside, rejecting the notion that each term must denote an object in D is the characteristic feature of what is called "free logic." Free logic is free of the supposition that all terms must denote existing objects. It is marked by having a use for the existence symbol, E, to designate the difference and by the employment of sentences of the form Et in derivation and tree rules. E was introduced into the vocabulary and syntax of PL^1 in chapter 10.3.5, but E and sentences of the form Et have not figured in the account of description theories given up to now. They will play an important role from here on.

Because supervaluationist and Meinongian theories are variants of free logic, it is illuminating to present them in parallel.[6]

The account that follows mixes denotation and satisfaction conditions together for the same reason that the syntax for PL^1 mixes formation rules for terms and sentences together. The values of complex terms can only be specified by appeal to prior determinations concerning the satisfaction of open sentences. Consider first the definition of an interpretation (or a "partial interpretation" on supervaluationist semantics).

Supervaluationist Interpretations

A **partial** interpretation, I, of **SPL[1] (supervaluationist description theory)** has **two** components, D and α.

(i) D is a **possibly empty,** possibly (but not necessarily) infinite set of objects, $\{o_1, o_2, o_3, \ldots\}$ called the domain of I.

(ii) α assigns:

- exactly one of T and F to **0 or more** zero-place predicates

- exactly one object, o, from D to **0 or more** names

- where n is greater than 0, a (possibly empty) set of lists of n (not necessarily distinct) objects from D to each n-place predicate, P.

Meinongian Interpretations

An interpretation, I, of **MPL[1] (Meinongian description theory)** has **four** components, $\mathbb{D}$, D, α, and α_2.

(i) **$\mathbb{D}$ is a possibly empty,** possibly (but not necessarily) infinite set of objects, $\{o_1, o_2, o_3, \ldots\}$, called the **outer** domain of I.

(ii) **D is a subset of $\mathbb{D}$, called the local domain of I.**

(iii) α assigns:

- exactly one of T and F to **each** zero-place predicate

- exactly one object, o, from $\mathbb{D}$ to **each** name

- where n is greater than 0, a (possibly empty) set of lists of n (not necessarily distinct) objects from $\mathbb{D}$ to each n-place predicate, P.

(iv) **α_2 is a secondary assignment of objects in $\mathbb{D}$ but not in D to terms selected by $(^1)^\wedge$. It and $(^1)^\wedge$ are discussed below.**

The differences between the theories start with the character of the interpretation. SPL[1] recognizes partial interpretations, which need not make assignments to all the zero-place predicates or all the names (though they can). MPL[1] requires α to assign a truth value to each zero-place predicate and an object to each name. The object need not come from D, providing for the possibility of names that do not denote existing objects. Though MPL[1] does not work with partial interpretations, the introduction of α_2 entails that it does work with a (single) extension on an original assignment.

SPL[1] takes improper terms to have no value and so has no need for an outer domain. MPL[1] assigns improper terms to objects in an outer domain. On the version of MPL given above, the outer domain includes all the objects in the local domain, so it is specified that improper terms are assigned objects that are in $\mathbb{D}$ but not in D.

Both SPL[1] and MPL[1] allow that domains can be empty. On SPL[1], when D is empty, α makes no assignments to names or higher-place predicates. The same holds on MPL[1] when $\mathbb{D}$ is empty. But on MPL[1], as long as there are objects in $\mathbb{D}$, α must assign one of them to each name, even if none of those objects is also in D.

Simple Denotation in SPL[1]

(p): **Either** $\alpha(p)$ is exactly one object, o, in D **or** $\alpha(\mathbf{p})$ **has no value.**

(χ): A variable assignment, δ, on an interpretation, I, assigns exactly one object from D to each variable, χ.

Simple Denotation in MPL[1]

(χ): A variable assignment, δ, on an interpretation, I, assigns exactly one object from D to each variable, χ.

MPL[1] has no need to specify the denotation of names. That is already taken care of by the definition of an interpretation. SPL[1] needs to comment on what happens when α makes no assignment to a name.

In both SPL[1] and MPL[1], δ is used to determine which descriptions are proper, so it is worth noting that δ's are in each case restricted to assigning objects from D to variables. In SPL[1] variable assignments cannot be partial. Each variable must receive an assignment on each δ. In MPL[1], the assignments must all be drawn from D, not from objects that are in $\mathbb{D}$ but not in D.

The satisfaction conditions for MPL[1] are identical to those given in section 7.7.3, but for the addition of (E).

Satisfaction in MPL[1]

(E): δ satisfies Et if and only if $\alpha/\delta(t)$ is in D; otherwise δ does not satisfy Et.

Though the other satisfaction conditions are drawn from section 7.7.3, note that MPL[1] allows α to assign objects that are in $\mathbb{D}$ but not in D to names and predicates. Consequently, MPL[1] countenances variable assignments that satisfy sentences like "Pegasus has wings" even when the object assigned to "Pegasus" is not in D.

SPL[1] does not go so far. It does not want any object to be assigned to an improper term. It insists that such terms simply lack a value, and it rewrites the satisfaction conditions of section 11.7.3 to specify what happens in this case.

Satisfaction in SPL[1]

($\bot$): No δ satisfies $\bot$.

(P): **If any item on $\langle\alpha/\delta(t_1),\ldots,\alpha/\delta(t_n)\rangle$ has no value $\delta(P(t_1\ldots t_n))$ is undetermined; otherwise,** δ satisfies $P(t_1\ldots t_n)$ if $\langle\alpha/\delta(t_1),\ldots,\alpha/\delta(t_n)\rangle$ is in $\alpha(P)$ and does not satisfy $P(t_1\ldots t_n)$ if $\langle\alpha/\delta(t_1),\ldots,\alpha/\delta(t_n)\rangle$ is not in $\alpha(P)$.

As a special case of (P), if a 0-place predicate, P, has no value on α, $\delta(P)$ is undetermined; otherwise δ satisfies P if $\alpha(P)$ is T and does not satisfy P if $\alpha(P)$ is F.

(=): **If neither $\delta(t)$ nor $\delta(s)$ has a value, $\delta(=ts)$ is undetermined; otherwise,** δ satisfies =ts if $\alpha/\delta(t)$ is $\alpha/\delta(s)$ and does not satisfy =ts if $\alpha/\delta(t)$ is not $\alpha/\delta(s)$.

(E): δ satisfies Et if and only if $\alpha/\delta(t)$ is in D; otherwise δ does not satisfy Et..

(~): **If $\delta(P)$ is undetermined, $\delta(\sim P)$ is undetermined; otherwise** δ satisfies ~P if it does not satisfy P and does not satisfy ~P if it satisfies P.

(bc): **If $\delta(P)$ or $\delta(Q)$ is undetermined, $\delta(P$ (bc) $Q)$ is undetermined where (bc) is any binary connective; otherwise,** (&), ($\vee$), ($\rightarrow$), and ($\equiv$) hold as stated in section 7.7.3.

With two exceptions, when a term lacks a value, a lack of determination percolates upwards, making sentences that contain those terms undetermined. The exceptions are E sentences, which are not satisfied when $\alpha/\delta(t)$ has no value, and = sentences, which are not satisfied when exactly one of the terms does not have a value. E is defined as being satisfied by all and only the objects in ID, so $I\alpha/\delta$ should not satisfy Et when t has no value. = is defined as a relation between terms that have the same value on $I\alpha/I\delta$, so if one term is assigned a value by $I\alpha/I\delta$ and the other is not, they do not have the same value, and $I\delta$ should not satisfy =ts. (MPL[1] reaches the same conclusion about E sentences for the same reason. It reaches and the same conclusion about = sentences on the premise that if one term denotes an object in D and the other does not, the two objects cannot be the same.)

Complex Denotation in SPL[1]

(^{1})x: If $^1\chi P$ is a definite description, then if there is exactly one object, o, in ID such that $I\delta[o/\chi]$ satisfies P, $I\delta(^1\chi P)$ is o; **otherwise $I\delta(^1\chi P)$ has no value.**

> ### Complex Denotation in MPL[1]
>
> $(^1)^\wedge$: If $^1\chi P$ is a definite description, then if there is exactly one object, o, in D such that $\delta[\alpha/\chi]$ satisfies P, and P does not contain any terms that denote an object that is not in D, $\delta(^1\chi P)$ is o; **otherwise, $^1\chi P$ denotes an object in $\mathbb{D}$ that is not in D as assigned by** α_2.

In applying $(^1)$x in cases where $^1\chi P$ contains names or lower-level descriptions that have no value, it is considered that if for each o $\delta[o/\chi](P)$ is undetermined (because P contains a term that has no value), then $\delta(^1\chi P)$ has no value. In applying $(^1)^\wedge$, the requirement that P not contain any terms that denote objects that are not in D likewise prevents δ from making an assignment to higher-level descriptions containing improper lower-level terms.

As presented so far, SPL[1] looks like the three-valued, Bochvar semantics described in appendix 5.2, but for using "is undetermined" where Bochvar semantics uses N. Were that the case, the semantics would dictate that =tt has no value when t is improper, and so that =tt is not valid. But in SPL[1], what has no value can have a supervalue. The semantics of partial interpretations is not the full semantics. The gaps left by I are (sometimes) filled by completions and by supervaluations based on those completions. To fill the gaps, SPL[1] takes three further steps.

A "completion," I′, of a partial interpretation, I, is defined as follows:

> ### (def cp)
>
> *(definition of a completion of a partial interpretation)*
>
> An interpretation, I′, is a completion of a partial interpretation, I, if and only if:
>
> (i)   ID is a subset of I′D
>
> (ii) I′α assigns:
>
>   (ii.a)   exactly one of T and F to each zero-place predicate that has no value on Iα
>
>   (ii.b)   exactly one object, o, from I′D to each name that has no value on Iα
>
>   (ii.c)   where n is greater than 0, a (possibly empty) set of lists of n (not necessarily distinct) objects from I′D to each n-place predicate, P, in such a way that Iα(P) is a subset of I′α(P)
>
>   (ii.d)   exactly one object, o, from I′D to each definite description that has no value on I.

In sum, (i) I′ can add objects to I′D that are not in ID, but it cannot remove any that are in ID; (ii.a) I′α can fill truth value gaps left by Iα, but it cannot change any truth values assigned by I′α; (ii.b) I′α must assign an object to each name without altering assignments of objects to names already made by Iα; (ii.c) I′α can add n-place lists of objects from I′D to the extension of n-place predicates, but it cannot remove or alter any lists already added by Iα. As a consequence, whatever predicate sentences are satisfied by Iδ must still be satisfied by I′δ, but predicate sentences that are not satisfied by Iδ can be satisfied by I′δ.

(ii.d) does the same job for SPL[1] that α_2 does for MPL[1] and that 0 does for Frege/Carnap semantics. Like α_2, (ii.d) assigns an arbitrarily selected object to each improper description. It just draws these objects from D rather than an outer domain. For each different object that might be selected from D, there is a different completion of I that selects that object.

The completions of an interpretation no longer determine a supervaluation, as they did on the account of appendix 5.1. Each completion must be corrected in light of a comparison of its verdicts with the verdicts made by I. A "correction," I⋆, of a completion, I′, is defined as follows:

> ### (def cc)
>
> *(definition of a correction of a completion)*
>
> A correction, I⋆, of a completion, I′, of an interpretation, I, is an interpretation such that for each atomic sentence, P
>
> • If Iδ satisfies P then I⋆δ satisfies P
>
> • if Iδ does not satisfy P then I⋆δ does not satisfy P
>
> • if I(P) is undetermined then I⋆δ(P) is I′δ(P).

Corrections are necessary because the existence of predicate, identity, and existence sentences gives rise to a situation that did not exist in SL. In SL, no completion of an interpretation could alter the verdicts already drawn by an interpretation. The completions just filled the gaps. But in predicate logic, values are not simply assigned to sentence letters, but determined by more fundamental assignments to names and predicates. Completions make further assignments to the domain, to names, and to predicates, and those assignments have an impact on satisfaction and so on truth. This makes it possible for a completion to undo some of the work done by the interpretation it completes. Corrections rectify that outcome wherever it occurs. When $I'\delta$ satisfies a predicate, identity, or existence sentence that was not satisfied by $I\delta$, or when it does not satisfy one that was satisfied by $I\delta$, that verdict is "corrected" by $I\star\delta$, which reinstates $I\delta$'s original verdict. ($I'\delta$'s other verdicts continue to be retained by $I\star\delta$). This further layer of valuation is in keeping with the project of restricting completions to filling gaps in what I has done and prohibiting them from changing what I has already decided.

Without corrections, (def supertruth) would validate Et, which says that each name and each description must denote an object in D (because by definition each completion assigns an object from D to each name and each description). But a principal purpose of SPL^1 is to serve as a semantics for a free logic, that is, a logic that denies that every term must denote an existing object. That is equivalent to denying the validity of Et. Correcting completions ensures that supervaluations will reflect that result.

Corrections also have implications for the treatment of predicate and identity sentences. Suppose o is the one object in ID that is in $\alpha(P)$ and that o is also in $\alpha(Q)$. Then $I\delta[o/x](x)$ is the one object in ID that is in $\alpha(P)$, so $I\delta(^1xPx)$ is o, which means that $I\delta$ satisfies Q^1xPx. A completion could add an extra object to the domain and expand the extension of $\alpha(P)$ to include that object, thereby making ^1xPx improper. It could then assign some object that is not in $\alpha(Q)$ to this improper description, which would mean that $I'\delta$ would not satisfy Q^1xPx. Similar shenanigans can be envisioned with identity sentences when both t and s are proper or one is proper and the other is not. Correcting completions cancels such results.

As a final step, supervaluations are defined by appeal to corrected completions, rather than completions.

(def supertruth)

A sentence, P, is:

- true on the supervaluation, SI, on an interpretation, I, (supertrue on I) if and only if δ satisfies P on each corrected completion of I. (Notation: SI(P) is T)

- false on SI (superfalse on I) if and only if δ does not satisy P on any corrected completion of I. (Notation: SI(P) is F)

- undetermined on SI in all other cases.

On this account, =tt continues to be true on any interpretation, even those on which t is improper. When t is improper on an interpretation, I, any completion, I', of I must assign it to exactly one object in ID. Under that condition, =tt must be satisfied on any completion of any interpretation. By the third bullet of (def cc), when I(P) is undetermined $I\star$ is allowed to follow the verdict reached by I'. By (=), when t is improper on an interpretation, I, I(=tt) is undetermined. So =tt must be true on any correction of any completion of any interpretation on which t is improper. Of course, it must also be true on any interpretation on which t is proper.

As noted in appendix 5.1, SPL^1 makes modifications to the definitions of intensional concepts to accommodate the fact that sentences can be undetermined on a supervaluation. (MPL^1 requires no such revisions.)

A sentence, P, is:

- S-valid (supervalid) if and only if there is no supervaluation on which it is not true (that is, on which it is either false or undetermined)

- S-unsatisfiable if and only if it there is no supervaluation on which it is true

- S-contingent if and only if there is at least one supervaluation on which it is true and at least one supervaluation on which it is not true.

A set, Γ, is:

- S-unsatisfiable if and only if there is no supervaluation on which each sentence Γ is true

> - S-satisfiable if and only if there is a supervaluation on which each sentence in Γ is true.
>
> A demonstration, Γ / P, is:
>
> - S-valid if and only if there is no supervaluation on which each sentence in Γ is true and P is not true
> - S-invalid if and only if there is a supervaluation on which each sentence in Γ is true and P is not true.
>
> Two sentences, P and Q, are:
>
> - S-equivalent if and only if there is no supervaluation on which one is true and the other is not true
> - S-nonequivalent if and only if there is a supervaluation on which one is true and the other is not true.

In sentential logic, any sentence that is undetermined on one supervaluation must be true on at least one completion and false on at least one completion and so true on at least one supervaluation and false on at least one supervaluation. But in predicate logic completions must be corrected before supervalues are determined. As instanced by some of the following exercises, this makes it possible for there to be sentences that are undetermined on a supervaluation but not false on any supervaluation, and sentences that are undetermined on a supervaluation but not true on any supervaluation. As already noted in appendix 5.1 (p.137), all the intensional concepts tabulated above "designate" truth. But it turns out that further categories need to be recognized, even if they are only described and not named.

Exercise 11.12

1. *Determine the value of the following sentences in (i) MPL¹ (ii) SPL¹ on the following system-specific interpretations. Also comment on what truth values the sentences would have on Russellian and Frege/Carnap semantics on the interpretation provided for SPL¹. For the latter, consider the result of taking each of 1, 2, and 3 in turn to be the designated object.*

   MPL¹:
   $\mathbb{D}$:　{1,2,3,4}
   D:　{1,2,3}
   α:

   　a: 2; b: 3
   　G: {<1,1>, <1,2>, <1,3>, <2,1> <2,3>}
   　H: {1}; K: {2,4}

   α_2:　All improper terms are 4

   SPL¹:
   D: {1,2,3}
   a: 2; b: 3
   G: {<1,1>, <1,2>, <1,3>, <2,1> <2,3>}
   H: {1}; K: {2}

   ★a. H¹yG(ya)
   　b. H¹yG(ay)
   ★c. G¹yG(ay)a
   　d. K¹yG(yy)
   ★e. = ¹x~Hx ¹yKy
   　f. = ¹xG(¹yG(ay)x) ¹x~Kx
   ★g. K¹x(G(¹yH(y)x) → Kb)
   　h. K¹x(Kx ≡ ~Hx)

2. *Establish the following in both MPL¹ and SPL¹. Do this by supposing that there is an interpretation of the right sort and reasoning back from assignments to compounds to assignments to components to discover the conditions this interpretation must satisfy. If a contradiction does not emerge, devise and verify an interpretation that satisfies the conditions. If a contradiction does emerge, it demonstrates that there is no such interpretation. Solutions to the ★ exercises in this set provide illustration.*

   ★a. G¹xGx is p-invalid / S-invalid.
   　b. G¹x~=xx is p-satisfiable / not false on at least one supervaluation.

★**c.** G^1xGx, Ga, Gb / =ab is p-invalid / S-valid. *(Hint: find a contradiction in the claim that it is S-invalid. What must I be like if it is not to have a completion on which a premise is false? The disagreement between MPL^1 and SPL^1 in this case is discussed in section 14.4.4.)*

   d. $= a \ ^1x=xa$ is p-invalid / S-invalid. *(This says that "a" is the one x that is "a." Note that, like definite descriptions, names need not have an object in D assigned to them. Though this sentence is S-invalid [not true on at least one supervaluation], it is not false on any supervaluation; explain why.)*

★**e.** $G^1xHx \rightarrow G^1yHy$ is p-invalid / S-invalid.

   f. $= \ ^1x=xx \ ^1x\sim=xx$ is p-satisfiable / not false on at least one supervaluation. *(Hint: $^1x=xx$ is improper on any interpretation with more than one object in its domain or an empty domain.)*

3. *Determine whether the following assertions are true on both MPL^1 and SPL^1 semantics.*

  ★**a.** $E^1xGx \vDash = \ ^1xGx \ ^1yGy$

    b. E^1xGx, Ga, Gb $\vDash$ =ab

  ★**c.** $\vDash = \ ^1x\sim=xx \ ^1x\sim=xx$

    d. Ea, $= a \ ^1xGx \vDash G^1xGx$ *(★solution for SPL^1)*

  ★**e.** Ea $\vDash = a \ ^1x=xa$ *(if a denotes an existing object, then "a" is the one x that is "a")*

    f. $E^1xGx \vDash G^1xGx$

Discussion of trees for sentences containing definite descriptions is postponed until section 16.5.4. On any semantics for definite descriptions, the tree rules are more perspicaciously formulated using a more powerful language than PL^1.

Notes

1 Preface any sentence, P, containing a description, $^1\chi Q$, with $(^1\chi Q)$. For example, formalize, "The present king of France is bald" as $(^1Kx)B^1xKx$. Denying that there is a bald present king of France is then formalized as $\sim(^1xKx)B^1xKx$ and asserting that there is a present king of France who is not bald as $(^1xKx)\sim B^1xKx$. Compare the syntax for $\forall\chi$ and $\exists\chi$ introduced in chapter 12.

2 Frege (1892: 40–1), Carnap (1956: 32–9). The account that follows is loosely based on Kalish, Montague, and Mar (1980: 306–45). Kalish, Montague, and Mar (1980: 395–402) offers a detailed contrast between the implications of this theory and Russell's.

3 Notably in Meinong (1904).

4 Russell (1920: 209–10); Quine (1948).

5 See, for instance, Routley (1966, 1980), and Priest (2005), both of whom respond to Russell and Quine at some length.

6 The supervaluationist semantics presented here is based on that found in Bencivenga, Lambert, and van Fraassen (1991).

References

Bencivenga, Ermanno, Lambert, Karel, and van Fraassen, Bas C, 1991, *Logic, Bivalence and Denotation*, 2nd edition, Ridgeview, Atascadero, CA.

Carnap, Rudolf, 1956, *Meaning and Necessity,* University of Chicago Press, Chicago, IL.

Chisholm, Roderick M, 1981, *Realism and the Background of Phenomenology*, reprint edition, Ridgeview, Atascadero, CA.

Frege, Gottlob, 1892, "Über Sinn und Bedeutung," *Zeitschrift für Philosophie und philosophische Kritik,* 100: 25–50. English translation by Max Black in Geach and Black, 1980.

Geach, Peter, and Black, Max, 1980, *Translations from the Philosophical Writings of Gottlob Frege,* 3rd edition, Blackwell, Oxford.

Kalish, Donald, Montague, Richard, and Mar, Gary, 1980, *Logic: Techniques of Formal Reasoning*, 2nd edition, Harcourt Brace Jovanovich, San Diego.

Meinong, Alexius, 1904, "Über Gegenstandstheorie," in *Untersuchung zur Gegenstandstheorie und Experimentalpsychologie,* JA Barth, Leipzig, 1–51. Translated in Chisholm (1981).

Priest, Graham, 2005, *Towards Non-Being,* Clarendon Press, Oxford.

Quine, Willard Van Orman, 1948, "On What There Is," *Review of Metaphysics* 2: 21–38.

Routley, Richard, 1966, "Some Things Do Not Exist," *Notre Dame Journal of Formal Logic,* 7: 251–76.

———, 1980, *Meinong's Jungle,* Research School of the Social Sciences, Canberra.

Russell, Bertrand, 1920, *Introduction to Mathematical Philosophy*, George Allen & Unwin, London.

A-5

Advanced Topics for PSL

The advanced topics taken up in this chapter deal only with PSL. The demonstration of parallel points for PLf requires going on at some length to address minor complications in ways that are not particularly instructive and that do not further illuminate the principal line of demonstration. The topics taken up here are either ancillary to those taken up in chapter A-6 (dealing with them now makes it unnecessary to deal with them later) or are important preliminaries. They are demonstrated by making modifications to the demonstrations of the corresponding principles of SL. In some cases, the demonstrations merely add clauses to cover the innovations introduced by PSL. In these cases, the innovations are in bold. Many of the demonstrations establish points that might be considered intuitively obvious. The one that may be of most concern is the demonstration of lemma 1 (the basis clause) of the demonstration of the completeness of Tp. It establishes that the bin method for constructing revised denotation assignments (chapter 11.4) will never yield incomplete or inconsistent results.

Following a policy instituted in section A-4.4, this chapter demonstrates only the soundness of Dp and the completeness of Tp. The fact that p-trees can be converted to derivations, which is a minor extension of a point demonstrated in chapter A-3.4, makes it possible to establish the soundness of Tp and the completeness of Dp without the need for direct demonstrations.

A-5.1 Extensionality and Variance

A-5.1.1 Extensionality

According to the extensionality principle for sentences of PSL, now called the sentence extensionality principle, if P contains one or more occurrences of Q and I(Q) is I(R) then I(P) is **I**(P(R ⫿ Q)), where P(R ⫿ Q) is the result of replacing one or more occurrences of Q in P with R. The demonstration that was given in section A-1.3 for the extensionality of the sentences of SL works just as well to prove that of sentences of PSL, with minor modifications to reflect the changed terminology (for instance, putting "p-equivalent" for "s-equivalent").

However, in PSL extensionality takes on a further form, that of name extensionality or n-extensionality. Name extensionality applies to names that have been assigned the same value rather than components that have been

DOI: 10.4324/9781003026532-19

assigned the same value. Take P to be a sentence containing zero or more occurrences of q. Take $P(r \mid q)$ to refer to any result of replacing zero or more occurrences of q in P with occurrences of r. Then according to the name extensionality principle, if q and r denote the same object on $I\alpha$, P and $P(r \mid q)$ must have the same value on I. For example, if $I\alpha(a)$ is $I\alpha(b)$, then $I(Caa)$ is T if and only if each of Cab, Cba, and Cbb is T on I.

> **Name Extensionality**
>
> If $I\alpha(q)$ is $I\alpha(r)$ then $I(P)$ is $I(P(r \mid q))$

Name extensionality is proven by mathematical induction on the sentences of PSL grouped by the number of occurrences of connectives in those sentences. The first group contains all the sentences with 0 occurrences of connectives (the atomic sentences). The second group contains all the sentences with one connective, e.g., ~Ba and =ab & Bc. The third group contains all the sentences with two occurrences of connectives, e.g., ~~=ab, ~Ha ∨ Ba. And so on.

> *Basis:* All sentences of PSL with 0 occurrences of connectives are n-extensional.
>
> *Induction:* If all sentences of PSL with from 0 to k occurrences of connectives are n-extensional, then all sentences with $k+1$ occurrences of connectives are n-extensional.
>
> ___
>
> *Conclusion:* All sentences of PSL are n-extensional.

Demonstration of the basis: Suppose P contains 0 occurrences of connectives. Suppose further that $I\alpha(q)$ is $I\alpha(r)$. Since P contains 0 occurrences of connectives it might be ⊥ or a zero-place predicate sentence, a higher-place predicate sentence, or an identity sentence.

> *Case one:* If P is ⊥ or a zero-place predicate sentence then it does not contain any occurrences of names and therefore P and $P(r \mid q)$ are identical, since substituting r for q does not make any changes to P. So, $I(P)$ is the same as $I(P(r \mid q))$ in this case.
>
> *Case two:* If P consists of an n-place predicate and n individual names where n is greater than 0, there are two possibilities: it might be that none of these names is q or that one or more of them is.
>
> > *Case two(a):* If q does not occur in P then P and $P(r \mid q)$ are identical since substituting r for q does not make any changes to P. So $I(P)$ is the same as $I(P(r \mid q))$ in this case.
> >
> > *Case two(b):* P contains one or more occurrences of q. In this case P is of the form $Pp_1 \ldots p_n$ where one or more of $p_1 \ldots p_n$ is q. Then the following chain of consequences holds in both directions (from 1 down to 4 and 4 back up to 1):

> > > 1. $I(Pp_1 \ldots p_n)$, where one or more of $p_1 \ldots p_n$ is q, is T.
> > > 2. $\langle \alpha(p_1), \ldots, \alpha(p_n) \rangle$, where one or more of $p_1 \ldots p_n$ is q, is in $\alpha(P)$.
> > > 3. $\langle \alpha(p_1(r \mid q)), \ldots, \alpha(p_n(r \mid q)) \rangle$ is in $\alpha(P)$.
> > > 4. $I(Pp_1 \ldots p_n)(r \mid q)$, is T.

1   is the case if and only if 2 is by (P).

2   is the case if and only if 3 is because each of $p_1 \ldots p_n$ either is q or it isn't. If it isn't then it is unchanged in $\langle \alpha(p_1(r \mid q)), \ldots, \alpha(p_n(r \mid q)) \rangle$. If it is q, then by supposition $\alpha(q)$ is $\alpha(r)$, so the same object is still denoted as occupying that place on the list, whether r replaces q or not. Consequently, $\langle \alpha(p_1(r \mid q)), \ldots, \alpha(p_n(r \mid q)) \rangle$ must be the same list of objects as $\langle \alpha(p_1), \ldots, \alpha(p_n) \rangle$. If the one is in $\alpha(P)$ the other must be in $\alpha(P)$ as well.

3   is the case if and only if 4 is by (P).

Because this chain of consequences holds in both directions, it follows that $I(P)$ is T if and only if $I(P(r \mid q))$ is T. That in turn means that it is impossible for these two sentences to have different values on I. If one is true, the other must be as well, and if one is false the other cannot be true. So, $I(P)$ is the same as $I(P(r \mid q))$ in this case.

Exercise A-5.1

Prove case three: P is a sentence of the form $=p_1p_2$.

Because cases one to three comprise an exhaustive list of all the possible forms that a sentence of PSL with 0 occurrences of connectives can have, and each case leads to the same consequence, that consequence follows in any case: if P contains 0 occurrences of connectives and $I\alpha(p)$ is $I\alpha(q)$ then $I(P)$ is the same as $I(P(r \mid q))$, that is, if P contains 0 occurrences of connectives then it is n-extensional.

Demonstration of the induction: To abbreviate work, the inductive step is demonstrated just for sentences of the lean language. Like the lean language for SL the lean language for PSL contains just one connective, $\rightarrow$.

Suppose for purposes of conditional proof that all the sentences of PSL with from 0 to k occurrences of connectives are n-extensional. Any sentence P with k+1 occurrences of connectives must contain at least one connective and so must have the form $Q \rightarrow R$. On any interpretation on which $I\alpha(q)$ is $I\alpha(r)$, the following chain of consequences holds in both directions:

1. $I(Q \rightarrow R)$ is T.
2. Either $I(Q)$ is F or $I(R)$ is T.
3. Either $I(Q(r \mid q))$ is F or $I(R(r \mid q))$ is T.
4. $I((Q \rightarrow R)(r \mid q))$ is T.

1   is the case if and only if 2 is by $(\rightarrow)$.
2   is the case if and only if 3 is because each of Q and R must contain k or fewer occurrences of connectives (so that the sum of the occurrences of connectives in both is exactly k). In that case, by the inductive hypothesis (all sentences of PSL with from 0 to k occurrences of connectives are n-extensional) both Q and R are n-extensional. Since $\alpha(p)$ is $\alpha(q)$, it follows that $I(Q)$ must have the same value as $I(Q(r \mid q))$ and $I(R)$ must have the same value as $I(R(r \mid q))$.
3   is the case if and only if 4 is by $(\rightarrow)$.

It follows by conditional proof that if $Q \rightarrow R$ contains $k+1$ occurrences of connectives, and $I\alpha(q)$ is $I\alpha(r)$ then $I(Q \rightarrow R)$ is T if and only $I((Q \rightarrow R)(r \mid q))$ is T, that is, if and only if $I(Q \rightarrow R)$ is $I((Q \rightarrow R)(r \mid q))$. By definition of n-extensionality, if $Q \rightarrow R$ contains $k+1$ occurrences of connectives, it is n-extensional.

To sum up, if all the sentences with from 0 to k occurrences of connectives are n-extensional then any sentence with $k+1$ occurrences of connectives is n-extensional.

A-5.1.2 Variance

Given a set of sentences, Γ, of PSL, and an interpretation, I, a variant, J, on I, is an interpretation that uses the same domain that I does, and that makes the same assignments to all the names and predicates in Γ that I does, but that makes zero or more different assignments to one or more names and predicates not in Γ. (It is useful to be able to consider any interpretation to be a variant on itself, hence the allowance that J might not differ from I in any way.)

A-5.1.2.1 The Variant Interpretation Principle

The variant interpretation principle for PSL states that if J is a variant on I with respect to a single sentence, P, then J(P) must be the same as I(P). This needs no demonstration. The value of a sentence, P, of PSL is entirely determined by the domain and the assignments to the names and predicates that occur in P. Where the assignments to the domain, names, and predicates do not vary, as they do not on I and J when J is a variant on I with respect to P, I and J must assign the same value to P.

A-5.1.2.2 The Variant Name Principle

The variant name principle is only slightly more interesting. It states that if a sentence, P, containing one or more occurrences of q is true on an interpretation, I, and r is a name that does not occur in P, then $P(r \mid q)$, the sentence that results from replacing each occurrence of q in P with r must be true on an interpretation, J, that is just like I but for the fact that Jα(r) is Iα(q) (Jα assigns the object that Iα assigns to q to r as well as to q, which it can do since it shares I's domain).

Demonstration of the variant name principle:

1. Suppose for purposes of conditional proof that (i) a sentence, P, containing one or more occurrences of a name, q, is true on an interpretation, I; (ii) r is a name that does not occur in P, (iii) J is an interpretation that has the same domain and makes the same assignments to all the names and predicates in P that I does, and (iv) Jα(r) is Iα(q).
2. From 1(iii) and the fact that q is in P, Jα(q) is Iα(q).
3. From lines 2 and 1(iv), Jα(r) is Jα(q).
4. From line 3 by n-extensionality, J(P) is J(P(r | q)).
5. Since (r | q), that is, putting r for each occurrence of q, is one form that (r | q) can take, from line 4, J(P) is J(P(r | q)).
6. From 1(iii) by the variant interpretation principle, J assigns the same value to P that I does.
7. From lines 6 and 5, J assigns the same value to P(r | q) that I does.
8. From 1(i) and line 7, J(P(r | q)) is T.
9. From lines 1–8 by conditional proof, if P contains one or more occurrences of q, I(P) is T, r is a name that does not occur in P, and J is an interpretation that is just like I except that Jα(r) is Iα(q), then J(P(r | q)) is T.

Exercise

Why do the variant interpretation principle and the variant name principle matter?

The variant interpretation principle matters because it is needed to demonstrate the variant name principle. The variant name principle underwrites (Tf), the characteristic rule of pf-trees, which permits identifying a functional term with a name, provided that name is new to the path. A name that is new to the path is like a name that denotes the same object that the functional term denotes on a variant interpretation. This has utility for demonstrating the soundness of Tpf. In chapters 13 and 14, it is shown that derivations and trees for quantified predicate logic must employ an analogous identification rule. This makes the variant interpretation principle central to demonstrating the soundness of those systems as well.

A-5.2 Soundness of Dp

> If L ⊢ P **in Dp** then $\Gamma_L \vDash_p$ P
> where Γ_L is the set of the sentences on L

Like Ds, Dp is shown to be sound by establishing that any derivation in bracket free notation begins with a sequent that is sound and proceeds to derive other sequents in accord with rules that preserve soundness. (Paralleling what was said in section A-2.1, to say that a sequent, L ⊢ P, "is sound" means that Γ_L, the set of sentences on L, p-entails P.) This makes it possible to argue by mathematical induction on the lines of a derivation that the sequent occurring on any line of any derivation in Dp must be sound. Notably the sequent occurring on the last line of any derivation, L ⊢ P, must be sound. That is, $\Gamma_L \vDash_p$ P.

1. Suppose that L ⊢ P in D**p**.
2. By definition of derivability in D**p**, there is a derivation in D**p** that ends with L ⊢ P.
3. The sequent on the first line of any derivation in D**p** is sound. *(Lemma 1)*
4. If the sequents on lines 1 to *k* of a derivation in D**p** are sound, the sequent on line *k*+1 is sound. *(Lemma 2)*
5. From lines 3 and 4 by mathematical induction, the sequent on the last line of any derivation in D**p** is sound.
6. From lines 5 and 2, L ⊢ P must be sound, that is, $\Gamma_L \vDash_p$ P.
7. From lines 1–6 by conditional proof, if L ⊢ P then $\Gamma_L \vDash_p$ P.

The highlighted portions do not indicate the extent of the difference between this version of the soundness demonstration and the version given in chapter A-2.1. Lemma 2 is justified by appeal to the rules of Dp, and Dp includes two rules not found in Ds. One of those rules, (=E), must be shown to preserve soundness. The other, (=I), must be included in the demonstration of lemma 1.

The demonstration of lemma 1 now opens with the observation that the only derivation rules that do not appeal to sequents established on prior lines are (A) and (=I). Accordingly, the sequent on the first line of any derivation in Dp has either the form P ⊢ P or the form ⊢ =pp. The (A) case is demonstrated as it was in chapter A-2.1. The demonstration of the (=I) case is a slightly embellished version of the solution to exercise 11.6#4. After line 6, the derivation is new.

1. Because the only derivation **rules** that do not appeal to sequents established on prior lines **are** (A) **and (=I),** the sequent on the first line of any derivation in Dp must be justified by (A) **or (=I).**
2. **Suppose for purposes of proof by cases on line 1 that the sequent on the first line is justified by (A).**
    3. By (A), the sequent on the first line has the form P ⊢ P.
    4. By the solution to exercise 5.12(a), if a set, Γ, contains a sentence, P, then Γ ⊨ P.
    5. As a special case of this general principle, when Γ is {P}, P ⊨ P.
    6. From lines 3 and 4–5 by definition of "is sound," the sequent on the first line of any derivation in Dp is sound.
7. Suppose for further purposes of proof by cases on line 1 that the sequent on the first line is justified by (=I).
    8. By (=I), the sequent on the first line has the form, ⊢ =pp.
    9. By the solution to exercise 11.6#4, ~=pp is p-unsatisfiable.
    10. By definition of p-unsatisfiability, there is no interpretation on which ~=pp is true.
    11. Given any set, Γ, there can be no interpretation on which all the sentences in Γ are true and ~=pp is true.
    12. By (~), there can be no interpretation on which all the sentences in Γ are true and =pp is false.
    13. By definition of p-entailment, Γ p-entails =pp.
    14. As a special case of this general principle, when Γ is ∅, ⊨ =pp.
    15. From lines 8 and 14 by definition of "is sound" the sequent derived on the first line of any derivation in Dp is sound.
16. Since, according to line 1, the sequent on the first line of any derivation in Dp must be justified by (A) or (=I), and since, from lines 2–6 and 7–15, either way that sequent must be sound, it follows from lines 1, 2–6, and 7–15 by proof by cases that the sequent on the first line of any derivation in Dp is sound.

Lemma 2 is established in the same way it was established in chapter A-2.1, by showing that, for each of the remaining rules, if the antecedent conditions specified by the rule are sound, the inference the rule permits must also be sound. Where the rules that Dp inherits from Ds are concerned, no alterations to the earlier demonstrations are required. Two further demonstrations are needed to cover applications of (=I) and (=E). As was the case in chapter A-2.1, the demonstration of each case involves an appeal to an entailment principle. In chapter A-2.1 those principles were justified by appeal to the solutions to the earlier exercises 5.12(a)–(l). The (=I) entailment principle (Γ ⊨ =pp where Γ is any set of sentences of PSL) is justified by lines 7–15 of the demonstration that was just given for lemma 1. The (=E) entailment principle (if Γ ⊨ =rq or =qr and Γ ⊨ P, then Γ ⊨ P(r⎪q)) is a corollary of the n-extensionality principle of section A-5.1.1.

1. Suppose for purposes of conditional proof that Γ ⊨ =rq or =qr and that Γ ⊨ P.
    2. By definition of p-entailment, on any interpretation, I, on which all the sentences in Γ are true, I(=qr) or I(=rq) and I(P) is T.
    3. By (=), either way, Iα(q) is Iα(r).
    4. By n-extensionality, I(P) is I(P(r⎪q)).
    5. From the last conjunct of line 2 and line 4, I(P(r⎪q)) is T.

6. Since I was previously defined to be any interpretation on which all the sentences in Γ are true, there can be no interpretation on which all the sentences in Γ are true and $P(r \mid q)$ is false.

7. By definition of p-entailment, $\Gamma \vDash P(r \mid q)$.

8. From lines 1–7 by conditional proof, if Γ p-entails =rq or =qr and $\Gamma \vDash P$, then $\Gamma \vDash P(r \mid q)$.

With these entailment principles established, the demonstration of lemma 2 found in section A-2.1 is completed with the addition of the following cases:

Case thirteen: The sequent on line $k+1$ is derived by (=I). Then it must have the form $L_{k+1} \vdash$ =pp (or it would not be justified by (=I)). By the (=I) entailment principle (justified over lines 7–15 of the demonstration of lemma 1 given above), for any set, Γ, $\Gamma \vDash$ =pp, so in the specific case where Γ is Γ_{k+1}, $\Gamma_{k+1} \vDash$ =pp. So, the sequent on line $k+1$ is sound in this case.

Case fourteen: The sequent on line $k+1$ is derived by (=E). Then it must have the form $L_{k+1} \vdash Q(r \mid p)$ and the earlier lines 1 to k must include a line, h, of either the form $L_{k+1} \vdash$ =pr or the form $L_{k+1} \vdash$ =rp, and a line, i, of the form $L_{k+1} \vdash Q$, where Q contains one or more occurrences of p (otherwise, (=E) could not be applied as it requires that the list at each of lines h, i, and $k+1$ be the same). Because lines h and i are prior to line $k+1$, it follows from the inductive hypothesis that $\Gamma_{k+1} \vDash$ =rp (or =pr as the case may be) and $\Gamma_{k+1} \vDash Q$. By the (=E) entailment principle, $\Gamma_{k+1} \vDash Q(r \mid p)$. So, the sequent on line $k+1$ is sound in this case.

A-5.3 Completeness of Tp

> If Γ is **p**-unsatisfiable, it has at least one closed **p**-tree

The completeness of Tp is demonstrated by contraposition. The demonstration proceeds by establishing that if each tree for Γ is open then, even if none has an exhausted path, Γ must be p-satisfiable. From this it follows that if Γ is p-unsatisfiable, it must have at least one closed tree.

1. Suppose for purposes of conditional proof that each tree for Γ is open.

...

n. By ?, Γ is **p**-satisfiable.

$n+1$. From lines 1 to n by conditional proof, if each tree for Γ is open it is **p**-satisfiable.

$n+2$. By contraposition, if Γ is **p**-unsatisfiable it must have a closed tree.

The demonstration is given by showing that if each tree for a set, Γ, is open, then each of the one-step extensions of trees, T_1, T_2, T_3, ... in the canonical series of trees for Γ is open. The demonstration proceeds to show that for each of these trees to be open, each must contain at least one path, θ, that is characterized by certain features that define a canonical tree model, I★. That I★ is a model for all the sentences on θ, and hence for Γ can be demonstrated either by mathematical induction on the number of connectives in sentences of the lean language for PSL (to save work), or by mathematical induction on the length of sentences of PSL if a demonstration for the full language is desired.

If the choice is made to give the demonstration for the full language, length must be defined in a way that ensures that all atomic sentences have the same length, and are shorter than any compound sentence. For Ts this requires excluding numerical subscripts from the length count. For Tp it also requires excluding names, to ensure that sentences like =ab and Aa are shorter than ~A.

Many of the details of the demonstration follow those of the completeness demonstrations given in chapter A-3.2, the solution to exercise A-3.3#2, and section A-4.2. The demonstration is complicated by the fact that in PSL values of higher-place predicate sentences and identity sentences are determined by assignments made to names and predicates. This requires doing some work to show that there will always be a model for the literals on θ, that is, an interpretation on which all the literals on that path are true. Because those literals include higher-place predicate sentences and identity sentences, they cannot just be considered to have T's assigned to them. It must be shown that they must have T's assigned to them as determined by the valuation rules and as determined by what sentences (=E) places on θ.

Extra clauses must also be added to the demonstration of the inductive step to cover the cases where the sentence on θ is a negated identity sentence or a negated higher-place predicate sentence. In the lean language, this means a sentence of the form $=pq \rightarrow \perp$, or a sentence of the form $P \rightarrow \perp$ where P is a higher-place predicate followed by the appropriate number of names.

The revised demonstration given here saves work by following the solution to exercise A-3.3#2 and section A-4.2 in considering just the lean language.

- The lean language for PSL is the lean language for SL supplemented by the identity symbol and the name symbols.
- Lean language trees use (MP), which must be applied as soon as possible after both P and $P \rightarrow \perp$ appear on a path, where P is atomic. (MP) is imported into Tp for this purpose.
- Sentences of the form $=pp \rightarrow \perp$ close a path. (Lean Tp retains ($\perp$I) for this purpose.)
- (T$\rightarrow$) is revised as one would expect, to derive $P \rightarrow \perp$ on a left path and Q on a right path. To prevent infinitely extendible paths, (T$\rightarrow$) is restricted to reducing conditionals that do not have $\perp$ as their consequents.
- When P is atomic, $P \rightarrow \perp$ is treated as a literal and so is not subject to (T$\rightarrow$).
- When $P \rightarrow \perp$ has the form $(Q \rightarrow R) \rightarrow \perp$ it is reduced by a modified version of ($\sim\rightarrow$), called ($\rightarrow\perp$). Unsurprisingly, given that $(Q \rightarrow R) \rightarrow \perp$ is $\sim(Q \rightarrow R)$, it places Q over $R \rightarrow \perp$ on each open path running up to $(Q \rightarrow R) \rightarrow \perp$.
- Because $P \rightarrow \perp$ is considered a literal when P is atomic, (=E) must be performed on it at stage 2 of the canonical method (as explained below).

Exercise A-5.2

Demonstrate that any sentence of the form $=pp \rightarrow \perp$ is p-unsatisfiable.

Revised opening portions of the demonstration of the completeness of Tp: *the canonical method and features a–e of* θ.

1. Suppose for purposes of conditional proof that each tree for Γ is open.
   2. Each tree in the canonical series of trees for Γ is open.

As for Ts, the canonical series of trees is generated by following a canonical method for making one-step extensions of trees. For Tp, the canonical method is as follows:

- T_1 places the sentence with the lowest catalogue number of all the sentences in Γ on top of the tree. Catalogue numbers are determined by assigning a unique two-digit number to each vocabulary element.

Symbol	Numeral	Symbol	Numeral	Symbol	Numeral	Symbol	Numeral
$\perp$	10	0	20	A	30	a	40
$\rightarrow$	11	1	21	B	31	b	41
(	12	•	•	C	32	c	42
)	13	•	•	G	33	d	43
□★	14	•	•	H	34	e	44
=	15	9	29	K	35	f	45

★ Though □ is not used by PSL, its number is left open for it.

(No one needs to know which sentence in Γ has the lowest catalogue number. There must be one, and whichever one it is, it is T_1. These are not instructions for generating the canonical series of trees. They are a definition of that series.)

- Each subsequent tree in the series is a one-step extension of the previous one produced by applying rules of Tp to sentences by repeatedly cycling through three successive stages. All work that can be done at a stage must be done before proceeding to the next stage. When all work at one stage has been exhausted, the next stage in order is taken up. When no work can be done at a stage, work proceeds to the next stage. Stages must be cycled through in order (from first to last and then back to first). It is not permissible to skip a stage if there is work to be done at that stage or to revert to do work at an earlier stage except by way of making a cycle through the later stages.

- At stage 1, all possible applications of (MP), (~→), and (T→) are made to sentences taken in the order they occur from the top of the tree down and including sentences resulting from work at this stage when their turn comes up. When different sentences occur on different paths on the same line they are reduced simultaneously even if this means using multiple rules. Stage 1 must be completed before proceeding to stage 2.

- At stage 2, all possible applications of (=E) are made to sentences taken in the order they occur from the top of the tree down, including = sentences created as a result of work at this stage when their turn comes up. This means going down the tree to the first identity sentence and applying that identity sentence as source to each literal to occur on each path that runs through that identity sentence's location, taking those literals in the order they occur from the top of the path down, including literals generated as a result of work at this stage when their turn comes up and applying (=E) just once to each literal to replace all occurrences of the target name in that literal. After this has been done using the topmost identity sentence as source, the process is repeated using the identity sentence next to the top, and this continues until each identity sentence on the tree has been used as source including identity sentences added to the bottom of paths as a consequence of work at this stage. Stage 2 must be completed before proceeding to stage 3.

- At stage 3, the sentence in Γ with the next lowest catalogue number is placed on the top of the tree. The sequence of stages then recommences. Cycling through the stages continues for as long as there are sentences in Γ to be added, and after that for as long as doing so continues to produce changes on at least one open path. Work stops if the tree closes or a complete cycle through the stages produces no changes on at least one open path. In the last of these cases the path is exhausted.

If none of the trees, T_1, T_2, T_3, … for a set, Γ, of sentences produced by following the canonical method is closed, then each tree for Γ must contain at least one path, θ, that has five features:

Features of θ

(a) ⊥ does not stand alone on any line on θ.

(b) No sentence of the form =pp → ⊥ occurs on θ.

(c) For each nonliteral sentence on θ, at least one of the up to two path extensions of reduction results for that sentence appears on θ in at least one of the subsequent trees in the series.

(d) For each sentence of the form =rq on θ and each literal, P, to occur anywhere on θ, the sentence P(r|q) obtained from P by replacing all occurrences of q in P with occurrences of r (including sentences of the form =rr), is on at least one extension of θ in at least one of the subsequent trees in the series.

(e) Each sentence in Γ occurs on θ in at least one of the subsequent trees in the series.

Features (a) and (b) must be present, because otherwise θ would be closed and the completeness demonstration begins with the supposition that θ is not closed.

Features (c), (d), and (e) must be present, because (i) the canonical method ensures that the turn of each nonliteral sentence on θ to be reduced, the turn of each identity substitution to be performed, and the turn of each sentence in Γ to be added to the head of the tree, will come up at some finite point, and (ii) the placement principle dictates that the results of reducing a sentence on θ or performing an identity substitution to sentences on θ must be entered on each open path that runs up to that sentence. Since the extensions of θ in each subsequent tree in the series are such a path, the results must appear on it.

Following the canonical method ensures that the turn of each nonliteral sentence on θ to be reduced, the turn of each identity substitution to be performed, and the turn of each sentence in Γ to be added to the head of the tree will come up at some finite point, because (1) the method dictates that each nonliteral on θ be reduced in the order it appears from the top down (so none can be overlooked), (2) the method dictates that each identity substitution be performed in the order the involved identity sentences and literals occur from the top down (so no identity substitution can be overlooked), (3) reducing any one nonliteral sentence is a finite process, (4) performing an identity substitution is a finite process, (5) there is only a finite amount of work that can be done at each of the stages, and

(6) the canonical method only allows returning to work at a prior stage by way of a complete cycle through all the stages (which, at each passage through stage 3, involves adding a further sentence from Γ to the head of the tree).

(1) and (2) are obvious. (3) is the case because sentences are reduced only once (and not at all if their complete reduction results already appear on the path) and the results of reducing a sentence are always finite. Each sentence is only finitely long (the demonstration of this result in section A-1.1 is readily updated for lean PSL) and is reduced to a finite number of sentences (never more than four) that are shorter than it is, entered on a finite number of new paths (never more than two[1]), on a finite number of pre-existing paths. Trees start with only one path, each one-step extension never does more than double the number of prior ones, and the product of finite quantities is always finite. So, the situation where there is an infinite task to complete before going on to reduce the next sentence never arises.

(4) is the case because any given source, =rq, is applied to any given target, P, only once, to replace all occurrences of q in P with occurrences of r. As already noted, sentences of PSL are only finitely long. There are consequently only finitely many occurrences of q in P. So, the process of rewriting P while substituting r for each occurrence of q in P must come to an end. As has already been demonstrated, the number of paths on which these results must be entered must be finite, (=E) does not increase their number, and no rule application adds further occurrences of q to P. So, the situation where there is an infinite task to complete before going to apply the source to the next target never arises.

(5.1) Work at stage 1 must come to an end because, when a sentence is reduced, it is replaced by sentences that, on any one path, contain fewer vocabulary elements than the sentence that was reduced. Thus, even though each reduction adds more sentences to be reduced by subsequent one-step extensions (other than (MP) which closes the path to further reductions), only finitely many one-step extensions can occur before all available sentences are reduced to literals, leaving no more work to be done at the stage in question. (T→) is not an exception. Though there could be as many vocabulary elements in the sentence being reduced, $(P \rightarrow Q)$, as there are in the sentence on the left path, $(P \rightarrow \perp)$, either P is atomic, in which case $(P \rightarrow \perp)$ cannot be further reduced, or it has the form $((P_1 \rightarrow P_2) \rightarrow \perp)$, in which case it must be reduced by $(\rightarrow\perp)$, which replaces $((P_1 \rightarrow P_2) \rightarrow \perp)$ with P_1 over $(P_2 \rightarrow \perp)$. In combination, these reduction results contain fewer vocabulary elements than the original $((P_1 \rightarrow P_2) \rightarrow Q)$. In this case, it just takes two rule applications to generate the reduction in number of vocabulary elements.

(5.2) Work at stage 2 must come to an end because the canonical method prohibits any work at stage 3 from being performed while work still remains to be done at stage 2. Since it is only at stage 3 that there is a chance of adding sentences containing new names to the tree, and since it has already been demonstrated that any tree can only contain finitely many finitely long sentences, there can only be finitely many names occurring in finitely many places, and so only finitely many identity substitutions that are possible at any point where work at stage 2 is in progress.

(5.3) Work at stage 3 must come to an end because it only involves doing one thing: adding a finitely long sentence to the head of a tree.

(6) As a consequence of these considerations, each nonliteral on θ must be reduced, each identity substitution must be performed, and each sentence in Γ must be added to the head of the tree. Even if Γ is infinite, since each of the infinitely many sentences in Γ is only finitely long, each has a finite catalogue number and so is only finitely far along in line. Because each of the stages must be completed after a finite number of one-step extensions, cycles through stage 3 must continue for as long as there are sentences in Γ to add to the tree. The turn of any given sentence in Γ to be reduced will therefore come up at some finite point. When Γ is infinite, there is just no end to the finite points at which the turn of the next sentence in line comes up.

Revised continuing portions of the demonstration of the completeness of Tp: *the canonical tree model,* I★, *and properties i–iv of* I★.

A path with features (a)–(e) determines the canonical tree model, I★, which is defined as having the following properties.

Properties of I★

(i) I★α assigns a T to every 0-place predicate that occurs on θ and an F to every other 0-place predicate of PSL.

(ii) I★ makes a provisional denotation assignment, α_1, of "1" to the alphanumerically earliest name to occur on θ, "2" to the next, "3" to the third, and so on. Notation: $\alpha_1(p_n)$ is n, where p_n is the alphanumerically n^{th} name to occur on θ. Where a name, p, does not occur on θ, $\alpha_1(p)$ is 1. I★ then makes a revised denotation assignment, α, that rewrites this initial assignment as follows: for each group of identity sentences, $=p_1q$, $=p_2q$, $=p_3q$, ... occurring on θ and containing the same name, q, in the second position, α reassigns q to the numeral that α_1 assigned to the alphanumerically earliest of $p_1, p_2, p_3, ...$ So $\alpha(q)$ is $\alpha_1(p_e)$, where p_e is the alphanumerically earliest of $p_1, p_2, p_3, ...$

(iii) I★D consists of just the numbers employed in making these assignments (in the case where no names occur on θ, all names are assigned to "1" and I★D is just $\{1\}$).

(iv) For each n-place predicate, P, I★α (P) is the set of all and only those n-place lists of objects that are denoted by n-place lists of names $<p_1...p_n>$ occurring after P in sentences of the form $Pp_1...p_n$ that stand alone (and unnegated) on θ. (If no sentence of the form $Pp_1...p_n$ stands alone on θ, I★α(P) is $\varnothing$.)

For I★ to be not just a tree model (as defined above) but a p-model (as defined in chapter 11), and hence a justification for claims about satisfaction, (1) I★D must contain at least one object, (2) I★α must assign exactly one of T and F to each zero-place predicate sentence, (3) I★α must assign exactly one object in I★D to each name, and (4) I★α must assign a (possibly empty) set of n-place lists of objects to each n-place predicate, where $n > 0$.

I★ satisfies all of these conditions. It has a domain with at least one object in it in virtue of property (iii), which ensures that even if no names appear in any sentence in Γ, all names will at least be assigned 1, which will be in I★D. Because any zero-place sentence must either stand alone on a line of θ or not stand alone on a line of θ, property (i) ensures that Iα★ must assign exactly one of T and F to each zero-place predicate sentence. By definition, I★α_1 assigns a different object to each name. I★α only alters these assignments for those names that appear in identity sentences on θ. In virtue of feature (d) of θ (which requires that $=rq$ be used as source in an $(=E)$ application to itself, yielding $=rr$), each name, p, mentioned in any identity sentence on θ must occur in the second place in at least one identity sentence on θ. By definition I★α assigns exactly one object to p, the same object I★α_1 assigned to the alphanumerically earliest name to occur in an identity sentence on θ ending with p. So each name must be assigned to exactly one object, and these objects must occur in I★D because by property (iii) the objects used by α_1 as revised by α must occur in I★D. Finally, I★ satisfies (4) in virtue of clause (iv).

It is a further question whether the canonical model is a model for the givens that head off θ. Answering that question is the job of the remainder of the completeness demonstration.

Revised completion of the demonstration of the completeness of Tp

Given features (a)–(e) of θ, and properties (i)–(iv) of I★, it can be demonstrated by mathematical induction on the number of connectives in sentences on θ that each sentence on θ must be true on I★.

1. Suppose for purposes of conditional proof that each tree for Γ is open.
2. Each tree in the canonical series of trees for Γ is open.
3. As already explained, each tree in the canonical series of trees for Γ must contain at least one path, θ, with features (a)–(e).
4. Each sentence on θ containing 0 occurrences of connectives is true on the canonical interpretation, I★. *(Lemma 1)*
5. If each sentence on θ containing from 0 to k occurrences of connectives is true on I★, each sentence on θ containing $k+1$ occurrences of connectives is true on I★. *(Lemma 2)*
6. From lines 4 and 5 by mathematical induction, each sentence on θ is true on I★.
7. By feature (e) of θ, all the sentences in Γ are true on I★.
8. By def. satisfaction, Γ is p-satisfiable.
9. From lines 1–8 by conditional proof, if each tree for Γ is open, Γ is p-satisfiable.
10. By contraposition, if Γ is p-unsatisfiable, it must have at least one closed tree.

Whether considering the lean language or the full language, the assertion on line 4 is no longer true by definition of a valuation and so is a lemma. Justifying the lemma requires establishing that I★ assigns a T to all the higher-place predicate sentences and all the identity sentences on θ. The latter requires some work, and incidentally demonstrates that the bin method for producing a revised denotation assignment (chapter 11.4) always makes assignments that verify each identity sentence on θ, provided it is backed up by a correct application of the systematic procedure for applying (=E).

> *Demonstration of lemma 1:* The sentences containing 0 occurrences of connectives are the atomic sentences: the zero-place predicate sentences, higher-place predicate sentences, and identity sentences. So, there are three cases to consider.
>
> *Case one*: P is a zero-place predicate sentence on θ. In this case it follows from property (i) of I★ that I★(P) is T.
>
> *Case two*: P is a higher-place predicate sentence on θ. Then P has the form $Qp_1...p_n$. By (P) and property (iv) of I★, which says that *all* those lists of objects denoted by lists of names following standalone occurrences of Q on θ are are in I★α(Q), $<$I★α(p_1),...,I★ α(p_n)$>$ is in I★α(Q). By (P), I★($Qp_1...p_n$) is T.
>
> *Case three:* P is an identity sentence on θ.

(For an identity sentence, =pq, that occurs on θ to be true on I★, I★α must assign each of p and q to the same object. This must be the case because feature (d) of θ ensures that each of p and q must occur to the right of an alphanumerically earliest name, p_e and q_e respectively, that lies to its left in an identity sentence on θ. q is at least preceded by p in =pq, and p must at least be preceded by itself, since feature (d) of θ requires applying (=E) to =pq to generate =pp. Both q and p must therefore be preceded by p. If p is not the alphanumerically earliest name to precede each of them, for the reason given below the alphanumerically earliest names that do precede each of them, p_e and q_e, must nonetheless be the same name. Consequently, I★α must take p and q to denote the same object, so I★(=pq) is T.)

> 1. Suppose for purposes of conditional proof that =pq is on θ.
>   2. $=q_eq$ is a sentence on θ, since q_e would at least have to be p.
>   3. $=p_ep$ is a sentence on θ since =pp would have to be on θ due to an (=E) application of =pq to itself, so p_e would at least have to be p.
>   4. $=p_eq$ is a sentence on θ from lines 3 and 1 by an (=E) application required by feature (d) of θ (take $=p_ep$ from line 3 as source and =pq from line 1 as target).
>   5. $=q_ep$ is a sentence on θ from lines 1 and 2 by an (=E) application required by feature (d) of θ (take =pq from line 1 as source and $=q_eq$ from line 2 as target).
>   6. p_e is not earlier than q_e from lines 2 and 4 because by definition q_e is the alphanumerically earliest name to occur to the left of q in an identity sentence on θ.
>   7. q_e is not earlier than p_e from lines 3 and 5 because by definition p_e is the alphanumerically earliest name to occur to the left of p in an identity sentence on θ.
>   8. p_e and q_e are the same from lines 6 and 7.
>   9. I★α(q) is $α_1(q_e)$ from line 2 by property (ii) of I★.
>   10. I★α(p) is $α_1(p_e)$ from line 3 by property (ii) of I★.
>   11. I★α(p) is I★α(q) from lines 9, 10, and 8.
>   12. I★(=pq) is T from line 11 by (=).
> 13. From lines 1 to 12 by conditional proof, if =pq is on θ then I★(=pq) is T.

Since cases one to three represent all the kinds of atomic sentences that can exist on θ, and in each case the sentence must be true on I★, it follows that the basis clause is correct: all the sentences with 0 occurrences of connectives on θ must be true on I★.

> *Demonstration of lemma 2:* Suppose for purposes of conditional proof that all the sentences on θ containing from 0 to k occurrences of connectives are true on I★. The aim is to show that making this supposition requires accepting that all the sentences on θ with $k+1$ occurrences of connectives are true on I★. The sentences with $k+1$ occurrences of connectives must contain at least one connective. Since there is only one connective in the lean language, $→$, they must be either (i) sentences of the form P $→$ ⊥ where P is atomic, that is, where P is ⊥ or a zero-place predicate sentence, an identity sentence or a higher-place

predicate sentence, (ii) sentences of the form $P \rightarrow \perp$ where P is compound, or (iii) sentences of the form $P \rightarrow Q$ where Q is not $\perp$. So there are five cases to consider. (The cases are distinguished because the sentences of these forms are either reduced by different rules or are literals that are true on $I^\star$ for different reasons.)

Case one: The sentence with $k+1$ occurrences of connectives has the form $P \rightarrow \perp$ where P is $\perp$ or a zero-place predicate sentence. Then P does not occur on θ. (If it did, an application of (MP) would be required which would result in $\perp$ occurring on θ, and that is ruled out by feature (a) of θ.) In virtue of either ($\perp$) or property (i) of $I^\star$, $I^\star(P)$ is F. So, by ($\rightarrow$), $I^\star(P \rightarrow \perp)$ is T.

Case two: The sentence with $k+1$ occurrences of connectives has the form $=pq \rightarrow \perp$. In this case, q cannot be p, because if it was, feature (b) of θ (no sentence of the form $=pp \rightarrow \perp$ can occur on θ) would be violated. Hence, α_1 must have provisionally assigned different objects to p and q. $I^\star\alpha$ could not have revised this provisional assignment to assign the same object to p and q. Any such revision would require that there be identity sentences of the form $=r_ep$ and $=r_eq$ on θ, where r_e is the alphanumerically earliest name to occur to the left of p and q in an identity sentence on θ. But there could be no such sentences. r_e would have to be either p, q, or some name alphanumerically earlier than either of them. In the first case, an identity sentence of the form $=pq$ occurs on the path; in the second, an identity sentence of the form $=qp$ occurs on the path; in the third, identity sentences of the form $=r_ep$ and $=r_eq$ occur on the path. The first case is impossible because $=pq \rightarrow \perp$ occurs on the path and feature (a) of θ specifies that θ cannot contain $\perp$, which it would (by (MP)) if both $=pq \rightarrow \perp$ and $=pq$ were to occur on θ. The second is also impossible because when both $=qp$ and $=pq \rightarrow \perp$ occur on the path, it follows by feature (d) of θ that $=qp$ will have been used as source in an (=E) application to $=pq \rightarrow \perp$ as target ($=pq \rightarrow \perp$ is a literal of the lean language) yielding $=qq \rightarrow \perp$ on θ, contrary to feature (b) of θ. Finally, the third is also impossible because in that case feature (d) would dictate using $=r_ep$ and $=r_eq$ as sources in (=E) applications to $=pq \rightarrow \perp$ as target eventually yielding $=r_er_e \rightarrow \perp$ on θ, again contrary to feature (b). It follows that $I^\star\alpha(p)$ cannot be the same object as $I^\star\alpha(q)$ and hence that $I^\star$ must assign an F to $=pq$. By ($\rightarrow$), $I^\star(=pq \rightarrow \perp)$, which in this case is $I^\star(P \rightarrow \perp)$, is T.

Case three: The sentence with $k+1$ occurrences of connectives has the form $Qp_1...p_n \rightarrow \perp$. Then it can be proven that for any sentence, $Qr_1...r_n$, that occurs on θ, $<I^\star\alpha(r_1)... I^\star\alpha(r_n)>$ must differ in at least one place from $<I^\star\alpha(p_1)... I^\star\alpha(p_n)>$ (that is, the list of objects denoted by $p_1...p_n$ in $Qp_1...p_n \rightarrow \perp$ cannot be the same as the list of objects denoted by any n names following any occurrence of the Q predicate that stands alone on θ). Consequently, by property (iv) of $I^\star$, which says that *only* those lists of objects denoted by lists of names following standalone occurrences of Q on θ can be in $I^\star\alpha(Q)$, $<I^\star\alpha(p_1)...I^\star\alpha(p_n)>$ is not in $I^\star\alpha(Q)$. By (P), $I^\star(Qp_1...p_n)$ is F. By ($\rightarrow$), $I^\star(Qp_1...p_n \rightarrow \perp)$, which in this case is $I^\star(P \rightarrow \perp)$, is T.

To prove that for any sentence, $Qr_1...r_n$, that occurs on θ the n-place list of objects, $< I^\star\alpha(r_1)...I^\star\alpha(r_n)>$ must differ in at least one place from $<I^\star\alpha(p_1)... I^\star\alpha(p_n)>$, suppose to the contrary that there is a predicate sentence, $Qr_1...r_n$, on θ that is just like $Qp_1...p_n$ except that one or more of $r_1...r_n$ is a different name from $p_1...p_n$, respectively. (All the names could not be the same because it is being supposed that $Qp_1...p_n \rightarrow \perp$ occurs on θ, so $Qp_1...p_n$ cannot occur on θ; otherwise, by (MP), $\perp$ would occur on θ, in violation of feature (a) of θ.) Suppose further that at each position, i, where p_i is not the same name as r_i, $I^\star\alpha(r_i)$ is $I^\star\alpha(p_i)$, that is, they denote the same object on $I^\star\alpha$. As noted when proving case 2, property (ii) of $I^\star$ stipulates that for $I^\star\alpha(r_i)$ to denote the same member of the domain as $I^\star\alpha(p_i)$, the same alphabetically earliest name must occur to the left of each of them in an identity sentence on θ. That alphabetically earliest name could be either r_i itself, p_i itself, or some third name, q_e. In the first case, an identity sentence of the form $=r_ip_i$ occurs elsewhere on θ; in the second, an identity sentence of the form $=p_ir_i$ occurs elsewhere on θ; in the third, identity sentences of the form $=q_er_i$ and $=q_ep_i$ occur elsewhere on θ.

But in each of these cases it follows by feature (d) of θ that the implied (=E) applications must have been made to the literals supposed to exist on θ: the conditional, $Qp_1...p_n \rightarrow \perp$, and the atomic sentence, $Qr_1...r_n$. If $=r_ip_i$ occurs, then r_i must have been substituted for p_i wherever it occurs in $Qp_1...p_n \rightarrow \perp$; if $=p_ir_i$ occurs then p_i must have been substituted for r_i wherever it occurs in $Qr_1...r_n$; and if $=q_er_i$ and $=q_ep_i$ occur then q_e must have been substituted for r_i wherever it occurs in $Qr_1...r_n$ and for p_i wherever it occurs in $Qp_1...p_n \rightarrow \perp$. Because of all these substitutions there would have to be literal sentences on θ of the form R and $R \rightarrow \perp$. But then an application of (MP) is required, resulting in an appearance of $\perp$ on θ, in violation of feature (a) of θ. Since this contradiction arises from supposing that there is a Q-sentence on θ that contains names $r_1...r_n$ that denote the same n-place list of obects as $<p_1...p_n>$ do on $I^\star\alpha$, that supposition must be rejected. It follows that for any sentence, $Qr_1...r_n$, that occurs on θ the n-place list $<I\star\alpha(r_1)... I\star\alpha(r_n)>$ must differ from $<I\star\alpha(p_1)... I\star\alpha(p_n)>$.

Case four: The sentence with $k+1$ occurrences of connectives has the form $(Q \rightarrow R) \rightarrow \perp$. Then it follows from feature (c) of θ that $(Q \rightarrow R) \rightarrow \perp$ has been reduced by $(\rightarrow\perp)$ and consequently that Q and R $\rightarrow \perp$ occur on at least one extension of θ in at least one of the subsequent trees in the canonical series. Since $(Q \rightarrow R) \rightarrow \perp$ contains $k+1$ occurrences of connectives, each of Q and R $\rightarrow \perp$ must contain k or fewer occurrences of connectives. And since it is being supposed that any sentence on θ that contains k or fewer occurrences of connectives is true on I$\star$, I$\star$(Q) and I$\star$(R $\rightarrow \perp$) are T. By ($\perp$), I$\star$($\perp$) is F, so, by (MT), I$\star$(R) is F. By ($\rightarrow$), I$\star$(Q $\rightarrow$ R) is F and I$\star$((Q $\rightarrow$ R) $\rightarrow \perp$) is T. So, in this case the sentence on θ with $k+1$ occurrences of connectives is true on I$\star$.

Case five: The sentence with $k+1$ occurrences of connectives has the form P $\rightarrow$ Q where P is compound and Q is not $\perp$. Then it follows from feature (c) of θ that P $\rightarrow$ Q must have been reduced by (T$\rightarrow$) and consequently that either P $\rightarrow \perp$ or Q occurs on at least one extension of θ in at least one of the subsequent trees in the canonical series.

Suppose P $\rightarrow \perp$ is the sentence that occurs on θ in at least one of the subsequent trees in the series. P must be either atomic or compound.

If P is atomic then, as established over the course of the demonstrations of cases one to three, I$\star$(P) is F. Alternatively, if P is compound then, as established over the course of case four, I$\star$(P), is F.
So, whether P is atomic or compound, I$\star$(P) is F. By ($\rightarrow$), I$\star$(P $\rightarrow$ Q) is T.

Now suppose that Q is the sentence that occurs on θ in one of the subsequent trees in the series. Then, because P $\rightarrow$ Q contains $k+1$ occurrences of connectives, Q must contain k or fewer occurrences of connectives. And since it is being supposed that any sentence on θ that contains k or fewer occurrences of connectives is true on I$\star$, it follows that Q is true on I$\star$. By ($\rightarrow$) that I$\star\alpha$(P $\rightarrow$ Q) is T.

So, either way, in this case the sentence on θ with $k+1$ occurrences of connectives is true on I$\star$.

In all cases, therefore, if all the sentences on θ containing 0 to k occurrences of connectives are true on I$\star$, all the sentences on θ with $k+1$ occurrences of connectives are true on I$\star$.

A-5.4 Tree Conversion; Soundness of Tp; Completeness of Dp

Section A-3.4 described how to convert s-trees into derivations. p-trees differ from s-trees only in the inclusion of results obtained by (=E) and in allowing $\perp$ to be derived directly from sentences of the form ~=pp. Since (=E) is also a derivation rule, any sentence derived on a tree path by (=E) can be derived at the corresponding point in a derivation based on the tree. The more liberal version of ($\perp$I) used on trees can be accommodated by rewriting the version of ($\perp$I) used in Dpt to also permit deriving $\perp$ directly from ~=pp. p-trees can therefore be converted to derivations using only a minor extension to the procedure for converting s-trees to derivations.

Since p-trees can be converted to derivations no dedicated demonstrations of either the soundness of Tp or the completeness of Dp are required. The soundness of Tp can be demonstrated by appeal to the soundness of Dp, and the completeness of Dp by appeal to the completeness of Tp.

Soundness of Tp

1. Suppose for purposes of conditional proof that a set, Γ, has at least one closed tree.
    2. By the tree conversion principle, that tree can be converted to a derivation in Dpt that derives $\perp$ from the initial assumption of a finite list, L, of the sentences in Γ (those that appear as givens on the head of the tree).
    3. By the soundness of Dp, $\Gamma_L \vDash \perp$.
    4. By the solution to exercise 5.12(b) and since Γ is a superset of Γ_L, $\Gamma \vDash \Gamma_L$.
    5. By the solution to exercise 5.11#2a, Γ is p-unsatisfiable.
6. From lines 1–6 by conditional proof, if a set, Γ, has at least one closed tree then Γ is p-unsatisfiable, that is Tp is sound.

Completeness of Dp

1. Suppose for purposes of conditional proof that $\Gamma \vDash_p P$.
2. By def $\vDash_p$, there is no interpretation on which all the sentences in Γ are true and P is false.
3. By (~), there is no interpretation on which all the sentences in Γ are true and ~P is true.
4. By def satisfaction, $\Gamma \cup$ ~P is p-unsatisfiable.
5. By the completeness of Tp, $\Gamma \cup$ ~P has at least one closed tree.
6. To be closed, the tree must be headed off by a finite subset, Γ_L, of sentences in Γ (it could only be headed off by an infinite set if at least one path never closes, allowing a continual addition of further sentences to the head of the tree with each cycle through the stages).
7. By the tree conversion principle, the assumption of each of the sentences on L followed by the assumption of ~P yields $\bot$ in Dpt, where L is any list of all the sentences in Γ_L.
8. By (IP), $\Gamma_L \vdash P$ in Dpt.
9. Whatever can be derived in Dpt can be derived in Dp, so $\Gamma_L \vdash P$ in Dp.
10. From lines 1–9 by conditional proof, if $\Gamma \vDash_p P$ then $L \vdash P$ where L is a finite subset of the sentences in Γ.

Exercise A-5.3

Convert any closed trees discovered in solutions to exercise 11.8#3–6 into derivations.

Answers for 4a, c, e; 5a, c, e; 6c

Note

1 Informal notational conventions are disregarded, so iterated conjunctions and iterated disjunctions are fully punctuated and reduced accordingly.

Part IV

Quantified Predicate Logic

12 Vocabulary, Syntax, and Formalization

Contents

12.1 Informal Vocabulary and Syntax

Whereas PSL formalizes relations between individual objects and predicates, QPL, the language for quantified predicate logic, also formalizes the relations between groups of objects and predicates. Since groups are defined by

DOI: 10.4324/9781003026532-21

predicates (a one-place predicate is a set of one-place lists of objects, that is, a group of objects), this reduces to formalizing relations between predicates. For PSL, the alternatives are few and simple. An object either satisfies a predicate or it does not. For QPL, the possibilities are multiplied. Each of the objects in a group may satisfy a predicate, or only some may, or none, or exactly one, at least one, at most one, at least two, and so on.

To capture this variation, QPL needs to be outfitted with symbols for quantities of objects, and it needs to be able to refer to some or all objects without having to name them.

12.1.1 *Symbols for Objects*

Like PL[1], QPL uses names. It also introduces lower-case x, y, z, into the language. If more than three are needed, x's can be numerically subscripted. These symbols were first used in chapter 10.1 as place holders for predicates. In PL[1] and QPL they are instead used as object variables. Each variable is uninterpreted beyond being taken to denote exactly one object in D. Different variables denote not necessarily distinct objects in D.

Because variables play the same syntactic role as names, the expression, "term," is used to refer to a class that includes both names and variables.

12.1.2 *Symbols for Quantities of Objects*

QPL also needs some way of representing how many of the objects in a group are being spoken of. It does this by introducing a quantity symbol, "∀," called "universal." When used in combination with "=" and the connectives, "∀" can represent any number.

"∀" is read as "All" or "every" or, preferentially, "each." The semantics to be given in chapters 15 and 16 emphasizes that the verdict that *all* the objects in the domain are a certain way is obtained by inspecting *each* individually. "Each" does more to emphasize that background operation.

∀ can be used together with ~ to say the opposite, "~∀," which should be read as "it is not the case that each is …" This is equivalent to saying "at least one is not …"

"∀…~" should be read as "each on its own proves not to be …" This is equivalent to saying "not even one is" or "none are."

"~∀…~" is read as "it is not the case that each is not." Double negative constructions are confusing, so QPL simplifies by introducing a second quantity symbol, ∃, called "existential," which can be read as "at least one is." ∃ is equivalent to ~∀…~.

12.1.3 *Informal Syntax*

Predicate sentences can have multiple places (as in Gx, Hxy, Kxyz), and identity sentences have two places (as in =xy). There needs to be a way of designating what place a quantity symbol refers to. QPL does this by tagging both the place and the quantity symbol with a variable, and then tagging the predicate or identity sentence with the tagged quantity symbol. Tagging the one place in the one-place predicate letter, G, with an x, tagging the universal symbol with an x, and putting the tagged universal symbol in front of the tagged predicate letter produces ∀xGx, which says that each object that the variable x might denote is G. More briefly, each of the objects in the domain is G. ∃yHay says that at least one object the variable y might denote stands in second place with the object named by "a" in an ordered pair in the extension of the H predicate. More briefly at least one of the objects in the domain stands in second place in the H relation to the object denoted by "a." ∃yKayb says that at least one of the objects that y might denote is flanked on the left by the object named by "a" and on the right by the object named b on a three-place list in the extension of the K predicate. ∃x∃y~=xy says that for at least one object that the variable x might denote, at least one object that that the variable y might denote is not the same. In other words, x does not denote the only object in the domain.

The combination of a quantity symbol tagged by a variable, ∀x, ∃y, …, is a quantifier. Syntactically, quantifiers like ∀x constitute a unit. The formal syntax prohibits ∀ and ∃ from occurring without being followed by exactly one variable. It is tempting to express this union by enclosing the quantifier and the following variable in parentheses, but this creates needless clutter.

Tildes may be placed before, after, or in between quantifiers, but never in between the quantity symbol and the variable. So all of ~∀x∀y, ∀x~∀y, and ∀x∀y~ are permissible, but ∀~x is not.

12.2 Formal Vocabulary and Syntax

Vocabulary of QPL	
Names:	a, b, c, d, e, f, a_1, a_2, a_3, …
Variables:	**x, y, z, x_1, x_2, x_3, …**
n-place predicate letters:	A, B, C, G, H, K, A_1, A_2, A_3, … followed by 0 or more places
Contradiction symbol:	⊥
Identity symbol:	=
Quantity symbols:	**∀, ∃**
Connectives:	~, &, ∨, →, ≡
Punctuation marks:	), (

For purposes of work at the keyboard, quantifiers that use ∀ can be replaced with the associated variable in parentheses. ∀x, ∀y, ∀z become (x), (y), (z), respectively. ∃ can be replaced with capital V on the principle (justified in the following chapter) that existentials are like big disjunctions.

The most significant change to the syntax is the addition of a new kind of expression. Up to now, expressions of a formal language have been divided into those that conform to formation rules and those that do not. QPL has two levels of formation rule. Expressions created by following the familiar formation rules are now called formulas. Those formulas need to meet a further condition, to be specified later, to be recognized as sentences.

Quantifiers can be added to formulas but they are not connectives. They do not build a compound sentence that has a value that is a function of the value of its component parts. To accommodate them, QPL recognizes a category of "operators." Operators are of two sorts, connectives and quantifiers.

The following statement of the formation rules for formulas uses Greek lower-case chi (χ), (later supplemented by psi (ψ) and zeta (ζ)) to stand for any variable.

Syntax of QPL
An *expression* is any vocabulary element or sequence of vocabulary elements.
A *quantifier* is a quantity symbol followed by a variable.
A *term* is either a name or a variable.
A *formula* is any expression formed in accord with the following rules:

(P):	If P is an *n*-place predicate and <t_1,…,t_n> is a list of *n* not necessarily distinct **terms**, then $Pt_1…t_n$ is a **formula**. As a special case of (P), if P is ⊥ or a 0-place predicate then P is a **formula**.
(=):	If **t** and **s** are two not necessarily distinct **terms** then =ts is a **formula**.
(~):	If P is a **formula**, then ~P is a **formula**.
(bc):	If P and Q are two (not necessarily distinct) **formulas**, then (P & Q), (P ∨ Q), (P → Q), and (P ≡ Q) are **formulas**.
(Q):	**If P is a formula that contains at least one occurrence of a variable, χ, and no χ quantifier then ∀χP and ∃χP are formulas**
(exclusion):	Nothing is a **formula** unless it has been formed by one or more applications of the preceding rules.

(P) and (=) make it possible to form formulas that contain variables. Whereas in PSL the places in predicates must be filled with names, in QPL they can be filled with names, a combination of names and variables, or variables only. Gab, Gax, and Gxy are all formulas, as are =ab, =ax, and =xy.

(Q) treats quantifiers as unary operators. They work the same way as ~, or □ and ◇ in MSL, or ¹x in PL¹. Provided the conditions stipulated by (Q) are satisfied, formulas can be prefaced with quantifiers in just the way they are prefaced with tildes. Any number of quantifiers may occur in succession in front of a formula and they may be a mixture of ∀ and ∃ quantifiers. Tildes may also be interspersed among them. However, the restrictions on (Q) rule out adding a χ quantifier to a formula that already contains a χ quantifier (∀y∃yGxy cannot be formed by (Q), for example) or a quantifier to a formula that does not contain the variable it quantifies (∀x⊥ and ∃yGx cannot be formed by (Q)). (Q) demands that when a χ quantifier is added to a formula, that formula contain a χ variable, and no previously added χ quantifier.

As with (~), punctuation is never used with quantifiers. If punctuation ever appears before or after a quantifier, it is only because there is a binary connective that uses that punctuation.

Exercise 12.1

Which of the following are formulas of QPL and which are only expressions? If an expression is not a formula, say why not.

★a. ∀∃xyGxy

b. (∀y)(∃x)Gxy

★c. ∃x∀y(Gxy)

d. ∃y(∀xGxy)

★e. ∀x∃yGyx

f. ∀z∃xGxaxy

★g. ∃y∃xGxax

h. ∃xGayx

★i. ∃x∀y∀xGayx

j. ∀x~Hx

★k. ∀x(~Hxy)

l. ~∀x~(~Hxy)

★m. ∀y~∃z~Gxyz

n. ∀x(Gx → ∃yHyx)

★o. (∀xGx) → (∃yHyx)

p. ∀xGx → ∃yHyx

★q. ∀x∃y(Gxy → Hy)

r. ∀x(∃yGxy → Hz)

★s. ∀x∃yGxy → Hz

t. ∀xGx → ∀xHx

★u. ∀x(Gx → ∀xHx)

v. ∃x(Gx → ∀yHy)

★w. ∀wGw

x. ∀x(=xa)

It remains to specify what makes a formula a sentence. This requires a preliminary expansion to the definition of scope, and the introduction of the concepts of a free and a bound variable.

> When ~, ∀χ, or ∃χ is followed by ⊥ or a predicate or identity formula, its scope is that ⊥ or predicate or identity formula.
>
> When ~, ∀χ, or ∃χ is followed by an opening punctuation mark, its scope extends to the corresponding closing punctuation mark.
>
> When ~, ∀χ, or ∃χ is followed by another ~, ∀χ, or ∃χ, its scope is that ~, ∀χ, or ∃χ, plus that ~, ∀χ, or ∃χ's scope.
>
> The scope of &, v, →, and ≡ begins and ends with the punctuation marks used in conjunction with that &, ∨, →, or ≡.
>
> **A *free variable* is a variable that does not fall under the scope of any quantifier naming that variable.**
>
> **A *bound variable* is a variable that falls under the scope of a quantifier naming that variable.**
>
> **A *sentence* of QPL is any formula that contains no free variables.**
>
> **An *open sentence* of QPL is any formula that contains at least one free variable.**

QPL uses all the same names for forms that were used by PSL, except "operator" replaces "connective," "formula" replaces "sentence," and "term" replaces "name" on the list of named forms. The following named forms are new. The notion of an instance is particularly important for chapters 13 and 14.

An expression of the form $\forall\chi$ is a *universal quantifier*.
An expression of the form $\exists\chi$ is an *existential quantifier*.
The connectives and the quantifiers are *operators*.

Formulas that have "~," "&," "∨," "→," or "≡" as their main operators are *connective compounds*.
A formula with $\forall x$ as its main operator is a universally quantified formula or $\forall$ formula. $\forall$ formulas have the form $\forall\chi P$ where "$\forall\chi$" is the main operator and P is the immediate subformula.
A formula with $\exists\chi$ as its main operator is an existentially quantified formula or $\exists$ formula. $\exists$ formulas have the form $\exists\chi P$ where "$\exists\chi$" is the main operator and P is the immediate subformula.
Formulas that have $\forall\chi$ or $\exists\chi$ as their main operators are *quantified formulas*.

An *instance* of a sentence of QPL of the form $\exists\chi P$ or $\forall\chi P$ is the result, $P[q\,|\,\chi]$, of removing the quantifier and replacing each occurrence of χ in P with some name, q. *(The same name must be used in place of each occurrence of χ.)*

$\forall\chi P$ and $\exists\chi\sim P$ are *oppositional duals*.
$\exists\chi P$ and $\forall\chi\sim P$ are *oppositional duals*.

QPL uses the same informal notational conventions as PSL: (b), (ip), (sc), and (op).

Exercise 12.2

1. *Demonstrate by means of syntactic trees and appeal to the syntactic formation rules that each of the following is a formula of QPL. Identify which formulas are sentences and which are open sentences.*
   * **a.** $\forall x Gaxy$
     b. $\forall x(Gx \vee Hx)$
   * **c.** $\forall x Gx \vee Hx$ *(interesting case)*
     d. $\forall x Gx \vee \forall x Hx$
   * **e.** $\forall x=xx$
     f. $\exists x\sim=ax$
   * **g.** $\sim\exists z\sim Gza$
     h. $\sim\exists z\sim\forall y=yz$
   * **i.** $\forall y\exists x Gxy \vee \exists x\forall y Gyx$
     j. $\forall y\forall x Gxy \rightarrow \exists z Hz \vee =x_1 c$
   * **k.** $\forall y\sim\forall x(Gxy \rightarrow \exists z Hz \vee =x_1 c)$
     l. $\forall y\sim(\forall x Gxy \rightarrow \exists z Hz \vee =x_1 c)$
   * **m.** $\forall y\sim\forall x Gxy \rightarrow \exists z Hz \vee =x_1 c$
     n. $(\forall y\sim\forall x Gxy \rightarrow \exists z Hfz) \vee =x_1 c$

2. *Identify the main operator of each of the following formulas.*
   * **a.** $\forall y\forall x Gxy$
     b. $\forall y(\sim Gy \vee Hyx)$
   * **c.** $\forall x Gx \rightarrow Hy$
     d. $\sim\exists x(Gx \& Hx)$
   * **e.** $=ax$
     f. $\exists x\sim Gx \& \sim H$

3. *Give the negation of each of the following formulas.*
   * **a.** $\forall x\sim Gx$
     b. $\sim\forall x Gx$
   * **c.** $\forall x(Gx \rightarrow \sim H)$

    d. ∀xGx → H
 ★e. ~∀xGx → H
    f. ~(~∀xGx → H)

4. *Give an instance of each of the following sentences using "a" as the instantiating name.*
 ★a. ∀xGbx
    b. ∀xGax
 ★c. ∀x∃yGyxx
    d. ∃y∀z∀x(Gax → Hyz)
 ★e. ∃yGy → ∀yHy *(trick question)*
    f. ∃y(Gy → ∀xHyx)

12.3 Formalizing English Sentences in Quantified Predicate Logic

12.3.1 Simply Quantified Sentences; Scope

Sentences of QPL are like sentences of PSL, except that variables can appear in the place of names, and those variables must fall under the scope of a quantifier. ∀ is used to refer to *each* object in the domain. ∃ is used to refer to at least one of them. "∀x" means "for each domain object that variable x might be taken to denote"; "∃x" means "for at least one of the domain objects that variable x might be taken to denote." Taking the domain to be restricted to persons, a sentence like "each person is happy" is formalized in the same way as "Alma is happy," except that the name is replaced with a variable and is universally quantified. Ha becomes ∀xHx. "Alma knows Boda," which might be formalized as Kab, becomes ∃yKyb if *at least one* person knows Boda and ∀zKaz if Alma knows each person.

Since variables stand for what can vary, it does not matter which variable is used in conjunction with ∀ or ∃. "Each person is happy" could just as well be formalized ∀xHx, ∀yHy, or ∀zHz. However, when more than one quantifier is in use, the syntactic rule that quantifiers naming same variables cannot fall within one another's scope must be observed. "Each person knows at least one person" may not be formalized as ∀x∃xKxx. A combination of different variables is required, such as ∀x∃yKxy.

Up to now, it has been a rule that within any one exercise or example, multiple uses of the same variable stand for the same variant. That rule is now restricted. Multiple uses of the same object variable only stand for the same object when they fall within the scope of the same quantifier. When an x variable, for example, falls outside of the scope of an x quantifier, it need not denote the same object as the x variables that fall within that quantifier's scope. Of course, it also goes the other way, as it always has: different variables can denote same variants so a y variable could denote the same object as an x variable, regardless of the scope of quantifiers, unless something is added to rule that out.

For example, ∃xGx & ∃xHx is a formula of QPL. Though it contains two x quantifiers, it satisfies (Q) because neither x quantifier falls within the scope of the other. Gx is a formula that contains an x variable and no x quantifier, so by (Q) ∃xGx is a formula, and a similar demonstration establishes that ∃xHx is a formula. Since each of them is a formula, (∃xGx & ∃xHx) is a formula by (bc), and ∃xGx & ∃xHx is by (op). The x in Hx does not fall under the scope of the ∃x quantifier in ∃xGx, and the x in Gx does not fall under the scope of the ∃x quantifier in ∃xHx. The x in ∃xGx and the x in ∃xHx therefore need not denote the same object.

Exercise

Take Gx to be the predicate "x has gold" (or "x is rich"), and Hx to be "x is happy." Take the domain to be persons. On that interpretation, what does ∃xGx & ∃xHx say? What does ∃xGx & ∃yHy say?

∃xGx & ∃xHx says that at least one of the persons that the variable x might denote is rich, and at least one of the persons that the variable x might denote is happy. This is a conjunction of two distinct sentences describing the objects that a variable might denote. It does not say that the variable must denote the same person in the one case that it does in the other, and so does not say that at least one person is both rich and happy. ∃xGx & ∃yHy says that at least one of the persons that the variable x might denote is rich and at least one of the persons that the variable y might denote is happy. This is again a conjunction of two distinct sentences describing the objects that a variable might denote. It does not say that the variable used in the one case cannot denote the same person as the variable used in the other case and so does not say at least one person is rich and at least one *other* person is happy. ∃xGx & ∃xHx and ∃xGx & ∃yHy both say the same thing: that at least one person is rich and at least one person is happy. The first does not promise that the two are the same (or rule it out), and the second does not promise that they are different (or rule it out).

Saying that at least one person is both rich and happy requires bringing both occurrences of the variable under the same quantifier, as in ∃x(Gx & Hx), which says that at least one of the persons that the variable x might denote is both rich and happy. Saying that at least one person is rich and at least one other person is happy requires adding a negated identity clause: ∃x[Gx & ∃y(~=yx & Hy)]. This says that at least one of the persons that the variable x might denote is rich and that for this person there is at least one person the variable y might denote who is not the same and who is happy. (It still does not rule out that the rich person is also happy and the other person also rich. That requires adding further conjuncts. This is left as an exercise.)

While "each" and "at least one" are the canonical readings for ∀ and ∃, English has many ways of expressing "each" and "at least one." Some of them have subtly different meaning or ambiguous meaning. "Some" might be read as meaning "at least one" but it could also be read as implying that there is more than one or as denying that all are a certain way. "A" or "an" could refer to at least one, as in "a cat is happy," or to each, as in "a cat is not an herbivore." "Any" refers to each one in certain contexts and at least one in others.

When sentences are lifted out of context, as they are in exercises, the default is to treat "all," "every," "everyone," and similar expressions as meaning "each," and to treat "some," "someone," and "there is" as meaning "at least one." "A," "an," "any," and "anyone" require thinking about what is intended.

Exercise 12.3

1. *Instantiate the following sentences on the interpretation:* D: *persons;* Gx − x *is rich;* Hx − x *is happy. Note that, as just used,* x *is a predicate place holder that may be replaced by any of the variables* x, y, z, x_1, *etc.*
   * **a.** ∀xGx
   b. ∃yHy
   * **c.** ∀xGx & ∀yHy
   d. ∀x(Gx & Hx)
   * **e.** ∃xGx & ∃xHx
   f. ∃x(Gx & Hx)
   * **g.** ∀yGy ∨ ∀yHy
   h. ∀y(Gy ∨ Hy)
   * **i.** ∃zGz ∨ ∃xHx
   j. ∃z(Gz ∨ Hz)
   * **k.** ∃zGz & ∀z(Gz ∨ Hz)
   l. ∃x(Gx & Hx) ∨ ∀xHx

2. *Formalize the following sentences using the interpretation* D: *persons;* Gx − x *is rich;* Hx − x *is happy. A formalization may not contain free variables.*
   * **a.** All are happy and some are rich.
   b. There are those who are happy, and there are those who are rich, and there are those who are both.
   * **c.** Anyone is rich and happy.
   d. Everyone is happy and rich.
   * **e.** Some are either rich or happy.
   f. Either someone is happy or everyone is rich.
   * **g.** Either all are rich or all are happy.
   h. All are either rich or happy.
   * **i.** Some are rich and some are happy.
   j. At least one person is rich and at least one other person is happy. *(Using two different variables is not good enough! Why not?)*
   * **k.** At least one person is rich and they are happy.
   l. At least one person is rich or happy.
   * **m.** Everyone is either rich or happy, but it is not the case that either everyone is rich or everyone is happy.
   n. Someone is rich and someone is happy, but it is not the case that anyone is rich and happy.

   *⋆o. Someone is either rich or happy if and only if either someone is rich or someone is happy.
   p. Everyone is rich and everyone is happy if and only if everyone is rich and happy.
   *⋆q. Some are happy and others are not, but no one is both happy and unhappy.
   r. Someone is rich and someone is happy, but none are rich and happy.

12.3.2 *Multiply Quantified Sentences; Scope Ambiguity*

As observed earlier, when one quantifier falls within the scope of another, the quantifiers must use different variables. Where the domain is restricted to persons, "Each person knows each person" cannot be formalized as ∀x∀xKxx (where Kxy is x knows y). Using just one quantifier to produce ∀xKxx does yield a formula of QPL, but this formula does not say that each person knows each person. In accord with the rule that variables that fall under the scope of the same quantifier mention the same object, ∀xKxx only says that each person the variable x might denote occurs with itself in an ordered pair in the extension of the K predicate. In brief, each person knows themselves. "Each person knows each person" must instead be formalized using two quantifiers with different variables, as in ∀x∀yKxy. However, because variables stand for what can vary, and one variant is that two different variables might stand for the same object, ∀x∀yKxy does not just say that each person knows each *other* person. It also says that each person knows themselves. The fact that two different variables are used does not suggest otherwise because different variables can stand for same objects. Saying that each person knows each other person requires placing a condition on the sentence: for each x and each y, if x is not the same person as y, then x knows y. This comes out as ∀x∀y(~=xy → Kxy). Saying not only that but ruling out that anyone knows themselves requires ∀x∀y(~=xy ≡ Kxy).

Sentences containing different overlapping quantifiers, like "everyone knows someone," "someone knows everyone," "everyone is known by someone," and "someone is known by everyone," raise special problems. Different English speakers understand these sentences differently, and same speakers understand them differently in different contexts. The challenges associated with formalizing them are best approached from the other end, by considering the meaning of the analogous sentences of QPL: ∀x∃yKxy, ∃y∀xKxy, ∀x∃yKyx, and ∃y∀xKyx. The definition of an instance dictates that each of ∀x∃yKxy, ∃y∀xKxy, ∀x∃yKyx, and ∃y∀xKyx have different instances. These instances are all sentences of PSL, and PSL semantics shows that these instances are not p-equivalent. Each of the sentences must therefore have its own meaning.

An instance of ∀x∃yKxy is formed by removing the main operator, ∀x, and replacing each occurrence of the variable x, in the resulting subformula, ∃yKxy, with a name. Since ∀ means "each," ∀x∃yKxy asserts that each of its instances, ∃yKay, ∃yKby, ∃yKcy, … is the case. These instances have their own instances. Because each of these instances is existentially quantified, each of them only promises that one of its instances is the case, without saying which one, and without promising that the name that appears in any one instance is the same name that appears in any other. The instances can be listed by using name metavariables to designate the unspecified names: Kap_1, Kbp_2, Kcp_3, … where any two of p_1, p_2, p_3, are possibly but not necessarily different names. The set, {Kap_1, Kbp_2, Kcp_3, …}, therefore represents all the instances of instances of ∀x∃yKxy.

The instances of instances of ∀x∃yKxy are {Kap_1, Kbp_2, Kcp_3, …}
where any two of p_1, p_2, p_3 are possibly but not necessarily distinct names.

The instances illustrate that the ∀x∃yKxy asserts that each person knows at least one person. However, there is no suggestion that each person knows the same person. The sentence would still be true if each person knew only themselves and no one else. Contrast this result with ∃y∀xKxy. An instance may only be formed by removing the main operator. In this case, that operator is ∃y. The existential quantifier only promises that one of its instances is the case, without saying which one. Using a single name variable to designate the single unspecified name, there is just one instance, ∀xKxp. That one instance is universally quantified, so it has multiple instances: Kap, Kbp, Kcp, … The set of these instances is quite different from the previous set.

The instances of instances of ∃y∀xKxy are {Kap, Kbp, Kcp, …},
where p denotes the same object in each instance.

These instances illustrate that ∃y∀xKxy asserts that there is some one person who is known by everyone. The sets of instances of instances of ∀x∃yKxy and ∃y∀xKxy are sets of all the cases they are saying are true. Since these sets are different, ∀x∃yKxy and ∃y∀xKxy say different things. The latter entails the former. If there is someone whom everyone knows, then everyone knows someone or other. But the former does not imply the latter. Everyone may know someone without that one being the same person in each case and so without there being someone who is known by everyone. Switching the order of the quantifiers changes the meaning.

There is a striking difference in the meaning of the existential quantifier in these two cases. In the second case, where the existential precedes the universal, it has the sense of "one for all." But the first case, where the existential follows the universal, does not say "all for one"; it says "each for some one or other." In the second case, where the existential precedes the universal, one object makes a pair with each object; in the first, where the existential follows the universal, each object makes a pair with at least one object, but no two need make a pair with the same one. The sense of the existential quantifier shifts from "some one or other" to "the same one" depending on whether it follows or precedes a universal. The instances make this clear. The existential quantifier is instantiated with p_1, p_2, p_3, ... in the first case and a single p in the second. Should an existential fall between two universals it would have both senses simultaneously, the one with reference to the universal that precedes it, the other with reference to the universal that follows it.

Now compare the first case, $\forall x \exists y Kxy$, with the effect of keeping the quantifiers in the same order but flipping the variables in the predicate formula to produce $\forall x \exists y Kyx$.

The instances of $\forall x \exists y Kyx$ are $\exists y Kya$, $\exists y Kyb$, $\exists y Kyc$, ... Each of these instances is existentially quantified and so only promises that one of its instances is the case, without saying which one. Accordingly,

The instances of instances of $\forall x \exists y Kyx$ are $\{Kp_1a, Kp_2b, Kp_3c, ...\}$,
where any two of p_1, p_2, p_3 are possibly but not necessarily distinct names.

Each person is known by someone or other, but it need not be the same one who knows everyone. By similar reasoning,

The instances of instances of $\exists y \forall x Kyx$ are $\{Kpa, Kpb, Kpc, ...\}$.

This does say that there is at least one person who knows everyone.

In each case, the sets of instances of instances are different. Each of $\forall x \exists y Kxy$, $\exists x \forall y Kxy$, $\forall x \exists y Kyx$, and $\exists x \forall y Kyx$ therefore says something different. Suppose it is resolved to describe what each of these formulas says with an English sentence that uses the same quantifier order. The result is:

$\forall x \exists y Kxy$:　each x knows some y or other

$\exists y \forall x Kxy$:　the same y or y's are known by each x

$\forall x \exists y Kyx$:　each x is known by some y or other

$\exists y \forall x Kyx$:　the same y or y's know each x

As the meaning of the existential quantifier changes, depending on whether it is before or behind the universal, so the mood of the verb changes depending on how the quantifier order is related to the order of the variables in the following predicate formula. When Kxy is a transitive predicate like "x knows y," and the first quantifier quantifies the first place in the predicate, the rendition uses the active voice of the verb (in this case, "knows"). When the first quantifier quantifies the second place, the rendition must use the passive voice (in this case, "is known by").

Stylists are hostile to the passive voice. Satisfying the peccadillos of the stylists would mean rewriting the English renditions given above as follows.

$\forall x \exists y Kxy$:　each x knows **some y or other**

$\exists y \forall x Kxy$:　each x knows **the same y or y's**

$\forall x \exists y Kyx$:　**some y or other** knows each x

$\exists y \forall x Kyx$:　**the same y or y's** know each x

There are two problems with the second and third of these English renditions. The two senses of the existential quantifier depend on its scope. When an existential falls within the scope of a universal, it has the sense of "some one or other." When it has a universal within its scope it has the sense of "the same one in each case." This makes it important to specify the scope of existential quantifiers. English does not have many resources for doing this. Whereas binary connectives are employed along with verbal and written punctuation marks, like "either," "neither," "both," and "then," English language unary operators do not have their own verbal or written punctuation marks. In their absence, one of the few recourses left for identifying the scope of a quantifier is position. Using position to indicate scope would mean adopting some convention, such as the convention operative in QPL, that the operator with wide scope (scope over all of the rest of the formula) is the one that is mentioned first. However, satisfying the peccadillos of the stylists means giving up on using position to identify scope. The "active voice" renditions given above sometimes mention the quantifier with wide scope first (in the first and fourth cases above), and sometimes second (in the second and third cases, repeated below).

$\exists y \forall x Kxy$:   each x knows the same y or y's

scope of "each x": knows

scope of "the same y or y's": each x knows

$\forall x \exists y Kyx$:   some y or other knows each x

scope of "some y or other": knows

scope of "each x": some y or other knows

In the second and third of the "active voice" renditions, the quantifier that the English rendition mentions second has scope over the remainder of the rendition, whereas the quantifier that is mentioned first only has scope over the predicate.

This would not be as much of a problem if some inflection were attached to wide scope and narrow scope uses of the existential quantifier. Above, inflections were used. "Some one or other" was attached to the narrow scope usage, and "the same one" was attached to the wide scope usage. But these inflections are rarely used in spoken or written English. This is the second problem with accepting the peccadillos of the stylists. The stylists have instituted a practice that has effectively made it impossible to use position to distinguish between wide scope and narrow scope senses of the existential quantifier, and English speakers tend not to use inflections to do the job.

Exercise 12.4

Unlike multiply quantified sentences of English, sentences of QPL are not ambiguous. Instantiate the following sentences of QPL on the interpretation: D: persons; Gx − x is rich; Hx − x is happy; Kxy − x knows y (alternatively, y is known by x). Inflect English instantiations of existential quantifiers where necessary to resolve any resulting ambiguity. Note that, as just used, x and y are predicate place holders that may be replaced by any of the variables x, y, z, x_1, etc.

⋆a. $\forall x \exists y Kxy$

  b. $\forall x \exists y Kyx$ *(Provide both an "active" and a "passive" instantiation; say which mentions the quantifier with wide scope first.)*

⋆c. $\exists x \forall y Kyx$ *(Provide both an "active" and a "passive" instantiation; say which mentions the quantifier with wide scope first.)*

  d. $\exists x \forall y Kyx$

⋆e. $\forall x Gx \rightarrow \forall x Hx$

  f. $\exists z Hz \rightarrow \exists y \forall z Kzy$ *(Provide an instantiation that mentions the quantifier with wide scope first.)*

⋆g. $\forall x \forall y Kxy$

  h. $\forall x Kxx$

⋆i. $\forall x \exists y (Kxy \ \& \sim=yx)$

  j. $\exists x \exists y Kxy$

⋆k. $\exists x \exists y Kyx$ *(Provide an instantiation that mentions the quantifier with wide scope first.)*

  l. $\forall y \forall x Kxy$ *(Provide an instantiation that mentions the quantifier with wide scope first.)*

Because English does not punctuate unary operators, because stylistic peccadillos have made it impossible to rely on position as an indication of which operator has the widest scope, and because English speakers tend not to inflect their uses of the existential quantifier, multiply quantified sentences of English often contain no indication of which quantifier is the main operator and hence no indication of which sense of the existential quantifier is intended. They exhibit "quantifier scope ambiguity." A sentence like "everyone loves someone" might be understood as saying that each person loves some person or other, but it might also be understood as saying that there is some one person who is loved by everyone. In QPL, $\forall x \exists y Kxy$ unambiguously says that each person stands in the K relation to some person or other, and not necessarily the same one in each case. Referring to the same one in each case requires putting the existential quantifier in front of the universal. But in English there are sentences, like "Archaeologists have determined that all the inhabitants were killed by some disease," that imply that everyone was killed by the same disease. In this case, the English quantifier, "some" comes after the quantifier "all" even though it has the sense of "the same one for each case."[1]

Similarly, a sentence like "someone loves everyone" might be read as saying that there is some one person who loves each person or as saying that there is someone who loves one person, someone who loves another, and so on without there having to be any one person who loves everyone. In QPL, $\exists x \forall y Kxy$ unambiguously says that there is some one person who stands in the K relation to each person. But in English there are sentences like "there is a coin in every pocket" or "there is a fork by every plate" that imply that there is a different coin or fork in each pocket or by each plate. Heroic measures to read these uses of "a" as meaning "the same one," like imagining a stack of plates with a single fork beside them or a fork-shaped coin that snakes into every pocket, are amusing. They amuse precisely because this is *not* the intuitive way of understanding "there is a fork by every plate" or "there is a coin in every pocket." These English sentences are not even ambiguous. They are flat out contrary to the practice endorsed by QPL of mentioning the existential quantifier first if and only if it has the sense of "the same one for each case."

This is an unfortunate situation. Because many multiply quantified sentences, like "everyone loves someone" and "someone loves everyone" are ambiguous, students of logic cannot rely on their intuitions about the meaning of associated English sentences to understand multiply quantified sentences of QPL, and instructors have little choice but to rely on the formal syntax and the formal semantics of QPL to explain how QPL works. Formalization exercises and examination questions are a disaster. Fairness and a recognition of the conflicting intuitions of others demand that the instructor accept almost any answer.

To address this problem as far as possible, it is best to institute a policy for how to disambiguate and formalize multiply quantified sentences of English.

Policy 12.3.2
(for interpreting and formalizing multiply quantified sentences of English)

Formalize an English multiply quantified sentence in the way that most closely approximates its syntax. (Put the quantifier that the English sentence mentions first in first place, the one it mentions second in second place, etc.)

Consider the meaning of an English sentence to be the meaning determined by the resulting QPL formalization.

Exception: When existential quantifiers are inflected with "the same one" or "some one or other" or other words or phrases to those effects, give the existential the scope required by its inflection.

According to this policy, English sentences are to be interpreted to mean what the QPL formalization that most closely approximates their syntax means, except when existentials are inflected. Where English sentences are ambiguous, this policy dictates how they are to be disambiguated. Where English sentences clearly do not mean what the policy dictates (e.g., "all the inhabitants were killed by some disease"; "there is a coin in every pocket") the English sentence is to be considered ungrammatical and should be rewritten to express the meaning using a quantifier order that is approved for that task by QPL.

For example, the English sentence, "everyone loves someone" puts the universal quantifier first, the existential second. Preserving this syntactic feature means putting the universal quantifier first in the QPL formalization, that is, making it the main operator. Because $\forall x \exists y$ unambiguously means "for each x there is some y or other" the English sentence is interpreted accordingly, as saying that everyone loves someone or other, and not necessarily the same one in each case. It is incumbent on English speakers who do not wish to be so interpreted to use a different sentence (at least when speaking to logicians or students of logic). If this means using the passive voice, so be it. Style cannot be allowed to prevail over precision.

The exception arises when the existential quantifier is inflected, as in "everyone loves the same one" or "someone or other is loved by everyone." Inflections are like construction signs that direct traffic out of its course (or, in some cases, along it). They designate the proper position of something that has been (or may have been) put out of its proper place. "The same one" indicates that the QPL formalization must give the existential scope over the universal, even if the existential is mentioned second, "some one or other" that QPL must give the existential scope under the universal, even if the existential is mentioned first.

Logic is in no position to dictate how English speakers should express themselves. But making further progress in the study of logic requires laying down some rules concerning how the English that is in use in the textbook is intended and how the English that appears in exercise and examination answers is expected to be used and will be understood. This is a provision for use in this context only. In all others, pester others to inflect their existential quantifiers or look to background circumstances for clues.

Exercise 12.5

Abiding by policy 12.3.2, formalize the following sentences using the interpretation D: *persons;* Gx − x *is rich;* Hx − x *is happy;* Kxy − x *knows* y. *A formalization may not contain free variables.*

⋆**a.** Everyone knows themselves.
 b. Everyone knows someone.
⋆**c.** Someone knows everyone.
 d. Someone is known by everyone.
⋆**e.** Everyone is known by someone.
 f. Everyone knows someone other than themselves.
⋆**g.** Someone knows someone.
 h. Everyone knows everyone.
⋆**i.** Someone is known by someone.
 j. Everyone is happy only if everyone knows someone.
⋆**k.** If someone is rich, someone is known by everyone.
 l. If someone is rich, they are known by everyone. *(Careful! The answer to k will not work here.)*

12.3.3 Negations of Quantified Claims; Duality; The Square of Opposition; "Any"

In QPL, placing a tilde before a universal quantifier alters what is said in a different way from placing a tilde after a universal quantifier. The same holds for placing a tilde before or after an existential quantifier. Taking the domain to be restricted to persons and ∀xHx to formalize "each person is happy," ~∀xHx says the opposite: that it is not the case that each person is happy.

Exercise

Suppose the domain contains two people, Alma and Boda. Suppose it is said that it is not the case that each person is happy. What needs to be the case for this to be true?

∀xHx says that each person that the variable x might be taken to denote is happy. This states a universal rule. A universal rule is falsified by is a single counterexample. If even one person is not happy, the assertion that all are happy is false, making the assertion that it is not the case that all are happy true. Conversely, if the assertion that it is not the case that all are happy is true at least one person is not happy. ~∀xHx, is accordingly true if and only if there is at least one person who is not happy. That is, it is true if and only if ∃x~Hx is true.

In contrast, ∀x~Hx says that each person that the variable x might be taken to denote, Alma, Boda, Crumb, …, is not in the extension of the predicate, "happy." In a domain restricted to persons, the group of those who are happy is empty. ∀x~Hx accordingly says that not even one person is happy. "Not even one" can be formalized as ~∃xP. The word "none" can be read as a contraction, "n'one," of "not one." It is literally what is formalized by ~∃xP. ∀x~Hx is true if and only if ~∃xHx is true, that is, if and only if none are happy.

~∀xHx (it is not the case that each is happy) allows for the possibility that some are happy whereas others are not. It does not rule out that none are happy, but it does not promise that any more than one is unhappy. ∀x~Hx does promise that none are happy.

~∀x~Hx says something different yet again: that ∀x~Hx, which says that none are happy, is false. ∀x~Hx asserts a universal rule. A universal rule is falsified by a single counterexample. If and only if even one person is happy, the assertion that all are not happy is false, making the assertion that it is not the case that all are not happy true. It follows that at least one person is happy, that is, that ∃xHx. It does not follow that all are, though this is not ruled out.

∀xHx, ~∀xHx, ∀x~Hx, and ~∀x~Hx have interesting relations to one another, often illustrated by placing them on the corners of a square, called the square of opposition.

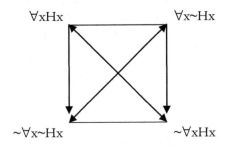

The sentences on the diagonally opposite corners of the square are opposites. As always, opposites are sentences that are the same but for the fact that one is prefaced by a tilde.

The sentences on the top two corners, ∀xHx and ∀x~Hx, are not opposites. They could both be false. The one says that each thing is H, the other that nothing is H. If some things are H and others are not, both sentences are false. The sentences on the bottom two corners, ~∀x~Hx and ~∀xHx, are not opposites either. They could both be true. The one says that it is not the case that each thing is not H, the other that it is not the case that each thing is H. In the case where some things are H and others are not, both sentences are true.

The sentences on the two top corners are contraries. While they can both be false, they cannot both be true. The sentences on the bottom two corners are subcontraries. While they can both be true, they cannot both be false.

Like PSL, the semantics for QPL classically insists that there be at least one object in the domain of any interpretation. Given that prerequisite, the sentence on the top left corner of the square intuitively entails the sentence on the bottom left: If each thing is H, then at least one thing is H. The sentence on the top right corner of the square likewise entails the sentence on the bottom right: If each thing is not H then at least one thing is not H.

∀x~P and ∃xP are oppositional duals (see chapter 8.3 and exercise 8.7). The negation of either one is equivalent to the other one: ~∀x~P to ∃xP, and ∀x~P to ~∃xP. The same holds for ∀xP and ∃x~P. ~∀xP is equivalent to ∃x~P and ∀xP to ~∃x~P. Our intuitions about the meanings of the corresponding English phrases confirm this. The phrase, "it is not the case that each one is" (~∀xP) is equivalent to "at least one is not" (∃x~P). ∀x~P means "not even one is," which may be further contracted to "none is," phrases that are literally the ones formalized as ~∃xP. "It is not the case that not even one is not" (~∀x~P) is equivalent to at least one is (∃xP). Finally, "each is" (∀xP) which states universal rule, is intuitively equivalent to denying that there is a counterexample to that rule, that is to "it is not the case that even one is not" (~∃x~P).

Because these equivalences hold, it is strictly correct to formalize English quantified sentences as if they were the negations of their duals.[2] Notably, since "none," which strictly says "not even one" (~∃xP), is the negation of the dual, ∃x~P, of ∀x~P, ∀x~P may just as well formalize "none" as ~∃xP. However, while this is strictly correct, it is a practice that should be avoided if possible. A good formalization of an English sentence clearly formalizes *that* sentence. Putting universal quantifiers where the English sentence has existentials, or existentials where it has universals, and situating tildes in a different place from where the English has negations obscures the connection between the formalization and its English instantiation.

This having been said, when negations are entered into the mix of unary operators, there are a number of cases where attempting to preserve an exact correspondence between the order of vocabulary elements of English and those of corresponding elements of QPL produces results that are incorrect, ambiguous, or needlessly difficult to understand. Some of these cases are surveyed below. Prior to doing so, it will be helpful to introduce a principle that governs how to shift the position of a tilde without changing the meaning of a sentence.

According to the tilde shift principle, moving a tilde from one side of a quantifier to the other, and changing the quantifier's sign produces an equivalent sentence. ∀x~∃yGxy can be rewritten as either ~∃x∃yGxy (shifting the tilde one place to the left and changing the ∀x quantifier over which the tilde jumps to ∃x) or ∀x∀y~Gxy (shifting the tilde one place to the right and changing the ∃y quantifier over which it jumps to ∀y). These three formulations are all equivalent.

> ### ~ Shift Principle
>
> When a quantifier is preceded or followed by a ~, shifting the ~ to the opposite side and replacing the quantity symbol with its dual (∀ with ∃ or ∃ with ∀) preserves the meaning of the original.

The correctness of the ~ shift principle can be easily confirmed by constructing negations of duals (or working back from already constructed negations of duals) and assuming (as will be demonstrated later) that negations of duals can be substituted for quantified subformulas that occur as parts of longer sentences of QPL. For example, ∀x~∃yGxy has the form ∀x~P. Its dual is ∃xP. The negation of the dual is ~∃xP. Taking P to be ∃yGxy gives the result ~∃x∃yGxy, identified earlier as a product of applying the ~ shift principle to ∀x~∃yGxy. Again, the same sentence, ∀x~∃yGxy can be taken to have the form [Q]~∃yP. ~∃yP is the negation of ∃yP which is the dual of ∀y~P. So [Q]~∃yP ends with the negation of the dual of the ending of [Q]∀y~P. Recalling that ∀x is [Q] and that P is Gxy transforms [Q]∀y~P into ∀x∀y~Gxy, identified earlier as a product of applying the ~ shift principle to ∀x~∃yGxy.

This section has so far considered just how negations work in QPL. English has only been used to transliterate or comment, as clearly as English allows, on what can be said and done in QPL and on the relations between various sorts of sentences of QPL. Once again, the way things are said in QPL is not perfectly reflected in English. Just as there are scope ambiguities in multiply quantified sentences of English, so there are scope ambiguities in English sentences that mix quantifiers and negations. Suppose someone says, "All swans are white," and someone else responds, "Each swan is not white," or "All swans are not white," or "Every swan is not white." In this context, "each is not" and "all are not" are just another way of denying that each is or that all are. They express what QPL expresses with ~∀xP. English here states "not" after it states the quantifier it means to negate ("each" or "all" or "every"). Another way to put this is to say that English gives "not" wide scope. It does not just negate the following predicate formula, "is white." Its scope extends back to make it negate the entire quantified formula, "all swans are white."

But English will also use "not" to just negate the following predicate formula. Someone who says, "Fish are not warm-blooded" means to talk about all fish, and most likely means to deny warm-bloodedness of each fish individually, not just to insist that something less than 100% of them are warm-blooded. Here "not" has narrow scope. This creates ambiguity. There is no structural difference between "All swans are not white" and "All fish are not warm-blooded" that would flag that the first means to negate the whole quantified formula whereas the second means to negate only the predicate subformula. This infects other sentences where context is not as decisive. Someone who says "all the restaurants in town are not open" could be understood either way. They might be denying the assertion that all are open, and so saying that at least one is not open, or lamenting that all are closed and so saying that none are open. Different auditors will have different intuitions about what is meant, and the same person may have different intuitions at different times. QPL has no such ambiguity. Its definition of scope is precise. ~∀xGx and ∀x~Gx say different things.

This looseness of fit poses the problem of how "all are not" is to be formalized in QPL. One way to deal with the problem is to avoid the issue. English has other ways to express the two different senses of "all are not." It can say "not all are" and it can say "none are." This makes it possible to deal with the ambiguity of "all are not" by refraining from using it, a policy only inadvertently neglected in this textbook.

However, one of the principal purposes of logic is to assess the implications of what others choose to say. The logician does not have the power to forbid others from using ambiguous expressions. It remains a problem how to understand those who use "all are not." When they are present, they can of course be asked what they mean (ideally by way of pestering them to such an extent that they give up on using the expression). But the speaker is not always present, not always willing to reply, or not always capable of giving a clear answer. Sometimes, background knowledge can indicate what the speaker must mean (as background knowledge of zoology dictates how to understand the swan and fish sentences). But context is not always decisive.

Where context is not decisive, the principle of charity dictates adopting the reading that is more likely to be true. "Not all are" is verified by a single negative case whereas "none are" requires that each case be negative. This suggests that the default formalization of "all are not" (the one used when no other consideration is decisive) should be ~∀x.

But charity is not the only default principle that might be invoked, and not clearly the best one. Others that might be used include simplicity and consistency. The principle that, in the absence of any further clue, the *operator* that is mentioned first in English should be formalized in first place in QPL has the advantage of simplicity. It is easy to apply. It only requires copying the English syntax. It is also a natural generalization of policy 12.3.2, which demands that the *quantifier* that is mentioned first in English occur first in formalization. When different policies work the same way, it makes for a simpler and more consistent system than when one policy needs to be crafted for one sort of case and a different one for another. The policy adopted in this textbook is accordingly:

Policy 12.3.3a
(for interpreting and formalizing "all are not" and similar phrases of English)

When the speaker is not explicit and context is not decisive, "each is not," "all are not," and similar phrases should be formalized as ∀x~ and understood accordingly.

Placing the operator that is mentioned first in English first in formalization is a default policy. It applies only in cases where no other considerations dictate otherwise. The case of "all are not" often calls for this default treatment. However, other pairings of quantifiers with negations resist it. Consider

12.1   *Someone* does *not* care for *someone*

12.1 places a negation between two existential quantifiers. Were it formalized in accord with that operator order the result would be ∃x~∃yGxy (taking Gxy to formalize the predicate, "x cares for y"). But this result says that for at least one individual (∃x) there is not even one person (~∃y) that individual cares for. In other words, there is someone who cares for no one. This is clearly not what is meant by the English sentence. Unlike "all are not," which is ambiguous, "Someone does not care for someone" lends itself to only one interpretation. It says that someone does not care for at least one person.

In this case, English wants to give "not" narrow scope, as if 12.1 were punctuated leaving the concluding quantifier lying outside of the scope of the negation:

12.2   Someone (does not care for) someone

QPL cannot handle this dangling quantifier. ∃x(~Gxy)∃y violates the formation rules. Respecting both policy 12.3.2, which dictates putting the quantifier that is mentioned second in English after the one mentioned first, and the narrow scope English wants to give to "not" produces a formalization that captures the sense of the original,

12.3   ∃x∃y~Gxy: for at least one individual, x, at least one person, y, is such
        that individual x does not care for person y

It is as if "does not care for" were amalgamated into a unit, like "dislikes" or "neglects." Taking Hxy to be "x dislikes y" or "x neglects y," the formalization of "Someone dislikes/neglects someone" is uncontroversially ∃x∃yHxy, which says that for at least one individual there is at least one person that individual dislikes or neglects.

It might be thought that this example could serve as the foundation for a variant formalization principle that preserves consistency with the scope of tildes in QPL: When a negation is followed by a predicate formula, consider the negation to have scope just over that predicate formula. But this principle does not hold in general. Consider

12.4   Someone *does not care for* everyone

Supposing the negation has narrow scope, it should be formalized as ∃x∀y~Gxy. But this sentence of QPL says that for at least one individual (∃x) each person (∀y) is such that the individual does not care for them. In other words, there is someone who cares for no one. There may be English speakers who intuitively accept that not caring for everyone means not caring for the first one, the second one, the third one, and so on up to the full 100%.[3] And perhaps no one would disagree with them when the negation is "welded" to the predicate by being made the same word with the predicate, as in "Someone dislikes everyone" or "Someone neglects everyone." But there are many English speakers who would insist that when the negation is made using a separate word or phrase the sentence means no such thing. It comes down to the question of whether someone who does not care for everyone is a devil or just not a saint. Someone who falls just short of sainthood, and cares for everyone except for one person, is someone of whom it may truly be said that they do not care for everyone. On this understanding, not caring for everyone means not caring for the full 100%; it does not mean caring for 0%.

On the latter account, English wants to give "not" wide scope, as if the sentence were punctuated as

12.5   Someone does not (care for everyone)

Recognizing that QPL needs to put the quantifier before the predicate formula it quantifies, the corresponding formalization is

12.6   ∃x~∀yGxy: at least one individual, x, is such that it is not the case that
        for each person, y, individual x cares for person y

Comparing "Someone does not care for someone" with "someone does not care for everyone" yields results that are surprising in more than one way. The two sentences are word-for-word identical, but for the fact that one ends with "someone" and the other ends with "everyone." Yet despite this extensive similarity, and even though the negation occupies the same position in both sentences, the former gives the negation narrow scope and the latter gives it wide scope. There is no clue that it does so: no inflection, no punctuation, no change in operator order or in location of the predicate formula relative to the negation. The only way to make a case for saying that the one sentence gives the negation narrow scope and the other gives it wide scope is to appeal to speaker intuitions.

This is not the only thing that is surprising. As careful readers will already have noticed, the two sentences say the same thing (if the second sentence is considered ambiguous, they at least say the same thing on one of two ways of reading the second sentence). Not caring for someone means not caring for at least one person and not caring for everyone means not caring for at least one person. And yet, the only *apparent* difference between the two sentences is the concluding words, "someone" and "everyone," which clearly do not mean the same thing. How is it possible that this difference should make no difference?

The answer is that while there is no *apparent* difference between the two sentences beyond the concluding quantifier, there is a nonapparent difference. The first sentence is intuitively read as giving narrow scope to the negation, the second as giving wide scope to the negation. Once again, only the QPL formalizations make the extent of the difference clear.

> 12.1   Someone does not care for someone: $\exists x \exists y \sim Gxy$
> 12.4   Someone does not care for everyone: $\exists x \sim \forall y Gxy$

QPL makes something else apparent as well. According to the $\sim$ shift principle, the two formalizations are equivalent. It is no wonder, therefore, that the two sentences should say the same thing. They only appear different because the scope of the negation is not considered. When it is, the one sentence is saying "at least one is not" and the other is saying "not all are," and those expressions are intuitively equivalent. But only QPL makes the equivalence and the reason for it clear. English on its own fails to make the scope explicit, making the comparison seem more paradoxical than it is.

What has just been said holds for "Everyone does not care for someone" and "Everyone does not care for everyone" when those sentences are read in accord with policy 12.3.3a, and so as having the form $\forall x \sim P$. This suggests a policy for all cases of this sort.

Policy 12.3.3b
(a policy governing the formalization and interpretation of English phrases of the form
[negation]-[predicate]-[quantifier]*)*

English phrases of the form [negation]-[predicate]-[existential] are to be parsed as giving narrow scope to the negation and formalized as $\exists x \sim P$.

English phrases of the form [negation]-[predicate]-[universal] are to be parsed as giving wide scope to the negation and formalized as $\sim \forall x P$.

Exception: When the negation is not a separate word from the predicate (as in negative predicates beginning with dis-, in-, non-, un-) it always has narrow scope.

It has been established that neither "Someone does not care for someone" nor "Someone does not care for everyone" clearly say that someone cares for no one. (The former sentence clearly does not say this, and the latter is at least ambiguous.) When English speakers want to unambiguously express this thought they say

> 12.7   Someone does not care for anyone

or just "someone cares for no one."[4] The latter English sentence is uninteresting, because it does not have the form, [negation]-[predicate]-[quantifier] shared by the other sentences. The former bears further scrutiny.

Exercise

What is the scope of "not" in "Someone does not care for anyone?" Does it have wide scope, as in "Someone does not (care for anyone)" or narrow scope, as in "Someone (does not care for) anyone?" Might there be some other variation in this case that English fails to signify?

Those who have pondered the exercise might have reached the conclusion that the scope of "not" in "Someone does not care for anyone" depends on how "anyone" is understood. Strictly, "any" has the meaning that it does in "Pick a card, any card." Reach into the domain, select one object, and whichever one is chosen, it should not make any difference to the result. In the case at hand, take the misanthropic person under consideration, reach into the domain, pick someone, and it should turn out that the misanthrope does not care for the chosen person. Moreover, this should always be this way regardless of who is chosen. So, there is *not one* ($\sim\exists x$) person that could be chosen that the evil person would care for (even themselves). And *each* one ($\forall x$, including the evil person themselves) must turn out to be one that the evil person would not ($\sim$) care for.

On this analysis, there are two ways of formalizing 12.7.

$$\exists x \sim \exists y G x y$$
$$\exists x \forall y \sim G x y$$

The two formalizations are equivalent according to the $\sim$ shift principle. They should be since they formalize the same sentence, and the sentence is (presumably) not ambiguous. On the first formalization, "anyone" has narrow scope (it has scope only over the predicate subformula, not over the negation), on the second, wide scope (scope over the negation as well as the predicate formula). "Anyone" has narrow scope when "not anyone" is read as "not even one," and so when "not" negates an existentially quantified formula. "Anyone" has wide scope when "not anyone" is read as "anyone is not [cared for]," and so when "not" falls under a universal quantifier. None of this is made clear in English. English does not indicate the scope of "not" and it uses a quantifier, "anyone" that can be formalized either as an existential or as a universal.

This suggests an extension of policy 12.3.3b.

Policy 12.3.3b (Continued)
(a policy governing the formalization and interpretation of English phrases of the form
[negation]-[predicate]-[quantifier]*)*

English phrases of the form [negation]-[predicate]-[any] are formalized as either
$\sim\exists x P$ or $\forall x \sim P$.

According to this principle, when "any" or "anyone" is given narrow scope it appears in QPL as an existential quantifier. When it is given wide scope, it appears as a universal. Whether there is a pattern here, and how far it extends if there is, are matters that are considered further in section 12.3.6. As a further note, in this case there is no exception for negative predicates like "dislikes" or "neglects."

Exercise 12.6

1. *Instantiate the following sentences on the interpretation: D: persons; Gx – x is rich; Hx – x is happy; Kxy – x knows y; a: Alma. Note that, as just used, x and y are predicate place holders that may be replaced by any of the variables x, y, z, x_1, etc. The answered questions first offer a close English paraphrase of the QPL formula and then step up to an instantiation that sounds like what people naturally say in English conversation. Try to do likewise.*
   ★**a.** $\forall x H x$
   b. $\sim\forall x H x$
   ★**c.** $\forall x \sim H x$ *(The answer is noteworthy.)*
   d. $\sim\forall x \sim H x$
   ★**e.** $\exists x H x$
   f. $\exists x \sim H x$
   ★**g.** $\sim\exists x H x$
   h. $\sim\exists x \sim H x$

  ★i. ∃xHx & ∃x~Hx

  j. ∀x(Hx ∨ ~Hx)

  ★k. ~∃x(Hx & ~Hx)

  l. ∃x[Hx & ∃y(Hy & ~=xy)]

  ★m. ∀xKxa ∨ ∀x~Kxa *(Apply the ~ shift principle to the second disjunct.)*

  n. ∀xKxa ∨ ~∀xKxa

  ★o. ~∀x∀yKxy

  ★p. ∀x~∀yKxy *(Apply the ~ shift principle.)*

  ★q. ∀x∀y~Kxy *(Apply the ~ shift principle twice; the consequences of not doing so are noteworthy.)*

  r. ~∃x∃yKxy

  s. ∃x~∃yKxy

  t. ∃x∃y~Kxy

  ★u. ∀x∃y~Kxy ∨ ∀x~∃yKxy *(Careful!)*

  v. ∃x~∀yKyx ∨ ∃x∀y~Kyx *(Hint: read the second disjunct as ∃x~∃y; use the ~ scope principle to devise two apparently different but equivalent instantiations of the first disjunct.)*

  ★w. ∀x(∃yKxy → Hx)

  x. ∀x∃y(Kxy → Hx) *(This is not saying the same thing as (w). Think of the difference between knowing anyone at all and knowing some special person.)*

  ★y. ~∀xGx ≡ ∃x~Gx

  z. ~(∃x~Gx → ~∃xGx)

2. *Abiding by policies 15.3.2 and 15.3.3, formalize the following sentences using the interpretation given in question 1. Begin with a paraphrase like those used in answer to question 1. A formalization may not contain free variables.*

  ★a. Everyone knows themselves.

  b. Not everyone knows themselves.

  ★c. Not everyone knows someone.

  d. Not everyone knows everyone.

  ★e. Not everyone knows anyone.

  f. Everyone does not know someone. *(Compare m.)*

  ★g. Everyone does not know everyone.

  h. Everyone does not know anyone. *(Provide two alternative, equivalent formalizations; compare o.)*

  ★i. No one knows everyone.

  j. No one knows anyone.

  ★k. Everyone knows no one.

  l. Someone knows no one.

  ★m. Someone does not know someone.

  n. Someone does not know everyone. *(Compare g.)*

  ★o. Someone does not know anyone.

  p. There is someone no one knows.

★3. *2c and 2e are intuitively equivalent and are formalized in the same way. 2f and 2g, as well as 2m and 2n are also equivalent (this may take a moment's reflection), but they should not have been formalized the same way. What explains this?*

4. *Formalize each of the following ambiguous English sentences in two different ways using the interpretation provided.*

  ★a. Everyone does not know themselves. (Kxy – x *knows* y; *take the domain to be persons.*)

  b. All are not rich. (Gx – x *is rich; take the domain to be persons.*)

  ★c. All politicians are not liars. (Gx – x *is a liar; take the domain to be politicians.*)

  d. Every athlete is not funded. (Gx – x *is funded; take the domain to be athletes.*)

  ★e. All the mechanics are not certified. (Gx – x *is certified; take the domain to be the mechanics in a shop.*)

  f. All inspectors are not unscrupulous. (Gx – x *is scrupulous; take the domain to be inspectors.*)

12.3.4 *Formalizing Relations between Predicates*

Quantifiers can be used to specify how many of the objects in a group satisfy a predicate or how many of the objects that satisfy one predicate satisfy another. Imagine the objects in a group are collected in a circle, G, and imagine the objects that satisfy a predicate are collected in another circle, H. There are five principal relations that a group of objects can have to a predicate, depicted by the five principal ways these circles can be situated relative to one another.[5] The G circle might be contained in the H circle; the H circle might be contained in the G circle; the two circles may be coextensive; they may be separate; or they may partially overlap.

Take the insects in a garden to constitute a domain of objects. Take G to represent the group of gnats. Take H to represent the property of being hooded. The first picture puts the G circle inside the H circle.

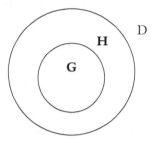

According to this picture, each gnat falls within the group of hooded insects. There may be hooded insects that are not gnats, but there are no gnats that are not hooded. This relation can be described in English by saying that

12.8   Each gnat is hooded

How might this relation be formalized in QPL? ∀xGx says that each insect that a variable, x, might denote is a gnat, but the diagram allows that there may be other kinds of insects. ∃xGx says that at least one insect that a variable, x, might denote is a gnat, which fails to mention the connection between being a gnat and being hooded. ∃xGx & ∃xHx says that at least one insect is a gnat and at least one insect is hooded, which likewise fails to mention the connection. ∃x(Gx & Hx) says that at least one insect is a gnat and hooded, but the diagram says that each is hooded. ∀x(Gx & Hx) says that each insect is a gnat and hooded, but the diagram allows that there may be insects that are hooded that are not gnats and insects that are neither gnats nor hooded.

The diagram says that each of those insects that is a gnat is among those insects that are hooded. Each insect is such that, if it is a gnat it is also hooded. One way to capture this relation using the vocabulary of QPL is

12.9   ∀x(Gx → Hx)

This says that for each insect that a variable, x, might denote, if that insect is a gnat, then it is hooded.

This way of formalizing the relation between the group of gnats and the property of being hooded puts → to a new use. Up to now, → has been used as a functional connective, that is, a connective used to build a compound sentence that has a value that is a function of the values of its components. But Gx and Hx are not sentences. → is here being used subsententially. In this context, it does not have an independent connective meaning of its own. It hangs together with the quantifier, ∀x, to make a hybrid operator, ∀x(…→…). This hybrid is best understood as describing the result of an operation performed on the objects in the domain. The operation is that of inspecting each object individually. The result is discovering that each (∀) of the objects the variable (x) might denote that proves upon inspection to be a gnat (G) also proves upon further inspection to be hooded (H).

The second principal way the group of gnats might be related to the predicate of being hooded, is also formalized using this hybrid operator.

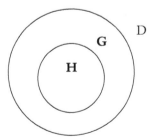

It is easy to assess this diagram as a minor variant on the previous one, and so as saying that each hooded insect is a gnat. But this way of putting things turns the property of being hooded into a name for a group of insects and

the group of gnats into a property. It is more illuminating to read the diagram in a way that preserves the perspective that the gnats are the subject and being hooded is the predicate. This means continuing to read it as describing how the group of gnats is related to the property of being hooded. The diagram puts all the hooded insects within the group of gnats. It does not promise that all the gnats are hooded. There may be some gnats that lie outside the H circle. But any hooded insect must lie within the G circle and so must be a gnat. No other insect can be hooded. Considered as depicting a relation between the group of gnats and the predicate of being hooded, this diagram is described by the English sentence

12.10   Only gnats are hooded

The ∀x(…→…) hybrid operator can be used to generate a sentence of QPL that captures this relation between the gnats and the property of being hooded. Imagine going through the domain and inspecting each insect. If an insect is taken up and found not to be hooded, it need not be examined any further because the diagram depicts nothing about the nature of the unhooded insects. It allows that they may either be gnats or not be gnats. Likewise, if an insect is taken up and found to be a gnat, it need not be examined any further because the diagram makes no promises about gnats. It allows that they may be either hooded or not hooded. But if an insect is found to be hooded it must prove upon further examination to also be a gnat.

12.11   ∀x(Hx → Gx)

Each (∀) insect the variable (x) might denote proves upon inspection to be hooded (H) only if it also proves to be a gnat (G).

The third principal form that the relation between the group of gnats and the predicate of being hooded can take is being coextensive.

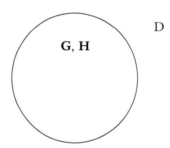

In keeping with the policy of reading these diagrams as making an assertion about the gnats, considered as subjects, and being hooded, considered as a predicate, the diagram depicts a situation in which each gnat is hooded and only gnats are hooded. It might be thought that this would be a situation in which the ampersand connective is properly employed to represent the relation between the subject and the predicate. And it is. But the conjunction does not have the form ∀xGx & ∀xHx or the form ∀x(Gx & Hx). These are two different ways of saying that each insect that a variable x might denote is a hooded gnat. However, the diagram allows that there may be insects in the domain that fall outside of either circle.

The conjunction depicted in the diagram is the conjunction of each gnat being hooded, earlier formalized as ∀x(Gx → Hx), and only gnats being hooded, earlier formalized as ∀x(Hx → Gx).

12.12   ∀x(Gx → Hx) & ∀x(Hx → Gx)

The hybrid operator, ∀x(…→…), is still doing the foundational work. Unsurprisingly, the description might be simplified using a new hybrid operator, ∀x(…≡…).

12.13   ∀x(Gx ≡ Hx)

Each (∀) insect the variable (x) might denote proves upon inspection to be a gnat (G) if and only if it is hooded (H). Equivalently,

12.14   All and only the gnats are hooded

The contrary situation, where the two circles lie outside one another,

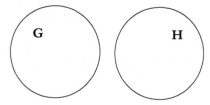

is the situation where no gnats are hooded. The ∀x(...→...) operator continues to be effective for this case, with the help of ~.

>   12.15   ∀x(Gx → ~Hx)

For each (∀) insect the variable (x) might denote, if that insect is a gnat (G), then it is not (~) hooded (H).

When this formalization is read back in English, it can come out as "Each gnat is not hooded." As noted in section 12.3.3, that English sentence is ambiguous. However, there is nothing ambiguous about ∀x(Gx → ~Hx), which (as already noted in chapter 10.2.1) is properly understood as a direct description of the state of affairs depicted on the diagram and not as a formalization of any English sentence. QPL sentences only manage to be formalizations of English sentences by describing the same states of affairs as those English sentences, and if the English sentences cannot manage that without ambiguity the only lesson to be drawn is to be careful about how to read the QPL sentence in English. The ambiguity can be avoided by reading ∀x(Gx → ~Hx) as

>   12.16   No gnats are hooded

~∃x(Gx & Hx), which says that it is not the case that there is even one insect the variable x might denote that is both a gnat and hooded, is syntactically closer to 12.16,[6] but when QPL is being used to directly describe the state of affairs depicted on the diagram there is no alternative syntax that needs to be approximated.

A minor variant on this situation expands the H circle to be coextensive with the domain outside the G circle, so that the boundary of the G circle is the inner rim of the H surface. (The gap between the two circles in the diagram below is present for visual clarity only. It is not intended to represent a portion of the domain that is not in either area.

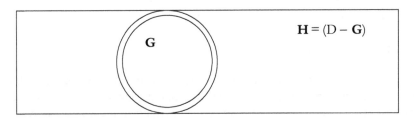

This represents the situation where all the insects but for the gnats are hooded,

>   12.17   All but the gnats are hooded

which is formalized as

>   12.18   ∀x(~Gx ≡ Hx)

Like "all and only" [∀x(Gx ≡ Hx)], "all but" or "all except for" [∀x(~Gx ≡ Hx)], may be divided into two conjuncts.

>   12.19   ∀x(~Gx → Hx) & ∀x(Hx → ~Gx)

The first of these conjuncts provides assurance that any insect that is not a gnat is hooded, but says nothing about the gnats. It does not rule out hooded gnats. Considered on its own, it would be depicted by a diagram like the one above, except that the H plane has no inner rim, allowing for the possibility of hooded insects inside the G circle, but providing no assurance that there are any in there. (The only assurance is that there is room for hooded insects outside the G circle.) The further assurance that the H circle has an inner rim, excluding any hooded insects there might be from the group of gnats, is added by the second conjunct (which is unsurprisingly equivalent to 12.15).

While 12.18 formalizes the state of affairs depicted on the diagram, it might be objected that the English 12.17 only expresses the first conjunct of 12.19. Other textbook authors have been divided over this matter, some saying that "all but" should be formalized using a $\forall x(\ldots \equiv \ldots)$ hybrid, others favouring $\forall x(\sim\ldots \rightarrow \ldots)$.[7] A diplomatic resolution is to follow chapter 4.7 in recognizing that exceptions (now expressed by "all but" or "all except for" rather than "unless") can be made in a strong or a weak sense. Strong exceptions promise that none of the excluded objects are that way (they add the second conjunct). Weak exceptions say nothing about the excluded objects and only promise that all the others are a certain way.

The remaining case, where the two circles partially overlap,

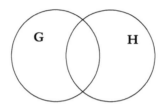

depicts the situation where some, but not all the gnats are hooded. The assertion that not all the gnats are hooded is simply the negation of the assertion that each is hooded.

12.20 $\sim\forall x(Gx \rightarrow Hx)$

The different assertion that some are hooded can be parsed as "There is at least one ($\exists$) insect the variable (x) might denote that is both a gnat (G) and hooded (H).

12.21 $\exists x(Gx \ \& \ Hx)$

This sentence contains a subsentential use of &, combined with $\exists x$ to make a third hybrid operator. The situation might alternatively be described by saying that it is not the case that no gnats are hooded ($\sim\forall x(Gx \rightarrow \sim Hx)$), but $\exists x(Gx \ \& \ Hx)$ is not as complicated.

The diagram depicts the conjunction of 12.20 and 12.21,

12.22 $\exists x(Gx \ \& \ Hx) \ \& \ \sim\forall x(Gx \rightarrow Hx)$

but it is possible to assert just one of the conjuncts on its own. The assertions made by each conjunct on its own cannot be diagrammed without introducing further ornaments, but they are clearly described by each conjunct. $\exists x(Gx \ \& \ Hx)$ says that some gnats are hooded without saying anything about whether they all are. $\sim\forall x(Gx \rightarrow Hx)$ implies that at least one gnat is not hooded without commenting on what they are all like.

Exercise 12.7

1. *Describe the following situations in QPL. The situations are described using English sentences (they must be described somehow) but the exercise is not to formalize the English sentences but to use QPL to describe the same situation. Use the following formalization key: Gx − x is rich; Hx − x is happy*
   - ⋆**a.** All who are rich are happy.
   - b. The rich are happy.
   - ⋆**c.** The rich are all happy.
   - d. Not all who are rich are happy.
   - ⋆**e.** The rich are not all happy.
   - f. Some who are rich are happy.
   - ⋆**g.** Some who are rich are not happy.

    h. None who are rich are happy.

*i. None who are happy are not rich.

    j. None but the rich are happy. *(Hint: draw a circle diagram first; according to what is said, there may be rich people who are not happy, but there are no happy people who are not rich. The diagram depicts a situation that has already been covered. What is it?)*

*k. Only those who are rich are happy.

    l. Those who are rich are the only ones who are happy.

*m. All who are rich are happy and all who are happy are rich.

    n. All and only those who are rich are happy.

*o. Not all who are rich are happy, but some are.

    p. There are not any who are rich who are happy.

*q. All who are rich are unhappy, but so are some who are not rich.

    r. Only those who are happy are rich, but not all the rich are happy.

    s. If some who are rich are not happy, and some who are happy are not rich, and none are both, then all the rich are unhappy.

2. *Instantiate the following sentences of QPL using the formalization key of question 1.*

    *a. $\forall x(Hx \rightarrow Gx)$ *(Give two answers, one using "only" the other using "all.")*

    b. $\forall x(Hx \rightarrow \sim Gx)$ *(Give two answers, one using "only those who" the other using "all.")*

    *c. $\forall x(Hx \rightarrow \sim Gx)$ *(Give two answers, one using "none," the other using "it is not the case that.")*

    d. $\sim\exists x(Hx \,\&\, \sim Gx)$ *(Give two answers, one using "none," the other using "it is not the case that.")*

    *e. $\forall xHx \rightarrow \forall xGx$ *(Give two answers, one using "if" the other using "only if.")*

    f. $\forall xGx \rightarrow \forall xHx$ *(Give two answers, one using "if" the other using "only if.")*

12.3.5 A, E, I, and O sentences; Existential Import

The basic formulas identified in section 12.3.4 are traditionally assembled under four headings. $\forall x(Gx \rightarrow Hx)$, $\forall x(Hx \rightarrow Gx)$, $\forall x(Gx \equiv Hx)$, $\forall x(\sim Gx \equiv Hx)$, and $\forall x(\sim Gx \rightarrow Hx)$ are treated as variants on one formula, while $\exists x(Gx \,\&\, Hx) \,\&\, \sim\forall x(Gx \rightarrow Hx)$ is treated as two basic formulas. $\forall x(Gx \rightarrow \sim Hx)$ continues to be distinctly counted to make up the four. The grouping is based on the forms of what are called "categorical" sentences of English or other natural languages. These are sentences that have a subject–predicate structure. They are analysed into two groups of two. Categorical sentences may say something of all the subjects (these are called universal sentences) or of just some of them (these are called particular sentences), and they may do so by affirming a predicate of the subject (these are called affirmative sentences) or denying a predicate of the subject (these are called negative sentences). This gives rise to a scheme according to which there are four principal kinds of formulas, traditionally called A, E, I, and O formulas.

		Natural Language Formulation	**QPL Equivalent**
A:	universal affirmative	All G's are H's	$\forall x(Gx \rightarrow Hx)$
E:	universal negative	No G's are H's	$\forall x(Gx \rightarrow \sim Hx)$ / $\sim\exists x(Gx \,\&\, Hx)$
I:	particular affirmative	Some G's are H's	$\exists x(Gx \,\&\, Hx)$
O:	particular negative	Some G's are not H's	$\exists x(Gx \,\&\, \sim Hx)$ / $\sim\forall x(Gx \rightarrow Hx)$

There is a substantive difference between an older way of doing logic, expressed by the natural language formulations of A, E, I, and O sentences, and modern logic, expressed by the QPL equivalents of those sentences. Suppose I am perfectly healthy. Suppose I say, "All my health problems are undiagnosed." Is what I have said true or false? For traditional logic, the sentence is false, because I have no health problems that could be undiagnosed. For modern logic, the sentence is true, and for the same reason: because I have no health problems, it is only to be expected that I would have no diagnosed health problems.

As traditionally understood, A and E sentences have existential import. If I say, "all my health problems are undiagnosed" or "none of my health problems is diagnosed," I imply that I have health problems. If I have no problems, my sentence is at least misleading.

In QPL, in contrast, the hybrid operator, ∀x(...→...) which expresses A and E sentences, has no existential import. ∀x(Gx → Hx) and ∀x(Gx → ~Hx) describe the result of a two-stage test that is performed on a domain of objects. ∀x(Gx → Hx) is not, in the first instance, a way of formalizing the English phrases, "all are," "everyone is," "each is" or other synonymous phrases, taken together with all their implications. They are in the first instance descriptions of the objects in the domain. The test is to pick an object from the domain. The object is then inspected to determine if it satisfies the G predicate. If it does not, it passes the test and need not be further considered. However, if it does satisfy the G predicate, it needs to be further examined to determine if it satisfies the H predicate. Provided it satisfies the H predicate it passes the test. In the case where an object satisfies the G predicate but does not satisfy the H predicate, that object fails the test. ∀x(Gx → Hx) says that each object in the domain passes the test. But each can do so in one or other of two ways: by not satisfying G or by satisfying H. Should the case arise where there are no objects that are G's, each object that is picked from the domain would pass the test "trivially," that is without needing to be further examined to determine whether it is an H. This makes ∀x(Gx → Hx) "trivially true" when there are no G's. That is why it has no existential import. It does not say that there are any objects that are G's. It only implies that if there were any, they would be H's. The same account applies to the QPL analogue of E sentences, ∀x(Gx → ~Hx).

Traditionally, A, E, I, and O formulas were also placed on the square of opposition (section 12.5.3). But QPL reduces the square to a pair of crossed diagonals.

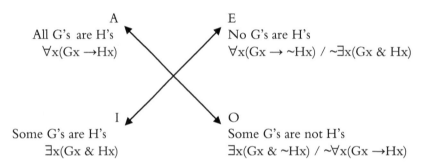

A and O formulas are clearly opposites, as are E and I formulas. (Consult the second way of formalizing E and O formulas in QPL.) But the QPL versions of A and E formulas are not contrary. Contraries cannot both be true, but ∀x(Gx → Hx) and ∀x(Gx → ~Hx) are both true when there are no G's. Likewise, the QPL versions of I and O formulas are not subcontrary. Subcontraries cannot both be false. But when there are no G's, both ∃x(Gx & Hx) and ∃x(Gx & ~Hx) are false, since both assert that there is at least one object that does satisfy G. For the same reason, the QPL versions of A and E formulas do not q-entail the QPL versions of I and O formulas, respectively. When there are no G's, A and E formulas are true, but I's and O's are false.

The analogous formulas discussed in section 12.5.3, ∀xGx, ∀x~Gx, ∃xGx and ~∀xGx, are exceptions (they do make a square) because, like PSL, classical QPL does not countenance empty domains. Since each domain must contain at least one object, the assertion that each object satisfies a predicate entails that at least one does so. The point does not apply to A, E, I, and O sentences because, while domains cannot be empty, predicates can have empty extensions. In particular, the subject predicate in categorical formulas can have an empty extension.

For traditional logic, in contrast, both the A assertion that all G's are H's and the E assertion that no G's are H's imply that there are objects that satisfy the subject (G) predicate. Since there are, it cannot be that all of them are H's and that none of them are. The formulas cannot both be true, though they can both be false (when some are H's and others are not). Likewise, since "all G's are H's" implies that there are G's, it follows that some G's are H's, and since "no G's are H's" implies that there are G's, it follows that some G's are not H's. Even I's and O's are subcontrary. Traditional logic maintains that they cannot both be false. I's are the opposites of E's, and E's entail O's. If an I sentence is false, its E opposite must be true, as must the entailed O, making it impossible for an I to be false and the corresponding O not to be true. A similar demonstration establishes that if an O is false the corresponding I must be true.

This last consequence is counterintuitive. Suppose the domain is the fruit in the refrigerator and it is said that some of the apples are rotten. Then if the refrigerator is opened and there are no apples there, rotten or sound, it would be natural to declare the sentence false. After all, it implies that there are apples there that are rotten. This would be even more so if it were said that there are apples in the refrigerator that are not rotten, and it turned out upon inspection that there were no apples there at all. It seems quite possible that both "some apples are rotten" and "some apples are not rotten" should both be false. They can both be false precisely because I and O formulas do have existential import and so assert the existence of the subjects they assert to have or not have those predicates.

This reflection highlights a further oddity in the traditional square of opposition. Like QPL, traditional logic accepts that A's and O's are contradictory, and that I's and E's are contradictory. But the strict opposite of an I sentence "some G's are H's" is "it is not the case that some G's are H's," which is a denial of there being G's that are H's without any attendant assertion to the effect that there are G's. Reading an E sentence "no G's are H's" as nonetheless implying that there are G's makes the E sentence say something more than a strict opposite of an I sentence can say. The same point can be made of A sentences. If they are the strict opposites of O sentences, they can say no more than that it is not the case that there are G's that are not H's. This is saying something less than that there are G's that are H's.[8]

This having been said, traditional logic is still widely employed, and the quantifiers used in natural languages do have existential import in many contexts. For both reasons it is good to be familiar with the traditional account and its implications.

Exercise 12.8

Identify which of the following are A, E, I, *or* O *sentences and say which have existential import according to modern logic. (Not all sentences are true.)*

⋆**a.** All animals with hearts are animals with kidneys.
  b. Not all sea creatures are fish.
⋆**c.** Some physicists are not astronomers.
  d. No cyclists are runners.
⋆**e.** All amateur athletes are impoverished.
  f. Some writers are illiterate.

12.3.6 Predicate Descriptions; Changing Scope

Most of the objects that exist lack names. When they are denoted at all, they are denoted by descriptions, called definite descriptions, that purport to uniquely identify them. These descriptions take the form of open sentences, which can be turned into complex terms (see sections 10.3.4–5) or embedded in longer, quantified sentences (to be discussed in section 12.3.8 below). Many predicates also lack names. The liquid in a bottle, for example, might be said to satisfy a predicate description, such as "fermented Chaptalized juice from a variety of Bordeaux red grapes, aged in oak barrels." Alternatively, it might be said to satisfy a predicate, such as "claret."

Whereas definite descriptions are ubiquitous, predicate descriptions are rare, but for two exceptions. People will not put up with them, and for good reason. They make any extended discussion intolerably convoluted. For this reason, many predicate descriptions appear only once. The one appearance is in a definition, which identifies the predicate description with a predicate name so that on all future occasions the name may be used in place of the description. For example, in section A-1.3, some sentences were said to satisfy a predicate described as "invariance in meaning under substitution of parts that have the same meaning." Section A-1.3 went on to provide a demonstration that all the sentences of SL satisfy this predicate. The demonstration mentioned the predicate many times. But the predicate description is 12 words long, comprising almost a line of printed text. It is so long that reading it interrupts any thought that was in progress before getting to it. Had the full description been used each time the predicate had to be mentioned, the demonstration would have been all but impossible to follow through the thicket of verbiage. To avoid that, the predicate description was used only once, to describe the meaning of the predicate names, "extensional" and "extensionality." After that, the names were used in its place.

Aside from appearing in definitions, predicate descriptions are largely confined to cases where predicates are described by two or three conjunctions of other predicates or negations of predicates. The truth conditions of conjunctions of literals are straightforward, so people tolerate working with them. And when the conjunctions are short, it is often easier to work with them than to invent and remember a new name for each minor variant on a group that might be described. Hence the proliferation of predicate descriptions such as "ruminant animal," "old antelope," "spotted cow," "aluminium alloy rim," "nonstick surface baking pan," and so on.

Like definite descriptions, predicate descriptions are formalized as open sentences. "Spotted cow" might be formalized as Gx & Hx, where Gx is "x is spotted" and Hx is "x is a cow"; "unwelcome intruder" as ~Kx & Cx, where Kx is "x is welcome" and Cx is "x is an intruder." These predicate descriptions can replace predicates wherever predicates might occur. For example, the A sentence, ∀x(Px → Qx) has as one of its instances ∀x[(Gx & Hx) → (~Kx & Cx)], "spotted cows are unwelcome intruders."

Not all predicate descriptions can be formalized as conjunctions of predicates. An old antelope is an object that is old and an antelope, but an egregious blockhead is not an object that is egregious and a blockhead, just someone who is a blockhead to a superior degree. Whereas "old antelope" might be formalized as "Gx & Hx," "egregious blockhead" can only be formalized as Gx, where Gx is "x is an egregious blockhead." One way to mark the difference is to remember that predicates are sets of objects. Predicate descriptions likewise identify sets of objects. Predicate descriptions differ in how they do this. Some predicate descriptions identify a set by appeal to relations between other sets, such as relations of intersection or containment. QPL is well suited to formalize such relations, as shown in section 12.3.4. But other predicate descriptions identify sets of objects by means of operations performed on a single set. A description that is confined to picking out those objects that satisfy a single predicate to a greater or lesser degree, like "egregious blockhead," calls for a more powerful formal language. QPL has to use a predicate letter.

Those predicate descriptions that QPL can formalize differ from one another in some important ways. A rich engineer is an object that occupies the intersection of the rich objects and the engineers. An electrical engineer is not an object that occupies the intersection of the electrical objects and the engineers. The electrical engineers make up their own smaller group within the larger group of engineers. A certified engineer is neither an object that occupies the intersection of the certified objects and the set of engineers nor a species of engineer. A certified engineer is a kind of certified individual, one certified as an engineer. An older brother might be considered to be an object that occupies the set of brothers, but it could not be an object that occupies the set of older objects. There might be a set of *old* objects, but a set of *older* objects is not well defined. "Older" is a relative term, so what is older changes depending on what it is related to what. The same might even be said of "brother." Someone is a brother only in relation to a sibling, and older in relation to some siblings but not others, so the contents of the set are not fixed. There is still such a thing as a set of older brothers, but it is a set of pairs of objects. The first object in each pair is older than the second and a brother of the second.

The details contained in these different kinds of predicate descriptions are formalized in different ways. Alma is a rich engineer might be formalized as

12.23   Ga & Ha

taking "a" to be Alma, Gx to be x is rich, and Hx to be x is an engineer. This formalization allows inference to "Alma is rich" and "Alma is an engineer" should that information be of any use.

In contrast, "Alma is an electrical engineer" and "Alma is a certified engineer" cannot be formalized as conjunctions. The genus/species relation that being an engineer has to being an electrical engineer or that being a certified professional has to being a certified engineer might be formalized as A sentences

12.24   Ka & ∀x(Kx → Hx)
12.25   Ba & ∀x(Bx → Cx)

where Kx is "x is an electrical engineer," Bx is "x is a certified engineer," and Cx is "x is a certified professional." But the second conjuncts in these formalizations are rarely stated. If they appear at all, it is only once, by way of definition. Generally, competent speakers are assumed to know these things without needing to be told, and the definitions are only inserted in demonstrations where required to establish the validity of the conclusion.

Relative predicates are different yet again. "Alma is an older brother" attributes a predicate to Alma that depends on the existence of a younger sibling. It is formalized as ∃x(Kax & Cax) where Kxy is "x is older than y" and Cxy is "x is a brother of y."

There are structural similarities between A, E, I, and O sentences that contain predicate descriptions and A, E, I, and O sentences that have been compounded using connectives. "Red currants are tart" is an A sentence containing a predicate description, appropriately formalized as ∀x[(Gx & Hx) → Kx], where Gx is "x is red," Hx is "x is a currant" and Kx is "x is tart." "Red currants and black currants are tart" is a conjunction of two A sentences, appropriately formalized as ∀x[(Gx & Hx) → Kx] & ∀x[(Bx & Hx) → Kx]. It is tempting to follow the English formulation in eliminating the repetition, but this requires caution. ∀x[(Gx & Bx & Hx) → Kx] amalgamates two different predicate descriptions into a description of a single predicate, producing nonsense. (It says that anything that is both red and black and a currant is tart.) In this case the distinction between the two predicate descriptions can be preserved by thinking that the assertion is that either of the two sorts of currant is tart. This is formalized as ∀x([(Gx v Bx) & Hx] → Kx).

Exercise 12.9

Formalize the following sentences in QPL. Determine what the domain should be, and what the name and predicate letters should refer to. If the sentence contains predicate descriptions that can be formalized as conjunctions, be sure to do so.

  ⋆**a.** Vermin are undesirable animals.
   b. Alma is an excellent speaker but not an excellent writer.
  ⋆**c.** Volunteer fire fighters and bicycle mechanics are urgently needed participants.
   d. An oblong steel container was abandoned.
  ⋆**e.** Some small rectangular objects with dots on them are for sale.
   f. Square iron nails and white bone buttons were among the pilfered artefacts.

Even though many predicate descriptions can be formalized as compound open sentences, it is not always necessary. QPL is primarily a language used to describe states of affairs and only secondarily a language used to formalize what is said in English. The fact that English speakers use a predicate description to identify a set is not by itself a reason why QPL should use a similarly complex description. QPL could just assign the objects or lists of objects that satisfy the described set to a predicate letter. Whether to "unpack" an English predicate description as an open sentence of QPL is often a judgement call, based on antecedent decisions about what to include in the domain and whether the information contained in the description is consequential. Consider the sentence,

> 12.26   Anyone with a bicycle lock distrusts someone, but only those with an
>   older brother distrust everyone.

12.26 includes the predicate descriptions, "has a bicycle lock," "distrusts someone," "has an older brother," and "distrusts everyone. One way to deal with these descriptions is to formalize the sets they describe as predicate letters: Hx for "x has a bicycle lock," Cx for "x distrusts someone," Bx for "x has an older brother," and so on. Another is to try to formalize as much of the information contained in the predicate description as possible, unpacking what it means for x to have a bicycle lock in terms of there being at least one object, y, that is a bicycle lock that x has, unpacking distrusting someone as there being at least one person, z, whom x does not trust, and so on.

It is always a question how much of the information that can be formalized should be formalized. The best approach is not a blind determination to formalize everything. It is better to identify what is likely to be consequential in the case at hand and just formalize that. "Too much information" can sometimes be as bad as too little, as the old joke goes. In the context of a demonstration, for example, missing information can make the demonstration invalid but extra information can make the validity of the conclusion impossible to intuit and more difficult to demonstrate.

In the case of 12.26, there is no larger context to judge from, but there is an intrinsic context. The sentence is devoted to drawing a distinction between two groups of people. It uses having a bicycle lock as a criterion for identifying the one group and having an older brother as a criterion for identifying the other. This suggests that there is no need to treat "having a bicycle lock" and "having an older brother" as anything more than two, different one-place predicates that people might satisfy. However, there is a contrast drawn between distrusting only someone and distrusting everyone. This suggests that it might be important to treat "distrusting" as a two-place predicate, rather than take "distrusts someone" and "distrusts everyone" to be two different one-place predicates.

Decisions about how much information to formalize are bound up with decisions concerning the domain for the formalization. Supposing 12.26 is just concerned with drawing a distinction between persons, limiting the domain to persons would be appropriate. A wider domain, including persons and bicycle locks, or just things in general, might be considered for safety's sake, but larger domains mean more work. When the domain is persons there is no need for a predicate, "x is a person," to appear in the formalization, but when the domain is things, each different sort of thing that is spoken of needs to first be identified by including a dedicated predicate in the formalization, such as "x is a person," or "y is a bicycle lock."

There are two recommendations for formalizing more complex sentences such as 12.26. First, approach the sentence as if it were a mapping project. Begin by producing a large-scale map. Then make another map at higher resolution. Continue until as much detail as is apparently relevant has been formalized. The largest scale map assigns the whole sentence to a zero-place predicate letter. The map at the next level of resolution down identifies the main operator and the immediate subformula or subformulas. In the case of 12.26, the comma before "but" suggests that "but" is the main operator. An appropriate formalization at this scale is therefore

12.26a   A & B

where A is "anyone with a bicycle lock distrusts someone" and B is "only those with an older brother distrust everyone." This formalization continues to suppress obviously relevant information, but it is a start, and it provides a guide to what to do next. Since the main operator is a connective, the two immediate components can be formalized in isolation. Nothing that is discovered when formalizing the one conjunct will have any bearing on how the other conjunct is formalized though, of course, any objects or predicates named in both conjuncts ought to be assigned to the same name or predicate letters.

Each of the conjuncts appears to have a quantifier as its main operator. This is where the second recommendation comes into play. Where the main operator is a quantifier, paraphrase quantified formulas prior to formalizing them. Do this by restating universal quantifiers using the phrase "each object that the variable (x, y, z, and so on, as needed) might denote is" and existential quantifiers using the phrase "at least one obect that the variable (x, y, z …) might denote." The phrases are cumbersome and may be abbreviated to "each x" and "at least one y."

When paraphrasing, attention also needs to be given to quantifier scope. As discussed in section 12.3.2, in the absence of inflections on existential quantifiers, when a universal is followed by an existential, the existential has the force of "some one or other," whereas when the existential precedes the universal it has the force of "the same one." Paraphrases need to make this order clear in order to make the sense of the existential quantifier clear. Paraphrases like "for each x and at least one y" and "for at least one x and each y" should be avoided because conjunctions are reversible and so imply no particular order. The order, universal − existential should be paraphrased as "for each x, at least one y is such that." The order, existential − universal should be paraphrased as "for at least one x, each y is such that." An existential sandwiched between two universals is paraphrased as "for each x at least one y is such that for each z." A universal sandwiched between two existentials is paraphrased as "for at least one x, each y is such that for at least one z."

Exercise 12.10

1. *Formalize each of the following paraphrases as sentences of QPL. Ensure that your answers do not contain free variables or punctuation that is not associated with a binary connective.*
    *   **★a.** For each x, each y is such that if Gxy then Gyx.
    *   b. Each x is such that, for each y, if Gxb and Gby then for at least one z, Gzz.
    *   **★c.** For at least one x, at least one y is such that it is not the case that for each z Gzxy.
    *   d. It is not the case that, for even one x, if for each y, Gy, then for at least one z, Hxz.
    *   **★e.** For each x, at least one y is such that, if Gyx then for each z it is not the case that for each x_1 Gx_1z
    *   f. For at least one x, Gx, and for each y if Hy then for at least one z, Gyz. *(The use of "and" does not violate the injunction on how to state quantifier pairings. Why not?)*

2. *Paraphrase each of the following to produce a result like those in exercise 1.*
    *   **★a.** $\exists x(\forall yGy \rightarrow \exists zHxz)$
    *   b. $\exists x\forall y(Gy \rightarrow \exists zHxz)$
    *   **★c.** $\forall y(\exists xGx \rightarrow \exists zHyz)$
    *   d. $\forall y\exists x(Gx \& \exists zHyz)$
    *   **★e.** $\exists x(\forall yGy \& \exists zHxz)$
    *   f. $\exists xGx \& \forall y(Hy \rightarrow \exists zKyz)$

3. *Paraphrase each of the following.*
    *   **★a.** Everyone who knows Alma knows someone.
    *   b. Someone who knows Alma knows everyone.
    *   **★c.** Someone who knows Alma knows everyone who knows Alma.
    *   d. Everyone who knows Alma knows everyone who knows Alma.
    *   **★e.** Everyone who knows Alma knows someone who does not know Alma.
    *   f. Someone who knows Alma knows someone who does not know Alma.

Each conjunct of 12.26 poses challenges for paraphrasing. There are no connectives in the first conjunct, "Anyone with a bicycle lock distrusts someone," other than the negation implicit in "distrusts," which is unlikely to be a main operator. However, there are two quantifiers. In accord with policy 12.3.2, when the main operator is not a connective, and any existential quantifiers are not inflected, the main operator is the first quantifier to be mentioned. That would be "anyone."

As discussed in section 12.3.3, "anyone" means "someone, but it does not matter to the result which one." However, the first conjunct does not just say, "Anyone distrusts someone." It lays a further condition on the result. It is as if the conjunct said, "Pick a person from the domain. Now check if that person has a bicycle lock. If they do, then they distrust someone. This will be the case for each person who is chosen from the domain." In paraphrase form: For each person the variable x might denote, if that person has a bicycle lock, then they distrust someone (otherwise, maybe they do, maybe they do not).

Subject to further refinement, this paraphrase suggests the following, more detailed formalization of the first conjunct, where the domain is restricted to persons, Hx is "x has a bicycle lock" and Cx is "x distrusts someone"

$$12.26b1 \quad \forall x(Hx \rightarrow Cx) \; \& \; ...$$

The second conjunct, "Only those with an older brother distrust everyone," also has two quantifiers, though some acquaintance with section 12.3.4 helps to appreciate why. "Only those" marks the sentence as having the form "only G's are H's" which is properly paraphrased as "for each person the variable x might denote, that person distrusts everyone only if they have an older brother."

Subject to further refinement, this paraphrase suggests the following, more detailed formalization of the second conjunct, where the domain is again restricted to persons, Ax is "x distrusts everyone" and Bx is "x has an older brother."

$$12.26b2 \quad ... \; \& \; \forall x(Ax \rightarrow Bx)$$

The combined result

$$12.26b \quad \forall x(Hx \rightarrow Cx) \; \& \; \forall x(Ax \rightarrow Bx)$$

comes much closer than 12.26a to formalizing obviously important information. It manages to draw a contrast between two groups of people, those with a bicycle lock and those with an older brother. It makes the one a sufficient condition on distrusting someone, and the other a necessary condition for distrusting everyone. But it does not capture the obviously relevant information that there is distrusting going on in both cases, varying only in the quantity of people distrusted. QPL can readily formalize this information. Cx might be paraphrased as

> 12.27   at least one person the variable, z, might denote is such that the x person distrusts the z person

and Ax as

> 12.28   each person the variable, z might denote is such that the x person distrusts them

"Distrusts" can be further expanded to "does not trust." But this requires caution. The original English uses "distrust" in both conjuncts. "Distrust" welds the negation to the predicate, giving it "narrow" scope over just the predicate. Paraphrasing "distrust" as "does not trust" distinguishes the negation from the predicate, thereby drawing its scope into question.[9] The paraphrases need to be careful to preserve the original intention to weld the negation to the predicate in both conjuncts. The information suppressed in Cx should be paraphrased as

> 12.27a   at least one person the variable, z, might denote is such that the x person does not trust the z person

and that suppressed in Ax should be paraphrased as

> 12.28a   each person the variable, z might denote is such that the x person does not trust them

The formalization of the whole sentence at this new level of detail is, accordingly,

12.26c $\forall x(Hx \rightarrow \exists z{\sim}Cxz) \text{ \& } \forall x(\forall z{\sim}Cxz \rightarrow Bx)$

where Cxy is "x trusts y."

12.26c strikes a balance between giving too little and too much information. However, the Hx and Bx predicates do contain further information QPL is capable of formalizing. Having a bicycle lock might be formalized as a relation between at least one person and at least one thing, a bicycle lock. Were the decision made to unpack this detail, the domain would need to be expanded, perhaps to things in general, and a special predicate would need to be added to specify that the bicycle lock is a thing and the owner is a person.

Doing this work on the first conjunct puts pressure on devoting similar attention to the second. The information contained in the predicate description, "x has an older brother," can be paraphrased as "there is at least one object the variable y might denote such that Byx and Ayx," where Byx is "y is a brother of x" and Ayx is "y is older than x."

There is no justification for going yet further. Having a bicycle lock does not presuppose the existence of some bicycle that it is used to lock. A bicycle lock would still be a bicycle lock if all the bicycles were destroyed. And while QPL can formalize the information that everything that is a bicycle lock is a lock, this is not information that is included in the original sentence or obviously pertinent. Likewise, while it is a feature of the "brother of" relation that if x is a brother of y then y is a sibling of x, and of the "older than" relation that if x is older than y then y is not older than x, and a feature of both that y is not x, and while QPL is capable of formalizing all of these assertions, they and others like them are not evidently important.

Confining efforts at supplementation just to paraphrasing the information that there is a bicycle lock and an older brother, the first conjunct is:

12.26d1   For each object the variable, x, might denote, if that object is a person, then if at least one object the variable y might denote is a bicycle lock and the person has this object, then at least one object the variable z might denote is such that it is a person and is not trusted by the x person & …

and the second conjunct is:

12.26d2   For each object the variable, x, might denote, if that object is a person then, if for each object the variable y might denote, if that object is a person then the x person does not trust them, then at least one object the variable z might denote is a person, a brother of the x person. and older than the x person.

Where the domain is things, the formalization is

12.26d $\forall x(Gx \rightarrow [\exists y(Ky \text{ \& } Hxy) \rightarrow \exists z(Gz \text{ \& } {\sim}Cxz)]) \text{ \& }$
$\forall x(Gx \rightarrow [\forall y(Gy \rightarrow {\sim}Cxy) \rightarrow \exists z(Gz \text{ \& } Bzx \text{ \& } Azx)])$

where Gx is "x is a person," Ky is "y is a bicycle lock" and Hxy is "x has y."

It may well be wondered whether the extra detail required by the domain of things is worth the added effort, particularly given that the details only make the main point more difficult to discern. 12.26d is a formalization for someone who wants to flex their muscles and prove how much complexity they can handle. 12.26c is for someone principally concerned to separate the important information from a forest of less important details.

Exercise 12.11

1. *Formalize each of the following sentences twice, once using a domain restricted to persons and a second time using a domain that includes everything. The use of = is not called for in any case. Universal quantifiers should always have conditionals as their immediate subformulas and existential quantifiers should always have conjunctions as their immediate subformulas. A sentence of QPL contains no free variables and no punctuation marks unless those punctuation marks are used in conjunction with a binary connective. Making a paraphrase prior to formalization will assist in discovering the correct answer but need not be included with the answer.*

   D: *persons*   D: *everything*
   d: *Boda*   d: *Boda*
                         Ax: *x is a person*

Bxy: x *loves* y   Bxy: x *loves* y
Cxy: x *despises* y   Cxy: x *despises* y
                          Gx: x *is a thing*
Hxy: x *owes something to* y   Hxyz: x *owes* y *to* z
Kxy: x *knows* y   Kxy: x *knows* y

  *a. If everyone loves everyone, then everyone is loved by everyone. *(The antecedent requires a different formalization than the consequent.)*

  b. If someone loves someone, then someone is loved by someone. *(The antecedent requires a different formalization than the consequent.)*

  *c. If everyone loves everyone then everyone loves someone and everyone is loved by someone.

  d. If someone loves everyone then everyone is loved by someone

  *e. Someone loves everyone, but not everyone loves someone and someone is not loved by anyone. *(The first and the last conjuncts are not contradictory in English; their formalizations in QPL should not be contradictory, either.)*

  f. Everyone loves someone, but someone is not loved by everyone and someone is not loved by anyone.

  *g. Everyone loves someone, but someone does not love everyone, and everyone is not loved by someone.

  h. Either everyone loves someone or not everyone loves someone.

  *i. Either everyone loves someone or everyone does not love someone.

  j. Everyone either loves someone or does not love someone.

  *k. Everyone either loves someone or does not love that person.

  l. Someone both loves and despises someone.

  *m. Everyone owes something to everyone.

  n. Everyone owes everyone something.

  *o. There is something that everyone owes to everyone.

  p. Everyone either loves or despises Boda, but it is not the case that either everyone loves her or everyone despises her.

  *q. Someone loves Boda and someone despises her, but no one both loves and despises her.

  r. Everyone who knows Boda both loves and despises her.

2. *Instantiate each of the following sentences in natural English on the second interpretation given for question 1 above. Crafting a paraphrase is an important first step to coming up with a natural English instantiation. Strive for a final result that is more natural than the paraphrase.*

  *a. $\forall x[Ax \rightarrow \forall y(Ay \rightarrow Bxy)] \rightarrow \forall x[Ax \rightarrow \forall y(Ay \rightarrow Byx)]$

  b. $\exists x[Ax \,\&\, \forall y(Ay \rightarrow Bxy)] \rightarrow \forall x[Ax \rightarrow \exists y(Ay \,\&\, Byx)]$

  *c. $\exists x[Ax \,\&\, \exists y(Ay \,\&\, Byx)] \rightarrow \exists x(Ax \,\&\, \exists y[Gy \,\&\, \exists z(Az \,\&\, Hzyx)])$

  d. $\forall x(Ax \rightarrow \forall y[(Ay \,\&\, Bxy) \rightarrow \exists z(Gz \,\&\, Hxzy)])$

  *e. $\forall x[(Ax \,\&\, Cxx) \rightarrow \sim\exists y(Ay \,\&\, Byx)]$

  f. $\forall x[(Ax \,\&\, Cxx) \rightarrow \sim\exists y(Ay \,\&\, Bxy)]$

  *g. $\exists x(Ax \,\&\, \forall y[Gy \rightarrow \forall z\,(Az \rightarrow Hzyx)])$

  h. $\forall x(Ax \rightarrow \forall y[Gy \rightarrow \exists z(Az \,\&\, Hxyz)])$

Sometimes the procedures that have been laid out above produce a formula of QPL that is not acceptable. "Anyone has a bicycle lock" is formalized as $\forall xHx$ (where Hx is, as before, "x has a bicycle lock") on the ground that "anyone" means "any one object in the domain, it does not matter which one." On this reading, it follows that each person has a bicycle lock. But not all occurrences of "anyone" are amenable to such treatment.

    12.29   If anyone has a bicycle lock, someone distrusts someone

is a conditional. It has the form,

    12.30   A → B

where A is "Anyone has a bicycle lock" and B is "Someone distrusts someone." Continuing to formalize the sentence represented by A as $\forall x Hx$ yields

12.31 $\forall x Hx \rightarrow B$

which is clearly incorrect. It makes everyone's having a bicycle lock a sufficient condition on someone distrusting someone. But the original English sentence places a much less demanding sufficient condition on the result: just that at least one person have a bicycle lock. The correct formalization is

12.32 $\exists x Hx \rightarrow B$

It appears that when "anyone" occurs as the main operator of the antecedent of a conditional sentence it must be formalized as an existential quantifier. This raises a problem for the formalization of sentences like

12.33   If anyone has a bicycle lock, they distrust someone

Given what has just been discovered, it would appear that this sentence ought to be formalized in the same way as 12.29/12.32, say as $\exists x Hx \rightarrow C$, where C is "they distrust someone." But when work proceeds to formalization of the information contained in the interpretation of the C predicate a difficulty emerges. C cannot be unpacked as either $\exists y Cy$ or $\forall y Cy$, where Cy is "y distrusts someone." The former says that someone distrusts someone and the latter says that everyone distrusts someone, but the English says that the person with the bicycle lock, specifically, distrusts someone.

Attempting to make a link between the person referred to in the antecedent and the person referred to in the consequent by formalizing the sentence as $\exists x Hx \rightarrow Cx$ is also impermissible. The x in Cx is free. It does not fall within the scope of the existential quantifier and so does not refer to the individual who has a bicycle lock. This is one respect in which QPL has a weakness that is not present in English or English paraphrases. The English pronoun "they" clearly refers back to the person who has a bicycle lock. The paraphrase, "if at least one person the variable x might denote has a bicycle lock then that person distrusts someone" also makes clear reference back to the person mentioned in the antecedent.

In what follows, two points are made about how this situation is to be addressed. The first is that it cannot be addressed by extending the scope of the existential quantifier over the whole sentence. The second is that it can be addressed by replacing the existential quantifier in the antecedent with a universal that has scope over the whole conditional. This is just 12.26b1, $\forall x (Hx \rightarrow Cx)$, the formalization proposed earlier for "Anyone with a bicycle lock distrusts someone."

The problem cannot be rectified by introducing punctuation to widen the scope of the quantifier. Punctuation cannot be inserted at will. QPL syntax only uses punctuation with binary operators. When the binary operator has scope over a quantifier, as it does in any sentence of the form "If anyone … then …," introducing punctuation to widen the scope of the existential quantifier is tantamount to narrowing the pre-existing scope of the binary connective. This changes the sentence from a sentence that places a sufficient condition on a result to a sentence that puts an existential quantifier on a predicate description. $\exists x (Hx \rightarrow Cx)$ says, "At least one person satisfies the predicate description, has-a-bicycle-lock-only-if-they-distrust-someone." This promises nothing more than that at least one person either does not have a bicycle lock, or distrusts someone. The original English sentence promises more than that. Even though "anyone" is formalized with an existential quantifier, when it occurs as the main operator of the antecedent of a conditional, it still means anyone who is picked from the domain.[10] 12.33 says that if person o_1 is picked from the domain, that person will either not have a bicycle lock or distrust someone." If o_2 is picked instead, the same must be true of them, and likewise for o_3, o_4, and all the others in the domain for however many there are.

The correct way of addressing the problem can be discovered by going back to 12.29, earlier formalized as 12.32, where B is "someone distrusts someone." In this case B can be unpacked as $\exists y Cy$ without giving rise to any problems of cross-reference. The whole sentence can therefore be formalized as

12.34 $\exists x Hx \rightarrow \exists y Cy$

Like 12.31

12.35 $\forall x Hx \rightarrow \exists y Cy$

is an incorrect formalization of 12.29. But

12.36 $\forall x(Hx \rightarrow \exists yCy)$

is correct. It is in fact equivalent to 12.34, and this holds in general.

$\exists xP \rightarrow Q$ is equivalent to $\forall x(P \rightarrow Q)$, where x does not occur in Q.

(The stipulation that x not occur in Q is needed to cover the right-to-left side of the equivalence. $\forall x(Hx \rightarrow Cx)$ is not equivalent to $\exists xHx \rightarrow Cx$ because the latter is not a sentence. In the other direction, if x does occur in Q and $\exists xP \rightarrow Q$ is a sentence, the x's in Q must be bound by their own x quantifier, as, for example, in $\exists xHx \rightarrow \exists xCx$. Converting $\exists xHx \rightarrow \exists xCx$ to $\forall x(Hx \rightarrow \exists xCx)$ would again produce a nonsentence. But in this case $\exists xCx$ can be rewritten as $\exists yCy$ prior to the conversion. Rewriting all occurrences of one variable with occurrences of some variable that does not appear anywhere else in the sentence produces an intuitively equivalent sentence.)

The equivalence can be demonstrated by appeal to intuitive truth conditions. $\exists xP \rightarrow Q$ asserts that if there is a person who satisfies the condition P, then Q is true. It does not promise that there is such a person. It only asserts that, going through the domain person by person, any person that is selected will prove upon inspection to either not satisfy the condition P, or Q will be found to be true. Of course, it would be ridiculous to attempt to establish this by running through the domain person by person. Just look to see if Q is true or false. If it is true, $\exists xP \rightarrow Q$ is "trivially" true (established as true with no need to run through the domain to see what anyone is like). But if Q is false, establishing the truth of $\exists xP \rightarrow Q$ would require running through the domain to show that no one satisfies the condition P. The same would be the case if establishing the truth of Q also requires running through the domain person by person. In that case, provided any who fail to satisfy Q also fail to satisfy P, $\exists xP \rightarrow Q$ is still confirmed.

Compare this with the truth condition for $\forall x(P \rightarrow Q)$. It asserts that each person satisfies the condition $P \rightarrow Q$. Keeping in mind that x does not occur in Q, this reduces to asserting that each person either does not satisfy the condition P, or Q is true. The truth conditions of $\exists xP \rightarrow Q$ and $\forall x(P \rightarrow Q)$, and so the falsity conditions, are identical.

This equivalence has an immediate practical implication for formalizing 12.33. At an intermediate stage, this sentence was formalized as $\exists xHx \rightarrow C$. When attention turns to unpacking the content in C, and it is noticed that C contains a reference to the object bound by the existential quantifier in the antecedent, $\exists xHx \rightarrow C$ can be converted to the equivalent $\forall x(Hx \rightarrow C)$. C can then be unpacked as Cx without creating a free variable. This policy can be generalized to any case where an existentially quantified subformula occurs as the antecedent of a conditional and the conditional's consequent contains a reference to the object bound by that existential quantifier.

Policy 12.3.6

When "anyone," "any," "a," "an," "someone," "some," or equivalent expressions occur as the main operator of the antecedent of a conditional, formalize the conditional as $(\exists xP \rightarrow Q)$.

If Q contains a reference to the object bound by $\exists x$ in $\exists xP$, replace $(\exists xP \rightarrow Q)$ with $\forall x(P \rightarrow Q)$ and go on to further unpack the information contained in Q.

Exercise 12.12

1. *Provide multiple, increasingly detailed formalizations for each of the following sentences. Include a paraphrase where necessary to explain the step from a less detailed to a more detailed formalization. Then formalize it as a sentence of QPL using the first interpretation provided for exercise 12.11#1.*
   ⋆**a.** A person loves everyone only if they love themselves.
     b. Someone loves everyone only if everyone loves someone.
   ⋆**c.** If everyone owes something to someone, everyone despises someone.
     d. Anyone who knows Boda loves her.
   ⋆**e.** Someone who knows Boda loves her.
     f. If someone loves someone, they owe them something.

2. *Redo the answers to question 1 using the second interpretation provided for exercise 12.11#1. Answers for* **a, c, e.**

3. *Some of the following cases pose special problems, discussed under the solution links.*
    ★**a.** Someone is happy if they are rich.
     b. Someone is happy only if they are rich.
    ★**c.** Anyone is happy if they are rich.
     d. Anyone who is rich is happy.
    ★**e.** Everyone is happy if they are rich.
     f. If everyone is rich then they are happy.

Policy 12.3.6 raises a question about a parallel case. Is $\forall x P \to Q$ also equivalent to $\exists x(P \to Q)$? The question can be taken up by asking a further question about the second conjunct of 12.26,

> 12.26   … but only those who have an older brother distrust everyone

earlier formalized as

> 12.26c   … & $\forall x(\forall z \sim Cxz \to Bx)$

Exercise

Why does $\forall x(\forall z \sim Cxz \to Bx)$ place the left parenthesis between the two quantifiers? Could the left parenthesis just as well be placed either before or behind the two of them?

The formalization begins "$\forall x(\forall z$" because the English original reads "only those with an older brother distrust everyone," and sentences of the form "only G's are H's" are appropriately formalized using the $\forall x(\ldots \to \ldots)$ hybrid connective, as discussed in section 12.3.4. That means confining $\forall z$ to the antecedent of the conditional subformula, since it is used in describing the "distrusts everyone" (H) group. Putting the left parenthesis to the left of $\forall x$ would make the arrow the main operator, freeing the x variable in Bx. Putting the left parenthesis to the right of $\forall z$ would change the meaning, making the formalization say something other than the original English sentence.

To see what is wrong with $\forall x \forall z(\sim Cxz \to Bx)$, consider one of its instances, $\forall z(\sim Caz \to Ba)$, where "a" denotes Alma, who does not have an older brother. (Neither the original English sentence nor the domain used for the formalization rule out people who do not have older brothers.) By PSL semantics, Ba is false. For $\forall z(\sim Caz \to Ba)$ to be true, each of its instances must be true. Because Ba is false, regardless of which instance, $\sim Cap \to Ba$ (where p is a name for any object), is chosen, $\sim Cap$ must be false and so Cap must be true. Consequently, Alma must trust everyone. The instance, $\forall z \sim Caz \to Ba$, of $\forall x(\forall z \sim Cxz \to Bx)$ is likewise true provided it has a false antecedent. But since $\forall z \sim Caz$ says that Alma distrusts everyone, it is false provided there is even one person whom Alma trusts (her mother, for instance, or herself).

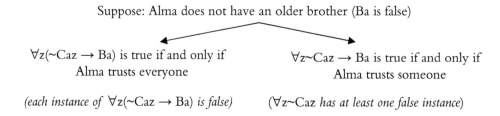

Suppose: Alma does not have an older brother (Ba is false)

$\forall z(\sim Caz \to Ba)$ is true if and only if $\forall z \sim Caz \to Ba$ is true if and only if
Alma trusts everyone   Alma trusts someone

(each instance of $\forall z(\sim Caz \to Ba)$ is false)   *($\forall z \sim Caz$ has at least one false instance)*

Now think of what the second conjunct of 12.26 says: only those who have an older brother distrust everyone. This has implications for those who do not have an older brother, like Alma. They cannot distrust everyone, on pain of making 12.26 false. Not distrusting everyone means trusting at least one person. It does not mean trusting everyone. $\forall z(\sim Caz \to Ba)$ implies more than what the original English sentence says. Since $\forall x \forall z(\sim Cxz \to Bx)$ affirms of each person, x, what $\forall z(\sim Caz \to Ba)$ affirms of Alma, it is likewise an incorrect formalization of the original English sentence.

Interestingly, ∃z(~Caz → Ba) reflects what the English original requires of people like Alma, who have no older brother. An existentially quantified sentence is true provided one of its instances is true. Since Ba is false, ~Caz must be false of at least one person z might denote, that is, Alma must trust at least one person. ∃z(~Cdz → Bd) is also true of anyone, denoted by the name letter d, who does have an older brother, in this case just because Bd is true. So, whether any given person, x, has an older brother or not, ∃z(~Cxz → Bz) is true of them. Since everyone in the domain is one or the other, ∃z(~Cxz → Bz) is true of everyone, making ∀x∃z(~Cxz → Bz) a correct alternative to ∀x(∀z~Cxz → Bz).

This having been said, there is not the same pressure to find a formalization that extends the scope of the quantifier in cases where the antecedent of a conditional is universally quantified.

> 12.37   If everyone who is rich is avaricious, then they are unhappy

has a consequent that refers to the objects quantified in the antecedent. But because the objects are quantified as all the objects that satisfy the description, the cross-reference is likewise to all the objects that satisfy the description. The sentence can therefore be formalized by simply repeating that "they" refers to all those individuals. Taking Gx to be "is rich," Ax to be "x is avaricious," and Hx to be "x is happy" the correct formalization is

> 12.38   ∀x(Gx → Ax) → ∀x(Gx → ~Hx)

English disapproves of the repetition, and uses "they" merely for stylistic reasons, to abbreviate discourse.

It is a different matter when the antecedent is existentially quantified. "If someone is rich, then they are unhappy" cannot be formalized as ∃xGx → ∃x~Hx, because there is no guarantee that the two existential quantifiers refer to the same object, whereas the English does mean to refer to the same object. This demands the alternative formalization ∀x(Gx → ~Hx). But when the rich people are all the people that there are, there is no chance of missing the target by quantifying the consequent reference a second time.

> 12.39   ∀x(Gx → Ax) → ∀y(Gy → ~Hy)

is still an acceptable formalization. All the G's are all the G's, wherever they are and by means of whatever variable they are designated.

Nonetheless, because ∀xP → Q and ∃x(P → Q) are equivalent, the latter could be used in the place of the former. It is important to be clear about what this means.

> 12.40   If everyone is rich then they are happy

is intuitively equivalent to

> 12.41   If everyone is rich then everyone is happy

because "they" refers to everyone. This makes

> 12.42   ∀xGx → ∀xHx

a correct formalization.[11] Replacing ∀xP → Q with ∃x(P → Q) therefore means replacing the variables in exactly one of the antecedent and the consequent with a different variable before making the substitution. This might produce

> 12.43   ∃y(Gy → ∀xHx) or ∃x(Gx → ∀yHy)

Neither ∃x(Gx → ∀xHx) nor ∃x(Gx → Hx) would be a proper replacement. The former violates the formation rules. The latter does not preserve the meaning of the English original. The latter would be true if even one of its instances were true, which requires no more than that one person be either not rich or happy. But the English original would not be true if only one person were happy.

Even the correct replacements may seem startling on this account. It is equally true of them that they are true if even one of their instances are true. But in this case there is no problem. If even one person is not rich, ∃y(Gy → ∀xHx) has a true instance and so is true, but the same holds of the correct formalization, ∀xGx → ∀xHx. If even one person is not rich, it is false that all are rich, giving the conditional a false antecedent and so making it true. But if everyone is rich, the only way ∃y(Gy → ∀xHx) could have even one true instance is if ∀xHx is true, that is, if everyone is happy. This is just what ∀xGx → ∀xHx, and the English original say: that if everyone is rich, then everyone is also happy.

Because the matter has come up, in other cases where a component of a conditional, conjunction, or disjunction is quantified, the quantifier can be given broad scope without changing the meaning. Consider a formula, Q, that does not contain a variable χ, and a formula, P, that contains occurrences of χ. The following equivalence principles hold, and can be relied upon in formalization. (The principles are interderivable in Dq and Tq, and justified by the semantics of chapter 15.)

Equivalence Principles Governing the Scope of Quantifiers

∀χP & Q =|= ∀χ(P & Q)

Q & ∀χP =|= ∀χ(Q & P)

∃χP & Q =|= ∃χ(P & Q)

Q & ∃χP =|= ∃χ(Q & P)

∀χP ∨ Q =|= ∀χ(P ∨ Q)

Q ∨ ∀χP =|= ∀χ(Q ∨ P)

∃χP ∨ Q =|= ∃χ(P ∨ Q)

Q ∨ ∃χP =|= ∃χ(Q ∨ P)

Q → ∀χP =|= ∀χ(Q → P)

Q → ∃χP =|= ∃χ(Q → P)

In cases where occurrences of Q appearing on the left side of each of these equivalences do contain a χ quantifier, the following principle can be invoked to allow the conversion.[12]

Quantifier Rewrite Principles

∀χP =|= ∀ψP(ψ|χ)

∃χP =|= ∃ψP(ψ|χ)

(where ψ does not occur in P and P(ψ|χ) is the result of replacing each occurrence of χ in P with ψ)

This having been said, the best policy is to follow the English syntax. When English quantifies just one conjunct or disjunct or just the consequent of a conditional, the formalization should do likewise. When it quantifies the whole conjunction, disjunction, or conditional, the formalization should do likewise. The one exception is when English quantifies just the antecedent of a conditional. In that circumstance, policy 12.3.6 should be applied. It is restated below, with an update to cover universally quantified antecedents.

Policy 12.3.6 (Amended)

When "anyone," "any," "a," "an," "someone," "some," or equivalent expressions occur as the main operator of the antecedent of a conditional, formalize the conditional as (∃xP → Q).

If Q contains a reference to the object bound by ∃x in ∃xP, replace (∃xP → Q) with ∀x(P → Q) and go on to further unpack the information contained in Q.

When "each," "every," "all," "everyone," or equivalent expressions occur as the main operator of the antecedent of a conditional, formalize the conditional as (∀xP → Q).

If Q contains a reference to the objects bound by ∀x in ∀xP, preface Q with its own universal quantifier to bind that reference.

The following equivalence principles govern conditionals with quantified antecedents. Only the second has practical application.

$$\forall \chi Q \rightarrow P =|= \exists \chi (Q \rightarrow P)$$
$$\exists \chi Q \rightarrow P =|= \forall \chi (Q \rightarrow P)$$

There are no equivalence principles for biconditionals. They can be rewritten as conjunctions of converse conditionals. Each conjunct is independently governed by the appropriate principle for conditionals.

When a conjunction, disjunction, or conditional with a quantified component is itself quantified, and the component quantifier or its dual is "moved out" in accord with the equivalence principles, it should be placed to the right of any pre-existing quantifiers. For example, $\forall x(\forall z \sim Cxz \rightarrow Bx)$ becomes $\forall x \exists z(\sim Cxz \rightarrow Bx)$, not $\exists z \forall x(\sim Cxz \rightarrow Bx)$. As already noted, the existential quantifier has a different meaning when it follows a universal from the meaning it has when it precedes that universal. This makes it important to preserve the order of the quantifiers. When all the quantifiers have the same sign, their order does not matter, and putting an existential that belongs in front of a universal after it produces a sentence that is a consequence of the proper formalization. These facts are summarized by the following principles.

$$\forall \chi \forall \psi P =|= \forall \psi \forall \chi P$$
$$\exists \chi \exists \psi P =|= \exists \psi \exists \chi P$$
$$\exists \chi \forall \psi P \vDash \forall \psi \exists \chi P$$

12.3.7 *Quantities and Superlatives*

QPL can formalize other quantities than "at least one," "each," and "none." "At most one object is G," is canonically formalized as

12.44 $\forall x[Gx \rightarrow \forall y(Gy \rightarrow =yx)]$

This can be paraphrased as, "for each object the variable x might denote, if it is a G then each object the variable y might denote is such that if it is also a G it must be the x object." This is not the most obvious way of expressing "at most one." A more intuitive, though objectionable rendition would be

12.45 $\exists x Gx \rightarrow \forall y(\sim Gy \vee =yx)$

This attempts to say that if, on going through the domain object after object, an object is found that is a G, any object that is subsequently inspected must either not be a G or must prove to be the object that was first found to be a G. This captures what "at most one is G" means. "At most one is G" does not promise that there are any G's, and neither does this attempted formalization, which would be true if it had a false antecedent. At the same time, "At most one is G" asserts that there cannot be two or more things that are G's, and the attempted formalization reflects this by stipulating that if the antecedent is true, and there is at least one object that is a G, all objects that are found to be G's must prove to be the first one found to be a G. Unfortunately, the formalization is unacceptable, because it leaves a free variable. As already discussed, extending the scope of the existential quantifier to cover the final occurrence of x requires that it be converted to a universal. This yields $\forall x[Gx \rightarrow \forall y(\sim Gy \vee =yx)]$. Given the equivalence of $\sim P \vee Q$ and $P \rightarrow Q$, it can be hoped that $\sim Gy \vee =yx$ would prove to be equivalent to $Gy \rightarrow =yx$ (as is indeed the case). Thus, the intuitive $\exists x Gx \rightarrow \forall y(\sim Gy \vee =yx)$ is rendered as $\forall x[Gx \rightarrow \forall y(Gy \rightarrow =yx)]$.

The formalization of "Exactly one object is G," rewrites "At most one is G with an existential quantifier and ampersand, to promise that there is indeed at least one object that is G and that any object that proves to be G must also prove to be the first one found to be G.

12.46 $\exists x[Gx \& \forall y(Gy \rightarrow =yx)]$

The formalization of "At least two objects are G," includes an important detail.

12.47 $\exists x[Gx \& \exists y(\sim =xy \& Gy)]$

Two existential quantifiers are not enough to express that there are two objects, because the two variables could denote the same object. To rule this out, a negated identity clause is required. Paraphrased, "at least one object the variable x might denote is G and at least one object the variable y might denote is not the same object but is also G." This is once again not a standard formalization. The standard formalization invokes one of the equivalence principles mentioned at the close of section 12.3.6 to move the second existential quantifier out of the conjunction and flips the conjuncts, yielding the more elegant $\exists x \exists y (Gx \& Gy \& \sim=xy)$.

Formalizing "Exactly two objects are G," requires adding a further detail:

12.48 $\exists x \exists y (Gx \& Gy \& \sim=xy \& \forall z[Gz \rightarrow (=zx \lor =zy)])$

In addition to saying that at least two objects are G, it must be added that there are no others. This is done by adding that for each object the variable z might denote, if that object is G then it is either the x object or the y object (in other words, any object is either not a G or is one or other of x and y).

Exercise 12.13

Apply what has just been said to formalize "Exactly three objects are G.". All of $\sim=xy$, $\sim=yz$, and $\sim=xz$, as well as a fourth variable, x_1, are necessary and a corresponding expansion is required for the disjuncts.

Exercise 12.13 illustrates the desirability of omitting internal punctuation in iterated conjunctions and disjunctions: As numbers increase, the sentences would otherwise become unreadable.

There are at most two G's is:

12.49 $\forall x \forall y [(Gx \& Gy \& \sim=xy) \rightarrow \forall z[Gz \rightarrow (=zx \lor =zy)]]$

Paraphrased, for each object the variable x might denote and each object the variable y might denote, if they are G and they are not the same (so, if there are two different things that are G), then any object the variable z might denote is such that if it is G then it is the same as one or other of them (so, there cannot be a third G). The consequent, that any object is either not G or is the same as one or other of some two that are, only holds if there are two G's, and the sentence does not say that there are that many. It only says that should there be that many, there could not be any more.

QPL can similarly formalize at least *n*, at most *n*, and exactly *n*, for any number *n*.

Exercise 12.14

Apply what has just been said to formalize "There are at least three G's" and "There are at most three G's."

The formalization of superlatives is another case where a further detail must be added. Superlatives say something about the individual at the top of some ranking, such as the first or the oldest or the best or the least. They are based on comparative relations, such as "is faster than," "is smarter than," "is older than," and so on. A first stab at formalizing "Alma is the oldest brother of Boda" using "a" for Alma, b for Boda, Gxy for "x is a brother of y," and Hxy for x is older than y" might be

12.50 $\forall x (Gxb \rightarrow Hax)$

But this has two untoward implications. First, the English promises that Boda has an oldest brother. But, as discussed in section 12.3.5, universally quantified sentences do not have existential import. The proposed formalization only manages to say that Alma would be the odest brother if Boda had any brothers. Second, a universally quantified sentence is true only if each of its instances is true. Among those instances is Gab $\rightarrow$ Haa, which says that if Alma is a brother of Boda, then he is older than himself. But background knowledge maintains that no one can be older than themselves. A formalization that rectifies both of these shortcomings is

12.51 $Gab \& \forall x (Gxb \& \sim=xa \rightarrow Hax)$

Paraphrased, "Alma is a brother of Boda and for each object the variable x might denote, if x is a brother of Boda who is not Alma, then Alma is older than x." The rectified paraphrase adds two conjuncts to address each problem. The first, Gab, provides assurance that Boda does have an older brother, notably Alma, and the second conjunct of the antecedent of the universally quantified component makes Alma an exception to the general rule that Alma is older than any brother of Boda.

Ordinal numbers can be formalized by appeal to a successor or predecessor relation, such as "before" or "after" or "lesser" or "greater." For example, "Alma is the first to have completed the test" might be formalized as follows, using Gxy for "x completed y," "Hxyz" for "x completed y before z," a for Alma, and "b" for the test.

> 12.52 Gab & ∀x(Gxb & ~=xa → Habx)

This is almost the same formalization that was provided for "Alma is Boda's oldest brother." The difference is only in the interpretation of the name and predicate letters. This goes to show that, unsurprisingly, "the first" is not distinct from "the oldest" as far as the logic of the relation is concerned.

"Alma was the second to have completed the test," can be formalized as

> 12.53 Gab & ∃x[Gxab & ~=xa & Hxba & ∀y(Gyb & ~=yx & ~=ya → Haby)]

Loosely paraphrased, Alma completed the test, and there is someone else who completed it before she did, but anyone else who completed the test did so after Alma did.

When formalizing sentences that mention relations that have special properties, it may be necessary to supplement the formalization to convey this information. Alma cannot be taller than herself. But "Someone in the room is taller than Alma," which might be formalized as ∃x(Gx & Hxa), does not by itself justify the inference that there is someone other than Alma in the room, which might be formalized as ∃x(Gx & ~=xa). The inference cannot be drawn without adding that H is an asymmetric relation, that is, without adding that ∀x∀y(Hxy → ~Hyx). Everyone knows that "taller than" is asymmetric, but this knowledge is not conveyed by formalizing "x is taller than y" as "Hxy." The fact that it is being used to formalize an asymmetric property needs to be made explicit to justify the inference.

When a sentence is formalized in isolation, it would impose an undue burden to demand that each property that any of its predicates bears be formalized. But when the consequence of a demonstration turns on such a property, it is necessary to formalize it (if possible; see chapter 17 for further discussion of properties of relations).

Exercise 12.15

Provide a quasi-English paraphrase for each of the following sentences. Then formalize it as a sentence of QPL using the formalization key provided.

D: everything
d: Boda
Ax: x is a person
Bxy: x loves y
Cxy: x is a sister of y
Gxy: x is older than y
Hxy: x is a brother of y

★**a.** At most one person loves themselves.
  b. At least one person loves Boda
★**c.** Boda loves exactly one person and it is not herself.
  d. At least two people other than Boda love her.
★**e.** Boda has (exactly) two sisters.
  f. Boda has at least one sister who is older than she is.
★**g.** Boda is the oldest of her siblings.
  h. Boda's oldest sister is not as old as she is.
★**i.** Neil Armstrong was the first person to walk on the Moon. *(Use: e: Neil Armstrong; f: the Moon; Ax: x is a person, Kxy: x walked on y; Kxyz: x walked on y after z.)*
  j. God is the most perfect being. *(Use: e: God; Kxy: x is more perfect than y; since D is everything, a "being" predicate is not required.)*

12.3.8 Definite Descriptions

Of the formalizations discussed in the previous subsection, those for "exactly one" and superlatives have a further application. They allow QPL to formalize definite descriptions without using the term forming operators introduced in chapter 10.3.4. In case that material was not studied, definite descriptions, such as "the English astronomer who designed St. Paul's cathedral," are descriptions that are intended to pick out exactly one object. PSL can only use names to stand for the objects picked out by definite descriptions. This comes at the cost of losing the information the descriptions contain.

The ability to formalize this information is valuable because it can be consequential. For example, "The English astronomer who designed St. Paul's cathedral was knighted in 1763" entails that an astronomer was knighted in 1763. But the inference cannot be formalized in a way that captures its validity if the definite description is formalized as a name. Take "a" to denote "the English astronomer who designed St. Paul's cathedral," Gx to stand for "x is an astronomer," and Kx to stand for "x was knighted in 1763." Then the resulting formalization,

12.54 $\dfrac{\text{Ka}}{\exists x(Gx \ \& \ Kx)}$

is not p-valid, even though the English demonstration it formalizes is valid.

One way to get around this difficulty, famously proposed by Bertrand Russell (1920: 207–23; 1956: 241–54), is to use the resources provided by QPL to represent a definite description as a subformula of an ∃ sentence. On Russell's proposal, "The English astronomer who designed St. Paul's cathedral was knighted in 1763" can be formalized as

12.55   ∃x[Hx & Gx & Cxb & ∀y(Hy & Gy & Cyb → =yx) & Kx]

where Hx stands for "x is English," Cxy stands for "x designed y," and b denotes St. Paul's cathedral.

The open sentence, Hx & Gx & Cxb, unpacks the information suppressed in "a" when "a" is used as a name to denote the English astronomer who designed St. Paul's cathedral. Placing this open sentence under an existential quantifier has the effect of (i) promising that there is at least one object that satisfies it. Including the conjunct, ∀y(... → =yx), within the existentially quantified subformula has the effect of (ii) promising that no other object satisfies the open sentence. Supplementing these two formulas with Kx (iii) identifies the object denoted by this description with someone knighted in 1763. These three components of Russell's formalization can be thought of as (i) the existence assertion, (ii) the uniqueness assertion, and (iii) an additional predication.

The immediate payoff for this complex approach is that it makes it possible to derive the information contained in a definite description from that description. ∃x(Gx & Kx), for instance, is derivable from the Russellian definite description displayed above. At the same time, Russell's approach only allows information to be derived from proper descriptions (those that denote an object), not from improper descriptions (those that do not denote an object or that denote more than one of them).

Sentences of the form "The (one) thing that is G is G" can seem valid, especially when the form is instantiated as "The English astronomer who designed St. Paul's cathedral designed St. Paul's cathedral" or "The cat is a cat." This is not so much the case when it is instantiated as "The round square is round" or "The assassin of Caesar was an assassin." These instantiations reveal that "The (one) thing that is G is G" is only plausible when it is assumed that there is exactly one thing that is G. When the description "the (one) thing that is G" is improper, the bare use of that description does not establish that there is any object in the extension of the predicate G, much less one denoted by the description "the (one) thing that is G." On Russell's approach, "The (one) thing that is G is G" is formalized as ∃x[Gx & ∀y(Gy → =yx)]. When more than one thing is G, the second conjunct is false, making the description false, and any further sentence of the form ∃x[Gx & ∀y(Gy → =yx) & Hx] containing a third conjunct that makes an additional predication is false as well. When nothing is G, nothing satisfies the first conjunct, with the same results.

Russell's approach also manages a difficulty that arises when improper descriptions appear in negations. The sentence

12.56   The present King of France is bald

is false, because there is no present King of France to be found in the extension of the "bald" predicate. It would seem to follow that

12.57 The present King of France is not bald

must be true. Yet many people would balk at accepting this on the ground that it also suggests that there is a present King of France. Reformulating the sentence as "It is not the case that the present King of France is bald" is of no help given the scope ambiguity of English uses of "not."

Russell's approach "spreads the formalization out," so to speak, allowing the "King of France" sentence to be formalized two different ways, depending on the intended scope of the negation. Take Kx to stand for "x is the present King of France," and Hx to stand for "x is bald." On the one formalization the sentence says (falsely) that there is a present King of France who is not bald:

primary (narrow scope negation): ∃x[Kx & ∀y(Ky → =yx) & ~Hx]

On the other, it says (truly) that there is no present King of France to be bald:

secondary (wide scope negation): ~∃x[Kx & ∀y(Ky → =yx) & Hx]

Russell referred to these as "primary" and "secondary" senses. Others have referred to them as *de re* and *de dicto* negations (the former denying that an object, or *res*, is in the extension of a predicate, the latter negating a sentence or *dictum*). These are not the most memorable labels. Consistently with terminology employed elsewhere in this chapter, they are better described as wide scope and narrow scope negations.

Russell's approach is the third of the five ways of developing a semantics for improper descriptions surveyed in chapter 11.7.6. It considers any predicate or identity sentence that contains an improper description to be false. This is a necessary consequence of putting an existential quantifier on the formalization of any sentence containing a definite description and making the description a conjunct of the immediate subformula.

As discussed in chapter 11.7.6, not everyone accepts that sentences containing improper descriptions ought to be considered false, merely on that account. One objection is that this approach does not reflect an intuitive assessment of such demonstrations as

12.58 The Loch Ness Monster is an aquatic animal.
   _____
   Something is an aquatic animal.

Many would consider this demonstration to be invalid. The fact that the Loch Ness Monster is an aquatic animal does nothing to establish that there are aquatic animals, since there is no Loch Ness Monster. On the Russellian account, in contrast, this is a valid demonstration. There either is a Loch Ness Monster or there is not. If there is, the conclusion is true. If there is not, the premise is false. Either way, the demonstration does not have a true premise and a false conclusion, and for Russell these are the only ways.

For those opposed to Russell's account, these are not the only ways because the fact that there is no Loch Ness monster does nothing to detract from the truth of the assertion that the Loch Ness monster is an aquatic animal.

The view that "The Loch Ness Monster is an aquatic animal" is true is accommodated by free logic, introduced in chapter 11.7.6 and further investigated in chapters 13.5 and 14.4.3.

Exercise 12.16

1. *Provide a quasi-English paraphrase for each of the following sentences. Then formalize it as a sentence of QPL using the formalization key provided. Universal quantifiers should always have conditionals as their immediate subformulas and existential quantifiers should always have conjunctions as their immediate subformulas. A sentence of QPL contains no free variables and no punctuation marks unless those punctuation marks are used in conjunction with a binary connective.*

   D: everything
   d: Boda; e: Elvis
   Ax: x is a person; Bxy: x loves y; Cxy: x knows y; Gx: x is a cook; Hxy: x is happier than y; Kxy: x is older than y; A₁xy: x is a brother of y

⋆**a.** The only person who loves Boda is Elvis.

 b. The only person who knows Boda is Elvis.

⋆**c.** The only person who knows Boda is the cook.

 d. The only person who knows Boda is the happiest cook.

⋆**e.** There is no cook.

 f. There is no happiest cook.

⋆**g.** It is not the case that there is exactly one cook.

 h. The happiest cook is not Boda's oldest brother.

⋆**i.** It is not the case that the cook is happier than Boda.

 j. It is not the case that the cook is not Boda.

2. *The principle "The (one) thing that is G is G" has been referred to as the characterization principle. While many would accept that the characterization principle does not hold for instances like "The round square is round," many would also accept that it holds in cases where more than one object satisfies the description. For these people, it is not intuitive that "The assassin of Caesar was an assassin" is false. What about the assertions that the Loch Ness monster is a monster, or that the Loch Ness monster inhabits Loch Ness? Can the intuition that the characterization principle fails for "The round square is round" be reconciled with the intuition that it holds in these other cases, or are the only alternatives to maintaining that it either fails for all definite descriptions (as Russell maintained) or holds for all of them, even "the round square is round?"*

12.3.9 Bare Existence; Limits of Formalization

As noted in section 12.3.5, while a universally quantified sentence can be true without implying that there are objects that satisfy its immediate subformula, negations of universally quantified sentences say that at least one object does not satisfy the immediate subformula. "All wolves are social," says that everything is either not a wolf or social, which is trivially true if there are no wolves to be asocial and provide a counterexample. "Not all wolves are social," in contrast, requires that there be an example, which means at least one lone wolf must be found.

QPL does not say that there is a lone wolf with an existence predicate. Instead, it uses an existential quantifier or a negated universal construction.

$$12.59 \quad \exists x(Gx \,\&\, {\sim}Hx) \text{ or } {\sim}\forall x(Gx \to Hx)$$

where Gx is "x is a wolf" and Hx is "x is social."

Even though the existential quantifier only says that at least one of the objects in the domain satisfies the description (and there are no constraints on what can be included in a domain), it is tempting to read existentially quantified sentences as asserting that something exists. A bare existence sentence uses a name, the identity symbol, and an existentially quantified variable to make what looks like an existence assertion. Take "a" to name Santa Claus. Then a bare existence sentence concerning Santa Claus would be:

$$12.60 \quad \exists x{=}ax$$

Similarly, "God exists," can be formalized as

$$12.61 \quad \exists x{=}bx$$

where "b" names God.

Though these bare existence sentences look meaningful, they are not. A sentence is only meaningful if there is a chance it could be false. Only then does it say something informative: that the chance happens not to be the case. But any sentence of QPL of the form $\exists x{=}px$ is q-valid. This does not mean that it is a logical truth that God exists. $\exists x{=}bx$ is true on any interpretation, and so true regardless of what b denotes, because by definition of an interpretation, each name must be assigned to exactly one of the objects in the domain. It is not a logical truth that God must be included in the domain. But it is a feature of QPL that each name must denote an object in the domain.

The existential quantifier is misnamed, and bare existence sentences are imposters. The existential quantifier only asserts that at least one of the objects in the domain satisfies the immediate subformula, not that this object exists. Drawing that further inference would require presuming that the contents of the domain are determined by what exists. But logic is not so restrictive. It does not presume to declare what belongs in the domain and is happy to consider domains that include objects that are not presumed to exist. Bare existence sentences are the opposite of what an existence sentence should be. If anything is a "brute fact," that is, something that could be otherwise, it ought to be an assertion that something exists. But bare existence sentences are q-valid. They do not affirm the brute fact that something exists. They merely repeat the stipulation that a name of QPL may only denote an object in the domain.

While the use of a name entails that there is an object in the domain denoted by that name, the use of a description does not. Taking Gxy to be "x is more perfect than y," "The most perfect being exists," can be formalized as

> 12.62 $\exists x \forall y (\sim=yx \rightarrow Gxy)$

Unlike $\exists x=bx$, this sentence is not q-valid, as demonstrated in exercise 16.8f.

In line with these results, there are certain limitations that need to be placed on formalization in QPL. As with PSL, domains and names need to complement one another. If an English sentence names an object that is not in the domain, either the domain must be expanded to include that object, or the name should not be formalized. Formalizing it would imply that it does denote an object in the domain. The name must instead be included in the interpretation of a predicate letter. For example, if Zeus is not in the domain but Mount Olympus is, then "Mount Olympus was the seat of Zeus" might be formalized as Ga, where "a" is Mount Olympus and Gx is "x was the seat of Zeus."

Definite descriptions can be treated differently. Speakers normally intend definite descriptions to refer to exactly one object, and listeners normally understand them to be intended in that way, but those intentions and assumptions can be incorrect. An interpretation on which they are incorrect will not include the described object in the domain, or will include more than one object that satisfies the description. In either of those cases, the description can still be formalized, either in the Russellian fashion outlined in section 12.3.8, or in an alternative formal language (for instance the one discussed in chapters 10.3.4–5 and 11.7). The Russellian formalization converts any atomic sentence that contains a definite description into an existentially quantified sentence, thereby ensuring that this sentence will be false if the description is improper. Other description theories have their own ways of managing improper descriptions (some discussed in chapter 11.7.6). Either way, definite descriptions can be formalized, even when they do not denote exactly one object.

Special care must be taken with English sentences that talk about people's thoughts, beliefs, assertions, desires, intentions, aims, and other attitudes. These sentences describe a relation between a person and an object, but in cases where the relation is thinking, believing, asserting, desiring, and so on, the object is an intentional object. Formalizing relations to intentional objects has untoward results when the object does not exist, and in some cases even when it does.

> 12.63   Virginia wondered whether there is a Santa Claus

names a person who actually existed, Virginia O'Hanlon (1889–1971), and describes a relation between her and an intentional object. Attempting to formalize the sentence as any of

> 12.64   Gac
> 12.65 $\exists x(Cx \ \& \ Gax)$
> 12.66 $\exists x[Cx \ \& \ \forall y(Cy \rightarrow =yx) \ \& \ Gax]$

where "a" denotes Virginia, c denotes Santa Claus, Cx is "x is a Santa Claus," and Gxy is "x wondered whether y exists" yields unacceptable results.

12.64 is based on an assignment of Santa Claus to c. Since every name must be assigned exactly one object in the domain, this only works if the domain is expanded to include Santa Clause. But Virginia meant to ask whether Santa Claus is a material object in the space and time of the real world. Her question is about a domain with an admission criterion. She was asking whether Santa Claus meets that criterion. 12.64 is not an adequate formalization, because it uses a different domain of discourse than the one she intended to ask about.

12.65 and 12.66 avoid this outcome, but both are false, since there is no object that satisfies the first conjunct of the immediate subformula. But the original English sentence is true. Virginia did wonder whether there is a Santa Claus. So they likewise do not capture the meaning of the original English sentence.

QPL can only handle this case by treating the "wondering" relation to an intentional object as an unanalysable mental state of Virginia.

12.67   Ha

where Hx is "x wondered whether Santa Claus exists." This solution comes at a cost: it suppresses information about what Virginia was wondering about under a predicate letter.

The same holds when the intentional relation is to some of the objects in a group.

12.68   There are witches in Salem

can be formalized as

12.69   ∃x(Gx & Hxa)

where "a" is Salem, Gx is "x is a witch," and Hxy is "x is in y." The English sentence is false of the real world, and its formalization is false on any interpretation on which the extension of the predicate Gx, "x is a witch," is empty. But

12.70   Cotton Mather was looking for witches

is true even though there were no witches. People can very well look for things that do not exist. On the assumption that Mather was looking for some witches, "Cotton Mather was looking for witches" needs to be read as asserting a one-place predicate of Cotton Mather, not a relation between Mather and other objects. The best formalization that QPL can manage in this case is

12.71   Hc

where c is Cotton Mather and Hx is "x is looking for witches." Again, this comes at the cost of losing information about what Mather was looking for.

The same does not hold for universals or negations of existentials, which are equivalent to universals. On the assumption that Mather was looking for all the witches in a restricted area (perhaps all the witches in Salem), and did not particularly care to find any there might be outside that area,

12.72   Cotton Mather was looking for witches (in Salem)

can be formalized as

12.73   ∀x(Gx & Hxa → Kcx)

where Kxy is "x was looking for y." For this sentence of QPL to be true, each object in the domain must either not be a witch in Salem or be something Mather was looking for. It is false if and only if there is at least one object that is witch in Salem whom Mather is not looking for. This captures the truth conditions of the original English sentence.

Similarly,

12.74   William Phips was *not* looking for witches

can be formalized as ~∃x(Gx & Hxa & Kex) or ∀x(Gx & Hxz → ~Kex), where e denotes William Phips. In this case, the English sentence is not attributing a relation to an intentional object to Phips. On the contrary, it is confined to denying that there are objects that stand in any such relation to Phips.

Even cases where the intentional relation is to a group that contains objects raise difficulties. Gammer Gurton wanted *her* needle. No other would do. Where "a" is Gammer Gurton, Gx is "x is a needle," and Hxy is "x wants y"

12.75   ∃x(Gx & Hax)

is an appropriate formalization of the assessment

12.76   Gammer Gurton wanted a needle

In this case, there was a needle, indeed a very special one, that Gammer Gurton wanted.

In contrast, standing on Bosworth Field, Richard III wanted *a* horse. Not *his* horse, which he would have been happy to abandon for any more readily available. Not *any two or more* of the available horses, since he could make no use of more than one of them. But also not any one of them in preference to another, since he would have seized any he could get.

Had there been no horses left on the field, Richard's case would have been like Mather's. But because Richard did not want all the available horses, a variant on 12.73 would not be a correct formalization of

12.77   Richard III wanted a horse

A variant on 12.71, where the name denotes Richard III and the one-place predicate is "x wants a horse," would be correct.

It might be thought that had there been horses left on the field, a variant on 12.75 would be a correct formalization of 12.77. Indeed, the identical formalization would serve. Just take "a" to denote Richard III rather than Gammer Gurton and Gx to be "x is a horse" rather than "x is a needle." Being otherwise identical, the formalizations say the same thing: that there is at least one object that is the object the person in question wants to have. But there was no special horse Richard wanted, as there was a special needle Gammer Gurton wanted. 12.76 is correct for 12.75, but overdetermined for 12.77. It claims to identify at least one object that is the object Richard wanted.

It was noted in section 12.3.2 that the existential quantifier has two senses: "the same one" and "some one or other." But it only has either of these senses when paired to the left or the right of a universal quantifier. On its own, it only says "at least one object in the domain is such that …."

This having been said, it might be thought that the difficulty could be overcome by a variant on 12.72 that puts the existential quantifier after a universal to give it the sense of "some one or other." Take Gx to be "x is a horse on Bosworth Field." Then 12.77 might be paraphrased as "for each object the variable x might denote, if that object is a horse on Bosworth Field, at least one object the variable y might denote is horse on Bosworth field, and Richard wants that horse.

12.78 $\forall x[Gx \rightarrow \exists y(Gy \ \& \ Hay)]$

This formalization has some attractive features. If there are no horses left, the antecedent of the conditional subformula is not satisfied, so the conditional subformula is satisfied. If there is exactly one left, it would be the one Richard wants. If there is more than one, for each one of them, at least one (not necessarily but perhaps another one) is the one Richard wants, but there is nothing to say that for each case (in the case of each horse) it is the same (other) horse he wants. The formalization in this way introduces a looseness of fit that approximates the notion that there is no special horse he is after.

Unfortunately, this still will not work. The formalization requires that for each horse there be a special one that is paired with it as the one Richard wants. But Richard does not want one horse relative to this horse, another (not necessarily distinct) horse relative to some other horse, and so on. He just wants a horse.

There is still something worth pursuing about 12.78. It brings up the notion of multiple different cases (the case of each horse) where the results are possibly different in each case. This is the sort of situation that modal logic is suited to handle. The modal logic studied in chapters 8–9 and A-4 is concerned with possible cases, suggesting that some combination of modal with quantificational languages like

12.79 $\exists x(Gx \ \& \ \Diamond Hax)$

might do the job. This particular combination is well off the mark. It is false if there are no horses, whereas the English sentence is still true. And Richard does not just possibly want a horse. This attempted formalization gets the scope of the operators wrong. It puts the modal operator under the existential quantifier. But the English sentence "Richard wants a horse" mentions a modal operator (wants) before the existential quantifier (a).

There are systems of modal logic that deal with knowledge, belief, desire, and other intentional predicates as if they were operators. (Modal logic is as much the logic of intensional operators as of modes of assertion.) In epistemic modal logic, KtP and BtP, where t is a term and P is a sentence, are used as operators on combinations of a person and a sentence. They apply to combinations of persons and sentences in the way $\Box$ and $\Diamond$ apply to sentences. $\exists x Kx P$ says that someone knows that P. BaP says that Richard believes that P. $\exists x Kx \exists x P$ says that someone knows that there is at least one thing that satisfies the condition, P. "Wants" can be dealt with in the same way. Taking Wt to be the modal operator "t wants it to be the case that,"

12.80   Wa∃x(Gx & Hax)

says that Richard wants it to be the case that there is a horse that he has. This is a successful formalization. It puts the existential quantifier under the scope of another operator, thereby giving the existential quantifier the sense of "some horse or other."

This has been an excursion beyond the bounds of QPL, which is not a language with the vocabulary or the syntax to handle this sort of formalization. Even in the case where there are horses, the best QPL can do is formalize "Richard III wants a horse" as Ha, where Hx is "x wants a horse." The remarks that have been made on how an intensional logic could express more of the information contained in the original English sentence are not intended to be applied in formalization exercises. They have been made to illustrate what would be required to capture the "some one or other" sense of the existential quantifier, and to make the point that QPL cannot do this with its own resources.

This having been said, for curiosity's sake, all cases that have been discussed in this section are cases that might be formalized using intensional operators. The Virginia case can be formalized as

12.81   W₁a∃xCx

where W_1tP is "t wonders whether P is true," "a" is Virginia, and Cx is "x is a Santa Claus." The Mather case is best formalized using a variant intensional predicate, Ltc, that operates on a term and what might be called a concept. Concepts are either individual concepts, formalized as terms, or categorical concepts, formalized as quantified predicates or quantified predicate descriptions. Using Ltc, "Cotton Mather was looking for witches" can be formalized as

12.82   Lc∃xGx

where c is Cotton Mather, and Gx is "x is a witch in Salem." In contrast "William Phips was not looking for witches," is

12.83   ~Le∃xGx or ∀x(Gx → ~Lex)

But QPL cannot do any of this. It must treat intensional operators as one-place predicates, and can do so only more or less successfully, with more or less loss of information in different cases.

Exercise 12.17

Devise a formalization key using the specified domain and formalize the following sentences in QPL using that key.

★**a.** The current President of France is French. *(Domain: currently existing objects)*

  b. The current King of France is French. *(Domain: currently existing objects)*

★**c.** Don Quixote is French. *(Domain: historically existing people)*

  d. Don Quixote is Spanish. *(Domain: historically existing people)*

★**e.** Bertrand Russell mentioned Don Quixote. *(Domain: historically existing people)*

  f. Bertrand Russell mentioned the current King of France. *(Domain: current and historically existing people)*

★**g.** Julius Caesar's assassin was a Roman Senator. *(Domain: historically existing people)*

  h. Jonathan Edwards wanted an egg. *(Domain: historically existing people and things, including a number of indistinguishable eggs in Edwards's pantry, between which he has no preference)*

★**i.** Egypt wants the inscribed stone in the British Museum. *(Domain: currently existing nations and objects)*

  j. Alexander the Great wanted to see a Yeti. *(Domain: historically existing people and things)*

Notes

1 Switching from the passive to the active voice ("Some disease killed all the inhabitants") puts the existential quantifier in the right place (that is, in what QPL considers to be the right place), but the problem is not the use of the passive voice. In the earlier "who knows whom" cases, insistence on using the active voice put the existential quantifier in the wrong place.

2 Since the only form of duality now under consideration is oppositional duality, the qualification "oppositional" is omitted from here on.

3 In that case, "not for all" would be another instance of the scope ambiguity that infects "all are not."

4 The ready availability of "someone does not care for anyone" is one reason for thinking that "Someone does not care for everyone" unambiguously says the same thing as "Someone does not care for someone." There is some pressure on those who want to say that someone cares for no one to use "Someone does not care for anyone" to express their thought, in preference to "Someone does not care for everyone."

5 Those familiar with Venn diagrams will be aware that the following depictions are not Venn diagrams. They are a variant on Euler diagrams. The G circle is always the "subject" circle and the H circle the "predicate" circle. Either circle may be empty. D represents an area that includes both circles rather than the area outside of them.

6 It is also intuitively equivalent to $\forall x(Gx \rightarrow \sim Hx)$ and is shown later to be both q-equivalent to it and interderivable with it.

7 Compare Leblanc and Wisdom (1976: 122) and Bergmann, Moor, and Nelson (2009: 333–4).

8 The thesis that A and E sentences lack existential import seems to have first been raised to prominence by the German philosopher and psychologist, Franz Brentano (1838–1917), for just this reason. Brentano observed that judgements have the logical form of affirming or denying existence (rather than combining subjects with predicates), and thus that A, E, I, and O sentences can all be rewritten as existence assertions without any change in meaning. In the case of A's and E's this means assertions to the effect that there is not any object that does not satisfy or that does satisfy a certain description. The relevant passages from Brentano's *Psychologie vom empirischen Standpunkt* are translated in Chisholm (1960: 62–70, see especially 66). See also Simons (2004: 45–65) and Kneale and Kneale (2008: 411, note 1). Some early reactions to Brentano's thesis were not positive, though it is now widely accepted. See Land (1876: 289–92). Land's report, which chiefly objected to the fact that Brentano's existential rewrites deprived A's and E's of existential import, originally acquainted English readers with Brentano's ideas on logic. See Orenstein (2002: 191, note 1).

9 As discussed in section 12.3.3, the paraphrase of "distrusts someone" as "does not trust someone" is intuitively understood as "does (not trust) someone," which continues to ascribe narrow scope to "not." But a paraphrase of "distrusts everyone" as "does not trust everyone" is (perhaps) ambiguous. There might be some who would read this assertion as giving similarly narrow scope to "not," and so as "does (not trust) everyone" ($\forall\chi\sim P$). But many would insist that in this case "not" unambiguously has "wide" scope and that the paraphrase can only be parsed as "does not (trust everyone)" ($\sim\forall\chi P$). On this account, paraphrasing "distrusts" as "does not trust" changes the meaning. The original meaning can only be preserved by rewriting "everyone" as "anyone" to produce "does not trust anyone." See section 12.3.3 for more on how to formalize "does not trust anyone."

10 While this is particularly clear of "anyone," the same is true for any of the English operators more closely associated with the existential quantifier, such as "at least one," "some," or "someone." "If someone has a bicycle lock they distrust someone" is no different from "If anyone has a bicycle lock they distrust someone."

11 $\forall x(Gx \rightarrow Hx)$ is not a correct formalization. It says that each person in the domain who is found to be rich must prove to also be happy. But the English original allows that there could be people who are rich but not happy. All it rules out is that *everyone* could be rich without everyone also being happy. As long as even one person is not rich, the English original has a false antecedent and so is true regardless of what any other people in the domain are like.

12 The quantifier rewrite principles are interderivable in Dq and Tq and justified by the semantics of chapter 15, but they are not mentioned here with a view to being used in any sort of demonstration. They are noticed to provide a guide to the ways formalizations of the same English sentence can differ from one another while still being correct. The intent is to provide some assurance about the sort of liberties that may be taken in formalization. Quantifiers tagged with different variables would ideally be chosen at the initial stages of formalization, were it anticipated that policy 12.3.6 would need to be applied.

References

Bergmann, Merrie, Moor, James, and Nelson, Jack, 2009, *The Logic Book*, 5th edition, McGraw-Hill, New York.

Chisholm, Roderick, 1960, *Realism and the Background of Phenomenology*, The Free Press, Glencoe, IL.

Kneale, William, and Kneale, Martha, 2008, *The Development of Logic*, Oxford University Press, Oxford.

Land, JPN, 1876, "Brentano's Logical Innovations," *Mind* 1: 289–92.

Leblanc, Hugues, and Wisdom, William A, 1976, *Deductive Logic*, 2nd edition, Allyn and Bacon, Boston.

Orenstein, Alex, 2002, *WV Quine*, Princeton University Press, Princeton.

Russell, Bertrand, 1920, *Introduction to Mathematical Philosophy*, 2nd edition, Allen & Unwin, London.

———, 1956, *Logic and Knowledge: Essays 1901–1950*, Allen & Unwin, London.

Simons, Peter, 2004, "Judging Correctly: Brentano and the Reform of Elementary Logic," *The Cambridge Companion to Brentano*, Cambridge University Press, New York, 45–65.

13 Derivations

Contents

13.1 Dq

Dq expands on Dp by adding a new assumption rule and four new derivation rules. Only two of the new derivation rules are intuitively obvious. The other two are intuitively invalid. Textbook authors go to some length to show why they should be accepted. That example is followed below. But these efforts only confirm that the rules are not intuitive. This makes Dq an exception to the derivation systems considered so far. It does not rest on intuition alone. It must appeal to a semantic system to demonstrate the soundness of some of its rules.

Fortunately, it is not necessary to agree with a rule to be able to follow it. Following a rule requires nothing more than the ability to recognize an instance of a form.

Dq uses all the rules of Dp, including the metatheorems and derived rules, but not the substitution principles.[1] The rules, metatheorems, and derived rules are unchanged but for the fact that they are extended to include sentences of QPL. This means that the following is a correct derivation in Dq.

1.	∃xGx & ∃xHx	given
2.	∃xHx	1 (&E)

But the following is not.

DOI: 10.4324/9781003026532-22

```
1. │ ∃x(Gx & Hx)     given
2. │ ∃xGx            1 (&E)   × WRONG!
```

(&E) can only be applied to conjunctions, and ∃x(Gx & Hx) is not a conjunction. Before any rules of Dp can be applied to quantified sentences, the quantifiers must be removed. This is not a straightforward procedure. Quantifiers cannot just be stripped off. The result of stripping a quantifier off the front of a sentence is an open sentence, that is, a formula containing one or more free variables. Derivations work with sentences, not with open sentences. Derivations in Dq characteristically begin by applying quantifier instantiation rules to convert quantified sentences to instances of those sentences. The rules of Dp are then applied to these instances. As needed, quantifier "generalization" rules may then be applied to convert instances into quantified sentences.

As a reminder, an instance of a quantified sentence, ∀χP or ∃χP, is formed by removing the quantifier, ∀χ or ∃χ as the case may be, and replacing each occurrence of the variable χ in P with an occurrence of a name, q. (There must be at least one occurrence of χ in P, otherwise ∀χP and ∃χP would not be sentences according to the formation rules.) The instance resulting from replacing each occurrence of χ in P with q is notated as P(q│χ)(read as "P q for chi"). The solid bar, │, means "put the symbol on the left in the place of each occurrence of the symbol on the right."

As a further reminder, only quantified sentences have instances. Their instances are formed by removing their main operator (which must be a quantifier if the sentence is a quantified sentence). Gaa and Gbb are instances of ∀xGxx. Gyy and Gab are not. Where the main operator is not a quantifier, there can be no instance. ∃xGx → Ha and ~∀xGx have no instances. Where the main operator is some other quantifier, instances can only be based on that other quantifier. ∀xGxa is not an instance of ∀x∀yGxy.

Exercise 13.1

1. *State whether the following formulas have instances. If they do, give an example of one such instance.*
    ⋆**a.** ∃yHcy → Gc
     b. ∃x(∀yGy → Hx)
    ⋆**c.** ∀z~∀x~Gxz
     d. ∀y∃x(Gxy → Hx & Ky)
    ⋆**e.** Gxa
     f. ~∀x(Hx → Gax)

2. *State whether the second formula in each pair is an instance of the first. If it is not, say why not.*
    ⋆**a.** ∀y(Hy → Kyy); Ha → Kaa
     b. ∃y∀x(Hx → Gy); ∃y(Ha → Gy)
    ⋆**c.** ∃x∃z∀y(Haxy → Gza); ∃z∀y(Haay → Gza)
     d. ∀x∀y(Gxy ∨ Kax); ∀y(Gay ∨ Kab)
    ⋆**e.** ∃xKxax; Kbax
     f. ∀x∃zHzx; Hab

Even when instances are properly formed, they cannot be derived or converted to quantified sentences at will. For the rules to be sound, restrictions must be put in place. The restrictions make use of the notion of an open assumption.

> An *assumption* is *open* at a line, *n*, of a derivation if and only if its assumption bracket continues down to line *n*.

When derivations are given using bracket free notation, the open assumptions at a line are the list of sentences to the left of the turnstile at that line. When they are given using standard notation, the open assumptions at a line are those that head off the assumption brackets that descend down to that line, taken in order from leftmost assumption bracket to rightmost. The concept is best grasped by doing an exercise.

Exercise 13.2

Identify which assumptions are open at lines ★3, 7, ★11, 12, ★16, and 19.

1.	$G \rightarrow \exists xHx$	given
2.	$\sim\exists x(G \rightarrow Hx)$	(A/IP)
3.	G	(A/CP)
4.	$G \rightarrow \exists xHx$	1 (R)
5.	$\sim\exists x(Gx \rightarrow Hx)$	2 (R)
6.	$\exists xHx$	3,4 (MP)
7.	Hb	(A/6$\exists$E)
8.	$\sim\exists x(Gx \rightarrow Hx)$	5 (R)
9.	$\sim Ha$	(A/IP)
10.	Hb	7(R)
10.1	$\sim\exists x(Gx \rightarrow Hx)$	8 (R)
10.2	G	(A/CP)
...	...	
11.	Hb	lemma for (CP) 10 (R)
12.	$G \rightarrow Hb$	lemma for ($\exists$G) 10.2–11 (CP)
13.	$\exists x(G \rightarrow Hx)$	lemma for ($\perp$I) 12 ($\exists$G)
14.	$\perp$	lemma for (IP) 13,10.1 ($\perp$I)
15.	Ha	lemma for ($\exists$E) 9–14 (IP)
16.	Ha	lemma for (CP) 6,7–15 ($\exists$E)
17.	$G \rightarrow Ha$	lemma for ($\exists$G) 3–16 (CP)
18.	$\exists x(G \rightarrow Hx)$	lemma for ($\perp$I) 17 ($\exists$G)
19.	$\perp$	lemma for (IP) 18,2 ($\perp$I)
20.	$\exists x(G \rightarrow Hx)$	2–19 (IP)

The most onerous restrictions are on instantiating existentially quantified sentences and converting instances to universally quantified sentences. Intuitively, existentially quantified sentences do not yield their instances. Just because someone is rich ($\exists xGx$) it does not follow that Alma is rich (Ga). An existentially quantified sentence says that at least one thing is a certain way, but it does not say which one or ones.

It might be thought that since an existentially quantified sentence promises that there is at least one object that is a certain way, that object could be baptized with a new name. We do this all the time. We say, "Someone is rich. Let's call that person 'Alma.'" This is unobjectionable by itself, but it needs to fit with the other derivation rules to make a sound system. Permitting any kind of instance to be derived from an existentially quantified sentence creates the risk that other derivation rules do too much with that instance. Part of what Dq does to prevent this from happening is stipulate that instances of existentially quantified sentences may only be assumed.

There is accordingly no rule for instantiating existentially quantified sentences. There is only a procedure to follow when dealing with them.

Procedure for Deriving Information from $\exists$ Sentences

If $L \vdash \exists \chi P$, apply (A) to derive $L, P(q|\chi) \vdash P(q|\chi)$, where q is a name that does not occur in any sentence on L or in $\exists \chi P$. Proceed using this expanded list.

When assumption brackets are used, the procedure has the following template:

	Procedure for Deriving Information from ∃ Sentences

$$
\begin{array}{ll}
 & \mid (\text{L}) \; \textit{(no q)} \\
\cdots & \mid \cdots \\
k. & \mid \exists\chi\text{P} \; \textit{(no q)} \quad ? \\
\cdots & \mid \cdots \\
n. & \mid\; \underline{\text{P}(q\,|\,\chi)} \qquad (\text{A}/k.\exists\text{E}) \\
\cdots & \mid\; \cdots
\end{array}
$$

On the template, (L) above the leftmost assumption bracket designates one or more assumptions that may head off one or more assumption brackets continuing down to lines k and n. *(no q)* means q does not occur in the sentence or in any sentence on the list.

In brief, the only thing that can be done with an existentially quantified sentence is assume an instance of that sentence, being careful to use a new name when doing so. The assumption is a special kind of assumption, an existential instantiation assumption, notated as (A/k.∃E). Like assumptions made for (PC) it is derived from a prior line, in this case line k, though it is derived as an assumption. A rule for extracting information from the ensuing subderivation, is provided later.

Exercise 13.3

State whether the sentence at line n *can be derived by* (A/∃E) *from the sentence at line* k. *If it cannot, say why not. In answering these questions, consider an assumption bracket headed off by* (a) *to stand for one or more subderivations headed off by assumptions that contain one or more occurrences of the name,* a.

★a.
$$
\begin{array}{ll}
 & \mid (a) \\
\cdots & \mid \cdots \\
k. & \mid \exists x Gx \quad ? \\
\cdots & \mid \cdots \\
n. & \mid Gx \qquad (A/k\exists E)
\end{array}
$$

b.
$$
\begin{array}{ll}
 & \mid (a) \\
\cdots & \mid \cdots \\
k. & \mid \exists x Gx \quad ? \\
\cdots & \mid \cdots \\
n. & \mid Gb \qquad (A/k\exists E)
\end{array}
$$

★c.
$$
\begin{array}{ll}
 & \mid (a) \\
\cdots & \mid \cdots \\
k. & \mid \exists x Gx \quad ? \\
\cdots & \mid \cdots \\
n. & \mid\; \underline{Ga} \qquad (A/k\exists E)
\end{array}
$$

d.
$$
\begin{array}{ll}
 & \mid (a) \\
\cdots & \mid \cdots \\
k. & \mid \exists x Gxx \quad ? \\
\cdots & \mid \cdots \\
n. & \mid\; \underline{Gca} \qquad (A/k\exists E)
\end{array}
$$

★e.
$$
\begin{array}{ll}
 & \mid (a) \\
\cdots & \mid \cdots \\
k. & \mid \exists x Gxb \quad ? \\
\cdots & \mid \cdots \\
n. & \mid\; \underline{Gbb} \qquad (A/k\exists E)
\end{array}
$$

f.
$$
\begin{array}{ll}
 & \mid (a) \\
\cdots & \mid \cdots \\
k. & \mid \exists x Gxx \quad ? \\
\cdots & \mid \cdots \\
n. & \mid\; \underline{Gbc} \qquad (A/k\exists E)
\end{array}
$$

★g.
$$
\begin{array}{ll}
 & \mid (a) \\
\cdots & \mid \cdots \\
k. & \mid \exists z Gza \quad ? \\
\cdots & \mid \cdots \\
n. & \mid\; \underline{Gca} \qquad (A/k\exists E)
\end{array}
$$

h.
$$
\begin{array}{ll}
 & \mid (a) \\
\cdots & \mid \cdots \\
k. & \mid \exists x \exists z Gzx \quad ? \\
\cdots & \mid \cdots \\
n. & \mid\; \underline{\exists x Gbx} \qquad (A/k\exists E)
\end{array}
$$

★i.
$$
\begin{array}{ll}
 & \mid (a) \\
\cdots & \mid \cdots \\
k. & \mid \exists x \exists z Gzx \quad ? \\
\cdots & \mid \cdots \\
n. & \mid\; \underline{\exists z Gzb} \qquad (A/k\exists E)
\end{array}
$$

It is very difficult to derive a universally quantified sentence. A universally quantified sentence says that each object is a certain way. Since there are infinitely many names, and domains can contain objects that have no names, even establishing that an infinite list of named objects is that way is inadequate to justify a universally quantified sentence. A workaround is to derive a "generic" instance, that is, an instance that is in no way special, meaning that, any other instance could have been derived instead. However, it is by no means obvious what it takes for an instance to be generic.

The rule for deriving universally quantified sentences, "universal generalization" or ($\forall$G), specifies two plausible conditions: the instantiating name must not occur in any sentence on L (that is, in any open assumption), and it must not occur in the universally quantified sentence. Under these conditions, ($\forall$G) declares that a universally quantified sentence can be derived from just one of its instances.

> ($\forall$G): If L $\vdash$ P(q|χ), where q is a name that does not occur in any sentence on L then,
> provided q does not continue to occur in $\forall\chi$P, L $\vdash$ $\forall\chi$P.

When assumption brackets are used, the sentences on L appear as sentences heading off assumption brackets that continue down to line *n,* that is, as open assumptions. The template for application of this rule is accordingly:

The restrictions rule out inferences such as the following:

The application of ($\forall$G) at line 3 is incorrect because the instance it is based on, Hab at line 2, uses an instantiating name, "a," that appears in an open assumption. The arrows chart the course of the mistake. The bottommost arrow shows that the universal quantifier (at line 3) quantifies the first place in the two-place predicate, H. The arrow from x to "a" identifies the instantiating name (the name used to make an instance of $\forall$xHxb in this case). The remaining arrow shows that this instantiating name occurs in an open assumption (at line 1). It does not matter that the arrow is not pointing to the occurrence of "a" in Hab (also at line 1). Any occurrence of the instantiating name anywhere in any open assumption is bad.

This is considered a mistake because Hcb, Hdb, etc. could not have been derived at line 2, so "Hab" at line 2 is not a *generic instance* of $\forall$xHxb. It is a *specific* one, derivable only because the instantiating name, "a," figures in the sentence assumed at line 1. The inference from Hab to $\forall$xHxb cannot be legitimate if it is only possible to derive Hab but not Hpb where p is any other name.

The restrictions also rule out inferences such as the following.

The bottommost arrow again shows that the universal quantifier quantifies the first place in the two-place predicate, H. The arrow from x to the first occurrence of "a" shows that the instantiating name is "a." The remaining arrow shows that the instantiating name continues to occur in the universally quantified sentence. This is a violation of the second restriction.

This is considered a mistake because the instance, Haa, is special. It contains occurrences of the instantiating name "a" that do not get replaced by x in ∀xHxa. No other instance, Hba, Hca, … is like that. If one of those other instances could have been derived, it should have been. If the only way to obtain ∀xHxa is to derive Haa, then it is not a generic instance. The inference from Haa to ∀xHxa cannot be legitimate if it is only possible to derive ∀xHxa from Haa, but not from Hpa, where p is any name.

While it is intuitively obvious that a universally quantified sentence is derivable from a generic instance, it is not intuitively obvious that the two conditions attached to (∀G) are either sufficient or even necessary to specify which instances are generic. It has been shown with two examples that the conditions rule out some unacceptable inferences, but it has not been shown that they rule out all of them, and it has not been shown that they do not cast too wide a net and also rule out some acceptable inferences.

In fact, the conditions are the correct ones. However, a rigorous demonstration can only be given by appeal to the semantic theory of chapter 15.

Exercise 13.4

State whether the sentence at line n can be derived by (∀G) from the sentence at line k. If it cannot, say why not. In answering these questions, consider an assumption bracket headed off by (a) to stand for one or more subderivations headed off by assumptions that contain one or more occurrences of the name, a.

★a.
```
   | (a)
...| ...
k. | Gbb        ?
...| ...
n. | ∀xGxx      k (∀G)
```

b.
```
   | (a)
...| ...
k. | Gbb        ?
...| ...
n. | ∀xGxb      k (∀G)
```

★c.
```
   | (a)
...| ...
k. | Gba        ?
...| ...
n. | ∀xGbx      k (∀G)
```

d.
```
   | (a)
...| ...
k. | Gba        ?
...| ...
n. | ∀xGxa      k (∀G)
```

★e.
```
   | (a)
...| ...
k. | Gbc        ?
...| ...
n. | ∀xGxx      k (∀G)
```

f.
```
   | (a)
...| ...
k. | ∀xGxb       ?
...| ...
n. | ∀x∀yGxy    k (∀G)
```

★g.
```
   | (a)
...| ...
k. | Gbc        ?
...| ...
n. | ∀xGxc      k (∀G)
h.  | ∀y∀xGxy   n (∀G)
```

★i.
```
   | (a)
...| ...
k. | Gb ∨ ∃xHx      ?
...| ...
n. | ∀xGx ∨ ∃xHx   k (∀G)
```

j.
```
   | (a)
...| ...
k. | Gb ∨ ∃xHx         ?
...| ...
n. | ∀x(Gx ∨ ∃xHx)    k (∀G)
```

The rule for deriving an instance from a universally quantified sentence (∀E) is permissive in all the ways the procedure for deriving information from an existentially quantified sentence is restrictive. ∀χP says that each object in the domain is a certain way. Intuitively, any instance of ∀χP ought to be derivable from it, with no requirement that the instance use a new name or that it be entered only as an assumption.

$$(∀E): \text{If } L \vdash ∀χP \text{ then } L \vdash P(q \mid χ)$$

The template for use with assumption brackets is:

Even though $\forall \chi P$ says that each object in the domain is a certain way, it is a bad idea to use new names with ($\forall$E). Sentences that do not match components of other sentences cannot figure in the application of other derivation rules. This makes it wise to use ($\forall$E) to create instances that match components of pre-existing sentences. This is so much the case that if more than one name occurs in a derivation, it can be wise to do ($\forall$E) more than once, each time using one of the names that have occurred elsewhere in the derivation.

Exercise 13.5

State whether the sentence at line n can be derived by ($\forall$E) from the sentence at line k. If it cannot, say why not. In answering these questions, consider an assumption bracket headed off by (a) to stand for one or more subderivations headed off by assumptions that contain one or more occurrences of the name, a.

★a. (a)

  k. | $\forall x G x$?

  n. | G x   k ($\forall$E)

b. (a)

  k. | $\forall x G x$?

  n. | Ga   k ($\forall$E)

★c. (a)

  k. | $\forall x G x x$?

  n. | Gcx   k ($\forall$E)

d. (a)

  k. | $\forall x G x$?

  n. | Gb   k ($\forall$E)

★e. (a)

  k. | $\forall x G x b$?

  n. | Gbb   k ($\forall$E)

f. (a)

  k. | $\forall x G x x$?

  n. | Gba   k ($\forall$E)

★g. (a)

  k. | $\forall z G z b$?

  n. | Gab   k ($\forall$E)

h. | Gbb   k ($\forall$E)

★i. (a)

  k. | $\forall x \forall z G z x$?

  n. | $\forall x G b x$ k ($\forall$E)

j. (a)

  k. | $\forall x \forall z G z x$?

  n. | $\forall z G z b$ k ($\forall$E)

★k. | Gbb   n ($\forall$E)

The rule for deriving an existentially quantified sentence, ($\exists$G) is similarly permissive in all the ways the rule for deriving a universally quantified sentence is restrictive. Intuitively, since $\exists \chi P$ only says that at least one object satisfies the description, P, any instance will justify it, even if the instantiating name continues to occur in the existentially quantified sentence or is present elsewhere in the derivation, including in open assumptions.

$$(\exists G): \text{If } L \vdash P(q|\chi) \text{ then } L \vdash \exists \chi P.$$

The template for use with assumption brackets is:

$$
\begin{array}{lll}
 & & (\exists G) \\
 & \Big| \,(L) & \\
\ldots & \ldots & \\
k. & \Big|\, P(q\,|\,\chi) & \text{lemma for } (\exists G) \\
\ldots & \ldots & \\
n. & \exists\chi P & k\ (\exists G)
\end{array}
$$

Exercise 13.6

State whether the sentence at line n *can be derived by* $(\exists G)$ *from the sentence at line k. If it cannot, say why not. In answering these questions, consider an assumption bracket headed off by (a) to stand for one or more subderivations headed off by assumptions that contain one or more occurrences of the name, a.*

★a.
$$
\begin{array}{lll}
 & \Big|\,(a) & \\
\ldots & \ldots & \\
k. & \Big|\, Gbb & ? \\
\ldots & \ldots & \\
n. & \exists x Gxx & k\ (\exists G)
\end{array}
$$

b.
$$
\begin{array}{lll}
 & \Big|\,(a) & \\
\ldots & \ldots & \\
k. & \Big|\, Gbb & ? \\
\ldots & \ldots & \\
n. & \exists x Gxb & k\ (\exists G)
\end{array}
$$

★c.
$$
\begin{array}{lll}
 & \Big|\,(a) & \\
\ldots & \ldots & \\
k. & \Big|\, Gba & ? \\
\ldots & \ldots & \\
n. & \exists x Gbx & k\ (\exists G)
\end{array}
$$

d.
$$
\begin{array}{lll}
 & \Big|\,(a) & \\
\ldots & \ldots & \\
k. & \Big|\, Gba & ? \\
\ldots & \ldots & \\
n. & \exists x Gxb & k\ (\exists G)
\end{array}
$$

★e.
$$
\begin{array}{lll}
 & \Big|\,(a) & \\
\ldots & \ldots & \\
k. & \Big|\, Gbc & ? \\
\ldots & \ldots & \\
n. & \exists x Gxx & k\ (\exists G)
\end{array}
$$

f.
$$
\begin{array}{lll}
 & \Big|\,(a) & \\
\ldots & \ldots & \\
k. & \Big|\, \exists x Gxb & ? \\
\ldots & \ldots & \\
n. & \exists x \exists y Gxy & k\ (\exists G)
\end{array}
$$

★g.
$$
\begin{array}{lll}
 & \Big|\,(a) & \\
\ldots & \ldots & \\
k. & \Big|\, Gbb & ? \\
\ldots & \ldots & \\
n. & \exists x Gxb & k\ (\exists G)
\end{array}
$$

★i.
$$
\begin{array}{lll}
 & \Big|\,(a) & \\
\ldots & \ldots & \\
k. & \Big|\, Gb \lor \exists x Hx & ? \\
\ldots & \ldots & \\
n. & \exists x Gx \lor \exists x Hx & k\ (\exists G)
\end{array}
$$

j.
$$
\begin{array}{lll}
 & \Big|\,(a) & \\
\ldots & \ldots & \\
k. & \Big|\, Gb \lor \exists x Hx & ? \\
\ldots & \ldots & \\
n. & \exists x (Gx \lor \exists x Hx) & k\ (\exists G)
\end{array}
$$

h.
$$
\begin{array}{ll}
\Big|\, \exists y \exists x Gxy & n\ (\exists G)
\end{array}
$$

The issue that was earlier left hanging (p.505) can now be addressed. The rule for deriving sentences from $(A/\exists E)$ subderivations is $(\exists E)$. It is only ever used in conjunction with a subderivation created by $(A/\exists E)$. $(A/\exists E)$ is always applied to assume an instance of an existentially quantified sentence. That instance strips off the existential quantifier and puts a name, the instantiating name, in the place of the variable named by the existential quantifier. According to $(\exists E)$, any sentence derived immediately to the right of the assumption bracket for an $(A/\exists E)$ subderivation that does not contain this instantiating name can be derived from the subderivation.

In bracket free notation, $(\exists E)$ is combined with the procedure for deriving information from an existentially quantified sentence to make a single rule statement.

> $(\exists E)$: If $L \vdash \exists\chi P$ and $L, P(q\,|\,\chi) \vdash R$, where q does not occur in any sentence on L, in $\exists\chi P$, or in R, then $L \vdash R$.

In practice, applying (∃E) in bracket free notation would entail using (A/∃E) to derive $L, P(q|\chi) \vdash P(q|\chi)$ as a prelude to deriving $L \vdash R$. The template for using the rule with assumption brackets makes this explicit.

$$
\begin{array}{ll}
 & \text{(A/∃E) / (∃E)} \\
 & \text{(L) } (no\ q) \\
\ldots & \ldots \\
h. & \exists\chi P\ (no\ q)\quad ? \\
\ldots & \ldots \\
i. & \quad|\ \underline{P(q|\chi)}\quad\text{(A/}h.\text{∃E)} \\
 & \quad| \\
\ldots & \quad|\ \ldots \\
k. & \quad|\ R\ (no\ q)\quad\text{lemma for (∃E)} \\
\ldots & \quad|\ \ldots \\
\ldots & \quad|\ \ldots \\
n. & \quad R\ (no\ q)\quad h, i{-}k\ \text{(∃E)}
\end{array}
$$

It is important to cite the existentially quantified sentence on line *h* as part of the justification for (A/∃E). $P(q|\chi)$ could contain other names than the one put in the place of χ. In that case, the only way to identify the instantiating name (and so the one that cannot continue to occur in R) is by consulting the original ∃ sentence.

The reason for stipulating that q not occur in R is also the reason for requiring that instances of existentially quantified sentences be assumed rather than derived, and one of the reasons for requiring that universally quantified sentences not be derived from instances that use names that appear in open assumptions: allowing q to occur in a sentence outside the $P(q|\chi)$ subderivation would open the door to applications of (∀G), making it possible to derive $\forall\chi P$ from $\exists\chi P$.

$$
\begin{array}{lll}
1. & |\ \exists x Gax & \text{given} \\
2. & |\ |\ Gab & \text{(A/1∃E)} \\
3. & |\ Gab & 1,2{-}2\ \text{(∃E)} \quad \textbf{\texttimes\ WRONG!}\ \textit{Sentence derived by (∃E) may not contain} \\
4. & |\ \forall x Gx & 3\ \text{(∀G)} \qquad\qquad\quad \textit{the instantiating name}
\end{array}
$$

The arrow at line 1 shows that the existential quantifier quantifies the second place in Gxy. The arrow from lines 1 to 2 shows that b is the instantiating name. The last arrow shows that b continues to occur in the sentence that has been derived by (∃E) (at line 3). This is not permitted because $\forall\chi P$ is not a legitimate inference from $\exists\chi P$. $\exists\chi P$ says that at least one thing is a certain way. From that it does not follow that each thing is that way, which is what $\forall\chi P$ says.

It is a further question why (∃E) should allow deriving *any* sentence that does not contain the instantiating name. Might this already be too much? The answer appeals to an affinity between (∃E) and (PC). $\exists\chi P$ says that at least one object is a certain way. This can be read as a long disjunction. Either the first object in the domain is that way, or the second, or the third, and so on for as many as there are. At least one of these virtual disjuncts is true, but it is not known which one. The strategy for deriving something from an existentially quantified sentence is to show that whichever disjunct is true, the same result is derivable. But rather than make a separate subderivation for each domain object, which is not feasible for large domains, or interpretations on which not all objects are named, the idea is to do the derivation only once, using a name that could stand for any object.

Exercise 13.7

State whether each of the following is a legitimate application of (∃E). If it is not, say why not. In answering these questions, consider an assumption bracket headed off by (a) to stand for one or more subderivations headed off by assumptions that contain one or more occurrences of the name, a.

★a.

	(a)	
...	...	
h.	∃xGax	?
...	...	
i.	Gab	(A/h∃E)
...	...	
k.	Ha	?
n.	Ha	h,i–k (∃E)

b.

	(a)	
...	...	
h.	∃xGbx	?
...	...	
i.	Gbc	(A/h∃E)
...	...	
k.	Hc	?
n.	∃xHx	h,i–k (∃E)

★c.

	(a)	
...	...	
h.	∃xGx	?
...	...	
i.	Gb	(A/h∃E)
...	...	
k.	⊥	?
n.	⊥	h,i–k (∃E)

d.

	(a)	
...	...	
h.	∃xGxb	?
...	...	
i.	Gab	(A/h∃E)
...		?
k.	Hc	
n.	Hc	h,i–k (∃E)

★e.

	(a)	
...	...	
h.	∃xGxb	?
...	...	
i.	Gcb	(A/h∃E)
...	...	
k.	Hb	?
n.	Hb	h,i–k (∃E)

f.

	(a)	
...	...	
h.	∃xGxb	?
...	...	
i.	Gcb	(A/h∃E)
...	...	
k.	Ha	?
n.	Ha	h,i–k (∃E)

★g.

	(a)	
...	...	
h.	∃xGx	?
...	...	
i.	Gc	(A/h∃E)
...	...	
k.	∃yGy	?
n.	∃yGy	h,i–k (∃E)

h.

	(a)	
...	...	
h.	∃xGx → H	?
...	...	
i.	Gx → H	(A/h∃E)
...	...	
k.	~Gb	?
n.	~Gb	h,i–k (∃E)

Dq inherits the strategies of Ds and supplements them with strategies for the application of each of the new rules. The (∃E) strategy occupies second place on that list of strategies, along with the (PC) strategy.

(∃E) *strategy:* For each existentially quantified sentence that appears above the gap, make an (A/∃E) assumption, using a name that has not occurred on any prior line and that does not occur in any sentence below the gap.

Enter the sentence that currently needs to be derived, P, on the last line of this subderivation, as a lemma for (∃E), and consider P to be derived from the existentially quantified sentence and its subderivation by (∃E). Aim to derive the lemma.

Since the (∃E) strategy shares a place with the (PC) strategy on the list of strategic priorities, it can be unclear which strategy should be applied first in cases where both existentially quantified sentences and disjunctions are present. Determining which to do first requires forethought and experiment.

If there is more than one existentially quantified sentence, the (∃E) strategy must be applied to each of them.

Consider the derivation of ∃x∃y(Ax & Bay) from {∃xAx, ∃x∃z(Cxb & Baz)}

1.	∃xAx	given
2.	∃x∃z(Cxb & Baz)	given
...	...	
20.	∃x∃y(Ax & Bay)	?

Because existentially quantified sentences exist at lines 1 and 2, the (∃E) strategy is called for. It does not matter which existentially quantified sentence is done first.

Since name b occurs in an assumption at line 2, and name "a" also occurs both in an assumption at line 2 and in the conclusion at line 20, neither can be used to make the instance. Using c on the first ∃ sentence gives:

1.	∃xAx	given
2.	∃x∃z(Cxb & Baz)	given
3.	**Ac**	**(A/1∃E)**
...	...	
19.	**∃x∃y(Ax &Bay)**	**lemma for (∃E)**
20.	∃x∃y(Ax & Bay)	**1,3–19 (∃E)**

In line with the strategy, whatever sentence currently needs to be derived is entered on the last line of the (A/∃E) subderivation as a lemma for (∃E), and (∃E) should be immediately used to justify the sentence on the last line. Above, the sentence on line 20 is copied on line 19, and that on line 20 is taken to be derived by 1, 3–19 (∃E). This should always be acceptable because any names occurring in the sentence on line 20 should have been noticed and rejected as candidates when making the instance at line 3. Looking down at line 20 and seeing an "a" in the sentence on that line means "a" cannot be used as the instantiating name at line 3.

Proceeding, the sentence on line 2 must be reduced from the outside in. Rules of Dq may only be applied to the main operators of sentences.

Since name c has already been used at line 3, it cannot be used to make an instance of the ∃ sentence on line 2. The alphanumerically earliest unused name is d.

1.	∃xAx	given
2.	∃x∃z(Cxb & Baz)	given
3.	Ac	(A/1∃E)
4.	**∃x∃z(Cxb & Baz)**	**2 (R)**
5.	**∃z(Cdb & Baz)**	**(A/4∃E)**
...	...	
18.	**∃x∃y(Ax & Bay)**	**lemma for (∃E)**
19.	∃x∃y(Ax & Bay)	lemma for (∃E) **2,4–18 (∃E)**
20.	∃x∃y(Ax & Bay)	1,3–19 (∃E)

Lines 18, 19, and 20 are all identical. This is a feature of derivations in Dq. The last lines will often end with multiple applications of (∃E), each deriving the same sentence.

Returning to the example, a further application of the (∃E) strategy is necessary. Though the exercise begins with just two existentially quantified sentences, a new existentially quantified sentence has since appeared on line 5. The strategy must be applied to it as well before turning to anything else.

At this point, all of names "a," b, c and d have been used. So e is used as the instantiating name.

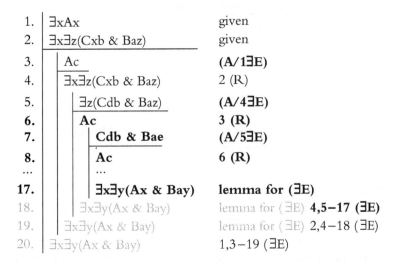

1.	∃xAx	given
2.	∃x∃z(Cxb & Baz)	given
3.	Ac	**(A/1∃E)**
4.	∃x∃z(Cxb & Baz)	2 (R)
5.	∃z(Cdb & Baz)	**(A/4∃E)**
6.	**Ac**	**3 (R)**
7.	**Cdb & Bae**	**(A/5∃E)**
8.	**Ac**	**6 (R)**
...	...	
17.	**∃x∃y(Ax & Bay)**	**lemma for (∃E)**
18.	∃x∃y(Ax & Bay)	lemma for (∃E) **4,5–17 (∃E)**
19.	∃x∃y(Ax & Bay)	lemma for (∃E) 2,4–18 (∃E)
20.	∃x∃y(Ax & Bay)	1,3–19 (∃E)

The derivation is still not done, though some progress has been made over lines 6 and 7. The (∃G) rule is required to complete it. But the derivation up to this point illustrates some main features of the use of the most restrictive of the quantifier rules, (∃E).

The strategy that is used with (∀G) is the bottom-up strategy, which puts (∀G) in the same group with (∨I), (&I), (MP), and (BMP).

> (∀G) *strategy:* when the aim is to derive a universally quantified sentence, make an instance of that sentence a lemma for (∀G) and attempt to derive that lemma. Be careful to use an instantiating name that does not occur in the universally quantified sentence or in any given or assumption that heads off an assumption bracket that continues down to the line at which the lemma is entered.

Suppose the goal is to derive is ∀x=xb. (It cannot be derived from Ø but set aside what it might be derived from for the moment.)

$$20. \quad \forall x{=}xb \ ?$$

Then =bb may not be entered as a lemma, because the instance may not be made with a name that already occurs in the universally quantified sentence.

19. | =bb   lemma for (∀G)
20. | ∀x=xb   19 (∀G)   ✗ *Wrong! Instantiating name may not occur in sentence derived by (∀G)*

The bottommost arrow shows that ∀x quantifies the first place in the identity sentence (at line 20). The arrow from x to b shows that this place is occupied by b in the instance at line 19. The last arrow points out the error. The instantiating name, b, may not continue to occur in the sentence derived by (∀G). Were =bb used as an instance for (∀G), the result would have to be ∀x=xx.

If "a" occurs in an open assumption, =ab may not be entered as a lemma either.

1. | ∀x=ax   Given
... | ...
19. | =ab   lemma for (∀G)
20. | ∀x=xb   19 (∀G)   ✗ *Wrong! instantiating name occurs in open assumption*

Following the chain of arrows from tail to head reveals the mistake.

In attempting to derive $\forall x{=}xb$ from $\{\forall x{=}ax\}$ an instance must be made using some name that does not occur either in $\forall x{=}xb$ or in any open assumption. "c" would work.

1.	$\forall x{=}ax$	given
...	...	
19.	=cb	lemma for ($\forall$G)
20.	$\forall x{=}xb$	19 ($\forall$G)

The derivation can be completed by applying a strategy for the use of ($\forall$E).

> ($\forall$E) *strategy:* once all (A/$\exists$E) assumptions have been made, apply ($\forall$E) repeatedly, using each name that appears in the derivation up to this point as the instantiating name.

While universally quantified sentences lend themselves to "top down" derivation, they should not be treated as "top down" sentences. This is because the wisest policy for applying ($\forall$E) is to do so repeatedly, using each name that has so far appeared in the derivation as the instantiating name. That makes it important to wait with applying ($\forall$E) until all possible assumptions for purposes of ($\exists$E) (which introduce new names), have been made. Accordingly, the ($\forall$E) strategy is placed after the ($\exists$E) strategy.

The ($\forall$E) strategy can be an expensive strategy to employ, especially when many names have been used. If there is a way of completing the derivation using just a few (ideally just one) of the names currently in use, only the requisite instances need be derived.

There are infinitely many different instances that may be derived from any universally quantified sentence. Sometimes more than one is needed. But whichever ones are created, they should look as much like sentences that already exist or as much like the sentence that needs to be derived as possible. The less an instance looks like anything else in the derivation, the less useful it will be.

The derivation that was partially completed earlier can be finished with two applications of ($\forall$E):

1.	$\forall x{=}ax$	given
2.	=ab	1 ($\forall$E)
3.	=ac	1 ($\forall$E)
...	...	
19.	=cb	lemma for ($\forall$G) 3,2 (=E)
20.	$\forall x{=}xb$	19 ($\forall$G)

The two ($\forall$E) applications use names that "already" appeared at line 19. ("Already" because derivations are properly done by working from the bottom up as well as the top down.) This creates a situation where (=E) can be applied to derive the lemma at line 19 and so complete the derivation.

There is nothing wrong with this move. ($\forall$E) can be applied as many times as desired to the same universally quantified sentence, and any name may be used as the instantiating name.

Notably, a name that already occurs in the universally quantified sentence may be used. Thus, =aa may be derived from $\forall x{=}ax$. In this case, =aa was not derived because doing so would have served no purpose.

The derivation that has just been completed might seem paradoxical. If everything is "a" how could everything also be b? Consider that the only way $\forall x{=}ax$ could be true is if there is only one object in the domain. Since each name must denote exactly one object, b must denote that object as well, and all names must denote the object any name, be it "a" or b, denotes.

($\exists$G) is applied in conjunction with a further bottom-up strategy.

> ($\exists$G) *strategy:* when the aim is to derive an existentially quantified sentence, make an instance of that existentially quantified sentence a lemma for ($\exists$G) and attempt to derive that lemma. Choose an instance that looks as much like sentences higher up in the derivation as possible.

This time there are no restrictions. The instantiating name may occur in the derived sentence or in open assumptions.

The lack of restrictions can be more of a curse than a blessing because it leaves too much choice.

The best policy is to attempt to derive an instance that looks as much as possible like sentences higher up in the derivation. The less the instance resembles any earlier sentence, the harder it is to derive from the earlier sentences.

As an illustration, consider the derivation that was abandoned earlier:

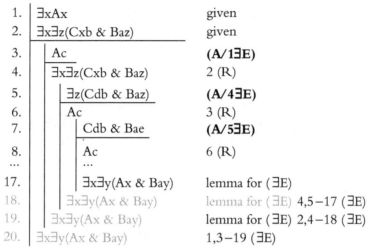

The (∃G) strategy suggests entering an instance of ∃x∃y(Ax & Bay) on line 16, that is, a sentence of the form ∃y(A_ & Bay). The instantiating name for the blank space should be the name that produces a sentence (in this case, a component sentence) that looks like one of the earlier sentences. That is the sentence at line 8, which has c in this spot.

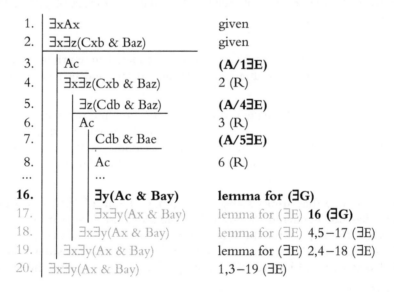

Now the question is how to derive the lemma at line 16. This means looking for another instance that looks as much as possible like something that can be derived from the earlier sentences. That would be the instance that puts e for y.

1.	∃xAx	given
2.	∃x∃z(Cxb & Baz)	given
3.	Ac	**(A/1∃E)**
4.	∃x∃z(Cxb & Baz)	2 (R)
5.	∃z(Cdb & Baz)	**(A/4∃E)**
6.	Ac	3 (R)
7.	Cdb & Bae	**(A/5∃E)**
8.	Ac	6 (R)
...	...	
15.	Ac & Bae	lemma for (∃E)
16.	∃y(Ac & Bay)	lemma for (∃E) **15 (∃G)**
17.	∃x∃y(Ax & Bay)	lemma for (∃E) 16 (∃G)
18.	∃x∃y(Ax & Bay)	lemma for (∃E) 4,5−17 (∃E)
19.	∃x∃y(Ax & Bay)	lemma for (∃E) 2,4−18 (∃E)
20.	∃x∃y(Ax & Bay)	1,3−19 (∃E)

Now the remaining lemma is readily derived by (&E) and (&I).

Strategic Summary

Stage 1 (Top Down)
Make all possible applications of (R) followed by all possible applications of (&E), (MP), (BMP), and (⊥I). Proceed to stage 1a.

Stage 1a (PC)/(∃E)
Make all possible applications of the (PC) and (∃E) strategies, then return to stage 1. When there is nothing to do at this stage after a cycle through stages 1 and 1a, proceed to stage 2.

(PC) Strategy
When a disjunction appears above the gap, split the derivation into two subderivations, each headed off by the assumption of one of the disjuncts. Enter the sentence that currently needs to be derived, P, on the last line of each subderivation, as a lemma for (PC) and consider P to have been derived from the disjunction and its subderivations by (PC). Aim to derive the lemmas.

(∃E) Strategy
For each ∃ sentence that appears above the gap, make an (A/∃E) assumption, using a name that has not occurred on any prior line and that does not occur in any sentence below the gap. Enter the sentence that currently needs to be derived, P, on the last line of this subderivation, as a lemma for (∃E), and consider P to be derived from the ∃ sentence and its subderivation by (∃E). Aim to derive the lemma.

Stage 1b (∀E)/(=E)
Apply (∀E) repeatedly, using each name that appears in the derivation up to this point as the instantiating name. Apply (=E) judiciously as needed to create sentences that look as much like other sentences or other sentential components as possible.

Stage 2 (CP)/(BP)
Apply the (CP)/(BP) strategy once and return to stage 1. When there is nothing more to do at stage 2 after a cycle through stage 1, proceed to stage 3.

(CP)/(BP) Strategy
When the aim is to derive a conditional, P → Q, assume P and make Q a lemma for (CP) on the last line of the assumption bracket for this assumption. When it is to derive a biconditional, P ≡ Q, split the prior derivation into two parts. In the first part assume P and make Q a lemma for (BP) on the last line of the assumption bracket for this assumption. In the second part, assume Q and make P a lemma for (BP) on the last line of the assumption bracket for this assumption.

Stage 3 (Bottom Up)
Make a single application of one of the (MP)/(BMP), (&I), (∨I), **(∀G) and (∃G)** strategies, as appropriate for the sentence that needs to be derived and return to stage 1. When there is nothing to do at stage 3 after a cycle through stages 1 to 2, proceed to stage 4.

(MP)/(BMP) Strategy

When the aim is to derive Q, look for a conditional, P → Q, that has Q as its consequent or a biconditional, P ≡ Q or Q ≡ P that has Q as one of its immediate components. Enter P as a lemma for deriving Q by (MP) or (BMP) and then attempt to derive P. If there is more than one conditional or biconditional that has Q as its consequent or immediate component, pick the one with the antecedent or other immediate component that that looks easiest to derive or that suggests making the most further assumptions or entering the most higher lemmas. Be prepared to repeat this experiment using one of the other conditionals or biconditionals should the chosen one not work. *Wrinkle:* if P → Q is the consequent of a compound conditional, R → (P → Q), R must be derived first. A similar point applies if P → Q, P ≡ Q, or Q ≡ P is a component of a larger biconditional. If P → Q, P ≡ Q or Q ≡ P is the antecedent of a compound conditional, forget about it; it cannot be used to get Q.

(⊥I) Strategy

When the aim is to derive ⊥, first attempt to derive it by work at stage 1. When this is not possible consider if it can be obtained by the (MP)/(BMP) strategy. When this is also not possible, pick one of the sentences that is above ⊥ and is placed immediately to the right of the same assumption bracket as ⊥. Enter the opposite of this sentence as a lemma for (⊥I) on the line immediately above ⊥ and attempt to derive this lemma. The best choice is a sentence that implies making further assumptions and entering further lemmas. Be prepared to repeat this experiment with a different sentence. Alternatively, consider whether these sentences contain opposite components that are derivable, or one derivable component that has a readily derivable opposite. In that case, enter these components as lemmas and attempt to derive them.

(~bc) Strategy

When the negation of a binary sentence, ~(P & Q), ~(P ∨ Q), ~(P → Q), or ~(P ≡ Q), exists above the gap, reiterate it as necessary to bring it into the subderivation that aims to derive ⊥ and enter its opposite as a lemma for deriving ⊥.

(&I) Strategy

When the aim is to derive P & Q and one or both of P and Q are not available, enter it/them as lemmas for (&I) and attempt to derive it/them.

(∨I) Strategy

When the aim is to derive is P ∨ Q, enter one of P or Q a lemma for (∨I) and attempt to derive it. If that proves unsuccessful, enter the other one as a lemma for (∨I) and attempt to derive that lemma instead.

(∀G) Strategy

When the aim is to derive an ∀ sentence, enter an instance of that ∀ sentence as a lemma for (∀G) and attempt to derive that lemma. Be careful to use an instantiating name that does not occur in the ∀ sentence or in any given or assumption that heads off an assumption bracket that continues down to the current line. Consistently with these restrictions, prefer an instantiating name that has been used before to one that has not.

(∃G) Strategy

When the aim is to derive an ∃ sentence, enter an instance of that ∃ sentence as a lemma for (∃G) and attempt to derive that lemma. Choose an instance that looks as much like other sentences higher up in the derivation as possible.

Stage 4 (Indirect Proof)
Apply the (IP) strategy: Assume the opposite of the sentence that currently needs to be derived and enter ⊥ as a lemma on the last line of this subderivation. Return to stage 1.

Exercise 13.8

1. *Establish each of the following in Dq.*

    ★a. $\forall x(Gx \rightarrow Hx), \exists y(Gy \,\&\, Ky) \vdash \exists x Hx$

    b. $\exists x Gxa, \forall x \forall y(Gxy \rightarrow Gyx) \vdash \exists y Gay$

    ★c. $\vdash (\forall x Gx \lor \forall x Hx) \rightarrow \forall x(Gx \lor Hx)$

    d. $\vdash \exists x(Gx \,\&\, Hx) \rightarrow (\exists x Gx \,\&\, \exists x Hx)$

    ★e. $\forall x(Gx \rightarrow {\sim}Hx) \vdash {\sim}\exists x(Gx \,\&\, Hx)$

    f. $G \rightarrow \forall x Hx, \exists x Hx \rightarrow G \vdash \forall x(Hx \equiv G)$

    ★g. $\vdash \forall x \exists y =xy$ *(Hint: begin with (=I).)*

    h. $\exists x \exists y(Gxy \,\&\, {\sim}Gyx) \vdash \exists y \exists x {\sim}{=}yx$

    ★i. $\exists x[Gx \,\&\, \forall y(Gy \rightarrow {=}yx)], Ga \,\&\, Gb \vdash {=}ab$

    j. $\forall x =xa \vdash {\sim}\exists x \exists y {\sim}{=}xy$

    ★k. $\exists x[Hxc \,\&\, \forall y(Hyc \rightarrow {=}yx) \,\&\, {=}xa] \,\&\, Gc, \forall x \forall y(Hxy \rightarrow Kxy) \vdash \exists x(Hax \,\&\, Gx)$

    l. $\forall x \forall y(Gxy \rightarrow Gyx), \forall x \forall y \forall z(Gxy \,\&\, Gyz \rightarrow Gxz) \vdash \forall x \forall y(Gxy \rightarrow Gxx)$

    m. $\exists x Gax, \forall x \forall y(Gxy \rightarrow {\sim}Gyx) \vdash \exists x {\sim}{=}ax$

    n. $\forall y(Gyc \,\&\, {\sim}{=}ya \rightarrow Hacy), \forall x \forall y \forall z(Hxyz \rightarrow {\sim}Hzyx) \vdash {\sim}\exists x(Gxc \,\&\, {\sim}{=}xa \,\&\, Hxca)$

    ★o. $\vdash \exists x \forall y Gxy \rightarrow \forall y \exists x Gxy$

    p. $\vdash \forall x(Gx \rightarrow Hx) \lor \exists x Gx$ *(Hint: assume the opposite, assume Ga, apply (∃G).)*

    ★q. $\vdash \forall x \exists y(Gy \rightarrow Gx)$ *(Hint: use (CP) to make an instance, do not use (IP).)*

    r. $\vdash \forall x(\forall y Gy \rightarrow Gx)$

    ★s. $\vdash \forall x(Gx \rightarrow \exists y Gy)$

    t. $\vdash \exists x(Gx \rightarrow \forall y Gy)$ *(Hint: assume the opposite; attempt to derive $Ga \rightarrow \forall y Gy$ under this assumption; apply (∃G); to derive $Ga \rightarrow \forall y Gy$ assume the antecedent; then assume the negation of an instance of the consequent [don't use "a" as the instantiating name]; look for a contradiction, remembering that $P \rightarrow Q$ is a consequence of ${\sim}P$; compare the solutions to u and 15.24#2m.)*

    ★u. $\vdash \exists x(\exists y Gy \rightarrow Gx)$

2. *Establish each of the following in Dq.*

    ★a. $\forall x Gx \dashv\vdash \forall y Gy$

    b. $\exists x Gx \dashv\vdash \exists y Gy$

    ★c. $\forall x \forall y Gxy \dashv\vdash \forall y \forall x Gxy$

    d. $\exists x \exists y Gxy \dashv\vdash \exists x \exists y Gyx$

    ★e. $\forall x Gx \dashv\vdash {\sim}\exists x {\sim}Gx$

    f. $\exists x Gx \dashv\vdash {\sim}\forall x {\sim}Gx$

    ★g. ${\sim}\exists x Gx \dashv\vdash \forall x {\sim}Gx$

    h. ${\sim}\forall x Gx \dashv\vdash \exists x {\sim}Gx$

    ★i. $\forall x(Gx \,\&\, Hx) \dashv\vdash \forall x Gx \,\&\, \forall x Hx$

    j. $\exists x(Gx \lor Hx) \dashv\vdash \exists x Gx \lor \exists x Hx$

    ★k. $\exists x Gx \rightarrow H \dashv\vdash \forall x(Gx \rightarrow H)$

    l. $\forall x Gx \rightarrow H \dashv\vdash \exists x(Gx \rightarrow H)$ *(Hint: assume the opposite; solving this will require aiming to derive both $Ga \rightarrow H$ and Gb, the latter in order to derive ∀xGx; use the derived rule, (T→). Compare the solution to m.)*

    ★m. $G \rightarrow \exists x Hx \dashv\vdash \exists x(G \rightarrow Hx)$

    n. $G \rightarrow \forall x Hx \dashv\vdash \forall x(G \rightarrow Hx)$

    ★o. $\forall x Gx \,\&\, H \dashv\vdash \forall x(Gx \,\&\, H)$

    p. $\exists x Gx \,\&\, H \dashv\vdash \exists x(Gx \,\&\, H)$

    ★q. $\forall x Gx \lor H \dashv\vdash \forall x(Gx \lor H)$

    r. $\exists x Gx \lor H \dashv\vdash \exists x(Gx \lor H)$

    ★s. $\exists x(Gx \rightarrow Hx) \dashv\vdash \forall x Gx \rightarrow \exists x Hx$

    t. $\exists x \forall y =xy \dashv\vdash \forall x \exists y =xy$

    u. $\exists x[Gx \,\&\, \forall y(Gy \rightarrow {=}yx)] \dashv\vdash \exists x \forall y(Gx \equiv {=}yx)$

3. *Establish each of the following in Dq.*

    ★a. $\forall x {\sim}{=}xa \vdash \bot$

    b. $\forall x(Gx \rightarrow Hx), \exists x(Gx \,\&\, {\sim}Hx) \vdash \bot$

    ★c. $\forall x(Gx \rightarrow {\sim}Hx), \exists x(Gx \,\&\, Hx) \vdash \bot$

    d. $\forall x[Gx \rightarrow (Hx \ \& \sim Hx)] \ \& \ \exists yGy \vdash \perp$

★e. $\sim\exists x(\forall yGy \rightarrow Gx) \vdash \perp$

    f. $\exists x[Gx \ \& \ \forall y(Gy \rightarrow =yx)], \exists x\exists y(Gx \ \& \ Gy \ \& \sim=xy) \vdash \perp$

★g. $\exists x[Gx \ \& \ \forall y(Gy \rightarrow =yx)], \forall y\sim Gy \vdash \perp$

    h. $\forall x(Ax \rightarrow Bxx), \exists x\forall y(Ay \ \& \sim Bxy) \vdash \perp$

    i. $\exists x\exists y[Gxy \ \& \ (Gyx \rightarrow Hy)], \forall x\forall y(=xy \ \& \sim Hx) \vdash \perp$

13.2 Extensions of Dq

13.2.1 Functional Terms

In QPL the rule for forming functional terms, (ctf), has broader application than it does in PSL, even though the wording is identical.

> (ctf): If f is an *n*-place function letter and $t_1...t_n$ are *n* (not necessarily distinct) terms,
>   then $f(t_1...t_n)$ is a term.

In QPL, variables are also terms, but they are not function letters. (ctf) therefore allows the creation of functional terms that contain variables, such as f(x). But since variables are not function letters, it does not recognize expressions like x(ab) as terms.

Functional terms that contain variables are open terms. Functional terms that contain no variables, including names, are closed terms. In what follows, the lower-case letter k is used to designate closed terms.

The addition of functional terms and open terms has ramifications for the identity and quantifier rules. Derivations only work with sentences, so (=I) cannot take the form $L \vdash =tt$, as that would allow deriving $=\chi\chi$, which is not a sentence. $\forall\chi P$ says that each object is a certain way and $\exists\chi P$ says that at least one is. Since objects can be denoted by closed terms, ($\forall$E) and ($\exists$G) should be extended to work with instances made from closed terms, but ($\forall$E) should not be extended so far as to allow deriving instances made from open terms. The revised quantifier rules are accordingly:

> (=I): $L \vdash =kk$
>
> (=E): If $L \vdash =k_1k_2$ or $L \vdash =k_2k_1$ and $L \vdash P$, then $L \vdash P(k_1|k_2)$
>
> ($\forall$E): If $L \vdash \forall\chi P$ then $L \vdash P(k|\chi)$
>
> ($\exists$G): If $L \vdash P(k|\chi)$ then $L \vdash \exists\chi(P)$

The restrictions on (=E) and ($\exists$G) are not strictly necessary. Givens and assumptions must be sentences, and the restrictions on (=I) and ($\forall$E) prevent deriving open sentences, so there can be no open sentences for (=E) or ($\exists$G) to be applied to. But for the sake of emphasis and simplicity, the rules are said to work only with closed terms.

While the less restrictive rules, ($\forall$E) and ($\exists$G) are extended to include inferences involving all closed terms, the more restrictive rules ($\forall$G) and (A/$\exists$E) are restricted to working only with names. $\forall\chi P$ cannot be inferred from $P(k|\chi)$, even when k does not occur in an open assumption or continue to occur in $\forall\chi P$.

1.	$\forall xGf(x)$	given
2.	$Gf(a)$	1 ($\forall$E)
3.	$\forall xGx$	2 ($\forall$G) **✗ WRONG!** *Cannot do ($\forall$G) on top of a functional term.*

The inference at line 2 is legitimate. ($\forall$E) can be applied "inside" a functional term. But the inference at line 3 does not follow from the one at line 2. The premise at line 1 says that the value that any object is assigned in $\alpha(f)$ is in $\alpha(G)$. From that it does not follow that each object is in $\alpha(G)$, which is what the incorrect inference at line 3 declares. $\alpha(f)$ could assign the same value, 1, to each object 1, 2, 3, ..., in D while not assigning any of those objects, other than 1, to the extension of G.

(A/$\exists$E) must be restricted for similar reasons. $\exists x P$ only says that at least one object satisfies the condition P. It does not say that this object is among those that *n*-place function f assigns as values to any list of *n* arguments.

Exercise 13.9

1. *State whether each of the following is a legitimate application of a rule of* Dqf. *If it is not, say why not.*

★**a.**	*i.*	=af(a)			**b.**	*i.*	=af(a)	
	...	...				...	...	
	k.	Gf(f(a))				*k.*	Gf(f(a))	
	...	...				...	...	
	n.	Gf(f(f(a)))	*i,k* (=E)			*n.*	Gf(a)	*i,k* (=E)

	k.	∀xGaxf(x)				*k.*	Gaf(f(a))	
	...	...				...	...	
★**c.**	n_1.	Gaaf(a)	*k* (∀E)	★**g.**	n_1.	∃xGxf(f(x))	*k* (∃G)
d.	n_2.	Gabf(b)	*k* (∀E)	h.	n_2.	∃xGaf(f(x))	*k* (∃G)
★**e.**	n_3.	Gaf(a)f(f(a))	*k* (∀E)	★**i.**	n_3.	∃xGaf(x)	*k* (∃G)
f.	n_4.	Gaf(b)f(b)	*k* (∀E)	j.	n_4.	∃xGax	*k* (∃G)
				★**k.**	n_5.	∃xGxf(x)	*i* (∃G)

For the following, assume that the list of open assumptions contains sentences that contain occurrences of a *and* f(b).

			(a), (f(b))					(a), (f(b))	
			...					...	
	k.		Gf(f(c))			*k.*		Gbcf(a) → Haf(c)	
			...					...	
l.	n_1.		∀xGf(f(x))	*k* (∀G)	n.	n_1.		∀x(Gxcf(a) → Haf(c))	*k* (∀G)
★**m.**	n_2.		∀xGf(x)	*k* (∀G)	★**o.**	n_2.		∀x(Gbcf(x) → Hxf(c))	*k* (∀G)
					p.	n_3.		∀x(Gbxf(a) → Haf(c))	*k* (∀G)
					★**q.**	n_4.		∀x(Gbxf(a) → Haf(x))	*k* (∀G)

			(a), (f(b))	
			...	
	k.		∃xGe(x)c	
			...	
r.	n_1.		Ge(a)c	*k* (∃E)
			...	
★**s.**	n_2.		Ge(b)c	*k* (∃E)
			...	
t.	n_3.		Ge(c)c	*k* (∃E)
			...	
★**u.**	n_4.		Ge(f(d))c	*k* (∃E)
			...	
v.	n_5.		Ge(d)c	*k* (∃E)

2. *Demonstrate the following in* Dqf.
   ★**a.** ∀xGx ⊢ ∃xGf(x)
   b. ∀xGf(x) ⊢ ∃xGx
   ★**c.** ∃xGf(x) ⊢ ∃xGx
   d. ∀xGf(x) ⊢ ∃x(Gx & Gf(x))
   ★**e.** ~=af(a) ⊢ ∃x∃y~=xy
   f. ⊢ ∀x∃y=yf(x) *(Hint: use (=I).)*
   ★**g.** ∀x=f(x)x ⊢ ∀x=f(f(x))x
   h. ⊢ ∀x∀y(=xy → =f(x)f(y))

13.2.2 *Intuitionistic Logic*

The derivation system for intuitionistic quantified logic, Diq, uses the same quantifier rules as Dq. It differs from Dq only in the way Dis differs from Ds: by not using (IP), which is replaced with (IP~I) and (EFQ).

(IP~I):	If L,P ⊢ ⊥, then L ⊢ ~P
(EFQ):	If L ⊢ ⊥ then L ⊢ P

Though the only differences are in the sentential rules, many results obtained in Diq are affected. Most notably, ∃ cannot be defined by ~∀~. While ∃χP ⊢ ~∀χ~P, the reverse does not hold. The same is the case for ∀χP and ~∃χ~P, and ∃χ~P and ~∀χP, though ∀χP and ~∃χP remain interderivable. Some of the principles covering how quantifiers distribute over conjunctions, disjunctions, and conditionals fail as well.

These failures indicate that even though Diq uses the classical quantifier rules, it understands them differently.

Like other systems of predicate logic, intuitionistic quantified logic uses object domains. But it uses more than one. For each evidential state, there is a domain of the objects that are evident at that state. Because evidence cannot decay, those objects continue to be in the domain of all later stages in the development of evidence. But other objects can be discovered at later stages, so domains can expand with passage from earlier to later stages. From the perspective of any earlier stage, s, there is a local domain, Ds, of evident objects. At any later stage, Dt, Ds is a subset of Dt. Dt contains all the objects in Ds. But Dt may contain others as well. Some of these objects might be conceivable at Ds, but not evident at that stage, because Ds sees alternative stages in the development of evidence that do not have the objects that are evident in Dt in their domains.

The existential quantifier is restricted to ranging over objects in Ds. This gives it a force that does not come out in formalization or in derivations but is made explicit when considering truth or satisfaction conditions. The horror film cliché, "there is something out there," is not true unless the thing that is out there is identified. As with the case of the pot of beans discussed in section 6.6, what makes an existential sentence true is not the existence of an unknown object. We have no access to that sort of truth. What makes an existential sentence true is evidence of an object. The complications this creates for the use of names are discussed in chapter 14.4.2.

The universal quantifier is not similarly local in its range. If it is evident that all objects satisfy P, then there cannot be any subsequent stage in the development of evidence where there is an object that does not satisfy P. The truth of universals is based on the evident impossibility, already apparent at s, of discovering a counterexample. Provided s sees a possible stage in the development of evidence at which there is a counterexample, a universally quantified sentence is not true. This is not to say it is false. That would require that s not see any alternative stage in the development of evidence at which there is no counterexample.

Systems of logic that recognize multiple domains sometimes make use of four quantifiers. ∀ and ∃ range over objects in the local domain. Two further quantifiers, Π and Σ (pi and sigma), range over all domains. The intuitionist universal quantifier might better be symbolized as Π, while retaining ∃ for the existential, but this innovation will not be adopted here.

Exercise 13.10

1. *One of the sentences in each of the following pairs is derivable from the other in* Diq *and the other is not. Determine which direction is impossible and identify the step in the corresponding* Dq *derivation that is not permitted in* Diq. *These are familiar exercises, so the answers can be given by consulting their earlier solutions.*

   ★a. ∀xGx; ~∃x~Gx *(compare 15.22#2e)*

   b. ∃xGx; ~∀x~Gx *(compare 15.22#2f)*

   ★c. G → ∃xHx; ∃x(G → Hx) *(compare 15.22#2m)*

   d. ~∀xGx; ∃x~Gx *(compare 15.22#2h)*

   ★e. ∀xGx ∨ H; ∀x(Gx ∨ H) *(compare 15.22#2q)*

   f. ∀xGx → H; ∃x(Gx → H) *(compare 15.22#2l)*

2. *One of the two following sentences is derivable from the other in* Diq *and the other is not. Give the derivation for the one that is. Remember that double negations cannot be eliminated in* Diq *and that it is not permissible to use indirect proof to derive* P *from the assumption of* ~P.

   ∀x~~Gx; ~~∀xGx

13.2.3 Free Logic

Free logic is free of the supposition that every term must denote an object (in D). This requires modifications to the quantifier rules. The quantifiers range over objects (in D), not over names. ∀xGx, for instance, says that each *object* is in α(G), not that each *name* is. On the supposition that not all terms denote objects (in D), ∀χP, does not justify the inference to P(k|χ), where k is a closed term, as defined in section 13.3.1. It only justifies the inference that if k denotes an object in D, then P(k|χ). Conversely, ∃χP, does not just say that at least one object is a certain way. It includes the assertion that there is at least one object (in D) that is this way.

The claim that there is object that a term, t, denotes can be formalized by adding an existence symbol, E, to the vocabulary for QPL and supplementing QPL syntax with the formation rule

$$\boxed{\text{(E):}\quad \text{If t is a term, then Et is a formula}}$$

The assertion that t denotes an object (in D) might just as well be formalized as ∃x=tx, but Et is cleaner. The free quantifier rules are accordingly,

(F∀E):	If L ⊢∀χP **and L ⊢ Ek** then L ⊢ P(k|χ).	
(F∀G):	If **L, Eq** ⊢ P(q|χ) then L ⊢ ∀χP, provided q does not occur in any sentence on L or in ∀χp.	
(F∃E):	If L ⊢∃χP and L, **Eq & P(q|χ)** ⊢ R, then L ⊢ R, provided q does not occur in any sentence on L, in ∃χP or in R.	
(F∃G):	If **L ⊢ Ek and** L ⊢ P(k|χ) then L ⊢ ∃χP.	

Templates for the use of these rules with assumption brackets are:

(F ∀E)		
	(L)	
...	...	
i.	Ek	?
...	...	
k.	∀χP	?
...	...	
n.	P(k|χ)	*i,k* (F∀E)

(F∃G)		
	(L)	
...	...	
i.	Ek	lemma for (F∃G)
...	...	
k.	P(k|χ)	lemma for (F∃G)
...	...	
n.	∃χP	*i,k* (F∃G)

(F ∀G)		
	(L) *(no q)*	
...	...	
i.	Eq	(A/F∀G)
...	...	
k.	P(q|χ)	lemma for (F∀G)
...	...	
n.	∀χP *(no q)*	*i–k* (F∀G)

(F∃E)		
	(L) *(no q)*	
...	...	
h.	∃χP *(no q)*	?
...	...	
i.	Eq & P(q|χ)	(A/*h* F∃E)
...	...	
k.	R *(no q)*	lemma for (F∃E)
...	...	
n.	R	*h,i–k* (F∃E)

Whatever is derivable in FDq is derivable in classical Dq, but there are some things that are derivable in classical Dq that are not derivable in FDq. Notably, ∀χP → ∃χP, which is a theorem of classical Dq, is not derivable in FDq.

1.	∀χP	given
2.	Ek	(A/CP)
3.	∀χP	1 (R)
4.	P(k|χ)	2,3 (∀E)
5.	Ek → P(k|χ)	2–4 (CP)
...	???	???
17.	Ek	lemma for (F∃G) / ???
18.	P(k|χ)	lemma for (F∃G) / ???
19.	∃χP	17, 18 (F∃G)
20.	∀χP → ∃χP	1–19 (CP)

Interestingly, classical Dq agrees with FDq in not providing for a way to derive an I sentence, ∃x(P & Q), from an A sentence, ∀χ(P → Q).

1.	∀χ(P → Q)	given
2.	(P → Q)(k|χ)	1 (∀E)
...	???	???
18.	(P & Q)(k|χ)	?
19.	∃χ(P & Q)	18 (∃G)
20.	∀χ(P → Q) → ∃χ(P & Q)	1–19 (CP)

Viewed from this perspective, free logic is more consistent than classical QPL. It rejects existential import for all universally quantified sentences, not just for A sentences. But its truly radical innovations are rejecting ∀χP → P(k\|χ) and P(k\|χ) → ∃χP.

Exercise 13.11

Derive the following in FDq *or* FDqf.
⋆a. ∀x(Gx → Hx), ∃xGx ⊢ ∃xHx
  b. ∀x(Gx → Hx), ∀x(Hx → Kx) ⊢ ∀x(Gx → Kx)
⋆c. ∀xGx, ∃x=xa ⊢ Ga
  d. ∃x=xa, ~Ga ⊢ ~∀xGx
⋆e. ~∀x~Gx ⊢ ∃xGx
  f. ∃x(Gx → H) ⊢ ∀xGx → H
⋆g. ⊢ ∀x=xx
  h. ⊢ ∀x∀y(=xy → =f(x)f(y))

13.2.4 Free Description Theory

Derivation rules for sentences containing definite descriptions vary depending on how those descriptions are formalized and what semantics is chosen for them. When the Russellian method for formalizing definite descriptions (section 12.3.8) is adopted, no extensions to Dq are required. Definite descriptions have the form ∃χ[P & ∀ψ(P(ψ\|χ) → =ψχ)], and are handled by the classical quantifier rules.

This having been said, the free quantifier rules, which are free specifically of the assumption that all terms must denote domain objects, are well suited to handle definite descriptions. Indeed, the development of free logic was in part motivated by the desire to offer an alternative to the Russellian approach to formalizing definite descriptions.[2] (Accommodating the ordinary use of names that do not denote an object was another motive.) When QPL is expanded to include the term forming operator introduced in section 10.4, the free rules for extracting information from a proper description and deriving a sentence containing a proper description are:

> (^{1}E): If L ⊢ Ek and L ⊢ =k^{1}χP then L ⊢ P(k|χ) and L ⊢ ∀ψ(P(ψ|χ) → =ψk)
>
> (^{1}I) : If L ⊢ P(k|χ) and L ⊢ ∀ψ(P → =ψk) then L ⊢ Ek → =k^{1}χP

(^{1}E) says that if k denotes an existing object, and this object is the one object that satisfies P, then it can be inferred that k denotes an object that satisfies P and that it denotes the only object that does so. (^{1}I) says that if k denotes an object that satisfies P, and denotes the only object that does so, then it can be inferred that if k denotes an existing object then it denotes the one object that satisfies P.

(^{1}E) could have been stated without reference to a closed term, as: If L ⊢ E^{1}χP then L ⊢ P^{1}χP and L ⊢ ∀ψ(P(ψ|x) → =ψ^{1}χP). On the assumption that =kk continues to be axiomatic, this is a corollary of the given version, arising when k is ^{1}χP. The given version is more general and so more useful.

Both (^{1}E) and (^{1}I) are consequences of an underlying description axiom:

$$∀ζ[=ζ^1χP ≡ P(ζ|χ) \ \& \ ∀ψ(P(ψ|ζ) → =ψζ)]$$

which says that any object a variable might denote is the one object to satisfy the description P if and only if it does indeed satisfy the description P and is indeed the only one to do so. (F∀E) and (CP) unpack this axiom as:

$$Ek → [=k^1χP ≡ P(k|χ) \ \& \ ∀ψ(P(ψ|χ) → =ψk)]$$

If L ⊢ Ek and L ⊢ =k^{1}χP, the information on the right side of the biconditional is derivable by (BMP), which is the operation codified in (^{1}E). And if L yields the information on the right side of the biconditional, it yields Ek → =k^{1}χP, which is the operation codified by (^{1}I). The associated derivations of these results are left as an exercise.

As is readily verified ∀ψ(Eψ → ~=ψ^{1}χP) is derivable in cases where it is established that ^{1}χP is improper, that is where ~∃ψ=ψ^{1}χP (nothing satisfies P) or ∃ψ∃ζ(P(ψ|χ) & P(ζ|χ) & ~=ψζ) (more than one thing satisfies P). This is also left as an exercise.

Garson (2013: 279–84) brings up a further rule that is useful for derivations involving improper descriptions.[3]

> (~p):   If L ⊢ ~=pk, where p does not occur in any sentence on L or
>   in k, then L ⊢ ⊥.

(~p) says that if a closed term cannot be baptized with a new name (as is the case when a definite description violates the conditions laid down by the description axiom), then something has gone wrong and an assumption must be abandoned. This rule is the foundation for a routine that enables many intuitively sound derivations that would otherwise not be possible with (^{1}E) and (^{1}I) as stated above. The routine begins by assuming the opposite of the conclusion and then entering ~=q^{1}χP as a lemma for deriving ⊥ under conditions where q does not occur on any sentence on L or in ^{1}χP. =q^{1}χP is then entered as an assumption for deriving ~=q^{1}χP by (IP). This has the effect of adding =q^{1}χP to the head of a derivation in circumstances where it would otherwise be underivable. Some of the following exercises use the strategy.

Exercise 13.12

Derive the following in FDq^1. This is the system containing Dp, the versions of (=I) and (=E) given in section 13.2.1, (^{1}E), (^{1}I), (~p), and the free quantifier rules.

★**a.** E^{1}xGx ⊢ G^{1}xGx

 b. ⊢ G^{1}xGx ∨ ~G^{1}xGx *(Hint: sometimes sentences are valid for reasons that have to do merely with their connectives.)*

★**c.** =a^{1}xGx, =b^{1}xGx ⊢ =ab *(Hint: or other reasons that do not depend on description theory.)*

 d. E^{1}xGx ⊢ ∀y(Gy → =y^{1}xGx) *(Hint: compare the solution to (a).)*

★**e.** ⊢ ~E^{1}x~=xx *(Hint: assume the opposite; make an assumption for (~p).)*

The following two exercises establish that (^{1}E) and (^{1}I) are consequences of the description axiom.

 f. ∀x[=x^{1}yGy ≡ Gx & ∀z(Gz → =zx)], Ea, =a^{1}yGy ⊢ Ga & ∀y(Gy → =ya)

★**g.** ∀x[=x^{1}yGy ≡ Gx & ∀z(Gz → =zx)], Ga, ∀y(Gy → =ya) ⊢ Ea → =a^{1}yGy

h. $\sim\exists x=x^1yGy \vdash \forall y\sim=y^1xGx$ *(Hint: look for a way to use (^{1}I).)*

★i. $\sim G^1xGx \vdash \sim\exists x=x^1yGy$

j. $\sim G^1xGx \vdash \sim E^1xGx$ *(Hint: assume the opposite, make an assumption for ($\sim$p), use (=E).)*

★k. $\exists x\exists y(Gx \mathbin{\&} Gy \mathbin{\&} \sim=xy) \vdash \sim E^1xGx$

l. $\exists x\exists y(Gx \mathbin{\&} Gy \mathbin{\&} \sim=xy) \vdash \sim\exists x=x^1yGy$

★m. $\exists x[Gx \mathbin{\&} \forall y(Gy \rightarrow =yx)] \vdash G^1xGx$

n. $\sim\exists x[Gx \mathbin{\&} \forall y(Gy \rightarrow =yx)] \vdash \sim\exists x=x^1Gy$

★o. $E^1xGx \vdash \exists y=y^1xGx$

p. $\exists y=y^1xGx \vdash \exists x[Gx \mathbin{\&} \forall y(Gy \rightarrow =yx)]$

★q. $E^1xGx, Ea \mathbin{\&} Ga \vdash =a^1xGx$

r. $E^1xGx, Ea \mathbin{\&} Ga \vdash \forall y(Gy \equiv =ya)$ *(Use the result of exercise q for the first half.)*

★s. $E^1xGx \vdash \forall y(Gy \equiv =y^1xGx)$ *(Use the result of exercise q for the first half.)*

t. $Gb \rightarrow Hb, =a^1xGx, Eb \mathbin{\&} Gb \vdash Ea \rightarrow H^1xGx$

★u. $E^1xGx, \forall x(Gx \equiv Hx) \vdash =^1xGx^1xHx$

★v. $E^1xGx \vdash = {}^1xGx\ {}^1yGy$

★w. $E^1x(Gx \vee Hx) \vdash E^1xGx \vee E^1xHx$

Notes

1   It needs to be established that substitution of equivalent subformulas preserves validity in $\forall$ and $\exists$ formulas. That can only be known after establishing a routine for performing such substitutions using just the basic rules of Dq. While it would still be correct to make substitutions of components that do not fall within the scope of quantifiers, it is simpler to disallow all substitutions.

2   A third approach worth acknowledging is the Fregean theory found in Kalish, Montague, and Mar (1980) and discussed in chapter 11.1.6. Supervaluational semantics and Meinongian semantics, also discussed in 11.1.6, fit well with free derivation systems.

3   As discussed in the appendix to chapter A-6, Garson's case for ($\sim$p) is based on its role in providing for the completeness of a derivation system for any modal logic that recognizes nonrigid terms (terms that denote different objects in different words). Nonrigid terms do not figure in QPL, but descriptions that use the ^{1} notation are paradigms of nonrigid terms in modal logic. ($\sim$p) is helpful for dealing with them even in Dq^1.

References

Garson, James W, 2013, *Modal Logic for Philosophers*, 2nd edition, Cambridge University Press, New York.

Kalish, Donald, Montague, Richard, and Mar, Gary, 1980, *Logic: Techniques of Formal Reasoning*, 2nd edition, Harcourt Brace Jovanovich, San Diego.

14 Trees and Tree Model Semantics for Quantified Predicate Logic

Contents

14.1 Rules

q-trees are p-trees expanded with four new rules governing the reduction of universally and existentially quantified sentences and negations of those sentences.

$\exists \chi P$ says that there is at least one object that satisfies the condition, P. It does not say which object that is. $\sim\forall \chi P$ says that not all objects satisfy P. In other words, at least one does not. But, again, $\sim\forall \chi P$ does not specify which object that is. Since it is assured, in the one case, that there is an object that satisfies P, and in the other, that there is one that does not, a way to proceed is to "baptize" these objects with new names. Since objects can have more than one name, using a new name does not preclude the possibility that the name refers to an object that has already been given a different name. But it does not illegitimately assume that the object that satisfies or does not satisfy P is one of those objects.

This gives the following forms to rules for reducing existential and negated universal sentences.

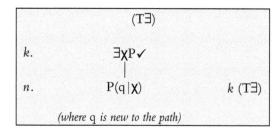

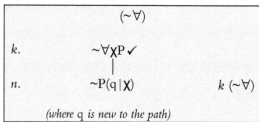

DOI: 10.4324/9781003026532-23

Each time (T∃) or (~∀) is applied a new name is called for. For example, ∃x∃yGyax has the following tree:

$$
\begin{array}{lll}
1. & \exists x \exists y Gyax \checkmark & \text{given} \\
2. & \quad \exists y Gyab \checkmark & 1\ (T\exists) \\
3. & \quad\quad Gcab & 2\ (T\exists)
\end{array}
$$

There is only one way to produce a tree for this sentence. The two different existential quantifiers may not be reduced with a single application of (T∃). And the ∃x quantifier must be dealt with first because it is the main operator. The only possible variation is in the choice of new names at lines 2 and 3. Whatever name is added at line 2 must be different from "a," which already appears at line 1, and whatever name is added at line 3 must be different both from "a" and the name that was added at line 2. By convention, the alphanumerically earliest unused name is added, so even that is not up for choice.

∀χP says that each object satisfies the condition, P. ~∃χP says that not even one of them satisfies this condition, which is another way of saying that each does not. "Each" means "each," so universal and negated existential sentences cannot be reduced just once. They must be reduced repeatedly, for each name that appears on the path. If new names are added to a path, as they could be by (T∃) or (~∀), any universal and negated existential sentences on the path would have to be further reduced for those new names. If no names have yet appeared, "each" still means "at least one," since any interpretation must have at least one object in its domain, so universal and negated existential sentences are reduced once, using "a" as the instantiating name. Because their complete reduction is not assured before all the paths that run up to them either close or are exhausted, they are not checked off. However, it helps to make a note of which names have so far been used as each instance is made.

This gives the following forms to the rules for reducing universal and negated existential sentences.

$$
\begin{array}{ll}
\textbf{(T\forall)} & \textbf{(\sim\exists)} \\[4pt]
k. \quad \forall\chi P_{q1\ldots qn} & k. \quad \sim\exists\chi P_{q1\ldots qn} \\
\quad\quad | & \quad\quad\quad | \\
m. \quad P(q_1\,|\!\chi) \quad k\ (T\forall) & \quad \sim P(q_1\,|\!\chi) \quad k\ (\sim\exists) \\
\quad\quad \ldots & \quad\quad\quad \ldots \\
m+n. \quad P(q_n\,|\!\chi) \quad k\ (T\forall) & \quad \sim P(q_n\,|\!\chi) \quad k\ (\sim\exists)
\end{array}
$$

where q₁–qₙ are each name to occur on the path
or "a" if no name occurs on the path

Consider a tree for {Ga, ~(Gb ∨ Kbb) ∨ ~(∀xKxa ∨ Ca), ∀x(Hx & ∃yKya)}

$$
\begin{array}{lll}
1. & Ga & \text{given} \\
2. & \sim(Gb \lor Kbb) \lor \sim(\forall xKxa \lor Ca)\checkmark & \text{given} \\
3. & \forall x(Hx\ \&\ \exists yKya\,) & \text{given} \\[6pt]
4. & \sim(Gb \lor Kbb)\checkmark \quad\quad \sim(\forall xKxa \lor Ca)\checkmark & 2\ (T\forall) \\
5. & \sim Gb \quad\quad\quad\quad\quad \sim\forall xKxa\checkmark & 4\ (\sim\lor) \\
6. & \sim Kbb \quad\quad\quad\quad\quad\ \sim Ca & 4\ (\sim\lor) \\
7. & \quad\quad\quad\quad\quad\quad\quad \sim Kca & 5\ (\sim\forall)
\end{array}
$$

At line 5, (~∨) is applied to the sentences on line 4 on each path, even though they are not the same. Whenever a rule applies to sentences on same lines on different paths, it should be applied simultaneously on each of those paths, even if the sentences involved are not the same. This avoids needlessly lengthening the tree.

At line 7 (~∀) is performed using c as the instantiating name. "a" and b already appear on the path and a new name is required with each (~∀) application.

At this point there is nothing left to do but perform (T∀) on line 3. Because there are two open paths running up to line 3, the (T∀) results must be entered on each path. But because different names occur on each path, the results are different.

1.	Ga	given
2.	~(Gb ∨ Kbb) ∨ ~(∀xKxa ∨ Ca)✓	given
3.	∀x(Hx & ∃yKya) **abc**	given

4.	~(Gb ∨ Kbb)✓	~(∀xKxa ∨ Ca)✓	2 (TV)
5.	~Gb	~∀xKxa✓	4 (~V)
6.	~Kbb	~Ca	4 (~V)
7.	|	~Kca	5 (~∀)
8.	**Ha & ∃yKya**	**Ha & ∃yKya**	**3 (T∀)**
9.	**Hb & ∃yKya**	**Hb & ∃yKya**	**3 (T∀)**
10.		**Hc & ∃yKya**	**3 (T∀)**

The left path only has instances using "a" and b because c does not occur on that path. The right path must include an instance using c. Now that the single ∀ sentence so far to occur on this tree has been fully reduced, work can recommence on other sentences.

1.	Ga	given
2.	~(Gb ∨ Kbb) ∨ ~(∀xKxa ∨ Ca)✓	given
3.	∀x(Hx & ∃yKya) **abc**	given

4.	~(Gb ∨ Kbb) ~Gb ~Kbb	~(∀xKxa ∨ Ca)✓ ~∀xKxa ~Ca	2 (TV)
5.	|	~Kca	5 (~∀)
6.	Ha & ∃yKya✓	Ha & ∃yKya✓	3 (T∀)
7.	Hb & ∃yKya✓	Hb & ∃yKya✓	3 (T∀)
8.	|	Hc & ∃yKya✓	3 (T∀)
9.	**Ha**	**Ha**	**6 (T&)**
10.	**∃yKya✓**	**∃yKya✓**	**6 (T&)**
11.	**Kda**	**Kda**	**10 (T∃)**
12.	**Hb**	**Hb**	**7 (T&)**
13.	**∃yKya✓₁₁**	**∃yKya✓₁₁**	**7 (T&)**
14.		**Hc**	**8 (T&)**
15.		**∃yKya✓₁₁**	**9 (T&)**

Only ∀, ~∃, and = sentences should be reduced more than once. Lines 10, 13, and 15 illustrate a situation that can often arise on q-trees. Applications of (T∀) and (~∃) can cause the same component to reappear multiple times on the same path, as is the case with ∃yKya. When that happens, the sentence should only be reduced once on each path. Further appearances of the sentence on the path can be checked off. A notation next to the checkmark indicating the line where the later appearance was reduced helps the reader to follow the tree. The subscripted 11 on the left path of line 13, for instance, indicates that the occurrence of ∃yKya at line 10 was reduced to Kda at line 11.

In this case, failing to notice that ∃yKya should only be reduced once would cause the tree to go on forever. Each subsequent (T∃) application would introduce a new name, and that would in turn require a subsequent reduction of the ∀ sentence at line 3, generating yet another occurrence of ∃yKya.

The tree illustrates a further strategic feature at line 11, where ∃yKya is reduced to Kda on both paths. d is used as the instantiating name because the name must be new to the path, and all of a, b, and c occur higher up on the right path. Only a and b occur on the left path. However, using c on the left path would confuse the indexing at line 3. The ∀ sentence at line 3, which sits above both paths, has already been indexed as having been reduced for a, b, and c. Reducing ∃yKya to Kca on the left path would illegitimately suggest that the ∀ sentence on line 3 has already been reduced for c on the left path, which is not the case. (Relying on memory to keep these matters straight would be unwise.) Customarily, the alphabetically earliest unused name is used to instantiate ∃ and ~∀ sentences. But it should be the alphanumerically earliest after all the names to appear anywhere on the tree. There are infinitely many names, so there is no chance of running out.

The observation that has just been made indicates that the tree is not finished. Reducing the ∃ sentence at line 10 has introduced a new name. It is necessary to return to the ∀ sentence and reduce it for this new name, adding d to the index at line 3.

1.		Ga	given
2.	~(Gb ∨ Kbb) ∨	~(∀xKxa ∨ Ca)✓	given
3.		∀x(Hx & ∃yKya) abcd	given
4.	~(Gb ∨ Kbb)	~(∀xKxa ∨ Ca)✓	2 (T∨)
	~Gb	~∀xKxa	
	~Kbb	~Ca	
5.	|	~Kca	5 (~∀)
6.	Ha & ∃yKya✓	Ha & ∃yKya✓	3 (T∀)
7.	Hb & ∃yKya✓	Hb & ∃yKya✓	3 (T∀)
8.	|	Hc & ∃yKya✓	3 (T∀)
9.	Ha	Ha	6 (T&)
10.	∃yKya✓	∃yKya✓	6 (T&)
11.	Kda	Kda	10 (T∃)
12.	Hb	Hb	7 (T&)
13.	∃yKya✓₁₁	∃yKya✓₁₁	7 (T&)
14.		Hc	8 (T&)
15.	|	∃yKya✓₁₁	9 (T&)
16.	**Hd & ∃yKya✓**	**Hd & ∃yKya✓**	**3 (T∀)**
17.	**Hd**	**Hd**	**12 (T&)**
18.	**∃yKya✓₁₁**	**∃yKya✓₁₁**	**12 (T&)**
19.	**e**	**e**	

The paths are declared to be exhausted because each sentence on them is either a literal, a non-∀ or non-~∃ sentence that has been checked off, or a ∀ or ~∃ sentence that has been indexed for each name on the path. (Had there been any identity sentences on the path there would have been a fourth condition to meet: all (=E) applications would need to be performed.)

(def ex)

A path of a q-tree is *exhausted* if and only if:

  (i) each sentence in the set the tree was made for has been placed on top of the tree

  (ii) ⊥ does not stand alone on any line of the path

  (iii) each sentence on the path is either (i) a literal, (ii) a nonliteral, **non-∀ or non-~∃** sentence that has been reduced (checked off), **or (iii) a ∀ or ~∃ sentence that has been reduced using each name to occur on each path that runs through it, or using "a" if there are no names on a path**

  (iv) for each sentence of the form =rq and each literal, P, a sentence of the form P(r | q) (including sentences of the form =rr), occurs on the path.

When applying (~∀) and (~∃) in the case where P is a negation, a tilde must still be added to P. For example, ~∀x~∀yGyax reduces to ~~∀yGyab.

A sentence that begins with a string of unary operators may only be reduced by the rule for the main operator.

$$1. \quad \sim \exists x \forall y \sim \sim Gxy \quad \text{given}$$

$\sim \exists x \forall y \sim \sim Gxy$ may not be reduced by applying (T∃), (T∀) or (DN).

1.	$\sim \exists x \forall y \sim \sim Gxy_{ab}$		given
2.	$\sim \forall y \sim \sim Gay$✓		1 (∼∃)
3.	$\sim \sim \sim Gab$✓		2 (∼∀)
4.	$\sim Gab$		3 (DN)
5.	$\sim \forall y \sim \sim Gby$		1 (∼∃)

...

As this tree suggests, some paths create an unending sequence of reductions. The measure that was taken to avoid this outcome on the tree done previously is not effective here because each subsequent (∼∃) application creates a new sentence. $\sim \forall y \sim \sim Gby$ at line 5 must be reduced using a new name, entering $\sim \sim \sim Gbc$ at line 6. Addition of this new name to the path requires a further (∼∃) application, creating a new sentence, $\sim \forall y \sim \sim Gcy$, which must then be reduced by adding yet another new name.

In some cases, an infinitely extendible path can be recognized. As with the tree above, the tree goes into a cycle and there is clearly no way to break it.

In such cases, a model can sometimes be extracted from a portion of the unfinished path. There are two ways this might be done.

(i) When q-trees go into a cycle, an infinite model can sometimes be extrapolated from how the tree is developing over two or three cycles.

(ii) q-tree models can have domains that are larger than necessary to verify the givens. Should a path go into an unbreakable cycle, a finite model can sometimes be based on the portion of the tree that runs up to the first, second, or third recycle point. (After the third, the tree is likely to have become too large to permit further work.)

The tree given above lends itself to both resolutions. Line 5, which replicates line 2 but for having a sentence on it with b in the place of "a," marks the start of a new cycle. Were the tree continued for two more cycles it would produce,

6.	$\sim \sim \sim Gbc$✓		5 (∼∀)
7.	$\sim Gbc$		6 (DN)
8.	$\sim \forall y \sim \sim Gcy$		1 (∼∃)
9.	$\sim \sim \sim Gcd$		8 (∼∀)
10.	$\sim Gcd$		9 (DN)

This makes it clear how the tree will continue. Literals of the form $\sim Gpq$ will continually be added, where q is a new name and p is the name that occurred in second place in the last literal to be added.

The procedure for extracting a tree model from a q-tree is the same one used for p-trees. (QPL only differs from PSL in the addition of quantifiers and variables, and tree models are based on literals, which do not contain either.) Extrapolation from the partially completed tree above yields the following model:

D: {1,2,3,...}
a: 1; b: 2; c: 3; ...
G: { }

The method for verifying q-tree models has yet to be discussed, so this model cannot yet be demonstrated to be a model for the given.

An evident feature of this model is that it makes no difference how many objects there are in the domain. The given is verified just by the fact that $\alpha(G)$ is empty. This suggests that a model for the given might be found by just considering the portion of the path that runs up to the first recycle point, which yields:

D: {1,2}
a: 1; b: 2
G: { }

This is also a model for the given, but it is unverifiable using the "tree model" semantics of section 14.3. That semantics only works for exhausted paths or (with the aid of object variables) extrapolations to infinitely extended paths. It is, however, readily verifiable using the "Tarski" semantics of chapter 16, which does not need to appeal to named objects.

Of these two recourses, the first is more generally applicable than the second. While q-trees sometimes look for infinite models where finite ones will do the job, sometimes only a model with an infinite domain can satisfy the givens. An example found in many textbooks is based on the sentences that specify that a relation, G, is serial ($\forall x \exists y Gxy$), irreflexive ($\forall x \sim Gxx$), and transitive ($\forall x \forall y \forall z (Gxy \ \& \ Gyz \rightarrow Gxz)$). Given seriality, any object, o, stands in first place in the G relation to at least one, second place object. Given irreflexivity, this second object must be some other object, n. By seriality, n must also be G-related to some object. Given irreflexivity, this object cannot be n itself. It also cannot be o, because if <n,o> and <o,n> were both in $\alpha(G)$, transitivity would require that <n,n> be in $\alpha(G)$ which violates irreflexivity. n must therefore be G-related to a third object, m, putting <n,m> in $\alpha(G)$. Now seriality requires that m be G-related to some object. By irreflexivity, it cannot be m itself. By transitivity and irreflexivity, it cannot be n, and by transitivity and irreflexivity it cannot be o (transitivity requires that <o,m> be in $\alpha(G)$, which means <m,o> cannot be). The stage is set for an infinite expansion to the domain.

A q-tree for this set is complex, but it serves to illustrate some finer points of tree construction. A tree for the givens might begin as follows.

1.	$\forall x \exists y Gxy_a$	given
2.	$\forall x \sim Gxx_a$	given
3.	$\forall x \forall y \forall z (Gxy \ \& \ Gyz \rightarrow Gxz)_a$	given
4.	$\exists y Gay$ ✓	1 (T$\forall$)
5.	$\sim Gaa$	2 (T$\forall$)
6.	$\forall y \forall z (Gay \ \& \ Gyz \rightarrow Gaz)_a$	3 (T$\forall$)
7.	$\forall z (Gaa \ \& \ Gaz \rightarrow Gaz)_a$	6 (T$\forall$)
8.	$Gaa \ \& \ Gaa \rightarrow Gaa$ ✓	7 (T$\forall$)
9.	Gab	4 (T$\exists$)
10.	$\sim(Gaa \ \& \ Gaa)$ ✓ Gaa	8 (T$\rightarrow$)
11.	$\bot$	10,5 ($\bot$I)
12.	$\sim Gaa$ $\sim Gaa$	10 ($\sim$ &)

Since the givens are all universally quantified sentences, and there are no names among them, one sentence is instantiated using "a," and the others are instantiated using that name. When a tree will not close, it is good practice to reduce all universal and negated existential sentences as a group, taking them in order from the top down (as over lines 4–6 above) and then continue with any further universal or negated existential sentences created as a result of this work (as over lines 7–8). Once this work is begun, it should not be interrupted to do any other reductions (that is, to apply any rules other than (T$\forall$) and ($\sim\exists$)). Interruptions make it more difficult to keep track of what remains to be done. Interrupting (T$\forall$) and ($\sim\exists$) applications to apply (T$\exists$) or ($\sim\forall$) is particularly unwise as it adds extra names to the path, confusing what remains to be done with the prior names with what must now be done with the new names. After this work has been completed, the newly introduced compound sentences on lines 4, 8, and 10 are reduced, and one path closes. The two others are unfinished since a new name, b, was introduced at line 9 (subsequent to completion of the first round of (T$\forall$) / ($\sim\exists$) applications) and none of the universally quantified sentences on its paths has yet been reduced for it.

Because the two unfinished paths are identical from the top of the tree down, nothing will appear on the one that will not appear on the other, so the tree can be continued by looking just at what happens on one of them. To make room for new work, the closed right path is also omitted.

1.	$\forall x \exists y Gxy_{ab}$	given
2.	$\forall x {\sim} Gxx_{ab}$	given
3.	$\forall x \forall y \forall z (Gxy \ \& \ Gyz \rightarrow Gxz)_{ab}$	given
4.	$\exists y Gay \checkmark$	1 (T$\forall$)
5.	${\sim}Gaa$	2 (T$\forall$)
6.	$\forall y \forall z (Gay \ \& \ Gyz \rightarrow Gaz)_{ab}$	3 (T$\forall$)
7.	$\forall z (Gaa \ \& \ Gaz \rightarrow Gaz)_{ab}$	6 (T$\forall$)
8.	$Gaa \ \& \ Gaa \rightarrow Gaa \checkmark$	7 (T$\forall$)
9.	Gab	4 (T$\exists$)
	$\cdots$	
12.	${\sim}Gaa$	10 (${\sim}\&$)
13.	$\exists y Gby \checkmark$	1 (T$\forall$)
14.	${\sim}Gbb$	2 (T$\forall$)
15.	$\forall y \forall z (Gby \ \& \ Gyz \rightarrow Gbz)_{ab}$	3 (T$\forall$)
16.	$\forall z (Gab \ \& \ Gbz \rightarrow Gaz)_{ab}$	6 (T$\forall$)
17.	$Gaa \ \& \ Gab \rightarrow Gab$	7 (T$\forall$)
18.	$\forall z (Gba \ \& \ Gaz \rightarrow Gbz)_{ab}$	15 (T$\forall$)
19.	$\forall z (Gbb \ \& \ Gbz \rightarrow Gbz)_{ab}$	15 (T$\forall$)
20.	$Gab \ \& \ Gba \rightarrow Gaa$	16 (T$\forall$)
21.	$Gab \ \& \ Gbb \rightarrow Gab$	16 (T$\forall$)
22.	$Gba \ \& \ Gaa \rightarrow Gba$	18 (T$\forall$)
23.	$Gba \ \& \ Gab \rightarrow Gbb$	18 (T$\forall$)
24.	$Gbb \ \& \ Gba \rightarrow Gba$	19 (T$\forall$)
25.	$Gbb \ \& \ Gbb \rightarrow Gbb$	19 (T$\forall$)
26.	Gbc	13 (T$\exists$)

Where there are multiple universal or negated existential sentences to be reduced, it is not only important to proceed from the top down but also to keep track of index letters to ensure that everything that needs to be done is done. The universally quantified sentences on lines 1–3 and 6–7 were originally reduced for "a." With the addition of the new name, b, at line 9, those sentences must be reduced a second time for b. This is done, taking them in order from the top down, over lines 13–17. That work creates two new universally quantified sentences at lines 15 and 16, so they must each be reduced for both "a" and b. That work is done over lines 18–21. That work also creates two new $\forall$ sentences at lines 18 and 19. They are reduced for both "a" and b over lines 22–25. Even though the first thing the work does is create a new existentially quantified sentence at line 13, that sentence is not reduced. It bears repeating that once a (T$\forall$) or (${\sim}\exists$) application has been made, only (T$\forall$) or (${\sim}\exists$) should be applied until there are no (T$\forall$) or (${\sim}\exists$) applications left to perform.

The existentially quantified sentence at line 13 is only reduced after each universal and negated existential sentence to appear on the tree has been reduced in order, from the top down. When the existentially quantified sentence is reduced, it adds another new name to the path at line 25. This means all the universal and negated existential sentences on the path from line 1 on must be reduced again for c, followed by any new universal or negated existential sentences created as a result of reducing the existing ones. However, before turning to that, there are multiple unreduced conditionals on the path. There is no hope that reducing them will produce an exhausted path, since all will branch out below line 25 and so all will have c on them, making them unfinished. (Refraining from producing Gbc will not help, because each conditional is still below $\exists y Gby$ on line 13, which reduces to Gbc on any path below it.) The only way a further round of universally quantified sentence reductions could be avoided is if reducing the conditionals closes the tree. But that does not happen. An optimal selection, picking conditionals that will produce the most closed paths for first reduction, might look like this. (To save space, the following continuation of the tree just focuses on the literals and the conditionals on the path.)

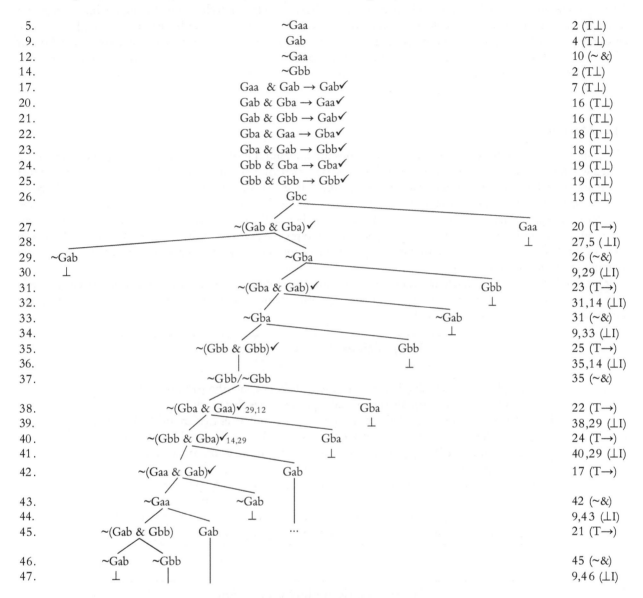

5.	~Gaa	2 (T⊥)
9.	Gab	4 (T⊥)
12.	~Gaa	10 (~ &)
14.	~Gbb	2 (T⊥)
17.	Gaa & Gab → Gab✓	7 (T⊥)
20.	Gab & Gba → Gaa✓	16 (T⊥)
21.	Gab & Gbb → Gab✓	16 (T⊥)
22.	Gba & Gaa → Gba✓	18 (T⊥)
23.	Gba & Gab → Gbb✓	18 (T⊥)
24.	Gbb & Gba → Gba✓	19 (T⊥)
25.	Gbb & Gbb → Gbb✓	19 (T⊥)
26.	Gbc	13 (T⊥)

line 27. ~(Gab & Gba)✓ .... Gaa — 20 (T→)
line 28. ⊥ — 27,5 (⊥I)
line 29. ~Gab .... ~Gba — 26 (~&)
line 30. ⊥ — 9,29 (⊥I)
line 31. ~(Gba & Gab)✓ .... Gbb — 23 (T→)
line 32. ⊥ — 31,14 (⊥I)
line 33. ~Gba .... ~Gab — 31 (~&)
line 34. ⊥ — 9,33 (⊥I)
line 35. ~(Gbb & Gbb)✓ .... Gbb — 25 (T→)
line 36. ⊥ — 35,14 (⊥I)
line 37. ~Gbb/~Gbb — 35 (~&)
line 38. ~(Gba & Gaa)✓ 29,12 .... Gba — 22 (T→)
line 39. ⊥ — 38,29 (⊥I)
line 40. ~(Gbb & Gba)✓ 14,29 .... Gba — 24 (T→)
line 41. ⊥ — 40,29 (⊥I)
line 42. ~(Gaa & Gab)✓ .... Gab — 17 (T→)
line 43. ~Gaa .... ~Gab — 42 (~&)
line 44. ⊥ — 9,43 (⊥I)
line 45. ~(Gab & Gbb) Gab ... — 21 (T→)
line 46. ~Gab ~Gbb — 45 (~&)
line 47. ⊥ | — 9,46 (⊥I)

The tree ends up with four unfinished paths. (The sentence on line 42 right should be considered to have copies of all the paths that appear on lines 43–47 underneath it.). At line 37, reduction of the ~& sentence at line 34 produces two paths, but because they are headed off by the same sentence, there is no point in pursuing them both, so they are amalgamated. Reduction of the ~& sentences on lines 38 and 40 would only produce paths that are headed off by sentences that already exist on the path above them, so they are checked off, as nothing could happen on the subsequent portions of the tree that would not happen in their absence.

All four unfinished paths contain the same two atomic sentences: Gbc and Gab, establishing that all the work that was done over lines 27–47 has added no more information to the tree than was already present at line 26. The portion of the tree up to line 26 defines a tree model where D is {1,2,3,…} and α(G) is {<1,2>, <2,3>,…} A further round of reductions for c would clearly add ~Gcc, ∃yGcy, and Gcd to the tree. Less obviously (but plausibly, given that one of the new instances of the sentence on line 16 will be Gab & Gbc → Gac), reducing the resulting conditionals would also add Gac to any unfinished paths, expanding D to {1,2,3,4,…} and α(G) to {<1,2>, <1,3>, <2,3>, <3,4>,…}. The tree is by now too complex to contemplate a third cycle to confirm this suspicion, though the ambitious reader with a large sheet of paper may attempt the exercise. It is easier to consider whether the model that has just been extracted from the partially completed tree verifies the givens. On that model D is the set of natural numbers and $\alpha(G)$ is the set of ordered pairs of natural numbers $<o,n>$ such that o is less than n. A verification can be based on the solution to exercise 16.8#6e, which deals with a variant on this problem.

The attempt to find tree models by using a portion of an unfinished path to extrapolate an infinite model or define a finite model can fail. A tree might become unmanageable before a cycle can be found, leaving it uncertain whether it has an infinitely extendible path. Even when a cycle is found, it may not be feasible to complete the tree up to the point where a portion can be found that suggests a verifiable tree model. q-trees are undecidable. Any set of sentences of QPL still has either at least one closed tree or at least one tree with at least one exhausted or infinitely extendible path. But, while many trees turn out one way or the other after a manageable number of one-step extensions, in some cases, it is not possible to discover which result obtains before exhausting the available resources.

14.2 Method

There are two methods for doing q-trees: the judicious method and the systematic method. The judicious method is used when it is anticipated that the tree will close. The systematic method must be used when it is anticipated that it will not close. The different methods are needed because q-trees can very quickly become unmanageably large. In such cases, if the tree will close, making a judicious choice of which sentences to reduce first, and which instances to enter on the path can be necessary to bring about closure before the tree becomes unmanageable. But if the tree will grow an exhausted or infinitely extendible path, failing to proceed systematically can make it so difficult to keep track of what still needs to be done that it is impossible to continue while still being confident that path closing sentences have not been overlooked.

It is often hard to tell in advance whether a tree will close. But a choice must be made between proceeding judiciously and proceeding systematically. Should the wrong choice be made, the tree will have to be scrapped to make a fresh start with the alternative approach.

The Judicious Reduction Method
(Follow the steps in order.)

(i)   Apply "straight" reduction rules (those that do not split the path) other than $(T\forall)$, $(\sim\exists)$, and $(=E)$. Also apply path-splitting rules that produce closed paths.

(ii) Apply $(T\forall)$, $(\sim\exists)$, and $(=E)$ to make only those instances that are most likely to close the tree or close paths. Make the instance that produces the most closures first and immediately proceed to apply the rules needed to produce those closures. Then go on to the next instance.

(iii) Apply those path-splitting rules that produce one or more open paths only when there are no other rules that can be applied. Choose the application that produces paths that are most likely to close with some further work and proceed to do that further work before applying any more path-splitting rules.

The Systematic Reduction Method

Stage 1 (Checkables)
- Reduce nonliteral sentences other than $\forall$ and $\sim\exists$ sentences following the judicious strategies. In cases where an application of $(T\forall)$, $(\sim\exists)$, or $(=E)$ will quickly close a path it is permissible to make these applications as well. When that happens, the rule should not only be applied on the path that it closes, but across the tree on any other paths where it applies.
- By the end of stage 1, all sentences that can be checked off should have been checked off. These are all sentences other than literals, $\forall$ sentences, $\sim\exists$ sentences, and $=$ sentences.
- Proceed to stage 2 only after completing stage 1.

Stage 2 (∀ and ~∃ Sentences)
- Starting at the top of the tree and proceeding in order from top to bottom, repeatedly apply (T∀) or (~∃) to each ∀ or ~∃ sentence, using each name to occur on the path on which reduction results are being entered in order from the alphanumerically earliest on. Also apply (T∀) and (~∃) to ∀ and ~∃ sentences entered on the bottom of paths by working at this stage.
- Do not go back to stage 1 or interrupt work at stage 2 to do stage 1 reductions that might arise from work at stage 2. Continue working at stage 2 until all ∀ and ~∃ sentences have been reduced for all names.
- When all ∀ and ~∃ sentences have been reduced, do not go back to stage 1. Proceed directly to stage 3.

Stage 3 (Identification of Names)
- If there are no identity sentences on the tree, return to stage 1; otherwise:
- Starting at the top of the tree and proceeding in order from top to bottom, repeatedly apply (=E) using each = sentence as source. Do this by going down to the first = sentence, =rq, to appear on the path. Taking =rq as source, go back up to the top of the path and take in turn each literal, P, from the top of the path down as a target for one (=E) application that puts r in the place of each occurrence of q in P. Include the application of the = sentence to itself when its turn comes up. Be careful to make applications to each literal to occur on an open path running up to the = sentence. Pass over applications that reproduce a literal that already exists on the path. Include literals added to paths as a consequence of work at this stage. When done, go down to the next identity sentence on the path and repeat this process, using it as source. Also use = sentences entered on the bottom of paths as the result of work at this stage as sources for (=E) when their turn comes up. Continue until the lowest = sentence on the tree has been used as source on all targets. Then go back to the top and repeat. Keep cycling through the = sentences until a complete cycle produces no changes to the tree. At this point return to stage 1.

Stop when either all paths close or a complete cycle through stages 1 to 3 produces no changes to at least one open path. In the second case, declare that path to be exhausted. Do not continue work on a tree that has produced an exhausted path.

When following the systematic method, it is permissible to focus work on the path most likely to turn into an exhausted path. But when sentences higher up on this path are reduced, the placement principle still applies: the reduction rule must be applied on each path that runs up to the sentence being reduced, not just on the path that will supposedly become an exhausted path. It is also wise to apply rules on all paths where they apply. For example, if 4,6 (=E) is being applied on the path that is most likely to be exhausted, and there is an identity sentence on line 4 on another path, and a suitable target on line 6 of that other path, (=E) should be applied on that path as well, even if the sentences appearing on the other path are different from the ones on the focal path. That way, if the path disappoints expectations and does not close, a portion of the work on the remainder of the tree will have been done at the point where it was in order, making it possible to continue the tree without having to backtrack.

Proceeding through the three stages of the systematic method ensures that all names that can be introduced through (T∃) and (~∀) get introduced before (T∀), (~∃), and (=E) commence. This in turn ensures that (T∀), (~∃), and (=E) reductions that might close a path or a tree are not inadvertently omitted.

(T∀) and (~∃) reductions will often produce nonliteral sentences. When proceeding systematically it is important to refrain from reducing these nonliterals when they first appear. Interrupting work at stage 2 can make it hard to remember where to resume it. Finishing the (T∀), (~∃), and (=E) reductions in order ensures that nothing is forgotten. It also avoids getting caught in an endless cycle when turning to other sentences would produce an exhausted path or, contrary to expectations, close the tree.

As an illustration of the systematic method, consider the use of the tree method to demonstrate that ∀xGx → H and ∀x(Gx → H) are not interderivable in Tq. As with Ts and Tp, doing this requires showing that at least one of the corresponding sets does not have a closed tree.

The exercise will fail to deliver the right result unless the trees are done for what really is one sentence and the negation of the other. This means that the negation needs to be formed correctly.

Exercise

What is the opposite of $\forall xGx \rightarrow Hx$?

In approaching this exercise, it is wisest to pick the set that appears most likely to produce multiple paths, as that is the set most likely to have a tree with an exhausted path. But there is no obvious difference between the sets in this case. Consider first a tree for $\forall x(Gx \rightarrow H)$ and the opposite of $\forall xGx \rightarrow H$.

1.	$\forall x(Gx \rightarrow H)$	given
2.	$\sim(\forall xGx \rightarrow H)$	given

There is no choice over how to proceed with this tree. The sentence at line 1 requires a stage 2 reduction (it is a universally quantified sentence), so, unless it can already be seen how reducing it will close the tree, it may not be reduced before all stage 1 reductions have been performed. Since the sentence at line 2 requires a stage 1 reduction, it must be done first.

1.	$\forall x(Gx \rightarrow H)$	given
2.	$\sim(\forall xGx \rightarrow H)$ ✓	given
3.	$\forall xGx$	2 ($\sim\rightarrow$)
4.	$\sim H$	2 ($\sim\rightarrow$)

Now, both the remaining nonliterals, that at line 1 and that at line 3, are universally quantified sentences. Work at stage 2 must commence.

1.	$\forall x(Gx \rightarrow H)_a$	Given
2.	$\sim(\forall xGx \rightarrow H)$ ✓	Given
3.	$\forall xGx_a$	2 ($\sim\rightarrow$)
4.	$\sim H$	2 ($\sim\rightarrow$)
5.	$Ga \rightarrow H$	1 (T$\forall$)
6.	Ga	3 (T$\forall$)

Universal and negated existential reductions do not split paths, do not add new names to paths, and cannot go on forever. Even if they create other universal or negated existential sentences, those sentences are shorter than their parents. Only a finite amount of work can be done before no universal or negated existential sentences remain to be reduced. It is best to clear that work before proceeding to anything else.

The universally quantified sentences at lines 1 and 3 are not checked off, since additional names could appear later.

As there are no names on the path as of line 4, the alphanumerically earliest unused name, "a," is used to make an instance at line 5. At line 6, there is already one name, "a," on the path, but there are no others, so the one existing name is used to make the instance. (T$\forall$) never introduces new names unless there are no names yet in existence. This means making one (T$\forall$) application when either none or only one name exists on the path, more when more than one name is on the path.

As of line 6, all (T$\forall$) reductions have been performed and stage 2 ends. After stage 2 ends, stage 3 must commence. However, there are no stage 3 reductions to be done on this tree. Work may therefore return to stage 1. Since the last time work was done at stage 1, a new stage 1 sentence has been entered at line 5. Now is the time for it to be reduced.

```
1.    ∀x(Gx → H)ₐ        given
2.    ~(∀xGx → H)✓       given
3.        ∀xGxₐ           2 (~→)
4.        ~H             2 (~→)
5.      Ga → H✓          1 (T∀)
6.        Ga             3 (T∀)

              /\
7.    ~Ga        H        5 (TV)
8.     ⊥         |        6,7 (⊥I)
9.               ⊥        7,4 (⊥I)
```

After reducing the sentence on line 5, the tree closes. It therefore fails to establish that one of the two corresponding sets does not have a closed tree. This makes it necessary to consider the trees for the other corresponding set, {∀xGx → H, ~∀x(Gx → H)}.

```
1.      ∀xGx → H        given
2.     ~∀x(Gx → H)      given
```

In this case, the sentences on both lines are stage 1 reductions. However, since the first sentence splits the path, the second should be done first.

```
1.      ∀xGx → H        given
2.     ~∀x(Gx → H) ✓    given
3.      ~(Ga → H)       2 (~∀)
```

(~∀) requires the use of a name that has not yet appeared on the path. By convention, the alphanumerically earliest unused name is always chosen. Since no names yet appear, "a" is chosen to make the instance.

The tree should be continued by reducing the sentence on line 3, as it does not split the path.

```
1.      ∀xGx → H        given
2.     ~∀x(Gx → H) ✓    given
3.      ~(Ga → H) ✓     2 (~∀)
4.          Ga          3 (~→)
5.          ~H          3 (~→)
```

Now only the sentence at line 1 remains unreduced.

```
1.      ∀xGx → H ✓      given
2.     ~∀x(Gx → H)✓     given
3.      ~(Ga → H)✓      2 (~∀)
4.          Ga          3 (~→)
5.          ~H          3 (~→)

              /\
6.   ~∀xGx        H      1 (T→)
7.               ⊥       6,5 (⊥I)
```

Reducing the sentence on line 1 closes the right path, but the left remains open.

$$
\begin{array}{lll}
1. & \forall xGx \rightarrow H\checkmark & \text{given} \\
2. & \sim\forall x(Gx \rightarrow H)\checkmark & \text{given} \\
3. & \sim(Ga \rightarrow H)\checkmark & 2\ (\sim\forall) \\
4. & Ga & 3\ (\sim\rightarrow) \\
5. & \sim H & 3\ (\sim\rightarrow) \\
\end{array}
$$

$$
\begin{array}{lll}
6. & \sim\forall xGx\checkmark \quad\quad H & 1\ (T\rightarrow) \\
7. & \quad\quad|\quad\quad\quad \perp & 6,5\ (\perp I) \\
8. & \mathbf{\sim Gb} & \mathbf{6\ (\sim\forall)} \\
& \mathbf{e} &
\end{array}
$$

($\sim\forall$) requires the use of a new name. So, after ($\sim\forall$) is applied to the sentence on line 6, the left path remains open. It is also exhausted. There are no universally quantified sentences and no identity sentences on the path. (The sentence on line 1 is a conditional.) Each other sentence is either a literal or has been checked off.

The exhausted path proves that $\forall xGx \rightarrow H$ and $\forall x(Gx \rightarrow H)$ are not interderivable in Tq. But does that mean that they are not q-equivalent? The result seems suspicious because the only difference between $\forall xGx \rightarrow H$ and $\forall x(Gx \rightarrow H)$ is punctuation that might seem pointless as it only extends the scope of the quantifier over a formula that does not contain an x variable. To establish that the result really is correct, the tree model defined by the exhausted path should be extracted and verified.

Tree models for q-trees are based on literals, which are sentences of PSL, so there are no changes to the procedure to extracting a tree model from an exhausted path as laid out in chapter 11.4. But verifying universally and existentially quantified sentences requires valuation rules for those sentences. This in turn requires a preliminary foray into QPL semantics.

14.3 Tree Model Semantics

Tree models have two features that make it possible to verify them using only a rudimentary expansion on PSL semantics. Only sentences appear on trees, and the procedure for extracting a tree model from an exhausted path ensures that there are no unnamed objects in the domain. Consequently, the instances for any existentially or universally quantified sentence pick out all and any objects that satisfy the sentence's immediate subformula.

These features make it possible to supplement PSL semantics with the following two "tree model" (TM) rules for quantified sentences:

Tree Model Valuation Rules

(FTM$\forall$):   A universally quantified sentence, $\forall\chi P$, is true on a tree model, I, if and only if, for each name, q, $I(P(q\,|\,\chi))$ is T; otherwise (if any instance of $\forall\chi P$ is F on I), $I(\forall\chi P)$ is F.

(FTM$\exists$):   An existentially quantified sentence, $\exists\chi P$, is true on a tree model, I, if and only if for at least one name, q, $I(P(q\,|\,\chi))$ is T; otherwise (if each instance is F on I), $I(\exists\chi P)$ is F.

A tree model is verified by proceeding up the exhausted path from the bottom to show that the truth of the literals follows from the tree model, and the truth of each sentence higher up on the path follows from the truth of the sentences into which it was reduced lower on at least one extension of the path. It is not always necessary to consider each sentence on the path. In particular:

- Sentences derived by (=E) can usually be ignored. Often, these sentences are only on the path to demonstrate that the other literals on the path are not contradictory. They play no role in verifying the tree model.
- Demonstrating that negations are true on the model can often be skipped in favour of appealing just to the fact that their nullations are false on the model.

By way of illustration consider the verification of the tree that was just completed.

1.	$\forall x Gx \rightarrow H$ ✓	given
2.	$\sim\forall x(Gx \rightarrow H)$ ✓	given
3.	$\sim(Ga \rightarrow H)$ ✓	2 ($\sim\forall$)
4.	Ga	3 ($\sim\rightarrow$)
5.	$\sim$H	3 ($\sim\rightarrow$)

```
             /\
```

6.	$\sim\forall x Gx$ ✓	H	1 (T$\rightarrow$)
7.	|	$\perp$	6,5 ($\perp$I)
8.	$\sim$Gb		6 ($\sim\forall$)
	e		

The tree model that comes off the exhausted path is:

D: {1,2}
a: 1; b: 2
G: {1}; H: F

The model is established by the fact that two names occur on the path and they are not identified with one another, so there are two objects in the domain, which are assigned to the names in alphanumeric order. The only unnegated literal on the path is Ga, which means α(G) must be {1}. Since H does not appear on the path, α(H) is F.

The model is verified by going up the exhausted path from literals to givens. Looking up at the justifications column for the tree, the lowest literal (on line 8) comes from the sentence on line 6, which in turn comes from the given on line 1. This traces out one path for bottom-up reasoning from the tree model. The next lowest literals on the exhausted path are on lines 5 and 4. They both come from the sentence on line 3 which comes from the given on line 2. This traces out a second path for bottom-up reasoning.

1.	α(b) is 2 and 2 is not in α(G)	given
2.	I(Gb) is F	1 (P) *Tree line 8 asks for a demonstration that $\sim$Gb is true on the model. But in this case the falsity of Gb is needed for the rest of the verification, so there is no need to mention that $\sim$Gb is true on I.*
3.	I($\forall x Gx$) is F	2 (TM$\forall$)
4.	I($\forall x Gx \rightarrow H$) is T	3 ($\rightarrow$) *verifying the given line 1*
5.	I(H) is F	given *(going on to infer that $\sim$H on tree line 5 is true is unnecessary for the rest of the verification.)*
6.	α(a) is 1 and 1 is in α(G)	given
7.	I(Ga) is T	6 (P)
8.	I(Ga $\rightarrow$ H) is F	7,5 ($\rightarrow$) *going on to infer that $\sim$(Ga $\rightarrow$ H) is true on I can can be skipped.*
9.	I($\forall x(Gx \rightarrow H)$) is F	8 (TM$\forall$)
10.	I($\sim\forall x(Gx \rightarrow H)$) is T	9 ($\sim$) *verifying the given on tree line 2*

This verification invokes the new rule, (TM$\forall$) twice over, at lines 3 and 9. In both cases, the rule is used to falsify a universally quantified sentence. A universally quantified sentence is easy to falsify. It requires just one counterexample, that is, just one false instance. Proving that universally quantified sentences are true and existentially quantified sentences false is more work. In accord with (TM$\forall$) and (TM$\exists$) it requires citing lines that show that each instance to appear on the path is true ($\forall$ sentences) or false ($\exists$ sentences). It is also necessary to add an observation that the cited instances use all the names that there are on the path.

The tree done earlier for {Ga, Gb ∨ ∃x~Kxa, ∀x(Hx & ∃yKya)} can serve for illustration.

1.		Ga	given
2.		~(Gb ∨ Kbb) ∨ ~(∀xKxa ∨ Ca)✓	given
3.		∀x(Hx & ∃yKya) ₐbc d	given
4.	~(Gb ∨ Kbb)	~(∀xKxa ∨ Ca) ✓	2 (TV)
	~Gb	~∀xKxa	
	~Kbb	~Ca	
5.	│	~Kca	5 (~ ∀)
6.	Ha & ∃yKya✓	Ha & ∃yKya✓	3 (T∀)
7.	Hb & ∃yKya ✓	Hb & ∃yKya ✓	3 (T∀)
8.	│	Hc & ∃yKya✓	3 (T∀)
9.	Ha	Ha	6 (T&)
10.	∃yKya ✓	∃yKya ✓	6 (T&)
11.	Kda	Kda	10 (T∃)
12.	Hb	Hb	7 (T&)
13.	∃yKya✓₁₁	∃yKya✓₁₁	7 (T&)
14.	│	Hc	8 (T&)
15.	│	∃yKya✓₁₁	9 (T&)
16.	Hd & ∃yKya ✓	Hd & ∃yKya✓	3 (T∀)
17.	Hd	Hd	12 (T&)
18.	∃yKya✓₁₁	∃yKya✓₁₁	12 (T&)
	e	e	

The tree model that comes off the leftmost exhausted path is:

D: {1,2,3}
a: 1; b: 2; d: 3
G: {1,2}; H: {1,2,3}; K: {<3,1>}

Verification of the tree model begins with the sentence on line 17 of the exhausted path, skipping the sentences on lines 18, 16, and 13. The sentences on lines 18 and 13 are forced repetitions of the sentence on line 10. That sentence was originally reduced at line 11, so the verification of all three must wait for verification of line 11. Since line 10 is also needed to verify the sentence on line 16, that verification must also be postponed.

1.	α(d) is 3 and 3 is in α(H)	given
2.	I(Hd) is T	1 (P)
3.	α(b) is 2 and 2 is in α(H)	given
4.	I(Hb) is T	3 (P)
5.	<α(d),α(a)> is <3,1> and <3,1> is in α(K)	given
6.	I(Kda) is T	5 (P)
7.	I(∃yKya) is T	6 (TM∃)
8.	I(Hd & ∃yKya) is T	2,7 (&)
9.	α(a) is 1 and 1 is in α(H)	given
10.	I(Ha) is T	9 (P)
11.	I(Hb & ∃yKya) is T	4,7 (&)
12.	I(Ha & ∃yKya) is T	10,7 (&)
13.	a, b, and d are all the names there are on the path	given
14.	I(∀x(Hx & ∃yKya)) is T	12,11,8,13 (TM∀) *verifying the given on line 3*
15.	α(b) is 2 and 2 is in α(G)	given
16.	I(Gb) is T	15 (P)

17. I(Gb ∨ ∃x~Kxa) is T	16 (∨) *verifying the given on line 2*
18. α(a) is 1 and 1 is in α(G)	given
19. I(Ga) is T	18 (P) *verifying the given on line 1*

Establishing that a universally quantified sentence is true can be laborious. For each name that appears on the path, an instance of the universally quantified sentence using that name must appear on the path. On a properly done exhausted tree path, that will always be the case. Each of those instances must be verified. If there are three names on the path, there are three instances to be verified, as at lines 12, 11, and 8 above. Then, it must be observed that those three instances have indeed used up all the names that appear on the path, as at line 13 above. Only then can (TM∀) be applied to establish the truth of the universally quantified sentence.

The same holds when aiming to establish that an existentially quantified sentence is false.

This is not to say that (TM∀) and (TM∃) always require four justifications for true ∀'s and false ∃'s respectively. They require as many justifications as there are names appearing on the path, plus one that notes that those are all the names on the path.

The situation is reversed when existentially quantified sentences are true or universally quantified sentences false. It only takes one true instance to establish the truth of an existentially sentence and one false instance to establish the falsity of a universally quantified sentence. It makes all the difference whether (TM∀) and (TM∃) are used to establish the truth or the falsity of the sentence. Those who have studied chapter 9 will notice the parallel with (□) and (◇), which have the same relation to worlds that (TM∀) and (TM∃) have to objects.

Exercise 14.1

1. *Determine using* Tq *whether each of the following sets is inconsistent in* Tq. *Say what the tree proves and why. If the set has a tree with an exhausted path, describe and verify the tree model defined by the path. If the set has a closed tree, verify this result by showing that the set yields* ⊥ *in* Dq.

   ⋆**a.** {∃x∃yGxy, ∃x∃y~Gxy}

   b. {∃x∃yGxy, ∀x∀y~Gxy}

   ⋆**c.** {∃xGx, ~∀xGx}

   d. {∃xGx, ∃xHx, ~∃x(Gx & Hx)}

   ⋆**e.** {∃xGx, ∃xHx, ∃x~(Gx & Hx)}

   f. {∀x(Gx → Hx), ∀x(Gx → ~Hx), ∃xGx}

   ⋆**g.** {∀x(Gx → Hx), ∀x~(Gx → Hx)}

   h. {∀x(Gx → Hx), ~∀x(Gx → Hx)}

   ⋆**i.** {∀x(Gx → Hax), ~∃x (Gx ∨ Hxa), ∃xHax}

   j. {∃xGx & ∃xHx, ∀x(Gx → ~Hx)}

   ⋆**k.** {∀x∀y=xy, ∀x(Gx → Hx) → ∃x(Hx & Kx), ∃x(~Gx & ~Hx)}

   l. {Ga, ∀x(Gx → Hx), ~∃x(Gx & Hx)}

2. *Use a judicious tree to show that each of the demonstrations of exercise 13.8#1a–b, e–f, and h–n is derivable in* Tq. *Also show that the following demonstrations are derivable in* Tq *and* Dq.
   Answers to a, e, i, k, m

   ⋆**o.** ∃x[Gx & ∀y(Gy → =yx) & Hx], ∃x(Gx & Kx) / ∃x(Hx & Kx)

   p. ∃x∀y(Gx → Hy) / ∀y∃x(Gx → Hy)

   ⋆**q.** ∀x(∃yGyx → ∀zHxz), ∀x∀y(Hxy → Hyx) / ∀x∀y(∃zGxz → ∃zHyz)

   r. ∃x∀y(∃zGyz → Gyx), ∀x∃yGxy / ∃x∀yGyx

   ⋆**s.** ∀x∃y(Gx → Hy) / ∃y∀x(Gx → Hy)

   t. ∀x∃y(Gy → Hx) / ∃y∀x(Gy → Hx) *(compare the answer to s)*

3. *Use a systematic tree to show that each of the following demonstrations is not derivable in* Tq. *Describe and verify the tree model defined by the leftmost exhausted path.*

   ⋆**a.** ∃x(Ax & Bcx), Ad / Bcd

   b. ∀x(Gx → Hx) / ∃x(Gx & Hx)

   ⋆**c.** ∀x(∀yGxy → Gxx) / ∀xGxx

   d. ∀x[Gx → ∃y(Hxy & =yx)] / ∀x~Gx

    ⋆e. ∀x(Gxx → =xa), Gaa & =ab / ∀x∀y=xy

    f. ∀x(=xa → =xb), ∃xGxa / ∃xGxx

    ⋆g. ∀x(Gx → ∃yHxy), Ga / ∀y~Hay

    h. ∀x(Gax → =xb), ∃xGax /~=ab

    ⋆i. ∀x[~Gx → ∃y(Hxy & =yx)] / ∃xGx

4. *Use judicious trees to prove each of the interderivability claims of exercise 13.8#2 in* Tq.
    Answers to a, c, e, g, i, k, m, o, q

5. *Use a systematic tree to show that the sentences in each of the following pairs are not interderivable in* Tq. *Describe and verify the tree model defined by the leftmost exhausted path.*
    ⋆a. ∀x~Gx, ~∀xGx
    b. ∀x(Gx ∨ Hx), ∀xGx ∨ ∀xHx
    ⋆c. ∃x(Gx & Hx), ∃xGx & ∃xHx
    d. ∃x(Gx → H), ∃xGx → H
    ⋆e. ∀x(Gx → Hx), ∃xGx → ∀xHx
    f. ∀x(Gx → Hx), ∀xGx → ∀xHx

6. *Use a judicious tree to show that each of the sentences of exercise 13.8#1c–d, g, and o–u is a theorem of* Tq. *Also show that the following sentences are theorems of both* Tq *and* Dq.
    Answers to c, g, o, q, s, u
    ⋆a. (∃xGx → ∀x~Hx) → ∀x(∃yGy → ~Hx)
    b. ∃x=ax
    ⋆e. (∃xGx → ∃xHx) → ∃x∀y(Gy → Hx)
    f. ∃x[Gx & ∀y(Gy → =yx)] ≡ ∃x∀y(Gy ≡ =yx)

7. *Use a judicious tree to show that each of the sentences of exercise 13.8#3⋆a, d, ⋆e is inconsistent in* Tq. *Also show that the following sentences are inconsistent in both* Tq *and* Dq.
    b. ∀x∀y(Gxy & ~Gyx)
    ⋆c. ∃x∀yGxy & ~∀y∃xGxy
    f. ∀x∀y=xy & ∃x∃y∃z[(Gyx & (~Gxx ∨ ~Gxz)]

8. *Use systematic trees to show that each of the following sentences is contingent in* Tq. *Describe and verify the tree models defined by the leftmost exhausted path of each tree.*
    ⋆a. ∃y∀x=yx
    b. ∃xGx & ∃x~Gx
    ⋆c. ∀xGx → ∀x~Gx
    d. ∀x(Gx → Hx) & ∀x(Gx → ~Hx)
    ⋆e. (∀xGx → ∀xHx) → ∀x(Gx → Hx)
    f. [∃x(Ax & Bx) & ∃x(Bx & Cx)] → ∃x(Ax & Cx)

14.4 Extensions of Tq

14.4.1 Functional Terms

Tqf, the tree method for determining the inconsistency of sets containing quantified sentences and functional terms, is a straightforward combination of Tq and Tpf. As such, it adds the extended closure and (=E) rules used by Tpf. (A restriction to closed terms is not necessary since =tt is not used as an axiom on trees.)

(⊥I)	(=E)
k. P *k.* ~=tt	*k.* =ts
⎮ ⎮	⎮
k⋆. ~P *or:* *n.* ⊥ *k* (⊥I)	*k⋆.* P
⎮	⎮
n. ⊥ *k,k⋆* (⊥I)	*n.* P(t⦙s) *k,k⋆* (=E)
(where P is atomic)	*(where P is a literal containing 0 or more occurrences of s)*

It also adds (T*f*).

> (T*f*): If $f(p_1...p_n)$ occurs in a literal on a path, and no sentence of the form $=qf(p_1...p_n)$, where q is a name, occurs on that path, enter $=rf(p_1...p_n)$ on each open extension of the path, where r is the alphabetically earliest name not yet to have appeared in any sentence on the path.

Paths are not just closed by opposite literals and by sentences of the form $\sim=pp$, where p is a name. They are closed by any sentence of the form $\sim=tt$ where t is a term. $\sim=f(a)f(a)$ closes a tree path. And (=E) can be used to put any identified term in the place of the term it is identified with, whether the "source" term and the target terms are names, complex terms, or a combination of both.

In T*qf*, rules of T*q* are used up to the point where all nonliterals on the tree have been reduced, and rules of T*pf* are used to identify the terms. (T∀) and ($\sim$∃) continue to require instantiation using each *name*. Since complex terms must be identified to the right of a name, it is unnecessary to instantiate universal or negated existential sentences with complex terms. Instantiation with complex terms is permitted, but doing so would be unwise except in the case where the instance quickly closes a path.

Because (T*f*) adds new names to the tree, it can also cause paths to become infinitely extendible. To take a simple example, any tree for $\forall xGf(x)$ has an infinitely extendible path.

1.	$\forall xGf(x)_{abc}$	given
2.	$Gf(a)$	1 (T∀)
3.	$=bf(a)$	2 (T*f*)
4.	Gb	3,2 (=E)
5.	$=bb$	3,3 (=E)
6.	$Gf(b)$	1 (T∀)
7.	$=cf(b)$	6 (T*f*)
8.	Gc	7,6 (=E)
9.	$=cc$	7,7 (=E)
10.	$Gf(c)$	1 (T∀)

…

The ways of basing a tree model on an infinitely extendible path that were discussed in section 14.1 can be employed on some of these paths.

As with T*q*, the possibility of unending cycles makes it necessary to impose restrictions on the order in which sentences may be reduced on a path that will not close. Without restrictions, the sentences involved in producing an unending cycle might be reduced to the exclusion of all others. But reducing other sentences might either close the path or produce an exhausted offshoot from the path. It is thus essential that cycles not prevent any sentence that appears on a path from getting its turn to be reduced (if it is a nonliteral) or identified (if it is subject to (=E) or (T*f*)) at some finite point. The following statement of the systematic reduction method achieves this goal by making an appropriate combination of the methods for T*q* and T*pf*.

The Systematic Reduction Method

Stages 1 and 2 are as stated in section 14.2.

Stage 3 (Identification of Functional Terms)
- **If there are no functional terms or none that have not yet been identified to the right of a name, proceed to stage 4; otherwise:**
- **Starting at the top of the tree identify each occurrence of a level-1 functional term to occur in a literal. Apply (=E) or (T*f*) as necessary to identify any of these terms that have not so far been identified to the right of a name. In cases where either (=E) or (T*f*) can be applied to make the identification, prefer (=E). In cases where multiple functional terms require identification, take them up in an order that maximizes the number of identifications that can be made by (=E).**

> • **When all level-1 functional terms have been identified, do not go back to stage 1 or 2. Proceed directly to stage 4.**
>
> **Stage 4** (Identification of Names)
> The remainder of the method is the same as stated in section 14.3.

Exercise 14.2

Determine whether the following sequents are true using Tqf. *If the tree produces an exhausted path, recover and verify the tree model defined by the leftmost such path.*

★**a.** $\vdash \forall x \exists y = f(x)y$

 b. $\vdash \forall x \forall y(=f(x)y \rightarrow = f(f(x)) f(y))$

★**c.** $\vdash \forall x \exists y = f(y)x$

 d. $\vdash \forall x(=f(x)x \rightarrow = f(f(x)) x)$

★**e.** $\vdash \forall x \forall y(=f(x)f(y) \rightarrow =xy)$

 f. $\forall x Gf(x) \vdash \exists x(Gx \ \& \ Gf(x))$ *(careful!)*

14.4.2 Semantics and Trees for Intuitionistic Logic

Interpretations and semantics for intuitionistic quantified logic are expanded to include object domains, predicate and identity rules, and quantifier rules.

Object domains are dynamic. As new evidence comes in, new objects are discovered or constructed, and the domain grows. There is no such thing as a finished domain of all the objects that will ever be discovered or constructed. There is only a domain of the objects that have so far been discovered or constructed. This domain is always finite, but also always subject to expansion. The object domain at any one stage, s, includes only those objects that are evident at s. However, there are many more objects that can be conceived at s than there are objects that are evident at s, and so than there are objects in s's object domain. When it is uncertain at s whether an object, o, exists it is because s sees subsequent stages of evidence, t_1 and t_2, such that o is in Dt_1 but not in Dt_2 (an object that is in all domains s sees is evident at s and so in s's object domain). Insofar as s sees other accessible stages, it sees *some* of the objects in the domains of those stages (not necessarily all, because objects may be discovered or constructed at later stages that are not conceived at s). This makes it helpful to distinguish between the object domain at s, which is the domain of the objects that are evident at s, and a more general domain at s that includes the object domain at s but also includes objects that s sees in some but not all accessible object domains. The former may be called s's local domain, the latter, which is the domain of objects that are conceived at s, may be called s's outer domain.

Identities also need to be discovered. When an identity is discovered, apparently different objects are discovered to be evidently one object. This makes object domains subject to a kind of contraction as well as expansion, though the contraction is, in a sense, only apparent. From the perspective of any later stage in the development of evidence, there never were any more objects in the domain than there are at that later stage. It simply becomes evident that their manifestations at different places and times are manifestations of the same object. This is a phenomenon that needs to be reflected in the semantics. A tentative proposal for doing so is made below.

As mentioned in chapter 13.2.2, the existential quantifier ranges only over objects in the local domain, that is, over evidently existing objects. $\exists \chi P$ does not just assert that there is something that satisfies P. It asserts that something that satisfies P has been discovered or constructed. $\exists \chi P$ never asserts that something satisfies P, though it is unknown what it is. That is just a way for $\exists \chi P$ to be nonevident.

$\forall \chi P$ asserts that it is evident that each object satisfies P. Because object domains can expand, this includes the claim that each object that could ever be discovered must satisfy P (perhaps because the contrary has been demonstrated to involve a contradiction). When $\forall \chi P$ is not true, it is not evident that each object satisfies P, which is cashed out as meaning that the current stage sees an alternative stage in the development of evidence at which there is an object that does not satisfy P. When $\forall \chi P$ is false, it is evident that there could never be evidence that each object satisfies P.

It follows that $\sim\forall \chi P$ does not say quite the same thing as $\exists \chi \sim P$. $\exists \chi \sim P$ asserts that it is evident that there is an object that does not satisfy P. $\sim\forall \chi P$ asserts that it is evident that there can be no evidence that each object satisfies P. This is not as strong as saying that it is evident that there is an object that does not satisfy P. It is only saying that it is established that such an object can never be ruled out. $\exists \chi \sim P$ entails $\sim\forall \chi P$, but the converse does not hold. Similarly,

~∀χ~P does not entail ∃χP. Evidence that there can be no evidence that each object does not satisfy P, is compatible with not being able to identify an object that does satisfy P. It can be established that an object that satisfies P cannot ever be ruled out without identifying any such object. ∀χP does entail ~∃χ~P. If it is evident that each object satisfies P, it is evident that there could be no evidence of an object that does not satisfy P. But ~∃χ~P does not entail ∀χP. ~∃χ~P claims that it is evident that there could be no evidence for an object that does not satisfy P. That is not as strong as asserting that it is evident that each object satisfies P. Duality fails for the intuitionist quantifiers. However, ~∃χP does entail ∀χ~P, and ∀χ~P entails ~∃χP. If it is evident that there could be no evidence for anything that satisfies P then any conceivable object must not satisfy P. And if any conceivable object does not satisfy P then it must be evident that there could be no evidence of an object that satisfies P. Trees for intuitionistic quantified logic confirm these results.

The following account of interpretations for intuitionistic quantified logic is driven by the consideration that an intuitionist ought to treat =pq ∨ ~=pq in the same way as A ∨ ~A or Rpq ∨ ~Rpq, that is, as contingent. Both =pq and ~=pq can be nonevident. =pq is true when it is evident that p and q denote the same object. ~=pq is true when it is evident that there could be no evidence that p and q denote the same object. But an object can be evident without it being evident that all its manifestations are identical. There was a time when Phosphoros and Hesperos were evident, but their identity was not. This makes it inappropriate for α to assign objects directly to names. If an identity sentence is nonevident, it could only be because the same object is not evidently assigned to both names. Any assignment of objects to each name would make all identity sentences either true or false. But leaving names that are in use without any denotation is not an acceptable alternative. Those who used "Phosphoros" and "Hesperos" used them to refer to things that were evident, even though the identity of those things was not evident. When someone wonders whether Hesperos is Phosphoros they are not puzzled because they do not know what one or both the names denote. The *names* already have referents, and the referents are different. If they were the same there would be no wondering going on. But were the referents different *objects* there would also be no wondering going on. Something else must be the target of names.

One way to manage this situation is to distinguish between objects and their manifestations. A manifestation of a physical object might be one of its temporal states or one of its spatial facets. As made evident at any one time or from any one perspective, an object satisfies a set of predicates that may be somewhat different from the set it satisfies at an earlier or later time, or when viewed from a different position. Something similar might be said of mathematical objects or other nonphysical objects. It might be discovered that an object that is constructed in accord with one definition, and so satisfies one set of predicates, also satisfies another set of predicates (or cannot do so). This is tantamount to discovering that different object manifestations are (or are not) manifestations of the same object. On the account that follows, domains contain object manifestations and manifestations of objects are assigned to names. The identity symbol is made part of the nonlogical vocabulary. Identity sentences do not have their own valuation rule. Instead, identity is treated as (reflexive, symmetric, transitive) predicate with an extension comprised of pairs of object manifestations. Identity sentences are satisfied in accord with (P), and so in accord with how the identity predicate is interpreted. At different stages of evidence, α(=) can have different extensions. As usual, evidence does not decay, so pairs of manifestations of objects that are in α(=) at earlier stages must continue to be in α(=) at all later stages. But later stages can contain pairs not found at earlier stages.

An interpretation, I, for intuitionistic sentential logic consists of:

  (i) a nonempty set, Ω, of stages of evidence $\{s_1, s_2, s_3, \ldots\}$
  (ii) a reflexive, transitive accessibility relation, S, between the stages of Ω
  (iii) a domain structure, $\mathbb{D}$, consisting of a finite object domain, Ds, (also called the "local domain" of s) of manifestations of objects for each stage in Ω, such that for any stage, s_k, if s_k sees s_n, Ds_k is a finite subset of Ds_n
  (iv) a stage-relative **but inherited** assignment, α, of
    • **$\underline{0}$** to ⊥ and **$\underline{1}$** (T) to a finite selection of **zero-place predicates**. Any sentence letter that is not assigned **$\underline{1}$** has the default value **$\underline{0}$**. α does not assign or inherit default values.
    • **a finite set of pairs of object manifestations from any domain that s sees to =, such that = is reflexive, symmetric, and transitive within each domain**

> • **a finite number of object manifestations in any domain that *s* sees to a finite number of names such that no two object manifestations, o and n, are assigned to one name unless <o,n> is in $\alpha_s(=)$**
> • **consistently with the assignments made to =, a finite set of *n*-place lists of object manifestations to a finite number of higher-place predicates.**

Because QPL uses numbers to designate domain objects, this statement bold underlines 1 and 0 when they are used to designate the two truth values. As before, **1** means "evident," and **0** means nonevident. Assigning **1** to a sentence is equivalent to considering it to be evidently true. Technically, **0** is only "assigned" to ⊥. It is a default value for zero-place predicates. The only "assignment" consists in converting it to **1**. (This means that α only ever makes a finite number of assignments [of **1**] at any given stage.) Having the value **0** is equivalent to being nonevident. Being nonevident is not the same as being false. Being false is the equivalent of assigning **1** to the negation of a sentence, and is understood as asserting the evidence of the impossibility of evidence.

The domain structure ensures that object manifestations that are in D*s* must be in the domains of all stages that *s* sees and the stipulation that α be inherited entails that assignments of **1** to zero-place predicates and assignments made by α_s to names, the identity predicate, and other higher-place predicates must continue to be made by α_t at all stages, *t*, that *s* sees.[1] Consequently, if $\alpha_s(P)$ is **1**, where P is atomic, $\alpha_t(P)$ must be **1** at any later stage, *t*, that *s* sees. The same does not hold for **0**. Additional object manifestations can be discovered and assigned previously unused names at later stages, the extension of = and other higher-place predicates can be expanded (either with lists containing new object manifestations or with lists entirely comprised of previously discovered object manifestations), and additional atomic sentences can be assigned **1** at later stages.

The conditions on assignments to = mean that if object manifestation, o, is in any domain, D*t*, for any stage that *s* sees (including in D*s* since *s* sees itself), <o,o> must be in $\alpha_t(=)$, that if <o,n> is in $\alpha_t(=)$, <n,o> must be as well, and that if <o,n> and <n,m> are in $\alpha_t(=)$, <o,m> must be as well.

As noted earlier a stage, *s*, may see object manifestations in the domains of other stages that are not in its own domain. This helps to account for what it means for an object manifestation to be conceivable at *s* but nonevident at *s*. Identity relations between merely conceived object manifestations can be merely conceived, as can identity relations between evident and merely conceived object manifestations, and identity relations between evident object manifestations. This is why α_s is said to assign pairs of object manifestations from any domain that *s* sees to = (without crossing domain boundaries, so the objects in any one pair both come from the same domain). These are conceivable identities at *s* but not evident identities unless they are present at each stage *s* sees. The condition should not be read as implying that *s* sees all the objects in all the accessible domains.

As with zero-place predicates, α does not make assignments to all the names or all the predicates. As noted in section 9.3, intuitionists do not accept results that require the completion of infinite tasks. Even specifying a default assignment for unused names is undesirable. Since further object manifestations can be discovered at later stages, it is useful to have a bank of unused names.

The comment, "consistently with the assignments made to =" means that α must ensure that object manifestations that have been identified with the same object all satisfy the same predicates. If α assigns <o,n> to = and α assigns an *n*-place list, <…,o,…>, containing one or more occurrences of o to an *n*-place predicate, P, then α also assigns the same list, with n in the place of one or more occurrences of o, to P.

In making assignments to compound formulas, I uses the following valuation rules:

> Abbreviation: if P is ⊥ or a sentence letter, I*s*(P) is Iα_s(P)
>
> (⊥):   I(⊥) is 0 at any stage.
>
> (P):   I*s*(Pq_1…q_n) is **1** if and only if <$\alpha_s(q_1)$…$\alpha_s(q_n)$> is in α_s(P); otherwise I*s*(Pq_1…q_n) is **0**; as a special case of (P), I*s*(=pq) is T if and only if <α_s(p),α_s(q)> is in α_s(=); otherwise I*s*(=pq) is **0**.
>
> (~):   I*s*(~P) is **1** if and only if for each stage, *t*, if *s* sees *t*, I*t*(P) is **0**; otherwise I*s*(~P) is **0**.
>
> (F):   I*s*(P) is F if and only if I*s*(~P) is **1**.
>
> (&):   I*s*(P & Q) is **1** if and only if I*s*(P) and I*s*(Q) are **1**; otherwise I*s*(P & Q) is **0**.
>
> (∨):   I*s*(P ∨ Q) is **1** if and only if at least one of I*s*(P) and I*s*(Q) is **1**; otherwise I*s*(P ∨ Q) is **0**.

> ($\rightarrow$): Is(P $\rightarrow$ Q) is **1** if and only if for each stage, t, if s sees t, either It(P) is **0** or It(Q) is **1**; otherwise Is(P $\rightarrow$ Q) is **0**.
>
> ($\equiv$): Is(P $\equiv$ Q) is **1** if and only if for each stage, t, if s sees t, It(P) is the same as It(Q); otherwise Is(P $\equiv$ Q) is **0**.
>
> ($\forall$): Is($\forall\chi$P) is **1** if and only if for each stage, t, if s sees t, for each name, q, in use at t, It(P(q$|\chi$)) is **1**; otherwise Is($\forall\chi$P) is **0**.
>
> ($\exists$): Is($\exists\chi$P) is **1** if and only if for at least one name, q, in use at s, Is(P(q$|\chi$)) is **1**; otherwise Is($\exists\chi$P) is **0**.

The valuation rules for universally quantified and existentially quantified sentences reflect the tree model semantics of section 14.3. The quantifiers range over finite domains of object manifestations. Each of those manifestations is evident and so can be assigned to an unused name as needed, since it is not required that all names be assigned values. (($\forall$) recognizes this by only mentioning names in use at t.)

Like (&) and ($\vee$), ($\exists$) applies just to the current stage of evidence, and so to objects that are currently evident, though by definition of $\mathbb{D}$ those objects must continue to be evident at all stages that s sees. ($\forall$) does not just require that currently evident objects satisfy P at all accessible stages, but that any objects conceived at later stages also do so.

Trees for intuitionistic quantified logic accept $\sim=$pp as an alternative justification for ($\bot$I) and use (=E) in the usual way. The quantifier rules are:

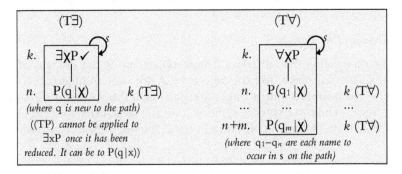

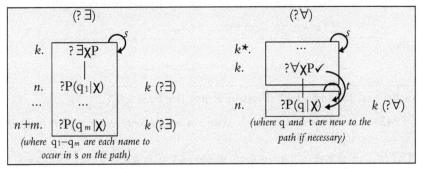

This statement of the tree rules is consistent with the semantics for intuitionistic quantified logic, but it does not fully reflect that semantics in the case of (T$\exists$) and (T$\forall$). As noted earlier, according to that semantics, $\exists\chi$P does not just assert that there must be something that satisfies P. It asserts that something that satisfies P has been identified. Accordingly, the object denoted by q in (T$\exists$) must be a known object. A new name is used for this object only to cover the possibility that it has not so far been named on the path.

Intuitionistic semantics also entails that evident universals make a claim about what is found at any subsequent stage in the development of evidence. For $\forall\chi$P to be evident at s, s cannot see any later stage of evidence at which an object emerges that fails to satisfy P. However, (T$\forall$) does not need to demand this because (TP) carries $\forall\chi$P into each accessible box. For practical purposes, it suffices to instantiate in s just using each name to appear on the path in s, to instantiate in t just using each name to appear on the path in t, and so on.

The "if necessary" notation on (?$\forall$) means that if ?P(r$|\chi$) already occurs in s or in some other accessible box on the path, ?$\forall\chi$P is reduced by that occurrence. A new box containing ?P(q$|\chi$) is only called for when that is not the case.

Exercise 14.3

1. *Establish the following. Remember to make a tree for the opposite, which is question marked.*

    ⋆**a.** ⊢ ∀xGx → ~∃x~Gx

    b. ⊢ ∃xGx → ~∀x~Gx

    ⋆**c.** ⊢ ∃x~Gx → ~∀xGx

    d. ⊢ ∀x~Gx → ~∃xGx

    ⋆**e.** ⊢ ~∃xGx → ∀x~Gx

    f. ⊢ ∃x(Gx → H) → (∀xGx → H)

2. *Establish that the following are not theorems of* Tiq. *Extract the tree model defined by the leftmost exhausted path and verify it using the semantics for intuitionistic quantified logic. If a path cannot be exhausted, attempt to base a model on a portion of the path.*

    ⋆**a.** ~∃x~Gx → ∀xGx

    b. ~∀x~Gx → ∃xGx

    ⋆**c.** ~∀xGx → ∃x~Gx

    d. (G → ∃xHx) → ∃x(G → Hx)

    ⋆**e.** (∀xGx → H) → ∃x(Gx → H)

    f. ∀x(G ∨ Hx) → G ∨ ∀xHx

    g. ∀x~~Gx → ~~∀xGx

14.4.3 Semantics and Trees for Free Logic

Free logic is free of the supposition that all terms denote objects in D, the domain of existing objects. This includes names. But the quantifiers range over the objects in D, not over all objects that might be named. Free logic accordingly modifies the quantifier rules to add the requirement that instantiating names denote an existing object. This is done by using adding an existence symbol, E, to the vocabulary for QPL. It could just as well be done by using ∃χ=pχ, which says that p is an object in D, but E is more elegant. To accommodate it, QPL syntax is supplemented.

> **Additional Formation Rule for Formulas of Free QPL**
>
> (E:)   If t is a term, then Et is a formula.

A valuation rule for E sentences is added to free tree model semantics.

> **Additional Tree Model Valuation Rules for Free QPL**
>
> **(TME):** **An E sentence, Ep is true on a tree model, I, if and only if α(p) is in D.**
>
> (FTM∀): A universally quantified sentence, ∀χP, is true on a tree model, I, if and only if, for each name, q, **if I(Eq) is T then** I(P(q|χ)) is T; otherwise (if **for any name, q, I(Eq) is T and I(P(q|χ)) is F**), I(∀χP) is F.
>
> (FTM∃): An existentially quantified sentence, ∃χP, is true on a tree model, I, if and only if for at least one name, q, **I(Eq) and** I(P(q|χ)) **are** T; otherwise (if **for each name, q, if I(Eq) is T then I(P(q|χ)) is F**), I(∃χP) is F.

These rules have an implication that will be familiar to those who have worked with the rules for □ and ◇ sentences (chapter 9). When there are no names that denote an object in D, any sentence of the form ∀χP is true. (TM∀) says, in part, that for I(∀χP) to be T it is necessary that if I(Eq) is T then I(P(qχ)) is T. When no name denotes an object in D, the condition, "if I(Eq) is T then I(P(qχ)) is T" is trivially satisfied, since it has a false antecedent.

For a similar reason, when no name denotes an object in D, any sentence of the form ∃χP is false. It follows that P(q|χ) → ∃χP is not a theorem of free logic and that Pa / ∃xPx is fq-invalid.

Trees for free quantified logic (called fq-trees) correspondingly use quantifier rules that add existence sentences. There are no other changes to the tree method.

(FT∃)

k. ∃χP✓
|
n. Eq   k (FT∃)
n+1. P(q|χ)   k (FT∃)
(where q is new to the path)

(FT∀)

k. ∀χP
k★. Eq
|
n. P(q|χ)   k,k★ (FT∀)
(where q is each name to occur in an E sentence on the path)

(F~∃)

k. ~∃χP
k★. Eq
|
n. ~P(q|χ)   k,k★ (FT∃)
(where q is each name to occur in an E sentence on the path)

(F~∀)

k. ~∀χP✓
|
n. Eq   k (FT∃)
n+1. ~P(q|χ)   k (FT∃)
(where q is new to the path)

(FT∀) and (F~∃) are better described as derivation rules than reduction rules. They place a condition on the reduction of ∀χP and ~∃χP. An E sentence must exist on the path before either rule can be applied. (If more than one E sentence exists on the path, the rule requires deriving an instance based on each one, and if different E sentences exist on different paths running up to ∀χP or ~∃χP, the correspondingly different instances must be derived on each path.) When an E sentence does not exist on the path, work on the ∀ and ~∃ sentences must be postponed until one appears. Should none appear, the ∀ and ~∃ sentences cannot be reduced.

Tree models for exhausted fq-tree paths have domains that are based exclusively on names that appear in sentences of the form Ep that stand alone on the path. Should Ea not appear on the path, "a" may not be considered when defining the contents of D, even if it occurs in other literals on the path. In the case where a ∀ or ~∃ sentence cannot be reduced because no E sentences stand alone on the path, the path defines a model with an empty domain. Under verification by (FTM∀) and (FTM∃), the unreduced ∀ or ~∃ sentences are declared true (in the case of ~∃ sentences this means the nullation is declared false) on the ground that D is empty. (Those who have studied chapter 9.2 will have noticed a similar result for □ and ~◇ sentences.)

This can produce some surprising results. Consider a tree for ∀x(Gx & ~Gx).

1. ∀x(Gx & ~Gx)   given
e

Since there are no E sentences on the single path of this tree, the sole ∀ sentence on the path is reduced, which means that the path is exhausted. The tree accordingly establishes that ∀x(Gx & ~Gx) is consistent in Tfq.

The result can be legitimated by extracting the tree model from the exhausted path and supplying a verification.

D: { } D is empty because only names occurring in E sentences on the path are used to determine its contents
G: { }

On this interpretation, the local domain is empty, which is one of the things free logic is deliberately written to countenance. Each term must still denote exactly one object, but it need not be an object in the local domain. Verification is:

1. D is empty   given
2. I(Eq) is F for each name, q   1 (E)

3.   I($\forall$x(Gx & ~Gx)) is T   2 (FTM$\forall$) *(since* I(Eq) *is not* T *for any name,* q, *it is trivially true that for each* q *if* I(Eq) *is* T *then* P(q|χ) *is* T; *since this condition is satisfied* $\forall\chi$P *is* T)

Exercise 14.4

Determine whether the following claims are true using Tfq. *If the tree produces an exhausted path, recover and verify the tree model defined by the leftmost such path.*

★a. ⊢ $\exists$x=ax

  b. ⊢ $\forall$x=xx

★c. ⊢ $\forall$xGx → $\exists$xGx

  d. ⊢ Ga → $\exists$xGx

★e. ⊢ ($\forall$xGx → H) → $\exists$x(Gx → H) *(Compare exercise 14.1#4l, based on exercise 13.8#2l.)*

  f. ⊢ $\forall$xGx → Ga

★g. $\exists$x(Gx & $\forall$y(Gy → =yx)) –|– $\exists$x$\forall$y(Gy ≡ =yx)

  h. Ga & $\forall$y(Gy → =ya) –|– $\forall$y(Gy ≡ =ya) *(Careful! One direction does not close. Why not?)*

14.4.4 *Semantics and Trees for Free Description Theories*

When the Russellian method for formalizing definite descriptions (section 12.3.8) is adopted, no modifications to Tq are required. Definite descriptions are embedded in sentences of the form $\exists\chi$[P & $\forall\psi$(P(ψ|χ) → =$\chi\psi$) & Q], where Q says something about the purported object of the description. Such sentences are reduced by (T$\exists$). This yields P(q|χ) and $\forall\psi$(P(ψ|χ) → =ψq), where q is new to the path. If there is evidence to the contrary (if ~P(q|χ) or P(r|χ) & ~=rq can be derived) the path will close; otherwise the path will define a tree model with a domain that includes a unique object denoted by the description.

While Russellian description theory is easy to apply, there are concerns that it does not adequately capture the logic of definite descriptions. As discussed in chapters 11.7.6, and 12.3.8, there are sentences and demonstrations involving definite descriptions that are not assessed in intuitively satisfactory ways by Russellian semantics. These concerns have motivated ongoing investigations into the feasibility of alternative description theories. Free description theory is a popular alternative.

Whereas Russellian description theory treats descriptions as $\exists$ sentences, free description theory treats them as complex terms, and, of course, it uses the free tree rules. Descriptions are formalized as terms using the term forming operator, ^{1}, introduced in chapter 10.3.4–5. A description like "the gnat" is formed by taking the predicate "x is a gnat," formalized as Gx, and turning this formula into something that looks like a quantified formula, ^{1}xGx, but that is read as a term "the x such that x is a gnat." (This is a term, rather than a formula, because it denotes an object rather than make a claim that might be true or false of an object.) ^{1}xGx figures in formulas in the way that terms like "a" or x figure in formulas. As Ha might be taken to formalize "Alma is an insect," and $\forall$x(Gx → Hx) might be taken to formalize "All gnats are insects," H^{1}xGx says "that gnat is an insect."

Chapter 11.7.7 presents two semantics for free description theories, SPL^1 and MPL^1, now called SQL^1 and MQL^1. (S is for "supervaluation" and M is for "Meinongian.") Each works with its own denotation condition for definite descriptions. They are repeated here in a modified form, to make for a better fit with the tree model semantics studied in this chapter.

The conditions draw on a preliminary definition of what it means for an object to "satisfy" a description. The definition is adequate because tree models assign each object to at least one name.

> **(Def satisfaction)**
> An object, o, satisfies a description, $^1\chi$P, if and only if, for any term, s, if I/α(s) is o then I(P(s|χ)) is T.

> **Description Condition for SQL[1]**
>
> (^{1})x: If $^1\chi P$ is a definite description, then if there is exactly one object, o, in ID that satisfies $^1\chi P$, then I($^1\chi P$) is o; otherwise, I($^1\chi P$) **has no value**.

> Description Condition for MQL[1]
>
> (^{1})^:   If $^1\chi P$ is a definite description, then if there is exactly one object, o, in D that satisfies $^1\chi P$ and P does not contain any terms that denote an object that is not in D, then I($^1\chi P$) is o; otherwise, I($^1\chi P$) **is an object in $\mathbb{D}$ that is not in D as assigned by α_2**

These two versions of (^{1}) divide descriptions into two sorts: those that are "proper," in the sense that there is exactly one object in D that satisfies the description, and those that are "improper" because either there is nothing in D that satisfies the description or there is more than one thing that does so. MQL[1] adds a clause to stipulate that a proper description is only based on lower level descriptions that are proper. For SQL[1] this is automatic. The versions differ over how they treat improper descriptions. The first takes them to create a "value gap" that is addressed by appeal to supervaluations (appendix 5.1 and chapter 11.7.7). The second assigns them values that are not drawn from the domain.

Treating descriptions as complex terms calls for an amendment to the free quantifier rules of section 14.4.3. MQL[1] requires no more than that references to names be replaced with references to terms.

> **Modified Free Quantifier Rules for MQL[1]**
>
> (FTM∀):   I($\forall\chi P$) is T if and only if, for each **term, t**, if I(Et) is T then I(P(**t**$|\chi$)) is T; otherwise (if for at least one **term, t**, I(Et) is T and I(P(**t**$|\chi$)) is F), I($\forall\chi P$) is F.
>
> (FTM∃):   I($\exists\chi P$) is T if and only if for at least one **term, t**, I(Et) and I(P(**t**$|\chi$)) are T; otherwise (if for each **term, t**, if I(Et) is T then I(P(**t**$|\chi$)) is F), I($\exists\chi P$) is F.

Tree model semantics for MQL[1] uses the other valuation rules of chapter 3.2, as supplemented by the following versions of (P), (=) and (E). The notation I/α is used to cover the possibility that t is a name, in which case its value is assigned by α, and the possibility that it is a definite description, in which case its value is assigned by I.

> (P):   I(P**t**$_1$...**t**$_n$) is T if and only if <I/α(t$_1$), ...,**I**/α(**t**$_n$)> is in α(P); otherwise, I(P**t**$_1$...**t**$_n$) is F.
>
> (=):   I(=**ts**) is T if and only if **I**/α(**t**) is **I**/α(**s**); otherwise I(=**ts**) is F.
>
> (E):   I(E**t**) **is T** if and only if I/α(**t**) is in D; otherwise I(Et) is F.

As noted in section 11.7.7, supervaluationist semantics works with slightly modified valuation rules. (E) is exceptional in being the same for both SQL[1] and MQL[1].

> **Modified Valuation Rules for SQL[1]**
>
> (P):   **If any of I/α(t$_1$),..., I/α(t$_n$) has no value I(P(t$_1$...t$_n$)) is undetermined; otherwise,** I(P**t**$_1$...**t**$_n$) is T if and only if <I/α(t$_1$), ...,I/α(t$_n$)> is in α(P) and F if and only if <I/α/δ(t$_1$),...,I/α/δ(t$_n$)> is not in α(P).
>
> (=):   **If neither I/α(t) nor I/α(s) has a value, I(=ts) is undetermined; otherwise,** I(=ts) is T if and only if I/α(t) is I/α(s) and F if and only if I/α(t) is not I/α(s).
>
> (E):   I(Et) is T if and only if α(t) is in D; otherwise I(Et) is F.
>
> (~):   **If I(P) is undetermined, I(~P) is undetermined; otherwise,** I(~P) is T if and only if I(P) is F and I(~P) is F if and only if I(P) is T.

> (bc):   **If I(P) or I(Q) is undetermined, I(P (bc) Q) is undetermined where (bc) is any binary connective; otherwise, (&), (∨), (→), and (≡) hold as stated in chapter 3.2.**
>
> (FTM∀/∃)   **If I(P(t|χ)) is undetermined for each term, t, such that I(Et) is T, then I(∀χP) and I(∃χP) have no value; otherwise, (FTM∀) and (FTM∃) hold as stated for MQL[1].**

(P(t|χ) could have no value for any proper term, t, if it contains some other term that has no value. Think of ∀xGx¹y~=yy.)

SQL[1] also works with a modified notion of a corrected completion of an interpretation.

> ### (def cc)
> *(definition of a correction of a completion)*
>
> A correction, I⋆, of a completion, I′, of an interpretation, I, is an interpretation that
>
> - assigns I(P) to P if I(P) is T or I(P) is F
>
> - assigns I′(P) to P if I(P) is undetermined.

These differing valuation rules only affect how tree models are verified. The tree reduction rules are the same in both systems. Trees for free description theory work like trees for sentences containing functional terms. (⊥I) and (=E) are updated to work with terms of all kinds.

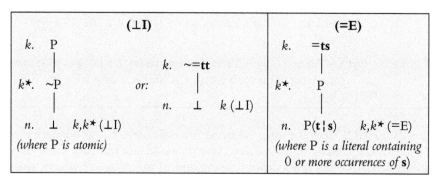

In Tfq[1] as in Tqf, the aim is to identify each complex term with a name, use (=E) to replace all occurrences of the term with occurrences of that name, and finish the tree using the replacement names. Like Tqf, Tfq[1] uses either (=E) or a dedicated identification principle to identify each level-1 definite description to the right of a name. But whereas (Tqf) can assume that there is exactly one object in D that is denoted by each functional term, (Tfq[1]) cannot make that assumption. There is no way to design formation rules that will forbid the formation of descriptions that do not denote an object, such as ¹x~=xx (the non-self-identical object) or ¹x(Gx & ~Gx) (the object that both is and is not in α(G)). (Tqf) can simply pick an unused name and take it to denote the one object in D that is denoted by *f*(t). (Tfq[1]) must search for a name that denotes such an object (if there is one). It does this by saying that a name, q, that denotes exactly one object in D described by ¹χP must satisfy three conditions: (i) the object is in D (that is, I(Eq) is T); (ii) α(q) does satisfy the description, P (that is, I(P(q|χ) is T); and (iii) it is the only one that does so (that is, for any other name, r, if I(P(r|χ)) is T then α(r) is α(q)).

(T¹)

k.   R

k⋆.   Eq
|

n.   =q¹χP ≡ P(q|χ) & ∀ψ(P(ψ|χ) → =ψq)   k,k⋆ (T¹)
(where R is a literal containing a level-1 definite description, ¹χP)

As indicated by the gap and the justifications column, (T[1]) does not generate the requisite E sentence. Like (FT∀) and (F~∃), it requires that it be given or obtained in some other way. (T[1]) has this feature because it is based on the description axiom, $\forall\zeta[=\zeta^1\chi P \equiv P(\zeta|\chi) \;\&\; \forall\psi(P(\psi|\chi) \rightarrow =\psi\zeta)]$. The description axiom says that a name, q, can be identified with the one thing that is P if and only if α(q) is the only object in D that satisfies the description, P, that is, if and only if I(P(q|χ) is T, and for any other name, r, either I(P(r|χ)) is F or α(r) is α(q). To save a line of demonstration, (T[1]) does not enter the axiom on trees. It enters instances of that axiom. By (FT∀) an instance of the axiom is derivable if Eq is given for the instantiating name, q.

The search for an object to identify with ^1xP is undertaken by testing each name to occur in an E sentence that stands alone on the path until one is found that satisfies the conditions set by (T[1]). If no E sentence stands alone on the path, (T[1]) cannot be applied. (FT∀) prevents instantiation of the background axiom, $\forall\zeta[=\zeta^1\chi P \equiv P(\zeta|\chi) \;\&\; \forall\psi(P(\psi|\chi) \rightarrow =\psi\zeta)]$. If the path does not close, become exhausted, or go on to infinity for other reasons, it defines a tree model on which there is no object in D that is denoted by $^1\chi P$.

If there are E sentences that stand alone on the path, the names they contain can be taken up in alphanumeric order, in their order of appearance from the top of the path down, or by picking the one most likely to close the tree or produce an exhausted path. A (T[1]) application produces a biconditional, which reduces to two paths, one headed off by $=q^1\chi P$, the other by $\sim=q^1\chi P$. If the wrong name is chosen, the path headed off by $=q^1xP$ closes. The remaining path, headed off by $\sim=q^1xP$, fails to satisfy the requirement that ^1xP be identified to the right of a name. If it does not also close, a new name must be chosen from the E sentences that stand alone on the path and entered by (T[1]) on all open paths that run up to R. Infinite regress threatens because one of the paths under $\sim=q^1\chi P$ introduces an existence sentence containing a new name.

As in T*qf*, each level-1 definite description to occur in a literal must be identified to the right of a name for an existing object, unless all paths running up to that literal close first.

(def ex)

A path of **an fq[1]-tree** is exhausted if and only if:

   (i)   each sentence in the set the tree was made for has been placed on top of the tree

   (ii) ⊥ does not stand alone on any line of the path

  (iii) each sentence on the path is either (i) a literal, (ii) a nonliteral, non-∀ or non-~∃ sentence that has been reduced (checked off), or (iii) a ∀ or ~∃ sentence that has been reduced using each name to occur on each path that runs through it, or using "a" if there are no names on a path

  (iv) for each sentence of the form =qt and each literal, P, a sentence of the form P(q|t) (including sentences of the form =qq), occurs on the path

   (v) **each term of the form $^1\chi P$ to occur in a literal that stands alone on a line of the path occurs in a sentence of the form $=q^1\chi P$ that stands alone on a line of path.**

(T[1]) is a laborious rule to apply. It need not be applied to descriptions that have been identified to the right of a name, so if there is any way to obtain such an identification without using (T[1]), that way should be preferred. The obvious alternative is (=E), but when a description has been identified to the left of a name, (sym), introduced in section 11.6, can be applied to reverse the order of the terms.

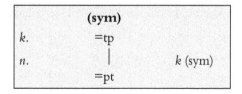

(sym)

k.   =tp

n. | k (sym)
       =pt

When E^1xP is given, an abbreviated version of (T[1]), (TE), may be employed.

$$
\begin{array}{lll}
\multicolumn{3}{c}{\textbf{(TE)}} \\
k. & E^1\chi P\checkmark & \\
& | & \\
n. & Eq & k \text{ (TE)} \\
n+1. & =q^1\chi P & k \text{ (TE)} \\
n+2. & P(q\,|\,\chi) & k \text{ (TE)} \\
n+3. & \forall\psi(P(\psi\,|\,\chi) \to\, =\psi q) & k \text{ (TE)} \\
\multicolumn{3}{c}{\textit{(where q is new to the path)}}
\end{array}
$$

(TE) is based on the fact that Et is equivalent to $\exists\zeta=\zeta t$ and so could be reduced accordingly, by adding Eq and $=q^1\chi P$ to the path (where q is a new name) as if (FT$\exists$) had been applied to $\exists\zeta=\zeta^1\chi P$. Were this reduction followed by applications of (=E) and (T^1), the stated version of (TE) would result, as indicated by the highlighted portions of the following tree.

$$
\begin{array}{ll}
\multicolumn{2}{c}{\textbf{(TE)}} \\
\multicolumn{2}{c}{\textit{(exploded view)}} \\
\end{array}
$$

k.	**E¹χP**	
	|	
n.	$\exists\zeta=\zeta^1 xP\checkmark$	definition of E
n+1.	**Eq**	*n* (FT∃)
n+2.	$=q^1\chi P$	*n* (FT∃)
n+3.	$=q^1\chi P \equiv P(q\,|\,\chi)\ \&\ \forall\psi(P(\psi\,|\,\chi) \to\, =\psi q)\checkmark$	*k,n*+1 (T¹)
n+4.	$=q^1xP$ $\sim=q^1\chi P$	*n*+3 (T≡)
n+5.	$P(q\,|\,\chi)\ \&\ \forall\psi(P(\psi\,|\,\chi) \to\, =\psi q)\checkmark$ $\sim[P(q\,|\,\chi)\ \&\ \forall\psi(P(\psi\,|\,\chi) \to\, =\psi q)]$	*n*+3 (T≡)
n+6.	| $\perp$	*n*+2, *n*+4 (⊥I)
n+7.	$P(q\,|\,\chi)$	*n*+5 (T&)
n+8.	$\forall y(P(\psi\,|\,\chi) \to\, =\psi q)$	*n*+5 (T&)

When no other way of identifying a description to the right of a name can be employed, (T^1) must be applied. Its application should be postponed until everything else that can be done has been done. At that point, one (T^1) application should be made, and all the consequences of that application should be derived before making a further application. (T^1) creates right paths that continually introduce sentences of the form Eq, where q is a new name, creating the potential for an unending cycle. However, these paths search for a model on which there is more than one object that satisfies the description. It is often possible to define a tree model based on the portion of the path that introduces two different names. That portion of the path suffices to establish that the description is improper, which should be all that is needed to verify a model.

Consider a tree used to determine whether E^1xGx / $E^1x(Gx \lor Hx)$ is derivable in Tfq^1.

$$
\begin{array}{lll}
1. & E^1xGx & \text{given} \\
2. & \sim E^1x(Gx \lor Hx) & \text{given} \\
3. & Ea & 1 \text{ (TE)} \\
4. & =a^1xGx & 1 \text{ (TE)} \\
5. & Ga & 1 \text{ (TE)} \\
6. & \forall y(Gy \to\, =ya)_{\,a} & 1 \text{ (TE)} \\
7. & Ga \to\, =aa & 3,6 \text{ (FT }\forall) \\
& \qquad \diagup\!\diagdown & \\
8. & \sim Ga \qquad =aa & 7 \text{ (T}\to) \\
9. & \perp \qquad\quad \cdots & 5,8 \text{ (⊥I)} \\
\end{array}
$$

The tree continues with an application of (T¹). It might be thought that the case where ¹xGx and ¹x(Gx ∨ Hx) name the same object would be precisely the one that would close the tree. That would dictate choosing "a" for the identification (though in this case there are no other choices, since Ea is the only E sentence on the path). However, the expectation that this instance will close the tree is not immediately realized.

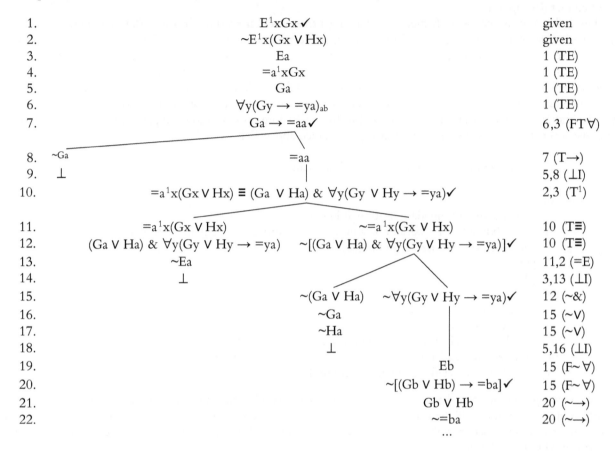

By this point, it is beginning to look like the tree might have defined a model for the givens. A few more lines reveal that the path is the start of an unending cycle.

The third path from the left is still unfinished. ¹x(Gx ∨ Hx) has not yet been identified. There are two names occurring in E sentences on the path, "a" and b, and (T¹) has so far only been attempted using "a." At this point, the tree is set to start a second cycle. Those who remain convinced that it ought to close may want to take up the exercise of entering =b¹x(Gx ∨ Hx) ≡ (Gb ∨ Hb) & ∀y[(Gy ∨ Hy) → =yb] at line 28 by 2,17 (T¹) and seeing what will happen. (The picture that has just been drawn will be reproduced with b in the place of "a" and a new name, c, in the place of b.) Perhaps surprisingly, the tree has an infinitely extendible path.

This may seem counterintuitive. It might be thought that if the one thing that is G exists, the one thing that is either G or H must exist. But the tree illustrates the error in this line of thinking. The unfinished path raises the possibility that there is a second object, named b, that is in α(H). I(Gb ∨ Hb) is also T. So even though there is exactly one object that is G, there is another that is H (but not G), which means there are two that are either G or H. The *Treatise of Human Nature* was written by David Hume. *The Adventures of Gil Blas* was written by Alain-René Lesage. From the fact that there was exactly one person who was the author of the *Treatise* it does not follow that there was exactly one person who was the author of either the *Treatise* or the *Adventures*. There were in fact two people who satisfied that description.

This indication should be confirmed by extracting a tree model from the portion of the tree completed above. The method for extracting a tree model from an exhausted path is the one used for Tfq in section 14.4.3 (p.549). It uses E sentences on the path to define the contents of D. That method needs to be supplemented by a way of determining the denotation of descriptions. Tpf and Tqf determine the denotation of functional terms by appeal to identity sentences on the path. An analogous procedure for Tfq^1 would use identity sentences to define the denotation of definite descriptions, where identity sentences are available and would otherwise diplomatically declare that the denotation of the description is "not in D." But that procedure is question-begging. Using it to define a model and give a verification based on the unfinished path studied above yields:

> D: $\{1,2\}$ (because of the E sentences at lines 3 and 17)
> a: 1
> b: 2
> ^{1}xGx: 1 (because of the identification at line 4)
> ^{1}x(Gx ∨ Hx): not in D (because it will not be identified with a name appearing in an E sentence, for however long the tree is prolonged)
> G: $\{1\}$
> H: $\{2\}$

> 1. I(^{1}x(Gx ∨ Hx)) is not in D   given
> 2. I(E^{1}x(Gx ∨ Hx)) is F   1 (E)
> 3. I(~E^{1}x(Gx ∨ Hx)) is T verifying the given on line 2   2 (~)
> 4. I(^{1}xGx) is 1 and 1 is in D   given
> 5. I(E^{1}xGx) is T, verifying the given on line 1   4 (E)

The verification is question-begging, because anyone who considers the inference from E^{1}xGx to E^{1}x(Gx ∨ Hx) to be intuitively appealing will demand an explanation of how ^{1}x(Gx ∨ Hx) could have a different denotation from ^{1}xGx, and so of how the latter could denote an object in D while the former does not. The verification does nothing to explain why this is the case.

An adequate verification must explain how the definite descriptions get the denotation that they do. That means appealing to the denotation condition for definite descriptions. That in turn means choosing between (^{1})x and (^{1})^ (or an alternative description condition appropriate for whatever description theory might be preferred instead). If (^{1})x is chosen, the tree model must include partial and complete interpretations and must use supervaluation semantics. If (^{1})^ is used, it must include an outer domain and the associated assignments.

These are not difficult tasks. Applications of (T^1) produce three principal paths, seen above at line 11 left and line 15. The leftmost path, headed off by =q$^1\chi$P, explores the possibility that q denotes the one object that satisfies the description. If it is exhausted, it defines a model with that feature. The middle path, headed off by ~P(q|χ), explores the possibility that α(q) does not satisfy the description. In case where α(q) does not satisfy the description, the path could go on forever looking for an object that does, but a tree model that ensures that there is nothing that satisfies the description could verify the givens. The third path, headed off by ∀y(P(ψ|χ) → =ψq) explores the possibility that α(q) is one of many objects that satisfy the description. Third paths are stupid in the sense that once they have established that there is a second object that satisfies the description, they go on forever, mindlessly testing one name after another to see if it might name the one and only object that satisfies the description. The infinite extension can generally be ignored in favour of taking the path to define a model on which there are two objects that satisfy the description. Tree models should be constructed accordingly. Working up the path from the bottom by going from literals to the sentences they were reduced from will reveal the details.

In the case at hand, the right path did not close. If the givens are verifiable it will be with an interpretation that allows two or more objects to satisfy the description. The path has two E sentences, Ea and Eb, and =ab does not occur. This mandates putting two objects in D, with the first assigned to "a" and the second to b. The only (unnegated, standalone) predicate sentences on the path are Hb and Ga. They define the contents of α(G) and α(H). The only (unnegated, standalone) identity sentences are =aa and =a^{1}xGx. The latter promises that ^{1}xGx will prove to be identified with α(a) by (¹). Since ¹x(Gx ∨ Hx) does not occur, it is likely improper. MQL¹ and SQL¹ will hopefully find that both α(a) and α(b) satisfy this description.

MQL¹ models and verifies the partially completed path as follows. The dashed line marks a distinction between what is drawn from the tree path and what is inferred only after applying the second clause of (¹)^.

D: {1,2,3}

D: {1,2}

α:

    a: 1; b: 2

    G: {1}, H: {2}

α₂:

    ¹x(Gx ∨ Hx): 3

1.	α(b) is 2 and 2 is in α(H)	given
2.	I(Hb) is T	1 (P)
3.	I(Gb ∨ Hb) is T	2 (∨)
4.	α(a) is 1 and 1 is in α(G)	given
5.	I(Ga) is T	4 (P)
6.	1 is the only object, in D that satisfies ¹xGx	given
7.	I(¹xGx) is 1, and (again) 1 is in D	6 (¹)^ and given
8.	I(E¹xGx) is T, verifying the given on line 1	7 (E)
9.	I(Ga ∨ Ha) is T	5 (∨)
10.	α(a) is not α(b) but both are in D, so there is not only one object in D that satisfies ¹x(Gx ∨ Hx)	given and 9,3
11.	α₂(¹x(Gx ∨ Hx)) is 3 and 3 is not in D	given as mandated by 10 (¹)^
12.	I(E¹x(Gx ∨ Hx)) is F	11 (E)
13.	I(~E¹x(Gx ∨ Hx)) is T, verifying the given on line 2	12 (~)

In this case the SQL¹ model leaves nothing unassigned and so constitutes its own single corrected completion.

D: {1,2}

α:

    a: 1; b: 2

    G: {1}, H: {2}

1.	α(b) is 2 and 2 is in α(H)	given
2.	I(Hb) is T	1 (P)
3.	I(Gb ∨ Hb) is T	2 (∨)
4.	α(a) is 1 and 1 is in α(G)	given
5.	I(Ga) is T	4 (P)
6.	1 is the only object, in D that satisfies ¹xGx	given
7.	I(¹xGx) is 1, and (again) 1 is in D	6 (¹)x and given
8.	I(E¹xGx) is T, verifying the given on line 1	7 (E)
9.	I(Ga ∨ Ha) is T	5 (∨)
10.	α(a) is not α(b) but both are in D, so there is not only one object in D that satisfies ¹x(Gx ∨ Hx)	given and 9,3
11.	I(¹x(Gx ∨ Hx)) has no value	10 (¹)x
12.	I(E¹x(Gx ∨ Hx)) is F	11 (E)
13.	I(~E¹x(Gx ∨ Hx)) is T, verifying the given on line 2	12 (~)

Even though I(¹x(Gx ∨ Hx)) has no value, in the case of E sentences, the underdetermination does not percolate up from terms to sentences containing those terms. I assigns an F to E sentences that contain terms that have no value.

The dashed line still marks a distinction between what is inferred from what is on the path and what is inferred from the special implications of the description rule when the path does not identify a description with a name.

This is a rosy picture of how the systems, Tfq[1], MQL[1], and SQL[1] work. The case of $G^1xGx \rightarrow \exists xGx$, which says that if the one thing that is G is G then something is G, is not quite so rosy. The sentence might seem intuitively valid, in which case any tree for the negation should close,

$$
\begin{array}{lll}
1. & \sim(G^1xGx \rightarrow \exists xGx)\checkmark & \text{given} \\
2. & G^1xGx & 1\ (\sim\rightarrow) \\
3. & \sim\exists xGx & 1\ (\sim\rightarrow) \\
& e &
\end{array}
$$

but it does not. There is no E sentence that would make it possible to apply either (T[1]) to the sentence on line 2 or (F~∃) to the sentence on line 3.

It might seem that Tfq[1] is not up to the job of closing a tree that should close, but some reflection shows that, on the contrary, no system of free logic should countenance the closure of this tree. Free logic is free of the supposition that every term must denote an existing object. But $\exists xGx$ asserts that there is exactly one object in the domain (of existing objects) that is in $\alpha(G)$. In the absence of assurance that ^1xGx denotes an existing object (given by E^1xGx), G^1xGx is not sufficient for $\exists xGx$. In light of this, the exhausted path defines an intuitive model: There is no domain object in $\alpha(G)$, which is what $\sim\exists xGx$ says, but ^1xGx denotes something that is in $\alpha(G)$, making G^1xGx and $\sim(G^1xGx \rightarrow \exists xGx)$ true on I.

MQL[1] can accommodate this intuition with a q-model that assigns an object that is in $\mathbb{D}$ but not in D to ^1xGx, adding this object to $\alpha(G)$, but being careful to ensure that no object in D is in $\alpha(G)$.

$$\mathbb{ID}: \{1\}$$

$$\text{ID}: \{\ \}$$
$$\text{I}\alpha:$$
$$\qquad \text{G}: \{1\}$$
$$\text{I}\alpha_2$$
$$\qquad ^1xGx: 1$$

1.	There is nothing in ID	given
2.	For any term, t, $\text{I}/\alpha(Et)$ is F	1 (E)
3.	$\text{I}(\exists xGx)$ is F	2 (FTM∃)
4.	There is no object in ID that satisfies ^1xGx	given
5.	$\text{I}\alpha_2(^1xGx)$ is 1 and 1 is in $\alpha(G)$	given as mandated by 4 (^{1})^
6.	$\text{I}(G^1xGx)$ is T	5 (P)
7.	$\text{I}(G^1xGx \rightarrow \exists xGx)$ is F	6,3 ($\rightarrow$)
8.	$\text{I}(\sim(G^1xGx \rightarrow \exists xGx))$ is T	7 ($\sim$)

It is not so easy for SQL[1]. In fact, it is demonstrable that there is no completion of a partial interpretation, and so no partial interpretation that verifies the given, $\sim(G^1xGx \rightarrow \exists xGx)$.

1. Suppose to the contrary that there is completion, I′, of an interpretation, I, on which $\sim(G^1xGx \rightarrow \exists xGx)$ is T
2. By ($\sim$), I′$(G^1xGx \rightarrow \exists xGx)$ is F
3. By ($\rightarrow$), I′(G^1xGx) is T and I′$(\exists xGx)$ is F
4. From the second conjunct of line 3 by (FTM∃) for any term, t, either I′(Et) is F or I′(Gt) is F
5. By definition, a completion of an interpretation must assign an object from D to each term, t, thereby verifying Et, so from line 4 by disjunctive syllogism, for any term, t, I′(Gt) is F
6. Since ^1xGx is a term, I′(G^1xGx) is F
7. Since the supposition at line 1 leads to a contradiction at lines 3 and 6, that supposition must be rejected: there is no completion of any interpretation on which $\sim(G^1xGx \rightarrow \exists xGx)$ is T

Unlike MQL[1], SQL[1] cannot consider $G^1xGx \rightarrow \exists xGx$ to be false on any completion of a partial interpretation. That would require that the completion assign a T to the antecedent and an F to the consequent, and that is not possible, since SQL¹ semantics does not permit making the antecedent true without an object in D to assign to ¹xGx as well as to α(G) and once both those things are done ∃xGx is verified. SQL¹ does not have the outer domain that MQL¹ can use to evade this consequence.

However, SQL¹ still has a recourse. A partial interpretation, I, can have an empty domain thereby making Et false (not undetermined!) where t is any term, and while no *completion* of such an interpretation can leave the domain empty or any term without a domain object as its value, a *corrected* completion must respect I's assignment of F to Et and so to ∃xGx, thereby verifying the tree.

$$
\begin{array}{ll}
\text{ID: } \{\ \} & \text{I'D: } \{1\} \\
\text{I}\alpha: & \text{I'}\alpha: \\
\quad \text{G: } \{\ \} & \quad \text{G: } \{1\} \\
 & \quad {}^1\text{xGx: } 1
\end{array}
$$

Just to be scrupulous, I' satisfies the conditions for being a completion of I.

- ID is a subset of I'D.
- there are no zero-place predicates or names needing assignment.
- the set of one-place lists of objects assigned to I'α(G) includes all the one-place lists of objects assigned to Iα(G).
- Exactly one object from I'D is assigned to each description that has no value on I (there is just one, ¹xGx).

I⋆ corrects I', verifies the tree, and assigns T to ~(G¹xGx → ∃xGx) in virtue of the following line of reasoning:

1.	There is no object in ID that satisfies ¹xGx	given
2.	I(¹xGx) has no value	1 (¹)x
3.	I(G¹xGx) is undetermined	2 (P)
4.	I'α(¹xGx) is 1 and 1 is in I'α(G)	2 (def cp) and given
5.	I'(G¹xGx) is T	4 (P)
6.	I⋆(G¹xGx) is T	3,5 (def cc)
7.	ID is empty, so for any term, t, I/α(t) has no value	given
8.	For any term, t, I(Et) is F	7 (E)
9.	For any term, t, I⋆(Et) is F	8 (def cc)
10.	I⋆(∃xGx) is F	9 (FTM∃)
11.	I⋆(G¹xGx → ∃xGx) is F	6,11 (→)
12.	I⋆(~(G¹xGx → ∃xGx)) is T	11 (~)

G¹xGx → ∃xGx turns out to be S-invalid. There is at least one corrected completion, I⋆, of at least one interpretation, I, on which it is false. It is therefore supervaluationally "not true" on I. This does not mean it is supervaluationally false on I. As is readily demonstrated, there are also corrected completions of I on which G¹xGx → ∃xGx is true, so SI(G¹xGx → ∃xGx) is unassigned. G¹xGx → ∃xGx cannot be false on any supervaluation on any interpretation. That would require an interpretation that has at least one completion on which G¹xGx → ∃xGx is false (and so is not liable to further correction), and it has already been demonstrated that there can be no such completion. The best that SQL¹ can come up with is a corrected completion on which G¹xGx → ∃xGx is false, and a corresponding supervaluation on which G¹xGx → ∃xGx is "not true."

This result points to an important difference between SQL¹ and MQL¹. MQL¹ allows that P(t|χ) can be true even when I/α(t) denotes an object that is not in D. SQL¹ does not. The most SQL¹ can countenance is that P(t|χ) is undefined when I/α(t) is undefined. This is why MQL¹ has little problem modelling the falsity of P(t|χ) → ∃χP, whereas SQL¹ can only manage this by correcting a completion against its partial interpretation. Perhaps this is not a bad thing. It establishes that MQL¹ and SQL¹ are not merely notationally different from one another. They take different stands on the metaphysically robust question of whether nonexistent objects can satisfy predicate sentences.

But there is an unsettling consequence. While SQL¹ denies the validity of P(t|χ) → ∃χP, it must accept the validity of the corresponding demonstration, P(t|χ) / ∃χP. By definition, a demonstration is supervalid if and only if there is no supervaluation on which the premise is true and the conclusion is not true. The definition of S-validity requires considering any supervaluation on which P(t|χ) is true. Beginning with a partial interpretation on which P(t|χ) is undetermined is not an option, as it is with the corresponding conditional. Under this constraint, the validity of P(t|χ) / ∃χP is demonstrable. But a tree for G^{1}xGx / ∃xGx is identical to the one given above for ~(G^{1}xGx → ∃xGx) minus the first line. Either the tree is correct and there is a problem with SQL^1 semantics or fq^1 trees are not closing in all cases where the givens are unsatisfiable according to SQL^1 semantics.[2]

Exercise 14.5

Determine whether the following sentences are theorems of Tfq^1, *inconsistent in* Tfq^1, *or contingent in* Tfq^1. *If a tree produces an exhausted path or a path goes into an unending cycle, recover and verify the tree model defined by the leftmost such path using* MQL^1 *semantics. Consider whether* SQL^1 *semantics supports the same result.*

★**a.** ∃x=xa & G^{1}x(Gx & ~Gx) *(The second conjunct might be read as "the thing that is both green and not green is green.")*

 b. = ^{1}x~=xx ^{1}x~=xx *(Hint: a tree for the negation derives ⊥ at line 2. Why?)*

★**c.** E^{1}xGx & ~E^{1}xHx → ~= ^{1}xGx ^{1}xHx

 d. E^{1}xGx & Ga → =a^{1}xGx

★**e.** Ea → = a ^{1}x=xa

 f. E^{1}xGx → G^{1}xGx

★**g.** ∃x∀y=yx & Ga → =a^{1}xGx

 h. E^{1}x(Gx & Hx) → E^{1}xGx

Notes

1 Later stages in the development of evidence only see earlier stages by seeing themselves. (They preserve whatever was evident at earlier stages.) α$_s$ inherits the domain and the assignments of **1** that were present at earlier stages as if they were preset. It does not look back at the earlier stages to redo what they did. To put the same point with another metaphor, the earlier assignments are its endowment and its work is confined to expanding on that endowment.

2 As noted in chapter 12.3.8 (p.495) a variant on this case also poses problems for Russell's theory of descriptions. See Bencivenga, Lambert, and van Fraassen (1991: 98–9 and 107–10) for further discussion.

References

Bencivenga, Ermanno, Lambert, Karel, and van Fraassen, Bas C, 1991, *Logic, Bivalence and Denotation*, 2nd edition, Ridgeview, Atascadero, CA.

15 Semantics for QPL without Mixed Multiple Quantification

Contents

15.1 Objectual Semantics

There are three popular ways of providing a semantics for quantified sentences. The "substitutional" approach bases the semantics for quantified sentences on that of their instances. The "hybrid" approach treats objects as if they were things that could occupy places in sentences. The "objectual" approach bases the semantics of sentences on that of their subformulas. The tree model semantics of chapter 14 is a version of substitutional semantics. Most of this chapter and the next focus on objectual semantics. This chapter develops objectual semantics for formulas that contain occurrences of one variable or less, and for connective compounds of such formulas. The following chapter expands this semantics to deal with formulas that contain quantifiers with overlapping scope. The remainder of this section applies to formulas of both sorts.

DOI: 10.4324/9781003026532-24

Objectual semantics is not a truth value semantics. It instead works with the more basic notion of satisfaction. PSL semantics lays the foundation for this move by declaring the value of higher-place predicate sentences to be determined by satisfaction. A higher-place predicate sentence, $Pt_1...t_n$, is true on an interpretation, I, if and only if the list of objects, $<\alpha(t_1),...,\alpha(t_n)>$, denoted by the list of terms, $<t_1,...,t_n>$, satisfies P. In PSL, satisfaction is a consequence of the inclusion of lists of objects in a set. $<\alpha(t_1),...,\alpha(t_n)>$ satisfies P if and only if $<\alpha(t_1),...,\alpha(t_n)>$ is in the set, $\alpha(P)$. Objectual semantics comes up with a way of extending this account to all formulas.

The foundations for this move are laid by generalizing the notion of a predicate description (section 12.3.6) to treat any open sentence as if it were a complex predicate. Like predicates, open sentences have "places," but their places are marked by the different free variables they contain. An open sentence like Gx & ∃yHxy is a one-place open sentence. (The y is bound, so the formula contains only one free variable, x, and only different free variables are counted when counting places, not multiple occurrences of the same free variable.) Gxy & Hyx is a two-place open sentence. Gxyyx is also a two-place open sentence, though G is a four-place predicate. Gxy → Haz is a three-place open sentence. ("a" is a name, not a free variable.)

In predicate sentences, places are ordered from left to right. In open sentences like Gxy & Hyx, same "places" occur in different spots, depending on where same free variables recur. The order of "places" in open sentences is not their order from left to right. It is instead determined by quantification. When the free variables in an open sentence are bound by quantifiers, the variable in first place in the order is the one that belongs to the quantifier with widest scope, the variable in second place is the one that belongs with next widest scope, and so on. (Formulas that do not have quantifiers as their main operators are not subject to this analysis.)

Exercise 15.1

1. *How many places are there in each of the following formulas?*
    ★**a.** ∀x(Ax → Bx)
    b. ∀x(Ax → By)
    ★**c.** Axx
    d. ∀x[Axy → ∃z(Byz ∨ Bzx)]
    ★**e.** Bax ∨ Bby
    f. ~=xx ∨ =xy

2. *Reduce each of the following quantified sentences to subformulas that do not have quantifiers as their main operators. (Do this by first identifying the immediate subformula. If that subformula has a quantifier as its main operator, identify its immediate subformula. Proceed to the point where the formula no longer has a main operator or no longer has a quantifier as its main operator.) Then state the order of the places in the reduced subformula by appeal to how it was originally quantified.*
    ★**a.** ∃x∃z∃y(Az & Bxy)
    b. ∀x∃y(Ax → Bxy)
    ★**c.** ∀x(Ax → ∃yBxy)
    d. ∀x∃yByxy
    ★**e.** ∀z∃y(∀xBx → Byz)
    f. ∃x∃z∃y(Az & Bxy) ∨ ∃xCax *(trick question)*
    ★**g.** ∀y∀x∀z(Ax & By → Czxy)

15.2 Denotation

15.2.1 Variable Assignments

Building on this understanding of the places and the order of places in an open sentence, objectual semantics specifies the conditions under which an *n*-place list of objects satisfies an *n*-place open sentence. Since the places in open sentences are marked by variables, this calls for a way of considering variables to denote objects.

To manage this, objectual semantics supplements PSL semantics with two further notions, that of a variable assignment, δ (delta), on an interpretation, and that of a variant on a variable assignment, δ[...o/χ ...].[1] A semantics for the formulas considered in this chapter can be given just by appeal to variable assignments. Variants are required to give a semantics for the formulas taken up in chapter 16.

(For work at the keyboard, δ might be replaced with lower-case "d," standing for "denotes." However, the English letter is suboptimal for verbal lectures and discussion, given that upper-case "D," which has the same verbal name, is also in play in contexts where variable assignments are likely to be discussed. Greek delta is pressed into service as a compromise.)

> **A *variable assignment*, δ, on an interpretation, I, assigns exactly one object in ID to each variable.**
>
> The *denotation of a variable*, χ, on **a variable assignment, δ, for** an interpretation, I, is the unique object, o, that χ denotes on δ. Notation: δ(χ) is o.

As is the case with names, ambiguity and vacuity are not allowed. No variable assignment can assign two different objects to the same variable, and no variable assignment can leave a variable without an assignment. However, the same object can be assigned to multiple variables.

This might seem objectionable. The variables of QPL are instituted to stand for one or more unspecified domain objects. A variable assignment makes each of them denote exactly one object, as if they were names, apparently depriving them of their purpose. However, the variety in what variables can refer to is preserved by the variety of assignments that can be made to them on any one interpretation. Whereas each interpretation works with only one assignment to the names and predicates of the language, there are as many different variable assignments on any one interpretation as there are different ways of assigning objects to variables.

Consider the following interpretation for the open sentence, Gxy → Haz.

D: {1, 2, 3}
a: 1
G: {<1,3>,<3,3>}; H: {<1,2>,<2,2>}

This abbreviated interpretation has a small domain and makes assignments to the single name and the two predicates that occur in the open sentence. A correspondingly abbreviated variable assignment expands on the interpretation by assigning exactly one object from D to each of the three variables occurring in the formula.

As there are three objects in D, and Gxy → Haz is a three-place open sentence, there are $3^3 = 27$ variable assignments to the three variables that mark the places in the open sentence.

δ_1: x is 1, y is 1, z is 1
δ_2: x is 1, y is 1, z is 2
δ_3: x is 1, y is 1, z is 3
δ_4: x is 1, y is 2, z is 1
δ_5: x is 1, y is 2, z is 2
δ_6: x is 1, y is 2, z is 3
δ_7: x is 1, y is 3, z is 1
δ_8: x is 1, y is 3, z is 2
δ_9: x is 1, y is 3, z is 3
δ_{10}: x is 2, y is 1, z is 1

and so on for 17 more.

Whereas interpretation I just considers the assignments made by α to "a," G and H, it must consider all 27 variable assignments.

Exercise 15.2

How many different variable assignments are there for:

★**a.** a formula containing one variable and an interpretation with a domain containing one object?
★**b.** a formula containing two variables and a domain containing one object?
★**c.** a formula containing one variable and a domain containing two objects?
★**d.** a formula containing two variables and a domain containing two objects?

  *e. a formula containing three variables and a domain containing two objects?
  *f. a formula containing two variables and a domain containing three objects?
  *g. What is the general rule for calculating the number of different possible variable assignments?

As exercise 15.2 illustrates, the number of variable assignments increases exponentially with increases in the number of variables. The valuation rules to be given shortly require that each variable assignment be polled before a ∀ formula can be satisfied or an ∃ formula not satisfied. (In this regard, variable assignments in QPL are like worlds in MSL.) This makes it important to keep the number of objects in the domain as low as possible. (Sentences say what they say, so there is no way of reducing the number of variables without changing what is said.) That will often be fewer objects than there are variables and other terms. (Almost all the exercises in this and the following chapter can be done with a domain of less than three objects.)

Whereas interpretations are described by specifying a domain and extensions for the predicates and names, variable assignments are never listed. Since all of them need to be considered, and for any number of objects, and any number of variables, the permutations on the variable assignments are obvious, there is no need to list them.

It is sometimes necessary to identify specific variable assignments. In anticipation of a notation to be used in chapter 16, this is done by tagging the variable assignment with a bracketed reference to the assignment it makes to one variable. For example, $\delta[1/x]$ (read as "delta 1 for x") is provisionally understood to be a variable assignment that assigns object 1 as the value of variable x.[2] In conformity with the definition of a variable assignment, each δ makes an assignment to each variable, so $\delta[1/x]$ must make infinitely many other assignments. In the current context, those other assignments do not matter.

Tags are not always used. Where it does not matter what assignments a variable assignment makes, it is referred to simply as δ. A δ that appears without a tag is not a δ that makes no assignments. It just makes no assignments that are taken note of.

Exercise 15.3

1. *State what* n-*place lists are named by each of the following predicate formulas on* $\delta[1/x]$ *on an interpretation that assigns 1 to a, 2 to b, and 3 to c.*
   *a. Axax
   b. Abxc
   *c. Axxb
   d. Acxa

2. *State what* n-*place lists are named by each of the following predicate formulas on* $\delta[\alpha(b)/x]$ *on an interpretation that assigns 1 to a, 2 to b, and 3 to c.*
   *a. Axax
   b. Abxc
   *c. Axxb
   d. Acxa

15.2.2 Names

Variable assignments respect all the assignments made by the interpretations they are on. For example, if $I\alpha(a)$ is 3, then any variable assignment on I will respect this assignment and treat "a" as denoting 3. It could be said that if $\alpha(a)$ is 3 then $\delta(a)$ is 3. But such descriptions are not employed. Assignments made by α are notated as made by α, understanding that any δ on I must respect those assignments. It does not go the other way. α does not recognize assignments made by δ. Variable assignments (δ's) expand on name assignments (α's) precisely by making assignments to variables, which name assignments never do.

Accordingly, the denotation conditions for names are unchanged:

> The denotation of a name, p, on an interpretation, I, is the unique object, o, in D that p denotes on α. Notation: $\alpha(p)$ is o.

In what follows, it will be useful to have an expression that speaks about the denotation of terms in circumstances where, for whatever reason, it is undesirable to specify whether the term is a name or a variable. α/δ will be used for this purpose. "$\alpha/\delta(t)$ is o" says that term t denotes object o (in virtue of having o assigned to it). If term t is a name, then the assignment is made by α. If it is a variable, the assignment is made by δ. When it is not determined whether t is a name or a variable, it cannot be said whether the assignment is made by α or instead by δ so it is said to be made by α/δ, which can be read as "α or δ as the case may be."

> **If t is a name, p, let $\alpha/\delta(t)$ refer to $\alpha(p)$**
> **If t is variable, χ, let $\alpha/\delta(t)$ refer to $\delta(\chi)$**

Exercise 15.4

1. *State whether the following claims are sense or nonsense, according to QPL semantics.*
   ★a. $\alpha(c)$ is 1
   b. $\delta(y)$ is 1
   ★c. $\alpha(y)$ is 1
   d. $\delta(c)$ is 1
   ★e. $\delta[1/y](y)$ is 1
   f. $\delta[1/y](y)$ is 3
   ★g. $\delta[\alpha(c)/y](y)$ is $\alpha(c)$
   h. $\alpha(\delta[1/y](y))$ is 1

2. *State whether the following are true or false.*
   ★a. When t is b, $\alpha/\delta(t)$ is $\alpha(b)$
   b. When t is z, $\alpha/\delta(t)$ is $\alpha(z)$
   ★c. When t is a, $\alpha/\delta(t)$ is $\delta(a)$
   d. When t is x, $\alpha/\delta(t)$ is $\delta(x)$
   ★e. When $\alpha(b)$ is 1, $\alpha/\delta(b)$ is $\delta[1/y](y)$
   f. When $\alpha(b)$ is 1, $\alpha(b)$ is not $\delta[2/x](x)$

15.3 Satisfaction

15.3.1 Satisfaction Conditions for Predicate and Identity Formulas

In PSL, an object satisfies a one-place predicate if and only if it is in the set of objects that defines that predicate. This notion can be expanded to one-place open sentences, which may be one-place predicate sentences like Gx, but which may just as well be higher-place predicate sentences like Gxax, or identity sentences such as =xx or =ax. However, whereas an object satisfies a one-place predicate, it takes a variable assignment to satisfy a one-place open sentence. One-place open sentences contain a variable rather than a name, and the relation between variables and objects is not fixed by an interpretation but differently determined by the different variable assignments. An object can only satisfy an open sentence (or not) on the variable assignment that assigns that object to the variable. This is why it is not properly said that object o or object n satisfies or does not satisfy Gxax or =ax. Instead, the variable assignments that assign o or n to the variable that marks the place (in the cases of Gxax and =ax that would be $\delta[o/x]$ or $\delta[n/x]$) satisfy or do not satisfy the open sentence.

The rest, however, is familiar from PSL. What it means for a variable assignment, $\delta[o/x]$ to satisfy a predicate or identity sentence is precisely what the (P) and (=) valuation rules for PSL would lead one to expect, after substituting references to satisfaction for references to truth. Suppose $\alpha(a)$ is 1 and δ assigns 2 to x. Then $\delta[2/x]$ satisfies Gxax if and only if the triplet, <2,1,2> is in the set of triplets that defines the predicate, G, that is, if and only if $<\delta[o/x](x),\alpha(a),\delta[o/x](x)>$ is in $\alpha(G)$.

Keeping with this example, $\delta[2/x]$ does not satisfy =ax. $\delta[2/x](x)$ is 2 (that is to say, $\delta[2/x]$ assigns 2 to x) whereas $\alpha(a)$ is 1, so $\delta[2/x](x)$ and $\alpha(a)$ are not the same object.[3] Given that $\alpha(a)$ is 1, there is only one variable assignment that satisfies =ax, namely, $\delta[1/x]$.

> (P): δ **satisfies** $Pt_1...t_n$ if and only if $<\alpha/\delta(t_1)...\alpha/\delta(t_n)>$ is in $\alpha(P)$
>
> (=): δ **satisfies** $=ts$ if and only if $\alpha/\delta(t)$ is $\alpha/\delta(s)$

Those with sharp eyes may notice what might be considered an untoward implication in these rule statements. Suppose $\alpha(a)$ is 1 and 1 is in $\alpha(G)$. Then according to (P), which says that if $\alpha/\delta(t)$ is in $\alpha(P)$, δ satisfies Pt, it does not follow that $I(Ga)$ is T. It follows that δ satisfies Ga. (More precisely, it follows that any δ on I satisfies Ga, since, as already observed, each δ must respect the assignments made by α to names and predicates.)

Similarly, if $\alpha(a)$ and $\alpha(b)$ are both 1, it does not follow that $I(=ab)$ is T. It follows that δ satisfies $=ab$. When t and s are names, $\alpha/\delta(t)$ is $\alpha(a)$ and $\alpha/\delta(s)$ is $\alpha(b)$. But that does nothing to change the fact that when $\alpha/\delta(t)$ is $\alpha/\delta(s)$ the sole consequence that is recognized is that δ satisfies $=ts$, that is, $=ab$ in this case.

There is no mistake in these statements. A δ is not limited to satisfying one-place open sentences. It can satisfy identity and predicate formulas even when the formula does not contain any variables and so has the denotations of all its terms fixed by α. The valuation rules for predicate and identity sentences extend the dominion of the δ's over all predicate and identity formulas, open or closed, atomic or compound.

Exercise 15.5

1. *State what conclusion follows from each of the following claims by (P).*
    *   **★a.** $\delta(x)$ is not in $\alpha(G)$
    *   b. $\alpha(a)$ is in $\alpha(G)$
    *   **★c.** $<\delta(x),\delta(x)>$ is in $\alpha(G)$
    *   d. $<\alpha(c),\delta(x)>$ is not in $\alpha(G)$
    *   **★e.** $<\delta(x),\alpha(a)>$ is not in $\alpha(G)$
    *   f. $<\alpha(b),\alpha(b)>$ is in $\alpha(G)$
    *   **★g.** $<\alpha(c),\delta(y),\delta(y)>$ is in $\alpha(G)$
    *   h. $<\delta(x),\alpha(c),\alpha(b)>$ is not in $\alpha(G)$
    *   **★i.** δ satisfies Gx.
    *   j. δ satisfies Ga
    *   **★k.** δ does not satisfy Gab
    *   l. δ does not satisfy Gxa

2. *State what conclusions follow from each of the following claims by (=).*
    *   **★a.** $\alpha(c)$ is not $\alpha(b)$ *(There are two conclusions to be drawn here and from similar claims.)*
    *   b. $\delta(x)$ is $\alpha(a)$
    *   **★c.** $\delta(y)$ is not $\delta(x)$
    *   d. $\delta(x)$ is not $\alpha(a)$
    *   **★e.** δ satisfies $=ay$ *(There is only one conclusion to be drawn here and from similar claims, though it can be stated in two different ways.)*
    *   f. δ satisfies $=xa$
    *   **★g.** δ does not satisfy $=ac$
    *   h. δ does not satisfy $=yy$

15.3.2 *Satisfaction Conditions for* $\perp$*, Zero-Place Predicates, and Connective Compounds*

The development of semantics from sentential through predicate logic resembles the history of European nations. It begins with monarchical authority, where interpretations magisterially dictate truth or falsity to the aristocratic sentences and where the commoners, the little lower-case names, are entirely suppressed. The first rumblings of a challenge to this authority appear with PSL, where the commoners assert their existence and overthrow the aristocrats, demanding to be the ones that determine the values of sentences in virtue of the land (the predicates) on which they have set up their little bourgeois establishments. But supreme power still rests with the ministerial α's, which retain the ultimate authority to determine which commoners will be allowed to set up their shops on which predicates. However, once the anonymous proletarian mob of variables appears on the scene, a true revolution sets in. The variables usurp sovereign power, setting it in the hands of their demagogues, the variable assignments. The α's, which deal only with names and predicates, retain their sovereign status in name only. The truth that they determine is decided for them by the legislative body of δ's, which despite their numbers are able to reach a surprising unanimity in all their major decisions.

Put less metaphorically, the semantics for open sentences forces itself on the semantics for sentences, in the process rewriting claims about truth on I as claims about satisfaction by δ. This is not a situation like that specified earlier for the denotation of terms, where δ and α divide their authority, with δ's determining the denotation of variables, and α's determining the denotation of names and the extension of predicates. With formulas, there is no way to neatly divide the provinces of authority. Consider "Ga." This is a sentence of QPL. But thinking that it should therefore have a truth value that is determined by an assignment to G and "a" raises a problem when Ga figures as a subformula in an open sentence, like Ga → Hx. This formula does not have a truth value, and its semantics is determined not by any assignment to names and predicates but by variable assignments. *Any* sentence can become part of an open sentence by being conjoined with an open sentence using a binary connective. If Ga does not lose its truth value when conjoined with Hx, then it becomes perplexing what happens to Ga → Hx. If its meaning is determined in part by a truth value and in part by a variable assignment, then the valuation rules will need to be more complex than they are about to be presented as being. Maintaining instead that the sentences of the realm are constantly switching their allegiance depending on where they put themselves (that Ga comes under the authority of α and truth value semantics as long as it occurs alone or in the good company of other sentences but comes under the authority of the δ's and satisfaction whenever it appears in the bad company of free variables) is still too complex. There is no practical way of dividing the realm of formulas up into two parts, one ruled by α and truth, the other by the δ's and by satisfaction. It is simpler to cede total control over all the formulas of QPL to the δ's, be those formulas sentences or open sentences.

The semantics for open sentences is promoted into a semantics for all the formulas of QPL. Sentences and truth are overthrown. Variable assignments, formulas, and satisfaction reign.

The triumph of the revolution is expressed right at the outset, where the δ's take power even in the very last bastion of the monarchy, the zero-place predicates, and the aristocratic α's are forced into ignoble servitude to the proletarian δ's.

(⊥):   **No δ satisfies ⊥ on any interpretation.**

(P):   **δ satisfies** $Pt_1...t_n$ **if and only if** $<\alpha/\delta(t_1)...\alpha/\delta(t_n)>$ **is in** α(P); **as a special case of (P), δ satisfies a** 0-place predicate sentence, P, **if and only if** α(P) **is** T; **δ does not satisfy** P **if and only if** α(P) **is** F.

The world is turned on its head. Truth value assignments establish satisfaction, rather than the other way around. After this triumph, the remaining valuation rules are not surprising.

(~):   **δ satisfies** ~P **iff δ does not satisfy** P; otherwise **δ does not satisfy** ~P

(&):   **δ satisfies** P & Q **iff δ satisfies** each of P and Q; otherwise **δ does not satisfy** P & Q

(∨):   **δ satisfies** P ∨ Q **iff δ satisfies** at least one of P or Q; otherwise **δ does not satisfy** P ∨ Q

(→):   **δ does not satisfy** P → Q **iff δ satisfies** P but not Q; otherwise **δ satisfies** P → Q

(≡):   **δ does not satisfy** P ≡ Q **iff δ satisfies** one of P and Q **but not the other**; otherwise **δ satisfies** P ≡ Q

Exercise 15.6

1. *State whether each of the following claims is in accord with QPL semantics. If it is not, say why not.*
    ★**a.** α(A) is T
     b. α satisfies A
    ★**c.** δ does not satisfy A
     d. δ(A) is T
    ★**e.** α satisfies Gab

    f. δ satisfies Gab

★**g.** δ(Gab) is T

    h. I satisfies Gab

★**i.** I satisfies =ab

    j. δ satisfies =xb

2. *Identify the variable assignment on which each of the following open sentences is satisfied on an interpretation that has domain {1,2} and that assigns 1 to a, and 2 to b. Do so both by identifying the variable assignment "directly" with the object assigned to the variable, as in exercise 15.3#1 and identifying it "obliquely" with a name that the interpretation assigns to the object, as in exercise 15.3 #2.*

★**a.** =ax

    b. =xb

★**c.** ~=xa

    d. =xa → ~=bb

★**e.** ~=xb ≡ ⊥

    f. =xb ≡ =ba

15.3.3 Satisfaction Conditions for Singly Quantified Formulas

The valuation rules for singly quantified formulas of QPL include two new satisfaction conditions for quantified formulas. Along with the denotation condition for variables, these are provisional rules. While the other rules and conditions are permanent, these will be rewritten in chapter 16 to accommodate formulas containing quantifiers with overlapping scope. They are called (S∀) and (S∃) for singly quantified universal and singly quantified existential.

> **(S∀): Each δ satisfies ∀χP iff for each object, o, δ[o/χ] satisfies P; otherwise, no δ satisfies ∀χP.**

In other words, it takes a unanimous vote by the legislative body of variable assignments before a universally quantified formula ∀χP can be satisfied. Each variable assignment must be polled on the question of whether it satisfies the subformula P, and each must vote "yes." A single variable assignment has a veto on the positive judgement of all the others, like the nations at the UN security council. If a single variable assignment does not satisfy the subformula P, then even though all the others do satisfy P, all must deny satisfaction to the universally quantified formula ∀χP. That is the mob politics that rules QPL semantics for universally quantified formulas. Those who have studied chapter 9 will recognize the affinity of (S∀) with (□), which similarly specifies that □P is true if and only if P is true in each accessible world, so that its being false in a single accessible world suffices to make □P false in any world that sees it, notwithstanding what else that other world sees.

(S∃) is the reverse of (S∀).

> **(S∃): Each δ satisfies ∃χP iff for at least one object, o, in D, δ[o/χ] satisfies P; otherwise, no δ satisfies ∃χP.**

Here, the mob politics goes the other way. A single positive verdict on the satisfaction of the subformula P overrides the rest of the mob on the question of the satisfaction of the existentially quantified formula ∃χP. It takes nothing less than unanimity against the subformula to reach a negative verdict about the existentially quantified formula, like a jury finding against the defendant in a court of law. Even though δ_1 does not satisfy the subformula P it might still be forced to satisfy the existentially quantified formula ∃χP because some other variable assignment δ_2 does satisfy P, just as, even if P is false in w, w might have to assign T to ◇P because P is true in some other accessible world, v. Consequently, the only way to show that any δ does not satisfy ∃χP is to poll all the δ's and verify that each one does not satisfy the subformula.

When applying these rules in specific contexts, it is useful to distinguish between four cases:

  i. inference from the claim that each δ satisfies ∀χP or does not satisfy ∃χP

  ii. inference from the claim that each δ satisfies ∃χP or does not satisfy ∀χP

  iii. inference from the claim that each δ satisfies or does not satisfy P

  iv. inference from the claim that at least one δ satisfies or does not satisfy P

(The case where just some δ's satisfy a quantified formula does not arise. Because of how (S∀) and (S∃) are written, either each does or none does.)

Suppose it is given that

i(a):   each δ satisfies ∀χP

Then it follows that δ[1/χ] must satisfy P, as must δ[2/χ], δ[3/χ], and so on, for however many objects there are in D. In general, **for each object, o, in D, δ[o/χ] must satisfy P**. Similarly, if

i(b):   no δ satisfies ∃χP

then it follows that **for *each* o, δ[o/χ] does not satisfy P.**

In contrast, if it is given that

ii(a):   each δ satisfies ∃χP

then it follows that *at least one* δ satisfies P. It could be any one or more of the δ's on I: δ[1/χ], δ[2/χ], δ[3/χ], etc. Speaking again in general terms, all that can be inferred is that **for *at least one* object, o, in D, δ[o/χ] satisfies P.**

Similarly, if

ii(b):   no δ satisfies ∀χP

then all that can be inferred is that **for *at least one* o, δ[o/χ] does not satisfy P.**

Now consider inferences in the reverse direction, from subformulas to formulas. Suppose it is given that,

iii(a):   for *each* o, δ[o/χ] satisfies P

Then **each δ satisfies ∀χP.**

It also follows that each δ satisfies ∃χP, but it does not take each δ to prove that. It is bad form to draw a conclusion from more premises than are strictly required to establish that conclusion. When one case suffices, all of them should not be cited. The proper conclusion from iii(a) is that each δ satisfies ∀χP. Just pick one that satisfies P to make the case that all satisfy ∃χP.

Similarly, if

iii(b):   for *each* o, δ[o/χ] does *not* satisfy P

then **no δ satisfies ∃χP.**

Again, it also follows that no δ satisfies ∀χP, but it does not take each δ to prove that. One counterexample refutes a general rule.

Accordingly, if it is given that

iv(a):   for *at least one* o, δ[o/χ] satisfies P

then it follows that **each δ satisfies ∃χP**, whether that δ satisfies P or not. That is because ∃χP just says that at least one object satisfies P. If even one among their number does satisfy P, all the δ's must acknowledge that ∃χP is satisfied.

Finally, if it is given that

iv(b):   for *at least one* o, δ[o/χ] does not satisfy P

then it follows that **no δ satisfies ∀χP.** As already noted, a single counterexample suffices to refute a general rule, and ∀χP states a general rule: that all the variable assignments satisfy P. If one among their number does not, all must acknowledge that the general rule is unsatisfied.

When conclusions are drawn about the subformulas of connective compounds, it is important not to presume that the variable assignment that does the job for one subformula also does the job for the other. For example, suppose it is given that

15.1   Each δ satisfies ∃xGx & ~∀xH

By (&), each δ must satisfy both ∃xGx and ~∀xHx, so by (~), each δ must satisfy ∃xGx but not satisfy ∀xHx. For ∃xGx to be satisfied, at least one δ must satisfy Gx. For ∀xHx not to be satisfied, at least one δ must not satisfy Hx. But it does not have to be the same one that does both jobs. The proper inference to draw is:

15.2   For at least one o, δ[o/x] satisfies Gx and for at least one n, δ[n/x]
       does not satisfy Hx

where o is possibly but not necessarily distinct from n.

Because of cases like this, it is not proper to infer that because each δ satisfies ∃xGx "some" δ satisfies Gx, or because each δ does not satisfy ∀xHx "some" δ does not satisfy Hx. This makes it too tempting to take the two occurrences of "some" to name the same variable assignment, and infer that there is one variable assignment that does both jobs. Using the more cumbersome "for at least one o" and "for at least one n" forestalls this mistake, though it needs to be kept in mind that the objects are not necessarily distinct.

Exercise 15.7

State what conclusions follow from each of the following claims in accord with a single application of (S∀) or (S∃).

  ⋆**a.** For at least one o, δ[o/x] satisfies Gx.
   b. δ[1/x] does not satisfy Gx.
  ⋆**c.** Both δ[1/x] and δ[2/x] satisfy Gx and D is {1,2}.
   d. For each o, δ[o/x] satisfies ~Gx.
  ⋆**e.** For each o, δ[o/x] does not satisfy Gx.
   f. δ[2/y] satisfies Gcy.
  ⋆**g.** For at least one n, δ[n/z] does not satisfy Gzz.
   h. Each δ satisfies ∃z(Gza & ~Hz)
  ⋆**i.** No δ satisfies ∀x(Gx → Hx)
   j. Each δ satisfies ∀y(Ga ≡ Hy).
  ⋆**k.** No δ satisfies ∃y~=ay.
   l. Why is it impossible for one δ to satisfy ∃xGx (say it is δ[1/x]) while at least one other δ (say δ[2/x]) does not satisfy ∃xGx?

15.4 Truth

Truth is not entirely set aside. Sentences are still said to be true or false. And the definitions of intensional concepts are still given in terms of truth on interpretations. As with PSL, truth is not assigned but determined. Only one valuation rule is required for sentences of all sorts:

> **A sentence, P, is true on an interpretation, I, if and only if each variable assignment on I satisfies P; it is false if and only if no variable assignment on I satisfies P.**

This definition appears to ignore the possibility that some variable assignments might satisfy P while others do not. However, provided P is a sentence, that cannot happen.

The reason why will have to be revisited in chapter 16. For now, it suffices to observe that the only sentences under consideration are atomic sentences, singly quantified sentences (sentences containing just one quantifier, which is the main operator of the sentence), and connective compounds of such sentences. Atomic sentences contain no variables, because they are sentences and the only way a sentence can contain a variable is if that variable is bound, in which case the sentence is not atomic. Since variable assignments only disagree about the assignments they make to the variables, all must agree when it comes to satisfying or not satisfying atomic sentences. All variable assignments must also agree about satisfying or not satisfying singly quantified sentences, since (S∀) and (S∃) force them into agreement. And the values of all connective compounds are ultimately determined by the values of their atomic or singly quantified subformulas, leaving no room for the variable assignments to dispute over them.

The application of the valuation rules is best learned by doing exercises. As a preliminary illustration, consider the interpretation

    D: {1, 2, 3}
    a: 1; b: 2; c: 2
    G: {<1,1>, <1,2>, <1,3>, <2,2>, <3,2>}

and the sentence,

    15.3 $\forall x(Gax \rightarrow \sim=bx)$

15.3 should receive exactly one of T and F on the interpretation. Which it receives can be established by determining the values of the atomic subformulas and applying the valuation rules to reason from values of subformulas to values of the formulas they compose. Those values, and the intermediate values determined by them, are not T or F. They are "is" and "is not"; "is in" and "is not in"; and "satisfied" (sat) and "not satisfied" (not sat) by one or more δ's. The determination of the truth value of the whole sentence is only drawn at the last step in the reasoning.

Consider the first atomic subformula, Gax. Since D is {1, 2, 3} the possible assignments to x are $\delta[1/x]$, $\delta[2/x]$, and $\delta[3/x]$.

Each of these variable assignments must respect the fact that $\alpha(a)$ is 1.

$\delta[1/x]$ satisfies Gax because $\alpha(a)$ is 1, $\delta[1/x](x)$ is obviously 1, and <1,1> is in $\alpha(G)$.
$\delta[2/x]$ and $\delta[3/x]$ satisfy Gax for similar reasons. <1,2> and <1,3> are also in $\alpha(G)$. So, each variable assignment satisfies Gax.

However, $\delta[2/x]$ does not satisfy $\sim=bx$. $\delta[2/x](x)$ is obviously 2, and $\alpha(b)$ is also 2. So $\delta[2/x]$ satisfies $=bx$, which means it does not satisfy $\sim=bx$. The other two variable assignments, however, do satisfy $\sim=bx$.

Because Gax $\rightarrow \sim=bx$ is a conditional, and there is one variable assignment, $\delta[2/x]$, that satisfies its antecedent but does not satisfy its consequent, this subformula is not satisfied by $\delta[2/x]$. Gax $\rightarrow \sim=bx$ is universally quantified, so it is governed by (S$\forall$). According to that rule, if even one variable assignment does not satisfy the immediate subformula, the universally quantified formula cannot be satisfied by any variable assignment. So, no δ satisfies $\forall x(Gax \rightarrow \sim=bx)$. According to the definition of truth, this is the condition under which I assigns an F to this sentence.

A formal demonstration of this result can be written up as follows. "Satisfies" is abbreviated "sat," and "does not satisfy" is abbreviated "not sat."

1.	$\alpha(a)$ is 1, $\delta[2/x](x)$ is 2 and <1,2> is in $\alpha(G)$, so $<\alpha(a),\delta[2/x](x)>$ is in $\alpha(G)$	given
2.	$\delta[2/x]$ sat Gax	1 (P)
3.	$\alpha(b)$ is 2 and $\delta[2/x](x)$ is 2 so $\alpha(b)$ is $\delta[2/x](x)$	given
4.	$\delta[2/x]$ sat $=bx$	3 (=)
5.	$\delta[2/x]$ not sat $\sim=bx$	4 (~)
6.	$\delta[2/x]$ not sat Gax $\rightarrow \sim=bx$	2,5 ($\rightarrow$)
7.	No δ sat $\forall x(Gax \rightarrow \sim=bx)$	6 (S$\forall$)
8.	I($\forall x(Gax \rightarrow \sim=bx)$) is F	7 def truth

As a further example, consider how to determine the value of

    15.4 $\exists y[(=yc \lor =ya) \& \sim Gyy]$

on the interpretation given earlier.

Since $\alpha(a)$ is 1 and $\alpha(c)$ is 2, $\delta[1/y]$ satisfies the second disjunct of $=yc \lor =ya$ and $\delta[2/y]$ satisfies the first, but $\delta[3/y]$ does not satisfy either disjunct. So two of three variable assignments satisfy the disjunction and one does not. By (&), the one that does not, does not satisfy the conjunction. Since both <1,1> and <2,2> are in $\alpha(G)$, it follows that the other two variable assignments satisfy Gyy. Hence, neither of them satisfies the second conjunct, $\sim Gyy$. So, none of the variable assignments satisfies the conjunction, the first two because they do not satisfy the second conjunct, and third because it does not satisfy the first conjunct. Since the conjunction falls under an existential quantifier, it is governed by (S$\exists$), which says that when no variable assignment satisfies the immediate subformula, none can satisfy the existentially quantified formula. So no δ satisfies 15.4. According to the definition of truth, this is the condition under which I assigns an F to 15.4.

In this case, the formal demonstration of the result must be careful to establish that each variable assignment fails to satisfy the subformula. This makes it necessary to include a reference to the fact that $\delta[1/y]$, $\delta[2/y]$, and $\delta[3/y]$ are all the variable assignments there are on I. This is done by appeal to the definition of the contents of D.

1.	$\delta[1/y](y)$ is 1 and $\delta[2/y](y)$ is 2 and $<1,1>$ and $<2,2>$ are in $\alpha(G)$, so $<\delta[1/y](y),\delta[1/y](y)>$ and $<\delta[2/y](y),\delta[2/y](y)>$ are in $\alpha(G)$	given
2.	$\delta[1/y]$ and $\delta[2/y]$ sat Gyy	1 (P)
3.	$\delta[1/y]$ and $\delta[2/y]$ not sat ~Gyy	2 (~)
4.	$\delta[1/y]$ and $\delta[2/y]$ not sat (=yc ∨ =ya) & ~Gyy	3 (&)
5.	$\delta[3/y](y)$ is 3, $\alpha(c)$ is 2 and $\alpha(a)$ is 1, so $\delta[3/y](y)$ is not $\alpha(c)$ or $\alpha(a)$	given
6.	$\delta[3/y]$ not sat =yc or =ya	5 (=)
7.	$\delta[3/y]$ not sat =yc ∨ =ya	6 (∨)
8.	$\delta[3/y]$ not sat (=yc ∨ =ya) & ~Gyy	7 (&)
9.	For each o, $\delta[o/x]$ not sat (=yc ∨ =ya) & ~Gyy	4,8 def D
10.	No δ sat ∃y[(=yc ∨ =ya) & ~Gyy]	9 (S∃)
11.	I(∃y[(=yc ∨ =ya) & ~Gyy]) is F	10 def truth

Take careful note of line 9. Justifications for unsatisfied existentials and satisfied universals must appeal to a claim that looks like the claim on line 9. They require an appeal to no δ or to each δ respectively, which means that the case must have been made for each δ in turn, supplemented by a claim to the effect that all the cases have indeed been considered. Hence the four justifications for line 9 (two at line 4, one at line 8, and def D). The justification appeals to the definition of D (def D), because that is what specifies how many objects there are in D and hence how many different variable assignments there are. The reader looking at line 9 will turn to see that D is {1, 2, 3} and then look to see that lines 4 and 8 make the point for each of $\delta[1/y]$, $\delta[2/y]$, and $\delta[3/y]$.

Exercise 15.8

Demonstrate the value of each of the following sentences on an interpretation that makes the following assignments.

D: {1, 2, 3}
a: 1; b: 2; c: 2
G: {<1,1>, <1,2>, <1,3>, <2,2>, <3,2>}
H: { }; K: {3}; A: {1, 2}

★a. ∀xKx
  b. ∀xGxb *(Hint: compare the solution to i.)*
★c. ∃xAx & Gaa
  d. ∃xHx ∨ =ba *(Hint: compare the solutions to c and u.)*
★e. ∀x~Hx
  f. ∃x~Ax *(Hint: Compare the solutions to e and q.)*
★g. ∃xKx & ∃x~Kx
  h. ∃x(Kx & ~Kx) *(Hint: Compare the solution to (i); argue in the same way that no δ sat the conjunction.)*
★i. ∀x(Kx ∨ Ax)
  j. ~∃x(Gxa & ~Kx)
★k. ∀y(Hy → Gby ∨ Ky)
  l. ~∀z(Gbz ∨ Kz)
★m. ∀x=xb → ∀xKx
  n. ~∀xKx → ∃y~Gyy
★o. ~∀xKx → ∀y~Gyy
  p. ∀z=az ≡ Kb
★q. ∃z~=az & ~∃y~Aay
  r. ∀y(Gya ∨ Gby)
★s. ∃xKx & ~∃zHz & (Kc ∨ ∀yAy)
  t. ∃x(Kx & Hx) ≡ ∀y(Gya → Ay)
★u. ∀y(=yc & Ay → Gby)
  v. ~∀y(Gya ∨ Gby) ∨ ∀y(=ya ∨ =yb)

15.5 Working with the Semantics

15.5.1 Discovering Interpretations

Intensional concepts are still defined in terms of truth or falsity on interpretations. The definitions are unchanged from section 3.4, except that "q" replaces "s."

q-invalidity, q-satisfiability, q-contingency, and q-nonequivalence are demonstrated by discovering and verifying an interpretation of the right sort. In simple cases, interpretations can be discovered in the same way that contradictions are discovered when attempting to demonstrate q-validity, q-unsatisfiability, and q-equivalence. Begin by assuming that there is an interpretation on which the sentence is false (q-validity), that there is an interpretation on which the sentence is true (q-unsatisfiability), or that there is one interpretation of each sort (q-contingency). Reason from values of compounds to values of components by appeal to (def truth) and the satisfaction conditions. When the sentence really is q-invalid, q-unsatisfiable, or q-contingent, this reasoning will not uncover a contradiction. Instead, it will "bottom out" in an assignment of lists of objects to predicates or of names to objects that is not obviously contradictory. An interpretation that makes these assignments should be verifiable as one that assigns F to a q-invalid sentence, T to a q-satisfiable sentence, or both to a q-contingent sentence. A similar procedure can be used to discover interpretations that demonstrate the q-equivalence of sentences, the q-satisfiability of sets, and the q-validity of demonstrations. However, where sentences have multiple subformulas, or when attempting to discover interpretations that demonstrate q-equivalence, q-satisfiability, or q-validity, it can be challenging to define an interpretation that makes all the assignments that are discovered. In these cases, it can be easier to discover interpretations using Tq.

To gain facility with the application of the new S-rules, and as a step to understanding the full semantics of chapter 16, open tree paths should be used to discover models appropriate to the semantics of this chapter and should be verified using this semantics. In practice, this means that names should not appear in models unless those names occur in the givens. Other names will of necessity appear on open paths, as a consequence of (T∃) and (~∀) applications. Only the numbers recovered from using the bin method to make assignments to these other names should appear in the interpretation (that is, in the domain and in the lists assigned to predicates) and in the verification. The solutions to the ★ questions in exercise 15.9#2–6 provide more guidance.

Exercise 15.9

1. *Demonstrate that the following sentences are q-contingent. Use reasoning from the satisfaction and denotation conditions to discover interpretations and verify those interpretations using the semantics of this chapter. The examples given by the solutions to the ★ questions illustrate how to approach these tasks. This exercise is an exhaustive survey of the inferences that ought to be drawn from the truth or falsity of the principal forms of quantified formula. More complex exercises do no more than apply sequences of the solutions to these simple exercises.*

 ★a. $\forall x Gx$
  b. $\exists x Gx$
 ★c. $\forall x{\sim}Gx$
  d. $\exists x{\sim}Gx$
 ★e. $\forall x(Gx \rightarrow Hx)$
  f. $\forall x(Gx \rightarrow {\sim}Hx)$
 ★g. $\forall x{\sim}(Gx \rightarrow Hx)$
  h. $\forall x(Gx \lor Hx)$
 ★i. $\forall x{\sim}(Gx \lor Hx)$
  j. $\forall x(Gx \mathbin{\&} Hx)$
 ★k. $\forall x{\sim}(Gx \mathbin{\&} Hx)$
  l. $\forall x(Gx \equiv Gx)$
 ★m. $\forall x{\sim}(Gx \equiv Hx)$
  n. $\exists x(Gx \mathbin{\&} Hx)$
 ★o. $\exists x(Gx \mathbin{\&} {\sim}Hx)$
  p. $\exists x{\sim}(Gx \mathbin{\&} Hx)$
 ★q. $\exists x(Gx \rightarrow Hx)$
  r. $\exists x(Gx \equiv Hx)$
 ★s. $\forall x{=}xa$
  t. $\exists x{\sim}{=}ax$

2. *Demonstrate with the help of trees that the following sentences are q-invalid.*

    ★a. $(\forall xGx \rightarrow \forall xHx) \rightarrow \forall x(Gx \rightarrow Hx)$

    b. $(\exists xGx \ \& \ \exists xHx) \rightarrow \exists x(Gx \ \& \ Hx)$

    ★c. $\exists xGx \rightarrow \forall x(Hx \rightarrow Gx)$

    d. $\forall x(Gx \vee Hx) \rightarrow (\forall xGx \vee \forall xHx)$

    ★e. $\sim\forall xGx \rightarrow \forall x(Gx \rightarrow Hx)$

    f. $\forall x(Gx \rightarrow Ga)$

3. *Demonstrate with the help of trees that the following sentences are q-satisfiable.*

    ★a. $\forall x(Gx \rightarrow Hx) \ \& \ \forall x(Gx \rightarrow \sim Hx)$

    b. $\exists xGx \ \& \ \exists x\sim Gx$

    ★c. $\exists xGx \ \& \ \exists xHx \ \& \ \sim\exists x(Gx \ \& \ Hx)$

    d. $\sim(\forall xGx \vee \forall x\sim Gx)$

    ★e. $\forall x(Gx \equiv Hx) \rightarrow \sim\exists x(Gx \ \& \ Hx)$

    f. $(\forall xGx \rightarrow \forall xHx) \rightarrow \exists x(Gx \ \& \ \sim Hx)$

4. *Demonstrate with the help of trees that the following sentences are not q-equivalent.*

    ★a. $\forall x\sim Gx, \sim\forall xGx$

    b. $\exists x\sim Gx, \sim\exists xGx$

    ★c. $\exists x(Gx \rightarrow Ha), \exists xGx \rightarrow Ha$

    d. $\forall x(Gx \rightarrow H), \forall xGx \rightarrow H$

    ★e. $\forall x(Gx \equiv Hx), \exists xGx \equiv \exists xHx$

    f. $\exists x(Gx \equiv Hx), \exists xGx \equiv \exists xHx$

5. *Demonstrate with the help of trees that the following sets are q-satisfiable.*

    ★a. $\{\exists xGx, \sim\forall xGx\}$

    b. $\{\exists xGx, \exists xHx, \exists x\sim(Gx \ \& \ Hx)\}$

    ★c. $\{\forall x(Gx \rightarrow Hx), \forall x(Hx \rightarrow Kx), \forall x(Gx \rightarrow \sim Kx)\}$

    d. $\{\exists xGx \vee \exists x\sim Hx, \forall x(\sim Gx \vee Hx)\}$

    ★e. $\{\exists xGax, \exists xHxa, \forall x(\sim Gax \vee \sim Hxa)\}$

    f. $\{\forall x(Gax \rightarrow Gxa), \exists xGxa, \sim\exists xGax\}$

6. *Demonstrate with the help of trees that the following demonstrations are q-invalid.*

    ★a. $\exists x(Gx \rightarrow Hx), \exists xGx \ / \ \exists xHx$

    b. $\exists xGx \ / \ Ga$ *(So how can (A/∃E) and (T∃) be sound?)*

    ★c. $\sim\forall xGx \ / \ \sim Ga$ *(So how can (~∀) be sound?)*

    d. $Ga \ / \ \forall xGx$ *(So how can (∀G) be sound?)*

    ★e. $\forall x(Ax \rightarrow \sim Bx), \exists x(Cx \ \& \ \sim Bx) \ / \ \exists x(Cx \ \& \ Ax)$

    f. $\forall x(Ax \rightarrow Bx), \forall x(Ax \rightarrow Cx) \ / \ \exists x(Ax \ \& \ Cx)$

    ★g. $\exists x(Ax \ \& \ Bx), \exists x(Bx \ \& \ Cx) \ / \ \exists x(Ax \ \& \ Cx)$

    h. $\forall x(Ax \rightarrow Bx), \exists x(Bx \ \& \ Cx) \ / \ \exists x(Ax \ \& \ Cx)$

15.5.2 Discovering Contradictions

As before, to establish that demonstrations, sets, and sentences are q-valid, unsatisfiable, and equivalent, assume there is a counterinterpretation and demonstrate by appeal to the valuation rules and definitions of the intensional properties that this supposition leads to a contradiction and so must be rejected. In doing this, apply the valuation rules only from left to right (formula to subformula), and look for a deeper problem than a contradiction in truth value assignments. The contradiction should be a contradiction in the assignment of objects to predicates, names to objects, or variables to objects, perhaps expressed as a contradiction in what variable assignments satisfy what predicate or identity formulas.

    While most of the demonstrations proving these points involve straightforward applications of the valuation rules, some inferences require caution.

Case 1: Distribution

When each δ satisfies a universally quantified sentence, like $\forall x(Gx \rightarrow Hx)$, (S∀) dictates inferring that each δ satisfies the subformula, $Gx \rightarrow Hx$. The next inference needs to be carefully stated and correctly understood. *Each δ either* does not satisfy Gx or does satisfy Hx. The term "each" is used in preference to "every" to stress that the claim is to be understood distributively rather than collectively. Each δ must individually do the one or the other. One δ could do the first, while another can do the second instead.

A similar situation arises when it is inferred that each δ satisfies (Gx ∨ Hx). The inference to draw is that *each* δ *either* satisfies Gx or Hx, which means that some could satisfy one, others the other, as long as each satisfies one or the other.

It is very easy to invert the scope, and think that *either each* δ satisfies Gx or it satisfies Hx. But that implies that all the δ's either do the one or do the other, which is not what follows. The instances of ∀x(Gx ∨ Hx) are $Ga_1 ∨ Ha_1$, $Ga_2 ∨ Ha_2$, $Ga_3 ∨ Ha_3$, and so on. For each of those instances to be satisfied, only one disjunct in each pair needs to be satisfied. It need not always be the first one. It need always be the second one. In some instances, i, Ga_i may be satisfied, in others, k, Ha_k may be satisfied.

It is different when the sentence is not a universally quantified sentence but a conditional or a disjunction. When each δ satisfies ∀xGx → ∃yHy, the inference to draw is that *either each* δ does not satisfy ∀xGx or each δ satisfies ∃yHy. Similarly, when each δ satisfies ∀xGx ∨ ∀xHx, the inference to draw is that either each δ satisfies ∀xGx or each δ satisfies ∀xHx.

The difference is a function of which operator is the main operator. When ∀χ is the main operator and → or ∨ occur in the immediate subformula, "each" has scope over "either," as in "each δ either …" When → or ∨ is the main operator and ∀χ occurs in the immediate subformula, "either" has scope over "each," as in "either each δ … or each δ …"

Case 2: Specification

Since truth is defined as satisfaction by each variable assignment, and falsity as satisfaction by none, and demonstrations begin with claims about which sentences are true or false, demonstrations begin with claims about what each or no variable assignment does.

When a universal sentence is true or an existential sentence is false, there is no problem. The transition is from each δ satisfying the universal sentence to each δ satisfying its immediate subformula, and from no δ satisfying the existential sentence to no δ satisfying its subformula. But when a universal sentence is false or an existential sentence is true, the transition needs to be managed more carefully. It is best not to use general expressions like "some" or "at least one." Instead, give a name to the δ in question by saying "for at least one o, δ[o/x]" or "for at least one n, δ[n/y]." In some cases, it might be known which object does the job, in which case the inference can name that object, as in δ[1/z], δ[3/y], and so on. When it is not known which object does the job, use different object variables to name the variable assignments that do different jobs. Using different object variables does not preclude the possibility that the different variables refer to the same object, but it does not invite the assumption that they must.

Vague use of "some δ" or "at least one δ" is to be avoided, because there are contexts where different δ's might be at play. Confusing them could lead to false inferences. For example, ∃xAx & ∃xBx does not q-entail ∃x(Ax & Bx), as is proven by an interpretation with D: {1,2} where α(A) is {1} and α(B) is {2}. But when due care is not taken to specify the δ's, a mistaken demonstration can be produced.

1. I(∃xAx & ∃xBx) is T
2. Each δ sat ∃xAx & ∃xBx   1 def truth
3. Each δ sat ∃xAx   2 (&)
4. Each δ sat ∃xBx   2 (&)
5. Some δ sat Ax   3 (S∃)
6. Some δ sat Bx   3 (S∃)
7. Some δ sat (Ax & Bx)   5,6 (&)   ✗ *WRONG!!*

The inference at line 7 is incorrect, because there is no reason to think that the δ at line 5 is the δ at line 6. The difference is obscured by describing both δ's as "some δ." Specifying the δ in question prevents the faulty inference.

1. α(∃xAx & ∃xBx) is T
2. Each δ sat ∃xAx & ∃xBx   1 def truth
3. Each δ sat ∃xAx   2 (&)
4. Each δ sat ∃xBx   2 (&)
5. For some o δ[o/x] sat Ax   3 (S∃)
6. For some n δ[n/x] sat Bx   3 (S∃)

This parallels what is done in Dq and Tq, where each application of (∃A) and (T∃) requires a foreign name.

Case 3: Extensionality

Suppose that $\alpha(a)$ is 1. Then $\delta[1/x]$ can be rewritten as $\delta[\alpha(a)/x]$. It follows that if $\alpha(G)$ is $\{1\}$ then the fact that $\alpha(a)$ is in $\alpha(G)$ can be rewritten as the fact that $\delta[\alpha(a)/x](x)$ is in $\alpha(G)$. This makes it possible to pass from the fact that δ satisfies Ga to the fact that $\delta[\alpha(a)/x]$ satisfies Gx, or the reverse. Such transitions can be useful. Consider the demonstration that Ga entails $\exists$xGx.

1. Suppose to the contrary that there is an interpretation, I, such that I(Ga) is T and I($\exists$xGx) is F.
   2. By def truth, each δ sat Ga and no δ sat $\exists$xGx.
   3. By (P), $\alpha(a)$ is in $\alpha(G)$.
   4. From line 2 by (S$\exists$), for each o, $\delta[o/x]$ not sat Gx, so $\delta[\alpha(a)/x]$ not sat Gx.
   5. By (P) $\delta[\alpha(a)/x](x)$ is not in $\alpha(G)$.
   6. Since $\delta[\alpha(a)/x](x)$ is by definition $\alpha(a)$, $\alpha(a)$ is not in $\alpha(G)$.
7. Since the supposition at line 1 leads to a contradiction at lines 3 and 6, that supposition must be rejected: there is no interpretation on which Ga is T and $\exists$xGx is F.
8. By def. q-entailment, Ga $\vDash$ $\exists$xGx.

Exercise 15.10

1. *Demonstrate that the following sentences are q-valid.*
   ⋆a. $\forall$xGx $\vee$ $\forall$xHx $\rightarrow$ $\forall$x(Gx $\vee$ Hx) *(compare 17.9#2d)*
   b. $\exists$x(Gx & Hx) $\rightarrow$ ($\exists$xGx & $\exists$xHx) *(compare 17.9#2b)*
   ⋆c. $\forall$x(Gx $\rightarrow$ Hx) $\rightarrow$ ($\forall$xGx $\rightarrow$ $\forall$xHx) *(compare 17.9#2a)*
   d. $\exists$xGx $\vee$ $\forall$x(Gx $\rightarrow$ Hx)
   ⋆e. Ga $\vee$ ($\forall$xGx $\rightarrow$ Ha)
   f. $\exists$x=ax
   ⋆g. $\forall$x=xx
   h. $\forall$x[=xa $\rightarrow$ (Gx $\equiv$ Ga)]

2. *Demonstrate that the following sentences are q-unsatisfiable.*
   ⋆a. $\forall$xGx & $\exists$x~Gx
   b. $\exists$xGx & $\forall$x~Gx
   ⋆c. ~$\forall$x(Gx $\rightarrow$ Gx)
   d. $\exists$x(Gx $\equiv$ ~Gx)
   ⋆e. $\forall$x=xa & $\exists$x(Gax & ~Gxa)
   f. ~$\exists$x=xa

3. *Demonstrate that the following sentences are q-equivalent.*
   ⋆a. $\forall$xGx, ~$\exists$x~Gx
   b. $\exists$xGx, ~$\forall$x~Gx
   ⋆c. $\forall$x(Gx $\rightarrow$ Hx), ~$\exists$x(Gx & ~Hx)
   d. $\exists$x(Gx & Hx), ~$\forall$x(Gx $\rightarrow$ ~Hx)
   ⋆e. $\forall$x(Gx $\rightarrow$ H), $\exists$xGx $\rightarrow$ H *(compare 17.9#4d)*
   f. $\exists$x(Gx $\rightarrow$ Ha), $\forall$xGx $\rightarrow$ Ha *(compare 17.9#4c)*

4. *Demonstrate that the following sets are q-unsatisfiable.*
   ⋆a. $\{\exists$x(Gx & Hx), $\forall$x~(Gx $\vee$ Hx)$\}$
   b. $\{\forall$xGx $\vee$ $\forall$x~Gx, $\exists$xGx $\equiv$ $\exists$x~Gx$\}$
   ⋆c. $\{\forall$x(Gx $\rightarrow$ Hx), $\forall$x(Hx $\rightarrow$ Kx), $\exists$y(Gy & ~Ky)$\}$ *(compare 17.10#5c)*
   d. $\{\forall$xGx $\vee$ $\forall$xHx, ~Ga, ~Hb$\}$
   ⋆e. $\{\forall$xGx $\rightarrow$ $\exists$yHy, ~$\exists$xHx, ~$\exists$x~Gx$\}$
   f. $\{\forall$x(Gx $\rightarrow$ Hx), $\forall$x(Gx $\rightarrow$ ~Hx), $\exists$xGx$\}$

5. *Demonstrate that the following demonstrations are q-valid.*
   ⋆a. Ga / $\exists$xGx *(compare 17.9#6b)*
   b. $\forall$xGx / Ga *(compare 17.9#6d)*
   ⋆c. ~$\exists$xGx / ~Ga *(compare 17.9#6c)*
   d. ~$\exists$xGx / $\forall$x(Gx $\rightarrow$ Hx)

*e. ~∀xGx / ∃x(Gx → Hx)
    f. ∀x(=xa ∨ =xb), ~Ga / ∃xGx → Gb

15.6 Demonstrating General Principles

Exercises 15.9#6b–d show that the derivation and tree rules are not obviously sound. It is clearly incorrect to infer a universally quantified sentence from a single instance. This is the fallacy of hasty generalization. Inferring an instance from an existentially quantified sentence, or the negation of an instance from a negated universal sentence, is also incorrect. This is a fallacy of overspecification. An existential or negated universal only says that at least one thing is a certain way. It does not identify which one. If the restrictions placed by Dq and Tq on (∀G), (∃E), (T∃), and (~∀) manage to avoid these fallacies, it is not obvious how. An informal soundness demonstration was offered when these rules were first introduced, but full assurance can only be obtained by showing that these derivation and tree rules are underwritten by the formal semantics for QPL.

Even though the semantics of this chapter is incomplete, it says enough to provide the requisite support. However, it needs to be supplemented by some principles concerning extensionality and variance.

15.6.1 Extensionality

Chapters A-1 and A-5 showed that SL and PSL are extensional in two ways: sentences that have the same value on an interpretation may be substituted for one another without changing the value the interpretation assigns to a compound containing one or other of those sentences; and names that have the same value on an interpretation may be substituted for one another without changing the value the interpretation assigns to a sentence containing one or other of those names. QPL introduces a third form of extensionality, variable extensionality.

This ought to seem impossible. In general, extensionality is the property of invariance under substitution of vocabulary elements that have the same meaning. Variables stand for what can vary and so have no fixed meaning. Of all things, extensionality ought not to apply to them. But it does, when the extension is suitably restricted.

Suppose each variable assignment satisfies an instance, $P(q|\chi)$, of an open sentence, P. For this to be the case, $P(q|\chi)$ must not contain any free variables. If it did, the variable assignments would disagree about what the free variables denote and there would be little chance they would all satisfy $P(q|\chi)$. However, the open sentence that $P(q|\chi)$ is an instance of, P, must contain free occurrences of the variable, χ. To take a simple example, suppose each δ satisfies Ga, which is an instance of the open sentence, Gx. The δ's will all disagree in the assignment they make to x, but they must all acknowledge the assignment to "a," because that is not up to them to make. Then q and χ are "extensional" in the sense that any variable assignment that assigns the same object to χ that α assigns to q must satisfy Gx. To continue with the example, if each δ satisfies Ga because α(a) is 1 and 1 is in α(G), then δ[1/x], which assigns the same object to x that α assigns to "a" must likewise satisfy Gx. Put in more general terms, if each δ satisfies Ga, then even without knowing what "a" denotes on α or what objects α assigns to G, it can be inferred that δ[α(a)/x] must satisfy Gx.

The implication holds in the other direction as well. If δ[1/x] satisfies Gx and α(a) is 1, meaning that δ[α(a)/x] satisfies Gx, then each δ must satisfy Ga, and it must do so independently of what assignment it makes to x. Of course, the other δ's do not satisfy Ga because δ[1/x] forces them to. They do so because α forces them to. But it is still accurate to say that if δ[α(a)/x] satisfies Gx, each δ must satisfy Ga.

> **Variable Extensionality (v-extensionality)**
>
> If P is an open sentence containing at least one free occurrence of a variable, χ, then $δ[α(q)/\chi]$ satisfies P if and only if each δ satisfies $P(q|\chi)$.

Suppose

    15.5 $δ[α(a)/x]$ satisfies Gx

Then by a left to right application of v-extensionality

    15.6   δ satisfies Ga

Going in the other direction, suppose

15.7   δ satisfies Gab

Then by right-to-left applications of v-extensionality

15.8   δ[α(a)/y] satisfies Gyb
15.9   δ[α(b)/x] satisfies Gax

To take a more complex case, suppose

15.10   δ satisfies Gb → Hab

Then

15.11   δ[α(b)/x] satisfies Gb → Hax

There is no typo here. Gb → Hab is an instance of Gb → Hax, so this is a legitimate application of the principle.

Exercise 15.11

Say what follows from each of the following claims by an application of the variable extensionality principle.

⋆**a.** δ[α(b)/y] sat Hy
  b. δ[α(c)/z] sat Hzcz
⋆**c.** δ[α(a)/x] sat =xb
  d. δ[α(a)/x] sat Gbx → =cx
⋆**e.** δ sat Gb
  f. δ not sat Gb

Variable extensionality is intuitively obvious, though complex enough that it needs to be illustrated before the intuition kicks in. That is enough for logicians to demand that the principle be demonstrated by appeal to the valuation rules. The demonstration is surprisingly long and complicated, and it contributes nothing to making the principle any more obvious than it has already been made to be, or to assisting in its application. It can be found in chapter A-6.

15.6.2 *Variance*

Given a set, Γ, of sentences, a variant, J, on an interpretation I, is an interpretation that makes all the same assignments to the names and predicates in sentences in Γ that I does, but that differs from I in 0 or more assignments made to names or predicates that do not occur in Γ. (The 0 case would be one in which J does not differ in any way from I. This is allowed because it is useful to be able to consider any interpretation to be a variant on itself.)

The variable assignments on an interpretation are the same as the variable assignments on any of its variants. This is because the only way variable assignments can differ is in what objects they assign to the variables. Each different way of assigning each variable to exactly one of the objects in the domain of an interpretation, I, is a variable assignment on I. Since any variant, J, on I must use the same domain, the complete list of variants on J must be identical to the complete list of variants on I.

The variant interpretation principle reports on an affinity in the results of the variable assignments made by interpretations and their variants.

Variant Interpretation Principle (variant-I)

A **formula**, P, of **QPL** is satisfied by a **variable assignment, δ, on an** interpretation, I, if and only if δ **satisfies** P on any variant, J, on I.

The principle is intuitively obvious. Since by definition of a variant, $J\alpha$ must make the same assignments to all the names and predicates in P that $I\alpha$ does, and since δ is the same assignment to all the variables in P on either I or J, there is nothing to lead δ to satisfy P on one of I and J but not the other.

As a corollary, if all the variable assignments on I satisfy P, all the variable assignments on J must satisfy P and vice versa. By definition of truth, this means that I(P) is T if and only if J(P) is T.

The variant interpretation principle and its corollary are obvious. But, as shown in exercise 15.12, they explain something that is not so obvious: why the restrictions on (A/∃E), (T∃) and (~∀) are necessary for these rules to be sound.

Exercise 15.12

Demonstrate (a) and (b) by appeal to v-extensionality, and (c)–(f) by appeal to variant-I and v-extensionality.

★**a.** If $\Gamma \vDash \forall\chi P$ then $\Gamma \vDash P(q|\chi)$ where q is any name.

  b. If $\Gamma \vDash P(q|\chi)$ then $\Gamma \vDash \exists\chi P$

★**c.** If all the sentences in $\Gamma \cup \exists\chi P$ are true on an interpretation, I, and q does not occur in any sentence in Γ or in P, then all the sentences in $\Gamma \cup \{\exists\chi P, P(q|\chi)\}$ are true on at least one variant, J, on I.

  d. If all the sentences in $\Gamma \cup \sim\forall\chi P$ are true on an interpretation, I, and q does not occur in any sentence in Γ or in P, then all the sentences in $\Gamma \cup \{\sim\forall\chi P, \sim P(q|\chi)\}$ are true on at least one variant, J, on I.

★**e.** If $\Gamma \vDash P(q|\chi)$ and q does not occur in any sentence in Γ or in $\forall\chi P$, then $\Gamma \vDash \forall\chi P$

  f. If $\Gamma \vDash \exists\chi P$ and $\Gamma \cup P(q|\chi) \vDash R$, and q does not occur in any sentence in Γ, in $\exists\chi P$, or in R, then $\Gamma \vDash R$

Notes

1 Variable assignments will be familiar to those who have studied section 11.7. What is said here repeats some of that information for those who may not have studied that material.

2 For future reference, chapter 16 will read $\delta[1/x]$ as a variant on δ rather than as a partial description of δ. In chapter 16, the tag is understood as saying "put 1 in place of whatever object δ assigns to x."

3 The claim, "$\delta[2/x](x)$ is 2" seems to stutter. Why not just say that $\delta[2/x]$ is 2? Why even bother to say that much when the 2/x already says that 2 is the value of x? The stuttering is forced by the semantics of chapter 16, which works with expanded variable assignments like $\delta[3/x,1/z,2/y]$. In any given context, which assignment is at issue, the one to x, the one to y, or the one to z? $\delta[2/x,1/z,3/y](z)$ says it is the assignment to z.

16 Semantics for QPL with Mixed Multiple Quantification

Contents

16.1 Variants on Variable Assignments; Denotation of Variables

A semantics for formulas that contain quantifiers with overlapping scope must be purely formal. Its rules are based on the concept of an instance of a quantified sentence. As discussed in chapter 12.3.2, that concept implies that the existential quantifier has two different meanings, depending on its position relative to a universal quantifier. When it precedes a universal, it means "(at least) one for all." It picks out at least one individual that works with each of the objects in the domain. When an existential follows a universal it means "some one or other for each one." In this case it is only promised that there is at least one individual that works with any one object, not that the same individual works with each. In the extreme, each object might work with a different individual and the claim would still be true. In chapter 12.3.2, these different senses were illustrated with the following lists of ordered pairs, where $1, 2, 3, \ldots$ designate each object, i designates an individual, and x_1, x_2, x_3 designate not necessarily identical individuals.

$$\exists y \forall z Gyz: \alpha(G) \text{ is: } \{<i,1>, <i,2>, <i,3>,\ldots\}$$
$$\forall z \exists y Gyz: \alpha(G) \text{ is: } \{<x_1,1>, <x_2,2>, <x_3,3>,\ldots\}$$

When an existential quantifier occurs between two universals, it has both meanings simultaneously, the second with reference to the universal quantifier to its left (in the second example above, flip the order of the variables after G and of the objects in the ordered pairs to make the combination easier to conceive), and the first with reference to the universal quantifier on its right.

DOI: 10.4324/9781003026532-25

$\forall x\exists y\forall zGxyz$: $\alpha(G)$ is: $\{<1,x_1,1>, <1,x_1,2>, <1,x_1,3>,\ldots$
$\{<2,x_2,1>, <2,x_2,,2>, <2,x_2,3>,\ldots$
$\{<3,x_3,1>, <3,x_3,,2>, <3,x_3,3>,\ldots$
$\ldots\}$

As further discussed in chapter 12.3.2, English is not sensitive to this distinction. English speakers are aware of it. But they have not developed, and do not employ, the English language in a way that adequately marks it. English sentences that use multiple quantifiers exhibit scope ambiguity. When the existential quantifier is mentioned first, it could have either of the two senses. Some English sentences that begin with an existential quantifier, like

16.1   There is someone who knows every answer

strongly suggest that the existential be read as picking out one for all, others, like

16.2   There is a fork by every plate

strongly suggest that it be read as picking out a different individual for each, and many, like

16.3   There is someone who loves everyone

lend themselves to either reading (the efforts of logic instructors to intimidate students into accepting that English always puts the quantifier with widest scope first notwithstanding). Because English cannot get straight what it means when it uses multiple quantifiers, a semantics for QPL must draw on its own resources. Attempting to illustrate the formal system with English language examples only invites confusion and mistakes. Those who have different intuitions about what the English sentence is saying, or different intuitions on different days, or no intuitions are not convinced by attempts to declare that an English sentence has the one meaning rather than the other. And they are all of us except for those who already understand formal QPL semantics and are determined to interpret English accordingly regardless of what others might in fact intend to say. This is why, beginning with chapter 5 and culminating with chapter 15, this textbook has provided incrementally advanced training in the use of formal semantic demonstrations. When sentences containing multiple quantifiers with overlapping scope come up for consideration, this is the only way to proceed. QPL is its own language and for this purpose it is a less ambiguous one than English. It needs to be understood on its own terms.

The core concept of what will be called "multiple" QPL semantics, that is, a semantics adequate for mixed multiple quantification, is that of a variant on a variable assignment. Variants are the semantic means of capturing the syntactic concept of an instance of a quantified sentence. An instance rewrites a sentence with a name in the place of a variable. Variable assignments, and variants on variable assignments consider the variable to denote an object.

> A *variant*, $\delta[o/\chi]$, on a variable assignment, δ, is a variable assignment that is exactly like δ except that it rewrites the assignment that δ makes to χ as an assignment of o to χ.

The notation, $\delta[o/\chi]$ is familiar from the "single" semantics of chapter 15, which is designed just for singly quantified sentences and connective compounds of such sentences. But single semantics uses it to specify what assignment δ makes to the single variable that is only ever at issue, whereas multiple semantics uses it to identify a different variable assignment from δ, one that is just like δ but for rewriting the assignment that δ makes to χ with a (not necessarily) different assignment. (It is useful to be able to consider each variable assignment to be a variant on itself, which is why it is noted that the object, o, that $\delta[o/\chi]$ assigns to χ need not necessarily be different from the one that δ already assigns to χ.)

Variants have a genealogical structure. Consider a domain, D, that contains three objects, 1, 2, 3, and a sentence, $\forall x\exists y\forall zGxyz$, that contains three variables. Then there are $o^{(v)}=27$ different variable assignments.

Consider just one of them, δ, which assigns 1 to x, 2 to y and 3 to z.

Considering just assignments to x, there are three variants on δ: $\delta[1/x]$, $\delta[2/x]$, and $\delta[3/x]$. (As just noted, it is useful to consider the variant that rewrites δ's assignment of 1 to x with an assignment of 1 to x as a variant on δ even though it makes no changes to δ.)

δ[2/x] and δ[3/x] assign objects to x that δ itself assigns to y and z. δ[2/x] and δ[3/x] nonetheless continue to also assign 2 to y and 3 to z, respectively. As variants on δ, they must make the same assignments that δ does, except for those that are specified on the bracketed list. But while they continue to assign 2 to y and 3 to z, δ[2/x] also assigns 2 to x and δ[3/x] also assigns 3 to x. There is nothing wrong with this. Different variables can have same objects assigned to them.

There are likewise three variants on δ with respect to y: δ[1/y], δ[2/y] and δ[3/y]. The same holds for z. These nine different variants can be considered the children of δ, notwithstanding that three of them, δ[1/x], δ[2/y], and δ[3/z] make no changes to δ.

Each of these children is a parent of its own children. The children of δ[2/y], for instance, are δ[2/y,1/x], δ[2/y,2/x], and δ[2/y,3/x], where x is concerned. There are also three children of δ[2/y] where z is concerned. Variants are quite promiscuous in their mating habits! Interestingly, they can also produce progeny by mating with themselves. δ[2/y] has three children by herself: δ[2/y,1/y], δ[2/y,2/y], and δ[2/y,3/y]. Just as δ[2/y] made no changes to δ, which already assigned 2 to y, so δ[2/y,2/y] makes no changes to either its parent or its grandparent. But δ[2/y,1/y] snubs both and rewrites their assignment of 2 to y with an assignment of 1 to y instead.

This is not a violation of the principle that no variable assignment can assign two or more different objects to the same variable. δ[2/y,1/y] does not assign both 2 and 1 to y. It only assigns 1 to y. Its parent, δ[2/y] assigned 2 to y, but δ[2/y,1/y] has changed that. The 2/y in δ[2/y,1/y] is not a representation of what δ[2/y,1/y] assigns to y. It is a record of what its parent did. Each variable assignment carries the record of the actions of its ancestors (but for the original δ) in its name.

Whereas ambiguity of names is ruled out by placing constraints on α, and single semantics rules out ambiguity of variables by placing constraints on δ, ambiguity is simply impossible for variants. δ[2/x,3/x] is a variant that takes x to denote 3 and only 3. Variants are made from left to right, so that any later assignment to the same variable, that is, any one further to the right, overwrites the earlier one.

These features of variants account for a new denotation condition for variables:

> The denotation of a **variable,** χ on a variable assignment, δ[...], **is the last (rightmost) object in D to be assigned to** χ **on the list,** [...]. **Notation:** δ[... o/χ ...](χ) **is o where o/χ contains the rightmost occurrence of** χ **on** [...]. **If** χ **is not mentioned on** [...], **or** δ **is not followed by** [...], **the denotation of** χ **is** δ(χ).

Exercise 16.1

State what object is denoted by each of the following.

*a. δ[3/x,2/y](x)
 b. δ[3/x,2/y,2/z](y)
*c. δ[3/x,1/x,2/x](x)
 d. δ[3/x,2/z,3/z](z)
*e. δ[3/z,2/y,2/x](z)
 f. δ[3/x,1/x,1/x](x)

The genealogical remarks of the previous section do not end with the grandchildren of δ. δ[2/y,1/y], as well as all the other grandchild variants that can be mentioned, have their own children by the different variables. For instance, the children of δ[2/y,1/y] with respect to x are δ[2/y,1/y,1/x], δ[2/y,1/y,2/x], and δ[2/y,1/y,3/x]. And even though there are only three variables, great grandchildren like δ[1/x,1/y,1/z] can continue to mate with any of x, y, and z and have progeny like δ[1/x,1/y,1/z,2/y]. When there are more variables under consideration or more objects in the domain, the possibilities are multiplied accordingly.

It is not always desirable to identify variants by identifying the objects that are reassigned to variables. It is often more important to consider some variant that makes some unspecified assignment, or each variant that makes any assignment. In these cases, the objects are designated by lower-case o, n, or m, or numerically subscripted o's. This is not a feature of the vocabulary of QPL. It is a convention of English used when talking about unspecified objects.

Like all other variables, the symbols o, n, and m do not necessarily stand for different objects. Thus, a reference to each o and each n will (naturally) include the case where o and n are the same object. ("Each" means "each," and so includes the case where o and n are the same.) Similarly, "for each o there is at least one n," does not exclude the possibility of o and n being the same object. The possibility that the objects may be distinct is always there. If it is meant to be precluded, words to that effect must be employed.

This discussion of variants lays the groundwork for an adequate understanding of multiple semantics. Consider the sentence mentioned earlier, $\forall x \exists y \forall z Gxyz$. Its main operator is a universal quantifier on the x variable. Single semantics would say that it is satisfied by each δ if and only if, for each object, o, $\delta[o/x]$ satisfies $\exists y \forall z Gxyz$. But it says nothing about how to determine whether each of these δ's satisfies a quantified open sentence.

Multiple semantics takes the next step. But first it takes a step back and makes a slight, but important change to what single semantics says. Rather than lay down a condition on which each δ satisfies a formula, it restricts itself to laying down a condition on which just one does.

$$\delta \text{ sat } \forall x \exists y \forall z Gxyz \text{ if and only if, for each o, } \delta[o/x] \text{ sat } \exists y \forall z Gxyz$$

The parent satisfies the $\forall$ sentence if and only if each of its children satisfies the immediate subformula. The next step is taken by noting that $\exists y \forall z Gxyz$ is $\exists$ quantified on variable y. So multiple semantics says that each of the $\delta[o/x]$ variants must itself be the parent of at least one y variant (not necessarily the same one in each case) that satisfies $\forall z Gxyz$.

$$\text{For each o, } \delta[o/x] \text{ sat } \exists y \forall z Gxyz \text{ if and only if for each o there is at least one n such that}$$
$$\delta[o/x,n/y] \text{ sat } \forall z Gxyz$$

Now, because $\forall z Gxyz$ is $\forall$ quantified on variable z, each z variant on each of the $\delta[o/x,n/y]$ variants that satisfies $\forall z Gxyz$ must satisfy Gxyz.

$$\text{For each o there is at least one n such that } \delta[o/x,n/y] \text{ sat } \forall z Gxyz \text{ if and only if}$$
$$\text{for each o there is at least one n such that for each m, } \delta[o/x,n/y,m/z] \text{ sat } Gxyz.$$

It gets rather complex when there are even as many as three quantifiers nested one within the scope of the other. But there is no reason to be daunted by the complexity because it is not necessary to keep the earlier parts of the formulation in mind. Work is only ever done with the last item on the list. However, it is important to retain the earlier list items in all subsequent formulations, because subsequent actions can remove the last item from the list, bringing up the next to last. A running account of all past list items must be retained for that eventuality.

Exercise 16.2

Expand the following into a claim about which variants on variants on variants must satisfy P for the formula to be satisfied. Consult the linked answers and learn by example. All the main variations for rows of three quantifiers are presented here, so this exercise exhausts this topic. Its solutions can be used as a reference key when writing up answers to subsequent exercise sets in this chapter.

★**a.** $\forall x \forall y \forall z P$
  b. $\forall x \forall z \exists y P$
★**c.** $\forall y \exists x \forall z P$
  d. $\forall y \exists z \exists x P$
★**e.** $\exists z \forall x \forall y P$
  f. $\exists z \forall y \exists x P$
★**g.** $\exists x \exists y \forall z P$
  h. $\exists x \exists y \exists z P$

16.2 Satisfaction Conditions for Quantified Formulas

The satisfaction conditions for quantified formulas are now stated in terms of variants.

> (∀):   δ[...] satisfies ∀χP if and only if for each o, δ[...,o/χ] satisfies P; otherwise
> δ[...] does not satisfy ∀χP.
>
> (∃):   δ[...] satisfies ∃χP if and only if for at least one o, δ[...,o/χ] satisfies P;
> otherwise δ[...] does not satisfy ∃χP.

"For each/at least one o, δ[...,o/χ]" now refers to each/at least one χ variant on δ[...], that is, to each/at least one variable assignment that makes all the same assignments δ[...] does, except (possibly) for the assignment to χ. It does not refer to each variable assignment whatsoever or any variable assignment of any sort. Correspondingly, δ[...] is just the parent of these variants, not each δ whatsoever. These rule statements are not as expansive as the (S∀) and (S∃) rules used by single semantics. They only talk about what is done by the family of one variable assignment, not what is done by all the families of all the variable assignments.

The rules are meant to be used in circumstances where ∀χP and ∃χP continue to contain free variables, and so are formulas about which different variable assignments can still disagree. Consequently, the rules no longer step up to the conclusion that all variable assignments reach the same decision. They only step up to the decision of the parentless parent. (The δ not followed by a variant list.) All parentless parents do still agree about all sentences. (Below, this is referred to as the exclusivity principle.) But this is no longer a direct consequence of the quantifier rules.

Working with these rules requires proceeding in order. When applying the rules from the left side of the biconditional to the right (from formula to subformula, and parent variant to child variant), a rule may only be applied to a main operator. For example, only (∀) can be applied to ∀x∃yGxy. (∃) may not be applied as ∃y is not the main operator. (∃) may only be applied to ∀x∃yGxy after (∀) has been applied. When (∃) is applied, the consequences of its application must be entered after the consequences of the (∀) application, both on the preliminary verbal statement about domain objects and on the variant list, as follows:

(i) δ sat ∀x∃yGyx

(ii) For each o, δ[o/x] sat ∃yGyx

(iii) for each o, at least one n is such that δ[o/x,n/y] sat Gyx

As illustrated by this case, the order is the quantifier order, from quantifier with widest scope to quantifier with next widest scope, not the order in which the variables appear in the predicate. It would be wrong to invert the order of application in any way.

Given: δ sat ∀x∃yGyx

It is wrong to infer: for at least one o, δ[o/y] sat ∀xGyx. The appropriate rule
must be applied to the main operator first.

Given: for each o, δ[o/x] sat ∃yGyx

It is wrong to infer: for at least one n, each o is such that δ[o/x,n/y] sat Gyx.
"For each o" comes first.

It is also wrong to infer: for each o, at least one n is such that δ[n/y,o/x] sat Gyx.
o/x comes first.

And it is wrong to infer: for at least one n, each o is such that δ[n/y,o/x] sat Gyx.
"For each o" and o/x come first.

There is one and only one place where each newly added piece goes: to the right of the previously assembled piece. The addition to the preliminary statement ("each is such that" / "at least one is such that") goes at the end of the preliminary statement; the addition to the variant list goes at the end of the variant list. And additions are made in the order in which quantifiers occur, from the one with widest scope in.

For purposes of comparison, the correct sequence of steps when δ does not satisfy ("not sat") ∀x∃yGyx is:

(i) δ not sat ∀x∃yGyx

(ii) for at least one o, δ[o/x] not sat ∃yGyx

(iii) for at least one o, each n is such that δ[o/x,n/y] not sat Gyx

These are the specific applications mandated by the rules:

δ sat ∀χP	leads to:	For each o, δ[o/χ] sat P	by (∀)
δ not sat ∀χP	leads to:	For at least one o, δ[o/χ] not sat P	by (∀)
δ sat ∃χP	leads to:	For at least one o, δ[o/χ] sat P	by (∃)
δ not sat ∃χP	leads to:	For each o, δ[o/χ] not sat P	by (∃)

When the main operator in P is a quantifier, the inference appropriate to that quantifier and the variable it quantifies is drawn next, with the preliminary statement being added to the right of the prior statement, and the supplement to the variant list being added to the right end of the variant list. After the first step, additional preliminary statements take on a slightly different form, as follows:

δ[...] sat ∀χP	leads to:	... each o is such that δ[...o/χ] sat P	by (∀)
δ[...] not sat ∀χP	leads to:	... at least one o is such that δ[...o/χ] not sat P	by (∀)
δ[...] sat ∃χP	leads to:	... at least one o is such that δ[...o/χ] sat P	by (∃)
δ[...] not sat ∃χP	leads to:	... each o is such that δ[...o/χ] not sat P	by (∃)

As more and more quantifiers are stripped off, the new preliminary statement is added to the end of the earlier statement, and the new variant is added to the end of the earlier variant list. Additions are never made at the front or middle of either list.

When multiple items are added to a list, it may seem more elegant to use "and." But this can wrongly change the satisfaction condition. The formulation,

For each o there is at least one n such that δ[o/x,n/y] sat Gyx

stipulates that satisfaction requires a set of lists of the form,

$$\{<n_1,1>, <n_2,2>, <n_3,3>, \ldots\}$$

where $\{1, 2, 3, \ldots\}$ are each object in D and $\{n_1, n_2, n_3, \ldots\}$ are not necessarily distinct objects drawn from anywhere in D. In contrast, the formulation,

For each o and at least one n δ[o/x,n/y] sat Gyx

is ambiguous between "some n or other" and "the same n for each one," that is, between the set described above and a set of the form

$$\{<i,1>, <i,2>, <i,3>, \ldots\}.$$

"And" is permissible when both quantifiers are the same: both universal or both existential. In such cases their order does not matter. But when universal and existential quantifiers quantify the same predicate or identity sentence, the order matters and the more expansive verbal formulation is required.

Exercise 16.3

1. *State what conclusions can be drawn from each of the following by a single, left to right application of a quantifier rule.*
    ★a. δ sat ∀x~Gx
    b. δ not sat ∃x~Gx
    ★c. δ sat ∀x∃yGxy
    d. δ sat ∃y∀xGxy
    ★e. δ not sat ∀x=cx
    f. δ sat ∃z(Gz & Hcz)
    ★g. δ[1/x] not sat ∃yGxy
    h. δ[1/x] not sat ∀yGxy
    ★i. δ[1/x] sat ∀yGxy

    j. For each o, $\delta[o/x]$ sat $\exists y Gxy$

★k. For each o, $\delta[o/y]$ not sat $\exists x Gxy$

    l. For at least one o, $\delta[o/z]$ not sat $\exists x Gzx$

★m. $\delta[1/x,2/y]$ sat $\forall z Gxzy$

    n. $\delta[2/y,1/x]$ sat $\forall z Gxzy$

★o. For each o, $\delta[2/y,o/x]$ not sat $\forall z Gxzy$

    p. For each n and each o, $\delta[n/y,o/x]$ does not satisfy $\forall z Gxzy$

2. *Draw all the conclusions that can be drawn by successive left to right applications of a quantifier rule. Do not draw any conclusions that require any other form of rule application.*

    ★a. δ sat $\forall z \exists y Gyz$

    b. δ not sat $\exists z \forall x Gxz$

    ★c. δ not sat $\forall x \exists y {\sim} \exists z (Gxy \lor {\sim}Hyz)$

    d. δ not sat $\forall z \forall x (\forall y Gy \to Hxz)$

    ★e. δ sat $\exists x \forall z \forall y {\sim}(Gzx \lor \exists x_1 {\sim}Hyx_1)$

    f. δ sat $\exists x \forall y \exists z (Gxz \lor {\sim}Gyx)$

3. *Above, it was said that the formulation "For each o there is at least one n such that $\delta[o/x,n/y]$ sat Gyx," stipulates that satisfaction requires a set of lists of the form, $\{<n_1,1>, <n_2,2>, <n_3,3>, \dots\}$.*

    Why does it require lists of that form rather than the form $\{<1,n_1>, <2,n_2>, <3,n_3>, \dots\}$?

When going in the opposite direction, that is, when reasoning from satisfaction conditions for subformulas to satisfaction of quantified formulas, the variant always shrinks in the opposite order from the order in which it was generated, so from right to left.

When reasoning from satisfaction conditions for subformulas to satisfaction conditions for quantified formulas, only the last (rightmost) variant on the list may (and must) be removed (no other variant may be removed), and only the last (rightmost) verbal description may (and must) be removed from the description (the description may not be altered in any other way). The removed variant determines what variable is quantified, and the removed verbal description determines how it is quantified. The new quantifier must always be added as the main operator. It may never be placed in any other position.

For example, the correct sequence of steps for drawing an upwards inference from the claim that for at least one o each n is such that $\delta[o/y,n/x]$ does not satisfy Gxy is

    (i) for at least one o each n is such that $\delta[o/y,n/x]$ not sat Gxy
    (ii) for at least one o, $\delta[o/y]$ not sat $\exists x Gxy$
    (iii) δ not sat $\forall y \exists x Gxy$

The first inference is to $\exists x Gxy$, because n/x is the last variant on the list, which means the x variable is the one that must be quantified. The x variable is existentially quantified, because each variable assignment (for each object, n) is said not to satisfy Gxy, and the condition under which each variable assignment fails to satisfy the subformula is the condition under which an existentially quantified formula is not satisfied.

It might be objected that if all fail it is that much more obvious that the universally quantified formula could not be satisfied. But, unless there is some special reason to do otherwise, when the same evidence allows both a stronger and a weaker conclusion to be drawn, the stronger one (the one that draws on all the evidence rather than just some of it) is the one that should be drawn. If there were some special reason to infer that $\forall x Gxy$ is not satisfied, then an intermediate inference should be drawn from the fact that since any D on any I must contain at least one object, when each variant fails to satisfy Gxy at least one must, and so for that reason $\forall x Gxy$ is not satisfied.

The second inference is to $\forall y \exists x Gxy$. It is not to $\exists x \forall y Gxy$, because the added quantifier must always be added as the main operator. And it is not to $\exists y \exists x Gxy$, because the verbal description only speaks of least one object that fails to satisfy $\exists x Gxy$. When there is a single exception, the $\forall$ formula is not satisfied. Each object must fail for an $\exists$ formula not to be satisfied.

Right-left inferences are more challenging than left-right inferences because the quantifier is not given but must be inferred from the verbal description. This means it is not possible to simply look up the rule for the quantifier. It is necessary to scan both rules in both their positive and negative variants to find the description and then, having identified the correct rule that way, apply the rule. It helps to have a summary for ease of reference.

... each o is such that δ[...o/χ] sat P	leads to:	... δ[...] sat ∀χP	by (∀)
... each o is such that δ[...o/χ] not sat P	leads to:	... δ[...] not sat ∃χP	by (∃)
... at least one o is such that δ[...o/χ] sat P	leads to:	... δ[...] sat ∃χP	by (∃)
... at least one o is such that δ[...o/χ] not sat P	leads to:	... δ[...] not sat ∀χP	by (∀)

Exercise 16.4

1. *State what conclusions can be drawn from each of the following by a single application of a quantifier rule.*

   ⋆**a.** δ[1/x] sat Gx

   b. For each o, δ[o/x] sat Gx

   ⋆**c.** δ[3/x] not sat Gx

   d. For each o, δ[o/x,3/y] sat Gxy

   ⋆**e.** For each o, δ[3/y,o/x] sat Gxy

   f. For each o, δ[3/x,o/y] sat Gxy

   ⋆**g.** For at least one o, δ[o/y,2/x] not sat Gxy

   h. For at least one o, δ[2/x,o/y] not sat Gxy

   ⋆**i.** For at least one o, δ[o/y,2/x] not sat Gyx

   j. For each o, at least one n is such that δ[o/z,n/y] sat Gayz

   ⋆**k.** For each n, at least one o is such that δ[n/y,o/z] sat Gayz

   l. For at least one n, each o is such that δ[n/y,o/z] sat Gayz

   ⋆**m.** δ[3/x,3/y] sat =xy

   n. For at least one n, δ[n/x] sat =ax

   ⋆**o.** For each o, at least one n is such that δ[o/y,n/x] not sat =xy

   p. For at least one o, each n is such that δ[o/x,n/y] sat =xy

2. *State what conclusions can be drawn from each of the following by a single application of a quantifier rule. In each case, there are two conclusions to be drawn, one by a right-to-left application of a quantifier rule, and the other by a left-to-right application. Draw both.*

   ⋆**a.** δ[1/x] not sat ∃yGxy

   b. δ[1/x] not sat ∀yGxy

   ⋆**c.** δ[1/x] sat ∀yGxy

   d. For each o, δ[o/x] sat ∃yGxy

   ⋆**e.** For each o, δ[o/y] not sat ∃xGxy

   f. For at least one o, δ[o/z] not sat ∃xGzx

   ⋆**g.** δ[1/x,2/y] sat ∀zGxzy

   h. δ[2/y,1/x] sat ∀zGxzy

   ⋆**i.** For each o, δ[2/y,o/x] not sat ∀zGxzy

   j. For each n and each o, δ[n/y,o/x] not sat ∀zGxzy

   ⋆**k.** For at least one o, δ[o/z] sat Gz & ∃xHzx *(Are there two conclusions to be drawn here or just one?)*

   l. For each o, δ[o/y] sat ∃x∀z(Gz → Hxy)

3. *State whether each of the following is a legitimate inference from the quantifier rules. If it is not, say why not.*

   ⋆**a.** δ[1/x,2/y] not sat Gxy therefore δ[2/y] not sat ∀xGxy

   b. δ[1/x,2/y] not sat Gxy therefore δ[1/x] not sat ∃yGxy

   ⋆**c.** δ[1/x,2/y] not sat Gxy therefore δ[1/x] not sat ∀xGxy

   d. δ[1/x,2/y] not sat Gxy therefore δ[1/x] not sat ∀yGxy

   ⋆**e.** δ[1/x] not sat ∃yGxy therefore δ not sat ∃y∀xGxy

   f. δ[1/x,2/y] sat Gxy therefore δ[1/x] sat ∀yGxy

   ⋆**g.** δ[1/x,2/y] sat Gxy therefore δ[2/y] sat ∃xGxy

   h. δ[1/x,2/y] sat Gxy therefore δ[1/x] sat ∃xGxy

   ⋆**i.** δ[1/x,2/y] sat Gxy therefore δ[1/x] sat ∃yGxy

   j. For at least one o each n is such that δ[o/x,n/y] sat Gxy therefore for at least one o, δ[o/x] sat ∀yGxy

   ⋆**k.** For at least one o each n is such that δ[o/x,n/y] sat Gxy therefore for at least one o, δ[o/x] sat ∃yGxy

l. For at least one o each n is such that $\delta[o/x,n/y]$ not sat Gxy therefore for at least one o, $\delta[o/x]$ not sat $\forall y$Gxy

★m. For each o at least one n is such that $\delta[o/x,n/y]$ not sat Gyx therefore for each o, $\delta[o/x]$ not sat $\forall y$Gyx

n. For at least one o each n is such that $\delta[o/x,n/y]$ sat =yx therefore for at least one o, $\delta[o/x]$ sat $\forall y$=yx

---

Formulations such as "for at least one o each n is such that for at least one m and at least one o_1, $\delta[o/y,n/x,m/z,o_1/y_1]$ not sat Gxyzy$_1$" are difficult to work with and hard to grasp. They can be abbreviated by taking 1 to stand for "At least one," ★ to stand for "each," and inserting 1 and ★ into the variant list. So,

for at least one o each n is such that for at least one m and at least one o_1
$\delta[o/y,n/x,m/z]$ not sat Gxyzy$_1$

can be abbreviated as

$$\delta[1o/y,\star n/x,1m/z,1o_1/y] \text{ not sat } Gxyzy_1$$

This having been said, a balance needs to be struck between clearing away verbiage that obscures the point, and offering a formulation that is so cryptic that it lends itself to misinterpretation. As noted at the outset of this chapter, the existential quantifier has different meanings depending on whether it is preceded or followed by universal. That sense is suppressed when only the variant list is presented. In what follows, the more expansive formulation is used in simpler situations. The more abbreviated formulation is adopted as a temporary measure, for long lists.

16.3 (P) and (=) Applications

Aside from replacing references to variable assignments with references to variants, there are no changes to the statement of the satisfaction conditions for atomic formulas.

However, since (P) and (=) are now applied in contexts where δ is a variant on a variable assignment, the applications have added complexity. The following exercises develop familiarity with work in those contexts.

Exercise 16.5

1. *State what lists of objects are denoted by each of the following variants. The first three questions are answered as an example.*

   a. $\delta[3/z,1/y,2/x](y)$
      Answer: <1>
   b. $<\delta[3/z,1/y,2/x](x), \delta[3/z,1/y,2/x](y)>$
      Answer: <2,1>
   c. $<\delta[3/z,1/y,2/x](z), \delta[3/z,1/y,2/x](x), \delta[3/z,1/y,2/x](y)>$
      Answer: <3,2,1>
   d. $<\delta[3/z,1/y,2/x](z), \delta[3/z,1/y,2/x](y), \delta[3/z,1/y,2/x](x)>$
   e. $<\delta[3/z,1/y,2/x](z), \delta[3/z,1/y,2/x](z)>$
   f. $\delta[2/x,3/y,1/x](x)$

2. *State whether each of the following formulas has been satisfied by the variant, $\delta[3/z,1/y,2/x]$, for the interpretation that has D: $\{1, 2, 3, \ldots\}$ and that assigns the extension, $\{<1,2,3>, <3,4,5>, <5,6,7> \ldots\}$ to G. Give the reasoning that justifies your conclusion.*

   ★a. Gxyz
   b. Gyxz
   ★c. Gxyx
   d. Gyyy
   ★e. Gyzx
   f. Gxyy

3. *Consider the following interpretation, I:*

D: {1, 2, 3, ...}
a: 1; b: 2
G: {<1,1,1>, <1,2,3>, <3,4,5>, <5,6,7> ...}

State whether each of the following claims is correct on this interpretation. If it is not correct say why not.

★**a.** <δ[1/x,2/y,3/z](x),δ[1/x,2/y,3/z](y),δ[1/x,2/y,3/z](z)> is in α(G)

b. <δ[1/x,2/y,3/z](x),δ[1/x,2/y,3/z](z),δ[1/x,2/y,3/z](y)> is in α(G)

★**c.** <α(a),α(b),δ[3/z](z)> is in α(G)

d. <δ[1/x,1/y,1/z](x),δ[1/x,1/y,1/z](y),δ[1/x,1/y,1/z](z)> is not in α(G)

★**e.** <δ[1/x](x),δ[1/x](x),δ[1/x](x)> is not in α(G)

f. <δ[1/x,3/z](x),α(b),δ[1/x,3/z](z)> is in α(G)

4. *State what follows from each of these claims by a single application of* (P). **The exercises from (f) to (i) teach an important lesson about the difference between quantifier order in a formula and variable order in a predicate sentence.** *See the annotation to the answers.*

★**a.** δ[1/x](x) is not in α(G)

b. α(a) is in α(G)

★**c.** δ[1/x,2/y](y) is in α(G)

d. δ[1/x,2/y](x) is in α(G)

★**e.** α(c) is in α(G)

f. <δ[1/x,2/y,3/z](x),δ[1/x,2/y,3/z](y),δ[1/x,2/y,3/z](z)> is in α(G)

★**g.** <δ[1/x,2/y,3/z](x),δ[1/x,2/y,3/z](y),δ[1/x,2/y,3/z](z)> is not in α(G)

h. <δ[1/z,2/y,3/x](x),δ[1/z,2/y,3/x](y),δ[1/z,2/y,3/x](z)> is in α(G)

★**i.** <δ[1/x,2/y,3/z](y),δ[1/x,2/y,3/z](x),δ[1/x,2/y,3/z](z)> is not in α(G)

j. <α(a),δ[1/x,2/y](y),δ[1/x,2/y](x)> is in α(G)

★**k.** <δ[1/x](x),α(c),δ[1/x](x)> is in α(G)

l. <δ[1/x,3/z](x),α(b),δ[1/x,3/z](z)> is in α(G)

5. *State whether each of the following claims is false by definition. If it is not false by definition, state what conclusion follows from it by an application of* (=).

★**a.** δ[2/y,2/z](y) is δ[2/y,2/z](z)

b. δ[1/x,1/y,2/z](x) is δ[1/x,1/y,2/z](z)

★**c.** δ[1/x,1/y,2/z](x) is not δ[1/x,1/y,2/z](z)

d. α(a) is not δ[2/x](x)

★**e.** α(a) is δ[1/x,2/y,3/z](x)

f. For at least one o and at least one n, δ[o/x,n/y] satisfies =xy.

★**g.** δ[1/x,2/y] satisfies =xy.

h. δ[1/x] satisfies =ax.

★**i.** δ satisfies =ab.

j. For each o and each n, δ[o/x,n/y] satisfies =xy.

16.4 Truth Conditions for Sentences

The truth condition is the same one used by single semantics.

Definition of Truth

A sentence, P, of QPL is true on an interpretation, I, if and only if each variable assignment on I satisfies P. It is false if and only if no variable assignment on I satisfies P.

The revised (∀) and (∃) rules make this definition questionable because they no longer imply that all the variable assignments must agree with one another. They only correlate conclusions drawn by variable assignments with conclusions drawn by the variants on those assignments. This raises the question of whether a sentence might be satisfied by some variable assignments but not by others.

This question is addressed by demonstrating the exclusivity principle.

Exclusivity

If P is a sentence of QPL, then either each variable assignment on any interpretation satisfies P or none do so.

Exclusivity excludes the possibility that some variable assignments might satisfy a sentence while others do not and legitimates inferring that if one variable assignment satisfies a sentence, all do, and if one does not, none do. The principle is rigorously proven in an appendix to this chapter. Of course, the principle only holds for sentences, which contain no free variables. As the solutions to the following exercises amply demonstrate, variants, which are all variable assignments in their own right, can disagree over whether to satisfy formulas that contain free variables.

While the proof of the principle can be taken for granted in what follows, it cannot be ignored. Even the most straightforward demonstrations of truth value assignments must now appeal to it, as shown in the solutions to the following exercises.

Exercise 16.6

Determine the value of each of the following sentences on an interpretation that makes these assignments:

   D: {1,2}
   a: 1
   G: {1}; H: {2}; K: {<1,1>, <1,2>}

★**a.** ∀xKxa
   b. ∃xKxa
★**c.** ∀xKax
   d. ∃xKxx
★**e.** ∃x(Hx & ∃yKyx)
   f. ∀x∀yKyx
★**g.** ∀x∃yKxy
   h. ∃y∀xKxy
★**i.** ∀x∃yKyx
   j. ∃y∀xKyx
★**k.** ∃x(Gx → ∀yKya)
   l. ∃x(Hx → ∀yKya)
★**m.** ∀x(Hx → ∃yKya) *(This solution is particularly instructive.)*
   n. ∀x(Hx → ∀yKya)
★**o.** ∀x(Hx → ∀yKyx)
   p. ∀x(Hx → ∃yKyx)
★**q.** ∃x∀y(=xy → Kxy)
   r. ∃x∃y(=xy & Kxy)
★**s.** ∀y∃x(=xy → Kxy)
   t. ∀x∀y(Gx & =xy → ~Hy)
★**u.** ∀x(Gx ∨ Hx → ∃yKxy)
   v. ∀x∀y(Gx ≡ Kxy)

16.5 Working with the Semantics

q-invalidity, satisfiability, contingency, and nonequivalence are still demonstrated by finding interpretations and demonstrating that those interpretations make the requisite truth value assignments to the sentence or sentences under consideration. q-validity, unsatisfiability, and equivalence are still demonstrated by assuming the opposite and finding a contradiction.

Interpretations can be discovered by reasoning from the valuation rules or by systematic trees. Systematic trees are automatic procedures that define a tree model in a straightforward fashion. But systematic trees for multiply quantified sentences can quickly become unmanageably complex, and can generate infinitely extendable paths even though the givens have a finite model. Reasoning from the valuation rules can be more direct and can discover a finite model when there is one, but it is not suited to cases where more than a few constraints on an acceptable interpretation need to be reconciled. The best approach is to attempt a tree first and have recourse to the semantics should the tree become unwieldy. Either way, the interpretation that is discovered should be verified using multiple semantics. While tree model semantics is adequate to verify tree models, it is better to take the opportunity to practice working with (∀) and (∃). As discussed in chapter 15.5, this requires replacing names introduced on tree paths by (∃) and (~∀) with the objects assigned to those names by the bin method.

For example, consider how to establish that $\forall x\exists y Gxy \rightarrow \exists y\forall x Gxy$ is q-invalid. In general, exercises involving sentences that contain connectives and collections of more than one sentence place multiple constraints on an interpretation. This makes Tq the preferred method for discovering an interpretation. But this is one of those cases where a tree does not yield a clear result.

1.	$\sim(\forall x\exists y Gxy \rightarrow \exists y\forall x Gxy)\checkmark$	given
2.	$\forall x\exists y Gxy_{abc}$	1 (~→)
3.	$\sim\exists y\forall x Gxy_{abc}$	1 (~→)
4.	$\exists y Gay\checkmark$	2 (T∀)
5.	$\sim\forall x Gxa\checkmark$	3 (~∃)
6.	Gab	4 (T∃)
7.	$\sim Gca$	5 (~∀)
8.	$\exists y Gby$	2 (T∀)
9.	$\exists y Gcy$	2 (T∀)
10.	$\sim\forall x Gxb$	3 (~∃)
11.	$\sim\forall x Gxc$	3 (~∃)

...

This systematic tree commences, as it must, at stage 1. Over lines 1–3, all possible stage 1 reductions are performed. As of line 4 stage 2 must commence, and as no names have yet appeared on the tree, the (T∀) and (~∃) reductions must introduce a new name. (Whichever reduction is done first introduces the new name and the following picks up with it.) These reductions are done in order from the top of the path down over lines 4 and 5, at which point there is nothing left to do at stage 2. As there are no identity sentences on the path, work reverts to stage 1. The work that was done at stage 2 has entered new ∃ and ~∀ sentences on the path, so there is new work to be done at stage 1. This second pass through stage 1 is completed as of line 7. It introduces two new names on the path, meaning there is new work to be done at stage 2 to reduce the ∀ and ~∃ sentences at lines 2 and 3 for these new names. This work is completed from the top of the path down, taking the new names in alphanumeric order, over lines 8–11. This new work has added four stage 1 sentences to the path, creating yet more work to be done on a third pass through stage 1. Rather than do this work, the tree is abandoned at this point. Obviously, the work will add four new names to the path, requiring yet more work to be done at stage 2, this time adding eight new ∃ and ~∀ sentences, and the cycle will continue forever, with numbers of names and sentences doubling at each pass. The path will not close (though this has not been rigorously proven) and will define a tree model with an infinite domain. Describing and verifying the tree model can be anticipated to be somewhat challenging.

Rather than attempt that, it is worth considering whether reasoning from the valuation rules will discover a finite and more readily verified interpretation.

Suppose that there is an interpretation, I, on which $\forall x\exists y Gxy \rightarrow \exists y\forall x Gxy$ is false. By (def truth), each δ on I satisfies $\forall x\exists y Gxy \rightarrow \exists y\forall x Gxy$. Since ID must contain at least one object, at least one δ must satisfy $\forall x\exists y Gxy \rightarrow \exists y\forall x Gxy$. By (→), this δ satisfies $\forall x\exists y Gxy$ but does not satisfy $\exists y\forall x Gxy$. Consider what is required for δ to do the first.

1. By ($\forall$), for each object, o, in ID, $\delta[o/x]$ satisfies $\exists yGxy$. By ($\exists$), for each o there is at least one (not necessarily distinct) object, n, that is such that $\delta[o/x,n/y]$ satisfies Gxy. By (P), for each o there is at least one n such that $<\delta[o/x,n/y](x),\delta[o/x,n/y](y)>$ is in $\alpha(G)$.

    Now consider what is required for δ to do the second.

2. By ($\exists$), for each o, $\delta[o/y]$ does not satisfy $\forall xGxy$. By ($\forall$), for each o there is at least one (not necessarily distinct) n such that $\delta[o/y,n/x]$ does not satisfy Gxy. By (P), for each o there is at least one n such that $<\delta[o/y,n/x](x),\delta[o/y,n/x](y)>$ is not in $\alpha(G)$.

Before proceeding further, two things about the reasoning that has just been presented merit careful note. First, it is important to carry the reasoning right down to the bottom level with an application of (P). It is only when (P) or (=) are applied that it becomes clear what lists must be in the extension of a predicate and what names must be identified with the same object. Second, it is important to be careful about the difference between quantifier order in a formula and variable order in a predicate subformula. Under 1 the quantifier order in the formula is $<\forall x, \exists y>$ and the variable order in the predicate sentence, Gxy, is $<x,y>$. But under 2 the quantifier order in the formula is $<\exists y, \forall x>$, whereas the variable order in the predicate sentence is still $<x,y>$. Any confusion or inversion over these matters will wreck the subsequent reasoning. Condition 1 is in effect saying that each object *is in first* place in at least one ordered pair in $\alpha(G)$. Condition 2 is saying that each object *is not in second* place in at least one ordered pair in $\alpha(G)$.

To return to the topic, the reasoning so far has uncovered the two conditions that any interpretation must meet to assign an F to the sentence. It only remains to consider whether these two conditions can both be satisfied by one and the same interpretation.

The best approach is to begin with the smallest and simplest interpretation possible and compromise on this starting point only to the extent necessary to satisfy all the conditions.

The smallest and simplest interpretation would be one with only one object in its domain and nothing in $\alpha(G)$. But that clearly will not work, because the first condition requires each object in D to occur in first place in an ordered pair in $\alpha(G)$.

This suggests compromising by adding $<1,1>$ to $\alpha(G)$. This satisfies the first condition, but the second condition requires that each object *not* occur in second place in at least one ordered pair in $\alpha(G)$. That means that there must be at least one object, n, such that $<n,1>$ is not in $\alpha(G)$.

This suggests further compromising by adding a second object, 2, to D, and being careful not to put $<2,1>$ in $\alpha(G)$. That new object must also satisfy both conditions. According to the first condition, it must occur in first place in an ordered pair in $\alpha(G)$, but it has just been stipulated that $<2,1>$ cannot occur in $\alpha(G)$.

This suggests yet another compromise: add $<2,2>$ to $\alpha(G)$. Now the first condition is satisfied as regards both 1 and 2 and the second condition is satisfied as regards 1. But is it satisfied as regards 2? Yes, it is. $<1,2>$ is not in $\alpha(G)$, so 2 does not occur in second place in at least one ordered pair in $\alpha(G)$.

If this reasoning is correct, $\forall x\exists yGxy \rightarrow \exists y\forall xGxy$ should be false on the following interpretation:

D: {1,2}
G: {$<1,1>,<2,2>$}

Far from requiring an infinite domain, as the tree model suggests, a domain with just two objects should be all that is needed to craft an interpretation on which $\forall x\exists yGxy \rightarrow \exists y\forall xGxy$ is false. However, the line of reasoning leading to this result has been complex enough to merit verification.

1.	$<\delta[1/y,2/x](x),\delta[1/y,2/x](y)>$ is $<2,1>$ and $<2,1>$ is not in $\alpha(G)$	given
2.	$\delta[1/y,2/x]$ not sat Gxy	1 (P)
3.	$\delta[1/y]$ not sat $\forall xGxy$	2 ($\forall$)
4.	$<\delta[2/y,1/x](x),\delta[2/y,1/x](y)>$ is $<1,2>$ and $<1,2>$ is not in $\alpha(G)$	given
5.	$\delta[2/y,1/x]$ not sat Gxy	4 (P)
6.	$\delta[2/y]$ not sat $\forall xGxy$	5 ($\forall$)

7.	For each o, δ[o/y] not sat ∀xGxy	3,6 def D
8.	δ not sat ∃y∀xGxy	7 (∃)
9.	<δ[1/x,1/y](x),δ[1/x,1/y](y)> is <1,1> and <1,1> is in α(G)	given
10.	δ[1/x,1/y] sat Gxy	9 (P)
11.	δ[1/x] sat ∃yGxy	10 (∃)
12.	<δ[2/x,2/y](x),δ[2/x,2/y](y)> is <2,2> and <2,2> is in α(G)	given
13.	δ[2/x,2/y] sat Gxy	12 (P)
14.	δ[2/x] sat ∃yGxy	13 (∃)
15.	For each o, δ[o/x] sat ∃yGxy	11,14 def D
16.	δ sat ∀x∃yGxy	15 (∀)
17.	δ not sat ∀x∃yGxy → ∃y∀xGxy	16,8 (→)
	-------- ↓ *boilerplate (can be omitted)* ↓ ----------	
18.	No δ sat ∀x∃yGxy → ∃y∀xGxy	17 exclusivity
19.	I(∀x∃yGxy → ∃y∀xGxy) is F	18 def truth
20.	∀x∃yGxy → ∃y∀xGxy is q-invalid	20 def q-invalidity

There are four challenges that frequently arise when writing demonstrations like this one.

16.5.1 *Order of List Items*

It is important to line up the parts of variants in the right order. (Lining up the parts of variants in the right order means deciding whether to do things like state the variant as δ[__/y, __/x] or δ[__/x, __/y]. The right order is the order in which the quantifiers are nested inside one another's scope from quantifier with widest scope to quantifier with narrowest scope. The variable that goes with the widest scope quantifier should be leftmost, the one that goes with the narrowest scope quantifier rightmost. This is illustrated over lines 2–3, 5–6, 10–11, and 14–15 above. Over those lines, the variant sometimes begins δ[__/y, __/x] and other times begins δ[__/x, __/y]. Which is used depends on the quantifier order of the sentences being aimed for at lines 8 and 16 respectively. To take another example, ∀y∃x∀z(Gzxy ∨ Hyx) requires a variant of the form δ[__/y,__/x,__/z]. It is important to look ahead to the quantified formula that is supposed to result from the process and line up the parts of the variant accordingly.

There is another kind of line up to keep an eye on. It is important to line up the terms that appear on lists in the order those terms occur after higher-place predicates. The formula just mentioned, ∀y∃x∀z(Gzxy ∨ Hyx), contains two higher-place predicate subformulas, Gzxy and Hyx. The variable order in Gzxy is unrelated to the variable order in Hyx, and each of them is unrelated to the quantifier order, ∀y∃x∀z. Since Gzxy is a three-place predicate, the corresponding list is an ordered triplet, <δ[…](z),δ[…](x),δ[…](y)> that specifies the assignment to each term in the order the terms occurring after G, that is, the order z-x-y. (The ellipses points within any one of the brackets would be filled with an expression of the form [__/y,__/x,__/z], reflecting the quantifier order.) The list for Hyx would similarly be the ordered pair <δ[…](y),δ[…](x)>. Compare the ordered pairs described at lines 1, 4, 9, and 12 of the demonstration given earlier. Why does each ordered pair specify δ[…](x) first and δ[…](y) second, regardless of whether the δ itself is expanded as δ[__/y,__/x] or δ[__/x,__/y]? Because xy is the variable order in Gxy, which is the predicate sentence under consideration in each case.

When three or more quantifiers fall within one another's scope, things can get complex, but knowing what to look for makes it possible to disregard all but what is important. The "guts" of the variant list – the parts between the square brackets – never change, except by way of addition of members on the right or loss of members from the right, and in either of these cases it only grows or shrinks as the result of an application of (∀) or (∃). Where (P) is applied, the variant list can be ignored in favour of focusing on the order of the terms in the *n*-place list and in the *n*-place predicate. For example, by (P) <δ[3/y,o/x,3/z]**(z)**,δ[3/y,o/x,3/z]**(x)**, δ[3/y,o/x,3/z]**(y)**> is not in α(G) if and only if δ[3/y,o/x,3/z] not sat G**zxy**. Where (∀) or (∃) are applied, the last item on the variant list is removed or added in concert with what quantifier is removed or added, and the variable order in the predicate can be ignored. For example, by (∀) δ[3/y,o/x,**3/z**] **not sat** Gzxy if and only if δ[3/y,o/x] **not sat** ∀zGzxy.

16.5.2 Embellishing the Variant List

Variant lists must be drawn up with an eye on the conclusion. This can mean including elements in the variant list that are irrelevant to the immediate project.

An example has already been encountered in the solution to exercise 16.6m. To take another example, consider the demonstration that the formula, $\forall x \exists y (Gx \rightarrow Hyx)$, is not satisfied by the interpretation,

D: {1,2}
G: {1}; H: { }

To make this point the demonstration first identifies a variant that satisfies Gx. The proper variant is one that may seem to contain irrelevant information. Rather than proceed by observing that $\delta[1/x](x)$ is in $\alpha(G)$, the demonstration instead observes that for each o, $\delta[1/x,o/y](x)$ is in $\alpha(G)$. There is no y in Gx, yet the demonstration proceeds by asking the reader to consider all the variants made by taking each domain member in turn to stand for y.

This approach is required because the goal is to draw a conclusion about $\forall x \exists y (Gx \rightarrow Hyx)$, which does contain a y (and a y that has to be dealt with before coming to the x, because the x quantifier operates on a y quantified subformula). A demonstration that the interpretation does not satisfy $\forall x \exists y (Gx \rightarrow Hyx)$ cannot be built up from isolated inferences about its subformulas. The quantifier order of the whole formula needs to be taken into consideration at the outset. Not satisfying the $\forall$ formula requires establishing the failure of each object in turn, put for y, to satisfy the $\exists$ subformula.

The demonstration proceeds as follows:

1.	1 is in $\alpha(G)$	given
2.	For each o $\delta[1/x,o/y]$ sat Gx	1 (P)
3.	For each o $<\delta[1/x,o/y](y),\delta[1/x,o/y](x)>$ is not in $\alpha(H)$	given
4.	For each o $\delta[1/x,o/y]$ not sat Hyx	3 (P)
5.	For each o $\delta[1/x,o/y]$ not sat Gx $\rightarrow$ Hyx	2,4 ($\rightarrow$)
6.	$\delta[1/x]$ not sat $\exists y(Gx \rightarrow Hyx)$	5 ($\exists$)
7.	δ not sat $\forall x \exists y(Gx \rightarrow Hyx)$	6 ($\forall$)
8.	No δ sat $\forall x \exists y(Gx \rightarrow Hyx)$	7 exclusivity
9.	$I(\forall x \exists y(Ax \rightarrow Hyx))$ is F	8 def truth

The claim at line 2 is really inferred just from the fact that since 1 is in $\alpha(G)$, it follows by definition that $\delta[1/x](x)$ is in $\alpha(G)$ and so that $\delta[1/x]$ sat Gx. But this conclusion is embellished by saying that for each o, $\delta[1/x,o/y]$ sat Gx. The idea is that if $\delta[1/x]$ sat Gx, then any variant on it that does not overwrite the assignment it makes to x will satisfy Gx as well. The embellishment is made for the sake of line 5, which would not follow if line 2 just spoke of $\delta[1/x]$, but which does follow when line 2 is embellished to refer to $\delta[1/x,\text{each } o/y]$.

16.5.3 Describing the Model at a More Abstract Level

Just as it is sometimes necessary to include apparently irrelevant information in a variant list, so it is sometimes necessary to present what is known at a higher level of abstraction. For example, $\forall x \forall y = xy$ is true on any model with a domain that contains only one object, and so is not q-unsatisfiable. But the demonstration should not be given too concretely, by saying,

Consider an interpretation with D: {1}. On this interpretation, $\delta[1/x,1/y](x)$ is $\delta[1/x,1/y](y)$, so by (=) $\delta[1/x,1/y]$ satisfies =xy, which means that $\delta[1/x]$ satisfies $\forall y = xy$ and δ satisfies $\forall x \forall y = xy$.

This would be a false inference even though 1 is the only object in D. It is false because justifying an $\forall$ formula requires establishing that each o satisfies the subformula. The demonstration must therefore be rewritten as follows

Consider an interpretation with D: {1}. On this interpretation, for each o and each n, $\delta[o/x,n/y](x)$ is $\delta[o/x,n/y](y)$. This is because D is {1}, so each o must be 1 and each n must also be 1. So by (=) for each o and each n $\delta[o/x,n/y]$ satisfies =xy, which by ($\forall$) means that for each o $\delta[o/x]$ satisfies $\forall y = xy$ and δ satisfies $\forall x \forall y = xy$.

16.5.4 Avoiding Inversion

It sometimes happens that a portion of a formula falls outside the scope of one of the quantifiers occurring in that formula, or that one quantifier falls within the scope of another even though their variables do not occur in the same predicate or identity formula.

$$16.1 \quad \forall x(Gx \rightarrow \exists yHxy)$$
$$16.2 \quad \forall x(Gx \rightarrow \exists yHy)$$

In 16.1, Hxy falls under the scope of both the universal and the existential quantifier, but Gx falls under the scope just of the universal. In 16.2, Hy falls under the scope of an x quantifier even though it does not contain an x variable. When working down from such sentences special care needs to be taken to avoid inverting operators. Exercises in chapter 15 demonstrate that the distribution of quantifiers over connectives fails in certain cases. Most notably, universals cannot be distributed over disjunctions (exercise 15.9#2d) and conjunctions cannot be distributed over I sentences (exercise 15.9#1b). That is reason enough to avoid any comparable inversion in informal demonstration, for example, from "for each ... either ... or" to "either for each ... or for each ..." The temptation to do this anyway is particularly strong in cases like those above. Demonstrations from the supposition of the truth of 16.1 and 16.2 are straightforward up to line 3.

16.1:
1. Suppose each δ sat $\forall x(Gx \rightarrow \exists yHxy)$.
2. By ($\forall$), for each o, $\delta[o/x]$ sat $Gx \rightarrow \exists yHxy$
3. By ($\rightarrow$), for each o, $\delta[o/x]$ either not sat Gx or sat $\exists yHxy$.

16.2:
1. Suppose each δ sat $\forall x(Gx \rightarrow \exists yHy)$
2. By ($\forall$), for each o, $\delta[o/x]$ sat $Gx \rightarrow \exists yHy$
3. By ($\rightarrow$), for each o, $\delta[o/x]$ either not sat Gx or sat $\exists yHy$

Proper continuations are as follows:

16.1:
4. By ($\exists$), for each o, $\delta[o/x]$ either not sat Gx or there is at least one n such that $\delta[o/x,n/y]$ sat Hxy.
5. By (P) for each o, $\delta[o/x](x)$ is either not in $\alpha(G)$ or there is at least one n such that $<\delta[o/x,n/y](x)$, $\delta[o/x,n/y](y)>$ is in Hxy, that is, for each object, o, either o is not in $\alpha(G)$ or there is at least one n such that $<o,n>$ is in $\alpha(H)$.

16.2:
4. By ($\exists$), for each o $\delta[o/x]$ either not sat Gx or there is at least one n such that $\delta[o/x,n/y]$ sat Hy.
5. By (P), for each o, $\delta[o/x](x)$ is either not in $\alpha(G)$ or there is at least one n such that $\delta[o/x,n/y](y)$ is in $\alpha(H)$, that is, for each object, o, either o not in $\alpha(G)$ or there is at least one object, n, such that n is in $\alpha(H)$.

The continuations are driven by the project of not arbitrarily inverting the distribution. The operator order in each sentence is $\forall x$ / $\rightarrow$, which unpacks first as "for each ... if," and then as "for each ... either not ... or ..." The continuations respect this by keeping "each" in front of "either." To do anything else would presume that inverting the order preserves the meaning, and that is a point that would need to be demonstrated. Exercise 16.8#3 is particularly challenging in this regard. The solved exercises merit careful scrutiny.

Exercise 16.7

1. *Demonstrate that the following sentences are q-invalid.*
   ★a. $(\forall xGx \rightarrow \exists yHy) \rightarrow \forall x(Gx \rightarrow \exists yHy)$
    b. $\forall x\exists yGyx \rightarrow \exists y\forall xGyx$
   ★c. $\forall x(Gx \rightarrow \forall yGy)$ *(The comment on the solution is important.)*
    d. $\exists x(Gxx \& \forall yGyx) \rightarrow \forall xGxx$
   ★e. $\exists x[Gx \& \forall y(Hxy \& =yx \rightarrow Hyx)]$
    f. $\exists x\forall y(\sim=yx \rightarrow Gxy)$

2. *Demonstrate that the following sentences are q-satisfiable.*
   ⋆**a.** ~∀x∃y~=xy
    b. ∀x(Gx → ∃y~Gy)
   ⋆**c.** ∀x(∃yGy → ~Gx)
    d. ∃y∀x(Gxy → ~Gyx)
   ⋆**e.** ∃y∀x(Gyx → ~Gxy)
    f. ~(∀x∀yGxy ≡ ∀xGxx)

3. *Demonstrate that the following sentences are q-contingent.*
   ⋆**a.** ∃x∀y=yx
    b. ∀y∃x~=yx
   ⋆**c.** ∃x(Gx & ∀y(Gy → =yx))
    d. ∀x∀y∀z(=xy ∨ =xz)
   ⋆**e.** ∀x∀y(Gxy ∨ Gyx → Gxx)
    f. ∀x∀y[(Gx ≡ Gy) → =xy]

4. *Demonstrate that the following sentences are not q-equivalent.*
   ⋆**a.** ∀x∃y(Gx → Hy), ∃x∃y(Gx → Hy)
    b. ∃x∀yGxy, ∀x∀yGxy
   ⋆**c.** ∀x∃y(Gx → Hxy), ∃x∀y(Gx → Hxy)
    d. ∀x∃y(Gx → Hxy), ∃y∀x(Gy → Hyx)
   ⋆**e.** ∀x(∀yGy → Hx), ∀x∀y(Gx → Hy)
    f. ∀x∃y([~=xy & (Gxy → ~Gyx)] ∨ =xy), ∀x∃yGyx *(refer to #1e)*

5. *Demonstrate that the following sets are q-satisfiable.*
   ⋆**a.** {∃x∃y~=xy, ∀x∃y=xy}
    b. {∃x∃y~=xy, ∃xGx, ∃yGy}
   ⋆**c.** {∀x(Gx → ∃yHxy), ∃xGx, ∀x~Hxx}
    d. {∃x∃y(~=xy & Gxy), ∀x∀y(Gxy → Gyx), ∀x~Gxx}
   ⋆**e.** {∀x[Gx → ∀y(Gy & ~=yx → Hxy)], ∀x∀y(Gx → Hxy), ∀x∀yHxy}
    f. {∀x[~Gx → ∃y(Hxy & =yx)], ∀x~Gx}

6. *Demonstrate that the following demonstrations are q-invalid.*
   ⋆**a.** ∀x[Gx → ∃y(Gy & Hxy)] / ∃x[Gx & ∀y(Gy → Hxy)]
    b. ∃x∃yGxy, ∃x∃yHxy / ∃x∃y(Gxy & Hxy)
   ⋆**c.** ∀x∃y(Gxy → Hxy), ∀x∃y(Hxy → Kxy) / ∀x∃y(Gxy → Kxy)
    d. ∀x∃y(Gx → Hy), ∀x∃y(Hx → Ky) / ∀xHx → ∀xKx
   ⋆**e.** ∀x∀y∀z(Gxy & Gyz → Gxz), ∀x∃yGxy / ∃xGxx
    f. ∃x∀y(Gxy ∨ Hxy), ∃x∀y~Gxy / ∃x∀yHxy

Demonstrations of q-validity, q-unsatisfiability, q-equivalence, and q-entailment begin by supposing to the contrary that there is an interpretation that demonstrates the opposite. Any such interpretation must make certain truth value assignments to the sentence or sentences under consideration. The demonstrations appeal to the definition of truth and the valuation rules to uncover what variable assignments must satisfy or not satisfy the atomic subformulas. Those assignments must be shown to be inconsistent. As in chapter 15, the inconsistency should not take the form of a claim that the same sentence is both true and false. It should take the form of a claim that a list of objects both is and is not in the extension of a predicate, or that an object both is and is not assigned to a name (by α) or a variable (by the same δ). Finding a contradiction in the assignment of truth values is an indication that the demonstration was not done properly. Common mistakes are applying the valuation rules from right to left (subformula to formula) or applying def truth anywhere else than at the start of the demonstration. The valuation rules should only be applied from left to right (formula to subformula). When that happens a contradiction in the assignment of truth values should not be discovered. It is not that such cases are impossible. But they are only genuine when the contradiction is found in the assignment to zero-place predicates, and exercises of that sort do not provide the right sort of instruction and so have not been included here.

Exercise 16.8

1. *Demonstrate that the following sentences are q-valid.*
   ★a. ∃y∀xGxy → ∀x∃yGxy
   b. ∃y∀xGyx → ∀x∃yGyx
   ★c. ∀x∃y=yx
   d. ∃x(Gx → ∀yGy)
   ★e. ∃x(∃yGy → Gx)
   f. ∀x∀y[=xy → (Gx ≡ Gy)]

2. *Demonstrate that the following sentences are q-unsatisfiable.*
   ★a. ∃x∀y~=xy
   b. ∀x∀y~=xy
   ★c. ∀x∀y(Gxy & ~Gyx)
   d. ∀x∃y(Gy & ~Gx)
   ★e. ∃x∀yGxy & ~∀x∃yGyx
   f. ∀x∀y=xy & ∃x∃y∃z[(Gyx & (~Gxx ∨ ~Gxz)]

3. *Demonstrate that the following sentences are q-equivalent.*
   ★a. ∀x∀y(Gx → Hy), ∃xGx → ∀yHy
   b. ∀x∃y(Gx → Hy), ∃xGx → ∃yHy
   ★c. ∀x∃y(Gy → Hx), ∀xGx → ∀yHy
   d. ∃x∃y(Gx → Hy), ∀xGx → ∃yHy
   ★e. ∃x(∃yGy → Hx), ∀x(Gx → ∃yHy)
   f. ∀x∀y(Gx → Hy), ∀y∀x(Gx → Hy)

4. *Demonstrate that the following sets are q-unsatisfiable.*
   ★a. {∀x∀yGxy, ∃y~Gyy}
   b. {∀x∀y=xy, ∃xFx, ∃x~Fx}
   ★c. {∃x∀yGxy, ∀x∀y~Gxy}
   d. {∃x∃y(Gxy ∨ Gyx), ~∃x∃yGxy}
   ★e. {∃x∀y(Gy → Hxy), ∀x∀y~Hxy, ∀xGx}
   f. {∃x∃y(Gxy & ~Gyx), ∀x∀y=yx}

5. *Demonstrate that the following demonstrations are q-valid.*
   ★a. Gab & ~Gba / ∃x∃y~=xy
   b. ∃xGxx / ∃x∃yGxy
   ★c. ∀x(∃yGy → Hx), Ga / ∀xHx
   d. ∀x(Gx → ∀yHy), Ga / ∀yHy
   ★e. ∃x[Gx & ∀y(Gy → =yx)] / ∀x∀y(Gx & Gy → =xy)
   f. ∃xGxa, ∀x∀y(Gxy → Gyx) / ∃yGay

Appendix Demonstration of the Exclusivity Principle

The truth condition for sentences of QPL, *a sentence, P, is true on an interpretation, I, if and only if each variable assignment satisfies P; it is false on I if and only if no variable assignment satisfies P*, appears to ignore the possibility that some variable assignments might satisfy P while others do not.

This is not a problem for single semantics, because (S∀) and (SE) force all the variable assignments to agree about the satisfaction of sentences. But (∀) and (∃) do not directly imply that the variable assignments must agree in their assessments of sentences. They only compel a "parent" variable assignment to satisfy or not satisfy a formula depending on the verdicts its variants deliver concerning the subformula, without saying that other parents must reach the same decision. δ₁ makes an assignment to each variable. δ₂ makes a different assignment, as does each other variable assignment. If δ₁ satisfies ∀χP because for each o, δ₁[o/χ] satisfies P, why should it follow that δ₂ must likewise satisfy ∀χP?

The answer rests on an observation about how variants work. Any two variable assignments, δ₁ and δ₂, will differ from one another in the assignment they make to at least one variable. At the extreme, they could differ from one another in the assignments they make to each variable. For example, δ₁ might only assign odd numbers to variables, while δ_2 only assigns even numbers to variables. But, however δ_1 and δ_2 might differ, the variants $\delta_1[1/x]$ and $\delta_2[1/x]$ must be the same in at least one respect: both must assign 1 to x. The same holds for expanded variant lists. For example, $\delta_1[1/x,2/y,3/z]$ and $\delta_2[1/x,2/y,3/z]$ must both assign 1 to x, 2 to y, and 3 to z. They must accordingly agree with one another about any results that follow just from those variants. Notably, they must agree with one another in their verdicts about any formula, P, that contains only the variables x, y, and z. But variable assignments, however they may differ from one another in the assignments they themselves make to variables, reach decisions about the satisfaction of formulas based on what their variants say. Their own assignments have no role to play in the decision. Since all the variable assignments have variants that begin with the same list (a list, like 1/x, describing a variant on any one variable assignment is paralleled by the same list attached to a variant on any other), of course they must all agree in any conclusions drawn just from those parallel list items.

This insight serves as the basis for the following, brief demonstration of the exclusivity principle, that If P is a sentence of QPL, then either each variable assignment on any interpretation satisfies P or none do so. As noted earlier, the exclusivity principle underwrites the definition of truth, by ruling out the possibility that some variable assignments might satisfy a sentence while others do not.

1. Suppose for purposes of conditional proof that P is a sentence.
2. By definition of a sentence, P contains no free variables.
3. Trivially, each δ on any interpretation, I, makes the same assignments to all the free variables in P.
4. On any interpretation, the δ's that make the same assignments to all the free variables in a formula either each satisfies that formula, or none satisfies it. *(Lemma)*
5. Since sentences are formulas, from lines 3 and 4, either each δ on any I satisfies P or none do so.
6. From lines 1–5 by conditional proof, if P is a sentence, either each δ on any I satisfies P or none do so.

This brief demonstration rests on a more involved demonstration of the lemma at line 4. While the insight behind the lemma has been informally described above, a rigorous demonstration requires induction on the number of operators in formulas of QPL, and so presumes familiarity with section A-1.1. (Those who have not studied that material can rest assured that the main line of demonstration is conveyed by the earlier, informal account.) To abbreviate discourse, the property described by the lemma is referred to as formula exclusivity.

Formula Exclusivity

On any interpretation, either each variable assignment that makes the same assignments to the free variables in a formula, P, satisfies P or none of them does so.

Basis: Any formula, P, that contains 0 occurrences of operators is formula exclusive.
Induction: If each formula, P_k, that contains from 0 to k occurrences of operators is formula exclusive, each formula, P_{k+1}, that contains $k+1$ occurrences of operators is formula exclusive.

Conclusion: All formulas are formula exclusive.

Demonstration of the basis: Suppose that P is a formula that contains 0 occurrences of operators. Then it is either (i) a 0-place predicate sentence, (ii) a higher-place predicate sentence, or (iii) an identity sentence. According to (P), and (=), whether a variable assignment satisfies formulas of each of these types is entirely determined by the assignments made by α to the predicate letters and names in P, and by δ to the variables in P. Any variable assignment must work with the assignments made by α to the predicate letters and names. Moreover, since P contains no quantifiers, any variables there are in P are free which means that any variable assignments that make the same assignments to the free variables in P must make assignments to all the variables in P. It follows that none of the variable assignments that make the same assignments to the free variables in P can treat P differently. (There is nothing for them to disagree about.) Either each satisfies P or none of them does. By definition of formula exclusivity, P must be formula exclusive. So, if P is a formula of QPL that contains 0 occurrences of operators, P is formula exclusive.

Demonstration of the induction: Suppose all the formulas of QPL that contain from 0 to k occurrences of operators are formula exclusive. The formulas containing $k+1$ occurrences of operators are either connective compounds or quantified formulas, and the quantified formulas are either universally quantified, or existentially quantified. So, there are three cases to consider.

Case 1: Suppose P is a connective compound. Then P has one of the forms, ~Q, Q & R, Q ∨ R, Q → R, or Q ≡ R. Because ~Q, Q & R, Q ∨ R, Q → R, and Q ≡ R are supposed to contain $k+1$ occurrences of operators, Q (and R, as the case may be) must contain k or fewer operators. So, they fall under the inductive hypothesis: any variable assignments that make the same assignments to the free variables in Q (and R, as the case may be) must agree about whether Q (and R, as the case may be) is (are) satisfied. According to (~), (&), (∨), (→), and (≡), whether a variable assignment, δ, on an interpretation, I, satisfies P is entirely determined by whether it satisfies or does not satisfy Q (and R, as the case may be). It follows that, since all the variable assignments that make the same assignments to the free variables in Q (and R, as the case may be) agree about whether Q (and R as the case may be) are satisfied, all must agree about whether ~Q, Q & R, Q ∨ R, Q → R, and Q ≡ R are satisfied. It follows by definition of formula exclusivity that ~Q, Q & R, Q ∨ R, Q → R, and Q ≡ R are formula exclusive. So, if P is a connective compound, it is formula exclusive.

Case 2: Suppose P is a universally quantified formula, ∀χQ. Any variable assignment, δ, either satisfies ∀χQ or it does not.

Suppose for purposes of proof by cases that δ satisfies ∀χQ. By (∀), for each o, δ[o/χ] satisfies Q. Consider any variable assignment, δ', that makes the same assignments to the free variables in ∀χQ that δ does. Because the only variable that is free in Q but not in ∀χQ is χ, and it is being supposed that δ' makes the same assignments to all the others that δ does, it follows that, for each o, δ'[o/χ] makes the same assignments to all the free variables in Q that δ[o/χ] does. Since it is being supposed that ∀χQ contains $k+1$ occurrences of operators, Q must contain k occurrences of operators. So, it falls under the inductive hypothesis: any variable assignments that make the same assignments to the free variables in Q must agree about whether Q is satisfied. So, for each o, δ'[o/χ] must agree with δ[o/χ] and also satisfy Q. By (∀), δ' must satisfy ∀χQ. Since δ' is any variable assignment that makes the same assignments to the free variables in ∀χQ that δ does, all the variable assignments that make the same assignments to the free variables in ∀χQ must satisfy ∀χQ, that is, all must agree about whether ∀χQ is satisfied.

Now suppose for further purposes of proof by cases that δ does not satisfy ∀χQ. By (∀), at least one o is such that δ[o/χ] does not satisfy Q. Consider any variable assignment, δ', that makes the same assignments to the free variables in ∀χQ that δ does. Because the only variable that is free in Q but not in ∀χQ is χ, and it is being supposed that δ' makes the same assignments to all the others that δ does, it follows that δ'[o/χ] makes the same assignments to all the free variables in Q that δ[o/χ] does. Since it is being supposed that ∀χQ contains $k+1$ occurrences of operators, Q must contain k occurrences of operators. So, it falls under the inductive hypothesis: any variable assignments that make the same assignments to the free variables in Q must agree about whether Q is satisfied. So, δ'[o/χ] must agree with δ[o/χ] that Q is not satisfied. By (∀), δ' does not satisfy ∀χQ. Since δ' is any variable assignment that makes the same assignments to the free variables in ∀χQ that δ does, none of the variable assignments that make the same assignments to the free variables in ∀χQ can satisfy ∀χQ, that is, all must agree about whether ∀χQ is satisfied.

Either way, therefore, if P is a universally quantified sentence, ∀χQ, all the variable assignments that make the same assignments to the free variables in ∀χQ must agree about whether ∀χQ is satisfied.

It follows by definition of formula exclusivity that ∀χQ is formula exclusive. So, if P is a universally quantified formula, it is formula exclusive.

Case 3: P is an existentially quantified formula. The proof of this case resembles that of case 2, with appropriate modifications, and is left as an exercise.

To sum up, regardless of which case is considered, P must be formula exclusive. So if each formula containing from 0 to k occurrences of operators is formula exclusive, each formula containing $k+1$ occurrences of operators is formula exclusive as well.

A-6

Advanced Topics for QPL

A-6.1 Extensionality and Variance

QPL requires an additional extensionality principle for variables, and supplements to the existing demonstrations of name extensionality and sentence extensionality (now called formula extensionality).

The notion of variance was introduced in chapter A-5. QPL works with an updated version of the variant interpretation principle. No updates are required to the demonstration of the variant name principle.

A-6.1.1 Name Extensionality

> **Name Extensionality**
>
> If $I\alpha(q)$ is $I\alpha(r)$, then **any variable assignment, δ, on** I **satisfies** P if and only if it **satisfies** $P(r \mid q)$.

The demonstration of n-extensionality runs as it did before, except that it is based on the number of occurrences of operators in formulas of lean QPL rather than the number of occurrences of connectives in sentences. The lean language for QPL adds ∀ and variables to the vocabulary for lean PSL. ∃ sentences are defined in terms of →, ⊥ and ∀. Though the demonstration of name extensionality mentions formulas rather than sentences, it still concerns the substitution of names for other names. Any variables occurring in formulas, including any free variables, are left untouched. Because the denotation of names is determined by α, there are no substantive changes required to

DOI: 10.4324/9781003026532-26

the demonstration beyond the occasional remark that no δ on I can alter the assignments made to names by Iα. The demonstration does require an addition. Because the lean language for QPL adds the universal quantifier and variables to the vocabulary, the formulas that contain $k+1$ occurrences of operators are of either the form P → Q or the form ∀χP. The demonstration of the inductive step is expanded to cover the second case.

Case two: P is of the form ∀χQ. Then for any variable assignment, δ on any interpretation, I, where α(p) is α(r) the following chain of consequences holds in both directions:

1. δ satisfies ∀χQ.
2. For each o, δ[o/χ] satisfies Q.
3. For each o, δ[o/χ] satisfies Q(r|p).
4. δ satisfies ∀χQ(r|p).

1 is the case if and only if 2 is by (∀).
2 is the case if and only if 3 is because Q must contain k occurrences of operators. So, by the inductive hypothesis it is name extensional.
3 is the case if an only if 4 is by (∀).

To sum up, if α(p) is α(r) then δ satisfies ∀χQ if and only it satisfies ∀χQ(r|p). In other words, P must be n-extensional in this case.

A-6.1.2 Variable Extensionality

A preliminary version of variable extensionality was discussed in chapter 15.6, where it was justified by appeal to intuition and used to demonstrate entailment principles that figure in demonstrating the soundness of the derivation and tree rules. That discussion is presupposed here and should be reviewed before proceeding further.

The preliminary version given in section 15.6 is updated as follows for conformity with the semantics of chapter 16.

Variable Extensionality

If P is an open sentence containing at least one free occurrence of a variable, χ, then δ[...,α(q)/χ] satisfies P if and only if δ[...] satisfies P(q|χ).

---

v-extensionality is demonstrated by mathematical induction on the open sentences of lean QPL grouped by the number of occurrences of operators in those open sentences. The first group contains all the open sentences with zero occurrences of operators (the atomic open sentences). The second group contains all the open sentences with one operator, e.g., ~Gz, ∀xHzx, and =ax & Gy. The third group contains all the open sentences with two occurrences of operators, e.g., ~~Hzx, ~Gy ∨ Hc. And so on.

> *Basis:* All the open sentences of QPL with 0 occurrences of operators are v-extensional.
> *Induction:* If all the open sentences of QPL with from 0 to k occurrences of operators are v-extensional, all the open sentences with $k+1$ occurrences of operators are v-extensional.
>
> ---
> *Conclusion:* All the open sentences of PL are v-extensional.

Demonstration of the basis: Consider any open sentence, P, of QPL with 0 occurrences of operators and at least one free occurrence of χ. P might be a higher-place predicate formula or an identity formula. So there are two cases to consider.

Case one: If P is a higher-place predicate formula, then it has the form, $Rt_1...t_n$, where as few as one and as many as all of $t_1,...,t_n$, are χ. Correspondingly, P(q|χ) has the form, $Rt_1...t_n(q|χ)$, which is to say that it is just like $Rt_1...t_n$ except for having q wherever χ occurs in $Rt_1...t_n$. Then the following chain of consequences holds in both directions (i.e., from 1 to 4 and from 4 to 1, establishing that 1 is the case if and only if 4 is the case):

1. $\delta[...,\alpha(q)/\chi]$ satisfies $Rt_1...t_n$.
2. $<\alpha/\delta[...,\alpha(q)/\chi](t_1), ..., \alpha/\delta[...,\alpha(q)/\chi](t_n)>$ is in $\alpha(R)$.
3. $<\alpha/\delta[...](t_1),...,\alpha/\delta[...](t_n)>(q|\chi)$ is in $\alpha(R)$.
4. $\delta[...]$ satisfies $Rt_1...t_n(q|\chi)$.

For example, suppose $Rt_1...t_n$ is Gaxy, χ is x, and q is "a." Then:

- $\delta[..., \alpha(q)/\chi]$ is $\delta[o/y, \alpha(a)/x]$, where o is some object in ID not necessarily distinct from $\alpha(a)$
- $<\alpha/\delta[...,\alpha(q)/\chi](t_1), ..., \alpha/\delta[...,\alpha(q)/\chi](t_n)>$ is $<\alpha(a), \delta[o/y,\alpha(a)/x](x), \delta[o/y, \alpha(a)/x](y)>$
- $<\alpha/\delta[...](t_1),...,\alpha/\delta[...](t_n)>(q|\chi)$ is $<\alpha(a), \alpha(a), \delta[o/y](y)>$
- The chain of consequences is:
  1. $\delta[o/y, \alpha(a)/x]$ satisfies Gaxy.
  2. $<\alpha(a), \delta[o/y,\alpha(a)/x](x), \delta[o/y,\alpha(a)/x](y)>$ is in $\alpha(G)$.
  3. $<\alpha(a), \alpha(a), \delta[o/y](y)>$ is in $\alpha(G)$.
  4. $\delta[o/y]$ satisfies Gaay.

   1 is the case if and only if 2 is by (P).
   2 is the case if and only if 3 is, because each t_i among $t_1...t_n$ is either χ or it is not.
   If t_i is not χ, then since $\alpha/\delta[...\alpha(q)/\chi]$ and $\delta[...]$ only differ from one another over the assignment $\delta[...\alpha(q)/\chi]$ makes to χ, $\alpha/\delta[...\alpha(q)/\chi](ti)$ is the same obect as $\alpha/\delta[...](t_i)$. To revert to the example given above, when t_i is a name, such as "a," its denotation is assigned by α, not by either by $\delta[...\alpha(q)/x]$ or $\delta[...]$, and when t_i is a variable other than x, such as y, $\delta[o/y,\alpha(a)/x](y)$ is $\delta[o/y](y)$ (both are o).
   On the other hand, if t_i is χ, then, because all occurrences of χ in $Rt_1...t_n(q|\chi)$ are overwritten by q, $\alpha/\delta[...\alpha(q)/\chi](t_i)$ is $\alpha/\delta[...](t_i)$. (To explain further, by definition, the assignment made by $\alpha/\delta[...\alpha(q)/\chi]$ to t_i [which is χ] is the object α assigns to q, and the assignment made by $\alpha/\delta[...](t_i)$ to t_i [which is q] must be the object α assigns to q since no δ can alter assignments made by any α.) To revert again to the example, $\delta[o/y,\alpha(a)/x](x)$ is by definition $\alpha(a)$, and, supposing all occurrences of x in G are replaced with occurrences of "a," $\delta[o/y](a)$ is also $\alpha(a)$, since no δ can change the assignments α makes to names.
   So, $<\alpha/\delta[...,\alpha(q)/\chi](t_1), ..., \alpha/\delta[...,\alpha(q)/\chi](t_n)>$ must denote the same list of objects as $<\alpha/\delta[...](t_1), ..., \alpha/\delta[...](t_n)>(q|\chi)$. If the one denotes a list of objects in $\alpha(G)$, the other must as well.
   3 is the case if and only if 4 is the case by (P).

So, $\delta[..., \alpha(q)/\chi]$ satisfies $Rt_1...t_n$ if and only if $\delta[...]$ satisfies $Rt_1...t_n(q|\chi)$, that is, P is v-extensional in this case.

Exercise A-6.1

Demonstrate case two: $\delta[..., \alpha(q)/\chi]$ satisfies $=t_1t_2$ if and only if $\delta[...]$ satisfies $=t_1t_2(q|\chi)$. The demonstration is so closely patterned on the one just given that the opening and closing sections need not be rewritten. It suffices to rewrite 2 and 3 in the chain of consequences for the = case, and explain why 2 is the case if and only if 3 is the case in the corresponding chain of consequences. Appeal to an example is not required, but may help to clarify the point of the demonstration.

Demonstration of the induction: The demonstration of the induction begins by assuming the inductive hypothesis: Suppose for purposes of conditional proof that all the open sentences of lean QPL with from 0 to k occurrences of operators are v-extensional. Any open sentence, P, with $k+1$ occurrences of operators must contain at least one operator and so must have either the form $Q \rightarrow R$ or the form $\forall\psi R$.

Case one: P is of the form $P_1 \rightarrow P_2$ where at least one of P_1 and P_2 contains at least one free occurrence of χ.
   Then the following chain of consequences holds in both directions (i.e., from 1 to 4 and from 4 to 1):

1. $\delta[..., \alpha(q)/\chi]$ sat $P_1 \rightarrow P_2$.
2. $\delta[..., \alpha(q)/\chi]$ either not sat P_1 or sat P_2.
3. $\delta[...]$ either not sat $P_1(q|\chi)$ or sat $P_2(q|\chi)$.
4. $\delta[...]$ sat $(P_1 \rightarrow P_2)(q|\chi)$.

1   is the case if and only if 2 is, by ($\rightarrow$).
2   is the case if and only if 3 is, because each of P_1 and P_2 must contain k or fewer occurrences of operators, so that the sum of the occurrences of operators in both is exactly k, and by the inductive hypothesis that means they must be v-extensional.
3   is the case if and only if 4 is the case, by ($\rightarrow$).

So, $\delta[\alpha(q)/\chi]$ satisfies $P_1 \rightarrow P_2$ if and only if δ satisfies $(P_1 \rightarrow P_2)(q \mid \chi)$. In other words, P must be v-extensional in this case.

Whereas case one is readily demonstrated by appeal to the inductive hypothesis, case two is not. It involves a kind of "leap-frogging" over the variant list that needs its own justification.

Case two: P is of the form $\forall\psi R$, where R contains at least one free occurrence of χ. Then the following chain of consequences holds in both directions:

1. $\delta[\dots, \alpha(q)/\chi]$ satisfies $\forall\psi R$.
2. For each o, $\delta[\dots, \alpha(q)/\chi, o/\psi]$ satisfies R.
3. For each o $\delta[\dots, o/\psi]$ satisfies $R(q \mid \chi)$.
4. $\delta[\dots]$ satisfies $\forall\psi R(q \mid \chi)$.

1 is the case if and only if 2 is by ($\forall$).
2 is the case if and only if 3 is because the only difference between $\delta[\dots, \alpha(q)/\chi, o/\psi]$ and $\delta[\dots, o/\psi]$ (if any) is in the assignment $\delta[\dots, \alpha(q)/\chi, o/\psi]$ makes to χ. That difference is erased where R and $R(q \mid \chi)$ are concerned because:

   (i) $\alpha(q)/\chi$ is the second last record on the variant list in $\delta[\dots, \alpha(q)/\chi, o/\psi]$, and the last record, o/ψ, does nothing to change this assignment to χ (even if $\alpha(q)$ is o, the record, o/ψ, only assigns o to ψ; it does not overwrite any assignment previously made to χ); it follows that all the occurrences of χ in R denote $\alpha(q)$ on $\delta[\dots, \alpha(q)/\chi, o/\psi]$

   (ii)   all the occurrences of χ in $R(q \mid \chi)$ have been overwritten by q, which denotes the same object on $\delta[\dots, o/\psi]$ that χ does on $\delta[\dots, \alpha(q)/\chi, o/\psi]$, because no δ can alter the assignment α makes to q.

It follows that the object that $\delta[\dots, \alpha(q)/\chi, o/\psi]$ assigns to χ in R is the same object that α assigns to the term that replaces each occurrence of χ in $R(q \mid \chi)$ (and so is an assignment that $\delta[\dots, o/\psi]$ cannot alter). Since these two variants do not differ in any other assignment, the former can satisfy R if and only if the latter satisfies $R(q \mid \chi)$.

3 is the case if and only if 4 is by ($\forall$).

So, $\delta[\alpha(q)/\chi]$ satisfies $\forall\psi R$ if and only if δ satisfies $\forall\psi R(q \mid \chi)$. In other words, P must be v-extensional in this case.

Since all the cases identified earlier lead to the same consequence, that consequence follows by proof by cases: any open sentence with $k+1$ occurrences of operators is v-extensional.

And since this consequence follows under the initial supposition of the inductive hypothesis, it further follows that this consequence can be affirmed provided that hypothesis is accepted: if all the open sentences of QPL containing from 0 to k occurrences of operators are v-extensional, all the open sentences containing $k+1$ occurrences of operators must be v-extensional.

A-6.1.3 *Formula Extensionality*

Formula extensionality is a minor expansion on the demonstration of sentence extensionality originally given in section A-1.4. But since quantified formulas of QPL do not have components, the entire demonstration needs to be rewritten in new terms. To abbreviate work, the demonstration is offered just for formulas of lean QPL.

Formula Extensionality

A **formula**, P, is extensional if and only if, if Q is a **subformula** of P and δ **satisfies Q if and only if it satisfies R** then δ **satisfies** P **if and only if it satisfies** $P(R \mid Q)$.

The demonstration of f-extensionality is based on mathematical induction on the number of operators in formulas of lean QPL; references to sentences are replaced with references to formulas; references to truth on interpretations are replaced with references to satisfaction by variable assignments; references to having the same value on an interpretation are replaced by references to biconditional satisfaction by a variable assignment, and the demonstration is expanded to include quantified formulas.

In what follows consider P to be a formula of lean QPL that contains one or more occurrences of some subformula, Q, and consider P(R | Q) to refer to the formula that results from taking P and replacing one or more of the occurrences of Q in P with occurrences of R.

Basis: All formulas of lean QPL with 0 occurrences of operators are f-extensional.
Induction: If all formulas of lean QPL with from 0 to k occurrences of operators
    are f-extensional, then all formulas with $k+1$ occurrences of operators are
    f-extensional.

Conclusion: All the formulas of lean QPL are f-extensional.

Demonstration of the basis:

1. Suppose for purposes of conditional proof that P has 0 occurrences of operators.
2. Suppose for purposes of a further conditional proof that any variable assignment, δ, satisfies Q if and only if it satisfies R.
3. From line 1, P can have no subformulas other than itself, so P must be the same as Q.
4. The result, P(R | Q), of putting R in the place of any occurrence of Q in P must therefore be the result of replacing P with R, so P(R | Q) is R.
5. From lines 3 (P is Q), 4 (P(R | Q) is R) and 2 (δ satisfies Q if and only if it satisfies R), δ satisfies P if and only if it satisfies P(R | Q).
6. From lines 2–5 by conditional proof, if δ satisfies Q if and only if it satisfies R then δ satisfies P if and only if it satisfies P(R | Q), that is, P is extensional.
7. From lines 1–6 by conditional proof, if P has 0 occurrences of operators, then it is extensional.

Demonstration of the induction: In demonstrating the induction there are two cases to consider: Since every formula is a subformula of itself, Q may just be P, or Q may be a "proper" subformula of P (a subformula other than P itself). In the first of these cases, P must be f-extensional for the reason given when demonstrating the basis (since Q is P, P(R | Q) is the same as R).

The demonstration of the remaining case begins by assuming the inductive hypothesis: Suppose for purposes of conditional proof that all the formulas with from 0 to k occurrences of operators are f-extensional. Any formula, P, with $k+1$ occurrences of operators, must contain at least one operator and so must be a sentence of either the form $P_1 \rightarrow P_2$ or the form $\forall \chi P_1$.

Case one: P is of the form $P_1 \rightarrow P_2$. Since $P_1 \rightarrow P_2$ contains $k+1$ operators, each of P_1 and P_2 must contain k or fewer operators, so that the sum of operators in both is k. So each of them falls under the inductive hypothesis: it is f-extensional. Suppose for purposes of conditional proof that any variable assignment, δ, satisfies Q if and only if it satisfies R. Then, regardless of whether R is put for Q in P_1, P_2, or both, or whether Q is a proper component of P_1 or P_2 or one or other of P_1 or P_2, δ satisfies P_1 if and only if it satisfies $P_1(R|Q)$, and δ satisfies P_2 if and only if it satisfies $P_2(R|Q)$. Since the satisfaction of a conditional is a function of the satisfaction of its subformulas, δ satisfies $P_1 \rightarrow P_2$ if and only if it satisfies $(P_1 \rightarrow P_2)(R|Q)$. It follows by conditional proof that if δ satisfies Q if and only if it satisfies R then it satisfies $P_1 \rightarrow P_2$ if and only if it satisfies $(P_1 \rightarrow P_2)(R|Q)$, that is, $P_1 \rightarrow P_2$ is f-extensional.

Case two: P is of the form $\forall \chi P_1$. By ($\forall$), (1) δ satisfies $\forall \chi P_1$ if and only if, for each o, $\delta[o/\chi]$ satisfies P_1. By supposition, $\forall \chi P_1$ has $k+1$ operators, so P_1 has k operators and so falls under the inductive hypothesis: it is f-extensional. Suppose for purposes of conditional proof that any variable assignment, δ, satisfies Q if and only if it satisfies R. Then, regardless of whether Q is a proper component of P_1 or is P_1, (2) for each o, $\delta[o/\chi]$ sat P_1 if and only if it sat $P_1(R|Q)$. By ($\forall$) again, (3) for each o, $\delta[o/\chi]$ sat $P_1(R|Q)$ if and only if δ sat $\forall \chi P_1(R|Q)$. From (1)–(3) by biconditional proof, δ satisfies $\forall \chi P_1$ if and only if it satisfies $\forall \chi P_1(R|Q)$. It follows by conditional proof that if δ satisfies Q if and only if it satisfies R then it satisfies $\forall \chi P_1$ if and only if it satisfies $\forall \chi P_1(R|Q)$, that is, $\forall \chi P_1$ is f-extensional.

Since all cases lead to the same consequence, that consequence follows by proof by cases: any formula of lean QPL containing $k+1$ occurrences of operators is f-extensional.

And since this consequence follows under the initial supposition of the inductive hypothesis, it further follows by conditional proof that if all the formulas of lean QPL containing from 0 to k occurrences of operators are f-extensional, all the formulas containing $k+1$ occurrences of operators are f-extensional.

A-6.1.4 Variance

PSL introduces two principles that deal with variant interpretations: the variant interpretation principle, and the variant name principle. The variant interpretation principle needs to be updated. According to the original variant interpretation principle, a sentence, P, is true on an interpretation if and only if it is true on every variant on that interpretation, where a variant is an interpretation that has the same domain and that makes all the same assignments to the names and predicates in P as the interpretation on which it varies.

That principle is now a corollary of a basic version.

(Base) Variant Interpretation Principle

A **formula**, P, is satisfied by **each variable assignment, δ, on** an interpretation, I, if and only if δ **satisfies** P on any variant, J, on I.

This principle is established by the consideration that, as variant interpretations, I and J have the same domain. Any variable assignment on the one must therefore be a variable assignment on the other, since the same objects are available to be assigned to the same variables. As variants, I and J also make the same assignments to all the names and predicates in P. So there is nothing for them to disagree about. A formula is satisfied as a consequence of the assignments made to the terms and predicates that occur in that formula. Where two interpretations make the same assignments to the names and predicates, the variable assignments on those interpretations cannot disagree over whether to satisfy the formula.

The corollary version is a special case of the base version, one where there are no free variables in the formula. It follows from the base version by appeal to def. truth.

(Corollary) Variant Interpretation Principle

A sentence, P, is true on an interpretation, I if and only if it is true on any variant on I.

A-6.2 Soundness of Dq

If $L \vdash_q P$ then $\Gamma_L \vDash_q P$
where Γ_L is the set of sentences on L.

Like Dp, Dq is shown to be sound by establishing that any derivation in bracket free notation begins with a sequent that is sound and proceeds to derive other sequents in accord with rules that preserve soundness. (Paralleling what was said in sections A-2.1 and A-5.2, to say that a sequent, $L \vdash P$, "is sound" means that Γ_L, the set of sentences on L, q-entails P.) This makes it possible to argue by mathematical induction on the lines of a derivation that the sequent occurring on any line of any derivation in Dq must be sound. Notably the sequent occurring on the last line of any derivation, $L \vdash P$, must be sound. That is, $\Gamma_L \vDash_q P$.

The soundness demonstration found in chapter A-5.2 serves here as well. It only needs to be modified by replacing Dp with Dq and $\vDash_p$ with $\vDash_q$. The demonstration appeals to two lemmas, the first being the basis and the second the induction for the conclusion that soundness must carry down to the last line of a derivation. No changes are needed to the demonstration of lemma 1 as found in chapter A-5.2.

The demonstrations of lemma 2 that were given in sections A-2.1 and A-5.2 need to be supplemented with four further cases, covering the quantifier rules. These cases appeal to the entailment principles established in the solutions to exercise 15.12a–b and e–f.

Case fifteen: The sequent on line $k+1$ is derived by ($\forall$E). Then it must have the form $L_{k+1} \vdash Q(r\,|\,\chi)$, and the earlier lines 1 to k must include a line, h, of the form $L_{k+1} \vdash \forall\chi Q$ (otherwise ($\forall$E) could not be applied, as it requires that the list at lines h and $k+1$ be the same). Because line h is prior to line $k+1$ it follows from the inductive hypothesis that $\Gamma_{k+1} \vDash \forall\chi Q$. By the solution to exercise 15.12(a), $\Gamma_{k+1} \vDash Q(r\,|\,\chi)$. So, the sequent on line $k+1$ is sound in this case.

Case sixteen: The sequent on line $k+1$ is derived by ($\exists$E). Then line $k+1$ must have the form $L_{k+1} \vdash R$ and the earlier lines 1 to k must include a line, i, of the form $L_{k+1} \vdash \exists\chi Q$, and a line h of the form $L_{k+1}, Q(p\,|\,\chi) \vdash R$ (otherwise, ($\exists$E) could not be applied, as it requires that the list at each of lines i and $k+1$ be the same and that line h use this list with the single addition of $Q(p\,|\,\chi)$.) Moreover, p may not occur in any sentence on L_{k+1}, in $\exists\chi Q$, or in R. Because lines i and h are prior to line $k+1$, it follows from the inductive hypothesis that $\Gamma_{k+1} \vDash \exists\chi Q$, and $\Gamma_{k+1} \cup Q(p\,|\,\chi) \vDash R$. Under these conditions, by the solution to exercise 15.12f, $\Gamma_{k+1} \vDash R$. So, the sequent on line $k+1$ is sound in this case.

Exercise A-6.2

Prove the cases for ($\forall$G) *and* ($\exists$G).

A-6.3 Completeness of Tq

> If Γ is **q**-unsatisfiable, it has at least one closed **q**-tree.

As noted in chapter 14, Tq is undecidable: in some cases it will not yield either a closed tree or a tree with an exhausted path after any finite number of one-step extensions. Nonetheless, it remains complete. If Γ is q-unsatisfiable, any tree for Γ will close after a finite number of one-step extensions. That closed tree may be so large that it may exhaust all resources before it is found, but it must exist.

The completeness of Tq is demonstrated by making the following modifications to the demonstration of the completeness of Tp found in section A-5.3.

- Since the demonstration begins by supposing for purposes of contraposition that Γ does not have a closed tree, the canonical method for generating trees for Γ is systematic, and reflects the three-stage system for applying reduction rules (see section 14.2).
- As a consequence of these changes, the features exhibited by θ are expanded from the five used to prove completeness of Tp to six for completeness of Tq.
- Two more clauses must be added to the demonstration of the inductive step, dealing with $\forall$ sentences and their negations.

As in chapter A-5.3, the demonstration is given for the lean language for QPL. On lean q-trees ($\sim\forall$) is replaced by ($\forall\bot$), which reduces sentences of the form $\forall\chi P \rightarrow \bot$ to sentences of the form $P(q\,|\,\chi) \rightarrow \bot$, where q is a name that is new to the path.

Exercise A-6.3

Define $\exists\chi P$ *in terms of a q-equivalent sentence using only* $\rightarrow$, $\bot$, $\forall$, χ, *and* P.

For lean QPL the canonical method for generating one-step extensions of trees is:

- T_1 consists of the sentence with the lowest catalogue number of all the sentences in Γ. Catalogue numbers are determined by assigning numerals to vocabulary elements as follows:

Symbol	Numeral	Symbol	Numeral	Symbol	Numeral	Symbol	Numeral
$\bot$	10	0	20	A	30	a	40
$\rightarrow$	11	1	21	B	31	b	41
(	12	.	.	C	32	c	42
)	13	.	.			**x**	**43**

□	14	•	•		y	44
=	15	9	29		z	45
∀	**16**					

(No one needs to know which sentence in Γ has the lowest catalogue number. There must be one, and whichever one it is, it is T_1. These are not instructions for generating the canonical series of trees. They are a definition of that series.)

- Each subsequent tree in the series is a one-step extension of the previous one produced by applying rules of **Tq** to sentences by repeatedly cycling through four successive stages. All work that can be done at a stage must be done before proceeding to the next stage. When all work at one stage has been exhausted, the next stage in order is taken up. When no work can be done at a stage, work proceeds to the next stage. Stages must be cycled through in order (from first to last and then back to first). It is not permissible to skip a stage if there is work to be done at that stage or to revert to do work at an earlier stage except by way of making a cycle through the stages.
- At stage 1, all possible applications of (MP), (∼→), (∀⊥), and (T→) are made to sentences taken in the order they occur from the top of the tree down and including sentences resulting from work at this stage when their turn comes up. When different sentences occur on different paths on the same line they are reduced simultaneously even if this means using multiple rules. Stage 1 must be completed before proceeding to stage 2.
- At stage 2, all possible applications of (T∀) are made to sentences taken in the order they occur from the top of the tree down, and including ∀ sentences created as a result of work at this stage when their turn comes up. Each ∀ sentence is reduced repeatedly for each name that has appeared on the path where its reduction results are entered, or once for "a" if no names have yet appeared. Stage 2 must be completed before proceeding to stage 3.
- At stage 3, all possible applications of (=E) are made to sentences taken in the order they occur from the top of the tree down, including = sentences created as a result of work at this stage when their turn comes up. This means going down the tree to the first identity sentence and applying that identity sentence as source to each literal to occur on each path that runs through that identity sentence's location, taking those literals in the order they occur from the top of the path down, including literals generated as a result of work at this stage when their turn comes up and applying (=E) just once to each literal to replace all occurrences of the target name in that literal. After this has been done using the topmost identity sentence as source, the process is repeated using the identity sentence next to the top, and this continues until each identity sentence on the tree has been used as source including identity sentences added to the bottom of paths as a consequence of work at this stage. Stage 3 must be completed before proceeding to stage 4.
- At stage 4, the sentence in Γ with the next lowest catalogue number is placed on the top of the tree. The sequence of stages then recommences. Cycling through the stages continues for as long as there are sentences in Γ to be added, and after that for as long as doing so continues to produce changes on at least one open path. Work stops if the tree closes or a complete cycle through the stages produces no changes on at least one open path. In the last of these cases the path is exhausted.

If none of the trees, $T_1, T_2, T_3, \ldots$ for a set, Γ, of sentences produced by following the canonical method is closed, then each tree for Γ must contain at least one path, θ, that has **six** features:

Features of θ

(a) ⊥ does not stand alone on any line on θ.

(b) No sentence of the form =pp → ⊥ occurs on θ.

(c) For each nonliteral, **non-∀** sentence on θ, at least one of the up to two paths of reduction results for that sentence appears on θ in at least one of the subsequent trees in the series.

(d) **For each sentence of the form ∀χP on θ, and each name, q, to occur in any sentence anywhere on θ in any subsequent tree in the series, or for "a" if no such name occurs, P(q|χ) (or P(a|χ) as the case may be) appears on θ in at least one of the subsequent trees in the series.**

(e) For each sentence of the form =rq on θ and each literal, P (or P → ⊥, where P is atomic), to occur anywhere on θ, the sentence P(r|q) that can be obtained from P (or P → ⊥) by replacing all occurrences of q in P with occurrences of r (including sentences of the form =rr), is on θ in at least one of the subsequent trees in the series.

(f) Each sentence in Γ occurs on θ in at least one of the trees in the series.

Demonstrating that θ has these features requires amending the case made for this result in section A-5.3 by showing that the application of the additional rules, (T$\forall$) and ($\forall\perp$), is always a finite process, and that they do nothing to prevent work at the stage at which they are applied from coming to an end. ($\forall\perp$) is a stage 1 reduction rule applied to conditionals of the form $\forall\chi P \rightarrow \perp$. The reasons already given in section A-5.3 for why the application of the other stage 1 reduction rules is a finite process apply to it as well without any need for further comment. Though ($\forall\perp$) introduces new names to the path, its doing so does nothing to increase or alter the work involved with other stage 1 reductions, including later applications of ($\forall\perp$), so the reasons given in section A-5.3 for why work at stage 1 must terminate also continue to apply without any need for further comment. The addition of new names does increase the amount of work to be done at stages 2 and 3, but on any pass through stage 1, only finitely many new names are added, creating only a finite amount of work for the upcoming passes through stages 2 and 3. The reasons why work at stage 3 (called stage 2 in section A-5.3) must terminate continue to hold. The reasons why work at what is now called stage 2 must terminate are considered below.

The new stage 2 of the canonical method is devoted to (T$\forall$) applications and is bound up with the new feature (d) of θ. Establishing (i) that reducing any one $\forall$ sentence is a finite process and (ii) that there is only a finite amount of work to be done on each cycle through stage 2 also establishes that θ must have feature (d). There are no further additions required to the reasons already given in section A-5.3 for concluding that θ must have the remaining features.

(i)   Unlike other nonliterals, $\forall$ sentences are reduced more than once, but, on any one pass through stage 2, the reduction of any one $\forall$ sentence is a finite process. Any pass through stage 2 begins at some finite point (that is, on some finite line number). Because any tree starts with a single path and the number of paths is only ever increased by some finite number by any one-step extension, there can only be finitely many paths with finitely many sentences on them at any finite point. Because sentences of QPL are only finitely long (the demonstration of this result in chapter A-1.1 is readily updated for lean QPL) there can only be finitely many names on the tree. Since each $\forall$ sentence is reduced only once for each name to appear on a path that runs through it, and each $\forall$ sentence is only finitely long, on any given pass through stage 2 the reduction of any one $\forall$ sentence must be a finite process.

(ii)   Work at stage 2 must come to an end because it begins at some finite point, which means that there can only be finitely many $\forall$ sentences on θ. It has just been established that, on any given pass through stage 2, reducing any one of them is a finite process. None of these applications introduces new names, except the very first in the case where no names yet exist on the path, and then only that first (T$\forall$) application adds a new name, which would in that case be the only name used by all other applications of (T$\forall$) at the current stage. The reduction of some $\forall$ sentences may create other $\forall$ sentences that are added to the bottom of θ and that must also be reduced at this stage when their turn comes up. But these new $\forall$ sentences are always shorter than their parents, which means that eventually only sentences will be produced that are too short to contain further $\forall$ quantifiers as main operators. So, an end must come to work at stage 2.

At each point where work at stage 2 comes to an end, all $\forall$ sentences have been completely reduced. As work continues, a subsequent cycle through stage 1 can cause new names to appear on θ but, because stage 1 work always comes to an end, only finitely many are ever introduced and a subsequent pass through stage 2 effects a new complete reduction of all $\forall$ sentences. θ therefore exhibits feature (d). Even if some $\forall$ sentences on θ are unreduced for some names at finite points in θ's construction, they are reduced for those names on θ in at least one of the subsequent trees in the series.

Given that θ has features (a)–(f), it can be proven by mathematical induction on the number of operators in sentences on θ that every sentence on θ must be true on the canonical tree model, I$\star$. I$\star$ is defined as it was in section A-5.3, and the completeness demonstration is also filled out as presented in that chapter with the usual rewrites (replacing "connective" with "operator," and so on). As noted there, the demonstration appeals to two lemmas, which form the basis clause and the inductive step for the conclusion that all the sentences on θ are true on I$\star$. Lemma 1 is justified as it was in section A-5.3. Lemma 2 needs to be updated.

Demonstration of lemma 2: Suppose for purposes of conditional proof that all the sentences on θ containing from 0 to k occurrences of operators are true on I$\star$. The sentences with $k+1$ occurrences of operators must contain at least one operator, and so must be either conditionals or $\forall$ sentences. The conditionals must be either (i) sentences of the form $P \rightarrow \perp$, where P is atomic, that is, where P is $\perp$ or a zero-place predicate sentence, an identity sentence or a higher-place predicate sentence, (ii) sentences of the form $P \rightarrow \perp$ where P is not atomic, that is, is a conditional or a universally quantified sentence, or (iii) sentences of the form P → Q where Q is not ⊥. So, there are seven cases to consider. Cases one to five were demonstrated in section A-5.3. Cases one to four need not be revisited here. Case five as presented in section A-5.3 needs to be revised and renamed case six. Its demonstration presupposes the following new case.

Case five: The sentence with $k+1$ occurrences of operators has the form $\forall\chi Q \to \bot$. Then it follows from feature (iii) of θ that $\forall\chi Q \to \bot$ has been reduced by (∀⊥), and consequently that for some name r, $Q(r\,|\,\chi) \to \bot$ occurs on at least one extension of θ in at least one of the subsequent trees in the canonical series. Because $\forall\chi Q \to \bot$ contains $k+1$ occurrences of operators, $Q(r\,|\,\chi) \to \bot$ contains k occurrences of operators. And since it is being supposed that any sentence on θ that contains k or fewer occurrences of operators is true on I⋆, it follows by definition of truth that on any δ, $\delta[\mathrm{I}^\star\alpha(r)/\chi]$ satisfies $Q(r\,|\,\chi) \to \bot$. By (⊥) no δ on any I satisfies ⊥. From these last two results by (MT), $\delta[\mathrm{I}^\star\alpha(r)/\chi]$ does not satisfy $Q(r\,|\,\chi)$. By (∀), δ does not satisfy ∀xQ, and so by (→) does satisfy ∀xQ → ⊥. By exclusivity and the definition of truth, ∀xQ → ⊥ is true on I⋆. So, in this case the sentence on θ with $k+1$ occurrences of operators is true on I⋆.

Case six: The sentence with $k+1$ occurrences of connectives has the form P → Q where P is compound and Q is not ⊥. Then it follows from feature (c) of θ that P → Q must have been reduced by (T→) and consequently that either P → ⊥ or Q occurs on at least one extension of θ in at least one of the subsequent trees in the canonical series.

Suppose P → ⊥ is the sentence that occurs on θ in at least one of the subsequent trees in the series. Then if P is atomic it follows by the argument of cases one to three that **no δ on I⋆ satisfies P**. Alternatively, if P is compound **it must have either the form R → P₁ or the form ∀xR. In the first case** it follows by the demonstration of case four that **no δ on I⋆ satisfies** R → P₁, which just is P in this case. **In the second case it follows by the demonstration of case 5 that no δ on I⋆ satisfies ∀xR, which just is P in this case.** So, whether P is atomic or compound, **it is not satisfied by any** δ on I⋆. But then it follows by (→) that **each δ on I⋆ satisfies P → Q. By def truth, I⋆(P → Q)** is T.

(The remainder of case six, which deals with the case where Q falls on θ, proceeds as it did in section A-5.3, with references to truth on I⋆ rewritten, as above, to follow from satisfaction by δ. The demonstration of lemma 2 concludes with a final case.)

Case seven: The sentence with $k+1$ occurrences of operators has the form $\forall\chi Q$. Since $\forall\chi Q$ is on θ, it follows from feature (d) of θ that for each name, r, that occurs in any sentence on θ, $Q(r\,|\,\chi)$ occurs on θ (or $Q(a\,|\,\chi)$ does if there is no such name). Since each of these instances has fewer than $k+1$ operators, and it is being supposed that any sentence on θ that contains k or fewer operators is true on I⋆, each of these instances is true on I⋆. By definition of truth, each variable assignment on I⋆ satisfies each of these instances. Now suppose to the contrary that at least one δ on I⋆ does not satisfy $\forall\chi Q$. By (∀) for at least one o, $\delta[o/x]$ does not satisfy Q. But according to clause (iii) of the definition of I⋆, each object in D is denoted by some name occurring on θ. So for some name, p_1, occurring on θ, $\mathrm{I}^\star\alpha(p_1)$ is o and $\delta[\mathrm{I}^\star\alpha(p_1)/\chi]$ does not satisfy Q. By v-extensionality, δ does not satisfy $Q(p_1\,|\,\chi)$, where p_1 is some name occurring on θ, contrary to what has just been established. It follows that the supposition that at least one δ does not satisfy $\forall\chi Q$ must be rejected: each δ on I⋆ satisfies $\forall\chi Q$. By the definition of truth $\mathrm{I}^\star(\forall\chi Q)$ is T. So, in this case the sentence on θ with $k+1$ occurrences of operators is true on I⋆.

A-6.4 Tree Conversion; Soundness of Tq; Completeness of Dq

Section A-5.4 described how to convert p-trees to derivations. q-trees differ from p-trees only in the inclusion of results obtained by (T∀), (T∃), (~∀), and (~∃). Applications of (T∀) on trees correspond to applications of (∀E) in derivations. Where (T∃) is applied on trees to derive $P(q\,|\,\chi)$ from $\exists\chi P$, the corresponding derivation enters $P(q\,|\,\chi)$ as an assumption for (∃E). Provided the tree closes, following the remainder of the tree under this assumption will yield ⊥, which can be derived outside of the scope of the assumption by (∃E). Applications of (~∀) and (~∃) on trees are mimicked in derivations by adding the following derived rules to Dqt:

(~∀): If L ⊢ $\sim\forall\chi P$, and L, $\sim P(q\,|\,\chi) ⊢ \bot$, where q does not occur in any sentence on L or in P, then L ⊢ ⊥.
(~∃): If L ⊢ $\sim\exists\chi P$ then L ⊢ $\sim P(q\,|\,\chi)$, where q is any name.

(~∀) works like (T∃). $\sim P(q\,|\,\chi)$ is entered as an assumption for (~∀), and ⊥ is derived outside this assumption by (~∀). The following tree establishes that $\forall x[Gx \to \exists y(Hyx \,\&\, \sim=yx)]$, ∃xGx / ∃x∃y~=xy is derivable in Tq. (The tree is judicious, rather than systematic, because it closes.) Its conversion is set to its right.

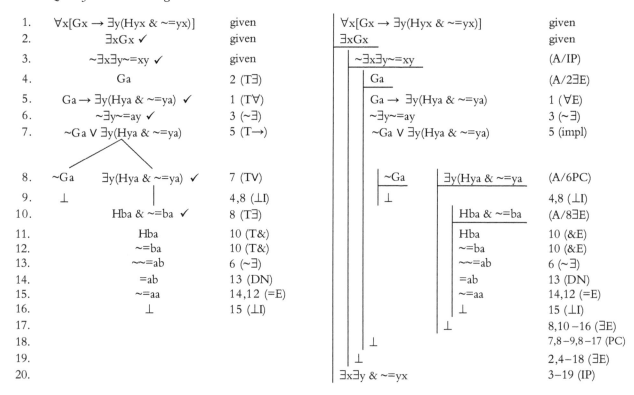

When the tree does not close, the derivation cannot be completed, unless at least one path is exhausted. In that case it is possible to derive an iterated conjunction of literals from the exhausted path. The iterated conjunction defines a tree model for the givens. However, the relevant point for purposes at hand is that any closed tree can be converted into a derivation of ⊥ from the givens. That makes it unnecessary to provide a dedicated demonstration of either the soundness of Tq or the completeness of Dq. Instead, those principles are established as they were in section A-5.4.

Exercise A-6.4

1. *Convert all the closed trees done in solutions to exercise 14.1 to derivations.*

   Answers for 14.1#1g, k; #2a, e, i, k, m, o, q, s; #4a, c, e, g, i, k, m, o, q; #6a, c, e, g, o, q, s, u; #7a, c, e

2. *Supply routines for deriving ⊥ from ~∀χP given that assuming P(q | χ), where q does not occur in P or in any open assumption, yields ⊥, and for deriving ~P(q | χ) from ~∃χP.*

Appendix Quantified Modal Logic

Attempting to combine MSL with QPL raises questions that have no intuitively obvious answers.

- Can the same object exist in different worlds?
- Can an object exist in one world but not another?
- How are names and definite descriptions related to objects in different worlds?
- What is the domain of the quantifiers: all objects in all worlds, or just all objects in the local world?

These questions are not logical but metaphysical or a matter of the philosophy of language. Logic does not answer them. But it does provide a set of tools for presenting them and for outlining different positions that might be taken on them. These tools make the questions, and the differences between the proposed answers to them, more precise.

A proper study of quantified modal logic is a topic for a course and a text of its own. This appendix is confined to surveying some of the more contentious issues. Garson (2013) is recommended for further study.

A-6.A.1 Objects and Worlds

In ordinary discourse about possibilities, people talk about alternative ways the same object might have been. They ask what would have become of someone had they made a different decision at a crucial point in their lives. People are envisioned dying old rather than young, staying single rather than marrying, having more or fewer children, being richer or poorer, and so on. People think this of themselves. They place themselves and others in other times or circumstances, and attribute different predicates to themselves and others in these contexts. Sometimes these predicates are radically different. Children imagine what it would be like if they had superpowers. The Pythagoreans believed that after death they might be reincarnated as animals or even as beans.

People also wonder what the world would have been like if certain objects had never existed. We wonder what the twentieth century would have been like if Hitler had not existed, or what would have happened if a tree that stood in the path of a skier had not existed.

This suggests that a system of logic that attempts to formalize how people reason about possibilities ought to recognize that same objects may exist in different worlds, and may often satisfy quite different predicates in those worlds. It also ought to recognize that objects may exist in some worlds but not in others.

A-6.A.1.1 Counterpart Theory

Philosophers have always had questions about our naïve attribution of identity to objects found in different contexts. The questions have focused on cases where the different contexts are different times and the question is what makes someone the same person over time. They become even harder to resolve when the contexts are different worlds, and nominally same objects are allowed to satisfy radically different predicates in those worlds, such as those that go along with being a human being and being a bean. What if there are contenders in one world for the title of identity with an object in the other world, and all of them are equally unrelated? Some philosophers, notably David Lewis (1941–2001), have claimed that we can make no sense of sameness of objects in different possible worlds. The best we can do is consider some of the objects in one world to have counterparts in another world.

Adopting this view when attempting to integrate MSL with QPL would mean that each world must have its own domain, and that no object in one domain could be in any other domain. Such a position might be supplemented by outfitting interpretations for QML with a set of counterpart relations. An interpretation for QML might consist of a set, Ω, of worlds $\{w_1, w_2, w_3, \ldots\}$, a set, D, of disjoint local domains $\{Dw_1, Dw_2, Dw_3, \ldots\}$ for each world, an assignment, α, of extensions to predicates in different worlds (same predicates would have different extensions in different worlds), and a counterpart relation, $\approx$ (squiggly identity), specifying which object in one world, if any, is a counterpart of an object in another world. (Assignments to names are another matter, considered below.) That objects must have counterparts in all worlds, or may not have more than one counterpart in any one world are further conditions that might be placed on $\approx$.

A-6.A.1.2 Haecceity Theory

One way to capture a more robust understanding of our naïve discourse about alternative possibilities for the same object is to identify some unique predicate or set of predicates that each counterpart must possess, and maintain that satisfying that predicate or set of predicates is what makes an object in one world the counterpart of an object in another. This recalls the Platonic–Aristotelian notion of a substantial form or essence. But as employed by Aristotle, an essence is what characterizes a species or kind of substance, not an individual. The analogous notion for individuals is that of a haecceity (from the Latin for *thisness*). A haecceity is a uniquely individuating property or set of properties. By definition, at most one object satisfies a haecceity in any world. There may be worlds in which nothing satisfies the haecceity, and objects that satisfy the haecceity in one world may satisfy different sets of other predicates as compared to objects that satisfy the haecceity in another world.

Understood in this way, haecceities are "diplomatic." Someone who denies that same objects can exist in different worlds can invoke haecceities to explain which object in one world (if any) is the counterpart of an object in another world. Someone who maintains that same objects can be found in different worlds can maintain that each object carries its haecceity with it wherever it is found.

Less diplomatic alternatives would, on the one side, take the counterpart relation to be defined by $\approx$ without the help of haecceities and, on the other side, postulate an outer domain, $\mathbb{D}$ (hollow D), of objects and take the local domains of various worlds to be subsets of $\mathbb{D}$. On the latter account, there is no more need to invoke a haecceity to explain what makes an object in one world be the same as an object in another world than there is to explain what makes an object in two intersecting subsets of the same superset be identical with itself. This is not to say that there is no problem of object individuation; it is just that there is no special problem of transworld identification.

A-6.A.2 Names and Predicates

Many objects have more than one name. Is this something that could have been otherwise? Might there be a world in which the person named Samuel Clemens does not also go by the name of Mark Twain? If so, then by the same token, might there be objects that go by one name in one world and a different name in another world? Telling against this is the principle that names must not be ambiguous under any one interpretation. If objects are allowed to be the same across worlds of an interpretation, and names are not allowed to be ambiguous on an interpretation, then same names must be used to name same objects in different worlds of an interpretation, and even when multiple names are used to name the same object, those multiple names must be employed in the same way in all worlds of that interpretation.

The principle that names may not be allowed to change their denotation from one world to the next is encapsulated in the claim that names are "rigid designators" and codified in the following two principles:

$$(\Box =): \quad =pq \vDash \Box =pq$$
$$(\Box \sim =): \quad \sim =pq \vDash \Box \sim =pq$$

An ironic consequence of these principles is that while an object that satisfies a predicate in one world could fail to satisfy that predicate in another world, and while this could be the case of any predicate the object satisfies (with the exception of its haecceity, if hacceity theory is accepted), the one thing it could not lose, and must retain from world to world, is its name. Pythagoras could be muscular in one world and gaunt in another. He could be a human being in one world and a bean in another. He could exist in one world and not in another. Across all these worlds there might not be one predicate he would constantly satisfy. But he could never lose his name, a thing we think is so inessential to us that it can be changed by legal fiat. Even if he goes by three different names, there could be no world in which he has any other aliases, or in which anyone else gets to use any of his.

This seems counterintuitive. "Mark Twain is Samuel Clemens" does not seem to be necessarily true. We think things could have been otherwise. But in modal logic, not all necessities are equal. $\Box P$ is not the same thing as $\vDash P$. "Mark Twain is Samuel Clemens" is not m-valid (true on all interpretations), unlike "Mark Twain is Mark Twain." Where p and q are distinct names it is always an option to devise alternative interpretations on which sentences of the form =pq are either true or false. The necessary truth of "Mark Twain is Samuel Clemens" is only truth in all worlds of any interpretation on which this sentence is true in any one world; it is not truth in all worlds of all interpretations. This is a weaker sense of "necessarily," and it is only in this weaker sense of "necessarily" that identities and nonidentities are necessary. It is always possible to appeal to alternative interpretations to establish that =pq is not modally necessary, when p and q are distinct names. It is however a consequence of the view that names are rigid designators that Samuel Clemens cannot have the pen name of Mark Twain in one world of one interpretation but not another of that same interpretation.

Taking names to be rigid while allowing that objects need not exist in all possible worlds raises a question about predicate sentences as well as identity sentences. Suppose Pegasus exists in v but not in w. Pegasus must have some name, "a," which, because names are rigid, denotes only Pegasus and so does not denote any object in w. But, by definition, α_w, assigns a (possibly empty) extension to each predicate. The question is what α_w draws on in doing so. May it only draw on objects in the local domain or may it draw on objects in a wider domain? If the latter, then it would be possible for claims about Pegasus to be satisfied or not satisfied in w, even though Pegasus does not exist in w.

The second route is naively appealing but epistemically and metaphysically objectionable. Naively, "Pegasus is a winged horse," and "Pegasus is a worm," are not equally true of Pegasus in this world, even though Pegasus does not exist in this world. But this naïve position raises the metaphysical question of what makes it true that Pegasus satisfies "winged" in this world if Pegasus does not exist in this world. It cannot be that Pegasus is winged because Greek myths describe Pegasus as winged, because the question is not about the translated contents of extant medieval copies of ancient Greek writings but about the nonexistent object the authors of those sources were writing about. Epistemically, our knowledge of what objects satisfy what predicates in this world (the actual world) is often only obtained by appeal to sense experience or testimony, which can only be had of objects that exist or existed in this world.

A response to these metaphysical and epistemological objections is that it is not the business of logic to determine matters of fact, and questions of what objects satisfy what predicates concern matters of fact. Logicians are happy to consider all the logical possibilities. While it is important to determine matters of fact, in modal logic there is nothing beyond sheer fiat that determines what objects satisfy what predicates in other possible worlds. The logician simply stipulates that such objects satisfy such predicates in w, that such objects satisfy such predicates in v and so on. If someone asks why those stipulations are as they are, the logician's answer is that there is no reason and anyone who wishes to stipulate differently is welcome to do so. All the different ways of distributing objects over predicates are instantiated by some world of some interpretation or other. Moreover, the question of which of these ways is the correct one, in the sense of the one that corresponds to the way things are in the actual world is one that does not arise for the logician, who need not recognize any one possible world as the actual world, but can focus on how things are in at least one or in all of them.

This still does not say why it should be accepted that Pegasus is winged in worlds in which Pegasus does not exist, but it does take some of the force out of the intuition that "Pegasus is winged" and "Pegasus is a worm" are equally false. It is but a small step from taking the satisfaction of predicates in other worlds to be up for stipulation by interpretations to taking the satisfaction of predicates by objects that do not exist in this world to be up for stipulation by interpretations. The answer to the epistemologist is that Pegasus is winged in this world by convention on the conventionally accepted interpretation. The community has traditionally agreed that this nonexistent object satisfies that predicate. Those who want to use a different interpretation are free to do so, because what is at issue is not a matter of fact (all are agreed that Pegasus does not satisfy E in this world) or a logical truth (because, taking G to be "winged" and "a" to denote Pegasus, Ga is not modally valid). But then the onus is on them to define their alternative interpretation, whereas there is no onus on those working with the accepted interpretation to even so much as advise others that they are doing so.

A-6.A.3   Quantifier Domains and the Barcan formulas

Supposing that there are distinct outer and local domains raises the question of which of these domains the quantifiers range over. Since ∀ means "all," and is not supposed to have existential import, there is reason to take ∀ to range over the objects in the outer domain. But speakers do not generally mean to include all possible objects when they say that everything is a certain way. On the contrary, they mean to make a robust claim just about what exists in their world. ∃ has a reverse ambiguity. While it is taken to be a specifically existential quantifier, and so to have existential import, as its name implies, it can be read merely numerically, as meaning "at least one," in which case there is no implication that the one or more things exist in the local domain. It is quite common for people to talk about what merely possible objects are like, as when project managers speak to designers about possible buildings or possible machines.

The view that the quantifiers should range over an outer domain of possible objects is called "possibilism." The view that they should range just over a domain of actually existing objects is called "actualism." Actualists fall into two camps. Variant domain theorists hold that while the quantifiers only range over actually existing objects, there is a different domain of actually existing objects for each world. The satisfaction conditions for quantified sentences are world-relative in the sense that they depend on what objects are in the local domain for that world. In opposition to both the variant domain theorists and the possibilists, constant domain theorists maintain that there is only one domain for all worlds (against the variant domain theorists) but also maintain that the objects in this domain all exist (against the possibilists).

The constant domain theory has an awkward implication: everything exists in all possible worlds, which is tantamount to saying that everything exists necessarily. All beings are necessarily existent beings, not just God. In fairness, there are various ways of avoiding this consequence. One is to maintain that even though everything exists in all worlds, the things that exist in a world need not satisfy any predicates in that world. Another is to observe that objects that are in the domain of one interpretation need not be included in the domain of another, so it is not *modally* necessary that any object exist.

A diplomatic alternative is to recognize an outer domain, various local domains, and four quantifiers. The two familiar ones, ∀χ and ∃χ are confined to the local domain. The broad quantifiers are commonly symbolized as Πχ and Σχ, (pi chi and sigma chi) for "each" and "at least one," respectively. The point to doing this is that quantification over just what exists is so common that being forced to further specify that the objects under consideration are just those in the local domain would be so irksome that it would impel the invention of dedicated local quantifiers.

This diplomatic solution does not resolve some of the most intriguing and stimulating questions about the range of the quantifiers. These are questions that arise from the fact that modal operators extend any statement they are applied to across worlds. When a modal operator is attached to a quantifier, it raises the question of how it extends the range of the quantifier. The pioneering work on this topic was done by Ruth Barcan Marcus (1921–2012), who asked what □ does to ∀ and what ∀ does to □. (Since □ and ◇ are interdefinable, and ∀ and ∃ are interdefinable, specifying how □ and ∀ interact means specifying how either modal operator interacts with either quantifier.) Is boxing a universally quantified formula the same as universalizing a boxed formula? Is saying that everything is necessarily P the same as saying that necessarily everything is P? The Barcan formula (BF) asserts ∀χ□P → □∀χP, whereas the converse Barcan formula (CBF) asserts □∀χP → ∀χ□P. Together, the two formulas assert that boxing a universally quantified formula is the same as universalizing a boxed formula. But are either or both of these formulas valid? The answer is they are if domains are constant, but they are not if domains are various. There are further interesting consequences for the relations between domains if one of them is accepted and the other rejected.

If domains are various but same objects can exist in different worlds, and if the universal quantifier has merely local scope, and so only means "all the objects in the local domain," whereas □ means "in all worlds," then "everything is necessarily P" does not mean the same thing as "necessarily, everything is P." One of ∀χ□P and □∀χP might be true while the other is false, and one or both of ∀χ□P → □∀χP and □∀χP → ∀χ□P might be rejected.

∀χ□P says that each object in the local domain satisfies □P, and so satisfies P in all accessible worlds. If ∀χ□P is true in one world, w, then all the objects in Dw must satisfy □P in w, which means all the objects in Dw must satisfy P in any accessible world, v. But even if all the objects in Dw are in Dv and continue to satisfy P in v (or even if any objects in Dw that are in Dv continue to satisfy P in v), if Dv contains objects that are not in Dw, and one or more of those further objects do not satisfy P in v, ∀χP will be false in v, the truth of ∀χ□P in w notwithstanding. Because ∀χP can be false in v, and v is accessible to w, □∀χP can be false in w. In sum, provided w has access to worlds that contain other objects in addition to the ones in Dw, ∀χ□P → □∀χP is invalid. (BF) affirms ∀χ□P → □∀χP. The only way it could be made a principle, therefore, is by imposing a restriction on an acceptable interpretation that stipulates that no accessible world, v, can contain objects that are not in the accessing world, w. Making (BF) a principle is tantamount to denying that domains could "expand" when moving from one world to another accessible world.

On the other hand, if □∀χP is true in one world, w, then ∀χP must be true in any accessible world, v. Consequently, each object in Dv must satisfy P in v. But if Dw contains objects that are not in Dv, and they do not satisfy P in v, then not all objects in w will satisfy P in all accessible worlds and ∀χ□P will be false in w. As long as w has access to worlds that are missing some of the objects in Dw, □∀χP → ∀χ□P is invalid. (CBF) affirms □∀χP → ∀χ□P. The only way it could be made a principle is if whatever objects are in the domain of a world must continue to be present in any accessible world. This is tantamount to denying that domains could "shrink" when moving from one world to another accessible world. (Those familiar with the discussion of intuitionistic logic from previous chapters will recognize this "no contracting domains" condition as a feature of intuitionistic semantics.)

Taken in combination, (BF) and (CBF) imply that domains can neither shrink nor expand. s5, one of the systems of modal logic studied in chapter 11, supposes that all worlds are "accessible" from all other worlds. On s5 and systems like it, accepting either one of (BF) and (CBF) entails accepting the other. The alternatives are either to reject both, or accept both. But on other systems it is possible for domains to "expand" while moving from accessible world to accessible world but not "contract," or to "contract" but not "expand."

(BF) and (CBF) have unquantified analogues that use the existence predicate. (BF), "no expanding domains," corresponds to ~Ep → □~Ep, which asserts that if α(p) does not exist in w, it cannot exist in any (accessible) world, and (CBF), "no contracting domains," corresponds to Ep → □Ep, which asserts that if α(p) exists in w it must exist in any (accessible) world.

A-6.A.4 Derivation and Tree Rules

Quantified modal logic raises problems for the standard formulation of the identity and quantifier rules.

Notoriously, (=E) can fail when applied to sentences that contain modal operators. The following example is due to Quine.

> The number of the planets is nine
>
> Nine is necessarily greater than seven
> _____
>
> The number of the planets is necessarily greater than seven

Taking "a" to denote "the number of the planets," b to denote 9, c to denote 7, and Gxy to refer to the predicate "x is greater than y," the demonstration can be formalized as:

$$=ab$$
$$\underline{\Box Gbc}$$
$$\Box Gac$$

These demonstrations are intuitively invalid. Yet the conclusions are derivable from the premises by (=E). Even in Tqm all that is required is a single application of (=E) to two of the givens followed by (⊥I).

Dq and Tq can turn a blind eye to such counterexamples because they formalize sentences containing modal operators as zero-place predicates. That makes the demonstrations formally invalid. But quantified modal logic cannot escape the difficulty.

One way for Dqm to avoid the counterexamples is to restrict (=E) to application to literals. Literals contain no modal operators so identity substitutions are safe there. This restriction has always been in force on trees in all systems.

Modifications are also needed for the quantifier rules. Constant domain theories can use the rules of Dq and Tq. But variant domain theories cannot. If objects need not exist in all worlds but objects that do not exist in this world nonetheless have names that no other object can assume, then the inference from $\forall\chi P$ to $P(q|\chi)$ could fail. All objects in w could satisfy P, so $\forall\chi P$ is true, but q could name an object that is not in w and that does not satisfy P in w, so $P(q|\chi)$ could be false. A variant domain theory must use different quantifier rules. The popular choice is the free rules, which have already been presented in chapters 15 and 16, and which are closely patterned on the classical rules. QML requires that a further restriction be placed on the free derivation rules as they were presented in chapter 15: (F∀E) and (F∃G) must be restricted to instantiation with names.

The restriction is motivated by sentences of the form $\exists\chi\Box=\chi k$, where k is any closed term, that is, any name, any functional term containing no variables or any definite description containing no free variables. Unlike names, functional terms and definite descriptions are uncontroversially nonrigid. They need not designate same objects in different words. In this world, it is true that David Hume was the author of the *Treatise of Human Nature*, and true that he had exactly one mother, Katherine Falconer. But questions of authorship and maternity can be disputed in court, which implies that a system of modal logic adequate to formalize legal reasoning must recognize other worlds in which someone else wrote the *Treatise* or someone else was the mother of David Hume. (□=) can be formulated as =pq → □=pq, but not as =ts → □=ts. Nonetheless, sentences of the form =kk, such as

The author of the *Treatise* is the author of the *Treatise*

The mother of David Hume is the mother of David Hume

are intuitively valid. Accepting that intuition, they are true in all worlds of all interpretations, which means that □=kk is true in all worlds of all interpretations. But if (F∃G) can be applied to P(k|x) when Ek is given, $\exists x\Box=xt$ can be derived from □=kk when Ek is given. Given that the author of the *Treatise* and the mother of David Hume existed in this world (and that historically existing objects are included in the domain), it follows by (F∃G) from the fact that the author of the *Treatise* is the author of the *Treatise* and that the mother of David Hume is the mother of David Hume that

There is someone who is necessarily the author of the *Treatise*

and that

There is someone who is necessarily the mother of David Hume

in violation of the intuitions that the *Treatise* could have been written by someone else in another world, or Hume could have had another mother in another world.

Avoiding this consequence calls for restrictions on the use of (F∀E) and (F∃G) with nonrigid terms. ((F∀E) must be restricted as well, because any application of (F∃G) can be replaced by a routine that uses (F∀E) instead.) One way of managing this, proposed by Garson (2013: 279–84), is to restrict (F∀E) and (F∃G) to instances made using names (which must be presumed to be rigid), and to supplement those restrictions with (~p). ((~p) was introduced in chapter 15 to deal with improper descriptions. But Garson proposed it to assist in governing inferences involving nonrigid terms.) On this proposal, the complete set of modified derivation rules is:

Modified Free Derivation Rules for Quantified Modal Logic

(=E):   If $L \vdash =k_1k_2$ or $=k_2k_1$, and $L \vdash P$ where **P is a literal containing** 0 or more occurrences of s, then $L \vdash P(k_1 | k_2)$.

(F∀E): If $L \vdash \forall\chi P$ and $L \vdash Eq$ then $L \vdash P(q | \chi)$.

(F∃G): If $L \vdash Eq$ and $L \vdash P[q | \chi]$, then $L \vdash \exists\chi P$.

(~p):   If $L \vdash \sim=pk$ where p does not occur in any sentence on L or in k, then $L \vdash \perp$.

(All other rules are unchanged from 15.5.3.)

There are no corresponding restrictions required on trees, because tree rules in all systems have always been restricted to working with names.

A-6.A.5 Substances

Up to now, objects have been treated as if they were atoms. They are either in a domain or they are not, and if an object is in multiple domains it is identical across those domains. However, modal logic has the resources to offer a more complex account of what an object is.

Consider a definite description such as "the author of the *Treatise*." In this world, David Hume was the author of the *Treatise*. In another world, it might have been Katherine Falconer or Henry Home or Adam Smith. In a third, it might have been coauthored. In a fourth, there might be no *Treatise* and so no author. The extension of a (possibly improper) term, t, at a world, w, is the object or (as in the case of co-authorship) set of objects that α_w assigns to that term. In contrast, the intension of a term is the pattern of assignments α makes to that term across worlds. The intension of a definite description can be unrestricted. In one world, it might denote nothing; in another, exactly one object; in a third, more than one object. Two different descriptions might denote the same object in one world but different objects in another.

In contrast, supposing names are rigid, the intension of names is restricted: there can be no world in which one name denotes more than one object, and if there is a world in which two names denote the same object, there can be no world in which those names denote two different objects. There can be no "splitting or joining," so to speak, when tracing the intensions of names from world to world. "Hesperus" and "Phosphorus" may both denote the same object in this world, but if they do, there can be no world in which either term denotes more than one object, that is, no world in which their intension "splits" and each denotes a different object. Conversely, if there is even one world in which "Hesperus" and "Phosphorus" denote different objects, there can be no world in which their intension is "joined" in the same object.

These reflections on the intensions of rigid terms open the door to a different understanding of objects. Take the special features that have just been ascribed to names (on the supposition that they track same objects from world to world) and take them to be created by a partial function f_o. f_o takes an object world pair, <o,w> as argument and returns an object manifestation in w as value. It is a partial function because it does not return a value for some worlds (those in which o does not exist). As a function it never assigns two different values to the same argument (the equivalent of "splitting"). It is further specially restricted to never assigning the same value to two different objects in the same world (which would be tantamount to "joining"). On this understanding, domains are domains of object manifestations rather than objects and an object is more than its manifestation in any one context or world. It is an individual substance, capable of persisting through change without loss of its individuality. As such, "object" is an exclusively intensional notion, defined by f_o. It is characterized on the one hand by the capacity of satisfying different predicates in different contexts, and on the other by "persistence" through these changes, which can be understood as the preservation of its individuality, cashed out in terms of the absence of splitting and joining.

Modal logic is well suited to capture this notion of an object. Consider worlds to be contexts (for instance, regions of space considered at moments of time) and consider local domains to be domains of object manifestations, that is, of objects as they manifest themselves in contexts (in a particular place at a particular time) by way of satisfying certain predicates in that context. In addition to being framed by such a domain of worlds, Ω, by an accessibility relation, S, and by domains of object manifestations, consider frames for interpretations for quantified modal logic to be outfitted with an object function.

When this account is adopted, the identity of objects across worlds or contexts is defined by f_o, so names need not be rigid. α might assign some names to object manifestations rather than to objects. For example, α might assign "Hesperus" and "Phosphorus" to object manifestations in the different contexts, w (yesterday evening) and v (this morning), without prejudicing the question of whether there is an object function that assigns the manifestation named "Hesperus" to w and the manifestation named "Phosphorus" to v. Given that $f_o(o,w)$ is α(Hesperus), it can remain a question whether $f_o(o,v)$ is α(Phosphorus) (from which it would follow that the object manifestations named "Hesperus" in w and "Phosphorus" in v are manifestations of the same object) or whether f_o takes α(Phosphorus) to be the value of some other object, n, in v.

This account makes room for the nonevidence of identity attributions required by intuitionistic quantified logic. It also allows the logician to model reasoning about the histories and possible states of objects without having to intrude on what is properly a metaphysical dispute between counterpart theorists, haecceity theorists, or champions of any other theory of the identity of objects. What determines the values assigned by f_o and how those determinations are ascertained is left, as it ought to be, to the metaphysician to resolve. Logic is able to proceed, as always, by being open to all possible interpretations.

Reference

Garson, James W, 2013, *Modal Logic for Philosophers*, 2nd edition, Cambridge University Press, New York.

17 Higher-Order Logic

Contents

17.1 Vocabulary and Syntax

Higher-order logic (HOL) expands on first-order logic (QPL and its extensions, QPL*f*, QPL[1], QML) in two ways. First, it permits quantification over predicates and over function letters. Ga, which might be read as "Alma is good," can not only be quantified as $\exists xGx$, "someone is good." It can also be quantified as $\exists XXa$, which says that "Alma has some quality," and as $\exists X\exists yXy$, which says that "some quality belongs to someone." Similarly, Gf(a), which might be read as "the square of one is odd," can not only be quantified as $\exists xGf(x)$, "the square of something is odd," or as $\exists xGx$, "something is odd." It can also be quantified as $\exists fGf(a)$, "the value of some function on one is odd," or as $\exists f\exists xGfx$, "the value of some function on something is odd," or even as $\exists X\exists f\exists yXfy$, "some quality belongs to the value of some function on something."

Secondly, higher-order logic recognizes predicates of predicates, as well as predicates of predicates of predicates, and so on.[1] Character traits and habits can be considered to be properties of individuals. A virtue is a character trait or habit of which people approve; a vice is one of which they disapprove. This makes virtue and vice predicates of predicates. "Being rational is better than being animate," asserts that the properties, rational and animate, stand in a relation to one another. So it asserts a relation between predicates.

Extensionally, predicates are sets of lists of objects. That makes predicates of predicates sets of sets of lists of objects. Seen in this way, numbers are predicates of predicates. The number five, for example, is a predicate of any set containing exactly five lists of objects, and so it is a predicate of a predicate. That makes properties and relations of numbers, like "x is integral" or "x is greater than y," predicates of predicates of predicates, or what might be called third-order predicates. Just as it is possible to quantify over "first-order" predicates like "is good," it is also possible to quantify over second- or higher-order predicates. The quantifiers are in this case called third- or higher-order quantifiers.

To accommodate these possibilities, HOL expands on the vocabulary of QPL to include predicate and function variables. The syntax is expanded to include formation rules for formulas containing higher-order predicates and predicate and function variables.

DOI: 10.4324/9781003026532-27

To keep the exposition as simple as possible while still illustrating the most important features of higher-order logic, the following statement of a vocabulary and syntax for HOL is confined to the second order. It also drops modal operators, the description operator, and functions from the language.

Vocabulary of HOL	
Object names:	a, b, c, d, e, f, a_1, a_2, a_3, …
Object variables:	x, y, z, x_1, x_2, x_3, …
Predicate **names**:	A, B, C, G, H, K, A_1, A_2, A_3, … followed by 0 or more places
Predicate variables:	**X, Y, Z, X_1, X_2, X_3, … followed by one or more places**
Second-order predicate names:	**$\underline{A}$, $\underline{B}$, $\underline{C}$, $\underline{G}$, $\underline{H}$, $\underline{K}$, $\underline{A}_1$, $\underline{A}_2$, $\underline{A}_3$, … followed by 0 or more places**
Contradiction symbol:	$\perp$
Identity symbol:	=
Connectives:	$\sim$, &, $\vee$, $\rightarrow$, $\equiv$
Quantity symbols:	$\forall$, $\exists$
Punctuation marks:	), (

The following statement of the formation rules for formulas uses variables as their own metavariables. Occurrences of x stand for any object variable (x, y, z, x_1, etc.) and likewise for occurrences of X and any predicate variable (X, Y, Z, X_1, etc.). Where a second or third metavariable is called for, y/Y and z/Z are likewise used. As always, different "variable metavariables" may stand for same variables, unless explicitly stated to the contrary. By now, the use of metavariables should be clear enough, and the contexts where they are called for should be obvious enough that it should not be necessary to mark the distinction.

Syntax of HOL
An expression is any vocabulary element or sequence of vocabulary elements.
A quantifier is a quantity symbol followed by **an object or predicate** variable.
A formula is any expression formed in accord with the following rules:

(P):	If P is an *n*-place predicate **name** and $<t_1,…,t_n>$ is a list of *n* not necessarily distinct terms, then $Pt_1…t_n$ is a formula. As a special case of (P), if P is $\perp$ or a 0-place predicate then P is a **formula. If $\underline{P}$ is an *n*-place second-order predicate name and $Q_1,…,Q_n$ are *n* (not necessarily distinct) predicate names or predicate variables, then $\underline{P}Q_1…Q_n$ is a formula.**
(X):	**If X is an *n*-place predicate variable and $t_1,…,t_n$ are *n* (not necessarily distinct) terms, then $Xt_1…t_n$ is a formula.**
(=):	If t and s are two not necessarily distinct terms then =ts is a formula. **If P and Q are two not necessarily distinct predicate names or predicate variables of the same number of places, then =PQ is a formula.**
($\sim$):	If P is a formula, then $\sim$P is a formula.
(bc):	If P and Q are two (not necessarily distinct) formulas, then (P & Q), (P $\vee$ Q), (P $\rightarrow$ Q), and (P $\equiv$ Q) are formulas.
(Q):	If P is a formula that contains at least one occurrence of **an object** variable, x, and no x quantifier then $\forall$xP and $\exists$xP are formulas, **and likewise for a predicate variable, X, and $\forall$XP and $\exists$XP.**
(exclusion):	Nothing is a formula unless it has been formed by one or more applications of the preceding rules.

A sentence is any formula that contains no free variables.

Named Forms

An expression of the form, ∀x, is a **first-order** universal quantifier.
An expression of the form ∀X is a second-order universal quantifier.
An expression of the form, ∃x, is a **first-order** existential quantifier.
An expression of the form, ∃X, is a second-order existential quantifier.

A formula with ∀x as its main operator is a **first-order** universally quantified formula **or first-order ∀ formula.**
A formula with ∀X as its main operator is a second-order universally quantified formula or second-order ∀ formula.
A formula with ∃x as its main operator is a **first-order** existentially quantified formula or **first-order ∃ formula.**
A formula with ∃X as its main operator is a second-order existentially quantified formula or second-order ∃ formula.
Formulas that have ∀x or ∃x as their main operators are **first-order** quantified formulas.
Formulas that have either ∀X or ∃X as their main operators are second-order quantified formulas.

Exercise 17.1

Determine whether each of the following is a sentence, a formula, or an expression of HOL. If it is not a sentence or not a formula, explain why not. If it is a formula, explain why it is in accord with the formation rules (supply a syntactic tree if it is built in accord with more than one of them). Consider predicate names and predicate variables to always be followed by the correct number of terms, predicates, or (in cases where following places are unoccupied) primes. Also consider all informal notational conventions to apply.

  ★**a.** Ga
   b. G̲H″
  ★**c.** G̲Ha
   d. G̲X′
  ★**e.** X̲G′
   f. Xab
  ★**g.** =GH
   h. =Xa
  ★**i.** =X′Y″
   j. =X′H′
  ★**k.** ∃XXa
   l. ∀AAa
 ★**m.** ∀aAa
   n. ∃XXx
  ★**o.** ∃X∀yXy
   p. ∃X(~Xa ∨ ∀yXy)
  ★**q.** ∃XHX
   r. ∃XG̲X
  ★**s.** ∃XXG
   t. ∃X∃yXy
  ★**u.** ∃y∃XXy
   v. ∃xGX

17.2 Formalization; Definitions of Higher-Order Predicates

Using the formal language that has just been described,

      17.1   Being rational is better than being animate

might be formalized as

17.2 $\underline{G}H'K'$

where $\underline{G}XY$ is the second-order relation, "X is better than Y," and Hx and Kx are the first-order predicates "rational" and "animate," respectively. In addition to being first-order predicates, "rational" and "animate" are both one-place predicates but, following the second clause of (P), when H and K fill the places of a second-order predicate, their own places are not filled. H and K are in this case followed by the appropriate number of primes ('). Without them, there would be nothing to indicate what number of places each of these predicates has.

More generally,

17.3   Some qualities are better than others

might be formalized as

17.4 $\exists X \exists Y \underline{G}X'Y'$

It is not always necessary to formalize sentences at the second order, even when they make claims about "unfilled" predicates. 17.1 might be read as equivalent to

17.5   Any*thing* that is rational is better than any*thing* that is (only) animate

and formalized in first-order logic as

17.6 $\forall x(Hx \rightarrow \forall y(Ky \rightarrow Gxy))$

where Gxy is the first-order relation, "better than." "Better than" can be treated as either a first-order or a second-order relation depending on whether it ranges over objects or predicates.

Alternatively, on an interpretation that works with a domain containing objects like "rationality" and "animality," 17.1 might be formalized as

17.7   Gab

where "a" is rationality and b is animality.

It is often a matter of choice whether to formalize a sentence at the first or second order. But when a predicate is both attributed to an object and said to have a second-order predicate, it can be necessary to formalize at the second order to capture all the logically relevant details. Capturing the details in a sentence like

17.8   Alma has some good qualities

requires existentially quantifying a first-order predicate variable to capture the notion that Alma has some quality

17.9a $\exists XXa$

and then using a second-order predicate to say that this quality is good.

17.9b $\exists X(Xa \ \& \ \underline{G}X')$

17.8 can also be formalized at the first order, but the cost is loss of detail.

17.10   Ga

is an acceptable formalization, where Gx is the first-order predicate "x has some good qualities." But it leaves out details that could bear on validity when the sentence occurs in a demonstration, or that could make a set containing the sentence unsatisfiable. Consider the demonstration,

17.11   Alma has some good qualities.
Generosity is not among them.
_____

Alma has some quality other than generosity.

Taking the second premise to imply that generosity is a good quality, but not a quality that Alma has, this demonstration is intuitively valid. But formalizing the first premise at the first order, as Ga, makes it impossible to formalize the remainder of the demonstration in a way that would be valid in QPL. However, as shown later, the second-order formalization

17.12 $\exists X(Xa \ \& \ \underline{G}X')$
$\underline{G}H' \ \& \ \sim Ha$
_____

$\exists X(Xa \ \& \ \sim =X'H')$

is valid in HOL.
Similarly, the set

17.13   {Alma has some good qualities; The only good quality is generosity;
Alma is an egregious miser; No egregious miser is generous}

is intuitively unsatisfiable. But there is no obvious way to formalize it as an unsatisfiable set of sentences of QPL. However, as will be shown later, the second-order formalization

17.14 $\{\exists X(Xa \ \& \ \underline{G}X'); \forall X(\underline{G}X' \rightarrow =X'H'); Ka; \forall x(Kx \rightarrow \sim Hx)\}$

is unsatisfiable.
The formalization just presented uses K to formalize the predicate description "x is an egregious miser." As discussed in section 12.3.6, breaking the complex into two parts and formalizing "Alma is an egregious miser" as "Ca & Ba" where Cx is "x is egregious" and Bx is "x is a miser" would be obviously inappropriate. "Egregious" describes the degree to which Alma satisfies the "miser" description. QPL does not permit objects to satisfy predicates to a greater or lesser degree. They are either in the extension of the predicate or they are not. HOL shares this feature. It would take further refinements to the vocabulary or the semantics to deal with degrees of satisfaction. (Multi–valued logic could provide the refinements.)
HOL has other features worthy of notice. It recognizes identity sentences made of predicates, for instance. Just as =ab says that "a" and b denote the same object, =G'H' says that G' and H' denote the same set of objects. Using the identity symbol to say that G' and H' denote the same set is not strictly necessary. The claim can be formalized at the first order, as $\forall x(Gx \equiv Hx)$. (If G and H are two-place predicates, $\forall x\forall y(Gxy \equiv Hxy)$ does the job, and similarly for higher-place predicates.)
The fact that the identity of two predicates can be expressed at the first order means that the second-order identity symbol can be defined at the first order. For one-place predicates the definition is

17.15 $\forall X\forall Y[=X'Y' \equiv \forall z(Xz \equiv Yz)]$

The definition for higher-place predicates can be gathered from this.
It follows that use of any instance of =XY could be dropped in favour of the corresponding instance of $\forall z(Xz \equiv Yz)$ (or its higher-place counterparts as appropriate). But it is convenient to have the more elegant second-order formulation available as well. It is especially useful for defining other second-order predicates. Since second-order predicates are sets of sets, any second-order predicate can be defined at the lower order using the identity symbol, provided all the lower-order predicates it includes have been named. For instance, if H and A are the only good qualities, the second-order quality, "good" can be defined as

17.16 $\forall X(\underline{G}X' \equiv =X'H' \vee =X'A')$

The first-order identity symbol can also be defined. The first-order definition is analogous to its second-order counterpart.

17.17 $\forall x \forall y[=xy \equiv \forall Z(Zx \equiv Zy)]$

This is an intuitive definition. Surprisingly, $\forall x \forall y[=xy \equiv \forall Z(Zx \rightarrow Zy)]$ serves just as well. This is because $\forall X(Xa \rightarrow Xb) \rightarrow \forall X(Xb \rightarrow Xa)$ is valid. The demonstration of this principle is left as an exercise. (It turns on the observation that if "a" does not satisfy a predicate, G, that b does satisfy, then "a" satisfies the predicate of not satisfying G. This yields $\bot$.)

According to 17.17, two terms denote the same object if and only if the object denoted by the one satisfies a predicate if and only if the object denoted by the other does so as well. The definition captures Leibniz's claim that indiscernible objects must be identical, as well as the converse claim that identical objects must be indiscernible.

Read from right to left, the definition provides a robust introduction rule for identity sentences: If $L \vdash \forall X(Xp \equiv Xq)$ then $L \vdash =pq$. The version of (=I) used up to now, $\vdash =pp$, is a consequence of the more limited fact that $\forall X(Xp \equiv Xp)$ is a theorem of Dh.

(=E) is a consequence of the left to right application of the definition of identity. If $L \vdash =pq$ then $L \vdash \forall X(Xp \equiv Xq)$, from which it follows that if $L \vdash =pq$ and $L \vdash Rp$ then $L \vdash Rq$.

Admitting "2" as a symbol for the second-order predicate, "two," two can be defined as follows:

17.18 $\forall X(2X' \equiv \exists x \exists y[Xx \,\&\, Xy \,\&\, {\sim}=xy \,\&\, \forall z(Xz \rightarrow =zx \lor =zy)])$

In other words, any one-place predicate, X, has the property of being a binary predicate (one that is satisfied by exactly two members of the domain) if and only if there are two distinct members of the domain that satisfy the predicate, and any other member of the domain either does not satisfy the predicate or is identical to one or the other of the two that do. Since predicates are sets, this is effectively a definition of any set that has the property of containing two objects, that is, of being two in number.

Similarly for zero, one, three …

17.19 $\forall X(0X' \equiv {\sim}\exists x Xx)$
17.20 $\forall X(1X' \equiv \exists x[Xx \,\&\, \forall y(Xy \rightarrow =yx)])$
17.21 $\forall X(3X' \equiv \exists x \exists y \exists z[Xx \,\&\, Xy \,\&\, Xz \,\&\, {\sim}=xy \,\&\, {\sim}=yz \,\&\, {\sim}=xz \,\&\,$
   $\forall w(Xw \rightarrow =wx \lor =wy \lor w=z)])$

… and so on for all the other integers.

Reflexivity ($\underline{R}$), symmetry ($\underline{S}$), transitivity ($\underline{T}$), and other predicates of predicates can be similarly defined in terms of quantification over first-order predicates.

17.22 $\forall X[\underline{R}X' \equiv \forall x Xxx]$
17.23 $\forall X[\underline{S}X' \equiv \forall x \forall y(Xxy \rightarrow Xyx)]$
17.24 $\forall X[\underline{T}X' \equiv \forall x \forall y \forall z(Xxy \,\&\, Xyz \rightarrow Xxz)]$

Exercise 17.2

Formalize the following sentences in HOL, using the formalization key provided.

D: objects
Ax: x is a person
Bx: x is good
GX: X is a good quality
HX; X is a bad quality
Kx: x is a good citizen

*a. There are at least two good qualities.
 b. Anyone has good qualities and bad qualities.
*c. Some people's good qualities are also their bad qualities.
 d. Everyone has some good qualities.
*e. Good citizens have good qualities.
 f. Good citizens have all the qualities of good people.
*g. Any two different things share something [i.e., some quality] in common.
 h. Any two things that share all qualities in common are the same thing.

17.3 Syntax II: Instances

The notion of an instance needs to be expanded to accommodate the addition of second-order quantified sentences. Instances for first-order quantified sentences substitute object names for object variables, but this is inadequate, except on interpretations where all objects have names. Because even the simplest quantified sentences, ∀xGx and ∃xGx, could refer to unnamed objects, QPL semantics works with variants on variable assignments as a way of capturing the range of objects a first-order ∀ or ~∃ sentence refers to. The same problem arises with second-order quantified sentences. Not all predicates (not all sets of lists of domain objects) need be assigned to predicate names. But second-order quantifiers range over all the predicates, not just those that have names. To deal with this, HOL permits instantiating predicate variables with predicate descriptions as well as predicate names. (As discussed in section 12.3.6, predicate descriptions are open sentences used to describe predicates.)

> A **strict** instance of a sentence of the form ∀XP or ∃XP is the result, **P(Q | X)**, of removing the main operator and replacing each occurrence of $Xt_1...t_n$ with **$Qt_1...t_n$, where Q is a predicate name of the same number of places as X.**
>
> A **general** instance of a sentence of the form ∀XP or ∃X is the result of removing the main operator and replacing each occurrence of $Xt_1...t_n$ in P with **$Q...(t_1 | y_1)...(t_n | y_n)...$, where Q is an open sentence of the same number of places as X, y_1 is each occurrence of the first free object variable to occur in Q, y_2 is each occurrence of the second free object variable to occur in Q, etc.**

When forming an instance of a second-order quantified sentence ∀XP or ∃XP, such as ∀X∀yXya, or ∃X∃y∃z(Xy & ~Xz), first identify how many places X has. The X in Xya is a two-place predicate variable, whereas the X in Xy & ~Xz is a one-place predicate variable. An instance substitutes a predicate or an open sentence with the corresponding number of places for each occurrence of the predicate variable, while slotting the terms that follow the predicate variable into the places in the predicate or open sentence.

(1) When predicates of the same number of places are substituted for predicate variables, the places in the predicate are filled with the terms following the predicate variable, taken in the order in which those terms occur after the predicate variable. Substituting the two-place predicate, G, for the two-place predicate variable X in ∀XXab yields the instance Gab. Making the substitution in ∀X∀yXya yields ∀yGya.

(2) A slight variation arises when substituting the two-place open sentence, Gxay, for Xab in ∀XXab. This yields Gaab, which is still an instance of ∀XXab. G is a three-place predicate, but Gxay is a two-place open sentence, since it contains only two variables. It can therefore be used to make an instance of ∀XXab, which quantifies a two-place predicate variable. According to the rule, the first and second terms following X, "a" and b, go in the first and second places, respectively, of Gxay, producing Gaab. A concrete example makes it easier to see why this is correct. ∀XXab refers to any relation between a and b. The sentence "Alma owes herself more than she owes to Boda" describes one such relation: a relation between Alma and Boda. Its formalization is an instance of ∀XXab, even though it can be formalized as Gaab. (It could just as well have been formalized as Gab, taking Gxy to be the predicate x owes Alma more than y.) Even though Gaab is a predicate sentence consisting of a three-place predicate and three object names, it is an instance of the open sentence Gxay nevertheless.

Similarly, stripping off the universal quantifier, ∀X, and substituting Gxay for each occurrence of X in ∀yXya yields ∀yGyaa.

(3) A further variation arises when Xab in ∀XXab is replaced with a two-place open sentence that contains multiple occurrences of the same place, like Gzy → ~Gyz, which might be read as saying that if z is taller than y, then y is not taller than z. As noted in chapter 15.1 and exercise 15.1#1, same places can occur in different spots in open sentences. In that case, the places are marked by occurrences of the same variable. In making general instances, the order of places in the open sentence is defined by which variable is mentioned first when reading from left to right. (Running through exercise 15.1#1 might be helpful at this point.) To make an instance of ∀XXab using Gzy → ~Gyz, strip off the initial quantifier, ∀X, put the whole open sentence in the place of the one occurrence of the predicate variable, X, and put the first term to occur after X, "a," in the first place in the open sentence while putting the second term, b, in the second place in the open sentence. This yields Gab → ~Gba. Similarly, the instance for ∀X∀yXya is ∀y(Gya → ~Gay). The first term to occur after X, y, goes in the first place in the open sentence, and the second term, "a," goes in the second place.

(4) It gets more difficult when a predicate variable itself occurs in more than one place. "∀X∀y(Xay → Xya)" contains two occurrences of the two-place predicate variable, X. An instance can be made using any two-place open sentence. For example, Gzd ∨ ~=zy is a two-place open sentence, as it contains two free variables, z and

y. In this case, the instance is made by replacing each occurrence of the predicate variable (X, in this case) with an occurrence of the entire open sentence. At the same time, whenever the open sentence is substituted for the predicate variable in one of the places where the variable occurs, the terms that follow the predicate variable in that place are put in the open places in the open sentence, taking the places as they are first mentioned from left to right. (In the example given, the terms following the predicate variable are "a" and y after the first occurrence of X, and y and "a" after the second occurrence.) Since there are two occurrences of X in the subformula Xay → Xya, and each is followed by a different list of terms, there are two substitutions that need to be performed when making the instance.

(4.1) In Xay the first term is the name "a," and the second is the variable, y. So when Gzd ∨ ~=zy replaces Xay, the first term in Xay, "a," goes in the first open place in Gzd ∨ ~=zy (the one marked by z), and the second term in Xay, y, goes in the second open place in Gxd ∨ ~=xy (the one marked by term y). This produces Gad ∨ ~=ay.

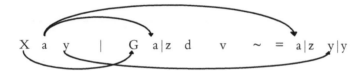

(4.2) In Xya the first term is the variable, y, and the second term is the name "a." So when Gzd ∨ ~=zy replaces this second occurrence of X, the first term in Xya, y, goes in the first open place in Gzd ∨ ~=zy (the one marked by z), and the second term in Xya, "a," goes in the second open place in Gzd ∨ ~=zy (the one marked by y). This produces Gyd ∨ ~=ya.

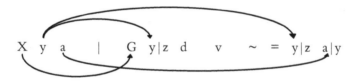

The complete result of making an instance for ∀X∀y(Xay → Xya) using Azd ∨ ~=zy is accordingly ∀y[(Aad ∨ ~=ay) → (Ayd ∨ ~=ya)].

The first of the four cases just discussed is a case of strict instantiation; the other three are general instantiations. The distinction is important for the statement of the derivation and tree rules.

Exercise 17.3

For each of the following sentences, make an instance using the specified open sentence.

*a. ∀XXa, Ax
  b. ∀XXa, =xb
*c. ∀XXa, =yy
  d. ∀XXa, Axa ∨ Bbx
*e. ∀X∃yXy, ∃z(Axz → ~Azx)
  f. ∀X∃y∀zXyz, Ax_1x_2
*g. ∀X∀z∃yXyz, $Ax_1x_2 ∨ Ax_2x_1$
  h. ∀X∃y∀z(Xyz → Ay), ~=x_1x_2
*i. ∀X∃y∀z(Xyz & ~Xzy), ~= x_1x_2
  j. ∃Y∃x (Yxa → ~Ybx), Gx ∨ Hy
*k. ∃Y∃x(Yxa → ~Ybx), Gya ∨ Hzy
  l. ∃Y∃x(Yab → ~Yxx), Gya ∨ Hzy

17.4 Derivations

The system of second-order derivation rules, Dh, includes all the rules of Dq. The quantifier rules are supplemented with the following cases for second-order quantifiers.

> (∀E): If L ⊢ ∀XP then L ⊢ any general instance, P(Q(t₁|y₁...t_n|y_n)|X(t₁...t_n)), of ∀XP.
>
> (∀G): If L ⊢ P(Q|X) where Q is a predicate of the same number of places as X that does not occur in any sentence on L or in ∀XP, then L ⊢ ∀XP.
>
> (∃E): If L ⊢ ∃XP and L, P(Q|X) ⊢ R, where Q is a predicate that does not occur in any sentence on L in ∃XP or in R, then L ⊢ R.
>
> (∃G): If L ⊢ any general instance, P(Q(t₁|y₁...t_n|y_n)|X(t₁...t_n)), of ∃XP, then L ⊢ ∃XP.

(∀E) and (∃G) use general instances whereas (∀G) and (∃E) are restricted to strict ones.

Exercise 17.4

Establish the following in Dh.

⋆**a.** ∀XXa –|– ~∃X~Xa

  b. ∀X~Xa –|– ~∃XXa

⋆**c.** ~∀X~Xa –|– ∃XXa

  d. ~∀XXa –|– ∃X~Xa

⋆**e.** ∀x∀YYx –|– ∀Y∀xYx

  f. ∃x∃YYx –|– ∃Y∃xYx

⋆**g.** ⊢ ∃x∀YYx –|– ∀Y∃xYx

  h. ⊢ ∃Y∀xYx –|– ∀x∃YYx

⋆**i.** ⊢ ∀X∀y(Xy ≡ Xy)

  j. ⊢ ∀x∃YYx

⋆**k.** ⊢ ∀x∃Y~Yx

  l. ⊢ ∀x∀y∃ZZxy *(Hint: make a general instance based on a disjunction.)*

⋆**m.** ⊢ ∀X(Xa → Xb) → ∀X(Xb → Xa) *(Hint: attempt to derive =ab from the antecedent.)*

  n. ∃X[Xa & G(X')]; G(H') & ~Ha ⊢ ∃X[Xa & ~=X'(H')]

⋆**o.** ∃X(Xa & G(X')); ∀X(G(X') → =X'H'); Ka; ∀x(Kx → ~Hx) ⊢ ⊥

  p. Ka; ∀x[Bx → ∀Y(G(Y') → ~Yx)]; ∀x(Kx → Bx) ⊢ ∀Y(G(Y') → ~Ya)

17.5 Semantics

The semantics for HOL adds an account of the meaning of second-order predicate variables and predicates to the semantics for QPL. The definitions of an interpretation, of a variable assignment, and of a variant on a variable assignment need to be updated. A denotation condition for predicate variables needs to be specified and the valuation rules for quantified formulas need to be supplemented.

An *n*-place predicate variable ranges over all the sets of *n*-place lists of domain objects that it is possible to form, whether those sets are assigned to *n*-place predicate names or not. An *n*-place second-order predicate is a set of *n*-place lists of sets of lists of domain objects.

> An interpretation, I, for **HOL** consists of a domain, D, and valuation, α.
>
> D is a nonempty and possibly (but not necessarily) infinite set, D, of objects. Notation: *D:* {o₁, o₂, o₃,...}.
>
> α assigns:
>
> (i) exactly one of T and F to each 0-place predicate **name**.
> (ii) exactly one object in D to each **object** name, p.
> (iii) where *n* > 0, α assigns a (possibly empty) set of *n*-place lists of objects in D to each *n*-place predicate **name**, P. Notation: <o₁,...,o_n> is / is not in α(P).

> **(iv) a (possibly empty) set of *n*-place lists of sets of lists of objects to each *n*-place second-order predicate, $\underline{P}$. Notation: $<\Gamma_1,...,\Gamma_n>$ is / is not in $\alpha(\underline{P})$, where $\Gamma_1,..., \Gamma_n$ are sets of lists of objects in D.**
>
> A *variable assignment*, δ, on an interpretation, I, assigns:
> (i) exactly one object in D to each **object variable**. Notation: $\delta(x)$ is o.
> **(ii) exactly one (possibly empty) set of *n*-place lists of objects to each *n*-place predicate variable, X. Notation: $<o_1,...,o_n>$ is / is not in $\delta(X)$.**
>
> The *denotation* of an *n*-place predicate variable, X, on a variable assignment, $\delta[...]$, is the last (rightmost) **set of *n*-place lists of objects** to be assigned to X on $[...]$. Notation: $\delta[...\Gamma/X\,...](X)$ is Γ, where Γ/X contains the rightmost occurrence of X on $[...]$. If X is not mentioned in $[...]$, or δ is not followed by $[...]$, the denotation of X is $\delta(X)$.

The denotation condition for object variables is unchanged from the one used by QPL. The valuation rules for quantified formulas are supplemented as follows:

> ($\forall$): δ satisfies $\forall XP$, where X is an *n*-place predicate variable, if and only if for each **set, Γ, of *n*-place lists of objects**, $\delta[\Gamma/X]$ satisfies P; otherwise δ does not satisfy $\forall XP$.
>
> ($\exists$): δ satisfies $\exists XP$, where X is an *n*-place predicate variable, if and only if for at least one **set, Γ, of *n*-place lists of objects**, $\delta[\Gamma/X]$ satisfies P; otherwise $\delta[\Gamma/X]$ does not satisfy $\exists XP$.

Exercise 17.5

1. *By reasoning from values of compounds to values of components using the semantic rules, discover and then verify interpretations that show that the following are* h-*invalid*.
   ⋆a. $\forall X \exists y Xy$
     b. $\forall X \exists y(Xy \rightarrow \forall Z Zy)$
   ⋆c. $\forall X \exists Y G(X'Y'') \,/\, \exists Y \forall X G(X'Y'')$
     d. $\exists X \exists y Xy \,/\, \exists x \forall Y Yx$
   ⋆e. $\forall X \forall y \forall z[(Xyz \rightarrow Xzy) \rightarrow Xyy]$
     f. $\forall X(\forall y Xyy \lor \forall y \sim Xyy)$

2. *Establish the following by appeal to the semantics for* HOL.
   ⋆a. $Ga \vDash \exists X \exists y Xy$
     b. $\forall X \exists y Xy \vDash \exists x Gx$
   ⋆c. $\vDash \forall x \exists Y \sim Yx$
     d. $\vDash \forall x \exists Y Yx$
   ⋆e. $\vDash \forall X(Xa \rightarrow Xb) \rightarrow {=}ba$
     f. $\vDash \forall x \forall y \exists Z Zxy$

17.6 Trees and Incompleteness

The tree method for second-order logic, Th, uses all the rules for Tq trees, with the addition of rules for second-order quantified sentences. The rules are embellishments of those for first-order quantified sentences.

$\exists XP$ says that there is at least one *n*-place predicate (that is, at least one set of *n*-place lists of objects) that satisfies the condition, P. It does not say which *n*-place predicate that is. $\sim\forall XP$ says that not all *n*-place predicates satisfy P. In other words, at least one does not. But, again, $\sim\forall XP$ does not specify which *n*-place predicate that is. Since it is assured in the one case that there is an *n*-place predicate that satisfies P, and in the other that there is one that does not, a way to proceed is to "baptize" these predicates with a predicate name that has not yet been used. Since predicates can have more than one name, using a new name does not preclude the possibility that the name refers to a predicate that has already been given a different name. But it does not illegitimately assume that the predicate that satisfies or does not satisfy P is one of those predicates.

This gives the following forms to rules for reducing second-order existential and negated universal sentences.

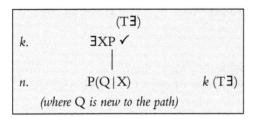
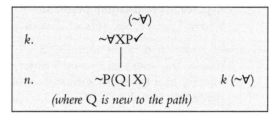

The rules dictate using the alphabetically first predicate name not yet to have occurred on the path to make a specific instance. ∃XXb reduces to Ab, supposing the one-place predicate name, A′, has not yet appeared on the path. ~∀Y∃zYzb reduces to ~∃zAzb, supposing the two-place predicate name, A″, has not yet appeared on the path.

For example, if Gbb and ∃X~Xbb are the two givens at the top of a tree, ∃X~Xbb reduces to ~Abb by (T∃). It is only reduced once and checked off. It may not be reduced to ~Gbb, as X is a two-place predicate variable and the two-place predicate G already occurs on the path. ∃X~Xbb may not be reduced to ~=bb. The identity symbol is not a predicate name. A two-place predicate name that has not yet occurred must be chosen to make the instance. Identity sentences have special features that other two-place predicate sentences need not share (for instance, they are reflexive, symmetric, and transitive). ∃X~Xbb refers to the negation of some two-place predicate sentence with occurrences of "b" in its two places, not necessarily one that shares the features of the identity sentences. A false closure could occur if it is assumed that ∃X~Xbb refers to a predicate sentence sharing all the features of an identity sentence. (Incidentally, Ø satisfies this sentence. It is a set that does not contain <α(b),α(b)>. (∃) does not stipulate that Γ be nonempty.)

∀XP says that each *n*-place predicate (that is, each set of *n*-place lists of objects that it is possible to form from domain objects) satisfies the condition, P. ~∃XP says that not even one set of *n*-place lists of objects satisfies this condition, which is another way of saying that each does not. "Each" means "each," so universal and negated existential sentences cannot be reduced just once. They must be reduced repeatedly, for each set of zero or more *n*-place lists comprised of objects that have so far been named on the path (so, including the empty set of such lists). If new object names are added to a path, as they could be by (T∃) or (~∀), further sets of *n*-place lists can be formed, so any universal and negated existential sentences on the path would have to be further reduced for all the further sets that can be formed using those new lists. If no object names have yet appeared, "each set of *n*-place lists of objects" still includes the empty set of such lists, since it, too, is a set of *n*-place lists of objects, as well as any sets that can be formed from lists of a single object, supposing any domain must contain at least one object.

Because not all sets of *n*-place lists of objects need be assigned to predicate names, ∀XP and ~∃XP must be reduced to general instances, understood to include strict instances as special cases. General instances are based on open sentences, which are infinite in number, even were they restricted to instances formed using object and predicate names appearing elsewhere on the tree. (That restriction is not made here because, as illustrated below, there are cases where a tree can be quickly closed with other instances.)

This gives the following forms to the rules for reducing universal and negated existential sentences.

	(T∀)				**(~∃)**	
k.	∀XP			*k.*	~∃XP	
	│				│	
m+1.	Q₁	*k* (T∀)		*m*+1.	~Q₁	*k* (~∃)
m+2.	Q₂	*k* (T∀)		*m*+2.	~Q₂	*k* (~∃)
m+3.	Q₃	*k* (T∀)		*m*+3.	~Q₃	*k* (~∃)
	…				…	
	where Q₁, Q₂, Q₃,… *are each general instance of* ∀XP				*where* Q₁, Q₂, Q₃,… *are each general instance of* ~∃XP	

Reduction of sentences of the forms ∀XP and ~∃XP goes on forever, except in the case where an instance can be found that closes all the paths running up to the sentence. As long as such an instance cannot be found, continuing to search for one would prevent doing other work that might close the tree or discover an exhausted path.

To manage this, Th mandates a systematic method for the application of rules on paths that cannot be closed or exhausted quickly. The method is like that used by Tq (see chapter 14), but it restricts stage 2 to reduction of first-order ∀ and ~∃ sentences. It then requires instantiating each sentence of the form ∀XP or ~∃XP once only, taking those sentences in the order they occur from the top of the tree down. Work then continues as usual. Further instances would only be entered upon completion of further cycles through each of the stages. An exception is made for cases where there is an instance of a ∀X or ~∃X sentence that would quickly close a path. In that case, other work may be put on hold to produce just that instance and obtain the anticipated closures.

It makes sense to prioritize entering instances based on open sentences that are most likely to close the tree or close as many paths as possible. These will often be instances that use only those object and predicate names that already appear on the path, but instances based just on identity formulas will often do the job. (While the identity symbol is not a predicate name, and so cannot be used to make a specific instance, it can figure in open sentences, which are used to make general instances.) ∀XP says that each *n*-place predicate (that is, each set of *n*-place lists of objects) satisfies the condition, P. It is important to remember that this includes the empty set of *n*-place lists of objects, which is elegantly described by unsatisfiable open sentences such as ~=xx.

To take an example, if Ga and ∀XXb are the two givens at the top of a tree, ∀XXb could be reduced to Ab by (T∀). However, (T∀) requires reducing ∀XXb to general as well as strict instances (strict instances are one kind of general instance). Any one-place open sentence may be used to make a general instance, including those made with any combination of predicate and object names that appear on the path, possibly including the identity symbol (even if it does not appear on the path). ~Gx is as good a one-place open sentence as Ax, as is ~=xx, which is also a one-place open sentence since it only contains one variable. Following these instructions and using ~=xx as the open sentence, an application of (T∀) produces ~=bb as the instance, which, instructively, closes the path. This is not "cheating." Using Gx as the one-place open sentence, an application of (T∀) produces Gb as the instance. Using ~Gx as the one-place open sentence, an application of (T∀) produces ~Gb as the instance. So, two applications of (T∀), one using Gx to make Gb, and another using ~Gx to make ~Gb, bring ⊥ onto the path and close the tree. Had the open sentence, Gx & ~Gx been chosen to make the instance, one application of (T∀) followed by (T&) would do that job. The path can be made to close even without drawing on ~=xx, though not as quickly. This is as it should be. ∀XXb says that "b" has every one-place predicate, which is intuitively false on any interpretation. On any interpretation, there is exactly one one-place predicate that is not satisfied by any object. That is because any set of one-place lists of objects is a one-place predicate. That includes the empty set, Ø, of one-place lists, which is among the one-place lists of objects, and so among the one-place predicates, on any interpretation. This predicate is described by infinitely many open sentences: ~=xx, Gx & ~Gx, ~(Gx ∨ ~Gx), and so on. These are all predicate descriptions that describe a one-place predicate that is not satisfied by any object, that is, that has Ø as its extension.

As another example, if ∀XXacb is the sole given appearing on line 1 of an h-tree, it cannot be reduced to general instances that use any predicate name, because no predicate names appear on the path. However, it can still be reduced by using the identity symbol to make an open sentence. Though the identity symbol has only two places, it can be used to make three-place open sentences, like ~(=xx ∨ =xy ∨ =xz). (This open sentence produces an instance that closes the tree.)

It can take some ingenuity to discover an instance of a second-order universal or negated existential sentence that will close a path, but understanding what the sentence is saying and having a sense for the changed context of second-order logic can help.

For example, in QPL, the distribution of ∃ over & fails in one direction: ∃xGx & ∃xHx does not yield ∃x(Gx & Hx). But the analogous claim in HOL, ∃XXa & ∃XXb ⊢ ∃X(Xa & Xb), is derivable. This is because ∃X(Xa & Xb) is a theorem, making the purported premises, ∃XXa and ∃XXb, irrelevant to its derivation. ∃X(Xa & Xb) says that there is some property that any two objects, α(a) and α(b), must share on any interpretation, and there are many of these, such as being in the domain, being in the set {α(a), α(b)}, being either α(a) or α(b), and being self-identical. The point is sometimes made more theatrically than it needs to be, by presenting ∃X(Xa & Xb) as a conclusion from an apparently invalid demonstration in the natural language such as

> Alma is a human being (Ga)
> 2 is a number (Hb)
> ———————————————————————————————
> Alma and 2 satisfy the same predicate (∃X(Xa & Xb))

The premises do not mention any predicate that Alma and 2 both satisfy, and so the conclusion seems unjustified. But an *n*-place predicate is any set of *n*-place lists that can be formed from objects found in the domain. As long as Alma and 2 are in the domain, a set that includes both is as good a set as any other, and so as good a one-place predicate as any other. The h-validity of this demonstration is a consequence of the vast range of predicates covered by the claim "a and b have some one-place predicate."

Th bears this out:

1.	Ga	given
2.	Hb	given
3.	~∃X(Xa & Xb) ✓	given
4.	~[(Ga ∨ Ha) & (Gb ∨ Hb)] ✓	3 (~∃) using Gx ∨ Hx
5.	~(Ga ∨ Ha) ✓ ~(Gb ∨ Hb) ✓	4 (~&)
6.	~Ga ~Gb	5 (~∨)
7.	~Ha ~Hb	5 (~∨)
8.	⊥	1,6 (⊥I)
9.	⊥	2,7 (⊥I)

=xx could just as well have been used as an instance at line 4. When justifying (~∃) the open sentence that was used to make the instance should be identified, as it is in the justification column here.

Another instructive example is provided by the tree establishing that the definition of identity is a principle of HOL.

1.	~∀x∀y[=xy ≡ ∀Z(Zx → Zy)] ✓	given
2.	~∀y[=ay ≡ ∀Z(Za → Zy)] ✓	1 (~∀)
3.	~[=ab ≡ ∀Z(Za → Zb)]	2 (~∀)
4.	=ab ∀Z(Za → Zb)	3 (~≡)
5.	~∀Z(Za → Zb) ~=ab	3 (~≡)
6.	~(Aa → Ab)	5 (~∀)
7.	Aa	6 (~→)
8.	~Ab	6 (~→)
9.	~Aa	4,8 (=E)
10.	⊥	7,9 (⊥I)

...

Up to this point, work on the tree has been almost routine. But as of line 10, it may seem like the tree will never close. The unfinished path describes a domain of at least two objects, and asserts that if one of those objects has any predicate then the other must as well. At first glance, these may seem like claims that could easily be modelled. But if one object has *any* predicate whatsoever that the other does, the principle of the identity of indiscernibles dictates that they must be the same.

Though this tenet may seem more metaphysical than logical, Th supports it. There is a way to continue the tree that closes the path.

1. $\sim\forall x\forall y[=xy \equiv \forall Z(Zx \to Zy)]$ ✓   given
2. $\sim\forall y[=a\,y \equiv \forall Z(Za \to Zy)]$ ✓   1 ($\sim\forall$)
3. $\sim[=ab \equiv \forall Z(Za \to Zb)]$ 2 ($\sim\forall$)

4.	$=ab$ $\forall Z(Za \to Zb)$	3 ($\sim\equiv$)
5.	$\sim\forall Z(Za \to Zb)$ $\sim=ab$	3 ($\sim\equiv$)
6.	$\sim(Aa \to Ab)$	5 ($\sim\forall$)
7.	Aa	6 ($\sim\to$)
8.	$\sim Ab$	6 ($\sim\to$)
9.	$\sim Aa$	4,8 (=E)
10.	$\bot$	7,9 ($\bot$I)
11.	$=aa \to\ =ab$	4 (T$\forall$) using =ax
12.	$\sim=aa$ $=ab$	11 (T$\to$)
13.	$\bot$	12 ($\bot$I)
14.	$\bot$	12,5 ($\bot$I)

The tree closes with the aid of the insight that the one-place predicate, "being the object denoted by "a," which is described by the open sentence, =ax, is an instance that closes the two right paths.

The closing of this and the previous tree may seem like pulling a rabbit out of a hat. The instance that closes the tree seems to have been found by guesswork rather than deductive reasoning. Given that the number of open sentences available to make instances is infinite, the prospects for reliably making such lucky guesses seem bleak.

This is more than just an appearance. The second-order (T$\forall$) and ($\sim\exists$) rules require reducing second-order n-place $\forall$ and $\sim\exists$ sentences to general instances because not all n-place predicates may be named. But can they even all be described? As it turns out, in cases where a sentence or a set of sentences has only infinite models (one such case was considered at the close of chapter 14.1), it is demonstrable that there are more n-place predicates than there are n-place predicate names or n-place predicate descriptions. In such cases, even if each specific instance and each general instance were to appear at some finite point on an infinitely extendible path, infinitely many n-place predicates would not have been considered.

In case further details are desired, the point can be gathered from the fact that the only difference between the vocabulary of HOL and that of QPL is the addition of X, Y, and Z. There is no problem slotting these new vocabulary elements into the cataloguing scheme for formulas of a lean language used earlier for QPL.

Symbol	Numeral	Symbol	Numeral	Symbol	Numeral	Symbol	Numeral
$\bot$	10	0	20	A	30	a	40
$\to$	11	1	21	B	31	b	41
(	12	2	22	C	32	c	42
)	13	3	23	G	33	d	43
□	14	4	24	H	34	e	44
=	15	5	25	K	35	f	45
^{1}	16	6	26	**X**	**36**	x	46
$\forall$	17	7	27	**Y**	**37**	y	47
		8	28	**Z**	**38**	z	48
		9	29				

This scheme defines a unique catalogue number for each sentence of HOL, the number created by the numerals assigned to each of its vocabulary elements, taken from left to right. For each sentence there is a natural number that is the catalogue number for that sentence. Consequently, there cannot be more sentences of HOL than there are natural numbers. But if there are as many objects in the domain as there are natural numbers, the set of n-place predicates that can be made from n-place lists of those objects is an order of infinity larger than the set of natural numbers.[2]

This circumstance raises large issues having to do with the undecidability of q-trees (and of QPL), with the incompleteness of h-trees and of HOL in general, and with where HOL fits among the disciplines.[3] These are topics for more advanced study.[4]

Exercise 17.6

Determine whether the following claims are true in Th. *State what your tree shows and why. If the tree has one or more exhausted paths, recover and verify the tree model defined by the leftmost such path and demonstrate that your interpretation works.*

★**a.** $\forall X \exists y Xy \vdash \exists y \forall XXy$

  b. $\vdash \forall X[\forall x \forall y \forall z(Xxy \ \& \ Xyz \rightarrow Xxz) \ \& \ \forall y \sim Xyy \rightarrow \forall y \forall z(Xyz \rightarrow Xzy)]$

★**c.** $\vdash \forall X \exists y(Xy \rightarrow \forall ZZy)$

  d. $Ka; \forall x[Bx \rightarrow \forall Y(G(Y') \rightarrow \sim Yx)] \vdash \forall Y(G(Y') \rightarrow \sim Ya)$

★**e.** $(\forall XXa \lor \forall XXb) \ -|- \ \forall X(Xa \lor Xb)$

  f. $\vdash \forall X(Xa \rightarrow Xb) \rightarrow \forall X(Xb \rightarrow Xa)$

Notes

1 This requires caution. Some ways of defining the notion of a predicate of a predicate have paradoxical results. This is notably the case if it is allowed that predicates might be predicated of themselves. Distinguishing between "orders" of predicate, as in what follows, is one way to avoid the paradoxes.

2 For a brief and elegant demonstration of this famous mathematical result, due to Georg Cantor (1845–1918), see Bell (2016: 35–6), preceded by a helpful background discussion beginning at 21.

3 Some have argued that HOL is more properly considered an aspect of set theory or mathematics, in part because incompleteness undermines the project of reducing mathematics to logic. For discussion and references, see Cohnitz and Estrada-González (2019: 65–87).

4 Jeffrey (1991) offers an accessible introductory treatment.

References

Bell, John L, 2016, *Oppositions and Paradoxes*, Broadview, Peterborough, ON.

Cohnitz, Daniel, and Estrada-González, Luis, 2019, *An Introduction to the Philosophy of Logic*, Cambridge University Press, Cambridge.

Jeffrey, Richard, 1991, *Formal Logic: Its Scope and Limits*, 3rd edition, McGraw-Hill, New York.

Main Appendix: Rule Summaries

This appendix is available to download from the book's product page at www.routledge.com/9780367460297

1 Foundational Definitions

A *sentence* of a language is any sequence of one or more symbols that the language recognizes as a sentence. As such a sentence must:
  (i) consist of symbols included in the vocabulary of the language
  (ii) list those symbols in an order approved by the syntax of the language

Two sentences are *the same* if and only if they consist of the same symbols, placed in the same order.

Two sentences are *different* if and only if they are not the same.

Two sentences are *opposite* if and only if they are the same but for the fact that one of them is qualified by "it is not the case that," or other words or phrases to that effect, or symbols recognized by the language in question as symbolizing words or phrases to that effect.

A *set* of sentences consists of 0 or more *different* sentences, collected in no particular order.

A *list* of sentences consists of 0 or more *not necessarily different* sentences listed one after another.

A *demonstration* is a list, $<\Gamma, A>$, consisting of a set of 0 or more sentences, Γ, followed by a further sentence, A. The sentences in Γ are called the *premises* of the demonstration and A is called its *conclusion*.

A *contradiction* arises when the same sentence is both affirmed and denied.

A sentence is *valid* if and only if it can*not* be *denied* without contradiction.
  A sentence is *invalid* if and only if it *can* be *denied* without contradiction.
A sentence is *unsatisfiable* if and only if it can*not* be *affirmed* without contradiction.
  A sentence is *satisfiable* if and only if it *can* be *affirmed* without contradiction.
A sentence is *contingent* if and only if it can be either affirmed or denied without contradiction.

A set of sentences is *unsatisfiable* if and only if there is a contradiction in affirming each sentence in the set.
  A set of sentences is *satisfiable* if and only if there is no contradiction in affirming each sentence in the set.
A demonstration is *valid* if and only if there is a contradiction in affirming the premises while denying the conclusion.

A demonstration is *invalid* if and only if there is no contradiction in affirming the premises while denying the conclusion.

Two sentences are *equivalent* if and only if there is a contradiction in affirming either one while denying the other.

Two sentences are *nonequivalent* if and only if there is no contradiction in affirming one of them one while denying the other.

2 Intensional Concepts

A sentence, P, is *true on an interpretation,* I, if and only if I(P) is T (that is, I assigns T to P).

An interpretation, I, *satisfies* a collection, Γ, if and only if I assigns T to each sentence in Γ.

A *model* for a collection of sentences, Γ, is an interpretation that satisfies Γ.

A collection of sentences, Γ, *entails* ($\vDash$) a sentence, P, if and only if $\Gamma \cup {\sim}P$ does not have a model.

Alternatively, $\Gamma \vDash P$ if and only if there is no interpretation on which all the sentences in Γ are true and P is false (equivalently, on any interpretation on which all the sentences in Γ are true, P is true).

(The bullet points under the following definitions are different ways of saying the same thing.)

A sentence, P, is *valid* if and only if

- there is no interpretation on which P is false (equivalently, P is true on each interpretation)
- ${\sim}P$ does not have a model
- $\varnothing \vDash P$

otherwise, P is *invalid*.

P is *unsatisfiable* if and only if

- there is no interpretation on which P is true (equivalently, P is false on each interpretation)
- P does not have a model
- $P \vDash \bot$

otherwise, P is *satisfiable*.

P is *contingent* if and only if

- there is at least one interpretation on which P is true and at least one on which P is false
- both P and ${\sim}P$ have models
- $\varnothing \nvDash P$ and $P \nvDash \bot$.

A set of sentences, Γ, is *unsatisfiable* if and only if

- there is no interpretation on which all the sentences in Γ are true
- Γ does not have a model
- $\Gamma \vDash \bot$

otherwise, Γ is *satisfiable*

A demonstration, Γ / P, is *valid* if and only if

- there is no interpretation on which all the sentences in Γ are true and P is false (equivalently, on any interpretation on which all the sentences in Γ are true, P is true)
- $\Gamma \cup {\sim}P$ does not have a model
- $\Gamma \vDash P$

otherwise, Γ / P is *invalid*.

Two sentences, P and Q, are *equivalent* if and only if

- there is no interpretation on which P and Q have different truth values
- neither $\{P, {\sim}Q\}$ nor $\{Q, {\sim}P\}$ has a model
- $P =|= Q$

otherwise, P and Q, are *nonequivalent*

3 Formation Rules

Chapters 2–7 use only (SL), (uo), (bc), (exclusion), (b), and (op). (uo) is named (~) and restricted to ~P.

Chapters 2–11 use "sentence" where "formula" appears and do not use (def sentence). (P) replaces (SL) as of chapter 10.

(ctf):   If f is an n-place function letter and $t_1,\ldots,t_n$ are n (not necessarily distinct) terms then $f(t_1\ldots t_n)$ is a *term*. (As a special case, if f is a 0-place function letter, f is a name.)

(st):   If t is a name or a variable, then t is a *term*.

(P):   If P is an n-place predicate letter and $t_1,\ldots,t_n$ are n (not necessarily distinct) terms then $P(t_1\ldots t_n)$ is a *formula*. (As a special case, if P is $\perp$ or a 0-place predicate letter then it is a formula.)

(SL):   **If P is $\perp$ or a 0-place predicate letter (a sentence letter) then P is a *formula*.**

(=):   If t and s are two (not necessarily distinct) terms then =ts is a *formula*.

(E):   If t is a term then Et is a *formula*.

(uo):   **If P is a sentence, then ~P, $\Box$P, and $\Diamond$P are *formulas*.**

(bc):   **If P and Q are two not necessarily distinct formulas, then (P & Q), (P ∨ Q), (P → Q), and (P ≡ Q) are *formulas*.**

(^{1}):   If P is a formula containing at least one occurrence of a name, q, and no χ variable then $^1\chi P(\chi \,|\, q)$ is a *term*.

(Q):   If P is a formula containing at least one occurrence of a variable, χ, and no χ quantifier then $\forall\chi P$ and $\exists\chi P$ are *formulas*.

(exclusion): Nothing is a *term* or a *formula* unless it has been formed by one or more applications of the preceding rules.

(Def sentence)

If P is a formula containing no free variables then P is a *sentence*.

A variable, χ, is *free* if it does not occur within the scope of an $\forall\chi$, $\exists\chi$, or $^1\chi$ operator.

If $\forall\chi$, $\exists\chi$, or $^1\chi$ is followed by a predicate, identity, or existence formula, then its *scope* is that predicate, identity, or existence formula.

If $\forall\chi$, $\exists\chi$, or $^1\chi$ is followed by a left parenthesis then its *scope* extends to the corresponding right parenthesis.

If $\forall\chi$, $\exists\chi$, or $^1\chi$ is followed by a unary operator ($\forall\psi$, $\exists\psi$, $^1\psi$, or ~) then its *scope* is that unary operator plus whatever falls within that unary operator's scope.

Informal Notational Conventions

(b):   **Brackets may be substituted for parentheses.**

(ip):   Internal punctuation may be omitted in iterated conjunctions and iterated disjunctions.

(sc):   Punctuation used to extend the scope of → or ≡ over & or ∨ may be omitted.

(op):   **Outermost parentheses may be coloured out.**

(Def instance)

An instance, $P(k \,|\, \chi)$, is the result of removing the initial operator from a formula of the form $\forall\chi P$, $\exists\chi P$, or $^1\chi P$ and replacing each occurrence of χ in P with a closed term, k. (A term is closed if it does not contain a free variable.)

4 Sentential Valuation Rules

(Chapters 3, 5, 9,11, and 14, excluding 11.7 and 14.4.4)

Chapters 2–7 do not recognize interpretations that contain Ω, S, or D. (There is only one world, and the only atomic sentences are $\perp$ and the sentence letters. No assignments are relativized to worlds.) (P), (=), ($\square$) and ($\lozenge$) are not recognized as valuation rules.

Chapter 9 does not recognize interpretations that contain D or assignments to objects or predicates. (P) and (=) are not recognized as valuation rules.

Chapters 11 and 14 do not recognize interpretations that contain Ω or S or assignments that are relativized to worlds. ($\square$) and ($\lozenge$) are not recognized as valuation rules.

An interpretation, I, consists of a set, Ω, of worlds, $\{w_1, w_2, w_3, \ldots\}$, a two-place relation, S, on the worlds of Ω, a set, D, of objects, $\{o_1, o_2, o_3, \ldots\}$, and a world-relative assignment, α, of:

- exactly one of T and F to each 0-place predicate relative to each world (Notation: $\alpha_w(P)$ is T or F)
- exactly one object from D to each name (Notation: $\alpha(p)$ is o)
- a (possibly empty) set of n-place lists of (not necessarily distinct) objects from D to each n-place predicate relative to each world (Notation: $<o_1,\ldots o_n>$ is in / is not in $\alpha_w(P)$)
- a world-relative function from n-place lists of objects from D onto objects in D to each n-place function letter

System k places no constraints on S.

System D requires that S is serial: for each world, w, there is at least one world, v, (not necessarily distinct from w) such that Swv.

System t requires that S is reflexive: for each world, w, Sww.

System 4 (s4) requires that S is reflexive and transitive: for each world, w, Sww and for any worlds, w, v, u, if Swv and Svu then Swu.

System B requires that S is reflexive and symmetric: for each world, w, Sww and for each world, w, if there is a world, v, such that Swv then Svw.

System 5 (s5) requires that S is reflexive and transverse: for each world, w, Sww and for any worlds w, v, u, if Swv and Swu then Svu and Suv.

(*f*):	Iw(*f*(t₁…tₙ) is the unique object o such that $<\text{Iw}/\alpha_w(t_1),\ldots,\text{Iw}/\alpha_w(t_n),o>$ is in $\alpha_w(f)$
(SL):	**If P is a sentence letter, Iw(P) is α_w(P).**
($\perp$):	**Iw($\perp$) is F.**
(P):	Iw(Pt₁…tₙ) is T if and only if $<\text{I}\alpha(t_1),\ldots,\text{I}\alpha(t_n)>$ is in Iα_w(P); otherwise, Iw(Pt₁…tₙ) is F.
(=):	Iw(=ts) is T if and only if Iα(t) is Iα(s); otherwise, Iw(=ts) is F.
(~):	**Iw(~P) is T if and only if Iw(P) is F; otherwise, Iw(~P) is F**
(&):	**Iw(P & Q) is T if and only if Iw(P) and Iw(Q) are T; otherwise, Iw(P & Q) is F.**
($\vee$):	**Iw(P $\vee$ Q) is T if and only if at least one of Iw(P) and Iw(Q) is T; otherwise Iw(P $\vee$ Q) is F.**
($\rightarrow$):	**Iw(P $\rightarrow$ Q) is F if and only if Iw(P) is T and Iw(Q) is F; otherwise Iw(P $\rightarrow$ Q) is T.**
($\equiv$):	**Iw(P $\equiv$ Q) is T if and only if Iw(P) is the same as Iw(Q); otherwise Iw(P $\equiv$ Q) is F.**
($\square$):	Iw($\square$P) is T if and only if, for each world, v, if Swv, Iv(P) is T; otherwise, Iw($\square$P) is F.
($\lozenge$):	Iw($\lozenge$P) is T if and only if, for at least one world, v, if Swv, Iv(P) is T; otherwise, Iw($\lozenge$P) is F.
(TM$\forall$):	Iw($\forall\chi$P) is T if and only if, for each name, q, Iw(P(q|χ) is T; otherwise, Iw($\forall\chi$P) is F.

(TM∃):   Iw(∃χP) is T if and only if, for at least one name, q, Iw(Pq|χ) is T;
otherwise, Iw(∃χP) is T.

5 Formulaic and Free Valuation Rules

(Chapters 11.7, 14.4.3-4, 15 and 16)

An interpretation, I, consists of a set, D, of objects, $\{o_1, o_2, o_3, \ldots\}$, and an assignment, α, of:

- exactly one of T and F to each 0-place predicate (Notation: $\alpha(P)$ is T or F)
- exactly one object from D to [free: 0 or more names] / [classical: each name] (Notation: $\alpha(p)$ is o)
- a (possibly empty) set of n-place lists of (not necessarily distinct) objects from D to each n-place predicate relative to each world (Notation: $<o_1, \ldots o_n>$ is in / is not in $\alpha_w(P)$)

A variable assignment, δ, on an interpretation, I, assigns exactly one object from D to each variable.
A variant $\delta[\ldots, o/\chi]$, on a variable assignment, $\delta[\ldots]$, overwrites whatever assignment $\delta[\ldots]$ makes to χ with a (not necessarily distinct) assignment of o to χ.

(*f*): $\delta(f(t_1 \ldots t_n))$ is the unique object o such that $<\alpha/\delta(t_1), \ldots, \alpha/\delta(t_n), o>$ is in $\alpha_w(f)$

(⊥):   No δ satisfies ⊥

(P): δ satisfies $Pt_1 \ldots t_n$ if and only if $<\alpha/\delta(t_1), \ldots, \alpha/\delta(t_n)>$ is in $\alpha(P)$; otherwise δ does not satisfy $Pt_1 \ldots t_n$; as a special case of (P), δ satisfies a 0- place predicate sentence, P, if and only if $\alpha(P)$ is T; δ does not satisfy P if and only if $\alpha(P)$ is F.

(=): δ satisfies =ts if and only if $\alpha/\delta(t)$ is $\alpha/\delta(s)$; otherwise, δ does not satisfy =ts.

(E): δ satisfies Et if and only if $\alpha/\delta(t)$ is in D.

(~): δ satisfies ~P if and only if δ does not satisfy P; otherwise δ does not satisfy ~P.

(&): δ satisfies P & Q if and only if δ satisfies both P and Q; otherwise δ does not satisfy P & Q.

(∨): δ satisfies P ∨ Q if and only if δ satisfies at least one of P and Q; otherwise δ does not satisfy P ∨ Q.

(→): δ does not satisfy P → Q if and only if δ satisfies P but does not satisfy Q; otherwise, δ satisfies P → Q.

(≡): δ does not satisfy P ≡ Q if and only if it satisfies one of P and Q but not the other; otherwise δ satisfies P ≡ Q.

(∀): $\delta[\ldots]$ satisfies ∀χP if and only if, for each o, $\delta[\ldots, o/\chi]$ satisfies P; otherwise $\delta[\ldots]$ does not satisfy ∀χP.

(∃): $\delta[\ldots]$ satisfies ∃χP if and only if, for at least one o, $\delta[\ldots, o/\chi]$ satisfies P; otherwise $\delta[\ldots]$ does not satisfy ∃χP.

(^{1}):   If there is exactly object, o, in D such that $\delta[o|\chi]$ satisfies P, then $\delta(^1\chi P)$ is o; otherwise δ does not satisfy $E^1\chi P$.

(exclusivity): If P is a sentence and I is an interpretation then either each variable assignment on I satisfies P or none do.

(def truth):   A sentence, P, of QPL is true on an interpretation, I, if and only if each variable assignment on I satisfies P. It is false if and only if no variable assignment on I satisfies P.

6 Derivation Rules

Lines k and k★ may occur in reverse order. Derivation rules for intuitionistic logic omit (IP) in favour of (IP~I) and (EFQ).

(CP)

i.	⌐ P	(A/CP)
...	...	
k.	Q	?
...	...	
n.	P → Q	*i−k* (CP)

(MP)

k.	P	?
...	...	
k★.	P → Q	?
...	...	
n.	Q	*k,k★* (MP)

(BP)

h.	⌐ P	(A/BP)
...	...	
i.	Q	?
k.	⌐ Q	(A/BP)
...	...	
m.	P	?
...		
n.	P ≡ Q	*h−i,k−m* (BP)

(IP)

i.	⌐ **P**	**(A/IP)**
...	...	
k.	⊥	**?**
...	...	
n.	**P− opposite**	***i−k* (IP)**

(⊥I)

k.	P	?
...	...	
k★.	~P	?
...	...	
n.	⊥	*k,k★* (⊥I)

(BMP)

k.	P	?
...	...	
k★.	P ≡ Q	?
...	...	
n.	Q	*k,k★* (BMP)

Or:

k.	Q	?
...	...	
k★	P ≡ Q	?
...	...	
n.	P	*k,k★* (BMP)

(PC)

h.	P ∨ Q		?
...	...		
i.	⌐ P	⌐ Q	(A/*h*PC)
...	...	...	
k.	R		?
...	...		
k★.		R	?
...	...		
n.	R		*h,i−k,i−k★* (PC)

(∨I)

k.	P	?
...	...	
n.	P ∨ Q	*k* (∨I)

Or:

k.	P	?
...	...	
n.	Q ∨ P	*k* (∨I)

(&E)

k.	P & Q	?
...	...	
n.	P	*k* (&E)

Or:

k.	P & Q	?
...	...	
n.	Q	*k* (&E)

(&I)

k.	P	?
...	...	
k★.	Q	?
...	...	
n.	P & Q	*k,k★* (&I)

(R)

k.	P	?
...	...	
...	...	
n.	P	*k* (R)

provided that:

i) the assumption bracket or box immediately to the left of P at line *k* continues unbroken down to line *n*

ii) P at line *n* lies exactly one *assumption bracket* to the right of P at line *k* *there may be no intervening box*

iii) P at line *k* and P at line *n* do not fall within parallel (PC) sub−derivations

---

(IP~I)

i.	⌐ **P**	**(A/IP~I)**
...	...	
k.	⊥	**?**
...	...	
n.	**~P**	***i−k* (IP~I)**

(EFQ)

k.	⊥	**?**
...	...	
n.	**P**	***k* (EFQ)**

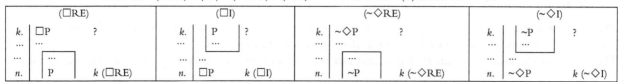

Dk is Ds + (□RE) + (□I) + (~◇RE) + (~◇I)   D is Dk + (D) axiom: □P → ◇P

(□RE)	(□I)	(~◇RE)	(~◇I)
k.　□P　　　?	k.　P │　?	k.　~◇P　　　?	k.　~P │　?
… …	… …	… …	… …
… │ …	… │ …	… │ …	… │ …
n.　│ P　　k (□RE)	n.　□P　　k (□I)	n.　│ ~P　　k (~◇RE)	n.　~◇P　　k (~◇I)

Dt is Dk + (□E)   Ds4 is Dt + (□R)   Ds5 is Dt + (□◇I)   DB is Dt + (B) axiom: P → □◇P

(□E)	(□R)	(□◇I)
k.　□P　　?	k.　□P　　　?	k.　◇P　　?
… …	… …	… …
n.　P　　k (□E)	n.　│ □P │　k (□R)	n.　□◇P　　k (□◇I)

(=I)	(∀E)	(∃G)
…│… n.　=kk　　　(=I)	│ (L) …│… k.　∀χP　　? …│… n.　P(k∣χ)　　k (∀E)	│ (L) …│… k.　P(k∣χ)　　? …│… n.　∃χP　　k (∃G)
(=E)	**(∀G)**	**(∃E)**
│ (L) …│… k.　=k₁k₂ [or =k₂k₁]　? …│… k★.　P　　? …│… n.　P(k₁∣k₂)　　k,k★ (=E)	│ (L) *(no q)* …│… k.　P(q∣χ)　　? …│… n.　∀χP *(no q)*　　k (∃G)	│ (L) *(no q)* …│… h.　∃χP *(no q)*　　? …│… i.　│ P(q∣χ)　　(A/h∃E) …│… … k.　│ R *(no q)*　　? …│… n.　R　　h,i–k (∃E)
	(F∀E)	**(F∃G)**
	│ (L) …│… i.　Ek　　? …│… k.　∀χP　　? …│… n.　P(k∣χ)　　i,k (F∀E)	│ (L) …│… i.　Ek　　? …│… k.　P(k∣χ)　　? …│… n.　∃χP　　i,k (F∃G)
	(F∀G)	**(F∃E)**
	│ (L) *(no q)* …│… i.　│ Eq …│… … k.　│ P(q∣χ) …│… n.　∀χP *(no q)*　　i–k (F∀G)	│ (L) *(no q)* …│… h.　∃χP *(no q)*　　? …│… i.　│ Eq & P(q∣χ)　　(A/h F∃E) …│… … k.　│ R *(no q)*　　? …│… n.　R　　h,i–k (F∃E)

(where k, k₁ and k₂ are closed terms and q is a name)

7 Tree Rules

Placement principle: The results of applying a rule to a sentence are to be completely and repeatedly entered on each path running up to its location, provided that ⊥ does not occur on that path.

They are not to be entered on any path that does not run up to its location or on any path on which ⊥ occurs.

Lines k and k★ may occur in reverse order

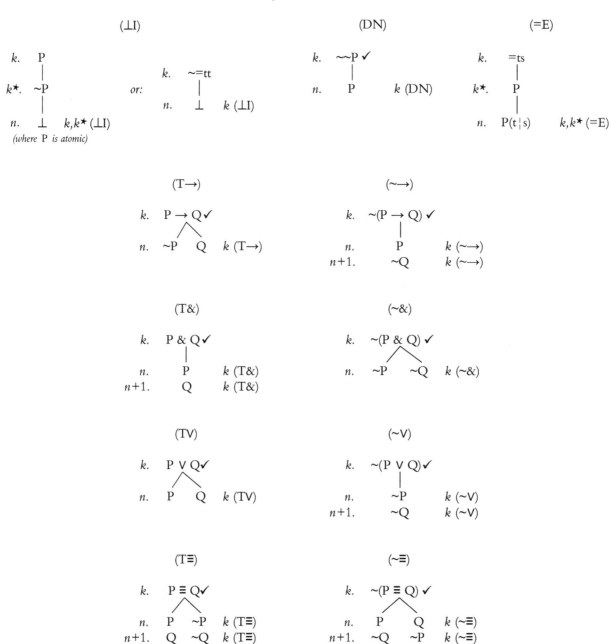

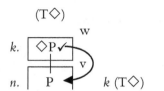

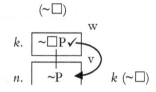

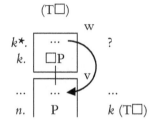

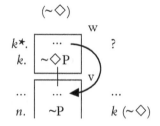

Tk: no arrows other than those produced by (T◇) and (~□)

Tt: add a reflexivity arrow to each box

Ts4: Tt + if there is an arrow from w to v and an arrow from v to u, add an arrow from w to u

Ts5: Tt + if there is an arrow from w to v and an arrow from w to u, add a double-headed arrow between v and u

(T∀)

k.	∀χP	
	|	
m.	P(q₁ | χ)	k (T∀)
...	...+...	...
m+n.	P(qₙ | χ)	k (T∀)

(where q₁ – qₙ are each name on the path
or "a" if no name occurs on the path)

(~∃)

k.	~∃χP	
	|	
m.	~P(q₁ | χ)	k (~∃)
...	...+...	...
m+n.	~P(qₙ | χ)	k (~∃)

(where q₁ – qₙ are each name on the path
or "a" if no name occurs on the path)

(~∀) / (F~∀)

k.	~∀χP ✓	
	|	
n.	**Eq**	**k (F~∀)**
n+1.	~P(q | χ)	k (~∀)/(F~∀)

(where q is new to the path and (F~∀) adds line n)

(T∃) / (F~∃)

k.	∃χP ✓	
	|	
n.	**Eq**	**k (F~∃)**
n+1.	P(q | χ)	k (T∃)/(F~∃)

(where q is new to the path and (F~∃) adds line n)

(FT ∀)

k.	Eq	
	|	
k★.	∀χP	
	|	
n.	P(q | χ)	k,k★ (FT ∀)

(where (FT ∀) is reapplied for each name
to occur in an E sentence on the path)

(F~∃)

k.	Eq	
	|	
k★.	~∃χP	
	|	
n.	~P(q | χ)	k,k★ (F~∃)

(where (F~∃) is reapplied for each name
to occur in an E sentence on the path)

Rules for Intuitionistic Sentential Trees

(TP)

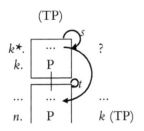

$k\star.$ ...   ?
$k.$ P
...   .
$n.$ P k (TP)

(~P)

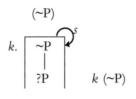

$k.$ ~P
    |
    ?P k (~P)

(?~)

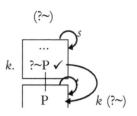

$k.$?~P ✓
    P k (?~)

(⊥I)

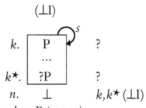

$k.$ P   ?
   ...
$k\star.$?P   ?
$n.$ ⊥ $k, k\star$ (⊥I)

where P is atomic
and lines k and k★ may occur in reverse
order

(T&)

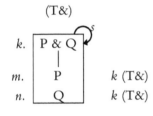

$k.$ P & Q
    |
$m.$ P k (T&)
$n.$ Q k (T&)

(?&)

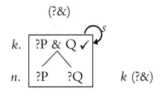

$k.$?P & Q ✓
$n.$?P   ?Q k (?&)

(T→)

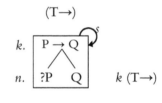

$k.$ P → Q
$n.$?P   Q k (T→)

(TV)

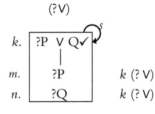

$k.$ P ∨ Q
$n.$ P   Q k (TV)

(?V)

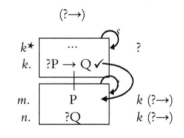

$k.$?P ∨ Q ✓
    |
$m.$?P k (? V)
$n.$?Q k (? V)

(?→)

$k\star$ ...   ?
$k.$?P → Q ✓
$m.$ P k (?→)
$n.$?Q k (?→)

(T≡)

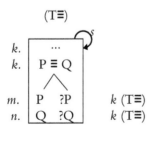

$k.$ ...
$k.$ P ≡ Q
$m.$ P   ?P k (T≡)
$n.$ Q   ?Q k (T≡)

(?≡)

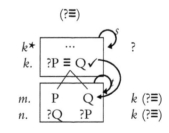

$k\star$ ...   ?
$k.$?P ≡ Q ✓
$m.$ P   Q k (?≡)
$n.$?Q   ?P k (?≡)

Index

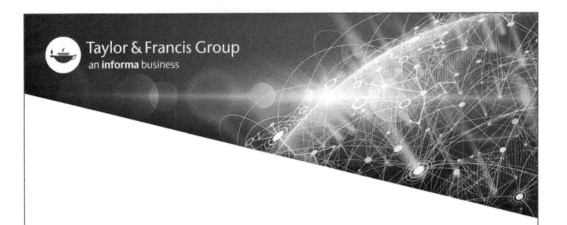

For Product Safety Concerns and Information please contact our EU
representative GPSR@taylorandfrancis.com
Taylor & Francis Verlag GmbH, Kaufingerstraße 24, 80331 München, Germany

www.ingramcontent.com/pod-product-compliance
Ingram Content Group UK Ltd.
Pitfield, Milton Keynes, MK11 3LW, UK
UKHW030829080625
459435UK00018B/598